KB186454

YBM 단기토익 700+

LC+RC

YBM
단기토익
700+

발행인	허문호
발행처	YBM

편집	이혜진
디자인	DOTS, 이현숙
마케팅	정연철, 박천산, 고영노, 박찬경, 김동진, 김윤하

초판발행	2019년 11월 1일
7쇄발행	2023년 6월 12일

신고일자	1964년 3월 28일
신고번호	제 300-1964-3호
주소	서울시 종로구 종로 104
전화	(02) 2000-0515 [구입문의] / (02) 2000-0436 [내용문의]
팩스	(02) 2285-1523
홈페이지	www.ybmbooks.com

ISBN	978-89-17-23214-1

토익 주관사가 제시하는 4주 완성 전략

YBM
단기토익 700+
이렇게 다릅니다!

각종 시험 응시 자격 취득을 위한 필독서

700점이라는 토익 점수는 토익 시험을 처음 시작하는 대부분의 학생들이 첫 번째 목표로 삼는 점수이며, 많은 관공서 및 전문직 자격 요건으로 요구되는 점수이기도 합니다. 특히 공무원 영어 시험이 토익으로 일부 대체되는 등의 변화와 함께 토익 700점은 더욱 더 많은 수험자들에게 있어 통과해야 하는 관문과 같은 대명사가 되었습니다. 이 책은 고득점을 최종 목표로 하는 시중의 단계별 학습 시리즈와는 달리, 단권으로 가장 빠르게 목표 점수에 도달하는 데 최적화된 토익 700 달성 최단거리 학습법을 제시합니다.

친절한 이론서이자 똑똑한 전략서

꼭 필요한 이론과 꼭 필요한 전략만을 담았습니다. 목표 점수에 맞게 설계된 문제 풀이 방식과 학습 포인트를 제시하여 단기간에 최대의 효율을 낼 수 있도록 커리큘럼을 구성하였습니다. 본 책의 타이틀에 부합하는 이론과 전략의 교과서라 자부합니다.

ETS 교재 출간 노하우를 담은 수험 종결서

출제기관 ETS의 토익 교재를 독점 출간하는 YBM이 그동안 쌓아온 노하우를 바탕으로 전 문항을 독자적으로 개발하였습니다. 본 책에 실린 모든 문항과 설명은 출제자의 의도를 정확히 분석하고 반영했기 때문에 타사의 어떤 교재와도 비교할 수 없는 퀄리티를 자랑합니다.

YBM의 모든 노하우가 집대성된 〈YBM 단기토익 700+〉는 최단 기간 목표 달성을 토익 수험자 여러분께 약속드립니다.

CONTENTS

LC

학습 플랜 A 20일 완성

Week 1

	Day 1	Day 2	Day 3	Day 4	Day 5
LC	Part 1 Unit 1	Part 1 Unit 2	Part 1 YBM TEST	Part 2 Unit 1, 2	Part 2 Unit 3, 4
RC	Part 5 문법 Unit 1, 2 어휘 Unit 1	Part 5 문법 Unit 3, 4 어휘 Unit 2	Part 5 문법 Unit 5, 6 어휘 Unit 3	Part 5 문법 Unit 7, 8 어휘 Unit 4	Part 5 문법 Unit 9, 10 어휘 Unit 5~7

Week 2

	Day 6	Day 7	Day 8	Day 9	Day 10
LC	Part 2 Unit 5, 6	Part 2 YBM TEST	Part 3 Unit 1, 2	Part 3 Unit 3, 4	Part 3 Unit 5, 6
RC	Part 5 문법 Unit 11, 12 어휘 Unit 8~10	Part 5 YBM TEST	Part 6 Unit 1, 2	Part 6 Unit 3, 4	Part 6 YBM TEST

Week 3

	Day 11	Day 12	Day 13	Day 14	Day 15
LC	Part 3 Unit 7, 8	Part 3 YBM TEST	Part 4 Unit 1	Part 4 Unit 2	Part 4 Unit 3
RC	Part 7 Unit 1, 2	Part 7 Unit 3, 4	Part 7 Unit 5, 6	Part 7 Unit 7, 8	Part 7 Unit 9, 10

Week 4

	Day 16	Day 17	Day 18	Day 19	Day 20
LC	Part 4 Unit 4	Part 4 Unit 5	Part 4 YBM TEST	오답 리뷰	FINAL TEST
RC	Part 7 Unit 11, 12	Part 7 Unit 13, 14	Part 7 YBM TEST	오답 리뷰	FINAL TEST

학습 플랜 B 28일 완성

	Day 1	Day 2	Day 3	Day 4
LC	Part 1 **Unit 1**	Part 1 **Unit 2**	Part 1 **YBM TEST**	Part 2 **Unit 1**
RC	Part 5 문법 **Unit 1**	Part 5 문법 **Unit 2**	Part 5 문법 **Unit 3**	Part 5 문법 **Unit 4**

	Day 5	Day 6	Day 7	Day 8
LC	Part 2 **Unit 2**	Part 2 **Unit 3**	Part 2 **Unit 4**	Part 2 **Unit 5**
RC	Part 5 문법 **Unit 5**	Part 5 문법 **Unit 6**	Part 5 문법 **Unit 7**	Part 5 문법 **Unit 8**

	Day 9	Day 10	Day 11	Day 12
LC	Part 2 **Unit 6**	Part 2 **YBM TEST**	Part 3 **Unit 1, 2**	Part 3 **Unit 3, 4**
RC	Part 5 문법 **Unit 9**	Part 5 문법 **Unit 10**	Part 5 문법 **Unit 11**	Part 5 문법 **Unit 12**

	Day 13	Day 14	Day 15	Day 16
LC	Part 3 **Unit 5, 6**	Part 3 **Unit 7, 8**	Part 3 **YBM TEST**	Part 4 **Unit 1**
RC	Part 5 어휘 **Unit 1**	Part 5 어휘 **Unit 2**	Part 5 어휘 **Unit 3**	Part 5 어휘 **Unit 4**

	Day 17	Day 18	Day 19	Day 20
LC	Part 4 **Unit 2**	Part 4 **Unit 3**	Part 4 **Unit 4**	Part 4 **Unit 5**
RC	Part 5 어휘 **Unit 5~7**	Part 5 어휘 **Unit 8~10**	Part 5 **YBM TEST**	Part 6 **Unit 1~4**

	Day 21	Day 22	Day 23	Day 24
LC	Part 4 **YBM TEST**	Part 1 **Review**	Part 2 **Review**	Part 3 **Review**
RC	Part 6 **YBM TEST**	Part 7 **Unit 1~3**	Part 7 **Unit 4~7**	Part 7 **Unit 8~10**

	Day 25	Day 26	Day 27	Day 28
LC	Part 3 **Review**	Part 4 **Review**	Part 4 **Review**	**FINAL TEST**
RC	Part 7 **Unit 11, 12**	Part 7 **Unit 13, 14**	Part 7 **YBM TEST**	**FINAL TEST**

TOEIC 소개

● **TOEIC**　Test of English for international Communication(국제적 의사소통을 위한 영어 시험)
의 약자로, 영어가 모국어가 아닌 사람들이 일상생활 또는 비즈니스 현장에서 꼭 필요한 실용적
영어 구사 능력을 갖추었는가를 평가하는 시험이다.

● **시험 구성**

구성	PART		유형	문항 수	시간	배점
Listening	Part 1		사진 묘사	6	45분	495점
	Part 2		질의응답	25		
	Part 3		짧은 대화	39		
	Part 4		짧은 담화	30		
Reading	Part 5		단문 빈칸 채우기	30	75분	495점
	Part 6		장문 빈칸 채우기	16		
	Part 7	독해	단일 지문	29		
			이중 지문	10		
			삼중 지문	15		
Total	**7 Parts**			**200문항**	**120분**	**990점**

● **평가 항목**

LC	RC
단문을 듣고 이해하는 능력	읽은 글을 통해 추론해 생각할 수 있는 능력
짧은 대화체 문장을 듣고 이해하는 능력	장문에서 특정한 정보를 찾을 수 있는 능력
비교적 긴 대화체에서 주고받은 내용을 파악할 수 있는 능력	글의 목적, 주제, 의도 등을 파악하는 능력
장문에서 핵심이 되는 정보를 파악할 수 있는 능력	뜻이 유사한 단어들의 정확한 용례를 파악하는 능력
구나 문장에서 화자의 목적이나 함축된 의미를 이해하는 능력	문장 구조를 제대로 파악하는지, 문장에서 필요한 품사, 어구 등을 찾는 능력

※ 성적표에는 전체 수험자의 평균과 해당 수험자가 받은 성적이 백분율로 표기되어 있다.

수험 정보

● **시험 접수 방법** 한국 토익 위원회 사이트(www.toeic.co.kr)에서 시험일 약 2개월 전부터
온라인으로 접수 가능

● **시험장 준비물**

신분증	규정 신분증만 가능 (주민등록증, 운전면허증, 기간 만료 전의 여권, 공무원증)
필기구	연필, 지우개 (볼펜이나 사인펜은 사용 금지)

● **시험 진행 시간**

09:20	입실 (9:50 이후 입실 불가)
09:30 ~ 09:45	답안지 작성에 관한 오리엔테이션
09:45 ~ 09:50	휴식
09:50 ~ 10:05	신분증 확인
10:05 ~ 10:10	문제지 배부 및 파본 확인
10:10 ~ 10:55	듣기 평가 (LISTENING TEST)
10:55 ~ 12:10	독해 평가 (READING TEST)

● **TOEIC 성적 확인** 시험일로부터 약 10-11일 후, 인터넷과 ARS(060-800-0515)로
성적을 확인 가능하며 성적표는 우편이나 온라인으로 발급 받을 수 있다.
우편으로 발급 받을 경우 성적 발표 후 대략 일주일이 소요되며,
온라인 발급을 선택하면 유효기간 내에 홈페이지에서 본인이 직접 1회에 한해
무료 출력할 수 있다. TOEIC 성적은 시험일로부터 2년간 유효하다.

● **토익 점수** TOEIC점수는 듣기 영역(LC)과 읽기 영역(RC)을 합계한 점수로 5점 단위로 구성되며
총점은 990점이다. TOEIC 성적은 각 문제 유형의 난이도에 따른 점수 환산표에 의해
결정된다.

LC 출제 경향 분석

● PART 1

문제 유형 및
출제 비율
(평균 문항 수)

사람을 주어로 하는 사람 묘사 문제가
가장 많은 비중을 차지하며 사람/사물 혼합
문제, 사물 묘사 문제가 각각 그 다음을
이룬다.

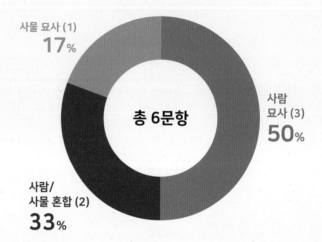

● PART 2

문제 유형 및
출제 비율
(평균 문항 수)

의문사 의문문이 거의 절반가량을 차지
하며 일반 의문문과 평서문이 그 다음을
이룬다. 부가/부정/선택 의문문은 평균
2문항씩 출제되며 간접 의문문은 간혹
1문제 출제된다.

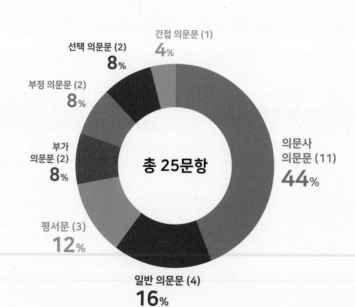

● PART 3
문제 유형 및
출제 비율
(평균 문항 수)

세부 사항을 묻는 문제가 가장 많은 비중을 차지하며 화자/장소 문제, 요청/제안/제공 문제, 다음에 할 일 문제, 주제/목적 문제가 그 다음을 차지한다. 문제점 및 걱정 거리 문제는 출제 빈도가 다소 낮다. 의도 파악 문제와 시각 정보 문제는 각각 2문항, 3문항 고정 비율로 출제된다.

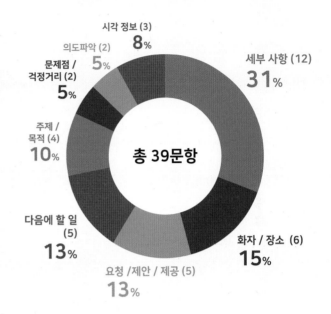

시각 정보 (3)
8%

의도파악 (2)
5%

문제점 /
걱정거리 (2)
5%

세부 사항 (12)
31%

주제 /
목적 (4)
10%

총 39문항

다음에 할 일 (5)
13%

화자 / 장소 (6)
15%

요청 /제안 / 제공 (5)
13%

● PART 4
지문 유형 및
출제 비율
(평균 지문 수)

전화 음성 메시지와 공지/안내/회의 발췌록이 가장 많이 출제된다. 광고/방송/보도가 그 다음을 차지하며 여행/견학/관람, 인물/강연/설명은 출제 빈도가 다소 낮다.

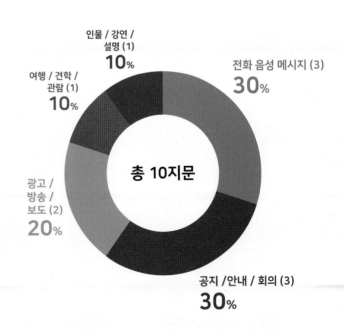

인물 / 강연 /
설명 (1)
10%

여행 / 견학 /
관람 (1)
10%

전화 음성 메시지 (3)
30%

광고 /
방송 /
보도 (2)
20%

총 10지문

공지 /안내 / 회의 (3)
30%

RC 출제 경향 분석

● PART 5

문법 문제 유형 및
출제 비율
(평균 문항 수)

전치사와 접속사를 구분하는 문제와 동사,
명사 등 품사 문제 출제 비중이 가장 높다.
기타 문법에서는 준동사가 1~2문항,
관계사가 매회 거의 1문항씩 출제된다.

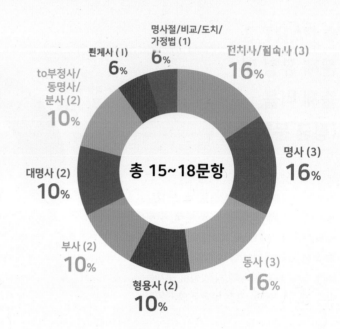

명사절/비교/도치/
가정법 (1)
6%

횐게시 (1)
6%

전치사/접속사 (3)
16%

to부정사/
동명사/
분사 (2)
10%

명사 (3)
16%

대명사 (2)
10%

총 15~18문항

부사 (2)
10%

동사 (3)
16%

형용사 (2)
10%

● PART 5

어휘 문제 유형 및
출제 비율
(평균 문항 수)

전치사, 명사, 부사 어휘 문제가 가장
많이 출제되며 형용사, 동사 어휘가 그
뒤를 잇는다.

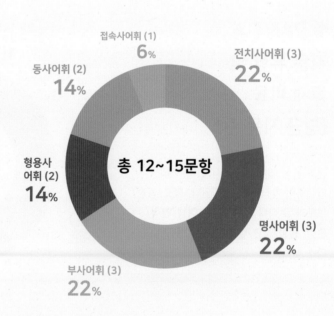

접속사어휘 (1)
6%

동사어휘 (2)
14%

전치사어휘 (3)
22%

형용사
어휘 (2)
14%

총 12~15문항

명사어휘 (3)
22%

부사어휘 (3)
22%

● PART 6

문제 유형 및
출제 비율
(평균 문항 수)

문법과 어휘 비중이 비슷하게 출제되며 접속부사가 1~2문항 출제된다. 문장 고르기 문제는 한 지문에 1문항씩 총 4문항이 고정 비율로 출제된다.

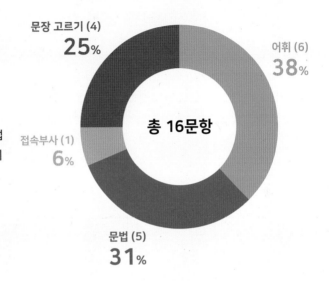

문장 고르기 (4)
25%

어휘 (6)
38%

접속부사 (1)
6%

총 16문항

문법 (5)
31%

● PART 7

문제 유형 및
출제 비율
(평균 문항 수)

세부 사항 문제가 가장 높은 비율을 차지하며 추론과 Not / True 문제가 그 다음으로 출제율이 높다. 문장 삽입 문제와 의도 파악 문제는 각각 2문항씩 고정 비율로 출제된다. 이중, 삼중 지문에서는 연계 문제가 8문항 정도 출제된다.

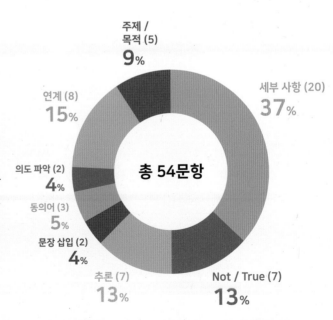

주제 /
목적 (5)
9%

연계 (8)
15%

세부 사항 (20)
37%

의도 파악 (2)
4%

동의어 (3)
5%

문장 삽입 (2)
4%

총 54문항

추론 (7)
13%

Not / True (7)
13%

1

● PART 1 풀이 전략

PART 1 이렇게 나온다

네 개의 보기를 듣고 그 중에서 사진을 가장 잘 묘사한 문장을 고르는 유형으로 총 6문제가 나온다. 주로 사람의 동작이나 인상착이, 사물의 위치나 장소, 배경 등을 묘사하는 문장이 나온다.

📖 시험지

1.

🔊 음원

1. Look at the picture marked number 1 in your test book.
   (A) She is entering a room.
   (B) She is moving a table.
   (C) She is holding a pen.
   (D) She is hanging a clock.

오답을 소거하자

음원을 듣기 전에 사람의 동작이나 상태, 사물의 위치 등을 눈여겨본 다음, 음원을 들으면서 오답들을 소거하면 정답을 쉽게 찾을 수 있다. 오답 유형은 크게 두 가지로 나뉜다.

❶ 사진과 다른 동작이나 상태 표현이 들리면 오답이다.

A man is ~~fixing~~ a car.   남자가 차를 수리하고 있다.
▸ **A man is washing a car.**   남자가 세차를 하고 있다.
He is ~~standing in front of~~ a car.   남자가 차량 앞에 서있다.
▸ **He is kneeling near a car.**   남자가 차량 근처에서 무릎을 꿇고 있다.

❷ 사진에 없는 단어가 들리면 오답이다.

The man is holding ~~some boxes~~.   남자가 상자들을 들고 있다.
▸ **The man is holding a basket.**   남자가 바구니를 들고 있다.
~~Crops~~ are placed on shelves.   농작물이 선반에 놓여 있다.
▸ **Items are placed on shelves.**   물건들이 선반에 놓여 있다.

동사의 형태에 주목하자

③ 현재 진행 시제 주로 사람의 동작을 묘사할 때 쓴다.

주어 + is/are + -ing	주어가 ~하고 있다

They **are playing** musical instruments. 사람들이 악기를 연주하고 있다.
They **are performing** outside. 사람들이 야외에서 공연을 하고 있다.

④ 현재 시제 현재의 상태를 나타낼 때 쓴다.

주어 + is/are + 형용사	주어가 ~한 상태이다
There is/are + 주어 + 전치사구	주어가 ~에 있다
주어 + is/are + 전치사구	주어가 ~에 있다

A chair **is** empty. 의자가 비어 있다.
There **is** a monitor on a desk. 책상 위에 모니터가 있다.
Some folders **are** on bookshelves. 책장에 서류철들이 있다.

⑤ 현재완료 시제 행동이나 움직임이 완료되었을 때 쓴다.

주어 + has/have p.p.	주어가 ~했다

A train **has arrived** at a station. 기차가 역에 도착했다.

⑥ 현재 수동태 / 현재완료 수동태 주로 사물의 위치나 상태를 묘사할 때 쓴다.

주어 + is/are + p.p.	주어가 ~되어 있다
주어 + has/have been p.p.	

Some flowers **are arranged** in a vase. 화병에 꽃꽂이가 되어 있다.
Cushions **have been set** on a couch. 쿠션들이 소파에 놓여 있다.

⑦ 현재진행 수동태 주어가 사물인 문장에서 사물에 행해지는 사람의 동작을 나타낼 때 쓴다.
따라서 사람이 없는 사진인데 'be being p.p.'가 들린다면 오답일 가능성이 높다.

주어 + is/are + being p.p.	주어가 ~되고 있다

A shopping cart **is being pushed**. (O) 쇼핑 카트가 밀리고 있다.
The floor **is being cleaned**. (X) 바닥이 청소되고 있다.
Some products **are being arranged**. (X) 제품들이 배치되고 있다.
주의 Some products **are being displayed**. (O) 제품들이 진열되어 있다.
be being displayed는 무언가를 전시하는 사람이 없더라도 진열된 상품을 묘사할 때 쓸 수 있는 표현이다.

전략 사람이 주어이므로 사람의 동작과 상태를 나타내는 다양한 동사 표현을 암기해 놓는 것이 중요하다. 동작을 나타내는 「be + -ing」 즉, 진행형 동사를 주의하여 듣고 오답을 소거하면서 푼다.

대표 동사 익히기

❶ 착용하고 있다 (상태)
wearing(O) *putting on(X)

❷ 보고 있다
looking / viewing / examining

❸ 기대어 있다 / 숙이고 있다
leaning / bending

❹ 짐을 싣고 / 내리고 있다
loading / unloading

❺ 연설하고 있다 / 모여 있다
addressing / gathered

❻ 손을 뻗고 있다
reaching (for)

❼ 끌고 있다
pushing / wheeling

❽ 걷고 있다
walking / strolling

❾ 붙잡고 있다
holding (onto) / grasping

❿ 오르고 있다
climbing / ascending

⓫ 작업 중이다 / 수리 중이다
working on / repairing

⓬ 치우고 있다 / 쓸고 있다
cleaning / sweeping

빈출 표현 익히기

사람을 묘사하는 사진에서는 사람의 동작을 나타내는 진행형 문장이 주로 정답이 된다.

picking up a box 상자를 들어올리고 있다
inspecting a vehicle 차량을 점검하고 있다
pouring a beverage 음료를 따르고 있다
handing out documents 문서를 나누어 주고 있다
boarding an airplane 비행기에 탑승하고 있다
carrying a briefcase 서류 가방을 들고 있다
facing each other 마주보고 있다
adjusting a device 장치를 조절하고 있다
resting arms on the desk 책상 위에 팔을 놓고 있다
browsing in a store 가게에서 둘러보고 있다
raking some leaves 낙엽을 긁어모으고 있다
mowing the lawn 잔디를 깎고 있다
wiping the window 창문을 닦고 있다

wrapping up a box 박스를 포장하고 있다
watering some plants 식물에 물을 주고 있다
studying a menu 메뉴판을 보고 있다
pointing at a screen 스크린을 가리키고 있다
sitting in rows 여러 줄로 앉아 있다
lifting some boxes 박스를 올리고 있다
distributing papers 종이를 나누어 주고 있다
operating a forklift 지게차를 운행 중이다
greeting each other 서로 인사하고 있다
waving to each other 서로에게 손을 흔들고 있다
applauding a speaker 연설자에게 박수를 치고 있다
assembling some shelves 선반을 조립하고 있다
polishing a countertop 조리대 상판을 닦고 있다

🎧 **P1_01** **Check Up**

문장을 듣고 빈칸에 들어갈 동사를 채워보자.   정답 및 해설 p.2

1.

A man is _____ some equipment.

2.

A man is _____ some documents.

3.

She is _____ some leaves.

4.

A woman is _____ a cart.

5.

They are _____ at a drawing.

6.

They are _____ some boxes into a vehicle.

LISTENING PRACTICE

사진을 묘사한 것으로 맞으면 O 틀리면 X로 표시해 보자.

1.

(A) O | X   (B) O | X   (C) O | X

2.

(A) O | X   (B) O | X   (C) O | X

3.

(A) O | X   (B) O | X   (C) O | X

4.

(A) O | X   (B) O | X   (C) O | X

5.

(A) O | X   (B) O | X   (C) O | X

6.

(A) O | X   (B) O | X   (C) O | X

---

wearing vs. putting on

착용한 상태를 나타낼 때는 wearing을 쓰고 착용 중인 동작을 나타낼 때는 putting on을 쓴다. 실제 시험에서는 착용 상태를 나타내는 wearing의 출제 빈도가 압도적으로 높으나 소매를 꿰고 있다든지 등의 동작을 하는 사진에서 putting on이 등장하기도 하므로 유의하자.

be seated / have gathered

사람 묘사 사진에서는 동작을 나타내는 진행형이 주로 정답이 되지만 다른 형태의 동사도 등장한다.

People **are seated** at a table.
사람들이 테이블에 앉아 있다.

A crowd **has gathered** near the entrance.
사람들이 입구 주변에 모여 있다.

정답 및 해설 p.3

1.

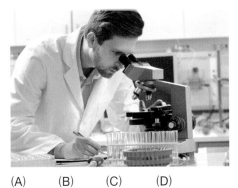

(A)   (B)   (C)   (D)

2.

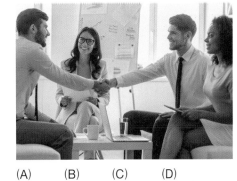

(A)   (B)   (C)   (D)

3.

(A)   (B)   (C)   (D)

4.

(A)   (B)   (C)   (D)

5.

(A)   (B)   (C)   (D)

6.

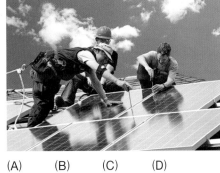

(A)   (B)   (C)   (D)

7.

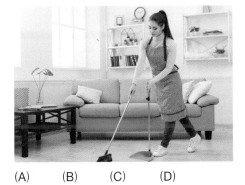

(A)   (B)   (C)   (D)

8.

(A)   (B)   (C)   (D)

사물 / 배경 / 혼합 사진

전략 사물의 상태를 나타내는 다양한 동사 표현을 암기해 놓는 것이 중요하다. 동사 형태를 주의하여 듣고 오답을 소거 하면서 푼다. 자주 등장하는 까다로운 사물 명칭은 암기하자.

대표 동사 익히기

① 놓여 있다
lying / sitting / resting

② 놓여 있다
placed / arranged / set

③ 줄지어 있다
lining / lined

④ 쌓여 있다
stacked / piled

⑤ (상품으로) 채워져 있다
stocked / filled

⑥ (배가) 정박해 있다
docked / tied / secured

⑦ (길이 / 계단이) 나 있다
leads / runs

⑧ 고정되어 있다
mounted / fastened

⑨ 받쳐져 있다, 기대어 있다
leaning / propped (against)

⑩ (다리가) 나 있다 / 뻗어 있다
extends / spans

⑪ 둘러싸고 있다
enclosing / surrounding

⑫ 접근하고 있다
approaching / pulling into

빈출 표현 익히기

사물 / 배경을 묘사할 때는 다양한 동사 형태로 표현이 가능하다.

being used 사용되고 있다
being operated 작동되고 있다
being worked on 작업이 되고 있다
being displayed 진열되어 있다
hanging on the wall 벽에 걸려 있다
suspended on the ceiling 천장에 매달려 있다
located in the corner 구석에 위치해 있다
casting a shadow 그림자를 드리우고 있다
growing in the garden 정원에서 자라고 있다
overlooking the river 강을 내려다보고 있다
standing in a row 일렬로 서 있다
erected near a building 건물 옆에 세워져 있다

left open 열린 채로 있다
spread out on a table 테이블에 펼쳐져 있다
floating in the water 물에 떠 있다
stopped at a traffic light 신호등에 멈춰 있다
surrounded by a fence 울타리로 둘러싸여 있다
hung on a wall 벽에 걸려 있다
positioned side by side 나란히 위치해 있다
attached to a pole 기둥에 부착되어 있다
covered with leaves 낙엽으로 덮여 있다
posted on the wall 벽에 게시되어 있다
reflected on the water 물에 반사되고 있다
scattered on the ground 바닥에 흩어져 있다

🎧 P1_04 **Check Up**

문장을 듣고 빈칸에 들어갈 단어를 채워보자.

정답 및 해설 p.5

1.

Some crops _____
_____ on a scale.

2.

Vehicles _____ near
the _____.

3.

Some electronic equipment
is _____.

4.

Tables _____
on an outdoor patio.

5.

A piece of furniture
_____.

6.

Some baked goods _____
_____ in a case.

사진을 묘사한 것으로 맞으면 O 틀리면 X로 표시해 보자.

1.

(A) O | X   (B) O | X   (C) O | X

2.

(A) O | X   (B) O | X   (C) O | X

3.

(A) O | X   (B) O | X   (C) O | X

4.

(A) O | X   (B) O | X   (C) O | X

5.

(A) O | X   (B) O | X   (C) O | X

6.

(A) O | X   (B) O | X   (C) O | X

사물 / 배경 / 혼합 사진 빈출 명사

curb 연석 (인도 경계석)	railing 난간	ramp 경사로	potted plant 화분
patio 테라스	forklift 지게차	staircase 계단	rack 거치대, 틀이, 선반
pier / dock 부두	counter 조리대	fence 울타리, 담장	lamppost / street light 가로등
fountain 분수대	podium 연단	cupboard 찬장	stool 등받이가 없는 의자
canopy 차양	statue 조각상	driveway 진입로	intersection 교차로
platform 승강장	artwork 예술 작품	runway 활주로	wheelbarrow 손수레

ACTUAL TEST 🎧 P1_06

정답 및 해설 p.7

1.

(A)　　　(B)　　　(C)　　　(D)

2.

(A)　　　(B)　　　(C)　　　(D)

3.

(A)　　　(B)　　　(C)　　　(D)

4.

(A)　　　(B)　　　(C)　　　(D)

5.

(A)　　　(B)　　　(C)　　　(D)

6.

(A)　　　(B)　　　(C)　　　(D)

7.

(A)　　　(B)　　　(C)　　　(D)

8.
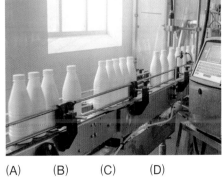
(A)　　　(B)　　　(C)　　　(D)

1.

2.

3.

4.

5.

6.

7.

8.

9.

10.

11.

12.

13.

14.

15.

16.

PART

2

● PART 2 풀이 전략

PART 2 이렇게 나온다

질문 1개와 보기 3개를 듣고 질문에 가장 적절한 답변을 고르는 유형으로, 총 25문제가 나온다.

📋 시험지

7. Mark your answer on your answer sheet.

🔊 음원

Where did you work before joining our firm?
(A) At a small company in Atlanta.
(B) I'd love to join you.
(C) As an executive assistant.

질문의 앞부분을 듣자

질문 전체를 정확히 듣는 것이 어렵다면 의문사, 주어, 동사 등 핵심 정보가 나오는 질문 앞부분이라도 최대한 듣고 질문의 요지를 기억한다. 정답으로는 직접적인 응답, 간접적인 응답 모두 가능하다.

Who was chosen to be keynote speaker at the seminar? 누가 선정되었나요?	❯ **The vice president.** 부사장님이오. ❯ **Let me check.** 알아볼게요.
Where did you put the draft of the magazine cover? 어디에 두셨어요?	❯ **It's in the cabinet.** 캐비닛 안에 있어요. ❯ **Ask Sarah.** 새라한테 물어보세요.
Would you measure the room before we order the furniture? 치수 좀 재주실래요?	❯ **Sure, I can handle that.** 그럼요, 제가 할 수 있어요. ❯ **Sorry, I have a meeting soon.** 죄송하지만 곧 미팅이 있어요.

오답을 소거하자

오답들을 소거하고 남은 하나가 정답이다. 다음 오답 유형들을 기억하자.

❶ 내용 오류

> **When** is your next business trip?
> 다음 출장은 언제 가세요?
>
> **With** my colleagues. (X) 제 동료들과 함께요.
> ❯ In two weeks. (O) 2주 뒤요.

❷ 의문사 질문에 Yes/No로 답변

> **How many** crates will be delivered?
> 나무 상자가 몇 개나 배달될까요?
>
> **No**, they are heavy.(X) 아뇨, 무거워요.
> ❯ At least fifteen. (O) 최소 15개요.

❸ 유사 발음이나 반복 어휘로 답변

> You cannot **enter** this area.
> 이 구역에 들어가실 수 없습니다.
>
> Near the **entrance**. (X) 입구 근처요.
> ❯ Sorry, I didn't know. (O) 죄송해요, 몰랐어요.

❹ 연상 어휘로 답변

> He's stuck in **traffic** at the moment.
> 그는 지금 교통체증에 묶여 있어요.
>
> The high **taxi** fare. (X) 비싼 택시 요금이요.
> ❯ How late will he be? (O) 얼마나 늦을 거래요?

만능답을 잡자

'모른다'라고 대답하면 정답이 된다.

> **Q. Who will manage the interns this year?**
> 올해는 누가 인턴 사원들을 관리하게 되나요?

모른다	I don't know.	I have no idea.	I'm not sure.
알아보겠다	I'll ask Tony.	Let me check.	Let me figure it out.
~에게 물어보라	Ask Chloe.	Check with Mr. Gupta.	
결정되지 않았다	I haven't decided.	It hasn't been decided yet.	
상황에 따라 다르다	It depends.		

Who / What / Which 의문문

출제 경향   who 의문문은 행위자, 업무 담당자를 묻는 질문이 많으며 what, which 의문문은 명사와 결합된 「what / which + 명사」 형태의 출제 빈도가 높다.

전략   who에 대한 답으로 자주 등장하는 직책명, 부서명을 익히자. what 질문에 명사구 단답형으로 답변하기, which 질문에 the one으로 답변하기와 같은 스킬을 적용할 수 있다. 의문사 의문문에는 Yes / No로 답변할 수 없음을 명심하자.

❶ Who

정답 패턴

Q. **Who** is in charge of arranging the conference?
회의 준비는 누가 담당하나요?

직접적으로 답하기
Mr. Ito in public relations. 홍보부 이토 씨요.
❷ 이름, 직책명, 부서명이 가장 대표적인 답변이다.

Q. **Who** can I speak to about a damaged wall?
파손된 벽에 대해 누구에게 말해야 하나요?

우회적으로 답하기
Here's the extension number. 내선번호를 드릴게요.
❷ 사람 대신 연락 방법이나 연락처를 줄 수 있다.

Q. **Who** is going to train the interns?
누가 인턴들을 교육시킬 건가요?

만능 답변
It hasn't been decided yet. 아직 결정되지 않았어요.
❷ '결정되지 않았다'는 어떤 질문에나 가능한 답변이다.

오답 패턴

Q. **Who** created this banner for our sales event?
누가 이 세일 행사용 배너를 만들었나요?

Yes / No 답변
Yes, William did. 네, 윌리엄이 했어요.
❷ 의문사 의문문에는 Yes, No로 답변할 수 없다.

Q. **Who** should I speak with to exchange a laptop?
노트북을 교환하려면 누구와 얘기해야 하나요?

유사 발음
I have change for 10 dollars. 잔돈이 10달러 있어요.
❷ exchange와 발음이 유사한 change를 이용했다.

Q. **Who** will take meeting minutes?
누가 회의록 기록을 누가 할 건가요?

내용 오류
Mr. Kyle found the key. 카일 씨가 열쇠를 찾았어요.
❷ 이름만 듣고 답하도록 유도하기도 한다.

직책 및 부서 관련 표현

assistant 보조, 비서	director/manager/supervisor 관리자	department head 부서장
human resources 인사부	accounting 회계부	payroll 경리부
maintenance 시설 관리부	personnel 인사부	publicity 홍보부
public relations 홍보부	administrative 총무부	customer service 고객서비스부
marketing 마케팅부	sales 영업부	the board of directors 이사회

질문을 듣고 적절한 응답을 고르자. 다시 듣기 하며 빈칸을 채우자.

1.
(A) (B) (C)

_____ _____ to change the work shift?
(A) Sarah, _____ _____.
(B) You'd _____ _____.
(C) Please _____ the _____ with me.

2.
(A) (B) (C)

_____ _____ _____ my loan application?
(A) I'll _____ _____ _____ later.
(B) _____ _____ be best.
(C) Let's _____ it together.

3.
(A) (B) (C)

_____ does this notebook _____ _____?
(A) A _____ must _____ _____ it there.
(B) The first and last _____.
(C) They _____ many books.

4.
(A) (B) (C)

_____ _____ the final guest list to the caterer?
(A) Ninety-eight people ____ _____.
(B) We're _____ _____ for a few responses.
(C) A _____ dinner would be best.

5.
(A) (B) (C)

_____ will _____ _____ of the broken light in the elevator?
(A) I'll _____ these boxes for you.
(B) Just _____ the street.
(C) _____ calling the maintenance _____.

6.
(A) (B) (C)

_____ _____ Mr. Carter _____ with at lunchtime?
(A) _____, it's _____ _____ in the morning.
(B) I'm sure they can _____ ___ _____.
(C) That was the _____ _____.

❷ What / Which

<table>
<tr><td>정답
패턴</td><td>

Q. **What** do we need to put on
before entering the laboratory?
실험실에 들어가기 전에 무엇을 착용해야 하나요?

</td><td>

직접적으로 답하기
Safety goggles and gloves. 안전 고글과 장갑이요.
❥ '무엇'에 해당하는 명사구만으로 짧게 답할 수 있다.

</td></tr>
<tr><td></td><td>

Q. **What** did you do during your
layover at the airport?
경유 시간 동안 공항에서 무엇을 했나요?

</td><td>

우회적으로 답하기
I had a direct flight. 직항을 탔어요.
❥ 해당사항이 없음을 돌려서 말할 수 있다.

</td></tr>
<tr><td></td><td>

Q. **Which** fitness center offers a
yoga class?
어떤 피트니스 센터가 요가 수업을 제공하나요?

</td><td>

만능 답변
The one on Main Street. 메인스트리트에 있는 거요.
❥ the one은 which 질문에 무조건 답이 된다.

</td></tr>
<tr><td>오답
패턴</td><td>

Q. **Which caterer** should we hire?
어떤 출장 요리 업체를 고용해야 할까요?

</td><td>

연상 어휘
They are my favorite <u>dishes</u>. 제가 좋아하는 요리예요.
❥ caterer를 듣고 연상 가능한 dishes를 이용했다.

</td></tr>
<tr><td></td><td>

Q. **What color** should we paint the
walls in the waiting room?
대기실 벽을 무슨 색으로 칠해야 할까요?

</td><td>

반복 어휘
About the <u>color</u> scheme. 색상 배합에 대해서요.
❥ 질문에 사용된 color를 그대로 사용했다.

</td></tr>
<tr><td></td><td>

Q. **What time** does the post office
open?
몇 시에 우체국이 문을 여나요?

</td><td>

내용 오류
Three or four <u>days</u>. 사흘이나 나흘이요.
❥ 시점 질문에 기간으로 답했다.

</td></tr>
</table>

What / Which 질문 형태

<table>
<tr><td>what 동사 + 주어</td><td>**What was the meeting** about?
회의는 무엇에 관한 것이었나요?</td><td>The new safety policy.
새로운 안전 정책이요.</td></tr>
<tr><td></td><td>**What should I bring** to the orientation session?
오리엔테이션에는 무엇을 가져가야 하나요?</td><td>Proof of employment.
사원증이요.</td></tr>
<tr><td>which of 명사 + 동사</td><td>**Which of these buses goes** to City Hall?
이 중에서 어떤 버스가 시청으로 가나요?</td><td>The green one stops there.
녹색 버스가 그쪽에 정차해요.</td></tr>
<tr><td></td><td>**Which of you attended** the workshop?
여러분 중에 누가 워크샵에 참여했나요?</td><td>All of us.
우리 모두요.</td></tr>
<tr><td>what / which + 명사</td><td>**What time** will the ferry leave?
몇 시에 배가 출항하나요?</td><td>At 4:45 P.M.
4시 45분이에요.</td></tr>
<tr><td></td><td>**Which airline** did you use?
어떤 항공사를 이용하셨나요?</td><td>The one I used last time.
지난번에 이용했던 항공사요.</td></tr>
</table>

질문을 듣고 적절한 응답을 고르자. 다시 듣기 하며 빈칸을 채우자.

1.

(A) (B) (C)

_____ _____ will the bank manager ____ _____ from lunch?

(A) At the _____ party.

(B) Yes, I have a _____ _____.

(C) ____ _____ twenty minutes.

2.

(A) (B) (C)

_____ _____ is Gary _____?

(A) A well-known _____.

(B) _____ _____ about time management.

(C) _____ ____ Central Shopping Plaza.

3.

(A) (B) (C)

_____ _____ in the box _____ today?

(A) Some _____ I ordered.

(B) To the _____.

(C) Let's _____ it tight.

4.

(A) (B) (C)

_____ _____ Mr. Phillips _____ _____ your report?

(A) I haven't _____ it yet.

(B) No, I don't _____ _____.

(C) You can _____ _____ to Mr. Ken.

5.

(A) (B) (C)

_____ company _____ ____ use for the hotel lobby's renovations?

(A) Yes, it looks _____ _____.

(B) It was _____ Ace Designs, I think.

(C) We _____ there _____ one week.

6.

(A) (B) (C)

_____ Chinese restaurant _____ the best _____ _____?

(A) Yes, there was a long _____.

(B) That building offers good _____.

(C) _____ _____ ____ Main Street.

1.	Mark your answer.	(A)	(B)	(C)
2.	Mark your answer.	(A)	(B)	(C)
3.	Mark your answer.	(A)	(B)	(C)
4.	Mark your answer.	(A)	(B)	(C)
5.	Mark your answer.	(A)	(B)	(C)
6.	Mark your answer.	(A)	(B)	(C)
7.	Mark your answer.	(A)	(B)	(C)
8.	Mark your answer.	(A)	(B)	(C)
9.	Mark your answer.	(A)	(B)	(C)
10.	Mark your answer.	(A)	(B)	(C)
11.	Mark your answer.	(A)	(B)	(C)
12.	Mark your answer.	(A)	(B)	(C)

13. Mark your answer.   (A)   (B)   (C)

14. Mark your answer.   (A)   (B)   (C)

15. Mark your answer.   (A)   (B)   (C)

16. Mark your answer.   (A)   (B)   (C)

17. Mark your answer.   (A)   (B)   (C)

18. Mark your answer.   (A)   (B)   (C)

19. Mark your answer.   (A)   (B)   (C)

20. Mark your answer.   (A)   (B)   (C)

21. Mark your answer.   (A)   (B)   (C)

22. Mark your answer.   (A)   (B)   (C)

23. Mark your answer.   (A)   (B)   (C)

24. Mark your answer.   (A)   (B)   (C)

25. Mark your answer.   (A)   (B)   (C)

출제 경향 when / where 발음 구분의 모호성을 이용한 문제가 출제되기도 한다.

전략 다양한 시간 표현과 장소 전치사를 익히자. 훈련을 통해 when과 where 발음을 정확하게 구분하자.

❶ When

Q. When is the quarterly budget proposal due?
분기 예산안은 언제까지 내야 하나요?

직접적으로 답하기
By next week. 다음 주 까지요.
❯ 시간 전치사와 특정 시간으로 답변할 수 있다.

Q. When are you going to work on the new layout?
새로운 배치도는 언제 작업하실 건가요?

우회적으로 답하기
I asked Ms. Han to do the job. 한 씨에게 넘겼어요.
❯ 답변할 수 있는 담당자가 아님을 돌려서 말할 수 있다.

Q. When did Ms. Wagner start working on the translation?
와그너 씨가 언제 번역 작업을 시작하셨나요?

만능 답변
Let me check her work log. 그녀의 업무 일지를 볼게요.
❯ '확인해 보겠다'는 어떤 질문에나 가능한 답변이다.

Q. When did they announce the merger plan?
언제 합병 계획을 발표했나요?

Yes / No 답변
Yes, I heard it, too. 네, 저도 들었습니다.
❯ 의문사 의문문에는 Yes, No로 답변할 수 없다.

Q. When are you going on vacation?
언제 휴가 가세요?

내용 오류
For two hours. 2시간 동안요.
❯ 시점 질문에 기간으로 답했다.

Q. When is our training scheduled to begin?
언제 교육이 시작될 예정인가요?

Sure로 답변
Sure, I will definitely attend. 물론이죠, 당연히 참석해요.
❯ Sure는 Yes로 답변한 것과 같은 오류이다.

시간 관련 표현

In about an hour. = In an hour or so. 한 시간쯤 후에요.
Not for another month or so. 앞으로 한 달은 더 있어야 해요.
By Monday at the latest. 늦어도 월요일까지요.
Anytime after lunch. 점심 이후 언제든지요.
Shortly after the meeting. 미팅 직후에요.
After the manager approves. 담당자가 승인한 후에요.
The sooner, the better. 빠를수록 좋아요.

In the next couple of days. 며칠 후에요.
Not until next week. 다음 주에요.
By the end of this week. 이번 주 내로요.
Sometime next week. 다음 주 중으로요.
At the next meeting. 다음 회의 때요.
As soon as possible. 가능한 한 빨리요.
Later this month. 이달 중으로요.

질문을 듣고 적절한 응답을 고르자. 다시 듣기 하며 빈칸을 채우자.

1.
(A) (B) (C)

_____ are you _____ _____ vacation?
(A) A _____ in Mexico.
(B) In the _____ of November.
(C) _____ two weeks.

2.
(A) (B) (C)

_____ is the registration _____ for the conference?
(A) _____ the organizer's Web site.
(B) Yes, it was very _____.
(C) Some newspaper _____.

3.
(A) (B) (C)

_____ _____ Robert _____ for Toronto?
(A) _____ his personal assistant.
(B) No, I've decided _____ ____ ____.
(C) I hope he has an _____ _____.

4.
(A) (B) (C)

_____ can I _____ the shuttle bus to the convention center?
(A) It's _____ _____.
(B) _____ the front of the hotel.
(C) It _____ every 20 minutes.

5.
(A) (B) (C)

_____ _____ _____ have the carpets cleaned in the lobby?
(A) _____ the check-in desk.
(B) The _____, the _____.
(C) Some cleaning _____.

6.
(A) (B) (C)

_____ _____ _____ _____ go see a dentist?
(A) No, I'm not _____ _____.
(B) _____ this month.
(C) As _____ ____ you could.

❷ Where

정답패턴

Q. **Where** is the job fair being held?
취업 박람회가 어디서 열리나요?

직접적으로 답하기

In the main auditorium. 주강당에서요.

◉ 장소 전치사구가 가장 대표적인 답변이다.

Q. **Where** do we keep the extra ink cartridges?
잉크 카트리지 여분을 어디에 두나요?

우회적으로 답하기

I think we used them up. 다 쓴 거 같아요.

◉ 해당 사항이 없음을 돌려서 말할 수 있다.

Q. **Where** is the publicity department located?
홍보부가 어디에 있나요?

만능 답변

Ask the receptionist. 안내 데스크 직원에게 문의하세요.

◉ '문의해 보세요'는 어떤 질문에나 가능한 답변이다.

오답패턴

Q. **Where** should we put the new supply closet?
새 사무용품 보관장을 어디에 두어야 할까요?

반복 어휘

We are in short supply. 공급이 부족합니다.

◉ 질문에 사용된 supply를 그대로 사용했다.

Q. **Where** is the nearest post office?
가장 가까운 우체국이 어디예요?

내용 오류 I

From the hardware store. 철물점에서요.

◉ 장소로 답해야 하는 질문에 출처로 답한 오류이다.

Q. **Where** will the annual conference take place this year?
연례 컨퍼런스가 올해는 어디에서 열리나요?

내용 오류 II

In the bottom drawer. 맨 아래 서랍에요.

◉ 질문 내용에 맞지 않는 장소이다.

Where 질문의 답으로 자주 쓰이는 전치사구

Where should we meet for lunch? 점심 식사하러 어디서 만날까요?	위치	**Outside** the office building. 사무실 건물 밖에서요.
Where did you get the document? 문서를 어디서 얻었나요?	출처	**From** Ms. Williams. 윌리엄스 씨로부터요.
Where can I find Mr. Peterson's office? 피터슨 씨의 사무실이 어디인가요?	방향	**Down** the hall and turn right. 복도를 따라가서 오른쪽으로 가세요.
Where is the closest pharmacy? 가장 가까운 약국이 어디인가요?	거리	Two blocks **away**. 두 블록 지나서요.
Where will you be going for your vacation? 휴가 때 어디로 가세요?	목적지	**To** my friend's house in Bangkok. 방콕에 있는 친구집이에요.
Where can I get the free samples? 무료 샘플을 어디서 구할 수 있을까요?	방법	**Simply register** for a membership. 멤버십에 가입만 하시면 돼요.

LISTENING PRACTICE 🎧 P2_05

질문을 듣고 적절한 응답을 고르자. 다시 듣기 하며 빈칸을 채우자.

1.
(A) (B) (C)

Where _____ I _____ these brochures for the trade show?
(A) Yes, they probably _____.
(B) Is that cash or _____?
(C) ____ the small _____ room.

2.
(A) (B) (C)

_____ ____ Dr. Peterson _____ his lecture?
(A) He's _____ ____ in room 103.
(B) Yes, I _____ that.
(C) _____ ____ seven o'clock.

3.
(A) (B) (C)

_____ _____ the tenant say there was a water _____?
(A) About twenty minutes _____.
(B) Yes, I've just _____ the _____.
(C) ____ the bathroom _____.

4.
(A) (B) (C)

_____ ____ ___ _____ the packing supplies?
(A) _____ ____ Tim in the mailroom.
(B) At least _____ _____ ____ _____.
(C) It's the older _____ design.

5.
(A) (B) (C)

_____ _____ the company retreat be taking place?
(A) ____ the Marina _____.
(B) It _____ _____ England, I guess.
(C) You should _____ it with extra care.

6.
(A) (B) (C)

_____ _____ ____ have my digital camera _____?
(A) Michael _____ _____.
(B) That's the _____ _____.
(C) The _____ quality is great.

1.	Mark your answer.	(A)	(B)	(C)
2.	Mark your answer.	(A)	(B)	(C)
3.	Mark your answer.	(A)	(B)	(C)
4.	Mark your answer.	(A)	(B)	(C)
5.	Mark your answer.	(A)	(B)	(C)
6.	Mark your answer.	(A)	(B)	(C)
7.	Mark your answer.	(A)	(B)	(C)
8.	Mark your answer.	(A)	(B)	(C)
9.	Mark your answer.	(A)	(B)	(C)
10.	Mark your answer.	(A)	(B)	(C)
11.	Mark your answer.	(A)	(B)	(C)
12.	Mark your answer.	(A)	(B)	(C)

13.	Mark your answer.	(A)	(B)	(C)
14.	Mark your answer.	(A)	(B)	(C)
15.	Mark your answer.	(A)	(B)	(C)
16.	Mark your answer.	(A)	(B)	(C)
17.	Mark your answer.	(A)	(B)	(C)
18.	Mark your answer.	(A)	(B)	(C)
19.	Mark your answer.	(A)	(B)	(C)
20.	Mark your answer.	(A)	(B)	(C)
21.	Mark your answer.	(A)	(B)	(C)
22.	Mark your answer.	(A)	(B)	(C)
23.	Mark your answer.	(A)	(B)	(C)
24.	Mark your answer.	(A)	(B)	(C)
25.	Mark your answer.	(A)	(B)	(C)

How / Why 의문문

출제 경향 의문사 의문문 중 질문의 형태가 가장 다양하다.

전략 다양한 질문 형태와 관용 표현을 암기하며 듣자마자 해석이 되도록 훈련하자.

❶ How

정답 패턴

Q. **How** do I get to the airport?
공항까지 어떻게 가야 하나요?

직접적으로 답하기
Take a shuttle bus. 셔틀버스를 타세요.
❷ 수단, 방법의 전치사구 또는 명령문으로 답할 수 있다.

Q. **How** did you like the new restaurant?
새로 생긴 식당 어땠어요?

우회적으로 답하기
I wouldn't recommend it. 추천하고 싶지는 않네요.
❷ 의견을 간접적으로 돌려서 말할 수 있다.

Q. **How often** should I change the filter?
필터를 얼마나 자주 교체해야 할까요?

만능 답변
It depends on the usage. 사용량에 따라 달라요.
❷ '상황에 따라 다르다'는 어떤 질문에나 가능한 답변이다.

오답 패턴

Q. **How** did the meeting with the clients **go**?
고객과의 미팅이 어떻게 진행되었나요?

내용 오류 Ⅰ
We took the subway. 지하철을 탔어요.
❷ 의견을 묻는 질문에 방법으로 답한 오류이다.

Q. **How long** will the musical performance last?
뮤지컬 공연 시간이 얼마나 될까요?

내용 오류 Ⅱ
It's about 10 kilometers. 약 10킬로미터요.
❷ 기간을 묻는 질문에 길이로 답한 오류이다.

Q. **How would you like** your steak?
스테이크를 어떻게 해드릴까요?

내용 오류 Ⅲ
It was great. 훌륭했어요.
❷ 선택을 요구하는 질문에 의견으로 답한 오류이다.

다양한 How 의문문

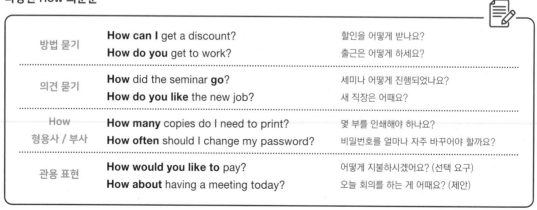

방법 묻기	**How can I** get a discount?	할인을 어떻게 받나요?
	How do you get to work?	출근은 어떻게 하세요?
의견 묻기	**How** did the seminar **go**?	세미나 어떻게 진행되었나요?
	How do you like the new job?	새 직장은 어때요?
How 형용사 / 부사	**How many** copies do I need to print?	몇 부를 인쇄해야 하나요?
	How often should I change my password?	비밀번호를 얼마나 자주 바꾸어야 할까요?
관용 표현	**How would you like to** pay?	어떻게 지불하시겠어요? (선택 요구)
	How about having a meeting today?	오늘 회의를 하는 게 어때요? (제안)

정답 및 해설 p.25

질문을 듣고 적절한 응답을 고르자. 다시 듣기 하며 빈칸을 채우자.

1.
(A) (B) (C)

_____ ____ I _____ ____ this printer?
(A) You can _____ it here.
(B) I need an _____ _____.
(C) _____ the red button.

2.
(A) (B) (C)

_____ _____ investors _____ yesterday's meeting?
(A) Of course, I'll ____ _____.
(B) _____ _____ of them.
(C) _____, it was very _____.

3.
(A) (B) (C)

_____ ____ _____ _____ your new home?
(A) I haven't _____ ____ yet.
(B) From a _____ colleague.
(C) Because of the _____ traffic.

4.
(A) (B) (C)

_____ _____ you _____ about our new campaign?
(A) It was better than _____.
(B) That's _____ ____ _____ it.
(C) I read about it in the company _____.

5.
(A) (B) (C)

_____ the customer service at Milton Apparel?
(A) Sorry, I was _____ _____ ____.
(B) That's _____ everyone thinks.
(C) The representatives were really _____.

6.
(A) (B) (C)

_____ _____ is your special sale _____ ____?
(A) At least 40 _____ _____.
(B) Today is the _____ _____.
(C) ____ _____ a coupon.

❷ Why

정답 패턴

Q. **Why** was the client meeting canceled?
왜 고객 미팅이 취소되었나요?

Because로 이유 답하기
(Because) Ms. Sato can't come. 사토 씨가 못 오신대요.
❯ Because를 생략하는 경우도 많다.

Q. **Why** are you going back to the conference room?
왜 회의실에 다시 가세요?

To 부정사로 목적 답하기
To look for my briefcase. 서류 가방을 찾으려고요.
❯ '하기 위해서'로 답할 수 있다.

Q. **Why don't you** join us for dinner?
저희와 같이 저녁 식사 같이 하시지 않을래요?

제안문에 답하기
Sorry, I have other plans. 죄송한데 다른 계획이 있어요.
❯ 제안을 승낙 또는 거절할 수 있다.

오답 패턴

Q. **Why** is Oxford Road closed today?
옥스포드 도로가 오늘 왜 폐쇄됐나요?

명사구 단답형
Alternative routes. 다른 경로들이요.
❯ 명사구 답단형은 what 질문에 가능한 답변이다.

Q. **Why** haven't you submitted the sales report?
왜 판매 보고서를 제출하지 않으셨나요?

내용 오류 I
For the board meeting. 이사회 미팅을 위해서요.
❯ 해명이 필요한 질문에 목적으로 답한 오류이다.

Q. **Why didn't you** join the meeting?
왜 어제 회의에 참석하지 않았나요?

내용 오류 II
That would be great. 그거 좋겠네요.
❯ Why don't you 제안문과 구분하지 못한 오류이다.

Why 의문문 구분하기

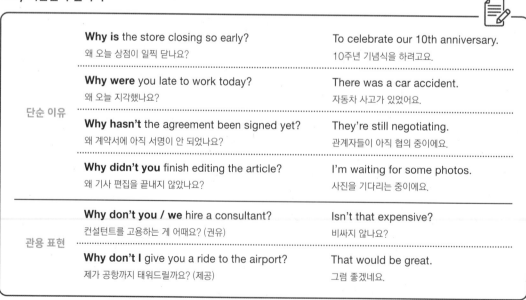

단순 이유	**Why is** the store closing so early? 왜 오늘 상점이 일찍 닫나요?	To celebrate our 10th anniversary. 10주년 기념식을 하려고요.
	Why were you late to work today? 왜 오늘 지각했나요?	There was a car accident. 자동차 사고가 있었어요.
	Why hasn't the agreement been signed yet? 왜 계약서에 아직 서명이 안 되었나요?	They're still negotiating. 관계자들이 아직 협의 중이에요.
	Why didn't you finish editing the article? 왜 기사 편집을 끝내지 않았나요?	I'm waiting for some photos. 사진을 기다리는 중이에요.
관용 표현	**Why don't you / we** hire a consultant? 컨설턴트를 고용하는 게 어때요? (권유)	Isn't that expensive? 비싸지 않나요?
	Why don't I give you a ride to the airport? 제가 공항까지 태워드릴까요? (제공)	That would be great. 그럼 좋겠네요.

질문을 듣고 적절한 응답을 고르자. 다시 듣기 하며 빈칸을 채우자.

1.
(A) (B) (C)

_____ _____ Steve _____ to _____ the conference room?
(A) He has a _____ to give.
(B) No, I won't be able to _____ ____.
(C) Which _____ is it ____?

2.
(A) (B) (C)

_____ _____ _____ have a chat about this month's sales?
(A) OK, let's ____ _____.
(B) _____ the room wasn't _____.
(C) _____ all new staff members.

3.
(A) (B) (C)

_____ _____ the new desks _____ yet?
(A) _____ ____ _____.
(B) _____ _____ a shipping _____.
(C) _____ office renovation.

4.
(A) (B) (C)

_____ _____ _____ so many extra chairs in the break room?
(A) It _____ _____ too often.
(B) The summer _____ start today.
(C) He's the _____.

5.
(A) (B) (C)

_____ _____ our team _____ its production goals?
(A) Yes, I _____ the _____.
(B) _____ _____ some machinery problems.
(C) The price _____.

6.
(A) (B) (C)

_____ _____ _____ _____ our ceremony at the Orlando hotel?
(A) From the _____ ____ _____.
(B) Lunch was _____, thanks.
(C) It's _____ _____, right?

1. Mark your answer.   (A)   (B)   (C)

2. Mark your answer.   (A)   (B)   (C)

3. Mark your answer.   (A)   (B)   (C)

4. Mark your answer.   (A)   (B)   (C)

5. Mark your answer.   (A)   (B)   (C)

6. Mark your answer.   (A)   (B)   (C)

7. Mark your answer.   (A)   (B)   (C)

8. Mark your answer.   (A)   (B)   (C)

9. Mark your answer.   (A)   (B)   (C)

10. Mark your answer.   (A)   (B)   (C)

11. Mark your answer.   (A)   (B)   (C)

12. Mark your answer.   (A)   (B)   (C)

13.	Mark your answer.	(A)	(B)	(C)
14.	Mark your answer.	(A)	(B)	(C)
15.	Mark your answer.	(A)	(B)	(C)
16.	Mark your answer.	(A)	(B)	(C)
17.	Mark your answer.	(A)	(B)	(C)
18.	Mark your answer.	(A)	(B)	(C)
19.	Mark your answer.	(A)	(B)	(C)
20.	Mark your answer.	(A)	(B)	(C)
21.	Mark your answer.	(A)	(B)	(C)
22.	Mark your answer.	(A)	(B)	(C)
23.	Mark your answer.	(A)	(B)	(C)
24.	Mark your answer.	(A)	(B)	(C)
25.	Mark your answer.	(A)	(B)	(C)

일반 의문문

출제 경향 조동사 의문문의 출제 빈도가 높다. Yes / No 답변이 가능하나 생략하거나 우회적인 답변을 준다.

전략 오답 패턴을 숙지하여 오답을 소거함으로써 정답을 찾는 풀이법을 적용하자.

---

❶ Be동사 의문문

Q. Are these decorations for sale?
이 장식품들은 판매용인가요?

Yes / No로 답하기
Yes, price tags are attached. 네, 가격표가 붙어 있어요.
❷ 가장 대표적인 답은 Yes, No이다.

Q. Is there a vacant room available?
빈 방이 있나요?

Yes / No 생략하기
(No) We're fully booked. (아니요) 예약이 다 찼어요.
❷ Yes, No를 생략하고 답변할 수 있다.

Q. Is office room 201 big enough for our meeting?
201호 사무실이 우리 회의하기에 충분히 큰가요?

우회적으로 답하기
Only a few will participate. 몇 명만 참석할 거예요.
❷ 직접적이지 않은 답변도 가능하다.

Q. Are you scheduled to arrive this afternoon?
오늘 오후에 도착할 예정인가요?

대명사 오류
Yes, he is. 네, 그는 그래요.
❷ Is he로 질문했을 때의 답변이다.

Q. Is the inspector coming to our office today?
조사관이 오늘 우리 사무실에 오나요?

동사 오류
Yes, he has. 네, 그는 그랬어요.
❷ Has he로 질문했을 때의 답변이다.

Q. Is our manager serious about quitting his job?
매니저가 정말 일을 그만 두시는 건가요?

연상 어휘
A new position as director. 부장으로서 새 직책이요.
❷ job을 듣고 연상 가능한 position을 이용했다.

Yes / No 답변을 대신하는 표현

Is Mr. Bernard going to retire next month? 버나드 씨가 다음 달에 은퇴하시나요?	**Yes 대신**	That's what I heard. 제가 들은 바로는 그렇습니다.
Is the copy machine broken again? 복사기가 또 고장인가요?		I think so. 제 생각에는 그렇습니다.
Are we getting additional funding from the city? 저희가 시로부터 추가 자금 지원을 받나요?	**No 대신**	Not that I know of. 제가 알기로는 아닙니다.
Are you going to finish the report by noon? 보고서를 정오까지 끝낼 건가요?		I'm afraid not. 유감이지만 아닙니다.

질문을 듣고 적절한 응답을 고르자. 다시 듣기 하며 빈칸을 채우자.

1.
(A) (B) (C)

_____ _____ _____ to _____ now?
(A) _____ ____ just a few minutes.
(B) _____ the window, ____ _____.
(C) I'll _____ _____ to you now.

2.
(A) (B) (C)

_____ your office desk _____ _____ to put a printer on?
(A) Yes, two _____.
(B) I don't _____ ____.
(C) Let me have 5 _____ of it.

3.
(A) (B) (C)

_____ _____ _____ ____ download the files you need?
(A) Yes, it was _____ _____ _____.
(B) You can _____ photos on the Web page.
(C) ____ duplicate, please.

4.
(A) (B) (C)

____ your _____ to the research database _____?
(A) To get a parking _____.
(B) Yes, I have _____ now.
(C) A research on product _____.

5.
(A) (B) (C)

____ _____ a battery charger I can borrow?
(A) ____ the library.
(B) We've tried everything.
(C) There's a _____ one in my bag.

6.
(A) (B) (C)

Are you _____ ____ the downtown music festival this weekend?
(A) In the financial _____.
(B) For another week ____ ____.
(C) I don't like big _____.

② 조동사 의문문

정답 패턴	**Q. Have you decided** on the place for the upcoming seminar? 다가오는 세미나를 위한 장소를 결정하셨나요?	**직접적으로 답하기** Yes, I can send you the map. 네, 약도를 드릴게요. ❺ 가장 대표적인 답변은 Yes, No이다.
	Q. Do you want me to help you with carrying those boxes? 상자들을 옮기는 것을 도와드릴까요?	**우회적으로 답하기** (No) These are fairly light. (아니요) 꽤 가벼워요. ❺ Yes, No를 생략하면 우회적인 답변이 될 수 있다.
	Q. Should I take the bus to the museum? 박물관까지 버스를 타야 하나요?	**회피성 답변** I'm new to this area, too. 저도 이곳이 처음이에요. ❺ '모른다'를 다양하게 돌려서 말할 수 있다.
오답 패턴	**Q. Has Mr. Peterson offered** you any feedback on your report? 피터슨 씨가 보고서에 대해 피드백을 주던가요?	**내용 오류** He won't be available then. 그는 그때 없을 거예요. ❺ 질문에 시점이 없으므로 then이라고 할 수 없다.
	Q. Do you like the new layout of our Web site? 새로운 웹사이트 레이아웃이 마음에 드세요?	**동사 오류** No, I haven't. 아니요, 저는 안 했어요. ❺ Have you로 질문했을 때의 답변이다.
	Q. Will you attend the awards <u>ceremony</u>? 시상식에 참석하실 건가요?	**반복 어휘** The opening <u>ceremony</u> begins at 9. ❺ 질문에 사용된 ceremony를 그대로 사용했다.

조동사로 시작하는 간접 의문문

Do you know 혹은 Can you tell me 뒤에 의문사 의문문이 오거나 일반 의문문이 올 수 있다.

• 의문사 의문문이 오는 경우 직접 의문문이 **의문사 + 주어 + 동사** 어순으로 바뀐다.
• 일반 의문문이 오는 경우 직접 의문문이 **if**[whether] **+ 주어 + 동사** 어순으로 바뀐다.

Do you know / **Can you tell me**	+ 직접 의문문	의문사 의문문 <u>Where is</u> the nearest bus stop? 일반 의문문 <u>Does</u> Mr. Brown <u>visit</u> us today?
	= 간접 의문문	**Do you know** <u>where</u> the nearest bus stop <u>is</u>? 가장 가까운 버스 정류장이 어디인지 아세요? **Can you tell me** if Mr. Brown <u>visits</u> us today? 브라운 씨가 오늘 저희를 방문하는지 알려주실 수 있어요?

※ 간접 의문문은 Yes / No로 답변할 수 있다.

ex Q. Do you know when the meeting will start? 미팅이 언제 시작하는지 아세요?
   A. Yes, as soon as everyone arrives. 네, 모두가 도착하면요.

LISTENING PRACTICE 🎧 P2_11

정답 및 해설 p.34

질문을 듣고 적절한 응답을 고르자. 다시 듣기 하며 빈칸을 채우자.

1.
(A) (B) (C)

_____ _____ _____ your passport?
(A) Thanks, I was looking _____ ____ it.
(B) I need to _____ my photo _____.
(C) Spain is nice _____ _____ ____ _____.

2.
(A) (B) (C)

_____ this video streaming service _____ a cancellation fee?
(A) I _____ _____ it.
(B) Let's _____ ____ now.
(C) Delivery is _____ ____ _____.

3.
(A) (B) (C)

Does Ms. Tina _____ that the workshop _____ has _____?
(A) In the _____.
(B) She was not _____ yet.
(C) Let's _____ it to April 7th.

4.
(A) (B) (C)

Should I _____ _____ _____ of the handouts?
(A) Yes, please.
(B) I have some _____ tickets.
(C) The book is _____ ____ _____.

5.
(A) (B) (C)

_____ this month's company newsletter been distributed?
(A) Once a month.
(B) No, not yet.
(C) I can _____ you _____ the _____.

6.
(A) (B) (C)

Do you _____ _____ _____ the basketball tickets cost?
(A) Six _____, please.
(B) No, I'm not _____ ____ a fan.
(C) Yes, at the _____ _____.

ACTUAL TEST 🎧 P2_12

정답 및 해설 p.35

1. Mark your answer. (A) (B) (C)

2. Mark your answer. (A) (B) (C)

3. Mark your answer. (A) (B) (C)

4. Mark your answer. (A) (B) (C)

5. Mark your answer. (A) (B) (C)

6. Mark your answer. (A) (B) (C)

7. Mark your answer. (A) (B) (C)

8. Mark your answer. (A) (B) (C)

9. Mark your answer. (A) (B) (C)

10. Mark your answer. (A) (B) (C)

11. Mark your answer. (A) (B) (C)

12. Mark your answer. (A) (B) (C)

13.	Mark your answer.	(A)	(B)	(C)
14.	Mark your answer.	(A)	(B)	(C)
15.	Mark your answer.	(A)	(B)	(C)
16.	Mark your answer.	(A)	(B)	(C)
17.	Mark your answer.	(A)	(B)	(C)
18.	Mark your answer.	(A)	(B)	(C)
19.	Mark your answer.	(A)	(B)	(C)
20.	Mark your answer.	(A)	(B)	(C)
21.	Mark your answer.	(A)	(B)	(C)
22.	Mark your answer.	(A)	(B)	(C)
23.	Mark your answer.	(A)	(B)	(C)
24.	Mark your answer.	(A)	(B)	(C)
25.	Mark your answer.	(A)	(B)	(C)

평서문 / 제안 및 요청문

25문항 중 평균 4~6문제 출제

출제 경향   평서문은 예측이 힘든 고난이도 유형에 속하는 반면, 제안 및 요청문은 전형적인 답변이 주를 이룬다.

전략   평서문은 오답 소거법을 이용하여, 제안 및 요청문은 승낙 또는 거절의 표현을 익혀 문제 풀이에 적용하자.

---

❶ 평서문

정답 패턴

Q. **Our supplier didn't meet** the delivery date again.	수락 / 동의 / 해결책 제시하기
공급 업체가 또 배송일을 어겼어요.	Let's file a complaint. 불만을 제기합시다. ▶ 문제점에 대한 해결책 제시는 가장 흔한 답변 패턴이다.

Q. **Everyone should attend** the safety training this Friday.	불응 / 반대 / 다른 의견 제시하기
금요일에 전직원이 안전 교육에 참석해야 해요.	I have a meeting then. 저는 그때 미팅이 있어요. ▶ 기타 의견으로 답변할 수 있다.

Q. **Mr. Lucas has been promoted** to branch manager.	되묻기
루카스 씨가 지점장으로 승진했어요.	Should we hold a party? 파티를 열어야 할까요? ▶ 주제와 관련해서 되묻는 답변 패턴도 종종 등장한다.

오답 패턴

Q. **I can switch shifts with you** if you'd like.	반복 어휘
원하시면 근무 교대를 바꿔줄 수 있어요.	Yes, I'd like some. 네, 조금 주세요. ▶ 질문에 사용된 **you'd like**를 사용했다.

Q. **There's a discount** on all the new arrivals this week.	유사 발음
모든 신상품에 대해 이번 주에 할인이 있습니다.	They are our rivals. 그들은 우리의 경쟁사예요. ▶ **arrivals**와 발음이 유사한 **rivals**를 이용했다.

Q. **Our year-end sale is only a week away**.	내용 오류
연말 세일이 일주일밖에 안 남았네요.	That's a good idea. 좋은 생각이네요. ▶ 제안문에 대한 답변이다.

평서문에 대한 답변의 특징

> **Yes / No로 답변할 수 있다. 특히 동의의 표현인 Yes가 자주 등장한다.**
> Ms. Wang's lecture was highly informative.   Yes, I was impressed with her knowledge.
> 왕 씨의 강연은 매우 유익했어요.   맞아요, 그녀의 지식에 감탄했어요.
>
> **But으로 답변할 수 있다. 동의하지 않음을 나타낸다.**
> We should order more food for our guests.   But, we had a lot of leftovers last time.
> 초대 손님들을 위한 음식을 좀 더 주문해야겠어요.   하지만 지난번에 음식이 많이 남았는 걸요.
>
> **Though(반론) / Then(해결책 제시)을 답변에 활용한다.**
> We need to set two more projectors.   I wonder if we can afford them, though.
> 2대의 프로젝터를 더 설치해야 해요.   하지만 재정이 허락할지 모르겠네요.
>
> We will have more guests than anticipated.   I should order more food then.
> 예상보다 더 많은 손님들이 올 거예요.   그렇다면 음식을 더 주문해야겠네요.

LISTENING PRACTICE 🎧 P2_13

질문을 듣고 적절한 응답을 고르자. 다시 듣기 하며 빈칸을 채우자.

1.
(A) (B) (C)

The new desks _____ _____.
(A) In the large _____ _____.
(B) I didn't know he was invited.
(C) I'll help you _____ _____ _____.

2.
(A) (B) (C)

We _____ _____ planning our year-end company party.
(A) _____ ____ too early?
(B) He _____ that company.
(C) No, they're the _____ results.

3.
(A) (B) (C)

The activation code _____ in three days.
(A) For _____ participation.
(B) You can _____ _____.
(C) Then I'd better _____ _____ ____ this soon.

4.
(A) (B) (C)

The housekeeping staff _____ _____ your room yet.
(A) No, I live in an apartment.
(B) _____ two beds.
(C) I don't _____ _____.

5.
(A) (B) (C)

____ _____ _____ souvenirs in Paris to give to our coworkers.
(A) A great deal of teamwork.
(B) Have you been there before?
(C) I think _____ _____ keychains.

6.
(A) (B) (C)

We won't be _____ ____ _____ the trail to the summit.
(A) Did you forget your password?
(B) _____ the park ranger said it was open.
(C) Yes, I enjoy _____ regularly.

❷ 제안 및 요청문

정답 패턴

Q. **Would you like to** go to the music festival with me this weekend?
주말에 저랑 음악 축제 가실래요?

수락하기
Sure, that sounds great. 네, 그거 좋죠.
❷ 수락은 가장 직접적이며 흔한 답변 패턴이다.

Q. **Can you** pick up my jacket from the dry cleaner's?
세탁소에서 자켓을 좀 찾아주시겠어요?

거절하기
I don't think I'll have time. 시간이 없을 것 같은데요.
❷ 거절의 이유가 곧 정답이 된다.

Q. **Please** send me the photos of the event.
행사 사진을 좀 보내 주세요.

되묻기
When do you need it by? 언제까지 필요하세요?
❷ 세부 사항을 확인하는 질문도 정답이 된다.

오답 패턴

Q. **Can you** set up the <u>projector</u> in the conference room?
회의실에 프로젝터를 설치해 주시겠어요?

유사 발음
It is <u>projected</u> to grow. 증가할 것으로 예상됩니다.
❷ projector와 발음이 유사한 project를 이용했다.

Q. **Would you like** some help with packing those bags?
가방 싸는 데 도움이 필요한가요?

동사 오류
Yes, I did. 네, 그랬어요.
❷ Did you로 질문했을 때의 답변이다.

Q. **Let's** take some <u>questions</u> from the audience.
청중에게 질문을 받읍시다.

연상 어휘
An unexpected <u>answer</u>. 예상하지 못한 답변이요.
❷ question을 듣고 연상 가능한 answer를 이용했다.

제안 및 요청문에 쓰이는 표현

요청	**Can you** forward the document to Ms. Wilson?	윌슨 씨에게 문서를 전달해주실 수 있나요?
	Could you e-mail me the breakdown of the costs?	비용 명세서를 보내주실 수 있나요?
	Would[Do] you mind giving me a ride to work?	직장까지 태워주실 수 있나요?
	Please remember to bring a receipt with you.	영수증을 꼭 가져오세요.
제안	**Will you** join us for lunch?	저희와 함께 점심 하실래요?
	Would you like to renew your membership?	멤버십을 갱신하시겠어요?
	Would you like me to send the package?	제가 소포를 보낼까요?
	Why don't we change our supplier?	공급 업체를 바꾸는 게 어떨까요?
	Let's throw a party for our manager.	매니저를 위해 파티를 열어줍시다.

※ 'Would[Do] you mind~?'에 대한 답변에 유의하기

Do you mind를 직역하면 '당신은 ~하는 것이 싫으신가요?'인데 '전혀 싫지 않다'라는 의미로
'Not at all.', 'Of course not.'과 같은 not이 포함된 표현으로 답할 수 있다.
또한 Do you mind를 '~해도 될까요'로 의역하여 수락의 뜻으로 'Sure(그러세요).'로 답할 수도 있다.

질문을 듣고 적절한 응답을 고르자. 다시 듣기 하며 빈칸을 채우자.

1.
(A) (B) (C)

_____ _____ _____ _____ seats with me?
(A) A computer _____.
(B) _____ and avenues.
(C) _____ _____.

2.
(A) (B) (C)

_____ _____ be _____ to help train Ms. Han, your replacement?
(A) I know a few good _____.
(B) _____ _____ will she start working?
(C) A storage _____.

3.
(A) (B) (C)

Do you _____ _____ out this survey?
(A) It's full.
(B) _____, I can do that.
(C) ____ alphabetical _____.

4.
(A) (B) (C)

_____ _____ _____ ____ attend the shareholders' meeting?
(A) She could _____ it.
(B) Yes, please ____ _____.
(C) _____ ____ ____?

5.
(A) (B) (C)

Would you _____ _____ _____ help with the _____?
(A) Sorry, I'm busy now.
(B) James will come ____ ____ _____.
(C) _____ the weekly inventory _____.

6.
(A) (B) (C)

_____ _____ _____ ____ ____ e-mail you my billing address?
(A) Thanks, but we _____ _____ ____ ____ _____.
(B) I'd love to have my _____ _____.
(C) I didn't think it would be _____ _____.

정답 및 해설 p. 43

1. Mark your answer.   (A)   (B)   (C)

2. Mark your answer.   (A)   (B)   (C)

3. Mark your answer.   (A)   (B)   (C)

4. Mark your answer.   (A)   (B)   (C)

5. Mark your answer.   (A)   (B)   (C)

6. Mark your answer.   (A)   (B)   (C)

7. Mark your answer.   (A)   (B)   (C)

8. Mark your answer.   (A)   (B)   (C)

9. Mark your answer.   (A)   (B)   (C)

10. Mark your answer.   (A)   (B)   (C)

11. Mark your answer.   (A)   (B)   (C)

12. Mark your answer.   (A)   (B)   (C)

13. Mark your answer.　　(A)　　(B)　　(C)

14. Mark your answer.　　(A)　　(B)　　(C)

15. Mark your answer.　　(A)　　(B)　　(C)

16. Mark your answer.　　(A)　　(B)　　(C)

17. Mark your answer.　　(A)　　(B)　　(C)

18. Mark your answer.　　(A)　　(B)　　(C)

19. Mark your answer.　　(A)　　(B)　　(C)

20. Mark your answer.　　(A)　　(B)　　(C)

21. Mark your answer.　　(A)　　(B)　　(C)

22. Mark your answer.　　(A)　　(B)　　(C)

23. Mark your answer.　　(A)　　(B)　　(C)

24. Mark your answer.　　(A)　　(B)　　(C)

25. Mark your answer.　　(A)　　(B)　　(C)

부가 / 부정 / 선택 의문문

출제 경향 부가/부정 의문문은 일반 의문문과 정답 형태가 동일하고, 선택 의문문은 전형적인 답변 패턴이 꾸준히 답으로 등장한다.

전략 부가 / 부정 의문문은 일반 의문문 풀이와 유사한 방식으로 오답 소거법을 적용하여 풀고, 선택 의문문은 답변 방식이 한정적이므로 답변에 자주 등장하는 표현을 익혀두자.

① 부가 의문문

 정답 패턴

Q. The lecture Dr. Travis gave us today was very informative, **wasn't it?**
트레비스 박사의 오늘 강연이 정말 유익했죠, 그렇죠?

Yes / No로 답하기
Yes, let's invite him again. 네, 그를 다시 초청합시다.
❸ 부가 의문문은 일반 의문문처럼 답변할 수 있다.

Q. There are no tickets for tonight's concert left, **right?**
오늘 밤 공연 티켓 남은 것 없죠, 그렇죠?

Yes / No 생략하기
(No) We've just sold out. 방금 매진됐어요.
❸ Yes, No를 생략하고 답을 하는 경우도 많다.

Q. You will lead the training session for the new employees, **won't you?**
신입사원들을 위한 교육을 맡으실 거죠? 그렇죠?

되묻기
Didn't Roy say he would? 로이가 하겠다고 안 했어요?
❸ 사실 확인을 위해 되묻는 답변도 정답이 된다.

 오답 패턴

Q. You have booked a flight for Ms. Carter, **right?**
카터 씨를 위해 비행기를 예약했죠, 그렇죠?

유사 발음
Yes, let me have the <u>flyer</u>. 네, 전단지를 주세요.
❸ flight와 발음이 유사한 flyer를 이용했다.

Q. Daniel has been working with us for quite a long time, **hasn't he?**
다니엘이 우리와 함께 일한 지 꽤 오래됐죠, 그렇죠?

반복 어휘
It shouldn't take <u>longer</u>. 더 오래 걸리진 않을 거예요.
❸ 질문에 사용된 long을 활용했다.

Q. The show begins at 6 o'clock, **correct?**
공연이 6시에 시작하죠, 맞나요?

연상 어휘
He is a famous <u>singer</u>. 그는 유명한 가수예요.
❸ show를 듣고 연상 가능한 singer를 이용했다.

부가 의문문의 답변 방식

사실 여부를 Yes, No로 답한 뒤 추가 의견을 덧붙이는 답변이 정답으로 자주 등장한다.

You can submit the expense report today, **right?** 비용 보고서를 오늘 제출하실 수 있죠, 그렇죠?	**Yes, but** not before lunch. 네, 하지만 점심 전에는 아니에요.
Mr. Ford is retiring next month, **isn't he?** 포드 씨가 다음 달에 은퇴하죠, 그렇죠?	**Yes, and** Ms. Turner will replace him. 네, 그리고 터너 씨가 그를 대신할 거예요.
You don't have this shirt in a larger size, **do you?** 이 셔츠 더 큰 사이즈로는 없는 거죠, 그렇죠?	**No, but** I can see if other stores have one. 네, 하지만 다른 매장에 있는지 알아봐 드릴 수 있어요.

LISTENING PRACTICE 🎧 P2_16

정답 및 해설 p. 48

질문을 듣고 적절한 응답을 고르자. 다시 듣기 하며 빈칸을 채우자.

1.
(A) (B) (C)

We should _____ buses, _____ _____?
(A) Sorry for the _____.
(B) It's _____ by bus.
(C) Yes, _____ Chicago.

2.
(A) (B) (C)

The furniture purchase has been _____, _____ ____?
(A) _____ of purchase.
(B) _____, _____ not the other decorations.
(C) I like the brown leather _____.

3.
(A) (B) (C)

The warranty is still ____ _____, _____?
(A) No, make a _____ _____ here.
(B) Digital scanning equipment.
(C) _____ the sales paperwork.

4.
(A) (B) (C)

We _____ ____ able to finish this project on time, _____ ____?
(A) At least two more classes.
(B) We'll need to _____.
(C) Probably the _____ train.

5.
(A) (B) (C)

The architect is finished _____ the building plans, _____ ____?
(A) I'll call and get a _____ report.
(B) The _____ shop near my home.
(C) I've never _____ a business before.

6.
(A) (B) (C)

You've _____ ____ the projection equipment before, _____?
(A) The _____ shipment.
(B) Their budget _____.
(C) That's Tony's _____.

부정 의문문

정답 패턴		

정답 패턴

Q. **Isn't Mr. Patel** going on a business trip tomorrow?
파텔 씨가 내일 출장 가시지 않나요?

Yes / No로 답하기
No, not until next week. 아니요, 다음 주에요.
◉ 부정 의문문은 일반 의문문처럼 답변할 수 있다.

Q. **Shouldn't we** put more chairs in the banquet hall?
연회장에 의자를 더 놓아야 하지 않을까요?

Yes / No 생략하기
(No) I've already taken care of it. 이미 처리했어요.
◉ Yes, No를 생략하고 답변할 수 있다.

Q. **Weren't you** supposed to give a demonstration of the item?
그 제품을 시연해 주시기로 하지 않았나요?

Yes / No + 'but'
Yes, but it's canceled. 그랬죠, 하지만 취소됐어요.
◉ Yes, but과 No, but은 정답 확률이 매우 높다.

오답 패턴

Q. **Didn't you** buy this coat online?
이 코트를 온라인으로 사지 않았어요?

반복 어휘
Yes, I registered online. 네, 온라인으로 등록했어요.
◉ 질문에 사용된 online을 그대로 사용했다.

Q. **Haven't you** checked the revised contract?
수정된 계약서를 확인하지 않으셨나요?

연상 어휘
Read terms and conditions. 계약 조건을 읽으세요.
◉ contract를 듣고 연상 가능한 어휘를 이용했다.

Q. **Hasn't the farewell party** been postponed until next week?
송별회가 다음 주로 연기되지 않았어요?

유사 발음
No, it was fairly brief. 아니요, 그것은 매우 간단했어요.
◉ farewell과 발음이 유사한 fairly를 이용했다.

부정 의문문의 풀이팁

> 부정 의문문은 긍정 의문문과 답변 방식이 같다. 즉, 긍정하려면 Yes, 부정하려면 No로 답한다.
> 따라서 부정 의문문에서 Not을 무시하고 긍정 의문문으로 해석해서 답변해도 무방하다.
>
> **Didn't you** replace the lock on the supply closet?
> 물품 보관장 자물쇠를 교체하셨나요?
> ◉ **Yes,** I did it yesterday.
> ◉ 했죠, 어제요.
>
> **Haven't you** finished writing a review?
> 후기 작성을 끝냈나요?
> ◉ **No,** but I'll do it later this afternoon.
> ◉ 안 했어요, 이따가 오후에 하려고요.
>
> 부정 의문문 Wouldn't you rather은 '~하는 게 낫지 않을까요?'의 뜻을 지닌 권유 문장이다.
>
> **Wouldn't you rather** include some illustrations?
> 차라리 삽화를 추가하는 게 낫지 않을까요?
> ◉ That might be too distracting.
> ◉ 그러면 너무 산만할지도 몰라요.

LISTENING PRACTICE 🎧 P2_17

정답 및 해설 p. 49

질문을 듣고 적절한 응답을 고르자. 다시 듣기 하며 빈칸을 채우자.

1.
(A) (B) (C)

_____ the post office _____ until 6 P.M.?

(A) _____ it on the bulletin board.

(B) _____ _____ national holidays.

(C) Yes, a _____ package.

2.
(A) (B) (C)

_____ _____ _____ that briefcase as a gift?

(A) Thanks, I really like it.

(B) She only spoke to us _____.

(C) Yes, _____ my team members.

3.
(A) (B) (C)

_____ the inspectors _____ ____ visit our factory this morning?

(A) _____ projectors from their Web site.

(B) At least one of those _____.

(C) They should be _____ _____.

4.
(A) (B) (C)

_____ _____ normally use your cell phone to call clients?

(A) _____, _____ I left it in my car by mistake.

(B) _____ _____ to give it back to me.

(C) Try to call after lunch.

5.
(A) (B) (C)

_____ ____ _____ for us to _____ our business software?

(A) Some of them _____ _____.

(B) The current version is _____ _____.

(C) In business _____.

6.
(A) (B) (C)

_____ _____ _____ to buy more office supplies?

(A) One of the business _____.

(B) It was a surprise party.

(C) Yes, we are _____ _____ on printer paper.

3 선택 의문문

정답 패턴

Q. Do you want to **call the client, or shall I?**
고객님께 전화하시겠어요, 아니면 제가 할까요?

둘 중에 선택하기
I will call after lunch. 점심식사 이후에 제가 할게요.
❍ 주어진 옵션 중 선택하는 것이 가장 대표적인 답변이다.

Q. Do you want me to send the application form **by e-mail or by fax?**
신청서를 이메일로 보낼까요, 팩스로 보낼까요?

제 3의 옵션 제시하기
I will pick it up myself. 제가 직접 찾아가겠습니다.
❍ 주어진 옵션 이외의 선택을 할 수도 있다.

Q. Should we **add more decorations, or** is it better to **leave it as it is?**
장식을 더 할까요, 이대로 두는 게 좋을까요?

되묻기
Do we even have time? 시간이 있긴 있나요?
❍ 선택하지 않는 것도 정답이 될 수 있다.

오답 패턴

Q. Do you work in **publicity or finance?**
홍보부에서 일하시나요, 아니면 재무부에서 일하시나요?

Yes / No 답변
Yes, I can work overtime. 네, 초과 근무할 수 있어요.
❍ 선택 의문문에 Yes, No로 답변할 수 없다.

Q. **Have you finished** correcting the errors, **or are you still working** on it?
오류 수정을 끝내셨나요, 아니면 아직 작업 중이신가요?

내용 오류 / 반복 어휘
During my work shift. 제 근무 시간 동안에요.
❍ 특정 의문문(when)에 할 수 있는 답변이다.
   또한, 질문에 사용된 working을 활용했다.

Q. Do you need this sales report **now, or can it wait until Thursday?**
이 매출 보고서가 지금 필요하신가요, 아니면 목요일까지 기다리실 수 있나요?

연상 어휘
Our profits have increased. 수익이 증가했어요.
❍ sales를 듣고 연상할 수 있는 profits를 이용했다.

선택 의문문에 대한 답변 유형

Either is fine with me. 어느 쪽이든 괜찮아요.	**Whichever** is convenient for you. 뭐든 당신이 편한 것으로요.	I don't have any **preference**. 아무거나 괜찮아요.
I'd prefer to do it now. 지금 하는 게 좋아요.	**I'd rather** take a taxi. 택시를 타는 편이 낫겠어요.	**Neither**, actually. 사실 둘 다 원하지 않아요.
Can I have **both**? 둘 다 가질 수 있을까요?	Taking a subway is **faster**. 지하철을 타는 게 더 빠르죠.	Can I have tea **instead**? 대신 차를 마셔도 될까요?

※ 선택 의문문에서는 질문에 나온 단어를 응답에 사용할 수 있으므로 반복 어휘에 해당하는 오답 소거법을 적용하지 않는다.

Q: Would you like to order **online** or over the phone?　　A: **Online**.
온라인으로 주문하시겠어요, 전화로 주문하시겠어요?　　온라인으로요.

질문을 듣고 적절한 응답을 고르자. 다시 듣기 하며 빈칸을 채우자.

1.
(A) (B) (C)

Is this form to be used ____ _____ ____ buyers?
(A) It's suitable for _____.
(B) We _____ a few of them.
(C) _____ at the bottom of the page.

2.
(A) (B) (C)

Should we print the invitations ____ _____ ____ black and white?
(A) I don't have a _____.
(B) For the anniversary party.
(C) Yes, the _____ has been repaired.

3.
(A) (B) (C)

Should we paint the hallway _____ ____ _____ a contractor?
(A) From some of the local _____.
(B) Who misplaced that _____?
(C) Let's have a _____ do it.

4.
(A) (B) (C)

Will you mail the package, ____ _____ ____ pick it up in person?
(A) Two to three _____ days.
(B) _____ one you prefer.
(C) I hope you feel better soon.

5.
(A) (B) (C)

Should we _____ to the meeting ourselves ____ _____ the subway?
(A) Let's _____ a few more.
(B) Do you want to deal with _____?
(C) ____ _____ the contract terms.

6.
(A) (B) (C)

Did you meet the _____, ____ _____ ____ too busy?
(A) He showed the _____.
(B) Yes, it will.
(C) The _____ is busy.

정답 및 해설 p.52

1. Mark your answer.   (A)   (B)   (C)

2. Mark your answer.   (A)   (B)   (C)

3. Mark your answer.   (A)   (B)   (C)

4. Mark your answer.   (A)   (B)   (C)

5. Mark your answer.   (A)   (B)   (C)

6. Mark your answer.   (A)   (B)   (C)

7. Mark your answer.   (A)   (B)   (C)

8. Mark your answer.   (A)   (B)   (C)

9. Mark your answer.   (A)   (B)   (C)

10. Mark your answer.   (A)   (B)   (C)

11. Mark your answer.   (A)   (B)   (C)

12. Mark your answer.   (A)   (B)   (C)

13.	Mark your answer.	(A)	(B)	(C)

14.	Mark your answer.	(A)	(B)	(C)

15.	Mark your answer.	(A)	(B)	(C)

16.	Mark your answer.	(A)	(B)	(C)

17.	Mark your answer.	(A)	(B)	(C)

18.	Mark your answer.	(A)	(B)	(C)

19.	Mark your answer.	(A)	(B)	(C)

20.	Mark your answer.	(A)	(B)	(C)

21.	Mark your answer.	(A)	(B)	(C)

22.	Mark your answer.	(A)	(B)	(C)

23.	Mark your answer.	(A)	(B)	(C)

24.	Mark your answer.	(A)	(B)	(C)

25.	Mark your answer.	(A)	(B)	(C)

정답은 본책 p.386 / 해설 PDF 무료 제공 / www.ybmbooks.com

1.	(A)	(B)	(C)		16.	(A)	(B)	(C)
2.	(A)	(B)	(C)		17.	(A)	(B)	(C)
3.	(A)	(B)	(C)		18.	(A)	(B)	(C)
4.	(A)	(B)	(C)		19.	(A)	(B)	(C)
5.	(A)	(B)	(C)		20.	(A)	(B)	(C)
6.	(A)	(B)	(C)		21.	(A)	(B)	(C)
7.	(A)	(B)	(C)		22.	(A)	(B)	(C)
8.	(A)	(B)	(C)		23.	(A)	(B)	(C)
9.	(A)	(B)	(C)		24.	(A)	(B)	(C)
10.	(A)	(B)	(C)		25.	(A)	(B)	(C)
11.	(A)	(B)	(C)		26.	(A)	(B)	(C)
12.	(A)	(B)	(C)		27.	(A)	(B)	(C)
13.	(A)	(B)	(C)		28.	(A)	(B)	(C)
14.	(A)	(B)	(C)		29.	(A)	(B)	(C)
15.	(A)	(B)	(C)		30.	(A)	(B)	(C)

NO TEST MATERIAL ON THIS PAGE

3

● PART 3 풀이 전략

PART 3 이렇게 나온다

대화문을 듣고 이에 딸린 세 개의 문제를 푸는 유형이다. 총 13개의 대화문에 39개의 문제가 출제되며, 시험지에 문제와 보기가 인쇄되어 나온다.

◁)) 음원

Questions 32 through 34 refer to the following conversation.

W Excuse me, I just wanted to let you know that I really like the music you have been playing here at this café. The style creates the perfect relaxing atmosphere. Who's the artist?

M Her name is Maria Martinez, and she's a singer from right here in Daynesville.

W Wow, she definitely has a lot of talent.

M If you like what you hear that much, you've got to see her live. She sings here regularly on the weekends. I'll get you a list of her upcoming shows.

32. What does the woman say she likes?
33. Who is Maria Martinez?
34. What does the man say he will do?

📄 시험지

32. What does the woman say she likes?
(A) The artwork on display
(B) The café's design
● (C) The background music
(D) The business's staff

33. Who is Maria Martinez?
● (A) A local performer
(B) A business owner
(C) A talent agent
(D) A café manager

34. What does the man say he will do?
(A) Bring the woman a menu
(B) Play a live video
(C) Check on an order
● (D) Give the woman a schedule

귀로 음원을 들으며   **동시에**   **눈으로는 시험지의 보기를 파악!**

PART 3 이렇게 푼다

❶ 대화문 듣기 전에 문제부터 읽기

문제를 먼저 읽는 것만으로도 앞으로 나올 대화의 흐름을 예상할 수 있다. 파트 3의 Directions를 읽어줄 때 32번~34번의 문제를 미리 읽어 둔다.

❷ 키워드 표시하기

키워드란 문제의 요지에 해당하는 단어들로, 의문사, 동사, 명사, 날짜, 시간 등이 이에 해당한다. 키워드를 표시하면 문제의 의미도 한눈에 들어오며, 정답의 단서가 들렸을 때 쉽게 포착할 수 있다.

> **32.** (What) does the (woman) say she (likes)? 여자가 좋아하는 것은?
> **33.** (Who) is (Maria Martinez)? 마리아 마르티네즈는 누구?
> **34.** (What) does the (man) say he (will do)? 남자가 할 일은?

❸ 화자 구분하기

문제를 읽고 정답을 말할 화자의 성별을 구분해 놓으면 해당 화자가 말할 때 집중해서 들을 수 있다.

> What does the **woman** say she likes? 여자가 정답을 말한다.
> What does the **man** say he will do? 남자가 정답을 말한다.
> According to the **man**, what will happen tomorrow? 남자가 정답을 말한다.
> What **is** the **man asked** to do? 여자가 정답을 말한다.

❹ 들으면서 정답 선택하기

정답의 단서는 문제 순서대로 나온다. 따라서 해당 문제의 단서를 들으면 바로 정답을 선택하고 다음 문제로 넘어가서 다음 단서를 기다린다.

❺ 문제를 읽어주는 동안 다음 대화문 준비하기

대화문이 끝나면 문제를 읽어주기 시작한다. 첫 번째 문제가 나오고 나서 8초 간격으로 다음 문제들을 읽어주기 때문에 이 시간을 활용하여 다음 대화문에 딸린 문제들을 읽어 둔다.

패러프레이징

Paraphrasing이란 말 바꾸기를 뜻하며 Part 3에서 패러프레이징은 핵심적인 역할을 한다. 대화문에서 들리는 단어가 보기에 그대로 등장하는 경우도 있지만 뜻이 통하는 다른 표현으로 바뀌어 나오는 경우가 많기 때문이다. 기본적으로 패러프레이징은 동의어와 상위어 개념을 사용한다.

유형 1. 동의어로 바꾸기
같은 뜻을 가진 대체어로 바꾸어 표현하는 방식 　예시　 **employees** 직원 ❯ **staff** 직원

not working 고장난	❯ malfunctioning	affordable 저렴한	❯ reasonable
submit 제출하다	❯ hand in / drop off	sold out 품절된	❯ out of stock
complete 작성하다	❯ fill out / fill in	expired 만료된	❯ not valid
review 검토하다	❯ go over / look over	cost estimate 견적서	❯ price quote
out of town 출장 중인	❯ on a business trip	price 가격	❯ rate
for free 무료로	❯ at no cost	manager 관리자	❯ supervisor
visit 방문하다, 들르다	❯ stop by / drop by	feedback 의견을 주다	❯ give an opinion
register 등록하다	❯ sign up for	short of 부족한	❯ not enough
move 옮기다	❯ relocate	revise 수정하다	❯ change / modify
contact 연락하다	❯ get in touch with	express (배송이) 빠른	❯ rush / expedited
discount 할인	❯ price reduction	delay 연기하다	❯ postpone
factory 공장	❯ manufacturing facility	contract 계약서	❯ agreement
receipt 영수증	❯ proof of purchase	team member 팀원	❯ colleague
organize 마련하다	❯ put together	discontinue 중단하다	❯ stop producing
coupon 쿠폰	❯ voucher	missing 빠져 있는	❯ incomplete

유형 2. 상위어로 바꾸기
포괄적인 뜻을 가진 상위 개념으로 바꾸어 표현하는 방식 　예시　 **envelops** 봉투 ❯ **stationery** 문구류

application form 신청서	❯ document 문서	shuttle 셔틀	❯ transportation 교통편
projector 프로젝터	❯ equipment 장비	bag 가방	❯ item 상품
blender 믹서기	❯ appliance 가전제품	banquet 연회	❯ event 행사
printing paper 용지	❯ office supply 사무용품	farewell 송별회	❯ gathering 모임
analyst 분석가	❯ expert 전문가	remodeling 리모델링	❯ project 작업, 공사, 업무
repair 수리	❯ service 서비스	caterer 출장 요리 업체	❯ supplier 제공 업체
water leak 누수	❯ damage 피해	restaurant 식당	❯ business 사업체
passport 여권	❯ identification 신분증	update 업데이트	❯ maintenance 유지, 보수

문장을 듣고 패러프레이징을 연습해보자.

1.

What problem does the man mention?

(A) An appliance is malfunctioning.

(B) A washing machine hasn't been delivered.

2.

What does the woman say she will do?

(A) Complete some paperwork

(B) Locate an application form

3.

What does the woman ask the man to do?

(A) Submit a report

(B) Review a document

4.

What does the woman say will be available?

(A) A form of transportation

(B) A meal coupon

5.

What does the man request?

(A) A form of identification

(B) Proof of purchase

6.

What problem does the woman mention?

(A) There is an insufficient number of items.

(B) Some furniture is not in good condition.

7.

What does the woman say she will do?

(A) Attend a celebratory gathering

(B) Organize a farewell party

8.

What problem does the man mention?

(A) Some information is wrong.

(B) An order is incomplete.

9.

What does the woman suggest?

(A) Finding a different supplier

(B) Hiring temporary staff

10.

What does the man like about the product?

(A) Its size is compact.

(B) Its price is reasonable.

11.

What does the woman ask the man to do?

(A) Provide feedback

(B) Create a new ad campaign

12.

What does the man say he will do?

(A) Make a revision to an article

(B) Submit a writing

13.

What does the man say about ink cartridges?

(A) They are sold out.

(B) They are discontinued.

14.

What does the woman offer to do?

(A) Provide expedited service

(B) Waive a fee

주제 / 목적 문제

전략 · 문제를 보자마자 주제, 목적 문제라는 것을 알 수 있도록 질문 형태에 미리 익숙해져야 한다. 주로 첫 문제로 등장하므로 초반부를 노려 듣자. 목적을 밝힐 때 등장하는 표현들을 숙지하여 정답이 나오는 포인트를 빠르게 포착하자.

문제 유형 · **What are the speakers** discussing / talking about? 화자들은 무엇에 관해 이야기 중인가?

What is the conversation mainly about? 대화는 주로 무엇에 관한 것인가?

Why is the woman calling? 여자는 왜 전화하고 있는가?

핵심 포인트 · **주제와 목적은 첫 두 문장을 듣고 파악하자.** 🎧 P3_02

M This is Ken from Cosmos Realty. I got your message saying that you plan to **move your insurance company**.

  ❯ 본인 소개 후 대화 주제가 바로 등장한다.

W That's right. We'd like to be moved into the new site by June 1, so the availability is important.

M I understand. I'll start researching properties now. I should have a few ready for you to view soon.

남 코스모스 부동산 켄이라고 합니다. 보험 회사를 이전하실 계획이라는 메시지 받았어요.

여 맞아요. 6월 1일까지 새로운 장소로 옮기려고 해요. 그래서 이 날짜가 가능한지가 중요해요.

남 알겠습니다. 지금 부동산을 알아보겠습니다. 곧 몇 군데 보여드릴 수 있을 거예요.

What is the conversation **mainly about?**

(A) Passing a building inspection

(B) Relocating a business

(C) Purchasing an insurance policy

(D) Assigning workers to a task

대화는 **무엇에 관한 것인가?**

(A) 건물 점검 통과하기

(B) 업체 이전하기

(C) 보험 가입하기

(D) 직원들에게 업무 할당하기

정답이 들리는 단서 표현

목적을 나타내는 도입부 표현을 들으면 정답을 포착할 수 있다.

I'm here for my regular checkup with Dr. Smith. · 스미스 박사님께 정기 점진 받으러 왔어요.

I came to drop off my application. · 신청서를 제출하려고 왔어요.

I'm calling to arrange an appointment. · 예약을 잡으려고 전화했어요.

I'd like to reserve a table for six people. · 6명 식사 예약을 하고 싶어요.

I'm wondering how to replace the ink cartridge. · 잉크 카트리지 교체 방법이 궁금해요.

I'm interested in renting a car. · 차를 렌트하고 싶어요.

LISTENING PRACTICE 🎧 P3_03

정답 및 해설 p.59

대화를 듣고 주제, 목적 문제를 풀어보자. 다시 듣고 빈칸을 채우자.

1.

What are the speakers **mainly discussing**?

(A) An upcoming job interview

(B) An advertising campaign

(C) A vacant position

(D) A hiring recommendation

W: Thank you for calling Indigo Publications. How may I help you?

M: Hello, I saw an advertisement for a _____ _____ position at your company, and I _____ _____ you could offer a few details about the position.

W: Oh, I need to _____ _____ through to Ms. Perez, our hiring manager. Hold on, please.

2.

What is the conversation **mainly about**?

(A) Finding a caterer

(B) Attending a conference

(C) Presenting a budget

(D) Opening a business

W: Russel, do you have a minute? I'm trying to find a _____ _____. Can you recommend one?

M: What's wrong with the current one?

W: Have you seen their recent prices? We need a _____ that _____ _____ _____ _____.

M: Well, let's ask other staff members then.

3.

What is the **purpose of the call**?

(A) To request time off

(B) To promote a service

(C) To change a schedule

(D) To negotiate a pay raise

M: Hello, this is Ron Vincent from Spotless Cleaners. I'm calling to _____ _____ the _____ that we visit your office to clean.

W: Mr. Gupta handles that, but he's _____ _____ _____ _____. I can give him a message, though.

M: Good. Please tell him we'd like to visit your building on Monday and Wednesday mornings.

4.

Why is the **man calling** the woman?

(A) To adjust an event's start time

(B) To inquire about a payment schedule

(C) To confirm a delivery of supplies

(D) To change a furniture arrangement

M: Hello, this is Alex calling from Polaris Insurance. We booked a banquet room at your site next week, and I'd like to make an _____ to our reservation.

W: Certainly. What do you have in mind?

M: I'd like the tables and chairs _____ _____ _____ _____ in small groups instead of long rows.

PART 3

UNIT 01 주제 / 목적 문제

77

화자 / 장소 문제

전략 의문사를 보고 화자, 장소 문제임을 파악한다. 특정 직업 관련, 혹은 업체 관련 어휘를 포착하여 신분과 장소를 유추해내자.

문제 유형 Who most likely is the woman? 여자는 누구인 것 같은가?

Where does the man most likely work? 남자는 어디에서 일하는 것 같은가?

Where is the conversation most likely taking place? 대화가 어디에서 일어나는 것 같은가?

핵심 포인트 **업무 관련 어휘로 화자와 장소를 파악하자.** 🎧 P3_04

W Excuse me, Manuel. Do you have time to **clean the suite 202** now?

❯ '스위트룸 청소'는 호텔에서 일어날 수 있는 일이다.

M I can, but that means the **third-floor rooms** won't be ready by **check-in** time at three.

❯ '3층 객실, 체크인'은 호텔 관련 어휘이다.

W We have a guest requesting an early check-in.

M Tina is supposed to prepare the first-floor ballroom, but if she puts that on hold, she can clean the suite.

여 마누엘, 지금 스위트룸 202호를 청소할 시간이 있나요?
남 네, 근데 그러면 3층 객실들은 3시 **체크인** 시간까지 준비가 안 될 텐데요.
여 조기 체크인을 요청하신 손님이 있어서요.
남 티나가 1층 연회장을 준비하기로 되어 있는데 그걸 미루면 스위트룸을 치울 수 있을 거예요.

Where is the conversation most likely **taking place?**

(A) At an airport
(B) At a car rental agency
(C) At a dining establishment
(D) At a hotel

대화는 **어디에서 일어나는 것** 같은가?

(A) 공항에서
(B) 자동차 렌탈 업체에서
(C) 식당에서
(D) 호텔에서

정답이 들리는 단서 표현

주제와 목적이 드러나는 대화 도입부에서 화자와 장소를 파악할 수 있다.

본인을 소개하면서	Hi James, this is Helen calling from Rosedale Dental. 안녕하세요, 로즈데일 치과의 헬렌입니다. ❯ **치과 접수원**과 **예약 환자** 간의 대화
대화 목적을 밝히면서	I'm interested in renting one of the office spaces you're advertising. 광고 내신 사무실 중 하나를 임대하고 싶은데요. ❯ **부동산 중개인**과 **잠재 고객** 간의 대화
대화 주제를 꺼내면서	It looks like the conveyer belt on the assembly line is malfunctioning. 조립 라인 컨베이어벨트가 고장인 것 같아요. ❯ **공장 조립 라인 직원**과 **책임자** 간의 대화

LISTENING PRACTICE 🎧 P3_05

대화를 듣고 화자, 장소 문제를 풀어보자. 다시 듣고 빈칸을 채우자.

1.

Who most likely is the **woman**?

(A) A factory worker

(B) A librarian

(C) A university faculty

(D) A supermarket manager

> M: Hello, I am here to _____ _____ _____
>
> ____ _____.
>
> W: Hmm... It looks like you need to pay a _____
>
> _____ of 6 dollars.
>
> M: I guess you're right. By the way, do you offer
>
> a _____ service? I want to avoid the
>
> same mistake next time.

2.

Who is **Barbara**?

(A) An intern

(B) A customer

(C) A supervisor

(D) A repairperson

> W: Welcome to Fairfax Print Shop.
>
> M: Hello. I have a digital file for an employee
>
> training manual I'd like printed. Do you do that?
>
> W: Yes, we do. _____ _____ _____
>
> Barbara, can _____ _____ _____ that.

3.

Where does the **woman work**?

(A) At a conference center

(B) At a dentist's office

(C) At a travel agency

(D) At a hair salon

> M: Hi. This is Oliver Wilson. I need
>
> to _____ a time ____ _____ Dr. Taylor
>
> for my _____ _____ _____.
>
> W: Hi, Mr. Wilson. The doctor will be out of town
>
> during the second week of July, but
>
> ____ _____ _____ should be fine.
>
> M: I see. How about the week after he gets back?
>
> I can come at three o'clock on Wednesday.

4.

Where is the conversation most likely **taking place**?

(A) At a laboratory

(B) At a public library

(C) At a post office

(D) At a pharmacy

> M: All right, Susan. Since it's your first day at
>
> work, I'll show you _____ ____ _____
>
> _____ _____ and _____ _____
>
> _____ ____ by customers.
>
> W: OK. I've completed the full training, but I
>
> haven't helped any actual customers yet.
>
> M: You'll _____ ____ quickly. Let's get started.

1. What kind of business is the man calling?
   (A) A design firm
   (B) A hotel
   (C) A restaurant
   (D) A fitness center

2. Why will the man visit the business?
   (A) To celebrate an anniversary
   (B) To conduct an inspection
   (C) To apply for a job
   (D) To promote a product

3. What does the man say he will do?
   (A) Confirm a time
   (B) Sign a check
   (C) Consult a supervisor
   (D) Give a recommendation

4. Why does the man ask to meet with the woman?
   (A) To resolve a disagreement
   (B) To provide some skills training
   (C) To discuss her job performance
   (D) To make plans for a celebration

5. Where most likely do the speakers work?
   (A) At a newspaper company
   (B) At a fashion design agency
   (C) At a television network
   (D) At an architectural firm

6. What does the man ask the woman to prepare?
   (A) A list of questions
   (B) A detailed timeline
   (C) A collection of her work
   (D) A marketing proposal

7. What is the conversation mainly about?
   (A) A company banquet
   (B) A recruitment event
   (C) A training session
   (D) An advertising campaign

8. What is the woman waiting for?
   (A) Confirmation of an upgrade
   (B) An itemized bill
   (C) Some promotional materials
   (D) A final guest list

9. What is the man asked to do?
   (A) Meet with a new client
   (B) Approve a proposal
   (C) Arrive at a site early
   (D) Purchase some decorations

10. Where do the speakers work?
    (A) At a restaurant
    (B) At a dental office
    (C) At an office supply store
    (D) At a bookstore

11. According to the woman, what will change at the business?
    (A) The return policy will be updated.
    (B) The staff will start receiving insurance coverage.
    (C) The hours of operation will be extended.
    (D) The services will become more expensive.

12. What information does the woman request?
    (A) The man's availability
    (B) The training requirements
    (C) The man's mailing address
    (D) The meeting agenda

13. Where most likely does the woman work?

(A) At a financial institution
(B) At a courier service
(C) At a utility company
(D) At a department store

14. What is the purpose of the man's call?

(A) To cancel an appointment
(B) To open a new account
(C) To report a lost item
(D) To make a payment

15. According to the woman, what should the man bring to the business?

(A) A confirmation code
(B) Completed complaint forms
(C) A sales receipt
(D) Proof of address

16. Where does the man work?

(A) At an insurance company
(B) At a caterer
(C) At a shipping company
(D) At a phone service company

17. According to the man, what happened last month?

(A) An advertising campaign was launched.
(B) Some programs were installed.
(C) An option was added.
(D) A business was relocated.

18. What does the woman ask about?

(A) The cost of a service
(B) The location of a business
(C) The availability of reservations
(D) Ways to reduce expenses

19. What does the man say about the woman?

(A) Her room is ready.
(B) Her speech was popular.
(C) Her schedule has changed.
(D) Her identification badge has an error.

20. What does the man say he will do for the woman?

(A) Inform others of her arrival
(B) Introduce her to a colleague
(C) Save a seat for her
(D) Loan her a book

21. Who most likely is Tony Ali?

(A) A corporate executive
(B) An event organizer
(C) An author
(D) A caterer

22. What most likely is the purpose of the man's visit?

(A) To file a complaint
(B) To sell a product
(C) To repair a machine
(D) To speak to a supervisor

23. What most likely will the man receive from the woman?

(A) A guidance map
(B) A guest pass
(C) An instruction manual
(D) A work uniform

24. What did the man bring with him?

(A) A bag of tools
(B) A security credential
(C) A production schedule
(D) A product catalogue

문제점 / 걱정거리 문제

전략 질문의 키워드를 보고 빠르게 문제 유형을 파악한다. 문제점이나 걱정을 제시할 때는 반전과 역접의 표현이 핵심 역할을 하므로 이를 잘 정리해두자.

문제 유형 What **problem** does the **man** mention? 남자는 어떤 문제점을 언급하는가?
What is the woman concerned about? 여자는 무엇에 대해 걱정하는가?
What **problem** is being discussed? 어떤 문제가 논의되고 있는가?

핵심 포인트 **반전과 역접의 표현 뒤에는 문제점이 언급된다.** 🎧 P3_07

M Excuse me, I purchased this **blender** here last week, **but** sometimes it **stops working** for no reason.

❯ 반전의 but에 바로 이어 문제점을 말하고 있다.

W That tends to happen if the pitcher isn't clicked into place correctly. Have you read the instructions in the user manual?

M Yes. I think it must be an issue with the blender's motor.

What **problem** does the **man** mention?
(A) A component is missing.
(B) An appliance is malfunctioning.
(C) She was overcharged for a device.
(D) She cannot find the item she needs.

남 실례합니다. 지난주에 이곳에서 믹서기를 구매했어요. **그런데 가끔 아무 이유 없이 작동을 멈춰요.**

여 용기가 제대로 안 꽂히면 그럴 때가 있어요. 사용자 매뉴얼에 있는 설명을 읽어보셨나요?

남 네. 제 생각에는 믹서기 모터 문제인 것 같아요.

여자는 어떤 문제점을 언급하는가?
(A) 부품이 하나 없다.
(B) 전자제품이 고장 났다.
(C) 기기 가격을 과다 청구 받았다.
(D) 필요한 물건을 찾을 수 없다.

정답이 들리는 단서 표현

반전과 역접, 걱정의 표현과 함께 정답이 등장한다.

I want to read reviews, **but** your Web site is down.	리뷰를 읽고 싶은데 웹 사이트가 다운됐네요.
I was issued an ID card. **Unfortunately**, I lost it.	신분증을 발급받았는데 유감스럽게도 분실했어요.
I ordered a printer. **However**, it hasn't arrived yet.	프린터를 주문했는데 아직 도착을 안 했어요.
It seems that we are running short of food.	음식이 부족할 것 같아요.
I am concerned we might be late.	늦을까 봐 걱정이에요.
I am worried we'll miss the train.	기차를 놓칠까 봐 걱정이에요.

W: Can you give me a ride to the office? 여: 사무실까지 태워주실 수 있나요?
M: **Actually**, it's in the repair shop. 남: 실은 차가 수리점에 있어요.

대화를 듣고 문제점, 걱정거리 문제를 풀어보자. 다시 듣고 빈칸을 채우자.

1.

What **problem** does the **man** mention about the chatting software?

(A) The audio is distorted.

(B) The video quality is poor.

(C) The text feature operates slowly.

(D) The group chat feature does not work.

> M: Hello. I'm trying to use your software to make video calls. The audio is OK, _____ the video is often _____.
>
> W: Usually, that problem is caused by a slow Internet connection. You should speak to your Internet service provider.
>
> M: Oh, I guess I'll need to do that. Thanks.

2.

What **problem** does the **woman** mention?

(A) She forgot her password.

(B) She cannot access a Web site.

(C) She cannot deliver a magazine.

(D) She cannot make an online purchase.

> W: I tried to log in to your Web site, but I got an error message saying my username was _____.
>
> M: I'm sorry. Our Web site is _____ maintenance right now, and it will be down for another few hours.
>
> W: Well, that's disappointing.
>
> M: To _____ you for the wait, we will give you free _____ to some of our popular media content.

3.

What is the **woman concerned about**?

(A) Investing too heavily in equipment

(B) Failing government inspections

(C) Finding qualified workers

(D) Keeping prices competitive

> M: Ms. Lucas, what do you think about adding a healthy line of yogurt to the food we produce?
>
> W: We're only _____ ____ make dry goods. _____ _____ we would _____ ____ _____ too much on machinery to add a dairy product.
>
> M: You know, it might be _____ ____. How about conducting a survey on this matter?

4.

What **concern** does the **man** mention?

(A) He may not be able to meet a deadline.

(B) He cannot access her online bank account.

(C) He has not been paid.

(D) He lives far away from a venue.

> W: Hi, James. Thanks for the excellent photographs. I'd like you to work for us again for the next project.
>
> M: That would be great, Amy. _____, I checked my bank account last night and my ____ from the last job _____ _____. Could you look into this for me?
>
> W: I apologize. I'll check it right away.

요청 / 제안 / 제공 문제

전략 키워드를 통해 요청, 제안, 제공 문제임을 파악한다. 문제의 키워드와 지문 속 단서 표현을 매치하여 정답이 나오는 구간을 놓치지 않도록 하자.

문제 유형 What does the man ask the woman to do? 남자는 여자에게 무엇을 하라고 요청하는가?

What does the woman suggest the man do? 여자는 남자에게 무엇을 하라고 제안하는가?

What does the woman offer to do? 여자는 무엇을 해주겠다고 하는가?

핵심 포인트 **요청, 제안문의 앞부분을 듣자.** 🎧 P3_09

M I would like to open a checking account with your bank.

W Please take this **application form** and **fill it out**.

❷ 부탁의 표현이 곧 정답으로 연결된다.

There are tables and chairs in our lobby.

M I also want to use the online banking service.

W OK. Let me have all the necessary forms ready for you.

What does the **woman ask** the man to do?

(A) Call a financial institution

(B) Complete some paperwork

(C) Visit a Web site

(D) Provide identification

남 은행 예금 계좌를 개설하고 싶어요.

여 **이 신청서를 가져가서 작성해주세요.** 로비에 테이블과 의자가 있어요.

남 온라인 뱅킹 서비스도 이용하고 싶어요.

여 네. 구비 서류를 준비해드릴게요.

여자는 남자에게 **무엇을 하라고 요청**하는가?

(A) 금융 기관에 전화하기

(B) 서류 작성하기

(C) 웹사이트 방문하기

(D) 신분증 제시하기

정답이 들리는 단서 표현

요청, 제안, 제공 문제는 다음과 같은 표현이 들릴 때 정답을 노려야 한다.

요청 문제	**Please** give us some advice.	조언 좀 부탁드려요.
	Could you cover my shift tomorrow?	내일 저 대신 일해주실 수 있을까요?
	I'd like you to lead the training.	교육을 맡아주시면 좋겠어요.
제안 문제	**I suggest** buying tickets online.	온라인으로 티켓을 구매하시기를 제안해요.
	I recommend you take a taxi.	택시를 타시기를 권해드려요.
	Why don't you start the meeting now?	지금 회의를 시작하는 것이 어때요?
제공 문제	**I can** go and take the inventory.	제가 가서 재고 조사를 할게요.
	I'll send you the instruction.	제가 설명서를 보내드릴게요.
	Why don't I take notes for you?	제가 기록을 해드리는 게 어떨까요?

LISTENING PRACTICE 🎧 P3_10

정답 및 해설 p.68

대화를 듣고 요청, 제안, 제공 문제를 풀어보자. 다시 듣고 빈칸을 채우자.

1.

What does the **woman ask** the man to do?

(A) Wait a few minutes

(B) Package a product

(C) Deliver a message

(D) Visit another office

M: Hi, I'm a delivery driver for BDL Shipping. I'm at your building with a package, but no one's here.

W: Really? A receptionist should be there.

M: Well, this package requires a signature. Should I come back later in the day?

W: _____ _____ _____ there for five minutes? I can be right over to sign for it.

2.

What does the **woman request**?

(A) A bulk discount

(B) A product catalog

(C) A sample item

(D) A business card

W: Hello. I'm interested in getting some water bottles made with my company's logo on them.

M: All right. We do _____ _____ for all kinds of merchandise.

W: That's great. _____ _____ _____ _____ _____ of the finished product before placing a large order?

3.

What does the **man suggest** doing?

(A) Postponing an event

(B) Attending an exhibition

(C) Checking availability online

(D) Applying for a job opening

M: Nina, our client just informed me that eight of them will be visiting our branch instead of five.

W: I was going to take them to see an opera, but I can't buy any more tickets. They're completely sold out.

M: Well, I know there's an _____ _____ at the Muse Gallery. _____ _____ _____ _____ _____ instead?

W: Good idea. Thanks for the suggestion.

4.

What does the **man offer to do** for the woman?

(A) Introduce her to a colleague

(B) Provide some equipment

(C) Take her to an office

(D) Write a recommendation letter

M: Hi, Lily. How are you settling in here? I'd like to do anything I can to help you get comfortable.

W: Thanks, Mr. Brown. There is one thing you could help with. I need a _____ to use the parking garage.

M: You can get that from security. If you want, _ _____ _____ _____ there.

1. Where does the woman work?
   (A) At an airport
   (B) At a retail store
   (C) At a taxi company
   (D) At a conference center

2. What problem does the man mention?
   (A) He forgot a phone number.
   (B) He lost a piece of luggage.
   (C) He cannot find a building.
   (D) He missed a flight.

3. What does the woman ask the man for?
   (A) A reservation number
   (B) A credit card payment
   (C) An account password
   (D) A taxi driver's name

4. What are the speakers discussing?
   (A) A corporate merger
   (B) A meeting with potential clients
   (C) A year-end celebration
   (D) A company excursion

5. What does the man suggest that the woman do?
   (A) Sign up for some activities
   (B) Arrange some transportation
   (C) Pack a specific clothing item
   (D) Arrive at a location early

6. What resort amenity does the man say he is most excited about?
   (A) The sauna
   (B) The swimming pool
   (C) The gym
   (D) The restaurant

7. What is mainly being discussed?
   (A) A CEO's retirement
   (B) A company expansion
   (C) A staff incentive program
   (D) A training course

8. What does the woman suggest?
   (A) Reading a document
   (B) Taking the train to work
   (C) Consulting family members
   (D) Applying for a transfer

9. What does the woman agree to do?
   (A) Find out some information
   (B) Send a memo to staff
   (C) Print a meeting itinerary
   (D) Conduct job interviews

10. Why did the man visit the business?
    (A) To exchange some merchandise
    (B) To make a purchase
    (C) To obtain some missing pieces
    (D) To arrange a delivery

11. What problem does Ms. Jones mention about a manufacturer?
    (A) It has slow processing times.
    (B) It will go out of business.
    (C) It has discontinued a product.
    (D) It does not allow returns.

12. What will the man do this afternoon?
    (A) Use an assembly service
    (B) Contact Ms. Jones
    (C) Call a manufacturing company
    (D) Bring an item to the business

13. What is the woman asked to do?

(A) Sign a contract

(B) Give someone a ride

(C) Order some goods

(D) Purchase an airline ticket

14. Why is the man busy this afternoon?

(A) He will conduct an interview.

(B) He has an urgent report due.

(C) He needs to inspect a shipment.

(D) He will visit a client's office.

15. What does the woman inquire about?

(A) A delivery address

(B) An arrival time

(C) An inspection result

(D) A payment method

16. What is the conversation mainly about?

(A) Relocating an office

(B) Practicing a presentation

(C) Reserving a booth

(D) Increasing event attendance

17. What does Marco express concern about?

(A) The participation costs

(B) The limited space

(C) The level of noise

(D) The outdated equipment

18. Why does the woman plan to call a manager?

(A) To get advice on decorations

(B) To request a budget change

(C) To give driving directions

(D) To ask for contract terms

19. What does the man say about the employee performance evaluations?

(A) They are done only for new employees.

(B) They are scheduled this week.

(C) They are done annually.

(D) They are divided into several steps.

20. What problem does the woman mention?

(A) She will go out of town.

(B) She has lost a file.

(C) A board meeting was canceled.

(D) A client made a complaint.

21. What does the woman offer to do?

(A) Give a presentation about a project

(B) Send some detailed instructions

(C) Update information on a Web site

(D) Stay at the office later than usual

22. According to the woman, why has the account been reassigned?

(A) A client did not like the previous work.

(B) A coworker will not be available.

(C) There was an error in the system.

(D) She volunteered to take on the job.

23. What does the woman inquire about?

(A) A project deadline

(B) A contract agreement

(C) A presentation method

(D) A business trip

24. What does the man offer to do?

(A) Approve overtime work

(B) Hold a staff meeting

(C) Contact a client

(D) Send some notes

전략   각 문제에서 요구하는 세부 사항이 무엇인지 키워드를 체크하여 노려 듣기 하자.

문제 유형   What **did the** man recently do? 남자는 최근에 무엇을 했는가?

How did the woman learn about the company? 여자는 회사에 대해 어떻게 알게 되었는가?

What does the man say about the conference? 남자는 회의에 대해 무엇이라고 말하는가?

핵심 포인트   **질문 속의 키워드는 그대로 나오거나 패러프레이징된다.**   🎧 P3_12

M   So, you said on the phone you are seeking ways to promote **your recently opened hair salon**, right?

❯ 질문의 키워드 recently가 대화에 그대로 등장했다.

W   Yes. A friend of mine who's running a restaurant spoke highly of your advertising agency.

M   We're always proud of our accomplishments. I brought some samples of our promotional materials you may find interesting to see.

남   최근 개업하신 미용실을 홍보할 방법을 찾고 계신다고 전화로 말씀하셨죠?

여   네. 친구가 식당을 운영하는데 당신의 광고 회사를 극찬하더라고요.

남   저희는 늘 저희의 업적에 자부심을 갖고 있습니다. 한번 보시고 싶으실 것 같아서 홍보 자료 샘플을 좀 가져왔습니다.

According to the **man**, what has the **woman recently done**?

(A) She opened a restaurant.

(B) She started her own business.

(C) She received an award.

(D) She submitted a manuscript.

남자의 말에 따르면 **여자는 최근에 무엇을 했는가?**

(A) 식당을 개업했다.

(B) 사업을 시작했다.

(C) 상을 받았다.

(D) 원고를 제출했다.

정답이 들리는 단서 표현

주요 세부 사항 문제는 다음과 같다.	
질문	정답 구간
What did the man **recently do**? 남자는 최근에 무엇을 했는가?	My book was **just** published. 제 책이 최근에 출판됐어요.
How did the woman **learn** about the sale? 여자는 할인에 대해 어떻게 알게 되었는가?	I **heard about** your promotion on the radio. 라디오에서 프로모션 행사에 관해 들었어요.
Why is the man **unavailable today**? 남자는 왜 오늘 시간이 없는가?	I'm **busy today** as a deadline is approaching. 마감일이 다가와서 오늘 저는 바쁩니다.
What is **unique** about the product? 제품은 어떤 점이 독특한가?	**Unlike others**, our product is extremely light. 다른 제품과 달리, 우리의 제품은 매우 가볍습니다.
Why is the woman **pleased**? 여자는 왜 기뻐하는가?	**That's great**! I could have more options, then. 잘됐네요! 그러면 옵션이 더 많아지겠네요.

LISTENING PRACTICE 🎧 P3_13

정답 및 해설 p. 74

대화를 듣고 세부 사항 문제를 풀어보자. 다시 듣고 빈칸을 채우자.

1.

Where did the **man learn about** a **service**?

(A) From the Internet

(B) From a newspaper

(C) From a television broadcast

(D) From an outdoor sign

> M: Hello. I _____ a _____ advertising your
> _____ service. My kitchen sink is _____
> very slowly, so I'm hoping you can help.
> W: Certainly. I can come by tomorrow afternoon.
> M: Well, I work all day so I won't be home. But I'll
> _____ the back door _____.

2.

Why does **Brenda recommend Re-Onics**
products?

(A) Their prices are reasonable.

(B) They have a unique smell.

(C) They are available in different packaging.

(D) Their ingredients are safe.

> M: Brenda, I'm looking for a new shampoo. Can
> you recommend one?
> W: I really like Re-Onics shampoos, because
> _____ _____ _____
> any _____ _____.
> M: Thanks! Oh, they're on sale now. I think I
> should get one.

3.

Why is the **woman unavailable** on the
weekend?

(A) She is playing a sport.

(B) She is leading a meeting.

(C) She is working on a marketing campaign.

(D) She is working on a report.

> M: Tina, could you help me prepare for my
> presentation?
> W: I'm afraid I'm a bit busy this week. I have to
> _____ a meeting this afternoon and I'm
> also taking part in a _____ tournament on
> Saturday.
> M: Do you know if anybody else is available?
> W: Possibly Susan. She's always helpful.

4.

What does the **man** say he has **already
done**?

(A) Delivered a package

(B) Made a complaint

(C) Changed a password

(D) Placed an order

> M: Sharon, ID cards for our new employees were
> supposed to have been delivered by now, but
> they haven't.
> W: Oh, no. They _____ _____ _____ _____
> _____ our lab areas then.
> M: ____ _____ _____ Human
> Resources and told them this is
> not _____.
> W: I agree. We might have to reschedule
> everything we planned for today.

다음에 할 일 문제

전략 미래 시제 또는 계획을 나타내는 표현, 질문에 등장하는 특정 시점이 그대로 등장하는 구간에서 정답을 구하자.

문제 유형 What does the man say he will do? 남자는 무엇을 할 것이라고 말하는가?

What will the woman most likely do next? 여자는 다음으로 무엇을 할 것 같은가?

What does the man say will happen next month? 남자는 다음 달에 무슨 일이 일어날 것이라고 하는가?

핵심 포인트 미래 시제 동사 또는 미래 시점을 포착하자. 🎧 P3_14

M I'd like to sign up for your art class.

W OK. Here's a registration form, and please pay in cash.

M Oh, you don't take credit cards? I'll need to **run to a cash machine**, then. I'll go and come right back.

❯ 'I'll'을 듣고 정답 구간을 포착한다.

What will the **man** most likely **do next?**

(A) Give the woman his business card

(B) Withdraw money from a machine

(C) Observe an art class

(D) Purchase painting supplies

남 미술 수업에 등록하고 싶어요.

여 여기 등록 양식서가 있어요. 현금으로 결제해주세요.

남 신용카드는 안 되나요? 그럼 **현금지급기에 들러야겠네요.** 금방 올게요.

남자는 다음으로 무엇을 할 것 같은가?

(A) 여자에게 명함을 준다.

(B) 기계에서 돈을 인출한다.

(C) 미술 수업을 참관한다.

(D) 미술 용품을 구매한다.

정답이 들리는 단서 표현

질문에 나오는 시점 표현은 패러프레이징이 되지 않고 대화에서 거의 그대로 등장한다.	
질문	정답 구간
What will happen **next year?** 내년에는 무슨 일이 일어날 것인가?	We should prepare for **next year's** office relocation. 내년 사무실 이전에 대비해야 합니다.
What will happen **later in the year?** 올해 말에는 무슨 일이 일어날 것인가?	Your lease will expire **later this year.** 임대가 올해 말에 만료됩니다.
What will happen **on Monday?** 월요일에는 무슨 일이 일어날 것인가?	**Starting on Monday,** we will be offering a discount. 월요일부터 할인을 제공할 것입니다.
Where is the man planning to go **today?** 남자는 오늘 어디에 갈 계획인가?	I'm going to a business expo **today.** 오늘 비즈니스 박람회에 갈 예정입니다.

정답 및 해설 p.75

대화를 듣고 다음에 할 일 문제를 풀어보자. 다시 듣고 빈칸을 채우자.

1.

What will the **man** most likely **do next**?

(A) Operate a cash register

(B) Search for a supervisor

(C) Post a warning notice

(D) Check a store's inventory

> M: Good afternoon. Are you looking for something in particular?
>
> W: I want to buy strawberry jam, but this bottle is a little big. Do you sell a sample size of this jam?
>
> M: __ ____ and _____ in our _____ in the back. It shouldn't take long.

2.

What will the **woman** most likely **do next**?

(A) File a complaint

(B) Submit a payment

(C) Put her name on a list

(D) Speak with some colleagues

> W: Hello. I'd like to book some tickets for this Thursday's show.
>
> M: I'm sorry but the show was already sold out. I can _____ _____ ___ the waiting list if you'd like.
>
> W: ____ ____ _____ ___ ___ _____ and see if they are _____ ___ _____.

3.

What does the **man** say he **will send** the woman?

(A) A video

(B) A contract

(C) An itinerary

(D) An e-mail address

> M: Susan. ABS News is sending a camera _____ this afternoon to get some _____. Can you give them a _____ of the plant?
>
> W: That's no problem, Is there anything in particular I should show them?
>
> M: Yes. They sent me their _____ _____ with a _____ of things they'd like to see. ____ _____ it to you.

4.

What does the **woman** say **will happen later today**?

(A) A grand opening will take place.

(B) New tables will be delivered.

(C) Workers will undergo training.

(D) A food critic will visit.

> W: Hi, Martin. Sorry to call you on your day off, but our restaurant is _____. Are you able to come in? We have a _____ _____ _____ _____ later today.
>
> M: I'm actually at a dental clinic at the moment. Why don't you contact Allstar, the temporary staffing agency?
>
> M: OK. I think I should do that.

1. What problem does the man mention?
   (A) A bill contained an error.
   (B) He missed a flight.
   (C) A meeting was postponed.
   (D) He lost a confirmation code.

2. What does the woman tell the man about?
   (A) A refund policy
   (B) A new service
   (C) A group reservation
   (D) A computer malfunction

3. What will the man probably do next?
   (A) Prepare his belongings
   (B) Call another business
   (C) Make a payment
   (D) Provide some information

4. What does the woman inquire about?
   (A) A business recommendation
   (B) A payment date
   (C) A project deadline
   (D) A travel plan

5. What is the man asked to do?
   (A) Contact the head of a company
   (B) Answer calls at the reception desk
   (C) Check for a piece of mail
   (D) Print a new copy of an invoice

6. What does the man plan to do?
   (A) Ask a colleague to do a task
   (B) Wait at the woman's office
   (C) Postpone a meeting
   (D) Review a budget report

7. What does the man say he wants to do?
   (A) Move to a new location
   (B) Change the hours of operation
   (C) Expand the size of the staff
   (D) Review some new designs

8. What does Sharon suggest doing?
   (A) Partnering with a competitor
   (B) Getting a recommendation
   (C) Holding a training session
   (D) Updating a Web site

9. What does Tiffany offer to prepare?
   (A) A job description
   (B) A rental contract
   (C) A business itinerary
   (D) A recruitment video

10. Why is the man excited?
    (A) He can enter a competition.
    (B) His submission will be published.
    (C) His sports team is gaining a sponsor.
    (D) He will be interviewed in a magazine.

11. What does the woman ask the man for?
    (A) Some uniforms
    (B) Some photos
    (C) An expense report
    (D) A registration form

12. What information does the woman give the man?
    (A) The rules of a contest
    (B) The date and time of a meeting
    (C) The e-mail address of a department
    (D) The proposed length of a piece of writing

13. Why is the woman running late?

(A) Her bus never came.

(B) There is traffic congestion.

(C) She woke up late.

(D) Her car would not start.

14. What kind of company do the speakers most likely work for?

(A) A beverage manufacturer

(B) A sports clothing producer

(C) A transportation company

(D) A recruitment agency

15. What does the man say he will try to do?

(A) Change a meeting location

(B) Take a different bus

(C) Visit the woman's workplace

(D) Postpone a presentation

16. What is the purpose of the phone call?

(A) To thank a donor

(B) To place an order

(C) To accept a job offer

(D) To extend an invitation

17. What does the man say happened last month?

(A) He retired from a job.

(B) He published a paper.

(C) He graduated from college.

(D) He changed his work schedule.

18. What will the man most likely do on Tuesday afternoon?

(A) Tour a facility

(B) Call a colleague

(C) Submit a document

(D) Watch a training video

19. What are the speakers mainly discussing?

(A) A new business deal

(B) A corporate restructuring

(C) An upcoming news story

(D) A supervisor's promotion

20. What will Tommy most likely do for Star Media?

(A) Upgrade their computer system

(B) Find an affordable printer

(C) Sell advertising spots

(D) Manage their online presence

21. What does the woman say is unusual?

(A) Hiring an outside contractor

(B) Merging with another company

(C) Having two people lead a project

(D) Working with news organizations

22. What does the man say about the clothing line?

(A) It is popular with customers.

(B) It is reasonably priced.

(C) It will be discontinued.

(D) It will be redesigned.

23. What did the woman recently purchase?

(A) Advertising space

(B) An article of clothing

(C) A training program

(D) A company car

24. What does the man say he will do?

(A) Promote an employee

(B) Cancel a subscription

(C) Call a colleague

(D) Forward an e-mail

의도 파악 문제

전략 주어진 문장을 확인하고 보기를 보면서 가능성을 따져 본다. 특정 단어를 노려 듣는 것이 아니라 제시 문구가 나올 때까지의 상황, 특히 앞뒤 문장을 잘 듣고 정답을 도출한다.

문제 유형 Why does the woman say, "this isn't the first time"? 왜 여자는 다음과 같은 말을 하는가?
What does the man mean when he says, "I know the city well"? 남자의 말의 의미는 무엇인가?
What does man imply when he says, "You can't do that"? 남자의 말이 암시하는 바는 무엇인가?

핵심 포인트 제시문 앞뒤 문맥으로 의도를 파악하자. 🎧 P3_17

M Do you have any ideas for your next feature article?

W Well, a new medical facility is scheduled to open next year, and I thought about writing a report on that.

M Oh, Sharon is already working on that.

W I guess I should think of something else, then.
❯ 업무 담당자가 이미 정해졌음을 알 수 있다.
Let me think about it and I'll let you know when I come up with another topic.

Why does the man say, "Sharon is already working on that"?
(A) To emphasize a deadline
(B) To compliment a worker
(C) To decline a proposal
(D) To suggest a collaboration

남 다음 특집 기사에 대한 아이디어 있어요?
여 새로운 의료 시설이 내년에 개원할 예정인데 **그것에 대한 보도를 쓸 생각이었어요.**
남 아, **그건 샤론이 이미 작업하고 있어요.**
여 그럼 다른 걸 **생각해야겠네요.** 생각해보고 다른 주제가 떠오르면 알려드릴게요.

남자가 "그건 샤론이 이미 작업하고 있어요"라고 말한 이유는 무엇인가?
(A) 마감일을 강조하기 위해
(B) 직원을 칭찬하기 위해
(C) 기획안을 거절하기 위해
(D) 협업을 제안하기 위해

정답이 들리는 단서 표현

제시문 바로 다음 문장에서 70% 이상 정답이 나온다.

M Isn't it supposed to rain today? ❯ 제시문
남 오늘 비 온다고 하지 않았어요?

W Yes, I don't think it's the best time to wash a car.
여 맞아요. 세차하기에 좋은 때는 아닌 것 같네요.

남자의 말은 무엇을 의미하는가?
(A) 행사 장소를 바꾸어야 한다.
(B) 가까운 식당을 추천한다.
(C) 작업을 미루어야 한다.
(D) 야외 진열 상품을 옮겨야 한다.

··

W Our annual clearance sale is approaching. ❯ 제시문
남 연례 재고 정리 세일이 다가오고 있어요.

M Don't worry. Everything is right on schedule.
여 걱정 마세요. 모든 것이 계획대로 되고 있어요.

여자는 이 말을 왜 했는가?
(A) 구매를 미룰 것을 제안하기 위해
(B) 업무를 도와 달라고 부탁하기 위해
(C) 직원들이 분주한 이유를 설명하기 위해
(D) 행사 준비를 재촉하기 위해

정답 및 해설 p.82

대화를 듣고 의도 파악 문제를 풀어보자. 다시 듣고 빈칸을 채우자.

1.

What does the **woman** mean when she says, "**It looks like it's going to rain**"?

(A) A project should be postponed.

(B) A weather report was inaccurate.

(C) A coworker should change clothes.

(D) A drive will take longer than usual.

> M: Maria, Bridge Hotel wants us to _____ their building. Let's load up the truck and head over.
>
> W: Right now? It looks like it's going to rain.
>
> M: Well, then we'd better _____ ____ our supplier to get paint and brushes.
>
> W: OK. Maybe we can start on the Bridge Hotel tomorrow.

2.

What does the **woman** mean when she says, "**This is a restricted event**"?

(A) She needs to check a form of identification.

(B) She has exclusive passes for sale.

(C) She cannot invite a colleague.

(D) She thinks a party will be fun.

> W: Excuse me, sir. May I help you? This is a restricted event.
>
> M: Oh, here is my _____ _____. I'm _____ the opening of the ceremony.
>
> W: Very good, Mr. Morris. You can pick up your press kit in the reporters' room down the hall.

3.

What does the **man** mean when he says, "**We've never done anything like that before**"?

(A) He wants to receive training.

(B) He is excited about a project.

(C) He is not comfortable taking a job.

(D) He thinks some contact information is wrong.

> M: Hi, you've reached Max Consulting. How may I help you?
>
> W: We're launching a new line of shoes this July. We need a marketing consultant to _____ _____ ___.
>
> M: We've never done anything like that before. Our firm _____ _____ consulting for _____. But I can recommend a company that offers the service.

4.

Why does the **man** say, "**they don't even fill a page**"?

(A) To explain that a task is easy

(B) To suggest changing suppliers

(C) To show disappointment with a report

(D) To select people for a project

> M: Julia, could you lead the new employee orientation next week?
>
> W: I'd love to help out, but I have a _____ _____ next week. Will it require a lot of preparation?
>
> M: I've got a copy of my _____ from last year here. As you can see, they don't even fill a page.
>
> W: OK. I can _____ that.

시각 정보 문제

전략 시각 정보에서 보기에 해당하는 항목은 직접적으로 언급되지 않으므로 보기에 대응하는 정보를 노려 듣는다.

문제 유형 Look at the graphic. What room does the man want? 시각 정보에 따르면 남자는 어떤 방을 원하는가?

Look at the graphic. What information is incorrect? 시각 정보에 따르면 어떤 정보가 잘못되었는가?

Look at the graphic. Where does the speaker work? 시각 정보에 따르면 화자는 어디에서 일하는가?

핵심 포인트 **대화에서 듣게 될 부분은 보기에 상응하는 시각 정보이다.** 🎧 P3_19

W Hello. I got your phone number from a friend, Sam Ford. I'd like to get a patio built in my backyard. Can you give me a price quote?

M Sure. What **type of material** would you like?

W I really like Sam's patio. **How much did that cost?**

M It was $150 per square meter.

❯ 가격을 듣고 표에서 상응하는 재질을 찾는다.

W That's not bad! When can you visit my place?

Material	Cost per Square Meter
Stone	$200
Brick	$150
Cement	$100
Gravel	$50

Look at the graphic. What is **Sam's patio made of**?

(A) Stone

(B) Brick

(C) Cement

(D) Gravel

> 보기 정보: 재질
> 들을 항목: 비용

여 안녕하세요. 당신의 번호를 제 친구 샘 포드한테 받았어요. 뒷마당에 테라스를 만들고 싶은데 견적서를 주실 수 있을까요?

남 물론이죠. **어떤 종류의 재질을** 원하세요?

여 샘의 테라스가 마음에 드는데 **그건 얼마였죠?**

남 제곱 미터당 **150달러요.**

여 나쁘지 않네요. 언제 방문하실 수 있으세요?

시각 정보에 따르면 샘의 테라스는 무엇으로 만들어졌는가?

(A) 돌

(B) 벽돌

(C) 시멘트

(D) 자갈

정답이 들리는 단서 표현

최상급을 사용하여 나타낼 수 있는 정보는 정답 가능성이 높다.

❯ the largest number 가장 큰 수치, the least amount 가장 적은 양, the most expensive 가장 비싼

※ 서수 + 최상급 표현에 유의하자 ❯ the second longest 두 번째로 긴

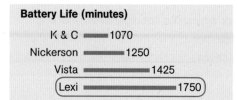

Battery Life (minutes)

K & C ━━1070
Nickerson ━━━1250
Vista ━━━━1425
Lexi ━━━━━━1750

❯ "We have **the longest** lasting battery in the industry."

우리는 업계에서 **가장 오래가는** 배터리를 가지고 있어요.

질문: 화자는 어떤 회사에서 일하는가?

정답: Lexi

LISTENING PRACTICE 🎧 P3_20

정답 및 해설 p.83

대화를 듣고 시각 정보 문제를 풀어보자. 다시 듣고 빈칸을 채우자.

1.

```
┌─────────────────────────────────┐
│   Waylon T11 Instruction Manual │
│        Table of Contents        │
├─────────────────────────────────┤
│ Part 1 ...............Charging the battery │
│ Part 2 ...............Emptying the bag     │
│ Part 3 ...............Connecting attachments │
│ Part 4 ...............Replacing the filter │
└─────────────────────────────────┘
```

Look at the graphic. Which part of the manual does the **woman mention**?

(A) Part 1   (B) Part 2

(C) Part 3   (D) Part 4

M: Thank you for calling Waylon Tech. How may I help you?

W: Hi. I just bought a Waylon Tech vacuum cleaner—the Waylon T11. But I'm having

_____ _____ _____.

M: I see. Have you tried visiting our Web site? There are _____ videos about how to use the features on all of our products.

W: I didn't realize that. I think that's exactly what I need. Thank you.

2.

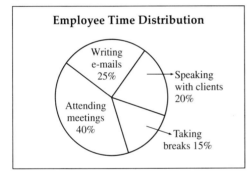

Employee Time Distribution

Writing e-mails 25%
Speaking with clients 20%
Attending meetings 40%
Taking breaks 15%

Look at the graphic. What figure does the **woman** think is **inaccurate** for her?

(A) 15%   (B) 20%

(C) 25%   (D) 40%

M: Here, take a look. Can you believe we spend so much of our time answering e-mails?

W: Actually, that doesn't surprise me. _____, this _____ ___ _____! There's ___ _____ I spend _____ _____ _____ in meetings.

M: Well, the numbers are averages for all the workers, so you might be an _____.

W: Can you e-mail this to me? I want to spend more time looking at it.

3.

```
┌─────────────────────────────────┐
│    Most Common Error Codes      │
├─────────────────────────────────┤
│ EC1: Paper jam                  │
│ EC2: Out of paper               │
│ EC3: Low toner                  │
│ EC4: Memory access error        │
└─────────────────────────────────┘
```

Look at the graphic. Which error code is the printer displaying?

(A) EC1   (B) EC2

(C) EC3   (D) EC4

W: I'm trying to copy some flyers, and I need some help with the copier.

M: What seems to be the problem?

W: It has started producing _____ _____ _____, and the _____ light is blinking.

M: Oh, I can take care of that. I'll be there in about fifteen minutes.

1. Why does the man congratulate the woman?
   (A) She submitted work early.
   (B) She found a new client.
   (C) She received a promotion.
   (D) She was given an award.

2. What is the woman working on now?
   (A) Preparing an informational brochure
   (B) Making travel arrangements
   (C) Recruiting new team members
   (D) Drafting a trade agreement

3. What does the man imply when he says, "Didn't Mr. Jackson work on it"?
   (A) He understands the reason for an error.
   (B) Mr. Jackson can provide some advice.
   (C) A task should have been completed.
   (D) The woman should pay Mr. Jackson.

4. Why will the woman travel to Dallas?
   (A) To deliver some items
   (B) To visit some relatives
   (C) To inspect a facility
   (D) To attend a business meeting

5. What does the woman mean when she says, "I know the city well"?
   (A) She is familiar with the man's company.
   (B) She has a lot of business connections in Dallas.
   (C) She does not need additional equipment.
   (D) She understands when to avoid rush hour.

6. What does the man say he will do in ten minutes?
   (A) Input the woman's details
   (B) Check a vehicle registry
   (C) Speak to a supervisor
   (D) Send a booking confirmation

Time	Activity
9:00 A.M.	Tour: Insect-Eating Plants
10:00 A.M.	Demonstration: Tree-Trimming
11:30 A.M.	Tour: Birdhouse Collection
12:30 P.M.	Demonstration: Caring for Roses

7. What has caused a cancellation?
   (A) Some computer errors
   (B) An absent employee
   (C) Some weather damage
   (D) A lack of participants

8. Look at the graphic. When will the man participate in an activity?
   (A) At 9:00 A.M.
   (B) At 10:00 A.M.
   (C) At 11:30 A.M.
   (D) At 12:30 P.M.

9. What does the woman give the man?
   (A) An updated schedule
   (B) An admission ticket
   (C) An informational pamphlet
   (D) A city map

10. What is the woman planning?

(A) A company outing
(B) A charity fundraiser
(C) A building restoration
(D) An awards ceremony

11. What does the man mention about the activity?

(A) The participation fee has recently increased.
(B) The tickets are not transferable.
(C) The booking must be made in advance.
(D) The size of the group varies.

12. What does the man imply when he says, "I don't see why not"?

(A) He is willing to provide a discount.
(B) He needs a situation explained again.
(C) He can accommodate a request.
(D) He is unable to provide more information.

13. What does the man say he needs to do?

(A) Install a computer program
(B) Write down an error message
(C) Take a lunch break
(D) Make some copies

14. What does the woman imply when she says, "this morning the computer automatically updated itself"?

(A) She has time to assist the man.
(B) She believes some work is unnecessary.
(C) She is experiencing technical difficulties.
(D) She is pleased with some software.

15. What does the woman offer to give the man?

(A) A user's manual
(B) A meal ticket
(C) A phone number
(D) A password

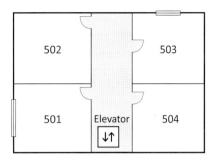

16. What is the purpose of the man's visit to the business?

(A) To make a delivery
(B) To attend an interview
(C) To lead a training session
(D) To sign a contract

17. Look at the graphic. Where does the man need to go?

(A) Room 501
(B) Room 502
(C) Room 503
(D) Room 504

18. What does the man inquire about?

(A) The hiring process
(B) The parking fee
(C) The closing time
(D) The security measures

19. Where does the man most likely work?
(A) At a bank
(B) At a clothing warehouse
(C) At a cell phone store
(D) At a catering company

20. What will the woman do next?
(A) Open a shipment
(B) Transfer some money
(C) Speak to a colleague
(D) Place an order

21. What does the man mean when he says, "I really appreciate that"?
(A) He is pleased that the woman will attempt to solve a problem.
(B) He is informing the woman her service will be upgraded.
(C) He is thanking the woman for postponing a payment date.
(D) He is encouraging the woman to open a new customer account.

22. Why does the woman say, "Mr. Han is working on many projects"?
(A) To promote an organization
(B) To request clarification
(C) To accept an offer
(D) To justify a cost

23. What is the man writing an article about?
(A) A method of financing
(B) A social media company
(C) A program for entrepreneurs
(D) A group of community organizers

24. What does the woman say she will send the man?
(A) Financial documents
(B) An appointment card
(C) Promotional materials
(D) An interview transcript

```
****************************
    Emerson Camping Goods
****************************
Customer Receipt 0158 / May 19


3-Person Tent x 1............. $145
Nylon Sleeping Bag x 1........ $95
Gas Lantern x 1.............. $50
Battery-Operated
Phone Charger X 1............ $30



                     TOTAL  $320
```

25. Look at the graphic. How much will the man receive as a refund?
(A) $145
(B) $95
(C) $50
(D) $30

26. What did the man do yesterday?
(A) Read some product reviews
(B) Returned from a camping trip
(C) Noticed some damage to a product
(D) Bought some camping gear

27. What does the man say he plans to do?
(A) Purchase some batteries for a device
(B) Browse the store for new merchandise
(C) Return to the business later
(D) Borrow an item from a friend

28. What problem does the man mention?

(A) A conference call was interrupted.

(B) A piece of equipment had a malfunction.

(C) An employee did not record her working hours.

(D) A technician could not install a software program.

29. Why does the man say, "This isn't the first time this has happened"?

(A) To apologize

(B) To express disapproval

(C) To comfort an employee

(D) To indicate he has a solution

30. What will Mr. Tyler help the woman do?

(A) Use a computer program

(B) Locate a missing item

(C) Apply for a promotion

(D) Submit an evaluation

---

31. What does the woman say about the lighting?

(A) She likes the color.

(B) It matches the theme of the event.

(C) It will help attract customers.

(D) A competitor used the same style.

32. Why does the woman say, "Many companies put most expensive products on the top shelf"?

(A) To provide information about a competitor

(B) To propose a different store layout

(C) To suggest some changes to a display

(D) To request that the man purchase a product

33. According to the woman, what will happen on Saturday?

(A) An event will finish.

(B) Items will be collected.

(C) A display will be set up.

(D) Some customers will arrive.

Valley Hiking Group				
Fall Hiking Trips Silver Mountains				
Sept. 3rd	Sept. 17th	Oct. 1st	Oct. 15th	Oct. 29th
Oak Trail	Holly Trail	Birch Trail	Pine Trail	Fern Trail

34. Who most likely is the man?

(A) A recruitment agent

(B) A store manager

(C) A personal trainer

(D) A local tour guide

35. What has the woman recently done?

(A) Started a new job

(B) Moved to a new city

(C) Gone on vacation

(D) Renewed a membership

36. Look at the graphic. When will the woman probably join the hiking group?

(A) September 17

(B) October 1

(C) October 15

(D) October 29

1. Where does the man work?

   (A) At a retail store
   (B) At a local theater
   (C) At a news publication
   (D) At a dining establishment

2. What does the woman want to do?

   (A) File a complaint
   (B) Receive a refund
   (C) Postpone a delivery
   (D) Cancel a subscription

3. What does the man offer to give the woman?

   (A) A free trial
   (B) A theater ticket
   (C) A restaurant coupon
   (D) An upgraded membership

4. What does the man want to record?

   (A) A social event
   (B) A press conference
   (C) A training session
   (D) A musical performance

5. What video camera feature does the woman say is important?

   (A) The option to connect a microphone
   (B) The ability to record in low light
   (C) The size of its memory card
   (D) The life of its battery

6. What does the woman suggest?

   (A) Buying another piece of equipment
   (B) Signing up for an Internet storage account
   (C) Installing professional lights
   (D) Renting a recording studio

7. Why does the woman apologize to the man?

   (A) She forgot to return his call.
   (B) She closed her store early.
   (C) She damaged a machine.
   (D) She sold an item.

8. What does the man say he needs?

   (A) A photo of a product
   (B) A security credential
   (C) An instruction manual
   (D) A repairperson's phone number

9. What will the woman most likely do next?

   (A) Call a colleague
   (B) Locate an item
   (C) Make a purchase
   (D) Wash some dishes

10. What is the man giving a presentation about?

   (A) Tourism
   (B) Marketing
   (C) Accounting
   (D) History

11. What does the woman give the man?

   (A) A city map
   (B) A bus ticket
   (C) A gift package
   (D) An identification badge

12. Why does the woman say, "It's in a lovely part of town"?

   (A) To make a recommendation
   (B) To thank the man for an offer
   (C) To agree with the man's opinion
   (D) To show her interest in history

13. What problem does the company have?

(A) It is unable to manufacture a clothing item.

(B) The jackets it sells are not waterproof.

(C) Delivery costs are too high.

(D) Sales have been decreasing.

14. What does the woman suggest?

(A) Contacting a local newspaper

(B) Running an advertising campaign

(C) Using a different supplier

(D) Closing a store

15. What does the woman ask Peter to do?

(A) Cancel a contract

(B) Arrange a meeting

(C) Order some materials

(D) Repair some machinery

16. What does the woman say about Maestro shoulder bags?

(A) They are very expensive.

(B) They are sold on the Internet.

(C) They are made out of leather.

(D) They are popular with students.

17. What does the man say he is eager for?

(A) Seeing reactions to some products

(B) Finishing a lengthy project

(C) Reading a magazine article

(D) Interviewing customers at a trade show

18. What will the man send the designer?

(A) Some fabrics

(B) Color samples

(C) Articles of clothing

(D) Promotional materials

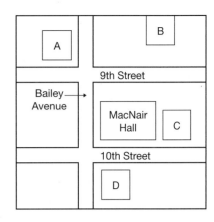

19. Who most likely is the man?

(A) A fitness instructor

(B) An academic lecturer

(C) A professional musician

(D) A theater critic

20. Look at the graphic. Where does the woman recommend parking?

(A) Lot A

(B) Lot B

(C) Lot C

(D) Lot D

21. What information will the woman check on?

(A) A billing address

(B) An entrance fee

(C) A mailing date

(D) A return policy

22. According to the woman, what will happen next week?

(A) A new product will be released.

(B) A company will open a new branch.

(C) A model will be discontinued.

(D) A store will hold a seasonal sale.

23. What does the woman ask about?

(A) Different models available

(B) Details of the promotion

(C) Delivery schedules

(D) Information about manufacturers

24. What does the man say the manager will do?

(A) Increase the inventory

(B) Visit a printing shop

(C) Distribute some leaflets

(D) Update some flyers

25. What does the man ask the woman about?

(A) A job candidate

(B) A business owner

(C) A keynote speaker

(D) A branch manager

26. In which department does the woman most likely work?

(A) Public relations

(B) Shipping and receiving

(C) Accounting

(D) Graphic design

27. What does the woman ask the man to do?

(A) Forward a message

(B) Review a contract

(C) Copy some documents

(D) Write a report

28. What is the woman trying to do?

(A) Receive legal assistance

(B) Relocate to a different city

(C) Sell an idea for a novel

(D) Apply for a permanent job

29. What does the man say the woman should do?

(A) Talking to an editor

(B) Visiting a place

(C) Keeping a journal

(D) Replacing a piece of equipment

30. What does the woman ask the man to do?

(A) Give her an advance payment

(B) Conduct a meeting remotely

(C) Leave a company some feedback

(D) Submit a sample product

31. Why is the woman at the store?

(A) To request a repair service

(B) To purchase a new item

(C) To make a complaint

(D) To pick up a delivery

32. What does the woman mean when she says, "there's a lot to wash every day"?

(A) She needs more employees.

(B) She cannot meet a deadline.

(C) She wants immediate repairs.

(D) She has a specific requirement in mind.

33. Why does the man recommend Astella's QM2 model?

(A) It is the most popular among customers.

(B) It is energy efficient.

(C) It makes less noise.

(D) It is offered at a reduced rate.

34. Why is the woman visiting Birmingham?

(A) To meet a client

(B) To attend a training session

(C) To give a presentation

(D) To purchase an upgraded machine

35. What does the woman say she is traveling with?

(A) Medical supplies

(B) Pieces of furniture

(C) Camera equipment

(D) Product catalogs

36. What does the man say about the room 901?

(A) It is reasonably priced.

(B) It is currently occupied.

(C) It is close to the elevator.

(D) It has been recently renovated.

---

37. What type of event are the speakers preparing for?

(A) An awards banquet

(B) A retirement party

(C) A product launch

(D) A charity dinner

38. What does the man say he saw earlier?

(A) A truck

(B) Some party supplies

(C) A former colleague

(D) Some audio-visual equipment

39. What does the man say he will do next?

(A) Contact a food vendor

(B) Distribute a schedule

(C) Finalize a guest list

(D) Revise a speech

Johnny Browning: Upcoming Events	
August 3	Bluelight Comedy Club
August 10	Hanover Plaza
August 17	Bluelight Comedy Club
August 18	Comedy Underground

40. Why will the man be busy?

(A) He will help a friend move.

(B) He will visit an art exhibition.

(C) He will go on vacation.

(D) He will attend a conference.

41. Look at the graphic. When do the speakers agree to attend a comedy show?

(A) On August 3

(B) On August 10

(C) On August 17

(D) On August 18

42. What does the woman say she will do next?

(A) Post a schedule

(B) Send a message

(C) Call her friends

(D) Reserve some seats

4

● PART 4 풀이 전략

PART 4 이렇게 나온다

한 사람이 말하는 담화문을 듣고 이에 딸린 세 개의 문제를 푸는 유형이다. 총 10개의 담화문을 듣고 30개의 문제를 풀게 되며, 파트 3와 마찬가지로 문제와 보기는 시험지에 인쇄되어 나온다.

🔊 음원

Questions 71 through 73 refer to the following telephone message.

Hi, Ms. Najera. This is Ron from the administration office. I'm making the arrangements for your upcoming trip for the assembly plant inspection in Mumbai. There are some vaccinations you'll need to get before your trip, so I've booked you an appointment next week with Dr. Herbert at the Central Clinic. That's for 2 P.M. on Tuesday.
Also, I want to purchase your airline tickets as soon as possible. Would you like to sit by the window or by the aisle? Please call me back to let me know. I'm at extension 22. Thanks.

71. Why will the listener visit Mumbai?
72. What should the listener do next week?
73. What information does the speaker request?

📖 시험지

71. Why will the listener visit Mumbai?
(A) To attend a conference
(B) To inspect a factory
(C) To set up an office
(D) To sign a contract

72. What should the listener do next week?
(A) Review an itinerary
(B) Visit a medical facility
(C) Book a hotel
(D) Renew a passport

73. What information does the speaker request?
(A) A seating preference
(B) An airline name
(C) A ticket number
(D) A hotel recommendation

귀로 음원을 들으며   동시에   눈으로는 시험지의 보기를 파악!

PART 4 이렇게 푼다

❶ 담화문 듣기 전에 문제부터 읽기

문제를 먼저 읽는 것만으로도 앞으로 나올 담화의 흐름을 예상할 수 있다. 파트 4의 Directions를 읽어줄 때 71번 ~ 73번의 문제를 미리 읽어 둔다.

❷ 키워드 표시하기

키워드란 문제의 요지에 해당하는 단어들로, 의문사, 동사, 명사, 시간, 숫자 등이 이에 해당한다. 키워드를 표시하면 문제의 의미도 한눈에 들어오며, 정답의 단서가 들렸을 때 쉽게 포착할 수 있다.

71. Why will the listener visit Mumbai?	청자는 왜 뭄바이에 가나?
72. What should the listener do next week?	청자가 다음 주에 할 일은?
73. What information does the speaker request?	화자가 요청한 정보는?

❸ 화자와 청자 구분하기

문제에서 묻고 있는 내용이 speaker에 관한 것인지 listener에 관한 것인지를 구분해야 한다.

What does the speaker ask the listener to do?	화자가 요청하는 것
What is the listener asked to do?	청자가 요청받은 것

❹ 들으면서 정답 선택하기

정답의 단서는 문제 순서대로 나온다. 따라서 해당 문제의 단서를 들으면 바로 정답을 선택하고 다음 문제로 넘어가서 다음 단서를 기다린다.

PART 4 담화 유형을 알아두자

다른 파트에 비해 어휘 수준이 높아 어렵게 느낄 수 있다. 담화 유형별 빈출 내용을 기억해 두자.

전화 메시지	전화 건 사람이 응답기에 남기는 메시지: 문의, 소식 전달, 예약 확인/취소/변경 등
	자동 응답 메시지(ARS): 업체 소개, 영업 시간 안내, 내선 번호 안내 등
공지 / 안내	인사 및 채용 결과, 새로운 시스템 도입, 공사, 행사, 시설물 이용 안내 등
관광 / 견학	방문 장소 소개, 일정 안내, 주의사항 등
광고 / 방송	신제품이나 서비스 광고, 지역사회 뉴스, 스포츠 뉴스, 일기예보 등
인물 / 강연	수상자/강연자/직원 소개, 환경이나 기술 등 특정 주제에 관한 강연 등

패러프레이징

패러프레이징은 Part 4에서도 중요하다. Part 3에서와 마찬가지로 패러프레이징의 기본 개념인 동의어로 바꾸기와 상위어로 바꾸기는 Part 4에서도 그대로 적용된다. 단, 지문이 대화 형식이 아니라 한 사람이 말하는 담화문이므로 한 문장의 길이는 대화문보다 길어질 수 있다.

유형 1 동의어로 바꾸기

같은 뜻을 가진 대체어로 바꾸어 표현하는 방식　예시 **revenue** 수익 ▸ **profit** 수익

hand out 나누어 주다	▸ distribute / pass out	survey 설문 조사	▸ questionnaire
taste 맛보다, 시음하다	▸ sample	retire 은퇴하다	▸ step down
detour 우회	▸ alternative route	short film 짧은 영상	▸ video
direction 설명, 안내	▸ instruction	easy to use 사용하기 쉬운	▸ user-friendly
free 무료의	▸ complimentary	snacks and drinks 다과	▸ refreshments
enlarge 확장하다	▸ expand	fundraiser 모금 행사	▸ charity event
gym 헬스클럽	▸ fitness center	collect money 돈을 걷다	▸ raise funds
entry form 신청서	▸ registration form	extra fee 추가 요금	▸ additional charge
launch 출시하다	▸ release	step 단계, 절차	▸ procedure
show 보여주다	▸ demonstrate	carry out 실시하다	▸ conduct
check (여부를) 확인하다	▸ verify	not allowed 허가되지 않은	▸ not permitted
specialist 전문가	▸ expert	call ~ back 회신 전화하다	▸ return a call
brainstorm 생각해내다	▸ come up with ideas	picnic 야유회	▸ outing
connect (전화를) 연결하다	▸ transfer a call	present 제시하다	▸ show / provide
match 시합, 대회	▸ competition	put together 조립하다	▸ assemble
schedule 일정을 잡다	▸ arrange	floor plan 평면도	▸ layout

유형 2. 상위어로 바꾸기

포괄적인 뜻을 가진 상위 개념으로 바꾸어 표현하는 방식　예시 **résumé** 이력서 ▸ **document** 서류

donation 기부	▸ contribution 기여	dentist 치과	▸ medical office 진료소
mayor 시장	▸ city official 시 공무원	hotel 호텔	▸ accommodation 숙소
vice president 부사장	▸ executive 임원	update 업데이트하다	▸ change 변경하다
storm 폭우	▸ bad weather 악천후	user review 고객 후기	▸ comment 의견
coffee / tea 커피, 차	▸ beverage 음료	TV / Radio TV, 라디오	▸ media 미디어, 매체
magazine 잡지	▸ publication 출판물	lunch 점심	▸ meal 식사
incentive 인센티브	▸ reward 보상	helmet 헬멧	▸ safety gear 안전 장비
warehouse 창고	▸ storage area 저장소	with a logo 로고가 있는	▸ customized 맞춤 제작된
keyboard 키보드	▸ accessory 부대용품	marathon 마라톤	▸ athletic event 운동 경기

문장을 듣고 패러프레이징을 연습해보자.

1.

What does the speaker ask the listener to do?

(A) Fill out a questionnaire

(B) Take part in a group exercise

2.

What does the speaker say is available?

(A) A price reduction

(B) Customized items

3.

What will be arranged by the company?

(A) Accommodation

(B) A luncheon

4.

What is Wyatt Morris planning to do?

(A) Relocate to a different branch

(B) Retire from the company

5.

What does the speaker recommend?

(A) Taking a detour

(B) Driving at a slow speed

6.

What does the speaker say she will do?

(A) Find some financial data

(B) Distribute some information

7.

What feature does the speaker mention?

(A) They are easy to assemble.

(B) They come ready to use.

8.

What does the speaker say is available?

(A) Some refreshments

(B) Product samples

9.

Who will visit the factory next week?

(A) A company executive

(B) A potential client

10.

What does the speaker say is available?

(A) Extra discount coupons

(B) Complimentary storage space

11.

What will happen next week?

(A) A facility tour

(B) A corporate outing

12.

Who held a press conference today?

(A) A city official

(B) An entrepreneur

13.

What feature does the speaker emphasize?

(A) It is durable.

(B) It is user-friendly.

14.

What does the speaker say she will do?

(A) Demonstrate some equipment

(B) Allocate funds

PART 4

INTRO 패러프레이징

전화 음성 메시지

출제 경향　병원 예약, 회사 생활, 주거, 일상 생활 등 가장 폭넓은 주제가 등장한다.

전략　화자의 신분, 전화 용건, 요청 사항에 포커스를 두어 청취하자.

● 지문의 흐름과 문제 구성　🎧 P4_02

번역 p. 94

인사 및 용건	Hi, this is Brenda Ahn. I'm scheduled to see the doctor for my annual checkup next month, **1 but I'm afraid I need to cancel.** I'll be moving out of state
추가 정보	very soon, and **2 I'm quite busy getting ready for the move.** Actually, I found a physician in the new
요청 사항	city, so **3 I would like you to send him my medical files.** Please give me a call back soon.

1 병원 정기 검사가 예약되어 있는데 취소해야 할 것 같아요.

2 곧 이사를 가게 되어 이사 준비로 바빠요.

3 이사하는 곳에 있는 병원 쪽으로 의료 기록을 보내주시면 좋겠어요.

주제 및 목적 문제	**1** What is the main **purpose of the call**? 전화의 목적은 무엇인가? **초반부 집중하기**	❷ **To cancel an appointment** 예약을 취소하기 위해
구체적 정보 문제	**2** **Why** does the speaker **say** she is **busy**? 화자는 왜 바쁘다고 말하는가? **키워드 busy 활용하기**	❷ **She is preparing for the relocation.** 이사 준비를 하고 있다.
요청 사항 문제	**3** What does the speaker **ask** the listener to do? 화자는 청자에게 무엇을 요청하는가? **요청의 단서 'I would like you to' 포착하기**	❷ **Send some records** 자료 보내기

질문의 단서가 되는 주요 표현

"**Thank you for calling** Eden Realty."	화자는 어디에서 일하는가?
"**Hi, this is** Alice **calling from** Northland Hospital."	청자는 누구인 것 같은가?
"**I'm calling about/regarding** your job application."	무엇에 관해 전화하는가?
"**I want to let you know that** your order is ready for pickup."	전화의 목적은 무엇인가?
"**I wonder if you could** write up a proposal."	화자는 무엇을 요청하는가?
"**Please call me back to** set up a time."	청자는 왜 전화해야 하는가?
"**You can reach me at** 555-1234/by e-mail."	화자는 어떻게 연락 받기를 원하는가?

LISTENING PRACTICE 🎧 P4_03

정답 및 해설 p.95

전화 음성 메시지를 듣고 다음 문제를 풀어보자. 다시 듣고 빈칸을 채우자.

1.

What is the **purpose** of the call?

(A) To confirm an agreement

(B) To make a payment

(C) To get driving directions

(D) To cancel an order

> Hello, this is Travis Anderson. I'm calling to let you know I've decided to _____ _____ _____ your business, using the _____ of the sample contract you gave me. Please call me back to discuss more in detail.

2.

What **problem** does the speaker mention?

(A) A patient missed an appointment.

(B) A form was delivered to the wrong recipient.

(C) A pharmacy is going out of business.

(D) A phone number is disconnected.

> Hi, I'm calling from Doctor Benson's office. We faxed you a _____ about an hour ago for one of our patients, Darryl Warren. He _____ _____ that he moved to the other side of town, but we _____ _____ you the _____. If you could give me a call back today to get this straightened out, I'd appreciate it.

3.

Why should the listener **call** the speaker **back**?

(A) To provide payment details

(B) To receive instructions for returns

(C) To arrange a time for a visit

(D) To set up delivery of some items

> Good morning, Ms. Hassan. This is Dustin Burns from Louis Contractors. I got your message saying that you're _____ _____ _____ the air conditioning system that we recently installed for you. I'll send someone to your home to do a check. Please call me back to _____ _____ _____ _____ _____ that would be best for you. Thanks.

4.

Why does the speaker say, "**now I don't know what to tell them**"?

(A) To express a regret

(B) To criticize a program

(C) To decline an invitation

(D) To request an instruction

> Mr. Ping, this is Ellen Donovan on the assembly floor. One of the conveyor belts stopped working. I have about fifteen workers _____ _____ _____, and now I don't know what to tell them. Until I _____ _____ _____ _____, I'm just going to send them to the cafeteria to _____ _____ _____.

1. Why does the speaker say there will be an additional charge to deliver an item?
   (A) It is large.
   (B) It is heavy.
   (C) It is fragile.
   (D) It is expensive.

2. What does the speaker ask the listener to do?
   (A) Make a payment online
   (B) Submit a paper document
   (C) Bring a piece of furniture outdoors
   (D) Specify a meeting time

3. What does the speaker recommend?
   (A) Joining a rewards program
   (B) Contacting a driver
   (C) Using an online service
   (D) Rescheduling a delivery time

4. What does the speaker say about Crystal Air Conditioning Services?
   (A) It no longer sells a certain brand.
   (B) It will open a new location soon.
   (C) It is having a holiday sale.
   (D) It is currently closed.

5. What can visitors to the Crystal Air Conditioning Services Web site do?
   (A) Look at merchandise
   (B) Download a coupon
   (C) Sign up for a newsletter
   (D) Extend a warranty

6. What should listeners do to obtain repair services?
   (A) Go to a store
   (B) Call a support line
   (C) E-mail a technician
   (D) Complete an online form

7. Why is the speaker calling the listener?
   (A) To request an invoice
   (B) To make a job offer
   (C) To gather contact information
   (D) To set up an interview

8. What is the listener asked to send?
   (A) A travel itinerary
   (B) Copies of a contract
   (C) A mailing address
   (D) Proof of certification

9. What does the speaker mention about Ms. Shim?
   (A) She can respond to questions.
   (B) She will conduct a training session.
   (C) She plans to contact the listener.
   (D) She is the newest employee.

10. Why does the speaker say, "We've sent those to Toronto"?
    (A) He wants to check whether items arrived.
    (B) He already dispatched some information.
    (C) He thinks a form may contain an error.
    (D) He wants to apologize for a delay.

11. What does the speaker plan to do?
    (A) Wait to process a request
    (B) Review an order online
    (C) Provide a partial refund
    (D) Send a new copy of a bill

12. What does the speaker say will happen next month?
    (A) A wider range of colors will be added.
    (B) The delivery area will be expanded.
    (C) More sizes will become available.
    (D) A loyalty program will be launched.

13. Who most likely is the listener?

(A) A park ranger

(B) A Web site developer

(C) A professional photographer

(D) A research scientist

14. What is the purpose of the call?

(A) To inquire about entrance fees

(B) To get advice about locations

(C) To set up an interview

(D) To schedule a group tour

15. What does the speaker say he plans to do?

(A) Attend a festival

(B) Lead a cleanup project

(C) Make a donation

(D) Attend a training session

16. Why does the speaker thank the listener?

(A) She helped to plan an anniversary party.

(B) She completed a task on short notice.

(C) She purchased an insurance policy.

(D) She waived a regular fee for a service.

17. What is Ms. Fletcher asked to do?

(A) Call the speaker back as soon as possible

(B) Assign a new task to her team

(C) Send some photographs of the options

(D) Share a compliment with her coworkers

18. What does the speaker imply when he says, "We've got lots of events in the coming months"?

(A) He would like to postpone a deadline.

(B) He is too busy to meet in person.

(C) He can provide future business.

(D) He will send an invitation to the listener.

Feature	C17	LR10	MH4	A9
Incline	✓	✓	✓	
Additional Cushioning	✓	✓		✓
Pre-Set Workout	✓			✓

19. Look at the graphic. Which model does the speaker think will be best?

(A) C17

(B) LR10

(C) MH4

(D) A9

20. What does the speaker inquire about?

(A) A setup procedure

(B) A delivery method

(C) A bulk discount

(D) A product warranty

21. What does the speaker say about Ms. Diaz?

(A) She must provide a signature.

(B) She is concerned about the budget.

(C) She will unload a shipment.

(D) She plans to meet with a supplier.

공지 / 안내 / 회의

출제 경향   회사 규정, 절차 변경사항 안내, 전략 회의 내용의 일부가 빈출된다.

전략   구체적인 변경 사항 및 변경 이유, 지시 전달 내용에 포커스를 두어 청취하자.

● 지문의 흐름과 문제 구성   🎧 P4_05   번역 p. 100

공지 사항

Good morning, everyone. I have a quick announcement to make. **¹ We would like to encourage all staff members to start carpooling to the office.** By doing so, **² you can take advantage of saving money on your commute.** To help you get organized for this activity, **³ I've put a sheet in the break room where you can sign up** if you're interested.

기대 효과

관련 정보

1	사무실 출근 시 카풀을 권장합니다.
2	교통비를 줄일 수 있을 거예요.
3	휴게실에 있는 신청서가 있어요.

주제 및 목적	**1** What is the announcement **mainly about?** 공지는 무엇에 관한 것인가? 초반부 집중하기	❯ **Sharing rides to work** 출근 시 차량 공유하기
구체적 정보 1	**2** What **benefit** does the speaker mention? 화자는 어떤 이점을 언급하는가? 키워드 **benefit** 활용하기 → **take advantage of**	❯ **Reducing personal expenses** 개인 비용을 줄이는 것
구체적 정보 2	**3** What is **available in the break room?** 휴게실에서 이용 가능한 것은 무엇인가? 키워드 **break room** 활용하기	❯ **A sign-up sheet** 신청서

질문의 단서가 되는 주요 표현

"**I have a few announcements before** we open our shoe store."	화자는 어디에서 일하는가?
"**As you may know**, a new alarm system was recently installed."	공지의 주제는 무엇인가?
"**I called this meeting to** discuss sales results."	회의의 목적은 무엇인가?
"**Please be advised to** check the board frequently."	화자는 무엇을 요청하는가?
"**Please note**, our office will be closed for renovations."	사무실은 왜 문을 닫는가?
"**All you have to do is** explain the new policy to customers."	청자는 무엇을 하도록 지시받는가?
"**If you have any questions about** the procedure, please call me."	청자는 왜 화자에게 전화하겠는가?

LISTENING PRACTICE 🎧 P4_06

정답 및 해설 p. 100

공지, 회의, 안내 메시지를 듣고 다음 문제를 풀어보자. 다시 듣고 빈칸을 채우자.

1.

What **are** the **passengers** of Flight 377 **asked** to do?

(A) Receive a new boarding document

(B) Agree to a security screening

(C) Form a line in front of a gate

(D) Remove certain items from their baggage

> Good evening, travelers. Queens Airlines Flight 377 to Dubai, _____ _____ at Gate D-12, has moved to Gate A-2 in the international terminal. Please note that Flight 377 passengers will _____ _____ _____ their boarding passes _____. Speak to an airline representative to receive your _____ boarding pass. We apologize for the inconvenience.

2.

What does the **speaker remind some employees** to do?

(A) Assist customers quickly

(B) Turn in some paperwork

(C) Check a price's accuracy

(D) Get a supervisor's help

> If there are no further questions, that's the end of our workshop on how to clean necklaces, rings, and bracelets. _____, these are _____ and expensive items, so if you are _____ about what to do, _____ _____ _____ _____ _____. I plan on holding more training like this in the future. I hope you'll find it helpful.

3.

What will the **listeners** most likely **do next**?

(A) Complete some paperwork

(B) Watch an educational video

(C) Meet some colleagues

(D) Vote on a suggestion

> Hello, and welcome to _____ _____ ___ at Alias Energy. You'll spend the next week going through our orientation program. _____ _____ _____ we're going to do is _____ _____ in a fun ice-breaking game. Let's all try to make a good impression. These are the people you'll likely work with for years to come.

4.

What does the **speaker encourage** the **listeners to do**?

(A) Attend a training session

(B) Send an e-mail to Ms. Bellani

(C) Participate in a competition

(D) View some images online

> To start off today's meeting, I'd like to congratulate one of our team members. Ms. Bellani was _____ the prestigious Angel Prize for design at an awards ceremony last night. Be sure to _____ _____ the photos of Ms. Bellani's _____ _____, which are posted on our company Web site. I'm sure you'll easily see why she was selected.

정답 및 해설 p. 101

1. Where is the announcement being made?
   (A) At a hotel
   (B) At a tourist information center
   (C) At a convention center
   (D) At an airport

2. What is the business now offering?
   (A) A guided tour
   (B) A range of discounts
   (C) A food court
   (D) A transportation service

3. Why are customers asked to fill in a form?
   (A) To enter a contest
   (B) To provide comments
   (C) To apply for a job
   (D) To make a payment

4. In which department do the listeners most likely work?
   (A) Purchasing
   (B) Human Resources
   (C) Finance
   (D) Quality Assurance

5. According to the speaker, what have employees requested?
   (A) An increase in vacation days
   (B) Higher pay for overtime hours
   (C) More options in an investment
   (D) Flexibility with a work schedule

6. What has Jennifer volunteered to do?
   (A) Lead an information session
   (B) Hire some temporary employees
   (C) Set up some equipment
   (D) Conduct a new survey

7. What is the speaker mainly discussing?
   (A) The delivery rates for a product
   (B) The closure of a warehouse
   (C) The results of a customer survey
   (D) The overtime rates for staff

8. Why does work need to be performed?
   (A) To enlarge storage space
   (B) To improve a manufacturing process
   (C) To make a building more accessible
   (D) To reduce delivery times

9. What will most likely happen in three weeks?
   (A) Some items will be on sale.
   (B) A new advertising campaign will begin.
   (C) Operating hours will change.
   (D) Some renovation work will be completed.

10. What event is the meeting mainly about?
    (A) An upcoming conference
    (B) An office assessment
    (C) A corporate merger
    (D) A new client

11. What does the speaker mean when he says, "Honestly, I can't find any reason to worry"?
    (A) He does not believe a rumor.
    (B) He believes a client is satisfied.
    (C) He does not understand a complaint.
    (D) He thinks the office is performing well.

12. What does the speaker say the listeners should do to report issues?
    (A) Speak directly to team leaders
    (B) Contact one of the inspectors
    (C) Send an e-mail to the speaker
    (D) File a report anonymously

13. Who most likely are the listeners?

(A) Athletes

(B) Journalists

(C) Artists

(D) Musicians

14. Why does the speaker recommend signing up quickly?

(A) A price increase is planned.

(B) Limited supplies are available.

(C) A lecture will begin soon.

(D) Early participants get a free gift.

15. Where should the listeners go for more information?

(A) To the front desk

(B) To the stage

(C) To the speaker's office

(D) To an entrance

16. What does the company plan to do?

(A) Have employees work from home

(B) Merge with a competitor

(C) Open a new site

(D) Improve staff productivity

17. What does the speaker imply when she says, "I haven't seen them all"?

(A) She will announce a decision later.

(B) She is worried about missing documents.

(C) She has more potential employees to interview.

(D) She wants to request a deadline extension.

18. What will the listeners hear about next?

(A) A group outing

(B) An annual bonus

(C) A prospective client

(D) A payment schedule

> ### Weekday Green Smoothies
>
> Monday .... Apple & Kale
>
> Tuesday.............. Melon & Mint
>
> Wednesday .... Spinach & Orange
>
> Thursday............ Avocado & Vanilla
>
> Friday.................. Kale & Pear

19. Look at the graphic. Which green smoothie does the speaker say will be available on two days this week?

(A) Apple & Kale

(B) Melon & Mint

(C) Spinach & Orange

(D) Kale & Pear

20. Who is Catherine Woods?

(A) A business owner

(B) A chef

(C) A food critic

(D) A customer

21. What has the speaker placed at the main entrance?

(A) Discount coupons

(B) Comment cards

(C) Promotional flyers

(D) Updated menus

여행 / 견학 / 관람

출제 경향   관광 여행, 공장/박물관 견학, 연극/영화 관람 안내가 빈출된다.

전략   견학 장소, 진행 순서, 유의 사항 및 권고 사항에 포커스를 두어 청취하자.

● 지문의 흐름과 문제 구성   🎧 P4_08

번역 p. 106

일정 안내

> Welcome to our factory tour. Let me briefly explain today's tour schedule. **¹ At 11 o'clock, you'll be taken to our laboratory area, where you can taste some of the new beverages.** After this, we will stop for lunch for an hour. **² Please come back here by 2 P.M.** When you come back, we'll watch a video of the history of our company. Okay, **³ I'm going to give you your wristbands next.** Please keep these on at all times.

요청 사항

다음에 할 일

> 1   11시에는 실험실로 가서 신제품 음료를 시음할 수 있어요.

> 2   점심 먹고 2시까지 복귀해주세요.

> 3   손목 밴드를 나눠드릴 테니 항상 착용해주세요.

구체적 정보	1	What **will** the **listeners do** at **11 o'clock**? 청자들은 11시에 무엇을 할 것인가? 키워드 **11 o'clock** 활용하기	❷ **Sample some products** 제품을 시식한다
요청 사항	2	What does the speaker **ask** the listeners do? 화자는 청자들에게 무엇을 하라고 요청하는가? 요청의 단서 '**please**' 포착하기	❷ **Return by a certain time** 특정 시간까지 돌아오기
다음에 할 일	3	What will the **speaker do next**? 화자는 다음으로 무엇을 할 것인가? 미래 표현 '**I'm going to**' 포착하기	❷ **Distribute some items** 물건을 나누어 준다.

질문의 단서가 되는 주요 표현

"**I'll be leading you through our exhibit today**."	화자는 누구인 것 같은가?
"**Welcome and thanks for visiting** our chocolate factory."	견학은 어디에서 일어나는가?
"**Before we begin our tour, please** put on safety goggles."	청자는 무엇을 하도록 요구되는가?
"**What's unique about our exhibition is** how we use light."	화자는 무엇이 특별하다고 말하는가?
"**Be sure to** stay with the group as we begin our tour."	화자는 무엇을 지시하는가?
"**I encourage you to** visit the souvenir shop."	화자는 무엇을 권장하는가?
"**Please avoid** using your mobile phone while in the museum."	화자는 청자에게 무엇을 금하는가?

LISTENING PRACTICE 🎧 P4_09

여행, 견학, 관람 메시지를 듣고 다음 문제를 풀어보자. 다시 듣고 빈칸을 채우자.

1.

According to the speaker, **what can the listeners do?**

(A) Watch some instructional videos

(B) Enjoy some refreshments

(C) Have some hands-on experiences

(D) Sell their hand-made items

> Welcome to our tour of the _____ Studio. Our facility has in-house artisans specializing in hand-made ceramics. Today they'll _____ the craft of making beautiful bowls, mugs, and many others. You will also have the opportunity ____ _____ your own clay pot on the potter's wheel. OK, let's begin.

2.

What should the **listeners ask permission to do?**

(A) Take flash pictures

(B) Record the show

(C) Feed animals

(D) Leave the group

> Now, we are passing through a natural habitat enclosure housing a variety of birds, the final course of our zoo tour today. Here, you can see over 70 _____ of birds, including parrots that can talk and sing. Please ____ _____ _____ any of the birds without the _____ of the zoo staff members.

3.

Who most likely is the **speaker?**

(A) A fitness center instructor

(B) A bicycle shop owner

(C) A factory manager

(D) A sports journalist

> OK, let's start today's tour. I'm Ted Benson, and I _____ all the operations here at this production facility. This is the Mach Cycle Company's largest _____ _____ — it produces more than 400 bicycles per day. First, we'll watch how our popular lines of mountain bikes are built. Come this way.

4.

Why is the **concert being held?**

(A) To decide the winner of a music contest

(B) To celebrate a historic event

(C) To raise money for a charity

(D) To promote tourism to a region

> Welcome to tonight's performance. This special _____ _____ is an annual event that is organized to benefit the City Music Foundation, which provides _____ _____ to aspiring music performers. All of the _____ from the event are donated to this _____ organization. Alright, let's begin our show.

1. Where is the announcement being made?
   (A) At a sports center
   (B) In an airport terminal
   (C) In a shopping mall
   (D) On a cruise ship

2. According to the speaker, what will be distributed shortly?
   (A) Meal vouchers
   (B) Activity schedules
   (C) Hotel coupons
   (D) Movie tickets

3. What does the speaker recommend doing?
   (A) Entering a prize drawing
   (B) Purchasing a health drink
   (C) Paying for items with cash
   (D) Posing for a group photo

4. Why does the speaker apologize to the listeners?
   (A) The group size was too large.
   (B) Some equipment was not working.
   (C) A tour had to be cut short.
   (D) An area of the museum was inaccessible.

5. According to the speaker, what can the listeners do at 2 P.M.?
   (A) Attend a lecture
   (B) Take another tour
   (C) Watch a movie
   (D) Meet a scientist

6. What will the speaker distribute?
   (A) A voucher
   (B) An event ticket
   (C) Some photos
   (D) Some postcards

7. Who most likely is the speaker?
   (A) A local playwright
   (B) A fundraising manager
   (C) A lighting technician
   (D) A photojournalist

8. What are the listeners invited to do?
   (A) Complete feedback surveys
   (B) Make video recordings
   (C) Participate in a discussion
   (D) Purchase a souvenir booklet

9. According to the speaker, what is available at no cost?
   (A) Seating upgrades
   (B) T-shirts
   (C) Magazines
   (D) Refreshments

10. Who most likely are the listeners?
    (A) New employees
    (B) Government inspectors
    (C) Tour participants
    (D) Building supervisors

11. Why does the speaker say, "There's nothing rare there"?
    (A) To explain that an area will be changed soon
    (B) To warn listeners that a site could be disappointing
    (C) To recommend meeting in a different place
    (D) To suggest that listeners may browse on their own

12. What can the listeners do at eleven o'clock?
    (A) Watch a demonstration
    (B) Enjoy some snacks and beverages
    (C) Listen to a historical lecture
    (D) Purchase some souvenirs

13. Who most likely is the speaker?
    (A) A museum curator
    (B) A waiter
    (C) An opera singer
    (D) A tour guide

14. According to the speaker, what has changed?
    (A) A start time
    (B) An event price
    (C) A ticketing policy
    (D) A menu item

15. What are the listeners advised to do?
    (A) Reserve some tickets
    (B) Take some photographs
    (C) Purchase some food
    (D) Buy some souvenirs

16. Where is the tour most likely taking place?
    (A) At a park
    (B) At a beach resort
    (C) At a restaurant
    (D) At a shopping mall

17. What does the speaker say has changed about the tour?
    (A) The price
    (B) The end location
    (C) The transportation method
    (D) The number of participants

18. What does the speaker offer to the listeners?
    (A) A complimentary drink
    (B) A lifejacket
    (C) A souvenir
    (D) A map

Royce Family Estate Tours

Groves and Grottoes	30 minutes
Native Wildlife	1 hour
Historical Walk	2 hours
Lunch Stroll	3 hours 30 minutes

19. What type of business did the Royce Family own?
    (A) A metal production facility
    (B) A gardening supply store
    (C) A national banking firm
    (D) A research laboratory

20. Look at the graphic. What tour are the listeners taking?
    (A) Groves and Grottoes
    (B) Native Wildlife
    (C) Historical Walk
    (D) Lunch Stroll

21. Where will the listeners go first?
    (A) To a butterfly house
    (B) To a body of water
    (C) To a rose garden
    (D) To a fruit orchard

광고 / 방송 / 보도

출제 경향 상품 광고, 교통 및 날씨 방송, 라디오 프로그램, 지역 뉴스가 빈출된다.

전략 광고 상품의 특징, 안내 방송이 나오는 장소 및 내용, 보도 주제에 포커스를 두어 청취하자.

● 지문의 흐름과 문제 구성 🎧 P4_11

번역 p. 111

방송 주제	¹ You're listening to Hong Kong's most trusted radio program for food lovers. This week we're talking about the unique recipes, straight from our listeners.	→	1 음식 애호가들을 위한 홍콩 최고 인기 라디오 방송을 듣고 계십니다.
참여 방법	² If there's a special dish you want to tell me how to make, call me here at the studio.	→	2 특별한 요리법을 알려주시려면 방송국으로 전화주세요.
세부 내용	³ The first recipe is a lasagna made without any cheese. What an idea! I always hear something new.	→	3 첫 번째는 치즈 없는 라자냐예요. 매번 새로운 것을 듣게 되는군요.

주제 및 목적	**1** What is the **topic** of the radio program? 라디오 프로그램의 주제는 무엇인가? **초반부 집중하기**	❷ **Food** 음식
구체적 정보	**2 Why** would a **listener call** the station? 청취자는 왜 방송국에 전화하겠는가? **키워드 'call' 주변 활용하기**	❷ **To share a recipe** 요리법을 공유하기 위해
의도 파악	**3** What does the speaker mean when he says, **"I always hear something new."**? 화자가 "매번 새로운 것을 듣게 되는군요." 라고 말하는 의미는 무엇인가? **제시문 앞뒤 문맥 파악하기**	❷ **He thinks an idea is interesting.** 아이디어가 흥미롭다고 생각한다.

질문의 단서가 되는 주요 표현

"**Are you having trouble** sleeping? **Then**, we're here to help you." 　무엇이 광고되고 있는가?

"**You'll be surprised at** how many options are available." 　화자는 무엇이 놀랍다고 말하는가?

"**Our guest tonight is** Lenny Smith, the renowned guitar player." 　레니 스미스는 누구인가?

"**A heavy rainstorm is expected** to arrive in Riverside tonight." 　방송은 무엇에 관한 것인가?

"**For more details about** the schedule, check the city's Web site." 　웹사이트에는 어떤 정보가 있는가?

"We will be taking your calls **after a short commercial break**." 　광고 후에는 무엇을 할 것인가?

"**Stay tuned for** the latest business updates." 　다음에 들을 방송은 무엇인가?

LISTENING PRACTICE P4_12

광고, 방송, 보도 메시지를 듣고 다음 문제를 풀어보자. 다시 듣고 빈칸을 채우자.

1.

Why does the speaker say, **"It's an exciting year for Boca Raton"**?

(A) It is celebrating an important anniversary.

(B) It will open a new conference center.

(C) It was recognized by a magazine.

(D) It is hosting many events.

> This is Gail Rodriguez, with your Boca Raton local update. It's an exciting year for Boca Raton, as a lot of _____ are _____ _____ _____. The Latin Food Festival, Summer Outdoor Concert, the annual Big Fish Competition, and more. Visit our Web site for details.

2.

Who is **Ms. Torres**?

(A) A salesperson

(B) A real estate agent

(C) An event organizer

(D) A news anchor

> Spring is coming, and that means the Auckland Garden Society is busy organizing their annual garden tour. If you live in the Historical District and have a yard you want to show off,
>
> _____ _____ _____ _____ the _____ _____, Sheila Torres, at 555-0111.

3.

What does the speaker **say about Outside the Box employees**?

(A) They come from many countries.

(B) They have certification.

(C) They change seasonally.

(D) They can make office visits.

> If you're looking for a fun adventure for your office, get in touch with Outside the Box. All of _____ _____ are _____ by the Alberta Board of Tourism, so you'll be _____ _____ _____ on your adventure. Sign up now to _____ your office's productivity with a unique experience.

4.

What will **happen next week**?

(A) A fundraiser will be held.

(B) An anniversary will be celebrated.

(C) A new show will debut.

(D) A winner will be announced.

> You're listening to WTRX Radio. Next week, on Thursday at 6 P.M., our station will _____ its _____ _____ _____, *Public Discourse* with host Tina Brown. This show will _____ a variety of topics that affect everyday society. Listeners can call the station to share their inquiries. Up next, let's see _____ _____ on the roadway is looking with an up-to-the-minute report.

1. What is the main topic of the show?
   (A) Construction
   (B) Fitness
   (C) Medicine
   (D) Finance

2. Who is Roy Benson?
   (A) A business creator
   (B) A politician
   (C) A course instructor
   (D) A business consultant

3. What will listeners hear immediately after the advertising?
   (A) Details about a job opening
   (B) An update on a product launch
   (C) Instructions for a contest
   (D) An interview with a business owner

4. According to the report, what may cause traffic delays in the downtown area?
   (A) An area of rain
   (B) A running contest
   (C) A road widening project
   (D) A tourism trade show

5. What are commuters encouraged to do that morning?
   (A) Leave their cars in a designated parking area
   (B) Use a ride share app for mobile phones
   (C) Travel to the city center by subway
   (D) Work from home via computer

6. Who is scheduled to gather at Lake Street on Friday?
   (A) House builders
   (B) Traffic engineers
   (C) Produce sellers
   (D) Ecology experts

7. What is scheduled to begin on June 1?
   (A) The introduction of a new fare card system
   (B) The opening of an expanded parking area
   (C) Construction of a new railway link
   (D) Renovations to a shopping center

8. According to Mr. Jones, what was a concern for residents?
   (A) Overcrowded trains
   (B) Delays in train services
   (C) Too few parking spaces for vehicles
   (D) Recent changes to train timetables

9. What did Mr. Jones invite residents to do?
   (A) Participate in a feedback survey
   (B) Explore a new railway station
   (C) Purchase monthly rail passes
   (D) Use an upgraded Web site

10. What is the broadcast mainly about?
    (A) An upcoming celebration
    (B) A new business opening
    (C) An art competition
    (D) A musical performance

11. What does the speaker say listeners should contact Kelly Walker for?
    (A) To receive a special discount
    (B) To register for an event
    (C) To purchase tickets
    (D) To offer support

12. What will listeners most likely hear next?
    (A) A weather report
    (B) An event schedule
    (C) A celebrity interview
    (D) A musical performance

13. Where is the speaker?

(A) At a sports venue

(B) At a recording studio

(C) At a movie theater

(D) At a public park

14. Why is the project manager pleased?

(A) A large private donation was made.

(B) A ceremony day had nice weather.

(C) A building is energy-efficient.

(D) A delay was avoided.

15. According to the speaker, why should listeners visit a Web site?

(A) To browse some photos

(B) To vote on a proposal

(C) To view tour times

(D) To purchase tickets

16. According to the advertisement, what do guests like about the Morris Hotel?

(A) Its friendly staff

(B) Its convenient location

(C) Its reasonable prices

(D) Its spacious rooms

17. What has the hotel recently added?

(A) A fitness facility

(B) An Internet connection

(C) An on-site restaurant

(D) A transportation service

18. Why does the speaker recommend visiting the hotel's Web site?

(A) To read customer comments

(B) To make a reservation

(C) To view a schedule

(D) To browse a photo gallery

Model	Type	Sale price
TS101	Diving shoes	$50
TS201	Volleyball shoes	$60
TS301	Comfort shoes	$70
TS401	Tennis shoes	$80

19. Why most likely is Zerox Shoes having a special sale?

(A) To reduce its unsold inventory

(B) To celebrate an anniversary

(C) To promote fitness walking

(D) To highlight a store opening event

20. Look at the graphic. What kind of product did Zerox Shoes most recently release?

(A) Diving shoes

(B) Volleyball shoes

(C) Comfort shoes

(D) Tennis shoes

21. According to the advertisement, how can listeners receive additional discounts?

(A) By paying via an app for mobile phones

(B) By participating in a sports contest

(C) By registering for a newsletter

(D) By completing a survey

인물 / 강연 / 설명

출제 경향 인사 이동 관련 인물, 특정 주제 강연, 제품 및 시설 사용 설명이 빈출된다.

전략 인물의 경력 및 업적, 강연의 주제, 설명 세부 사항에 포커스를 두어 청취하자.

● 지문의 흐름과 문제 구성 🎧 P4_14

번역 p. 117

강연 목적	Welcome to the seminar on business trends. We have several guest speakers today, and ¹ **we will learn some great tips that you can apply to your own businesses** from them. Let me start off by
연설자 소개	introducing our first speaker, Olivia Gail. ² **She is well known for her best-selling book** about how
강연 주제	to effectively run a company. ³ **Today she'll be telling us about a number of unique approaches to online marketing.** Come on up, Olivia.

1 여러분의 사업에 적용할 수 있는 훌륭한 팁들을 배워보겠습니다.

2 첫 강연자는 베스트셀러 책으로 유명하신 올리비아 게일입니다.

3 오늘은 게일 씨가 독특한 온라인 마케팅 전략을 알려주시겠습니다.

강연 대상	<u>1</u> **Who is** the **audience** for the talk? 강연의 청중은 누구인가? **인사말 및 강연 주제 주목하기**	❷ **Business owners** 사업주들
구체적 정보 1	<u>2</u> **Who** most likely is **Olivia Gail**? 올리비아 게일은 누구이겠는가? **고유명사 키워드 및 소개 내용에 주목하기**	❷ **An author** 저자
구체적 정보 2	<u>3</u> **What will Ms. Gail** most likely **talk about**? 게일 씨는 무엇에 관해 말할 것 같은가? 키워드 **talk about** 활용하기 ❷ **telling us about**	❷ **Advertising on the Internet** 인터넷 광고

질문의 단서가 되는 주요 표현

"I'm here to give business tips to **entrepreneurs like you**."	청자는 누구인가?
"**This seminar is aimed at** raising awareness of data protection."	강의의 주제는 무엇인가?
"**Now, I'm going to demonstrate how to** set a password."	화자는 무엇을 할 것이라고 하는가?
"**The next presenter is** Bon Howitt, **an award-winning** author."	휴이트 씨는 누구인가?
"**Mr. Palmer has recently** developed a new application."	팔머 씨는 최근에 무엇을 했는가?
"**Congratulate Ms. Serra on** generating the most revenue."	화자는 왜 세라를 축하하는가?
"**Now, let's begin by** watching a short video."	청자들은 다음에 무엇을 할 것인가?

LISTENING PRACTICE 🎧 P4_15

인물, 강연, 설명 메시지를 듣고 다음 문제를 풀어보자. 다시 듣고 빈칸을 채우자.

1.

What does the speaker say **he will give** participants?

(A) Some registration forms
(B) Some food samples
(C) Some copies of his book
(D) Some résumé templates

> Welcome to the workshop, where job seekers learn how to write a good résumé. Let's get started by looking at some of the _____ _____ which I'll be _____ _____ in a moment. Please read them through carefully. Also, please _____ that there is a section where you can _____ your top three choices.

2.

What most likely is the **purpose** of the **gathering**?

(A) To name nominees for an award
(B) To announce recent job promotions
(C) To honor a retiring employee
(D) To seek input on a sales campaign

> We are gathered here tonight to _____ our _____ Marketing Director, Fred Costas. During his _____ at our company, he developed many successful sales strategies—including our award-winning social media campaign. Congratulations, Mr. Costas, on a wonderful career, and best of luck on the next _____ in your life.

3.

According to the speaker, what **will the listeners do** after the talk?

(A) Evaluate newspaper advertisements
(B) Complete feedback surveys
(C) Participate in a role play
(D) Meet a local entrepreneur

> Welcome to my lecture, "Building Negotiation Skills." Today, I will provide you with valuable advice on business negotiations. After I finish my talk, I will _____ you _____ _____ for a _____ _____.
> Each pair will have a goods "seller" and a goods "buyer", and you will negotiate until you _____ on a mutually acceptable price point.

4.

According to the speaker, **what happened last month**?

(A) Some research findings were released.
(B) An ad campaign was launched.
(C) An IT specialist was featured in a publication.
(D) Some training sessions were canceled.

> As you will be using a new banking software system starting next week, I invited IT expert James Han, who will provide training on the _____ _____ of the program. Mr. Han has led several training sessions for our company. In fact, his professionalism and friendly attitude _____ _____ in the company newsletter last month. Now, let's welcome James Han.

1. What kind of company most likely is Canopus Ltd.?

   (A) A construction company

   (B) A clothing maker

   (C) A financial institute

   (D) An Interior design company

2. What is Ms. Shields being recognized for?

   (A) Increasing factory productivity

   (B) Improving customer satisfaction

   (C) Reducing entertainment costs

   (D) Recruiting new employees

3. According to the introduction, what will Ms. Shields receive?

   (A) Tickets for a music performance

   (B) An immediate job promotion

   (C) A gift card for a local store

   (D) Personalized coffee cups

4. What does the speaker say about the workshop?

   (A) It will be longer than planned.

   (B) It is the last one in a series.

   (C) It is provided free of charge.

   (D) It is being held at a fitness center.

5. What topic will be highlighted in a video?

   (A) Dressing for an interview

   (B) Types of body language

   (C) Improving job résumés

   (D) Speaking with confidence

6. What will the speaker distribute next?

   (A) Snack boxes

   (B) Carrying bags

   (C) Printed lists

   (D) Name tags

7. What type of book is the speaker discussing?

   (A) A travel guide

   (B) A self-help book

   (C) A fantasy novel

   (D) A biography

8. What does the speaker mean when she says, "I know I'm not alone"?

   (A) A book has many fans.

   (B) Mr. Pascal is known as a slow writer.

   (C) Other people are also confused.

   (D) The broadcast has a large audience.

9. What inspired Mr. Pascal to write the book?

   (A) A visit to a school

   (B) An overseas trip

   (C) The results of a survey

   (D) The release of a movie

10. What does the speaker sell?

    (A) Software

    (B) Real estate

    (C) Automobiles

    (D) Camping gear

11. Why does the speaker thank Mr. Phil?

    (A) He increased a department budget.

    (B) He provided some scheduling assistance.

    (C) He bought some new stoves.

    (D) He offered a spare tent.

12. What will the speaker do next?

    (A) Emphasize a point

    (B) Give an approval

    (C) Suggest a proposal

    (D) Object to an idea

13. Where most likely is the introduction being given?

(A) At a publishing company

(B) At an art museum

(C) At a used bookstore

(D) At a film studio

14. What is mentioned about *The Wind and the Rain*?

(A) It is based on a true story.

(B) It is well received by critics.

(C) It will be made into a movie.

(D) It was written by university students.

15. What most likely will happen after the book signing?

(A) A performance of a stage play

(B) A meal with organizers

(C) A practical demonstration

(D) A guided nature walk

---

16. What type of event is the talk for?

(A) A retirement party

(B) A welcome dinner

(C) A grand opening

(D) A corporate merger

17. What does the speaker say is special about the company?

(A) Its long history

(B) Its high-profile projects

(C) Its growing client base

(D) Its demonstrated teamwork

18. What does the speaker say he will do next month?

(A) Publish a book

(B) Launch a Web site

(C) Visit a tourist destination

(D) Make a donation

Step 1	Enter employee ID number
⇩	
Step 2	Enter user name
⇩	
Step 3	Enter employee e-mail address
⇩	
Step 4	Enter password

19. What kind of company do the listeners most likely work for?

(A) An interior design company

(B) A cooking equipment supplier

(C) An event planning firm

(D) A business software maker

20. Look at the graphic. Which step in the login process was removed?

(A) Step 1

(B) Step 2

(C) Step 3

(D) Step 4

21. What will the speaker probably demonstrate next?

(A) Responding to customer inquiries

(B) Restoring accidentally deleted files

(C) Logging into a computer system

(D) Entering data for a new customer account

정답은 본책 p.386 / 해설 PDF 무료 제공 / www.ybmbooks.com

1. What problem does the speaker mention?

(A) Regulations have been changed recently.

(B) Overhead costs have increased.

(C) It is difficult to find qualified employees.

(D) Competition in the field is getting heavier.

2. What does the speaker suggest doing?

(A) Raising ticket prices

(B) Tracking profits carefully

(C) Running more advertisements

(D) Forming a partnership

3. What does the speaker ask the listeners to do?

(A) Conduct some research

(B) Book a hotel room

(C) Review a business plan

(D) Form discussion groups

4. What type of event is the message about?

(A) A charity dinner

(B) A retirement party

(C) An employee training

(D) A business conference

5. What does the speaker suggest?

(A) Scheduling an earlier delivery

(B) Signing up for a membership

(C) Reviewing an online menu

(D) Make a change to an order

6. What does the speaker say about beef stew dishes?

(A) They are popular with children.

(B) They are made from local ingredients.

(C) They can be delivered a day before an event.

(D) They can be returned for free if they are not eaten.

7. Who is the speaker?

(A) An editor

(B) A photographer

(C) A spokesperson

(D) An athlete

8. What mistake did the speaker make?

(A) She misidentified someone.

(B) She called the wrong number.

(C) She went to the wrong location.

(D) She lost some photographs.

9. What will the speaker most likely do in the evening?

(A) Edit a portfolio

(B) Publish an article

(C) Attend a special event

(D) Watch a sports match

10. Why does the speaker think that the listeners will be pleased?

(A) They will be eligible to receive pay raises.

(B) They are permitted to leave the office early.

(C) They will have additional help for a task.

(D) They are invited to a company retreat.

11. In which department do the listeners most likely work?

(A) Public relations

(B) Shipping

(C) Customer service

(D) Accounting

12. According to the speaker, how can the listeners get more information?

(A) By speaking to a colleague

(B) By reading a memo

(C) By performing an online search

(D) By attending a meeting

13. Where most likely is this announcement being made?

    (A) At a cleaning company

    (B) At a restaurant

    (C) At a supermarket

    (D) At a care hire company

14. What problem does the speaker mention?

    (A) Some items are out of stock.

    (B) Some customers have complained.

    (C) The power supply is faulty.

    (D) A staff member is off sick.

15. What will employees be informed about the following morning?

    (A) Alterations to a cleaning schedule

    (B) Changes to opening hours

    (C) A new safety procedure

    (D) A machine installation

16. What does the speaker say Westport has many of?

    (A) Bus stops

    (B) New businesses

    (C) Outdoor venues

    (D) Takeout restaurants

17. What does Pulse do for its customers?

    (A) Offer advice

    (B) Schedule meetings

    (C) Deliver medicine

    (D) Create blogs

18. Who is Kevin Doyle?

    (A) A business founder

    (B) A medical professional

    (C) A radio personality

    (D) A software designer

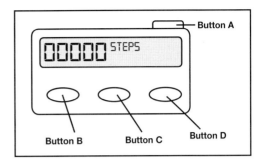

19. What is Ms. Wellington preparing for?

    (A) A gym grand opening

    (B) A product launch

    (C) An overseas vacation

    (D) An athletic competition

20. Look at the graphic. Which button is the speaker talking about?

    (A) Button A

    (B) Button B

    (C) Button C

    (D) Button D

21. What has the speaker sent to the listener?

    (A) A set of instructions

    (B) A partial refund

    (C) A new battery

    (D) An access code

22. Who most likely are the listeners?

(A) Apartment tenants

(B) New employees

(C) Construction workers

(D) Real estate agents

23. What does the speaker imply when he says, "I'm with you"?

(A) He will meet the listeners at 9.

(B) He agrees with a criticism.

(C) He was assigned to a new group.

(D) He is familiar with the crew members.

24. What will the listeners be able to do tomorrow?

(A) Attend a board meeting

(B) Watch an elevator repair

(C) Tour a fitness center

(D) View an updated schedule

25. What type of service does Zimmerly offer?

(A) Recruiting skilled employees

(B) Designing Web sites

(C) Running a security system

(D) Creating ad campaigns

26. What is unique about the business?

(A) It provides a money-back guarantee.

(B) Its representatives visit customers in person.

(C) It offers a free follow-up consultation.

(D) Its employees undergo intensive training.

27. What does the speaker recommend doing?

(A) Viewing past projects

(B) Using an online coupon

(C) Attending a feedback session

(D) Taking advantage of a sale

28. Where is the talk taking place?

(A) At a gym

(B) At a restaurant

(C) At a hospital

(D) At a bank

29. According to the speaker, what has Dan Hewitt recently done?

(A) Purchased a membership

(B) Offered a discount

(C) Broken a record

(D) Repaired some equipment

30. What does the speaker recommend that the listeners do?

(A) Sign up for a class

(B) Purchase a product

(C) Make a payment

(D) Visit a restaurant

31. Why is the meeting being held?

(A) To detail a new marketing strategy

(B) To inform staff about new safety rules

(C) To announce company sales figures

(D) To discipline staff members

32. Why does the speaker say, "There's going to be a quiz at the end"?

(A) To suggest the listeners perform research

(B) To inform listeners of a schedule change

(C) To describe a promotion opportunity

(D) To encourage participants to listen

33. What are the listeners asked to do?

(A) Locate a document

(B) Divide into teams

(C) Prepare a presentation

(D) Perform a demonstration

34. What type of business is Zen Brothers?

(A) A group of grocery stores

(B) A catering service

(C) A farm

(D) A restaurant chain

35. What is Zen Brothers now offering?

(A) Cooking classes

(B) Discounts on large purchases

(C) Takeout meals

(D) A loyalty program

36. What limitation to the offer does the speaker mention?

(A) It cannot yet be accessed at all locations.

(B) It can be enjoyed only on weekdays.

(C) It requires the use of a mobile app.

(D) It is available to a limited number of people.

37. What type of event will happen on Monday?

(A) A special presentation

(B) A contract negotiation

(C) An employee training

(D) A company outing

38. What does the speaker say about Mr. Brown?

(A) He won an award.

(B) He hosted a party.

(C) He received a promotion.

(D) He took a vacation.

39. What does the speaker remind listeners to do?

(A) Take home personal belongings

(B) Register for a social event

(C) Congratulate a coworker

(D) Turn off their computers

Company	Best Feature
Starr Events	Live music included
Glitz Inc.	25 years of experience
Gold Services	New client discount
Event Plus	Catering included

40. What type of business is being launched?

(A) An electronics store

(B) A coffee shop

(C) An art gallery

(D) A theater

41. What does the speaker say she is pleased about?

(A) A building layout

(B) A Web site design

(C) An event schedule

(D) A customer review

42. Look at the graphic. Which company does the speaker want to use?

(A) Starr Events

(B) Glitz Inc.

(C) Gold Services

(D) Event Plus

PART

5

문법편

어휘편

● PART 5 문장 성분

주어   문장의 주체

우리말로 '-은/-는/-이/-가'에 해당하는 말로, 주로 문장의 맨 앞에 온다. 명사(구/절)나 대명사가 주어로 쓰인다.

명사	**Access** is limited.	이용이 제한되어 있다.
명사구	**Access to the lab** is limited.	실험실 이용이 제한되어 있다.
대명사	**It** is limited.	그것은 제한되어 있다.

동사   주어의 동작이나 상태를 나타내는 말

우리말로 '-하다/-이다'에 해당하는 말로, 주어 다음에 온다. 동사에는 be동사, 일반동사, 조동사가 있다.

be동사	Registration **is** free.	등록은 무료이다.
일반동사	Registration **begins** this week.	등록은 이번 주에 시작한다.
조동사	Registration **will last** until Friday.	등록은 금요일까지 지속될 것이다.

목적어   동작의 대상이 되는 말

'-을/-를/-에게'에 해당하는 말로, 동사나 전치사 뒤에 온다. 명사(구/절)나 대명사가 목적어로 쓰인다.

동사 뒤	We met **the client** yesterday.	우리는 어제 고객을 만났다.
전치사 뒤	We sent a sample to **them**.	우리는 그들에게 견본을 보냈다.

보어   주어나 목적어를 보충하는 말

명사나 형용사가 보어로 쓰인다. 동사 뒤에서 주어를 보충하는 주격 보어와 목적어 뒤에서 목적어를 보충하는 목적격 보어가 있다.

주격 보어	Ms. Fonda is **a director**.	폰다 씨는 부장이다.
	Ms. Fonda is **competent**.	폰다 씨는 유능하다.
목적격 보어	The movie made Hue Sadler **a star**.	그 영화는 휴 새들러를 스타로 만들었다.
	The ending made the audience **surprised**.	그 결말은 관객들을 놀라게 만들었다.

● PART 5 문장 형식

1형식 문장   주어 + 동사

주어와 동사만으로도 완전한 문장이 되며, 수식어가 붙어도 형식은 변하지 않는다.

> An error occurred. 에러가 발생했다.
>   주어   동사
>
> A serious error occurred last night. 심각한 에러가 지난밤에 발생했다.

◉ **1형식 동사**   rise 오르다   arrive 도착하다   occur 발생하다   emerge 드러나다

2형식 문장   주어 + 동사 + 주격 보어

주어와 동사만으로도 의미가 불완전하므로 동사 뒤에 명사나 형용사가 주격 보어로 온다.

> The grocery store became popular. 그 식료품점이 인기가 높아졌다.
>   주어   동사   보어

◉ **2형식 동사**   be ~이다/~에 있다   become ~이 되다   remain 남아 있다   seem ~처럼 보이다

3형식 문장   주어 + 동사 + 목적어

가장 많이 쓰이는 문장 형태로, 대부분의 동사는 3형식으로 쓸 수 있다.

> Our marketing team revised the project schedule.   마케팅 팀이 프로젝트 일정을 수정
>   주어   동사   목적어   했다.

4형식 문장   주어 + 동사 + 간접목적어 + 직접목적어

'주다'를 의미하는 수여동사 뒤에 사람 목적어와 사물 목적어가 차례로 오는 구조이다.

> The shop offers new customers a discount. 그 상점은 신규 고객들에게 할인을 제공한다.
>   주어   동사   간접목적어   직접목적어

◉ **4형식 동사**   give 주다   send 보내다   offer 제공하다   award 수여하다   inform 알리다

5형식 문장   주어 + 동사 + 목적어 + 목적격 보어

3형식 문장 뒤에 목적어를 보충하는 목적격 보어가 오는 구조이다.

> All employees should keep the office [clean / ~~cleanly~~]. 모든 직원은 사무실을 청결하게
>   주어   동사   목적어   목적격 보어   유지해야 한다.

◉ **5형식 동사**   keep ~하게 유지하다   find ~라고 생각하다   consider ~로 간주하다
                 make ~하게 만들다

명사

기본 개념 잡기

명사란?

사람, 사물, 추상적 개념 등을 지칭하기 위해 정해 놓은 이름을 명사라고 한다.

employee	office	information	relationship
직원	사무실	정보	관계

명사의 형태

명사는 기본적으로 다음과 같은 어미를 가진다.

pay**ment** 지불	aware**ness** 인지	direc**tion** 안내	revi**sion** 개정
custom**er** 고객	advis**or** 조언자	fin**ance** 금융	leader**ship** 리더십
stor**age** 보관	enthusi**asm** 열정	iden**tity** 신분	plea**sure** 즐거움

명사의 종류

가산명사 vs. 불가산명사

가산명사 셀 수 있으므로 a/an을 붙일 수 있고 복수형이 있는 명사
  ❯ a client 고객, items 물건

불가산명사 셀 수 없으므로 a/an을 붙일 수 없고 복수형이 없는 명사
  ❯ access 이용, permission 허가

사람명사 vs. 사물명사/추상명사

사람명사 an employee 직원 / applicants 지원자들
  ❯ 사람명사는 가산명사

사물/추상명사 employment 고용 / application(s) 지원, 지원서
  ❯ 사물/추상명사는 가산 또는 불가산명사

출제 공식 1 　　　명사 자리

명사는 문장에서 주어, 보어, 목적어 자리에 온다.

주어 자리	The **price** rose significantly. 가격이 상당히 올랐다.
보어 자리	Mr. Bauer is an **author** of several books. 바우어 씨는 다수의 책 저자이다.
동사의 목적어 자리	We discussed the **details**. 우리는 세부사항을 논의했다.
전치사의 목적어 자리	This book is for **educators**. 이 책은 교육자들을 위한 것이다.

명사는 형용사와 소유격의 수식을 받는 자리에 온다.

형용사 + 명사	Ms. Diaz is a **qualified candidate**. 디아즈 씨는 자격을 갖춘 지원자이다.
소유격 + 명사	Customers like **our products**. 고객들은 우리의 제품을 좋아한다.

CHECK-UP
정답 및 해설 p. 124

1. The [effective / effectiveness] of the new flu remedy was exaggerated.
2. Supervisors are expected to make the right [decision / decisive] on a timely basis.
3. The organizers informed us of [restricts / restrictions] on the use of recordings.

출제 공식 2 　　　가산명사 vs. 불가산명사

명사는 셀 수 있는 명사와 셀 수 없는 명사로 구분된다.

가산명사	불가산명사	기타 불가산명사	
a permit 허가증	permission 허가	access 이용, 접근	advice 조언
a process 과정	processing 처리	information 정보	furniture 가구
a plan 계획	planning 계획	equipment 장비	baggage 수하물
a fund 자금	funding 자금 조달	news 뉴스	research 연구

가산명사	You need a [**permit** / ~~permission~~] to park here. 이곳에 주차하려면 주차증이 필요합니다. ❍ 가산명사의 단수형은 관사 또는 소유격과 함께 쓴다.
불가산명사	Enjoy unlimited [**access** / ~~accesses~~] to any article. 기사 무제한 이용을 누리세요. ❍ 불가산명사는 관사 없이 쓰거나, 정관사 the가 붙을 수 있다.

CHECK-UP
정답 및 해설 p. 124

1. Careful [plan / planning] is vital to ensure the project is completed on time.
2. Only a few employees have [access / accesses] to the company archives.
3. After a lengthy discussion, the allocation of [fund / funds] was finally approved.

출제 공식 3　　　　사람명사 vs. 사물/추상명사

명사 자리에는 사람명사와 사물/추상명사가 올 수 있는데 의미에 맞게 선택해야 한다.

an applicant 지원자	application 지원서	a participant 참여자	participation 참여
a producer 생산자(업체)	production 생산	a manufacturer 제조업자	manufacture 제조업
an enthusiast 팬, 지지자	enthusiasm 열의, 열광	a correspondent 통신원	correspondence 서신
a contributor 기여자	contribution 기여	a distributor 유통업자	distribution 유통
an employee 직원	employment 고용	a consultant 상담사	consultation 상담

사람명사　　　[**Applicants** / ~~Applications~~] should send an e-mail to Mr. Liu.
　　　　　　　지원자는 류 씨에게 이메일을 보내야 한다.
　　　　　　　❯ 동사 send(보내다)의 주체가 되는 사람명사가 올 자리이다.

사물/추상명사　We will soon resume [~~producer~~ / **production**]. 우리는 곧 **생산**을 재개할 것이다.
　　　　　　　❯ 동사 resume(재개하다)의 대상이 되는 사물 / 추상명사가 올 자리이다.

※ 사람명사는 가산명사이므로 단수형으로 쓸 때는 반드시 관사나 소유격이 붙는다.
　The science magazine is ready for [~~distributor~~ / **distribution**]. 그 과학 잡지는 **유통** 준비가 되어 있다.

CHECK-UP　　　　　　　　　　　　　　　　　　　　　　　　　정답 및 해설 p. 124

1. [Employees / Employment] of Pentel Ltd. will receive a bonus at the end of the year.
2. Survey respondents will be financially rewarded for their [participant / participation].
3. Recruits will be working in [consultant / consultation] with their direct supervisors.

출제 공식 4　　　　복합 명사

명사는 다른 명사와 결합하여 복합명사를 만들 수 있다.

명사 + 명사　There are few **job openings**. 일자리 공석이 거의 없다.
　　　　　　❯ 복합명사의 앞 명사에는 's'가 붙지 않는다. (예외: sales department)

대표 복합명사

job openings 일자리 공석	safety regulations 안전 규칙	mailing address 우편 주소
retail price 소매가	expiration date 만기일	office supplies 사무용품
employee productivity 직원 생산성	return policy 환불 정책	sales revenue 판매 수익
registration form 등록 양식	rental agreement 임대 계약(서)	safety reasons 안전상의 이유

CHECK-UP　　　　　　　　　　　　　　　　　　　　　　　　　정답 및 해설 p. 124

1. For [secure / security] reasons, all data entered is encrypted.
2. Companies strive to find new ways to increase employee [produce / productivity].
3. The Web site provides some useful tips on how to get the best [rent / rental] car.

이것도 알면 플러스 10점!

예외적인 형태의 명사

❶ -al로 끝나는 명사

renewal 갱신	appraisal 평가	referral 소개, 추천	withdrawal 철회, 인출
disposal 처분	proposal 제안(서)	arrival 도착(사람, 사물)	rental 임대
approval 승인	removal 제거	trial 시도, 시험	refusal 거절

Requests for the budget increase received [~~approve~~ / **approval**] from the management.
예산 인상 요청이 경영진으로부터 승인을 받았다.

❷ -tive형 명사

alternative a.대안의 n.대안	objective a.객관적인 n.목표	perspective 관점
initiative 계획(안), 주도권	representative 대표(자)	

The proposed [~~initiation~~ / **initiative**] aims to promote responsible business practices.
그 발의안은 책임 있는 비즈니스 관행을 장려하는 것을 목표로 한다.

두 가지 품사로 출제되는 명사

❶ 명사 & 동사

recruit / hire v.채용하다 n.신입	permit v.허가하다 n.허가증	fund n.자금 v.자금을 대다
document n.문서 v.문서화하다	limit n.제한 v.제한하다	lack n.부족 v.부족하다
delegate v.위임하다 n.대표자	associate v.관련시키다 n.직원	process n.과정 v.처리하다
access n.이용, 접근 v.이용하다	measure v.재다, 측정하다 n.조치	finance n.재정 v.자금을 대다
function n.기능 v.~로 기능하다	feature n.특징 v.특징으로 삼다	schedule n.일정 v.일정을 잡다

[~~Recruiter~~ / **Recruits**] will undergo intensive training in their respective fields.
신입사원들은 각자의 분야에서 집중 훈련을 받을 것이다.

❷ 명사 & 형용사

specific a.구체적인 / specifics n.세부사항	particular a.특정한 / particulars n.세부사항
professional a.전문적인 n.전문가	individual a.개인의, 각각의 n.개인

Members can network with other [~~professions~~ / **professionals**] in the area.
회원들은 그 분야의 다른 전문가들과 교류할 수 있다.

ACTUAL TEST

1. The ------- of Dr. Porter's speech may change depending on how the audience members react.
   (A) length
   (B) lengthy
   (C) lengthen
   (D) lengthened

2. Following a brief -------, the nutritionist will make diet recommendations to the patient.
   (A) consults
   (B) consultant
   (C) consulted
   (D) consultation

3. Some novice runners may get frustrated early in their training program, as it takes time to build -------.
   (A) endured
   (B) endurance
   (C) enduring
   (D) enduringly

4. In her role as Human Resources Director, Ms. Wong has always shown ------- in the workplace.
   (A) dedicated
   (B) dedicating
   (C) dedication
   (D) dedicates

5. As the current lease on his office building will expire next year, Mr. McCray has already started looking for a new -------.
   (A) placement
   (B) placing
   (C) place
   (D) placed

6. This poster is intended to inform passengers of ------- on items contained in carry-on luggage.
   (A) restricts
   (B) restricting
   (C) restrictive
   (D) restrictions

7. As Sales Manager, Ms. Lu has shown tremendous ------- to her team and its ongoing success.
   (A) committed
   (B) commits
   (C) being committed
   (D) commitment

8. The leak was discovered after a thorough and complete -------.
   (A) investigator
   (B) investigation
   (C) investigational
   (D) investigate

9. The company's annual Platinum Achievement Award recognizes ------- in management.
   (A) excellent
   (B) excellence
   (C) excelled
   (D) excellently

10. The elevators in the main lobby are shut down temporarily for ------- on the first day of each month.
    (A) cleaning
    (B) clean
    (C) cleaned
    (D) cleaner

11. The park expansion project was delayed because planners had difficulty securing -------.

(A) fundraise
(B) fund
(C) fundraiser
(D) funding

12. The campus sports center provides ------- to basketball and volleyball courts, as well as a large gym facility with a weight room.

(A) access
(B) accesses
(C) accessible
(D) accessing

13. After a long period of losses, Waterloo Ltd. expects a return to ------- this quarter.

(A) profitably
(B) profitable
(C) profitability
(D) profited

14. Ms. Rodrigues in the finance department is a highly competent ------- always showing the utmost attention to detail.

(A) associating
(B) association
(C) associate
(D) associated

15. There have been some ------- regarding privacy since the financial institute adopted the open-office concept.

(A) concern
(B) concerns
(C) concerned
(D) concerning

16. *Health Guide for Youth Magazine* is written by medical ------- in cooperation with child welfare organizations.

(A) professional
(B) professionally
(C) professionals
(D) profession

17. Overtime work will be allowed only with ------- of a supervisor.

(A) permit
(B) permissive
(C) permission
(D) permitted

18. Mr. Yamamoto's proposal lacks the ------- needed to determine whether the goals are achievable within the budget.

(A) specify
(B) specific
(C) specifics
(D) specifically

19. All assembly line workers were asked to work extra hours to meet the ------- schedule.

(A) produce
(B) production
(C) produces
(D) productivity

20. Q-Rex Tech recently announced price ------- on its D117 brand of mobile phone.

(A) reduce
(B) reduced
(C) reductions
(D) reduces

대명사

기본 개념 잡기

● 대명사란?

명사를 대신해서 지칭하는 말을 대명사라고 한다.

Mr. Cowell's duties are on the list.
코웰 씨의 임무들은 목록에 있다.

⋯⋯⋯➤

They are on the list.
그것들은 목록에 있다.

● 대명사의 종류

인칭대명사 사람 또는 사물을 대표하는 대명사

| we 우리는 | it 그것은 | they 그들은, 그것들은 |

We need to revise our contract. **우리는** 우리 계약을 수정해야 한다.

지시대명사 사람 또는 사물을 가리키는 대명사

| this 이것 | that 저것 | those ~하는 사람들 |

This is a common misconception. **이것은** 흔히 있는 오해이다.

부정대명사 불특정한 사람 또는 사물을 지칭하는 대명사

| another 또 다른 하나 | some 일부 | others 다른 것들, 다른 사람들 |

Some might disagree with the proposal. **일부 사람들은** 그 제안에 동의하지 않을 수도 있다.

● 인칭대명사의 격

인칭	격	주격 ~은, ~는, ~이, ~가	소유격 ~의	목적격 ~을, ~에게	소유대명사 ~의 것	재귀대명사 ~ 자신
1인칭	단수	I	my	me	mine	myself
	복수	we	our	us	ours	ourselves
2인칭	단수	you	your	you	yours	yourself
	복수	you	your	you	yours	yourselves
3인칭	단수	he	his	him	his	himself
		she	her	her	hers	herself
		it	its	it	–	itself
	복수	they	their	them	theirs	themselves

146

출제 공식 1　　　대명사의 격

인칭대명사는 위치에 따라 격이 달라진다.

주격　　　[**We** / ~~Our~~ / ~~He~~] strive to provide the best service. 우리는 최고의 서비스를 제공하기 위해 노력합니다.

　　　　　❷ 주어 자리에는 주격이 쓰이며 동사와 수 일치를 이루어야 한다.

소유격　　Workers do [**their** / ~~them~~ / ~~its~~] best to meet the deadline. 직원들은 마감을 맞추기 위해 최선을 다한다.

　　　　　❷ 명사 앞에는 소유격이 쓰이며 인칭대명사의 소유격 앞에는 관사를 붙이지 않는다.

목적격　　Samples were mailed to [**us** / ~~ours~~] as we requested [~~their~~ / **them**].

　　　　　견본품을 신청하자 그것들이 우리에게 발송되었다.

　　　　　❷ 타동사 뒤, 전치사 뒤에는 목적격이 쓰인다.

소유대명사　Lynn sent her report, but Tom didn't send [**his** / ~~him~~].

　　　　　린은 보고서를 보냈으나 톰은 자신의 것을 보내지 않았다.

　　　　　❷ 소유대명사는 「소유격 + 명사」이며 주어, 보어, 목적어 자리에 쓰인다. (his 그의 것 = his report)

CHECK-UP　　　　　　　　　　　　　　　　　　　정답 및 해설 p. 127

1. We encourage you to renew your membership before [it / they] expires.
2. Customers must present [them / their] original receipt to receive a full refund.
3. Most divisions cut their expenses, but the sales department could not reduce [it / theirs].

출제 공식 2　　　재귀대명사

재귀대명사는 재귀, 강조, 관용 표현으로 쓰인다.

재귀　　　Employees should familiarize [~~them~~ / **themselves**] with the manual. 직원들은 매뉴얼을 숙지해야 한다.

　　　　　❷ 동사의 주체와 목적어가 같을 때 타동사 뒤, 또는 전치사 뒤에 재귀대명사를 쓴다.

강조　　　Mr. Bernard will write the article [**himself** / ~~his own~~]. 버나드 씨는 직접 기사를 작성할 것이다.

　　　　　❷ 명사를 강조하기 위해 명사 뒤 또는 문장 끝에 쓰이며 생략할 수 있다.

관용　　　The team members analyzed the data **by themselves**. (=on their own)

　　　　　팀 멤버들은 데이터를 직접 분석했다.

　　　　　❷ by oneself는 '직접, 스스로'를 뜻하는 관용 표현으로, 강조 용법의 재귀대명사와 의미가 같다.

※ by oneself는 on one's own으로도 표현할 수 있다.

　Ms. Kang finished the work **on her own**.(=by herself) 강 씨는 업무를 스스로 마무리했다.

CHECK-UP　　　　　　　　　　　　　　　　　　　정답 및 해설 p. 127

1. Interns often need to carry out some important tasks by [them / themselves].
2. Survey participants were not allowed to talk among [theirs / themselves].
3. Mr. Maxwell was unable to do the job [his own / himself].

출제 공식 3   '~하는 사람들'을 뜻하는 지시대명사 those

지시대명사 those는 '~하는 사람들'로 쓰이며 who(se), -ing, p.p., 전치사구의 수식을 받는다.

those + who	Meals are available for **those who** pre-registered. 식사는 **미리 신청한 사람들**에게 제공됩니다.
those + -ing	**Those wishing** to register should call Ms. Gail. 등록하고 싶은 사람들은 게일 씨에게 연락해야 한다.
those + p.p.	**Those interested** in hiking can join us. 하이킹에 관심 있는 사람들은 저희와 함께할 수 있습니다.
those + 전치사구	Only **those with permission** can watch the videos. 허가된 사람들만 비디오를 시청할 수 있다.

※ those 대신 대명사 anyone이 들어갈 수 있는데, 이때 **수 일치**에 유의해야 한다.

[**Anyone** / ~~Those~~] who <u>wants</u> to participate should sign here. 참석을 원하는 **누구든지** 이곳에 서명해야 한다.

❷ anyone: 단수 취급 / those: 복수 취급

CHECK-UP
정답 및 해설 p. 127

1. Video recordings are available for [them / those] who did not attend the conference.
2. [They / Those] wishing to apply for the vacant position should contact Ms. Gail.
3. Online registration forms are available for [them / those] interested in participating.

출제 공식 4   부정대명사

one(s), another, the other(s), others는 불특정한 대상을 지칭한다.

one	The M4 tennis racket is the lightest **one**. M4 테니스 라켓은 가장 가벼운 **것**(라켓)이다. ❷ 앞에서 언급된 명사와 동일한 종류의 것을 지칭한다. 복수명사를 지칭할 때는 ones를 쓴다.
another	We have six branches and we will open **another**. 6개의 지점이 있으며 **또 다른 지점 하나**를 열 것이다. ❷ 정해지지 않은 가산 단수명사를 가리키며 an을 내포하고 있다. (another branch = another)
the other	Of the two, one is better than **the other**. 둘 중에서 하나가 **나머지 하나**보다 더 낫다. ❷ 범위가 주어졌을 때 남은 것을 가리킨다.
the others	Of the three, one is better than **the others**. 셋 중에서 하나가 **나머지들**보다 더 낫다. ❷ 범위가 주어졌을 때 남은 것들을 가리킨다.
others	Ms. Browning works well with **others**. 브라우닝 씨는 **다른 사람들**과 잘 협업한다. ❷ 「other + 복수명사」를 가리킨다. (other + people = others)

CHECK-UP
정답 및 해설 p. 128

1. The new microchip developed by SanTech is the smallest [one / that] ever created.
2. Some people enjoy working in a team while [other / others] avoid group activities.
3. If you are not satisfied with the item, you can exchange it for [another / ones].

이것도 알면 플러스 10점!

some 약간(의), 몇몇(의) vs. any 아무것도, 어느 것이든

> some은 주로 긍정문에, any는 주로 부정문, 의문문, 조건문에 쓰인다.
> 단, any가 긍정문에 쓰이면 '어느 것이든'을 뜻한다.

[**Some** / ~~One~~] of our policies have been revised. 우리 정책 중에 **일부는** 수정되었다.

You should not change [**any** / ~~none~~] of the settings. 설정 중 **어느 것도** 바꾸어서는 안 된다.

The coupon is valid at [**any** / ~~each other~~] of our locations. 그 쿠폰은 우리 지점 **어디에서나** 유효하다

수량을 나타내는 대명사

단수 취급	복수 취급	단·복수 둘 다 가능
much / little	many / few / several	all / most / none

[**All** / ~~Every~~] of the clients have different needs.
고객 **모두는** 각기 다른 요구사항을 가진다.

Mr. Stern knows the system better than [**most** / ~~other~~].
스턴 씨는 그 시스템을 **대부분의 사람들**보다 잘 안다.

※ every와 other는 수량 대명사로 쓰이지 않으며, 따라서 주어나 목적어 자리에 올 수 없다.

each other / one another 서로 (상호대명사)

Employees are encouraged to help [~~other~~ / **one another**].
직원들은 **서로를** 돕도록 권장된다.

[~~Each other~~ / **None**] of the managers will attend the seminar.
매니저 중 **아무도** 세미나에 참석하지 않을 것이다.

❷ 상호대명사는 목적어 자리에만 쓰이므로 주어 자리에 오지 못한다.

같은 명사의 반복을 피하기 위한 지시대명사 that / those

The length of Course A is shorter than [~~this~~ / **that**] of Course B.
A코스의 길이가 B코스의 **길이**보다 짧다.

❷ 명사 length의 반복을 피하기 위해 대명사 that 사용 (that = the length)

Our prices are below [~~them~~ / **those**] of comparable brands.
우리의 가격은 유사 브랜드들의 **가격**보다 낮다.

❷ 명사 prices의 반복을 피하기 위해 대명사 those 사용 (those = the prices)

ACTUAL TEST

정답 및 해설 p. 128

1. The crew members were surprised that the building restoration work took longer than ------- had expected.

   (A) they
   (B) them
   (C) their
   (D) theirs

2. When starting his new job, Mr. Rhodes found ------- under a great deal of pressure to meet the sales quotas.

   (A) ourselves
   (B) himself
   (C) themselves
   (D) itself

3. Ms. Velez has a lot of experience, so she can handle the account by -------.

   (A) she
   (B) her
   (C) hers
   (D) herself

4. Hotel guests joining the trip to the safari park are advised to bring ------- cameras.

   (A) them
   (B) theirs
   (C) they
   (D) their own

5. Depending on ------- availability, some part-time employees may be asked to work extra hours during the holiday period.

   (A) themselves
   (B) they
   (C) them
   (D) their

6. ------- who have completed the journalism course will first be considered for the editorial positions.

   (A) They
   (B) These
   (C) Everyone
   (D) Those

7. The clients seem enthusiastic about riding the city's new subway line, but it may not be the fastest option for ------- to use.

   (A) themselves
   (B) their
   (C) them
   (D) they

8. The lawyer hired an assistant to help ------- with digitizing client data.

   (A) him
   (B) his
   (C) himself
   (D) his own

9. Ms. Browning and Mr. Kato are currently working as a team, but Mr. Tanaka will be joining ------- as an intern.

   (A) they
   (B) their
   (C) them
   (D) themselves

10. By following the marked signs in the area, visitors can explore the city's historical district on -------, without using a guide.

    (A) theirs
    (B) their
    (C) themselves
    (D) their own

11. If any of our customers find lower prices elsewhere, we will lower ------- to match them.

    (A) us
    (B) our
    (C) ours
    (D) ourselves

12. While other firms are still working on bids, the senior planner expedited -------.

    (A) we
    (B) us
    (C) our
    (D) ours

13. Everyone at the dinner party, including ------- with particular nutritional needs, could enjoy the meal.

    (A) it
    (B) they
    (C) them
    (D) those

14. Ms. Sato, the new employee in accounting, would like the manager to give ------- more detailed instructions.

    (A) her
    (B) hers
    (C) herself
    (D) her own

15. The city official admitted that the unemployment rates this year have far surpassed ------- of the previous year.

    (A) those
    (B) it
    (C) they
    (D) these

16. As both candidates were highly qualified, the human resources director could not choose one over -------.

    (A) other
    (B) each
    (C) the other
    (D) those

17. While there was no fee for delivery of Mr. Lee's gas stove -------, professional installation incurred a small charge.

    (A) itself
    (B) yourself
    (C) himself
    (D) themselves

18. Builders of custom computers should make sure that all the components are compatible with -------.

    (A) each other
    (B) other
    (C) few
    (D) itself

19. Mr. Raul stopped by the shop in person to buy replacement ink cartridges because his department did not have -------.

    (A) any
    (B) few
    (C) every
    (D) other

20. During our fall clearance sale, ------- of our inventory will be sold at heavily discounted prices.

    (A) other
    (B) something
    (C) much
    (D) few

형용사

기본 개념 잡기

● 형용사란?

명사의 수, 성질, 상태를 나타내기 위해 명사를 꾸며 주는 수식어를 형용사라고 한다.

many 많은	lengthy 긴	possible 가능한	skilled 능력 있는

● 형용사의 형태

형용사는 기본적으로 다음과 같은 어미를 가진다.

avail**able** 이용가능한	**active** 활동적인	**various** 다양한	skill**ful** 숙련된
organ**ic** 유기농의	poten**tial** 잠재적인	prim**ary** 주요한	spot**less** 무결점의
confid**ent** 자신 있는	delic**ate** 섬세한	**handy** 유용한	ultim**ate** 궁극적인

● 형용사의 역할

형용사는 주어나 목적어의 상태를 보충하는 서술적 역할과 명사 앞이나 뒤에 놓여 명사의 성질을 한정 지어 주는 한정적 역할로 쓰인다.

서술적 기능

(주어 보충) The manager is **competent**. 그 매니저는 유능하다.
❯ 주어로 나온 명사 The manager를 보충

(목적어 보충) We found the task **easy**. 우리는 그 업무가 쉽다고 생각했다.
❯ 목적어로 나온 명사 task를 보충

한정적 기능

(명사 앞에서 수식) Mr. Williams is my **immediate** supervisor. 윌리엄스 씨는 나의 직속 상관이다.
❯ 뒤에 오는 명사 supervisor를 수식

(명사 뒤에서 수식) It is the cheapest item **possible**. 그것은 가능한 가장 싼 제품이다.
❯ 앞에 오는 명사 item을 수식

출제 공식 1   형용사 자리

형용사는 보어 자리에 쓰인다.

주격 보어 자리   The task became [**difficult** / ~~difficultly~~]. 그 업무는 **어려워졌다**.

목적격 보어 자리   We must <u>keep</u> the files [**confidential** / ~~confidentially~~]. 우리는 문서를 **기밀로** 유지해야 한다.

❥ 부사는 보어 자리에 올 수 없다.

- ◯ **주격 보어가 필요한 대표 동사: 2형식 동사:** be, become, remain, stay, appear, seem, prove 등
- ◯ **목적격 보어가 필요한 대표 동사: 5형식 동사:** keep, find, consider, make, leave, prove 등

CHECK-UP   정답 및 해설 p. 130

1. Employees seemed [calm / calmly] during the fire drill.
2. Many critics found director James's new movie [impressive / impressively].
3. Personal information will be kept [confidential / confidentially].

출제 공식 2   형용사의 수식 관계

형용사는 명사를 수식하며 부사의 수식을 받는다.

관사 + 형용사 + 명사   His idea had **a positive effect**. 그의 생각은 **긍정적인 영향을** 미쳤다.

관사 + 부사 + 형용사 + 명사   There is **an unusually high demand** for ice. 얼음에 대한 **유난히 높은 수요가** 있다.

명사 + 형용사   They used the cheapest **paint available**. 그들은 **이용 가능한** 가장 저렴한 **페인트를** 사용했다.

❥ –able, –ible이 붙는 형용사는 명사 뒤에서 수식할 수 있다.

형용사 + 형용사 + 명사   We work with **professional financial advisors**. 우리는 **전문 금융 고문과** 협력한다.

❥ 해석상 두 형용사가 모두 명사를 꾸밀 때는 형용사를 겹쳐 쓸 수 있다.

CHECK-UP   징답 및 해설 p. 130

1. We decided to employ a completely [fresh / freshly] design.
2. There are several compact car options [available / availability] on the market.
3. The company needs to hire a [new / newly] legal consultant.

출제 공식 3 수량 형용사

수량 형용사는 뒤따르는 명사와 수 일치를 이루어야 한다.

가산 단수	가산 복수	불가산	가산 복수 / 불가산	가산 단복수 / 불가산
each / every / another	(a) few / many / various / numerous / several / both / a number of	(a) little / much	all / some / more / most / a lot of / lots of / plenty of	any / no

※ few와 little은 a가 붙을 때 '약간의', a가 붙지 않을 때 '거의 없는'의 뜻을 가진다.

가산 단수 Please read [**every** / ~~all~~] question carefully.
　　　　　　모든 질문을 주의 깊게 읽으세요.

가산 복수 We had [~~another~~ / **several**] setbacks during the past years.
　　　　　　우리는 지난 몇 년간 **몇 가지** 차질을 겪었다.

불가산 The new policy has [~~few~~ / **little**] influence on overall sales.
　　　　개정된 정책은 판매에 **거의** 영향을 미치지 **않았다**.

CHECK-UP
정답 및 해설 p. 130

1. [All / Each] orders placed before noon will be shipped the same day.
2. [A few / A little] electronic banking services will be suspended next week.
3. Please visit our Web site for [another / more] information regarding the return policy.

출제 공식 4 혼동 형용사

어미 변화에 따라 뜻이 달라지는 형용사는 혼동하지 않도록 유의해야 한다.

considerable 상당한	considerate 사려 깊은	reliable 믿을 수 있는	reliant 의존하는
respectable 존경할 만한	respective 각각의	dependable 믿을 수 있는	dependent 의존하는
successful 성공적인	successive 연속적인	sizable 상당한	-sized (복합어로) 크기가 ~인
favorable 호의적인	favorite 가장 좋아하는	extensive 광범위한	extended 연장된

We provide the most [**reliable** / ~~reliant~~] computers at low prices.
우리는 가장 **믿을 수 있는** 컴퓨터를 저가에 제공합니다.

A [~~considerate~~ / **considerable**] amount of time was needed to finish the work.
그 업무를 완수하는 데 **상당한** 시간이 요구되었다.

CHECK-UP
정답 및 해설 p. 131

1. The hotel has three [sized / sizable] conference rooms.
2. *Economy Weekly* is renowned for its [reliable / reliant] market analysis.
3. Please be [considerable / considerate] of others by keeping your voice down.

-ly형 형용사

costly 비용이 비싼 timely 시기적절한 orderly 질서정연한 friendly 친근한 likely 있음직한

※ 형용사에 -ly를 붙이면 부사가 되지만 명사에 -ly를 붙이면 형용사가 된다.

It was a **costly** error.
그것은 **비용이 많이 드는** 오류였다.

Initial errors were corrected in a **timely** manner. (=in a timely fashion)
초기 오류는 **시기적절하게** 수정되었다.

J. Express is well known for its environmentally **friendly** packaging.
제이 익스프레스는 **친환경적인** 포장으로 유명하다.

that절을 받는 형용사

aware 잘 아는 confident 확신하는 likely ~할 것 같은 glad / pleased / delighted 기쁜

We are **confident that** you will be satisfied.
저희는 당신이 만족할 것이라고 확신합니다.

당위성을 나타내는 형용사 ('중요한, 필수적인'을 뜻하는 형용사)

important, necessary, essential, vital, imperative
+ that 주어 + (should) + 동사원형

It is imperative that all collected information [**remain** / ~~remains~~] confidential.
모든 수집된 정보는 기밀로 유지되어야 한다.　　　❸ 3인칭 단수 주어이지만 should가
　　　　　　　　　　　　　　　　　　　　　생략되어 동사원형을 쓴다.

분사형 형용사 (-ing / p.p.)

revised 수정된	expired 만료된	demanding 까다로운	remaining 남아 있는
desired 바라는, 희망하는	designated 지정된	challenging 어려운	existing 기존의
experienced 숙련된	detailed 자세한	leading 선도하는	rewarding 보람 있는

The research team has finally achieved a **desired** result.
연구팀은 마침내 **바라는** 결과를 얻었다.

ACTUAL TEST

정답 및 해설 p. 131

1. Genco Ltd.'s hand tools offer ------- durability.
   - (A) exception
   - (B) exceptional
   - (C) exceptionally
   - (D) excepted

2. Our office is located in the business district, so salespeople are always ------- to corporate clients.
   - (A) accessible
   - (B) accessibly
   - (C) more accessibility
   - (D) accesses

3. ------- contact with both the buyer and the seller of the property ensures that both sides are fully satisfied.
   - (A) Frequent
   - (B) Frequency
   - (C) Frequencies
   - (D) Frequently

4. The ------- language used in the novel helped readers to imagine the scene.
   - (A) descriptively
   - (B) descriptive
   - (C) description
   - (D) describe

5. Bao Inc., offers a ------- benefits package to new employees to attract high quality candidates.
   - (A) competitive
   - (B) competitively
   - (C) competed
   - (D) competition

6. At Alfonso's Solutions, we have our customer service available at ------- times.
   - (A) every
   - (B) much
   - (C) all
   - (D) a lot

7. Team members respect Ms. Choi because she has a number of qualities that are -------.
   - (A) admiration
   - (B) admiring
   - (C) admirable
   - (D) admire

8. The elevator is still -------, even after being damaged during the earthquake that occurred yesterday.
   - (A) function
   - (B) functional
   - (C) functionally
   - (D) functioned

9. The new documentary film by Paul Winter has created ------- interest in the director's previous work.
   - (A) substance
   - (B) substances
   - (C) substantial
   - (D) substantially

10. Novak Ltd. has gained a reputation for supplying ------- equipment to the metal industries.
    - (A) depended
    - (B) dependably
    - (C) dependable
    - (D) depends

11. Austin is the best location ------- for startup technology businesses due to the ease of attracting a qualified workforce.

(A) availability
(B) availabilities
(C) available
(D) availably

12. Lacking ------- efforts to keep the park free from litter, the problem may get worse over time.

(A) intention
(B) intentional
(C) intentionally
(D) intend

13. The installation of ------- accounting software would streamline the billing process and save a lot of time.

(A) numerous
(B) both
(C) any
(D) few

14. If the weather conditions become more -------, an alert message will be sent to the residents.

(A) hazard
(B) hazards
(C) hazardous
(D) hazardously

15. ------- rooms are currently available, but there will be some vacancies in the early afternoon.

(A) No
(B) None
(C) Never
(D) Not

16. ------- vehicles that are left on Braxton Avenue after midnight will be towed by the city.

(A) Each
(B) Whenever
(C) All
(D) Either

17. Due to the importance of keeping the financial statement -------, attention must be paid to every detail.

(A) accuracy
(B) accurate
(C) accurately
(D) accuracies

18. Griffin Jang proves himself ------- by always keeping deadlines as well as producing the best results.

(A) reliable
(B) relied
(C) relying
(D) reliability

19. Alcon Pictures witnessed an ------- 15% increase in its market share after releasing its new film, *Aurora*.

(A) impress
(B) impressive
(C) impression
(D) impressively

20. The views expressed in the articles are those of the ------- authors and do not necessarily reflect the positions of *Star Telegraph*.

(A) successive
(B) respective
(C) likely
(D) enormous

부사

기본 개념 잡기

● 부사란?

문장을 이루고 있는 각각의 품사 및 문장 전체를 꾸며 주는 수식어를 부사라고 한다.
부사는 형용사, 또 다른 부사, 동사, 문장 전체를 수식한다.

| **currently** available
현재 이용 가능한 | **very** quickly
매우 빨리 | respond **promptly**
신속하게 응답하다 |

| to **better** implement
더 잘 실행하기 위해 | **Fortunately**, we closed the deal.
운 좋게도, 우리는 그 계약을 성사시켰다. |

● 부사의 형태

부사는 기본적으로 형용사에 **-ly**를 붙여서 만든다.

easy 쉬운 ◐ eas**ily** 쉽게   brief 짧은 ◐ brief**ly** 짧게   recent 최근의 ◐ recent**ly** 최근에

● 부사의 수식

부사는 다양한 요소를 수식한다.

We **greatly** appreciate your help.	동사 수식	도움에 **매우** 감사드립니다.
The office is **relatively** new.	형용사 수식	사무실이 **비교적** 새것이다.
The project was done **extremely** fast.	부사 수식	프로젝트는 **매우** 빠르게 완료되었다.
We expect him to come **early**.	기타 수식	우리는 그가 **일찍** 올 것이라고 예상한다.
Fortunately, there are alternative routes.	문장 전체 수식	**다행히,** 다른 경로가 있습니다.

출제 공식 1   부사 자리

부사는 다양한 위치에서 동사를 수식한다.

주어 + 부사 + 동사	Mr. Liu **consistently** meets the sales goals. 류 씨는 **꾸준히** 판매 목표를 충족시킨다.
be동사 + 부사 + p.p.	The temperature in our warehouse is **strictly** controlled. 창고의 온도는 **엄격하게** 통제된다.
be동사 + 부사 + -ing	The deadline is **rapidly** approaching. 마감일이 **빠르게** 다가오고 있다.
have + 부사 + p.p.	Our company has **recently** released a new product. 우리 회사는 **최근** 신상품을 출시했다.
조동사 + 부사 + 본동사	Anyone can **easily** assemble the shelving unit. 누구든지 그 선반을 **쉽게** 조립할 수 있다.
자동사 + 부사	The two companies work **collaboratively**. 그 두 회사는 **협력하여** 일한다.
타동사 + 목적어 + 부사	Please read the instructions **carefully**. 그 지시 사항을 **주의 깊게** 읽으세요.

※ 타동사와 목적어 사이에 빈칸이 있을 때는 부사 자리가 아님에 유의하자.

The city made [**significant** / ~~significantly~~] progress. 그 도시는 **엄청난** 발전을 이루었다.

CHECK-UP
정답 및 해설 p. 133

1. The two companies have [final / finally] agreed on contract.
2. We [regret / regretfully] inform you that Ms. Han is leaving our company.
3. Please read the details [thorough / thoroughly] before you sign the lease.

출제 공식 2   부사의 수식 관계

부사는 형용사, 부사, 문장의 일부, 문장 전체를 수식한다.

형용사 수식	The office space is **temporarily** unavailable. 사무실 공간이 **일시적으로** 이용이 불가능하다.
부사 수식	The repair work has been completed **extremely** fast. 수리 작업이 **매우** 빠르게 끝났다.
전치사구 수식	That style is **totally** out of date. 그 스타일은 **완전히** 구식이다.
문장 일부 수식	**Shortly** after the meeting began, the room was closed. 회의가 시작한 **직후** 문이 닫혔다.
문장 전체 수식	**Unfortunately**, the item you ordered is out of stock. 유감스럽게도 주문하신 물품이 품절입니다.

CHECK-UP
정답 및 해설 p. 133

1. The demand for healthy beverages remains [consistent / consistently] stable.
2. [Immediate / Immediately] after earning a degree, Mr. Taylor joined a marketing firm.
3. The temperature can be controlled [relative / relatively] easily.

출제 공식 3 　　　 기타 부사의 수식

부사는 동명사, to부정사, 분사를 수식한다.

부사 + 동명사	We congratulated ourselves on **finally** closing the deal.
	우리는 **마침내** 계약을 성사시킨 것을 축하했다.
to부정사 + 부사	We keep our prices low to **best** serve our customers
	우리는 고객들에게 **최고로** 서비스하기 위해 가격을 낮게 유지한다.
부사 + 분사	We use less energy, **thereby** cutting costs.
	우리는 에너지를 덜 사용하고 **그렇게 함으로써** 비용을 줄인다.

CHECK-UP 정답 및 해설 p. 134

1. Mr. Palmer was commended for [continual / continually] surpassing sales goals.
2. The director decided to change the text [slight / slightly] on the front page.
3. [Former / Formerly] located on the top floor, the sales division is now on the 7th floor.

출제 공식 4 　　　 뜻에 유의할 부사

형용사 + -ly의 형태지만 형용사와는 완전히 다른 의미를 가지는 부사들이 있다.

> hardly 거의 ~ 않다 　　 shortly 곧 　　 highly 매우 　　 nearly 거의 　　 closely 자세히, 긴밀하게

The shuttle bus **hardly** arrives on time. 셔틀버스는 **거의** 제때 도착하지 **않는다**.

Our representative will contact you **shortly**. 저희 직원이 **곧** 연락을 드리도록 하겠습니다.

We interviewed **highly** qualified candidates. 우리는 **매우** 자격을 갖춘 지원자들을 인터뷰했다.

There are graphics on **nearly** every page. **거의** 모든 페이지에 그림이 있다.

We work **closely** with our local governments. 우리는 지역 정부들과 **긴밀하게** 협력한다.

CHECK-UP 정답 및 해설 p. 134

1. James Clark is best known for his [high / highly] regarded book, *Outer Space*.
2. The press conference took [nearly / shortly] twice as long as expected.
3. Vending machines are [closely / conveniently] located near the entrance.

이것도 알면 플러스 10점!

숫자 수식 부사

about, almost, nearly, approximately, around 대략
up to 최대 ~까지   just 단지   over, more than ~ 이상

Ms. Lobo has worked as an accountant for **over** 10 years.
로보 씨는 회계사로 10년 **넘게** 일했다.

The number of visitors to our Web site has **more than** doubled.
우리 웹사이트 방문자 수가 두 배 **이상** 늘었다.

증감 동사 수식 부사

dramatically, significantly, considerably, substantially, noticeably, remarkably,
markedly, sharply 상당히   gradually, steadily, incrementally 점점   slightly, marginally 약간

The demand for skilled workers has **significantly** increased.
기술직 직원에 대한 수요가 **상당히** 증가했다.

※ highly는 '매우'라는 뜻으로 의미는 비슷하지만 증감 동사를 수식하지 않는다.

비교급 수식 부사

even, much, far, a lot, still, significantly, considerably, substantially, noticeably 훨씬

The latest model is **much** thinner than the previous one.
최신 모델은 이전 모델보다 **훨씬** 더 얇다.

접속부사

however 그러나	moreover 게다가	therefore 따라서	nevertheless 그럼에도 불구하고
furthermore 게다가	consequently 그 결과	besides 게다가	otherwise 그렇지 않으면
then 그리고 나서	in fact 사실	meanwhile 그 동안에	likewise 마찬가지로

Payment should be made within 7 days. **Otherwise**, your order will be canceled.
7일 이내에 지불이 이루어져야 합니다. **그렇지 않으면** 주문이 취소될 것입니다.

※ 접속부사는 부사이므로 두 문장을 하나로 연결하지 못한다. 따라서 Part 6에서 주로 출제된다.

정답 및 해설 p. 134

1. Caron Motors ------- recalled its latest hybrid model due to a possible fault with the breaks.
   (A) to volunteer
   (B) voluntarily
   (C) voluntary
   (D) volunteer

2. Consumers have responded ------- to the release of the new Dingo vacuum cleaner.
   (A) enthusiasm
   (B) enthusiastic
   (C) enthusiastically
   (D) enthusiast

3. Dolman Living's kitchen utensils may be purchased ------- or in sets of three.
   (A) individual
   (B) individualize
   (C) individuals
   (D) individually

4. The new parking fines caused controversy and ------- divided voters.
   (A) sharpness
   (B) sharply
   (C) sharper
   (D) sharp

5. Morelli's Bistro features an ------- decorated dining area that is perfect for special occasions.
   (A) attract
   (B) attracted
   (C) attractively
   (D) attracting

6. All members should note that Pony Gym sends out membership renewal notices ------- via text message.
   (A) automate
   (B) automatic
   (C) automation
   (D) automatically

7. Surveys indicate that many young job seekers prefer to get their résumés ------- written by an expert.
   (A) professional
   (B) professionalized
   (C) professionally
   (D) professionalism

8. The streamlined product development process may ------- reduce the company's production costs.
   (A) significance
   (B) significantly
   (C) signify
   (D) significant

9. A recent study revealed that some popular juice drinks contain ------- low amounts of nutrients.
   (A) surprised
   (B) surprisingly
   (C) surprises
   (D) to surprise

10. The Arremax A10 digital camera offers more features than any other ------- priced model.
    (A) correspondence
    (B) corresponded
    (C) corresponding
    (D) correspondingly

11. Rigel Supply Co. offers a line of hardware tools with handles ------- designed for left-handed users.

(A) specify
(B) specified
(C) specifying
(D) specifically

12. The company's new factory is capable of producing kitchen appliances on an ------- large scale.

(A) impressed
(B) impressions
(C) impresses
(D) impressively

13. Laura's Bistro has been ------- ranked among the most popular restaurants in the region.

(A) consistent
(B) consistency
(C) consistently
(D) consistencies

14. The number of residents ------- seeking employment declined last quarter, a sign of a healthy local economy.

(A) activate
(B) active
(C) actions
(D) actively

15. The first-class section of the ten o'clock train was fully booked, so Ms. Sharon decided to take a later train -------.

(A) seldom
(B) instead
(C) however
(D) altogether

16. Our current business plan is not sustainable, and ------- we need to find more effective ways to stay afloat.

(A) therefore
(B) since
(C) why
(D) otherwise

17. Participants at the design festival were impressed by how ------- Bella Son incorporated art into her shoes.

(A) skillful
(B) skilled
(C) skill
(D) skillfully

18. The construction work is scheduled for completion by May, but it is ------- ahead of schedule thanks to the good weather.

(A) present
(B) presence
(C) presently
(D) presenting

19. ------- decorated by a top interior designer, every guest room at the Eiffel Hotel provides ample comfort.

(A) Elegant
(B) Elegance
(C) Elegantly
(D) More elegant

20. The upcoming seminar will focus ------- on ways for businesses to help local communities thrive.

(A) hardly
(B) primarily
(C) formerly
(D) relatively

동사

기본 개념 잡기

● 동사란?

주어의 상태나 동작을 서술하기 위한 문장 필수 성분을 동사라고 하며 동사에는 자동사와 타동사가 있다.

자동사			
rise	happen	remain	emerge
오르다	발생하다	남아있다	나타나다

타동사			
discuss	explain	mention	introduce
논의하다	설명하다	언급하다	도입하다

● 동사의 형태

동사의 형태를 결정하는 요소는 수 일치, 태, 시제 세 가지이다.

1. 수 일치 주어의 수에 따라 동사의 단/복수가 결정된다.

단수	It **is**	The CEO **has**	The director **intends**	The client **wishes**
복수	The items **are**	We **have**	The executives **intend**	They **wish**

Mr. Taylor [~~need~~ / **needs**] to attend monthly meetings. 테일러 씨는 월별 회의에 참석해야 한다.

Managers [**need** / ~~needs~~] to attend monthly meetings. 매니저들은 월별 회의에 참석해야 한다.

2. 태 능동태 문장의 목적어를 주어로 빼고 동사를 「**be동사 + p.p.**」 형태로 바꾸면 수동태가 된다.
수동태 문장에서 행위자는 「**by + 목적격**」으로 나타낸다.

능동태 We hold weekly meetings. 우리는 주별 회의를 연다.

수동태 Weekly meetings **are held** (by us). 주별 회의가 열린다.

3. 시제 단순 시제에 진행형(be동사 + -ing)과 완료형(have + p.p.)이 결합되어 진행 및 완료 시제를 만든다.

	현재	과거	미래
단순 시제	write	wrote	will write
진행 시제	is writing	was writing	will be writing
완료 시제	have written	had written	will have written

출제 공식 1 주어와 동사의 수 일치

단수 수어는 단수 동사와, 복수 수어는 복수 동사와 수 일치한다.

단수 The customer [**has** / ~~have~~] inquiries about the return policy. 그 고객은 반품 정책에 대해 문의사항이 있다.

복수 All participants [~~needs~~ / **need**] to submit entries by noon. 모든 참여자들은 출품작을 정오까지 제출해야 한다.

수식어구가 붙으면 수식어구 앞에 놓인 명사에 수 일치한다.

단수 The schedule (of events) [**is** / ~~are~~] on the Web site. 행사 스케줄은 웹사이트에 있습니다.

복수 Executives (from Dom Pharmaceuticals) [~~is~~ / **are**] visiting us. 돔 제약회사 임원들이 방문할 것이다.

동명사 주어는 단수 취급하여 단수 동사로 수 일치한다.

단수 Recruiting qualified workers [**is** / ~~are~~] a challenging task. 자격 있는 직원들을 채용하는 것은 어려운 일이다.

CHECK-UP
정답 및 해설 p. 136

1. Each lunch also [include / includes] a small salad, a banana, and an energy bar.
2. Members of the city council [has agreed / have agreed] to hold a convention.
3. Having frequent meetings [lead / leads] to some negative consequences.

출제 공식 2 유의해야 하는 수 일치

「수량 표현 + of」가 오는 경우 of 뒤에 오는 명사에 수 일치한다.

단수 Much of the information [**has** / ~~have~~] not been published. 많은 정보가 아직 발표되지 않았다.

복수 A number of workers [~~supports~~ / **support**] the policy. 많은 직원들이 그 정책을 지지한다.

> **수량 표현** all 모두 some 일부 most 대부분 none 아무(것)도 many 대다수 (a) few 약간 several 몇몇
> much 다량 (a) little 약간 a number of 많은

※ each는 「each of 복수명사 + 단수동사」 형태로 쓴다.

단수 Each of the presenters [**has** / ~~have~~] 15 minutes to speak. 발표자 각각은 15분의 발언권을 갖는다.

주격 관계대명사절 내에서의 동사는 선행사의 수에 일치한다.

Rules which [~~is~~ / **are**] outdated need to be revised. 시대에 뒤떨어진 규칙은 개정되어야 한다.

CHECK-UP
정답 및 해설 p. 137

1. All of the company executives [has acted / have acted] as a judge.
2. Each of the training sessions [is / are] expected to last for an hour.
3. Only those who [operate / operates] complex machinery will receive training.

출제 공식 3   능동태 vs. 수동태

동사 뒤에 목적어가 있으면 능동태, 목적어가 없으면 수동태를 선택한다.

능동태   Our new product [**earned** / ~~was earned~~] positive reviews. 우리의 신제품이 호평을 받았다.
                                            명사구 목적어 O

수동태   The book [~~published~~ / **was published**] in seven languages. 그 책은 7개국어로 출판되었다.
                                                  목적이 X

자동사는 목적어를 가지지 않으므로 수동태로 쓰지 않는다.

The shipment [**arrived** / ~~was arrived~~] yesterday. 배송품이 어제 도착했다.

4형식 동사의 수동태 뒤에는 목적어가 있다.

The association **awarded** Dr. Yoon the Norton Prize. 협회는 윤 박사에게 노튼상을 **수여했다**.
                                  목적어 1   목적어 2

Dr. Yoon **was awarded** the Norton Prize. 윤 박사는 노튼상을 **수여받았다**. ❯ 4형식 동사는 능동태일 때 목적어를 두 개
              수동태   목적어   가지므로 수동태가 되어도 하나의 목적어가 남는다.

CHECK-UP   정답 및 해설 p. 137

1. Ms. Juliet [has recorded / was recorded] the meeting minutes to post them online.
2. The presentation [cancelled / was cancelled] due to low public interest.
3. Macqueen's share price [has risen / was risen] recently.

출제 공식 4   수동태가 포함된 빈출 숙어

수동태 동사 + by 이외의 전치사

be satisfied with ~에 만족하다	be faced with ~에 직면하다	be engaged in ~에 관여하다
be associated with ~와 관련되다	be based on ~에 근거하다	be interested in ~에 관심 있다
be equipped with ~이 갖추어지다	be related to ~에 관련되다	be dedicated to ~에 전념하다

Ms. Porter's latest book is [**based** / ~~related~~] on her life story. 포터 씨의 최신 책은 그녀의 전기를 바탕으로 한다.

수동태 동사 + to부정사

be allowed to ~하도록 허락되다	be encouraged to ~하도록 권장되다	be expected to ~하도록 예상되다
be pleased to ~해서 기쁘다	be invited to ~하도록 요청되다	be asked to ~하도록 요청되다
be advised to ~하도록 권고되다	be urged to ~하도록 촉구되다	be scheduled to ~하기로 예정되다

Volunteers are [~~allowing~~ / **allowed**] to watch the performance. 자원봉사자들은 공연을 보도록 허용된다.

CHECK-UP   정답 및 해설 p. 137

1. We are [pleasing / pleased] to offer a new service to our customers.
2. The hotel is [equipping / equipped] with a large laundry area.
3. Over 20 authors were [inviting / invited] to attend the book signing event.

출제 공식 5 단순 시제

현재 시제는 습관, 반복, 일반적인 사실, 현재 상태를 나타낸다.

현재 시제의 단서   usually, generally, every day, each month, currently, presently 등

Delivery <u>usually</u> **takes** no more than 3 days. 배송은 보통 3일 이내로 **걸린다**.

※ 시간과 조건을 나타내는 접속사가 이끄는 절에서는 미래 시제 대신 현재(완료) 시제를 쓴다.

<u>When</u> the item [**arrives** / ~~will arrive~~], we **will notify** you. 상품이 **도착하면** 알려 드리겠습니다.

과거 시제는 이미 지난 일을 나타낸다.

과거 시제의 단서   previously, last, ago, yesterday, recently 등

Mr. Kato <u>previously</u> **worked** for a leading pharmaceutical firm. 카토 씨는 **이전에** 일류 제약 회사에서 **일했다**.

미래 시제는 앞으로 일어날 일을 나타낸다.

미래 시제의 단서   soon, tomorrow, shortly, upcoming, next month, later 등

Mr. Donovan **will conduct** a training session <u>next month</u>. 도노반 씨가 **다음 달에** 교육을 **실시할 것이다**.

CHECK-UP

정답 및 해설 p. 137

1. Engineers [have been educated / will be educated] in the upcoming workshop.
2. Recently, the company [decides / decided] to revise its vacation policy.
3. As soon as the station [opens / will open], traffic congestions will be relieved.

출제 공식 6 진행 시제

현재진행 시제는 현재 일어나고 있는 일을 나타낸다.

We **are** <u>currently</u> **accepting** bids for a new campaign. 우리는 **현재** 새로운 광고에 대한 입찰을 **받고 있다**.

※ 현재진행은 가까운 미래에 예정된 일을 나타내기도 한다.

We **are hosting** a special exhibit <u>next month</u>. 우리는 **다음 달에** 특별 전시회를 **개최할 것이다**.

과거진행 시제는 과거 특정 시간 동안에 일어났던 일을 나타낸다.

Mr. Ryu **was helping** customers while stocking shelves. 류 씨는 물건을 채우는 **동안** 고객들을 응대하고 있었다.

미래진행 시제는 미래에 진행될 이미 계획된 일을 나타낸다.

We **will be celebrating** Ms. Alba's promotion <u>next week</u>. 우리는 **다음 주에** 알바 씨의 승진을 **기념할 것이다**.

CHECK-UP

정답 및 해설 p. 137

1. Currently, we [are undergoing / were undergoing] extensive renovation.
2. The CEO [was visiting / will be visiting] our production facility later this month.
3. The café on Main Street [is closing / will be closed] its doors next month.

출제 공식 7 　　　완료 시제

현재 완료 시제는 ① 현재까지 지속적인 일, ② 최근 완료된 일을 나타낸다.

현재 완료 시제의 단서　　recently, lately, for+기간, over the last/past+기간, since+과거 시점

지속: **Since** Mr. Liu **joined** our team, sales **have increased**. 류 씨가 팀에 합류한 **이래** 판매가 **상승해왔다.**

완료: Our branch **has recently changed** operating hours. 저희 지점은 **최근** 운영 시간을 **변경했습니다.**

과거 완료 시제는 과거보다 더 앞선 지난 일을 나타낸다.

과거 완료 시제의 단서　　과거에 일어난 비교되는 두 시점

By the time Mr. Ito **arrived**, the train **had left** already. 이토 씨가 **도착했을 무렵** 기차는 **이미 떠나고 없었다.**

미래 완료 시제는 미래 시점에 이르러 완료될 일을 나타낸다.

미래 완료 시제의 단서　　by+미래 시점

By the end of the month, we **will have finished** the repair work. 이달 말 무렵이면 보수를 완료해 있을 것이다.

CHECK-UP
정답 및 해설 p. 138

1. The number of tourists in Japan [will decline / has declined] since last year.
2. Mr. Pascal [had lived / has lived] in Singapore before he moved to Hong Kong.
3. By the time the rehearsal starts, all booths [had been / will have been] set up.

출제 공식 8 　　　수 일치 + 태 + 시제

동사 문제는 수 일치, 태, 시제가 부분적으로 섞인 문제로 주로 출제된다.

동사 자리임이 판단되면 수 일치 ❷ 태 ❷ 시제 순서로 따져서 정답을 고르도록 하자.

수 일치		태		시제
단수 주어에 단수 동사, 복수 주어에 복수 동사 쓰기	❷	목적어가 있으면 능동태, 없으면 수동태 쓰기 (단, 4형식 동사는 예외)	❷	시제의 단서 표현 포착하기

The Bros Bistro ------- a new menu starting next week. 브로스 식당은 다음 주부터 신메뉴를 제공할 것이다.
(A) have offered　(B) are offering　(C) will be offering　(D) offered

❶ 수 일치 판단하기　　단수 주어 뒤 단수 동사 자리 → 복수 동사인 (A), (B)는 소거한다.
❷ 태 판단하기　　　　남은 둘 다 능동태이므로 소거 대상이 없다.
❸ 시제 판단하기　　　미래 시제의 단서인 next week가 있으므로 미래형인 (C)를 고른다.

CHECK UP
정답 및 해설 p 138

1. The release date [is delaying / has been delayed] due to unexpected problems.
2. Mr. Reynolds [returned / is returning] to his office yesterday.
3. The client [has been signed / will have signed] the contract by the end of the month.

빈출 자동사

rise 오르다	arrive 도착하다	happen 발생하다	occur 발생하다
appear 나타나다	emerge 등장하다	function 기능하다	last 지속되다
consist 구성되다	remain 남아 있다	work 일하다	proceed 진행되다

An unexpected error [**occurred** / ~~was occurred~~] during the operation.
작업 도중 예상치 못한 오류가 발생했다.

❷ 자동사는 목적어를 가지지 않으므로 수동태로 쓰지 않는다.

비슷한 의미의 자동사와 타동사

뜻	자동사	타동사	뜻	자동사	타동사
말하다	talk about	discuss	응답하다	respond to	answer
따르다, 준수하다	comply with	observe	참여하다	participate in	attend
다루다	deal with	address	참조하다	refer to	consult
설명하다	account for	explain	초래하다	lead to	cause

All employees should [~~attend~~ / **participate**] in the upcoming meeting.
전직원은 곧 있을 회의에 참석해야 한다.

Tourists must [**observe** / ~~comply~~] local standards. 관광객들은 지역 규범을 준수해야 한다.

❷ 자동사는 목적어를 받기 위해 전치사가 필요하고, 타동사는 목적어가 바로 나온다.

빈출 자동사 + 전치사

depend (up)on ~에 의존하다	rely (up)on ~에 의존하다	benefit from ~로부터 이익을 얻다
collaborate with ~와 협력하다	concentrate on ~에 집중하다	focus on ~에 집중하다
specialize in ~을 전문으로 하다	work as / serve as ~로서 일하다	inquire about ~에 대해 문의하다
refrain from ~을 삼가다	remark on ~에 대해 언급하다	comment on ~에 대해 언급하다
proceed with ~을 진행하다	adhere to ~을 따르다, 준수하다	coincide with ~와 동시에 일어나다
consist of ~로 구성되다	dispose of ~을 버리다, 처분하다	react to ~에 반응하다

Employees [**benefit** / ~~depend~~] from collaborating with each other.
직원들은 상호 협력으로 이익을 얻는다.

We [~~perform~~ / **specialize**] in commercial real estate.
저희는 상업용 부동산을 전문으로 합니다.

❷ 자동사를 외울 때 함께 쓰이는 전치사를 같이 외우면 빠르고 정확한 문제 풀이가 가능하다.

1. All orders ------- via the most efficient method from our main factory.
   (A) to be shipping
   (B) will be shipped
   (C) being shipped
   (D) is shipping

2. A cash award of $1,000 ------- to the winner of next quarter's sales contest.
   (A) was given
   (B) to give
   (C) is giving
   (D) will be given

3. To get reimbursed for travel expenses, all staff members must ------- original paper receipts to the accounting department.
   (A) be submitted
   (B) submitting
   (C) submits
   (D) submit

4. Betel Ltd. will ship all orders as soon as payment -------.
   (A) to receive
   (B) will receive
   (C) has been received
   (D) is receiving

5. Staffing issues ------- Silverado Department Store to reduce its business hours on weekdays.
   (A) forcing
   (B) forced
   (C) to force
   (D) are forced

6. Repairs on the laptop computer -------, but the technician was unable to get it working again.
   (A) attempted
   (B) were attempted
   (C) are attempting
   (D) have attempted

7. New Life Pharmaceuticals, ------- seemingly impossible solutions to major health problems.
   (A) was created
   (B) has created
   (C) to create
   (D) will be created

8. Now that Mr. Benson ------- to our headquarters in London, we must promote someone internally to fill his position.
   (A) has transferred
   (B) transfer
   (C) transferring
   (D) to transfer

9. Whenever there are subzero temperatures, Vance Department Store ------- complimentary tea.
   (A) providing
   (B) provides
   (C) provisions
   (D) are providing

10. Sage Bistro makes its signature dishes using recipes that ------- over many years.
    (A) being perfected
    (B) was perfected
    (C) have been perfected
    (D) to be perfecting

11. For nearly half a century, Midas Shopping Mall ------- for its great values and famous brands.

(A) is knowing
(B) being known
(C) has been known
(D) will have known

12. The new juice flavors introduced by Coweta Beverages ------- to young adult consumers who prefer natural ingredients.

(A) has appealed
(B) appeal
(C) appeals
(D) appealing

13. Silvia Wedding Gowns ------- free dress fittings since it opened last October.

(A) is offering
(B) has been offering
(C) will be offering
(D) would have been offering

14. New computer programmers ------- when our company merges with Ace Solutions early next year.

(A) were recruited
(B) recruiting
(C) to recruit
(D) will be recruited

15. By the time Mr. Bernard became the chief operating officer, he ------- at the company for almost 25 years.

(A) has served
(B) will served
(C) had served
(D) serves

16. Dealing with dissatisfied customers ------- one of the most demanding tasks.

(A) consider
(B) is considered
(C) have been considered
(D) is considering

17. Once an appointment -------, the patient will receive an e-mailed confirmation notice from the clinic.

(A) is scheduling
(B) was scheduled
(C) has been scheduled
(D) will schedule

18. Failing to ------- food safety regulations may result in a number of unfavorable consequences.

(A) observe
(B) function
(C) remark
(D) comply

19. Spico is a small printing company which ------- in design and production of promotional materials.

(A) experiences
(B) specializes
(C) dedicates
(D) displays

20. ------- the living space in your home or apartment with Arex Co.'s shelves and storage cabinets.

(A) Maximizing
(B) Maximize
(C) Maximized
(D) Maximization

to부정사와 동명사

기본 개념 잡기

● to부정사란?

「to + 동사원형」으로 나타내며 문장에서 기능이 한 가지로 정해져 있지 않다 하여 부정사라고 한다.

to부정사는 문장에서 명사, 형용사, 부사 기능을 하며 '~하는 것', '~할', '~하기 위해' 등의 뜻을 가진다.

want **to participate** 참여하는 것을 원하다	an opportunity **to participate** 참여할 기회	pay a fee **to participate** 참여하기 위해 돈을 내다

● 동명사란?

동사에 -ing를 붙인 형태로 나타내며 문장에서 명사 역할을 하는 것을 동명사라고 한다.

동명사는 '~하는 것'이라는 뜻을 가진다.

avoid **using** a flash 플래시를 **사용하는 것**을 피하다	**working** with others 다른 사람들과 **일하는 것**	refrain from **talking** **말하는 것**을 삼가다

● to부정사와 동명사의 동사적 성질

to부정사와 동명사는 동사의 형태에서 파생되어 동사와 비슷한 성질을 지니므로 준동사라고 한다.

준동사는 동사로 기능할 수는 없지만 동사처럼 보어나 목적어를 가질 수 있고 부사의 수식을 받을 수 있다.

준동사 + 보어

The company strives **to stay** competitive. 그 회사는 경쟁력을 유지하기 위해 노력한다.
　　　　　　　동사　　준동사　　보어

준동사 + 목적어

Customers will receive rewards for **using** the card. 고객들은 카드를 사용한 것에 대해 보상을 받을 것이다.
　　　　　　　동사　　　　　　　준동사　목적어

준동사 + 부사

Participants should plan **to arrive** promptly. 참석자들은 신속하게 도착하도록 계획해야 한다.
　　　　　　　동사　　　준동사　　부사

출제 공식 1   to부정사의 역할

to부정사는 명사 역할를 하여 문장에서 주어, 보어, 목적어 자리에 올 수 있다.

주어 역할   **To try** a new strategy is worthwhile. 새로운 전략을 시도하는 것은 가치 있다.

           = It is worthwhile to try a new strategy.

           ❷ 가주어 it을 주어자리에 사용하는 경우가 더 흔하다.

목적어 역할   We want **to have** a meeting once a week. 우리는 일주일에 한 번 회의하는 것을 원한다.

보어 역할   The aim of the meeting is **to discuss** the merger plan. 회의의 목적은 합병 계획을 논의하는 것이다.

           ❷ 목표, 목적을 나타내는 aim, goal, purpose, objective, mission은 to부정사를 보어로 가진다.

to부정사는 형용사 역할을 하여 문장에서 명사를 수식할 수 있다.

명사 수식   The seminar provides chances **to meet** with experts. 그 세미나는 전문가와 만날 기회를 제공한다.

           ❷ 앞 명사를 수식하며, 이때 해석은 '~할', '~하는'이 된다.

to부정사는 부사 역할을 하여 문장에서 기타 품사 또는 문장 전체를 수식할 수 있다.

문장 수식   We are working overtime **to fulfill** the order. 우리는 주문을 맞추기 위해 초과 근무를 하고 있다.

           ❷ 앞 문장을 수식하며 '~하기 위해서'로 해석된다. in order to 또는 so as to로 표현할 수 있다.

CHECK-UP   정답 및 해설 p. 140

1. The objective of the fundraiser is [support / to support] local businesses.
2. Visitors can pick up a copy of questionnaires [to fill out / filling out] near the entrance.
3. [To regain / Regain] the reputation it once enjoyed, Cresco, Ltd. hired marketing experts.

출제 공식 2   to부정사를 취하는 동사

to부정사를 목적어로 취하는 동사

want, wish 원하다	hope 바라다	aim ~하기를 목표하다	expect 기대하다	decide 결정하다
agree 동의하다	intend 의도하다	offer 제공하다	promise 약속하다	fail 실패하다

Two companies <u>decided</u> **to join** forces. 두 회사는 협력하기로 결정했다.

to부정사를 목적격 보어로 취하는 동사

ask 요청하다	require 요구하다	allow 허락하다	invite 요청하다	encourage 권장하다
expect 기대하다	remind 상기시키다	enable 가능하게 하다	cause 유발하다	advise 권고하다

They <u>asked</u> participants **to complete** the form. 그들은 참여자들에게 양식을 작성하라고 요청했다.

CHECK-UP   정답 및 해설 p. 141

1. The proposed initiative [aims / considers] to support scientific research.
2. New technologies have enabled us [maximize / to maximize] our production capacity.
3. The interviewees were [encouraged / remembered] to wear formal attire.

출제 공식 3　　　　동명사의 역할

동명사는 명사 역할을 하여 ~'하는 것'으로 해석되며 문장에서 주어, 목적어, 보어 자리에 올 수 있다.

주어 자리　**Renting** a car <u>is</u> becoming easier than ever before. 차를 렌트하는 것은 이전보다 쉬워지고 있다.
　　　❷ 주어 자리에 오는 동명사는 단수 취급하여 단수 동사로 수 일치한다.

동사의 목적어　Wo will <u>discontinue</u> **producing** our iconic S4 model. 우리는 대표 모델인 S4 생산을 중단할 것이다.
　　　❷ consider, avoid, suggest, recommend는 동명사를 목적어로 취하는 대표 동사이다.

전치사의 목적어　Receive 10 percent off <u>by</u> **purchasing** two or more items.
　　　2개 이상 **구매함으로써** 10퍼센트 할인을 받으세요.
　　　❷ to부정사는 전치사의 목적어로 쓸 수 없다는 점과 구분된다.

보어 자리　The next step <u>is</u> **removing** the stains on the surface. 다음 단계는 표면의 얼룩을 **제거하는 것**이다.
　　　❷ '주어가 ~하는 중이다'라는 진행형으로 해석하지 않도록 유의한다.

CHECK-UP　　　　　　　　　　　　　　　　　　　　　　　정답 및 해설 p. 141

1. [Meeting / For meeting] numerous deadlines is critical in the field of publishing.
2. Please avoid [to park / parking] on Jackson Road during the street festival.
3. Jenco Electronics is committed to [provide / providing] the best technical service.

출제 공식 4　　　　동명사 자리 vs. 명사 자리

동명사는 명사 역할을 하지만 동사적인 성질을 그대로 가지므로 목적어를 가질 수 있다.

명사 자리　The city official announced [**suspension** / ~~suspending~~] of the railway construction.
　　　시 공무원은 철도 공사의 **중단**을 발표했다.
　　　❷ 빈칸 뒤 목적어가 없으므로 동명사를 쓰지 않는다.

동명사 자리　The deadline for [~~submission~~ / **submitting**] <u>the expense report</u> is approaching.
　　　경비 보고서 **제출** 마감일이 다가온다.
　　　❷ 빈칸 뒤 목적어가 있으므로 동명사를 쓴다.

※ 단, 자동사는 목적어를 갖지 않으므로 「동명사 + 목적어」 규칙에 적용되지 않는다.
　　Participating in the survey is not required. 설문조사에 **참여하는 것**은 필수적이진 않다.

CHECK-UP　　　　　　　　　　　　　　　　　　　　　　　정답 및 해설 p. 141

1. Please tell us your preferred method for [return / returning] the completed form.
2. By [limitations / limiting] unnecessary purchases, JL Ltd, reduces the overall expenses.
3. You can greatly benefit from [subscriber / subscribing] to our newsletter.

이것도 알면 플러스 10점!

to부정사 관용 표현

too ... to 너무 …해서 ~할 수 없다	**enough ... to** ~하기에 충분한	**have yet to** 아직 ~ 않다
seem / appear to ~처럼 보이다	**remain to be seen** 두고 볼 일이다	**in an effort to** ~하려는 노력으로

The supplies **have yet to** arrive. 그 물품들은 **아직** 도착하지 **않았다.**
In an effort to increase profits, we hired an advisor. 수익을 늘리려는 **노력으로** 우리는 고문을 고용했다.

원형부정사

사역동사 let, have, make, 준사역동사 help는 목적격 보어로 원형부정사(동사원형)를 가진다.
We **let** senior managers **handle** customer complaints.
저희는 상급 관리자들이 고객 불평을 **관리하도록** 합니다.

help는 목적격 보어로 to부정사가 올 수도 있다. 또한 목적어를 생략하고 목적격 보어가 바로 올 수도 있다.
A distinctive logo will **help** your business **(to) stand out**. 독특한 로고는 회사를 **돋보이게** 해 줄 것이다.
A distinctive logo will **help (to) stand out**. 독특한 로고는 **돋보이게** 해 줄 것이다.

동명사 관용 표현

by -ing ~함으로써	**spend** (시간·돈) **(in) -ing** ~하느라 (시간·돈)을 쓰다
(up)on -ing ~하자마자	**have trouble[difficulty] (in) -ing** ~에 어려움을 겪다
be capable of -ing ~할 수 있다	**prevent[discourage] ~ from -ing** …이 ~하는 것을 막다

We **had difficulty finding** a suitable replacement. 우리는 적합한 대체자를 찾는 데 어려움을 겪었다.

to부정사와 전치사 to가 포함된 숙어

to부정사	전치사 to
be eager to 동사 ~하기를 열망하다	**be committed to** 명사 / -ing ~에 헌신하다, 전념하다
be likely to 동사 ~할 것 같다	**be devoted to** 명사 / -ing ~에 헌신하다, 전념하다
be hesitant to 동사 ~하기를 주저하다	**be dedicated to** 명사 / -ing ~에 헌신하다, 전념하다
be supposed to 동사 ~하기로 되어 있다	**be subject to** 명사 / -ing ~을 조건으로 하다, ~의 대상이다
be about to 동사 막 ~하려고 하다	**be opposed to** 명사 / -ing ~에 반대하다

All employees are [**expected** / ~~opposed~~] to attend the workshop.
모든 직원은 워크숍에 참석하도록 **기대된다.**

Shareholders were opposed to [~~negotiate~~ / **negotiating**] further.
주주들은 더 이상 협상하기를 **반대했다.**

❷ to 앞에 오는 어휘를 선택하거나 to 뒤에 나오는 형태를 고르는 문제로 출제된다.

1. The goal of the Ninth Street bridge widening project is ------- accessibility to the downtown area.
   (A) improve
   (B) to improve
   (C) that improves
   (D) being improved

2. Experts agree that it is important ------- the company and its corporate values before your job interview.
   (A) researched
   (B) to research
   (C) research
   (D) to be researched

3. ------- employees' vacation requests has become much simpler for our office manager, thanks to a software upgrade.
   (A) Approving
   (B) Approve
   (C) Being approved
   (D) Approval

4. ------- renewable energy, solar panels were installed on the roof of the public library.
   (A) Promotion
   (B) Promote
   (C) To promote
   (D) Promotes

5. The employee handbook lists several ways of ------- professionalism in the workplace.
   (A) maintain
   (B) maintenance
   (C) maintaining
   (D) to maintain

6. ------- accuracy in data entry is very important, because even one error can be costly to a business.
   (A) Improve
   (B) Improvement
   (C) Improving
   (D) Improves

7. Those affected by the changes in government funding are encouraged ------- their opinions at the town hall meeting.
   (A) voicing
   (B) voice
   (C) to voice
   (D) voices

8. Housing sales are expected ------- this spring, when Belmont Ltd. opens a new distribution center in the region.
   (A) rising
   (B) risen
   (C) to rise
   (D) rises

9. Some of our salespeople decided ------- a two-day marketing conference at the last minute.
   (A) attendance
   (B) being attended
   (C) attending
   (D) to attend

10. Freelance writers and editors should avoid ------- too many projects at once.
    (A) accepts
    (B) accepted
    (C) to accept
    (D) accepting

11. A private investor is providing more than 3 million dollars ------- developing the city's waterfront area.

(A) began
(B) begins
(C) to begin
(D) has begun

12. Even our smallest banquet hall is large enough ------- huge industrial gatherings.

(A) to host
(B) hosting
(C) being hosted
(D) to be hosted

13. Jambi Furniture is dedicated to ------- the highest level of customer service.

(A) offering
(B) offered
(C) offer
(D) offers

14. Build client loyalty with less effort by ------- the most talented customer service representatives possible.

(A) hires
(B) hire
(C) hiring
(D) hired

15. Polaris-Dec photo editing software allows users ------- the quality of their digital images in just a few simple steps.

(A) enhancement
(B) enhance
(C) to enhance
(D) enhancing

16. The property developer stated that ------- the deadlines for each phase was critical to the success of the construction project.

(A) meet
(B) meets
(C) meeting
(D) met

17. Many voters believe that the proposed measures for food safety will be too difficult -------.

(A) enforcement
(B) enforcing
(C) to enforce
(D) enforced

18. Though details of the merger plan have ------- to be announced, analysts are optimistic about the deal's potential.

(A) enough
(B) many
(C) already
(D) yet

19. Organizers of the photography contest may consider ------- the submission deadline, as few entries have been received so far.

(A) extends
(B) extending
(C) extension
(D) extended

20. This weekend's training workshop will help managers ------- the skills and potential of all company employees.

(A) evaluates
(B) evaluated
(C) evaluate
(D) evaluation

분사

기본 개념 잡기

● 분사란?

동사에 -ing 또는 -ed를 붙인 것으로, 문장에서 형용사 기능을 하는 것을 분사라고 한다.
-ing 형태의 분사를 현재분사, -ed 형태(또는 불규칙 형태)의 분사를 과거분사라 일컫는다.
현재분사는 능동, 과거분사는 수동의 의미를 갖는다.

현재분사				과거분사		
leading 선도하는	existing 기존의	lasting 지속적인	VS.	detailed 자세한	written 서면의	skilled 숙련된

● 분사구문이란?

접속사가 있는 문장에서 접속사와 주어를 생략하고 분사만 남기는 형태의 구문을 분사구문이라고 한다.

능동태로 쓰인 분사구문

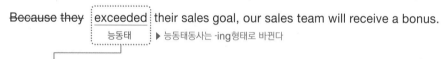

~~Because they~~ [exceeded] their sales goal, our sales team will receive a bonus.

능동태 ▶ 능동태동사는 -ing형태로 바뀐다

❯ **Exceeding** their sales goal, our sales team will receive a bonus.
　자신들의 판매 목표를 초과한 우리 판매팀은 보너스를 받을 것이다.

수동태로 쓰인 분사구문

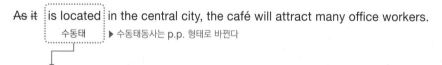

~~As it~~ [is located] in the central city, the café will attract many office workers.

수동태 ▶ 수동태동사는 p.p. 형태로 바뀐다

❯ **Located** in the central city, the café will attract many office workers.
　시 중심에 위치한 그 카페는 많은 회사원들을 끌어들일 것이다.

※ 접속사의 의미를 명확하게 해 주기 위해 접속사를 생략하지 않고 쓸 수도 있다.

　While staying at our hotel, you can have free access to the Internet.
　저희 호텔에 머무시는 동안 무료 인터넷을 이용하실 수 있습니다.

출제 공식 1   분사 자리

분사는 형용사처럼 명사 앞뒤에서 명사를 수식하거나 보어 자리에서 주어나 목적어를 수식한다.

명사 앞   Sales clerks have to deal with **demanding** <u>customers</u>. 판매 직원들은 **까다로운 고객**을 상대해야 한다.

     ❯ customers 앞에 놓여서 customers를 수식한다.

명사 뒤   The <u>e-mail</u> **sent** to Ms. Sato contains a link. 사토 씨에게 **보내진 이메일**은 링크를 포함하고 있다.

     ❯ e-mail 뒤에 놓여서 e-mail을 수식한다.

주격 보어   <u>The package</u> appeared **damaged**. 그 **소포는 파손된** 것 같아 보였다.

     ❯ 분사가 주어를 수식한다. (damaged의 주체: The package)

목적격 보어   The manager kept <u>the client</u> **waiting** for over 10 minutes. 매니저는 **고객을** 10분 이상 **기다리게** 했다.

     ❯ 분사가 목적어를 수식한다. (waiting의 주체: the client)

CHECK-UP   정답 및 해설 p. 144

1. The debate group has one [remain / remaining] issue to deal with.
2. The promotion does not apply to items [purchases / purchased] online.
3. The procedure for assembling the bookshelf seemed [challenge / challenging].

출제 공식 2   현재분사 vs. 과거분사

현재분사(-ing)는 능동, 과거분사(p.p.)는 수동의 의미를 나타낸다.

능동   The shop offers a free gift for **returning** customers. 그 가게는 **재방문하는** 고객에게 선물을 준다.

     ❯ customers가 재방문을 '하는' 것이므로 능동인 -ing 형태가 필요하다.

수동   All **returned** items undergo a full quality control check. 모든 **반품된** 상품은 철저한 품질 검수를 받는다.

     ❯ items가 반품이 '되는' 것이므로 수동인 p.p. 형태가 필요하다.

분사가 명사보다 뒤에 놓일 때(후치 수식)는 목적어의 유무가 분사의 형태를 결정하기도 한다.

We received an e-mail [~~outlined~~ / **outlining**] the schedule. 우리는 일정을 **요약한** 이메일을 받았다.

❯ e-mail을 뒤에서 수식하며 목적어 the schedule이 있으므로 -ing 형태가 필요하다.

Please refer to the e-mail [**sent** / ~~sending~~] on May 1. 5월 1일에 **발송된** 이메일을 참조해 주세요.

❯ e-mail을 뒤에서 수식하며 목적어가 없으므로 p.p. 형태가 필요하다.

CHECK-UP   정답 및 해설 p. 144

1. Most companies ask job candidates to write their [desiring / desired] salary.
2. Tenants should obtain [writing / written] permission to remodel their house.
3. We will hold a banquet [honored / honoring] our outgoing president.

출제 공식 3   감정 분사

감정을 나타내는 동사

satisfy 만족시키다	surprise 놀라게 하다	fascinate 매료시키다	disappoint 실망시키다
overwhelm 압도하다	interest 흥미를 끌다	please 기쁘게 하다	impress 감명을 주다
gratify 기쁘게 하다	distract 산란하게 하다	encourage 용기를 주다	depress 낙담시키다
discourage 좌절시키다	exhaust 고갈시키다	confuse 혼란스럽게 하다	frustrate 좌절시키다

감정을 나타내는 동사를 분사 형태로 바꿀 경우 감정을 유발할 때는 -ing, 감정을 느낄 때는 p.p.를 쓴다.

감정을 유발할 때   The performance was [~~fascinated~~ / **fascinating**]. 그 공연은 매혹적이었다.

감정을 느낄 때   The audience was [**fascinated** / ~~fascinating~~]. 청중은 매료되었다.

※ 대부분의 감정 분사 문제는 사람/기관을 수식할 때 p.p., 그 밖의 것을 수식할 때 -ing로 풀 수 있도록 출제된다.

CHECK-UP 정답 및 해설 p. 144

1. The three-day training session was very [satisfying / satisfied].
2. The ending of his latest novel was [disappointed / disappointing].
3. Interviewers were [impressive / impressed] with Mr. Gifford's résumé.

출제 공식 4   분사구문

주어와의 관계가 능동이면 -ing, 주어와의 관계가 수동이면 (being) p.p.를 쓴다.

능동   [**Passing** / ~~Passed~~] the exam, Ms. Mei got a certificate. 시험에 **통과하여** 메이 씨는 수료증을 받았다.

     ❷ 해석적 풀이   주어인 Ms. Mei가 통과한 것이므로 능동태
        구조적 풀이   목적어 the exam이 있으므로 능동태

수동   [~~Building~~ / **Built**] in the 1820s, the house became a landmark. 1820년대에 **지어진** 그 집은 명소가 되었다.

     ❷ 해석적 풀이   주어인 the house가 지어진 것이므로 수동태
        구조적 풀이   목적어가 없으므로 수동태

※ 분사구문에서 having p.p.는 분사의 시제를 표현한 것이다.

     단, 분사구문의 시제는 토익의 출제 범위가 아니므로 having p.p.가 능동태라는 것만 기억하자.

     Having earned a degree in marketing, Roy joined our company. 마케팅 학위를 **딴 후**, 로이는 우리 회사에 합류했다.

     ❷ 학위를 딴 것(능동태)이 회사에 합류한 것보다 시간적으로 우선함을 나타낸다.

CHECK-UP 정답 및 해설 p. 144

1. [Locating / Located] near several landmarks, Vincent Inn is the best choice for tourists.
2. The layout helps to use more natural light, [reducing / reduced] energy consumption.
3. [Having exceeded / Being exceeded] the sales goal, Mr. Bauer received a bonus.

분사형 형용사

분사형 형용사는 형태 그대로 암기하는 것이 좋다.

leading 선도하는	existing 기존의	desired 희망하는	detailed 상세한
rewarding 보람 있는	lasting 지속되는	expired 만료된	dedicated 헌신적인
demanding 까다로운	challenging 어려운	qualified 자격을 갖춘	written 서면의
remaining 남아 있는	promising 전도유망한	accomplished 뛰어난	skilled 숙련된
outstanding 뛰어난	emerging 신흥의, 떠오르는	distinguished 뛰어난	established 자리잡은

Golden House has become a [**leading** / ~~establishing~~] food supplier.
골든 하우스는 **주요** 식품 판매 업체가 되었다.

You can find [~~detailing~~ / **detailed**] information on our Web site.
당사의 웹사이트에서 **자세한** 정보를 찾을 수 있습니다.

현재분사와 짝을 이루는 명사

existing facility 기존 시설	demanding task 까다로운 업무	outstanding balance 미지불 잔고
leading expert 주요 전문가	growing business 성장하는 사업	outgoing executive 퇴임하는 임원
emerging market 신흥 시장	preceding year 지난해	missing luggage 분실된 수하물
winning entry 우승작	remaining inventory 남은 재고	long-lasting battery 오래 가는 전지

We should deal with [**remaining** / ~~remained~~] problems.
우리는 **남아 있는** 문제들을 해결해야 한다.

Some of the [**emerging** / ~~emerged~~] retailers will attend the fair.
신흥 소매 업체들이 박람회에 참여할 것이다.

과거분사와 짝을 이루는 명사

designated area 지정 구역	limited access 제한된 이용	written permission 서면 허가
revised proposal 수정안	experienced employee 경력자	customized item 고객 맞춤형 상품
reserved seat 지정석	attached file 첨부 파일	enclosed garden 담장이 있는 정원
preferred method 선호 수단	finished product 완제품	detailed information 자세한 정보

Put the trash in the [~~designating~~ / **designated**] bins.
쓰레기를 **지정된** 휴지통에 버리시오.

No [**customized** / ~~customizing~~] items can be returned or refunded.
주문 제작된 상품은 반품 및 환불이 불가합니다.

1. From the ------- products, it is clear that Mr. Benson takes great pride in his work as a furniture maker.
    (A) finishing
    (B) finish
    (C) finished
    (D) finishes

2. To recover a ------- password, click the "password reset" link and follow the instructions.
    (A) forgetting
    (B) forgotten
    (C) forgetful
    (D) to forget

3. Newer computers can run ------- gaming applications smoothly.
    (A) advancing
    (B) advancement
    (C) advanced
    (D) advances

4. Some revisions were made to several architectural drawings ------- to city planners.
    (A) submit
    (B) submitting
    (C) submitted
    (D) submission

5. To improve sales, the company will offer a few of its ------- beverage products in new flavors and sizes.
    (A) existed
    (B) existing
    (C) exists
    (D) having existed

6. Journalists should be aware that using too many technical terms can be ------- to readers.
    (A) confusing
    (B) confusion
    (C) confuse
    (D) confused

7. Although overseas travel can be quite -------, there are also many benefits to exploring your own country.
    (A) rewards
    (B) rewarded
    (C) rewarding
    (D) reward

8. All of our products must pass thorough inspections by our ------- quality assurance team.
    (A) certified
    (B) certifying
    (C) certification
    (D) certify

9. ------- painter Fred Ortega will discuss how he sells his artworks to the public.
    (A) Accomplishing
    (B) Accomplishment
    (C) Accomplished
    (D) Accomplishes

10. Mr. Bailey will make minor adjustments to the Web site design based on the client's feedback after ------- the prototype.
    (A) test
    (B) tested
    (C) testing
    (D) tests

11. A wide variety of ------- costs, such as taxes and insurance fees, can sharply increase the price of a car rental.

(A) hide
(B) hiding
(C) hidden
(D) being hidden

12. The number of bicycle trails in city parks has increased due to the ------- popularity of cycling for fitness.

(A) growth
(B) grows
(C) growing
(D) grown

13. Hiring a consultant can help ------- businesses identify weak points and then make necessary improvements.

(A) establish
(B) established
(C) establishing
(D) establishment

14. Thanks to its ------ plot and characters, *World Journey* is a film that can be recommended to all audiences.

(A) fascinate
(B) fascinating
(C) fascinated
(D) fascination

15. Central Business University is holding an information session for those ------- in applying to the school in the future.

(A) interest
(B) interesting
(C) interested
(D) interests

16. The Museum of Digital Technology has a timeline ------- famous inventions in the world of computer science.

(A) show
(B) showed
(C) shown
(D) showing

17. ------- friendly service and a comfortable atmosphere, Dahlia's Café has become a popular neighborhood gathering place.

(A) Been offered
(B) Offers
(C) Offered
(D) Offering

18. ------- nearly 100 years ago, Rossfort Stadium still serves as a venue for important sporting events.

(A) To build
(B) Built
(C) Building
(D) Builder

19. Hiring a qualified personal trainer will help you stay ------- to reach your fitness goals.

(A) motivates
(B) motivation
(C) motivated
(D) motivationally

20. A new series of online seminars gives advice on how to keep customers ------- with your company's services.

(A) satisfaction
(B) satisfactory
(C) satisfying
(D) satisfied

전치사

30문항 중 평균 2~3문제 출제

기본 개념 잡기

● 전치사란?

명사(구) 앞에 놓여 시간, 장소, 목적, 이유 등을 나타낼 수 있게 하는 품사를 전치사라고 한다.

during ~ 동안	on ~ 위에	for ~을 위해	due to ~ 때문에	by ~함으로써	to ~에게

시간	**during** shipment 배송 중에	이유	**due to** weather conditions 날씨 조건 때문에
장소	**on** the table 테이블 위에	목적	**for** your convenience 편의를 위해
방법	**by** pressing a red button 빨간 버튼을 눌러서	대상	**to** them 그들에게

● 전치사구란?

「전치사 + 명사(구)」 형태를 전치사구라고 하며 전치사구는 형용사나 부사처럼 수식하는 역할을 한다.

The president did not say much **during the press conference.** 사장은 기자회견 동안 말을 아꼈다.
　　　　　　　　　　　　　　　　전치사　　　　명사구　　　　▶ 전치사구

1. 형용사 역할

The items are **on sale**. 그 상품들은 **할인 판매 중**이다.
　　할인 판매 중인 ❸ 명사 The item 수식

2. 부사 역할

The flight will depart **on schedule**. 비행기는 **예정대로** 출발합니다.
　　예정대로 ❸ 동사 will depart 수식

출제 공식 1 시점 전치사 / 기간 전치사

시점 전치사 (시점을 나타내는 명사 앞)	기간 전치사 (기간을 나타내는 명사 앞)
since, from, until, by, before, prior to	for, during, over, in, within, throughout

※ 대표적인 기간 전치사를 암기하면 시점 전치사와 구분하는 문제를 쉽게 접근할 수 있다.

시점 We should sign the contract [**before** / ~~within~~] May 21. 지원자들은 양식서를 5월 21일 **이전에** 보내야 한다.

> ❶ May 21은 특정 시점을 나타내므로 시점 전치사와 함께 쓴다.

기간 The sales figures have increased [~~since~~ / **over**] the last 2 months. 판매 수치가 지난 두 달 **동안** 증가했다.

> ❶ two months는 일정 기간을 나타내므로 기간 전치사와 함께 쓴다.

CHECK-UP
정답 및 해설 p. 147

1. Applicants should submit their résumé and cover letter [before / within] March 5.
2. All orders made online will be shipped [until / within] the next 48 hours.
3. [In / Until] August 31st, our library will be closed for renovations.

출제 공식 2 장소와 방향 전치사

장소 전치사

at (특정 지점) ~에	in (공간) ~에	on (접촉) ~ 위에	next to ~ 옆에
throughout 전역에	near ~ 근처에	from ~에서부터	past ~을 지나
across from 맞은편에	opposite 맞은편에	across ~을 가로질러	through ~을 통과하여
inside ~ 안에	outside ~ 밖에	beside ~ 옆에	behind ~ 뒤에

Smoking is not allowed [~~into~~ / **throughout**] the building. 건물 **전 구역에서** 흡연이 금지됩니다.

❶ into는 go into the building '건물 안으로 들어가다'에서와 같이 방향성을 나타내는 동사와 함께 쓰인다.

방향 전치사

to ~(쪽)으로, ~에게	Please submit this form **to** Ms. Lobo. 로보 씨에게 이 서류를 보내 주세요.
toward(s) ~ 쪽으로	Proceeds will go **towards** child support. 수익금은 아동 지원 쪽으로 보내집니다.
into ~ 안으로	The company has recently expanded **into** Asia. 그 회사는 최근 아시아로 진출했다.

You should present your report [**to** / ~~between~~] your supervisor. 보고서를 **상관에게** 제출해야 한다.

❶ present의 대상인 your supervisor가 있으므로 '~에게 제출하다'로 써야 한다.

CHECK-UP
정답 및 해설 p. 147

1. The reception desk is located [next / near] the main entrance.
2. We want to increase our sales [throughout / past] European countries.
3. Customers should direct all inquiries [to / outside] the Customer Service Department.

출제 공식 3   기타 전치사

기타 빈출 전치사

of ~의, ~에 대한, ~ 중에서	due to ~ 때문에	for 동안, ~을 위해	within ~ 이내에 (거리·범위)
despite ~에도 불구하고	in spite of ~에도 불구하고	by (~함으로써 (수단)	regardless of ~에 관계없이
except (for) ~을 제외하고	without ~없이	along with ~와 함께	with ~을 가지고, ~와 함께
as ~로서 (자격)	as a result of ~의 결과로	instead of ~ 대신에	in addition to ~뿐만 아니라
apart from ~ 이외에	aside from ~ 이외에	through ~을 통해 (수단)	across ~ 전반에 걸쳐
based on ~에 근거하여	on account of ~ 때문에	besides ~뿐만 아니라	according to ~에 따르면
between (둘) 사이에	among (셋 이상) 사이에	unlike ~와는 달리	on behalf of ~을 대신해서

We attracted customers **by** offering big discounts. 우리는 대폭 할인을 **제공함으로써** 고객을 유치했다.

All deliveries are free of charge **regardless of** the package size. 포장 크기에 **상관없이** 모든 배송은 무료이다.

We reduced the prices **without** sacrificing the quality. 우리는 품질을 떨어뜨리지 **않고** 가격을 내렸다.

Please mail your application form **along with** the registration fee. 등록비와 **함께** 신청서를 우편으로 보내 주세요.

CHECK-UP
정답 및 해설 p. 147

1. The recreation facility is open every day [except / without] Monday.
2. The couch can also function perfectly [between / as] a bed.
3. Ticketing is available [through / on behalf of] apps on mobile phones.

출제 공식 4   전치사 관용 표현

빈출 전치사 관용 표현

at no cost 무료로	**on** a regular basis 정기적으로	**in** writing 서면으로
in detail 자세히	**in** advance 미리	**in** duplicate 2통으로
until further notice 추후 공지까지	**under** the direction 지휘 하에	**under** construction 공사 중인
ahead of schedule 일정보다 일찍	**behind** schedule 일정보다 늦게	**without** delay 지체 없이
upon receipt 받자마자	**upon** arrival 도착하자마자	**without** permission 허가 없이

All articles are updated [**on** / ~~with~~] a weekly basis. 모든 기사들은 **주 단위로** 업데이트됩니다.

The gym is closed [**until** / ~~on~~] further notice. **추후 공지가 있을 때까지** 헬스장이 문을 닫습니다.

The representatives are still [~~upon~~ / **under**] negotiations. 대표자들은 아직 **협상 중이다.**

All customer inquiries will be addressed [~~except~~ / **without**] delay. 모든 고객 문의는 **지체 없이** 처리될 것이다.

CHECK-UP
정답 및 해설 p. 148

1. All purchase requests must be submitted [in / for] writing.
2. The road construction was completed [beforehand / ahead of] schedule.
3. A signature confirmation is required [upon / as soon as] receipt of your parcel.

이것도 알면 플러스 10점!

by / until: ~까지

by	완료적 의미의 동사와 함께 (일회성)	submit, send, finish, complete 등
until	계속적 의미의 동사와 함께 (지속성)	postpone, continue, last, wait 등

Monthly reports should be **submitted** [**by** / ~~until~~] May 21.
월별 보고서는 5월 21일**까지 제출**되어야 한다.

The construction will be **postponed** [~~by~~ / **until**] next month.
공사가 다음 달**까지 연기**될 것이다.

for / during / over / in: ~ 동안

for	숫자와 함께	for an hour 한 시간 동안
during, over	기간 명사와 함께	during the holiday 휴가 동안 over the weekend 주말 동안
in	the last, past, next 와 함께	in the last 2 weeks 지난 2주 동안

※ [the last / past / next + 시점]은 for, during, over와 함께 쓸 수도 있다.
❯ for the next 2 years 향후 2년 동안

The community festival will be held **for** two days.
지역 축제는 **이틀 동안** 개최될 것이다.

Mr. Cowell showed initiative **during** his job interview.
코웰 씨는 **면접 동안** 적극성을 보였다.

Enrollment has been processed **in** the last two weeks.
등록은 **지난 2주 동안** 진행되었다.

분사형 전치사 (형태는 분사이지만 전치사로 쓰이는 단어)

including ~을 포함하여	regarding ~에 대하여	concerning ~에 대하여
excluding ~을 제외하고	following ~ 후에	considering ~을 고려(감안)하면
starting / beginning ~부터	given ~을 고려(감안)하면	notwithstanding ~에도 불구하고

An e-mail was sent [**regarding** / ~~among~~] overtime payment.
초과 근무 급여에 **관한** 이메일이 발송되었다.

[~~Upon~~ / **Following**] months of negotiations, we finally reached a mutual agreement.
수개월 동안의 협상 **후에** 우리는 마침내 상호 합의에 도달했다.

[**Given** / ~~Giving~~] the increase in demand, we should expand our production capabilities.
수요의 증가를 **감안하면**, 우리는 생산력을 증대시켜야 한다.

ACTUAL TEST

정답 및 해설 p. 148

1. The autumn music festival was canceled
   ------- heavy rain across the area.
   (A) according
   (B) consequently
   (C) due to
   (D) as to

2. ------- the rainy summer season, the
   beach resort communities reported good
   tourism revenue.
   (A) As a result
   (B) In spite of
   (C) Provided that
   (D) In contrast

3. The City Nature Center's guided nature
   walks are open to everyone, ------- age or
   hiking ability.
   (A) accordingly
   (B) in case
   (C) regardless of
   (D) whereas

4. More and more consumers are using
   mobile payment applications ------- cash
   to make purchases.
   (A) among
   (B) unlike
   (C) instead of
   (D) in the event of

5. If your merchandise arrives damaged in
   any way, you may return it ------- a refund.
   (A) for
   (B) to
   (C) at
   (D) by

6. ------- research, a high percentage of the
   residents living in Greenville are recent
   university graduates.
   (A) Recent
   (B) On behalf of
   (C) According to
   (D) Along with

7. Providing an incomplete or incorrect
   address will delay the shipment -------
   your merchandise.
   (A) during
   (B) of
   (C) into
   (D) from

8. Employees are encouraged to use the new
   on-site fitness center to exercise -------
   the start of the workday.
   (A) in that
   (B) such as
   (C) prior to
   (D) as long as

9. All the volunteers at the City Art Festival
   stayed motivated throughout the event
   ------- the rainy weather.
   (A) while
   (B) even if
   (C) regarding
   (D) despite

10. To be considered for employment at
    Central Post Office, all applicants must
    submit their résumés ------- May 1.
    (A) until
    (B) under
    (C) by
    (D) in

11. Unless stated otherwise on our Web site, all orders are processed and shipped ------- three to four business days.

    (A) until
    (B) on
    (C) about
    (D) within

12. Participants in our trekking tours should bring all the necessary equipment for hiking, ------- boots and a rain jacket.

    (A) about
    (B) as to
    (C) including
    (D) notwithstanding

13. Yoga classes continue to show strong growth in popularity ------- people of all ages.

    (A) across from
    (B) along with
    (C) upon
    (D) among

14. The City Finance Office has attendants on duty to answer residents' questions ------- proper completion of tax forms.

    (A) besides
    (B) how
    (C) concerning
    (D) under

15. Organizers have decided to postpone Friday's parade ------- the forecast for inclement weather.

    (A) until
    (B) except for
    (C) because of
    (D) as soon as

16. Tourism to Bailey City has increased remarkably ------- the completion of the new fashion district.

    (A) as a result
    (B) even as
    (C) since
    (D) beyond

17. ------- recent customer feedback, Dalamart Grocery Co. has decided to expand its organic food selection.

    (A) Inside
    (B) Based on
    (C) Unless
    (D) Whereas

18. The price of every Dubarnic Lake boat tour includes lunch and refreshments, ------- a souvenir photo.

    (A) within
    (B) as well
    (C) in case of
    (D) in addition to

19. The Lexton Model C electric car will go into limited production ------- in November.

    (A) start
    (B) starting
    (C) started
    (D) starts

20. Due to the monsoon rains, our restaurant's outdoor patio is closed ------- further notice.

    (A) on
    (B) into
    (C) until
    (D) during

접속사

기본 개념 잡기

● 접속사란?

단어와 단어, 구와 구, 혹은 문장과 문장을 연결해 주는 접속어를 접속사라고 한다.

and 그리고	**so** 그래서	**because** 왜냐하면	**although** 비록 ~지만	**as soon as** ~하자마자

● 부사절 접속사

접속사가 이끄는 문장이 부사 역할을 할 때 이를 부사절이라 하며, 해당 접속사를 부사절 접속사라 한다.

You should hurry <u>because space is limited.</u> 자리가 제한되어 있으므로 서두르셔야 합니다.
　문장 (주절)　　　부사절 접속사　　　　　　▶ 부사절

❷ 부사절이 빠져도 문장은 성립하며, 주절과 부사절은 위치를 바꿀 수 있다.
　부사절로 문장을 시작할 때는 콤마로 주절과 구분해 준다.

● 등위접속사와 상관접속사

등위접속사 대등하게 연결해주는 접속사

등위접속사는 단어와 단어, 구와 구, 절과 절을 대등하게 연결한다.

The movie was <u>educational</u> and <u>entertaining</u>. 그 영화는 교육적이고 재미있었다.
　　　　　　　　형용사　　　　　　　형용사

❷ 등위접속사로 연결된 두 항목은 같은 품사이거나 같은 형태를 이루어야 한다.

상관접속사 짝을 이루어 쓰는 접속사

상관접속사는 단어와 단어, 구와 구, 절과 절이 짝을 이루도록 연결한다.

Ms. Gifford is fluent in **both** English **and** Spanish. 기포드 씨는 영어와 스페인어 둘 다 유창하다.
　　　　　　　　　　　　　명사　　　　　명사

❷ 상관접속사로 연결된 두 항목은 같은 품사이거나 같은 형태를 이루어야 한다.

출제 공식 1 　　　 부사절 접속사의 종류

부사절 접속사는 부사절을 이끌어 양보, 시간, 이유 등을 의미하며 주절 앞 또는 뒤에 놓을 수 있다.

양보	although, though, even though, even if 비록 ~일지라도
시간	when ~할 때　before ~전에　after ~후에　until ~할 때까지　since ~이래로 once 일단 ~하면, ~하자마자　as soon as ~하자마자
이유	because, as, since, now that ~때문에, ~이므로
조건	if, provided (that) 만약 ~한다면　as long as ~하는 한　unless ~하지 않는 한
목적	so that, in order that ~하기 위해서, ~하도록

<u>**Although** the concert is free</u>, <u>donations are welcome</u>. 공연은 **무료이지만** 기부금은 환영합니다.
　　　　부사절　　　　　　　　　　　　주절
<u>You will be notified</u> **as soon as** <u>the item is shipped</u>. 물건이 **발송되자마자** 알림을 받으실 것입니다.
　　주절　　　　　　　　　　　　　　부사절

CHECK-UP
정답 및 해설 p. 150

1. [Because / Although] the concert is free, seating is limited.
2. The shareholders' meeting will begin [although / as soon as] all executives arrive.
3. Non-residents can attend the event [if / so that] they register in advance.

출제 공식 2 　　　 접속사 vs. 전치사

절을 연결하는 것은 접속사이며, 구를 연결하는 것은 전치사이다. 의미가 비슷한 접속사와 전치사를 구분하자.

접속사 + 절　[~~Despite~~ / **Although**] a mistake was made, it was corrected. 실수가 **발생했지만** 수정되었다.

전치사 + 구　[**During** / ~~While~~] the seminar, all speeches will be recorded. 세미나 **동안** 모든 연설은 녹음될 것이다.

	접속사	전치사
양보	although / even though 비록 ~일지라도	despite / in spite of ~에도 불구하고
시간	as soon as / once ~하자마자 before ~ 이전에 after ~ 이후에 while ~ 동안 until ~까지 since ~이래로	on / upon ~하자마자 before / prior to ~ 이전에 after / following ~ 이후에 during ~동안 until ~까지 since ~ 이래로
이유	because / since / as ~ 때문에	because of / due to / owing to ~ 때문에

CHECK-UP
정답 및 해설 p. 150

1. [During / While] the repair work is underway, staff members may not use the elevators.
2. At Dallas, employees use interoffice mail [although / despite] it is not mandatory.
3. [Once / Upon] we receive the returned item, our quality control team will inspect it.

출제 공식 3   부사절 접속사의 축약

부사절 접속사의 주어를 생략하고 분사만 남길 수 있다. 능동일 때는 -ing, 수동일 때는 p.p.를 쓴다.

능동   **When visiting** us, you can use the side door. 방문하실 **때** 옆문을 이용하실 수 있습니다.

         = When you visit us, you can use the side door.

         ❯ 주어인 you가 '방문하는' 것이므로 능동태이며 「접속사 + -ing」 형태로 축약하여 쓸 수 있다.

수동   The reception will be held on Tuesday **as planned**. 환영회는 **계획된 대로** 화요일에 열릴 것이다.

         = The reception will be held on Tuesday as it is planned.

         ❯ 주어인 reception은 '계획되는' 것이므로 수동태이며 「접속사 + p.p.」 형태로 축약하여 쓸 수 있다.

※ 빈출 형태: when -ing ~할 때   as p.p. ~된 대로   unless p.p. ~되지 않는다면

CHECK-UP   정답 및 해설 p. 151

1. [Since / When] leaving the train, make sure you haven't left anything behind.
2. Our office has become more productive [since / as] adopting the new software.
3. [Before / Unless] stated otherwise, all recyclable waste should be collected in green bins.

출제 공식 4   등위접속사와 상관접속사

등위접속사는 절과 절, 구와 구, 단어와 단어를 대등하게 연결할 수 있다.

and 그리고	but / yet 그러나	or 또는	so 따라서

The lecture was <u>lengthy</u> **yet** <u>informative</u>. 그 강연은 꽤 길었지만 매우 유익했다.

You can keep working **or** (you can) take a rest for a while. 계속 일하거나 잠시 쉬어도 됩니다.

❯ 등위접속사로 절과 절을 이을 때 반복되는 주어와 동사는 생략할 수 있다.

<u>Seating is limited</u>, **so** <u>you should hurry</u>. 자리가 제한되어 있으므로 서두르셔야 합니다.

❯ 등위접속사 so는 완전한 절과 절만 연결한다.

상관접속사는 A와 B가 짝을 이루도록 연결해 주는 접속사이다.

both A and B   The event is for **both** <u>adults</u> **and** <u>children</u>. 그 행사는 성인과 어린이 모두를 위한 것이다.

not only A but (also) B   James is **not only** <u>competent</u> **but also** <u>hard-working</u>. 제임스는 유능할 뿐만 아니라 근면하다.

B as well as A   We provide <u>free gifts</u> **as well as** <u>a light meal</u>. 간단한 식사뿐 아니라 선물도 제공합니다.

(n)either A (n)or B   Customers can **either** <u>e-mail</u> **or** <u>call</u> us. 고객들은 이메일을 보내거나 전화로 연락할 수 있습니다.

not A but B   We decided to travel **not** <u>by bus</u> **but** <u>by train</u>. 우리는 버스가 아니라 기차로 여행하기로 결정했다.

CHECK-UP   정답 및 해설 p. 151

1. Mr. Kyle has an urgent matter to attend to, [yet / so] we need to reschedule the meeting.
2. The special rates are available for [both / either] in-store and online purchases.
3. The class is [not only / nor] for beginners but also for intermediate learners.

이것도 알면 플러스 10점!

기출 부사절 접속사

❶ as: ~할 때 (시간), ~하면서 (경과), ~때문에 (이유)

As our business grew, the customer base became diverse.
우리 사업이 **번창하면서** 고객층이 다양해졌다.

As the host arrived late, the show was delayed.
사회자가 늦게 도착했기 **때문에** 공연이 지연되었다.

❷ now that: ~이므로, ~이기 때문에 (이유)

Now that Mr. Palmer is retired, he has more time for writing.
팔머 씨가 **은퇴했으므로**, 그에게는 글을 쓸 시간이 더 많다.

❸ in case: ~의 경우에 대비해서 (조건)

We will keep your résumé **in case** a position becomes available.
공석이 생길 때를 **대비하여** 귀하의 이력서를 보관하겠습니다.

❹ as long as: ~하는 한 (조건)

As long as you possess proper identification, you can have access to the lab.
적합한 신분증을 **소지하는 한**, 실험실을 이용할 수 있습니다.

❺ unless: ~하지 않는다면 (조건)

Your subscription will be automatically renewed **unless** service is cancelled.
서비스가 취소되지 **않는다면** 귀하의 구독은 자동 갱신될 것입니다.

❻ provided (that): **만약 ~한다면 (조건)**

You are qualified for a full refund **provided that** your order arrived damaged.
만약 주문품이 파손되어 **도착한다면** 전액 환불을 받으실 수 있습니다.

❼ in order that: ~하기 위해서 (목적)

We took a taxi **in order that** we would not be late for the meeting.
우리는 회의에 늦지 않기 **위해서** 택시를 탔다.

❽ whereas: 반면에 (양보)

We provide a price quote for free, **whereas** our competitors charge for the service.
우리의 경쟁사는 서비스 요금을 청구하는 **반면에** 우리는 견적을 무료로 제공합니다.

❾ considering (that) **/ given that: ~을 고려할 때, 고려하여 (기타)**

Mr. Morris was chosen to lead the team **given that** he is the most experienced.
모리스 씨가 가장 경력이 많다는 것을 **고려하여** 그 팀을 이끌도록 정해졌다.

❿ whether A or B A이든 B이든

Whether your travel is related to work or pleasure, we can accommodate your needs.
귀하의 여행이 **업무적이든 관광이든** 저희가 귀하의 요구 사항을 충족시켜 드리겠습니다.

1. The workers had to temporarily suspend their project ------- a heavy snowstorm hit the area.

   (A) due to
   (B) since
   (C) although
   (D) upon

2. The production team managed to meet all its deadlines last month, ------- it was quite understaffed.

   (A) as well as
   (B) despite
   (C) during
   (D) even though

3. Because of heavy traffic, the bus will not reach the city center ------- the parade is over.

   (A) until
   (B) since
   (C) past
   (D) after all

4. Your order will be processed ------- we receive your payment in full.

   (A) even if
   (B) according to
   (C) as soon as
   (D) during

5. ------- the general public nor the critics seemed to have a thorough understanding of the recent movie directed by John Miller.

   (A) Both
   (B) Each other
   (C) Neither
   (D) None

6. ------- the city is hosting its annual marathon race this Friday, parking in the downtown area will be very limited.

   (A) In order to
   (B) So that
   (C) Therefore
   (D) Because

7. The password will become invalid ------- your online membership ends.

   (A) once
   (B) until
   (C) upon
   (D) rather

8. We would take a taxi to the convention center ------- there are no other transportation options available.

   (A) except for
   (B) whereas
   (C) only if
   (D) until

9. The organizer of the Tech Conference, Ms. Choi, is attending a conference in Paris, ------- can still answer e-mail inquiries.

   (A) but
   (B) nor
   (C) also
   (D) so

10. Oil paint dries much more slowly than other types of paint, ------- it is an ideal choice for novice artists.

    (A) in fact
    (B) so
    (C) therefore
    (D) why

11. ------- we have digital photographs of our newest products, we can finally post them on our Web site.

(A) Now that
(B) In other words
(C) Before
(D) Whereas

12. The restaurant is busy today ------- the nearby theater has a show this evening.

(A) so
(B) since
(C) so that
(D) due to

13. The department store accepts returns on merchandise ------- the customer is able to present the original receipt.

(A) because of
(B) even though
(C) provided
(D) in order that

14. ------- there is an extreme weather event such as a blizzard, the tour bus will depart from Elton Station at 8 A.M.

(A) Despite
(B) Unless
(C) Likewise
(D) Until

15. Employee attendance at monthly department meetings is mandatory ------- stated in the employee handbook.

(A) regarding
(B) even though
(C) apart from
(D) as

16. The furniture wax should be evenly applied to the entire surface ------- all parts can be equally protected.

(A) so that
(B) in order to
(C) thereby
(D) but also

17. Some of the region's camping areas operate on a first come, first served basis, ------- others require reservations.

(A) whereas
(B) in case
(C) as well as
(D) rather than

18. Customers can change the shipping method ------- the items have not yet been packed for delivery.

(A) as long as
(B) prior to
(C) so that
(D) as to

19. ------- we anticipate any long delays in processing an order, we will notify the customer as soon as possible.

(A) Except
(B) Before
(C) If
(D) In fact

20. ------- developing the prototype of our new product, a major problem occurred, which caused considerable delays.

(A) In case
(B) While
(C) Besides
(D) After all

관계사

30문항 중 평균 1문제 출제

기본 개념 잡기

● 관계사란?

앞에 나온 명사를 수식하면서 두 문장을 연결해주는 접속사를 관계사라고 한다.
관계사가 이끄는 절을 관계절이라고 하며 관계절의 수식을 받는 명사를 선행사라고 한다.
관계사에는 관계대명사와 관계부사가 있다.

우리말: 제품을 구매한 모든 분께 쿠폰을 드려요.

영어식: 쿠폰을 드려요 / 모든 분께 / **who 제품을 구매한**
　　　　　　　　　　　 선행사　　　관계사　　　　▶ 관계절

● 관계대명사

두 문장을 이어 줄 때 「접속사 + 대명사」 기능을 하는 것을 관계대명사라고 한다.

We decided to hire Mr. Kim. + **He** is already skilled.

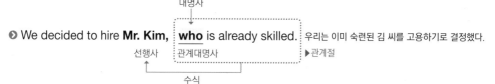

❯ We decided to hire **Mr. Kim**, **who** is already skilled. 우리는 이미 숙련된 김 씨를 고용하기로 결정했다.
　　　　　　　　　 선행사　　관계대명사　　　　　　▶ 관계절
　　　　　　　　　　　　　　수식

관계대명사의 격

선행사 ＼ 격	주격	소유격	목적격
사람	who	whose	whom
사물	which	whose	which
혼용	that	–	that

● 관계부사

두 문장을 이어 줄 때 「접속사 + 부사」 기능을 하는 것을 관계부사라고 한다.

You should visit <u>the branch</u>. + You bought your laptop **there**. (there = at the branch)

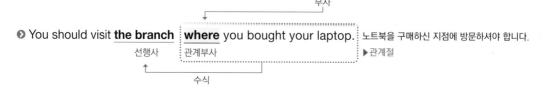

❯ You should visit **the branch** **where** you bought your laptop. 노트북을 구매하신 지점에 방문하셔야 합니다.
　　　　　　　　　 선행사　　관계부사　　　　　　　▶ 관계절
　　　　　　　　　　　　　　수식

출제 공식 1　　　　관계대명사의 격

관계대명사는 선행사와 격에 따라 바뀐다.

주격　This is the list of <u>employees</u> [**who** / **that** / ~~whose~~] will receive a raise.
　　　이것은 임금 인상을 받을 직원 목록이다.
　　　❱ 선행사가 사람이며 동사 앞에 위치하므로 주격 자리이다.

　　　We found an error [**which** / **that** / ~~whose~~] needs to be revised. 우리는 수정되어야 할 오류를 발견했다.
　　　❱ 선행사가 사물이며 동사 앞에 위치하므로 주격 자리이다.

소유격　We have <u>a guest</u> [~~who~~ / **whose**] name has yet to be disclosed.
　　　이름이 아직 공개되지 않은 초대 손님이 있습니다.
　　　❱ 선행사가 사람이며 명사 앞에 위치하므로 소유격 자리이다.

　　　We should find <u>a firm</u> [~~which~~ / **whose**] services are reliable. 우리는 서비스가 믿을 만한 회사를 찾아야 한다.
　　　❱ 선행사가 사물이며 명사 앞에 위치하므로 소유격 자리이다.

목적격　Mr. Teo is <u>the CEO</u> [~~whose~~ / **whom** / **that**] we met at the fair. 테오 씨는 우리가 박람회에서 만났던 CEO이다.
　　　❱ 선행사가 사람이며 주어와 동사 뒤에 met의 목적어가 없으므로 목적격 자리이다.

　　　Please refer to <u>the e-mail</u> [~~whose~~ / **which** / **that**] you received yesterday.
　　　어제 받은 이메일을 참조하세요.
　　　❱ 선행사가 사물이며 주어와 동사 뒤에 received의 목적어가 없으므로 목적격 자리이다.

CHECK-UP　　　　　　　　　　　　　　　　　　　　　　정답 및 해설 p. 153

1. Most participants [who / which] attended the workshop found it helpful.
2. Peter Miller [whom / whose] paintings are on display agreed to sell his artwork.
3. Dr. Bauer teaches at the university [that / whose] he graduated from.

출제 공식 2　　　　관계대명사의 생략

목적격 관계대명사는 생략할 수 있다.

Earn points for each purchase (**which**) you make. 각 구매에 대해 적립금을 받으세요.
These are the issues [**we** / ~~ours~~] discussed yesterday. 이것들은 우리가 어제 논의했던 그 문제들입니다.
❱ issues와 we 사이에 목적격 관계대명사 which가 생략된 구조를 파악하여 주격을 선택한다.

「주격 + be동사」는 생략할 수 있다.

We sell products (**which are**) made from recycled materials. 우리는 재활용 재료로 만든 상품을 판매한다.
Those [~~wait~~ / **waiting**] in line can order food in advance. 줄을 서 있는 사람들은 미리 음식을 주문할 수 있다.
❱ Those (who are) waiting에서 생략된 구조를 파악하여 분사를 선택한다.

CHECK-UP　　　　　　　　　　　　　　　　　　　　　　정답 및 해설 p. 154

1. Dairy products [are distributed / distributed] by La-Q are guaranteed to be fresh.
2. Coogee Electronics agreed to sign the contract [we / ours] discussed last week.
3. Anyone [will search / searching] for a writing job should refer to this Web site.

출제 공식 3　　　관계부사

관계부사는 선행사에 따라 when, where, why, how로 구분된다.

시간	**when**	The deadline is <u>10 May</u> **when** there is official assessment. 마감일은 공식 평가가 있는 5월 10일이다.
장소	**whoro**	Thic ic <u>tho placo</u> **whero** the annual conference was held. 이곳이 연례 회의가 열렸던 장소이다.
이유	**why**	Mr. Stern did not tell us <u>the reason</u> **why** he is leaving the company. 스턴 씨는 자신이 퇴사하는 이유를 말해 주지 않았다.
방법	**how**	We focus on **the way[how]** we can improve productivity. 우리는 생산성을 향상시키는 방법에 주목하고 있다. ❷ the way와 how는 함께 쓰지 않고 둘 중 하나만 쓴다.

CHECK-UP　　　　　　　　　　　　　　　　　　　　　정답 및 해설 p. 154

1. A new shopping mall was built on the site [where / which] a factory was once located.
2. Mr. Taylor was on a business trip during the time [when / whose] clients visited us.
3. The letter includes the reason [how / why] we request your collaboration.

출제 공식 4　　　관계대명사 vs. 관계부사

관계대명사 뒤에는 불완전한 절이 오고, 관계부사 뒤에는 완전한 절이 온다.

관계대명사 + 불완전　Participants will receive a cookbook [**which** / ~~where~~] <u>contains simple recipes</u>.
　　　　　　　　　　참석자들은 간단한 조리법이 담긴 요리책을 받을 것이다.

관계부사 + 완전　　　The CEO returned to London [~~which~~ / **where**] <u>he began his career</u>.
　　　　　　　　　　그 CEO는 그가 직장 생활을 시작했던 런던으로 돌아왔다.

관계부사는 「전치사 + 관계대명사」로 쓸 수 있다.

This is the hotel **where** Mr. Benson stayed. 이곳은 벤슨 씨가 머물렀던 호텔이다.

= This is the hotel **which** Mr. Benson stayed **at**. = This is the hotel **at which** Mr. Benson stayed.

CHECK-UP　　　　　　　　　　　　　　　　　　　　　정답 및 해설 p. 154

1. The auditorium, [which / where] was built last month, can accommodate 400 people.
2. The Web page explains [which / how] you can activate your account.
3. We have more than 30,000 employees in 32 countries in [which / where] we operate.

관계대명사 what

관계대명사 what은 선행사를 가지지 않으며 '~한 것'으로 해석된다.

These are the items [**that** / ~~what~~] we have in stock.
이것들은 저희가 재고로 가지고 있는 물품들입니다.

These are [~~that~~ / **what**] we have in stock.
이것들은 저희가 재고로 가지고 있는 것입니다.

복합관계사

관계사에 -ever를 붙인 것을 복합관계사라고 하며 복합관계사는 선행사를 가지지 않는다.

복합관계대명사	whoever 누구든지	whatever 무엇이든지	whichever 어떤 것이든지
복합관계부사	whenever 언제든지	wherever 어디든지	however 아무리 ~할지라도

Customers [**who** / ~~whoever~~] need assistance may contact us.
도움이 필요하신 고객은 저희에게 연락하실 수 있습니다.
❷ 선행사 Customers가 있으므로 관계대명사 자리이다.

[~~Who~~ / **Whoever**] needs assistance may contact us.
도움이 필요한 **누구든지** 저희에게 연락하실 수 있습니다.
❷ 선행사가 없고, '든지'라는 의미가 필요하므로 복합관계대명사 자리이다.

Customers may contact us [**whenever** / ~~whatever~~] they need assistance.
고객들은 도움이 필요하면 **언제든지** 저희에게 연락하실 수 있습니다.
❷ 완전한 절이 이어지므로 복합관계부사 자리이다.

[**Whoever** / ~~Anyone~~] wishes to use the lab must have an ID.
실험실을 이용하려는 **누구든지** 신분증이 있어야 한다.
❷ 동사 개수가 2개이므로 접속사 역할을 하는 복합관계부사 자리이다.

수량 표현 + 관계대명사

동사가 두 개인 문장에서 「수량 표현+of」 뒤에는 목적격 관계대명사를 쓴다.

선행사가 사람일 때
We invited several speakers, all of [~~them~~ / **whom**] are well-known in their field.
우리는 여러 연사를 초청했으며 **그들 모두는** 자신의 분야에서 유명하다.
❷ We invited several speakers. + All of them are well-known in their field.

선행사가 사물일 때
Several measures were discussed, none of [~~them~~ / **which**] received approval.
몇 가지 조치가 논의되었으나 **그것들 중 아무것도** 승인을 받지 못했다.
❷ Several measures were discussed. + None of them received approval.

1. Jeff Landers, ------- recently led our staff teambuilding workshop, will transfer to the operations department next month.

   (A) who
   (B) whose
   (C) which
   (D) whom

2. The event planning company will choose the best seating arrangement ------- will help ensure the success of our banquet.

   (A) who
   (B) which
   (C) what
   (D) it

3. The Transit Authority introduced a reduced-fare subway pass ------- is designed to promote the use of public transportation.

   (A) what
   (B) whom
   (C) where
   (D) that

4. The city's recycling program, ------- has been a success so far, is expected to have current high levels of participation.

   (A) it
   (B) that
   (C) which
   (D) what

5. Lexco's new CEO is Robert Farmer, ------- tenure begins next week.

   (A) whoever
   (B) whose
   (C) what
   (D) that

6. The Donarandic Mini is a compact travel umbrella ------- fits easily in small hand luggage.

   (A) whose
   (B) in which
   (C) that
   (D) what

7. The Greeny Club is volunteer organization ------- members pursue a variety of interests related to the natural world.

   (A) what
   (B) whom
   (C) who
   (D) whose

8. The Blue Trail in Katman Mountain Park is a steep route ------- will challenge even experienced hikers.

   (A) whose
   (B) whom
   (C) that
   (D) what

9. According to sales data, homes ------- are professionally landscaped can have up to 10% higher resale value.

   (A) those
   (B) they
   (C) what
   (D) that

10. Samson Express, Inc. has a package tracking system ------- allows you to view the progress of your shipment online.

    (A) what
    (B) where
    (C) which
    (D) how

11. Computer hardware and computer software are complementary products ------- are typically sold in the same store.

(A) those
(B) they
(C) that
(D) whose

12. The special exhibit features rare sculptures, some of ------- have never been displayed in this museum.

(A) whose
(B) where
(C) which
(D) whom

13. On March 27th, a special banquet, ------- will mark the 20th anniversary of our company's founding, will be held.

(A) which
(B) that
(C) where
(D) it

14. Ms. Wing's main responsibility is to send renewal letters to members ------- membership expires soon.

(A) who
(B) whose
(C) which
(D) what

15. The company recently started a staff blog through ------- employees can share their work experiences with others.

(A) whose
(B) where
(C) which
(D) whom

16. The X-Through display case ------- ensures excellent product visibility will be on sale for a limited time.

(A) where
(B) which
(C) whose
(D) it

17. Each high quality Rolocony watch contains 210 small parts, ------- require special tools to produce.

(A) what
(B) in which
(C) which
(D) whose

18. DMI employees have to commute to a suburb ------- the traffic is unfavorable.

(A) which
(B) where
(C) whose
(D) what

19. Ms. Janssen, ------- design concept was used for the new logo, is known for creating appealing images and graphics.

(A) where
(B) whose
(C) which
(D) whom

20. Survey participants were university students, many of ------- had not been engaged in similar activities before.

(A) them
(B) whom
(C) who
(D) which

명사절 접속사

30문항 중 평균 1문제 출제

기본 개념 잡기

명사절 접속사란?

문장을 주어, 목적어, 보어 자리에 오도록 명사화시켜 주는 접속사를 명사절 접속사라고 한다.

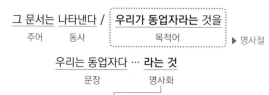

그 문서는 나타낸다 / 우리가 동업자라는 것을
　　주어　　　 동사　　　　　　목적어　　　　　 ▶ 명사절

우리는 동업자다 … 라는 것
　　　　문장　　　 　명사화

The document indicates **that** we are business partners.
　　　　　　　　　　명사절 접속사

명사절 접속사의 종류

that	~라는 것		
whether / if	~인지 아닌지		
의문사	who 누가 ~하는지	what 무엇이[무엇을] ~하는지	which 어느 것이[것을] ~하는지
	when 언제 ~하는지	where 어디서 ~하는지	why 왜 ~하는지
	how 어떻게 ~하는지		

Our records show **that** your order was shipped on June 15.
저희의 기록은 귀하의 주문이 6월 15일에 발송되었다는 것을 나타냅니다.

Let us know **whether[if]** you are available tomorrow.
내일 시간이 되시는지 알려 주세요.

We don't know **who** will join our team.
우리는 누가 우리의 팀에 합류할지 모른다.

출제 공식 1   that '라는 것'

명사절 접속사 that은 완전한 문장을 이끌어 주어, 목적어, 보어로 쓰인다.

주어   <u>**That** the CEO is going to retire</u> <u>came</u> as a surprise. CEO가 직위에서 물러날 예정이라는 것은 놀라운 소식이었다.
                S   V

목적어   <u>Customers</u> <u>should ensure</u> **that** <u>their addresses are correct</u>. 고객들은 **주소가 정확한지를** 확인해야 합니다.
           S   V   O

보어   <u>The problem</u> <u>is</u> **that** <u>nobody is interested in the project</u>. 문제는 아무도 그 프로젝트에 관심이 없다는 것이다.
          S   V   C

CHECK-UP
정답 및 해설 p. 156

1. A study indicates [it / that] working from home may increase employee productivity.
2. Kentac announced [that / what] it will recall all of its X-series laptop computers.
3. The recent trend is [that / how] many people are choosing to read e-books.

출제 공식 2   whether '~인지 아닌지'

명사절 접속사 whether는 완전한 문장을 이끌어 주어, 목적어, 보어 자리에 쓰인다.

주어   <u>**Whether** we will relocate</u> <u>depends</u> on our budget. 우리가 이전할지 아닐지는 우리 예산에 달려 있다.
                             S   V

동사의 목적어   <u>They</u> <u>asked</u> **whether[if]** <u>we could fulfill their order</u>. 그들은 우리가 주문을 처리할 수 있는지 물었다.
                S   V   O

       ❯ 동사의 목적어가 되는 절을 이끄는 whether의 경우에만 if로 대체할 수 있다.

전치사의 목적어   There is a dispute as to **whether** <u>a bonus will be paid</u>. 보너스가 지급될 것인지에 대한 논쟁이 있다.
                         전치사   O

보어   <u>The issue</u> <u>is</u> **whether** <u>we should expand overseas</u>. 쟁점은 우리가 해외 진출을 해야 하는가이다.
                 S   V   C

※ 명사절 접속사 whether는 or not의 의미를 포함하고 있으며 or not을 생략할 수 있다.

We are not sure about whether we could achieve the goal (or not).
우리는 그 목표를 달성할 수 있을지 없을지에 대해 확실하지 않다.

CHECK-UP
정답 및 해설 p. 157

1. Please let us know [that / whether] you can come or not.
2. The meeting was about [those / whether] we should expand into the Asian market.
3. The event coordinator asked [them / if] audio-visual equipment will be used.

PART 5

UNIT 11 명사절 접속사

203

출제 공식 3　　　의문사

의문사 who, what, which는 불완전한 문장, when, where, how, why는 완전한 문장을 이끈다.

불완전　The management will decide **which** is best. 경영진은 **어느 것이 최선인지** 결정할 것이다.

❷ 주어가 빠진 불완전한 문장

　　What Mr. Porter suggested was not accepted. 포터 씨가 제안한 것은 받아들여지지 않았다.

❷ 목적어가 빠진 불완전한 문장

완전　Please inform us **when** you will arrive. 언제 도착할지 우리에게 알려주세요.

　　We should know **how** the merger will affect us. 우리는 **합병이 어떻게 우리에게 영향을 미칠지** 알아야 한다.

※ 완전/불완전과 같은 구조적인 차이가 없을 때는 해석으로 풀이한다.

　　[**Who** / ~~What~~] will be available to work on weekend is uncertain.
　　누가 주말에 일할 수 있을지는 불확실하다. (**O**)　　무엇이 주말에 일할 수 있을지는 불확실하다. (**X**)

CHECK-UP　　　　　　　　　　　　　　　　　　　　정답 및 해설 p. 157

1. The editor was struggling to find out [what / why] was wrong with the first draft.
2. The architect explained [what / how] he would upgrade the space.
3. Mr. Kato knows [who / what] the next step is in addressing the problem.

출제 공식 4　　　명사절 접속사 – 복합관계대명사

복합관계대명사는 불완전한 문장을 이끄는 명사절 접속사로 쓰일 수 있다.

Whoever is on the list will receive a coupon. 목록에 있는 누구든지 쿠폰을 받을 것이다.

❷ 주어가 빠진 불완전한 문장

We will do **whatever** we can. 저희는 **할 수 있는 무엇이든지** 할 것입니다.

❷ 목적어가 빠진 불완전한 문장

You can choose **whichever** is convenient for you. 어느 것이든지 편한 것을 선택하실 수 있습니다.

❷ 주어가 빠진 불완전한 문장

CHECK-UP　　　　　　　　　　　　　　　　　　　　정답 및 해설 p. 157

1. Survey participants can comment on [whatever / whenever] they are concerned about.
2. Both of the watches are excellent, so you can choose [if / whichever] you prefer.
3. [Whenever / Whoever] wishes to work extra hours should obtain permission to do so.

동격절 that을 취하는 명사

fact that ~라는 사실	opinion that ~라는 의견	rumor that ~라는 소문
idea that ~라는 생각	news that ~라는 소식	speculation that ~라는 추측
evidence that ~라는 증거	claim that ~라는 주장	

We appreciate <u>the fact **that**</u> you met the tight deadline.
빠듯한 마감일을 맞춰 주셨다는 사실에 감사드립니다.

명사절 접속사 that을 취하는 형용사

be aware that ~을 잘 알다	be confident that ~을 확신하다
be imperative that ~이 필수적이다	be certain / obvious that ~은 분명하다
be pleased that ~해서 기쁘다	be delighted that ~해서 기쁘다

We <u>are delighted **that**</u> our monthly goal has been met. 월 목표량이 달성되어 기쁩니다.

※ 감정을 나타내는 형용사와 함께 that절이 자주 쓰인다.

형용사 역할을 하는 명사절 접속사

명사절 접속사 what과 which는 명사를 꾸미는 형용사로 기능할 수 있다.

We should determine **which plans** are more feasible. 우리는 **어떤 계획**이 더 실행 가능할지 결정해야 한다.

Please indicate **what color** you would like. **무슨 색상**을 원하는지 표시해주세요.

to부정사구와 결합하는 명사절 접속사

명사절 접속사가 반드시 문장을 이끄는 것은 아니다. 명사절 접속사는 to부정사구와 함께 쓰일 수 있다.

The audience didn't know **how they should respond**. 관객들은 어떻게 반응해야 할지 몰랐다.

= The audience didn't know **how to respond**.

ACTUAL TEST

정답 및 해설 p. 157

1. A study found ------- part-time workers are less likely to receive any chance for career progression.
   (A) whose
   (B) which
   (C) if
   (D) that

2. ------- is chosen to lead the Planning Committee will need to create the agenda for the monthly meetings.
   (A) Whomever
   (B) Whoever
   (C) Anyone
   (D) What

3. Dextron Clothing Store can provide ------- you are looking for to match your fashion needs.
   (A) how
   (B) whenever
   (C) whether
   (D) whatever

4. The meeting will focus on ------- we can strengthen international trade in coming years.
   (A) what
   (B) which
   (C) who
   (D) how

5. The Moore Foundation has promised ------- they will provide funds to meet the needs of the city's public library system.
   (A) what
   (B) that
   (C) which
   (D) whom

6. A survey will be conducted to determine ------- there is enough demand for a late night bus service.
   (A) whatever
   (B) whether
   (C) however
   (D) whenever

7. The unique feature of the Marden X10 smartphone is ------- it has a battery life of 12 hours per charge.
   (A) what
   (B) that
   (C) which
   (D) how

8. It is recommended ------- computer users save their documents frequently to avoid unexpected system failure.
   (A) that
   (B) what
   (C) whether
   (D) which

9. ------- will lead the quality-control training has yet to be decided.
   (A) When
   (B) Who
   (C) Whoever
   (D) Whether

10. Knowing ------- to encourage teamwork is an important business skill for all supervisors.
    (A) what
    (B) if
    (C) how
    (D) that

11. ------- we will hold our annual banquet depends on the number of participants as well as the availability of the space.

(A) Where

(B) What

(C) Which

(D) Whenever

12. The survey will help us determine ------- we should continue to produce our Hugo series wireless hair driers.

(A) whatever

(B) whichever

(C) wherever

(D) whether

13. Tourists are often unaware ------- there are many things to do on Monticello Island besides visiting the beach.

(A) of

(B) that

(C) however

(D) what

14. The new advertising campaign will focus on ------- sets our company apart from the competition.

(A) where

(B) whom

(C) what

(D) that

15. The plumber explained ------- the dark stains on the ceiling were indicative of water leakage on the floor above.

(A) what

(B) that

(C) which

(D) whenever

16. The video tutorial will show computer users ------- to merge several word processing documents into one.

(A) that

(B) how

(C) what

(D) which

17. Customers should note ------- items from multiple orders may be combined and shipped in single package.

(A) whenever

(B) which

(C) that

(D) however

18. In a recent interview for *Books and Pages Magazine*, author Amanda Weller revealed ------- she finds inspiration for her writing.

(A) what

(B) which

(C) who

(D) how

19. The R&D team was disappointed ------- it did not get much positive feedback from product testers.

(A) with

(B) which

(C) that

(D) whatever

20. Although Hannah's café accepts reservations, customers cannot decide ------- tables to occupy.

(A) which

(B) why

(C) how

(D) if

207

비교 / 가정법 / 도치

기본 개념 잡기

● 비교 구문이란?

대상을 비교하기 위해 상태나 정도를 '만큼', '더', '가장' 등으로 표시해 주는 구문을 비교 구문이라고 한다.
비교 구문에는 원급, 비교급, 최상급이 있다.

원급	비교급 (-er / more)	최상급 (-est / most)
large 큰	larger 더 큰	largest 가장 큰
frequent 빈번한	more frequent 더 빈번한	most frequent 가장 빈번한
recently 최근에	more recently 더 최근에	most recently 가장 최근에
important 중요한	less important 덜 중요한	least important 가장 덜 중요한

● 가정법이란?

접속사 if를 사용하여 현재 사실과 반대되는 상황을 가정하여 나타내는 것을 가정법이라고 한다.
가능성이 희박한 미래를 가정할 때는 should를 사용한다.

시간이 있다면 자세히 볼 텐데	가정법 과거 ▸	If we **had** more time, we **would take** a closer look.
연설자가 제때 **도착했다면** 행사가 더 일찍 시작했을 텐데	가정법 과거완료 ▸	If the speaker **had arrived** on time, the event **would have started** sooner.
혹시 문제가 발생하면 연락주세요	가정법 미래 ▸	If a problem **should arise**, **please contact** us.

● 도치 구문이란?

문장 성분이 원래의 어순이 아닌 뒤바뀐 어순으로 놓이는 것을 도치라고 한다.
주어 동사가 동사와 주어 순서로 바뀌는 도치 구문이 가장 흔하다.
주로 강조하고 싶은 대상을 문장 맨 앞에 놓기 위해 도치 구문을 쓴다.

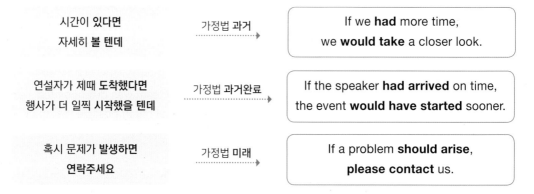

Photographs from the fundraiser are **attached.** 기금 마련 행사 사진이 첨부되어 있습니다.
주어 · 동사

❯ **Attached** are photographs from the fundraiser.
▸ 첨부 파일이 · 동사 · 주어
있음을 강조

출제 공식 1　　　비교급

'(~보다) 더'를 뜻하는 비교급 표현은 '-er' 또는 more로 나타내며 비교급 뒤에는 than이 올 수 있다.

비교급 + than　The new version is [**more reliable** / ~~reliably~~] than the previous one.
　　　　　　　신규 버전은 이전 버전보다 더 믿을 만하다.
　　　　　　　❯ be동사의 보어가 필요하고 형용사 자리이며 than이 있으므로 비교급이 어울린다.

　　　　　　　The speaker arrived [~~late~~ / **later**] than scheduled. 연설자는 예정보다 더 늦게 도착했다.
　　　　　　　❯ arrived를 꾸미는 부사 자리이며 than이 있으므로 비교급이 어울린다.

even, much, far, a lot, still, significantly 등의 부사는 비교급 앞에 놓여 비교급을 수식한다.

비교급 수식　We produced [~~highly~~ / **much**] less waste. 우리는 **훨씬 적은** 쓰레기를 생성했다.
　　　　　　❯ 비교급 표현 less가 있으므로 비교급을 수식하는 much를 고른다.

　　　　　　Our new menu was far [~~popular~~ / **more popular**]. 우리의 신메뉴는 **훨씬 더** 인기가 많았다.
　　　　　　❯ 비교급 수식 부사 far가 있으므로 비교급을 고른다.

CHECK-UP　　　　　　　　　　　　　　　　　　　　　　　　　정답 및 해설 p. 160

1. Use the reference code so that we can process your inquiry [efficient / more efficiently].
2. The Silverstone Stadium is [very / much] larger than any other stadium in the city.
3. The new rubber pipes are much [flexible / more flexible].

출제 공식 2　　　최상급과 원급

'가장'을 뜻하는 최상급 표현은 '-est' 또는 most로 나타내며 최상급 앞에는 the가 붙는다.

the + 최상급　TS 500 is the [**cheapest** / ~~cheaply~~] blender. TS 500은 가장 저렴한 믹서기이다.
　　　　　　　　　❯ blender를 수식하는 형용사 자리이며 the가 있으므로 최상급이 어울린다.

even, by far, single, very, ever, possible은 최상급을 수식하며, 수식 위치가 각각 다르다.

---❶--- + the 최상급	the ---❷--- + 최상급	the 최상급 + ---❸---
even, by far	single, very	ever, possible

최상급 수식　❶ **Even** the most skilled technician failed to fix it. 가장 숙련된 기술자**조차** 그것을 고치지 못했다.
　　　　　　❷ Mr. Palmer came up with the very best solution. 팔머 씨는 **단연** 최고의 해결책을 생각해 냈다.
　　　　　　❸ The event was the largest one ever. 그 행사는 **지금까지 중에서** 가장 큰 행사였다.

동등함을 나타내는 원급은 「as 형용사 / 부사 as」로 나타낸다.

as 원급 as　The hotel was as [**comfortable** / ~~more comfortably~~] as expected. 그 호텔은 예상**만큼** 안락했다.
　　　　　　　　❯ be동사의 보어가 필요한 자리이며 as ~ as 사이이므로 원급이 어울린다.

CHECK-UP　　　　　　　　　　　　　　　　　　　　　　　　　정답 및 해설 p. 160

1. There is a list of questions that are asked [frequent / most frequently].
2. Please send us the estimate as [prompt / promptly] as possible.
3. [Even / Ever] the most complex tasks have become easy thanks to the latest technology.

출제 공식 3　　　가정법

가정법은 시제 문제로 등장하며 공식만으로 풀이가 가능하다.

가정법 과거	If + 과거	S + [would / could / might] + 동사원형
가정법 과거완료	If + 과거완료 (had p.p.)	S + [would / could / might] + have p.p.
가정법 미래	If + should + 동사원형	S + [will / can / may] + 동사원형 또는 명령문

과거　　If we **had** a better option, we **would change** our supplier. 더 나은 옵션이 있다면 공급처를 바꿀 텐데.
　　　　❷ if절의 과거 동사 자리, 또는 주절의 동사 자리를 출제한다.

과거완료　If I **had been** there, I **would have signed** the contract. 내가 거기 있었다면 계약에 서명했을 텐데.
　　　　❷ if절의 과거완료 동사 자리, 또는 주절의 동사 자리를 출제한다.

미래　　If you **should** find any problem, **please let** us know. 혹시라도 문제를 발견하시면 저희에게 알려 주세요.
　　　　❷ 가능성이 희박한 경우를 나타내며, should 자리를 주로 출제한다.

CHECK-UP　　　　　　　　　　　　　　　　　　　　정답 및 해설 p. 160

1. If our team had more time, we [must / would] come up with better outcomes.
2. If you [should / would] cancel your order, your deposit will not be refunded.
3. If we [receive / had received] the grants, our project would not have been stopped.

출제 공식 4　　　도치

부정어구 never, hardly, seldom, not until, nor가 문두로 오면 도치가 일어난다.

부정어구 도치　**Seldom** has the team missed the deadline. 그 팀은 마감일을 거의 넘긴 적이 없었다.
　　　　　　　　　　동사　　주어
　　　　　　❷ 원문: The team has **seldom** missed the deadline.

보어 enclosed, attached, included를 강조하기 위해 문두로 보내면 도치가 일어난다.

보어 도치　**Enclosed** are a résumé and a list of references. 이력서와 추천인 목록이 동봉되어 있습니다.
　　　　　　　　　　동사　　　　　　주어
　　　　　　❷ 원문: A résumé and a list of references are **enclosed**.

가정하는 문장에서 if를 생략하면 도치가 일어난다.

가정법 도치　**Should** there be any changes, we will inform you. 혹시라도 변동이 있으면 알려 드리겠습니다.
　　　　　　　동사　주어
　　　　　　❷ 원문: If there **should** be any schedule changes, we will inform you.

CHECK-UP　　　　　　　　　　　　　　　　　　　　정답 및 해설 p. 160

1. [Never / Nearly] has Ms. Palmer missed deadlines, however tight they are.
2. [Attachment / Attached] are sample writings Ms. Hamilton sent us to review.
3. [Could / Should] Mr. Taylor cancel the appointment, Dr. Liu will replace him.

비교급 / 최상급 관용 표현

❶ as long as: ~하는 한 (조건)

A replacement part will be provided for free **as long as** the warranty is valid.
보증서가 유효한 한 교체 부품이 무료로 제공될 것입니다.

❷ as far as: ~하는 한 (범위)

As far as I know, the invoice has not been submitted yet.
제가 아는 한, 청구서가 아직 제출되지 않았습니다.

❸ as well as: ~뿐만 아니라 (첨가)

This course is designed to develop leadership skills **as well as** communication skills.
이 수업은 의사소통 능력뿐만 아니라 리더십 능력을 발전시키기 위해 마련되었다.

❹ more than: ~ 이상 / less than ~ 이하 (숫자 수식)

The fundraiser has received contributions from **more than** 2,500 donors.
그 기금 마련 행사는 2,500명 이상의 기부자들로부터 기부금을 받았다.

❺ at least: 최소, 적어도 (숫자 수식)

Invitations to the annual fair should be mailed **at least** two weeks before the event.
그 연례 박람회 초대장은 적어도 행사 2주 전에 발송되어야 한다.

❻ no later than: 늦어도 ~까지 (시점)

All application forms must be postmarked **no later than** August 16.
모든 신청서는 늦어도 8월 16일까지 우편 소인이 찍혀야 한다.

❼ at the latest: 늦어도 ~까지 (시점)

The construction of the shopping mall will be completed by March 18 **at the latest**.
쇼핑몰 건설은 늦어도 3월 18일까지 마무리될 것이다.

❽ no longer: 더 이상 ~ 않다

Marbel Manufacturing announced that they will **no longer** produce energy drinks.
마블사는 더 이상 에너지 음료를 생산하지 않겠다고 발표했다.

❾ rather than: ~라기보다

The delivery system error was caused by an update **rather than** a failed address.
배송 시스템의 오류는 잘못된 주소 때문이 아니라 업데이트로 인해 발생되었다.

❿ the 비교급, the 비교급: 더 ~할수록 …하다

The more we work with Mr. Benson, **the more** impressed we are with his abilities.
벤슨 씨와 더 일하면 일할수록 우리는 그의 능력에 더 놀란다.

1. Housing in Rosedale is not as ------- as it was a decade ago.

    (A) affordable

    (B) more affordable

    (C) most affordably

    (D) affordably

2. The City International Airport, now among the world's -------, operates 24 hours a day.

    (A) busily

    (B) busier

    (C) busiest

    (D) busy

3. After testing 30 food mixers, the editors of *Pro Kitchen Magazine* found the Teo T5 the ------- versatile machine of all of them.

    (A) many

    (B) most

    (C) more

    (D) much

4. The banquet facility we selected for the awards ceremony is the ------- one in the region.

    (A) largest

    (B) largely

    (C) more largely

    (D) most largely

5. This past spring's temperatures have been ------- warmer than average across the entire region.

    (A) less

    (B) much

    (C) very

    (D) too

6. Although the sales director is ------- with e-mail services, we will use whatever tools of communication the client prefers.

    (A) familiarity

    (B) familiarize

    (C) most familiar

    (D) more familiarity

7. Last year the company recorded the ------- sales in its 25 year history, far surpassing expectations.

    (A) stronger

    (B) more strength

    (C) strongest

    (D) most strengthen

8. Before implementing the new recycling regulations, ------- larger amounts of trash were produced in that district.

    (A) more significant

    (B) significant

    (C) significantly

    (D) significance

9. If we had received a lot of cost estimates for the building project, we ------- more time to choose a contractor.

    (A) needed

    (B) will need

    (C) had needed

    (D) would have needed

10. Now in its 50th year of operation, Artrax Hat Company is ------- older than many other businesses in the city.

    (A) too

    (B) a lot

    (C) so

    (D) just

11. ------- does the Art Museum have the honor to host a lecturer as distinguished as Robert Vanini.

(A) Enough
(B) Seldom
(C) Yet
(D) Much

12. ------- any resident of Fairdell City require an additional bin for recyclables, one will be provided free of charge.

(A) Could
(B) Should
(C) May
(D) That

13. If the prototypes ------- by October 5, we could have displayed them at the fall trade show.

(A) were completing
(B) had been completed
(C) complete
(D) are completed

14. Those interested in attending the Regional Medical Conference (RMC) should register ------- May 10.

(A) at least
(B) no later than
(C) lately
(D) as long as

15. Soft Design has been committed to providing the ------- best design solutions over the past 10 years.

(A) so
(B) very
(C) much
(D) more

16. All the rental items you requested for your private event should be returned to us by December 10th -------.

(A) later
(B) lately
(C) the last
(D) at the latest

17. ------- is a welcome packet with information you will need as a conference attendee.

(A) Enclosure
(B) Enclosing
(C) Enclosed
(D) Encloses

18. Many diners at our restaurant still request the spicy chicken platter even though the item is ------- available on our menu.

(A) anymore
(B) no longer
(C) not enough
(D) at least

19. ------- has the amusement park had a Saturday that was not busy.

(A) Nearly
(B) Hardly
(C) Ever
(D) Quite

20. In general, the ------- luggage you carry, the more comfortable your travels will be.

(A) little
(B) least
(C) less
(D) fewest

1 **access** 이용, 접근
gain access 이용권을 얻다
free access to ~에 대한 무료 이용

2 **permit** 허가증
a parking permit 주차증
a building permit 건축 허가증

3 **receipt** 영수증, 수령
present the original receipt 원본 영수증을 제시하다
upon receipt 받자마자

4 **initiative** 주도권, 계획
take the initiative 주도권을 잡다
the building restoration initiative 건물 복원 계획

5 **progress** 진전, 진행 상황
in progress 진행 중인
make continuous progress 지속적인 진전을 이루다

6 **usage** 사용(량)
heavy usage 많은 사용량
reduce energy usage 에너지 사용량을 줄이다

7 **asset** 자산
a valuable asset 귀중한 자산
become an asset to a company 회사의 자산이 되다

8 **revision** 개정, 변경
proposed revisions 제안된 변경 사항
the revision to the menu 메뉴 변경

9 **objective** 목표, 목적
an achievable objective 달성 가능한 목표
meet the objective 목표를 달성하다

10 **vacancy** 공석
a job vacancy 일자리 공석
fill a vacancy 공석을 채우다

11 **priority** 우선(권)
a top priority 최우선 사항
take priority over ~보다 우선권를 가지다

12 **exposure** 노출
increase exposure 노출을 증가시키다
excessive exposure to ~로의 과도한 노출

13 **term** 조건, 기간, 용어
terms and conditions 계약 조건, 약정
long-term outlook 장기적인 전망

14 **component** 구성 요소, 부품
a central component 핵심 구성 요소
vehicle components 차량 부품

15 **recognition** 인지, 인정
in recognition of ~을 인정하여
earn recognition 인정받다

16 **phase** 단계
the final phase 최종 단계
the initial design phase 초기 디자인 단계

17 **reference** 참조, 추천서, 언급
reference code 참조 번호
a reference letter 추천서

18 **occasion** 경우, 때, 행사
a special occasion 특별한 행사
on that occasion 그러한 경우에

19 **scope** 범위, 규모
the scope of the project 프로젝트의 규모/범위
beyond the scope of ~의 범위를 벗어난

20 **expertise** 전문 지식
areas of expertise 전문 분야
expertise in machinery 기계에 대한 전문 지식

ACTUAL TEST

정답 및 해설 p. 163

1. The digital subscription offers unlimited ------- to all of *The News Tribune*'s online content.

(A) approach

(B) reservation

(C) access

(D) publication

2. Our keynote speaker, the prize-winning journalist Jenny Huffman, will share her ------- on reporting and writing.

(A) capacity

(B) expertise

(C) insurance

(D) deadline

3. The ------- of the renovation project includes upgrades to the building's electrical system.

(A) scope

(B) inside

(C) enrollment

(D) director

4. The final ------- of the shopping mall construction involves installing the decorative fountains.

(A) way

(B) phase

(C) impact

(D) posture

5. Our store manager earned ------- for increasing quarterly sales by 10 percent.

(A) exception

(B) diversity

(C) recognition

(D) vacancy

6. Gary Lightfoot, the city's newly elected mayor, said he will make job creation his top -------.

(A) shortage

(B) incident

(C) manner

(D) priority

7. Engineered to the highest standards, Elton, Inc.'s ------- are the product of choice for the aerospace industry.

(A) suggestions

(B) evaluations

(C) components

(D) policies

8. Mr. Bowers clearly likes to take ------- at work, as he often volunteers to help his colleagues with projects.

(A) relaxation

(B) initiative

(C) absence

(D) compensation

9. Clearly inspired by his music, the author made numerous ------- to Billy Dawe in her novel.

(A) permission

(B) perspectives

(C) references

(D) creations

10. Ms. Sanders asked for a ------- to the contract for the new client, as the original form had a piece of inaccurate information.

(A) presentation

(B) revision

(C) nomination

(D) relocation

1 **basis** 단위
on a regular basis 정기적인 단위로
on a first-come-first-served basis 선착순으로

2 **capacity** 수용력, 능력
production capacity 생산력
operate in full capacity 최대치로 가동하다

3 **shift** 변화, 교대 근무
a significant shift 상당한 변화
work the overnight shift 철야 근무하다

4 **perspective** 관점
unique perspective 독특한 관점
see from a different perspective 다른 관점에서 보다

5 **transaction** 거래, 처리
business transactions 비즈니스 거래
payroll transactions 급여 처리

6 **emphasis** 강조
with an emphasis on ~에 강조점을 두어
put [place] an emphasis on ~을 강조하다

7 **replacement** 교체, 대체물, 대체자
replacement parts 교체 부품
find a replacement for ~의 대체자를 찾다

8 **shortage** 부족
inventory shortages 재고 부족
a shortage of funds 자금 부족

9 **alternative** 대안, 대체자
an affordable alternative to ~에 대한 저렴한 대안
search for an alternative 대안/대체자를 찾다

10 **reputation** 평판
have a reputation for ~에 대한 평판을 가지다
presence and reputation 입지와 평판

11 **admission** 가입, 입장
admission price 입장료
admission to a museum 박물관 입장

12 **concentration** 집중, 밀도, 농도
the largest concentration 가장 높은 밀도
concentration and productivity 집중력과 생산력

13 **consent** 동의
without written consent 서면 동의 없이
express consent 동의를 표하다

14 **patronage** 후원, 애용
continued patronage 지속적인 후원
appreciate one's patronage 후원에 감사하다

15 **accomplishment** 업적, 성취
remarkable accomplishments 놀라운 업적
the accomplishments of the objectives 목표 달성

16 **coverage** 범위, 보도, 보장
provide full coverage 완전한 보장을 제공하다
extensive media coverage 대대적인 언론 보도

17 **factor** 요인, 요소
a key factor 핵심 요소
consider external factors 외부 요인을 고려하다

18 **consequence** 결과
as a consequence of ~의 결과로
unexpected consequences 예상치 못한 결과

19 **intention** 의도
have no intention 의도가 없다
announce one's intention 의도를 밝히다

20 **range** 범위
a price range 가격대
a wide range of 다양한 ~

1. Despite the -------- of in-house staff, we were able to complete the project on time.
   (A) privilege
   (B) shortage
   (C) market
   (D) atmosphere

2. Collecting recyclable waste is done on a weekly ------- by the city, without charge to residents.
   (A) quantity
   (B) focus
   (C) basis
   (D) approach

3. During last Friday's staff meeting, Mr. Park officially announced his ------- to retire.
   (A) intention
   (B) structure
   (C) completion
   (D) employer

4. Although it is only in its fourth month of operations, Dana D's Bistro has already earned a ------- for excellent food.
   (A) acquisition
   (B) privilege
   (C) feature
   (D) reputation

5. Armytek, Inc. confirmed that the new airport was an important ------- in its decision to open a branch office in Clover City.
   (A) title
   (B) factor
   (C) supply
   (D) replacement

6. The new line of furniture is attractively designed, with a strong ------- on simplicity.
   (A) combination
   (B) procedure
   (C) comment
   (D) emphasis

7. Medical records are confidential, so they may not be released without a patient's -------.
   (A) merger
   (B) sensitivity
   (C) consent
   (D) reward

8. The warranty plan provides full ------- against damage to your mobile phone.
   (A) coverage
   (B) prediction
   (C) consumer
   (D) defect

9. For many commuters, cycling to work has become a healthy ------- to driving a car.
   (A) restriction
   (B) discovery
   (C) alternative
   (D) timetable

10. Sending out coupons is a simple way to thank loyal store customers for their continued -------.
    (A) shipment
    (B) reduction
    (C) revisions
    (D) patronage

PART 5

UNIT 01 빈출 명사 어휘

1 **acquisition** 인수
merger and acquisition (M&A) 기업 인수 합병
announce the acquisition of ~을 인수함을 발표하다

2 **approach** 접근(법)
a fresh approach 신선한 접근법
a new approach to ~에 대한 새로운 접근법

3 **service** 재직, 서비스
years of service as ~로서의 수년간의 재직
dedicate years of service to ~에 수년간 봉사하다

4 **dimension** 치수, 규모
the dimension of a site 현장의 크기
measure the dimensions 치수를 재다

5 **procedure** 절차
a safety procedure 안전 절차
implement new procedures 새로운 절차를 이행하다

6 **enthusiasm** 열정, 열의
with enthusiasm 열정적으로
show enthusiasm 열의를 보이다

7 **assessment** 평가
categories of the assessment 평가 항목
performance assessment 업무 평가

8 **portion** 부분
a significant portion 상당한 부분
a portion of the proceeds 수익금의 일부

9 **excess** 과잉, 초과(량)
in excess of ~을 초과하는
lead to an excess of ~의 과잉을 초래하다

10 **setting** 환경, 배경
work setting 업무 환경
a beautiful mountain setting 아름다운 산 배경

11 **nature** 성질, 특성
confidential nature 기밀성
sensitive nature of the contract 계약의 민감한 특성

12 **consensus** 합의
the consensus among members 멤버들 간의 합의
reach a consensus 합의에 도달하다

13 **circumstance** 환경, 상황
unforeseen circumstances 예상치 못한 상황
under no circumstance 어떠한 상황에도 ~가 아니다

14 **tendency** 경향
growing tendency 늘어나는 추세
have a tendency to ~하는 경향이 있다

15 **presence** 입지, 존재(감)
establish a presence 입지를 확립하다
the online presence 온라인에서의 입지

16 **proximity** 근접
in the proximity of ~ 가까이에 있는
the proximity to ~와의 근접성

17 **practice** 실행, 관행
hands-on practice 실습
environmentally friendly practice 친환경적 관행

18 **setback** 차질
a massive financial setback 상당한 금전적인 차질
weather-related setbacks 날씨로 인한 차질

19 **correspondence** 서신
business correspondence 비즈니스 서신
send official correspondence 공식 서신을 보내다

20 **appraisal** 평가
a formal appraisal 공식 평가
performance appraisals 업무 평가

ACTUAL TEST

정답 및 해설 p. 165

1. The research assistant position involves working with chemicals in a lab -------.
   (A) paper
   (B) setting
   (C) discovery
   (D) explanation

2. Before renting new space for a business, it is necessary to conduct a thorough ------- of the property's condition.
   (A) tour
   (B) proof
   (C) assessment
   (D) standard

3. Business travelers often prefer the North-Star Hotel because of its ------- to the airport.
   (A) elevation
   (B) selection
   (C) luxury
   (D) proximity

4. To maintain your ------- for a sport, it is advisable to add variety to your exercise routine.
   (A) enthusiasm
   (B) character
   (C) completion
   (D) occasion

5. A ------- of the national park's entrance fee will go toward maintaining the hiking trails.
   (A) promise
   (B) portion
   (C) seller
   (D) coverage

6. Hiring a personal trainer will give you a fresh ------- to your fitness routine.
   (A) neighborhood
   (B) approach
   (C) collection
   (D) reason

7. Employees should ensure that any written information of a confidential ------- is not left out on their desks.
   (A) recognition
   (B) advice
   (C) importance
   (D) nature

8. Despite some early -------, Delco Manufacturing grew to become one of the region's largest companies.
   (A) memberships
   (B) distances
   (C) abilities
   (D) setbacks

9. An anniversary party was held to celebrate Ms. Park's 20 years of ------- to the company.
   (A) distance
   (B) element
   (C) process
   (D) service

10. Customer service representatives must respond quickly to all ------- from current and potential clients.
    (A) processing
    (B) incentive
    (C) correspondence
    (D) participation

1 **lengthy** 장황한, 긴
a lengthy discussion 긴 논의
lengthy yet informative 길지만 유익한

2 **valid** 유효한
be valid until ~까지 유효하다
a valid form of identification 유효 신분증

3 **renowned** 유명한
be renowned for ~로 유명하다
world renowned artists 세계적으로 유명한 예술가들

4 **adjacent** 인접한
the adjacent building 인접한 건물
adjacent to the train station 기차역에 가까운

5 **confidential** 기밀의
a confidential document 기밀 문서
remain confidential 기밀로 유지되다

6 **specific** 구체적인
specific needs 구체적인 요구 사항
specific areas of interest 구체적인 관심 분야

7 **sincere** 진심 어린
a sincere apology 진심 어린 사과
extend one's sincere gratitude 진심으로 감사하다

8 **rigorous** 엄격한
rigorous standards 엄격한 기준
undergo rigorous tests 엄격한 시험을 거치다

9 **substantial** 상당한
a substantial increase 상당한 증가
have a substantial impact 상당한 영향력을 갖다

10 **external** 외부의
an external auditor 외부 감사자
external influences 외부 영향

11 **exceptional** 뛰어난, 특별한
exceptional service 뛰어난 서비스
with exceptional care 특별한 관리로

12 **demanding** 까다로운
a demanding task 까다로운 업무
a demanding customer 까다로운 고객

13 **durable** 견고한
durable materials 튼튼한 재질
lightweight yet durable 가볍지만 견고한

14 **fragile** 부서지기 쉬운
fragile items 깨지기 쉬운 상품
fragile documents 찢어지기 쉬운 문서

15 **sizable** 상당한
a sizable market 큰 시장
a sizable amount of information 상당한 양의 정보

16 **competent** 유능한
a highly competent employee 매우 유능한 직원
competent enough to ~할 만큼 충분히 유능한

17 **profitable** 수익성이 좋은
profitable enterprises 수익성이 좋은 기업
become profitable 수익이 나기 시작하다

18 **contrary** 반대되는
on the contrary 이와 반대로
contrary to popular opinion 일반적인 생각과는 달리

19 **confident** 확신하는
be confident that ~임을 확신하다
be confident of/in ~에 대해/~에 있어 확신하다

20 **unattended** 방치된
unattended vehicles 방치된 차량들
leave items unattended 물건을 방치된 채로 두다

ACTUAL TEST

정답 및 해설 p. 166

1. Use special care when packing ------- items to ensure that they do not break during shipping.
   (A) fragile
   (B) casual
   (C) productive
   (D) extensive

2. Shortening wait times at check-out lines can produce ------- improvements in customer satisfaction.
   (A) anonymous
   (B) impatient
   (C) substantial
   (D) contingent

3. It is best to hire a ------- professional to paint a large house or office.
   (A) competent
   (B) repeated
   (C) widespread
   (D) removable

4. Even in airline lounges, travelers should never leave their luggage -------.
   (A) unfolded
   (B) unfinished
   (C) unopened
   (D) unattended

5. Exhibiting at a trade show can cost a ------- amount of money, especially in cities where lodging is expensive.
   (A) sizable
   (B) responsible
   (C) rentable
   (D) stylish

6. Tour participants can enjoy ------- sunsets while trekking along the ridge of the Blue Mountain range.
   (A) exceptional
   (B) useful
   (C) tentative
   (D) progressive

7. The Securing Plus application will protect all of your passwords and other ------- personal information.
   (A) punctual
   (B) proficient
   (C) confidential
   (D) unauthorized

8. Frequent air travelers should choose luggage that is both lightweight and -------.
   (A) swift
   (B) durable
   (C) eventual
   (D) customary

9. The new Italian restaurant on First Street became ------- after only a few weeks.
   (A) deliberate
   (B) leisurely
   (C) profitable
   (D) respective

10. The Skymawr Tower office building was designed by a ------- team of architects from a top firm.
    (A) scenic
    (B) habitual
    (C) renowned
    (D) spacious

PART 5

UNIT 02 빈출 형용사 어휘

221

빈출 형용사 어휘 2

1 **authentic** 진짜의
authentic pottery 진품 도자기
an authentic Italian dish 정통 이탈리아 요리

2 **designated** 지정된
designated seats 지정석
designated parking space 지정된 주차 공간

3 **vulnerable** 취약한
vulnerable to ~에 취약한
vulnerable to staining 때가 묻기 쉬운

4 **delicate** 섬세한, 까다로운
delicate matters 민감한 문제
delicate items 깨지기 쉬운 물건

5 **prospective** 장래의, 예비의
prospective customers 잠재 고객
prospective tenants 예비 세입자

6 **punctual** 시간을 엄수하는
punctual service 시간을 엄수하는 서비스
punctual and reliable 시간을 잘 지키고 신뢰할 만한

7 **extensive** 광범위한
extensive experience 폭넓은 경험
extensive repairs 대대적인 수리

8 **practical** 실용적인
practical experience 실무 경험
luxurious yet practical 고급스러우면서도 실용적인

9 **sufficient** 충분한
sufficient amount of time 충분한 시간
sufficient notice 충분한 기한을 둔 공지

10 **sound** 견실한, 타당한
financially sound 재정적으로 견실한
a sound reason 타당한 이유

11 **spacious** 널찍한
a spacious workplace 넓은 작업 공간
modern and spacious 현대적이고 넓은

12 **overdue** 기한이 지난
overdue payment 기한이 지난 지불
overdue items 반납 기한을 넘긴 품목

13 **mandatory** 의무적인
a mandatory training session 의무 교육 시간
Attendance is mandatory. 참석은 필수입니다.

14 **proficient** 능숙한
proficient in[at] ~에 능숙한
proficient in speaking French 프랑스어 회화에 능숙한

15 **desirable** 바람직한
desirable time and place 좋은 시간과 장소
it is desirable that ~은 바람직하다

16 **persistent** 끈질긴, 끊임없는
a persistent stain 잘 안 지는 얼룩
persistent effort 끊임없는 노력

17 **prolonged** 연장된, 장기적인
prolonged road construction 장기적인 도로 공사
a prolonged lifespan 연장된 수명

18 **accessible** 이용할 수 있는
readily accessible 쉽게 이용할 수 있는
accessible to members only 회원만 이용할 수 있는

19 **satisfactory** 만족스러운
a satisfactory agreement 만족스러운 합의
satisfactory to both parties 양쪽 모두에게 만족스러운

20 **outdated** 구식의
an outdated version 구 버전
outdated equipment 낡은 장비

1. All of the hotel's banquet rooms are ------- enough to hold at least 100 people.

   (A) spacious
   (B) eventful
   (C) separate
   (D) rewarding

2. The free arts and crafts class is set to begin soon thanks to ------- funds.

   (A) sufficient
   (B) economical
   (C) foreseeable
   (D) definite

3. The construction work on Waterloo Street caused ------- road closures and delays.

   (A) dissatisfied
   (B) expandable
   (C) prolonged
   (D) insufficient

4. The company's phone system has a main information line, and ------- extensions for the offices of each department.

   (A) approving
   (B) designated
   (C) competitive
   (D) hesitant

5. ------- via mobile phone, Cadic Supermarket's delivery service is fast and easy to use.

   (A) Reversible
   (B) Necessary
   (C) Accessible
   (D) Ultimate

6. Candidates for the administrative assistant position should be ------- with a variety of office software programs.

   (A) absent
   (B) outgoing
   (C) proficient
   (D) streamlined

7. ------- renovation work, including upgrades to the plumbing and electrical systems, is planned for DRM Tower.

   (A) Extensive
   (B) Skilled
   (C) Vacant
   (D) Inviting

8. To remove ------- stains from delicate clothing items, it is best to use a professional cleaning service.

   (A) innovative
   (B) efficient
   (C) supportive
   (D) persistent

9. The park's vegetation is ------- to damage from hikers, so we ask all visitors to stay on marked trails.

   (A) dangerous
   (B) considerate
   (C) vulnerable
   (D) attentive

10. The tour bus leaves at exactly 9:00 A.M., so all participants must be -------.

    (A) punctual
    (B) automated
    (C) recurrent
    (D) seasonable

PART 5

UNIT 02 빈출 형용사 어휘

223

1 relevant 관련된
be relevant to ~에 관련되다
relevant information 관련 정보

2 versatile 다재다능한, 다용도의
a versatile blender 다용도 믹서기
versatile enough to ~할 만큼 다재다능한

3 unforeseen 예상치 못한
unforeseen circumstances 예상치 못한 상황
due to unforeseen delays 예상치 못한 지연 때문에

4 equivalent 동등한
equivalent results 동일한 결과
equivalent to ~에 맞먹는

5 unprecedented 전례 없는
unprecedented growth 전례 없는 성장
an unprecedented 50% 유례없는 50퍼센트

6 introductory 입문용의, 출시의
introductory courses 입문자를 위한 수업
introductory rates 출시 특가

7 utmost 최고의
utmost efforts 최선의 노력
with the utmost care 지극정성으로

8 successive 연속적인
three successive years 3년 연속
third successive year 3년 연속

9 subsequent 그 다음의
subsequent to ~ 다음으로
in subsequent years 차후 몇 년간

10 immediate 즉각적인, 직속의
immediate changes 즉각적인 변동 사항
an immediate supervisor 직속 상관

11 optimal 최적의
optimal conditions 최적의 조건
for optimal performance 최적의 성능을 위해

12 imperative 필수적인
it is imperative that ~하는 것은 필수적이다
an imperative duty 필수 임무

13 genuine 진짜의, 진심 어린
genuine leather 진짜 가죽
genuine concerns 진심 어린 걱정

14 controversial 논란이 많은
a controversial topic 논란이 많은 주제
remain controversial 논란인 채로 남아 있다

15 certified 공인된
a certified technician 공인 기술자
the certified service center 공인 서비스 센터

16 distinctive 독특한
distinctive accessories 독특한 장신구
distinctive characteristics 특징

17 adequate 충분한, 적절한
an adequate supply 충분한 공급
adequate for one's needs ~의 요구 사항에 맞는

18 distinguished 뛰어난, 저명한
a distinguished author 뛰어난 작가
a distinguished prize 저명한 상

19 welcome 환영받는, ~해도 좋은
a welcome addition to a team 반가운 충원
welcome to use 사용해도 되는

20 pending 미결의, 임박한
a pending order 보류 상태에 있는 주문
pending changes 곧 있을 변화

ACTUAL TEST

정답 및 해설 p. 169

1. Even if you are not a student at Walford Arts University, you are ------- to attend the annual student film festival.
   - (A) possible
   - (B) exciting
   - (C) welcome
   - (D) pending

2. It is sometimes difficult to distinguish the differences between a ------- designer handbag and an imitation.
   - (A) courteous
   - (B) grateful
   - (C) genuine
   - (D) sturdy

3. Customers are entitled to receive a refund, or an ------- amount of credit, if they receive faulty goods.
   - (A) pleasant
   - (B) wishful
   - (C) equivalent
   - (D) productive

4. It is ------- that you install a virus protection program on any new computer.
   - (A) voluntary
   - (B) imperative
   - (C) ambitious
   - (D) considerable

5. Today's smartphones are ------- devices that can do much more than make calls.
   - (A) optimistic
   - (B) satisfied
   - (C) versatile
   - (D) unavailable

6. A candidate's ------- experience is a key factor to consider when hiring a new software developer.
   - (A) adjacent
   - (B) numerous
   - (C) relevant
   - (D) impartial

7. Due to ------- circumstances, the keynote speaker will be unable to attend Thursday's conference.
   - (A) unforeseen
   - (B) occasional
   - (C) sound
   - (D) inviting

8. The speakers at the Digital Marketing Conference are some of the most ------- professionals in their fields.
   - (A) seasonal
   - (B) extensive
   - (C) distinguished
   - (D) reliant

9. Please note that the property sale is still -------, so the transaction is not yet complete.
   - (A) searching
   - (B) pending
   - (C) incoming
   - (D) resisting

10. To become a ------- yoga instructor, the completion of a 200-hour training course is required.
   - (A) prolonged
   - (B) certified
   - (C) projected
   - (D) assorted

1 typically 전형적으로

Training sessions typically take an hour.
교육 시간은 보통 한 시간 걸린다.

2 highly 매우

Making a reservation is highly recommended.
예약을 하는 것이 매우 권장된다.

3 heavily 심하게

The road is heavily congested with traffics.
도로는 교통으로 심하게 혼잡하다.

4 briefly 짧게, 간단히

The area is closed briefly for cleaning.
그 구역은 청소로 인해 잠시 문을 닫고 있다.

5 promptly 신속하게

We reacted promptly to the issue.
우리는 그 문제에 신속하게 대응했다.

6 extremely 극도로, 매우

The venue is extremely popular with tourists.
그 장소는 관광객들에게 매우 인기가 좋다.

7 eventually 결국, 마침내

The issue was eventually resolved.
문제는 마침내 해결되었다.

8 primarily 주로

We rely primarily on renewable energy.
우리는 주로 재생 에너지에 의존하고 있다.

9 routinely 일상적으로, 정기적으로

The mobile application is routinely updated.
그 모바일 애플리케이션은 주기적으로 업데이트된다.

10 fairly 상당히, 공평하게

The assembly process is fairly simple.
조립 과정은 상당히 간단하다.

11 frequently 자주

The photocopier frequently broke down.
복사기가 자주 고장 났다.

12 lately 최근에

The stock price has increased lately.
주가가 최근에 올랐다.

13 properly 제대로

The appliance is functioning properly.
가전제품이 제대로 작동하고 있다.

14 currently 현재

We are currently accepting applications.
우리는 현재 지원서를 받고 있습니다.

15 remarkably 두드러지게

Our revenues have remarkably grown.
우리의 수익이 상당히 늘었다.

16 rarely 거의 ~ 않다

We rarely have problems with any of our products.
저희는 어떤 제품과 관련해서도 문제가 거의 없습니다.

17 relatively 비교적

The new laptop is relatively lightweight.
새로운 노트북은 비교적 가볍다.

18 respectively 각각

The prices are $50, $75 respectively.
가격은 각각 50달러와 75달러이다.

19 shortly 곧, 즉시

The package will be mailed shortly.
소포가 곧 우편 발송될 것입니다.

20 thoroughly 철저히, 완전히

All returned items are thoroughly inspected.
모든 반품된 상품은 철저히 검수된다.

ACTUAL TEST

정답 및 해설 p. 170

1. Installing a new ink cartridge in the printer is a ------- simple task that takes about 10 minutes.
   (A) some
   (B) much
   (C) fairly
   (D) closely

2. In order to keep sales staff motivated, Mr. Ito ------- sets targets and offers incentives to the best performers.
   (A) frequently
   (B) extremely
   (C) subsequently
   (D) greatly

3. Tourists ------- visit the city's Museum of Industry because it is located far from the downtown area.
   (A) nearly
   (B) locally
   (C) finally
   (D) rarely

4. Each editorial intern will, when ------- trained, be assigned tasks such as writing press releases.
   (A) properly
   (B) formerly
   (C) probably
   (D) severely

5. The term "essentials" refers to products that shoppers purchase ------- without planning.
   (A) lately
   (B) routinely
   (C) unusually
   (D) inaccurately

6. ------- our tours of Dove Mansion include a visit to its outdoor gardens, although sometimes this area is closed for maintenance.
   (A) Productively
   (B) Largely
   (C) Typically
   (D) Easily

7. Organic fruits and vegetables have become more and more popular -------.
   (A) freshly
   (B) newly
   (C) lately
   (D) shortly

8. The award ceremony will begin ------- at 7:00 P.M., so everyone should be seated at that time.
   (A) extremely
   (B) promptly
   (C) solely
   (D) markedly

9. Hotel room rates are ------- inexpensive in every part of the city except for the Historic District.
   (A) approximately
   (B) repeatedly
   (C) relatively
   (D) exactly

10. The "About Us" section of the Web site will ------- explain our organization's objectives and values.
    (A) briefly
    (B) previously
    (C) whenever
    (D) alongside

1 entirely 완전히
We are funded entirely by donations.
우리는 전적으로 기부금으로 사금이 소날본나.

11 ideally 이상적으로
Mr. Gifford is ideally suited for the job.
기포드 씨는 그 일에 이상적으로 적합하다.

2 formerly 이전에
The building was formerly a factory.
그 건물은 이전에 공장이었다.

12 accidentally 우연히, 뜻하지 않게
The customer accidentally took off the price tag. 고객이 실수로 가격표를 떼어 냈다.

3 exclusively 전적으로
Tickets are sold exclusively online.
표는 온라인을 통해서만 판매됩니다.

13 temporarily 일시적으로
The office chair is temporarily out of stock.
사무실용 의자가 일시적으로 품절입니다.

4 customarily 통상적으로, 관례적으로
Executives customarily visit in June.
임원들은 통상적으로 6월에 방문한다.

14 unusually 이례적으로, 비정상적으로
The turnout was unusually large.
참석자 수가 이례적으로 많았다.

5 officially 공식적으로
The restaurant officially opens next month.
그 식당은 공식적으로 다음 달에 개업한다.

15 normally 보통, 정상적으로
Delivery normally takes a week.
배송이 보통 일주일 걸린다.

6 seldom 좀처럼 ~않다
We seldom receive complaints from our customers. 우리는 좀처럼 고객들로부터 불평을 받지 않습니다.

16 solely 오로지, 단독으로
Those photos are available solely in print form. 그 사진들은 프린트 형식으로만 이용 가능하다.

7 significantly 상당히
The new battery lasts significantly longer.
새로운 배터리는 상당히 더 오래간다.

17 periodically 주기적으로
The window displays are periodically changed. 상품 진열이 주기적으로 변경된다.

8 precisely 정확하게
The show will begin precisely at 9 A.M.
공연이 정각 9시에 시작될 것이다.

18 totally 완전히, 전적으로
We have totally different opinions.
우리는 완전히 다른 의견을 가지고 있다.

9 directly 직접, 바로
You can contact directly to the hiring manager.
채용 담당자에게 직접 연락하실 수 있습니다.

19 occasionally 가끔
The shop occasionally offers special deals.
그 상점은 가끔 특별 할인가를 제공한다.

10 steadily 꾸준히
Sales have steadily increased in the last year.
지난해 동안 판매가 꾸준히 올랐다.

20 increasingly 점점
The book is becoming increasingly popular.
그 책은 점점 인기를 얻고 있다.

1. The funding for the youth orchestra depends ------- on donations from local residents.

    (A) accurately
    (B) carefully
    (C) finely
    (D) entirely

2. Contrary to last year, this year's property prices have been falling -------.

    (A) agreeably
    (B) steadily
    (C) resistantly
    (D) potentially

3. -------, we should open our new restaurant in the waterfront entertainment district.

    (A) Virtually
    (B) Habitually
    (C) Ideally
    (D) Barely

4. Greeny Grocery ------- offers items at reduced prices to make room for new arrivals.

    (A) tightly
    (B) occasionally
    (C) carelessly
    (D) respectively

5. Market research indicates that customers ------- specify a brand preference when shopping for exercise equipment.

    (A) slightly
    (B) recently
    (C) moderately
    (D) seldom

6. The marathon runner requested a customized training program that is ------- focused on improving endurance.

    (A) adversely
    (B) quarterly
    (C) nearby
    (D) solely

7. Potential suppliers should note that Fresh Supermarket deals ------- with makers of organic food products.

    (A) previously
    (B) exclusively
    (C) markedly
    (D) accidentally

8. Cara Loomis, our company's new sales director, was ------- a product manager in the technology division.

    (A) moderately
    (B) formerly
    (C) shortly
    (D) perfectly

9. Some of Tucana's goods are ------- overpriced in Asian countries.

    (A) remotely
    (B) distantly
    (C) negatively
    (D) significantly

10. Tour groups ------- visit the oceanfront area in the morning to watch the sun rise.

    (A) exceedingly
    (B) customarily
    (C) vaguely
    (D) slightly

PART 5

UNIT 03 빈출 부사 어휘

빈출 부사 어휘 3

1 **noticeably** 주목할 만하게, 눈에 띄게
Our productivity improved <u>noticeably</u>.
우리의 생산성이 눈에 띄게 향상되었다.

2 **skillfully** 솜씨 좋게
The statue was <u>skillfully</u> crafted.
그 조각상은 솜씨 좋게 제작되었다.

3 **aggressively** 적극적으로, 공격적으로
We are <u>aggressively</u> seeking investors.
우리는 적극적으로 투자자들을 찾고 있다.

4 **prominently** 눈에 띄게
Some items are <u>prominently</u> displayed.
일부 상품들은 눈에 띄게 진열되어 있다.

5 **enormously** 엄청나게
We benefitted <u>enormously</u> from the seminar.
우리는 그 세미나에서 엄청나게 도움을 받았다.

6 **moderately** 적당히, 알맞게
The tour package is <u>moderately</u> priced.
그 관광 패키지는 적당하게 가격이 책정되어 있다.

7 **reportedly** 보도에 따르면
The firm was <u>reportedly</u> sold for $55 million.
그 회사는 보도에 따르면 5천5백만 달러에 매각됐다.

8 **preferably** 가급적, 되도록
Please reply, <u>preferably</u> within a week.
가급적이면 일주일 내로 회신 부탁드립니다.

9 **specifically** 구체적으로
We commented <u>specifically</u> on their service.
우리는 그들의 서비스에 대해 구체적으로 언급했다.

10 **intentionally** 의도적으로
The brand name was <u>intentionally</u> removed.
브랜드명이 고의적으로 제거되었다.

11 **presently** 현재
<u>Presently</u>, we are running at full capacity.
현재 우리는 풀가동 중이다.

12 **arguably** 틀림없이
The idea is <u>arguably</u> the most innovative.
그 생각은 단연코 가장 혁신적인 것이다.

13 **altogether** 아예, 완전히
The old machines stopped <u>altogether</u>.
낡은 기계들이 아예 작동을 멈췄다.

14 **deliberately** 고의로
Some information was <u>deliberately</u> removed.
일부 정보가 고의적으로 제거되었다.

15 **unexpectedly** 예상치 못하게
Some executives <u>unexpectedly</u> resigned.
일부 임원들이 예상치 못하게 사임했다.

16 **initially** 처음에
It took longer than we <u>initially</u> had expected.
그것은 우리가 처음에 예상했던 것보다 오래 걸렸다.

17 **subsequently** 그 다음으로
<u>Subsequently</u>, Dr. Liu was introduced.
그 다음으로 류 박사가 소개되었다.

18 **simultaneously** 동시에
Two events were held <u>simultaneously</u>.
두 행사가 동시에 개최되었다.

19 **markedly** 두드러지게, 눈에 띄게
Overall sales have risen <u>markedly</u>.
전체 판매량이 눈에 띄게 상승했다.

20 **marginally** 약간
The initiative was <u>marginally</u> successful.
그 계획은 미미하게나마 성공했다.

ACTUAL TEST

해설 p. 172

1. The company's president ------- canceled his planned tour of the new production facility in Pittsburgh.
   (A) greatly
   (B) unexpectedly
   (C) biweekly
   (D) loosely

2. Prices for air tickets are ------ higher during the busy summer vacation season.
   (A) noticeably
   (B) extremely
   (C) favorably
   (D) generously

3. Owned by celebrity chef Drew Khan, Fusion Max is ------- the city's best new restaurant.
   (A) gradually
   (B) portably
   (C) arguably
   (D) neutrally

4. The music festival will feature two bands playing ------- throughout the event, in different parts of the city park.
   (A) accidentally
   (B) simultaneously
   (C) doubly
   (D) precisely

5. Tuscan Motor GR-6 sedan was ------- criticized for its bland look, but it is now respected for.
   (A) initially
   (B) equally
   (C) conversely
   (D) superbly

6. With its large tables and open spaces, the new office was ------- designed to promote collaboration.
   (A) simultaneously
   (B) similarly
   (C) intentionally
   (D) namely

7. The cost of living can vary ------- across the region, with small towns being the most affordable places.
   (A) enormously
   (B) carelessly
   (C) consequently
   (D) purely

8. Thanks to mobile payment technology, some countries could eliminate paper money ------- in the future.
   (A) rather
   (B) altogether
   (C) freely
   (D) ever since

9. The Human Resources team would like to start interviewing candidates as soon as possible, ------- within two weeks.
   (A) immediately
   (B) accidentally
   (C) preferably
   (D) willingly

10. Ms. Xu viewed several of our storage spaces, and ------- decided to rent the largest unit.
    (A) subsequently
    (B) considerably
    (C) timely
    (D) currently

1 **enhance** 향상시키다
enhance the relationship 관계를 향상시키다
enhance corporate image 기업 이미지를 향상시키다

2 **attend** 참석하다, 돌보다
attend a seminar 세미나에 참석하다
attend to an urgent matter 급한 문제를 처리하다

3 **designate** 임명하다, 지정하다
designate A (as) B A를 B로 임명하다, 지정하다
be designated for bicycles 자전거 전용이다

4 **encounter** 직면하다
encounter problems 문제에 직면하다
encounter challenges 난관에 직면하다

5 **accompany** 동반하다
A accompany B A가 B와 동반하다
be accompanied by ~을 동반하다

6 **worsen** 악화시키다
worsen the congestion 혼잡을 악화시키다
worsen the relationship 관계를 악화시키다

7 **generate** 발생시키다
generate interest 관심을 유발하다
generate profits 수익을 발생시키다

8 **process** 처리하다
process the order 주문을 처리하다
process deposits 입금을 처리하다

9 **suspend** 중단시키다
suspend production 생산을 중단하다
suspend a service 서비스를 중단하다

10 **acknowledge** 감사를 표하다, 인정하다
acknowledge the support 후원에 감사하다
acknowledge the receipt 수령했음을 확인하다

11 **ensure** 확실하게 하다, 보장하다
ensure safety 안전을 보장하다
ensure that ~하는 것을 보장하다

12 **exceed** 초과하다
exceed the expectation 기대를 넘어서다
exceed a limit 제한을 초과하다

13 **surpass** 능가하다
surpass a goal 목표치를 능가하다
surpass one's competitors 경쟁사들을 능가하다

14 **indicate** 나타내다, 표시하다
indicate preference 선호도를 표시하다
indicate that ~라고 나타내다

15 **specialize** 전문으로 하다
specialize in women's apparel 여성복을 전문으로 하다
a business specializing in ~을 전문으로 하는 업체

16 **decline** 감소하다, 거절하다
The revenue declined. 수익이 감소했다.
decline the offer 그 제안을 거절하다

17 **notify** 알리다
notify A of B A에게 B에 대해 알리다
notify … that …에게 ~을 알리다

18 **retain** 간직하다, 보유하다
retain a receipt 영수증을 간직하다
retain competent staff 유능한 직원을 보유하다

19 **specify** 나타내다, 명시하다
specify the model 모델명을 명시하다
specify that ~을 나타내다

20 **accommodate** 수용하다
accommodate the requests 요구 사항을 수용하다
accommodate large groups 대규모 그룹을 수용하다

ACTUAL TEST

정답 및 해설 p. 174

1. The editorial team holds weekly brainstorming sessions to ------- ideas for future content.
   (A) prove
   (B) generate
   (C) conduct
   (D) dispose

2. The Springfield Banquet Room can ------- groups of up to 50 guests for sit-down meals.
   (A) accommodate
   (B) measure
   (C) transport
   (D) request

3. Thanks to innovative techniques, the salespeople expect to ------- their previous sales record by nearly twenty percent.
   (A) overhaul
   (B) surpass
   (C) compile
   (D) solicit

4. Highway 15 will be closed for expansion and motorists will ------- detours for the duration of the project.
   (A) encounter
   (B) relocate
   (C) require
   (D) occupy

5. The product brochure should ------- all the color and style options for the new line of office chairs.
   (A) specify
   (B) attain
   (C) exceed
   (D) decide

6. We will always ------- our customers if we expect any delays in shipping an item.
   (A) rely
   (B) qualify
   (C) strive
   (D) notify

7. As a trusted supplier of packaging for more than 30 years, Nelson Ltd. ------- in shipping boxes and mailing envelopes.
   (A) draws
   (B) appeals
   (C) specializes
   (D) appears

8. An expert guide will ------- every tour group that visits the historic Blanc House.
   (A) participate
   (B) accompany
   (C) emerge
   (D) consist

9. The costs of attending all the regional trade shows may ------- our current budget.
   (A) exceed
   (B) compete
   (C) analyze
   (D) evaluate

10. In his role as manager, Mr. Bailey is developing new strategies to ------- his department's most valuable employees.
    (A) resume
    (B) retain
    (C) connect
    (D) delegate

빈출 동사 어휘 2

1 **utilize** 이용하다
utilize skills 기술을 이용하다
utilize resources 자원을 이용하다

2 **accumulate** 축적하다
accumulate points 포인트를 쌓다
Snow is accumulated. 눈이 쌓여 있다.

3 **withstand** 견뎌[이겨] 내다
withstand high temperature 고온을 견뎌 내다
withstand the rigors (추위·고난 등의) 혹독함을 버티다

4 **commend** 칭찬하다, 추천하다
commend A for B B에 대해 A를 칭찬하다
commend A to B B에게 A를 추천하다

5 **eliminate** 제거하다
eliminate viruses 바이러스를 제거하다
eliminate stains 얼룩을 제거하다

6 **restore** 복구하다, 복원하다
restore a service 서비스를 복구하다
restore a traditional building 전통 건물을 복원하다

7 **finance** 자금을 대다
finance a business 사업에 자금을 대다
finance the renovation work 보수 작업에 자금을 대다

8 **terminate** 끝내다
terminate the lease agreement 임대차 계약을 끝내다
terminate the service 서비스를 종료하다

9 **settle** 해결하다, 결정하다
settle the account 정산하다, 결제하다
settle an issue 문제를 해결하다

10 **enforce** 시행하다
enforce a regulation 규칙을 시행하다
enforce a ban 금지령을 시행하다

11 **broaden** 넓히다, 확장하다
broaden one's knowledge 지식을 넓히다
broaden production capabilities 생산력을 늘리다

12 **disclose** 공개하다
disclose personal information 개인 정보를 공개하다
disclose one's intention 의도를 밝히다

13 **accelerate** 가속화하다
accelerate production 생산을 가속화하다
accelerate the growth 성장을 가속화하다

14 **undergo** 겪다, 받다
undergo maintenance 관리 점검을 받다
undergo a significant change 큰 변화를 겪다

15 **interfere** 방해하다, 참견하다
interfere with construction 공사에 지장을 주다
interfere in a situation 상황에 개입하다

16 **grant** 주다, 승인하다
grant scholarships 장학금을 주다
grant permission 허가를 승인하다

17 **consult** 참고하다, 상담하다
consult the manual 매뉴얼을 참고하다
consult with an expert 전문가와 상담하다

18 **reserve** 예약하다, 보유하다
reserve a conference room 회의실을 예약하다
reserve the right 권한을 보유하다

19 **feature** 특징으로 하다, 출연시키다
feature a panel of experts 전문가단을 출연시키다
feature academic topics 학문적인 주제를 다루다

20 **solidify** 확고히 하다
solidify one's position 입지를 굳히다
solidify a plan 계획을 확고히 하다

1. For information regarding the company's vacation policy, please ------- the employee manual.

   (A) educate
   (B) consult
   (C) exist
   (D) shift

2. It is important to ------- the social media when designing a marketing campaign to attract new customers.

   (A) excel
   (B) utilize
   (C) respond
   (D) yield

3. Every customer service representative must ------- a training course that focuses on communication skills.

   (A) assist
   (B) depend
   (C) undergo
   (D) spend

4. The company's newest factory uses automated assembly lines to ------- production.

   (A) rise
   (B) retreat
   (C) interfere
   (D) accelerate

5. *The Nutritious Meal Plans* cookbook ------- more than 50 creative recipes for healthy vegetarian dishes.

   (A) reaches
   (B) features
   (C) performs
   (D) attracts

6. Written permission from the landlord is required if a tenant wishes to ------- the lease agreement early.

   (A) concentrate
   (B) disconnect
   (C) terminate
   (D) remain

7. Working holiday programs can help young travelers ------- their stays in overseas cities.

   (A) assemble
   (B) finance
   (C) enlarge
   (D) occupy

8. In the wake of the storm, power service will be ------- as soon as the electric lines are repaired.

   (A) interrupted
   (B) diversified
   (C) restored
   (D) intended

9. XP Gaming recently acquired Reo Tech Ltd. to ------- its position as a top video game developer.

   (A) donate
   (B) solidify
   (C) consent
   (D) enter

10. We will reserve a conference room for the meeting as soon as the date is -------.

    (A) settled
    (B) departed
    (C) answered
    (D) appeared

1 **unveil** 공개하다, 발표하다
unveil a new model 신규 모델을 공개하다
unveil a plan 계획을 발표하다

2 **appoint** 임명하다
appoint a person to a post 사람을 직책에 임명하다
appoint him (as) president 그를 사장으로 임명하다

3 **delegate** 위임하다
delegate duties to 임무를 ~에게 위임하다
delegate authority to 권한을 ~에게 위임하다

4 **dispose** 버리다
dispose of used batteries 다 쓴 배터리를 처분하다
dispose of waste 쓰레기를 버리다

5 **strive** 노력하다, 애쓰다
strive to meet expectations 기대에 부응하려고 애쓰다
strive to ensure ~을 보장하려고 애쓰다

6 **stimulate** 자극하다
stimulate interest 관심을 불러일으키다
stimulate competitiveness 경쟁을 자극하다

7 **benefit** 이익을 주다, 이익을 얻다
benefit the environment 환경을 이롭게 하다
benefit from the merger 합병으로부터 이익을 얻다

8 **facilitate** 용이하게 하다
facilitate the transition 변화를 용이하게 하다
facilitate communication 의사소통을 용이하게 하다

9 **exercise** 발휘하다
exercise caution 주의하다
exercise influence 영향력을 행사하다

10 **direct** 보내다, 지휘하다
direct A to B A를 B로 보내다
direct the project 프로젝트를 지휘하다

11 **compile** 모으다, 편찬하다
compile data 데이터를 모으다
compile statistics 통계 자료를 모으다

12 **recognize** 인지하다, 인정하다
recognize the difference 차이를 인지하다
recognize the achievement 업적을 인정하다

13 **commence** 시작하다
commence at noon 정오에 시작하다
commence with a speech 연설과 함께 시작하다

14 **convene** 모이다
convene in Tokyo 도쿄에서 모이다
convene to discuss 논의하기 위해 모이다

15 **deliberate** 심사숙고하다
deliberate for hours 여러 시간 심사숙고하다
deliberate (up)on ~에 대해 심사숙고하다

16 **coincide** 동시에 일어나다
coincide with the opening 개막과 동시에 일어나다
coincide with the release 출시와 동시에 일어나다

17 **resume** 재개하다
resume one's duties 임무를 재개하다
Negotiations will resume. 협상이 재개될 것이다.

18 **thrive** 번성하다, 번영하다
grow and thrive 발전하다
Businesses will thrive. 기업들이 번영할 것이다.

19 **emerge** 드러나다, 나오다
emerge as a top designer 일류 디자이너로 부상하다
A problem emerged. 문제점이 드러났다.

20 **confront** 직면하다, 맞서다
be confronted with ~에 직면하다
confront the challenges 난관에 맞서다

ACTUAL TEST

정답 및 해설 p. 176

1. At Geo Adventure Tour Co., our expert guides ------- to make every trip a memorable one.
   (A) bring
   (B) handle
   (C) strive
   (D) undertake

2. Due to increasing oil prices, stocks in energy companies may ------- as favorites for investors.
   (A) emerge
   (B) operate
   (C) reveal
   (D) enable

3. The start of the region's rainy season often ------- with the summer vacation period for universities.
   (A) invites
   (B) demands
   (C) coincides
   (D) activates

4. Players at the Valley City golf tournament had to ------- windy weather during the entire match.
   (A) annoy
   (B) refrain
   (C) sacrifice
   (D) confront

5. This spring, more than 700 information technology experts will ------- at the Data Security Conference.
   (A) hold
   (B) arrange
   (C) convene
   (D) accumulate

6. Wyatt Goldberg has recently been ------- to serve as chairperson of the board of directors.
   (A) conducted
   (B) planned
   (C) appointed
   (D) appealed

7. Our manager ------- certain writing tasks to Ms. Yoon, as she has strong skills in written communication.
   (A) engages
   (B) delegates
   (C) approves
   (D) assists

8. Please ------- all billing inquires to our customer service department.
   (A) cause
   (B) direct
   (C) instruct
   (D) encourage

9. The city has opened a new recycling center where residents can ------- of unwanted electronic waste.
   (A) reduce
   (B) dispose
   (C) yield
   (D) delete

10. A supportive environment will improve morale and enable employees to ------- at work.
    (A) shorten
    (B) compile
    (C) thrive
    (D) oversee

1 **in an effort to V** ~하려는 노력으로

We carpool in an effort to save money.

우리는 돈을 아끼기 위해 승용차 함께 타기를 한다.

11 **in preparation for** ~에 대한 준비로

We set up signs in preparation for the race.

경주 준비로 우리는 푯말을 설치했다.

2 **in writing** 서면으로

All complaints must be submitted in writing.

모든 불만 사항들은 서면으로 제출되어야 한다.

12 **under the supervision of** ~의 지휘 하에

The project is under the supervision of Mr. Liu.

그 프로젝트는 리우 씨의 지휘 하에 있다.

3 **in exchange for** ~에 대한 교환으로

We give a coupon in exchange for any opinions.

의견을 주시면 쿠폰을 드립니다.

13 **with the exception of** ~은 제외하고

With the exception of Joe, everyone came.

조만 제외하고 모두 왔다.

4 **in detail** 상세히

All procedures are explained in detail on page 7.

모든 절차들은 7쪽에 상세히 설명되어 있다.

14 **ahead of schedule** 예정보다 앞선

The project was finished ahead of schedule.

프로젝트가 예정보다 일찍 끝났다.

5 **in advance** 미리

The registration fee must be paid in advance.

등록비는 선불로 지급되어야 한다.

15 **until further notice** 추후 공지까지

All flights will be postponed until further notice.

모든 항공편은 추후 공지가 있을 때까지 연기됩니다.

6 **in accordance with** ~에 따라

Everything went in accordance with plans.

모든 것은 계획대로 진행되었다.

16 **upon receipt** 받자마자

Please sign upon receipt of the item.

물건을 받자마자 서명해 주세요.

7 **in compliance with** ~을 준수하여

We act in compliance with the law.

우리는 법을 준수한다.

17 **a wide range of** 다양한

All bags are available in a wide range of colors.

모든 가방은 다양한 색상으로 이용 가능합니다.

8 **in charge of** ~을 담당하는

Ms. Gail is in charge of all bookings.

게일 씨가 모든 예약을 담당한다.

18 **take advantage of** ~을 이용하다

Members can take advantage of the perks.

회원들은 혜택을 이용할 수 있다.

9 **in response to N** ~에 대응하여

This is in response to your request.

이는 귀하의 요청 사항에 대한 응답입니다.

19 **have difficulty (with)** ~에 어려움을 겪다

We have difficulty (with) finding investors.

우리는 투자자를 찾는 데 어려움을 겪고 있다.

10 **in favor of** ~을 찬성하여, 지지하여

Residents are in favor of the proposal.

주민들은 그 제안을 지지한다.

20 **have access to N** ~에 대한 이용권을 갖다

We can have access to the data.

우리는 정보를 이용할 수 있다.

1. In a sincere ------- to improve its customer service, Dunne-Tekk Ltd. distributed feedback surveys via e-mail.

   (A) force
   (B) result
   (C) effort
   (D) stress

2. In ------- to increased demand, Bevardic Auto Ltd. will boost production of its electric car models.

   (A) ceremony
   (B) response
   (C) opportunity
   (D) difference

3. The City Art Museum will be closed until further ------- so that its galleries may be renovated.

   (A) circulation
   (B) removal
   (C) invention
   (D) notice

4. Shoppers are encouraged to take ------- of discounted prices during the clearance sale.

   (A) nomination
   (B) advantage
   (C) permission
   (D) inquiry

5. Upon ------- of full payment for your tour, a trip itinerary will be e-mailed to you.

   (A) security
   (B) ambition
   (C) receipt
   (D) honor

6. Lab assistants at the University Tech Center work under the ------- of full-time research scientists.

   (A) vacation
   (B) supervision
   (C) renovation
   (D) extension

7. Handrex Chemical Manufacturing Co. takes all the necessary measures to remain in ------- with the city's environmental laws.

   (A) transfer
   (B) compliance
   (C) allowance
   (D) satisfaction

8. The store's management will offer some associates overtime pay in ------- for working over the holiday weekend.

   (A) postponement
   (B) coupon
   (C) exchange
   (D) revision

9. Dentall's Sports Store has a wide ------- of products in stock, from bicycles to workout apparel.

   (A) range
   (B) time
   (C) hope
   (D) contest

10. In ------- for the sales presentation, Mr. Martin is reviewing the charts and graphs he will use.

    (A) availability
    (B) excitement
    (C) preparation
    (D) strictness

PART 5

UNIT 05 빈출 어구 / 명사

1   be eager to V ~하기를 열망하다
I am eager to attend the event.
서는 배우 ㄱ 행사에 참여하고 싶습니다.

2   be about to V 막 ~하려고 하다
We are about to launch a new campaign.
우리는 새로운 캠페인을 막 시작하려고 하고 있다.

3   be willing to V 기꺼이 ~하려고 하다
I am willing to donate some amount of money.
저는 일부 금액을 기꺼이 기부하려고 합니다.

4   be reluctant to V ~하기를 꺼리다
Ms. Han was reluctant to take the job.
한 씨는 그 일을 맡기를 꺼렸다.

5   be hesitant to V ~하기를 주저하다
They were hesitant to make a decision.
그들은 결정하기를 꺼렸다.

6   be bound to V 반드시 ~하다
The price is bound to increase.
가격이 반드시 오르게 되어 있다.

7   be likely to V ~할 것 같다
Ms. Henderson is likely to decline the offer.
헨더슨 씨는 그 제안을 거절할 것 같다.

8   be responsible for ~에 대한 책임이 있다
Ms. Diaz is responsible for the project.
디아즈 씨는 그 프로젝트를 담당한다.

9   be eligible for ~에 대한 자격이 있다
Mr. Ito is eligible for promotion.
이토 씨는 승진 자격이 있다.

10   be exempt from ~에서 면제되다
All orders are exempt from shipping fees.
모든 주문은 배송료가 면제된다.

11   be capable of ~할 능력이 있다
We are capable of handling more work.
우리는 더 많은 일을 치리힐 수 있다.

12   be committed to N ~에 전념하다
We are committed to meeting your needs.
우리는 귀하의 요구를 충족시키는 데 전념합니다.

13   be dedicated to N ~에 전념하다
The organization is dedicated to public health.
그 기관은 국민 건강에 전념한다.

14   be devoted to N ~에 전념하다, 바치다
Half of the grant was devoted to research.
보조금의 절반이 연구에 쏟아졌다.

15   be subject to N ~의 대상이다
All transactions are subject to a service fee.
모든 거래는 수수료가 붙는다.

16   be attributed to N ~ 때문이다
Our success is attribute to the new design.
우리의 성공은 새로운 디자인 때문이다.

17   be opposed to N ~에 반대하다
Shareholders are opposed to the acquisition.
주주들은 인수를 반대한다.

18   be related to N ~에 관련되다
Mr. Lewis's area of expertise is related to IT.
루이스 씨의 전문 분야는 IT와 관련되어 있다.

19   be limited to N ~으로 제한되다
Enrolment is limited to 50 people.
등록은 50명으로 제한되어 있다.

20   be compatible with ~와 호환되다
The app is compatible with most devices.
그 앱은 대부분의 기기와 호환된다.

1. All Nocturne Shops, Inc. employees are
------- for discounts when they purchase
any store item.

   (A) possible
   (B) eligible
   (C) flexible
   (D) essential

2. Based on a recent survey, many residents
are ------- to use City Park's expanded
hiking trails this summer.

   (A) eager
   (B) costly
   (C) potential
   (D) sympathetic

3. Folk singer Katrina Kiley announced that
she is ------- to release a new music video
soon.

   (A) necessary
   (B) likely
   (C) insisted
   (D) evident

4. In general, about half of our advertising
budget is ------- to online marketing
campaigns.

   (A) caring
   (B) claimed
   (C) denying
   (D) devoted

5. Under the country's new tax program,
foreign visitors are ------- from paying
sales taxes on most purchases.

   (A) eliminated
   (B) distinct
   (C) exempt
   (D) deducted

6. Goods that are not obtained legally from
the home country may be ------- to seizure
by customs agents.

   (A) opposed
   (B) reluctant
   (C) subject
   (D) admitted

7. Because they cannot inspect an item
beforehand, some consumers may be
------- to purchase clothing online.

   (A) sizable
   (B) hesitant
   (C) neutral
   (D) apparent

8. Mr. Karnov said his speaking ability in
Russian is ------- to only a few words and
phrases.

   (A) prevented
   (B) taken
   (C) limited
   (D) relaxed

9. Thanks to greater environmental
awareness, demand for eco-friendly
products is ------- to increase.

   (A) equal
   (B) subject
   (C) visible
   (D) bound

10. The Protek Plus anti-virus program is
------- with nearly every computer
operating system.

   (A) compatible
   (B) sociable
   (C) achievable
   (D) capable

PART 5

UNIT 06 빈출 어구 / 형용사

빈출 어구 / 동사

1 provide A with B 제공하다

We provide new hires with intensive training.
우리는 신입 사원들에게 집중 교육을 제공한다.

2 replace A with B 교체하다

Please replace your password with a new one.
암호를 새로운 것으로 교체하세요.

3 exchange A for B 교환하다

You can exchange the item for another.
그 물건을 다른 상품과 교환하실 수 있습니다.

4 prevent A from B 막다

Proper storage prevents items from spoiling.
적절한 보관은 상품이 상하는 것을 막는다.

5 discourage A from B 낙담시키다

Doctors discourages people from smoking.
의사들은 사람들이 흡연하는 것을 막는다.

6 honor A for B 상을 주다

We honor designers for their creative work.
우리는 디자이너들의 창의적인 작품에 대해 상을 줍니다.

7 familiarize A with B 익숙하게 하다

Familiarize yourself with the new policies.
새로운 정책을 숙지하시오.

8 transform A into B 변형하다, 바꾸다

We transformed the land into a garden.
우리는 터를 정원으로 바꾸었다.

9 add A to B 추가하다

The head chef added a new dish to the menu.
주방장은 메뉴에 새로운 요리를 추가했다.

10 direct A to B 보내다

Please direct all deliveries to the main room.
모든 배송품을 우편 보관실에 보내주세요.

11 refer A to B 보내다

Please refer all inquiries to Mr. Stern.
모든 문의는 스턴 씨에게 보내 주세요.

12 compensate A for B 보상하다

We will compensate you for any loss.
손해를 보상해 드리겠습니다.

13 distinguish A from B 구별하다

The logo distinguishes us from others.
로고가 우리를 다른 이들과 구별해 준다.

14 substitute A for B 대체하다

We substituted cheaper materials for metal.
우리는 금속을 더 저렴한 재료로 대체했다.

15 convert A into B 바꾸다, 전환하다

We converted a meeting room into a cafeteria.
우리는 회의실을 간이식당으로 바꾸었다.

16 reimburse A for B 환급하다

We will reimburse you for travel expenses.
저희가 출장 경비를 환급해 드릴 것입니다.

17 take into account 고려하다, 참작하다

We take customer privacy into account.
우리는 고객 프라이버시를 고려합니다.

18 present A to B 수여하다, 제시하다

We will present monetary prizes to the winners.
우리는 우승자들에게 상금을 수여할 겁니다.

19 inform A of B 알리다

Your manager will inform you of any updates.
매니저들이 추가 소식에 대해 여러분께 알려 줄 것입니다.

20 refrain from 삼가다

Please refrain from using mobile phones.
휴대폰 사용을 삼가 주시기 바랍니다.

ACTUAL TEST

정답 및 해설 p. 180

1. It is important to ------- the catering staff of any dietary restrictions the banquet's attendees may have.
   (A) talk
   (B) inform
   (C) discuss
   (D) claim

2. Because we no longer repair mobile phones at this store, we will ------- all requests for service to a local technician.
   (A) vary
   (B) seek
   (C) refer
   (D) moderate

3. The access card system is designed to ------- unauthorized personnel from entering the building.
   (A) caution
   (B) circle
   (C) modify
   (D) prevent

4. Employees will be ------- for fuel expenses when they use their own vehicle to travel to branch offices on business.
   (A) reimbursed
   (B) exchanged
   (C) attracted
   (D) influenced

5. Deccron Property Development is preparing to ------- an old, empty factory into a modern art gallery.
   (A) eliminate
   (B) transform
   (C) substitute
   (D) replace

6. The country's complex requirements for obtaining a tourist visa may ------- some travelers from visiting.
   (A) afford
   (B) avoid
   (C) discourage
   (D) terminate

7. The moving company's Web site offers tips on how to ------- yourself with a new city quickly.
   (A) cooperate
   (B) accompany
   (C) standardize
   (D) familiarize

8. The Library Association plans to ------- author Anna Grisdale for her contribution to children's literature.
   (A) honor
   (B) happen
   (C) express
   (D) deserve

9. When planning an outdoor picnic, be sure to take the weather forecast into -------.
   (A) calendar
   (B) account
   (C) storage
   (D) transcript

10. Members of the audience are asked to ------- from talking during the orchestra performance.
   (A) refrain
   (B) prevent
   (C) oppose
   (D) escape

1 **meet** 충족시키다
need / requirement / expectation
수요를 / 요구 사항을 / 기대를

2 **implement** 시행하다, 실시하다
policy / change / program
정책을 / 변화를 / 제도를

3 **conduct** 실시하다
study / survey / interview
연구를 / 설문 조사를 / 인터뷰를

4 **fulfill** 이행하다, 처리하다
duty / obligation / order
책임을 / 의무를 / 주문을

5 **perform** 수행하다
task / duty / role
업무를 / 임무를 / 역할을

6 **address** 다루다
complaint / issue / concern
불평을 / 문제를 / 걱정을

7 **observe** 따르다, 준수하다
policy / regulation / instruction
정책을 / 규칙을 / 지시 사항을

8 **deliver** 전달하다 [발표하다]
speech / presentation / talk
연설을 / 발표를 / 담화를

9 **assume** 떠맡다
title, position / responsibility
직책을 / 책임을

10 **undertake** 떠맡다
task / project
업무를 / 프로젝트를

11 **renew** 갱신하다
contract / membership / subscription
계약을 / 멤버십을 / 구독을

12 **evaluate** 평가하다
task / progress / performance
업무를 / 진행 상황을 / (업무) 수행을

13 **issue** 발행하다, 지급하다
permit / coupon / refund
허가증을 / 쿠폰을 / 환불을

14 **take** 취하다
action, measure / precaution
조치를 / 예방 조치를

15 **impose** 부과하다
tax / fine
세금을 / 벌금을

16 **determine** 알아내다, 밝히다
cause / feasibility / whether
원인을 / 실행 가능성을 / ~인지 아닌지를

17 **gain** 얻다
access / reputation / recognition
이용(권)을 / 명성을 / 인지도를

18 **simplify** 간소화하다
process / procedure / design
과정을 / 절차를 / 디자인을

19 **extend** 연장하다, 베풀다
deadline / membership / gratitude
마감 기한을 / 멤버십을 / 감사를

20 **express** 표하다
appreciation / interest / concern
감사를 / 관심을 / 걱정을

1. Zoani Apparel ------- coupons to first-time customers whose purchases are over $50.
   (A) allows
   (B) exchanges
   (C) receives
   (D) issues

2. With her latest promotion, Ms. Lynch will ------- the position of Chief Marketing Officer.
   (A) react
   (B) assume
   (C) decrease
   (D) arrive

3. The town hall meetings provide a forum in which residents can ------- concerns about various issues.
   (A) comment
   (B) express
   (C) speak
   (D) remark

4. Small business owners must ------- whether to lease or purchase office equipment for their enterprises.
   (A) hesitate
   (B) determine
   (C) stimulate
   (D) repair

5. Some of our customers have indicated that placing orders online is complex, so we should ------- the process.
   (A) consist
   (B) dispose
   (C) simplify
   (D) interview

6. In his talk, Mr. Mooney plans to ------- the issue of motivating teams in the workplace.
   (A) address
   (B) enroll
   (C) speculate
   (D) insist

7. Rosen National University will ------- a new recycling program thanks to a $10,000 grant from the local government.
   (A) reduce
   (B) implement
   (C) transport
   (D) succeed

8. Visitors should note that the city ------- a fine for littering in any public park.
   (A) imposes
   (B) resources
   (C) intervenes
   (D) confronts

9. Mr. Singh, the festival's organizer, would like to ------- his gratitude to the volunteers who helped out during the event.
   (A) extend
   (B) notify
   (C) comply
   (D) specialize

10. Your antivirus software subscription will be ------- automatically until we receive notice of your wish to cancel the service.
    (A) signed
    (B) renewed
    (C) suspended
    (D) corrected

빈출 Collocation / 동사 + 부사

1 **affect** 영향을 미치다
adversely / negatively / favorably
불리하게 / 부정적으로 / 유리하게

11 **closely** 밀접하게, 면밀히
work / review / examine
일하다 / 검토하다 / 심심하다

2 **divide** 분배하다, 나누다
equally / evenly
똑같이 / 균등하게

12 **thoroughly** 철저하게, 빠짐없이
review / inspect / examine
검토하다 / 검수하다 / 점검하다

3 **state** 언급하다
clearly / expressly / explicitly
분명히 / 명확히 / 명백하게

13 **strongly** 강력하게
encourage / recommend
권장하다 / 추천하다

4 **contribute** 기여하다
substantially / generously / financially
상당히 / 아낌없이 / 금전적으로

14 **evenly** 고르게, 균일하게
divide, distribute / apply
분배하다 / (뭉치지 않게) 바르다

5 **apologize** 사과하다
deeply / sincerely
깊이 / 진심으로

15 **accordingly** 그에 따라, 그에 알맞게
adjust / update / plan
조절하다 / 업데이트하다 / 계획하다

6 **appreciate** 감사하다
deeply / greatly / truly
깊이 / 대단히 / 진심으로

16 **smoothly** 순조롭게
go / proceed / progress
진행되다

7 **work** 일하다
closely / collaboratively
밀접하게 / 협력하여

17 **properly** 제대로
work / function
작동하다

8 **increase / decrease** 증가하다 / 감소하다
dramatically / substantially / steadily
엄청나게 / 상당히 / 꾸준히

18 **slightly** 약간
vary, differ / 비교급
다르다 / 더 ~하다

9 **respond** 응답하다, 대응하다
promptly / quickly
신속하게 / 빠르게

19 **generously** 아낌없이
donate / offer / contribute
기부하다 / 제공하다 / 기여하다

10 **arrive** 도착하다
punctually / promptly
시간을 엄수하여 / 신속하게

20 **regularly / routinely** 정기적으로
check / monitor
확인하다 / 감시하다

1. We will ------- review all of the service proposals before determining which is most suitable for our needs.

   (A) durably
   (B) closely
   (C) recently
   (D) respectfully

2. Most of what we included on the agenda was examined ------- at the last week's meeting.

   (A) relatively
   (B) thoroughly
   (C) exceedingly
   (D) rather

3. When eaten cold, pea soup has a ------- thicker texture and milder taste.

   (A) exclusively
   (B) carefully
   (C) slightly
   (D) deliberately

4. In the interest of fairness, supervisors should ensure that tasks are ------- distributed among team members.

   (A) firmly
   (B) noticeably
   (C) evenly
   (D) apparently

5. Traffic in the downtown area will be heavy during the parade, so drivers should plan -------.

   (A) similarly
   (B) accordingly
   (C) eventually
   (D) constantly

6. The musical's director announced she would ------- offer to host a question-and-answer session after Friday's performance.

   (A) overly
   (B) partially
   (C) correctly
   (D) generously

7. Interns will have the opportunity to work ------- with our product developers at every stage of the design process.

   (A) hardly
   (B) collaboratively
   (C) extremely
   (D) previously

8. Our workshop starts at 10:30 A.M., and participants are expected to arrive -------.

   (A) confidently
   (B) alongside
   (C) punctually
   (D) extensively

9. The delivery company will raise its shipping rates because fuel costs continue to increase -------.

   (A) restrictedly
   (B) substantially
   (C) largely
   (D) mainly

10. The company's exchange policies state ------- that customized products may not be returned for a refund.

    (A) either
    (B) neither
    (C) expressly
    (D) scarcely

1 fully operational 풀가동하는

The system is fully operational.

시스템이 풀가동하고 있다.

2 readily available 쉽게 이용 가능한

Details are readily available on the Web site.

자세한 사항은 웹사이트에서 쉽게 이용 가능합니다.

3 highly regarded 높이 평가되는

Mr. Redding is highly regarded by peers.

레딩 씨는 동료들에 의해 높이 평가된다.

4 mutually beneficial 상호 이익이 되는

Two firms reached a mutually beneficial deal.

두 회사가 상호 이익이 되는 거래를 성사시켰다.

5 conveniently located 편리하게 위치한

The conference venue is conveniently located.

그 회의 장소는 편리하게 위치해 있다.

6 rigorous inspection 엄격한 검사

All items will undergo rigorous inspection.

모든 상품은 엄격한 검사를 거칠 것이다.

7 reasonably priced 합리적 가격의

We provide reasonably priced beverages.

우리는 합리적 가격의 음료를 제공한다.

8 environmentally friendly 친환경적인

We only sell environmentally friendly products.

우리는 친환경 제품만 판매한다.

9 strictly confidential 절대 기밀인

Patient records are kept strictly confidential.

환자 기록은 엄격하게 기밀 상태로 유지된다.

10 consistently high 꾸준히 높은

The figures have been consistently high.

수치는 꾸준히 높았다.

11 widely known 널리 알려진

James Lee is widely known in the industry.

제임스 리는 업계에서 널리 알려져 있다.

12 immediately after 직후에

Sales rose immediately after the merger.

판매는 합병 직후에 상승했다.

13 critically acclaimed 비평가의 극찬을 받은

Mr. Wilson directed the critically acclaimed film.

윌슨 씨는 비평가의 극찬을 받은 영화를 감독했다.

14 routine maintenance 정기 점검

We are closed for routine maintenance.

정기 점검으로 인해 문을 닫습니다.

15 primarily due to 주로 ~ 때문에

The delay was primarily due to design flaws.

지연은 주로 디자인 결함 때문이었다.

16 randomly chosen 무작위로 선정된

The respondents were randomly chosen.

응답자는 무작위로 선정되었다.

17 welcome addition 환영받는 추가물[사람]

Ms. Lee is a welcome addition to our team.

이 씨는 우리의 팀의 환영받는 추가 인력이다.

18 not necessarily 반드시 ~은 아닌

Leaders are not necessarily managers.

리더가 반드시 관리자인 것은 아니다.

19 unless otherwise 달리 ~하지 않는다면

Unless otherwise stated, delivery is free.

별도로 언급이 없다면, 배송은 무료이다.

20 tentatively scheduled 잠정 예정된

The meeting is tentatively scheduled for noon.

회의는 정오로 잠정 예정되어 있다.

1. All of the summer interns have been working hard, so they are a ------- addition to our staff.
   (A) close
   (B) welcome
   (C) mutual
   (D) fascinated

2. The managers meeting is ------- scheduled for May 7, subject to further confirmation.
   (A) gradually
   (B) impressively
   (C) unknowingly
   (D) tentatively

3. Alpha Movers has earned positive customer reviews for its ------- high quality service.
   (A) potentially
   (B) consistently
   (C) eventually
   (D) adversely

4. The Home Basics package is Zoom Telecom's most ------- priced cable TV and Internet package.
   (A) readily
   (B) similarly
   (C) reasonably
   (D) barely

5. The lower attendance at last fall's music festival was ------- due to the rainy weather.
   (A) severely
   (B) primarily
   (C) highly
   (D) popularly

6. All of the used vehicles we sell must first pass a ------- inspection by a trained mechanic.
   (A) wealthy
   (B) polite
   (C) luxurious
   (D) rigorous

7. Most of the stock in our warehouse is ------- accessible and does not require the use of a ladder to reach.
   (A) voluntarily
   (B) loosely
   (C) readily
   (D) loudly

8. Tina Calo is a ------- regarded educator who has written award winning children's books.
   (A) profitably
   (B) densely
   (C) closely
   (D) highly

9. Snacks and refreshments will be served ------- after the afternoon seminar.
   (A) historically
   (B) presently
   (C) mannerly
   (D) immediately

10. Unless ------- instructed, please submit your employment application to the Human Resources Department.
    (A) else
    (B) diversely
    (C) moreover
    (D) otherwise

1. A recent survey showed that residents of the Valley Hills region show a strong ------- in outdoor recreational activities.

   (A) interest
   (B) interested
   (C) interesting
   (D) interestingly

2. At Lala Catering, we can tailor our menu offerings to ------- the needs of any group.

   (A) share
   (B) meet
   (C) remark
   (D) persist

3. The beauty of the redeveloped downtown area ------- many visitors to Greenberg City.

   (A) to surprise
   (B) surprising
   (C) surprisingly
   (D) surprises

4. According to research, most wealthy people ------- their success to education.

   (A) enter
   (B) describe
   (C) commute
   (D) attribute

5. ------- of use is said to be the most important factor in choosing a new software program.

   (A) Easy
   (B) Ease
   (C) Easily
   (D) Easier

6. Ms. Chiu ------- a detailed explanation of our new sales campaign to the board members.

   (A) engaged
   (B) presented
   (C) retreated
   (D) indicated

7. Mr. Loren will pack all of the product samples before we ------- for the trade show in Miami.

   (A) departing
   (B) departed
   (C) depart
   (D) will depart

8. Manteca Equipment Co.'s new line of backpacks, sold ------- at our physical stores, all feature side pockets for water bottles.

   (A) exclusive
   (B) exclusively
   (C) exclusivity
   (D) excluding

9. The hiring process for technical workers at IOS Systems is a ------- one, so applicants need to be patient.

   (A) durable
   (B) personal
   (C) portable
   (D) lengthy

10. A farewell gathering will be held at the company's cafeteria to ------- Mr. Gordon's ten years of service.

    (A) recognize
    (B) notice
    (C) determine
    (D) authorize

11. The Drayden Tourist Hotel can ------- easily from Central Highway.
    (A) reach
    (B) reached
    (C) reaching
    (D) be reached

12. Some of the services ------- are proud to offer include engine repair, brake repair, and windshield replacement.
    (A) ourselves
    (B) ours
    (C) we
    (D) us

13. The Big mart Pro app for mobile phones allows customers to check product ------- online and avoid unnecessary trips to the stores.
    (A) availably
    (B) available
    (C) availability
    (D) avails

14. Istase Motors plans to ------- its new electric car at the City Auto Show.
    (A) grant
    (B) occur
    (C) unveil
    (D) rely

15. Having a clear ------- for your team will help employees know what they are expected to achieve.
    (A) amount
    (B) appearance
    (C) objective
    (D) expense

16. This week's in-house seminar ------- advice on how to become a more decisive manager.
    (A) has been offered
    (B) offer
    (C) will offer
    (D) offering

17. We should ------- one associate to answer incoming calls when our receptionist is on vacation.
    (A) compare
    (B) merge
    (C) designate
    (D) perform

18. In the new film *Adventures in Alaska*, Todd Reaves gives a ------- performance in the lead role.
    (A) commending
    (B) commendable
    (C) commendation
    (D) commends

19. To ensure that we meet the food needs of future generations, our goal should be ------- sustainable agriculture.
    (A) to promote
    (B) promoted
    (C) promote
    (D) promotion

20. Some consumers are ------- to shop during holiday periods because they are concerned about large crowds.
    (A) exclusive
    (B) steady
    (C) reluctant
    (D) discreet

21. This month's edition of *Marketing Forum Magazine* shows ------- inventive advertisements that won industry awards.

(A) each
(B) either
(C) several
(D) another

22. Thanks to a ------- donation by a local business, the Town Children's Museum can add new interactive exhibits.

(A) profitable
(B) various
(C) resistant
(D) generous

23. The sales speech was delivered ------- by our marketing manager, Mr. Corbett.

(A) persuasive
(B) persuasively
(C) persuaded
(D) persuades

24. Members of the sales team will take a short break this afternoon ------ their computers can be updated.

(A) whereas
(B) even so
(C) so that
(D) nevertheless

25. ------- numbers of runners have signed up for the city's half marathon and marathon races.

(A) Direct
(B) Impending
(C) Impressed
(D) Unprecedented

26. The original *Games of Magic* was a ------- successful film, yet its remake enjoyed record earnings.

(A) simultaneously
(B) moderately
(C) fluently
(D) equally

27. To encourage additional customer spending, many stores have promotional merchandise ------- placed near the check-out lines.

(A) strategy
(B) strategized
(C) strategically
(D) strategic

28. To complete the merger deal, officials from both companies must negotiate to reach a ------- beneficial agreement.

(A) coincidentally
(B) mutually
(C) shortly
(D) vastly

29. As there is much to see in Ridge Valley National Park, allow ------- two or three days to explore the entire area.

(A) you
(B) your
(C) of yours
(D) yourself

30. A skilled salesperson can ------- prospective buyers' interest in a company's products or services.

(A) relocate
(B) stimulate
(C) attach
(D) involve

31. The business plan only gave a general idea, without addressing any -------.

(A) attachments
(B) particulars
(C) dimensions
(D) individuals

32. Delton Ltd. has developed an industrial robot ------- can learn new tasks without programming.

(A) it
(B) what
(C) which
(D) whose

33. Experts strongly recommend ------- office employees who work at desk-based jobs take short breaks every hour.

(A) which
(B) whenever
(C) what
(D) that

34. The orientation session for the interns will ------- with a welcoming speech by the company's founder.

(A) enter
(B) introduce
(C) commence
(D) undertake

35. All workers on the factory floor must ------- caution when using the machinery.

(A) interact
(B) exercise
(C) assist
(D) focus

36. Surveys show that online shopping is ------- becoming popular with consumers of all ages.

(A) increasingly
(B) necessarily
(C) thoughtfully
(D) approximately

37. The Moriana Heights Sports Center is now closed ------- it is being renovated.

(A) due to
(B) once
(C) since
(D) until

38. ------- flexible work schedules is a simple way of increasing employee retention in any department.

(A) Offer
(B) Offering
(C) Being offered
(D) Offered

39. Once you have arrived at Wilshire Airport, proceed ------- to the Swift Rental desk to obtain the keys to your vehicle.

(A) regularly
(B) directly
(C) closely
(D) firmly

40. Despite higher than expected costs, we will ------- with the construction project as planned.

(A) carry
(B) interrupt
(C) proceed
(D) depend

● PART 6 풀이 전략

PART 6 이렇게 나온다

Part 6는 총 4세트 출제된다. 한 세트는 4문제로 구성되어 있으며 어휘 2문제, 문법 1문제, 문장 고르기 1문제로 구성되기나 이휘의 문법 문항 수기 시로 비밀 수 있다. Part 6는 Part 5와는 달리 한 문장 인에시 칭립의 근거를 찾지 못하는 경우가 많다. 따라서 빈칸 바로 앞뒤만 보고 해당 문장 내에서만 정답을 구하려고 하면 오답을 선택할 확률이 크다. 크게는 전체 주제를, 작게는 문장 앞뒤 유기적 관계를 파악하며 읽는 것이 Part 6의 핵심임을 기억하자.

Questions 1-4 refer to the following information.   번역 p. 185

Wall-Dale Mart Co. delivery policies

Most of the time, your items ------- within one to five business days. -------, for larger items,
        1.   **2.**
we will e-mail you to confirm the day and time of delivery. If the date is inconvenient for
you, you may ask for a ------- of your shipment by calling our Customer Service.
                   3.
All deliveries require the signature of an adult recipient. -------. We will not leave unsigned
                                          4.
packages outside your door. Note that you should not sign the delivery receipt until you
have inspected the item for damage. Please ensure that you check the item while the
delivery person is still at your home.

---

1. 문법 문제
   (A) will have arrived
   (B) would have arrived
   (C) have arrived
   (D) will arrive

2. 접속부사 문제
   (A) For example
   (B) However
   (C) Therefore
   (D) Otherwise

3. 어휘 문제
   (A) recall
   (B) relocation
   (C) reschedule
   (D) receipt

4. 문장 고르기 문제
   (A) We would like to apologize for the delay in shipping your products.
   (B) Children should use this product only under adult supervision.
   (C) Someone should be available to accept your delivery.
   (D) We use recycled products in all of our packaging.

PART 6 이렇게 푼다

❶ 문법 문제　문제 종류와 상관없이 항상 지문 처음부터 읽기

> 월데일 마트 배송 규정
> 보통의 경우 고객님의 상품은 영업일 1일에서 5일 이내에 [도착했습니다 / **도착할 것입니다**].

❥ Part 6의 시제 문제는 Part 5와는 달리, 시제의 단서가 해당 문장 내에 존재하지 않을 수 있다. 이때 글의 종류 및 주제, 앞뒤 문맥이 시제를 결정한다. 이 글은 배송 정책을 알리는 정보성을 띠며 문제에 해당하는 문장의 바로 다음 문장에서 회사 방침을 미래 시제로 설명하고 있으므로 문맥상 미래 시제인 (D) will arrive가 정답이 된다.

❷ 접속부사 문제　문장 앞뒤 관계 파악하기

> ① **보통의 경우** 상품은 영업일 1일에서 5일 이내로 도착할 것입니다. [예컨대 / **하지만** / 따라서 / 그렇지 않으면],
> ② **부피가 큰 물품의 경우** 고객님께 이메일을 드려 배송 날짜와 시간을 확인합니다.

❥ 보통의 경우와 특수한 경우의 차이점을 구분해서 설명하고 있으므로 역접의 접속부사가 필요하다.
　보통의 경우: 5일 이내 도착 (B) However, 특수한 경우: 배송 날짜 이메일 발송

❸ 어휘 문제　주변 단어 활용하기

> 만약 **해당 날짜**가 맞지 않으실 경우 고객 서비스 센터로 연락하셔서 [회수를 / 재배치를 / **일정 변경을** / 영수증을] 요청하실 수 있습니다.

❥ 앞에서 배송 요일(the day), 시간(the time of delivery), 날짜 (the date)를 언급하고 있으므로 주제에 맞는 어휘는 일정 변경 (C) reschedule이다.

❹ 문장 고르기 문제　빈칸 앞뒤로 읽고 주제에 초점 맞추기 + 오답 소거하기

> ① 모든 **배송에는** 성인인 **수령인의 서명**이 필요합니다. **[빈칸]** ② **서명**되지 않은 물품은 문 밖에 두지 않습니다.

❥ 빈칸 앞뒤 문장의 주제는 서명이다.

　(C) Someone should be available to accept your delivery.
　　　배송을 수령할 수 있는 분이 반드시 계셔야 합니다.

　❥ (서명을 위해) 수령인이 필요함을 언급하므로 정답이다.
　　　나머지 오답 보기들은 배송, 서명, 수령인이라는 키워드에 맞지 않는 문장이므로 소거한다

접속부사는 문장과 문장을 논리적으로 연결하는 부사이다. 해석을 통해 논리적 관계에 따라 역접, 인과, 첨가, 대조 등 알맞은 접속부사를 선택해야 한다.

핵심 포인트 ## 빈칸 앞뒤를 꼼꼼하게 해석하여 상관 관계를 파악하자

번역 p. 185

How to Prepare International Parcels

❶ Rules for shipping parcels internationally differ from country to country. -------, ❷ it is important for customers to prepare their parcels according to the rules. No writing should appear on the outside of the parcel other than the name and address. Having additional writing could slow down the delivery process.

(A) Nevertheless   그럼에도 불구하고
(B) Therefore   **따라서**
(C) In contrast   이와 대조적으로
(D) Even so   그렇다고 해도

제목: 국제 우편물을 준비하는 방법
❶ 국제 배송 규칙은 국가마다 다르다.
따라서
❷ 고객이 본인의 소포를 규칙에 맞게 준비하는 것이 중요하다.

접속부사 therefore는 인과 관계를 나타낼 때 쓰는 연결어이다. 국제 배송 규칙이 국가마다 각각 다르기 때문에 규칙에 맞추어야 한다는 인과 관계로 연결하는 것이 자연스럽다.

정답률을 높이는 학습 노트

1. 빈출 접속부사

however 그러나	nevertheless 그럼에도 불구하고	still 그럼에도 불구하고	therefore 따라서
thus 그러므로	consequently 결과적으로	as a result 그 결과	likewise 마찬가지로
in addition 게다가	furthermore 게다가	moreover 게다가	alternatively 또는
in fact 사실	in contrast 이와 대조적으로	on the other hand 반면에	instead 대신
in particular 특히	otherwise 그렇지 않으면	for instance 예를 들어	meanwhile 한편

2. 접속부사 vs. 접속사 및 전치사

접속부사가 들어갈 자리에는 접속사나 전치사가 들어갈 수 없다.

There was a setback. [**However** / ~~Although~~ / ~~Despite~~], we proceeded with the plan.

차질이 있었다. **그러나** 우리는 계획을 진행했다.

❯ 접속부사는 두 문장을 직접 연결하지는 못하므로 앞 문장에 마침표를 찍고 두 문장으로 나누어 쓴다.

cf. **전치사의 쓰임** Despite a setback, we proceeded with the plan.

    접속사의 쓰임 Although there was a setback, we proceeded with the plan.

READING PRACTICE

정답 및 해설 p. 185

1.

Thank you for your purchase of a Matlock cast-iron frying pan. Cleaning and caring for the pan properly after every use will ensure its performance. To clean, first remove any oil or left-behind food by wiping the interior with a paper towel. Next, rinse the pan under hot water. Then dry the pan completely by using a paper towel. ------, dry the pan by placing it over medium heat on the stove top. Finally, coat the pan's surface with a half teaspoon of oil to prepare it for the next use.

(A) If so   (B) Alternatively   (C) Thus   (D) Consequently

2.

Gold Scientific Supply, a leading manufacturer of scientific instruments, is proud to announce that its VS-7 View model of microscope won the Best Design Award at the International Digital Microscope Trade Show (IDMTS). The award recognizes original design elements and ease of use. -------, the VS-7 View was praised for its stability under challenging operating conditions. For more information on the VS-7 View, go to www.ende-mark.com.

(A) In particular   (B) Still   (C) Even so   (D) Instead

3.

Starting on July 1, Dream Office Products will be located in the Greenview Shopping Plaza at 160 Maple Street. With more floor space and a larger parking area, this new facility will offer customers a wider selection of goods and more shopping convenience. To celebrate this expansion, we will hold a clearance sale at our old location during the week of June 21. Take up to 40% off specially marked items! -------, we will have another sale on the weekend of July 3 to promote our grand opening on Maple Street. We hope to see you soon!

(A) Nevertheless   (B) Specifically   (C) Moreover   (D) In addition to

어휘 문제

16문제 중 6~8문제 출제

Part 6의 어휘 문제를 풀기 위해서는 전체 글을 읽고 내용의 흐름을 파악해야 하며 특히 빈칸 주변에 놓인 힌트를 정답의 근거로 활용하는 것이 중요하다.

핵심 포인트 **앞뒤 주변 단어를 활용하자.**

번역 p. 186

Thank you for purchasing a KG Electronics power drill. **❶** The product is guaranteed to be free of defects from one year of purchase, provided that it is used according to instructions. **❷** This limited ------- does not cover damage caused by improper use or maintenance. A product found to be defective under these conditions may be sent to a service center for repair or replacement.

(A) discount 할인
(B) training 교육
(C) warranty **보증**
(D) profession 직업

❶ 이 제품은 구매 후 1년간 결함이 생기지 않음을 보장합니다.

❷ 이러한 제한적 **보증**은 소비자 과실에 대해서는 보상하지 않습니다.

품질 보증 기간이 1년이라고 하였으므로 뒤따르는 문장의 limited에 해당하는 것은 1년으로 제한된 '보증'을 뜻한다. 빈칸 뒤 동사가 cover(보상하다)인 것도 주어를 결정하는 힌트가 된다.

정답률을 높이는 학습 노트

> 1. 때로는 힌트가 멀리 떨어져 있다.
>
> > 저희 호텔에 [예약해 / 관심 가져] 주셔서 감사합니다. 저희 호텔은 각 방 사우나실을 갖추고 있으며…
> > – 호텔 소개 중략 –
> > 만약 지금 예약하시면 10퍼센트 할인권을 제공해 드리겠습니다.
>
> ❯ 근거가 마지막 부분에 있을 수 있으니 성급하게 답을 고르지 않도록 하자.
>
> 2. 주제와 연결되기도 한다.
>
> > 대중교통 사고가 늘고 있다. 정부는 이에 대한 조치로 대중교통 법규 위반 차량에 대한 벌금을 인상하기로 했다. 시민들은 정부의 이러한 [노력 / 자원]에 박수를 보내고 있다.
>
> ❯ 주제: 대중교통 사고 감소를 위한 정부의 대책 방안 마련 → 정부의 노력

READING PRACTICE

정답 및 해설 p. 186

1.

The Port of Delvin Shores is proud to announce a major expansion. The port's owner, the Delvin Shores Port Corporation (DSPC) recently purchased an adjacent block of vacant land. The site had previously been used for the Lawndale Mills factory, which was demolished last year. "To meet strong growth in the shipping industry, we must ------- our port facility," said Jeff Lee, chairman of the DSPC. A timeline for developing the land is being discussed by DSPC planners.

(A) relocate   (B) sell   (C) enlarge   (D) lend

2.

A recent study on landfills revealed that recyclable materials account for approximately seventy percent of waste. However, our community is only recycling about 30% of household trash. We would like to increase this ------- to get it in line with the national average for recycling, which is 40%. To assist residents with this goal, we will increase curbside pickup of recyclable goods to once a week from October 1. You can view a list of recycling regulations on the city's Web site.

(A) aim   (B) promise   (C) change   (D) figure

3.

On behalf of Castillo Bank, I would like to thank you for being a loyal customer for the past year. This is to inform you that you have qualified for Silver Rewards status. You are now eligible to earn 1 reward point for every dollar spent on qualifying purchases on your Castillo Bank credit card. Your status will be upgraded automatically, so no further action is required on your part. Check how much you've earned at any time by logging on to your online account. The ------- will appear on the main page.

(A) balance   (B) schedule   (C) invoice   (D) charge

시제 문제

Part 6의 시제 문제는 Part 5와 풀이법이 다르다. Part 5에서는 시제의 단서가 되는 시간 부사(구/절)가 문장 내에 존재하는 반면에 Part 6의 시제 문제는 해당 문장 내에 단서가 없는 것이 보통이다. 따라서 주변 문장에 쓰인 시제와 전체 문맥을 통해 정답을 고르는 것이 필요하다.

핵심 포인트 **날짜, 글의 종류, 앞뒤 문맥이 시제를 결정한다.** 번역 p. 187

REDWOOD HEIGHTS ❶ (April 7) – Van Croft Gallery, the largest gallery in the southwest region, ------- amateur artists with a platform to showcase their work. ❷ From May 1 to May 14, the gallery will hold an exhibition that openly accepts work from artists at any level. The pieces will be on display for public viewing during the gallery's regular hours of operation.

(A) would have provided   제공했을 텐데
(B) was providing   제공하고 있었다
(C) is to provide   **제공할 예정이다**
(D) has provided   제공해 왔다

4월 7일자 기사

❶ 반 크로프트 미술관이 아마추어 화가들에게 자신의 작품을 선보일 수 있는 발판을 **제공할 예정이다.**

❷ 5월 1일부터 5월 14일까지 이 미술관이 전시회를 개최할 것이다.

기사가 발행된 날짜는 4월 7일이며 주변 문장에 미래 시점(5월 1일 ~ 5월 14일)과 미래 시제(will hold)가 나오므로 빈칸에 어울리는 시제는 미래 시제이다. 「be + to」는 '예정'을 나타낼 수 있다.

정답률을 높이는 학습 노트

1. 시제의 쓰임새를 똑바로 알자.

한 가지 시제가 한 가지 역할만 할 수 있는 것은 아니다.

현재완료 have p.p.	❶ ~했다 (완료된 상황) → have shipped 이미 발송했다
	❷ ~해왔다 (현재까지 계속되는 상황) → have contributed 지금껏 기여해 왔다
현재진행 be -ing	❶ ~하고 있는 중이다 (현재 상황) → is being formed 만들어지고 있는 중이다
	❷ ~할 것이다 (정해진 미래) → is opening 곧 열 것이다

2. 유의해야 할 시제

Part 6에서 오답으로 자주 등장하는 시제가 있다.

would have p.p. 가정법에서 나오는 시제이므로 가정법 공식 적용이 안 될 시 소거하자.

will have p.p. 미래 시제를 써야 할 때 will만 보고 미래 시제와 동일하다고 착각해서는 안 된다.

※ 현재진행(be -ing), 미래진행(will be -ing), be to 용법(~할 예정이다)은 미래를 나타낼 수 있다.

❯ The museum <u>is hosting</u> a special exhibition on May 21. 박물관이 5월 21일에 특별 전시회를 개최할 것이다.
We <u>will be expanding</u> our delivery service. 우리는 배송 서비스를 확대할 것이다.
Access codes <u>are to be used</u> for security reasons. 접속 비밀번호가 보안상의 이유로 사용될 것이다.

READING PRACTICE

정답 및 해설 p. 187

1.

Business professionals know it is stressful to work on a tight deadline, and losing files due to equipment malfunctions or forgetting to save the word only makes the situation worse. Garnet Cloud Storage is the solution you need! Our system uses the latest technology to guarantee your information's security, and you no longer have to worry about data backup, as the process is automatic. In the default setting, open files are saved to our server every fifteen minutes. This period ------- to suit your needs. Visit www.garnet.com today to sign up for a free trial.

(A) was adjusted   (B) can be adjusted   (C) has been adjusted   (D) is being adjusted

2.

We always strive to improve our communication with our country club members, and we are pleased to announce the launch of a brand new newsletter that will be distributed through e-mail. Like some other members, you ------- an e-mail address. You can rectify this by updating your personal records on our Web site's Members' Portal, or by visiting our administration office in person. One of the clerical assistants will be able to assist you.

(A) have not provided   (B) may not provide   (C) will not provide   (D) cannot provide

3.

Flores Avenue will be closed to traffic for approximately five days for a repaving project. Meanwhile, residents living on that street will have to find alternative parking. "I wish the city had planned to do this project in sections instead of in one piece," said neighborhood resident Jackie Ford. "People ------- from several blocks away." Regina Croft, a Transit Authority representative said they will do their best to limit disruptions. "As soon as everything is completed, I think that residents will appreciate the smooth road surface."

(A) had to walk   (B) used to walk   (C) will have to walk   (D) was walking

문장 고르기 문제

Part 6의 문장 고르기 문제는 논리적인 흐름에 맞는 문장을 선택하는 문제로, 주제를 먼저 파악하고 보기에서 오답 요소들을 하나씩 소거하여 정답을 골라내는 방법으로 접근한다.

핵심 포인트 **주제문과 연결되는지 파악하자.**   번역 p. 187

Don't miss the 27th annual Milton City Art Fair. More than 200 local artists are expected to participate and they will sell their art directly to fair attendees. Booth space for exhibiting artists is still available — visit www.fair.org for more information. ❶ Please note that all art works must be original pieces designed and created by the actual artists. ❷ -------.

(A) Enrollment in the class is limited, so please register soon.
(B) Some of these booths will be staffed by festival volunteers.
(C) The display and sale of art reproductions is not allowed.
(D) His sculptures were also widely praised by art critics.

(A) 수업 등록자 수가 제한되어 있으므로 서둘러 등록하세요.
(B) 이 부스들 중 일부는 축제 자원봉사자들이 업무를 담당할 것입니다.
(C) 복제품의 전시나 판매는 허용되지 않습니다.
(D) 그의 조각품들은 미술 비평가들에 의해서도 널리 호평을 받습니다.

❶ 모든 작품은 반드시 실제 화가에 의해 디자인되고 만들어진 **원본 작품**이어야 합니다.

> **주제: 원본 작품**

❷ (C) 복제품의 전시나 판매는 허용되지 않습니다.

(A)는 수업 등록 제한에 관한 글이다.
(B)는 부스 담당자에 관한 글이다.
(C)는 복제품 금지에 관한 글이다.
(D)는 조각품에 대한 호평에 관한 글이다.

반드시 original pieces(원본 작품)이어야 함을 강조하며 reproduction (복제품)을 불허하는 내용이므로 주제문과 연결된다.

정답률을 높이는 학습 노트

1. 정관사, 대명사, 지시어, 부사의 활용

❶ Consumer interest is higher in <u>those</u> areas. 소비자 관심은 <u>그런</u> 지역에서 더 높다. ❶ **지시어**
❷ <u>The</u> technology is often used in building construction. <u>그</u> 기술은 건축에 자주 사용된다. ❷ **정관사**
❸ <u>Her</u> latest model is being tested. <u>그녀의</u> 최신 모델은 테스트되고 있다. ❸ **대명사**
❹ An original receipt may <u>also</u> be required. 원본 영수증 <u>또한</u> 요구된다. ❹ **부사 (첨가)**

▶ 지시어, 정관사, 대명사, also 등은 앞 문장에 관련 표현이 없을 시 오지 못하므로 앞 문장과의 연관성이 없는 경우 오답 처리, 연관성이 있는 경우 정답 처리할 수 있게 하는 핵심적 역할을 한다.

2. 빈칸의 위치에 유의하기
언뜻 주제와 개연성이 있는 듯 보이지만 위치상으로는 맞지 않는 문장에 유의하자.

> 공연 취소에 따른 환불금이 지급될 것입니다. -------. 환불 완료는 영업일 5~7일 정도 소요됩니다.

(A) 이해해 주셔서 감사합니다. vs. (B) 환불 처리가 현재 진행 중에 있습니다.
▶ (A) 문장은 맨 마지막에 위치해야 하므로 오답, (B)는 주제, 위치 모두 맞으므로 정답이다.

READING PRACTICE

정답 및 해설 p. 188

1.

Local author Ken Spina will give a talk this Saturday, April 23, at 2:00 P.M. at the Selby City's Public Library. He will read from his newly-published novel, *Sunshine Memories*, and talk about the challenges he faced while writing it. -------. Attendees will "no doubt" want to learn more about Mr. Spina's creative process, Posen said.

(A) These signed books will be offered to some of the participants.
(B) He plans to take these writing courses as soon as he can.
(C) Many newer books are also printed on recycled paper products.
(D) He will, of course, allow audience members to ask questions.

2.

The Prescott Music Festival is an annual event held in Prescott that attracts musical groups from across the country. The numerous positive reviews for the festival year after year show that the event planners always choose the bands well, and this year will be no exception. -------. Consequently, there is sure to be something for everyone. A few slots for bands are still available. Please e-mail director@prescottmusic.org to show your interest in giving a performance.

(A) You can purchase tickets in advance or at the entrance.
(B) The genres represented include jazz, pop, and folk music.
(C) The final list of bands has been posted on the event's Web site.
(D) Cancellations may take place if the weather is bad.

3.

On occasion, the furniture we display on our showroom floor is made available for purchase at reduced prices. These items are in no way damaged or defective. However, all sales of floor items are final. We will not accept any returns or refund requests on this furniture. -------. Customers are required to load and transport these items on their own.

(A) We regret that we cannot offer delivery service on floor items.
(B) We offer generous discounts on these floor models to encourage fast sales.
(C) In addition, our staff will pick up floor items for recycling.
(D) We are proud to offer consulting services on interior design.

About our shuttle services

Airhubs-Express Co. offers an affordable way to travel from the region's international airport to the downtown area and back again. We always tell riders the exact fare before they request a ride. This removes any uncertainty from the process and ensures there are no surprises. What's more, our high level of customer service **4. [distinguishes / transforms]** us from other shuttle companies. Visit our "testimonials" page to read about customers' positive experiences with our Airhubs-Express Co. -------. We look forward to
5.
serving your transportation needs.

---

5. (A) To apply for this position, submit a résumé.
   (B) Then book your next shuttle ride with us.
   (C) Note that some flights may be canceled.
   (D) Please remove your valuables from the car.

Announcement for customers

At Penny Lane Bookstore, we are continuously looking for new ways to provide the best service to our customers. For instance, we are planning to launch a new mobile phone application that will keep our customers informed about store promotions and sales as well as special in-store appearances by well-known authors. -------. Once you have chosen a
6.
user name and password, you will have full access to all of the **7. [features / models]** of the application. If you have any questions, you can visit the FAQ section included in the app.

---

6. (A) We value our customers' opinions and your feedback is greatly appreciated.
   (B) You can do this by leaving a review on one of the app stores.
   (C) This can be downloaded free of charge from the usual sources.
   (D) We have redesigned our Web site to make it easier to navigate.

NOTICE TO RIDGEMOOR EMPLOYEES

From September 1, after-hours access in and out of Viscount Tower will be permitted solely through the main entrance, even for those with keys to other entrances. We resisted changing the policy at first due to the proximity of other entrances to the parking areas. -------. We consulted an expert on cost-cutting measures, who recommend reducing the
8.
number of overnight security guards. By keeping movement through the main entrance only, we can maintain the same level of safety. **9. [In contrast / Furthermore]**, it may reduce the confusion among after-hours couriers, as they often have difficulty determining the fastest way to locate a member of staff.

---

8. (A) Meanwhile, the keys we distributed should be working again immediately after the repairs.

(B) There are several openings for new commercial tenants in some areas of the facility.

(C) However, the new policy is expected to reduce the company's expenses.

(D) Please contact the security office to be issued a new key for the side entrances.

Warehouse Manager Wanted

Sirocco Electronics currently has a vacancy for a Warehouse Manager at its distribution facility in Westbrook. The Warehouse Manager **10. [ensures / ensured]** that the receiving, storage, and shipping of merchandise is carried out properly and efficiently. While this is a management position, the successful candidate will also be required to lift heavy objects and climb ladders unassisted, so applicants should be physically capable. We would prefer to interview and potentially hire individuals with at least five years of experience in a similar role. Accordingly, it is important that you provide us with your full employment history when you fill out the application form. To apply, simply visit our careers center at www.sirocco. com/careers. -------.
11.

---

11. (A) We would be happy to contact you should any vacancies open up in the future.

(B) You made the right choice in accepting a position at Sirocco Electronics.

(C) Details about new Sirocco merchandise can be obtained from our sales team.

(D) For the position outlined above, enter reference number WM053 on your form.

정답은 본책 p. 386 / 해설 PDF 무료 제공 / www.ybmbooks.com

Questions 1-4 refer to the following notice.

Important Update

Due to the heavy snowfall from recent storms, our city's crews have been unable to

------- their normal schedule of collecting recyclable waste from residential areas.
   1.

They are currently about one week behind. Although today's warmer weather should melt

some of the snow, a few streets may remain slippery and present a challenge for the

workers' vehicles to travel on. -------. Currently, our crews anticipate waste pick-up
       2.

------- on Thursday, December 6 in District One. They will ------- begin the second round
 3.   **4.**

of collection in District Two, which is expected to continue through next week.

---

1. (A) delay
    (B) forecast
    (C) change
    (D) maintain

2. (A) The city also invites residents to attend public meetings.
    (B) It is advisable to stay indoors while road conditions are not safe.
    (C) Please share these tips with all drivers in your household.
    (D) Please be patient with us as we try to get to these areas.

3. (A) completing
    (B) being completed
    (C) was completing
    (D) has been completed

4. (A) instead
    (B) now
    (C) consequently
    (D) then

Job Fair Targets University Graduates

Fernald City will host its fourth annual Job Fair this Friday, May 24, from 10 A.M. to 3 P.M. at the downtown civic center. The yearly event will feature over 40 companies ------- are
5.
interested in hiring qualified candidates. "In the past, companies have ------- job offers
6.
on the spot," said organizer Gus Parkson. "So it's a great opportunity for recent university graduates seeking immediate -------." Attendees are asked to bring a résumé and wear
7.
appropriate attire for an interview. To get candidates ready for the fair, the city will also provide free preparation workshops between 9 and 11 A.M. this Wednesday and Thursday at the civic center. -------.
8.

5. (A) what
   (B) they
   (C) where
   (D) that

6. (A) recruited
   (B) proceeded
   (C) remained
   (D) extended

7. (A) employment
   (B) registration
   (C) supervision
   (D) fitness

8. (A) Remember to limit your résumé to a single page.
   (B) They will provide tips on how to answer interview questions.
   (C) They had a much higher turnout than officials had predicted.
   (D) They require a fee to cover the costs of instructional materials.

Questions 9-12 refer to the following e-mail.

To: Joseph Neuman <j.neuman@bonitamail.com>
From: Radio 106 <info@radio106.com>
Date: July 8
Subject: Radio 106 Summer Picnic

Dear Ms. Neuman,

Radio 106's annual summer picnic is scheduled for July 29 at Laguna Park. On that day, we ------- a series of activities. Participants can enjoy sports games, a singing
9.
contest, and prize drawings. Our staff members plan to be on site ------- light snacks and
10.
beverages. Local performers have been scheduled to give live performances on Laguna Park's outdoor stage. -------. Visitors are advised to bring their own chairs, which can be
11.
set up near the stage on a first-come, first-served basis. Further details of the event will be announced ------- our station's regular programming.
12.

The Radio 106 Team

---

9. (A) hosted
(B) will have hosted
(C) will host
(D) have hosted

10. (A) supplying
(B) containing
(C) redeeming
(D) dining

11. (A) Listeners voted for their favorite program.
(B) We will interview you on the air.
(C) You can win cash or gift certificates.
(D) The show is set to begin at 1 P.M.

12. (A) unlike
(B) towards
(C) during
(D) against

Gary Borego
3111 Oakridge Lane
San Gabriel, CA 91775

Dear Mr. Borego,

On behalf of TMA Apparel, I would like to thank you for your understanding of our --------.
13.

We are dedicated to selling high-quality clothing at a reasonable cost. -------, sometimes
14.

we fall short of our customer service goals. To apologize for sending you the wrong

clothing items, please ------- the enclosed coupon for twenty-five percent off a regularly
15.

priced item of your choice. You may use it at your leisure in our retail stores or online.

-------.
16.

Sincerely,
The TMA Apparel Team

13. (A) concern
(B) mistake
(C) complaint
(D) delay

15. (A) input
(B) ensure
(C) indicate
(D) accept

14. (A) In short
(B) To that end
(C) However
(D) Instead

16. (A) Please update your contact
information.
(B) Sales on merchandise are held
regularly.
(C) It does not have an expiration date.
(D) Each one comes with a warranty.

Questions 17-20 refer to the following press release.

Author Shane Roth is the first foreigner to receive the Stylo, a prestigious French literary award, for his novel *Amelia*. No ------- authors from Longmont Publishing, Roth's
17.
publisher, have had such honor bestowed upon them from another country. -------, Roth
18.
chose to have his book translated into French last year after meeting talented translator Tristan Fortin at an industry event.

"To have my work shared more widely is extremely satisfying," said Roth at a press conference yesterday. -------. However, it's not impossible to obtain one. ------- editions
19. **20.**
are selling for great prices online.

17. (A) another
    (B) little
    (C) other
    (D) these

18. (A) In fact
    (B) If so
    (C) In contrast
    (D) Namely

19. (A) Copies of the popular book are sold out across the country.
    (B) Roth plans to write another novel.
    (C) Critics are commenting on the plot.
    (D) Roth will release a digital version in the coming year.

20. (A) Use
    (B) Used
    (C) Using
    (C) To use

November 3
Jason Musgrave
Personnel Manager
Rutherford Gas & Electric

Dear Mr. Musgrave,

I am writing to you regarding the Customer Service Manager position at Rutherford

Gas & Electric. I am confident that I could be an invaluable ------- to your company's
21.

Customer Service Department. --------. My current role as the head of customer services
22.

at Brightman Energy has equipped me well to handle the responsibilities at your firm.

------- that, I worked at Comnet Telecom, where I was responsible for devising strategies
23.

to increase customer satisfaction. I hope you will take the time to look over my enclosed

résumé. It contains details of specific projects and ------- I have developed and
24.

implemented throughout my career.

I hope to hear from you soon regarding the position.

Best regards,
John Carlson
Enclosure

---

21. (A) profit
(B) incentive
(C) asset
(D) effort

22. (A) I'm pleased to hear you will consider the position.
(B) The project would not have been a success without you.
(C) Competition in the energy sector has never been so intense.
(D) I have worked for leading firms in the industry.

23. (A) Among
(B) Such as
(C) In advance
(D) Prior to

24. (A) initiatives
(B) mortgages
(C) revenues
(D) challenges

Questions 25-28 refer to the following Web page.

---

www.pelleterluggage.com

Pelleter Ltd.'s bags and backpacks are designed to last through a lifetime of travel.

-------. If you discover any defect in any of our products, you may return it to us and we
   25.

will replace it with an identical item at no cost. To make a return, ------- call our customer
                          26.

service line at 555-0006 for a return authorization number. Then return the ------- item
                              27.

in a sturdy box. Please make sure that your mailing address and return authorization

number ------- with the product you send us.
    28.

---

25. (A) The forum allows customers to
     discuss various topics.
  (B) There are many other benefits of
     traveling abroad.
  (C) Customer satisfaction is our highest
     priority.
  (D) It is best to leave some space for
     souvenirs.

26. (A) simple
  (B) simply
  (C) simplicity
  (D) simplify

27. (A) improved
  (B) unwanted
  (C) discounted
  (D) restored

28. (A) are included
  (B) were including
  (C) will have included
  (D) to have been included

Questions 29-32 refer to the following memo.

From: Edith Wagner, Operations Manager

To: All Branch Managers

Date: January 10

Re: New Procedure

I would like to bring to your attention a new procedure that ------- in all branches of Astro
                                                              29.

Burger. Starting February 1, for the final hour of business, we will no longer hold food

items in the warming station. -------, between 9 P.M. and 10 P.M., we will only cook items
                                            30.

to order on a customer-by-customer basis. This will help us cut down on unnecessary

waste, as we will not need to dispose of ------- items when the stores close at 10 P.M.
                                              31.

-------. If you have any questions regarding this new approach, please direct them to
32.

Angela Hayes at head office.

29. (A) is implementing
    (B) had been implemented
    (C) to implement
    (D) will be implemented

30. (A) Similarly
    (B) However
    (C) Instead
    (D) Although

31. (A) necessary
    (B) faulty
    (C) popular
    (D) excess

32. (A) This is our latest step in becoming
        a more environmentally-friendly
        company.
    (B) We are sure the new equipment will
        help reduce our monthly energy
        costs.
    (C) Additional staff will be hired in order
        to cope with the rising number of
        customers.
    (D) We believe that the new product
        range will succeed.

PART

7

● PART 7 풀이 전략

PART 7 이렇게 나온다

Part 7은 단일 지문이 10세트 총 29문항, 복수 지문이 5세트 총 25문항 출제된다. 어떤 순서로 읽는 것이 정답률과
속도 향상에 효과적일지에 대한 전략 확립은 기본적인 독해력과 어휘력 다지기만큼 점수에 결정적인 요소가 될 수 있다.
효과적인 독해 방식을 익혀 다양한 질문과 지문에 적용해보자.

❶ **Questions 1-2** refer to the following job advertisement. 구인 광고   번역 p. 191

---

❸
> **Paper Seeks New Division Lead** 신문사 구인
>
> The *Boulder Post-Gazette* is seeking a qualified
> journalist. Video capturing and editing abilities are a
> big plus, as **we are striving to raise the number of
> videos and other pieces we post to our Web site.**

··········● 역량 있는 경력 기자 구함

··········● 영상 촬영, 편집 기술 우대
　　　　　당사 웹사이트 게시물 수 늘리는 중

❻
> **Responsibilities** will include **proofreading** and
> **revising articles, interviewing elected officials and
> other local personalities**, and **coordinating a group
> of journalists** to maximize coverage of the events that
> Boulder residents care about.
> Contact Vicki Grimes at (791) 555-0122 if interested in
> applying.

··········● 업무 내용
　　　　　– 기사 교정, 수정
　　　　　– 당선인, 지역 인사 인터뷰
　　　　　– 기자단 관리

---

❷ **1.** What is the *Boulder Post-Gazette* trying to **increase**?
　　B사가 늘리려고 하는 것은?

❹
- (A) The quality of its streaming videos 스트리밍 영상 품질
- (B) The size of the region it reports on 보도 지역 규모
- **(C) The amount of content it puts online 콘텐트 분량**
- (D) The range of sections it publishes 출간 범위

> ❶ 지문의 종류를 읽는다.
> ❷ 문제를 읽는다.
> ❸ 본문을 처음부터 읽는다.
> ❹ 답이 나올 때까지 읽고 답한다.

❺ **2.** What is **NOT** a stated **responsibility** of the job?
　　업무 내용이 아닌 것은?

❼
- (A) Editing news articles 신규 기사 편집
- (B) Managing a news team 뉴스팀 관리
- (C) Speaking with politicians 정치인 인터뷰
- **(D) Maintaining a Web site 웹사이트 관리**

> ❺ 다음 문제를 읽는다.
> ❻ 본문을 이어서 읽는다.
> ❼ 답이 나올 때까지 읽고 답한다.

PART 7 이렇게 푼다

1 지문의 종류를 읽는다.

이 글은 **구인 광고**이므로 구인 광고 지문이 가지는 내용적 특성을 인지하고 문제 풀이에 임해야 한다.

❯ 자격 요건, 우대 조건, 업무 사항, 복리후생 등의 주요 내용을 예상할 수 있다.

2 문제를 읽는다.

〈볼더 포스트-가제트〉는 무엇을 **증가**시키려고 하는가?

❯ 고유명사 + '증가시키다'에 주목

3 본문을 처음부터 읽는다.

질문 포인트와 관련된 내용이 나올 때까지 요약하며 읽는다.

❯ 신문사에서 경력자를 뽑는다.
❯ 영상 촬영 및 편집 기술이 우대된다.

4 답이 나올 때까지 읽고 답한다.

본문의 키워드 **raise**(질문의 **increase**)를 포착하여 늘리려고 하는 것 고르기

웹사이트에 게시할 영상 및 기사를 늘리려고 한다.

❯ (C) 온라인에 올릴 콘텐츠 분량

5 다음 문제를 읽는다.

언급된 업무가 아닌 것은?

❯ 업무 내용 열거에 주목

6 본문을 이어서 읽는다.

본문의 키워드 **responsibilities**를 포착하여 업무 사항 체크하기

7 답이 나올 때까지 읽고 답한다.

언급된 세 가지 업무 확인하기

❯ (A) 교정과 수정 업무, (B) 기자 관리 업무, (C) 인터뷰 업무

패러프레이징

Part 7의 정답은 본문의 근거가 되는 문장을 Paraphrasing한 것이다. online ⊜ Web site처럼 자주 출제되는 짝도 있지만 모든 영어 문장은 다른 어휘나 다른 문장 구조를 사용하여 재표현이 가능하다는 것을 염두에 두어야 한다. 따라서 문제를 풀면서 나올 때마다 짝을 지어 표시해 두고 다양하게 바꾸어 말하기가 가능하다는 점을 인지하며 실전에 임하는 것이 중요하다.

유형 1. 동의어로 바꾸기

패러프레이징의 가장 기본 형태는 비슷한 뜻을 가진 다른 단어로 바꾸어 말하기이다.

질문	What is a required **qualification** for the position?	이 직책에 대해 요구되는 **자질**은?
지문	I have the Yoga instructor **license** listed as a **requirement** for the position, and I also have over five years of experience in Bronson Community Center.	저는 **필수 자격 요건으로 언급된** 요가 강사 **면허증**을 가지고 있으며 브론슨 커뮤니티 센터에서 5년 이상 일한 경력 또한 있습니다.
정답	**A professional certification**	전문 자격증

⊜ 질문의 키워드 qualification(자질)이 동의어인 requirement로 패러프레이징되었다.
지문의 license(면허증)가 동의어인 certification(자격증)으로 패러프레이징되었다.

> 추가 예시 • decade ⊜ 10 years 십 년
> • contract ⊜ agreement 계약서

유형 2. 상위어로 바꾸기

구체적인 단어는 포괄적인 단어로 패러프레이징될 수 있다.

질문	What should people avoid placing on the table?	무엇을 테이블에 두지 말아야 하는가?
지문	High temperatures can damage the wood's finish, so do not set **hot coffee mugs or dishes** on the table top.	고온은 나무 마감재를 손상시킬 수 있습니다. 따라서 **뜨거운 커피잔이나 접시**를 테이블 위에 두지 마십시오.
정답	**Hot items**	뜨거운 물건

⊜ 뜨거운 컵(mugs)이나 접시(dishes) 같은 구체적인 예시가 hot items로 패러프레이징되었다.

> 추가 예시 • hotel 호텔 ⊜ accommodation 숙박시설
> • repaint 페인트 칠을 다시하다 ⊜ renovate 개조하다

유형 3. 풀어 쓰기와 요약하기

단어를 구나 문장으로 풀어 쓰거나 반대로 구나 문장을 짧게 요약하는 형태로 패러프레이징될 수 있다.

질문	What does the writer **apologize** for?	글쓴이는 무엇에 대해 **사과**하는가?
지문	Thank you for your patronage during the construction of our patio. **We are sorry** that we must **eliminate part of our parking area** to accommodate this addition.	테라스 공사 동안에도 이용해 주셔서 감사드립니다. 증축을 위한 공간을 마련하기 위해 주차장의 일부를 없애게 되어 최송합니다.
정답	**A reduction of parking spots**	**주차 공간의 감소**

> 질문의 키워드 apologize(사과하다)를 지문에서 We are sorry로 풀어 썼다.
> 지문의 eliminate part(일부를 없애다)를 보기에서 reduction(감소)으로 요약했다.

> **추가 예시** • popular 인기 있는 ❯ attract many people 많은 사람을 끌어들이다
> • not everyone can have access 모든 사람이 이용할 수는 없다 ❯ limited 한정된, 제한적인

유형 4. 추론 유형

질문에 most likely, suggest about, imply와 같은 추론을 요구하는 표현이 들어가면 정답은 추론적 판단이 포함된 형태로 패러프레이징된다.

질문	What will **most likely happen** in the spring?	봄에는 무슨 일이 **일어날 것 같은가**?
지문	We are working closely with our contractors to **complete the patio** by the spring so that customers can enjoy eating under the trees when the weather warms up.	저희는 날씨가 따뜻해지면 고객들이 나무 아래에서 식사를 즐기실 수 있도록 **봄까지 테라스를 완성하기 위해** 건설업자들과 긴밀히 협력하고 있습니다.
정답	**Outdoor seating will become available.**	**야외 좌석 이용이 가능해질 것이다.**

> 테라스가 완성(complete)되면 이용가능해질 것(become available)이라는 것은 추론적 판단이 포함된 형태의 패러프레이징이다.

> **추가 예시** • open around the clock 24시간 운영한다 ❯ can contact anytime 언제든 연락할 수 있다
> • All sales are final. 모든 판매는 교환/환불 불가이다. ❯ non-refundable 반품할 수 없다

1.

> I have greatly enjoyed reading your magazine, *Every Weekend*. I particularly enjoy the pieces with advice for new travelers. It gives valuable suggestions on how to explore cities like a local.

What is indicated about *Every Weekend*?
(A) It is a magazine written by a local.
(B) It gives travel tips.

2.

> I wanted to extend my credit limit, but I was informed that credit limits can only be extended by placing a phone call. This does not make any sense to me. I think I should be able to accomplish the same tasks through the online support desk as I can by contacting the call center. I recommend you expand the online support center's capabilities so it can become a truly useful service.

What does the writer suggest that the company do?
(A) Expand the support center's hours of operation
(B) Allow the online support center to offer more services

3.

> Whether you like racing or mountain biking, Digby's has the latest bikes from the biggest brands at the best prices, guaranteed. If you find a better deal, we'll beat it by 10%.

What is stated about Digby's Bicycle Shop?
(A) It promises to offer the lowest prices.
(B) It offers 10% discount on bike brands.

4.

> Please help the library improve its services by filling out this survey.
>
> | | |
> |---|---|
> | Are the library staff friendly and knowledgeable? | ★★★★★ |
> | Is it easy for you to find books or other materials? | ★★★★☆ |
> | Are the study rooms well equipped? | ★★★★★ |
> | Is the book rental reasonably priced? | ★★☆☆☆ |

What is suggested about the library?
(A) All study rooms are wireless network accessible.
(B) It charges a fee for checking out books.

5.

> Requirements
> • Must have a valid state-issued license for massage therapy
> • Must have worked in a spa, clinic, or similar setting for no less than twelve months

What is required for the position?
(A) A master's degree
(B) A minimum of one year of experience

6.

> Tenants at Beacon Apartments are allowed to use the recreation room on the first floor of Tower A for private functions. It is equipped with a flat-screen television, several tables and chairs, and three sofas. Previously, the room could be booked by calling the property management office. However, starting from today, tenants must use an online system to make a booking.

What has changed about the recreation room?
(A) The equipment provided to renters
(B) The way to make a reservation

7.

> We have a growing client base of customers and a friendly working environment.
> We offer generous hourly wages as well as bonuses for hitting performance targets.
> Employees also receive ten percent of all product sales they make to their customers.

What benefit is mentioned?
(A) Generous paid vacation time
(B) Commission on merchandise sales

8.

> While You Were Out
>
> Message for: Amy Preston   From: Gordon Reaves   Company: Alpha Sales
> Contact Details: 555-0195   Date: Sept. 4   Time: 1:05 P.M.
>
>   Called   [ ]   Visited   [✓]
>   Please Call [✓]   Will Call Later [ ]
>
> Message: Mr. Reaves is creating a brochure to pass out at the next trade fair. Please prepare the annual sales amounts so that they can be included.

What is indicated about Mr. Reaves?
(A) He stopped by the business in person.
(B) He cannot attend the trade fair.

PART 7

INTRO 파트프레이징

주제 / 목적 문제

54문항 중 평균 3~5문제 출제

문제 유형
What does the article discuss? 이 기사는 무엇에 대해 논의하는가?
What is the purpose of the letter? 이 편지의 목적은 무엇인가?
Why was the message sent? 이 메시지는 왜 보내졌는가?

전략
대부분의 경우 주제 및 목적은 글의 도입부에서 드러나므로 앞 부분을 공략하자. 긴 서론을 두고 본론을 나중에 꺼내는 목적 문제도 있으므로, 초반부를 읽고 답을 구할 수 없는 경우 다음 문제를 먼저 해결하고 돌아오는 방식을 적용할 수도 있다.

문제 풀이 과정

번역 p. 193

Dear Ms. Juliet,

I heard that you were looking for ideas for improving worker productivity at our office. **I would like you to consider replacing our current cubicle setup with an open office plan.** ❷
I've put together a diagram of a possible arrangement. I've posted it on the bulletin board in the break room. Please have a look and give me feedback.

Q. Why was the letter written? ❶
(A) **To suggest changing an office layout** ❸
(B) To introduce a potential client
(C) To follow up on a furniture order
(D) To report performance evaluation results

STEP ❶ 문제를 읽고 목적 문제임을 확인한다.

STEP ❷ 단서 문장이 나올 때까지 읽고 목적이 드러나는 근거 문장을 포착한다.
"사무실 배치를 칸막이에서 개방형으로 바꿔 주셨으면 좋겠습니다."

STEP ❸ 패러프레이징된 정답을 고른다.
• I would like you to consider
  ❱ suggest
• replace ··· an office plan
  ❱ change an office layout

주제와 목적을 나타내는 문장

We are pleased to announce that our office is expanding.	사무실 확장을 알리게 되어 기쁩니다.
We regret to inform you that we cannot fulfill your order.	주문 처리 불가를 알리게 되어 유감입니다.
This is to acknowledge receipt of payment.	납입금을 수령했음을 알려 드립니다.
I would like to extend an invitation to you.	귀하를 초대하고자 합니다.
I would appreciate if you could send an updated invoice.	새로 송장을 보내 주시면 감사하겠습니다.
Please note that our office will be closed on Monday.	월요일은 휴무임을 알아두세요.

READING PRACTICE

정답 및 해설 p. 193

1. 문자 메시지

AUTOMATED MESSAGE. DO NOT REPLY.

Passengers on flight RW509 to Boston departing at 9:05 A.M. should note that the departure gate is no longer C24. Boarding will commence approximately one hour before the departure time at gate C30 instead. Any further changes to this flight will appear on the monitors throughout the terminal, so please refer to them to confirm flight details.

Q. Why was the message sent?

(A) To apologize for a delay in a departure

(B) To give notification about a gate change

(C) To confirm that a passenger has checked in

(D) To announce that a flight has begun boarding

2. 편지

Dear Mr. Sanchez,

Thank you for your coverage of Lake Penrose news and events. I have enjoyed reading your articles over the past several years. However, I noticed a mistake in your December 9 article about the restoration of the historic John Hevy Lodge. You stated that the project was being entirely funded by public subsidies and grants, but in fact, almost 50% of the financing for the restoration has been generously provided by private donors. It is important to give credit and thanks to those that support this vision. I look forward to seeing your correction in tomorrow's paper.

Thank you,

Imogene Finnley
Chief Financial Officer
Lake Penrose Historical Society

Q. Why did Ms. Finnley send the letter?

(A) To suggest a topic for an in-depth article

(B) To extend an event invitation

(C) To identify a factual error

(D) To ask for a donation

PART 7

UNIT 01 주제 / 목적 문제

세부 사항 문제

문제 유형   What information **does** Mr. Stern provide? 스턴 씨는 어떤 정보를 제공하는가?

How **has** Genco Group improved **its** corporate image? 젠코 그룹은 기업 이미지를 어떻게 개선했는가?

Why **has** the schedule of a project been postponed? 왜 프로젝트의 일정이 미뤄졌는가?

전략   문제에서 키워드를 잡고 지문을 빠르게 읽어 내려오다가 키워드가 등장하면 그 주변을 정독한다. 문제에서 요구하는 정보가 나오면 보기를 읽고 답한다.

● 문제 풀이 과정

번역 p. 194

It is my pleasure to notify you that our judges have selected you as one of the contest finalists. Congratulations!

You are invited to attend the awards banquet, at which **the first place winner will be revealed**, at the Royal Reception Hall in Ottawa on **March 3.** ❷

We have enclosed your tickets to the event.

Q. What will happen **on March 3**? ❶

  (A) A contest winner will be announced. ❸

  (B) Judges will conduct interviews.

  (C) A submission period will end.

  (D) A gallery exhibition will take place.

STEP ❶ 문제를 읽고 키워드를 확인한다.
특정 시점 키워드 – **March 3**

STEP ❷ 단서 문장이 나올 때까지 읽고 키워드가 포함된 문장을 포착한다.
"3월 3일 연회에서 우승자가 발표됩니다."

STEP ❸ 패러프레이징된 정답을 고른다.
- the first place winner
  ❷ a contest winner
- will be revealed
  ❷ will be announced

의문사와 핵심 키워드 파악하기

	세부 사항 관련 질문	포착할 키워드
누가	Who will **facilitate** the event? 사회자	고유명사 사람 이름, 직책명, host(사회자)
언제	When is the **submission due**? 제출일	특정 날짜, by, no later than(~까지), deadline
어디서	Where is Lama Ltd. **based**? 본사 위치	고유명사 도시명, headquarters(본사)
무엇을	What is **offered free of charge**? 무료 제공	provide, give away, receive, complimentary
어떻게	How can the **contest be entered**? 신청 방법	simply+명령문, by + -ing(~함으로써)
왜	Why is the **road** being **closed**? 폐쇄 이유	road closure, because, due to, so that, in order to

READING PRACTICE

정답 및 해설 p. 194

1. 일정표

Claremont Library Special Activities Schedule

Sunday	Closed
Monday	10 A.M. Children's Storytime, 4 P.M. Homework Help
Tuesday	7 P.M. Young Adult Book Club
Wednesday	10 A.M. Children's Storytime, 4 P.M. Homework Help
Thursday	11 A.M. Computer Basics for Senior Citizens
Friday	10 A.M. Children's Storytime, 4 P.M. Homework Help
Saturday	1 P.M. Craft Corner, 3 P.M. Shakespeare Read-Along

All activities are provided to library patrons at no charge. If you do not have a library card, you may sign up for one at the registration. If you would like to share your time assisting or leading one of the activities, please call Rhonda Stewart at 555-0132.

Q. On what day of the week is there an event specially for elderly people?

(A) Monday   (B) Tuesday

(C) Thursday   (D) Saturday

2. 기사

Ramondi Resort has finally opened for the season after weeks of delays. The resort typically opens in mid-November, but that was not possible. Although temperatures were well below freezing, there was not enough precipitation to produce sufficient levels of snow for skiing.

"We're pleased to be open to skiers now," said resort manager Billie Estes. "Now that we have a good base layer of snow, we expect good skiing conditions for the rest of the season."

Estes stated that the resort has already allocated funding to purchase additional snow machines next year. By using them, the site can begin producing artificial snow as soon as the weather becomes cold enough.

Q. According to Mr. Estes, what has the resort already done?

(A) Extended its daily operating hours   (B) Increase its entrance fees

(C) Installed more equipment   (D) Budgeted for a purchase

Not / True 문제

54문항 중 평균 7~8문제 출제

문제 유형　What is NOT stated as a benefit of the membership? 멤버십의 혜택으로 언급된 것이 아닌 것은?

What is true about Bluebird Hotel? 블루버드 호텔에 대해 사실인 것은?

What is mentioned in the article? 기사에서 언급된 것은?

진략　질문에 등장하는 핵심 명사를 주제로 하는 단락 전체를 읽고 답한다. 특정 키워드가 없는 문제의 경우 다른 문제를 먼저 해결하고 마지막으로 푸는 방식을 적용할 수도 있다.

● 문제 풀이 과정

번역 p. 195

An internal vacancy is open for the position of marketing manager. **To be considered for the position, applicants must have worked for three years or longer and taken at least one leadership role on their team. They will also need a letter of recommendation from their direct supervisor.** ②

If the above describes you, please send your résumé, and your letter of recommendation to Ms. Gregory.

Q. What is **NOT mentioned** as a basic **requirement** for applicants? ①
(A) An employment history
(B) A written endorsement from a supervisor
(C) An experience in a leadership role
(D) A portfolio of past projects ③

STEP ① 문제를 읽고 키워드를 확인한다.
　키워드 – 지원 자격 요건이 아닌 것

STEP ② 단서 문장이 나올 때까지 읽고 키워드가 포함된 문장을 포착한다.
　"지원하려면… 3년 경력, 리더십 경험, 상사의 추천서 필요"

STEP ③ 패러프레이징된 언급 사항들을 소거하여 언급되지 않은 정답을 남긴다.
　• must have worked for three years
　　❷ employment history 경력
　• must have taken at least one leadership role
　　❷ experience in a leadership role 팀장 역할 경험
　• letter of recommendation 추천서
　　❷ written endorsement 서면 보증

사실 관계 문제의 오답 유형

지문　I have worked as a professional singer in stage musicals for the past ten years.
저는 지난 10년간 뮤지컬 전문 가수로 일했습니다.

문제　What is true about the writer? 글쓴이에 대해 사실인 것은?

오답 유형 1 사실과 다른 정보 (False)	**오답 유형 2** 알 수 없는 정보 (Not Given)
She has been a dancer for a decade.	She has never changed her career.

정답　She is an experienced stage performer. 그녀는 숙련된 무대 공연가이다.

❷ 보기에는 Not Given 오답 유형처럼 지문에 없는 정보가 포함될 수 있으므로 지문을 먼저 읽고 정답을 가려낸다.

READING PRACTICE

정답 및 해설 p. 195

1. 기사

Cooking Contest to Mark 40th Anniversary of Antonio's Restaurant

Redville (August 30) – Antonio Borrello, the long-term owner of Antonio's Restaurant, is hosting a series of events in honor of his 40th year of being in business. Mr. Borrello is known to be particularly proud of the award for excellent service given to him 10 years ago by the *Redville* Gazette. With his son working in the kitchen and his wife now in charge of table service, Antonio can be sure his high standards are maintained.

Mr. Borrello intends for the main event during the celebrations to be a cooking competition. Local residents are invited to submit recipe ideas for consideration, and the owners of the top three ideas will be invited to cook their meals at Antonio's.

Further information about this competition is available on the City Hall Web site.

Q. According to the article, what is true about Antonio's restaurant?

(A) It has been nominated for an upcoming award.

(B) It serves food from a range of countries.

(C) Mr. Borrello's family work in the restaurant.

(D) It has had several different owners.

2. 공지

Attention residents of the Sunbury neighborhood:

The Pine City Planning Commission is considering modifying Sunbury zoning classification from "residential" to "commercial/residential". This change could have major effects on the neighborhood's citizens. Here are some potential effects that have been pointed out so far:

Positive	Negative
• Convenient access to businesses • Accompanying increase in bus service	• More car traffic • Noise from new construction projects

Please visit www.rcpc.gov/tfzs to take a survey on this issue.

Q. What is NOT mentioned as a possible change for the Sunbury neighborhood?

(A) House prices might increase.

(B) More vehicles might use the roads.

(C) Construction projects might begin.

(D) Public transportation might be improved.

추론 문제

문제 유형　Where would the memo most likely be seen? 어디에서 볼 수 있는 메모일 것 같은가?
　　　　　What is suggested about the new policy? 새로운 정책에 대해 암시되는(알 수 있는) 것은 무엇인가?
　　　　　What does the letter imply about the workshop? 이 편지글은 워크숍에 대해 무엇을 암시하는가?

선략　　시문에서 직접적으로 언급하지는 않으나 근거 문장이 반드시 존재하므로, 근거 문장에 철저히 의존해서
　　　　　내포하는 의미를 캐치해야 한다.

● 문제 풀이 과정

번역 p. 196

Dear Mr. Cowell,

Since you recently purchased our product, we want to invite you and a guest to a special event at our headquarters.

At the event, there will be snacks, live music, and demonstrations of various products by our engineers. **Bring this card to the event to gain entrance. ②**

Please visit our Web site for the details.

Q. What is **suggested about** the **event**? ❶
　(A) It is an annual event.
　(B) Pre-registration is required.
　(C) It will be held at a private venue.
　(D) It is by invitation only. ❸

STEP ❶ 문제를 읽고 키워드를 확인한다.
　　　　키워드 - 행사

STEP ❷ 단서 문장이 나올 때까지 읽고
　　　　키워드가 포함된 문장을 포착한다.
　　　　"행사에서는…
　　　　… 입장하려면 이 카드를 가져오세요."

STEP ❸ 근거 문장을 재해석한 보기를 고른다.
　　　　근거문: 입장하려면 카드를 가져와야
　　　　　　　한다.
　　　　재해석: 카드가 없으면 입장할 수 없다.
　　　　추론: 이 행사는 초대된 사람만 입장할
　　　　　　수 있는 행사이다.

추론의 범위

근거 문장	추론
단골 고객 할인을 받으셔서 총 구매 금액은 420달러입니다.	❷ 이 상점은 **고객 보상 프로그램**이 있다.
정기 연말 세일 기간 동안 연장 근무할 신청자를 받습니다.	❷ 이 상점은 **연례 판촉 행사**를 한다.
죄송하지만 스낵 바는 **회원 전용 시설**이므로 **이용하실 수 없습니다**.	❷ Ms. OO는 **비회원** 이용자이다.
표기된 **메뉴**는 재료 유무에 따라 달라질 수 있습니다.	❷ **일부 메뉴**는 주문이 **불가능할 수** 있다.

❷ 추론은 근거 문장을 바탕으로 2차적인 판단을 이끌어 내는 것이며 이 또한 넓은 의미의 패러프레이징에
　해당한다. 근거 문장을 반드시 찾아서 표시하고 정답과 비교하여 추론의 범위에 익숙해지는 것이 중요하다.

READING PRACTICE

정답 및 해설 p.196

1. 광고

Thanks for shopping at Top Marks Market!

We're so happy to have you as a customer that we want to offer you a special gift. Use coupon code WELCOME15 on your next order to receive a 15% discount. Just enter it into the box that says "Special Offer" when you check out on our Web site. This discount is valid for our entire store catalog, from small essentials like dry erase markers to exciting educational software programs that will make your classroom a school favorite.

*Coupons can be used only on orders totaling less than $300 before the discount is applied. Expires January 1. Cannot be combined with free shipping offers.

Q. Who most likely would shop at Top Marks Market?

(A) A writer

(B) An artist

(C) A teacher

(D) An athlete

2. 양식

Sorrento Enterprises: Reimbursement Request Form

Employee: Richard Donovan	**Employee Number:** 01468
Date: November 20	**Amount:** $237.50

Expense Type (check all that apply)

[ ] Flight(s) [✓] Meal(s) [✓] Taxi(s) [ ] Equipment [ ] Other _____

Details: The expenses (receipts attached) are for a business trip to Atlanta to sign the merger agreement with Delano Industries.

FOR OFFICE USE ONLY

Approved by: Stephen Trejo

To be issued: [ ] Immediately [✓] On next payday [ ] Other _____

Q. What is suggested about the payment?

(A) It cannot exceed a certain amount.

(B) It must be approved by a manager.

(C) It will be issued with the salary.

(D) It is for an equipment purchase.

문장 삽입 문제

문제 유형 In which of the positions marked [1], [2], [3], and [4] does the following sentence best belong?

"Then, wait until it gets dry."

[1], [2], [3], [4]로 표시된 곳들 중 다음 문장이 들어가기에 가장 적절한 곳은?

전략 주어진 문장의 요지를 잡고 같은 주제를 다루는 단락을 찾는다. 지시어, 연결어 등이 있을 시 이를 활용한다.

● 문제 풀이 과정

번역 p. 197

— [1] —. I have to ask you to adjust your schedule.

— [2] —. We have a shipment of coffee beans coming in on Friday. As you might be aware, **that truck arrives around 5 A.M. — [3] —.** ❷

Could you be here to receive it? ❸

Let me know your availability before leaving for the day. Thanks. — [4] —.

Q. In which of the positions marked [1], [2], [3], and [4] does the following sentence best belong?
"Usually, Regina is here to meet **the driver**, but she's on business trip now." ❶

(A) [1]

(B) [2]

(C) [3]

(D) [4]

STEP ❶ 주어진 문장을 읽고 요지를 확인한다.
"보통은 레지나가 기사님을 마중 나가지만 지금 출장을 갔어요."
• 문장 위치 힌트: **the driver**
❯ 지문 속에 '기사'와 관련된 표현이 등장한 이후에 주어진 문장이 들어갈 수 있다.

STEP ❷ 지문을 처음부터 읽어 내려와서 트럭이 올 것이라는 문장까지 도달한다.

STEP ❸ 주어진 문장을 넣고 앞뒤 연결이 자연스러운지 확인한다.
"배송 트럭이 오전 5시에 오는데요. 〈담당자가 출장 가고 지금 없어요.〉 오셔서 당신이 받아 줄 수 있을까요?"

※ 지시어(this, that, such), 대명사(they, them), 연결어(therefore, however, that way 등), 정관사 the는 앞의 말을 받는 말이므로 위치를 결정하는 힌트가 된다.

주어진 문장 속의 힌트 활용하기

지시어	this, that, such, both	지시어가 가리키는 대상을 찾아 연결 관계 확인
대명사	they, them, he	대명사의 인칭, 단/복수에 유의하여 가리키는 대상을 찾아 연결
부사(구)	therefore, that way, also	부사의 의미가 앞뒤 상관 관계를 논리적으로 만들어 주는지 확인
정관사	the plan, the item, the CEO	해당 명사, 또는 관련어를 본문에서 찾아 주변 빈칸 공략

READING PRACTICE

정답 및 해설 p. 197

1. 기사

Boston Business Insider

McCoy's Home Solutions will soon release a new line of high-end furniture. — [1] —.

McCoy's CEO, Jenny Aya, explains the strategy. — [2] —. "We've established ourselves as the number one producer of affordable furnishings across the country, so now it's time to expand into new markets and niches," says Ms. Aya. — [3] —.

Real Style products are scheduled for release in the fourth quarter of this year.

— [4] —.

Q. In which of the positions marked [1], [2], [3], and [4] does the following sentence best belong?

"Called "Real Style", the line is different from the company's usual cost-conscious products."

(A) [1]　　　　　　　　　　　(B) [2]

(C) [3]　　　　　　　　　　　(D) [4]

2. 편지

Dear Ms. Spiros,

I am pleased to inform you that the Foundation for British Arts (FBA) has reviewed your grant application and has decided to award you the Glover Grant. — [1] —. As you know, the grant was founded by Ms. Glover 45 years ago to ensure that young people would always have opportunities to learn about art. — [2] —.

We are confident that you are a worthy recipient of the Glover Grant. — [3] —. The work your program has done so far is truly inspiring. — [4] —.

We look forward to seeing what else you and your students can do.

Most kindly,

Jude Erwan
Jude Erwan
Chairperson

Q. In which of the positions marked [1], [2], [3], and [4] does the following sentence best belong?

"Your afterschool program that helps young people create and produce stage plays is perfectly in line with this goal."

(A) [1]　　　　　　　　　　　(B) [2]

(C) [3]　　　　　　　　　　　(D) [4]

동의어 문제

문제 유형   The word "cover" in paragraph 1, line 3, is closest in meaning to
첫 번째 단락의 세 번째 줄 "cover"와 의미가 가장 가까운 것은?

전략   주어진 단어의 단순 사전적 의미가 아닌 문장 내에서의 의미를 파악하는 것이 중요하다. 주어진 단어가
빈칸이라고 생각하고 빈칸에 들어갈 어휘 문제로 접근하자.

● 문제 풀이 과정

번역 p. 198

Good morning, Ms. Gail. Your Regel Q3 sedan is available at 14 Biltmore Street. The access code to retrieve your key is 7513.

Please don't hesitate to contact us anytime.

Thanks for choosing Harmond Rental Cars! ②

STEP ① 문제를 읽고 제시어의 위치를 확인한다.

STEP ② 제시어가 속한 문장을 해석해 본 후 제시어를 빈칸 처리하여 보기를 대입해 본다.
Thanks for ------- Harmond Rental Cars!
"하몬드 렌탈 카를 ○○해 주셔서 감사합니다!"

Q. The word "choosing" in paragraph 3, line 1 is closest in meaning to ①
(A) appointing
(B) volunteering
(C) giving an award to
(D) doing business with ③

STEP ③ 고객의 거래에 대한 감사 멘트이므로 "거래(이용)"를 정답으로 고른다.

필수 다의어

cover	address	reflect	bear	settle	term
덮다	연설하다	반사하다	(색채 등을) 띠다	정착하다	기간
포함하다, 다루다	다루다	반영하다	참다, 견디다	해결하다	용어
대신하다	보내다	반성하다	(책임을) 떠맡다	결정하다	조건
practice	**suspect**	**critical**	**figure**	**draw**	**recognize**
실행하다	의심하다	비판적인	수치	그리다	인지하다
영업하다	추측하다	결정적인	형상	끌다	알아차리다
연습, 관행	~라고 생각하다	중대한	인물	뽑다	(공을) 인정하다
account	**direct**	**decline**	**contact**	**room**	**run**
계좌, 계정	향하다	자. 감소하다	접촉	방, -실	운영하다
거래	지시하다	자. 쇠퇴하다	연락	자리, 공간	작동하다
단골 손님	보내다	타. 거절하다	연출	여지	계속 진행되다

◆ 기본적인 다의어는 출제 가능성이 높으므로 숙지하는 것이 유리하다.

READING PRACTICE

정답 및 해설 p. 198

1. 편지

Dear Mr. Reynolds,

I am excited to offer you the position of senior software developer at RSI. Many qualified programmers expressed interest in this position, and it was not easy to select just one out of the large field. In the end, however, your stellar professional experience made you stand out.

I have enclosed a form detailing the terms of our offer. Please review it and call me at 555-0136 if you have any question.

Q. The word "field" in paragraph 1, line 3 is closest in meaning to

(A) grassy area

(B) applicant pool

(C) academic subject

(D) text entry box

2. 이메일

FROM: <barrysherrill@tcc.edu>
TO: <esmerelda@esmereldaspottery.com>
SUBJECT: Great class!
DATE: October 12

Hello, Ms. Lopez.

I am not sure if you remember me, but I attended your free class on Saturday. I was so impressed with your enthusiasm as an instructor and skill as an artist that, as the hiring director at Toledo Technical College, I want to invite you to teach an evening course at our school. I think it would be valuable for community members, as well as good exposure for your business.

I would like to talk more in person if you are interested. When would be a good time to visit you at your studio?

Sincerely,
Barry Sherrill

Q. The word "exposure" in paragraph 1, line 4 is closest in meaning to

(A) publicity

(B) risk

(C) scenery

(D) discovery

의도 파악 문제

문제 유형   At 4:30 P.M., what does Shirley mean when she writes, "I had no other choices"?
오후 4시 30분에 셜리가 "다른 선택권이 없었어요"라고 쓴 것은 무엇을 의미하는가?

전략   제시문에 표시된 시간으로 해당 문장의 위치만 찾아 먼저 표시한 후, 처음부터 읽으며 대화자들의 관계와 상황을 파악한다. 제시문 앞뒤를 읽어 문맥적인 의미를 판단하자.

● 문제 풀이 과정

번역 p. 198

9:44 A.M.   Gerry, my flight has been delayed.

9:45 A.M.   When are you scheduled to arrive, Saul?

9:47 A.M.   I won't land until 12:10. **I'll try to grab a taxi and get to the office as soon as I can.**

9:49 A.M.   **Don't worry about that. I can come and get you. ②**

9:52 A.M.   I really appreciate it.

Q. At 9:49 A.M., what does Gerry mean when he writes, "Don't worry about that"? **①**
(A) The meeting is canceled.
(B) They will not need to rent a vehicle.
(C) Saul does not need to take a taxi. ③
(D) The office is very close.

STEP ①   문제를 읽고 제시문의 위치를 확인한다.

STEP ②   제시문의 앞뒤 상황으로 의도를 파악한다.
"A: 최대한 빨리 택시를 잡아 타고 갈게요."
"B: 그건 걱정 마요. 제가 데리러 갈게요."
● 그건 걱정 마요.
   = 택시를 타지 않아도 된다.

STEP ③   보기를 읽고 의도를 가장 잘 나타낸 정답을 고른다.

대화 주제 및 인물 관계 파악하기

A: 제임스, **우리가** 광고 회사에 **의뢰했던 디자인**이 이메일로 도착했어요. ────► 대화 주제: 디자인

B: 결과물이 어떻게 나왔던가요?   인물 관계: 회사 동료

A: 직접 보셔야 할 것 같아요.

B: 이런, 제가 원하던 게 아니네요. ·····················► 의도: **디자인**에 대해 염려하고 있다.

● 제시문의 앞뒤 문장만으로는 상황 파악이 어려울 수 있다. 대화의 맥락을 이해하기 위해서는 초반부에 설정된 대화 주제와 대화자들 간의 관계를 파악하는 것 또한 중요하다. 여러 명이 대화하는 경우 이름에 주의해서 읽자.

READING PRACTICE

정답 및 해설 p. 199

1. 분사 메시지

Chen Ning [9:45 A.M.]

Frankie, Mr. Hewitt told me you have the company car.

Frankie Carter [9:48 A.M.]

Yes. I'm visiting our factory on Elmore Street to deliver some product specifications.

Do you need it?

Chen Ning [9:48 A.M.]

Well, I'm meeting a client for lunch, and I thought I might drive.

Frankie Carter [9:49 A.M.]

Oh. Well... I'll be here at least until two.

Chen Ning [9:50 A.M.]

OK. I'll call a taxi, then.

Q. At 9:49 A.M., what does Ms. Carter most likely mean when she writes, "I'll be here at least until two"?

(A) Mr. Ning cannot use a vehicle.

(B) She cannot attend a meeting.

(C) She does not mind waiting for Mr. Ning.

(D) Mr. Ning does not need to order a meal for her.

2. 온라인 채팅

Elaine Alves [2:03 P.M.]

Jin-Woo, Mr. Teo just called to ask if he could get free shipping for bulk orders.

Jin-Woo Kang [2:04 P.M.]

But that promotion ended last week.

Elaine Alves [2:05 P.M.]

Well, Mr. Teo has been with us for a long time.

Jin-Woo Kang [2:06 P.M.]

You're right. It's important to keep loyal customers happy. Just be sure to make a note on the system about the change. Otherwise, it might confuse other employees.

Elaine Alves [2:07 P.M.]

No problem. I'll take care of it now.

Q. At 2:05 P.M., what does Ms. Alves most likely mean when she writes, "Mr. Teo has been with us for a long time"?

(A) She thinks that a fee should be waived.

(B) Mr. Teo is qualified for a job promotion.

(C) She is surprised that an error was made.

(D) Mr. Teo should know about a policy.

이메일 / 편지 지문

출제 경향 수신인/발신인의 관계에 따라 주제의 폭이 매우 넓으므로 질문 또한 다양하게 구성될 수 있다. 이메일이나 편지를 쓴 목적 문제가 단골 문제로 출제되며 요청 사항, 첨부/동봉된 것 등을 묻는 세부 사항 문제도 빈출된다.

● 지문의 흐름 및 독해 전략

번역 p. 199

수/발신인
To: Graham Vincent <g_williams@info.com>
From: Jane Liston <jliston@odellaudio.com>

보낸 날짜 Date: December 2

제목 Subject: Invitation Request

인사말 Dear Mr. Vincent,

목적 I enjoyed your book on marketing. It has many useful tips. **I am wondering whether you would be available to deliver a lecture** at our offices in

세부 사항 Seattle. Please see the attached map.

요청 사항 If you want to contact me, reply to this e-mail or call me at 555-0168, extension 47.
I hope we can discuss the matter further.

Sincerely,

Jane Liston

직책/소속 Director, Human Resources Department,
Odell Audio

Q. Why did Ms. Liston **send the e-mail**?
(A) To invite Mr. Vincent to give a talk
(B) To thank Mr. Vincent for assisting her company
(C) To offer a full-time position to Mr. Vincent
(D) To request that Mr. Vincent attend an interview

지문 확인 사항

① 수신인, 발신인, 보낸 날짜
❥ 사내 업무 이메일일 수 있으므로 같은 도메인을 쓰는지 확인하자. 날짜는 이메일이 쓰여진 시점을 기준으로 과거 및 미래 특정 시점 관련 세부 사항을 질문할 수 있다.

② 제목
❥ 내용을 압축해 놓은 핵심 문구이므로 반드시 확인하자.

③ 본문
❥ 단락 요지를 파악하면서 읽자.

귀하의 서적을 재미 있게 읽었습니다.
혹시 강연을 해주실 수 있는지 궁금합니다.
사무실 지도를 첨부했습니다.
이메일이나 전화로 연락주세요.

주제 / 목적 문제 **이메일의 목적**

• 목적을 드러내는 표현
I am wondering whether you would be available to V
~을 할 수 있는지 궁금하다

• 패러프레이징
deliver a lecture
❥ give a talk

정답: (A)

ACTUAL TEST

정답 및 해설 p. 200

Questions 1-2 refer to the following e-mail.

To:	Warehouse staff
From:	Joe Cardimon
Subject:	Recent events
Date:	October 3

I would like to thank all staff for their recent hard work. Due to the flooding of our warehouse, it has not been an easy few months working out of alternative storage facilities. However, I am delighted to report that the cleanup operation has been completed and we are now able to start using it again to house goods.

We anticipate this will allow us to meet orders at a faster rate and deal with an increased volume of orders as the faith of customers in our business returns. As such, our management team view this as a significant moment for the future of our company. To celebrate this landmark and thank you for your dedication, we will hold a celebration in the cafeteria next Tuesday after work. We hope to see you all there. A wide range of refreshments and food will be provided.

Warm regards,

Jane Dobson

Facilities Manager

1. What does the e-mail indicate about the warehouse?

   (A) It has run out of stock.
   (B) It has been closed for several months.
   (C) It has recently been enlarged.
   (D) It has been relocated to a new site.

2. What will happen next Tuesday?

   (A) A large volume of orders will be processed.
   (B) Staff will gather for a training workshop.
   (C) A party for employees will be held.
   (D) Customers will be permitted to enter the premises.

Questions 3-5 refer to the following e-mail.

```
┌─────────────────────────────────────────────────────────────────────┐
│                              *E-mail*                                 │
├──────────┬──────────────────────────────────────────────────────────┤
│ To:      │ Anita Davies <a.davies@smart-clips.com>                   │
├──────────┼──────────────────────────────────────────────────────────┤
│ From:    │ Brian Nichols <b.nichols@smart-clips.com>                 │
├──────────┼──────────────────────────────────────────────────────────┤
│ Date:    │ January 28                                                │
├──────────┼──────────────────────────────────────────────────────────┤
│ Subject: │ Waiting area changes                                      │
└──────────┴──────────────────────────────────────────────────────────┘
```

Dear Anita,

The preparations for improving our hair salon's waiting area are going smoothly. I'm glad we've decided to do this, as the newly opened salon across the street has a very impressive waiting area, and we need to match their level of sophistication. — [1] —. I've changed our old coffee maker with a new one that brews individual cups. I think both the staff and the customers will appreciate the wider variety of flavors, and we won't have to keep making new pots of coffee that may or may not be consumed. — [2] —.

I've ordered a new sofa and two oak side tables, which will arrive on Friday around lunchtime. — [3] —. I think our current armchairs will look fine after getting steam-cleaned. I'll rent a steam cleaner next week. I'm sure everyone will love our fresh new look. — [4] —.

Brian

---

3. Why is the business making some changes?

(A) To accommodate more customers

(B) To attract talented employees

(C) To respond to customer requests

(D) To keep up with a competitor

4. What will happen at the end of the week?

(A) Some furniture will be delivered.

(B) Mr. Nichols will steam-clean items.

(C) A machine will be installed.

(D) Ms. Davies will approve a plan.

5. In which of the positions marked [1], [2], [3], and [4] does the following sentence best belong?

"That way, we can also reduce unnecessary waste."

(A) [1]

(B) [2]

(C) [3]

(D) [4]

Questions 6-9 refer to the following letter.

Patel, David
Milton Inn
424 Canyon Road
Wellingville, California

Dear Mr. Patel,

I was advised to contact you regarding my recent stay at your hotel. I normally stay at the Milton Inn every time I visit Wellingville on business and I usually enjoy my stay. However, on this occasion, there were a number of issues that left me unsatisfied.

First of all, the shower in my en suite bathroom had no hot water supply when I first arrived. This was eventually fixed, but was a bit of an inconvenience. I was also disappointed that I couldn't use the swimming facilities, as these were closed for maintenance. The tennis courts, although I didn't personally use them, appeared poorly maintained. This meant that I could not maintain my workout routine during my stay.

A colleague is visiting Wellingville next week. My experience with you was so negative that I am seriously considering recommending that he stay at the Plaza Hotel. I can see online that although they are further from the airport than you, they offer a member point system which can be redeemed for free accommodation.

Please don't hesitate to contact me if you would like to discuss the above issues.

Kara Richards

6. Why was the letter sent?
(A) To inquire about hotel rates
(B) To make a complaint
(C) To change a reservation
(D) To request a room upgrade

7. What is suggested about Ms. Richards?
(A) She used to work for the hotel.
(B) She is planning to move to Wellingville.
(C) She played tennis during her stay.
(D) She has visited Wellingville before.

8. What is NOT mentioned as being a feature of the Milton Inn?
(A) Sports facilities
(B) A swimming pool
(C) An airport shuttle bus
(D) En suite bathrooms

9. According to the letter, what is indicated by the Web site of the Plaza Hotel?
(A) It offers cheaper room prices than the Milton Inn.
(B) It operates a customer reward scheme.
(C) It has several job vacancies it is looking to fill.
(D) It is located next to the airport.

광고 / 공지 지문

54문항 중 평균 3~4문제 출제

출제 경향   상품 광고, 구인 광고, 업무 공지, 행사 및 공사 공지, 규칙 변경 사항 공지, 이용 안내 및 유의 사항 공지가 주된 내용이다. 광고 대상자를 유추하거나, 공지문이 목격될 만한 장소를 유추하는 추론 문제, 상품의 특징, 할인 혜택 적용 방법 등을 묻는 세부 사항 문제, 나열성 정보에 따른 Not / True문제가 주로 출제된다.

● 지문의 흐름 및 독해 전략

번역 p.202

제목	**HELP WANTED**
모집 부문	A part-time server is needed for lunch and dinner shifts at Wolfpen Café.
자격 요건/우대 조건	**You must be free to work daytime, evenings, weekends, and holidays.** Previous serving experience, especially in a fast-paced environment, is strongly preferred.
업무 내용	Your main responsibilities include greeting customers, taking orders, and handling payment.
업무 특성	All servers receive an hourly wage plus tips. Promotion to a full-time position is possible after three months of working with us.
지원 방법	Apply in person, and you will have a preliminary on-the-spot interview with a manager.

Q. What is indicated as a **requirement** of the position?
  (A) Availability on holidays
  (B) Previous experience
  (C) A certain education level
  (D) Ability to lift heavy items

지문 확인 사항

① **제목**
➋ 업체 상품 광고인 경우 상품명이나 업체명이 제목에 포함될 때가 많으며 구인 광고인 경우 직책명이 포함되는 경우가 많다. 공지문의 경우 글머리에 대상자를 언급한다.

② **본문**
➋ 단락 요지를 파악하고 나열성 정보에 주목하자.

- -

• 시간제 근무자 모집
• **평일, 저녁, 주말, 휴일 근무 가능자**
• 서빙 업무 유경험자 선호
• 주요 업무
  손님 맞이, 주문 받기, 계산
• 3개월 후 정규직 전환 가능
• 직접 방문 지원, 면접 있음

세부 사항 문제 **자격 요건**

• 자격 사항과 우대 사항 구분하기
  must / required ➋ 자격 요건
  preferred / plus ➋ 우대 조건

• 패러프레이징
  must be free to work holidays
  ➋ availability on holidays

정답 (A)

ACTUAL TEST

정답 및 해설 p. 202

Questions 1-2 refer to the following advertisement.

Photography by Giovanni

Giovanni and his team of skilled photographers have proudly served Scranton for 15 years. We can take headshots, group portraits, and candid photos that portray your company in its best light. Receive all of your photos as beautiful prints to hang on your wall or, at no extra cost, as convenient digital files for use in your official publications and promotional materials.

Call us at 555-0163 today to learn more about our services and obtain a price quote!

PHOTO STUDIO

---

1. What is NOT indicated about Photography by Giovanni?

(A) Multiple photographers work there.

(B) A publication gave it special recognition.

(C) It provides digital copies of photographs.

(D) It was founded over a decade ago.

2. What does Photography by Giovanni most likely specialize in?

(A) Family photography

(B) School photography

(C) Fashion photography

(D) Corporate photography

Hale Art Museum: Notice to Visitors

Hale Art Museum is a popular site for photographers, as we house an extensive collection of contemporary art from around the world. We would like to inform all visitors that photography is allowed within the museum, with some exceptions. The flash should be turned off at all times, and tripods are not permitted.

Visitors may photograph all parts of the permanent collection. However, photography is prohibited for special exhibits. That is because these pieces are on loan from other museums, so the Hale Art Museum has no ownership rights. In these cases, signs will be prominently displayed.

Photos taken at the Hale Art Museum must be for personal use only. They may not be sold or used for commercial purposes of any kind. This is in part due to copyright protections that may be in place for some of the pieces. Additionally, this practice could harm the museum's income from the sale of posters, framed prints, and other merchandise sold in our first-floor gift shop, which is needed to raise funds for ongoing expenses. By taking photographs at the museum, you are consenting to the above regulations. Thank you!

3. What is the purpose of the notice?

(A) To explain the history of a museum

(B) To give tips for taking good photos

(C) To outline a museum policy

(D) To apologize for an unavailable service

4. Why are some items restricted from being photographed?

(A) They do not belong to the museum.

(B) They are currently up for sale.

(C) They have very delicate components.

(D) They are being stored in a private area.

5. What is indicated about Hale Art Museum?

(A) It houses both ancient and modern art.

(B) It failed to meet its fundraising goals.

(C) It is looking for more volunteers.

(D) It has some images for sale on site.

 **Ergo Future**

Anyone who sits at a desk for more than six hours a day is likely to be familiar with the aches and pains that come from spending time in an uncomfortable chair, typing on a keyboard at funny angles, and staring at a computer screen. — [1] —.

Ergo Future sells chairs and desks custom-fitted to your body, so you can work longer and be more comfortable. After a short session with one of our specialists, we'll build you a chair that conforms to the unique shape of your spine, and a desk that sits at the perfect level for your height. — [2] —. There's no comparison between one of our master-crafted office sets and a generic, one-size-fits-all workstation.

We make long-lasting products that support overall health. — [3] —. In fact, we think it is so important for everyone to use Ergo Future goods that we offer more payment plans than any other furniture company. Our sales representatives will find a way for you or your company to purchase our products, which come with all the same warranties and guarantees standard across furniture manufacturers. — [4] —. Athletes would never settle for inferior equipment, so why should office workers?

Call us today at (820) 555-0139 and tell us that you saw this ad to receive 10% off your first order.

6. What type of products does Ergo Future make?
   (A) Office furniture
   (B) Sports equipment
   (C) Personal computers
   (D) Household appliances

7. According to the advertisement, what is special about Ergo Future?
   (A) The way it acquires its raw materials
   (B) The extent of its satisfaction guarantee
   (C) The range of its financing options
   (D) The amount of training of its employees

8. How can customers receive a discount?
   (A) By joining a rewards program
   (B) By referring a friend to Ergo Future
   (C) By purchasing a large group of items
   (D) By mentioning an advertisement

9. In which of the positions marked [1], [2], [3], and [4] does the following sentence best belong?

   "Ergo Future understands this issue, and we have a solution."
   (A) [1]
   (B) [2]
   (C) [3]
   (D) [4]

문자 / 채팅 지문

출제 경향　두 사람이 문자 메시지를 주고받거나 셋 이상이 온라인에서 채팅하는 형식을 갖는다. 문제점 및 요청 사항, 다음에 할 일 등을 묻는 세부 사항 문제와, 대화 내용을 통해 대화자들이 어떤 업계에 종사하는지 추론하는 문제가 종종 출제된다. 대화 중간에 쓰인 한 문장을 발췌하여 글쓴이의 의도를 묻는 의도 파악 문제는 각 지문에 1문제씩 총 2문항 출제된다.

● 지문의 흐름 및 독해 전략

번역 p. 204

Shirley Lowell	9:38 A.M.
인사말　Charles, are you busy?	
Charles Miller	9:38 A.M.
No, I'm not. What's up?	
Shirley Lowell	9:39 A.M.
대화 목적　I realized I forgot to bring some important files. They are probably sitting on my desk. Can you scan and	
요청 사항　send them to me?	
Charles Miller	9:40 A.M.
세부 사항　**Sure. I'll get a key from Security to get into your office.**	
Shirley Lowell	9:41 A.M.
I left the door unlocked.	
Charles Miller	9:42 A.M.
요청 수락　OK, then. I'll take care of that right now.	

지문 확인 사항

① 대화 형태 및 특징
- 지문이 대화로만 이루어지므로 구어체가 등장한다.
- 사내 동료 간, 고객센터와 고객 간 대화가 많다.
- 의도 파악 문제가 출제된다.

② 주요 대화 주제
- 업무 상황 및 스케줄 공유, 업무 역할 분담
- 문제점 제시 및 해결 방안

③ 본문
▶ 인물 관계와 전체 스토리를 파악하자.

- -

A: 제 책상 위에 문서가 있을
　거예요. 스캔해서 보내 주실
　수 있나요?
B: 네. **사무실 열쇠를**
　받아올게요.
A: **문은 잠그지 않았어요.**
B: 지금 바로 처리할게요.

Q. At 9:41 A.M., what does Ms. Lowell **most likely mean** when she writes, "I left the door unlocked"?
(A) Mr. Miller cannot work from home.
(B) Mr. Miller does not need a key.
(C) Mr. Miller is at the wrong office.
(D) Mr. Miller should lock the door.

의도 파악 문제
"문은 잠그지 않았어요."

- 앞뒤 상황 파악하기
　A: 문서 스캔 요청
　B: 사무실 열쇠가 필요하다고 판단
　A: 문을 열어 두었다고 고지

▶ 열쇠가 필요 없는 상황

정답 (B)

ACTUAL TEST

정답 및 해설 p. 206

Questions 1-2 refer to the following text-message chain.

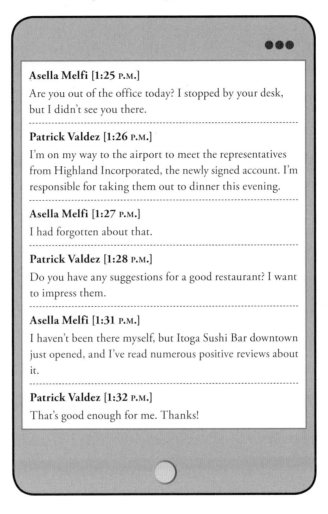

Asella Melfi [1:25 P.M.]
Are you out of the office today? I stopped by your desk, but I didn't see you there.

Patrick Valdez [1:26 P.M.]
I'm on my way to the airport to meet the representatives from Highland Incorporated, the newly signed account. I'm responsible for taking them out to dinner this evening.

Asella Melfi [1:27 P.M.]
I had forgotten about that.

Patrick Valdez [1:28 P.M.]
Do you have any suggestions for a good restaurant? I want to impress them.

Asella Melfi [1:31 P.M.]
I haven't been there myself, but Itoga Sushi Bar downtown just opened, and I've read numerous positive reviews about it.

Patrick Valdez [1:32 P.M.]
That's good enough for me. Thanks!

1. What is Mr. Valdez in charge of doing?

   (A) Recruiting some representatives
   (B) Booking some airline tickets
   (C) Entertaining some clients
   (D) Opening a bank account

2. At 1:32 P.M., what does Mr. Valdez suggest when he says, "That's good enough for me"?

   (A) He is willing to try a new business.
   (B) He liked the quality of some items.
   (C) He is pleased with Ms. Melfi's paperwork.
   (D) He thinks a review is ready to print.

Questions 3-6 refer to the following online chat discussion.

난이도 ● ● ●

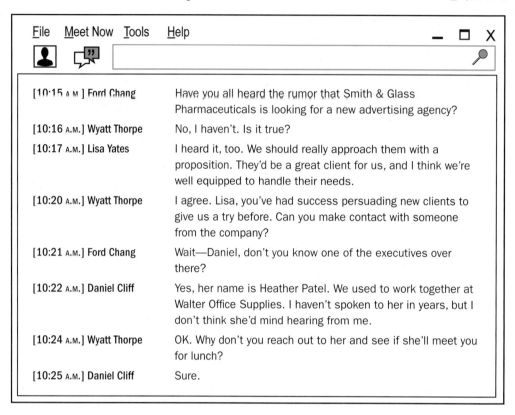

File Meet Now Tools Help	— ☐ X

[10:15 A.M.] Ford Chang	Have you all heard the rumor that Smith & Glass Pharmaceuticals is looking for a new advertising agency?
[10:16 A.M.] Wyatt Thorpe	No, I haven't. Is it true?
[10:17 A.M.] Lisa Yates	I heard it, too. We should really approach them with a proposition. They'd be a great client for us, and I think we're well equipped to handle their needs.
[10:20 A.M.] Wyatt Thorpe	I agree. Lisa, you've had success persuading new clients to give us a try before. Can you make contact with someone from the company?
[10:21 A.M.] Ford Chang	Wait—Daniel, don't you know one of the executives over there?
[10:22 A.M.] Daniel Cliff	Yes, her name is Heather Patel. We used to work together at Walter Office Supplies. I haven't spoken to her in years, but I don't think she'd mind hearing from me.
[10:24 A.M.] Wyatt Thorpe	OK. Why don't you reach out to her and see if she'll meet you for lunch?
[10:25 A.M.] Daniel Cliff	Sure.

3. Where do the writers most likely work?

(A) At a pharmaceutical company

(B) At an employment agency

(C) At an office supplies vendor

(D) At an advertising firm

4. What is indicated about Ms. Yates?

(A) She has worked at several companies.

(B) She heard some news from Mr. Chang.

(C) She has secured new clients in the past.

(D) She has finished drawing up a proposal.

5. At 10:21 A.M., what does Mr. Chang most likely mean when he writes, "Daniel, don't you know one of the executives over there"?

(A) Mr. Cliff did not include an important detail in a document.

(B) Mr. Cliff should not be part of a selection committee.

(C) Mr. Cliff should contact a former coworker.

(D) Mr. Cliff can describe a corporate culture.

6. What does Mr. Thorpe suggest arranging?

(A) A business lunch

(B) An equipment inspection

(C) A planning meeting

(D) An office tour

CLAIRE SANCHEZ [8:24 A.M.]
Hi, Michael. I've been working on our presentation slides. I'll send them to you right after they're done. I'm sorry they weren't with you yesterday as planned.

MICHAEL TURNER [8:41 A.M.]
Don't sweat it—we don't need them until this afternoon. And I've booked out the Lowry Suite.

CLAIRE SANCHEZ [8:48 A.M.]
Okay, I heard Robert Dean is coming along. I heard he provided some feedback on our work last time.

MICHAEL TURNER [8:54 A.M.]
Yes, he can be a bit difficult to please. I'm sure this time will go a lot better though.

CLAIRE SANCHEZ [9:06 A.M.]
Let's hope so. Okay, I'll meet you in the Lowry Suite after lunch. It is currently unfurnished, so we'll need to get the room ready.

MICHAEL TURNER [9:11 A.M.]
Okay, I'll head over at 12:00 sharp and help to set up.

7. What is suggested about Ms. Sanchez?

(A) She came into work early.

(B) She could not access some files.

(C) Her idea was disapproved.

(D) Her work took longer than expected.

8. At 8:41 A.M., what does Mr. Turner mean when he writes, "Don't sweat it"?

(A) He will allow Ms. Sanchez to miss a presentation.

(B) He recommends that Ms. Sanchez take some leave.

(C) He wants Ms. Sanchez to perform more research.

(D) He is not in a hurry to receive the presentation slides.

9. What is suggested about Robert Dean?

(A) He might not attend a meeting.

(B) He can be quite critical.

(C) He has collaborated with Mr. Turner.

(D) He is the owner of the company.

10. What is indicated about The Lowry Suite?

(A) It is located on the top floor.

(B) The nearby toilets are out of order.

(C) It can hold over ten people.

(D) It currently has no chairs inside.

기사 지문

출제 경향 지문의 난이도가 높으며, 지역 뉴스, 업계 뉴스, 인물 뉴스를 주요 내용으로 다룬다. 세부 사항 문제와 Not / True 문제가 주로 출제된다.

● 지문의 흐름 및 독해 전략

번역 p. 207

제목   **Local Woman Wins State Award**

지역
발행일   ARLINGTON (March 10) – At a press conference yesterday, a spokesperson for the law firm Nichols & Malone announced that Rena McKean is the recipient of the Kai Prize.

일반 정보   The prestigious award is presented each year to an educator who has shown dedication to language education.

세부 정보   Ms. McKean was recognized for her hard work and dedication to her class and her place of employment will receive a cash prize of $10,000. As it is a public site, **taxpayers are invited to attend the district meeting on March 17 to discuss how the money will be spent.**

Q. What are **taxpayers encouraged** to do?
(A) Nominate a candidate for an award
(B) Vote for a new district representative
(C) Make a financial contribution to a program
(D) Express a preference for a spending plan

지문 확인 사항

① 제목

❯ 기사 제목에는 주제가 드러난다. 시제와 관계없이 핵심만 파악한다.
ex "지역 여성, 상 받다"

② 본문

❯ 첫 문단은 육하원칙에 따른 주요 소식, 나머지 문단은 관련 정보 및 세부 소식을 담고 있다.

레나 맥킨, 카이상 수상
언어 교육자에게 매년 수여
학교: 현금 1만 달러 수상
3월 17일 납세자 회의에서 수상금 사용처 논의

세부 사항 문제
납세자들이 할 일

• 키워드 포착
taxpayer / encouraged

• 패러프레이징
discuss how the money will be spent ❯ express a preference for a spending plan

정답 **(D)**

정답 및 해설 p.207

Questions 1-2 refer to the following article.

Barton City Arts Corner

Barton City (May 7) — Donna Lopez did not intend to open her own ceramics studio so early in her career, but when she saw a workshop for rent at a bargain price in Porter Warehouse Complex, she reconsidered. "I've been using the facilities at the Arts Center downtown to make my pieces. I didn't think I would be able to afford my own space for a few more years, but my corner of Porter is a great deal," said Ms. Lopez. Ms. Lopez is funding the studio with proceeds from selling her plates, bowls and other kitchen ceramics on the Internet and from a series of classes she offers. These include "Practicum" on weekdays, which teaches advanced ceramics techniques, and "Foundations", a free class for beginning ceramics enthusiasts. More information can be found on her Web site, www.esmereldaspottery.com.

1. Why was Ms. Lopez able to open an art studio earlier than she expected?

   (A) She was granted a loan.

   (B) She won a competition.

   (C) She graduated from university early.

   (D) She found an inexpensive space.

2. According to the article, what does Ms. Lopez make?

   (A) Stained glass

   (B) Dinnerware

   (C) Statues

   (D) Tile mosaics

Denniton Labs Receives $130,000 from Council on Ohio's Future

DAYTON – The Council on Ohio's Future (COF) has chosen pharmaceuticals manufacturer Denniton Labs as the recipient of a $130,000 grant to enable high school students to be successful in the workplace after graduation. The COF's mission is to assist students to prepare for the future, and chairperson Rhonda Reynolds says they are always looking for partners in this goal. "Denniton Labs has a proven history of employing large numbers of Ohio students directly after graduation from high school, so we believe they'll be a valuable ally,"

explained Ms. Reynolds.

Denniton Labs will use the funds to provide weekend courses in which students can learn technical skills and participate in workshops that will offer advice and direction for their post-school work lives.

The first course will begin on November 5. The courses are open to all high school students in the Montgomery County School District. Students can register by signing up directly on the Denniton Labs Web site. There is no cost to attend, and food will be provided.

3. What group of people does the COF try to help?

(A) Scientists
(B) Students
(C) Teachers
(D) Businesspeople

4. Why was Denniton Labs chosen as a grant recipient?

(A) It hires many high school graduates.
(B) It makes educational products.
(C) It holds public lectures on important topics.
(D) It finances community development projects.

5. According to the article, what will happen at Denniton Labs on weekends in November?

(A) Technicians will install new machinery.
(B) Inventions will be exhibited.
(C) Career guidance will be provided.
(D) Staff will receive special skills training.

Wilshire Hall Transformation Goes Forward

TENNY HEIGHTS, April 5 – After two years of planning, Wilshire Hall is finally ready to undergo an ambitious renovation project. The project is aimed at transforming the hall into a modern performance venue. — [1] —. The closure will last for 18 months, and an exact grand opening date will be announced later.

Through a combination of private and corporate donations, federal arts grants, and ticket charges, the hall was able to raise $18.5 million for the work. — [2] —. Theater manager Davis Palmer praised the work of John Reynolds, the architect who designed the new auditorium. "After the project is completed, we will have nearly double the number of seats for audience members," Palmer explained. "In addition, the stage will be expanded to accommodate more performances. That way, we won't miss out on potential shows. For example, last year Arianne Fontaine didn't stop in Tenny Heights on her national concert tour because our stage was not large enough for her set. That won't be an issue after the renovations."— [3] —.

In addition to interior upgrades, work will be done on the exterior of the building, including planting flower beds near the main entrance and covering the on-site parking lot with a new layer of asphalt.

The final performance at Wilshire Hall before the closure will be a dramatic play entitled *Across the Road*. The play will be performed by Wilshire Hall's own in-house theater troupe. — [4] —.

6. How long will Wilshire Hall be closed?

(A) For six months

(B) For one and a half years

(C) For two years

(D) For three years

7. What is NOT mentioned as a part of the project?

(A) Repaving a parking lot

(B) Enlarging a stage

(C) Upgrading a sound system

(D) Adding more seats

8. Who most likely is Arianne Fontaine?

(A) An actress

(B) An architect

(C) A theater manager

(D) A musician

9. In which of the positions marked [1], [2], [3], and [4] does the following sentence best belong?

"It is certainly a fitting end to the site's first phase."

(A) [1]

(B) [2]

(C) [3]

(D) [4]

웹페이지 / 기타 양식 지문

출제 경향 웹페이지는 업체 소개, 고객 리뷰, 서비스 안내 페이지로 주로 구성되며, 기타 양식은 주문서, 영수증, 설문지, 일정표, 초대장 등으로 구성된다. 표가 어떤 정보를 담고 있는지를 묻는 간단한 정보 매칭형 문제(세부 사항 문제)와 Not / True 문제가 주로 출제된다.

● 지문의 흐름 및 독해 전략

번역 p. 209

웹주소/탭   www.thefreelancerpenplus.com

About	Jobs	Membership	Contact

Welcome!

소개말 The Freelancer Penplus is the best Web site to develop your writing skills and make connections with others that write for a living.

To get the most out of The Freelancer Penplus, consider becoming a paying member.

Members enjoy these great benefits:

세부정보
- **Respond to conversations on the forums or start your own.**
- **Members are informed of writing jobs and positions before anyone else.**
- **Our smartphone app is only available to our members.**

Interested in joining? Click on the "Membership" tab.

지문 확인 사항

① 웹주소 / 탭 / 제목
❺ 해당 웹페이지가 어떤 내용에 대해 다루는지 대략적으로 알 수 있다.
　※ 탭에서 About은 회사를 소개하는 내용을 담고 있는 섹션이다.

② 본문
❺ 단락 요지를 파악하고 나열성 정보에 주목한다.
　※ 별표(*) 또는 'Note'에 표기된 내용은 문제로 출제될 확률이 매우 높다.

프리랜서 펜플러스는?
글쓰기 실력을 연마하고 작가들과 소통할 수 있는 웹사이트

멤버십 혜택
- 포럼 이용 가능
- 일자리 정보 우선권
- 전용 스마트폰 앱 이용 가능

가입 – 멤버십 탭 클릭

Q. What is **NOT mentioned** as something **members can do**?

(A) See job listings earlier than nonmembers
(B) Start new discussions on message boards
(C) Use software designed for mobile devices
(D) Communicate privately with other members

Not / True 문제 회원 혜택

- 나열된 정보 패러프레이징하기
  ① 포럼 이용 ❺ (B)
  ② 일자리 정보 우선권 ❺ (A)
  ③ 전용 스마트폰 어플 ❺ (C)

정답 (D)

정답 및 해설 p. 200

Questions 1-2 refer to the following form.

Bao Computer Repair

Computer drop-off date:	October 14
Repair technician:	Abdul Khan
Repair ticket:	1114BL3
Client:	Donita Partridge
Phone number:	(413) 555-0189

Problem:

The computer makes a loud noise sometimes. The problem generally happens when the user loads large apps.

Diagnosis and repair procedure:

One of the cooling fans was out of alignment, so it made a funny sound whenever it turned on. The strain on the system from loading apps caused the fan to turn on. I replaced the fan and the problem disappeared.

Notes:

The computer is protected by our shop's extended warranty, which fully covers the fee for this repair.

Completed:	October 14
Technician signature:	Abdul Khan
Client signature:	

1. What is one purpose of the form?

   (A) To request a payment
   (B) To explain problems with a new system
   (C) To provide details of work carried out
   (D) To give feedback on a posting

2. What is stated about the repair?

   (A) It took several days to complete.
   (B) It required a complicated procedure.
   (C) It was done at no charge to the client.
   (D) It did not solve the reported problem.

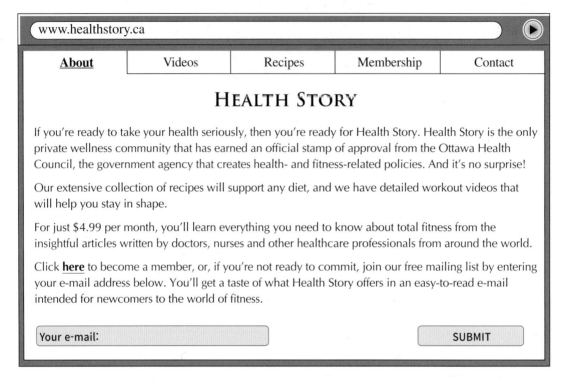

www.healthstory.ca

| **About** | Videos | Recipes | Membership | Contact |

HEALTH STORY

If you're ready to take your health seriously, then you're ready for Health Story. Health Story is the only private wellness community that has earned an official stamp of approval from the Ottawa Health Council, the government agency that creates health- and fitness-related policies. And it's no surprise!

Our extensive collection of recipes will support any diet, and we have detailed workout videos that will help you stay in shape.

For just $4.99 per month, you'll learn everything you need to know about total fitness from the insightful articles written by doctors, nurses and other healthcare professionals from around the world.

Click **here** to become a member, or, if you're not ready to commit, join our free mailing list by entering your e-mail address below. You'll get a taste of what Health Story offers in an easy-to-read e-mail intended for newcomers to the world of fitness.

Your e-mail: [   ]   SUBMIT

3. What is indicated about Health Story?

(A) It was featured on a television broadcast.

(B) It was originally a social media site for doctors.

(C) It offers discounted trial memberships.

(D) It is endorsed by a government body.

4. According to the Web page, what can be seen in Health Story videos?

(A) Celebrity interviews

(B) Exercise activities

(C) Cooking lessons

(D) News stories

5 Where do articles on Health Story come from?

(A) They are linked from other Web sites.

(B) They are chosen from popular forum posts.

(C) They are provided by competition winners.

(D) They are submitted by health-care experts.

Thank you for using Travel World's mobile application!
Please take a moment to fill out this survey.

What do you use the Travel World app for? Select all that apply.

☐ Making hotel reservations   ☐ Buying flight tickets

☑ Obtaining dining information   ☐ Arranging ground travel

Please indicate whether or not you agree with the following statements.

The Travel World app is easy to use.	☑ Yes	☐ No
The Travel World app meets all my traveling needs.	☑ Yes	☐ No
The Travel World app is reasonably priced.	☐ Yes	☑ No

Do you have any comments or suggestions for us? If so, write them below.

> Your app's range of features is convenient, but I find the functionality is superior on apps that dedicate themselves to one function. Actually, since I don't use most of your app's features, I'm going to switch to another one that I think is tailored more specifically to what I'll use it for.

Thanks for your feedback! Is it OK to contact you about your responses on this survey?

☑ Yes   ☐ No

Name: _Jane Peretti_

E-mail: _j.peretti@cnkomail.com_

---

6. What would Ms. Peretti most likely use the Travel World app to do?

(A) Book lodgings

(B) Research air travel

(C) Plan a driving route

(D) Decide where to eat

7. What is indicated about the Travel World app?

(A) It is compatible with all mobile devices.

(B) It is frequently updated.

(C) It is not free to use.

(D) It is not helpful in some countries.

8. Why does Ms. Peretti say she will stop using the Travel World app?

(A) She intends to travel less in the future.

(B) Its latest version does not include a certain feature.

(C) Her company purchased a different app.

(D) She will switch to a more specialized app.

이중 연계 지문

출제 경향 이중 연계 지문은 서로 관련이 있는 두 개의 지문과 5문항으로 구성되며, 반드시 한 문제는 연계 문제로 출제된다. 연계 문제는 각 지문에서 단서를 찾아내어 두 정보를 조합하여 답을 구하는 형태로 출제된다.

● 지문 구성

> **지문1** To Sales Team,
>
> I have heard from our CEO that **we will pull out of any country where we have done less than £25,000 in sales over the past year.** ②
>
> Please keep this in mind and prepare accordingly for the meeting.

> **지문2** CoCo Bedding Annual Sales Report
>   for the previous year
>
> | Switzerland | £33,000 | Spain | £56,000 |
> |---|---|---|---|
> | Germany | £78,000 | **France** | **£21,000** ❸ |

Q. Which country will CoCo Bedding most likely **stop selling** its products in? ①
(A) Swiss (B) Germany (C) Spain **(D) France** ❹

영업 팀에게

CEO께서 **지난해 매출이 2만 5천 파운드 미만인 국가에서는 판매를 중단하시겠다고 하셨습니다.**

이를 참고하여 회의 준비를 하십시오.

코코 베딩 전년 연매출 보고서

스위스	£33,000	스페인	£56,000
독일	£78,000	**프랑스**	**£21,000**

Q. 코코 베딩은 어떤 국가에서 상품 판매를 중단할 것 같은가?
(A) 스위스 (B) 독일
(C) 스페인 (D) 프랑스

● 문제 풀이 과정

STEP ① 문제를 읽고 찾아야 할 정보를 확인한다.
      "어느 국가에서 판매 중단?"

STEP ② 키워드가 드러나는 근거 문장을 포착한다.
      "매출 £25,000 미만인 국가에서 생산 중단"
      ↳ 국가명은 알 수 없음

STEP ③ 다음 지문에서 추가 정보를 확인한다.
      "작년 매출 £21,000 in France"

STEP ④ 두 가지 정보를 조합해서 답을 구한다.

※ 연계 문제를 알아보는 Tip
• 보기가 단답형 구성인 경우 연계 문제일 가능성이 높다.
• 추론 문제, Not / True 문제인 경우 연계 문제일 가능성이 높다.
• 지문에 표가 있는 경우 연계 문제로 반드시 출제된다.

READING PRACTICE

정답 및 해설 p.212

Q. 웹페이지 + 편지

---

www.redhillroofing.net

| HOME | PHOTO GALLERY | OUR PRODUCTS | MEET THE TEAM | CONTACT |

Redhill Roofing is the area's premier roofing company. We have been providing top-quality services for both residential and commercial properties for the past twenty-five years.

We have recently launched our Roofing Connect referral program. Current and previous customers can tell their friends about our business, providing them with a unique referral code. The friend will be given $50 off their bill.

A new roof can raise the value of your property, improve the energy efficiency of your home, and help you to avoid potential health hazards such as mold. Call us today at 679-555-0133, or click on the Contact tab above for a list of other ways to get in touch.

A.J. Costanza, 3007 Vesta Avenue
Marysville, PA 17053
October 12

Dear Mr. Costanza,

It was a pleasure meeting you yesterday to discuss the replacement of your home's roof. Enclosed you will find a statement of the approximate charges for this project. Please be aware that the price reflects the cost of replacing the entire roof of the structure, counting the garage. Through the Roofing Connect program, you will receive a $50 discount on the work, which is noted on the enclosed document.

Crews are available to start the work anytime. Call us at 550-0158 to schedule a time for the work.

Sincerely,
Danny Quintero

Q. What is suggested about Mr. Costanza?

(A) His requested project will take about sixty days.

(B) His current roofing tiles are still under warranty.

(C) He needs to have a new roof for his business.

(D) He found out about the business through a friend.

Questions 1-5 refer to the following Web page and e-mail.

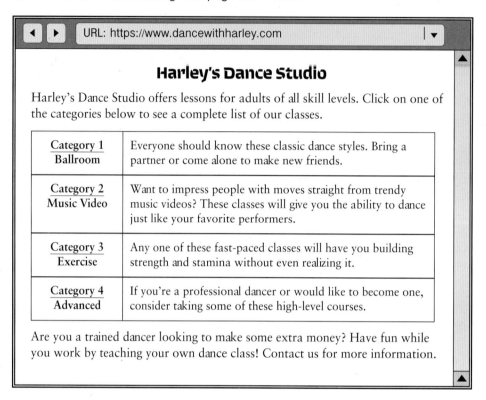

Harley's Dance Studio

Harley's Dance Studio offers lessons for adults of all skill levels. Click on one of the categories below to see a complete list of our classes.

Category 1 **Ballroom**	Everyone should know these classic dance styles. Bring a partner or come alone to make new friends.
Category 2 **Music Video**	Want to impress people with moves straight from trendy music videos? These classes will give you the ability to dance just like your favorite performers.
Category 3 **Exercise**	Any one of these fast-paced classes will have you building strength and stamina without even realizing it.
Category 4 **Advanced**	If you're a professional dancer or would like to become one, consider taking some of these high-level courses.

Are you a trained dancer looking to make some extra money? Have fun while you work by teaching your own dance class! Contact us for more information.

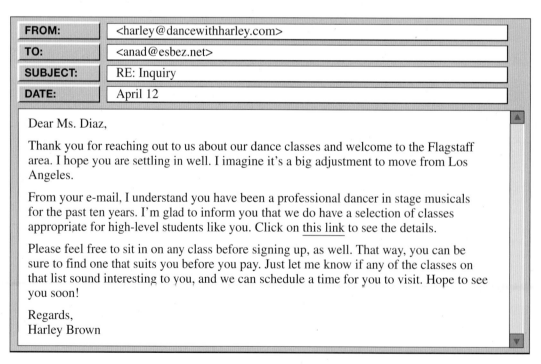

FROM:	\<harley@dancewithharley.com\>
TO:	\<anad@esbez.net\>
SUBJECT:	RE: Inquiry
DATE:	April 12

Dear Ms. Diaz,

Thank you for reaching out to us about our dance classes and welcome to the Flagstaff area. I hope you are settling in well. I imagine it's a big adjustment to move from Los Angeles.

From your e-mail, I understand you have been a professional dancer in stage musicals for the past ten years. I'm glad to inform you that we do have a selection of classes appropriate for high-level students like you. Click on this link to see the details.

Please feel free to sit in on any class before signing up, as well. That way, you can be sure to find one that suits you before you pay. Just let me know if any of the classes on that list sound interesting to you, and we can schedule a time for you to visit. Hope to see you soon!

Regards,
Harley Brown

1. What is NOT mentioned as a benefit of taking a dance class?

   (A) The acquisition of an impressive skill
   (B) Improved physical fitness
   (C) Temporary stress relief
   (D) A wider social network

2. What does the Web page indicate about Harley's Dance Studio?

   (A) It posts dance videos online.
   (B) It is seeking new employees.
   (C) It will open a new location.
   (D) It puts on public performances.

3. What is probably true about Ms. Diaz?

   (A) She is applying for a teaching job.
   (B) She owns a dance studio.
   (C) She recently moved to a new city.
   (D) She works for an entertainment company.

4. Which category of classes does Ms. Brown most likely provide a link to?

   (A) Category 1
   (B) Category 2
   (C) Category 3
   (D) Category 4

5. What does Ms. Brown encourage Ms. Diaz to do?

   (A) Try a class for free
   (B) E-mail some instructors
   (C) Read some student reviews
   (D) Sign up for an audition

www.armstronginst.com/awakeretreat

Reconnect to your vision with the Awake Retreat!

The Awake Retreat, sponsored by the Armstrong Institute, helps teachers and professors to bring back their passion and find renewed purpose in their work. The program is taught by specialists whose insights and experiences will help guide participants in maximizing their effectiveness in the classroom. The Awake Retreat is a two-day program including small-group discussions, lectures, and periods of self-reflection.

One of our four full-time, highly-qualified instructors will lead the entire retreat. Our instructors are Patrick Armstrong and Janice Shields (cofounders of the Armstrong Institute), Hannah Kim (program facilitator), and Gabrielle Melo (senior trainer). During the retreat, you'll learn about using your past experiences to drive policy changes, identifying the leadership categories in which you excel, creating a mission for your staff, and more. We are continually improving our program based on comments from participants who filled out the questionnaire we sent to them after completing the program. Don't miss this opportunity to take your career to the next level!

The fee for the Awake Retreat—which includes all meals as well as one night of accommodation in our cabins, is $595—and it can be divided into three payments.

Armstrong Institute
Customer Receipt

Customer:	Bruno Cardoso
Session:	Awake Retreat
Dates/ Instructor:	May 7-8 / Hannah Kim
Amount paid:	$595.00
Payment:	Royalcard XXXX-XXXX-XXXX-7638

Please bring this receipt as proof of payment when you check in for the session. For cancellations, please call Janice Shields at 555-0161.

6. What is NOT true about the Awake Retreat?

(A) Its fee can be paid in installments.

(B) Its target audience is people in the education field.

(C) Its participants stay two nights at the site.

(D) Its sessions are led by experts.

7. What is mentioned as a topic covered at the retreat?

(A) Managing time efficiently

(B) Getting feedback about policies

(C) Identifying leadership strengths

(D) Hiring experienced staff members

8. What does the Armstrong Institute send to participants?

(A) A coupon for other programs

(B) A follow-up survey

(C) A certificate of completion

(D) A list of participants

9. What is suggested about Mr. Cardoso?

(A) He will be trained by the program facilitator.

(B) He was eligible for a discount on the session.

(C) He has attended Armstrong Institute workshops before.

(D) He wants to cancel his original booking.

10. What is indicated on the receipt?

(A) Ms. Shields assisted Mr. Cardoso with the reservation.

(B) Mr. Cardoso will attend the event with a coworker.

(C) The registration was made by Mr. Cardoso's company.

(D) The amount was paid in full.

삼중 연계 지문

출제 경향   삼중 연계 지문은 서로 관련이 있는 세 개의 지문과 5문항으로 구성되며, 5문항 중 반드시 두 문제는 연계 문제로 출제된다. 연계 문제는 두 지문씩 연계되어 출제된다.

● 지문 구성

지문1   The Greendale Flea Market will open this Saturday. If you want to set up your booth, please check what items you can sell and send an e-mail to us.

Section A Home Appliances	Section B Books ❸
Section C Clothing	Section D Baby Products

지문2   Hello, My name is Ben Warren.
I would like to rent a stall in section B, ❷ and I want to use it for 2 days. ❷
Please let me know if it is available. Thank you.

지문3   Rental Costs for Booth Spaces

Section A $30 per day	Section B $35 per day ❸
Section C $40 per day	Section D $45 per day

Q1. What does **Mr. Warren intend to sell**? ❶
     Books ❹
Q2. **How much** should **Mr. Warren pay in total**? ❶
     $70 ❹

그린데일 벼룩시장이 이번 주 토요일에 개장합니다. 부스 설치를 원하면 어떤 품목을 판매할 수 있는지 확인하고 신청하려면 이메일을 보내세요.

구역 A 가전제품	구역 B 도서
구역 C 의류	구역 D 유아용품

안녕하세요, 저는 벤 워렌입니다. B구역에서 가판대를 빌리고 싶어요. 그리고 이틀간 사용하고 싶어요. 가능한지 연락 주세요. 감사합니다.

부스 임대료

구역 A 1일 $30	구역 B 1일 $35
구역 C 1일 $40	구역 D 1일 $45

Q1. 워렌 씨는 무엇을 팔려고 하는가?
     도서
Q2. 워렌 씨는 총 얼마를 내야 하는가?
     $70

● 문제 풀이 과정

첫 번째 연계 문제

STEP ❶ 문제를 읽고 찾아야 할 정보를 확인한다.
     "워렌 씨가 팔고자 하는 품목은?"

STEP ❷ 키워드가 드러나는 근거 문장을 포착한다.
     "D구역 기판메를 빌리고 싶어요."

STEP ❸ 관련된 추가 정보를 확인한다.
     "B 구역 – 도서"

STEP ❹ 두 가지 정보를 조합해서 답을 구한다.

두 번째 연계 문제

STEP ❶ 문제를 읽고 찾아야 할 정보를 확인한다.
     "워렌 씨가 지불해야 하는 총액은?"

STEP ❷ 키워드가 드러나는 근거 문장을 포착한다.
     "B구역 가판대를 이틀간 사용하고 싶어요."

STEP ❸ 관련된 추가 정보를 확인한다.
     "B구역 대여료 – $35 per day"

STEP ❹ 두 가지 정보를 조합해서 답을 구한다.

READING PRACTICE

정답 및 해설 p.215

1-2. 안내책자 + 공지 + 고객 상품평

Artmoor Furniture / Victorian Table (product no. 2NJI890)

- Description: Sturdy pine wood dinner table with elegant carved legs. Comfortably seats six, or can be extended (with use of optional extension leaf) to seat eight.
- Size: 63 X 36 X 31 (inch)
- Finishes: Oak, cherry, natural, maple
- Replacement/Accessory parts:
· Table legs (part no. 100-A) · Extension leaf (part no. 103-A) · Chairs (product no. N220)
· Mounting hardware (parts no. 101-A and 102-A)

Attention Sales Team:

I have some updates on the Victorian Table, product no. 2NJI890. I contacted the manufacturer, and apparently the oak-finished table is selling beyond expectations across the country, so there will be a fulfillment delay for any customers ordering that one.
Also, the manufacturer notified me that they stopped making the optional leaf, so take that piece out of your sales pitches. Please let me know if you have any questions.

Raul Santiago

---

www.artmoorfurniture.com/reviews

Vanessa Aya – March 20

I love my Victorian Table! Multiple guests have commented on how attractive it is. I'm not surprised to hear there is a backorder on the finish I got.

The only negative thing I can say about the table is that it is not easy for the average person to put together. It was too complicated for me, so I had to hire outside help.

Still, I highly recommend the table!

---

1. What did the table manufacturer stop producing?
(A) part no. 101-A
(B) part no. 102-A
(C) part no. 103-A
(D) product no. N220

2. Which finish did Ms. Aya choose for her table?
(A) Oak
(B) Cherry
(C) Natural
(D) Maple

정답 및 해설 p.216

Questions 1-5 refer to the following advertisement, letter, and e-mail.

FREE SPACE AVAILABLE!

A 500-square-foot meeting room on the top floor of Parkdale Library may now be reserved for one-time or regular use. In addition to the lovely view of Parkdale that is visible out of its windows, the room offers a whiteboard, 25 seats, and four tables that can be pushed together or separated as needed.

As Parkdale Library is committed to promoting a sense of community among Parkdale citizens, we will only consider reservation applications from persons and organizations that share this goal. Please provide evidence of this in your application. Applications may be submitted to our community outreach coordinator, Linda Armisen, in person or at this address:

Parkdale Public Library
312 Main Street
Parkdale, WI 53090

Linda Armisen
Parkdale Public Library
312 Main Street
Parkdale, WI 53090

Dear Ms. Armisen,

I am writing to apply to reserve the meeting space you advertised in the *Parkdale Daily Reader*. I am the president of Parkdale Tabletop Gaming (PTG), a friendly and welcoming community of people who like to play board games, card games, etc. on Saturday afternoons. Since we had our first meeting ten months ago, our treasurer has graciously hosted us in his home every week. However, our group has grown, and now needs a larger space. I believe your meeting room is exactly what we are looking for.
I have enclosed our application with this letter. To satisfy your special requirement, I have also attached to it an article that the *Parkdale Gazette* wrote about our group.
Thank you,

Kimmy Kang
Kimmy Kang

President, Parkdale Tabletop Gaming
Enclosure

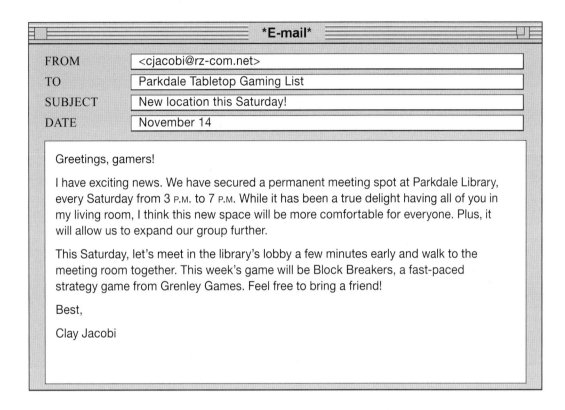

E-mail

FROM	<cjacobi@rz-com.net>
TO	Parkdale Tabletop Gaming List
SUBJECT	New location this Saturday!
DATE	November 14

Greetings, gamers!

I have exciting news. We have secured a permanent meeting spot at Parkdale Library, every Saturday from 3 P.M. to 7 P.M. While it has been a true delight having all of you in my living room, I think this new space will be more comfortable for everyone. Plus, it will allow us to expand our group further.

This Saturday, let's meet in the library's lobby a few minutes early and walk to the meeting room together. This week's game will be Block Breakers, a fast-paced strategy game from Grenley Games. Feel free to bring a friend!

Best,

Clay Jacobi

---

1. What is indicated about Parkdale Library?

(A) Its hours are different on weekends.

(B) Its staff produce a newsletter.

(C) Its building has multiple floors.

(D) Its meeting room has a projector.

2. What does Ms. Kang mention has changed about PTG?

(A) How many members it has

(B) What its membership fee is

(C) How often it meets

(D) What types of games it plays

3. What does the attachment that Ms. Kang sent most likely say about PTG?

(A) It is sponsored by a local company.

(B) It is beneficial to Parkdale residents.

(C) It has strict requirements for membership.

(D) It has purchased an insurance policy.

4. In the e-mail, the word "spot" in paragraph 1, line 1, is closest in meaning to

(A) commercial

(B) place

(C) stain

(D) sight

5. Who is Mr. Jacobi?

(A) A public relations specialist at a game company

(B) A community outreach coordinator at a library

(C) The founder of a community organization

(D) The treasurer of a gaming group

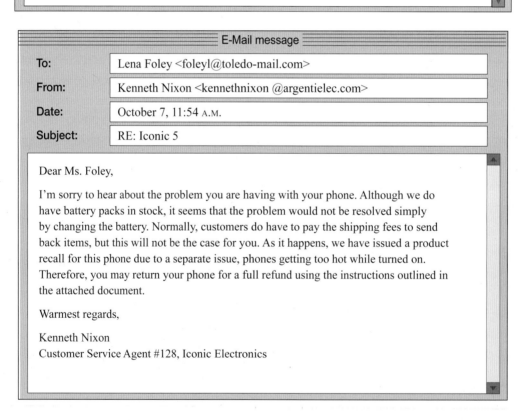

To:	Iconic Electronics <inquiries@argentielec.com>
From:	Lena Foley <foleyl@toledo-mail.com>
Date:	October 7, 8:29 A.M.
Subject:	Iconic 5

To Whom It May Concern:

I'm having a problem with my Iconic 5 smartphone, which I purchased last month at the Iconic retail store in the Canton Mall. When I press the Power button, it takes up to a minute for the screen to light up. Do you sell separate battery packs? If so, I am wondering purchasing a new battery would resolve this issue. Also, could you tell me when the next software update is? If I do send back the phone, would the company pay for the shipping costs, or must I cover those costs myself? Please reply as soon as possible.

Thank you,

Lena Foley

	E-Mail message
To:	Lena Foley <foleyl@toledo-mail.com>
From:	Kenneth Nixon <kennethnixon @argentielec.com>
Date:	October 7, 11:54 A.M.
Subject:	RE: Iconic 5

Dear Ms. Foley,

I'm sorry to hear about the problem you are having with your phone. Although we do have battery packs in stock, it seems that the problem would not be resolved simply by changing the battery. Normally, customers do have to pay the shipping fees to send back items, but this will not be the case for you. As it happens, we have issued a product recall for this phone due to a separate issue, phones getting too hot while turned on. Therefore, you may return your phone for a full refund using the instructions outlined in the attached document.

Warmest regards,

Kenneth Nixon
Customer Service Agent #128, Iconic Electronics

Product Recall: Iconic 5

How to Return Your Device

To request your recovery box, visit our Web site at www.argentielec.com. Please call 1-800-555-0167 if any of the components listed below are not in your recovery box.ℭ

-----

1. Make sure the phone is powered off so that the battery is not active while in transit.
2. Open the inner box, whose interior is lined with a special heat-resistant paper. Some people may be sensitive to this paper, so you should wear gloves or be careful not to touch it.
3. Place the phone in a plastic bag and then in the inner box, securing the box's lid with tape.
4. Place the inner box inside the shipping box and tape it shut.
5. Attach the pre-printed shipping label. Alternatively, if you purchased the item at an Iconic retail store, you may drop it off at the store.

-----

6. What problem does Ms. Foley mention?

(A) Her phone is slow to turn on.

(B) Her phone overheats while in use.

(C) She is missing some phone accessories.

(D) She broke her phone's screen.

7. What topic raised by Ms. Foley is NOT addressed by Mr. Nixon?

(A) Product availability

(B) Shipping costs

(C) Battery replacement

(D) A software update

8. Why should customers call the number provided?

(A) To check a refund's status

(B) To request a recovery box

(C) To report missing items

(D) To inquire about the steps

9. What is mentioned as one preparation step for returning the phone?

(A) Taping the plastic bag shut

(B) Printing a return shipping label

(C) Removing the phone's battery

(D) Avoiding touching a certain material

10. What is true about Ms. Foley?

(A) She will request a replacement device.

(B) She is permitted to return an item in person.

(C) She should send a receipt to Mr. Nixon.

(D) She purchased her smartphone in October.

Northline Country Club

Northline Country Club houses a perfect 18-hole golf course, an indoor Olympic-size swimming pool, a modern clubhouse, and more. Our site has been rated "Best Golf Course in Maine" for three consecutive years. Our on-site restaurant is available exclusively to members and their guests, and it can be booked for private events (Ultimate-level members only).

★ ★ ★ ★ ★ ★ ★ ★ ★ ★

Off-Peak Membership: Access to the golf course during off-peak times (weekdays after 2 P.M., weekends 6 P.M. to closing) [$175/month]

Standard Membership: Access to the golf course during any opening hours, 5% discount at clubhouse bar [$275/month]

Enhanced Membership: Access to the golf course during any opening hours with priority booking ahead of Standard and Off-Peak members, 10% discount at clubhouse bar [$300/month]

Ultimate Membership: Access to the golf course during any opening hours with priority booking ahead of all other memberships, 15% discount at clubhouse bar, private event booking [$375/month]

To:	Spencer Morris <s.morris@pinepost.ca>
From:	Peter Benson <bensonp@northlinecc.com>
Date:	June 24
Subject:	Lessons at Northline Country Club

Dear Mr. Morris,

You were put on a waiting list for golf lessons with Ryan Brodie when you first joined our club, and I'm pleased to say that a space has now opened up. You are very lucky to get this spot because there are a lot of people on the list, but you were the only person available at the open time slot. All of Mr. Brodie's other students have been training with him for a minimum of 24 months, and these lessons have yielded impressive results. They are preparing to compete in the Regional Golf Tournament next month. His goal is to drive them to reach their full potential.

Your first lesson will take place on July 1 at 3 P.M. You should meet Mr. Brodie at the clubhouse.

Please note that you will be billed $175 per two-hour lesson. This is in addition to the $300 in monthly fees that you pay for your membership.

Best regards,

Peter

Northline Country Club

Golf Lessons Schedule: Tuesday, July 1

Times & Instructors	Dorothy Santiago	Ryan Brodie	Avery Walsh
8 A.M.	Elizabeth Ferguson	Donna Karen	Sarah Wagner
10 A.M.	—	Ann Curtis	—
1 P.M.	Michael Smith	Jessica Hwang	—
3 P.M.	—	Spencer Morris	—
5 P.M.	Teen Group Lesson	Will Stern	Melanie Grenon

Meeting location: Clubhouse, unless otherwise arranged with the client.

11. What is true about Northline Country Club?

(A) It offers free golf cart use to members.

(B) Its swimming pool is closed in the winter.

(C) It has recently expanded its clubhouse.

(D) Its members have access to a dining facility.

12. What membership level does Mr. Morris most likely have?

(A) Off-peak Membership

(B) Standard Membership

(C) Enhanced Membership

(D) Ultimate Membership

13. What does Mr. Benson suggest about Mr. Brodie?

(A) He joined the club after Mr. Morris.

(B) He had to cancel some lessons.

(C) His services are in high demand.

(D) His lessons are for groups and individuals.

14. In the e-mail, the word "drive" in paragraph 1, line 6, is closest in meaning to

(A) motivate

(B) swing

(C) travel

(D) operate

15. What is implied about Ms. Curtis?

(A) Her lesson time has recently changed.

(B) Her membership provides priority booking.

(C) She has learned from Mr. Brodie for at least two years.

(D) She won the Regional Golf Tournament last year.

Questions 1-2 refer to the following e-mail.

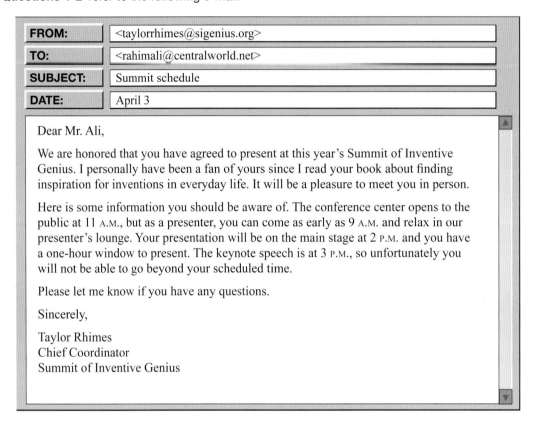

FROM:	<taylorrhimes@sigenius.org>
TO:	<rahimali@centralworld.net>
SUBJECT:	Summit schedule
DATE:	April 3

Dear Mr. Ali,

We are honored that you have agreed to present at this year's Summit of Inventive Genius. I personally have been a fan of yours since I read your book about finding inspiration for inventions in everyday life. It will be a pleasure to meet you in person.

Here is some information you should be aware of. The conference center opens to the public at 11 A.M., but as a presenter, you can come as early as 9 A.M. and relax in our presenter's lounge. Your presentation will be on the main stage at 2 P.M. and you have a one-hour window to present. The keynote speech is at 3 P.M., so unfortunately you will not be able to go beyond your scheduled time.

Please let me know if you have any questions.

Sincerely,

Taylor Rhimes
Chief Coordinator
Summit of Inventive Genius

1. What is indicated about Mr. Ali?

   (A) He will present an award.
   (B) He is a published author.
   (C) He will be a keynote speaker.
   (D) He invented a kitchen appliance.

2. By what time must Mr. Ali finish his presentation?

   (A) 9 A.M.
   (B) 11 A.M.
   (C) 2 P.M.
   (D) 3 P.M.

Questions 3-4 refer to the following notice.

Notice to Valleyview Residents:

Posted September 1 by George Zeigler

I am posting on this noticeboard for the first time in the hope that I can find a mutually beneficial arrangement with those seeking to dispose of their antique furniture. As the owner of Valleyview Collectibles, I am always on the lookout for items to add to my shop's collection. Regardless of the condition, you can sell your antique toys, watches, vintage postcards, and more. Save the time and hassle of taking your goods to a festival—I'll come right to your door. Throughout this month, I can visit your home and give you a quote for the value of your goods at no charge. Call me today at 555-0163. Please leave a message if there is no answer, and I will get back to you as quickly as possible.

---

3. Why did Mr. Zeigler post the notice?

(A) To sell some rare furniture
(B) To advertise a local business
(C) To announce a job opening
(D) To find items for purchase

4. According to the notice, what is available for free in September?

(A) A price estimate
(B) An art workshop
(C) Festival admission
(D) Transportation of goods

YBM TEST

Questions 5-7 refer to the following review.

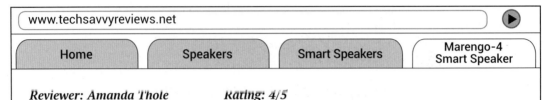

www.techsavvyreviews.net

| Home | Speakers | Smart Speakers | Marengo-4 Smart Speaker |

Reviewer: Amanda Thole   **Rating: 4/5**

After setting up the Marengo-4 Smart Speaker, I was somewhat disappointed that the volume of the speaker was not very loud in the music setting, even at the maximum level. It's not a problem if you plan to sit near your speaker—for example, if you have it positioned on your desk. However, if you like to have it playing constantly like I do, you might be frustrated that the sound doesn't carry into other rooms. Despite this drawback, I found the Marengo-4 Smart Speaker to be genuinely useful. It can perform online searches by voice command, give you the latest news headlines, remind you about your appointments, and more. The company has improved upon the appearance of the earlier Marengo-3 by offering metal, wood, and fabric exteriors, so you can easily coordinate it to your home's interior. Before making a purchase, please be aware that the price is for the device only. A monthly subscription to a smart assistant app is required, and this can cost from five to ten dollars per month.

5. What is suggested about the reviewer?
   (A) She thinks the device is too big.
   (B) She listens to a lot of music.
   (C) She uses the device at work.
   (D) She enjoys playing computer games.

6. What has changed about the Marengo-4 compared to the previous model?
   (A) It has a more lightweight design.
   (B) It can be used indoors and outdoors.
   (C) It comes in a wider variety of finishes.
   (D) It starts up more quickly.

7. What does Ms. Thole warn readers about?
   (A) The device is difficult to set up.
   (B) A service has ongoing costs.
   (C) The warranty does not last long.
   (D) A price has recently increased.

NEW SERVICE AT HUDSON DRY CLEANING!

Hudson Dry Cleaning, the best business in town for fast and reliable dry cleaning delivered right to your home, is pleased to offer a new service for customers. Now, in addition to removing stubborn stains and cleaning your clothing with environmentally friendly chemicals, our staff can shorten or lengthen your trousers, skirts, and suit jackets. Measurements are taken in the store, and the work can be done while you wait.

And don't forget that we give a discount to customers of our partner, Warner Hardware. Simply show your receipt, dated within the past week, to get five percent off your entire bill.

Hudson Dry Cleaning • 1584 Franklin Avenue • 555-0120

8. What new service has Hudson Dry Cleaning recently added?

(A) Home delivery
(B) Clothing alterations
(C) Eco-friendly cleaning
(D) Online ordering

9. The word "stubborn" in paragraph 1, line 3, is closest in meaning to

(A) determined
(B) unwilling
(C) tough
(D) not flexible

10. How can customers get a five percent discount?

(A) By having a certain number of items cleaned
(B) By bringing in clothing during the low period
(C) By proving a purchase from a partner business
(D) By being a member of a community group

Riverside, February 16 – The Riverside Society for Innovation (RSI) is once again hosting its annual drawing for local residents, offering a chance to win a five-day luxury cruise for two in the Caribbean as well as other fabulous prizes. The drawing is to be held at RSI's upcoming monthly meeting on Wednesday, February 19, but participants do not need to be present to win. — [1] —. All proceeds from the drawing will be donated to nonprofit organizations selected by RSI's board of directors.

RSI was formed fifteen years ago in an effort to assist in financing health and wellness studies that benefit the general public. Since its founding, the group has grown from eight members to over fifty. — [2] —.

Tickets for the drawing cost $1.50 each or ten for $12. They can be purchased at the Kovar Institute, Riverside Public Library, Riverside City Hall, Turnpike Hotel, and Soltis Department Store. — [3] —. RSI is offering several locations for purchases so that people do not have to go much out of their way to obtain tickets. This is in direct response to the feedback survey responses from last year. For questions or comments, call 555-0177. — [4] —.

11. What is the purpose of the article?

(A) To declare a winner
(B) To introduce a fundraiser
(C) To promote a new service
(D) To recruit new members

12. According to the article, what is RSI dedicated to doing?

(A) Supporting medical research
(B) Developing community activities
(C) Training local residents
(D) Providing financial advice

13. Why has the organization most likely made a change from last year?

(A) Businesses negotiated better deals.
(B) The price was considered to be unreasonable.
(C) The group's size has grown considerably.
(D) Participants did not want to travel far.

14. In which of the positions marked [1], [2], [3], and [4] does the following sentence best belong?

"However, they should provide their contact information."

(A) [1]
(B) [2]
(C) [3]
(D) [4]

Questions 15-18 refer to the following letter.

January 11
Farth County Historical Society
119 Magnolia Lane, Bowersville, GA

Dear Farth County Historical Society Board of Directors,

I am writing on behalf of the Farth County Forest Committee. — [1] —. The Farth County Forest, a 4,000-acre wooded area designated to be used for recreation and ecological conservation, is a treasured feature of Farth County. In order to both maintain and enhance its offerings, we hereby apply for the Farth County Historical Society's Henderson Grant. — [2] —.

I have enclosed the application form describing in detail how we propose to use the funds. — [3] —. First, we hope to acquire 600 acres of vacant land to extend our walking trails. Second, with your help, we would be able to develop and better preserve historical structures on our land. Finally, the additional funding would make it possible for us to offer classes such as cooking with local plants, wilderness first aid, and even theater, on our outdoor stage.

We hope that you share our vision and decide to support it with the Henderson Grant. — [4] —. Thank you again for your consideration.

Most sincerely,
Deborah Bella
Director, Farth County Forest Committee
Enclosure

15. Why did Ms. Bella write the letter?
   (A) To promote some community programs
   (B) To explain some county regulations
   (C) To request financial support
   (D) To accept a sales offer

16. What is indicated about Farth County Forest?
   (A) It has bicycle trails.
   (B) Its land has two official purposes.
   (C) Its trees are sometimes cut down and sold.
   (D) It is visited by over 4,000 people per year.

17. What is NOT a focus of the classes that Ms. Bella mentions?
   (A) Local history
   (B) Stage acting
   (C) Medical care
   (D) Food preparation

18. In which of the positions marked [1], [2], [3], and [4] does the following sentence best belong?

   "But, I would like to take this opportunity to introduce the key points."
   (A) [1]
   (B) [2]
   (C) [3]
   (D) [4]

Questions 19-22 refer to the following online chat discussion.

Daniel Lynch [3:21 P.M.]

Great news! Representatives from Shawo Department Store are considering selling our firm's clothing in their retail stores.

Sita Kumar [3:23 P.M.]

Fantastic! Having our apparel in a chain that large would be a wonderful opportunity for growth in the Asian market.

Daniel Lynch [3:24 P.M.]

Exactly. Because of this, I'm looking for someone who can translate the contract into Chinese. It's important that the agreement be accurate. Any ideas?

Carla Barros [3:25 P.M.]

What about Yan Geng? He has worked on projects for us before.

Daniel Lynch [3:26 P.M.]

I called him before lunch, but he said that he is fully booked for the next month. We can't wait for his schedule to free up.

Alan Almeida [3:28 P.M.]

Doesn't Melissa Yao in the sales department speak Chinese? Maybe she could help.

Carla Barros [3:29 P.M.]

She's too inexperienced for something this important. We need to make a good impression on Shawo's representatives.

Daniel Lynch [3:30 P.M.]

You've got that right. This may be our only chance.

Sita Kumar [3:31 P.M.]

I know that my former company used to use freelance translators from time to time. I'd be happy to call some of my old coworkers to see if they can give me some advice.

Daniel Lynch [3:32 P.M.]

That would be really helpful. Thanks, Sita!

19. In what industry do the writers most likely work?

(A) Construction

(B) Fashion design

(C) Auto manufacturing

(D) Marketing

20. What does Mr. Lynch ask the other writers to do?

(A) Meet with some representatives

(B) Check a translation's accuracy

(C) Recommend a worker for a task

(D) Negotiate a contract

21. What is mentioned about Mr. Geng?

(A) He is no longer working in the field.

(B) He does not have enough experience.

(C) He is away on a business trip.

(D) He is too busy to accept a project.

22. At 3:30 P.M., what does Mr. Lynch mean when he writes, "You've got that right"?

(A) He wants to assign work to Ms. Yao.

(B) It is important to impress a client.

(C) Some errors have now been corrected.

(D) The deadline is approaching soon.

Diego's Superstore Order Invoice				
Customer: Fontez Restaurants			Order#: ZZ78B1	
Item #	Description	Price	Quantity	
Q71	Mobley stainless steel range and oven	$1200.00	?	
C99	7-piece set of pots and pans	$300.00	3	
R19	Vacuum powered food processor	$400.00	1	
Q46	Goldstar 2000-watt microwave	$350.00	1	

Questions or comments?

Contact us at orders@diegosss.com.
And don't forget to check out our redesigned Web page, now with a virtual showroom that allows you to see three-dimensional images of all our products: www.diegosss.com.

Subtotal:	$4050.00
10% tax:	$405.00
Discount:	N/A
Balance due:	$4455.00

From:	<catrina@fontezrestaurants.com>
To:	<orders@diegosss.com>
Subject:	Order # ZZ78B1
Date:	April 3

Hello,

On behalf of Fontez Restaurants, I want to first thank your company for being our supplier for almost three decades. Our success in expanding our brand is in large part thanks to partners like you.

However, I also wanted to make a friendly suggestion. Every time we order from you, we hire a technician to install the equipment. If you trained your delivery drivers to do that instead, it would be convenient for customers, and an extra source of revenue for you.

One more thing. We meant to take advantage of your promotion for KES Express credit card users. I believe we can take 20% off of any Mobley-brand products in our order if we pay with an KES Express card. We meet the criteria for that discount, but I forgot to put the coupon code into the Web page when I checked out. Please let me know whether you'll be able to update the order with that discount.

Thanks for everything,

Catrina Morgan
Fontez Restaurants

23. Where will the items listed on the invoice most likely be used?

(A) In an office space

(B) In a kitchen

(C) In a warehouse

(D) In a waiting area

24. According to the invoice, what can be found on a Web site?

(A) Customer reviews

(B) A detailed search feature

(C) Special images of products

(D) A live chat function

25. According to the e-mail, which item may be eligible for a discount?

(A) Q71

(B) C99

(C) R19

(D) Q46

26. What does Ms. Morgan recommend to Diego's Superstore?

(A) Offering delivery service on weekends

(B) Increasing its range of payment options

(C) Training its employees to set up equipment

(D) Giving discounts on large orders

27. What does Ms. Morgan indicate about her order?

(A) She paid for it with a credit card.

(B) She needs to cancel it.

(C) It will be repeated in the future.

(D) It is her first purchase from Diego's Superstore.

Questions 28-32 refer to the following Web page, e-mail, and survey.

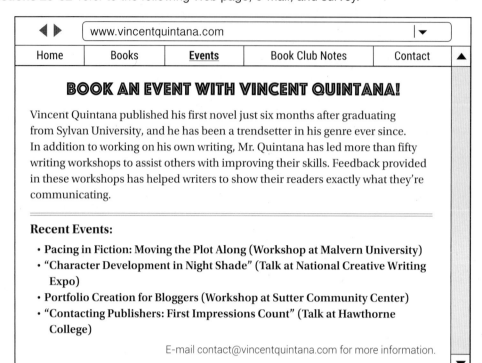

www.vincentquintana.com

| Home | Books | **Events** | Book Club Notes | Contact |

BOOK AN EVENT WITH VINCENT QUINTANA!

Vincent Quintana published his first novel just six months after graduating from Sylvan University, and he has been a trendsetter in his genre ever since. In addition to working on his own writing, Mr. Quintana has led more than fifty writing workshops to assist others with improving their skills. Feedback provided in these workshops has helped writers to show their readers exactly what they're communicating.

Recent Events:

- Pacing in Fiction: Moving the Plot Along (Workshop at Malvern University)
- "Character Development in Night Shade" (Talk at National Creative Writing Expo)
- Portfolio Creation for Bloggers (Workshop at Sutter Community Center)
- "Contacting Publishers: First Impressions Count" (Talk at Hawthorne College)

E-mail contact@vincentquintana.com for more information.

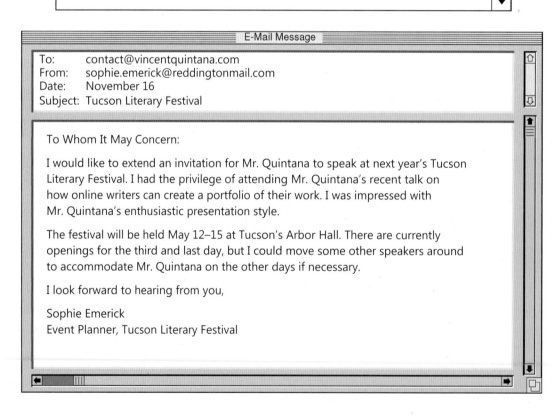

E-Mail Message

To: contact@vincentquintana.com
From: sophie.emerick@reddingtonmail.com
Date: November 16
Subject: Tucson Literary Festival

To Whom It May Concern:

I would like to extend an invitation for Mr. Quintana to speak at next year's Tucson Literary Festival. I had the privilege of attending Mr. Quintana's recent talk on how online writers can create a portfolio of their work. I was impressed with Mr. Quintana's enthusiastic presentation style.

The festival will be held May 12–15 at Tucson's Arbor Hall. There are currently openings for the third and last day, but I could move some other speakers around to accommodate Mr. Quintana on the other days if necessary.

I look forward to hearing from you,

Sophie Emerick
Event Planner, Tucson Literary Festival

TUCSON LITERARY FESTIVAL ATTENDEE SURVEY

Name: _Jackie Renfro_

How did you find out about the festival? _online advertisement_

Which day(s) did you attend the festival? Check all that apply.

☐ Day 1   ☑ Day 2   ☐ Day 3   ☐ Day 4

Please rate the speakers on a scale of 1 to 10: _9_
Comments: _The speakers were entertaining, and I felt like I learned a great deal. I was particularly inspired by Mr. Quintana's talk, and I thought it was helpful of him to take questions from the audience at the end._

Please rate your overall experience at the festival on a scale of 1 to 10: _7_
Comments: _Signing up to participate was not easy. Enrollment was only open for two weeks, which does not leave much time for advance planning. Also, the speakers should make sure that they have enough handouts for everyone._

---

28. What is implied about Mr. Quintana?
(A) He is a former employee of Sylvan University.
(B) He started his own publishing company.
(C) He has experience educating others.
(D) He has fifty books on the best-seller list.

29. Where did Ms. Emerick see Mr. Quintana speak?
(A) At Malvern University
(B) At the National Creative Writing Expo
(C) At Sutter Community Center
(D) At Hawthorne College

30. When did Mr. Quintana give a talk at the Tucson Literary Festival?
(A) May 12
(B) May 13
(C) May 14
(D) May 15

31. On the survey, the word "leave" in paragraph 4, line 3, is closest in meaning to
(A) depart
(B) allow
(C) abandon
(D) produce

32. What change would address one of Ms. Renfro's concerns?
(A) Making the registration period longer
(B) Reducing the cost of participation
(C) Providing the speaker schedule online
(D) Adding question-and-answer sessions

FINAL TEST

LISTENING TEST

In the Listening test, you will be asked to demonstrate how well you understand spoken English. The entire Listening test will last approximately 45 minutes. There are four parts, and directions are given for each part. You must mark your answers on the separate answer sheet. Do not write your answers in your test book.

PART 1

Directions: For each question in this part, you will hear four statements about a picture in your test book. When you hear the statements, you must select the one statement that best describes what you see in the picture. Then find the number of the question on your answer sheet and mark your answer. The statements will not be printed in your test book and will be spoken only one time.

Statement (C), "They're sitting at a table," is the best description of the picture, so you should select answer (C) and mark it on your answer sheet.

1.

2.

GO ON TO THE NEXT PAGE

3.

4.

5.

6.

GO ON TO THE NEXT PAGE

PART 2

Directions: You will hear a question or statement and three responses spoken in English. They will not be printed in your test book and will be spoken only one time. Select the best response to the question or statement and mark the letter (A), (B), or (C) on your answer sheet.

7. Mark your answer on your answer sheet.

8. Mark your answer on your answer sheet.

9. Mark your answer on your answer sheet.

10. Mark your answer on your answer sheet.

11. Mark your answer on your answer sheet.

12. Mark your answer on your answer sheet.

13. Mark your answer on your answer sheet.

14. Mark your answer on your answer sheet.

15. Mark your answer on your answer sheet.

16. Mark your answer on your answer sheet.

17. Mark your answer on your answer sheet.

18. Mark your answer on your answer sheet.

19. Mark your answer on your answer sheet.

20. Mark your answer on your answer sheet.

21. Mark your answer on your answer sheet.

22. Mark your answer on your answer sheet.

23. Mark your answer on your answer sheet.

24. Mark your answer on your answer sheet.

25. Mark your answer on your answer sheet.

26. Mark your answer on your answer sheet.

27. Mark your answer on your answer sheet.

28. Mark your answer on your answer sheet.

29. Mark your answer on your answer sheet.

30. Mark your answer on your answer sheet.

31. Mark your answer on your answer sheet.

PART 3

Directions: You will hear some conversations between two or more people. You will be asked to answer three questions about what the speakers say in each conversation. Select the best response to each question and mark the letter (A), (B), (C), or (D) on your answer sheet. The conversations will not be printed in your test book and will be spoken only one time.

32. Where are the speakers?

    (A) At a bus station
    (B) At an airport
    (C) At an arena
    (D) At a bank

33. What does the man ask for help with?

    (A) Taking a personal photo
    (B) Making travel arrangements
    (C) Tuning in to a news broadcast
    (D) Repairing a mechanical device

34. What does the woman ask the man for?

    (A) A receipt
    (B) A cash payment
    (C) A travel itinerary
    (D) An identification card

35. What problem does the woman mention?

    (A) An item was not delivered.
    (B) An appointment was missed.
    (C) A package was not picked up.
    (D) A payment was not received.

36. What does the woman ask the man to do?

    (A) Contact a supervisor
    (B) Reschedule a meeting
    (C) Increase a future order
    (D) Waive a subscription fee

37. Why does the man give the woman some free items?

    (A) To honor a coupon
    (B) To apologize for a mistake
    (C) To thank her for her business
    (D) To promote a new product line

38. Who most likely are the speakers?

    (A) Publicists
    (B) Musicians
    (C) Journalists
    (D) Gardeners

39. What does the man say he likes to do?

    (A) Record performances
    (B) Listen to the radio
    (C) Meet celebrities
    (D) Visit a park

40. What is Dorothy having trouble doing?

    (A) Finding directions to a venue
    (B) Setting up an interview
    (C) Preparing some equipment
    (D) Memorizing a script

41. What about a Web page surprised the woman?

    (A) Its ease of use
    (B) Its maintenance costs
    (C) Its advertising revenue
    (D) Its popularity with visitors

42. What idea does the man propose?

    (A) Modifying a budget request
    (B) Changing a Web page name
    (C) Hiring a new technical director
    (D) Charging users to view articles

43. What group of people will the woman meet in the afternoon?

    (A) Executives
    (B) Journalists
    (C) Customers
    (D) Technicians

GO ON TO THE NEXT PAGE

44. What is the purpose of the woman's visit?

(A) To submit a résumé
(B) To open a bank account
(C) To update a document
(D) To join a library

45. What does the man mention about his company?

(A) It only accepts local customers.
(B) It offers some services online.
(C) It will move to a new location.
(D) It has a new security policy.

46. What does the man ask the woman to return with?

(A) A letter of reference
(B) Proof of her address
(C) Payment for a service
(D) Completed paperwork

---

47. What does the woman say will happen at the end of April?

(A) A social event
(B) A store opening
(C) A seasonal sale
(D) A training seminar

48. What does the man suggest to the woman?

(A) Downloading a video file
(B) Speaking to a supervisor
(C) Buying a performance ticket
(D) Playing a musical instrument

49. What does the woman tell the man to send her?

(A) An event invitation
(B) An itinerary
(C) A media file
(D) An attendance list

---

50. Why is the man calling?

(A) To request a refund
(B) To advertise a service
(C) To give some feedback
(D) To schedule an appointment

51. What does the woman mention about Mr. Adams?

(A) He is good at his job.
(B) He is out of the office.
(C) He is a new employee.
(D) He is unhappy with a service.

52. What type of service did the man's office receive?

(A) A budget review
(B) A Web page update
(C) An employee training
(D) A marketing consultation

---

53. What is the purpose of the call?

(A) To sell insurance
(B) To conduct a survey
(C) To confirm an address
(D) To announce a policy change

54. What does the woman mean when she says, "I'm just about to walk out the door"?

(A) She can visit a retail outlet.
(B) She will not attend a meeting.
(C) She will be on time for a flight.
(D) She does not have time to talk.

55. What does the woman instruct the man to do?

(A) Meet her in person
(B) Send her an e-mail
(C) Contact her colleague
(D) Add her to a mailing list

56. Who is Dylan?

(A) A customer
(B) A supervisor
(C) A new employee
(D) A software expert

57. Where most likely are the speakers?

(A) At a corporate office
(B) At a research laboratory
(C) At a dining establishment
(D) At a manufacturing facility

58. What will the woman most likely do next?

(A) Learn a computer program
(B) Hear a sales pitch
(C) Assist a customer
(D) Interview a job applicant

---

59. Why are the speakers surprised?

(A) A test score was low.
(B) A projector malfunctioned.
(C) An employee called in sick.
(D) A report was completed early.

60. What does the man offer to do?

(A) Distribute a document
(B) Schedule a meeting
(C) E-mail a consultant
(D) Correct a mistake

61. What does the woman mean when she says, "I better take a look at it first"?

(A) She can repair a malfunctioning device.
(B) Some information might be incorrect.
(C) The man made a good decision.
(D) A product costs too much.

Discounts on Select Brands	
Everett	10%
Coolidge	15%
Biltmore	20%
Corkman	25%

62. What is the woman shopping for?

(A) A piece of sports equipment
(B) A food storage container
(C) A gardening tool
(D) A print publication

63. What does the man mention about the store he works in?

(A) It hosts an annual picnic.
(B) It sells locally produced food.
(C) It displays some goods outdoors.
(D) It no longer carries a particular brand.

64. Look at the graphic. What discount will the woman most likely receive?

(A) 10%
(B) 15%
(C) 20%
(D) 25%

GO ON TO THE NEXT PAGE

FINAL TEST

Welcome to the Youth Science Summit!	
Presentation	**Location**
Sports Physics	Grand Ballroom
Food Safety	Old Durban
Hidden Computers	Visionaries' Center
Responsible Forestry	Charlotte Hotel Lobby

Sorry I missed you!
My name is *Ben Meyer*.
Your package *requires a signature*.
Call (281) 555-0116 to retrieve it.

65. What is the woman's role at the Youth Science Summit?

(A) Teacher
(B) Assistant
(C) Presenter
(D) Attendee

66. Look at the graphic. What presentation will the man give?

(A) Sports Physics
(B) Food Safety
(C) Hidden Computers
(D) Responsible Forestry

67. What does the man say he is currently doing?

(A) Reading a book
(B) Preparing a speech
(C) Speaking to colleagues
(D) Making a hotel reservation

68. Why does the man say he returned so quickly?

(A) He forgot a package.
(B) Road traffic was light.
(C) A colleague helped him.
(D) There were few customers.

69. Look at the graphic. What company is the card for?

(A) Compton Hiring Services
(B) All Way Shipments
(C) Simon's Smoothies
(D) Houston Cooling

70. What did the man begin this week?

(A) A new job
(B) A training class
(C) A fitness program
(D) A holiday vacation

PART 4

Directions: You will hear some talks given by a single speaker. You will be asked to answer three questions about what the speaker says in each talk. Select the best response to each question and mark the letter (A), (B), (C), or (D) on your answer sheet. The talks will not be printed in your test book and will be spoken only one time.

71. What is the purpose of the call?

(A) To ask for advice
(B) To thank a colleague
(C) To request vacation time
(D) To respond to an invitation

72. What does the speaker say is confusing?

(A) Enrolling a client
(B) Hiring an employee
(C) Navigating a Web page
(D) Completing an application

73. What does the speaker offer to do for the listener?

(A) Write a recommendation
(B) Fill out a document
(C) Visit an office
(D) Buy a meal

74. What type of company does the speaker work for?

(A) A plastics manufacturer
(B) A dining establishment
(C) A news publication
(D) A consulting firm

75. What is the announcement about?

(A) A social event
(B) A policy change
(C) A writing opportunity
(D) A new line of products

76. What does the speaker mean when she says, "I'm not asking for volunteers"?

(A) A job is mandatory.
(B) A job is already complete.
(C) Payment will be provided.
(D) Many volunteers have already registered.

77. What business does the speaker work at?

(A) A financial institution
(B) A car rental company
(C) A Web design agency
(D) An event-organizing firm

78. What does the speaker offer the listener?

(A) A price quote
(B) A cash refund
(C) A free upgrade
(D) A gift voucher

79. According to the speaker, what can a visitor to a Web page do?

(A) Browse an inventory
(B) Review a contract
(C) Make a payment
(D) Ask a question

80. What is being advertised?

(A) A radio show
(B) A computer game
(C) A training seminar
(D) A corporate retreat

81. According to the advertisement, why can listeners trust Modern Team, Inc.?

(A) They are a nonprofit organization.
(B) They have a professional certification.
(C) They have operated for several decades.
(D) They receive high ratings from customers.

82. How can listeners receive a discount?

(A) By using a coupon code
(B) By making multiple purchases
(C) By joining a rewards program
(D) By signing up early

GO ON TO THE NEXT PAGE

83. What type of product is the news report about?

    (A) A home computer
    (B) A print publication
    (C) A piece of furniture
    (D) A piece of software

84. What does the speaker mean when he says, "I know I have seen something like this before"?

    (A) Most people are unfamiliar with a product.
    (B) A product was featured in a magazine.
    (C) He forgets how to use a product.
    (D) Similar products already exist.

85. What will listeners hear next?

    (A) A product review
    (B) A weather report
    (C) An advertisement
    (D) A celebrity interview

86. What does the speaker mention about an audit?

    (A) It produces unreliable results.
    (B) It will influence promotions.
    (C) The company's budget is not big enough to finish it.
    (D) The same agency from the previous year will conduct it.

87. What does the speaker ask listeners to do?

    (A) Complete a questionnaire
    (B) Review some test results
    (C) Add their names to a list
    (D) Write peer evaluations

88. Why does the speaker tell listeners not to e-mail her?

    (A) To test a new system
    (B) To hide their identities
    (C) To improve productivity
    (D) To increase face-to-face time

89. What does the speaker say about an employee training?

    (A) It will be rescheduled.
    (B) It requires an invitation.
    (C) It is mandatory to attend.
    (D) It has a cost of admission.

90. What caused Ms. Kim's travel delay?

    (A) Scheduling errors
    (B) Malfunctioning equipment
    (C) Poor weather conditions
    (D) Heavy traffic

91. According to the speaker, why should listeners contact Mr. Willis?

    (A) To enroll in a class
    (B) To watch some videos
    (C) To get a travel voucher
    (D) To report working hours

92. What has the listener recently done?

    (A) Sold a product
    (B) Taken a vacation
    (C) Applied for a job
    (D) Prepared for a speech

93. What does the speaker mean when she says, "Personally, I'm ready to make a decision"?

    (A) She wants to accept an offer.
    (B) She does not need more evidence.
    (C) She does not agree with the listener.
    (D) She wants the listener to submit a document.

94. Why does the speaker ask the listener to return her call?

    (A) To provide an e-mail address
    (B) To schedule an interview
    (C) To confirm some details
    (D) To complete an order

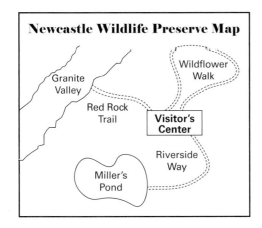

Newcastle Wildlife Preserve Map

Granite Valley
Wildflower Walk
Red Rock Trail
Visitor's Center
Riverside Way
Miller's Pond

Long Arc LLC

Date: **December 27**
Client ID: **CZ-20**
Order No. **61B8**

Products	Quantity
Auto-Clean Vacuum	3

---

95. What does the speaker say is not available?

(A) Visiting special gardens
(B) Going through all paths by car
(C) Having a group photo taken
(D) Picking up unusual rocks

96. Look at the graphic. What path will the tour start on?

(A) Red Rock Trail
(B) Granite Valley
(C) Riverside Way
(D) Wildflower Walk

97. What does the speaker encourage listeners to do?

(A) Buy a souvenir shirt
(B) Get a warm beverage
(C) Write a positive review
(D) Take a wildlife photograph

98. Where does the speaker work?

(A) At a financial institution
(B) At a retail store
(C) At a legal firm
(D) At a production facility

99. Why does the speaker apologize?

(A) He cannot cancel the order.
(B) He cannot meet a deadline.
(C) He cannot attend a meeting.
(D) He cannot approve a request.

100. Look at the graphic. What company is the order form for?

(A) Le Mans Technology
(B) Bluemont Capital
(C) Living Plus Outlet
(D) Thomas Law Offices

This is the end of the Listening test. Turn to Part 5 in your test book.

GO ON TO THE NEXT PAGE

READING TEST

In the Reading test, you will read a variety of texts and answer several different types of reading comprehension questions. The entire Reading test will last 75 minutes. There are three parts, and directions are given for each part. You are encouraged to answer as many questions as possible within the time allowed.

You must mark your answers on the separate answer sheet. Do not write your answers in your test book.

PART 5

Directions: A word or phrase is missing in each of the sentences below. Four answer choices are given below each sentence. Select the best answer to complete the sentence. Then mark the letter (A), (B), (C), or (D) on your answer sheet.

101. To help ------- provide the best possible customer service, please take a few minutes to answer some survey questions.

(A) we
(B) ourselves
(C) ours
(D) us

102. It is necessary to obtain ------- from the City Heritage Committee (CHC) before modifying a historical structure.

(A) approves
(B) approved
(C) approval
(D) approvingly

103. The city subway system's new Orange Line is expected to become ------- on September 1.

(A) operated
(B) operates
(C) operation
(D) operational

104. In job interviews, candidates are often asked about their ability to work ------- as a member of a team.

(A) cooperatively
(B) cooperative
(C) cooperates
(D) cooperation

105. Derex Ltd. has strengthened its management with the recent ------- of a new Senior Vice President.

(A) appointment
(B) appointed
(C) appoints
(D) to appoint

106. Freelance Web designers can easily work from home, ------- they have a reliable Internet connection.

(A) because of
(B) as long as
(C) thanks to
(D) regardless

107. Hikers in the national park should follow the trails ------- on the map and not venture into remote areas.

(A) illustrate
(B) illustrating
(C) illustration
(D) illustrated

108. As a member of the hotel's Frequent Guest Program, you are ------- for a room upgrade during your next stay.

(A) eligible
(B) noticeable
(C) constant
(D) associated

109. ------- of the positions at Agnon Tech Ltd. offer competitive salaries and benefit packages.

(A) All
(B) Each
(C) Everything
(D) Little

110. The City Finance Department has launched a new Web site to help eliminate ------- regarding tax payments.

(A) confusing
(B) confused
(C) confusingly
(D) confusion

111. ------- all the new merchandise was placed on display, the store had already opened for the day.

(A) By the time
(B) As soon as
(C) In addition to
(D) Along with

112. ------- providing clear, high quality sound, Namitec Ltd.'s model N10 headphones are lightweight and portable.

(A) In fact
(B) In addition to
(C) Whereas
(D) As a result of

113. It becomes prohibitively expensive to alter the design ------- the flooring has been installed.

(A) unless
(B) even though
(C) once
(D) since

114. Telemon Electronics Store will no longer ------- refunds for computer games or apps for mobile phones.

(A) providing
(B) provide
(C) provides
(D) provided

115. Leslie Houston is an emerging designer ------- interest lies in the intersection between craft and technology.

(A) who
(B) which
(C) whose
(D) what

116. The office manager is responsible for ensuring that old paper documents are ------- stored in an off-site warehouse.

(A) secure
(B) secured
(C) securing
(D) securely

117. Our City Bus Tours fill up quickly, so we encourage you to ------- your spot early.

(A) imply
(B) assemble
(C) reserve
(D) benefit

118. According to our shipping policy, all packages from Queen Spiders Co. ------- a signature upon delivery.

(A) inquire
(B) invest
(C) require
(D) locate

119. The production manager is responsible for ------- the company's manufacturing process from start to finish.

(A) depending
(B) overseeing
(C) corresponding
(D) contributing

120. On average, about 25% of our new customers come to us via a ------- from an existing client.

(A) referring
(B) referred
(C) refers
(D) referral

GO ON TO THE NEXT PAGE

121. A magazine survey about residents' food choices revealed some ------- trends, including more interest in healthy eating.

(A) surprises
(B) surprised
(C) surprising
(D) surprisingly

122. The company's new logo is ------- more modern and easier to read.

(A) noticed
(B) noticing
(C) noticeable
(D) noticeably

123. The company picnic will likely be postponed, as heavy rain is expected to fall ------- the region this weekend.

(A) between
(B) across
(C) among
(D) given

124. The hotel is a popular spot for nature enthusiasts because it is ------- to the city's largest park.

(A) renowned
(B) fortunate
(C) utmost
(D) adjacent

125. The sculptures should be packaged securely in order to ------- breakages during shipping.

(A) delay
(B) prevent
(C) refrain
(D) prohibit

126. At this time of year, farmers tend to spend long hours in the field while ------- their crops.

(A) harvest
(B) has harvested
(C) to harvest
(D) harvesting

127. While many people find it ------- to shop online, many others still prefer the in-store shopping experience.

(A) simply
(B) simple
(C) simplify
(D) simplicity

128. Restaurants that are ------- reviewed by food critic Jamal Cohen usually experience a boost in business.

(A) dividedly
(B) favorably
(C) extremely
(D) tightly

129. Once you have arrived at Wilshire Airport, proceed ------- to the Swift Rental desk to obtain the keys to your vehicle.

(A) regularly
(B) directly
(C) closely
(D) firmly

130. Young and old ------- will enjoy the Marmonk Theater Company's upcoming stage performances.

(A) each other
(B) alike
(C) exactly
(D) in common

PART 6

Directions: Read the texts that follow. A word, phrase, or sentence is missing in parts of each text. Four answer choices for each question are given below the text. Select the best answer to complete the text. Then mark the letter (A), (B), (C), or (D) on your answer sheet.

Questions 131-134 refer to the following press release.

FOR IMMEDIATE RELEASE

Ultimate Palm Ltd., a respected maker of camping equipment, recently got the news that its popular Pro-Tekk backpack was ------- by an important industry organization. The product won the "Top **131.** Design" prize at the Outdoor Recreation Association's awards event. -------, the association's judges **132.** were enthusiastic about the backpack's comfort, noting that its thickly-padded straps can be adjusted easily for a perfect fit. They also noted that the backpack has 28 different pockets of various sizes. -------. In all, the product was judged superior to backpacks from 60 ------- **133.** **134.** manufacturers. For more information, go to www.ultimatepalm.com.

131. (A) delivered
(B) discontinued
(C) recognized
(D) manufactured

132. (A) Nevertheless
(B) As a result
(C) Namely
(D) In particular

133. (A) This feature makes it simple to keep loose items organized.
(B) Experts recommend wearing sturdy shoes or hiking boots.
(C) Generally, there is enough space for all of this equipment.
(D) The backpack was promoted in several magazines.

134. (A) competed
(B) competing
(C) competitively
(D) competes

GO ON TO THE NEXT PAGE

For expert carpet cleaning, call on Sheenatec Solutions today. We offer customers upfront, guaranteed price quotes on all of our cleaning services. ------. What's more, our prices include
<u>135.</u>
removal of all stains. It is also our goal to promote environmental responsibility. We always use cleaning products with natural ingredients ------ harmful chemicals. Book your appointment by
<u>136.</u>
visiting www.sheen-atec.com. To find out ------ customers are saying about our service, we
<u>137.</u>
encourage you to view our Web site's testimonial page. We are proud of our customer ------ rate of
<u>138.</u>
94%.

135. (A) Pease find your latest invoice included.
(B) The crew undergoes intensive training courses.
(C) There are never any hidden fees or taxes.
(D) Some refund requests take longer to process.

136. (A) instead of
(B) such as
(C) rather
(D) except

137. (A) that
(B) either
(C) what
(D) another

138. (A) satisfied
(B) satisfactorily
(C) satisfies
(D) satisfaction

Mossdale City is this region's premier travel destination. ------- your trip is for business or pleasure,
139.
our city has all the amenities you need. We offer a wide selection of hotels, shops, and restaurants
for every preference. -------, our newly renovated Mossdale Convention Center has the area's most
140.
spacious exhibit space and can accommodate over 6,000 visitors at a time. -------. In the convention
141.
center's North Hall, a variety of conference and seminar rooms are available for rental. These
meeting spaces have flexible layout options, ------- for any kind of seating arrangement you may
142.
require.

139. (A) Even
(B) Whichever
(C) Either
(D) Whether

140. (A) Rather
(B) Thus
(C) In addition
(D) Alternatively

141. (A) Open air markets are also popular here.
(B) It is an ideal venue for large events.
(C) It was built before the hotel opened.
(D) The region's tourism is improving.

142. (A) allows
(B) allowed
(C) allowing
(D) have allowed

GO ON TO THE NEXT PAGE

Questions 143-146 refer to the following Web site.

Canovia Tech Ltd. Employment

How to prepare for a phone interview

Some teams at our company interview job candidates by telephone. ------. When the recruiter calls
143.
you, make sure you are in a quiet place with no ------. Remember to have your résumé on hand for
144.
quick ------, and have a pen and paper available for note taking. You ------ to ask your recruiter
145.   146.
questions as the interview progresses. If you have additional questions after the interview, do not

hesitate to contact your recruiter with a follow-up call.

---

143. (A) Usually the results are available within
two or three business days.
(B) Before your interview, take some time to
learn about our company.
(C) Team leaders should always seek to
improve their team's performance.
(D) They may be required to motivate staff
from other departments as well.

144. (A) strategies
(B) distractions
(C) possibilities
(D) signals

145. (A) to refer
(B) referred
(C) reference
(D) referential

146. (A) encourage
(B) are encouraged
(C) will be encouraging
(D) had been encouraged

PART 7

Directions: In this part you will read a selection of texts, such as magazine and newspaper articles, e-mails, and instant messages. Each text or set of texts is followed by several questions. Select the best answer for each question and mark the letter (A), (B), (C), or (D) on your answer sheet.

Questions 147-148 refer to the following directory.

Welcome to **Atelier Community Bank**
For deposits and withdrawals, please use the automated banking machines found on the first floor.

Office 201	Dylan Engles **Loans**	→
Office 202	Gina Hoffman **Debit and credit card replacement**	→
Office 203	Taylor Penfield **Account openings**	→
Office 204	Marina Laura **Online banking support**	→

147. What can customers do on the first floor?

(A) Put money into a checking account
(B) Apply for a business loan
(C) Obtain a banking card
(D) Pay a credit card bill

148. Who would a potential customer most likely speak to first?

(A) Mr. Engles
(B) Ms. Hoffman
(C) Mr. Penfield
(D) Ms. Laura

GO ON TO THE NEXT PAGE

FINAL TEST

Questions 149-150 refer to the following notice.

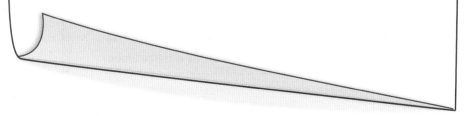

Attention patrons and staff of Gracie Lou's Books:

On Saturday, April 14, I accidentally left my mobile phone on one of the tables at the back of the store at around 3 P.M. I returned an hour later, but it was not there. I am offering a reward for any help getting it back.

It is a very common phone, so I believe someone mistook it for their own and picked it up. It is a Voltor 6G, released this year. It has a black body and is covered by a black leather flip case. It has contact information for my students in it, as well as information that I use to prepare for my classes, so it is very valuable to me.

You can contact me with any information at estebanbarillo@gper.com. Thank you!

Esteban Barillo

149. What is the purpose of the notice?

(A) To warn patrons of a store closure
(B) To advertise the sale of a used item
(C) To request help finding a lost item
(D) To announce a job opening

150. What is suggested about Mr. Barillo?

(A) He is employed at a bookstore.
(B) He is a business owner.
(C) He designs electronics.
(D) He is a teacher.

Questions 151-152 refer to the following text-message chain.

Ji-Min Lee   7:24 P.M.
Hi, Raphael. I just landed.

Raphael Moralez   7:25 P.M.
Oh, you're a little early! Great. I just parked, and now I'm heading to the terminal. I'll come to the baggage carousel and wait with you.

Ji-Min Lee   7:28 P.M.
I didn't check any bags.

Raphael Moralez   7:29 P.M.
Where should I meet you, then?

Ji-Min Lee   7:29 P.M.
I'm walking towards the exit now. Can you pick me up out front?

Raphael Moralez   7:32 P.M.
Sure. I'll drive up to the main terminal and wait for you by the exit.

| | Send |

151. At 7:28 P.M., what does Ms. Lee most likely mean when she writes, "I didn't check any bags"?

(A) She should not have to pay a fee.
(B) She is ready to leave immediately.
(C) She forgot to bring an item.
(D) She can assist Mr. Moralez.

152. What will Mr. Moralez most likely do next?

(A) Go to a convenience store
(B) Speak to an airline representative
(C) Check a display board
(D) Get into his car

GO ON TO THE NEXT PAGE

MEMBERSHIP CHANGES

This year has been a successful year for Reynolds Office Rentals, with our business expanding faster than we could ever have imagined. As a result, we have been forced to make some changes to enable us to keep up with the increased demand.

At the moment, customers are able to place orders through our telephone hotline service. It has been decided that this method is too inefficient. As such, customers will now need to select their goods using the members' area of our Web site. The items will then be delivered the next working day provided that the order is submitted by 5 P.M.

We appreciate this may be an inconvenience to some of you. As a way of showing that we value your business, please find attached a personalized number that provides you with 10% off the total of your next order. Simply enter this at checkout to redeem your savings.

We look forward to serving you and helping you meet your office furniture needs.

---

153. What is stated about the ordering system?

(A) Customers will still be able to place orders over the phone.
(B) The acceptance of orders has been temporarily suspended.
(C) It has experienced technical difficulties recently.
(D) Customers will only be able to order through the Web site.

154. What was sent to customers along with the notice?

(A) Some store directions
(B) A discount code
(C) A monthly invoice
(D) Product samples

Reed County Reader

AUGUST 26—Reed County Recreation Center (RCRC) will close to the public on September 14 and reopen on March 10 of next year. — [1] —. The swimming area on the lake will close a week earlier, at 6 P.M. on September 7, but visitors will be able to fish or enjoy the dozens of miles of hiking trails on the property for an additional week.

The manager of the recreation center, Jeff Perkins, has requested that community members visit on Saturday, September 17 to help winterize the grounds. "There's a lot of work to be done to get our docks and picnic areas ready for the heavy snows in January and February. — [2] —. We could really use some help."

Mr. Perkins emphasizes that volunteers will be able to become lifetime members of RCRC for free, a privilege which normally costs $100. — [3] —. "We don't have the resources to pay volunteers, but we're glad we can make it easier for them to enjoy our facilities this way," he says.

Those interested should gather at the center's Winston Street entrance by 9 A.M. on September 17. — [4] —. All the food service facilities will be closed, so Mr. Perkins says volunteers should bring their own lunch and snacks. For any questions about volunteering or general inquiries, please call the recreation center at 555-0172.

155. What is mentioned about RCRC?

(A) It offers annual passes.
(B) It has many walking paths.
(C) It has boats for rent.
(D) It does not permit outside food.

156. What is Mr. Perkins requesting assistance with?

(A) Picking up trash in a park
(B) Preparing facilities for winter
(C) Selling community center memberships
(D) Providing supplies for a fundraising
    event

157. In which of the positions marked [1], [2], [3], and [4] does the following sentence best belong?

"Members are able to enter the center for a discounted price."

(A) [1]
(B) [2]
(C) [3]
(D) [4]

FINAL TEST

GO ON TO THE NEXT PAGE

Durham Moving Company

The Relocation Specialists ›››››

These days, it's not unusual to relocate your business to a new venue once, twice, or even three times. Don't let this change upset your entire operation. Hire professionals that can make the transition totally painless.

If you want to be back in business as quickly as possible after your move, consider Durham Moving Company's Professional Grade Service Package. We'll come to your office, take photos, pack all your belongings, move them to your new location, unload them, and—unlike any other moving company—even unpack and place them in the same relative locations they occupied before. In fact, you'll be able to resume business-as-usual in less than 24 hours.

One moving challenge that no one wants to tackle is packing up a research laboratory— no one except the pros at Durham Moving Company, that is! Our movers are specially licensed to move and install research instruments, computers, delicate materials, and anything else you want to bring with you to your new location.

›››

There's no task we can't handle. Call 555-0172 and tell us that you saw this ad to receive 10% off your next move.

---

158. What is mentioned as a special feature of the Professional Grade Service Package?

(A) Clients pay a flat fee for an unlimited number of moves.
(B) Clients can observe the moving process on a Web site.
(C) Movers will arrange work spaces according to their original layout.
(D) Packing supplies for breakable items are provided at no charge.

159. What is indicated about Durham Moving Company employees?

(A) They have special certifications.
(B) Some of them are part-time contractors.
(C) Some of them work mainly at night.
(D) They are given frequent safety training.

160. How can customers receive a discount?

(A) By scheduling an appointment before a certain date
(B) By selecting a newly created service
(C) By mentioning an advertisement
(D) By writing a positive review

Questions 161-164 refer to the following e-mail.

```
══════════════════ E-Mail message ══════════════════
  From:     <employeerelations@fitzconnorhotel.com>

  To:       Staff

  Subject:  A special invitation

  Date:     February 26
```

Good evening, Fitz-Connor Hotel employees.

You might have heard that Tony Moriarty has selected our hotel as the location for his newest art exhibition. Though I doubt he needs an introduction, Mr. Moriarty is a world-famous, award-winning sculptor, known best for portraying human feelings in hyper-realistic, life-sized sculptures of faces. We expect many visitors coming just to see Mr. Moriarty's work. This will be an excellent opportunity to show off the newly improved ballroom now that all of the construction projects on our hotel have been finished.

The happy news for all of you is that you have been invited to the opening night celebration for the show. Visiting a Tony Moriarty exhibition is a rare treat, and the chance to meet the man himself is truly an opportunity that can't be missed. I am attaching the invitation to the event. It has all the pertinent information, such as the time and dress code. I highly encourage everyone that can come to do so. If you're scheduled to work that night, please stop by on your break.

Regards,
Sveta Markov
Director of Employee Relations
Fitz-Connor Hotel

161. What is Mr. Moriarty's artwork known for?

(A) Being displayed outdoors
(B) Being colorful
(C) Depicting emotions
(D) Educating viewers about social issues

162. According to the e-mail, what is true about the hotel?

(A) It was recently renovated.
(B) It is popular with tourists.
(C) It will host an art class.
(D) It won an industry award.

163. What does Ms. Markov indicate about an opening event?

(A) A famous artist will be there.
(B) The cost of admission will be high.
(C) Attendees may dress casually.
(D) It will be broadcast online.

164. What did Ms. Markov send with the e-mail?

(A) A floor plan
(B) A sign-up sheet
(C) A work schedule
(D) An event invitation

GO ON TO THE NEXT PAGE ➡

From:	<octaviamoran@stapersglobal.com>
To:	<archiestapers@stapersglobal.com>
Date:	October 28
Subject:	An investment proposal
Attachment:	📎 Information

Hello, Mr. Stapers,

I am writing to you about our office's latest performance results. While we have reached our sales targets, it seems that most of our tour bookings have been made through our Web site or over the phone, and the number of tours we're booking in our office is actually declining. I believe I know why that is.

Our presentation equipment is old, and the amplification system in particular is unreliable. We fill our meeting room with potential tourists who are excited to book a trip to Italy or Ecuador, but when we deliver our sales pitch, they lose faith in our organization because of the poor quality of our presentation.

Therefore, I think it would be worthwhile to invest in some new technology. I did some research on the Internet and created the attached list of some low-cost options that I think would make our presentations more effective, which would lead to better sales. If you can approve the purchase of some of the items on the list, I will go ahead and place the orders.

Best,

Octavia Moran

165. What type of company does Ms. Moran work for?

(A) An advertising firm
(B) A travel agency
(C) A theater group
(D) A recording studio

166. According to Ms. Moran, what would improve sales?

(A) A better office location
(B) Updates to a Web site
(C) A promotional campaign
(D) Some new equipment

167. What does Ms. Moran ask Mr. Stapers to do?

(A) Forward an attachment
(B) Attend a presentation
(C) Authorize some purchases
(D) Confirm some sales figures

CLIFFORD CITY, May 14 — A number of doctors and nurses at Solana Hospital took to the streets yesterday in support of the State Health Care Act, a proposal aimed at reducing the cost of prescription drugs. Supporters marched with signs and passed out leaflets outlining the proposed changes. — [1] —.

"Politicians need to understand that getting this proposal passed is essential to the long-term care of our citizens," said Roger Gifford, a physician at Solana Hospital. "The price of prescription drugs has been steadily rising, and we need the government to step in and make these goods more affordable. In some extreme cases, families with limited incomes must choose between purchasing much-needed medicines or spending their money on other essentials such as food and utilities. — [2] —."

If passed, the proposal would put price regulations on certain products. It would also allow imports from other countries, creating a more competitive market. Opponents of the bill say that it restricts the free market and does not offer a long-term solution. "The testing process is lengthy, and numerous safety procedures are required," said Niko Ulmer, a spokesperson for the Rosa Corporation, a pharmaceutical producer. "When taking these factors into consideration, it is easy to see that our products are fairly priced. — [3] —."

Legislators will vote on the proposal on May 31. Local citizens should have their voices heard on this matter by writing a letter or e-mail to the representative of their local district. — [4] —. Contact information is provided on the state's homepage.

168. What is the purpose of the proposal?

(A) To decrease the number of imported goods
(B) To improve staff training at hospitals
(C) To lower the price of medications
(D) To raise the salaries of health care workers

169. Who is Roger Gifford?

(A) A medical professional
(B) A hospital board member
(C) A prominent politician
(D) A company spokesperson

170. What are people encouraged to do?

(A) Shop for cheaper brands
(B) Vote on a proposal
(C) Contact local lawmakers
(D) Attend a feedback session

171. In which of the positions marked [1], [2], [3], and [4] does the following sentence best belong?

"People shouldn't have to make that kind of decision."

(A) [1]
(B) [2]
(C) [3]
(D) [4]

FINAL TEST

GO ON TO THE NEXT PAGE

Susan Quinn 11:42 A.M.	
Looks like we're finally getting some new neighbors.	
Jim Sarco 11:43 A.M.	
In that vacant office on this floor? I thought we were going to use it.	
Pam Watts 11:43 A.M.	
Yeah, I noticed movers have been busy all morning bringing in boxes.	
Susan Quinn 11:44 A.M.	
No, Jim. Management decided against expanding our office space since so much of our team telecommutes from home. It's actually over half of our workforce, now.	
Jim Sarco 11:45 A.M.	
Oh, wow. I didn't realize that.	
Pam Watts 11:45 A.M.	
I wonder what company is moving in, though. Does anyone know?	
Susan Quinn 11:46 A.M.	
The supervisor for this office complex might. I'll ask. Hold on.	
··· **Tommy Grohl joined the conversation** ···	
Susan Quinn 11:47 A.M.	
Hi, Tommy. By any chance, do you know who's moving into Suite B?	
Tommy Grohl 11:48 A.M.	
Hi, Sue. It's Albany Trucking Support. They're a big East Coast shipper, and they're putting in a regional office here.	
Susan Quinn 11:49 A.M.	
OK. Good to know. Thanks, Tommy. Say, do you all remember when we moved in? Discus Financial gave us a welcome basket.	
Pam Watts 11:50 A.M.	
Yes, I do remember that. I guess it's our turn now, isn't it?	
Tommy Grohl 11:52 A.M.	
I hope I'm not overstepping by suggesting this, but — my friend works for Vartago Events, and she does that sort of thing all the time. Would you like her phone number?	

172. What is indicated about the company Ms. Quinn works for?

(A) Its employees mostly work from home.
(B) It manufactures packaging materials.
(C) It will merge with another company.
(D) It is reducing its office space.

173. Who is Mr. Grohl?

(A) A building manager
(B) A receptionist
(C) A truck driver
(D) An accountant

174. At 11:49 A.M., what does Ms. Quinn most likely mean when she writes, "Discus Financial gave us a welcome basket"?

(A) She wants to know where a container is.
(B) Her company should send a thank-you note.
(C) She recommends doing business with Discus Financial.
(D) Her company should give a gift to a new neighbor.

175. What does Mr. Grohl offer to do?

(A) Transport a delivery
(B) Make a list of suggestions
(C) Share some contact information
(D) Design some invitations

GO ON TO THE NEXT PAGE

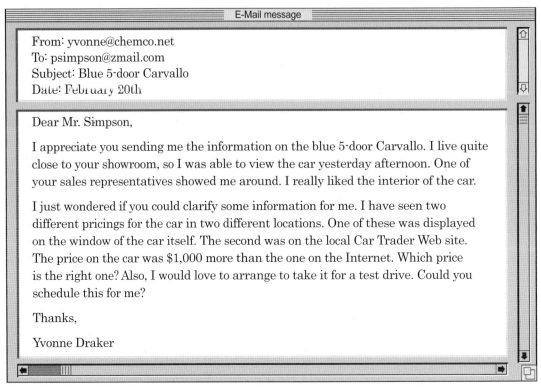

E-Mail message

From: yvonne@chemco.net
To: psimpson@zmail.com
Subject: Blue 5-door Carvallo
Date: February 20th

Dear Mr. Simpson,

I appreciate you sending me the information on the blue 5-door Carvallo. I live quite close to your showroom, so I was able to view the car yesterday afternoon. One of your sales representatives showed me around. I really liked the interior of the car.

I just wondered if you could clarify some information for me. I have seen two different pricings for the car in two different locations. One of these was displayed on the window of the car itself. The second was on the local Car Trader Web site. The price on the car was $1,000 more than the one on the Internet. Which price is the right one? Also, I would love to arrange to take it for a test drive. Could you schedule this for me?

Thanks,

Yvonne Draker

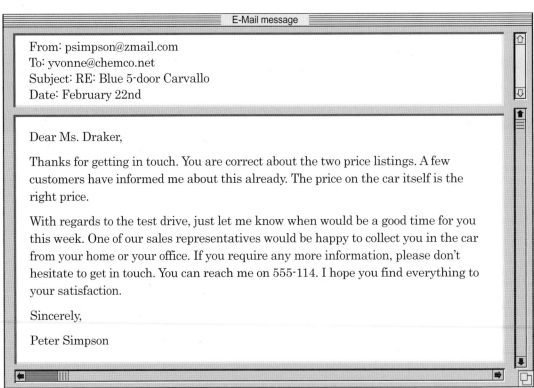

E-Mail message

From: psimpson@zmail.com
To: yvonne@chemco.net
Subject: RE: Blue 5-door Carvallo
Date: February 22nd

Dear Ms. Draker,

Thanks for getting in touch. You are correct about the two price listings. A few customers have informed me about this already. The price on the car itself is the right price.

With regards to the test drive, just let me know when would be a good time for you this week. One of our sales representatives would be happy to collect you in the car from your home or your office. If you require any more information, please don't hesitate to get in touch. You can reach me on 555-114. I hope you find everything to your satisfaction.

Sincerely,

Peter Simpson

176. Why did Ms. Draker write to Mr. Simpson?

(A) To complain about a staff member
(B) To ask about a particular vehicle
(C) To ask for directions
(D) To arrange payment on an item

177. What problem does Ms. Draker have?

(A) Her bank account is overdrawn.
(B) She lives too far away from the showroom.
(C) The showroom was closed when she visited.
(D) She is uncertain over the price.

178. What does Ms. Draker ask Mr. Simpson to do?

(A) Schedule a test drive of a vehicle
(B) Send her his business address
(C) Change the car's interior
(D) Set up a payment plan

179. What piece of information contains an error?

(A) Details displayed on the car windscreen
(B) A list of instructions in a manual
(C) An advertisement on a Web site
(D) Information provided by a sales associate

180. What does Mr. Simpson request from Ms. Draker?

(A) Information about her availability
(B) Her bank details
(C) Details of her current vehicle
(D) Her driving license number

GO ON TO THE NEXT PAGE

Become part of the Freemans Family

Freemans is an up-and-coming new business venture! Freemans develops and sells a range of quality men's and women's fragrances at affordable prices. Our ambition is to establish ourselves as true market leaders. We are currently searching for driven and determined new employees interested in the following opportunities to help us reach this aim.

✦ **Chief Sales Associate:** Must have prior experience working in the industry. Must be able to take business trips in order to visit several branches around the country. Must be present at annual board meetings.

✦ **Product Developer:** Must be familiar with the computer software package NICE. Must have a professional qualification.

✦ **Marketing Director:** Must have strong teamwork and leadership skills. Will be responsible for leading Freemans advertising campaigns. Must possess a Master's degree and have previously worked in a similar role.

✦ **Human Resources:** Starter salary. A Bachelor's in Communications essential. Successful applicants will work under the direction of several senior staff members.

To submit your application, please e-mail your completed form to Edna Kweller at e.kweller@freemans.com or fax them at 555-682-6321.

From:	Kate Stone <kslowston@highmail.net>
To:	Edna Kweller <e.kweller@freemans.com>
Date:	September 17
Subject:	Vacancy
Attachment:	📎 Kate_slowston_doc.

Dear Ms. Kweller,

I am writing in regards to your job vacancies I saw listed in the *Bradfield Gazette* this evening. I would like to express my interest in the position of Marketing Director.

I believe my skillset helps make me the ideal candidate for this role. I meet all the requirements of the job specification. I have attached a list of references to this e-mail. They all agreed to provide a letter if requested. I look forward to hearing from you soon.

Regards,

Kate Stone

181. What type of product does Freemans most likely produce?

(A) Furniture
(B) Electronics
(C) Clothing
(D) Perfume

182. In the advertisement, the word "reach" in paragraph 1, line 5, is closest in meaning to

(A) contact
(B) raise
(C) accomplish
(D) examine

183. What is a listed requirement of the chief sales associate position?

(A) Ability to deliver presentations
(B) Flexibility to allow for travel
(C) Familiarity with a particular computer package
(D) Strong teamwork skills

184. What is suggested about Ms. Stone?

(A) She has been unemployed for a long time.
(B) She lives far from company headquarters.
(C) She is interested in several vacancies.
(D) She has achieved a Master's degree.

185. What did Ms. Stone send with her e-mail?

(A) A cover letter
(B) A portfolio
(C) A recommendation letter
(D) A list of names

GO ON TO THE NEXT PAGE

▶ ◀ http://www.bunellofoods.com/menus/0942

| Home | Subscription Plans | Menus | Contact |

Langley Foods

A Ready-to-Cook-Meals Delivery Service

August Menu

Our August meals have been decided! Once you fill out your order card, we'll package the recipes and ingredients for the main dishes, side dishes, and desserts you want into a box that will be delivered right to your door.

Main Dishes

Parmesan Bake	Ingredients: Tomato sauce, chicken tenders, breading, parsley, noodles Preparation time: 15 minutes Cooking time: 10 minutes
Hearty Stew	Ingredients: Carrots, celery, onion, red potatoes, lamb shoulder Preparation time: 20 minutes Cooking time: 2 hours
7-Layer Lasagna	Ingredients: Ground beef, tomato sauce, eggs, mozzarella cheese, ricotta cheese, noodles Preparation time: 1 hour Cooking time: 1 hour
Italian Pizza	Ingredients: Pizza dough, pizza sauce, pork sausage, mozzarella cheese Preparation time: 15 minutes Cooking time: 10 minutes

From:	<bentalley@langleyfoods.com>
To:	All customers
Date:	July 28
Subject:	Notice

Dear Langley Foods Customers,

I'm sorry to inform you that, because of a miscommunication with a supplier, we won't be able to provide red potatoes to customers in August. If you ordered a dish that was supposed to include them and would now like to modify your order, please notify me by writing back to this e-mail as soon as possible. Sorry for the inconvenience, and thank you for being a Langley Foods customer!

Ben Talley

Langley Foods Customer Service

Thank you for your ordering from Langley Foods!
Would you mind filling out this satisfaction survey?

Name Sitara Indrani
Phone number (802) 555-0116
How long have you been a Langley Foods customer? 3 months
Have you ever subscribed to another food delivery service? No
How satisfied are you with Langley Foods? Very satisfied!

Comments

Your deliveries are quick, and the meals are delicious! My family and I particularly enjoy your pizzas. The only thing I can suggest is allowing certain ingredient substitutions. For example, I really wanted to try August's 7-Layer Lasagna, but my son is allergic to the meat in that dish, so I ordered the Parmesan Bake instead. Otherwise I've very much enjoyed subscribing to your ready-to-cook-meals delivery service. Thank you!

---

186. What is mentioned about all of the dishes listed on the Web page?

(A) They come with complimentary desserts.
(B) They will be delivered on August 1.
(C) They must be cooked.
(D) They are of Italian origin.

187. How many main dishes will be affected by a supply issue?

(A) One
(B) Two
(C) Three
(D) Four

188. What does Mr. Talley ask customers to do?

(A) Alert him to desired changes to their orders
(B) Complete a customer feedback survey
(C) Submit their order forms for next month
(D) Buy an ingredient from their local store

189. What does Ms. Indrani imply her son is allergic to?

(A) Chicken
(B) Lamb
(C) Beef
(D) Pork

190. What is true about Ms. Indrani?

(A) She is unhappy with Langley Foods's service.
(B) She orders from several meal delivery companies.
(C) She has tried Langley Foods's pizzas before.
(D) She made a dish with an alternative ingredient.

Schorr Publishing
913 Dale Avenue
Philadelphia, PA 19103

Dear Ms. Woodley,

I would like to thank you once again for choosing Bluefield Incorporated's services. I understand that you have already been approved for a loan for a larger home, so I will do my best to help you sell your current residence quickly. Your home should be cleaned thoroughly before the open house, which is scheduled for Saturday, September 4, from 2 P.M. to 5 P.M. Although using a professional cleaning service is a viable option, you could also do it yourself. I highly recommend shampooing all eight of the carpeted rooms, and I have enclosed a brochure for the business we recommend. I will visit the property on September 3 to check the appearance of the home and make sure nothing was missed.

Warmest regards,

Marilyn Prisco

Marilyn Prisco

Bluefield Incorporated, 555-0136

Deep clean your home for a great price!

Rent the Rug-Master carpet cleaner for do-it-yourself cleaning at a fraction of the cost of hiring a professional service. Our standard package comes with one Rug-Master cleaning device, which can be rented for one day ($39.95), two days ($65.95), or one week ($124.95).

Shampoo Guide

	1-liter bottle (up to 2 rooms)	2-liter bottle (up to 4 rooms)	4-liter bottle (up to 8 rooms)	8-liter bottle (up to 16 rooms)
Regular	$12.95	$24.95	$44.95	$74.95
Pet-Pro*	$14.95	$26.95	$46.95	$77.95

*Specially designed for stains and odors left behind by pets.

Optional Accessories (additional fees apply)

✛ **Mini Steamer:** For cleaning curtains easily without removing them from the rod
✛ **Hand Steamer:** Designed for cleaning the upholstery on sofas and armchairs
✛ **Turbo Fan:** For accelerating the drying time of rooms after being cleaned

191. Where does Ms. Prisco most likely work?

(A) At a financial institution
(B) At a housekeeping service
(C) At a real estate agency
(D) At a moving company

192. In the letter, the word "missed" in paragraph 1, line 8, is closest in meaning to

(A) declined
(B) disappointed
(C) unused
(D) overlooked

193. How much shampoo will Ms. Woodley most likely buy?

(A) 1 liter
(B) 2 liters
(C) 4 liters
(D) 8 liters

194. What is suggested about Ms. Woodley?

(A) She has pets living in her home.
(B) She will shampoo some of her curtains.
(C) She wants the rooms to dry quickly.
(D) She plans to clean her furniture.

195. When will the device be picked up?

(A) On August 27
(B) On September 1
(C) On September 2
(D) On September 3

FINAL TEST

GO ON TO THE NEXT PAGE

Underground Water Pipe Project Introduced

GLENWAY, January 20 – A proposal to divert water from the Kingston Canal to the Glenway Pumping Station via an underground pipe is being considered by the city council. Samples taken by Danielle Bennett of Sutton University have shown slight increases in contamination over the past few years. The pipeline will allow for the movement of water in a more controlled environment. Residents of the Bonner neighborhood will be affected most, as digging will occur within their property boundaries. The change may also affect agricultural sites in the region, especially during the dry season. "I'm concerned about how this will affect the irrigation of my crops," said Nicholas Nolen.

To address public concerns, the city will hold a number of meetings that are open to the public. Particular groups will receive formal invitations, depending on the focus of the meeting as follows: February 3 Bonner neighborhood residents, February 10 environmental groups, February 17 business owners, and February 24 contractors bidding for the work.

Phase 1, which began this month, involves gathering feedback from the public as well as experts. Phase 2, digging trenches for the pipeline, is set to begin in April. Phase 3, the installation of the pipe, is scheduled for November of this year.

To: Ms. Jocelyn Riley

The Glenway City Council cordially invites you to discuss the Underground Water Pipe Project. Your opinions will be taken into consideration by decision-makers.

When:	Tuesday, February 3, 7:00 P.M.
Where:	Glenway City Hall, Room 103
Agenda:	Opening talk by City Council Chairperson Joan Webber, Environmental Impact Report, Presentation of Proposed Timeline, Q&A Session, Closing Remarks

Topic: Underground Water Pipe Project

Sort by: Newest First ▾   *Posted 2 days ago*

I would like to thank the city council for holding their very informative meeting. I was particularly impressed with the question-and-answer session, as the moderator was able to handle a lot of inquiries in a short period of time. I am in support of this project because cleaner water will provide many health benefits to residents, and the pipe will ensure that fertilizers and pesticides do not leach into the water while it is traveling to the treatment plant. My only concern about the project is that it is already behind schedule. Planners reported that Phase 2 will start one month late, and that is likely to delay Phase 3 as well.

Jocelyn Riley

196. What is the reason for the proposed change?

(A) Water quality has declined.
(B) The town's population has grown.
(C) Floods happen more frequently.
(D) Previous infrastructure was damaged.

197. Who most likely is Mr. Nolen?

(A) A local farmer
(B) A city planner
(C) A university professor
(D) A climate scientist

198. What is implied about Ms. Riley?

(A) She is a member of an environmental group.
(B) She plans to submit a bid for some work.
(C) She owns a business in Glenway.
(D) She lives in the Bonner neighborhood.

199. What does Ms. Riley mention about the question-and-answer session?

(A) It was led by Ms. Webber.
(B) It included experts.
(C) It was efficient.
(D) It had to be cut short.

200. When will the trenches begin to be created?

(A) In March
(B) In April
(C) In May
(D) In November

FINAL TEST

Stop! This is the end of the test. If you finish before time is called, you may go back to Parts 5, 6, and 7 and check your work.

정답

YBM TEST - PART 1
교재 p. 24

1.(C)	**2.**(C)	**3.**(C)	**4.**(A)	**5.**(C)	**6.**(A)	**7.**(C)
8.(A)	**9.**(C)	**10.**(C)	**11.**(D)	**12.**(A)	**13.**(B)	**14.**(D)
15.(A)	**16.**(C)					

YBM TEST - PART 2
교재 p. 68

1.(C)	**2.**(C)	**3.**(B)	**4.**(A)	**5.**(C)	**6.**(B)	**7.**(B)
8.(A)	**9.**(B)	**10.**(A)	**11.**(A)	**12.**(C)	**13.**(C)	**14.**(C)
15.(A)	**16.**(C)	**17.**(B)	**18.**(B)	**19.**(A)	**20.**(A)	**21.**(B)
22.(C)	**23.**(A)	**24.**(B)	**25.**(B)	**26.**(C)	**27.**(B)	**28.**(A)
29.(B)	**30.**(A)					

YBM TEST - PART 3
교재 p. 102

1.(C)	**2.**(D)	**3.**(A)	**4.**(C)	**5.**(B)	**6.**(A)	**7.**(D)
8.(C)	**9.**(B)	**10.**(C)	**11.**(C)	**12.**(A)	**13.**(A)	**14.**(C)
15.(B)	**16.**(C)	**17.**(A)	**18.**(B)	**19.**(D)	**20.**(A)	**21.**(C)
22.(D)	**23.**(B)	**24.**(C)	**25.**(A)	**26.**(C)	**27.**(B)	**28.**(C)
29.(A)	**30.**(B)	**31.**(B)	**32.**(D)	**33.**(B)	**34.**(C)	**35.**(B)
36.(C)	**37.**(B)	**38.**(A)	**39.**(A)	**40.**(B)	**41.**(C)	**42.**(B)

YBM TEST - PART 4
교재 p. 132

1.(B)	**2.**(D)	**3.**(A)	**4.**(A)	**5.**(D)	**6.**(D)	**7.**(B)
8.(A)	**9.**(C)	**10.**(C)	**11.**(D)	**12.**(C)	**13.**(B)	**14.**(C)
15.(B)	**16.**(B)	**17.**(C)	**18.**(A)	**19.**(D)	**20.**(C)	**21.**(A)
22.(A)	**23.**(B)	**24.**(D)	**25.**(B)	**26.**(C)	**27.**(A)	**28.**(A)
29.(D)	**30.**(B)	**31.**(B)	**32.**(D)	**33.**(A)	**34.**(A)	**35.**(C)
36.(A)	**37.**(D)	**38.**(C)	**39.**(A)	**40.**(C)	**41.**(B)	**42.**(C)

YBM TEST - PART 5
교재 p. 250

1.(A)	**2.**(B)	**3.**(D)	**4.**(D)	**5.**(B)	**6.**(B)	**7.**(C)
8.(B)	**9.**(D)	**10.**(A)	**11.**(D)	**12.**(C)	**13.**(C)	**14.**(C)
15.(C)	**16.**(C)	**17.**(C)	**18.**(B)	**19.**(A)	**20.**(C)	**21.**(C)
22.(D)	**23.**(B)	**24.**(C)	**25.**(D)	**26.**(B)	**27.**(C)	**28.**(B)
29.(D)	**30.**(B)	**31.**(B)	**32.**(C)	**33.**(D)	**34.**(C)	**35.**(B)
36.(A)	**37.**(C)	**38.**(B)	**39.**(B)	**40.**(C)		

YBM TEST - PART 6
교재 p. 268

1.(D)	**2.**(D)	**3.**(B)	**4.**(D)	**5.**(D)	**6.**(D)	**7.**(A)
8.(B)	**9.**(C)	**10.**(A)	**11.**(D)	**12.**(C)	**13.**(B)	**14.**(C)
15.(D)	**16.**(C)	**17.**(C)	**18.**(A)	**19.**(A)	**20.**(B)	**21.**(C)
22.(D)	**23.**(D)	**24.**(A)	**25.**(C)	**26.**(B)	**27.**(B)	**28.**(A)
29.(D)	**30.**(C)	**31.**(D)	**32.**(A)			

YBM TEST - PART 7
교재 p. 332

1.(B)	**2.**(D)	**3.**(D)	**4.**(A)	**5.**(B)	**6.**(C)	**7.**(B)
8.(B)	**9.**(C)	**10.**(C)	**11.**(B)	**12.**(A)	**13.**(D)	**14.**(A)
15.(C)	**16.**(B)	**17.**(A)	**18.**(C)	**19.**(B)	**20.**(C)	**21.**(D)
22.(B)	**23.**(B)	**24.**(C)	**25.**(A)	**26.**(C)	**27.**(A)	**28.**(C)
29.(C)	**30.**(B)	**31.**(B)	**32.**(A)			

FINAL TEST LC
교재 p. 346

1.(A)	**2.**(B)	**3.**(B)	**4.**(D)	**5.**(D)	**6.**(A)
7.(C)	**8.**(B)	**9.**(B)	**10.**(B)	**11.**(B)	**12.**(A)
13.(C)	**14.**(C)	**15.**(A)	**16.**(A)	**17.**(C)	**18.**(A)
19.(B)	**20.**(C)	**21.**(B)	**22.**(B)	**23.**(C)	**24.**(A)
25.(C)	**26.**(A)	**27.**(A)	**28.**(B)	**29.**(A)	**30.**(A)
31.(A)	**32.**(B)	**33.**(B)	**34.**(D)	**35.**(A)	**36.**(C)
37.(B)	**38.**(C)	**39.**(A)	**40.**(B)	**41.**(B)	**42.**(D)
43.(A)	**44.**(B)	**45.**(C)	**46.**(B)	**47.**(A)	**48.**(D)
49.(C)	**50.**(C)	**51.**(C)	**52.**(C)	**53.**(B)	**54.**(D)
55.(B)	**56.**(D)	**57.**(C)	**58.**(A)	**59.**(D)	**60.**(A)
61.(B)	**62.**(B)	**63.**(C)	**64.**(D)	**65.**(B)	**66.**(B)
67.(C)	**68.**(B)	**69.**(D)	**70.**(A)	**71.**(A)	**72.**(D)
73.(D)	**74.**(A)	**75.**(D)	**76.**(C)	**77.**(B)	**78.**(C)
79.(A)	**80.**(B)	**81.**(B)	**82.**(A)	**83.**(D)	**84.**(D)
85.(A)	**86.**(D)	**87.**(A)	**88.**(B)	**89.**(A)	**90.**(C)
91.(B)	**92.**(C)	**93.**(B)	**94.**(B)	**95.**(B)	**96.**(C)
97.(B)	**98.**(D)	**99.**(B)	**100.**(D)		

FINAL TEST RC
교재 p. 358

101.(D)	**102.**(C)	**103.**(D)	**104.**(A)	**105.**(A)	**106.**(B)
107.(D)	**108.**(A)	**109.**(A)	**110.**(D)	**111.**(A)	**112.**(B)
113.(C)	**114.**(B)	**115.**(C)	**116.**(D)	**117.**(C)	**118.**(C)
119.(B)	**120.**(D)	**121.**(C)	**122.**(D)	**123.**(B)	**124.**(D)
125.(B)	**126.**(D)	**127.**(B)	**128.**(B)	**129.**(B)	**130.**(B)
131.(C)	**132.**(C)	**133.**(A)	**134.**(B)	**135.**(C)	**136.**(A)
137.(C)	**138.**(D)	**139.**(D)	**140.**(C)	**141.**(B)	**142.**(C)
143.(B)	**144.**(B)	**145.**(C)	**146.**(B)	**147.**(A)	**148.**(C)
149.(C)	**150.**(D)	**151.**(B)	**152.**(D)	**153.**(C)	**154.**(B)
155.(B)	**156.**(C)	**157.**(C)	**158.**(C)	**159.**(A)	**160.**(C)
161.(C)	**162.**(A)	**163.**(A)	**164.**(D)	**165.**(B)	**166.**(D)
167.(C)	**168.**(C)	**169.**(A)	**170.**(C)	**171.**(B)	**172.**(A)
173.(A)	**174.**(C)	**175.**(C)	**176.**(B)	**177.**(C)	**178.**(A)
179.(C)	**180.**(D)	**181.**(D)	**182.**(C)	**183.**(B)	**184.**(D)
185.(D)	**186.**(C)	**187.**(A)	**188.**(A)	**189.**(C)	**190.**(D)
191.(C)	**192.**(D)	**193.**(C)	**194.**(D)	**195.**(C)	**196.**(A)
197.(A)	**198.**(D)	**199.**(C)	**200.**(C)		

YBM 단기 토익 700⁺

정답 및 해설

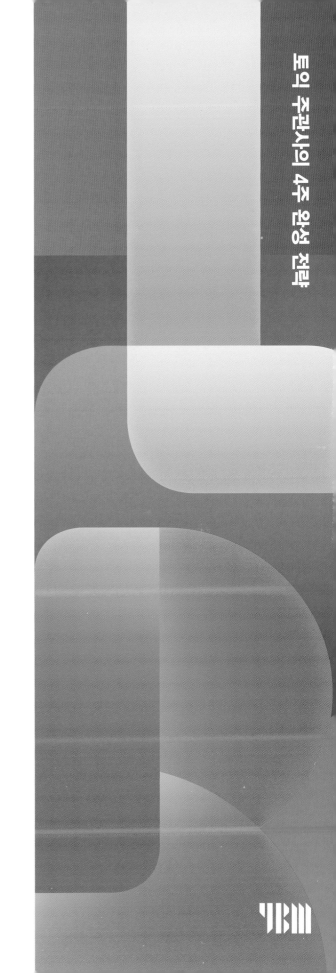

YBM
단기
토익
700+

LC+RC

정답 및 해설

PART 1

● UNIT 01 사람 중심 사진

CHECK-UP

교재 p. 17

1. examining	**2.** handing out	**3.** raking
4. wheeling	**5.** pointing	**6.** loading

M-Cn

1. A man is examining some equipment.
2. A man is handing out some documents.
3. She is raking some leaves.
4. A woman is wheeling a cart.
5. They are pointing at a drawing.
6. They are loading some boxes into a vehicle.

어휘 examine 살펴보다, 점검하다 equipment 장비
hand out 나눠주다 rake 갈퀴로 모으다
wheel (바퀴 달린 것을) 밀다, 끌다 point at ~을 가리키다
load 싣다 vehicle 차량

1. 남자가 장비를 점검하고 있다.
2. 남자가 서류를 나눠주고 있다.
3. 여자가 갈퀴로 나뭇잎들을 모으고 있다.
4. 여자가 카트를 끌고 있다.
5. 사람들이 그림을 가리키고 있다.
6. 사람들이 차에 상자들을 싣고 있다.

LISTENING PRACTICE

교재 p. 18

1. (A) X (B) X (C) O	**2.** (A) X (B) O (C) X
3. (A) O (B) X (C) O	**4.** (A) O (B) X (C) X
5. (A) X (B) O (C) X	**6.** (A) O (B) O (C) X

1 W-Am

(A) They are putting on helmets. (X)
(B) The woman is pointing at a computer screen.
 (X)
(C) She is holding a laptop computer. (O)

put on 입다, 쓰다, 걸치다

번역 (A) 사람들이 헬멧을 쓰는 중이다.
   (B) 여자가 컴퓨터 화면을 가리키고 있다.
   (C) 여자가 노트북 컴퓨터를 들고 있다.

해설 **사람 중심 사진 – 실내 작업장**
   (A) X : 두 사람이 이미 헬멧을 착용한 상태이지 쓰고 있는
      (are putting on) 중은 아니다.
   (B) X : 여자가 가리키고 있는(is pointing at) 동작을 하
      고 있지만 컴퓨터 화면을 가리키고 있지는 않다.
   (C) O : 여자가 노트북 컴퓨터(a laptop computer)를
      들고 있는 모습이므로 맞는 묘사이다.

2 M-Cn

(A) They are facing the same direction. (X)
(B) He is carrying a box. (O)
(C) He is stacking some boxes. (X)

face ~을 향하다 direction 방향 stack 쌓다

번역 (A) 사람들이 같은 방향을 향하고 있다.
   (B) 남자가 상자를 나르고 있다.
   (C) 남자가 상자들을 쌓고 있다.

해설 **사람 중심 사진 – 집안**
   (A) X : 두 사람이 같은 방향을 향하고 있는(are facing
      the same direction) 모습이 아니다.
   (B) O : 남자가 상자를 나르고(is carrying) 있으므로 맞
      는 묘사이다.
   (C) X : 사진에 상자들이 보이지만 남자가 상자들을 쌓고
      있는(is stacking) 것은 아니다.

3 W-Br

(A) He is inspecting the pipe. (O)
(B) He is writing a memo on a board. (X)
(C) He is kneeling on the floor. (O)

inspect 점검하다 kneel 무릎을 꿇다

번역 (A) 남자가 배관을 점검하고 있다.
   (B) 남자가 칠판에 메모를 하고 있다.
   (C) 남자가 바닥에 무릎을 꿇고 있다.

해설 **사람 중심 사진 – 부엌**
   (A) O : 남자가 배관을 점검하고(inspecting the pipe)
      있는 모습이므로 맞는 묘사이다.
   (B) X : 사진에는 칠판이 보이지 않는다.
   (C) O : 남자가 바닥에 무릎을 꿇고(is kneeling) 있으므
      로 맞는 묘사이다.

4 M-Au

(A) They are rowing a boat. (O)
(B) They are wearing hats. (X)
(C) They are throwing away their oars. (X)

row 노를 젓다   throw away 버리다   oar 노

번역 (A) 사람들이 배를 젓고 있다.
　　 (B) 사람들이 모자를 쓰고 있다.
　　 (C) 사람들이 노를 버리고 있다.

해설 **사람 중심 사진 – 강**
　　 (A) O: 두 남자가 배를 젓고 있는(are rowing) 모습이므
　　　　 로 맞는 묘사이다.
　　 (B) X : 한 남자는 모자를 쓰고 있지만 또 다른 남자는 모
　　　　 자를 쓰고 있지 않다.
　　 (C) X : 사진에 노가 보이지만, 노를 버리는(are throwing
　　　　 away their oars) 것은 아니다.

5 M-Cn

(A) He is exiting a room. (X)
(B) He is pulling a suitcase. (O)
(C) He is holding onto a railing. (X)

exit 나가다, 떠나다   hold onto ~을 붙잡다   railing 난간

번역 (A) 남자가 방에서 나가고 있다.
　　 (B) 남자가 여행 가방을 끌고 있다.
　　 (C) 남자가 난간을 붙잡고 있다.

해설 **사람 중심 사진 – 복도**
　　 (A) X : 남자는 방에서 나가고(is exiting) 있지 않다.
　　 (B) O: 여행 가방을 끌고 있는(is pulling) 모습이므로 맞
　　　　 는 묘사이다.
　　 (C) X : 사진에는 난간(railing)이 보이지 않는다.

6 W-Am

(A) People are seated at a table. (O)
(B) Some people are applauding a speaker. (O)
(C) All of the people are sitting on chairs. (X)

applaud 박수를 치다, 갈채를 보내다

번역 (A) 사람들이 탁자에 앉아 있다.
　　 (B) 사람들이 연설자에게 박수를 보내고 있다.
　　 (C) 모든 사람들이 의자에 앉아 있다.

해설 **사람 중심 사진 – 회의실**
　　 (A) O : 사람들이 탁자에 앉아(are seated) 있으므로 맞
　　　　 는 묘사이다.
　　 (B) O : 몇몇 사람들이 발표자로 보이는 여자에게 박수를
　　　　 보내고 있는(are applauding a speaker) 모습
　　　　 이므로 맞는 묘사이다.
　　 (C) X : 여자 한 명은 앉아 있지 않다.

ACTUAL TEST
교재 p. 19

1. (C)	2. (C)	3. (D)	4. (D)	5. (D)
6. (A)	7. (B)	8. (B)		

1 M-Cn

(A) A man is moving some equipment.
(B) A man is looking into a mirror.
(C) A man is using a microscope.
(D) A man is assembling a machine.

microscope 현미경   assemble 조립하다

번역 (A) 남자가 장비를 옮기고 있다.
　　 (B) 남자가 거울을 들여다보고 있다.
　　 (C) 남자가 현미경을 사용하고 있다.
　　 (D) 남자가 기계를 조립하고 있다.

해설 **사람 중심 사진 – 연구실**
　　 (A) 동작 묘사 오답: 사진에 장비가 보이지만 남자가 장비
　　　　 를 옮기고 있는(is moving) 것은 아니다.
　　 (B) 사진에 없는 명사 사용 오답: 사진에는 거울(mirror)
　　　　 이 보이지 않는다.
　　 (C) 정답: 현미경을 사용하고 있는(is using a microscope)
　　　　 모습이므로 정답이다.
　　 (D) 동작 묘사 오답: 사진에 기계가 보이지만 남자가 기계를
　　　　 조립하고 있는(is assembling) 것은 아니다.

3

2 W-Am

(A) One of the people is holding a cup.
(B) Some people are posting a memo.
(C) The men are greeting each other.
(D) They are seated in a row.

post 게시하다   in a row 한 줄로, 연이어

번역 (A) 사람들 중 한 명이 컵을 들고 있다.
(B) 사람들이 메모를 게시하고 있다.
(C) 남자들이 인사를 나누고 있다.
(D) 사람들이 한 줄로 앉아 있다.

해설 **사람 중심 사진 – 실내**
(A) 동작 묘사 오답: 사진에 컵이 보이지만 사람들 중 한 명이 컵을 들고(is holding) 있지는 않다.
(B) 동작 묘사 오답: 사진에 메모가 보이지만, 게시하는 (are posting) 것은 아니다.
(C) 정답: 남자들이 인사를 나누고 있는(are greeting) 모습이므로 정답이다.
(D) 상태 묘사 오답: 사람들이 한 줄로 앉아 있는(seated in a row) 것이 아니라 테이블에 둘러 앉아 있는 모습이다.

3 M-Au

(A) A man is pushing a stroller.
(B) A man is trimming some trees.
(C) A man is lifting a basket.
(D) A man is mowing the lawn.

stroller 유모차   trim 다듬다   mow (잔디를) 깎다

번역 (A) 남자가 유모차를 밀고 있다.
(B) 남자가 나무들을 다듬고 있다.
(C) 남자가 바구니를 들어올리고 있다.
(D) 남자가 잔디를 깎고 있다.

해설 **사람 중심 사진 – 마당**
(A) 사진에 없는 명사 사용 오답: 사진에는 유모차 (stroller)가 보이지 않는다.
(B) 동작 묘사 오답: 남자가 나무들을 다듬고 있는(is trimming) 모습이 아니다.
(C) 사진에 없는 명사 사용 오답: 사진에는 바구니 (basket)가 보이지 않는다.
(D) 정답: 남자가 잔디를 깎고 있는(is mowing the lawn) 모습이므로 정답이다.

4 M-Cn

(A) Some people are hanging some images.
(B) Some people are admiring artwork.
(C) Some people are taking notes on a whiteboard.
(D) Some people are viewing a chart.

admire 감탄하며 바라보다   artwork 예술 작품

번역 (A) 사람들이 그림들을 걸고 있다.
(B) 사람들이 예술 작품을 감상하고 있다.
(C) 사람들이 화이트보드에 메모를 하고 있다.
(D) 사람들이 차트를 보고 있다.

해설 **사람 중심 사진 – 실내**
(A) 동작 묘사 오답: 사진에 그림들(some images)이 보이지만 사람들이 그림들을 걸고 있는(are hanging) 것은 아니다.
(B) 사진에 없는 명사 사용 오답: 사진에는 미술품 (artwork)이 보이지 않는다.
(C) 사진에 없는 명사 시용 오답: 시진에는 화이트보드가 보이지 않는다.
(D) 정답: 사람들이 차트를 보고(are viewing) 있으므로 정답이다.

5 W-Br

(A) He is resting near a building.
(B) He is repairing a broken window.
(C) He is unfolding an umbrella.
(D) He is adjusting an awning.

unfold 펼치다   adjust 조정하다, 바로잡다   awning 차양

번역 (A) 남자가 건물 근처에서 쉬고 있다.
(B) 남자가 부서진 창문을 고치고 있다.
(C) 남자가 우산을 펴고 있다.
(D) 남자가 차양을 바로잡고 있다.

해설 **사람 중심 사진– 실외**
(A) 동작 묘사 오답: 남자는 건물 근처에서 작업을 하고 있지 쉬고 있는(is resting) 것은 아니다.
(B) 사진에 없는 명사 사용 오답: 사진에는 부서진 창문 (broken window)이 보이지 않는다.
(C) 사진에 없는 명사 사용 오답: 사진에는 우산이 보이지 않는다.

(D) 정답: 차양을 바로잡고 있는(is adjusting an awning) 모습이므로 정답이다.

6 W-Am

(A) They are working on a device.
(B) They are packing some tool belts.
(C) They are putting up some signs.
(D) They are stacking some frames.

work on ~에 공들여 작업하다 device 기구, 장치 pack (짐, 꾸러미 따위를) 싸다 put up 설치하다 stack 쌓다

번역 (A) 사람들이 장치에 작업을 하고 있다.
　　(B) 사람들이 공구 벨트를 싸고 있다.
　　(C) 사람들이 표지판을 설치하고 있다.
　　(D) 사람들이 틀을 쌓고 있다.

해설 **사람 중심 사진 – 실외**
　　(A) 정답: 사람들이 장치에 작업을 하고(are working on a device) 있으므로 정답이다.
　　(B) 동작 묘사 오답: 공구 벨트를 허리에 찬 사람은 보이지만, 싸고 있는(are packing some tool belts) 모습은 보이지 않는다.
　　(C) 사진에 없는 명사 사용: 사진에는 표지판(signs)이 보이지 않는다.
　　(D) 동작 묘사 오답: 사람들이 쌓는(are stacking) 동작을 하고 있지 않다.

7 M-Cn

(A) She is removing some furniture.
(B) She is sweeping the floor.
(C) She is placing a vase on a table.
(D) She is walking through a hallway.

remove 치우다 sweep 쓸다 hallway 복도, 통로

번역 (A) 여자가 가구를 치우고 있다.
　　(B) 여자가 바닥을 쓸고 있다.
　　(C) 여자가 탁자에 꽃병을 놓고 있다.
　　(D) 여자가 복도를 걸어가고 있다.

해설 **사람 중심 사진 – 실내**
　　(A) 동작 묘사 오답: 사진에 가구가 보이지만 여자가 가구를 치우는(is removing) 것은 아니다.

(B) 정답: 바닥을 쓸고 있는(is sweeping) 모습이므로 정답이다.
(C) 동작 묘사 오답: 사진에 탁자와 꽃병이 보이지만 여자가 탁자에 꽃병을 놓는(is placing a vase) 것은 아니다.
(D) 사진에 없는 명사 사용: 사진에는 복도(hallway)가 보이지 않는다.

8 W-Am

(A) They are getting off a vehicle.
(B) They are boarding an aircraft.
(C) They are waving to each other.
(D) Some people are checking in their luggage.

board 탑승하다 aircraft 비행기 luggage 수하물, 짐

번역 (A) 사람들이 차량에서 내리고 있다.
　　(B) 사람들이 비행기에 탑승하고 있다.
　　(C) 사람들이 서로에게 손을 흔들고 있다.
　　(D) 사람들이 짐을 부치고 있다.

해설 **사람 중심 사진 – 비행장**
　　(A) 동작 묘사 오답: 사람들은 차량에서 내리고(are getting off) 있지 않다.
　　(B) 정답: 사람들이 비행기에 탑승하고(are boarding) 있으므로 정답이다.
　　(C) 동작 묘사 오답: 사람들은 서로에게 손을 흔들고(are waving) 있지 않다.
　　(D) 동작 묘사 오답: 사진에 짐이 보이지만 사람들이 짐을 부치고 있는(are checking in their luggage) 것은 아니다.

●Unit 02 사물 / 배경 / 혼합 사진

CHECK-UP　　　　　　교재 p. 21

1. are being weighed　**2.** are parked / curb
3. being adjusted　　　**4.** have been arranged
5. is being moved　　　**6.** are being displayed

W-Am

1. Some crops <u>are being weighed</u> on a scale.
2. Vehicles <u>are parked</u> near the <u>curb</u>.
3. Some electronic equipment is <u>being adjusted</u>.
4. Tables <u>have been arranged</u> on an outdoor patio.
5. A piece of furniture <u>is being moved</u>.
6. Some baked goods <u>are being displayed</u> in a case.

어휘 crop 농산물 weigh 무게를 달다 scale 저울 curb 연석
adjust 조절하다, 정돈하다 arrange 배열하다 baked
goods 제과류

1. 저울에서 농산물의 무게가 측정되고 있다.
2. 연석 가까이에 차들이 주차되어 있다.
3. 전자기기가 조절되고 있다.
4. 탁자들이 야외 테라스에 놓여 있다.
5. 가구 한 점이 옮겨지고 있다.
6. 제과류가 진열장에 진열되어 있다.

LISTENING PRACTICE

교재 p. 22

1. (A) X (B) O (C) O   **2.** (A) O (B) O (C) X
3. (A) O (B) X (C) X   **4.** (A) O (B) O (C) X
5. (A) X (B) X (C) O   **6.** (A) X (B) X (C) O

1 M-Cn

(A) Some crops are being picked up. (X)
(B) Shelves are stocked with some produce. (O)
(C) Some fruits are being displayed in a
supermarket. (O)

crop 작물 pick up 들어올리다. 수확하다 stock (재고 등을)
채우다 produce 농산물

번역 (A) 농작물이 수확되고 있다.
(B) 선반들이 농산물로 채워져 있다.
(C) 과일이 슈퍼마켓에 진열되어 있다.

해설 **사물 사진 – 슈퍼마켓**
(A) X : 사진에는 농작물(crops)를 수확하는 동작을 하는
사람이 없다.
(B) O : 선반들이 농산물(produce)로 채워져 있으므로
맞는 묘사이다.
(C) O : 과일이 슈퍼마켓에 진열되어 있는(are being
displayed) 모습이므로 맞는 묘사이다.

2 W-Br

(A) The lights have been turned on. (O)
(B) Light fixtures are suspended from the ceiling.
(O)
(C) Some lamps are being fixed. (X)

light fixture 조명기구 suspend 매달다 fix 수리하다

번역 (A) 조명이 켜져 있다.
(B) 조명기구들이 천장에 매달려 있다.
(C) 램프들이 수리되고 있다.

해설 **사물 사진 – 조명**
(A) O : 조명들이 켜져 있으므로 맞는 묘사이다.
(B) O : 조명기구들(light fixtures)이 천장에 매달려 있는
모습이므로 맞는 묘사이다.
(C) X : 사진에는 램프들을 수리하는 동작을 하는 사람이
없다.

3 M-Au

(A) Dishware is being organized in a machine. (O)
(B) A woman is opening the door of an oven. (X)
(C) She is washing the dishes. (X)

dishware 식기류

번역 (A) 식기들이 기기에 정리되고 있다.
(B) 여자가 오븐 문을 열고 있다.
(C) 여자가 설거지를 하고 있다.

해설 **사람·사물 혼합 사진 – 주방**
(A) O : 식기들(dishware)이 여자에 의해 기기에 정리되
고 있으므로 맞는 묘사이다.
(B) X : 사진에는 오븐이 없다.
(C) X : 여자가 설거지를 하고 있는(is washing the
dishes) 모습이 아니다.

4 W-Am

(A) The floor is being mopped. (O)
(B) Some items are resting on a desk. (O)
(C) Some bookcases are being assembled. (X)

mop 대걸레질 하다 rest 놓다. 놓여 있다 assemble 조립하다

번역 (A) 바닥이 걸레질 되고 있다.
(B) 물건들이 책상에 놓여 있다.
(C) 책장들이 조립되고 있다.

해설 **사람·사물 혼합 사진 – 실내**

(A) O : 바닥이 여자에 의해 걸레질 되고 있으므로 맞는 묘사이다.

(B) O : 물건들이 책상에 놓여 있는(are resting) 상태이므로 맞는 묘사이다.

(C) X : 책장들을 조립하는 동작을 하는 사람은 없다.

5 M-Cn

(A) A piece of jewelry is being picked up. (X)

(B) Items are being removed from the case. (X)

(C) Some jewelry is on display. (O)

remove 꺼내다   on display 진열되어 있는

번역 (A) 보석이 들어올려지고 있다.

(B) 물건들이 진열장에서 꺼내어지고 있다.

(C) 보석들이 진열되어 있다.

해설 **사람·사물 혼합 사진 – 실내**

(A) X : 보석(a piece of jewelry)을 들어올리는 동작을 하는 사람은 없다.

(B) X : 물건들을 꺼내는 사람은 없다.

(C) O : 보석들이 진열되어 있는(is on display) 상태이므로 맞는 묘사이다.

6 W-Br

(A) Trees are being planted. (X)

(B) Street lights are lining a street. (X)

(C) Some bushes are growing in a garden. (O)

plant 심다   line ~을 따라 늘어서다

번역 (A) 나무들이 심어지고 있다.

(B) 가로등들이 거리를 따라 늘어서 있다.

(C) 관목들이 정원에서 자라고 있다.

해설 **사물 사진 – 관목**

(A) X : 사진에는 나무를 심는 동작을 하는 사람이 없다.

(B) X : 가로등들이 거리를 따라 늘어서 있지(are lining a street) 않다.

(C) O : 정원에서 관목들이 자라고(are growing) 있으므로 맞는 묘사이다.

ACTUAL TEST
교재 p. 23

1. (A)	**2.** (D)	**3.** (D)	**4.** (B)	**5.** (D)
6. (C)	**7.** (A)	**8.** (C)		

1 W-Am

(A) A train is stopped at a platform.

(B) People are stepping down from a train.

(C) Some railroad tracks are being fixed.

(D) A line is being painted on the ground.

platform 승강장

번역 (A) 기차가 승강장에 멈춰 있다.

(B) 사람들이 기차에서 내리고 있다.

(C) 철로 일부가 수리되고 있다.

(D) 바닥에 선이 그려지고 있다.

해설 **배경 사진 – 승강장**

(A) 정답: 기차가 승강장에 멈춰 있는(is stopped at a platform) 상태이므로 정답이다.

(B) 동작 묘사 오답: 기차에서 내리는(stepping down from a train) 동작을 하는 사람은 없다.

(C) 진행 묘사 오답: 사진에는 철로를 수리하는 동작을 하는 사람이 없다.

(D) 진행 묘사 오답: 사진에는 바닥에 선을 그리는 동작을 하는 사람이 없다.

2 W-Br

(A) Some equipment is being reassembled.

(B) A vehicle is being towed.

(C) Workers are putting on uniforms.

(D) A roadway is being repaved.

reassemble 재조립하다   tow 견인하다   repave 재포장하다

번역 (A) 일부 장비가 재조립되고 있다.

(B) 차량이 견인되고 있다.

(C) 근로자들이 유니폼을 입는 중이다.

(D) 도로가 재포장되고 있다.

해설 **사람·사물 혼합 사진 – 도로**

(A) 진행 묘사 오답: 사진에 일부 장비를 재조립하는 동작을 하는 사람은 없다.

(B) 진행 묘사 오답: 사진에 차량을 견인하는 동작을 하는
사람은 없다.

(C) 동작 묘사 오답: 근로자들은 유니폼을 착용한 상태이
지 입고 있는(are putting on) 중은 아니다.

(D) 정답: 도로가 재포장되고 있는(is being repaved) 모
습이므로 정답이다.

3 M-Cn

(A) A table is being set up.
(B) A sofa is being positioned in the corner.
(C) Cushions have been removed.
(D) A room is illuminated by some candles.

position 놓다, 배치하다   illuminate 밝히다

번역 (A) 탁자가 세팅되고 있다.
(B) 소파가 구석에 놓이고 있다.
(C) 쿠션들이 치워지고 없다.
(D) 방이 촛불들로 밝혀져 있다.

해설 **배경 사진 – 방**

(A) 진행 묘사 오답: 사진에는 탁자를 세팅하는 동작을 하
는 사람이 없다.

(B) 진행 묘사 오답: 사진에는 소파를 놓고 있는 동작을 하
는 사람이 없다.

(C) 상태 묘사 오답: 쿠션은 치워지고 없는(have been
removed) 상태가 아니다.

(D) 정답: 방이 촛불로 밝혀져 있는(is illuminated) 상태
이므로 정답이다.

4 W-Br

(A) Shelves are being stocked with books.
(B) All the seats are unoccupied.
(C) Some items are being put on a table.
(D) Curtains have been pulled closed.

be stocked with ~로 채워지다   unoccupied 비어 있는

번역 (A) 선반이 책들로 채워지고 있다.
(B) 모든 좌석이 비어 있다.
(C) 물건들이 탁자 위에 놓이고 있다.
(D) 커튼이 닫혀져 있다.

해설 **배경 사진 – 서재**

(A) 진행 묘사 오답: 사진에는 선반을 책들로 채우는 동작
을 하는 사람이 없다.

(B) 정답: 모든 좌석이 비어 있는(are unoccupied) 모습
이므로 정답이다.

(C) 진행 묘사 오답: 사진에는 물건들을 탁자에 놓는 동작
을 하는 사람이 없다.

(D) 상태 묘사 오답: 커튼은 닫혀져 있지(have been
pulled closed) 않고 열려져 있다.

5 M-Au

(A) He is paying a cashier.
(B) The floor is being wiped.
(C) A man is drinking a beverage.
(D) Vending machines are standing in a row.

wipe 닦다   beverage 음료수   vending machine 자판기
in a row 일렬로, 연달아

번역 (A) 남자가 계산원에게 지불하고 있다.
(B) 바닥이 닦이고 있다.
(C) 남자가 음료수를 마시고 있다.
(D) 자판기가 일렬로 서 있다.

해설 **사람·사물 혼합 사진 – 자판기**

(A) 동작 묘사 오답: 남자가 계산원에게 지불하고 있는(is
paying a cashier) 모습이 아니다.

(B) 진행 묘사 오답: 사진에 바닥을 닦는 동작을 하는 사람
은 없다.

(C) 동작 묘사 오답: 남자가 음료수를 마시는 (is drinking
a beverage) 모습이 아니다.

(D) 정답: 자판기(vending machines)가 일렬(in a
row)로 서 있는 상태이므로 정답이다.

6 W-Am

(A) Some poles are being replaced.
(B) A cyclist is stopped at a park.
(C) A bike has been propped against a structure.
(D) Some road directions are being rearranged.

replace 교체하다   prop against ~에 기대어 놓다, 받쳐 놓다
rearrange 재배치하다, 재배열하다

번역 (A) 기둥들이 교체되고 있다.

(B) 자전거를 탄 사람이 공원에 멈춰 있다.

(C) 자전거가 구조물에 기대어져 있다.

(D) 도로 표지판들이 재배치되고 있다.

해설 **배경 사진 – 야외**

(A) 사진에 없는 명사 사용·진행 묘사 오답: 사진 속에 기둥들(poles)은 보이지 않으며 기둥들을 교체하는 동작을 하는 사람도 없다.

(B) 사진에 없는 명사 사용·연상 단어 사용 오답: 사진 속에 자전거를 탄 사람(cyclist)은 보이지 않는다.

(C) 정답: 자전거가 구조물에 기대어져 있는(has been propped against a structure) 상태이므로 정답이다.

(D) 진행 묘사 오답: 사진에 도로 표지판들을 재배치하는 동작을 하는 사람이 없다.

7 M-Cn

(A) Gardening is being carried out.

(B) The men are watering the plants.

(C) A fence is enclosing a yard.

(D) A pathway leads to a warehouse.

carry out 실행하다   enclose 둘러싸다   warehouse 창고

번역 (A) 조경 작업이 이루어지고 있다.

(B) 남자들이 화분에 물을 주고 있다.

(C) 울타리가 마당을 둘러싸고 있다.

(D) 길이 창고까지 나 있다.

해설 **사람·사물 혼합 사진 – 야외**

(A) 정답: 조경 작업을 하고 있는 사람들이 있다.

(B) 동작 묘사 오답: 화분에 물을 주는(are watering the plants) 동작을 하는 사람은 없다.

(C) 사진에 없는 명사 사용 오답: 사진 속에 울타리(fence)는 보이지 않는다.

(D) 사진에 없는 명사 사용 오답: 사진 속에 창고(warehouse)는 보이지 않는다.

8 W-Am

(A) Bottles are being removed from a case.

(B) A beverage is being poured.

(C) Some items are lined up in a row.

(D) Products have been piled up.

pour 붓다, 따르다   pile up 쌓아 올리다

번역 (A) 병들이 상자에서 꺼내지고 있다.

(B) 음료가 따라지고 있다.

(C) 물건들이 일렬로 정렬되어 있다.

(D) 제품들이 쌓여 있다.

해설 **사물 사진 – 병**

(A) 진행 묘사 오답: 사진에 병들을 상자에서 꺼내는 동작을 하는 사람이 없다.

(B) 진행 묘사 오답: 사진에 음료를 따르는 동작을 하는 사람이 없다.

(C) 정답: 물건들이 일렬로 정렬되어 있는(are lined up) 상태이므로 정답이다.

(D) 상태 묘사 오답: 사진에 제품들이 쌓여 있지 않다.

PART 2

●UNIT 01
Who / What / Which 의문문

❶ Who

LISTENING PRACTICE

1. (A) **2.** (A) **3.** (A) **4.** (B) **5.** (C) **6.** (C)

1

W-Am Who wants to change the work shift?
W-Br (A) Sarah, I guess.
(B) You'd better not.
(C) Please shift the seats with me.

> work shift 근무 교대 shift 바꾸다

번역 누가 근무 교대를 바꾸고 싶어하죠?
(A) 사라 씨인 것 같아요.
(B) 그러지 않는 편이 좋겠어요.
(C) 저와 자리를 바꿔 주세요.

해설 **Who 의문문**
(A) 정답: 교대 희망자를 묻는 질문에 사람 이름으로 답하고 있다.
(B) 내용 오류: 조언이 필요한 질문이나 평서문에 어울릴 수 있는 답변이다.
(C) 반복 어휘 오답: 질문의 shift를 반복 사용한 오답이다.

2

W-Br Who will review my loan application?
M-Au (A) I'll let you know later.
(B) That would be best.
(C) Let's load it together.

> loan 대출 application 신청, 신청서 load 싣다

번역 제 대출 신청서는 누가 검토할 예정인가요?
(A) 나중에 알려드릴게요.
(B) 그게 최선일 것 같아요.
(C) 그것도 같이 실읍시다.

해설 **Who 의문문**
(A) 정답: 담당자를 묻는 질문에 나중에 알려주겠다며 직접적인 답변을 미루는 상황이다.
(B) 내용 오류: 제안문에 어울리는 답변이다.

(C) 유사 발음 오답: 질문의 loan과 발음이 유사한 load를 이용한 오답이다.

3

M-Au Who does this notebook belong to?
W-Am (A) A trainee must have left it there.
(B) The first and last chapters.
(C) They publish many books.

> trainee 교육생

번역 이 노트는 누구의 것입니까?
(A) 교육생이 거기에 두고 갔을 겁니다.
(B) 첫 번째와 마지막 장이요.
(C) 그들은 많은 책을 출간했어요.

해설 **Who 의문문**
(A) 정답: 물건이 누구의 것인지 묻는 질문에 사람명사(trainee)로 답하고 있다.
(B) 내용 오류: which chapter로 물었을 때 어울리는 답변이다.
(C) 반복 어휘 오답: 질문의 notebook에서 book을 반복 사용한 오답이다.

4

W-Am Who sent the final guest list to the caterer?
M-Cn (A) Ninety-eight people in total.
(B) We're still waiting for a few responses.
(C) A buffet dinner would be best.

> caterer 출장 요리 업체 response 회신

번역 누가 출장 요리 업체에 최종 손님 명단을 보냈습니까?
(A) 총 98명입니다.
(B) 아직 회신을 좀 더 기다리고 있습니다.
(C) 뷔페식 저녁 식사가 제일 좋을 것 같아요.

해설 **Who 의문문**
(A) 내용 오류: how many 의문문에 어울리는 답변이다.
(B) 정답: 최종 손님 명단 발송자를 묻는 질문에 아직 회신을 기다리고 있다며 명단이 확정되지 않았음을 답하고 있다.
(C) 연상 어휘 오답: 질문의 caterer에서 연상할 수 있는 buffet dinner를 이용한 오답이다.

5

M-Cn Who will take care of the broken light in the elevator?
W-Am (A) I'll take these boxes for you.
(B) Just across the street.
(C) Try calling the maintenance crew.

> maintenance 유지 보수 crew 팀, 반

번역 엘리베이터의 고장 난 등은 누가 처리할 건가요?
(A) 제가 당신을 위해 이 상자들을 가져갈게요.
(B) 바로 길 건너편이에요.
(C) 관리 팀에 전화해 보세요.

해설 **Who 의문문**
(A) 반복 어휘 오답: 질문의 take를 반복 사용한 오답이다.
(B) 내용 오류: where 의문문에 어울리는 답변이다.
(C) 정답: 고장 처리 담당자를 묻는 질문에 담당 부서로 답하고 있다.

6

W-Am Who was Mr. Carter arguing with at lunchtime?
M-Cn (A) No it's taking place in the morning.
(B) I'm sure they can work it out.
(C) That was the HR manager.

argue with ~와 언쟁을 벌이다　work ~ out 해결하다
HR (Human Resources) 인사부

번역 카터 씨는 점심 시간에 누구와 언쟁을 했나요?
(A) 아니요, 그 일은 아침에 일어났어요.
(B) 그들이 해결할 수 있을 거라고 확신해요.
(C) 인사부장이었어요.

해설 **Who 의문문**
(A) Yes/No 답변 불가 오답: 의문사 의문문에는 Yes/No로 대답할 수 없다.
(B) 연상 어휘 오답: 질문의 argue에서 연상할 수 있는 work it out을 이용한 오답이다.
(C) 정답: 논쟁 상대를 묻는 질문에 직책명으로 답변하고 있다.

❷ What / Which

LISTENING PRACTICE　교재 p. 33

1. (C)　**2.** (B)　**3.** (A)　**4.** (A)　**5.** (B)　**6.** (C)

1

W-Am What time will the bank manager be back from lunch?
M-Cn (A) At the retirement party.
(B) Yes, I have a savings account.
(C) In about twenty minutes.

retirement 은퇴, 퇴직　savings account 예금 계좌

번역 은행 지점장은 점심을 먹고 몇 시에 돌아올 예정인가요?
(A) 퇴직 기념 파티에서요.
(B) 네, 저는 예금 계좌가 있어요.
(C) 약 20분 후에요.

해설 **What 의문문**
(A) 내용 오류: where 의문문에 어울리는 답변이다.
(B) 연상 어휘 오답: 질문의 bank에서 연상할 수 있는 savings account를 이용한 오답이다.
(C) 정답: 점심 후 복귀 시각을 묻는 질문에 「in+시간」으로 답하고 있다.

2

W-Br Which workshop is Gary leading?
M-Cn (A) A well-known author.
(B) The one about time management.
(C) Next to Central Shopping Plaza.

management 관리

번역 개리 씨는 어떤 워크숍을 주재하나요?
(A) 잘 알려진 작가요.
(B) 시간 관리에 관한 워크숍요.
(C) 센트럴 쇼핑 플라자 옆이요.

해설 **Which 의문문**
(A) 내용 오류: who 의문문에 어울리는 답변이다.
(B) 정답: 주재하는 워크숍이 어떤 것인지 묻는 질문에 「the one+주제」로 답하고 있다.
(C) 내용 오류: where 의문문에 어울리는 답변이다.

3

M-Au What was in the box delivered today?
M-Cn (A) Some books I ordered.
(B) To the upstairs.
(C) Let's wrap it tight.

upstairs 위층

번역 오늘 배송된 상자 안에 무엇이 있었나요?
(A) 제가 주문한 책들이요.
(B) 위층으로요.
(C) 단단히 포장합시다.

해설 **What 의문문**
(A) 정답: 상자 내용물을 묻는 질문에 대해 구체적인 품목으로 답변하고 있다.
(B) 내용 오류: where 의문문에 어울리는 답변이다.
(C) 연상 어휘 오답: box에서 연상할 수 있는 wrap을 이용한 오답이다.

4

W-Br What did Mr. Phillips think about your report?
M-Cn (A) I haven't submitted it yet.
(B) No, I don't think so.
(C) You can report directly to Mr. Ken.

submit 제출하다　directly 직접

번역 필립스 씨는 당신의 보고서를 어떻게 봤나요?

(A) 아직 제출하지 않았어요.

(B) 아니요, 그렇게 생각하지 않습니다.

(C) 켄 씨에게 직접 보고해도 됩니다.

해설 **What 의문문**

(A) 정답: 제 3자의 의견을 묻는 질문에 아직 제출하지 않았다며 반전의 답변을 주고 있다.

(B) Yes/No 답변 불가 오답: 의문사 의문문에는 Yes/No로 대답할 수 없다.

(C) 반복 어휘 오답: 질문의 report를 반복 사용한 오답이다.

5

W-Am What company did we use for the hotel lobby's renovations?

M-Cn (A) Yes, it looks much better.

(B) It was called Ace Designs, I think.

(C) We stayed there for one week.

renovation 개조, 수리

번역 호텔 로비 개조 공사에 어떤 업체를 썼죠?

(A) 네, 전보다 훨씬 좋아 보입니다.

(B) 에이스 디자인이라는 곳이었던 것 같아요.

(C) 우리는 1주일간 그곳에 머물렀어요.

해설 **고용한 업체를 묻는 What 의문문**

(A) Yes/No 답변 불가 오답: 의문사 의문문에는 Yes/No로 답할 수 없다.

(B) 정답: 개조 공사를 위해 고용한 업체를 묻는 질문에 구체적인 업체 이름으로 답변하고 있다.

(C) 연상 어휘 오답: 질문의 hotel에서 연상할 수 있는 stayed를 이용한 오답이다.

6

M-Au Which Chinese restaurant got the best online reviews?

W-Am (A) Yes, there was a long line.

(B) That building offers good views.

(C) The one on Main Street.

review 후기

번역 어떤 중식당의 온라인 후기가 가장 좋았나요?

(A) 네, 줄이 길었어요.

(B) 저 건물은 전망이 좋아요.

(C) 메인 스트리트에 있는 거요.

해설 **Which 의문문**

(A) Yes/No 답변 불가·유사 발음 오답: 의문사 의문문에 Yes/No로 답변한 오답이다. 또한 질문의 online과 발음이 유사한 long line을 이용한 오답이다.

(B) 유사 발음 오답: 질문의 reviews와 일부 발음이 동일한 views를 이용한 오답이다.

(C) 정답: 어떤 중식당의 온라인 후기가 가장 좋은지를 묻는 질문에 「the one+장소」로 답하고 있다.

ACTUAL TEST

교재 p. 34

1. (C)	2. (C)	3. (C)	4. (A)	5. (A)
6. (C)	7. (C)	8. (A)	9. (C)	10. (B)
11. (B)	12. (B)	13. (B)	14. (A)	15. (B)
16. (A)	17. (B)	18. (C)	19. (B)	20. (B)
21. (A)	22. (C)	23. (B)	24. (C)	25. (C)

1

M-Cn What did you think of the meal?

W-Am (A) An Italian restaurant.

(B) I'll have the steak, please.

(C) It was great.

번역 식사는 어땠나요?

(A) 이탈리아 음식점이요.

(B) 저는 스테이크 주세요.

(C) 아주 좋았습니다.

해설 **의견을 묻는 What 의문문**

(A) 연상 어휘 오답: 질문의 meal에서 연상할 수 있는 restaurant를 이용한 오답이다.

(B) 연상 어휘 오답: 질문의 meal에서 연상할 수 있는 steak를 이용한 오답이다.

(C) 정답: 식사는 어땠는지 묻는 질문에 아주 좋았다고 대답하고 있다.

2

W-Br Who was Katrina talking to at lunchtime?

M-Cn (A) Sure, let's discuss it.

(B) Thanks, but I've already eaten.

(C) The regional manager.

regional 지역의

번역 카트리나 씨는 점심 시간에 누구에게 이야기를 하고 있었나요?

(A) 물론이죠. 얘기해 봅시다.

(B) 감사합니다만 이미 먹었어요.

(C) 지역 관리자요.

해설 **Who 의문문**

(A) 연상 어휘 오답: 질문의 talking에서 연상할 수 있는 discuss를 이용한 오답이다.

(B) 내용 오류: 권유문에 어울리는 답변이다.

(C) 정답: 대화 상대를 묻는 질문에 직책명으로 답하고 있다.

3

W-Am Who made these charts and tables?

M-Cn (A) By noon at the latest.

　　(B) At the large buffet table.

　　(C) Probably Dan's assistant.

tables 표　at the latest 늦어도

번역 이 도표와 표는 누가 만들었죠?

(A) 늦어도 정오까지요.

(B) 큰 뷔페 테이블에요.

(C) 아마 댄의 비서일 겁니다.

해설 Who 의문문

(A) 내용 오류: when 의문문에 어울리는 답변이다.

(B) 반복 어휘 오답: 질문의 tables을 반복 사용한 오답이다.

(C) 정답: 문서 작성자를 묻는 질문에 사람 이름과 직책명으로 답하고 있다.

4

M-Au Who's in charge of editing our company newsletter?

W-Br (A) Ask Rachel in Human Resources.

　　(B) Both regular and express mail.

　　(C) Around November 9th.

express mail 특급우편

번역 회사 소식지 편집은 누가 맡고 있습니까?

(A) 인사부서의 레이첼 씨에게 물어보세요.

(B) 보통우편과 특급우편 둘 다요.

(C) 11월 9일경에요.

해설 Who 의문문

(A) 정답: 편집 담당자를 묻는 질문에 다른 사람에게 물어보라(Ask Rachel ~)며 만능 답변 형태로 답하고 있다.

(B) 연상 어휘 오답: 질문의 newsletter에서 연상할 수 있는 mail을 이용한 오답이다.

(C) 내용 오류: when 의문문에 어울리는 답변이다.

5

M-Cn What time should we leave to go to the picnic?

W-Am (A) I was thinking around 2.

　　(B) No, he's still here.

　　(C) It should be easier by now.

번역 소풍을 가려면 몇 시에 출발해야 할까요?

(A) 대략 2시경으로 생각하고 있어요.

(B) 아니요, 그는 아직 여기 있어요.

(C) 지금쯤은 더 쉬울 겁니다.

해설 What 의문문

(A) 정답: 출발 시간을 묻는 질문에 구체적인 시간으로 답하고 있다.

(B) Yes / No 답변 불가 오답: 의문사 의문문에는 Yes / No로 답할 수 없다.

(C) 연상 어휘 오답: 질문의 what time에서 연상할 수 있는 now를 이용한 오답이다.

6

W-Am Who is the first speaker at the seminar?

M-Cn (A) I'll speak to her about it.

　　(B) At the conference center.

　　(C) Check the event schedule.

번역 세미나의 첫 번째 연설자는 누구죠?

(A) 그녀에게 그것에 대해 얘기해 볼게요.

(B) 회의장에서요.

(C) 행사 일정을 확인해 보세요.

해설 Who 의문문

(A) 유사 발음 오답: 질문의 speaker와 일부 발음이 동일한 speak를 이용한 오답이다.

(B) 연상 어휘 오답: 질문의 speaker와 seminar에서 연상할 수 있는 conference center를 이용한 오답이다.

(C) 정답: 연설자를 묻는 질문에 행사 일정을 확인해 보라(Check ~)며 만능 답변 형태로 답하고 있다.

7

W-Am Which dress looks better on me?

M-Au (A) Use my e-mail address.

　　(B) Yes, I can see that.

　　(C) The green one is nice.

번역 어떤 옷이 저에게 더 잘 어울려요?

(A) 제 이메일 주소를 사용하세요.

(B) 네, 알 것 같아요.

(C) 녹색 옷이 멋지네요.

해설 Which 의문문

(A) 유사 발음 오답: 질문의 dress와 일부 발음이 동일한 address를 이용한 오답이다.

(B) Yes / No 답변 불가 오답: 의문사 의문문에는 Yes / No로 답할 수 없다.

(C) 정답: 어떤 옷이 자신에게 잘 어울리는지를 묻는 질문에 「the one + 색상」으로 답하고 있다.

8

M-Au What was Mr. Donovan's presentation about?

W-Am (A) I didn't see it.
(B) He is a competent employee.
(C) At conference room 11.

competent 유능한   conference 회의

번역 도노반 씨의 발표는 무엇에 관한 것이었나요?
(A) 저는 보지 못했어요.
(B) 그는 유능한 직원입니다.
(C) 11번 회의실에서요.

해설 **What 의문문**
(A) 정답: 발표의 주제를 묻는 질문에 발표를 보지 못했다며 모른다는 의미를 우회적으로 전달하고 있다.
(B) 내용 오류: 인물에 대해 묻거나 의견을 구할 때 가능한 답변이다.
(C) 내용 오류: where 의문문에 어울리는 답변이다.

9

W-Am Who parked the bicycle in front of the building?

M-Cn (A) Both jogging and cycling.
(B) I've never been to that park.
(C) A delivery person, I believe.

번역 누가 건물 앞에 자전거를 댔나요?
(A) 조깅과 자전거 타기 둘 다요.
(B) 저는 그 공원에 간 적이 없어요.
(C) 배달원일 겁니다.

해설 **Whose 의문문**
(A) 유사 발음 오답: 질문의 bicycle과 일부 발음이 동일한 cycling을 이용한 오답이다.
(B) 반복 어휘 오답: 질문의 parked를 변형한 park를 변형하여 반복 사용한 오답이다.
(C) 정답: 행위자를 묻는 질문에 직업명으로 답하고 있다.

10

W-Br Who should I speak with to get an updated employee directory?

M-Cn (A) Not that I am aware of.
(B) Ms. Goldberg is in charge.
(C) Try the other direction.

directory 명부, 안내 책자   be aware of ~을 알다
be in charge 담당하다, 맡다   direction 방향

번역 업데이트된 직원 명부를 구하려면 누구에게 얘기해야 하죠?
(A) 제가 알기로는 그렇지 않습니다.
(B) 골드버그 씨가 담당하고 있어요.
(C) 다른 방향으로 가 보세요.

해설 **Who 의문문**
(A) 내용 오류: "Not that I am aware of."는 부정의 뜻을 밝힐 때 사용하는 No와 같은 의미이며, 따라서 의문사 의문문에 맞지 않는 답변이다.
(B) 정답: 담당자를 묻는 질문에 사람 이름으로 답하고 있다.
(C) 유사 발음 오답: 질문의 directory와 일부 발음이 유사한 direction을 이용한 오답이다.

11

M-Au What did the client say about our revised design?

M-Cn (A) For the board meeting.
(B) I haven't been told yet.
(C) At the proposed site.

revise 수정하다   board meeting 이사회   proposed 제안된   site 부지, 장소

번역 고객은 수정된 디자인에 대해 뭐라고 하던가요?
(A) 이사회를 위해서요.
(B) 아직 듣지 못했어요.
(C) 제안된 장소에서요.

해설 **What 의문문**
(A) 연상 어휘 오답: 질문의 client에서 연상할 수 있는 meeting을 이용한 오답이다.
(B) 정답: 수정된 디자인에 대한 고객의 의견을 묻는 질문에 아직 듣지 못했다며 만능 답변 형태로 답하고 있다.
(C) 내용 오류: where 의문문에 어울리는 답변이다.

12

W-Am Who left these application forms on my desk?

M-Cn (A) A position in marketing.
(B) That was David.
(C) Yes, they're in my drawer.

application form 지원서   drawer 서랍

번역 누가 제 책상에 이 지원서를 두었나요?
(A) 마케팅 직책이요.
(B) 데이비드 씨였어요.
(C) 네, 그것들은 제 서랍에 있어요.

해설 **Who 의문문**
(A) 연상 어휘 오답: 질문의 application(지원)에서 연상할 수 있는 position(직책)을 이용한 오답이다.

(B) 정답: 행위자를 묻는 질문에 사람 이름으로 답하고 있다.

(C) Yes/No 답변 불가 오답: 의문사 의문문에는 Yes/No로 답할 수 없다.

13

M-Au Who received the delivery of office supplies this morning?

W-Am (A) Just some red pens.

(B) I think it was Jake.

(C) No, in the afternoon.

번역 오늘 아침에 누가 사무용품 배송을 받았습니까?

(A) 빨간 펜 몇 자루요.

(B) 제이크 씨였던 것 같아요.

(C) 아니요, 오후에요.

해설 **Who 의문문**

(A) 연상 어휘 오답: 질문의 office supplies에서 연상할 수 있는 pens를 이용한 오답이다.

(B) 정답: 수신인을 묻는 질문에 사람 이름으로 답하고 있다.

(C) Yes/No 답변 불가 연상 어휘 오답: 의문사 의문무에 Yes/No로 답변한 오답이다. 또한 질문의 morning에서 연상할 수 있는 afternoon을 이용한 오답이다.

14

W-Br Who will lead the training session tomorrow?

M-Cn (A) Amy said she'd do it.

(B) I think a bus would be faster.

(C) From 9 until 11.

번역 내일 교육은 누가 주관할 예정이죠?

(A) 에이미 씨가 한다고 했어요.

(B) 버스가 더 빠를 것 같아요.

(C) 9시부터 11시까지요.

해설 **Who 의문문**

(A) 정답: 교육 주관자를 묻는 질문에 사람 이름으로 답하고 있다.

(B) 연상 어휘 오답: 질문의 train에서 연상할 수 있는 bus를 이용한 오답이다.

(C) 내용 오류: how long 의문문에 어울리는 답변이다.

15

W-Am Which bus goes to the baseball stadium?

M-Cn (A) I went there yesterday.

(B) Number 22.

(C) It's an important game.

번역 어떤 버스가 야구 경기장으로 가죠?

(A) 저는 어제 거기 갔어요.

(B) 22번이요.

(C) 중요한 경기였어요.

해설 **Which 의문문**

(A) 내용 오류: when 의문문에 어울리는 답변이다.

(B) 정답: 어떤 버스가 야구 경기장으로 가는지 묻는 질문에 버스 번호로 답하고 있다.

(C) 연상 어휘 오답: 질문의 baseball stadium에서 연상할 수 있는 game을 이용한 오답이다.

16

M-Cn Who took these photos?

W-Am (A) They're from several of the attendees.

(B) To download the newest software.

(C) Individually and in a group.

attendee 참석자   individually 개별적으로, 각각

번역 이 사진들은 누가 찍었나요?

(A) 참석자 여러 명이 찍은 겁니다.

(B) 최신 소프트웨어를 다운로드하려고요.

(C) 개별적으로, 그리고 단체로요.

해설 **Who 의문문**

(A) 정답: 사진 촬영자를 묻는 질문에 여러 명이라고 대답하고 있다.

(B) 내용 오류: why 의문문에 어울리는 답변이다.

(C) 연상 어휘 오답: 질문의 photos에서 연상할 수 있는 group을 이용한 오답이다.

17

M-Au What should we include in the gift basket for the client?

W-Am (A) No, I didn't wear a jacket today.

(B) Anything that can be personalized.

(C) Thank you for the compliment.

personalize 개인화하다   compliment 칭찬

번역 고객을 위한 선물 바구니에 무엇을 넣어야 할까요?

(A) 아니요, 저는 오늘 재킷을 입지 않았어요.

(B) 개인 맞춤형이 될 수 있는 건 뭐든지요.

(C) 칭찬해 주셔서 감사합니다.

해설 **What 의문문**

(A) Yes/No 답변 불가 오답: 의문사 의문문에는 Yes/No로 답할 수 없다.

(B) 성답: 포함할 물품을 묻는 질문에 포괄적인 답변을 주고 있다.

(C) 연상 어휘 오답: 질문의 gift에서 연상할 수 있는 Thank you를 이용한 오답이다.

18

W-Br Who lost this access card?
M-Au (A) Sure, I shop there quite often.
     (B) Only for a specific building.
     (C) It should have a name on it.

---

access 입장, 접근   specific 특정한

번역 누가 이 출입 카드를 잃어버렸나요?
     (A) 물론입니다. 저는 거기서 꽤 자주 쇼핑을 해요.
     (B) 특정 건물만요.
     (C) 이름이 쓰여 있을 거예요.

해설 **Who 의문문**
     (A) 내용 오류: "Sure"는 질문에 긍정의 뜻을 밝힐 때 사용하는 Yes와 같은 의미이며, 따라서 의문사 의문문에 맞지 않는 답변이다.
     (B) 연상 어휘 오답: 질문의 access card(출입 카드)에서 연상할 수 있는 building(건물)을 이용한 오답이다.
     (C) 정답: 카드 분실자를 묻는 질문에 이름이 쓰여 있을 것이라며 간접적으로 답변하고 있다.

19

W-Am Who'll be responsible for forming a search committee?
M-Cn (A) Some research projects.
     (B) The personnel director.
     (C) No, I will inform the staff about the change.

---

search committee 조사 위원회   research 연구
personnel 인사과

번역 누가 조사 위원회 조직을 맡을 예정이죠?
     (A) 몇몇 연구 프로젝트요.
     (B) 인사 부장이요.
     (C) 아니요, 제가 직원들에게 변경사항을 알릴게요.

해설 **Who 의문문**
     (A) 유사 발음 오답: 질문의 search와 일부 발음이 동일한 research를 이용한 오답이다.
     (B) 정답: 책임자를 묻는 질문에 직책명으로 답하고 있다.
     (C) Yes/No 답변 불가 오답: 의문사 의문문에는 Yes/No로 답할 수 없다.

20

M-Cn What was your previous job like?
W-Am (A) I'd love to.
     (B) I didn't get paid as I expected.
     (C) I quit them a while ago.

---

previous 이전의   quit 그만두다

번역 이전 일자리는 어땠어요?
     (A) 그러고 싶어요.
     (B) 기대한 만큼 보수를 받지 못했어요.
     (C) 얼마 전에 그만뒀어요.

해설 **What 의문문**
     (A) 내용 오류: 권유문에 어울리는 답변이다.
     (B) 정답: 이전 직장에 대한 의견을 묻는 질문에 보수와 관련하여 답하고 있다.
     (C) 연상 어휘 오답·대명사 오류: 질문의 job에서 연상할 수 있는 quit을 이용한 오답이다. 또한 질문에 복수명사가 없으므로 답변에서 them으로 지칭할 수 없다.

21

W-Br Which logo design should we use?
M-Au (A) I don't like any of them.
     (B) We put up some signs earlier.
     (C) No, it's brand new.

---

brand new 신품의

번역 어떤 로고 디자인을 사용해야 할까요?
     (A) 다 마음에 들지 않아요.
     (B) 이전에 팻말들을 걸었어요.
     (C) 아니요, 그건 신상품이에요.

해설 **Which 의문문**
     (A) 정답: 어떤 로고 디자인을 사용해야 할지 묻는 질문에 아무것도 선택하지 않는 답변이다.
     (B) 유사 발음 오답: 질문의 design과 일부 발음이 유사한 signs를 이용한 오답이다.
     (C) Yes/No 답변 불가 오답: 의문사 의문문에는 Yes/No로 답할 수 없다.

22

W-Am What's the local time in Singapore right now?
M-Cn (A) Much farther than I thought.
     (B) He speaks both English and Mandarin.
     (C) Let me check the app on my mobile phone.

---

farther 더 먼

번역 지금 싱가포르 현지 시간으로 몇 시죠?
     (A) 생각했던 것보다 훨씬 더 멀어요.
     (B) 그는 영어와 중국어를 다 해요.
     (C) 휴대전화 앱으로 확인해 볼게요.

해설 **What 의문문**
     (A) 내용 오류: 시간을 묻는 질문에 거리로 답하고 있으므로 오답이다.
     (B) 연상 어휘 오답: 질문의 Singapore에서 연상할 수 있는 English and Mandarin을 이용한 오답이다.

(C) 정답: 싱가포르 현지 시간을 묻는 질문에 휴대전화 앱으로 확인하겠다(Let me check ~)며 만능 답변 형태로 답하고 있다.

23

M-Au Which photos should we use for the brochure?

W-Am (A) I agree, they are informative.
(B) Let's ask Brian what he thinks.
(C) Over 100 photos.

brochure 안내 책자   informative 유익한

번역 안내 책자에 어떤 사진들을 사용해야 할까요?
(A) 그것들이 유익하다는 데 동의해요.
(B) 브라이언 씨가 어떻게 생각하는지 물어봅시다.
(C) 사진 100장 이상요.

해설 Which 의문문
(A) 연상 어휘 오답: brochure(안내 책자)에서 연상할 수 있는 informative(유익한)를 사용한 오답이다.
(B) 정답: 안내 책자에 어떤 사진들을 사용해야 할지 묻는 질문에 브라이언 씨에게 물어보자(Let's ask ~)며 만능 답변 형태로 답하고 있다.
(C) 반복 어휘 오답: 질문의 photos를 반복 사용한 오답이다.

24

W-Br Who will be presenting our proposal to the board of directors?

M-Cn (A) She turned down our proposal.
(B) No thanks, I'm full.
(C) I think I should do the job.

proposal 제안

번역 누가 이사회에 우리의 제안서를 발표할 건가요?
(A) 그녀는 우리 제안을 거절했어요.
(B) 괜찮습니다. 배가 불러요.
(C) 제가 해야 하는 것 같아요.

해설 Who 의문문
(A) 반복 어휘 오답·대명사 오류: 질문의 proposal을 반복 사용한 오답이다. 또한 질문에 she를 지칭할 대상이 없다.
(B) 내용 오류: 권유문에 어울리는 답변이다.
(C) 정답: 발표자를 묻는 질문에 자신이라고 답하고 있다.

25

W-Am What does our company policy say about the travel expenses?

M-Au (A) A few of us will take part.
(B) I didn't know he said so.
(C) Ms. Larson will know better than I do.

policy 정책   travel expense 출장 경비   take part 참가하다

번역 회사 정책에 출장 경비에 대해 뭐라고 나와 있습니까?
(A) 우리 중 몇 명이 참가할 거예요.
(B) 그가 그렇게 얘기한 줄 몰랐어요.
(C) 라슨 씨가 저보다 잘 알 거예요.

해설 What 의문문
(A) 내용 오류: who 의문문에 어울리는 답변이다.
(B) 반복 어휘 오답·대명사 오류: 질문의 say를 반복 사용한 오답이다. 또한 질문에 사람이 없으므로 답변에서 he로 지칭할 수 없다.
(C) 정답: 출장 경비를 묻는 질문에 다른 사람에게 물어보라는 것을 우회적으로 나타내고 있다.

●Unit 02 When / Where 의문문

❶ When

LISTENING PRACTICE
교재 p. 37

1. (B) **2.** (A) **3.** (A) **4.** (C) **5.** (B) **6.** (B)

1

W-Am When are you going on vacation?

M-Cn (A) A resort in Mexico.
(B) In the middle of November.
(C) For two weeks.

번역 언제 휴가를 떠날 예정인가요?
(A) 멕시코에 있는 리조트요.
(B) 11월 중순에요.
(C) 2주 동안요.

해설 When 의문문
(A) 연상 어휘 오답: 질문의 vacation에서 연상할 수 있는 resort를 이용한 오답으로 where 의문문에 어울리는 답변이다.
(B) 정답: 휴가 일정을 묻는 질문에 「in+시점」으로 답하고 있다.
(C) 내용 오류: how long 의문문에 어울리는 답변이다.

2

M-Au When is the registration deadline for the conference?

W-Am (A) Check the organizer's Web site.
(B) Yes, it was very helpful.
(C) Some newspaper headlines.

registration 등록

번역 회의 등록 마감기한은 언제입니까?
   (A) 주최측 웹사이트를 확인해 보세요.
   (B) 네, 매우 유용했어요.
   (C) 신문 헤드라인이요.

해설 **When 의문문**
   (A) 정답: 마감 기한을 묻는 질문에 웹사이트를 확인해 보라(Check ~ Web site)며 만능 답변 형태로 답하고 있다.
   (B) Yes/No 답변 불가 오답: 의문사 의문문에는 Yes/No로 답할 수 없다.
   (C) 유사 발음 오답: 질문의 deadline과 일부 발음이 동일한 headlines를 이용한 오답이다.

3

> M-Cn When will Robert depart for Toronto?
> W-Br (A) Ask his personal assistant.
>   (B) No, I've decided not to go.
>   (C) I hope he has an enjoyable trip.
>
> depart for ~로 떠나다

번역 로버트 씨는 언제 토론토로 떠날 예정인가요?
   (A) 로버트 씨의 개인 비서에게 물어보세요.
   (B) 아니요, 저는 가지 않기로 결정했어요.
   (C) 그가 즐거운 여행을 했으면 좋겠어요.

해설 **When 의문문**
   (A) 정답: 떠나는 시기를 묻는 질문에 비서에게 물어보라(Ask ~)며 만능 답변 형태로 답하고 있다.
   (B) Yes/No 답변 불가 오답·대명사 오류: 의문사 의문문에는 Yes/No로 답할 수 없다. 또한 질문의 주어가 Robert이므로 답변에서 I로 지칭할 수 없다.
   (C) 연상 어휘 오답: 질문의 depart에서 연상할 수 있는 trip을 이용한 오답이다.

4

> W-Am When can I catch the shuttle bus to the convention center?
> M-Cn (A) It's completely free.
>   (B) From the front of the hotel.
>   (C) It leaves every 20 minutes.
>
> completely 완전히

번역 회의장으로 가는 셔틀버스를 언제 탈 수 있을까요?
   (A) 완전히 무료입니다.
   (B) 호텔 앞에서요.
   (C) 20분마다 출발해요.

해설 **When 의문문**
   (A) 연상 어휘 오답: 질문의 shuttle bus에서 연상할 수 있는 free를 이용한 오답이다.

(B) 연상 어휘 오답: 질문의 shuttle bus에서 연상할 수 있는 hotel을 이용한 오답으로 where 의문문에 어울리는 답변이다.
   (C) 정답: 버스 시간을 묻는 질문에 배차 간격으로 답하고 있다.

5

> W-Br When should we have the carpets cleaned in the lobby?
> M-Cn (A) From the check-in desk.
>   (B) The sooner, the better.
>   (C) Some cleaning supplies.
>
> supplies 용품

번역 로비 카펫은 언제 청소해야 하죠?
   (A) 체크인 데스크에서요.
   (B) 빠를수록 좋아요.
   (C) 청소용품들이요.

해설 **When 의문문**
   (A) 연상 어휘 오답: 질문의 lobby에서 연상할 수 있는 check-in desk를 이용한 오답이다.
   (B) 정답: 청소를 해야 하는 시기를 묻는 질문에 빠를수록 좋다(The sooner, the better)는 관용 표현으로 답하고 있다.
   (C) 반복 어휘 오답: 질문의 cleaned를 변형한 cleaning을 반복 사용한 오답이다.

6

> M-Au When did you last go see a dentist?
> W-Am (A) No, I'm not available now.
>   (B) Earlier this month.
>   (C) As often as you could.

번역 치과에 언제 마지막으로 갔죠?
   (A) 아니요, 저는 지금 시간이 안 돼요.
   (B) 이번 달 초에요.
   (C) 가능하신 만큼 자주요.

해설 **When 의문문**
   (A) Yes/No 답변 불가 오답: 의문사 의문문에는 Yes/No로 답할 수 없다.
   (B) 정답: 치과 방문 시기를 묻는 질문에 구체적인 시점으로 답하고 있다.
   (C) 내용 오류: 빈도를 묻는 how often 의문문에 어울리는 답변이다.

❷ Where

LISTENING PRACTICE 교재 p, 39

1. (C) **2.** (A) **3.** (C) **4.** (A) **5.** (A) **6.** (A)

1

W-Am Where should I keep these brochures for the trade show?
M-Cn (A) Yes, they probably will.
(B) Is that cash or credit?
(C) In the small storage room.

trade show 무역 박람회 storage 보관

번역 이 무역박람회 안내 책자는 어디에 두어야 할까요?
(A) 네, 아마 그럴 거예요.
(B) 현금인가요, 아니면 신용카드인가요?
(C) 작은 보관실에요.

해설 Where 의문문
(A) Yes / No 답변 불가 오답: 의문사 의문문에는 Yes / No로 답할 수 없다.
(B) 연상 어휘 오답: brochures에 대한 지불 방법과 관련해서 연상할 수 있는 cash or credit을 이용한 오답이다.
(C) 정답: 안내 책자를 둘 위치를 묻는 질문에 「in + 장소」로 답하고 있다.

2

M-Au Where is Dr. Peterson giving his lecture?
W-Am (A) He's setting up in room 103.
(B) Yes, I enjoyed that.
(C) Promptly at seven o'clock.

lecture 강의 set up 준비하다 promptly 정각에

번역 피터슨 박사는 어디에서 강의를 하나요?
(A) 103호에서 준비 중입니다.
(B) 네, 즐거웠어요.
(C) 7시 정각에요.

해설 Where 의문문
(A) 정답: 강의 장소를 묻는 질문에 구체적인 강의실 호수로 답하고 있다.
(B) Yes / No 답변 불가 오답: 의문사 의문문에는 Yes / No로 답할 수 없다.
(C) 내용 오류: when 또는 what time 의문문에 어울리는 답변이다.

3

M-Cn Where did the tenant say there was a water leak?
W-Br (A) About twenty minutes ago.
(B) Yes, I've just signed the lease.
(C) In the bathroom sink.

tenant 세입자 water leak 누수 lease 임대 계약

번역 세입자가 누수가 있다고 말한 곳이 어디죠?
(A) 20분쯤 전에요.
(B) 네, 임대 계약서에 막 서명했어요.
(C) 욕실 개수대요.

해설 Where 의문문
(A) 내용 오류: when 의문문에 어울리는 답변이다.
(B) Yes / No 답변 불가 오답: 의문사 의문문에는 Yes / No로 답할 수 없다.
(C) 정답: 누수 위치를 묻는 질문에 「in + 장소」로 답하고 있다.

4

W-Am Where do we keep the packing supplies?
W-Br (A) Talk to Tim in the mailroom.
(B) At least three days in advance.
(C) It's the older package design.

at least 최소한 in advance 미리

번역 포장용품은 어디에 보관합니까?
(A) 우편물실 팀 씨에게 얘기하세요.
(B) 최소한 3일 전에요.
(C) 그건 예전 포장 디자인이에요.

해설 Where 의문문
(A) 정답: 보관 장소를 묻는 질문에 팀 씨에게 얘기하라(Talk to Tim ~)며 만능 답변(Ask + 사람)의 변형 형태로 답하고 있다.
(B) 내용 오류: when 의문문에 어울리는 답변이다.
(C) 유사 발음 오답: 질문의 packing과 일부 발음이 동일한 package를 이용한 오답이다.

5

W-Br Where will the company retreat be taking place?
M-Cn (A) At the Marina Resort.
(B) It came from England, I guess.
(C) You should treat it with extra care.

retreat 야유회 take place 열리다, 개최되다

번역 회사 야유회는 어디서 열릴 예정인가요?

(A) 마리나 리조트에서요.

(B) 영국에서 온 것 같아요.

(C) 특별히 더 주의해서 다루어야 해요.

해설 Where 의문문

(A) 정답: 야유회가 열릴 장소를 묻는 질문에 「at+장소」로 답하고 있다.

(B) 내용 오류: 출처를 묻는 where 의문문에 어울리는 답변이다.

(C) 유사 발음 오답: 질문의 retreat과 일부 발음이 동일한 treat을 이용한 오답이다.

6

W-Am **Where can I have my digital camera fixed?**
M-Au (A) Michael might know.

(B) That's the sale price.

(C) The picture quality is great.

번역 제 디지털 카메라를 어디에서 수리할 수 있을까요?

(A) 마이클 씨가 알 거예요.

(B) 그건 할인 가격입니다.

(C) 사진 회질이 아주 좋습니다.

해설 Where 의문문

(A) 정답: 수리 장소를 묻는 질문에 마이클 씨가 알 것 (Michael might know)이라며 만능 답변(Ask+사람)의 변형 형태로 답하고 있다.

(B) 내용 오류: 가격과 관련된 질문에 어울리는 답변이다.

(C) 연상 어휘 오답: 질문의 digital camera에서 연상할 수 있는 picture quality를 이용한 오답이다.

ACTUAL TEST
교재 p. 40

1. (B)	2. (B)	3. (A)	4. (C)	5. (C)
6. (C)	7. (A)	8. (B)	9. (A)	10. (B)
11. (C)	12. (A)	13. (C)	14. (C)	15. (C)
16. (C)	17. (B)	18. (B)	19. (B)	20. (A)
21. (C)	22. (C)	23. (B)	24. (B)	25. (A)

1

W-Am **When will the new assignment be given?**
W-Br (A) I'll sign it for you.

(B) Sometime next week.

(C) By the department manager.

assignment 과제, 임무   sometime 언젠가

번역 새로운 임무는 언제 주어질까요?

(A) 제가 대신 서명할게요.

(B) 다음 주 중에요.

(C) 부서 관리자요.

해설 When 의문문

(A) 유사 발음 오답: 질문의 assignment와 일부 발음이 동일한 sign을 이용한 오답이다.

(B) 정답: 업무 할당 시점을 묻는 질문에 구체적인 시점 명사로 답하고 있다.

(C) 연상 어휘 오답: assignment(임무)에서 연상할 수 있는 department manager(부서 관리자)를 사용한 오답이다.

2

W-Am **When is our year-end banquet?**
M-Au (A) Delicious, thanks.

(B) On Friday the 17th.

(C) At the Branmoor Hotel.

year-end 연말   banquet 연회

번역 송년회는 언제입니까?

(A) 맛있네요. 감사합니다.

(B) 17일 금요일요.

(C) 브랜무어 호텔에서요.

해설 When 의문문

(A) 연상 어휘 오답: banquet의 음식과 관련해서 연상할 수 있는 delicious를 사용한 오답이다.

(B) 정답: 송년회 시기를 묻는 질문에 「on+요일 및 날짜」로 답하고 있다.

(C) 내용 오류: where 의문문에 어울리는 답변이다.

3

W-Am **Where did this cake come from?**
M-Cn (A) Jeff brought it for the welcome party.

(B) By baking them for about 20 minutes.

(C) I thought so, but I wasn't sure.

번역 이 케이크는 어디에서 난 건가요?

(A) 제프 씨가 환영 파티를 위해 가져왔어요.

(B) 약 20분 동안 구워서요.

(C) 그렇게 생각했는데 확실하진 않아요.

해설 Where 의문문

(A) 정답: 케이크의 출처를 묻는 질문에 사람 이름으로 답하고 있다.

(B) 내용 오류: how 의문문에 어울리는 답변이다.

(C) 내용 오류: : "I thought so"는 질문에 긍정의 뜻을 밝힐 때 사용하는 Yes와 같은 의미이며, 따라서 의문사 의문문에 맞지 않는 답변이다.

4

M-Cn When will the City Orchestra have its next concert?

W-Br (A) In the downtown auditorium.
(B) Classical music, as always.
(C) Try checking their Web site.

auditorium 강당   as always 늘 그렇듯

번역 시립 오케스트라는 언제 다음 연주회를 열 예정입니까?
(A) 시내 강당에서요.
(B) 항상 그렇듯 클래식 음악이요.
(C) 거기 웹사이트를 확인해보세요.

해설 When 의문문
(A) 연상 어휘 오답: 질문의 concert에서 연상할 수 있는 auditorium을 이용한 오답으로 where 의문문에 어울리는 답변이다.
(B) 연상 어휘 오답: 질문의 Orchestra와 concert에서 연상할 수 있는 Classical music을 이용한 오답이다.
(C) 정답: 연주회 개최 시점을 묻는 질문에 웹사이트를 확인해보라(check ~)며 만능 답변 형태로 답하고 있다.

5

W-Am When will Ms. Jansen be back from lunch?

M-Cn (A) It launches on March 1st.
(B) At the bakery downstairs.
(C) Usually by 1 P.M.

launch 시작하다, 개시하다

번역 잰슨 씨는 점심 식사를 하고 언제 돌아옵니까?
(A) 3월 1일에 시작됩니다.
(B) 아래층에 있는 제과점에서요.
(C) 보통 오후 1시까지요.

해설 When 의문문
(A) 유사 발음 오답: 질문의 lunch와 발음이 유사한 launches를 이용한 오답이다.
(B) 내용 오류: where 의문문에 어울리는 답변이다.
(C) 정답: 돌아오는 시점을 묻는 질문에 「by+시점」으로 답하고 있다.

6

M-Au Where are the employee records?

W-Am (A) The part-time workers.
(B) Sure, take one.
(C) In the filing cabinet.

번역 직원 기록은 어디에 있나요?
(A) 시간제 근로자들요.
(B) 물론이죠, 하나 가져가세요.
(C) 문서 보관함에요.

해설 Where 의문문
(A) 연상 어휘 오답: 질문의 employee에서 연상할 수 있는 workers를 이용한 오답이다.
(B) 내용 오류: 요청문에 어울릴 수 있는 답변이다.
(C) 정답: 문서의 소재를 묻는 질문에 「in+장소」로 답하고 있다.

7

M-Cn When did you get your new mobile phone?

W-Am (A) A few days ago.
(B) There are good deals online.
(C) My old one broke.

번역 새 휴대전화는 언제 샀나요?
(A) 며칠 전에요.
(B) 온라인에 좋은 가격의 제품들이 있어요.
(C) 예전 전화기가 고장 났어요.

해설 When 의문문
(A) 정답: 구입 시점을 묻는 질문에 시점 부사구로 답하고 있다.
(B) 연상 어휘 오답: 질문의 new mobile phone에서 연상할 수 있는 good deals를 이용한 오답이다.
(C) 내용 오류: why 의문문에 어울릴 수 있는 답변이다.

8

M-Cn When are you moving to your new home?

M-Au (A) The best moving company.
(B) At the end of the month.
(C) Just past Asbury Street.

번역 새 집으로 언제 이사하세요?
(A) 최고의 이사업체예요.
(B) 이번 달 말에요.
(C) 애즈버리 스트리트를 막 지나서요.

해설 When 의문문
(A) 반복 어휘 오답: 질문의 moving을 반복 사용한 오답이다.
(B) 정답: 이사 시기를 묻는 질문에 「at+시점」으로 답하고 있다.
(C) 내용 오류: 길을 찾는 how 의문문에 어울릴 수 있는 답변이다.

9

W-Am Where did you find the information about the return policy?

M-Cn (A) On the last page of the booklet.
(B) Later this month.
(C) Within 2 weeks.

return policy 반품 규정   booklet 소책자

번역 반품 규정에 관한 정보를 어디서 찾으셨나요?

(A) 소책자 마지막 페이지에서요.

(B) 이번 달 중으로요.

(C) 2주 이내에요.

해설 **Where 의문문**

(A) 정답: 정보 출처를 묻는 질문에 「on + 책자 페이지」로 답하고 있다.

(B) 내용 오류: when 의문문에 어울리는 답변이다.

(C) 내용 오류: when 의문문에 어울리는 답변이다.

10

W-Br	When will my vehicle's engine be fixed?
W-Am	(A) About two hundred dollars.
	(B) By Tuesday afternoon.
	(C) Some metal components.

component 부품

번역 제 차 엔진은 언제 고쳐질까요?

(A) 약 200달러입니다.

(B) 화요일 오후까지요.

(C) 금속 부품들이요.

해설 **When 의문문**

(A) 내용 오류: how much 의문문에 어울리는 답변이다.

(B) 정답: 수리 완료 시점을 묻는 질문에 「by + 시점」으로 답하고 있다.

(C) 연상 어휘 오답: vehicle's engine(차 엔진)에서 연상할 수 있는 metal components(금속 부품들)를 사용한 오답이다.

11

W-Am	Where did Sally leave the shipping invoice?
M-Cn	(A) Yes, I made the payment.
	(B) She's leaving at 4.
	(C) I believe it's on your desk.

invoice 송장, 청구서

번역 샐리 씨가 선적 송장을 어디에 두었죠?

(A) 네, 제가 지불했습니다.

(B) 그녀는 4시에 떠날 거예요.

(C) 당신 책상에 있을 겁니다.

해설 **Where 의문문**

(A) Yes / No 답변 불가 오답: 의문사 의문문에는 Yes / No로 답할 수 없다.

(B) 반복 어휘 오답: 질문의 leave를 변형한 leaving을 반복 사용한 오답이다.

(C) 정답: 물건을 둔 장소를 묻는 질문에 「on + 위치」로 답하고 있다.

12

W-Br	When should we head off to the music festival?
W-Am	(A) Right after breakfast.
	(B) Once a year.
	(C) I enjoyed his performance.

head 향하다   performance 공연

번역 음악 축제를 보러 언제 떠나야 하죠?

(A) 아침 먹고 바로요.

(B) 1년에 한 번요.

(C) 그의 공연이 좋았어요.

해설 **When 의문문**

(A) 정답: 출발 시점을 묻는 질문에 「after + 시점」으로 답하고 있다.

(B) 내용 오류: 빈도를 묻는 how often 의문문에 어울리는 답변이다.

(C) 연상 어휘 오답: 질문의 music festival에서 연상할 수 있는 enjoyed와 performance를 이용한 오답이다.

13

M-Cn	When is Ms. Allen's flight supposed to arrive?
W-Br	(A) I suppose she will.
	(B) At Terminal 2.
	(C) Just after 4.

be supposed to ~하기로 되어 있다
suppose 생각하다, 추측하다

번역 앨런 씨가 탄 비행기는 언제 도착하기로 되어 있나요?

(A) 그녀는 그렇게 할 것 같아요.

(B) 2번 터미널에서요.

(C) 4시 막 지나서요.

해설 **When 의문문**

(A) 반복 어휘 오답: 질문의 supposed에서 suppose를 반복 사용한 오답이다.

(B) 연상 어휘 오답: 질문의 flight에서 연상할 수 있는 Terminal을 이용한 오답으로 where 의문문에 어울리는 답변이다.

(C) 정답: 도착 시점을 묻는 질문에 「after + 시점」으로 답하고 있다.

14

W-Am	Where should we eat dinner tonight?
M-Cn	(A) I'd love to join you.
	(B) The dessert was the best part.
	(C) Let's go to the pizza place.

번역 어디에서 오늘 저녁 식사를 할까요?
(A) 당신과 함께 가고 싶어요.
(B) 디저트가 가장 좋았어요.
(C) 피자 먹으러 갑시다.

해설 **Where 의문문**
(A) 내용 오류: 제안문에 어울릴 수 있는 답변이다.
(B) 연상 어휘 오답: 질문의 dinner에서 연상할 수 있는 dessert를 이용한 오답이다.
(C) 정답: 식사 장소를 묻는 질문에 구체적인 음식점 종류로 답하고 있다.

15

W-Br Where is the company's headquarters located?
W-Am (A) Several branches.
(B) To a larger building.
(C) In New York City.

headquarters 본사

번역 그 회사의 본사는 어디에 있나요?
(A) 지점 여러 곳이요.
(B) 더 큰 건물로요.
(C) 뉴욕이에요.

해설 **Where 의문문**
(A) 연상 어휘 오답: 질문의 headquarters에서 연상할 수 있는 branches를 이용한 오답이다.
(B) 내용 오류: 현재 위치를 묻는 질문에 방향으로 답변한 오답이다.
(C) 정답: 본사 위치를 묻는 질문에 「in + 도시명」으로 답하고 있다.

16

M-Au When will Mr. Hodges retire from the firm?
W-Am (A) The replacement CEO.
(B) Let's take a break then.
(C) He decided to stay.

retire from ~에서 은퇴하다, 퇴직하다 firm 회사
replacement 대체, 후임자

번역 호지스 씨는 언제 퇴직할 예정인가요?
(A) 후임 CEO예요.
(B) 그럼 쉬는 시간을 갖죠.
(C) 그는 회사에 남기로 결정했어요.

해설 **When 의문문**
(A) 연상 어휘 오답: 질문의 retire에서 연상할 수 있는 replacement CEO를 이용한 오답으로 who 의문문에 어울리는 답변이다.
(B) 내용 오류: 해결책이 필요한 질문이나 평서문에 어울릴 수 있는 답변이다.

(C) 정답: 퇴직 시기를 묻는 질문에 회사에 남기로 결정했다며 반전의 답변을 주고 있다.

17

W-Br Where can I get the materials for the upcoming seminar?
M-Au (A) Anytime between 9 and 6.
(B) You can download them online.
(C) For a different time and place.

material 자료 upcoming 앞으로 있을, 다가오는

번역 다가오는 세미나 자료는 어디서 받나요?
(A) 9시에서 6시 사이 아무 때나요.
(B) 온라인에서 다운로드할 수 있어요.
(C) 다른 때와 장소요.

해설 **Where 의문문**
(A) 내용 오류: when 의문문에 어울리는 답변이다.
(B) 정답: 자료를 구할 수 있는 곳을 묻는 질문에 출처 및 방법으로 답변하고 있다.
(C) 연상 어휘 오답: seminar에서 연상할 수 있는 time and place를 이용한 오답이다.

18

W-Am When was the photocopier repaired?
M-Cn (A) On the third floor.
(B) Sometime this week.
(C) At least 50 copies.

photocopier 복사기 sometime 언젠가
at least 최소한

번역 복사기는 언제 고쳤나요?
(A) 3층에서요.
(B) 이번 주중에요.
(C) 최소 50부요.

해설 **When 의문문**
(A) 내용 오류: where 의문문에 어울리는 답변이다.
(B) 정답: 복사기 수리 시점을 묻는 질문에 시점 부사구로 답하고 있다.
(C) 유사 발음 오답: 질문의 photocopier와 일부 발음이 동일한 copies를 이용한 오답이다.

19

M-Au Where will the company banquet be held this year?
W-Am (A) There's a bank on Main Street.
(B) At a 5-star hotel.
(C) On December 29th.

번역 올해 회사 연회는 어디에서 열리나요?
- (A) 메인 스트리트에 은행이 있어요.
- (B) 5성 호텔에서요.
- (C) 12월 29일에요.

해설 **Where 의문문**
- (A) 유사 발음 오답: 질문의 banquet과 일부 발음이 유사한 bank를 이용한 오답이다.
- (B) 정답: 연회 장소를 묻는 질문에 「at+호텔」로 답하고 있다.
- (C) 내용 오류: when 의문문에 어울리는 답변이다.

20

W-Br **Where should we put the new copy machine?**
M-Cn (A) I didn't know we ordered one.
(B) That's what we were told.
(C) Not until next week.

번역 새 복사기는 어디에 두어야 할까요?
- (A) 주문한 줄 몰랐어요.
- (B) 저희는 그렇게 얘기 들었어요.
- (C) 다음 주나 되어야 해요.

해설 **Where 의문문**
- (A) 정답: 새 복사기를 놓을 위치를 묻는 질문에 주문한 줄 몰랐다며 불확실함을 우회적으로 전달하고 있다.
- (B) 내용 오류: "That's what we were told"는 질문에 긍정의 뜻을 밝힐 때 사용하는 Yes와 같은 의미이며, 따라서 의문사 의문문에 맞지 않는 답변이다.
- (C) 내용 오류: when 의문문에 어울리는 답변이다.

21

W-Am **When did you start working at this company?**
W-Br (A) I commute by train.
(B) Yes, I'm settling in well.
(C) Last July.

commute 통근하다 settle in 적응하다

번역 언제 이 회사에서 근무하기 시작하셨나요?
- (A) 저는 기차를 타고 통근해요.
- (B) 네, 잘 적응하고 있습니다.
- (C) 지난 7월요.

해설 **When 의문문**
- (A) 연상 어휘 오답: 질문의 working과 company에서 연상할 수 있는 commute를 이용한 오답이다.
- (B) Yes/No 답변 불가 오답: 의문사 의문문에는 Yes/No로 답할 수 없다.
- (C) 정답: 근무 시작 시점을 묻는 질문에 구체적인 시점으로 답하고 있다.

22

M-Cn **When can I see the revised prototype of our hybrid vehicle?**
W-Am (A) I use public transportation.
(B) No, the due date has already passed.
(C) At our next meeting.

revised 수정된 prototype 시제품. 샘플 public transportation 대중교통

번역 수정된 하이브리드 차량 시제품은 언제 볼 수 있나요?
- (A) 저는 대중교통을 이용해요.
- (B) 아니요, 기한이 이미 지났어요.
- (C) 다음 회의 때요.

해설 **When 의문문**
- (A) 연상 어휘 오답: 질문의 vehicle에서 연상할 수 있는 transportation을 이용한 오답이다.
- (B) Yes/No 답변 불가 오답: 의문사 의문문에는 Yes/No로 답할 수 없다.
- (C) 정답: 시제품을 볼 수 있는 시기를 묻는 질문에 「at+시점」으로 답하고 있다.

23

M-Cn **Where can I find the outline of Mr. Smith's presentation?**
W-Br (A) From left to right.
(B) Did you miss the meeting?
(C) Sometime in mid-March.

outline 개요 miss 놓치다

번역 스미스 씨 발표 개요는 어디에서 볼 수 있나요?
- (A) 왼쪽에서 오른쪽으로요.
- (B) 회의에 참석을 못 하셨나요?
- (C) 3월 중순 중에요.

해설 **Where 의문문**
- (A) 내용 오류: 방향 또는 방법을 묻는 질문에 어울릴 수 있는 답변이다.
- (B) 정답: 질문에 답변하는 대신 질문하는 이유를 되묻고 있다.
- (C) 내용 오류: when 의문문에 어울리는 답변이다.

24

W-Am **When are we planning to launch our new laptop?**
M-Cn (A) That's a great plan.
(B) In the third quarter.
(C) It's selling well.

launch 시작하다, 개시하다 quarter 분기

번역 새 노트북 컴퓨터는 언제 출시할 계획입니까?
  (A) 좋은 계획이네요.
  (B) 3분기에요.
  (C) 잘 팔리고 있어요.

해설 **When 의문문**
  (A) 반복 어휘 오답: 질문의 planning에서 plan을 반복 사용한 오답이다.
  (B) 정답: 출시 시점을 묻는 질문에 「in + 시점」으로 답하고 있다.
  (C) 연상 어휘 오답: new laptop의 판매와 관련해서 연상할 수 있는 selling well을 사용한 오답이다.

25

M-Cn Where can I get the information on your calling plans?
W-Am (A) I can send it to you by e-mail.
  (B) As soon as you get there.
  (C) I really appreciate it.

calling plan 전화 요금제 appreciate 감사하다

번역 사용하시는 전화 요금제 관련 정보는 어디에서 얻을 수 있나요?
  (A) 이메일로 보내드릴 수 있어요.
  (B) 도착하자마자요.
  (C) 정말 감사합니다.

해설 **Where 의문문**
  (A) 정답: 정보를 구할 수 있는 곳을 묻는 질문에 직접 도움을 제공하고 있다.
  (B) 반복 어휘 오답: 질문의 get을 반복 사용한 오답이다.
  (C) 내용 오류: 호의 제공에 대해 할 수 있는 답변이다.

●Unit 03 How / Why 의문문

❶ How

LISTENING PRACTICE
교재 p. 43

1. (C) **2.** (B) **3.** (A) **4.** (C) **5.** (C) **6.** (B)

1

W-Am How do I turn on this printer?
M-Cn (A) You can return it here.
  (B) I need an extra copy.
  (C) Try the red button.

번역 이 프린터는 어떻게 켜나요?
  (A) 여기에 반납하시면 됩니다.
  (B) 한 부 더 필요해요.
  (C) 빨간 버튼을 눌러보세요.

해설 **How 의문문**
  (A) 유사 발음 오답: 질문의 turn과 일부 발음이 동일한 return을 이용한 오답이다.
  (B) 연상 어휘 오답: printer에서 연상할 수 있는 copy를 사용한 오답이다.
  (C) 정답: 프린터를 켜는 방법을 묻는 질문에 해당 버튼을 알려주고 있다.

2

W-Br How many investors attended yesterday's meeting?
W-Am (A) Of course, I'll be there.
  (B) Almost all of them.
  (C) Yes, it was very productive.

investor 투자자 productive 생산적인

번역 얼마나 많은 투자자가 어제 회의에 참석했나요?
  (A) 물론 저는 거기 참석할 겁니다.
  (B) 거의 모든 투자자가요.
  (C) 네, 매우 생산적이었어요.

해설 **How many 의문문**
  (A) 내용 오류: 참석 여부를 물었을 때 어울리는 답변이다.
  (B) 정답: 인원수를 묻는 질문에 수량을 나타내는 대명사로 답하고 있다.
  (C) Yes / No 답변 불가 오답: 의문사 의문문에는 Yes / No로 답할 수 없다.

3

W-Am How do you like your new home?
M-Cn (A) I haven't moved in yet.
  (B) From a former colleague.
  (C) Because of the loud traffic.

former 이전의 colleague 동료

번역 새 집은 어때요?
  (A) 아직 이사를 하지 못했어요.
  (B) 이전 동료에게서요.
  (C) 시끄러운 차량들 때문에요.

해설 **How 의문문**
  (A) 정답: 새 집에 대한 의견을 묻는 질문에 아직 이사를 하지 못했다며 반전의 답변을 주고 있다.
  (B) 내용 오류: 방법이나 경로를 묻는 how 의문문에 어울릴 수 있는 답변이다.
  (C) 내용 오류: why 의문문에 어울리는 답변이다.

4

M-Cn	How did you learn about our new campaign?
W-Br	(A) It was better than expected.
	(B) That's how I learned it.
	(C) I read about it in the company newsletter.

newsletter 소식지

번역 저희 신규 캠페인에 대해 어떻게 아셨나요?
(A) 예상보다 더 좋았어요.
(B) 그렇게 해서 제가 알게 됐어요.
(C) 회사 소식지에서 읽었어요.

해설 **How 의문문**
(A) 연상 어휘 오답: 질문을 이해하지 못한 채 의문사 How 만 들었을 경우 의견을 묻는 질문으로 착각하여 연상할 수 있는 better than expected를 이용한 오답이다.
(B) 반복 어휘 오답: 질문의 learn을 변형한 learned를 반복 사용한 오답이다.
(C) 정답: 알게 된 경로를 묻는 질문에 매체로 답하고 있다.

5

W-Am	How's the customer service at Milton Apparel?
M-Cn	(A) Sorry, I was told not to.
	(B) That's what everyone thinks.
	(C) The representatives were really helpful.

representative 직원, 대표자

번역 밀튼 어패럴의 고객 서비스는 어때요?
(A) 죄송하지만 하지 말라고 당부 받았어요.
(B) 모두가 그렇게 생각해요.
(C) 상담원들이 적극적으로 도와줍니다.

해설 **How 의문문**
(A) 내용 오류: 요청문을 거절할 때 할 수 있는 답변이다.
(B) 내용 오류: "That's what ~ think(s)"는 질문에 긍정의 뜻을 밝히거나 의견에 동의할 때 쓸 수 있는 표현이므로 질문에 맞지 않는 답변이다.
(C) 정답: 고객 서비스에 대한 의견을 묻는 질문에 긍정적인 평가로 답하고 있다.

6

W-Br	How long is your special sale going on?
M-Cn	(A) At least 40 percent off.
	(B) Today is the final day.
	(C) By presenting a coupon.

present 제시하다, 보여주다

번역 특별 할인은 얼마나 오래 하나요?
(A) 최소 40% 할인입니다.
(B) 오늘이 마지막 날입니다.
(C) 쿠폰을 제시해서요.

해설 **How long 의문문**
(A) 연상 어휘 오답: 질문의 sale에서 연상할 수 있는 40 percent off를 이용한 오답이다.
(B) 정답: 할인 기간을 묻는 질문에 종료일을 알려 주며 답하고 있다.
(C) 내용 오류: 방법을 묻는 how 의문문에 어울리는 답변이다.

❷ Why

LISTENING PRACTICE 교재 p. 45

1. (A) **2.** (A) **3.** (B) **4.** (B) **5.** (B) **6.** (C)

1

M-Cn	Why does Steve want to use the conference room?
W-Am	(A) He has a presentation to give.
	(B) No, I won't be able to make it.
	(C) Which floor is it on?

make it 시간 맞춰 가다

번역 스티브 씨는 왜 회의실을 사용하고 싶어합니까?
(A) 해야 할 발표가 있거든요.
(B) 아니요, 저는 시간 맞춰 가지 못할 거예요.
(C) 몇 층에 있나요?

해설 **Why 의문문**
(A) 정답: 회의실 사용 이유를 묻는 질문에 발표가 있다고 답하고 있다.
(B) Yes/No 답변 불가 오답: 의문사 의문문에는 Yes/No로 답할 수 없다.
(C) 연상 어휘 오답: 질문의 conference room에 대해 위치와 관련해서 연상할 수 있는 floor를 사용한 오답이다.

2

W-Br	Why don't we have a chat about this month's sale?
M-Cn	(A) OK, let's do that.
	(B) Because the room wasn't available.
	(C) For all new staff members.

번역 이번 달 판매량에 대해 이야기를 좀 나눌까요?
(A) 네, 그렇게 하시죠.
(B) 그 방은 이용이 불가능했거든요.
(C) 모든 신입 직원을 위해서요.

해설 **제안문**
(A) 정답: 판매량에 대해 이야기를 나누자는 제안에 동의의 뜻(OK)을 밝히고 있다.
(B) 내용 오류: 제안문을 이유를 묻는 의문문으로 착각했을 때 할 수 있는 오답이다.

(C) 내용 오류: 이유를 묻는 why 의문문에 어울릴 수 있는
답변이다.

3

W-Am Why haven't the new desks arrived yet?
W-Br (A) Two of them.
(B) There was a shipping delay.
(C) For office renovation.

shipping 배송   renovation 개조, 보수

번역 새 책상들이 왜 아직 도착하지 않았죠?
(A) 그것들 중 두 개요.
(B) 배송 지연이 있었습니다.
(C) 사무실 개조를 위해서요.

해설 Why 의문문
(A) 내용 오류: how many 의문문에 어울리는 답변이다.
(B) 정답: 물품이 도착하지 않은 이유를 묻는 질문에 배송
지연이 있었다고 답하고 있다.
(C) 연상 어휘 오답: 질문의 desks에서 연상할 수 있는
office를 사용한 오답이다.

4

M-Cn Why are there so many extra chairs in the
break room?
W-Am (A) It breaks down too often.
(B) The summer interns start today.
(C) He's the chairman.

break down 고장 나다   chairman 의장

번역 휴게실에 여분의 의자가 왜 그렇게 많이 있죠?
(A) 그건 너무 자주 고장이 나요.
(B) 오늘 하계 인턴들이 일을 시작해요.
(C) 그는 의장입니다.

해설 Why 의문문
(A) 반복 어휘 오답: 질문의 break를 반복 사용한 오답이다.
(B) 정답: 의자가 많은 이유를 묻는 질문에 의자를 사용하
게 될 사람들이 있음을 전달하고 있다.
(C) 유사 발음 오답·대명사 오류: 질문의 chairs와 일부
발음이 동일한 chairman을 이용한 오답이다. 또한 질
문에 사람이 없으므로 답변에서 he로 지칭할 수 없다.

5

W-Br Why did our team miss its production
goals?
W-Am (A) Yes, I watched the game.
(B) Because of some machinery problems.
(C) The price reductions.

production 생산   machinery 기계
reduction 감소, 인하

번역 왜 우리 팀은 생산 목표를 맞추지 못했나요?
(A) 네, 저는 경기를 봤습니다.
(B) 기계 문제 때문이에요.
(C) 가격 인하요.

해설 Why 의문문
(A) Yes/No 답변 불가 오답: 의문사 의문문에는 Yes/
No로 대답을 할 수 없다.
(B) 정답: 생산 목표가 미달인 이유를 묻는 질문에 기계 결
함을 이유로 들고 있다.
(C) 유사 발음 오답: 질문의 production과 일부 발음이
동일한 reductions를 이용한 오답이다.

6

M-Au Why don't we hold our ceremony at the
Orlando hotel?
W-Br (A) From the board of directors.
(B) Lunch was tasty, thanks.
(C) It's big enough, right?

hold a ceremony 식을 개최하다
board of directors 이사회

번역 올랜도 호텔에서 식을 개최하면 어떨까요?
(A) 이사회로부터요.
(B) 점심이 맛있었어요. 감사합니다.
(C) 그곳은 충분히 크죠, 그렇죠?

해설 제안문
(A) 연상 어휘 오답: 질문의 hold에서 연상할 수 있는
board of directors를 이용한 오답이다.
(B) 연상 어휘 오답: 질문의 ceremony에서 연상할 수 있
는 Lunch를 이용한 오답이다.
(C) 정답: 제안문에 대해 조건이 맞는지 되묻는 답변이다.

ACTUAL TEST

교재 p. 46

1. (C)	**2.** (B)	**3.** (B)	**4.** (C)	**5.** (C)
6. (B)	**7.** (C)	**8.** (C)	**9.** (B)	**10.** (B)
11. (C)	**12.** (A)	**13.** (A)	**14.** (C)	**15.** (A)
16. (B)	**17.** (B)	**18.** (A)	**19.** (C)	**20.** (C)
21. (B)	**22.** (C)	**23.** (A)	**24.** (A)	**25.** (A)

1

W-Am How was your commute to work today?
M-Au (A) I don't think it was.
(B) It suddenly stopped working.
(C) It was smooth as usual.

commute 통근   as usual 늘 그렇듯이, 평상시처럼

번역 오늘 통근길은 어땠어요?
  (A) 그랬던 것 같지 않아요.
  (B) 갑자기 작동을 멈췄어요.
  (C) 평소대로 원활했어요.

해설 **How 의문문**
  (A) 내용 오류: "I don't think it was"는 질문에 부정의 뜻을 밝힐 때 사용하는 No와 같은 의미이며, 따라서 의문사 의문문에 맞지 않는 답변이다.
  (B) 반복 어휘 오답: 질문의 work를 변형한 working을 반복 사용한 오답이다.
  (C) 정답: 통근길의 상태를 묻는 질문에 상태를 나타내는 형용사로 답하고 있다.

2

M-Cn Why was the oven taken out of the kitchen?
W-Br (A) We will take the clients for dinner.
  (B) It needs some repairs.
  (C) To the employee lounge.

번역 오븐을 왜 주방 밖으로 꺼냈죠?
  (A) 고객들을 저녁 식사에 모실 겁니다.
  (B) 수리해야 해서요.
  (C) 직원 휴게실로요.

해설 **Why 의문문**
  (A) 반복 어휘 오답: 질문의 taken을 변형한 take를 반복 사용한 오답이다.
  (B) 정답: 오븐이 부엌 밖으로 나와 있는 이유를 묻는 질문에 수리해야 한다고 답하고 있다.
  (C) 내용 오류: where 의문문에 어울리는 답변이다.

3

W-Am How did Ms. Sanchez feel about your budget proposal?
M-Cn (A) By April 25th.
  (B) She seemed quite impressed.
  (C) Let's look at the figures.

  budget 예산   figures 수치

번역 산체스 씨는 당신의 예산 제안서를 어떻게 생각했나요?
  (A) 4월 25일까지요.
  (B) 꽤 인상 깊게 여기는 것처럼 보였어요.
  (C) 수치를 봅시다.

해설 **How 의문문**
  (A) 내용 오류: when 의문문에 어울리는 답변이다.
  (B) 정답: 제안서에 대한 제 3자의 의견을 묻는 질문에 긍정적이었다고 답하고 있다.
  (C) 연상 어휘 오답: budget에서 연상할 수 있는 figures를 이용한 오답이다.

4

M-Au How do I retrieve an e-mail I deleted?
W-Cn (A) I am delighted to do so.
  (B) It was a good experience.
  (C) You can find the instructions online.

번역 제가 삭제한 이메일을 어떻게 회수하나요?
  (A) 그렇게 하게 되어 기쁩니다.
  (B) 좋은 경험이었어요.
  (C) 온라인에서 설명을 찾을 수 있을 겁니다.

해설 **How 의문문**
  (A) 유사 발음 오답: 질문의 deleted와 발음이 유사한 delighted를 이용한 오답이다.
  (B) 내용 오류: 의견을 묻는 how 질문에 어울리는 답변이다.
  (C) 정답: 방법을 묻는 질문에 해결책을 제시한 답변이다.

5

M-Cn Why did you bring a salad for lunch?
W-Am (A) Okay, I'll have the same.
  (B) I doubt it will fill me up.
  (C) To lose some weight.

  doubt 확신하지 않다   fill up 배가 부르다   lose weight 살이 빠지다, 체중을 감량하다

번역 점심 식사로 왜 샐러드를 가져오셨어요?
  (A) 좋아요, 저도 같은 걸로 할게요.
  (B) 그걸로 배가 부를지 모르겠어요.
  (C) 살을 빼려고요.

해설 **Why 의문문**
  (A) 연상 어휘 오답: 질문의 lunch에서 연상할 수 있는 have the same(같은 걸로 먹다)을 이용한 오답이다.
  (B) 연상 어휘 오답: 질문의 salad for lunch에서 연상할 수 있는 fill me up(배가 부르다)을 이용한 오답이다.
  (C) 정답: 이유를 묻는 질문에 「to부정사＋목적」으로 답하고 있다.

6

M-Au How much do I have to pay to rent a bicycle here?
M-Cn (A) We have lots of bike brands.
  (B) Five dollars per hour.
  (C) There's a rental shop by the river.

  rental shop 대여점

번역 여기서 자전거를 대여하는 데 얼마를 내야 하나요?
  (A) 많은 상표의 자전거를 갖고 있습니다.
  (B) 시간당 5달러입니다.
  (C) 강 옆에 대여점이 있습니다.

해설 **How much 의문문**

(A) 연상 어휘 오답: bicycle에서 연상할 수 있는 bike를 사용한 오답이다.

(B) 정답: 자전거 대여 비용을 묻는 질문에 구체적인 가격을 제시하고 있다.

(C) 반복 어휘 오답: 질문의 rent를 변형한 rental을 반복 사용한 오답이다.

7

W-Am Why are these boxes sitting beside the elevator?

M-Au (A) I'll take the stairs instead.

(B) You can use this chair.

(C) They're being delivered to a customer.

take the stairs 계단을 이용하다   instead 대신

번역 이 상자들은 왜 엘리베이터 옆에 놓여 있나요?

(A) 저는 대신 계단을 이용할게요.

(B) 이 의자를 사용하시면 됩니다.

(C) 고객에게 배송 중입니다.

해설 **Why 의문문**

(A) 연상 어휘 오답: 질문의 elevator에서 연상할 수 있는 stairs를 이용한 오답이다.

(B) 연상 어휘 오답: 질문의 sitting에서 연상할 수 있는 chair를 사용한 오답이다.

(C) 정답: 상자들이 엘리베이터 옆에 놓여 있는 이유를 묻는 질문에 고객에게 배송 중이라고 이유를 제시하고 있다.

8

M-Au How many employees will attend Mr. Hendrix's retirement party?

W-Am (A) I believe not.

(B) I'm glad he liked it.

(C) I passed the figures on to Ms. Lynn.

retirement 은퇴, 퇴직   pass 전달하다   figures 수치

번역 헨드릭스 씨의 은퇴 기념 파티에 직원이 몇 명이나 참석할 건가요?

(A) 아닐 겁니다.

(B) 그가 마음에 들어하니 좋네요.

(C) 린 씨에게 수치를 전달했어요.

해설 **How many 의문문**

(A) 내용 오류: "I believe not."은 질문에 부정의 뜻을 밝힐 때 사용하는 No와 같은 의미이며, 따라서 의문사 의문문에 맞지 않는 답변이다.

(B) 내용 오류: how many에 대한 답변도 아니며 시제도 맞지 않다.

(C) 정답: 인원수를 묻는 질문에 다른 사람에게 정보를 전달했다고 우회적으로 답변하고 있다.

9

M-Cn How soon will this warranty expire?

W-Am (A) A mechanical fault.

(B) In six months.

(C) That's a relief.

warranty 품질 보증서   expire 만료되다   relief 안도

번역 이 품질 보증서는 언제 만료됩니까?

(A) 기계적 결함입니다.

(B) 6개월 후요.

(C) 그거 다행입니다.

해설 **How soon 의문문**

(A) 연상 어휘 오답: 질문의 warranty에서 연상할 수 있는 mechanical fault를 이용한 오답이다.

(B) 정답: 품질 보증서 만료 시점을 묻는 질문에 「in+지속 기간」으로 답하고 있다.

(C) 내용 오류: 긍정적인 소식을 들었을 때, 또는 문제가 해결되었을 때 할 수 있는 답변이다.

10

M-Cn Why don't we ask the senior designer for some advice?

W-Br (A) No, just a few tips.

(B) I don't think he's available today.

(C) We don't have any left.

번역 선임 디자이너에게 조언을 구하면 어떨까요?

(A) 아니요. 그냥 몇 가지 조언이요.

(B) 오늘 시간이 되실 것 같지 않네요.

(C) 우리에겐 아무것도 남지 않았어요.

해설 **제안문**

(A) 연상 어휘 오답: 질문의 advice에서 연상할 수 있는 tips를 이용한 오답이다.

(B) 정답: 조언을 구하자는 제안에 거절의 뜻을 간접적으로 나타내고 있다.

(C) 내용 오류: 상대방이 물질적인 것을 요구했을 때 할 수 있는 답변이다.

11

W-Am How long does the advanced computing class take?

M-Cn (A) I took it last week.

(B) Spaces are limited.

(C) That one has been canceled.

advanced 고급의, 상급의   limited 제한된
cancel 취소하다

PART 2

29

번역 컴퓨터 고급반은 시간이 얼마나 걸리나요?
번역 컴퓨터 고급반은 시간이 얼마나 걸리나요?

(A) 지난주에 들었어요.

(B) 자리가 제한되어 있습니다.

(C) 그 수업은 취소됐습니다.

해설 **How long 의문문**

(A) 반복 어휘 오답: 질문의 take를 변형한 took을 반복 사용한 오답이다.

(B) 연상 어휘 오답: 질문의 class에서 연상할 수 있는 spaces와 limited를 이용한 오답이다.

(C) 정답: 수업 진행 시간을 묻는 질문에 수업이 취소되었다며 반전의 답변을 주고 있다.

12

M-Au How did you travel to Vancouver last month?

W-Br (A) By train.

(B) For a sales meeting.

(C) On the 23rd.

번역 지난달에 밴쿠버까지 어떻게 가셨나요?

(A) 기차로요.

(B) 영업회의를 위해서요.

(C) 23일이에요.

해설 **How 의문문**

(A) 정답: 여행 방법을 묻는 질문에 「by+교통 수단」으로 답하고 있다.

(B) 내용 오류: why 의문문에 어울리는 답변이다.

(C) 내용 오류: when 의문문에 어울리는 답변이다.

13

W-Am Why has this year's film festival been postponed?

M-Au (A) Ticket sales were too low.

(B) At a movie theater downtown.

(C) Until the end of July.

번역 올해 영화제는 왜 연기됐죠?

(A) 티켓 판매량이 너무 저조했어요.

(B) 시내에 있는 영화관에서요.

(C) 7월 말까지요.

해설 **Why 의문문**

(A) 정답: 영화제가 연기된 이유를 묻는 질문에 저조한 판매량을 이유로 들고 있다.

(B) 연상 어휘 오답: 질문의 film에서 연상할 수 있는 ticket을 이용한 오답이다.

(C) 내용 오류: when 의문문에 어울리는 답변이다.

14

W-Br How did you enjoy your stay?

W-Am (A) Until about 8.

(B) I think he will like it.

(C) It was great, thanks.

번역 머무신 소감이 어떠신가요?

(A) 8시 정도까지요.

(B) 그가 그것을 좋아할 것 같습니다.

(C) 좋았어요. 감사합니다.

해설 **How 의문문**

(A) 내용 오류: How long에 어울릴 수 있는 답변이다.

(B) 대명사 오류: 질문의 주어가 you이므로 답변에서 he로 지칭할 수 없다.

(C) 정답: 의견을 묻는 질문에 호감을 나타내고 있다.

15

M-Cn How can I sign up for a membership at Platinum Gym?

W-Am (A) You can do it online.

(B) I've been coming here for a year.

(C) Sure, I'll remember.

sign up for ~을 신청하다

번역 플래티넘 짐 회원은 어떻게 신청하면 되죠?

(A) 온라인으로 하시면 돼요.

(B) 1년간 여기 다녔어요.

(C) 물론이죠. 기억할게요.

해설 **How 의문문**

(A) 정답: 회원 신청 방법을 묻는 질문에 온라인으로 할 수 있다는 전형적인 답변을 주고 있다.

(B) 내용 오류: how long 의문문에 어울리는 답변이다.

(C) 유사 발음 오답: 질문의 membership과 일부 발음이 동일한 remember를 이용한 오답이다.

16

M-Cn Why is Hailey leaving work early?

W-Br (A) Around 5 P.M. on weekdays.

(B) For a dentist appointment.

(C) You'll need the manager's permission.

appointment 예약   permission 승인

번역 헤일리 씨는 오늘 왜 일찍 퇴근하죠?

(A) 평일엔 오후 5시경이에요.

(B) 치과 예약을 위해서요.

(C) 관리자 승인이 필요할 겁니다.

해설 **Why 의문문**
(A) 연상 어휘 오답: 질문의 leaving work early에서 연상할 수 있는 5 P.M.을 이용한 오답이다
(B) 정답: 이른 퇴근 이유를 묻는 질문에 치과 예약을 이유로 들고 있다.
(C) 연상 어휘 오답: leaving work early에서 연상할 수 있는 manager's permission을 이용한 오답이다.

17

M-Cn Why are our sales so low this month?
W-Am (A) A discount of 20 percent.
(B) They aren't too bad.
(C) He's our top salesperson.

번역 이번 달 우리 매출이 왜 이렇게 저조합니까?
(A) 20퍼센트 할인이요.
(B) 그리 나쁘지 않은데요.
(C) 그는 영업사원 중 최고입니다.

해설 **Why 의문문**
(A) 연상 어휘 오답: 질문의 sales에서 연상할 수 있는 discount of 20 percent를 이용한 오답이다.
(B) 정답: 매출이 저조한 이유를 묻는 질문에 그렇게 나쁘지 않다고 반대되는 의견을 제시하고 있다.
(C) 반복 어휘 오답·대명사 오류: 질문의 sales를 반복 사용한 오답이다. 또한 질문에 he를 지칭할 대상이 없다.

18

M-Au Why don't you come to the Indian restaurant with us after work?
M-Cn (A) I have to finish a report.
(B) On Eleventh Avenue.
(C) I'm glad you enjoyed the food.

번역 퇴근 후에 저희와 함께 인도 음식점에 갈래요?
(A) 보고서를 끝마쳐야 해요.
(B) 11번가예요.
(C) 맛있게 드셨다니 좋습니다.

해설 **제안문**
(A) 정답: 퇴근 후 식사 제안에 보고서를 끝내야 한다고 거절의 의사를 간접적으로 밝히고 있다.
(B) 내용 오류: where 의문문에 대한 답변이다.
(C) 연상 어휘 오답: 질문의 restaurant에서 연상할 수 있는 food를 이용한 오답이다.

19

W-Am How often do you clean the air conditioner in the office?
M-Cn (A) Call the repair technician.
(B) It was getting too hot in here.
(C) At least once a week.

---

technician 기술자　at least 최소한

번역 사무실에 있는 에어컨은 얼마나 자주 청소하나요?
(A) 수리공에게 연락하세요.
(B) 이곳은 너무 더워지고 있었어요.
(C) 적어도 1주일에 한 번요.

해설 **How often 의문문**
(A) 연상 어휘 오답: 질문의 air conditioner에서 연상할 수 있는 repair technician을 이용한 오답이다.
(B) 연상 어휘 오답: 질문의 air conditioner에서 연상할 수 있는 getting too hot을 이용한 오답이다.
(C) 정답: 빈도를 묻는 질문에 구체적인 횟수로 답하고 있다.

20

W-Am How did you like the dessert?
M-Cn (A) Coffee with sugar.
(B) One would be enough.
(C) It was good.

번역 디저트는 어땠어요?
(A) 커피에 설탕을 넣어서요.
(B) 하나로 충분합니다.
(C) 맛있었어요.

해설 **How 의문문**
(A) 연상 어휘 오답: 질문의 dessert에서 연상할 수 있는 coffee를 이용한 오답이다.
(B) 내용 오류: how many 의문문에 대한 답변이다.
(C) 정답: 디저트에 대한 의견을 묻는 질문에 긍정적인 평가로 답하고 있다.

21

W-Am How was the food at that new Italian restaurant?
M-Au (A) Either online or by telephone.
(B) I haven't been there yet.
(C) No, but he'll visit Paris.

번역 새로 생긴 이탈리아 음식점의 음식은 어땠어요?
(A) 온라인이나 전화로요.
(B) 아직 가 보지 못했어요.
(C) 아니요, 하지만 그는 파리에 갈 겁니다.

해설 **How 의문문**
(A) 내용 오류: 방법을 묻는 how 질문에 어울리는 답변이다.
(B) 정답: 음식점에 대한 의견을 묻는 질문에 아직 가 보지 못했다며 모른다는 의미를 우회적으로 전달하고 있다.
(C) Yes/No 답변 불가 오답: 의문사 의문문에는 Yes/No로 대답할 수 없다.

22

W-Am How many people have enrolled in the yoga class?

M-Au (A) Don't worry, you have enough experience.
(B) Every Tuesday and Thursday.
(C) We're already at full capacity.

---
enroll in ~에 등록하다 full capacity 정원

번역 요가반에 몇 명이 등록했습니까?
(A) 걱정 마세요. 경험이 충분하시니까요.
(B) 매주 화요일과 목요일요.
(C) 이미 정원이 꽉 찼어요.

해설 **How many 의문문**
(A) 연상 어휘 오답: 질문의 how many에서 연상할 수 있는 enough를 이용한 오답이다.
(B) 내용 오류: when 또는 how often 의문문에 어울리는 답변이다.
(C) 정답: 등록 인원수를 묻는 질문에 구체적인 수치 대신 정원이 다 찼다고 간접적으로 답하고 있다.

23

M-Cn How did you learn about the vacant position at ABS Corporation?

W-Am (A) It is posted on their Web site.
(B) To assistant supervisor.
(C) The programs were quite informative.

---
vacant 비어 있는 post 게시하다 informative 유익한

번역 ABS 코퍼레이션의 공석에 대해 어떻게 아셨습니까?
(A) 회사 웹사이트에 게시됐어요.
(B) 부관리자에게요.
(C) 프로그램들은 꽤 유익했습니다.

해설 **How 의문문**
(A) 정답: 알게 된 경로를 묻는 질문에 정보가 게시된 곳을 알려주고 있다.
(B) 연상 어휘 오답: 질문의 position에서 연상할 수 있는 supervisor를 이용한 오답이다.
(C) 내용 오류: 의견을 묻는 how 의문문에 어울리는 답변이다.

24

W-Br Why didn't you submit your proposal to the manager?

M-Au (A) It requires some revisions.
(B) Please hand it in by Friday.
(C) Sure, I'd be glad to.

---
proposal 제안 revision 수정 hand in 제출하다

번역 제안서를 관리자에게 제출하지 않은 이유가 뭡니까?
(A) 수정해야 합니다.
(B) 금요일까지 제출하세요.
(C) 물론입니다. 그렇게 하겠습니다.

해설 **Why 의문문**
(A) 정답: 제안서를 제출하지 않은 이유를 묻는 질문에 수정해야 한다는 이유를 제시하고 있다.
(B) 연상 어휘 오답: 질문의 submit에서 연상할 수 있는 hand it in을 이용한 오답이다.
(C) 내용 오류: 제안문으로 착각했을 때 할 수 있는 오답이다.

25

M-Au How can I get access to our company's data center?

W-Am (A) Just sign in at the security desk.
(B) Last November, most likely.
(C) Several columns and rows.

---
access 접근, 이용 security 보안 most likely 아마도
column 세로단 row 줄, 열

번역 우리 회사 데이터 센터에 어떻게 들어가죠?
(A) 보안 데스크에서 서명하기만 하면 됩니다.
(B) 아마 지난 11월일 겁니다.
(C) 여러 개의 열과 행이요.

해설 **How 의문문**
(A) 정답: 이용 방법을 묻는 질문에 절차를 알려주고 있다.
(B) 내용 오류: when 의문문에 어울리는 답변이다.
(C) 연상 어휘 오답: 질문의 data에서 연상할 수 있는 columns and rows를 이용한 오답이다.

●Unit 04 일반 의문문

❶ Be동사 의문문

LISTENING PRACTICE   교재 p. 49

1. (A) **2.** (B) **3.** (A) **4.** (B) **5.** (C) **6.** (C)

1

W-Br Are you ready to order now?

M-Cn (A) Give us just a few minutes.
(B) Near the window, if possible.
(O) I'll bring thooo to you now.

번역 지금 주문하시겠어요?
(A) 몇 분만 더 기다려주세요.
(B) 가능하다면 창가 근처로요.
(C) 지금 가져다 드릴게요.

해설 **Be동사 의문문**

(A) 정답: 식당 주문을 받기 위한 질문에 주문을 미루고 있는 상황이다.

(B) 내용 오류: where 의문문에 어울리는 답변이다.

(C) 반복 어휘 오답·대명사 오류: 질문의 now를 반복 사용한 오답이다. 또한 질문에 복수명사가 없으므로 답변에서 those로 지칭할 수 없다.

2

M-Au Is your office desk big enough to put a printer on?

W-Br (A) Yes, two drawers.

(B) I don't think so.

(C) Let me have 5 copies of it.

drawer 서랍

번역 사무실 책상은 프린터를 둘 수 있을 만큼 큰가요?

(A) 네, 서랍 두 개요.

(B) 그럴 것 같지 않아요.

(C) 다섯 부 가져갈게요.

해설 **Be동사 의문문**

(A) 연상 어휘 오답: 질문의 desk에서 연상할 수 있는 단어 drawers를 이용한 오답이다.

(B) 정답: 책상이 충분히 큰지 묻는 질문에 그럴 것 같지 않다며 No를 대신하는 부정의 표현으로 답하고 있다.

(C) 연상 어휘 오답: 질문의 printer에서 연상할 수 있는 명사 copies를 이용한 오답이다.

3

M-Cn Were you able to download the files you need?

W-Am (A) Yes, it was simple and easy.

(B) You can upload photos on the Web page.

(C) In duplicate, please.

in duplicate (서류 등이) 두 통으로

번역 필요한 파일들을 다운로드하실 수 있었나요?

(A) 네, 간단하고 쉬웠어요.

(B) 웹페이지에 사진을 올리셔도 됩니다.

(C) 두 통 주세요.

해설 **Be동사 의문문**

(A) 정답: 다운로드 여부를 묻는 질문에 긍정의 뜻(Yes)과 부연 설명으로 답하고 있다.

(B) 연상 어휘 오답: 질문의 download에서 연상할 수 있는 upload를 이용한 오답이다.

(C) 연상 어휘 오답: 질문의 files에서 연상할 수 있는 in duplicate를 이용한 오답으로 how many 의문문에 어울리는 답변이다.

4

W-Br Is your password to the research database working?

M-Cn (A) To get a parking pass.

(B) Yes, I have access now.

(C) A research on product packaging.

parking pass 주차권   packaging 포장

번역 조사 데이터베이스 패스워드가 맞나요?

(A) 주차권을 받기 위해서요.

(B) 네, 지금 접속됐어요.

(C) 제품 포장에 관한 조사요.

해설 **Be동사 의문문**

(A) 반복 어휘 오답: 질문의 password에서 pass를 반복 사용한 오답이다.

(B) 정답: 비밀번호가 맞는지 묻는 질문에 긍정으로 답하고 부연 설명하고 있다.

(C) 반복 어휘 오답: 질문의 research를 반복 사용한 오답이다.

5

M-Au Is there a battery charger I can borrow?

W-Br (A) To the library.

(B) We've tried everything.

(C) There's a spare one in my bag.

battery charger 충전지

번역 제가 빌릴 수 있는 충전기가 있나요?

(A) 도서관으로요.

(B) 모든 걸 다 해 봤어요.

(C) 제 가방에 여분으로 한 개 있어요.

해설 **Be동사 의문문**

(A) 연상 어휘 오답: 질문의 borrow에서 연상할 수 있는 library를 이용한 오답이다.

(B) 내용 오류: 문제 해결을 위한 조언 또는 무엇을 했는지 묻는 질문에 할 수 있는 답변이다.

(C) 정답: 충전기 유무를 묻는 질문에 Yes를 생략하고 긍정으로 답하고 있다.

6

M-Cn Are you going to the downtown music festival this weekend?

W-Am (A) In the financial district.

(B) For another week or so.

(C) I don't like big crowds.

financial 금융의   district 구역, 지역   or so 쯤, 정도

번역 이번 주말에 시내 음악축제에 가실 건가요?

(A) 금융가에서요.

(B) 한 주 정도 더요.

(C) 인파가 많은 것을 좋아하지 않아요.

해설 Be동사 의문문

(A) 내용 오류: where 의문문에 어울리는 답변이다.

(B) 반복 어휘 오답: 질문의 weekend에서 week를 반복 사용한 오답이다.

(C) 정답: 축제 참여 여부를 묻는 질문에 No를 생략하고 가지 않는 이유로써 부정의 의미를 간접적으로 전달하고 있다.

❷ 조동사 의문문

LISTENING PRACTICE

교재 p. 51

1. (B) **2.** (A) **3.** (B) **4.** (A) **5.** (B) **6.** (B)

1

M-Cn Have you renewed your passport?

W-Am (A) Thanks, I was looking forward to it.

(B) I need to get my photo taken.

(C) Spain is nice this time of year.

renew 갱신하다　look forward to ~을 고대하다

번역 여권을 갱신했나요?

(A) 감사합니다. 기대하고 있었어요.

(B) 사진을 찍어야 해요.

(C) 스페인은 연중 이맘때가 좋아요.

해설 조동사(Have) 의문문

(A) 내용 오류: 제안문에 어울릴 수 있는 답변이다.

(B) 정답: 여권 갱신 여부를 묻는 질문에 No를 생략하고 사진을 찍어야 한다며 아직 하지 않았음을 간접적으로 나타내고 있다.

(C) 연상 어휘 오답: 질문의 passport에서 연상할 수 있는 Spain을 이용한 오답이다.

2

W-Am Does this video streaming service charge a cancellation fee?

M-Cn (A) I haven't used it.

(B) Let's watch it now.

(C) Delivery is free of charge.

charge 청구하다　cancellation 취소
free of charge 무료로

번역 이 동영상 스트리밍 서비스는 해지 수수료가 부과되나요?

(A) 저는 사용한 적이 없어요.

(B) 지금 한 번 봅시다.

(C) 배송은 무료입니다.

해설 조동사(Do) 의문문

(A) 정답: 서비스의 해지 수수료 부과 여부를 묻는 질문에 사용한 적이 없다며 반전의 답변을 주고 있다.

(B) 연상 어휘 오답: 질문의 video에서 연상할 수 있는 watch를 이용한 오답이다.

(C) 반복 어휘 오답: 질문의 charge를 반복 사용한 오답이다.

3

M-Au Does Ms. Tina know that the workshop venue has changed?

W-Am (A) In the ballroom.

(B) She was not informed yet.

(C) Let's change it to April 7th.

venue 장소　inform 알리다

번역 티나 씨는 워크숍 장소가 변경된 걸 알고 있나요?

(A) 연회장에서요.

(B) 그녀는 아직 전달받지 못했어요.

(C) 4월 7일로 변경합시다.

해설 조동사(Do) 의문문

(A) 내용 오류: where 의문문에 어울리는 답변이다.

(B) 정답: 티나 씨가 워크숍 장소가 변경된 것을 알고 있는지 묻는 질문에 No를 생략한 뒤 아직 전달받지 못했다고 부연 설명하고 있다.

(C) 반복 어휘 오답: 질문의 change를 반복 사용한 오답이다.

4

W-Br Should I print extra copies of the handouts?

M-Cn (A) Yes, please.

(B) I have some extra tickets.

(C) The book is out of print.

handout 인쇄물, 유인물　out of print 절판된

번역 유인물 사본을 추가로 출력해야 할까요?

(A) 네, 그래주세요.

(B) 저에게 여분의 티켓이 몇 장 있습니다.

(C) 그 책은 절판됐어요.

해설 조동사 (Should) 의문문

(A) 정답: 제안문에 대해 수락(Yes, please)으로 답변하고 있다.

(B) 반복 어휘 오답: 질문의 extra를 반복 사용한 오답이다.

(C) 반복 어휘 오답: 질문의 print를 반복 사용한 오답이다.

5

W-Am Has this month's company newsletter been distributed?
W-Br (A) Once a month.
　　(B) No, not yet.
　　(C) I can help you with the writing.

distribute 배포하다, 배부하다

번역　이번 달 회사 소식지가 배포됐나요?
　　(A) 한 달에 한 번요.
　　(B) 아니요, 아직요.
　　(C) 제가 집필을 도와드릴 수 있어요.

해설　**조동사(Have) 의문문**
　　(A) 반복 어휘 오답: 질문의 month를 반복 사용한 오답이다.
　　(B) 정답: 완료 여부를 묻는 have 의문문에 아직 아니다 (not yet)라며 전형적인 답변 패턴으로 답하고 있다.
　　(C) 연상 어휘 오답: 질문의 newsletter에서 연상할 수 있는 writing을 이용한 오답이다.

6

M-Cn Do you know how much the basketball tickets cost?
W-Am (A) Six seats, please.
　　(B) No, I'm not much of a fan.
　　(C) Yes, at the ticket office.

번역　농구 경기 입장권이 얼마인지 아세요?
　　(A) 여섯 장이요.
　　(B) 아니요, 저는 그다지 좋아하지 않아요.
　　(C) 네, 매표소에서요.

해설　**How much 간접 의문문**
　　(A) 연상 어휘 오답: 질문의 basketball tickets에서 연상할 수 있는 six seats를 이용한 오답이다.
　　(B) 정답: 농구 경기 입장권의 가격을 묻는 질문에 No로 답하고, 가격을 모르는 이유(그다지 좋아하지 않는다)를 덧붙여 답변한 정답이다.
　　(C) 반복 어휘 오답: 질문의 tickets을 반복 사용한 오답이다.

ACTUAL TEST
교재 p. 52

1. (A)	2. (B)	3. (C)	4. (B)	5. (C)
6. (B)	7. (A)	8. (C)	9. (C)	10. (A)
11. (A)	12. (B)	13. (C)	14. (A)	15. (C)
16. (B)	17. (C)	18. (C)	19. (C)	20. (A)
21. (C)	22. (C)	23. (B)	24. (B)	25. (A)

1

W-Am Is this the right subway stop for City Hall?
M-Cn (A) No, it's the next one.
　　(B) We can stop for a rest.
　　(C) About 5 kilometers.

번역　여기가 시청으로 가는 지하철역이 맞나요?
　　(A) 아니요, 다음 역이에요.
　　(B) 우리는 잠시 쉬었다 갈 수 있어요.
　　(C) 약 5킬로미터요.

해설　**Be동사 의문문**
　　(A) 정답: 정거장이 맞는지 확인하는 질문에 부정으로 답하며 정보를 정정해주고 있다.
　　(B) 반복 어휘 오답: 질문의 stop을 반복 사용한 오답이다.
　　(C) 내용 오류: How long 또는 How far에 어울리는 답변이다.

2

M-Au Was your presentation a success?
W-Am (A) Yes, at 3 P.M. today.
　　(B) No, things could've gone better.
　　(C) With the Japanese investors.

investor 투자자

번역　발표는 잘 했어요?
　　(A) 네, 오늘 오후 3시에요.
　　(B) 아니요, 더 잘 할 수 있었는데 말이죠.
　　(C) 일본 투자자들과 같이요.

해설　**Be동사 의문문**
　　(A) 내용 오류: 발표를 했는지 물었을 때 할 수 있는 답변이다.
　　(B) 정답: 발표가 잘 되었는지 묻는 질문에 아쉬움을 나타내는 표현으로 답하고 있다.
　　(C) 내용 오류: 발표 성공 여부와 관련 없는 답변이다.

3

M-Cn Did you book the conference room?
W-Br (A) They were excellent speakers.
　　(B) Mostly non-stop flights.
　　(C) Do we need such a big space?

non-stop flight 직항편

번역　회의실을 예약했습니까?
　　(A) 그들은 훌륭한 연설자입니다.
　　(B) 대부분 직항편입니다.
　　(C) 그렇게 큰 장소가 필요합니까?

해설 **조동사(Do) 의문문**

(A) 연상 어휘 오답·대명사 오류: 질문의 conference room에서 연상할 수 있는 speakers를 이용한 오답이다. 또한 질문에 they를 지칭할 대상이 없다.

(B) 연상 어휘 오답: 질문의 book에서 연상할 수 있는 flights를 이용한 오답이다.

(C) 정답: 회의실을 예약했는지 묻는 질문에 그렇게 큰 장소가 필요한지 되물어 예약을 하지 않았음을 우회적으로 전달하고 있다.

4

W-Br	Has the assistant accountant position been filled?
M-Cn	(A) Please fill it up halfway. (B) There's one more round of interviews. (C) No, I work as an accountant.

accountant 회계사 halfway 중간에, 가운데쯤

번역 보조 회계사 직책은 채용됐나요?

(A) 절반쯤 채우세요.
(B) 면접이 한 차례 더 있어요.
(C) 아니요, 저는 회계사로 근무해요.

해설 **조동사(Have)의문문**

(A) 반복 어휘 오답: 질문의 fill을 반복 사용한 오답이다.
(B) 정답: 채용이 완료되었는지 묻는 질문에 면접이 더 있다며 부정의 뜻을 우회적으로 나타내고 있다.
(C) 반복 어휘 오답: 질문의 accountant를 반복 사용한 오답이다.

5

M-Cn	Am I supposed to submit the sales report by this Friday?
W-Am	(A) Sure, I will. (B) Thanks for your efforts. (C) No, Monday is fine.

be supposed to ~하기로 되어 있다 effort 수고, 노력

번역 이번 금요일까지 매출보고서를 제출해야 합니까?

(A) 네, 그렇게 하겠습니다.
(B) 노고에 감사드립니다.
(C) 아니요, 월요일에 제출하면 됩니다.

해설 **Be동사 의문문**

(A) 대명사 오류: 질문의 주어가 I이므로 답변에서 다시 I로 답할 수 없다.
(B) 내용 오류: 이미 제출한 사람에게 할 수 있는 답변이다.
(C) 정답: 제출 기한이 금요일이 맞는지 확인하는 질문에 다른 요일을 제시하며 정정해주고 있다.

6

W-Br	Were the clients impressed with the blueprints?
M-Cn	(A) For the new museum extension. (B) Yes, they loved the designs. (C) I sent them a copy.

blueprint 설계도 extension 확대, 증축

번역 고객들이 설계도를 마음에 들어 하던가요?

(A) 새 박물관 증축을 위해서요.
(B) 네, 디자인을 아주 마음에 들어했어요.
(C) 그들에게 사본을 보냈습니다.

해설 **Be동사 의문문**

(A) 연상 어휘 오답: blueprints에서 연상할 수 있는 museum extension을 이용한 오답이다.
(B) 정답: 고객들의 반응이 호의적이었는지 묻는 질문에 긍정으로 답하고 부연 설명하고 있다.
(C) 내용 오류: 고객의 만족 여부와 관련 없는 답변이다.

7

W-Am	Is Mr. Lewis attending a convention in Las Vegas?
M-Au	(A) No, a training seminar. (B) It's an annual event. (C) You can register online.

convention 협의회 annual 연례의 register 등록하다

번역 루이스 씨는 라스베이거스에서 열리는 협의회에 참석할 예정입니까?

(A) 아니요, 교육 세미나에요.
(B) 연례행사입니다.
(C) 온라인으로 등록하실 수 있어요.

해설 **Be동사 의문문**

(A) 정답: 참석하는 행사가 컨벤션인지 묻는 질문에 부정으로 답하고 다른 행사에 참석함을 알려주고 있다.
(B) 연상 어휘 오답: 질문의 convention에서 연상할 수 있는 annual event를 이용한 오답이다.
(C) 연상 어휘 오답: 질문의 convention에서 연상할 수 있는 register를 이용한 오답이다.

8

M-Cn	Do you think you can meet the deadline this week?
W-Am	(A) No, twice a week. (B) It's due this Friday. (C) Yes, I'm staying late tonight.

due ~하기로 되어 있는

번역 이번주 마감 기한을 지킬 수 있을 것 같아요?
(A) 아니요, 일주일에 두 번요.
(B) 이번 금요일이 마감입니다.
(C) 네, 오늘 저녁 늦게까지 남을 거예요.

해설 **조동사(Do) 의문문**
(A) 반복 어휘 오답: 질문의 week를 반복 사용한 오답이다.
(B) 연상 어휘 오답: 질문의 deadline에서 연상할 수 있는 due를 이용한 오답이다.
(C) 정답: 마감 기한을 지킬 수 있는지 묻는 질문에 긍정으로 답하며 계획을 말하고 있다.

9

M-Cn Have the shareholders been informed about the meeting?
W-Am (A) I'll prepare the forms.
(B) In the conference room upstairs.
(C) No, but I'll let them know.

shareholder 주주

번역 주주들에게 회의에 내해 고시했나요?
(A) 제가 서류를 준비할게요.
(B) 위층 회의실에서요.
(C) 아니요, 제가 고지하겠습니다.

해설 **조동사(Have) 의문문**
(A) 유사 발음 오답: 질문의 informed와 일부 발음이 유사한 forms를 이용한 오답이다.
(B) 연상 어휘 오답: 질문의 meeting에서 연상할 수 있는 conference room을 이용한 오답이다.
(C) 정답: 회의 고지 여부를 묻는 질문에 부정으로 답하고 계획을 밝히고 있다.

10

M-Cn Will the ventilation system be installed this weekend?
W-Am (A) I hope so.
(B) I often go to the movies.
(C) In installments.

ventilation 환기 install 설치하다
in installments 할부로, 분납으로

번역 환기 시스템이 이번 주말에 설치되나요?
(A) 그러면 좋겠어요.
(B) 저는 영화 보러 자주 갑니다.
(C) 할부로요.

해설 **조동사(Will) 의문문**
(A) 정답: 환기 시스템을 설치할 예정인지 묻는 질문에 불확실한 긍정으로 답하고 있다.
(B) 연상 어휘 오답: 질문의 weekend에서 연상할 수 있는 go to the movies를 이용한 오답이다.

(C) 반복 어휘 오답: 질문의 installed를 변형한 installments를 반복 사용한 오답이다.

11

W-Br Has the shipment of promotional flyers arrived yet?
M-Cn (A) Yes, check the storeroom.
(B) His flight departs at 10.
(C) For the store's grand opening.

flyer 전단 storeroom 창고 depart 출발하다, 떠나다
grand opening 개장, 개점

번역 판촉 전단이 이제 배송됐나요?
(A) 네, 창고를 확인해 보세요.
(B) 그가 탈 항공편은 10시에 출발합니다.
(C) 매장 개점을 위해서요.

해설 **조동사(Have) 의문문**
(A) 정답: 배송 여부를 묻는 질문에 긍정으로 답하고 부연 설명하고 있다.
(B) 유사 발음 오답: 질문의 flyers와 발음이 유사한 flight를 이용한 오답이다.
(C) 내용 오류: why 의문문에 어울릴 수 있는 답변이다.

12

W-Br Do you think our department is understaffed?
M-Au (A) Just above the research room.
(B) We could use some part-time help.
(C) I'd prefer a larger apartment.

understaffed 인력이 부족한

번역 우리 부서 인력이 부족하다고 생각하세요?
(A) 연구실 바로 위요.
(B) 시간제 직원을 써도 될 것 같아요.
(C) 저는 더 큰 아파트가 좋아요.

해설 **조동사(Do) 의문문**
(A) 내용 오류: where 의문문에 어울리는 답변이다.
(B) 정답: 인력이 부족한지 묻는 질문에 인력 보충이 필요함을 우회적으로 답변하고 있다.
(C) 유사 발음 오답: 질문의 department와 일부 발음이 동일한 apartment를 이용한 오답이다.

13

M-Cn Do you know where the nearest grocery store is?
W-Am (A) A wide range of products.
(B) Yes, he's always busy.
(C) There's one around the corner.

grocery store 식료품점 a wide range of 다양한

번역 가장 가까운 식료품점이 어디에 있는지 아세요?

    (A) 다양한 제품요.

    (B) 네, 그는 항상 바쁩니다.

    (C) 모퉁이를 돌면 하나 있어요.

해설 **Where 간접 의문문**

    (A) 연상 어휘 오답: 질문의 store에서 연상할 수 있는 products를 이용한 오답이다.

    (B) 대명사 오류: 질문에 he를 지칭할 대상이 없다.

    (C) 정답: 가까운 식료품점 위치를 아는지 묻는 간접 의문문에 구체적인 위치를 알려주고 있다.

14

M-Cn Is it OK if I put all your items in one bag?

W-Am (A) Sure, if they'll all fit.

    (B) No, they didn't come.

    (C) The quality control team has one.

quality control 품질 관리

번역 당신의 물건들을 가방 하나에 넣어도 될까요?

    (A) 물론이죠, 다 들어간다면요.

    (B) 아니요, 그들은 오지 않았어요.

    (C) 품질 관리팀이 하나 갖고 있어요.

해설 **Be동사 의문문**

    (A) 정답: 허락을 구하는 질문에 긍정적으로 답하고 있다.

    (B) 내용 오류: 허락을 구하는 질문에 도착 여부로 답변한 오답이다.

    (C) 반복 어휘 오답: 질문의 one을 반복 사용한 오답이다.

15

M-Cn Does this hotel have a fitness room?

W-Am (A) No, we don't offer upgrades.

    (B) Press 2 for room service.

    (C) Yes, on the fourth floor.

번역 이 호텔에는 피트니스 시설이 있나요?

    (A) 아니요, 저희는 업그레이드를 해드리지 않습니다.

    (B) 룸서비스는 2번을 누르세요.

    (C) 네, 4층에요.

해설 **조동사(Do) 의문문**

    (A) 내용 오류: 업그레이드 여부를 묻는 질문에 어울리는 답변이다.

    (B) 반복 어휘·연상 어휘 오답: 질문의 room을 반복 사용, 질문의 hotel에서 연상할 수 있는 room service를 이용한 오답이다.

    (C) 정답: 피트니스 시설 유무를 묻는 질문에 긍정으로 답하고 위치를 알려주고 있다.

16

M-Cn Will the awards banquet end before 9 P.M.?

W-Am (A) By the end of the month.

    (B) I guess so.

    (C) Mr. Williams is the recipient.

banquet 연회   recipient 수상자, 수신인

번역 시상 연회는 밤 9시 전에 끝날 예정인가요?

    (A) 이번 달 말까지요.

    (B) 그럴 것 같아요.

    (C) 윌리엄스 씨가 수상자예요.

해설 **조동사(Will) 의문문**

    (A) 반복 어휘 오답: 질문의 end를 반복 사용한 오답이다.

    (B) 정답: 시상식이 9시 이전에 끝나는지 묻는 질문에 불확실한 긍정으로 답하고 있다.

    (C) 연상 어휘 오답: 질문의 awards에서 연상할 수 있는 recipient를 이용한 오답이다.

17

W-Br Is there a way to download the product photos on our Web site?

M-Cn (A) Down Oxford Street.

    (B) You can delete it.

    (C) Sandra might know about that.

번역 제품 사진을 웹사이트에 다운로드할 방법이 있습니까?

    (A) 옥스포드 스트리트 아래로요.

    (B) 삭제해도 됩니다.

    (C) 산드라 씨가 알고 있을 거예요.

해설 **Be동사 의문문**

    (A) 연상 어휘 오답: 질문의 way에서 연상할 수 있는 down ~ street을 이용한 오답이다.

    (B) 연상 어휘 오답: 질문의 download에서 연상할 수 있는 delete를 이용한 오답이다.

    (C) 정답: 사진을 웹사이트에 다운로드할 방법의 유무를 묻는 질문에 다른 사람에게 물어보라는 것을 우회적으로 나타내고 있다.

18

M-Au Are the interns invited to the year-end celebration?

W-Am (A) It was held at Magenta Hotel.

    (B) Thanks for the invitation.

    (C) Yes, everyone is welcome.

year-end celebration 송년회

번역 인턴들이 송년회에 초대되나요?

(A) 마젠타 호텔에서 열렸어요.

(B) 초대해 주셔서 감사합니다.

(C) 네, 누구나 환영합니다.

해설 Be동사 의문문

(A) 내용 오류: where 의문문에 어울릴 수 있는 답변이며 시제도 맞지 않다.

(B) 반복 어휘 오답: 질문의 invited를 변형한 invitation을 반복 사용한 오답이다.

(C) 정답: 초대 여부를 묻는 질문에 긍정으로 답하고 있다.

19

W-Am Are we celebrating Ms. Patterson's retirement with a party?

M-Au (A) I will take her place.

(B) A few parts are still missing.

(C) Yes, at Rose Banquet Hall.

retirement 은퇴, 퇴직 take one's place ~을 대체하다, ~의 자리를 맡다

번역 패터슨 씨의 은퇴를 축하하는 파티를 여나요?

(A) 제가 그녀의 직책을 대신 맡아요.

(B) 부품 몇 개가 아직 없어요.

(C) 네, 로즈 연회장에서요.

해설 Be동사 의문문

(A) 연상 어휘 오답: 질문의 retirement에서 연상할 수 있는 take her place를 이용한 오답이다.

(B) 유사 발음 오답: 질문의 party와 발음이 유사한 parts를 이용한 오답이다.

(C) 정답: 패터슨 씨의 은퇴 축하 파티를 여는지 묻는 질문에 긍정으로 답하고 구체적인 장소를 알려주고 있다.

20

W-Am Did you discuss the safety regulations with the board members?

M-Au (A) No, was that on the agenda?

(B) It's a regular size.

(C) Mr. Smith is.

regulation 규정, 수칙 agenda 회의 안건

번역 이사회 위원들과 안전 수칙에 대해 논의했습니까?

(A) 아니요, 회의 안건에 있었나요?

(B) 보통 크기입니다.

(C) 스미스 씨입니다.

해설 조동사(Do) 의문문

(A) 정답: 안전 수칙을 논의했는지 묻는 질문에 부정으로 답하고 논의의 필요성을 되묻고 있다.

(B) 내용 오류: how large 의문문에 어울리는 답변이다.

(C) 내용 오류: who is 의문문에 어울리는 답변이다.

21

M-Cn Do you know when we will get our pay raise?

W-Am (A) I'm afraid they're not.

(B) No, let me try it again.

(C) Did you miss the meeting?

pay raise 임금 인상

번역 임금 인상이 언제 이뤄질지 아세요?

(A) 그들은 아닌 것 같습니다.

(B) 아니요, 다시 해 볼게요.

(C) 회의에 빠지셨나요?

해설 When 간접 의문문

(A) 대명사 오류: 질문에 they를 지칭할 대상이 없다.

(B) 내용 오류: 답변의 it이 가리키는 것이 our pay raise에 해당하게 되므로 다시 시도한다는 내용과 맞지 않다.

(C) 정답: 질문에 답변하는 대신 질문하는 이유를 되묻고 있다.

22

M-Cn Was Mr. Gifford appointed head of sales?

W-Br (A) They're ahead of schedule.

(B) It's the best price of the year.

(C) Yes, he's an excellent choice.

appoint 임명하다 ahead of schedule 일정보다 일찍

번역 기퍼드 씨가 영업부장으로 임명됐나요?

(A) 그들은 예정보다 앞서 있습니다.

(B) 1년 중 가장 좋은 가격입니다.

(C) 네, 기퍼드 씨는 탁월한 선택이었어요.

해설 Be동사 의문문

(A) 유사 발음 오답: 질문의 head of와 일부 발음이 동일한 ahead of를 이용한 오답이다.

(B) 연상 어휘 오답: 질문의 sales에서 연상할 수 있는 price를 이용한 오답이다.

(C) 정답: 임명 여부를 묻는 질문에 긍정으로 답하고 있다.

23

W-Br Has the final draft been printed yet?

M-Cn (A) Leave it on my desk.

(B) I'm waiting for Ms. Hanson's approval.

(C) To oversee the company's activities.

approval 승인 oversee 감독하다

번역 최종안이 출력됐나요?

(A) 제 책상에 올려 두세요.

(B) 한슨 씨의 승인을 기다리고 있습니다.

(C) 회사 활동을 감독하기 위해서요.

해설 조동사(Have) 의문문

(A) 내용 오류: 질문 내용으로 볼 때 질문자가 할 수 있는 말이다.

(B) 정답: 회의 안건을 출력했는지 묻는 질문에 No를 생략하고 승인을 기다리고 있다며 이유를 제시한 정답이다.

(C) 내용 오류: why 의문문에 어울리는 답변이다.

24

W-Br Do you know how to use this document scanner?

M-Cn (A) Who wrote it?
(B) Debbie can help you.
(C) The other editing software.

editing 편집

번역 이 문서 스캐너 사용법을 아세요?
(A) 그걸 누가 썼나요?
(B) 데비 씨가 도와드릴 수 있어요.
(C) 다른 편집 소프트웨어요.

해설 조동사(Do) 의문문

(A) 연상 어휘 오답: 질문의 document에서 연상할 수 있는 wrote를 이용한 오답이다.

(B) 정답: 스캐너 사용법을 아는지 묻는 질문에 다른 사람에게 물어보라는 것을 우회적으로 나타내고 있다.

(C) 연상 어휘 오답: 질문의 document에서 연상할 수 있는 editing을 이용한 오답이다.

25

W-Br Have you been to the new café on Elm Street?

M-Au (A) No, but I heard the food is excellent.
(B) A new reservation system.
(C) We once met before.

번역 엘름 스트리트에 새로 생긴 카페에 가 보셨나요?
(A) 아니요, 하지만 음식이 아주 맛있다고 들었어요.
(B) 새로운 예약 시스템이요.
(C) 우린 전에 한 번 만났어요.

해설 조동사(Have) 의문문

(A) 정답: 새로 생긴 카페에 가본 적이 있는지 묻는 질문에 부정으로 답하고 반전의 부연 설명을 덧붙이고 있다.

(B) 반복 어휘 오답: 질문의 new를 반복 사용한 오답이다.

(C) 내용 오류: 특정 장소에 가본 경험을 묻는 질문에 만난 경험으로 답하고 있으므로 오답이다.

●Unit 05 평서문 / 제안 및 요청문

❶ 평서문

LISTENING PRACTICE
교재 p. 55

1. (C) **2.** (A) **3.** (C) **4.** (C) **5.** (C) **6.** (B)

1

M-Cn The new desks have arrived.

W-Br (A) In the large file folder.
(B) I didn't know he was invited.
(C) I'll help you set them up.

set up 놓다, 설치하다

번역 새 책상들이 도착했어요.
(A) 더 큰 파일 폴더예요.
(B) 그가 초대받은 줄 몰랐어요.
(C) 설치하시는 걸 도와드릴게요.

해설 평서문

(A) 연상 어휘 오답: 질문의 desks에서 연상되는 file folder를 이용한 오답이다.

(B) 대명사 오류: 질문에 사람이 없으므로 답변에서 he로 지칭할 수 없다.

(C) 정답: 책상들이 도착했다는 말에 설치를 도와주겠다며 도움을 제공하는 답변이다.

2

W-Am We should start planning our year-end company party.

M-Cn (A) Isn't it too early?
(B) He founded that company.
(C) No, they're the quarterly results.

found 설립하다 quarterly 분기의

번역 회사 연말 파티 계획을 시작해야 합니다.
(A) 너무 이르지 않아요?
(B) 그는 그 회사를 설립했어요.
(C) 아니요, 그것들은 분기별 결과입니다.

해설 평서문

(A) 정답: 연말 파티 계획을 시작해야 한다는 말에 반대 의견을 제시하고 있다.

(B) 반복 어휘 오답: 질문의 company를 반복 사용한 오답이다.

(C) 연상 어휘 오답·대명사 오류: 질문의 year-end에서 연상할 수 있는 quarterly를 이용한 오답이다. 또한 복수명사가 없으므로 답변에서 they로 지칭할 수 없다.

3

M-Au The activation code expires in three days.

W-Am (A) For active participation.

(B) You can stay longer.

(C) Then I'd better take care of this soon.

activation 활성화   expire 만료되다

번역 활성화 코드는 3일 후 만료됩니다.

(A) 적극적인 참여를 위해서요.

(B) 더 오래 머물러도 좋아요.

(C) 그럼 곧 처리하는 편이 좋겠네요.

해설 평서문

(A) 유사 발음 오답: 질문의 activation과 일부 발음이 동일한 active를 이용한 오답이다.

(B) 연상 어휘 오답: 질문의 three days에서 연상할 수 있는 stay longer를 이용한 오답이다.

(C) 정답: 활성화 코드가 3일 후에 만료된다는 말에 곧 행동을 취하겠다는 답변을 하고 있다.

4

W-Am The housekeeping staff hasn't prepared your room yet.

M-Au (A) No, I live in an apartment.

(B) With two beds.

(C) I don't mind waiting.

housekeeping (호텔의) 객실 관리

번역 객실 관리 직원들이 아직 귀하의 객실 준비를 마치지 못했습니다.

(A) 아니요, 저는 아파트에 삽니다.

(B) 침대 두 개요.

(C) 기다려도 괜찮습니다.

해설 평서문

(A) 내용 오류: 주거 형태를 확인하는 질문에 어울릴 수 있는 답변이다.

(B) 연상 어휘 오답: 질문의 room에서 연상할 수 있는 beds를 이용한 오답이다.

(C) 정답: 직원들이 아직 객실 준비를 못했다는 말에 기다려도 괜찮다고 호의적으로 답변하고 있다.

5

W-Am We should buy souvenirs in Paris to give to our coworkers.

M-Cn (A) A great deal of teamwork.

(B) Have you been there before?

(C) I think they'd like keychains.

souvenir 기념품   coworker 동료

a great deal of 상당한

번역 파리에서 동료들에게 줄 기념품을 사야 해요.

(A) 엄청난 팀워크요.

(B) 전에 거기 가본 적이 있나요?

(C) 동료들이 열쇠고리를 좋아할 것 같아요.

해설 평서문

(A) 내용 오류: 제안문에 명사구 단답형으로 답할 수 없다.

(B) 연상 어휘 오답: 질문의 Paris에서 연상할 수 있는 been there before(전에 그곳에 가본 적이 있는)를 이용한 오답이다.

(C) 정답: 파리에서 동료들에게 줄 기념품을 사야 한다는 말에 구체적인 품목을 제시하고 있다.

6

W-Br We won't be able to access the trail to the summit.

W-Am (A) Did you forget your password?

(B) But the park ranger said it was open.

(C) Yes, I enjoy hiking regularly.

trail 산길, 코스   summit 정상   park ranger 공원 관리자

번역 우리는 정상으로 가는 등산로를 이용할 수 없을 거예요.

(A) 패스워드를 잊어버렸습니까?

(B) 하지만 공원 관리인이 등산로가 개방되어 있다고 했는데요.

(C) 네, 저는 정기적으로 산행을 즐깁니다.

해설 평서문

(A) 연상 어휘 오답: 질문의 access에서 연상할 수 있는 password를 이용한 오답이다.

(B) 정답: 정상으로 가는 코스를 이용할 수 없을 거라는 말에 관리인으로부터 들은 상반되는 정보를 제공하는 답변이다.

(C) 연상 어휘 오답: 질문의 trail에서 연상할 수 있는 hiking을 이용한 오답이다.

❷ 제안 및 요청문

LISTENING PRACTICE   교재 p. 57

1. (C)   **2.** (B)   **3.** (B)   **4.** (C)   **5.** (B)   **6.** (A)

1

W-Am Would you mind switching seats with me?

M-Cn (A) A computer switch.

(B) Streets and avenues.

(C) No problem.

switch 바꾸다

번역 저와 자리를 바꿔 주실 수 있나요?
  (A) 컴퓨터 스위치요.
  (B) 스트리트와 애비뉴요.
  (C) 그럼요.

해설 요청문
  (A) 반복 어휘 오답: 질문의 switching에서 switch를 반복 사용한 오답이다.
  (B) 내용 오류: 요청문에 명사구 단답형으로 답할 수 없다.
  (C) 정답: 요청의 질문에 수락하는 답변이다.

2

> W-Br Will you be able to help train Ms. Han, your replacement?
> W-Am (A) I know a few good places.
>   (B) How soon will she start working?
>   (C) A storage compartment.
>
> replacement 대체, 후임자   storage 보관
> compartment 칸

번역 후임자인 한 씨를 교육하는 것을 도와주실 수 있어요?
  (A) 좋은 곳을 몇 군데 알아요.
  (B) 그녀가 언제 일을 시작할 예정인가요?
  (C) 보관함요.

해설 요청문
  (A) 유사 발음 오답: 질문의 replacement와 일부 발음이 유사한 places를 이용한 오답이다.
  (B) 정답: 후임자 교육을 도와 달라는 요청에 일의 시작 시기를 묻고 있다.
  (C) 유사 발음 오류: 질문의 replacement와 일부 발음이 동일한 compartment를 이용한 오답이다.

3

> M-Cn Do you mind filling out this survey?
> M-Au (A) It's full.
>   (B) Sure, I can do that.
>   (C) In alphabetical order.
>
> fill out 작성하다   survey 설문 조사

번역 이 설문 조사를 작성해 주실 수 있을까요?
  (A) 꽉 찼어요.
  (B) 물론 해 드릴 수 있습니다.
  (C) 알파벳 순서대로요.

해설 요청문
  (A) 연상 어휘 오답: 질문의 filling에서 연상할 수 있는 full을 이용한 오답이다.
  (B) 정답: 설문 조사를 작성해 달라는 요청을 수락하는 답변이다.
  (C) 내용 오류: 정렬 방식을 묻는 질문에 어울리는 답변이다.

4

> W-Am Would you like to attend the shareholders' meeting?
> M-Cn (A) She could share it.
>   (B) Yes, please be seated.
>   (C) When is it?
>
> shareholder 주주   share 공유하다   be seated 앉다

번역 주주총회에 참석하시겠습니까?
  (A) 그녀는 그것을 공유할 수 있어요.
  (B) 네, 앉아 주십시오.
  (C) 언제죠?

해설 제안문
  (A) 반복 어휘 오답 · 대명사 오류: 질문의 shareholders에서 share를 반복 사용한 오답이다. 또한 질문에 she를 지칭할 대상이 없다.
  (B) 내용 오류: 참석한다는 의미의 yes와 뒤따르는 내용이 어울리지 않는다.
  (C) 정답: 회의 참석 제안에 회의가 언제인지 되묻고 있다.

5

> W-Br Would you like me to help with the inventory?
> M-Cn (A) Sorry, I'm busy now.
>   (B) James will come in a minute.
>   (C) On the weekly inventory list.
>
> inventory 재고, 물품 목록

번역 재고 조사를 도와 드릴까요?
  (A) 죄송합니다만 지금 바빠요.
  (B) 제임스 씨가 금방 올 겁니다.
  (C) 주간 재고 목록이에요.

해설 제안문
  (A) 내용 오류: 요청문에 어울리는 답변이다.
  (B) 정답: 도움을 베풀고자 하는 호의에 도와줄 수 있는 다른 사람이 있다고 밝히며 우회적으로 거절하고 있으므로 정답이다.
  (C) 내용 오류: where 의문문에 어울릴 수 있는 답변이다.

6

> M-Cn Would you like me to e-mail you my billing address?
> W-Am (A) Thanks, but we already have it on file.
>   (B) I'd love to have my own office.
>   (C) I didn't think it would be that much.

번역 제 청구서 발송지를 이메일로 보내드릴까요?
(A) 감사합니다만 이미 파일에 있습니다.
(B) 제 사무실을 갖고 싶습니다.
(C) 그렇게 많을 거라고 생각하지 않았어요.

해설 **제안문**
(A) 정답: 제안의 표현에 정중하게 거절하며 거절의 이유를 밝히고 있다.
(B) 연상 어휘 오답: 질문의 Would you like ~?에서 연상할 수 있는 I'd love to를 이용한 오답이다.
(C) 내용 오류: that much(그렇게 많이)라고 지칭할 수 있는 대상이 없다.

번역 여기는 좀 덥네요.
(A) 저도 못 들었어요.
(B) 에어컨을 더 세게 틀게요.
(C) 누기 그것들을 비웠나요?

해설 **평서문**
(A) 유사 발음 오답: 질문의 here와 발음이 동일한 hear를 이용한 오답이다.
(B) 정답: 덥다는 의견에 에어컨을 세게 틀겠다는 해결책을 제시하는 답변이다.
(C) 대명사 오류: 질문에 them을 지칭할 대상이 없다.

ACTUAL TEST

교재 p. 58

1. (C)	2. (B)	3. (B)	4. (A)	5. (B)
6. (C)	7. (B)	8. (B)	9. (B)	10. (C)
11. (B)	12. (C)	13. (B)	14. (B)	15. (C)
16. (C)	17. (C)	18. (A)	19. (B)	20. (C)
21. (C)	22. (C)	23. (B)	24. (C)	25. (C)

1

M-Cn Would you like a pastry?
W-Br (A) He wrote it in his notes.
(B) A large vase of flowers.
(C) I had one already, thanks.

번역 페이스트리 드실래요?
(A) 그는 메모에 그걸 썼어요.
(B) 큰 꽃병요.
(C) 이미 하나 먹었어요. 감사합니다.

해설 **제안문**
(A) 대명사 오류: 질문의 주어가 you이므로 답변에서 he로 지칭할 수 없다.
(B) 연상 어휘 오답: 질문의 pastry를 듣고 답변의 flowers(꽃)를 flour(밀가루)로 착각하도록 유도하는 오답이다.
(C) 정답: 음식을 권하는 제안에 정중히 거절하는 답변이다.

2

W-Br It feels a little warm in here.
M-Cn (A) I didn't hear that either.
(B) I'll turn up the air conditioner.
(C) Who emptied them?

turn up (소리, 온도 등을) 높이다, 올리다 empty 비우다

3

M-Cn Let's book our conference tickets today.
W-Am (A) It was very informative.
(B) Have they gone on sale yet?
(C) I never borrow books from there.

informative 유익한

번역 오늘 컨퍼런스 표를 예약합시다.
(A) 굉장히 유익했어요.
(B) 벌써 판매하고 있나요?
(C) 저는 거기에선 절대 책을 빌리지 않아요.

해설 **제안문**
(A) 연상 어휘 오답: 질문의 conference에서 연상할 수 있는 informative를 이용한 오답이다.
(B) 정답: 컨퍼런스 표를 예약하자는 제안에 판매중인지 되묻고 있다.
(C) 반복 어휘 오답: 질문의 book을 반복 사용한 오답이다.

4

M-Au I love the poster you designed for the upcoming musical.
W-Br (A) Ryan supplied the photographs.
(B) No, the tickets were sold out.
(C) Next Tuesday at Harmony Hall.

upcoming 다가오는, 앞으로 있을 supply 제공하다, 공급하다 sold out 매진된

번역 다가오는 뮤지컬 공연을 위해 디자인해 주신 포스터가 마음에 듭니다.
(A) 라이언 씨가 사진을 제공해 주셨어요.
(B) 아니요, 표는 매진됐어요.
(C) 다음 화요일에 하모니홀에서요.

해설 **평서문**
(A) 정답: 포스터에 대한 긍정적인 의견에 대해 협력자를 밝히며 공을 돌리는 답변이다.
(B) 연상 어휘 오답: 질문의 musical에서 연상할 수 있는 tickets를 이용한 오답이다.
(C) 내용 오류: when 의문문에 어울리는 답변이다.

5

M-Cn The freight elevator is out of order.
W-Am (A) Yes, in order of priority.
　　　(B) It broke down again?
　　　(C) To call the shipping firm.

　　　freight 화물　priority 우선 사항　break down 고장 나다

번역　화물용 엘리베이터가 고장 났어요.
　　　(A) 네, 우선순위에 따라서요.
　　　(B) 또 고장이 났어요?
　　　(C) 배송업체에 전화하려고요.

해설　평서문
　　　(A) 반복 어휘 오답: 질문의 order를 반복 사용한 오답이다.
　　　(B) 정답: 엘리베이터가 고장났다는 말에 실망하는 표현으로 답하고 있다.
　　　(C) 연상 어휘 오답: 질문의 freight에서 연상할 수 있는 shipping을 이용한 오답이다.

6

W-Br The air conditioner is making loud noises.
M-Cn (A) We told him to speak more softly.
　　　(B) Because of an exciting sports match.
　　　(C) I already called the technician.

번역　에어컨에서 큰 소음이 나고 있어요.
　　　(A) 그에게 더 부드럽게 말하라고 했습니다.
　　　(B) 신나는 스포츠 경기 때문에요.
　　　(C) 이미 기술자에게 전화했어요.

해설　평서문
　　　(A) 연상 어휘 오답: 질문의 loud에서 연상할 수 있는 softly를 이용한 오답이다.
　　　(B) 내용 오류: why 의문문에 어울리는 답변이다.
　　　(C) 정답: 소음에 대한 불평의 말에 해결책을 제시하고 있다.

7

M-Cn Could you repair some machinery on the production floor?
W-Br (A) He works on the fifth floor.
　　　(B) Which devices are having trouble?
　　　(C) Six pairs of them.

　　　machinery 기계(류)　production floor 생산 작업장
　　　pair 짝, 쌍

번역　생산 작업장의 기계를 수리해 주실 수 있어요?
　　　(A) 그는 5층에서 일합니다.
　　　(B) 어떤 기기에 문제가 있나요?
　　　(C) 여섯 쌍요.

해설　요청문
　　　(A) 반복 어휘 오답: 질문의 floor를 반복 사용한 오답이다.
　　　(B) 정답: 기계 수리 요청에 대해 필요한 정보를 되묻고 있다.
　　　(C) 유사 발음 오류: 질문의 repair와 일부 발음이 동일한 pairs를 이용한 오답이다.

8

W-Am Could you put up these signs near the entrance?
M-Cn (A) Next to the front desk.
　　　(B) Sure, I'd be happy to.
　　　(C) Sign at the bottom, please.

　　　put up a sign 팻말을 세우다, 간판을 내걸다

번역　이 표지판들을 입구 근처에 세워주시겠습니까?
　　　(A) 프런트 데스크 옆이요.
　　　(B) 네, 그렇게 할게요.
　　　(C) 맨 아래 서명해 주세요.

해설　요청문
　　　(A) 내용 오류: where 의문문에 어울리는 답변이다.
　　　(B) 정답: 설치 요청에 수락하는 답변이다.
　　　(C) 반복 어휘 오답: 질문의 signs에서 sign을 반복 사용한 오답이다.

9

W-Am Our online banking site is getting very popular.
M-Cn (A) No, I'd prefer to visit him in person.
　　　(B) Yes, customers like its convenience.
　　　(C) It's our standard checking account.

　　　in person 직접　convenience 편리함
　　　checking account 당좌 예금 계좌

번역　우리 온라인 뱅킹 사이트의 인기가 치솟고 있어요.
　　　(A) 아니요, 저는 그를 직접 방문하고 싶어요.
　　　(B) 네, 고객들은 사이트 편의성을 맘에 들어해요.
　　　(C) 그건 우리 보통 당좌 예금 계좌예요.

해설　평서문
　　　(A) 연상 어휘 오답·대명사 오류: 질문의 online과 site에서 연상할 수 있는 visit과 in person을 이용한 오답이다. 또한 질문에 him을 지칭할 대상이 없다.
　　　(B) 정답: 온라인 뱅킹 사이트의 인기가 치솟고 있다는 말에 동의하며 추가 의견을 덧붙이고 있다.
　　　(C) 연상 어휘 오답: 질문의 banking에서 연상할 수 있는 account를 이용한 오답이다.

10

W-Am Would you like to purchase additional insurance?

M-Cn (A) A magazine subscription.
(B) Both coffee and tea.
(C) How much would that cost?

insurance 보험   subscription 구독

번역 보험을 추가로 구매하시겠어요?
(A) 잡지 구독요.
(B) 커피와 차 둘 다요.
(C) 비용이 얼마나 들죠?

해설 **제안문**
(A) 내용 오류: what 의문문에 어울리는 답변이다.
(B) 내용 오류: 선택 의문문에 어울리는 답변이다.
(C) 정답: 보험 추가 구매 제안에 대해 비용을 되묻는 답변이다.

11

M-Cn These office windows need to be cleaned.

M-Au (A) Close them, if you feel cold.
(B) Let's ask Frank to do it.
(C) I'll lock up before I leave.

lock up 문단속을 하다

번역 사무실 창문을 닦아야겠네요.
(A) 추우면 닫으세요.
(B) 프랭크 씨에게 해 달라고 요청합시다.
(C) 제가 나가기 전에 문단속을 할게요.

해설 **평서문**
(A) 연상 어휘 오답: 질문의 windows에서 연상할 수 있는 close를 이용한 오답이다.
(B) 정답: 창문을 닦아야 한다는 말에 다른 사람에게 업무를 맡기자고 제안하고 있다.
(C) 연상 어휘 오답: 질문의 windows에서 연상할 수 있는 lock up을 이용한 오답이다.

12

W-Am The warranty on this running machine has already expired.

M-Cn (A) It comes with the product as standard.
(B) Three years from the purchase date.
(C) We'd better look after it then.

warranty 품질 보증서   expire 만료되다   as standard 기본적으로   purchase date 구입일자

번역 이 러닝머신의 품질 보증기한은 이미 만료됐어요.
(A) 제품에 기본적으로 딸려 옵니다.
(B) 구입일자로부터 3년요.
(C) 그럼 잘 관리해야겠군요.

해설 **평서문**
(A) 연상 어휘 오답: warranty에서 연상할 수 있는 comes with the product(제품에 딸려 오다)를 이용한 오답이다.
(B) 연상 어휘 오답: expired에서 연상할 수 있는 three years와 date를 이용한 오답이다.
(C) 정답: 러닝머신의 품질 보증기한이 만료되었다는 말에 잘 관리해야겠다는 의견을 말하고 있다.

13

M-Au Please sign both copies of the contract and return one to me.

W-Am (A) I'll contact her to find out.
(B) Sure, you'll have it by tomorrow.
(C) Both of them were very satisfied.

번역 계약서 두 부에 모두 서명하시고 한 부는 저에게 돌려주십시오.
(A) 제가 그녀에게 전화해서 알아볼게요.
(B) 알겠습니다. 내일까지 드릴게요.
(C) 둘 다 매우 만족스러워했어요.

해설 **요청문**
(A) 유사 발음 오답: 질문의 contract와 발음이 유사한 contact를 이용한 오답이다.
(B) 정답: 서명 요청을 수락하는 답변이다.
(C) 반복 어휘 오답: 질문의 both를 반복 사용한 오답이다.

14

W-Br I would like directions to City Hall.

M-Cn (A) No, it's a direct flight.
(B) Take this information booklet.
(C) I would be delighted.

directions 길 안내   booklet 소책자

번역 시청 가는 길 안내를 받고 싶습니다.
(A) 아니요, 직항편입니다.
(B) 이 안내책자를 가져가세요.
(C) 그렇다면 매우 기쁘겠습니다.

해설 **평서문**
(A) 반복 어휘 오답: 질문의 directions를 direct로 변형하여 반복 사용한 오답이다.
(B) 정답: 길 안내를 받고 싶다는 요청에 안내책자를 제공하고 있으므로 정답이다.
(C) 내용 오류: 제안문에 어울릴 수 있는 답변이다.

15

W-Am Mr. Miller is looking for volunteers to attend the convention.
M-Cn (A) I appreciate your help.
　　 (B) A three-day event.
　　 (C) I'd be happy to go.

> volunteer 자원봉사자, 지원자　convention 협의회

번역　밀러 씨는 협의회에 참석할 지원자를 찾고 있어요.
　　 (A) 도와주셔서 감사합니다.
　　 (B) 3일간의 행사입니다.
　　 (C) 제가 갈게요.

해설　평서문
　　 (A) 연상 어휘 오답: 질문의 volunteers에서 연상할 수 있는 help를 이용한 오답이다.
　　 (B) 연상 어휘 오답: 질문의 convention에서 연상할 수 있는 event를 이용한 오답이다.
　　 (C) 정답: 지원자를 찾고 있다는 말에 대해 적극적인 지원 의사를 표시하고 있다.

16

W-Am Do you mind if I borrow your company handbook?
M-Cn (A) I'll definitely keep that in mind.
　　 (B) Oh, did you?
　　 (C) It's sitting on my desk.

> handbook 편람, 안내서　definitely 분명히, 틀림없이
> keep in mind ~을 명심하다

번역　회사 편람을 빌려주실 수 있나요?
　　 (A) 꼭 명심하겠습니다.
　　 (B) 아, 그러셨어요?
　　 (C) 제 책상 위에 있습니다.

해설　요청문
　　 (A) 반복 어휘 오답: 질문의 mind를 반복 사용한 오답이다.
　　 (B) 내용 오류: 평서문에 어울릴 수 있는 답변이다.
　　 (C) 정답: 대여를 요청하는 말에 Yes를 생략하고 수락의 뜻을 간접적으로 나타내고 있다.

17

M-Au It feels a bit chilly in the reception area.
W-Br (A) They're exceptional in all areas.
　　 (B) Sure, I'd love to.
　　 (C) I'll turn the heat up.

> exceptional 뛰어난

번역　로비가 약간 쌀쌀해요.
　　 (A) 그들은 모든 부분에서 뛰어납니다.
　　 (B) 물론이죠, 그리고 싶어요.
　　 (C) 제가 히터 온도를 높일게요.

해설　평서문
　　 (A) 유사 발음·반복 어휘 오답: 질문의 reception과 발음이 유사한 exceptional을 이용, 질문의 area를 반복 사용한 오답이다.
　　 (B) 내용 오류: 제안하는 질문에 할 수 있는 답변이다.
　　 (C) 정답: 로비가 쌀쌀하다는 말에 히터 온도를 높이겠다는 해결책을 제시하고 있다.

18

M-Cn My cellphone isn't getting a signal in here.
W-Am (A) Use the office phone.
　　 (B) That's not my number.
　　 (C) Sorry, we don't sell them.

번역　이 곳에선 제 휴대전화에 신호가 안 잡히네요.
　　 (A) 사무실 전화기를 쓰세요.
　　 (B) 그건 제 전화번호가 아닙니다.
　　 (C) 죄송하지만 저희는 판매하지 않습니다.

해설　평서문
　　 (A) 정답: 휴대전화 신호가 안 잡힌다는 말에 대안을 제시하고 있다.
　　 (B) 연상 어휘 오답: 질문의 cellphone에서 연상할 수 있는 number를 이용한 오답이다.
　　 (C) 유사 발음 오답: 질문의 cellphone과 일부 발음이 유사한 sell을 이용한 오답이다.

19

M-Cn Ms. Serra was offered the senior accountant position.
W-Am (A) The account was closed.
　　 (B) Yes, and she accepted it.
　　 (C) A team of five.

> accountant 회계사　accept 수락하다

번역　세라 씨는 선임 회계사 직책을 제안받았어요.
　　 (A) 그 계좌는 해지됐어요.
　　 (B) 네, 그리고 그녀가 수락했고요.
　　 (C) 5명으로 이뤄진 팀입니다.

해설　평서문
　　 (A) 유사 발음 오답: 질문의 accountant와 일부 발음이 동일한 account를 이용한 오답이다.
　　 (B) 정답: 세라 씨가 선임 회계사 직책을 제안 받았다는 말에 동조하며 그녀가 수락했다는 추가 정보를 주고 있다.
　　 (C) 내용 오류: how many 의문문에 어울리는 답변이다.

20

M-Cn Could I empty that trash bin for you?

W-Br (A) No, we use recycling bins.

(B) You're welcome to borrow one.

(C) Thanks, but I'll take it out in a moment.

trash bin 쓰레기통   recycling bin 분리수거함

번역 제가 쓰레기통을 비워드릴까요?

(A) 아니요, 우리는 분리수거함을 사용합니다.

(B) 하나 빌려셔도 됩니다.

(C) 감사하지만 제가 곧 가지고 나갈 거예요.

해설 **제안문**

(A) 반복 어휘 오답: 질문의 bin을 반복 사용한 오답이다.

(B) 내용 오류: 요청문에 어울릴 수 있는 답변이다.

(C) 정답: 쓰레기통을 비워주겠다는 제안에 자신이 곧 가지고 나갈 것이라며 정중히 거절하고 있다.

21

M-Cn I heard that the new historical movie is 3 hours long.

W-Am (A) We're short of gas.

(B) Even before the 19th century.

(C) It's quite interesting, though.

short of ~이 부족한

번역 새 역사 영화가 3시간짜리라고 들었어요.

(A) 연료가 부족해요.

(B) 19세기도 되기 전입니다.

(C) 그런데 꽤 재미있어요.

해설 **평서문**

(A) 연상 어휘 오답: 질문의 long에서 연상할 수 있는 short를 이용한 오답이다.

(B) 연상 어휘 오답: 질문의 historical movie에서 연상할 수 있는 19th century를 이용한 오답이다.

(C) 정답: 새 영화가 길다는 의견에 다른 의견을 제시하고 있다.

22

M-Cn Why don't I inform the hotel that we'll be checking in late?

W-Am (A) An automated payment system.

(B) Which airline did he use?

(C) That would be a good idea.

automated 자동화된   payment 결제

번역 우리가 체크인을 늦게 한다고 호텔에 알릴까요?

(A) 자동 결제 시스템입니다.

(B) 그는 어느 항공사를 이용했나요?

(C) 좋은 생각이네요.

해설 **제안문**

(A) 내용 오류: 제안문에 명사구 단답형으로 답할 수 없다

(B) 연상 어휘 오답·대명사 오류: 질문의 checking in에서 연상할 수 있는 airline을 이용한 오답이다. 또한 질문에 he를 지칭할 대상이 없다.

(C) 정답: 체크인이 늦음을 호텔 측에 알리겠다는 제안에 동의하는 답변이다.

23

M-Cn The international bank transfer has not shown up in our account.

W-Br (A) Sure, I can show you.

(B) It usually takes a few days.

(C) Over ten thousand euros.

transfer 이체

번역 우리 계좌에서 해외 이체 건은 안 보이는데요.

(A) 물론이죠. 제가 알려드릴게요.

(B) 보통 며칠 걸립니다.

(C) 10,000유로 이상요.

해설 **평서문**

(A) 반복 어휘 오답: shown을 변형한 show를 반복 사용한 오답이다.

(B) 정답: 계좌와 관련된 걱정을 해소해 주는 답변이다.

(C) 연상 어휘 오답: account에서 연상할 수 있는 ten thousand euros를 이용한 오답이다.

24

W-Am That new coffee shop on Broadway got good reviews.

M-Cn (A) I only met him once.

(B) A view of the riverfront.

(C) We should give it a try.

give it a try 시도해보다

번역 브로드웨이에 새로 생긴 저 커피숍은 평이 좋아요.

(A) 저는 그를 딱 한 번 만나봤어요.

(B) 강 전망입니다.

(C) 우리도 한번 가봐야겠네요.

해설 **평서문**

(A) 대명사 오류: 질문에 사람이 없으므로 답변에서 him으로 지칭할 수 없다.

(B) 유사 발음 오답: 질문의 reviews와 일부 발음이 동일한 view를 이용한 오답이다.

(C) 정답: 새로 생긴 커피숍 평이 좋다는 말에 이용 의사를 밝히고 있다.

25

M-Cn	I'd recommend practicing your presentation in advance.
W-Am	(A) I joined an advanced class.
	(B) Yes, I signed up early.
	(C) I'd appreciate some feedback.

in advance 미리   sign up 신청하다, 등록하다

번역 미리 발표 연습을 하실 것을 권합니다.
(A) 저는 상급자반에 들어갔어요.
(B) 네, 저는 일찍 신청했어요.
(C) 피드백을 좀 주시면 감사하겠습니다.

해설 **제안문**
(A) 반복 어휘 오답: 질문의 advance를 변형한 advanced를 반복 사용한 오답이다.
(B) 연상 어휘 오답: 질문의 in advance에서 연상할 수 있는 early를 이용한 오답이다.
(C) 정답: 제안의 의견을 간접적으로 수용하고 있다.

●Unit 06 부가/부정/선택 의문문

❶ 부가 의문문

LISTENING PRACTICE
교재 p. 61

1. (C)   **2.** (B)   **3.** (C)   **4.** (B)   **5.** (A)   **6.** (C)

1

W-Am	We should transfer buses, shouldn't we?
M-Au	(A) Sorry for the delay.
	(B) It's faster by bus.
	(C) Yes, in Chicago.

번역 우리 버스를 갈아타야 하죠, 그렇죠?
(A) 지연되어 죄송합니다.
(B) 버스를 타는 게 더 빨라요.
(C) 네, 시카고에서요.

해설 **부가 의문문**
(A) 연상 어휘 오답: 질문의 bus에서 연상할 수 있는 delay를 이용한 오답이다.
(B) 반복 어휘 오답: 질문의 bus를 반복 사용한 오답이다.
(C) 정답: 버스를 갈아타야 하는지 묻는 질문에 긍정으로 답하며 추가 정보를 제공하고 있다.

2

W-Br	The furniture purchase has been approved, hasn't it?
M-Cn	(A) Proof of purchase.
	(B) Yes, but not the other decorations.
	(C) I like the brown leather sofa.

approve 승인하다   proof of purchase 구매 증빙
leather 가죽

번역 가구 구입 건은 승인됐죠, 그렇죠?
(A) 구매 증빙이요.
(B) 네, 하지만 다른 장식품들은 안 됐어요.
(C) 저는 갈색 가죽 소파가 마음에 들어요.

해설 **부가 의문문**
(A) 반복 어휘 오답: 질문의 purchase를 반복 사용한 오답이다.
(B) 정답: 가구 구입 승인 여부를 묻는 질문에 긍정으로 답하며 추가 정보를 제시하고 있다.
(C) 연상 어휘 오답: 질문의 furniture에서 연상할 수 있는 sofa를 이용한 오답이다.

3

M-Au	The warranty is still in effect, right?
W-Am	(A) No, make a left turn here.
	(B) Digital scanning equipment.
	(C) Check the sales paperwork.

warranty 품질 보증서   in effect 효력이 있는
equipment 장비

번역 품질 보증서는 아직 유효하죠, 그렇죠?
(A) 아니요, 여기서 좌회전하세요.
(B) 디지털 스캐닝 장비입니다.
(C) 판매 서류를 확인해 보세요.

해설 **부가 의문문**
(A) 연상 어휘 오답: 질문의 right에서 연상할 수 있는 left를 이용한 오답이다.
(B) 내용 오류: what 의문문에 어울릴 수 있는 답변이다.
(C) 정답: 품질 보증서가 유효한지 묻는 질문에 판매 서류를 확인해 보라(Check ~)며 만능 답변 형태로 답하고 있다.

4

M-Cn	We won't be able to finish this project on time, will we?
W-Am	(A) At least two more classes.
	(B) We'll need to hurry.
	(C) Probably the express train.

on time 제 시간에   express train 급행열차

번역 우리는 이 프로젝트를 제때 끝내지 못하겠죠, 그렇죠?

(A) 적어도 강의 2개는 더요.

(B) 서둘러야 할 겁니다.

(C) 아마 급행열차일 겁니다.

해설 **부가 의문문**

(A) 내용 오류: how many에 어울릴 수 있는 답변이다.

(B) 정답: 시간 내 프로젝트 마감 가능성을 묻는 질문에 서둘러야 한다고 우회적으로 답하고 있다.

(C) 내용 오류: 가능성을 묻는 질문에 명사구 단답형으로 답할 수 없다.

5

> W-Br The architect is finished revising the building plans, isn't he?
>
> M-Au (A) I'll call and get a progress report.
>
> (B) The plant shop near my home.
>
> (C) I've never started a business before.
>
> revise 수정하다   progress report 경과 보고서

번역 그 건축가는 공사 계획 수정을 끝마쳤죠, 그렇죠?

(A) 제가 연락해서 경과 보고를 받을게요.

(B) 저희 집 근처 꽃가게요.

(C) 저는 전에 창업한 적이 없어요.

해설 **부가 의문문**

(A) 정답: 수정 완료 여부를 확인하는 질문에 확인 의사를 밝히며 모른다는 것을 간접적으로 나타내고 있다.

(B) 유사 발음 오답: 질문의 plans와 발음이 유사한 plant를 이용한 오답이다.

(C) 연상 어휘 오답: 질문의 finished에서 연상할 수 있는 started를 이용한 오답이다.

6

> W-Am You've set up the projection equipment before, right?
>
> M-Au (A) The overdue shipment.
>
> (B) Their budget projections.
>
> (C) That's Tony's area.
>
> projection equipment 프로젝터   overdue 기한이 지난

번역 프로젝터 기기를 설치해 본 적이 있으시죠, 그렇죠?

(A) 기한이 지난 배송품입니다.

(B) 그들의 예산안이요.

(C) 그건 토니 씨의 업무입니다.

해설 **부가 의문문**

(A) 유사 발음 오답: 질문의 equipment와 일부 발음이 동일한 shipment를 이용한 오답이다.

(B) 반복 어휘 오답: 질문의 projection을 반복 사용한 오답이다.

(C) 정답: 특정 업무 경험 유무를 확인하는 질문에 다른 사람의 임무라며 경험이 없음을 우회적으로 전달하고 있다.

❷ 부정 의문문

LISTENING PRACTICE   교재 p. 63

1. (B)   **2.** (C)   **3.** (C)   **4.** (A)   **5.** (B)   **6.** (C)

1

> W-Am Isn't the post office open until 6 P.M.?
>
> M-Cn (A) Post it on the bulletin board.
>
> (B) Not on national holidays.
>
> (C) Yes, a fragile package.
>
> bulletin board 게시판   fragile 깨지기 쉬운

번역 우체국은 오후 6시까지 열지 않나요?

(A) 게시판에 올리세요.

(B) 국경일에는 아닙니다.

(C) 네, 깨시기 쉬운 심입니다.

해설 **부정 의문문**

(A) 반복 어휘 오답: 질문의 post를 반복 사용한 오답이다.

(B) 정답: 우체국 운영이 6시까지 맞는지 확인하는 질문에 예외인 경우를 알려주고 있다.

(C) 연상 어휘 오답: 질문의 post office에서 연상할 수 있는 package를 이용한 오답이다.

2

> W-Am Didn't you receive that briefcase as a gift?
>
> M-Au (A) Thanks, I really like it.
>
> (B) She only spoke to us briefly.
>
> (C) Yes, from my team members.
>
> briefcase 서류 가방   briefly 간단히

번역 그 서류 가방을 선물로 받지 않으셨어요?

(A) 감사합니다. 무척 마음에 들어요.

(B) 그녀는 우리에게 간단하게만 얘기했어요.

(C) 네, 저희 팀원들로부터요.

해설 **부정 의문문**

(A) 연상 어휘 오답: 질문의 gift에서 연상할 수 있는 Thanks를 사용한 오답이다.

(B) 유사 발음 오답: 질문의 briefcase와 일부 발음이 동일한 briefly를 이용한 오답이다.

(C) 정답: 선물로 서류 가방을 받았는지 묻는 질문에 긍정으로 답하며 누구에게서 받았는지 구체적으로 밝히고 있다.

3

W-Am Aren't the inspectors supposed to visit our factory this morning?

M-Cn (A) Order projectors from their Web site.

(B) At least one of those factors.

(C) They should be arriving soon.

inspector 조사관, 감독관 be supposed to ~하기로 되어 있다 factor 요인

번역 감독관들이 오늘 아침 우리 공장을 방문하기로 되어 있지 않나요?

(A) 웹사이트에서 프로젝터를 주문하세요.

(B) 적어도 이 요인들 중 하나입니다.

(C) 그들이 곧 도착할 겁니다.

해설 부정 의문문

(A) 유사 발음 오답: 질문의 inspectors와 일부 발음이 동일한 projectors를 이용한 오답이다.

(B) 유사 발음 오답: 질문의 factory와 발음이 유사한 factors를 이용한 오답이다.

(C) 정답: 감독관들의 공장 방문 여부를 묻는 질문에 Yes를 생략하고 긍정으로 답하고 있다.

4

M-Cn Don't you normally use your cell phone to call clients?

W-Am (A) Yes, but I left it in my car by mistake.

(B) Make sure to give it back to me.

(C) Try to call after lunch.

normally 대개 by mistake 실수로

번역 고객들에게 전화를 거는 데 보통 휴대전화를 사용하지 않나요?

(A) 네, 하지만 실수로 차에 두고 내렸어요.

(B) 저에게 꼭 돌려주세요.

(C) 점심 식사 이후에 전화해 보세요.

해설 부정 의문문

(A) 정답: 휴대폰 사용 여부를 묻는 질문에 긍정으로 답하며 부연 설명을 덧붙이고 있다.

(B) 내용 오류: 사용 여부를 묻는 질문에 돌려 달라는 답변은 어울리지 않는다.

(C) 반복 어휘 오답: 질문의 call을 반복 사용한 오답이다.

5

W-Br Isn't it time for us to update our business software?

M-Cn (A) Some of them arrived late.

(B) The current version is running fine.

(C) In business journals.

current 현재의

번역 우리 회사 소프트웨어를 업데이트할 시기 아닌가요?

(A) 그것들 중 일부가 늦게 도착했어요.

(B) 현재 버전이 잘 작동하고 있습니다.

(C) 비즈니스 전문지들에서요.

해설 부정 의문문

(A) 연상 어휘 오답: 질문의 time에서 연상할 수 있는 late를 이용한 오답이다.

(B) 정답: 업데이트 제안에 반대하는 의견을 제시하고 있다.

(C) 반복 어휘 오답: 질문의 business를 반복 사용한 오답이다.

6

W-Am Don't we need to buy more office supplies?

M-Au (A) One of the business leaders.

(B) It was a surprise party.

(C) Yes, we are running low on printer paper.

office supply 사무용품 run low 고갈되다, 떨어져 가다

번역 사무용품을 더 사야 하지 않을까요?

(A) 기업주 중 한 명요.

(B) 깜짝 파티였어요.

(C) 네, 프린터 종이가 다 떨어져 가요.

해설 부정 의문문

(A) 내용 오류: who 의문문에 어울리는 답변이다.

(B) 유사 발음 오답: 질문의 supplies와 발음이 유사한 surprise를 이용한 오답이다.

(C) 정답: 사무용품 구입 필요성을 묻는 질문에 동의하며 구체적인 필요 물품을 제시하고 있다.

❸ 선택 의문문

LISTENING PRACTICE
교재 p. 65

1. (A)   2. (A)   3. (C)   4. (B)   5. (B)   6. (A)

1

W-Br Is this form to be used by vendors or buyers?

M-Au (A) It's suitable for both.

(B) We bought a few of them.

(C) Sign at the bottom of the page.

vendor 판매 회사 suitable 적합한

번역 이 서류는 판매업체에서 사용하나요, 아니면 구매자가 사용하나요?
(A) 모두에게 적합합니다.
(B) 우리는 그것들 중 몇 개를 샀어요.
(C) 페이지 맨 아래에 서명하세요.

해설 **선택 의문문**
(A) 정답: 선택 의문문에서 주어진 선택 사항을 둘 다 고른 답변이다.
(B) 연상 어휘 오답: 질문의 buyers에서 연상되는 bought를 이용한 오답이다.
(C) 연상 어휘 오답: 질문의 form에서 연상할 수 있는 sign을 이용한 오답이다.

2

W-Br Should we print the invitations in color or black and white?
M-Cn (A) I don't have a preference.
(B) For the anniversary party.
(C) Yes, the printer has been repaired.

anniversary 기념일

번역 초대장을 컬러로 출력해야 할까요, 아니면 흑백으로 출력해야 할까요?
(A) 저는 특별히 선호하는 쪽이 없어요.
(B) 기념 파티를 위해서요.
(C) 네, 프린터는 수리되었어요.

해설 **선택 의문문**
(A) 정답: 선택 사항을 묻는 질문에 어느 것이든 상관없다는 의미로 답하고 있다.
(B) 연상 어휘 오답: 질문의 invitations에서 연상할 수 있는 anniversary party를 이용한 오답이다.
(C) 반복 어휘 오답: 질문의 print를 변형한 printer를 사용한 오답이다.

3

W-Am Should we paint the hallway ourselves or hire a contractor?
M-Cn (A) From some of the local artists.
(B) Who misplaced that contract?
(C) Let's have a professional do it.

contractor 도급업자   misplace 제자리에 두지 않다
professional 전문가

번역 복도를 우리가 칠해야 할까요, 아니면 하청업체를 고용해야 할까요?
(A) 지역 예술가들로부터요.
(B) 누가 그 계약서를 딴 곳에 뒀나요?
(C) 전문가가 하도록 합시다.

해설 **선택 의문문**
(A) 연상 어휘 오답: paint에서 연상할 수 있는 artists를 이용한 오답이다.
(B) 반복 어휘 오답: 질문의 contractor에서 contract를 반복 사용한 오답이다.
(C) 정답: 선택 의문문에서 주어진 선택 사항 중 후자를 간접적으로 고른 답변이다.

4

M-Au Will you mail the package, or should I pick it up in person?
W-Am (A) Two to three working days.
(B) Whichever one you prefer.
(C) I hope you feel better soon.

in person 직접   working day 영업일

번역 소포를 우편으로 보내실래요, 아니면 제가 직접 찾아갈까요?
(A) 영업일 기준 이삼일이요.
(B) 어느 쪽이든 원하시는 대로요.
(C) 곧 회복하시길 바랍니다.

해설 **선택 의문문**
(A) 내용 오류: how long 의문문에 어울리는 답변이다.
(B) 정답: 선택 사항을 묻는 질문에 어느 것이든 상관없다는 의미로 답하고 있다.
(C) 내용 오류: 선택 의문문에 비교급이 정답으로 자주 등장한다는 것을 역이용한 오답이다.

5

M-Cn Should we drive to the meeting ourselves or take the subway?
W-Br (A) Let's take a few more.
(B) Do you want to deal with traffic?
(C) To discuss the contract terms.

deal with ~을 다루다, 상대하다
contract terms 계약 조건

번역 회의에 우리가 운전을 해서 갈까요, 아니면 지하철을 탈까요?
(A) 몇 개 더 가져갑시다.
(B) 교통체증을 겪고 싶어요?
(C) 계약 조건을 논의하려고요.

해설 **선택 의문문**
(A) 반복 어휘 오답: 질문의 take를 반복 사용한 오답이다.
(B) 정답: 두 가지 선택 사항 중 후자를 간접적으로 고른 정답이다.
(C) 내용 오류: why 의문문에 어울리는 답변이다.

6

W-Am Did you meet the architect, or was he too
busy?
M-Au (A) He showed the blueprint.
  (B) Yes, it will.
  (C) The line is busy.

architect 건축가 blueprint 설계도

번역 건축가를 만나셨나요, 아니면 그가 너무 바빠서 못 만나셨
나요?
(A) 그가 설계도를 보여줬어요.
(B) 네, 그럴 겁니다.
(C) 통화 중이네요.

해설 **선택 의문문**
(A) 정답: 선택 의문문에서 주어진 선택 사항 중 전자를 간
접적으로 고른 답변이다.
(B) 대명사 오류: 질문에 쓰인 명사가 사람명사이므로 답
변에서 it으로 지칭할 수 없다.
(C) 반복 어휘 오답: 질문의 busy를 반복 사용한 오답이다.

ACTUAL TEST

교재 p. 66

1. (B)	**2.** (A)	**3.** (C)	**4.** (B)	**5.** (B)
6. (A)	**7.** (C)	**8.** (A)	**9.** (B)	**10.** (B)
11. (B)	**12.** (A)	**13.** (A)	**14.** (C)	**15.** (B)
16. (C)	**17.** (B)	**18.** (B)	**19.** (C)	**20.** (B)
21. (B)	**22.** (C)	**23.** (A)	**24.** (B)	**25.** (A)

1

W-Br Mandy is training the new employees, isn't
she?
M-Cn (A) The earlier departure.
  (B) I'm not really sure.
  (C) I started there two years ago.

departure 출발

번역 맨디 씨가 신입사원들을 교육하고 있죠, 그렇죠?
(A) 더 이른 출발이요.
(B) 잘 모르겠어요.
(C) 저는 2년 전에 거기서 시작했어요.

해설 **부가 의문문**
(A) 연상 어휘 오답: training을 train(기차)으로 착각하는
경우 연상할 수 있는 departure를 사용한 오답이다.
(B) 정답: 사실을 확인하는 질문에 만능 답변(I'm not
sure) 형태로 답하고 있다.
(C) 대명사 오류: 질문의 주어가 Mandy이므로 답변에서
I로 지칭할 수 없다.

2

M-Cn Is this meeting room available now, or is
someone planning to use it?
W-Am (A) Check the reservation list.
  (B) I'm free to meet after lunch.
  (C) That's an interesting plan.

번역 이 회의실은 지금 쓸 수 있나요, 아니면 누군가 쓸 계획인
가요?
(A) 예약 목록을 확인해 보세요.
(B) 점심 시간 후에는 만날 시간이 있어요.
(C) 흥미로운 계획이군요.

해설 **선택 의문문**
(A) 정답: 선택 사항을 묻는 질문에 만능 답변(Check ~)
형태로 답하고 있다.
(B) 반복 어휘 오답: 질문의 meeting에서 meet을 반복
사용한 오답이다.
(C) 반복 어휘 오답: 질문의 planning에서 plan을 반복
사용한 오답이다.

3

W-Br Aren't you in charge of handling customer
complaints?
M-Cn (A) No, there's no charge.
  (B) Because of some construction noise.
  (C) Yes, what's the problem?

in charge of ~을 담당하는 handle 다루다, 처리하다
complaint 불만 charge 요금

번역 고객 불만사항 처리를 맡고 계시지 않나요?
(A) 아니요, 요금이 부과되지 않습니다.
(B) 공사 소음 때문에요.
(C) 네, 무슨 문제이시죠?

해설 **부정 의문문**
(A) 반복 어휘 오답: 질문의 charge를 반복 사용한 오답
이다.
(B) 연상 어휘 오답: 질문의 complaints에서 연상할 수
있는 noise를 이용한 오답이다.
(C) 정답: 담당자인지 묻는 질문에 긍정으로 답하며 문제
가 무엇인지 되묻는 답변이다.

4

W-Am Wouldn't it be better to hold the seminar in
a smaller room?
M-Cn (A) They were quite informative.
  (B) Well, we're expecting a high turnout.
  (C) Some free space on the hard drive.

informative 유익한 turnout 참가자의 수

번역 세미나를 더 작은 회의실에서 여는 게 낫지 않을까요?
(A) 그것들은 꽤 유익했어요.
(B) 음, 우리는 참석자가 많을 거라고 예상하고 있어요.
(C) 하드 드라이브의 여유 공간요.

해설 **부정 의문문**
(A) 연상 어휘 오답: 질문의 seminar에서 연상할 수 있는 informative를 이용한 오답이다.
(B) 정답: 세미나를 더 작은 회의실에서 열자는 제안에 참석자가 많을 것이라며 우회적으로 거절하고 있다.
(C) 연상 어휘 오답: 질문의 room에서 연상할 수 있는 space를 이용한 오답이다.

5

W-Br Don't we have enough time to finish the project this week?
M-Cn (A) The one who rejected them.
(B) Only if we work extra hours.
(C) Because of the heavy traffic.

reject 거절하다   work extra hours 초과 근무하다

번역 이번 주에 프로젝트를 마무리할 시간이 넉넉하지 않나요?
(A) 그것들을 거절한 사람요.
(B) 초과 근무를 해야 가능해요.
(C) 교통체증 때문에요.

해설 **부정 의문문**
(A) 유사 발음 오답: 질문의 project와 일부 발음이 동일한 rejected를 이용한 오답이다.
(B) 정답: 프로젝트 마무리 시간이 충분하지 않은지 묻는 질문에 초과 근무를 해야 한다고 우회적으로 답변하고 있다.
(C) 내용 오류: why 의문문에 대한 답변이다.

6

W-Am You can pick up the sales director at the airport, can't you?
M-Cn (A) I'm getting ready to go there now.
(B) An upgrade to business class.
(C) Those figures are in the report.

figures 수치

번역 공항에 영업 부장을 태우러 갈 수 있죠, 그렇죠?
(A) 지금 가려고 준비 중입니다.
(B) 비즈니스석으로 업그레이드요.
(C) 그 수치들은 보고서에 있습니다.

해설 **부가 의문문**
(A) 정답: 공항에 영업 부장을 태우러 갈 수 있는지 묻는 질문에 긍정으로 답변하고 있다.
(B) 연상 어휘 오답: 질문의 airport에서 연상할 수 있는 business class를 이용한 오답이다.
(C) 유사 발음 오답: 질문의 airport와 일부 발음이 동일한 report를 이용한 오답이다.

7

M-Cn The warranty covers the repair costs, doesn't it?
W-Am (A) This pair of glasses.
(B) It was lost in transit.
(C) Yes, but you'll need to show your receipt.

warranty 품질 보증서   in transit 운송 중에

번역 품질 보증에는 수리 비용이 포함되죠, 그렇죠?
(A) 이 안경요.
(B) 배송 중에 분실됐습니다.
(C) 네, 하지만 영수증을 보여주셔야 합니다.

해설 **부가 의문문**
(A) 유사 발음 오답: 질문의 repair와 일부 발음이 동일한 pair를 이용한 오답이다.
(B) 내용 오류: 답변의 it이 가리키는 것이 질문의 warranty에 해당하게 되므로 배송 중 분실되었다는 내용과 맞지 않다.
(C) 정답: 무상 수리 가능 여부 질문에 긍정으로 답하며 조건을 제시하는 답변이다.

8

W-Br Would you like to book an afternoon or an evening flight?
M-Cn (A) I'd prefer a morning departure.
(B) In the magazine section.
(C) Last month's sightseeing tour.

sightseeing 관광

번역 오후 항공편을 예약하시겠습니까, 아니면 저녁 항공편을 예약하시겠습니까?
(A) 아침 출발편이 좋습니다.
(B) 잡지 구역에서요.
(C) 지난달 관광 여행요.

해설 **선택 의문문**
(A) 정답: 선택 의문문에서 주어진 선택 사항을 고르지 않고 제3의 대안을 제시한 답변이다.
(B) 연상 어휘 오답: 질문의 book을 '서적'으로 착각하는 경우 연상할 수 있는 magazine을 이용한 오답이다.
(C) 연상 어휘 오답: flight에서 연상할 수 있는 sightseeing tour를 이용한 오답이다.

9

M-Cn Isn't it time to get the windows cleaned?
W-Am (A) The housekeeping manager.
　　 (B) They do look rather dusty.
　　 (C) They're cleaning solutions.

rather 상당히, 꽤 dusty 먼지 낀 solution 용액

번역 창문 청소를 할 때가 되지 않았나요?
　　 (A) 객실 관리 책임자요.
　　 (B) 먼지가 꽤 낀 것 같네요.
　　 (C) 그것들은 세척 용액입니다.

해설 부정 의문문
　　 (A) 연상 어휘 오답: 질문의 cleaned에서 연상할 수 있는 housekeeping을 이용한 오답이다.
　　 (B) 정답: 청소할 때가 되지 않았는지 묻는 질문에 먼지가 꽤 낀 것 같다며 청소할 때가 되었음을 우회적으로 전달하고 있다.
　　 (C) 반복 어휘 오답: 질문의 cleaned를 동명사로 바꿔서 반복 사용한 오답이다.

10

W-Am Julia will be training the interns, won't she?
M-Cn (A) The six o' clock shuttle bus.
　　 (B) I'll check the orientation schedule.
　　 (C) At the trade fair last month.

trade fair 무역박람회

번역 줄리아 씨는 인턴들을 교육할 예정이죠, 그렇죠?
　　 (A) 6시 정각 셔틀버스요.
　　 (B) 제가 오리엔테이션 일정을 확인해 보겠습니다.
　　 (C) 지난달 무역박람회에서요.

해설 부가 의문문
　　 (A) 내용 오류: what 또는 which 의문문에 어울릴 수 있는 답변이다.
　　 (B) 정답: 담당자 및 담당 업무를 확인하는 질문에 만능 답변(I'll check ~)의 형태로 답하고 있다.
　　 (C) 내용 오류: where 또는 when 의문문에 어울릴 수 있는 답변이다.

11

M-Cn The outgoing mail was already picked up, wasn't it?
W-Br (A) For our outgoing CEO.
　　 (B) The carrier just left with it.
　　 (C) They gave me a ride there.

outgoing (특정 장소에서) 나가는, 퇴임하는 give ~ a ride ~을 태워주다

번역 발신 우편물은 이미 수거해 갔죠, 그렇죠?
　　 (A) 퇴임하는 저희 CEO를 위해서요.
　　 (B) 배달원이 막 가지고 갔습니다.
　　 (C) 그들이 거기서 저를 태워줬어요.

해설 부가 의문문
　　 (A) 반복 어휘 오답: 질문의 outgoing을 반복 사용한 오답이다.
　　 (B) 정답: 우편물 수거 여부를 확인하는 질문에 긍정으로 답하고 있다.
　　 (C) 연상 어휘 오답: 질문의 picked up에서 연상할 수 있는 ride를 이용한 오답이다.

12

W-Am Are they holding the sports day indoors or outdoors?
M-Au (A) It'll take place at Dawson Park.
　　 (B) That's what I heard, too.
　　 (C) Yes, I'll be there all day.

take place 열리다, 개최되다

번역 그들은 운동회를 실내에서 개최하나요, 야외에서 개최하나요?
　　 (A) 도슨 공원에서 개최될 겁니다.
　　 (B) 저도 그렇게 들었어요.
　　 (C) 네, 저는 하루 종일 거기 있을 거예요.

해설 선택 의문문
　　 (A) 정답: 선택 의문문에서 주어진 선택 사항 중 후자를 간접적으로 고른 답변이다.
　　 (B) 내용 오류: "That's what I heard"는 질문에 긍정의 뜻을 밝힐 때 사용하는 Yes와 같은 의미이며, 따라서 선택 의문문에 맞지 않는 답변이다.
　　 (C) Yes / No 답변 불가 오답: or 앞뒤가 구로 이루어진 선택 의문문에는 Yes / No로 대답할 수 없다.

13

W-Am We can dispose of batteries in the regular trash, can't we?
M-Au (A) No, there's a special container.
　　 (B) How about posing as a group?
　　 (C) It's running out of power.

dispose of ~을 버리다 pose 포즈를 취하다
run out of ~을 다 써버리다

번역 일반 쓰레기통에 건전지를 버려도 되죠, 그렇죠?
　　 (A) 아니요, 특별 용기가 있어요.
　　 (B) 그룹으로 포즈를 취하면 어때요?
　　 (C) 그것은 방전됐어요.

PART 2

해설 **부가 의문문**

(A) 정답: 건전지 폐기와 관련된 정보가 맞는지 확인하는 질문에 부정으로 답하며 정보를 정정해주고 있다.

(B) 유사 발음 오답: 질문의 dispose와 일부 발음이 동일한 pose를 이용한 오답이다.

(C) 연상 어휘 오답: batteries에서 연상할 수 있는 running out of power를 이용한 오답이다.

14

M-Cn Should we contact the lawyer today or tomorrow?

W-Am (A) A signature is needed.

(B) For the whole month.

(C) Actually, he's visiting us this afternoon.

lawyer 변호사, 법률가 signature 서명

번역 변호사에게 오늘 연락을 해야 할까요, 아니면 내일 해야 할까요?

(A) 서명이 필요합니다.

(B) 한 달 내내요.

(C) 실은 오늘 오후에 변호사가 우리를 방문할 예정입니다.

해설 **선택 의문문**

(A) 연상 어휘 오답: 질문의 contact를 듣고 contract(계약서)로 착각하여 연상할 수 있는 signature를 이용한 오답이다.

(B) 내용 오류: how long에 어울릴 수 있는 답변이다.

(C) 정답: 연락 시기를 선택 사항으로 묻는 질문에 연락하지 않아도 된다는 반전의 답변을 주고 있다.

15

M-Cn Shouldn't we update this software program?

W-Br (A) The latest news updates.

(B) Tony can help you with that.

(C) No, they are mine.

번역 이 소프트웨어 프로그램을 업데이트해야 하지 않아요?

(A) 최신 뉴스 업데이트요.

(B) 토니 씨가 도와드릴 수 있을 겁니다.

(C) 아니요, 그것들은 제 것이에요.

해설 **부정 의문문**

(A) 반복 어휘 오답: 질문의 update를 반복 사용한 오답이다.

(B) 정답: 업데이트를 해야 하지 않는지 묻는 질문에 담당자 이름을 제공하여 간접적으로 업데이트가 필요함을 나타내고 있다.

(C) 대명사 오류: 질문에 they를 지칭할 대상이 없다.

16

W-Am The maintenance work will begin tomorrow, right?

M-Cn (A) To avoid unnecessary expenses.

(B) Some complaints from tenants.

(C) It's been postponed.

maintenance 유지 보수 avoid 피하다 expense 지출 tenant 세입자

번역 유지보수 작업이 내일 시작되죠, 그렇죠?

(A) 불필요한 비용 지출을 피하려고요.

(B) 세입자들의 불만사항요.

(C) 연기됐어요.

해설 **부가 의문문**

(A) 내용 오류: why 의문문에 어울리는 답변이다.

(B) 연상 어휘 오답: 질문의 maintenance work에서 연상할 수 있는 complaints from tenants를 이용한 오답이다.

(C) 정답: 작업이 내일 시작하는지 묻는 질문에 No를 생략하고 작업이 미루어졌음을 밝히고 있다.

17

M-Au Shouldn't our business plan have more detailed financial forecasts?

W-Am (A) Those plants grew quickly.

(B) I think it has enough data.

(C) The regional weather forecast.

detailed 자세한 financial 금융의, 재무의 forecast 예측 regional 지역의

번역 우리 사업 계획에 더 자세한 재무 예측 내용이 있어야 하지 않을까요?

(A) 그 식물들은 빨리 자랐어요.

(B) 자료가 충분하다고 생각해요.

(C) 지역 일기 예보요.

해설 **부정 의문문**

(A) 유사 발음 오답: 질문의 plan과 발음이 유사한 plants를 이용한 오답이다.

(B) 정답: 자세한 정보의 필요성을 묻는 질문에 No를 생략하고 필요하지 않음을 간접적으로 밝히고 있다.

(C) 반복 어휘 오답: 질문의 forecast를 반복 사용한 오답이다.

18

M-Cn Isn't there a question-and-answer session after the lecture?
W-Am (A) As often as I can.
(B) Yes, for 15 minutes.
(C) It is supposed to be up there.

번역 강의 후에 질의응답 시간이 있지 않나요?
(A) 가능한 한 자주요.
(B) 네, 15분간요.
(C) 그것은 거기 있어야 해요.

해설 부정 의문문
(A) 내용 오류: how often 의문문에 어울리는 답변이다.
(B) 정답: 질의응답 시간이 있지 않는지 묻는 질문에 긍정으로 답하고 구체적인 시간을 알려주고 있다.
(C) 반복 어휘 오답: 질문의 there를 반복 사용한 오답이다.

19

W-Am We should submit relocation requests to Mr. Khan, shouldn't we?
M-Cn (A) Thanks, I already received it.
(B) It's located downtown.
(C) No, Ms. Reid handles those.

relocation 이전, 재배치

번역 칸 씨에게 이전 요청서를 제출해야 하죠, 그렇죠?
(A) 감사합니다. 이미 받았어요.
(B) 그것은 시내에 있습니다.
(C) 아니요, 그건 라이드 씨가 처리해요.

해설 부가 의문문
(A) 연상 어휘 오답: 질문의 submit에서 연상할 수 있는 receive를 이용한 오답이다.
(B) 유사 발음 오답: 질문의 relocation과 일부 발음이 동일한 located를 이용한 오답이다.
(C) 정답: 신청서 제출을 칸 씨에게 하는 것이 맞는지 확인하는 질문에 부정으로 답하며 정보를 정정해주고 있다.

20

W-Br Should we hold our meeting in person or via conference call?
M-Cn (A) From a software company.
(B) It depends on others' schedules.
(C) No, I haven't met him before.

in person 직접 via ~을 통해
conference call 다자간 회의 통화

번역 대면 회의를 해야 할까요, 아니면 컨퍼런스 콜을 할까요?
(A) 소프트웨어 업체로부터요.
(B) 다른 사람들의 일정에 달렸어요.
(C) 아니요, 저는 전에 그를 만난 적이 없어요.

해설 해설 선택 의문문
(A) 연상 어휘 오답: 질문의 meeting에서 연상할 수 있는 company를 사용한 오답이다.
(B) 정답: 선택 사항을 묻는 질문에 만능 답변(It depends ~) 형태로 답하고 있다.
(C) Yes/No 답변 불가 오답: or 앞뒤가 구로 이루어진 선택 의문문에 Yes/No로 대답할 수 없다.

21

M-Cn The technology workshop is going to be held in Barcelona, isn't it?
W-Br (A) Experts from all over the world.
(B) That's what I heard.
(C) From the warehouse.

warehouse 창고

번역 기술 워크숍이 바르셀로나에서 개최될 예정이죠, 그렇죠?
(A) 전 세계에서 온 전문가들요.
(B) 저는 그렇게 들었어요.
(C) 창고에서요.

해설 부가 의문문
(A) 내용 오류: who 의문문에 어울리는 답변이다.
(B) 정답: 워크숍 개최 장소가 맞는지 묻는 질문에 그렇게 들었다며 Yes를 대신하는 긍정의 표현으로 답하고 있다.
(C) 내용 오류: where 의문문에 어울리는 답변이다.

22

W-Am Is Mr. Morris meeting with the consultant today or tomorrow?
M-Cn (A) At an intersection.
(B) No, it's not.
(C) Ask his assistant.

intersection 교차로

번역 모리스 씨는 컨설턴트를 오늘 만나요, 아니면 내일 만나나요?
(A) 교차로에서요.
(B) 아닙니다.
(C) 그의 비서에게 물어보세요.

해설 **선택 의문문**

(A) 내용 오류: where 의문문에 어울리는 답변이다.

(B) Yes/No 답변 불가 오답: or 앞뒤가 구로 이루어진 선택 의문문에는 Yes/No도 대답일 수 없다.

(C) 정답: 주어진 선택 사항을 고르지 않고 비서에게 물어보라(Ask his assistant)며 만능 답변 형태로 답하고 있다.

23

W-Br Delivery of these kitchen appliances is free, right?

M-Au (A) Yes, but there's a charge for rush service.

(B) I need a new oven and refrigerator.

(C) It will take two to three days.

kitchen appliance 주방 기기   charge 요금

번역 이 주방용품 배송은 무료죠, 그렇죠?

(A) 네, 하지만 빠른 배송은 요금이 있어요.

(B) 저는 새 오븐과 냉장고가 필요해요.

(C) 이삼일 걸릴 겁니다.

해설 **부가 의문문**

(A) 정답: 무료 배송 여부를 묻는 질문에 긍정으로 답하고 무료가 아닌 경우에 대해 추가 설명을 덧붙이고 있다.

(B) 연상 어휘 오답: kitchen appliances에서 연상할 수 있는 oven과 refrigerator를 이용한 오답이다.

(C) 연상 어휘 오답: Delivery에서 연상할 수 있는 take two to three days를 이용한 오답이다.

24

M-Cn Won't the sales report be released soon?

W-Am (A) It's more stable.

(B) I don't think so.

(C) It begins at noon.

release 발표하다   stable 안정적인

번역 매출보고서가 곧 발표되지 않나요?

(A) 더 안정적입니다.

(B) 아닌 것 같은데요.

(C) 정오에 시작합니다.

해설 **부정 의문문**

(A) 내용 오류: 보고서 발표 여부를 묻는 질문에 안정적이라는 답변은 어울리지 않는다.

(B) 정답: 영업보고서가 곧 발표되지 않는지 묻는 질문에 그렇게 생각하지 않는다며 No를 대신하는 부정의 표현으로 답변하고 있다.

(C) 연상 어휘 오답: 질문의 soon에서 연상할 수 있는 begins at noon을 이용한 오답이다.

25

W-Br You can join us for Friday's business lunch, can't you?

M-Au (A) Sure, I'm planning to come along.

(B) He is one of the gym members.

(C) At the product launch event.

come along 함께 가다   launch 출시, 개시

번역 금요일 점심 회식에 오실 수 있죠, 그렇죠?

(A) 네, 함께 가려고 생각하고 있습니다.

(B) 그는 체육관 회원 중 한 명입니다.

(C) 제품 출시 행사에서요.

해설 **부가 의문문**

(A) 정답: 회식 참석 여부를 확인하는 질문에 긍정으로 답하고 있다.

(B) 대명사 오류: 질문에 he를 지칭할 대상이 없다.

(C) 유사 발음 오답: 질문의 lunch와 발음이 유사한 launch를 이용한 오답이다.

PART 3

● 패러프레이징

LISTENING PRACTICE

1. (A) **2.** (A) **3.** (B) **4.** (A) **5.** (B)
6. (A) **7.** (A) **8.** (B) **9.** (A) **10.** (B)
11. (A) **12.** (B) **13.** (A) **14.** (A)

1 M-Cn

My washing machine suddenly stopped working.

번역 제 세탁기가 갑자기 작동이 안 됩니다.

문제 남자는 어떤 문제점을 언급하는가?
(A) 가전제품이 제대로 작동하지 않는다.
(B) 세탁기가 배송되지 않았다.

패러 washing machine ❯ appliance
stop working ❯ malfunctioning

2 W-Am

I will fill out this application form right away.

번역 제가 지금 바로 신청서를 작성할게요.

문제 여자는 무엇을 하겠다고 말하는가?
(A) 문서 작업 완료하기 (B) 신청서 찾기

패러 fill out ❯ complete
application form ❯ paperwork

3 W-Br

Can you go over the budget proposal before I submit it to the manager?

번역 제가 예산 제안서를 관리자에게 제출하기 전에 검토해 주실 수 있나요?

문제 여자는 남자에게 무엇을 해달라고 요청하는가?
(A) 보고서 제출하기   (B) 문서 검토하기

패러 go over ❯ review
budget proposal ❯ document

4 W-Am

Moreover, free shuttle service to and from the hotel will be available.

번역 또한 호텔로 가거나 호텔에서 출발하는 무료 셔틀 서비스가 이용가능해질 것입니다.

문제 여자는 무엇이 이용 가능할 것이라고 말하는가?
(A) 교통편   (B) 식권

패러 shuttle service ❯ transportation

5 M-Cn

Be sure to bring the original receipt with you when you stop by our store.

번역 상점에 들르실 때 반드시 원본 영수증을 가져오세요.

문제 남자는 무엇을 요청하는가?
(A) 신분증   (B) 영수증

패러 receipt ❯ proof of purchase

6 W-Br

We will have more attendees than expected. It seems we don't have enough chairs.

번역 예상보다 참석자가 더 많을 거예요. 의자가 충분하지 않은 것 같군요.

문제 여자는 어떤 문제점을 언급하는가?
(A) 물품의 개수가 충분하지 않다.
(B) 가구의 상태가 좋지 않다.

패러 not enough ❯ insufficient
chairs ❯ items

7 W-Am

This evening, I'll go to the farewell party for our outgoing vice president Mr. Benson.

번역 오늘 저녁 저는 퇴임하는 부사장 벤슨 씨를 위한 송별회 파티에 갈 거예요.

문제 여자는 무엇을 할 것이라고 말하는가?
(A) 기념하는 모임에 참석한다.
(B) 송별회를 마련한다.

패러 farewell party ❯ celebratory gathering

8 M-Au

I've just received the bookshelves I ordered. But it looks like some parts are missing

번역 제가 주문했던 책장을 방금 받았어요. 그런데 부품 몇 개가 빠져 있네요.

문제 남자는 어떤 문제점을 언급하는가?
(A) 일부 정보가 잘못되었다.
(B) 주문품에 빠진 것이 있다.

(패러) missing ➤ incomplete

9 W-Am

> If they keep letting us down, we should consider hiring another caterer.

번역 만약 그들이 계속해서 우리를 실망시킨다면 다른 출장 요리 업체를 고용하는 것이 좋겠어요.

문제 여자는 무엇을 제안하는가?
(A) 다른 공급 업체를 찾는 것
(B) 임시 직원을 고용하는 것

(패러) caterer ➤ supplier

10 M-Au

> I recommend the K4 model. It's more affordable compared to other brands of similar size.

번역 저는 K4 모델을 추천해요. 비슷한 크기의 다른 제품들에 비해 가격이 더 적당합니다.

문제 남자는 제품의 어떤 점을 마음에 들어하는가?
(A) 크기가 작다.
(B) 가격이 적당하다.

(패러) affordable ➤ reasonable

11 W-Am

> Ben, do you have a minute? I'd like you to give some opinions about the new advertising campaign.

번역 벤 씨, 잠깐 시간이 되세요? 새 광고 캠페인에 대해 의견을 주셨으면 합니다.

문제 여자는 남자에게 무엇을 해달라고 요청하는가?
(A) 피드백 제공하기   (B) 새로운 광고 캠페인 만들기

(패러) give some opinions ➤ provide feedback

12 M-Au

> I've finished writing the article. I'll drop it off at your office tomorrow.

번역 기사 작성을 막 끝마쳤습니다. 내일 사무실로 갖다 드릴게요.

문제 남자는 무엇을 하겠다고 말하는가?
(A) 기사 수정하기
(B) 원고 제출하기

(패러) drop off ➤ submit
article ➤ writing

13 M-Cn

> Ms. Browning, a customer ordered some ink cartridges, but they are temporarily out of stock. What should I do?

번역 브라우닝 씨, 고객이 잉크 카트리지를 주문했는데 현재 재고가 없습니다. 어떻게 해야 할까요?

문제 남자는 잉크 카트리지에 대해 뭐라고 말하는가?
(A) 다 팔렸다.
(B) 생산이 중단됐다.

(패러) temporarily out of stock ➤ sold out

14 W-Am

> If you'd like, I can send the package by express delivery for a small extra fee.

번역 원하신다면 소정의 추가 금액을 받고 빠른 우편으로 소포를 보내드릴 수 있습니다.

문제 여자는 무엇을 하겠다고 제안하는가?
(A) 긴급 서비스 제공
(B) 수수료 면제

(패러) express delivery ➤ expedited service

●UNIT 01 주제/목적 문제

LISTENING PRACTICE   교재 p. 77

1. (C)   **2.** (A)   **3.** (C)   **4.** (D)

1

> W-Br Thank you for calling Indigo Publications. How may I help you?
> M-Cn Hello, I saw an advertisement for a senior editor position at your company, and I wondered if you could offer a few details about the position.
> W-Br Oh, I need to put you through to Ms. Perez, our hiring manager. Hold on, please.
>
> publication 출판   put through to ～로 연결하다

번역 여 인디고 출판사에 전화 주셔서 감사합니다. 어떻게 도와 드릴까요?
남 안녕하세요. 귀사의 선임 편집자 직책 공고를 보았습니다. 해당 직책에 대한 세부 사항을 알려주실 수 있는지 궁금합니다.
여 아, 저희 채용 관리자 페레즈 씨에게 연결해 드려야 할 것 같아요. 잠시만요.

화자들은 주로 무엇에 대해 이야기하는가?
(A) 앞으로 있을 면접
(B) 광고 캠페인
(C) 공석
(D) 채용 추천

해설 **전체 내용 – 대화 주제**
남자가 첫 대사에서 선임 편집자 직책 공고를 보았다(I saw an advertisement ~ at your company)고 했고 이 후 관련 대화가 이어지므로 정답은 (C)이다.

어휘 upcoming 다가오는, 앞으로 있을 advertising 광고 vacant 비어 있는 recommendation 추천

2

W-Am Russel, do you have a minute? I'm trying to find a new caterer. Can you recommend one?
M-Au What's wrong with the current one?
W-Am Have you seen their recent prices? We need a caterer that fits in our budget.
M-Au Well, let's ask other staff members then.

caterer 출장 요리 업체 recommend 추천하다 current 현재의 budget 예산

번역 여 러셀 씨, 잠시 시간 되세요? 새로운 케이터링 업체를 찾고 있는데요. 하나 추천해주시겠어요?
남 현재 케이터링 업체에 문제가 있나요?
여 최근 가격을 보셨나요? 우리 예산에 맞는 케이터링 업체가 필요해요.
남 음, 그럼 다른 직원들에게 물어보죠.

문제 대화는 주로 무엇에 관한 것인가?
(A) 케이터링 업체 찾기 (B) 회의 참석하기
(C) 예산 제시하기 (D) 회사 개업하기

해설 **전체 내용 – 대화 주제**
여자가 첫 대사에서 새로운 케이터링 업체를 찾고 있다 (I'm trying to find a new caterer)고 하자 남자가 현재 업체에 문제가 있는지 물은 후 이에 관련한 대화가 이어지므로 (A)가 정답이다.

어휘 attend 참석하다 conference 회의 present 제시하다, 보여주다

3

M-Cn Hello, this is Ron Vincent from Spotless Cleaners. I'm calling to discuss changing the time that we visit your office to clean.
W-Am Mr. Gupta handles that, but he's gone for the day. I can give him a message, though.
M-Cn Good. Please tell him we'd like to visit your building on Monday and Wednesday mornings.

번역 남 여보세요. 저는 스팟리스 클리너스의 론 빈센트입니다. 사무실 청소를 위한 방문 시간 변경에 관해 논의하고 싶어서 전화 드렸습니다.
여 굽타 씨가 그 건을 담당하는데 오늘은 퇴근했어요. 메시지는 전해드릴 수 있습니다.
남 좋습니다. 월요일과 수요일 오전에 건물을 방문하고 싶다고 전해주세요.

문제 전화를 건 목적은?
(A) 휴가를 요청하기 위해
(B) 서비스를 홍보하기 위해
(C) 일정을 변경하기 위해
(D) 임금 인상을 협상하기 위해

해설 **전체 내용 – 전화한 목적**
대화 초반부 남자가 사무실 청소 방문 시간 변경에 관해 논의하고 싶다(I'm calling ~ your office to clean)고 하므로 정답은 (C)이다.

어휘 request 요청하다 promote 홍보하다, 촉진하다 negotiate 협상하다 pay raise 임금 인상

4

M-Au Hello, this is Alex calling from Polaris Insurance. We booked a banquet room at your site next week, and I'd like to make an adjustment to our reservation.
W-Br Certainly. What do you have in mind?
M-Au I'd like the tables and chairs to be set up in small groups instead of long rows.

insurance 보험 banquet 연회 make an adjustment 조정하다, 변경하다 row 열, 줄

번역 남 여보세요. 저는 폴라리스 보험의 알렉스라고 합니다. 다음 주에 귀하의 장소에 연회장을 예약했는데 예약 사항을 변경했으면 합니다.
여 그러시죠. 어떤 걸 염두에 두고 계신가요?
남 테이블과 의자가 긴 열 대신 소그룹으로 배치됐으면 합니다.

문제 남자가 여자에게 전화를 건 이유는?
(A) 행사 시작 시간을 조정하기 위해
(B) 지급 일정에 대해 문의하기 위해
(C) 용품 배송을 확인하기 위해
(D) 가구 배치를 변경하기 위해

해설 **전체 내용 – 남자가 전화한 이유**
남자가 첫 대사에서 예약 조정을 원한다고 했고 마지막 대사에서 테이블과 의자 배치 변경이라고 조정의 내용을 구체화하고 있으므로 (D)가 정답이다.

어휘 adjust 조정하다 inquire 알아보다, 문의하다 delivery 배송 supplies 용품 arrangement 배열

●UNIT 02 화자 / 장소 문제

LISTENING PRACTICE
교재 p. 79

1. (B) **2.** (C) **3.** (B) **4.** (C)

1

> M-Cn Hello, I am here to return the books I borrowed.
>
> W-Am Hmm... It looks like you need to pay a late fee of 6 dollars.
>
> M-Cn I guess you're right. By the way, do you offer a notification service? I want to avoid the same mistake next time.
>
> late fee 연체료   notification 알림, 통지

번역   남 안녕하세요. 빌린 책을 반납하러 왔습니다.
　　　여 음, 연체료 6달러를 내셔야 할 것 같은데요.
　　　남 그럴 겁니다. 그런데 알림 서비스를 제공하시나요? 다음번엔 같은 실수를 하지 않도록 하려고요.

문제   여자는 누구이겠는가?
　　　(A) 공장 근로자　　　(B) 사서
　　　(C) 대학교수　　　　(D) 슈퍼마켓 관리자

해설   **전체 내용 – 여자의 신분**
　　　대화 초반부 남자가 책을 반납하러 왔다고 하자 여자가 도와주겠다고 말하므로 여자는 도서관 사서임을 알 수 있다. 따라서 정답은 (B)이다.

어휘   librarian 사서   faculty 교수진

2

> W-Am Welcome to Fairfax Print Shop.
>
> M-Au Hello. I have a digital file for an employee training manual I'd like printed. Do you do that?
>
> W-Am Yes, we do. Our store manager, Barbara, can help you with that.
>
> manual 설명서

번역   여 페어팩스 인쇄소에 오신 것을 환영합니다.
　　　남 안녕하세요. 출력하려는 직원 교육 설명서를 디지털 파일로 갖고 있어요. 출력해 주시나요?
　　　여 네. 저희 매장 관리자 바바라 씨가 도와주실 거예요.

문제   바바라 씨는 누구인가?
　　　(A) 인턴　　　　　(B) 고객
　　　(C) 관리자　　　　(D) 수리공

해설   **세부 내용 – 바바라의 신분**
　　　여자가 마지막 대사에서 매장 관리자 바바라(our store manager, Barbara)라고 했으므로 정답은 (C)이다.

3

> M-Au Hi. This is Oliver Wilson. I need to schedule a time to see Dr. Taylor for my annual teeth cleaning.
>
> W-Br Hi, Mr. Wilson. The doctor will be out of town during the second week of July, but any other week should be fine.
>
> M-Au I see. How about the week after he gets back? I can come at three o'clock on Wednesday.
>
> annual 매년의, 연례의

번역   남 안녕하세요. 저는 올리버 윌슨입니다. 매년 하는 치아 스케일링 때문에 테일러 박사님 진료 일정을 잡아야 해요.
　　　여 안녕하세요, 윌슨 씨. 선생님께서 7월 둘째 주에는 출장을 가세요. 하지만 나머지 주는 모두 괜찮습니다.
　　　남 알겠습니다. 돌아오신 다음 주는 어떨까요? 수요일 3시에 갈 수 있습니다.

문제   여자는 어디에서 일하는가?
　　　(A) 회의장　　　　(B) 치과
　　　(C) 여행사　　　　(D) 미용실

해설   **전체 내용 – 여자의 근무 장소**
　　　대화 초반부 남자가 치아 스케일링 진료 일정을 잡아야 한다고 하자 여자는 담당 의사의 부재를 알리며 가능한 날짜를 제시하고 있다. 따라서 정답은 (B)이다.

어휘   travel agency 여행사

4

> M-Au All right, Susan. Since it's your first day at work, I'll show you how we deal with packages and other mail brought in by customers.
>
> W-Am OK. I've completed the full training, but I haven't helped any actual customers yet.
>
> M-Au You'll catch on quickly. Let's get started.
>
> deal with ~을 다루다, 취급하다   complete 완료하다
> actual 실제의   catch on 이해하다

번역   남 그럼 수잔 씨. 오늘 근무 첫 날이니 고객이 접수한 소포와 우편을 어떻게 취급하는지 알려드릴게요.
　　　여 네. 교육을 다 이수했는데 실제 고객은 아직 응대해 보지 못했어요.
　　　남 금방 이해하실 겁니다. 시작해 보죠.

문제   대화는 어디에서 이루어지겠는가?
　　　(A) 실험실　　　　(B) 공립도서관
　　　(C) 우체국　　　　(D) 약국

해설   **전체 내용 – 대화 장소**
　　　남자가 첫 대사에서 여자에게 근무 첫 날이니 소포와 우편 취급 방법을 알려주겠다(Since it's your first day at

work ~ mail brought in by customers)고 하므로 정답은 (C)이다.

어휘 laboratory 실험실 pharmacy 약국

ACTUAL TEST

1. (C)	**2.** (A)	**3.** (C)	**4.** (C)	**5.** (A)
6. (C)	**7.** (B)	**8.** (A)	**9.** (D)	**10.** (D)
11. (C)	**12.** (A)	**13.** (A)	**14.** (C)	**15.** (D)
16. (D)	**17.** (C)	**18.** (A)	**19.** (B)	**20.** (A)
21. (C)	**22.** (C)	**23.** (B)	**24.** (A)	

1-3

W-Br Good evening. You've reached Julie's Dining. How may I help you?

M-Cn Hello. **1**I'd like to reserve a table for twelve people for this Friday at seven P.M. under the name Robert Kono. **2**Our department is celebrating the company's twenty-year anniversary.

W-Br Let's see… we're fully booked in the main dining room, but I could put you in one of our private rooms. There's an additional forty-dollar charge, though.

M-Cn **3**I'll check with my manager to see if that's all right. Just a moment, please.

---
reserve 예약하다 celebrate 축하하다 anniversary 기념일 be fully booked 예약이 꽉 차다 charge 요금

번역 여 안녕하세요. 줄리스 다이닝입니다. 어떻게 도와드릴까요?

남 안녕하세요. 이번 금요일 저녁 7시에 로버트 코노 이름으로 12명 식사를 예약하고 싶습니다. 저희 부서에서 회사 창립 20주년을 기념할 예정이에요.

여 한 번 볼게요. 주 식사실은 예약이 꽉 찼지만 저희 개인실 중 한 곳에 배정해 드릴 수 있습니다. 그런데 40달러의 추가 요금이 있어요.

남 괜찮을지 저희 관리자께 확인해 보겠습니다. 잠시만요.

1. 남자는 어떤 업체에 전화하는가?
(A) 디자인 업체   (B) 호텔
(C) 음식점   (D) 피트니스 센터

해설 전체 내용 – 남자가 전화한 업체
남자가 첫 대사에서 전화를 받은 여자에게 식사 예약을 문의하고 있으므로 정답은 (C)이다.

2. 남자가 업체를 방문하는 목적은?
(A) 기념일을 축하하기 위해
(B) 검사를 실시하기 위해

(C) 일자리에 지원하기 위해
(D) 제품을 홍보하기 위해

해설 전체 내용 – 남자의 업체 방문 목적
대화 중반부 남자가 식사 예약의 목적으로 회사 창립을 기념할 예정(Our department is ~ twenty-year anniversary)이라고 하므로 정답은 (A)이다.

어휘 conduct (특정한 활동을) 하다 inspection 검사 apply for ~에 지원하다 promote 홍보하다, 촉진하다

3. 남자는 무엇을 하겠다고 말하는가?
(A) 시간 확정하기   (B) 수표에 서명하기
(C) 관리자와 상의하기   (D) 추천하기

해설 세부 내용 – 앞으로 할 일
대화 후반부 여자가 추가 요금 40달러를 말하자, 남자는 이를 관리자에게 확인하겠다고 했으므로 관리자와 상의할 것임을 알 수 있다. 따라서 정답은 (C)이다.

어휘 confirm 확정하다 consult 상담하다 recommendation 추천

4-6

M-Au Hi, Olivia. Your annual evaluation is coming up soon. **4**I'd like to schedule some time to talk about your work one-on-one. Are you free this afternoon?

W-Am Yes, Mr. Sanders. **5**I'm working on the front-page article about the new park, but the deadline's not until tomorrow. Should I prepare anything for the meeting?

M-Au **6**If you can put together a file with a few articles you're proud of, that would be helpful. And don't be nervous. Everyone has been very happy with your work.

---
evaluation 평가 put together 준비하다, 만들다

번역 남 안녕하세요, 올리비아 씨. 연례 평가가 곧 다가오네요. 업무에 대해 일대일로 이야기할 시간을 잡고 싶은데요. 오늘 오후에 시간이 되세요?

여 네, 샌더스 씨. 새로운 공원에 관한 1면 기사를 쓰고 있긴 하지만, 마감 기한이 내일까지입니다. 회의를 위해 준비해야 할 것이 있을까요?

남 자신 있는 기사 몇 개로 파일을 준비해 오시면 도움이 될 것 같군요. 긴장하지 마세요. 모두가 올리비아 씨의 업무에 굉장히 만족스러워했으니까요.

4. 남자가 여자에게 만나자고 요청한 이유는?
(A) 의견 차이를 해결하기 위해
(B) 기술 훈련을 해 주기 위해
(C) 여자의 업무 성과를 논의하기 위해
(D) 기념 행사 계획을 짜기 위해

해설 전체 내용 – 남자가 만나자고 한 이유
남자가 첫 대사에서 연례 평가가 다가온다며 업무에 대해 이야기할 시간을 잡자고 했으므로 정답은 (C)이다.

어휘 resolve 해결하다 disagreement 의견 차이 celebration 기념 행사

5. 화자들은 어디에서 일하겠는가?
(A) 신문사　　　(B) 패션 디자인 업체
(C) TV 방송국　　(D) 건축업체

해설 전체 내용 – 근무 장소
업무에 대해 얘기하자는 남자의 말에 여자는 공원 관련 기사를 쓰고 있다는 얘기를 꺼내고 있으므로 신문사에서 근무한다고 추론할 수 있다. 따라서 정답은 (A)이다.

어휘 television network TV 방송국 architectural 건축의

6. 남자는 여자에게 무엇을 준비해 달라고 요청하는가?
(A) 질문 목록
(B) 세부 시간표
(C) 작품 모음집
(D) 마케팅 제안서

해설 세부 내용 – 남자의 요청 사항
남자가 마지막 대사에서 자신 있는 기사를 파일로 묶어 가져오면 좋겠다고 하므로 정답은 (C)이다.

어휘 timeline 일정표, 시각표 proposal 제안

7-9

M-Cn Angela, ⁷have you reserved a booth for our company at the regional career fair yet?

W-Br ⁸I originally booked us a standard booth but then decided to upgrade to a premium booth. The event planner said she would find a spot for us. I'm just waiting to hear back from her.

M-Cn All right. Is there anything that I can help you with? One of my client meetings was canceled, so I have some extra time.

W-Br ⁹Would you mind buying some colored paper and balloons so we can decorate the booth? They should be navy blue and silver, like our company colors.

regional 지역의 career fair 취업박람회 originally 원래 decorate 장식하다

번역 남 안젤라 씨, 지역 취업박람회에 우리 회사 부스를 예약했나요?
여 원래 일반 부스를 예약했는데 프리미엄 부스로 업그레이드하기로 결정했습니다. 행사 기획자가 우리를 위한 자리를 찾아주겠다고 했어요. 회신이 오기를 기다리고 있는 중입니다.

남 좋아요. 도와드릴 일이 있나요? 고객 회의 중 하나가 취소돼서 시간이 있어요.
여 부스를 장식할 수 있도록 색종이와 풍선을 좀 사 주시겠어요? 회사 색상처럼 진한 남색과 은색이어야 해요.

7. 대화는 주로 무엇에 관한 것인가?
(A) 회사 연회
(B) 채용 행사
(C) 교육 시간
(D) 광고 캠페인

해설 전체 내용 – 대화 주제
남자가 첫 대사에서 여자에게 취업박람회 부스를 예약했는지(have you reserved ~ career fair yet?) 묻는 질문으로 대화가 시작되고 있다. 따라서 정답은 (B)이다.

어휘 banquet 연회 recruitment 채용 advertising 광고

8. 여자는 무엇을 기다리는가?
(A) 업그레이드 확정
(B) 명세서
(C) 홍보 자료
(D) 최종 고객 명단

해설 세부 내용 – 여자가 기다리는 것
대화 초반부 여자가 프리미엄 부스로 업그레이드하기로 했고, 행사 기획자가 자리를 찾아주겠다고 해서 회신을 기다리는 중이라고 했으므로 정답은 (A)이다.

어휘 confirmation 확인, 확정 itemized 항목별로 구분된 promotional 홍보의, 판촉의 material 자료

9. 남자는 무엇을 하라고 요청 받았는가?
(A) 신규 고객 만나기
(B) 제안서 승인하기
(C) 현장에 일찍 도착하기
(D) 장식품 구입하기

해설 세부 내용 – 남자가 받은 요청 사항
대화 후반부 여자가 남자에게 부스 장식용 색종이와 풍선 구입을 요청했으므로 정답은 (D)이다.

어휘 approve 승인하다 proposal 제안 site 현장 purchase 구입하다 decoration 장식

10-12

M-Cn Hi, Sonya. Since I'm leaving early for my dental appointment, ¹⁰I'm wondering if there is anything important I'll miss from our bookstore's weekly meeting.

W-Am Actually, yes. ¹¹Starting from next month, we're going to close at 9 P.M. instead of 7 P.M. We're hoping that will bring in more customers who work late.

M-Cn Does that mean our usual shifts will change?

W-Am Yes. ¹²You should let me know which shifts you will be able to work. Give it some thought and get back to me about it sometime next week.

---

appointment 약속   weekly meeting 주간 회의
actually 사실   instead of ~ 대신   shift 교대 근무(시간)

번역 남 안녕하세요, 소냐 씨. 치과 예약 때문에 오늘 일찍 퇴근해서, 제가 서점 주간 회의에서 듣지 못할 중요한 일이 있는지 궁금합니다.
여 네, 사실 있어요. 다음 달부터 오후 7시가 아닌 오후 9시에 문을 닫을 예정입니다. 늦게까지 일하는 고객을 더 많이 유치하게 되길 바라고 있어요.
남 평상시 교대근무시간이 변경된다는 건가요?
여 네. 어떤 근무시간에 일할 수 있는지 알려주셔야 해요. 생각을 좀 해 보시고 다음 주 중에 답해주세요.

10. 화자들은 어디에서 일하는가?
(A) 음식점   (B) 치과
(C) 사무용품점   (D) 서점

해설 **전체 내용 – 근무 장소**
대화 초반부 남자가 our bookstore(서점)라고 언급하므로 정답은 (D)이다.

어휘 office supply 사무용품

11. 여자에 따르면 회사에 어떤 변화가 있을 것인가?
(A) 환불 정책이 개선될 것이다.
(B) 직원들이 보험 보장을 받기 시작할 것이다.
(C) 영업시간이 연장될 것이다.
(D) 서비스 요금이 더 올라갈 것이다.

해설 **전체 내용 – 회사에 있을 변화**
대화 중반부 여자가 폐점 시간을 7시에서 9시로 바꿀 예정(Starting from next month, we're going to close at 9 P.M. instead of 7 P.M.)이라고 했으므로 정답은 (C)이다.

어휘 policy 정책   insurance coverage 보험 보장   hours of operation 영업시간   extend 연장하다

12. 여자는 어떤 정보를 요청하는가?
(A) 남자가 일할 수 있는 시간
(B) 교육 요건
(C) 남자의 우편 주소
(D) 회의 안건

해설 **세부 내용 – 여자가 요청하는 정보**
여자가 마지막 대사에서 가능한 근무시간을 알려 달라(You should let me know which shifts you will be able to work)고 했으므로 (A)가 정답이다.

어휘 availability 이용 가능성   requirement 요건   agenda 안건

13-15

W-Br ¹³Thank you for calling First Wealth Bank. How may I direct your call?
M-Cn Hi, my name is Christopher Wilson, and ¹⁴I've lost my credit card. I need to cancel it right away.
W-Br Let me just find you in the system. OK, I've canceled the card. A new one will be sent to you within three business days.
M-Cn Would it be possible to change my mailing address over the phone? I haven't updated my contact details there, and I don't have an online account.
W-Br For security reasons, you'll have to come to the branch in person if you don't have an online account. ¹⁵You'll need proof of your new address such as a recent utility bill.

---

cancel 취소하다   business day 영업일   account 계정
security 보안   in person 직접   proof 증명   recent 최근의   utility bill 공과금 고지서

번역 여 퍼스트 웰스 은행에 전화 주셔서 감사합니다. 전화를 어디로 연결해 드릴까요?
남 안녕하세요. 제 이름은 크리스토퍼 윌슨입니다. 신용카드를 분실했어요. 바로 취소해야 합니다.
여 시스템에서 이름을 찾아보겠습니다. 네, 제가 카드를 취소해 드렸습니다. 새 카드가 영업일 기준 3일 이내에 발송됩니다.
남 전화로 제 우편물 배송지를 변경할 수 있을까요? 제 연락처를 업데이트하지 않았는데 저는 온라인 계정이 없어요.
여 보안상의 이유로 온라인 계정이 없으신 경우 직접 지점을 방문해 주셔야 합니다. 최근 공과금 고지서 등 새 주소지 증빙이 필요합니다.

13. 여자는 어디에서 일하겠는가?
(A) 금융기관   (B) 택배 회사
(C) 공익 기업   (D) 백화점

해설 **전체 내용 – 여자의 근무 장소**
여자가 첫 대사에서 퍼스트 웰스 은행에 전화 주어 감사하다(Thank you for calling First Wealth Bank)고 했으므로 정답은 (A)이다.

어휘 financial 금융의   courier 택배 회사   utility company 공익 기업

14. 남자가 전화를 건 목적은?
(A) 약속을 취소하기 위해
(B) 계좌를 새로 개설하기 위해
(C) 분실물을 신고하기 위해
(D) 지불하기 위해

64

해설 **전체 내용 – 전화한 목적**

대화 초반부 남자가 신용카드를 분실했다(I've lost my credit card)고 했으므로 정답은 (C)이다.

어휘 appointment 약속   open an account 계좌를 개설하다 make a payment 지불하다. 결제하다

15. 여자에 따르면 남자는 업체에 무엇을 가져가야 하는가?

(A) 확정 코드
(B) 작성된 불만 신고 양식
(C) 판매 영수증
(D) 주소지 증빙 자료

해설 **세부 내용 – 남자가 업체로 가져가야 하는 것**

여자가 마지막 대사에서 남자에게 공과금 고지서 등 새 주소지 증빙을 요청(You'll need proof of your new address such as a recent utility bill)했으므로 정답은 (D)이다.

어휘 confirmation 확인, 확정   complete a form 서식을 작성하다

16-18

M-Cn **16**Thank you for calling the EOS Telecommunications. How can I help you?

W-Am Hi, I'd like to change my mobile phone plan. Could you recommend one?

M-Cn OK, I can offer you the best plan based on your calling patterns. Would you like to continue using our prepaid options?

W-Am No, I don't mind changing to any of the monthly payment options if it's still within my budget.

M-Cn That's great. **17**We launched a new calling plan last month that allows users to have unlimited data usage.

W-Am That's good to hear. **18**How much is the new plan?

---

recommend 추천하다   based on ~에 기반하여 prepaid 선불된   monthly payment 월별 지불, 월 납부 budget 예산   unlimited 무제한의

번역 남 EOS 통신에 전화해 주셔서 감사합니다. 어떻게 도와 드릴까요?

여 안녕하세요. 제 휴대전화 요금제를 바꾸고 싶어요. 하나 추천해 주실 수 있을까요?

남 네. 통화 패턴에 기반해 가장 잘 맞는 요금제를 제공해 드릴 수 있습니다. 선불 옵션을 계속 사용하고 싶으신가요?

여 아니요. 제 예산 한도 내에 있다면 월 요금제 중 하나로 바꿔도 괜찮습니다.

남 좋습니다. 저희가 지난달에 사용자가 데이터를 무제한으로 이용할 수 있도록 하는 새 요금제를 출시했습니다.

여 그거 괜찮네요. 새 요금제는 얼마인가요?

16. 남자는 어디에서 일하는가?

(A) 보험회사   (B) 출장 요리 업체
(C) 배송업체   (D) 통신업체

해설 **전체 내용 – 남자의 근무 장소**

남자가 첫 대사에서 EOS 통신에 전화 주어 고맙다고 했고 여자가 전화 요금제 변경을 요청했으므로 정답은 (D)이다.

어휘 insurance 보험   shipping 배송, 선적

17. 남자에 따르면 지난달에 어떤 일이 있었는가?

(A) 광고 캠페인이 시작됐다.
(B) 일부 프로그램이 설치됐다.
(C) 옵션이 추가됐다.
(D) 업체가 이전했다.

해설 **세부 내용 – 지난달에 있었던 일**

대화 중반부 남자가 지난달에 새 요금제를 출시했다고 했다. 요금제 옵션이 추가된 것이므로 정답은 (C)이다.

어휘 launch 착수하다, 시작하다   install 설치하다   relocate 이전하다

18. 여자는 무엇에 대해 질문하는가?

(A) 서비스 요금   (B) 회사 위치
(C) 예약 가능 여부   (D) 경비 절감 방법

해설 **세부 내용 – 여자가 질문하는 것**

여자가 마지막 대사에서 새 요금제(new plan)는 얼마인지 물었으므로 정답은 (A)이다.

어휘 availability 이용 가능성   reservation 예약   reduce 줄이다   expense 비용, 경비

19-21

M-Au Hi, Ms. Hanson. Thank you for agreeing to present at this year's conference. **19**Your speech last year was very well received, so everyone is excited to hear you again.

W-Am I'm flattered. By the way, I just arrived, so I still need to contact the other conference organizers.

M-Au Oh, no problem. **20**I'll call them and tell them you've arrived. I actually have a copy of tonight's schedule right here. You'll be presenting right after Tony Ali.

W-Am **21**Tony Ali? Didn't he write *Best Choices for Hard Situations*? That's one of my favorite books. I can't believe I'll get to meet him.

---

present 참석하다, 출석하다   conference 회의   be flattered 어깨가 으쓱해지다   organizer 주최자, 조직자

번역 남 안녕하세요, 핸슨 씨. 올해 회의에 참석하는 데 동의해 주셔서 감사합니다. 작년에 해 주신 연설의 반응이 굉장히 좋아서 모두가 다시 듣고 싶어합니다.

여 정말 기쁩니다. 그런데 제가 이제 막 도착해서 다른 회의 주최자들에게 연락을 해 봐야 해요.

남 네, 괜찮습니다. 제가 전화해서 도착하셨다고 얘기할게요. 제가 오늘 저녁 일정표 사본을 갖고 있는데요. 토니 알리 씨 바로 뒤에 발표하시겠네요.

여 토니 알리 씨요? 〈난관에 처했을 때 최선의 선택〉을 쓰시지 않았나요? 제가 가장 좋아하는 책 중 하나예요. 만나뵙게 되다니 믿을 수가 없네요.

19. 남자는 여자에 대해 뭐라고 말하는가?
(A) 여자가 쓸 방이 준비되어 있다.
(B) 여자의 연설이 인기가 높았다.
(C) 여자의 일정이 변경됐다.
(D) 여자의 신분 확인 명찰에 오류가 있다.

해설 **세부 내용 – 여자에 대해 언급된 사항**
대화 초반부 남자가 여자에게 작년에 한 연설의 반응이 아주 좋았다(Your speech last year was very well received)고 하므로 정답은 (B)이다.

어휘 identification 신원 확인

20. 남자는 여자에게 무엇을 해 주겠다고 말하는가?
(A) 다른 사람들에게 여자가 도착했다고 알리기
(B) 여자를 동료에게 소개하기
(C) 여자의 자리를 맡아두기
(D) 여자에게 책을 빌려주기

해설 **세부 내용 – 남자의 제안 사항**
대화 중반부 남자가 여자의 도착을 전화로 알리겠다(I'll call them and tell them you've arrived)고 했으므로 (A)가 정답이다.

어휘 inform 알리다 colleague 동료

21. 토니 알리 씨는 누구이겠는가?
(A) 회사 임원 (B) 행사 기획자
(C) 저자 (D) 케이터링 담당자

해설 **세부 내용 – 토니 알리 씨의 신분**
여자가 마지막 대사에서 토니 알리의 저서를 언급하므로 (C)가 정답이다.

어휘 corporate 회사의 executive 임원 author 저자

22-24

M-Cn Good morning. I'm Mike Lincoln. I got a call yesterday about a malfunctioning conveyor belt, so ²²I'm here to fix it.

W-Br Oh, thanks for coming, Mr. Lincoln. Can you follow me to the security desk? ²³I need to sign you in and give you a visitor card.

M-Cn Sure. ²⁴Is it OK if I leave my bag here? It has a lot of heavy tools in it, so I'd rather not carry it around unnecessarily.

malfunctioning 오작동 fix 고치다, 수리하다 security 보안 sign in 이름을 적다 unnecessarily 불필요하게

번역 남 안녕하세요. 저는 마이크 링컨입니다. 어제 컨베이어 벨트 오작동에 관해 전화를 받고 고치러 왔습니다.

여 아, 와 주셔서 감사합니다, 링컨 씨. 보안 데스크까지 저를 따라오실래요? 성함을 기록하고 방문자 카드를 드려야 합니다.

남 네. 제 가방을 여기 둬도 될까요? 안에 무거운 공구가 많아서 불필요하게 가지고 돌아다니고 싶지 않아서요.

22. 남자가 방문한 목적은 무엇이겠는가?
(A) 불만을 제기하려고 (B) 제품을 판매하려고
(C) 기계를 수리하려고 (D) 관리자에게 이야기하려고

해설 **전체 내용 – 남자의 방문 목적**
남자가 첫 대사에서 기기 오작동 전화를 받고 고치러 왔다 (I'm here to fix it)고 했으므로 정답은 (C)이다.

어휘 file a complaint 불만을 제기하다, 고소하다 supervisor 감독관, 관리자

23. 남자는 여자에게서 무엇을 받겠는가?
(A) 안내도 (B) 방문자 출입증
(C) 사용설명서 (D) 직장 유니폼

해설 **세부 내용 – 남자가 받을 것**
대화 중반부 여자가 남자에게 이름을 쓰고 방문자 카드를 주어야 한다(I need to sign you in and give you a visitor card)고 하므로 정답은 (B)이다.

어휘 guidance 안내 instruction 설명

24. 남자는 무엇을 가지고 왔는가?
(A) 공구 가방 (B) 보안 인증서
(C) 생산 일정표 (D) 제품 카탈로그

해설 **세부 내용 – 남자가 가지고 온 것**
남자가 마지막 대사에서 무거운 공구가 든 가방을 맡겨도 될지 물었으므로 정답은 (A)이다.

어휘 security 보안 credential 자격 인증서

●UNIT 03 문제점 / 걱정거리 문제

LISTENING PRACTICE 교재 p. 83

1. (B) **2.** (B) **3.** (A) **4.** (C)

1

M-Au Hello. I'm trying to use your software to make video calls. The audio is OK, but the video is often blurry.

W-Br Usually, that problem is caused by a slow Internet connection. You should speak to your Internet service provider.

M-Au Oh, I guess I'll need to do that. Thanks.

> video call 화상통화 blurry 흐릿한, 모호한 connection 연결, 접속

번역 남 안녕하세요. 화상통화를 하기 위해 귀사의 소프트웨어를 사용 중인데요. 음향은 괜찮은데 영상이 종종 흐릿해요.

여 보통 그 문제는 인터넷 접속이 느려서 생기는데요. 인터넷 서비스 공급업체에 한번 얘기해보세요.

남 아, 그래야겠네요. 감사합니다.

문제 남자는 채팅 소프트웨어의 어떤 문제점을 언급하는가?
(A) 오디오가 손상됐다.
(B) 비디오 화질이 좋지 않다.
(C) 텍스트 기능이 느리게 작동한다.
(D) 그룹 채팅 기능이 작동하지 않는다.

해설 **세부 내용 – 남자가 언급하는 문제점**
대화 초반부 남자가 음향은 괜찮은데 영상이 흐릿하다(The audio is OK, but the video is often blurry)고 했으므로 정답은 (B)이다.

어휘 distort 왜곡하다

2

W-Am I tried to log in to your Web site, but I got an error message saying my username was invalid.

M-Au I'm sorry. Our Web site is undergoing maintenance right now, and it will be down for another few hours.

W-Am Well, that's disappointing.

M-Au To compensate you for the wait, we will give you free access to some of our popular media content.

> invalid 인식이 불가능한, 유효하지 않은 undergo 겪다 maintenance 유지 보수 disappointing 실망스러운 compensate 보상하다

번역 여 웹사이트에 로그인하려고 시도했는데 제 사용자명이 인식되지 않는다는 오류 메시지를 받았어요.

남 죄송합니다. 저희 웹사이트는 현재 보수 작업이 진행되고 있어서 앞으로 몇 시간 동안 연결이 안 될 겁니다.

여 음, 실망스럽네요.

남 기다리시게 한 것에 대한 보상으로 저희 인기 미디어 콘텐츠의 무료 이용권을 드리겠습니다.

문제 여자는 어떤 문제점을 언급하는가?
(A) 패스워드를 잊어버렸다.
(B) 웹사이트에 접속이 안 된다.
(C) 잡지를 배송할 수 없다.
(D) 온라인 구매를 할 수 없다.

해설 **세부 내용 – 문제점**
여자가 첫 대사에서 웹사이트 로그인 시도 중 오류 메시지를 받았다(I tried to log in ~ my username was invalid)고 했으므로 정답은 (B)이다.

어휘 access 접속하다. 접근하다 make a purchase 구입하다

3

M-Cn Ms. Lucas, what do you think about adding a healthy line of yogurt to the food we produce?

W-Br We're only equipped to make dry goods. I'm worried we would have to spend too much on machinery to add a dairy product.

M-Cn You know, it might be worth it. How about conducting a survey on this matter?

> produce 생산하다 equipped 갖춘 dairy product 유제품 conduct a survey 설문조사를 실시하다

번역 남 루카스 씨, 저희가 생산하는 식료품에 건강한 요거트 제품을 추가하는 것에 대해 어떻게 생각하세요?

여 우리는 건조 식품을 만들 장비만 갖췄습니다. 유제품 추가를 위한 기계류에 돈을 너무 많이 써야 하는 건 아닌지 우려스럽습니다.

남 그럴 만한 가치가 있을 겁니다. 이 문제에 대해 설문조사를 실시하면 어떨까요?

문제 여자는 어떤 점을 우려하는가?
(A) 장비에 지나치게 투자하는 것
(B) 정부 검사에 불합격하는 것
(C) 자격을 갖춘 근로자를 찾는 것
(D) 가격 경쟁력을 유지하는 것

해설 **세부 내용 – 여자의 걱정거리**
대화 중반부 여자가 유제품 기계류에 너무 많은 돈을 써야 하는 건 아닌지 우려스럽다고 했으므로 정답은 (A)이다.

어휘 invest 투자하다 equipment 장비 inspection 검사 qualified 자격을 갖춘 competitive 경쟁력 있는

4

W-Br Hi, James. Thanks for the excellent photographs. I'd like you to work for us again for the next project.

M-Cn That would be great, Amy. However, I checked my bank account last night and my wages from the last job haven't arrived. Could you look into this for me?

W-Br I apologize. I'll check it right away.

> account 계좌 wage 임금. 급여 apologize 사과하다

번역 여 안녕하세요, 제임스 씨. 멋진 사진 감사합니다. 다음 프로젝트에서도 저희와 다시 일해 주셨으면 합니다.

남 그랬으면 좋겠습니다, 에이미 씨. 그런데 어젯밤에 은행 계좌를 확인했는데 지난번 일에 대한 급여가 들어오지 않았어요. 알아봐주실 수 있나요?

여 죄송합니다. 바로 확인해볼게요.

문제 남자는 어떤 우려 사항을 언급하는가?
(A) 마감 기한을 지키지 못할 수도 있다.
(B) 여자의 온라인 계좌에 접속이 안 된다.
(C) 지불을 받지 못했다.
(D) 어떤 장소에서 먼 곳에 산다.

해설 **세부 내용 – 남자의 우려 사항**
대화 중반부 남자가 급여가 안 들어왔다(my wages from the last job haven't arrived)고 하므로 정답은 (C)이다.

어휘 meet a deadline 기한을 맞추다 venue 장소

●UNIT 04 요청 / 제안 / 제공 문제

LISTENING PRACTICE
교재 p. 85

1. (A) **2.** (C) **3.** (B) **4.** (C)

1

M-Au Hi, I'm a delivery driver for BDL Shipping. I'm at your building with a package, but no one's here.
W-Am Really? A receptionist should be there.
M-Au Well, this package requires a signature. Should I come back later in the day?
W-Am Can you stay there for five minutes? I can be right over to sign for it.

shipping 운송 receptionist 안내 데스크 직원

번역 남 안녕하세요, 저는 BDL 운송의 배달 기사입니다. 배송 물품을 가지고 건물에 왔는데 아무도 안 계시네요.
여 정말요? 안내 데스크 직원이 있어야 하는데요.
남 음, 이 배송물품은 서명이 필요한데요. 이따가 다시 와야 할까요?
여 5분만 거기 계실 수 있나요? 제가 바로 가서 서명할 수 있어요.

문제 여자는 남자에게 무엇을 해 달라고 요청하는가?
(A) 몇 분 기다리기
(B) 제품 포장하기
(C) 메시지 전달하기
(D) 다른 사무실 방문하기

해설 **세부 내용 – 여자의 요청 사항**
대화 후반부 남자가 다시 와야 하는지 묻자, 여자는 5분만 거기 있어 줄 수 있는지(Can you stay there for five minutes?) 묻고 있다. 따라서 정답은 (A)이다.

어휘 deliver 전달하다

2

W-Am Hello. I'm interested in getting some water bottles made with my company's logo on them.
M-Au All right. We do custom printing for all kinds of merchandise.
W-Am That's great. Could I get a sample of the finished product before placing a large order?

custom 맞춤형의, 주문 제작의 merchandise 상품
finished product 완제품 place an order 주문을 넣다

번역 여 안녕하세요. 저희 회사 로고를 넣어 물병을 제작하는데 관심이 있어요.
남 알겠습니다. 저희는 모든 종류의 상품에 맞춤형 인쇄를 합니다.
여 좋아요. 대량 주문을 하기 전에 완제품 견본을 받아볼 수 있나요?

문제 여자는 무엇을 요청하는가?
(A) 대량 구입 할인
(B) 제품 카탈로그
(C) 견본 제품
(D) 명함

해설 **세부 내용 – 여자가 요청하는 것**
대화 후반부 여자가 주문 전에 완제품 견본을 받을 수 있는지(Could I get a sample of the finished product before placing a large order?) 묻고 있으므로 정답은 (C)이다.

어휘 bulk discount 대량 구입으로 인한 할인

3

M-Au Nina, our client just informed me that eight of them will be visiting our branch instead of five.
W-Am I was going to take them to see an opera, but I can't buy any more tickets. They're completely sold out.
M-Au Well, I know there's an art exhibit at the Muse Gallery. Why don't you go there instead?
W-Am Good idea. Thanks for the suggestion.

instead of ~ 대신 completely 완전히 sold out
매진된 exhibit 전시 suggestion 제안

번역 남 니나 씨, 고객 다섯 명이 아닌 여덟 명이 저희 지점을 방문할 예정이라고 방금 연락을 받았어요.

여 음… 오페라를 관람하러 모시고 갈 예정이었는데 티켓을 더 구입할 수가 없어요. 완전히 매진됐거든요.

남 뮤즈 갤러리에서 미술 전시회가 있는 것으로 알고 있는데요. 대신 거기 가면 어때요?

여 좋은 생각이네요. 제안해 주셔서 감사합니다.

문제 남자는 무엇을 하자고 제안하는가?
(A) 행사 연기하기
(B) 전시회 참석하기
(C) 온라인으로 이용 가능 여부 확인하기
(D) 구인공고에 지원하기

해설 **세부 내용 – 제안 사항**
대화 후반부 남자가 미술 전시회가 있다며 가자(Why don't you go there instead?)고 제안하고 있으므로 (B)가 정답이다.

어휘 postpone 연기하다, 미루다 exhibition 전시 apply for ~에 지원하다 job opening 구인, 공석

4

M-Cn Hi, Lily. How are you settling in here? I'd like to do anything I can to help you get comfortable.

W-Br Thanks, Mr. Brown. There is one thing you could help with. I need a permit to use the parking garage.

M-Cn You can get that from security. If you want, I can take you there.

---

settle in 적응하다 permit 허가증 parking garage 주차장 security 보안

번역 남 안녕하세요, 릴리 씨. 여기서 적응하시기에 어때요? 편해지시는 데 도움이 될 수 있는 일이 있다면 해 드릴게요.

여 감사합니다, 브라운 씨. 도와주실 일이 한 가지 있어요. 주차장 사용 허가증을 받아야 해요.

남 보안팀에서 받으시면 돼요. 원하신다면 데려다 드릴게요.

문제 남자는 여자에게 무엇을 해 주겠다고 제안하는가?
(A) 여자에게 동료 소개해 주기
(B) 장비 제공하기
(C) 여자를 사무실로 데려가기
(D) 추천서 써 주기

해설 **세부 내용 – 남자의 제안 사항**
남자가 마지막 대사에서 여자가 찾아가야 할 사무실을 알려주며 원하면 데려다 주겠다(I can take you there)고 제안하고 있다. 따라서 정답은 (C)이다.

어휘 colleague 동료 recommendation letter 추천서

PART 3

1. (C)	**2.** (B)	**3.** (D)	**4.** (D)	**5.** (C)
6. (B)	**7.** (B)	**8.** (D)	**9.** (A)	**10.** (C)
11. (A)	**12.** (D)	**13.** (B)	**14.** (C)	**15.** (D)
16. (C)	**17.** (C)	**18.** (B)	**19.** (B)	**20.** (A)
21. (D)	**22.** (B)	**23.** (C)	**24.** (D)	

1-3

W-Am [1]You've reached Golden Taxi Cabs, taxi service with a smile. Can I help you?

M-Au Yes. I took one of your cabs from the airport yesterday, and I'm afraid [2]I left my suitcase in the back seat. It has my credit card in it, so it's a little urgent. Did a driver turn one in?

W-Am Oh dear. I'm afraid not. It's possible that it's still in the car and he hasn't noticed it, though. [3]Do you remember the driver's name?

M-Au Unfortunately, I don't. He was a younger gentleman with blond hair, though. I hope that helps.

---

cab 택시 urgent 긴급한 turn in 돌려주다, 반납하다 notice 알아차리다

번역 여 미소로 모시는 택시 서비스, 골든 택시입니다. 어떻게 도와드릴까요?

남 네. 어제 골든 택시를 공항에서 탔는데 뒷자리에 여행 가방을 놓고 내린 것 같아요. 안에 신용카드가 들어 있어서 좀 급해요. 운전기사가 갖다 주신 것이 있나요?

여 아, 없는 것 같아요. 그런데 아직 차 안에 있고 운전기사가 알아차리지 못했을 수도 있어요. 운전기사 이름을 기억하세요?

남 안타깝게도 기억하지 못해요. 금발의 젊은 남자분이긴 했는데요. 도움이 됐으면 좋겠어요.

1. 여자는 어디에서 일하는가?
(A) 공항
(B) 소매점
(C) 택시 회사
(D) 회의장

해설 **전체 내용 – 여자의 근무 장소**
여자가 첫 대사에서 미소로 모시는 택시 서비스, 골든 택시(You've reached Golden Taxi Cabs, taxi service with a smile)라고 인사말을 하므로 정답은 (C)이다.

어휘 retail store 소매점 conference center 회의장

2. 남자는 어떤 문제점을 언급하는가?
(A) 전화번호를 잊어버렸다.
(B) 짐 하나를 분실했다.
(C) 건물을 찾지 못하고 있다.
(D) 비행기를 놓쳤다.

해설 **세부 내용 – 문제점**
남자가 첫 대사에서 택시에 가방을 놓고 내렸다(I left my suitcase in the back seat)고 했으므로 정답은 (B)이다.

3. 여자는 남자에게 무엇을 요청하는가?
(A) 예약번호　　　　(B) 신용카드 결제
(C) 계좌 비밀번호　　(D) 택시 운전기사 이름

해설 **세부 내용 – 여자의 요청 사항**
여자는 두 번째 대사에서 기사 이름을 기억하는지(Do you remember the driver's name?) 물었다. 따라서 정답은 (D)이다.

어휘 reservation 예약　account 계좌

4-6

M-Au ⁴Are you looking forward to the summer retreat at Glade Mountain next week? It will have to be really special to match last year's trip.

W-Br ⁴Yes, I am. I agree, I really enjoyed it last year. Our company really puts on fantastic events for the employees.

M-Au It sure does. I've been asked to help plan it this year. I have to keep the activities a secret, but ⁵you should pack some sturdy walking boots.

W-Br How mysterious! Okay, I'll do that. We're staying at the Glade Mountain Resort, right?

M-Au That's right. It has a sauna and gym facilities on site. ⁶I'm mostly looking forward to visiting the rooftop pool, though.

---

look forward to 고대하다　retreat 피정, 야유회　match 필적하다, 맞먹다　employee 직원　activity 활동　sturdy 견고한, 튼튼한　facility 시설　rooftop 옥상

번역 남 다음 주 글레이드 마운틴에서 있을 하계 야유회가 기대되세요? 작년 야유회에 필적하려면 굉장히 특별해야 할 거예요.
여 네, 기다려져요. 저도 동의해요. 작년 야유회가 무척 좋았거든요. 우리 회사는 직원들을 위해 정말 멋진 행사를 많이 열어요.
남 맞아요. 올해 기획을 도와 달라는 요청을 받았는데요. 활동들은 비밀에 부쳐야 하지만 견고한 워킹화를 준비해야 할 겁니다.
여 정말 알 수가 없네요! 좋아요, 그럴게요. 글레이드 마운틴 리조트에 투숙하죠, 그렇죠?

남 맞습니다. 사우나와 운동 시설이 갖춰져 있어요. 그런데 저는 옥상 수영장에 정말 가 보고 싶어요.

4. 화자들은 무엇에 대해 이야기하는가?
(A) 회사 합병
(B) 잠재 고객들과의 회의
(C) 송년회
(D) 회사 야유회

해설 **전체 내용 – 대화 주제**
남자가 첫 대사에서 야유회가 기대되는지(Are you looking forward to ~ next week?) 묻자 여자가 그렇다고 한 후 야유회 관련 대화가 이어지므로 정답은 (D)이다.

어휘 corporate 회사의　merger 합병　potential 잠재적인　excursion 짧은 단체 여행

5. 남자는 여자에게 무엇을 하라고 제안하는가?
(A) 일부 활동 신청하기
(B) 교통편 마련하기
(C) 특정 의류품 챙기기
(D) 장소에 일찍 도착하기

해설 **세부 내용 – 남자의 제안 사항**
대화 중반부 남자가 여자에게 견고한 워킹화를 준비하라(you should ~ walking boots)고 제안하므로 정답은 (C)이다.

어휘 sign up for ~을 신청하다　arrange 마련하다, 주선하다　specific 특정한

6. 남자는 리조트의 어떤 시설이 가장 기대된다고 말하는가?
(A) 사우나
(B) 수영장
(C) 체육관
(D) 음식점

해설 **세부 내용 – 남자가 가장 기대하는 시설**
남자가 마지막 대사에서 옥상 수영장에 정말 가고 싶다(I'm mostly looking forward to visiting the rooftop pool, though)고 하므로 정답은 (B)이다.

어휘 amenity 편의 시설

7-9

M-Cn Hi, Susan. Did you hear the news that our CEO announced this morning? ⁷It seems we are going to open another office in Marble City.

W-Am Oh, you live in Marble City, don't you? ⁸You should consider asking for a move to the new branch.

M-Cn That's not a bad idea. Actually, I have to go and meet a client now. ⁹Could you read the memo and find out how many staff members they need?

W-Am **⁹Sure, I can do that for you. I'll let you know** this afternoon.

---

announce 발표하다, 알리다 branch 지점

번역 남 안녕하세요, 수잔 씨. 저희 CEO께서 오늘 아침 발표한 소식을 들었나요? 마블 시티에 새 사무실을 열 것 같아요.

여 아, 마블 시티에 사시죠, 그렇죠? 새 지점으로 전근 요청을 고려해 보시면 좋겠네요.

남 나쁘지 않죠. 사실 제가 지금 고객을 만나러 가야 해서요. 회람을 읽어 보시고 몇 명의 직원이 필요한지 알려주실 수 있어요?

여 네, 그렇게 해 드릴게요. 오늘 오후에 알려드리겠습니다.

7. 대화의 주제는?
(A) CEO의 은퇴
(B) 회사 확장
(C) 직원 장려금 제도
(D) 교육 과정

해설 **전체 내용 – 대화 주제**
대화 초반부 남자가 마블 시티에 새 사무실을 오픈할 것 같다(It seems ~ in Marble City)고 했으므로 정답은 (B)이다.

어휘 retirement 은퇴, 퇴직 expansion 확장 incentive 장려금

8. 여자는 무엇을 제안하는가?
(A) 서류 읽기
(B) 기차를 타고 출근하기
(C) 가족 일원들과 상의하기
(D) 전근 신청하기

해설 **세부 내용 – 여자의 제안 사항**
새 지점을 열 것 같다는 남자에게 여자는 새 지점으로 전근 요청을 고려해보라고 하므로 정답은 (D)이다.

어휘 transfer 이동, 전근

9. 여자는 무엇을 하는 데 동의하는가?
(A) 정보 알아내기
(B) 직원들에게 회람 보내기
(C) 회의 일정 출력하기
(D) 면접 진행하기

해설 **세부 내용 – 여자가 동의하는 것**
대화 후반부 남자가 필요한 직원 수를 알려달라고 요청하자, 여자가 그러겠다고 했으므로 정답은 (A)이다.

어휘 itinerary 일정 conduct (특정한 활동 등을) 하다

10-12 3인 대화

M-Au Good afternoon. **¹⁰I purchased a self-assembly cabinet here, but two of the components were not in the box. Can I get those?**

W-Am I'm not sure. **¹¹Let me check with my manager.** Ms. Jones, can we replace individual parts that weren't in a self-assembly furniture box?

W-Br They can be requested directly from the manufacturer. But **¹¹it will take quite some time. ¹²You're better off bringing the item back and exchanging it for a new one.**

M-Au All right. I'll do that. **¹²I don't have it with me now, so I'll come back after lunch.**

---

purchase 구입하다 assembly 조립 component 부품
replace 교체하다 individual 각각의, 개개의 parts 부품
request 요청하다 manufacturer 제조업자 be better
off 더 낫다 exchange 교환하다

번역 남 안녕하세요. 여기서 셀프 조립 캐비닛을 구입했는데 부품 두 개가 상자에 들어있지 않습니다. 받을 수 있을까요?

여1 잘 모르겠습니다. 관리자와 확인해 보겠습니다. 존스씨, 셀프 조립 가구 상자에 들어있지 않았던 개별 부품을 교체할 수 있나요?

여2 부품은 제조업체에서 바로 요청할 수 있어요. 하지만 시간이 좀 걸립니다. 물건을 다시 가져와서 새 걸로 교환하는 편이 더 낫습니다.

남 알겠습니다. 그렇게 할게요. 지금은 갖고 있지 않으니 점심 시간 이후에 다시 오겠습니다.

10. 남자가 업체를 방문한 목적은?
(A) 일부 제품을 교환하기 위해
(B) 구입하기 위해
(C) 빠진 부품들을 구하기 위해
(D) 배송을 처리하기 위해

해설 **전체 내용 – 남자의 업체 방문 목적**
남자가 첫 대사에서 구입품의 일부 부품이 없다며, 받을 수 있는지(Can I get those?) 물었으므로 정답은 (C)이다.

어휘 merchandise 상품, 물품 make a purchase 구입하다
obtain 얻다, 구하다

11. 존스 씨는 제조업체의 어떤 문제점을 언급하는가?
(A) 절차가 오래 걸린다.
(B) 도산할 것이다.
(C) 제품 생산을 중단했다.
(D) 환불 처리가 안 된다.

해설 **세부 내용 – 제조 업체의 문제점**
대화 중반부 첫 번째 여자가 관리인인 존스에게 부품 교체 가능 여부를 묻자, 두 번째 여자가 존스가 시간이 좀 걸린다(But it will take quite some time)고 했으므로 정답은 (A)이다.

어휘 processing 가공, 처리   go out of business 도산하다 discontinue 생산을 중단하다

12. 남자는 오늘 오후에 무엇을 할 것인가?
(A) 조립 서비스 이용하기
(B) 존스 씨에게 연락하기
(C) 제조업체에 전화하기
(D) 업체로 제품 가져오기

해설 **세부 내용 – 남자가 오후에 할 일**
대화 후반부 두 번째 여자가 새 제품으로의 교환을 제안했고, 남자가 지금은 없으니 다시 오겠다(I don't have it with me now, so I'll come back after lunch)고 했으므로 정답은 (D)이다.

어휘 manufacturing 제조

13-15

M-Cn Amanda, **13**do you have time this afternoon to pick up our client, Mr. Liu, from the airport and take him to his hotel? I was supposed to do it, but the shipment from the Atlanta Corporation has arrived, so **14**I have to help with unloading the goods and check if there's any damage.

W-Am Sure, I can handle that. There will be some parking fees at the airport. **15**Should I just pay cash for those?

M-Cn It would be better to use the company credit card. I'll get it for you.

---

be supposed to ~하기로 되어 있다. ~할 예정이다
shipment 적하물, 수송품   unload 내리다   damage 훼손
handle 처리하다   pay cash 현금으로 지불하다

번역 남 아만다 씨, 오늘 오후에 공항에서 고객 리우 씨를 픽업해 호텔로 모셔다 드릴 시간이 되나요? 제가 하기로 되어 있었는데 애틀랜타 코퍼레이션에서 보낸 수송품이 도착해서 물건을 내리고 훼손 물품이 있는지 확인하는 일을 도와야 하거든요.
여 네, 제가 할 수 있어요. 공항에서 주차요금이 나올 텐데요. 현금으로 지불해야 하나요?
남 회사 신용카드를 이용하는 편이 나을 겁니다. 제가 구해 드릴게요.

13. 여자는 무엇을 요청 받았는가?
(A) 계약서에 서명하기
(B) 누군가를 차로 태워주기
(C) 제품 몇 가지를 주문하기
(D) 항공권 구입하기

해설 **세부 내용 – 여자가 받은 요청**
남자가 첫 대사에서 여자에게 리우 씨를 픽업해 호텔에 내려 줄 수 있는지(do you have time ~ to his hotel?) 물었으므로 정답은 (B)이다.

어휘 sign a contract 계약서에 서명하다   give ~ a ride ~을 차로 태워주다   purchase 구입하다

14. 남자가 오늘 오후에 바쁜 이유는?
(A) 면접을 실시할 것이다.
(B) 긴급한 보고서 마감이 있다.
(C) 수송품을 점검할 것이다.
(D) 고객 사무실을 방문할 것이다.

해설 **세부 내용 – 남자가 오후에 바쁜 이유**
대화 중반부 남자가 부탁 이유로 물건을 내리고 물품 검사를 도와야 한다(I have to help ~ any damage)고 했으므로 정답은 (C)이다.

어휘 urgent 긴급한   inspect 점검하다, 검사하다

15. 여자는 무엇에 대해 문의하는가?
(A) 배송 주소   (B) 도착 시간
(C) 검사 결과   (D) 결제 방법

해설 **세부 내용 – 여자가 문의하는 내용**
대화 후반부 여자가 주차요금을 현금으로 지불해야 하는지 묻고 있으므로 정답은 (D)이다.

어휘 inspection 검사, 점검

16-18 3인 대화

M-Cn Thank you both for stopping by. I heard you're interested in participating in our annual technology expo.

W-Br Yes, that's right. **16**It's our company's first time operating a booth, so we're not sure what spot to book. Marco, what was the point you made on the way here?

M-Au Well, **16,17**I was worried about being close to the main stage because it could be too loud to have conversations with participants.

M-Cn We still have a few more of our premium spots available. They're near the entrance, far from the stage.

W-Br They're a higher price, though. **18**I'll call my supervisor to ask for an increase in funds.

---

stop by 들르다   participate in ~에 참가하다   expo 박람회   operate 운영하다   spot 자리, 장소   book 예약하다   available 이용 가능한   entrance 입구   fund 자금, 기금

번역 남1 두 분 모두 들러주셔서 감사합니다. 저희 연례 기술 박람회 참석을 원하신다고 들었습니다.
여 네, 맞아요. 저희 회사는 부스를 처음 운영하는 터라 어떤 자리를 예약해야 하는지 잘 모르겠어요. 마르코 씨,

여기 오는 길에 얘기한 의견이 뭐였죠?

남2 음, 주 무대에 가깝게 있는 것이 걱정돼요. 참가자들과 대화를 나누기에 너무 시끄러울 수도 있으니까요.

남1 아직 프리미엄 부스 자리가 몇 개 더 남아 있습니다. 입구 근처이고 무대와는 멀리 떨어져 있어요.

여 그럼 가격이 더 높겠네요. 저희 상사에게 전화해서 비용 인상을 요청해 볼게요.

16. 대화의 주제는?
(A) 사무실 이전   (B) 발표 연습
(C) 부스 예약   (D) 행사 참석률 증진

해설 **전체 내용 – 대화 주제**
대화 초반부 여자가 부스 운영이 처음이라 어떤 자리를 예약할지 모르겠다(It's our~ what spot to book)고 했으므로 정답은 (C)이다.

어휘 relocate 이전하다, 이동시키다 attendance 참석자 수, 참석률

17. 마르코 씨는 어떤 우려를 표현하는가?
(A) 참여 비용   (B) 한정된 공간
(C) 소음 정도   (D) 낡은 장비

해설 **세부 내용 – 마르코 씨의 걱정거리**
여자가 마르코를 호명하며 의견을 묻자, 주 무대와 가까워 참가자들과 대화 시 시끄러울 수 있다고 하므로 (C)가 정답이다.

어휘 participation 참여 limited 한정된, 제한된 outdated 구식의, 낡은

18. 여자가 관리자에게 전화를 하려는 목적은?
(A) 장식에 관한 조언을 얻으려고
(B) 예산 변경을 요청하려고
(C) 운전 길 안내를 하려고
(D) 계약 조건을 요청하려고

해설 **세부 내용 – 여자가 전화하려는 목적**
여자가 마지막 대사에서 상사에게 비용 인상 요청을 위해 전화하겠다(I'll call my supervisor to ask for an increase in funds)고 하므로 정답은 (B)이다.

어휘 request 요청하다 budget 예산 terms 조건

19-21

M-Cn Ms. Moore, I know we were supposed to meet next week for the employee performance evaluations, but I just found out that I had the wrong information. ¹⁹They're due this Thursday.

W-Br But ²⁰I have to fly to Frankfurt tomorrow to attend the board meeting. I won't be back until Friday.

M-Cn That probably means you'll be busy wrapping up some projects today, right?

W-Br Yes, but I should be finished by six, the time I normally go home. ²¹I can work overtime and meet you then.

evaluation 평가 board meeting 이사회 probably 아마 wrap up 마무리짓다 work overtime 초과근무를 하다

번역 남 무어 씨, 직원 업무 평가를 위해 다음 주에 만나야 하는 것으로 알았는데, 방금 잘못 알고 있다는 사실을 발견했습니다. 이번주 목요일이 마감 기한입니다.
여 하지만 저는 내일 이사회 참석을 위해 프랑크푸르트로 가요. 금요일까지는 없을 텐데요.
남 오늘 프로젝트들을 마무리하느라 바쁘시겠군요, 그렇죠?
여 네, 하지만 제가 보통 퇴근하는 시간인 6시까지는 끝날 겁니다. 초과근무를 하고 그 때 만날 수 있어요.

19. 남자는 직원 업무 평가에 대해 뭐라고 말하는가?
(A) 신입사원들에 한해 실시한다.
(B) 이번 주로 예정되어 있다.
(C) 일 년에 한 번 실시한다.
(D) 여러 단계로 나뉜다.

해설 **전체 내용 – 남자가 평가에 대해 하는 말**
남자가 첫 번째 대사에서 직원 업무 평가 미팅을 다음 주로 알았는데, 이번주 목요일이 마감 기한이다(They're due this Thursday)라고 하므로 (B)가 정답이다.

어휘 be scheduled 예정되다 annually 일 년에 한 번 be divided into ~로 나뉘다

20. 여자는 어떤 문제점을 언급하는가?
(A) 출장을 갈 예정이다.
(B) 파일을 잃어버렸다.
(C) 이사회가 취소됐다.
(D) 고객이 불만을 제기했다.

해설 **세부 내용 – 여자가 언급한 문제점**
대화 중반부 여자가 이사회 참석차 프랑크푸르트로 간다(But I have to fly ~ the board meeting)고 하므로 정답은 (A)이다.

어휘 make a complaint 불만을 제기하다

21. 여자는 무엇을 하겠다고 제안하는가?
(A) 프로젝트에 관한 발표하기
(B) 자세한 설명 보내기
(C) 웹사이트에 정보 업데이트하기
(D) 평소보다 늦게까지 회사에 남기

해설 **세부 내용 – 여자가 제안하는 것**
여자가 마지막 대사에서 초과근무를 하면 만날 수 있다(I can work overtime and meeting you then)고 제안했으므로 정답은 (D)이다.

어휘 give a presentation 발표하다 instruction 설명

22-24

W-Am Richard, do you have a minute? I need some help on the advertising account for Como Industries.

M-Au The last I heard, Sandra was handling that account.

W-Am ²²It's been reassigned to me because Sandra has a lot of business trips coming up this month.

M-Au I see. What do you need assistance with?

W-Am Well, I'm not sure about the best way to present our plan to the clients. ²³Should I use a slideshow or just give a talk?

M-Au You know, ²⁴I have some notes that I used in a meeting with a similar company. I'll forward them to you.

> advertising 광고   account 고객   the last I heard 최근에 듣기로는   reassign 다시 배정하다   assistance 도움, 조력   give a talk 말하다   similar 비슷한, 유사한

번역 여 리처드 씨, 잠시 시간이 있나요? 코모 인더스트리즈 광고주에 대해 도움을 좀 받아야 해요.
남 제가 최근에 듣기로는 산드라 씨가 그 광고주를 맡고 있다고 했는데요.
여 산드라 씨가 이번 달에 출장이 많아서 저에게 다시 배정됐어요.
남 그렇군요. 어떤 도움이 필요하세요?
여 음, 저희 기획을 고객에게 가장 잘 설명할 방법을 모르겠어요. 슬라이드쇼를 이용할까요, 아니면 그냥 설명만 할까요?
남 유사한 업체와의 회의에서 사용한 기록이 있어요. 전달해 드릴게요.

22. 여자에 따르면 고객이 다시 배정된 이유는?
(A) 고객이 이전 작업을 마음에 들어하지 않았다.
(B) 동료가 시간이 되지 않는다.
(C) 시스템 오류가 있었다.
(D) 여자가 그 일을 맡겠다고 자진했다.

해설 **세부 내용 – 고객이 다시 배정된 이유**
여자가 두 번째 대사에서 산드라가 출장이 많아서 자신에게 다시 배정됐다고 하므로 (B)가 정답이다.

어휘 reassign 다시 할당하다   previous 이전의   coworker 동료

23. 여자는 무엇에 대해 문의하는가?
(A) 프로젝트 마감 기한
(B) 계약서
(C) 발표 방법
(D) 출장

해설 **세부 내용 – 여자의 문의 사항**
대화 중반부 여자가 슬라이드쇼를 활용할지 설명만 할지

(Should I use ~ or just give a talk?) 묻고 있으므로 정답은 (C)이다.

어휘 deadline 기한   method 방법

24. 남자는 무엇을 하겠다고 제안하는가?
(A) 초과 근무 승인하기
(B) 직원 회의 개최하기
(C) 고객에게 연락하기
(D) 기록 보내기

해설 **세부 내용 – 남자의 제안 사항**
대화 후반부 남자가 유사 업체와의 회의에서 사용한 기록을 전달해 주겠다(I'll forward them to you)고 했으므로 정답은 (D)이다.

어휘 approve 승인하다   hold a meeting 회의를 개최하다

●UNIT 05 세부 사항 문제

LISTENING PRACTICE

1. (D)　**2.** (D)　**3.** (A)　**4.** (B)

1

M-Cn Hello. I saw a billboard advertising your plumbing service. My kitchen sink is draining very slowly, so I'm hoping you can help.

W-Br Certainly. I can come by tomorrow afternoon.

M-Cn Well, I work all day so I won't be home. But I'll leave the back door unlocked.

> billboard (옥외) 광고판   advertising 광고   plumbing 배관   drain 물이 내려가다   unlocked 잠겨 있지 않은

번역 남 안녕하세요. 배관 서비스 옥외 광고를 봤어요. 저희 주방 개수대에 물이 굉장히 늦게 내려가서 도와주셨으면 합니다.
여 네. 내일 오후까지 갈 수 있습니다.
남 음, 제가 온종일 일을 해서 집에 없을 겁니다. 하지만 뒷문을 열어두겠습니다.

문제 남자는 어디에서 서비스에 대해 알게 되었는가?
(A) 인터넷
(B) 신문
(C) TV 광고
(D) 옥외 광고판

해설 **세부 내용 – 남자가 정보를 얻은 경로**
남자가 첫 대사에서 서비스 옥외 광고를 봤다(I saw a billboard advertising your plumbing service)고 밝히고 있으므로 정답은 (D)이다.

어휘 broadcast 방송   outdoor 옥외의, 야외의

2

M-Au Brenda, I'm looking for a new shampoo. Can you recommend one?

W-Am I really like Re-Onics shampoos, because they don't contain any harmful chemicals.

M-Au Thanks! Oh, they're on sale now. I think I should get one.

---

contain 포함하다   harmful 해로운   chemical 화학물질

번역 남 브렌다, 제가 샴푸를 새로 찾고 있는데, 하나 추천해 주실 수 있나요?
여 저는 리오닉스 샴푸를 무척 좋아해요. 해로운 화학물질이 전혀 들어있지 않거든요.
남 고맙습니다. 아, 지금 할인을 하네요. 하나 사야겠어요.

문제 브렌다 씨가 리오닉스 제품을 추천하는 이유는?
(A) 가격이 적당하다.
(B) 독특한 향이 있다.
(C) 다양한 포장에 담겨 있다.
(D) 안전한 성분이다.

해설 **세부 내용 – 리오닉스 제품의 추천 이유**
대화 중반부 여자가 리오닉스 샴푸를 추천하며 해로운 화학물질이 없다(they don't contain any harmful chemicals)고 했으므로 정답은 (D)이다.

어휘 reasonable 합리적인. 가격이 적당한   ingredient 성분

3

M-Au Tina, could you help me prepare for my presentation?

W-Am I'm afraid I'm a bit busy this week. I have to chair a meeting this afternoon and I'm also taking part in a golf tournament on Saturday.

M-Au Do you know if anybody else is available?

W-Am Possibly Susan. She's always helpful.

---

presentation 발표   chair 의장을 맡다   take part in ~에 참가하다   available 시간이 되는

번역 남 티나 씨, 발표 준비를 도와주실 수 있나요?
여 이번주는 좀 바쁠 것 같아요. 오늘 오후 회의 의장을 맡아야 하고 토요일엔 골프 토너먼트에도 참가하거든요.
남 가능한 다른 사람이 혹시 있을까요?
여 아마 수잔 씨가 될 거예요. 항상 기꺼이 도와주시죠.

문제 여자가 주말에 시간이 안 되는 이유는?
(A) 스포츠 경기를 한다.
(B) 회의를 주관한다.
(C) 마케팅 캠페인 관련 일을 한다.
(D) 보고서를 작성한다.

해설 **세부 내용 – 여자가 주말에 바쁜 이유**
대화 초반부 여자가 토요일에 골프 대회에 참가한다

(I'm also taking part in a golf tournament on Saturday)고 했으므로 정답은 (A)이다.

4

M-Cn Sharon, ID cards for our new employees were supposed to have been delivered to us by now, but they haven't.

W-Am Oh, no. They won't be able to access our lab areas then.

M-Cn I've already phoned Human Resources and told them this is not acceptable.

W-Am I agree. We might have to reschedule everything we planned for today.

---

be supposed to ~하기로 되어 있다. ~할 예정이다   deliver 배달하다, 배송하다   acceptable 받아들일 수 있는

번역 남 샤론 씨, 신입 사원들을 위한 새 ID 카드가 지금쯤은 배송되어야 했는데 오지 않았어요.
여 이런, 큰일이네요. 그럼 실험실 구역에 출입할 수가 없거든요.
남 인사부서에 이미 전화해서 이러면 안 된다고 얘기했습니다.
여 맞아요. 오늘 계획한 모든 일정을 다시 잡아야 할지도 몰라요.

문제 남자는 무엇을 이미 했다고 말하는가?
(A) 소포 배달하기   (B) 불만 제기하기
(C) 패스워드 변경하기   (D) 주문하기

해설 **세부 내용 – 남자가 이미 한 것**
대화 중반부 남자가 이미 인사부에 이러면 안 된다고 알렸다(I've already phoned ~ this is not acceptable)고 했으므로 정답은 (B)이다.

어휘 make a complaint 항의하다. 불만을 제기하다   place an order 주문하다

●UNIT 06 다음에 할 일 문제

LISTENING PRACTICE   교재 p. 91

1. (D)   **2.** (D)   **3.** (C)   **4.** (D)

1

M-Cn Good afternoon. Are you looking for something in particular?

W-Br I want to buy strawberry jam, but this bottle is a little big. Do you sell a sample size of this jam?

M-Cn I'll go and look in our storeroom in the back. It shouldn't take long.

번역 남 안녕하세요. 특정 물품을 찾고 계신가요?

여 딸기잼을 사고 싶은데, 병이 좀 크네요. 샘플 크기의 잼도 판매하세요?

남 뒤편에 있는 창고에 가서 확인해보겠습니다. 오래 걸리진 않을 거예요.

문제 남자가 다음으로 할 것 같은 일은?

(A) 금전 등록기 작동시키기

(B) 관리자 찾기

(C) 경고문 게시하기

(D) 매장의 재고 확인하기

해설 **세부 내용 – 남자가 다음에 할 일**

남자가 마지막 대사에서 창고에 가서 확인해 보겠다(I'll go and look in our storeroom in the back)고 했으므로 정답은 (D)이다.

어휘 cash register 금전 등록기   post 게시하다   inventory 재고

2

W-Am Hello. I'd like to book some tickets for this Thursday's show.

M-Cn I'm sorry but the show was already sold out. I can put you on the waiting list if you'd like.

W-Am Let me talk to my coworkers and see if they are willing to wait.

book 예약하다   coworker 동료   be willing to 기꺼이 ~하다

번역 여 안녕하세요. 이번주 목요일 공연 표를 예매하고 싶은데요.

남 죄송하지만 이미 매진됐습니다. 원하시면 대기 명단에 넣어드릴 수 있어요.

여 동료들에게 대기할 의향이 있는지 물어볼게요.

문제 여자가 다음으로 할 것 같은 일은?

(A) 불만 제기하기

(B) 납입금 내기

(C) 자신의 이름을 명단에 올리기

(D) 동료들과 이야기하기

해설 **세부 내용 – 여자가 다음에 할 일**

여자가 마지막 대사에서 동료들의 의향을 묻겠다(Let me talk to my coworkers ~)고 했으므로 정답은 (D)이다.

어휘 file a complaint 불만을 제기하다, 고소하다   submit 제출하다   colleague 동료

3

M-Cn Susan, ABS News is sending a camera crew this afternoon to get some footage. Can you give them a tour of the plant?

W-Br That's no problem. Is there anything in particular I should show them?

M-Cn Yes. They sent me their proposed schedule with a list of things they'd like to see. I'll forward it to you.

footage (자료) 화면   give a tour of ~을 안내하다   plant 공장

번역 남 수잔, ABS 뉴스가 오늘 오후 자료 화면을 얻기 위해 카메라 담당자를 보낼 예정인데요. 공장 견학을 시켜 주실 수 있나요?

여 그렇게 할게요. 특별히 보여드려야 할 것이 있나요?

남 네. 저에게 보고 싶은 것들의 목록과 함께 일정 제안을 보냈어요. 전달해 드릴게요.

문제 남자는 여자에게 무엇을 보낼 것이라고 말하는가?

(A) 동영상

(B) 계약서

(C) 일정

(D) 이메일 주소

해설 **세부 내용 – 남자가 여자에게 보낼 것**

남자가 마지막 대사에서 그쪽에서 일정을 보냈다(They sent me their proposed schedule)며 전달해 주겠다(I'll forward it to you)고 했으므로 정답은 (C)이다.

어휘 itinerary 일정

4

W-Am Hi, Martin. Sorry to call you on your day off, but our restaurant is understaffed. Are you able to come in? We have a food critic visiting us later today.

M-Cn I'm actually at a dental clinic at the moment. Why don't you contact Allstar, the temporary staffing agency?

W-Am OK. I think I should do that.

day off (근무를) 쉬는 날   understaffed 인원이 부족한   critic 비평가, 평론가   at the moment 지금   temporary 임시의, 일시적인   staffing 인력 파견

번역 여 안녕하세요, 마틴 씨. 쉬시는 날에 전화 드려서 죄송하지만 저희 음식점에 일손이 부족해서요. 와 주실 수 있나요? 오늘 오후에 음식 비평가가 방문할 겁니다.

남 사실 지금 치과에 있어요. 올스타에 연락해 보시는 거 어떠세요? 임시 인력 파견업체요.

여 네, 그래야 하겠네요.

문제 여자는 오늘 오후 어떤 일이 있을 것이라고 말하는가?
(A) 개업식이 열릴 것이다.
(B) 새 탁자들이 배송될 것이다.
(C) 직원들이 교육을 받을 것이다.
(D) 음식 평론가가 방문할 것이다.

해설 **세부 내용 - 오늘 오후에 있을 일**
여자가 첫 대사에서 오늘 오후 음식 비평가가 방문한다
(We have a food critic visiting us later today)고 했
으므로 정답은 (D)이다.

어휘 grand opening 개장, 개점 undergo 겪다

ACTUAL TEST
교재 p. 92

1. (C)	**2.** (C)	**3.** (A)	**4.** (B)	**5.** (C)
6. (A)	**7.** (C)	**8.** (B)	**9.** (A)	**10.** (B)
11. (B)	**12.** (C)	**13.** (B)	**14.** (A)	**15.** (D)
16. (D)	**17.** (C)	**18.** (A)	**19.** (A)	**20.** (D)
21. (C)	**22.** (A)	**23.** (A)	**24.** (C)	

1-3

M-Cn Hello, this is Tim Holmes calling from room 408.

W-Am Hello, Mr. Holmes. How can I help you?

M-Cn I'd like to extend my reservation by two more nights. Unfortunately, **¹**one of my meetings here in Seattle was changed to Friday.

W-Am **²**The entire fourth floor has been booked for a group reservation. We have another room available on the fifth floor, though.

M-Cn All right. By when do I have to be out of my room?

W-Am Eleven A.M. I can send someone to help you move your items.

M-Cn Thank you. That would be great. **³**I'll get my luggage and personal items ready now.

extend 연장하다 reservation 예약 personal 개인의

번역 남 안녕하세요. 저는 408호 팀 홈스라고 합니다.
여 안녕하세요, 홈스 씨. 어떻게 도와드릴까요?
남 이틀 밤 더 예약을 연장하고 싶습니다. 안타깝게도 시애틀에서 열리는 회의 한 건이 금요일로 변경됐어요.
여 4층 전체가 단체 예약됐는데요. 그런데 5층에 다른 객실이 있긴 합니다.
남 좋습니다. 언제까지 방을 비워드려야 할까요?
여 오전 11시입니다. 물건을 옮기시는 걸 돕도록 사람을 보내드릴 수 있어요.
남 감사합니다. 그러면 좋겠네요. 지금 짐과 개인 물품을 꾸리겠습니다.

---

1. 남자는 어떤 문제점을 언급하는가?
(A) 계산서에 오류가 있다.
(B) 비행기를 놓쳤다.
(C) 회의가 연기됐다.
(D) 확정 코드를 잊어버렸다.

해설 **세부 내용 - 문제점**
남자가 두 번째 대사에서 예약 연장을 요청하여 회의 날짜
가 변경되었다(Unfortunately, one of my meetings ~
changed to Friday)고 했으므로 정답은 (C)이다.

어휘 contain 포함하다 postpone 연기하다, 미루다
confirmation 확인, 확정

2. 여자는 남자에게 무엇에 대해 말하는가?
(A) 환불 정책
(B) 새로운 서비스
(C) 단체 예약
(D) 컴퓨터 오작동

해설 **세부 내용 - 여자가 남자에게 말하는 내용**
여자의 두 번째 대사에서 남자가 머무는 4층 전체의 단체
예약에 대해 언급하므로, 정답은 (C)이다.

어휘 refund 환불 policy 정책 malfunction 오작동

3. 남자가 다음으로 할 일은?
(A) 소지품 준비하기
(B) 다른 업체에 전화하기
(C) 결제하기
(D) 정보 제공하기

해설 **세부 내용 - 남자가 다음에 할 일**
남자가 마지막 대사에서 지금 짐을 꾸리겠다(I'll get my
luggage and personal items ready now)고 했으므
로 정답은 (A)이다.

어휘 belongings 소유물 make a payment 지불하다,
결제하다

4-6

W-Am Hi, Phillip. I saw that the rest of the landscaping work out front has been completed. **⁴**Do you know when we have to settle the bill?

M-Cn I was expecting to receive an invoice by mail yesterday.

W-Am It might be at the reception desk. **⁵**Would you mind going there to look for it?

M-Cn Okay, but I'm just on my way out for a meeting. If it's there, **⁶**I'll ask one of the receptionists to take it to your office.

landscaping 조경 out front 입구 쪽에 complete
완료하다 settle the bill 계산하다 invoice 청구서, 송장

여 안녕하세요, 필립 씨. 입구 쪽 조경 작업 나머지가 마무리된 걸 봤습니다. 언제 계산해야 하는지 아세요?

남 어제 우편으로 청구서를 받기를 기다리고 있었어요.

여 안내 데스크에 있을 겁니다. 가서 찾아봐 주실 수 있어요?

남 네, 그런데 제가 지금 회의하러 나가는 길입니다. 안내 데스크 직원 중 한 명에게 사무실로 가져다 드리라고 요청할게요.

4. 여자는 무엇에 대해 문의하는가?
(A) 업체 추천   (B) 지불일자
(C) 프로젝트 마감 기한   (D) 여행 계획

해설 전체 내용 – 여자의 문의 사항
여자가 첫 대사에서 조경 작업 비용을 언제 지불해야 하는지(when we have to settle the bill) 물었으므로 정답은 (B)이다.

어휘 deadline 기한

5. 남자는 무엇을 요청 받았는가?
(A) 회사 대표에게 연락하기
(B) 안내데스크에서 전화 응대하기
(C) 우편물 확인하기
(D) 청구서 사본 새로 출력하기

해설 세부 내용 – 남자가 받은 요청 사항
우편물 도착을 기다리고 있었다는 남자의 말에 여자가 안내 데스크에 있을 거라며 가서 찾아봐달라(Would you mind going there to look for it?)고 요청했으므로 정답은 (B)이다.

6. 남자는 무엇을 하려고 계획하는가?
(A) 동료에게 업무 수행 부탁하기
(B) 여자의 사무실에서 기다리기
(C) 회의 연기하기
(D) 예산 보고서 검토하기

해설 세부 내용 – 남자의 계획
남자가 마지막 대사에서 안내 데스크 직원에게 서류 전달할 것(I'll ask one of the receptionists to take it to your office)이라고 했으므로 정답은 (A)이다.

어휘 colleague 동료   postpone 연기하다, 미루다   budget 예산

7-9 3인 대화

M-Cn Tiffany, Sharon, [7]I think we need to hire more workers as our design services are in high demand.

W-Am You're right. We're having trouble keeping up.

M-Cn There are so many recruiters out there, so it would be difficult to know which one is best. What do you think, Sharon?

W-Br [8]How about I talk to my former colleague at G & S Incorporated to see if she can recommend a company? Does that seem reasonable, Tiffany?

W-Am Yes. Good idea. While you're working on that, [9]I can write up a list of job duties to send to the recruiter.

> hire 채용하다   be in high demand 수요가 높다   keep up 따라가다   recruiter 채용업체   former 이전의 reasonable 합리적인, 타당한

번역 남 티파니 씨, 샤론 씨, 제 생각엔 직원을 더 채용해야 할 것 같아요. 저희 디자인 서비스의 수요가 많아서요.

여1 맞아요, 수요를 맞추기가 힘들어요.

남 채용 대행업체가 많아서 어떤 업체가 최선인지 확인하기가 어려워요. 어떻게 생각해요, 샤론?

여2 제가 G & S 인코퍼레이티드의 예전 동료에게 업체를 추천해 줄 수 있는지 물어보는 건 어때요? 괜찮아 보이나요, 티파니?

여1 네, 좋은 생각이네요. 그렇게 해 주시는 동안 저는 채용업체에 보낼 직무 목록을 작성할 수 있어요.

7. 남자는 무엇을 하고 싶다고 말하는가?
(A) 새로운 곳으로 이사하기
(B) 운영시간 변경하기
(C) 직원 규모 늘리기
(D) 새로운 디자인 검토하기

해설 세부 내용 – 남자가 원하는 것
남자가 첫 대사에서 직원을 더 채용해야 할 것 같다(I think we need to hire more workers)고 했으므로 정답은 (A)이다.

8. 샤론 씨는 무엇을 하자고 제안하는가?
(A) 경쟁업체와 제휴하기
(B) 추천 받기
(C) 교육 진행하기
(D) 웹사이트 업데이트하기

해설 세부 내용 – 샤론 씨의 제안
대화 중반부 남자가 샤론을 호명했고 샤론이 이전 동료에게 추천을 해줄 수 있는지 알아보자(How about ~ see if she can recommend a company)고 했으므로 정답은 (B)이다.

어휘 partner with ~와 협력하다

9. 티파니 씨는 무엇을 준비하겠다고 제안하는가?
(A) 직무기술서   (B) 임대차 계약서
(C) 사업 일정   (D) 채용 동영상

해설 세부 내용 – 티파니가 준비할 것
여자가 마지막 대사에서 채용 대행업체에 보낼 직무 목록을 작성하겠다(I can write up a list of job duties to send to the recruiter)고 했으므로 정답은 (A)이다.

어휘 job description 직무기술서 itinerary 일정
recruitment 채용

10-12

W-Br Hello, this is Jenna White calling from *Outdoor Sports Magazine*. I'm trying to reach Dylan Carter.

M-Cn Yes, speaking.

W-Br Good afternoon, Mr. Carter. ¹⁰We received your article about your experiences learning to surf, and we'd love to publish it.

M-Cn That's great news! I'm excited to hear that. Thank you.

W-Br It's our pleasure. ¹¹Do you happen to have any photos that we can print along with the article?

M-Cn Yes, I have some. How should I send them to you?

W-Br ¹²Please e-mail them to our photo department at photos@os-magazine.com. We'll expect them by noon tomorrow.

article 글, 기사 publish 출판하다. 게재하다 along with ~와 함께 department 부서

번역 여 안녕하세요. 저는 아웃도어 스포츠 매거진의 제나 화이트입니다. 딜런 카터 씨와 통화하고 싶습니다.

남 네, 접니다.

여 안녕하세요, 카터 씨. 서핑을 배우신 경험에 관한 글은 잘 받았습니다. 게재를 했으면 합니다.

남 좋은 소식이네요! 그러시다니 무척 기뻐요. 감사합니다.

여 저희가 감사드립니다. 글과 함께 실을 수 있는 사진을 갖고 계신가요?

남 네, 있습니다. 어떻게 보내드리면 될까요?

여 저희 사진 부서 이메일 photos@os-magazine.com으로 보내주세요. 내일 정오까지 받겠습니다.

10. 남자가 기뻐하는 이유는?
(A) 시합에 나갈 수 있다.
(B) 남자의 제출물이 게재될 예정이다.
(C) 남자가 속한 스포츠팀이 후원자를 구했다.
(D) 잡지 인터뷰를 할 예정이다.

해설 **세부 내용 – 남자가 기뻐하는 이유**
대화 초반부 여자가 남자의 글을 잡지에 게재하고 싶다고 하자 남자가 좋은 소식(That's great news!)이라고 하므로 정답은 (B)이다.

어휘 enter a competition 시합에 나가다. 경연에 참가하다 submission 제출

11. 여자는 남자에게 무엇을 요청하는가?
(A) 유니폼 (B) 사진
(C) 지출품의서 (D) 신청서

해설 **세부 내용 – 여자의 요청 사항**
대화 중반부 여자가 글과 함께 실을 수 있는 사진이 있는지 (Do you happen to have ~ with the article?) 물어봤으므로 (B)가 정답이다.

어휘 expense report 지출품의서 registration 등록. 신청

12. 여자는 남자에게 어떤 정보를 주었는가?
(A) 시합 규정 (B) 회의 날짜와 시간
(C) 부서 이메일 주소 (D) 글의 길이 제안

해설 **세부 내용 – 여자가 제공한 정보**
대화 후반부 여자가 사진 송부 방법을 묻는 남자에게 부서 이메일 주소를 알려주었으므로 정답은 (C)이다.

어휘 propose 제시하다. 제안하다

13-15

W-Br Hi, Jeff. I'm afraid I'm running a little late. ¹³My bus was supposed to depart at 9 o'clock, but it's been held up due to bad road conditions.

M-Au Oh, I'm sorry to hear that. ¹⁴We told the potential client that we'd present our new range of energy drinks at 11. But, I guess you won't make it on time.

W-Br There's still a slight chance. The journey should only take around one hour.

M-Au Even so, ¹⁵I'm going to ask if we can push the presentation back to this afternoon, just in case. The client also wants to show us around his store, so we can probably just do that this morning.

depart 출발하다 be held up 지연되다 due to ~때문에 potential 잠재적인 make it (시간 맞춰) 가다 on time 제시간에. 늦지 않고 slight chance 약간의 가능성 presentation 발표

번역 여 안녕하세요, 제프 씨. 제가 조금 늦을 것 같아요. 버스가 9시 정각에 출발해야 하는데 도로 상황이 좋지 않아 지연됐어요.

남 아, 안타깝군요. 잠재 고객에게 우리 새 에너지 음료 제품들을 11시에 발표하겠다고 했거든요. 그런데 제시간에 못 오실 것 같네요.

여 아직 약간 가능성이 있긴 해요. 가는 데 한 시간 정도밖에 안 걸리거든요.

남 그렇다고 해도 만약을 대비해서 오늘 오후로 발표를 미룰 수 있는지 물어볼게요. 고객은 우리에게 매장도 보여주고 싶어하니 오전엔 그걸 하면 될 거예요.

13. 여자가 늦는 이유는?
(A) 여자가 탈 버스가 오지 않았다.
(B) 교통 체증이 발생했다.
(C) 늦게 일어났다.
(D) 여자의 차에 시동이 걸리지 않았다.

세부 내용 – 여자가 늦는 이유

여자가 첫 대사에서 늦은 이유를 도로 상황으로 인한 버스 지연 때문(My bus was supposed to ~ due to bad road conditions)이라고 했으므로 정답은 (B)이다.

어휘 congestion 혼잡

14. 화자들은 어떤 종류의 회사에서 일하겠는가?
(A) 음료 제조업체　　(B) 스포츠 의류 생산업체
(C) 운수업체　　(D) 채용 대행업체

해설 **전체 내용 – 근무 장소**

남자가 첫 번째 대사에서 자신들의 새 음료 제품 발표를 언급하고 있으므로 정답은 (A)이다.

어휘 beverage 음료　manufacturer 생산자

15. 남자는 무엇을 해 보겠다고 말하는가?
(A) 회의 장소 변경하기
(B) 다른 버스 타기
(C) 여자의 직장 방문하기
(D) 발표 연기하기

해설 **세부 내용 – 남자가 할 일**

남자가 마지막 대사에서 발표를 미룰 수 있는지 물어보겠다(I'm going to ask if we can push the presentation back to this afternoon)고 하므로 정답은 (D)이다.

어휘 workplace 직장

16-18

W-Br　Good afternoon. This is Sylvia Pine calling from Kensington Pharmaceuticals.
M-Cn　Hi, Ms. Pine.
W-Br　First, thanks for interviewing with us last week. Your interviewer was very impressed. [16]We want to invite you for a second interview. The department head would like to speak to you.
M-Cn　That's fantastic. [17]I finished my college course last month, so my schedule is flexible. When should I come?
W-Br　[18]How about Tuesday? You can come for the interview in the morning, and then take the afternoon to look around our laboratory.
M-Cn　I'd love that. I can come at nine A.M. Will that be OK?
W-Br　That sounds good.

pharmaceuticals 제약회사　flexible 유연성이 있는, 융통성 있는　laboratory 실험실

번역　여 안녕하세요. 저는 켄싱턴 제약회사의 실비아 파인입니다.
남 안녕하세요, 파인 씨.

여 먼저 지난 주 면접에 참여해 주셔서 감사합니다. 면접 진행자가 깊은 인상을 받았습니다. 2차 면접을 제안하고 싶은데요. 부서장님께서 이야기를 나누고 싶어하십니다.
남 좋습니다. 지난달에 대학교 과정을 끝마쳐서 일정에 여유가 있습니다. 언제 가면 될까요?
여 화요일 어떠세요? 오전에 면접을 보시고 오후에 실험실을 돌아보시면 됩니다.
남 좋습니다. 오전 9시에 갈 수 있습니다. 괜찮을까요?
여 좋습니다.

16. 전화를 건 목적은?
(A) 기부자에게 감사를 전하기 위해
(B) 주문하기 위해
(C) 일자리 제안을 수락하기 위해
(D) 초대하기 위해

해설 **전체 내용 – 전화를 건 목적**

여자가 두 번째 대사에서 만족스러운 면접 결과를 언급하며 2차 면접을 제안하고 있으므로 정답은 (D)이다.

어휘 donor 기부자　place an order 주문하다　extend an invitation 초대하다, 초대장을 보내다

17. 남자는 지난달에 무슨 일이 있었다고 말하는가?
(A) 퇴직했다.　　(B) 논문을 출판했다.
(C) 대학교를 졸업했다.　(D) 근무 일정을 바꿨다.

해설 **세부 내용 – 지난달 남자에게 있었던 일**

대화 중간에 남자가 지난달에 대학교 과정을 마쳤다고 하므로 정답은 (C)이다.

어휘 retire 퇴직하다, 은퇴하다　publish 출판하다, 출간하다 graduate from ~을 졸업하다

18. 남자는 화요일 오후에 무엇을 하겠는가?
(A) 시설 견학하기　　(B) 동료에게 전화하기
(C) 서류 제출하기　　(D) 교육 동영상 시청하기

해설 **세부 내용 – 남자가 화요일 오후에 할 일**

대화 후반부 여자가 화요일에 면접과 실험실 돌아보기를 제안했고, 남자가 수락했으므로 정답은 (A)이다.

어휘 facility 시설　submit 제출하다

19-21 3인 대화

M-Au　Hi, Victoria. Good morning, Tommy. [19]Did you hear Star Media hired us to manage their corporate rebranding?
M-Cn　[19]Of course. It's a huge account.
M-Au　That's why I want the two of you to jointly oversee it. [20]Tommy, you'll be in charge of their social media accounts on the Internet.
M-Cn　OK, no problem.
M-Au　And Victoria, you will make all the art decisions.

W-Am You mean logos, graphics, and other visual content?

M-Au Yes. Can you handle them?

W-Am **²¹**It's not very common that both of us work on the same account together, **but if you think it's a good idea, I'm willing to try.**

---

corporate 회사의　account 고객　jointly 공동으로　oversee 감독하다　be in charge of ~을 담당하다　be willing to 기꺼이 ~ 하다

번역 남1 안녕하세요, 빅토리아 씨. 안녕하세요, 토미 씨. 스타 미디어가 회사 리브랜딩을 위해 우리를 고용했다는 얘기 들으셨어요?

남2 물론이죠. 그곳은 중요 고객이잖아요.

남1 그래서 두 분이 공동으로 그곳을 관리해 주셨으면 합니다. 토미 씨는 인터넷 소셜미디어 계정을 맡으실 겁니다.

남2 네, 알겠습니다.

남1 그리고 빅토리아 씨는 모든 미술 관련 결정을 내리시게 됩니다.

여 로고와 그래픽, 기타 시각적 콘텐츠를 말씀하시는 건가요?

남1 네, 하실 수 있을까요?

여 저희 둘이 한 고객을 맡는 일은 매우 드물지만 괜찮다고 생각하시면 해 보겠습니다.

19. 화자들은 무엇에 대해 이야기하는가?
(A) 새로운 사업 거래 건
(B) 회사 구조조정
(C) 앞으로 있을 보도 기사
(D) 관리자의 승진

해설 **전체 내용 – 대화 주제**
남자가 첫 대사에서 빅토리아와 토미를 호명하며 스타 미디어가 자신들을 고용했다는 소식을 들었는지 묻고 있으므로 정답은 (A)이다.

어휘 restructuring 구조조정　upcoming 다가오는, 앞으로 있을　promotion 승진

20. 토미 씨는 스타 미디어를 위해 무엇을 하겠는가?
(A) 컴퓨터 시스템 업그레이드하기
(B) 가격이 적당한 프린터 찾기
(C) 광고 스팟 판매하기
(D) 온라인 인지도 관리하기

해설 **세부 내용 – 토미가 할 일**
대화 중반 남자가 토미에게 인터넷 소셜미디어 계정을 맡게 될 것(Tommy, you'll be in charge of their social media accounts on the Internet)이라고 하므로 정답은 (D)이다.

어휘 affordable 가격이 적당한　advertising 광고　manage 관리하다　presence 존재, 존재감

---

21. 여자는 무엇이 드문 일이라고 말하는가?
(A) 외부 도급업체를 채용하는 것
(B) 다른 회사와 합병하는 것
(C) 두 명이 프로젝트를 진행하도록 하는 것
(D) 언론사와 협력하는 것

해설 **세부 내용 – 여자가 말하는 드문 일**
여자가 마지막 대사에서 두 사람이 한 고객을 맡는 일은 드문 일이다(It's not very common ~ account together)라고 했으므로 정답은 (C)이다.

어휘 contractor 계약자, 도급업자　merge 합병하다

22-24

W-Am Phil, did you see this e-mail about our advertising budget? It's going to be cut in half.

M-Au Yes. **²²**Our clothing line is selling pretty well, so the executives must have assumed we didn't need more advertising. We have the potential to reach a lot more customers still, though.

W-Am I agree. Plus, **²³**I just bought a package of advertising space in the paper from *Rosedale Times*. They're expecting a large payment each month.

M-Au **²⁴**I'll give Mr. Stern in management a call. Maybe he can give us a few more months with our current budget.

---

cut in half 절반으로 줄이다, 삭감하다　executive 임원　assume 추정하다　potential 잠재력　management 관리　current 현재의

번역 여 필 씨, 광고 예산에 관한 이메일 보셨어요? 절반으로 삭감될 거예요.

남 네, 의류 제품이 상당히 잘 팔려서 임원진이 광고가 더 필요하지 않을 거라고 추정한 것 같습니다. 아직 훨씬 더 많은 고객을 확보할 잠재력이 있는데 말이죠.

여 동의해요. 게다가 저는 〈로즈데일 타임즈〉의 지면 광고 자리를 샀거든요. 매월 많은 비용을 지불해야 해요.

남 제가 관리부서 스턴 씨에게 전화할게요. 아마 현 예산을 몇 달 더 배정해 주실 수 있을 겁니다.

22. 남자는 의류 상품에 대해 뭐라고 말하는가?
(A) 고객에게 인기가 많다.
(B) 가격이 적당하게 매겨졌다.
(C) 단종될 것이다.
(D) 디자인이 다시 이뤄질 것이다.

해설 **세부 내용 – 남자가 상품에 대해 하는 말**
남자가 첫 번째 대사에서 제품이 상당히 잘 팔리고 있다(Our clothing line is selling pretty well)고 했으므로 정답은 (A)이다.

어휘 reasonably 합리적으로　discontinue 생산을 중단하다

23. 여자는 최근 무엇을 구입했는가?
(A) 광고 지면　　　　(B) 의류 한 점
(C) 교육 프로그램　　(D) 회사 차량

해설 세부 내용 – 여자가 구입한 것
여자가 두 번째 대사에서 지면 광고 자리를 샀다고 하므로 정답은 (A)이다.

어휘 article (같은 종류의 것의) 한 개

24. 남자는 무엇을 하겠다고 말하는가?
(A) 직원 승진시키기　　(B) 구독 취소하기
(C) 동료에게 전화하기　　(D) 이메일 전달하기

해설 세부 내용 – 남자가 할 일
마지막 대사에서 남자가 예산 배정 연장을 위해 관리 부서 스턴 씨에게 전화하겠다(I'll give Mr. Stern in management a call)고 하므로 정답은 (C)이다.

어휘 promote 승진시키다　subscription 구독, 가입
forward 전달하다

●UNIT 07 의도 파악 문제

LISTENING PRACTICE 교재 p. 95

1. (A)　　**2.** (A)　　**3.** (C)　　**4.** (A)

1

M-Au Maria, Bridge Hotel wants us to paint their building. Let's load up the truck and head over.
W-Am Right now? It looks like it's going to rain.
M-Au Well, then we'd better head to our supplier to get paint and brushes.
W-Am OK. Maybe we can start on the Bridge Hotel tomorrow.

load up 짐을 싣다　supplier 공급업자

번역 남 마리아 씨, 브리지 호텔이 건물 페인트칠을 해 달라고 합니다. 트럭에 짐을 싣고 출발합시다.
여 지금요? 비가 올 것 같은데요.
남 음, 그럼 공급업체에 가서 페인트와 붓을 사는 게 좋겠어요.
여 좋아요. 아마 브리지 호텔 일은 내일 시작할 수 있을 겁니다.

문제 여자가 "비가 올 것 같은데요"라고 말할 때 그 의도는 무엇인가?
(A) 프로젝트가 연기되어야 한다.
(B) 일기예보가 맞지 않았다.
(C) 동료가 옷을 갈아입어야 한다.
(D) 운전하는 데 평소보다 오래 걸릴 것이다.

해설 세부 내용 – 화자의 의도
인용문 앞에서 남자가 페인트칠을 하자고 했을 때 여자가 비가 올 것 같다고 했고 두 사람이 일을 미루는 데 동의하는 상황이 이어지므로 여자의 말은 업무를 미루려는 의도로 볼 수 있다. 따라서 정답은 (A)이다.

어휘 weather report 일기예보　inaccurate 부정확한
coworker 동료

2

W-Br Excuse me, sir. May I help you? This is a restricted event.
M-Cn Oh, here is my press pass. I'm covering the opening of the ceremony.
W-Br Very good, Mr. Morris. You can pick up your press kit in the reporters' room down the hall.

restricted 제한된　press pass 기자증　cover 취재하다, 보도하다　press kit 보도 자료

번역 여 실례합니다. 도와드릴까요? 입장이 제한된 행사입니다.
남 아, 여기 기자증이 있어요. 저는 개막식을 취재합니다.
여 좋습니다, 모리스 씨. 복도 끝에 있는 기자실에서 보도 자료를 가져가시면 됩니다.

문제 여자가 "입장이 제한된 행사입니다"라고 말할 때 그 의도는 무엇인가?
(A) 신분증을 확인해야 한다.
(B) 전용 출입증을 판매한다.
(C) 동료를 초대할 수 없다.
(D) 파티가 재미있을 것이라고 생각한다.

해설 세부 내용 – 화자의 의도
여자가 첫 대사에서 입장이 제한된 행사라고 하자 인용문 뒤에서 남자가 개막식을 취재한다며 기자증을 제시한 것으로 보아 여자의 말은 입장을 위해 신분증 확인을 요구하기 위한 것이었음을 알 수 있다. 따라서 정답은 (A)이다.

어휘 a form of identification 신분증　exclusive 독점적인, 전용의

3

M-Cn Hi, you've reached Max Consulting. How may I help you?
W-Br We're launching a new line of shoes this July. We need a marketing consultant to help guide us.
M-Cn We've never done anything like that before. Our firm normally offers consulting for startups. But I can recommend a company that offers the service.

launch 개시하다, 출시하다　firm 회사　startup 신규 업체

번역　남　안녕하세요, 맥스 컨설팅입니다. 무엇을 도와드릴까
　　　　요?

　　　여　저희는 올 7월에 새로운 신발을 출시하는데요. 저희를
　　　　도와줄 마케팅 컨설턴트가 있었으면 합니다.

　　　남　저희는 이런 일을 맡아본 적이 없습니다. 저희 회사는
　　　　보통 신규 업체에 컨설팅 서비스를 제공하죠. 하지만
　　　　그 서비스를 제공하는 업체를 추천해드릴 수는 있어요.

문제　남자가 "저희는 이런 일을 맡아본 적이 없습니다"라고 말
　　　할 때 그 의도는 무엇인가?

　　　(A) 교육을 받고 싶어한다.
　　　(B) 프로젝트에 대해 기대하고 있다.
　　　(C) 일을 맡는 것이 쉽지 않다.
　　　(D) 연락처 정보가 잘못됐다고 생각한다.

해설　**세부 내용 – 화자의 의도**
　　　인용문 앞에서 여자가 마케팅 컨설턴트를 찾는다고 하자
　　　남자가 그런 일을 맡아본 적이 없다며 전문 분야가 따로 있
　　　음을 언급한다. 따라서 정답은 (C)이다.

어휘　take a job 일을 맡다, 취직하다

4

M-Au Julia, could you lead the new employee
orientation next week?

W-Am I'd love to help out, but I have a report
due next week. Will it require a lot of
preparation?

M-Au I've got a copy of my notes from last year
here. As you can see, they don't even fill a
page.

W-Am OK. I can handle that.

due (~까지) 하기로 되어 있는, 예정된

번역　남　줄리아 씨, 다음 주 신입 사원 오리엔테이션을 맡아주
　　　　실 수 있나요?

　　　여　도와드리고 싶지만 다음 주가 기한인 보고서가 있어요.
　　　　준비를 많이 해야 할까요?

　　　남　여기 작년에 썼던 기록이 있어요. 보다시피 한 장도 안
　　　　됩니다.

　　　여　좋아요, 할 수 있겠어요.

문제　남자가 "한 장도 안 됩니다"라고 말한 이유는 무엇인가?
　　　(A) 일이 쉽다는 것을 설명하려고
　　　(B) 공급업체를 바꾸는 것을 제안하려고
　　　(C) 보고서에 대한 실망감을 표시하려고
　　　(D) 프로젝트 인원을 선발하려고

해설　**세부 내용 – 화자의 의도**
　　　인용문 앞에서 남자가 도움을 요청하자 여자가 다음 주 기
　　　한인 보고서가 있다며 준비할 것이 많은지 물었다. 이에 남
　　　자가 샘플을 보여주며 한 장도 안 된다고 한 것은 일이 쉬
　　　워서 준비할 것이 많지 않다는 것을 설명하려는 의도로 볼
　　　수 있다. 따라서 정답은 (A)이다.

어휘　supplier 공급업자　disappointment 실망

●UNIT 08 시각 정보 문제

LISTENING PRACTICE
교재 p. 97

1. (C)　　**2.** (D)　　**3.** (C)

1

M-Au Thank you for calling Waylon Tech. How
may I help you?

W-Am Hi. I just bought a Waylon Tech vacuum
cleaner—the Waylon T11. But I'm having
trouble connecting attachments.

M-Au I see. Have you tried visiting our Web site?
There are instructional videos about how to
use the features on all of our products.

W-Am I didn't realize that. I think that's exactly
what I need. Thank you.

vacuum cleaner 진공청소기　attachment 부속품
feature 기능

번역　남　웨일런 테크에 전화 주셔서 감사합니다. 어떻게 도와드
　　　　릴까요?

　　　여　안녕하세요. 웨일런 테크의 진공청소기 웨일런 T11을
　　　　막 구입했는데요. 부속품을 연결하는 데 어려움을 겪고
　　　　있어요.

　　　남　알겠습니다. 저희 웹사이트에 가 보셨나요? 전 제품 기
　　　　능 사용법에 관한 교육용 동영상이 올라와 있습니다.

　　　여　몰랐어요. 저에게 딱 필요한 것이네요. 감사합니다.

웨일런 T11 설명서 목차	
Part 1 .... 배터리 충전	
Part 2 .... 주머니 비우기	
Part 3 .... 부속 장치 연결하기	
Part 4 .... 필터 교체	

문제　시각 정보에 따르면, 여자는 설명서의 어떤 부분을 언급하
　　　고 있는가?
　　　(A) 파트 1
　　　(B) 파트 2
　　　(C) 파트 3
　　　(D) 파트 4

해설　**세부 내용 – 시각 정보 연계**
　　　여자가 첫 번째 대사에서 부속품을 연결하는 데 어려
　　　움을 겪고 있다(I'm having trouble connecting
　　　attachment)고 하였다. 표에서 부속 장치연결을 찾아 확
　　　인하면 정답은 (C)이다.

어휘　instruction 설명　table of contents 목차　charge
　　　충전하다　replace 교체하다

2

M-Cn Here, take a look. Can you believe we spend so much of our time answering e-mails?

W-Am Actually, that doesn't surprise me. But, this can't be right! There's no way I spend that much time in meetings.

M-Cn Well, the numbers are averages for all the workers, so you might be an exception.

W-Am Can you e-mail this to me? I want to spend more time looking at it.

---
no way 절대 ~이 아니다   exception 예외

번역 남 여기를 한 번 보세요. 우리가 이메일 답신을 하느라 시간을 이렇게 많이 보낸다는 사실이 믿어지세요?

여 사실 그 부분은 놀랍지 않습니다. 하지만 이건 분명 잘못됐어요! 제가 이렇게 많은 시간을 회의하는 데 쓸 리가 없어요.

남 음, 수치는 모든 직원의 평균치이니, 예외이실 수 있죠.

여 저에게 이것을 이메일로 보내주실 수 있어요? 시간을 갖고 좀 더 보고 싶어요.

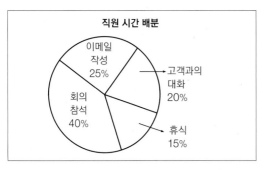

직원 시간 배분

이메일 작성 25%
고객과의 대화 20%
회의 참석 40%
휴식 15%

문제 시각 정보에 따르면, 여자는 어떤 수치가 자신의 경우에 맞지 않다고 생각하는가?
(A) 15%   (B) 20%
(C) 25%   (D) 40%

해설 세부 내용 – 시각 정보 연계
대화 초반부 여자가 자료가 잘못되었다며 자신은 회의에 많은 시간을 쓰지 않는다고 했다. 시각 정보에서 회의 참석을 찾아서 확인하면 정답은 (D)이다.

어휘 figure 수치   inaccurate 부정확한

3

W-Br I'm trying to copy some flyers, and I need some help with the copier.

M-Cn What seems to be the problem?

W-Br It has started producing poor quality copies, and the toner light is blinking.

M-Cn Oh, I can take care of that. I'll be there in about fifteen minutes.

---
flyer 전단지   copier 복사기   blink 깜빡이다

번역 여 전단지를 복사하려고 하는데요. 복사기 좀 봐주셨으면 해요.

남 무슨 문제예요?

여 흐리게 인쇄되기 시작했어요. 토너 표시가 깜빡이고 있고요.

남 오, 제가 그걸 해결할 수 있어요. 15분쯤 후에 그쪽으로 갈게요.

가장 흔한 오류 코드
EC1: 종이 걸림
EC2: 용지 부족
EC3: 토너 부족
EC4: 메모리 액세스 오류

문제 시각 정보에 따르면, 프린터는 어떤 에러 코드를 표시하고 있는가?
(A) EC1   (B) EC2
(C) EC3   (D) EC4

해설 세부 내용 – 시각 정보 연계
대화 중반부 여자가 인쇄가 흐리고 토너 표시가 깜빡인다고 했다. 표에서 토너 부족을 찾아 확인하면 정답은 (C)이다.

ACTUAL TEST
교재 p. 98

1. (C)	**2.** (A)	**3.** (B)	**4.** (B)	**5.** (C)
6. (D)	**7.** (C)	**8.** (B)	**9.** (C)	**10.** (A)
11. (D)	**12.** (C)	**13.** (A)	**14.** (B)	**15.** (D)
16. (A)	**17.** (C)	**18.** (D)	**19.** (B)	**20.** (C)
21. (A)	**22.** (B)	**23.** (A)	**24.** (C)	**25.** (C)
26. (A)	**27.** (D)	**28.** (C)	**29.** (B)	**30.** (A)
31. (C)	**32.** (C)	**33.** (B)	**34.** (C)	**35.** (B)
36. (C)				

1-3

M-Au [1]Ms. Lopez, I read in a memo that you've been promoted to senior graphic designer. Congratulations! You truly deserve it.

W-Br Thank you! There are a lot of new things to learn, though. [2]Right now, I need to design the brochure that tells about our services.

M-Au How is it going so far?

W-Br Well, [3]I want it to be informative but not too complicated. I'm not sure how much text was used last year.

M-Au Didn't Mr. Jackson work on it?

W-Br [3]You're right. I'll see what he has to say.

---
promote 승진시키다   deserve ~을 받을 만하다, 자격이 되다   informative 유익한   complicated 복잡한

84

번역 남 로페즈 씨, 선임 그래픽 디자이너로 승진하셨다는 회람을 읽었습니다. 축하합니다! 자격이 정말 충분하십니다.

여 감사합니다! 하지만 배운 것들이 많아요. 지금은 우리 회사 서비스에 관해 설명하는 안내책자를 디자인해야 해요.

남 현재까지 어떻게 진행되고 있나요?

여 음, 유익하지만 너무 복잡하지 않게 만들고 싶습니다. 작년에 문구가 얼마나 들어갔는지 잘 모르겠어요.

남 잭슨 씨가 작업하지 않았나요?

여 맞습니다. 잭슨 씨 이야기를 들어봐야겠어요.

1. 남자가 여자를 축하하는 이유는?
(A) 작품을 일찍 제출했다.
(B) 새로운 고객을 찾았다.
(C) 승진했다.
(D) 상을 받았다.

해설 **세부 내용 – 남자가 여자를 축하한 이유**
남자가 첫 번째 대사에서 승진했다는 회람을 읽었다(Ms. Lopez, I read in a memo ~ senior graphic designer)며 축하하고 있으므로 (C)가 정답이다.

어휘 submit 제출하다   promotion 승진   award 상

2. 여자는 지금 어떤 일을 하고 있는가?
(A) 정보 안내책자 준비하기
(B) 여행 준비하기
(C) 새로운 팀원 채용하기
(D) 무역 협정서 초안 잡기

해설 **세부 내용 – 여자가 하고 있는 일**
여자의 첫 번째 대사에서 지금은 서비스 관련 안내책자를 디자인해야 한다(Right now, I need to design the brochure that tells about our services)고 말한다. 따라서 (A)가 정답이다.

어휘 make arrangements 준비하다   draft 초안을 작성하다
trade agreement 무역 협정

3. 남자가 "잭슨 씨가 작업하지 않았나요?"라고 말할 때 그 의도는 무엇인가?
(A) 오류가 발생한 이유를 알고 있다.
(B) 잭슨 씨가 조언을 해 줄 수 있다.
(C) 업무를 완료했어야 했다.
(D) 여자는 잭슨 씨에게 돈을 지불해야 한다.

해설 **세부 내용 – 화자의 의도**
인용문 앞에서 여자가 작업 방식에 대해 언급하며 잘 모르겠다고 하자 남자는 잭슨 씨가 그 작업을 했다고 했다. 남자의 말을 들은 여자가 잭슨 씨 이야기를 들어보겠다고 했으므로 남자가 한 말은 잭슨 씨가 작업 경험이 있으므로 해 줄 말이 있을 것이라는 뜻으로 이해할 수 있다. 따라서 정답은 (B)이다.

어휘 complete 완료하다

4-6

W-Am Hi, **4**I'm flying to see my cousins in Dallas next week, and I'd like to rent a car for one week. Do you have one available for pickup on the morning of March 16 at Terminal B?

M-Au Yes. The cost for a one-week rental is four hundred eighty dollars. **5**For an additional twenty dollars, we will include a satellite navigation device so you can get around easily.

W-Am Actually, I know the city well.

M-Au All right. Let me get your contact details now, and then **6**I'll e-mail you to confirm your reservation in about ten minutes.

---

available 이용 가능한   additional 추가의   satellite 인공위성   confirm 확정하다, 확인하다

번역 여 안녕하세요. 저는 다음 주에 댈러스에 있는 사촌들을 만나러 가서 1주일간 차량을 대여하고 싶어요. 3월 16일 아침에 터미널 B에서 픽업 가능한 차량이 있나요?

남 네. 1주 대여료는 480달러입니다. 추가 20달러를 지불하시면 위성 내비게이션 장치가 포함되어 쉽게 돌아다니실 수 있어요.

여 사실 저는 그 도시를 잘 알아요.

남 좋습니다. 지금 연락처 정보를 주시면 약 10분 후 예약 확정 이메일을 보내드릴게요.

4. 여자가 댈러스로 가는 이유는?
(A) 상품을 전달하기 위해
(B) 친척을 방문하기 위해
(C) 시설을 점검하기 위해
(D) 사업상의 회의에 참석하기 위해

해설 **세부 내용 – 여자가 댈러스에 가는 이유**
여자는 첫 번째 대사에서 다음 주에 댈러스에 있는 사촌들을 만나러 간다고 하므로 (B)가 정답이다.

어휘 relative 친척   inspect 점검하다, 시찰하다   facility 시설

5. 여자가 "저는 그 도시를 잘 알아요"라고 말할 때 그 의도는 무엇인가?
(A) 남자의 회사를 잘 안다.
(B) 댈러스에 사업상의 인맥이 많다.
(C) 추가 장비가 필요 없다.
(D) 혼잡 시간대를 언제 피할 수 있는지 안다.

해설 **세부 내용 – 화자의 의도**
인용문 앞에서 남자가 내비게이션 장치를 소개했는데 여자가 그 도시를 잘 안다고 말했으므로 내비게이션이 필요하지 않다는 뜻으로 이해할 수 있다. 따라서 정답은 (C)이다.

어휘 be familiar with ~을 아주 잘 알다, ~에 익숙하다   avoid 피하다

85

6. 남자는 10분 후 무엇을 하겠다고 말하는가?
(A) 여자 관련 세부사항 입력하기
(B) 차량 등록부 확인하기
(C) 관리자에게 이야기하기
(D) 예약 확정 보내기

해설 세부 내용 – 남자가 10분 후에 할 일
대화 마지막에 남자가 10분 후 예약 확정 이메일을 보내겠다고 했으므로 정답은 (D)이다.

어휘 registry 등록 booking 예약 confirmation 확정, 확인

7-9 대화＋스케줄

W-Am Welcome to Cleo Botanical Gardens. May I see your admission ticket, please?

M-Cn Yes, here it is. And I'm interested in seeing the tour of insect-eating plants.

W-Am I'm sorry, sir. **7**That activity has been canceled. There was some damage to our greenhouse due to last week's storm.

M-Cn That's too bad. **8**I guess I'll wait around for the demonstration on cutting off some branches. I might be able to pick up some tips to use at home.

W-Am All right. **9**In the meantime, here's one of our brochures. It has a detailed map of the grounds.

---

botanical garden 식물원 admission ticket 입장권 greenhouse 온실 demonstration 시연 in the meantime 그사이에 grounds 부지 trim 다듬다, 손질하다

번역 여 클레오 식물원에 오신 것을 환영합니다. 입장권을 보여 주시겠어요?
남 네, 여기 있습니다. 저는 곤충을 먹는 식물 투어를 보고 싶은데요.
여 죄송합니다. 그 투어는 취소됐어요. 지난 주 폭풍우로 인해 저희 온실이 훼손됐거든요.
남 안타깝네요. 가지치기 시연을 기다려야겠어요. 집에서 활용할 몇 가지 조언을 얻을 수 있을 것 같아요.
여 맞습니다. 안내책자가 여기 있으니 그사이에 보세요. 구내 상세 안내도가 있습니다.

시간	활동
오전 9:00	투어: 곤충을 먹는 식물
오전 10:00	시연: 나무 가지치기
오전 11:30	투어: 새집 수거
오후 12:30	시연: 장미 가꾸기

7. 취소가 된 이유는?
(A) 컴퓨터 오류   (B) 직원 결근
(C) 기상 재해   (D) 참가자 수 부족

해설 세부 내용 – 취소 이유
대화 중반부 여자가 폭풍우로 온실이 훼손되어 투어가 취소되었다(That activity ~ due to last week's storm)고 하므로 정답은 (C)이다.

어휘 absent 결근한, 결석한 weather damage 기상 재해 lack 부족, 결핍

8. 시각 정보에 따르면, 남자는 언제 활동에 참여할 예정인가?
(A) 오전 9:00   (B) 오전 10:00
(C) 오전 11:30   (D) 오후 12:30

해설 세부 내용 – 시각 정보 연계
남자가 두 번째 대사에서 가지치기 시연을 기다리겠다고 했고, 시각 정보에서 가지치기 시연을 찾아서 확인하면 있으므로 정답은 (B)이다.

어휘 participate in ~에 참가하다

9. 여자는 남자에게 무엇을 주었는가?
(A) 변경된 일정표   (B) 입장권
(C) 정보 안내책자   (D) 시 지도

해설 세부 내용 – 여자가 남자에게 준 것
여자가 마지막 대사에서 안내도를 포함한 안내책자가 있다고 하므로 정답은 (C)이다.

어휘 admission 입장

10-12

W-Am Good afternoon. This is Tina Wilson from Creeds Publishing. **10**I'm in charge of organizing an excursion for our staff members, and I'm wondering about your guided tours of Central Park.

M-Cn We offer four tours a day, and **11**there are usually between fifteen and twenty-five people in each tour group.

W-Am **12**We'll have twenty-three people, but we'd really like to have a private tour with only members of our own group. Would that be possible?

M-Cn I don't see why not. I can make the booking for you now.

---

be in charge of ~을 담당하다 organize 기획하다, 주관하다 excursion 소풍, 야유회

번역 여 안녕하세요. 저는 크리드 출판사의 티나 윌슨입니다. 직원 야유회 기획을 맡고 있어요. 센트럴 파크 가이드 투어에 대해 알고 싶은데요.
남 하루에 4회 투어를 제공합니다. 보통 한 그룹당 15~25명이 참여해요.

여 저희는 23명인데 저희 직원으로만 구성된 개인 투어를 원합니다. 가능할까요?

남 안 될 이유가 없지요. 지금 예약해 드릴 수 있습니다.

10. 여자는 무엇을 계획하는가?

(A) 회사 야유회　　　　(B) 자선 기금 모금 행사

(C) 건물 복구　　　　　(D) 시상식

해설 **전체 내용 – 여자가 계획하는 것**

여자가 첫 대사에서 직원 야유회 기획을 맡고 있다(I'm in charge of ~ staff members)고 했으므로 정답은 (A)이다.

어휘 outing 야유회, 여행　charity 자선　fundraiser 모금 행사　restoration 복원, 복구　awards ceremony 시상식

11. 남자는 활동에 대해 뭐라고 말하는가?

(A) 참가비가 최근 인상됐다.

(B) 표는 양도할 수 없다.

(C) 미리 예약해야 한다.

(D) 단체 규모는 각기 다르다.

해설 **세부 내용 – 남자의 활동에 대한 언급**

대화 중반부 남자가 투어 그룹이 15~25명으로 구성된다(there are usually between ~ in each tour group)고 했으므로 정답은 (D)이다.

어휘 recently 최근　transferable 양도 가능한　in advance 미리　vary 각기 다르다

12. 남자가 "안 될 이유가 없지요"라고 말할 때 그 의도는 무엇인가?

(A) 기꺼이 할인해 줄 것이다.

(B) 상황 설명을 다시 들어야 한다.

(C) 요청을 수용할 수 있다.

(D) 추가 정보를 제공할 수 없다.

해설 **세부 내용 – 화자의 의도**

인용문에서 여자가 투어에 대한 요청 사항이 가능한지 묻자 남자가 안 될 이유가 없다고 했으므로 남자가 한 말의 의도는 요청 수용이라고 볼 수 있다. 따라서 정답은 (C)이다.

어휘 provide a discount 할인해 주다　accommodate 수용하다

13-15

M-Cn Hi, I'm here from the tech support department. ¹³,¹⁴We're installing a new security program, so I need to work on your computer for a bit. Is now a good time?

W-Br Oh, but this morning the computer automatically updated itself.

M-Cn Yes, the computers keep themselves up-to-date with certain software, but I'll be installing an entirely new program. I can come back later, if you're busy.

W-Br Well, it's almost lunch time. Do you need my computer password? ¹⁵I can write it down for you, if you like.

- -

support 지원　department 부서　install 설치하다　security 보안　automatically 자동으로　up-to-date 최신의　entirely 전적으로, 완전히

번역 남 안녕하세요. 기술지원부서에서 왔습니다. 새 보안 프로그램을 설치하고 있는데요. 잠시 귀하의 컴퓨터에 작업이 필요합니다. 지금 괜찮으세요?

여 아, 그런데 오늘 아침 컴퓨터가 자동으로 업데이트됐는데요.

남 네, 컴퓨터는 특정 소프트웨어를 통해 계속 스스로 업데이트하지만 저는 완전히 새로운 프로그램을 설치하려고 합니다. 바쁘시면 나중에 다시 올 수 있습니다.

여 점심 시간이 다 됐네요. 제 컴퓨터 비밀번호가 필요하세요? 원하시면 적어드릴게요.

13. 남자는 무엇을 해야 한다고 말하는가?

(A) 컴퓨터 프로그램 설치하기

(B) 오류 메시지 기록하기

(C) 점심 식사하러 가기

(D) 몇 부 복사하기

해설 **세부 내용 – 남자가 해야 할 일**

대화 초반부 남자가 여자의 컴퓨터에 프로그램을 설치해야 한다(We're installing a new security program, so I need to work on your computer for a bit)며 시간이 괜찮은지 물었으므로 정답은 (A)이다.

어휘 make a copy 복사하다

14. 여자가 "오늘 아침 컴퓨터가 자동으로 업데이트됐어요"라고 말할 때 그 의도는 무엇인가?

(A) 남자를 도울 시간이 있다.

(B) 일부 작업이 필요하지 않다고 생각한다.

(C) 기술적인 문제점을 겪었다.

(D) 소프트웨어에 만족한다.

해설 **세부 내용 – 화자의 의도**

인용문 앞에서 남자가 새 보안 프로그램을 설치해야 한다고 했을 때, 여자가 오늘 아침 컴퓨터가 자동으로 업데이트됐다고 한 것으로 보아 작업의 불필요성을 전달하려는 것임을 추론할 수 있다. 따라서 정답은 (B)이다.

어휘 assist 돕다　technical 기술적인

15. 여자는 남자에게 무엇을 주겠다고 제안하는가?

(A) 사용 설명서　　　　(B) 식권

(C) 전화번호　　　　　(D) 비밀번호

해설 **세부 내용 – 여자가 남자에게 줄 것**

여자가 마지막 대사에서 비밀번호가 필요한지 묻고 원하면 적어주겠다고 했으므로 정답은 (D)이다.

16-18 대화 + floor plan

M-Au Hello. Do you know where Mr. Turner's office is? **16**I've got a parcel for him.

W-Br I can accept it and bring it up to him myself.

M-Au Thanks, but actually I need him to sign for it.

W-Br I understand. In that case, take the elevator to the fifth floor. **17**Mr. Turner's office is at the end of the hallway, the last one on the right.

M-Au Thank you. **18**And do I need to get a security pass while I'm in the building?

W-Br That's only for the top two floors.

M-Au All right. I appreciate your help.

parcel 소포   hallway 복도   security pass 보안 출입증
appreciate 감사하다

번역　남　안녕하세요. 터너 씨의 사무실이 어딘지 아세요? 터너 씨 소포를 가져왔습니다.
　　　여　제가 받아서 전달해 드릴 수 있습니다.
　　　남　감사합니다만, 터너 씨가 서명을 하셔야 해요.
　　　여　알겠습니다. 그렇다면 엘리베이터를 타고 5층으로 가세요. 터너 씨 사무실은 복도 끝, 오른쪽 끝에 있는 사무실입니다.
　　　남　감사합니다. 건물에 있는 동안 보안 출입증이 있어야 하나요?
　　　여　그건 맨 꼭대기 두 층에만 해당됩니다.
　　　남　알겠습니다. 도와주셔서 감사합니다.

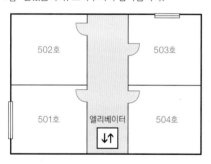

16. 남자가 업체를 방문한 이유는?
　　(A) 배송하기 위해
　　(B) 면접에 참석하기 위해
　　(C) 교육을 진행하기 위해
　　(D) 계약서에 서명하기 위해

해설　**세부 내용 – 남자가 업체를 방문한 이유**
남자가 첫 대사에서 터너의 사무실 위치를 물으며 소포를 가져왔다(I've got a parcel for him)고 하므로 정답은 (A)이다.

어휘　attend 참석하다   sign a contract 계약서에 서명하다

17. 시각 정보에 따르면 남자는 어디로 가야 하는가?
　　(A) 501호　　　　(B) 502호
　　(C) 503호　　　　(D) 504호

해설　**세부 내용 – 시각 정보 연계**
대화 중반부 여자가 터너의 사무실 위치를 묻는 남자에게 엘리베이터에서 내려 복도 끝 오른쪽으로 가라(Ms. Turner's office is at the end of the hallway, the last one on the right)고 했다. 시각 정보에서 복도 끝 오른쪽 방을 찾아서 확인하면 정답은 (C)이다.

18. 남자는 무엇에 대해 문의하는가?
　　(A) 채용 절차
　　(B) 주차 요금
　　(C) 폐장 시간
　　(D) 보안 조치

해설　**세부 내용 – 남자의 문의 사항**
대화 후반부 남자가 보안 출입증이 필요한지(And do I need to get a security pass while I'm in the building?) 물었으므로 정답은 (D)이다.

어휘　process 절차   measures 조치, 대책

19-21

M-Cn Hi, is that Paula? I'm just calling to inform you that your payment on your account is now overdue. **19**We won't be able to deliver any more T-shirts until it is paid off.

W-Am Oh, really? Thanks for letting me know. **20,21**I'll get in touch with George in our accounting department and ask him to send the payment immediately.

M-Cn I really appreciate that. You have been a loyal customer of ours for many years, so I'm sure it was just a misunderstanding. We look forward to doing business with you for many years to come.

payment 지불   account 계좌   overdue 기한이 지난
deliver 배송하다   pay off 다 갚다   accounting 회계
immediately 즉시   loyal customer 단골 고객
misunderstanding 오해   look forward to ~을 고대하다

번역　남　안녕하세요, 폴라 씨인가요? 계좌 입금 기한이 지나서 알려드리려고 전화했습니다. 지불이 완료될 때까지 티셔츠를 더 배송해 드릴 수 없습니다.
　　　여　아, 정말요? 알려주셔서 감사합니다. 저희 회계부서 조지 씨에게 연락해서 즉시 지급해 달라고 요청할게요.
　　　남　정말 감사합니다. 몇 년간 저희 단골 고객이시니, 착오가 있었을 거라고 생각합니다. 앞으로도 오랫동안 계속 거래가 이뤄지길 바랍니다.

19. 남자는 어디에서 일하겠는가?
　　(A) 은행
　　(B) 의류 창고
　　(C) 휴대전화 매장
　　(D) 출장 요리 업체

해설 **전체 내용 – 남자의 근무 장소**
남자가 첫 대사에서 지불이 완료될 때까지 티셔츠를 보낼 수 없다고 하므로 의류 관련 업계에서 근무하고 있음을 알 수 있다. 따라서 (R)가 정답이다.

어휘 warehouse 창고

20. 여자는 다음으로 무엇을 하겠는가?
(A) 수송품 열어보기
(B) 송금하기
(C) 동료에게 이야기하기
(D) 주문하기

해설 **세부 내용 – 여자가 다음에 할 일**
대화 중반부 여자가 회계부서 조지에게 연락해 지급을 요청하겠다(I'll get in touch ~ payment immediately)고 했으므로 정답은 (C)이다.

어휘 shipment 수송품 transfer money 송금하다 place an order 주문하다

21. 남자가 "정말 감사합니다"라고 말할 때 그 의미는 무엇인가?
(A) 여자가 문제를 해결하려고 해줘서 기쁘다.
(B) 여자에게 서비스가 업그레이드될 것임을 알리고 있다.
(C) 여자가 납부 기한을 미뤄준 데 대해 고마워하고 있다.
(D) 여자에게 새 고객 계좌를 개설하라고 권하고 있다.

해설 **세부 내용 – 화자의 의도**
인용문 앞에서 여자가 회계부서 조지에게 연락해서 지급하도록 하겠다고 하자 남자가 감사 인사를 했다. 이는 여자가 지급 문제 해결을 도와줘서 고맙다는 뜻이므로 정답은 (A)이다.

어휘 attempt 시도하다 payment date 납부 기한 encourage 권장하다, 독려하다 open an account 계좌를 개설하다

22-24

M-Au Good afternoon. This is Greg Smith calling from the *Business Daily*. I'd like to invite Mr. Han for an interview about his work.
W-Am That shouldn't be a problem, but Mr. Han is working on many projects.
M-Au Oh, right. ²²Specifically, I want to speak to him about his role as CEO of Vivid Technology Solutions. ²³I'm writing a piece on how new companies finance themselves.
W-Am Oh, yes, He'll be happy to talk about it. ²⁴Let me send you some marketing brochures for Vivid Technology Solutions, so you can go over them while you wait to hear from Mr. Han.

specifically 구체적으로 말하면 finance 자금을 대다

번역 남 안녕하세요. 저는 〈비즈니스 데일리〉의 그레그 스미스입니다. 한 사장님을 업무에 관한 인터뷰에 초청하고 싶습니다.
여 좋습니다만, 한 사장님은 지금 많은 프로젝트를 진행하고 계신데요.
남 아, 그렇군요. 구체적으로 말씀드리자면, 저는 비비드 테크놀로지 솔루션스의 CEO로서 역할에 대해 이야기를 하고 싶습니다. 신생업체들이 어떻게 스스로 자금을 마련하는지 글을 쓰고 있거든요.
여 아, 네. 기꺼이 이야기해 주실 겁니다. 사장님과의 인터뷰를 기다리시는 동안 훑어보실 수 있도록 비비드 테크놀로지 솔루션스의 마케팅 책자를 보내드릴게요.

22. 여자가 "한 사장님은 지금 많은 프로젝트를 진행하고 계신데요"라고 말한 이유는?
(A) 조직을 홍보하기 위해
(B) 명확한 설명을 요청하기 위해
(C) 제안을 수락하기 위해
(D) 비용을 정당화하기 위해

해설 **세부 내용 – 화자의 의도**
인용문 앞에서 남자가 한 사장님을 업무 관련으로 인터뷰하고 싶다고 말하자 여자는 사장님이 많은 프로젝트를 진행하고 있다고 하였다. 이에 남자는 구체적으로 CEO로서의 역할에 대한 것이라고 하나를 명시해준다. 즉, 여자의 말은 사장의 여러 업무 중에 정확하게 어떤 것에 대해 인터뷰하려는 것인지 알기 위한 것임을 알 수 있다. 따라서 정답은 (A)이다.

어휘 promote 홍보하다 clarification 명확한 설명, 명시 justify 정당화하다

23. 남자는 무엇에 관해 기사를 쓰는가?
(A) 자금 조달 방법
(B) 소셜미디어 업체
(C) 기업가를 위한 프로그램
(D) 공동체 기획자 단체

해설 **세부 내용 – 남자 기사의 내용**
대화 중반부 남자가 자금 마련 방법에 대해 글을 쓴다(I'm writing a piece on how new companies finance themselves)고 했으므로 정답은 (A)이다.

어휘 financing 자금 조달 entrepreneur 기업가

24. 여자는 남자에게 무엇을 보내겠다고 말하는가?
(A) 금융 서류 (B) 예약 카드
(C) 홍보 자료 (D) 인터뷰 전사

해설 **세부 내용 – 여자가 남자에게 보내줄 것**
여자가 마지막 대사에서 회사의 마케팅 책자를 보내주겠다(Let me send you ~ Vivid Technology Solutions)고 하므로 정답은 (C)이다.

어휘 financial 금융의 promotional 홍보의, 판촉의 material 자료 transcript 말을 글로 베낀 것, 전사

25-27 대화+영수증

W-Am Good afternoon. May I help you?

M-Au Well, I bought some camping gear here a few days ago, **25**but I'd like to return one of the items, this lantern.

W-Am Was there a problem with it?

M-Au I didn't even open the box. **26**I was reading some camping lantern reviews yesterday and most people recommend battery-operated ones instead of gas.

W-Am Would you like to exchange it rather than get a refund?

M-Au **27**Actually, my friend is going to lend me what I need, so I'd just like to make a return. Here's my receipt.

> gear 장비 recommend 추천하다 battery-operated 건전지로 작동하는 exchange 교환하다 get a refund 환불받다 sleeping bag 침낭

번역
여 안녕하세요. 도와드릴까요?
남 음, 여기서 며칠 전에 캠핑 장비를 샀는데요. 물품 중 하나인 이 랜턴을 환불하고 싶어서요.
여 문제가 있었나요?
남 상자를 열지도 않았어요. 어제 캠핑 랜턴 후기를 읽었는데 대부분 가스 대신 건전지로 작동하는 랜턴을 추천하더라고요.
여 환불보다는 교환을 원하시나요?
남 사실 제 친구가 필요한 걸 빌려줄 예정이라 환불하고 싶습니다. 영수증이 여기 있습니다.

```
***************************
        에머슨 캠핑용품
***************************
    고객 영수증 0158/5월 19일


3인용 텐트 x 1 ....................145달러
나일론 침낭 x 1 ....................95달러
가스 랜턴 x 1 .....................50달러
건전지 작동 전화 충전기 X 1 ..........30달러


                    합계 320달러
```

25. 시각 정보에 따르면 남자는 얼마를 환불받겠는가?
(A) 145달러   (B) 95달러
(C) 50달러   (D) 30달러

해설 세부 내용 – 시각 정보 연계
남자가 첫 대사에서 랜턴을 환불하겠다고 했다. 시각 정보에서 랜턴의 가격을 찾아서 확인하면 정답은 (C)이다.

26. 남자는 어제 무엇을 했는가?
(A) 상품평 확인   (B) 캠핑 여행에서 복귀
(C) 제품 손상 발견   (D) 캠핑 장비 구입

해설 세부 내용 – 남자가 어제 한 일
대화 중반부 남자가 어제 캠핑 랜턴 후기를 읽었다 (I was reading some camping lantern reviews yesterday)고 했으므로 정답은 (A)이다.

어휘 product review 상품평

27. 남자는 무엇을 할 계획이라고 말하는가?
(A) 기기를 위한 배터리 구입하기
(B) 매장에서 새 상품 둘러보기
(C) 나중에 업체에 다시 오기
(D) 친구에게 제품 빌리기

해설 세부 내용 – 남자의 계획
남자가 마지막 대사에서 친구가 필요한 것을 빌려줄 예정(Actually, my friend is going to lend me what I need)이라고 했으므로 정답은 (D)이다.

어휘 browse 둘러보다, 훑어보다

28-30

M-Cn Hi, Olivia. Did you work late last night?

W-Br No, Mr. Watson. I left right at five.

M-Cn I see. **28**I noticed you didn't clock out yesterday.

W-Br Oh, no. **29**The new time management software is confusing. I must have logged my time incorrectly.

M-Cn This isn't the first time this has happened.

W-Br I'm sorry, Mr. Watson. It won't happen again.

M-Cn OK. It's important for all employees to accurately record their working hours. **30**I'm going to send our technical support manager, Andrew Tyler, to your desk so he can show you how to use the software again.

> clock out 퇴근 시간을 기록하다 incorrectly 부정확하게 accurately 정확하게

번역
남 안녕하세요, 올리비아 씨. 어젯밤 늦게까지 일하셨어요?
여 아니요, 왓슨 씨. 5시에 바로 퇴근했어요.
남 그렇군요. 어제 퇴근 시간을 기록하지 않으셨더군요.
여 아, 그렇네요. 새로운 시간 관리 소프트웨어가 헷갈려서요. 시간을 잘못 입력한 것 같습니다.
남 이런 일이 이번이 처음이 아니라서요.
여 죄송합니다, 왓슨 씨. 다시 이런 일이 없도록 할게요.
남 알겠습니다. 모든 직원이 정확하게 근무시간을 기록하는 것은 중요한 일입니다. 기술지원 관리자인 앤드류 타일러 씨를 자리로 보내드릴게요. 소프트웨어 사용법을 다시 알려주실 겁니다.

28. 남자는 어떤 문제점을 언급하는가?
(A) 컨퍼런스 콜이 중단됐다.
(B) 장비 한 점이 제대로 작동하지 않았다.
(C) 직원이 근무 시간을 기록하지 않았다.
(D) 기술자가 소프트웨어 프로그램을 설치하지 않았다.

해설 **세부 내용 – 문제점**
대화 초반부 남자가 퇴근 시간을 기록하지 않은 여자의 행동을 문제 삼고 있으므로 정답은 (C)이다.

어휘 interrupt 중단시키다   malfunction 오작동   technician 기술자   install 설치하다

29. 남자가 "이런 일이 이번이 처음이 아니라서요."라고 말한 이유는?
(A) 사과하려고
(B) 못마땅함을 나타내려고
(C) 직원을 위로하려고
(D) 자신에게 해결책이 있음을 내비치려고

해설 **세부 내용 – 화자의 의도**
인용문 앞에서 여자가 헷갈려서 시간을 잘못 입력했다고 했는데 이에 대해 남자가 "이런 일이 이번이 처음이 아니다."라고 응답했다. 즉, 남자는 여자의 반복된 실수에 못마땅함을 나타내려는 것이므로 정답은 (B)이다.

어휘 apologize 사과하다   disapproval 반감. 못마땅함   indicate 내비치다. 시사하다

30. 타일러 씨는 여자가 무엇을 하는 것을 도울 것인가?
(A) 컴퓨터 프로그램 사용하기
(B) 없어진 물건 찾기
(C) 진급 신청하기
(D) 평가 제출하기

해설 **세부 내용 – 타일러 씨가 도울 일**
남자가 마지막 대사에서 소프트웨어 사용법을 알려줄 타일러 씨를 여자에게 보내주겠다고 했으므로 정답은 (A)이다.

어휘 promotion 승진. 진급   evaluation 평가

31-33

W-Br Mike, thanks for setting up our booth at the trade fair. **31**The lighting style you've used will definitely draw customers' attention.

M-Cn Thanks, I want to showcase our products in a way that stands out.

W-Br Sure. **32**I do have some feedback about the display, though. Many companies put most expensive products on the top shelf. And their cheapest on the bottom.

M-Cn I understand. **32**I'll look into that right away. By the way, when do we need to pack everything up by?

W-Br Well, **33**the event ends on Friday, so right after that. I have arranged for a courier to pick up our unsold items the following morning.

---

set up 설치하다   trade fair 무역박람회   definitely 분명히, 틀림없이   draw attention 관심을 끌다   stand out 눈에 띄다   pack up (짐을) 꾸리다   courier 택배 회사

번역 여 마이크 씨, 무역박람회에서 우리 부스를 설치해 주셔서 감사합니다. 사용하신 조명 스타일은 분명 고객의 관심을 끌 거예요.
남 감사합니다. 우리 제품을 눈에 띄게 전시하고 싶어서요.
여 네. 그런데 전시에 관한 피드백이 있어요. 많은 회사들이 가장 비싼 제품을 선반 맨 위칸에 두잖아요. 가장 저렴한 제품을 아래 두고요.
남 알겠습니다. 지금 바로 살펴볼게요. 그런데 제품을 언제까지 모두 싸야 하나요?
여 음, 행사가 금요일에 끝나니 그 직후예요. 다음날 오전에 판매되지 않은 제품을 수거해 갈 택배 회사를 섭외해 뒀어요.

31. 여자는 조명에 대해 뭐라고 말하는가?
(A) 색상이 마음에 든다.
(B) 행사 주제와 어울린다.
(C) 고객 유치에 도움이 될 것이다.
(D) 경쟁업체에서 똑 같은 스타일을 사용했다.

해설 **세부 내용 – 여자가 조명에 대해 언급한 사항**
여자가 첫 대사에서 조명이 고객의 관심을 끌 것(The lighting style you've used will definitely draw customers' attention)이라고 했으므로 정답은 (C)이다.

어휘 attract 끌다. 유치하다   competitor 경쟁자

32. 여자가 "많은 회사들이 가장 비싼 제품을 선반 맨 위칸에 두잖아요"라고 말한 이유는?
(A) 경쟁업체 관련 정보를 제공하기 위해
(B) 다른 매장 배치를 제안하기 위해
(C) 진열을 바꾸자고 제안하기 위해
(D) 남자가 제품을 살 것을 요청하기 위해

해설 **세부 내용 – 화자의 의도**
인용문 앞에서 여자가 전시에 대한 피드백이 있다며 "많은 회사들이 가장 비싼 제품을 선반 맨 위칸에 둔다"고 했다. 화자들의 회사는 다수의 회사들과 다른 방식으로 물건을 진열했다는 것으로 볼 수 있고 남자도 살펴보겠다고 하므로 진열을 바꾸자는 제안을 하려는 의도임을 알 수 있다. 따라서 정답은 (C)이다.

어휘 propose 제안하다   layout 배치

33. 여자에 따르면, 토요일에 어떤 일이 있을 것인가?
(A) 행사가 종료된다.
(B) 제품들이 수거될 것이다.
(C) 진열대가 설치될 것이다.
(D) 고객들이 도착할 것이다.

해설 **세부 내용 – 토요일에 있을 일**
대화 후반부 남자가 제품을 언제까지 싸야 하는지 물었고 여자가 금요일 직후라며 다음날 제품 수거를 위해 택배 회사를 섭외했다고 하므로 정답은 (B)이다.

어휘 collect 모으다, 수거하다

34-36 대화+스케줄

M-Cn **34**Well, I hope you enjoyed your first training session with me. To be honest, you are already in much better shape than most of my clients here at the gym. What do you do to keep fit?

W-Am Well, I used to hike near my hometown. **35**But I just moved here, and I can't find anyone to go hiking with.

M-Cn Well, we do have a local hiking group. **36**In fact, I'm planning to join the group for the Pine Trail hike next month. Why don't you come along?

W-Am That sounds great! I'd love to see the local mountains.

in good shape 체형이 좋은, 건강한 몸을 유지하는   keep fit 건강을 유지하다   come along 함께 가다

번역 남 자, 저와 함께 한 첫 번째 트레이닝 시간이 즐거우셨기를 바랍니다. 솔직히 이 헬스클럽의 제 고객 대다수보다 이미 몸 상태가 훨씬 더 좋습니다. 건강 유지를 위해 무엇을 하시나요?
여 음, 고향 근처에서 등산을 하곤 했어요. 하지만 이곳으로 이사 와서 같이 등산할 사람을 찾지 못했어요.
남 지역 등산팀이 있습니다. 사실 저는 다음 달에 소나무길 등반팀에 합류할 계획이 있는데요. 같이 하시면 어때요?
여 그럼 좋겠네요! 지역에 있는 산에 가 보고 싶거든요.

밸리 하이킹 그룹				
가을 하이킹 여행 – 실버 마운틴즈				
9월 3일	9월 17일	10월 1일	10월 15일	10월 29일
떡갈 나무길	호랑가시 나무길	자작 나무길	소나무길	양치 식물길

34. 남자는 누구이겠는가?
(A) 채용 대행업체 직원
(B) 매장 관리자
(C) 개인 트레이너
(D) 현지 투어 가이드

해설 **전체 내용 – 남자의 신분**
남자가 첫 대사에서 자신과의 트레이닝 시간을 즐겼기를 바란다며 여자의 몸상태가 이 헬스클럽의 다른 고객보다도 좋다(Well, I hope you enjoyed ~ my clients here at the gym)고 하므로 정답은 (C)이다.

35. 여자가 최근에 한 일은?
(A) 새로운 일 시작
(B) 새로운 도시로 이사
(C) 휴가
(D) 회원 갱신

해설 **세부 내용 – 여자가 최근에 한 일**
여자가 첫 번째 대사(I just moved here, and I can't find anyone to go hiking with)에서 최근에 이사했음을 언급했다. 따라서 정답은 (B)이다.

어휘 go on vacation 휴가 가다   renew 갱신하다

36. 시각 정보에 따르면 여자는 언제 등반팀에 참여할 것인가?
(A) 9월 17일
(B) 10월 1일
(C) 10월 15일
(D) 10월 29일

해설 **세부 내용 – 시각 정보 연계**
대화 중반에 남자가 소나무길 등반을 제안했고 여자가 동의했다. 시각 정보에서 소나무길 등반팀을 찾아서 확인하면 정답은 (C)이다.

PART 4

● 패러프레이징

LISTENING PRACTICE

교재 p. 111

1. (A) **2.** (B) **3.** (A) **4.** (B) **5.** (A)
6. (B) **7.** (A) **8.** (A) **9.** (A) **10.** (B)
11. (B) **12.** (A) **13.** (B) **14.** (A)

---

1 M-Cn

In the meantime, I'd like you to take part in our customer survey, which will help us improve our services and enhance your experiences with us.

번역 그 동안에 저는 여러분이 고객 설문조사에 참여해 주시기를 바랍니다. 이는 우리의 서비스를 개선하고 여러분의 서비스 이용을 향상시키는 것을 도와줄 것입니다.

문제 화자는 청자에게 무엇을 하라고 요청하는가?
(A) 설문 조사를 작성하기
(B) 그룹 활동에 참여하기

패러 survey ❯ questionnaire

---

2 W-Am

For a small additional fee, we can make promotional mugs with your company logo on them, and you can give them away to your customers.

번역 소액의 추가 비용을 내면 귀사의 로고가 찍힌 홍보용 머그잔을 만들어 드려요. 그것들을 귀사의 고객들께 배포할 수 있을 거고요.

문제 화자는 무엇이 이용 가능하다고 말하는가?
(A) 가격 할인
(B) 고객 맞춤형 아이템

패러 mugs with ~ logo ❯ customized items

---

3 W-Br

I'm pleased to let you know that the company will cover all travel expenses associated with the workshop including airfare and hotel lodging.

번역 항공료, 호텔 숙박비를 포함한 워크숍과 관련된 모든 출장 경비를 회사가 지원할 것임을 알리게 되어 기쁩니다.

문제 회사에 의해 무엇이 준비될 것인가?
(A) 숙박   (B) 오찬

패러 hotel lodging ❯ accommodation

---

4 M-Au

Our advertising director Wyatt Morris has decided to step down from his position at the end of the month.

번역 저희 광고 부장인 와이어트 모리스 씨는 이달 말 은퇴하시기로 결정했습니다.

문제 와이어트 모리스는 무엇을 하려고 계획하는가?
(A) 다른 지사로 전근을 간다.
(B) 회사를 은퇴한다.

패러 step down ❯ retire

---

5 W-Am

As traffic is slow on Highway 17, I suggest you take an alternate route to avoid delays.

번역 교통이 17번 고속도로에서 더디므로 지연을 피하기 위해 다른 경로로 가실 것을 제안합니다.

문제 화자는 무엇을 추천하는가?
(A) 우회할 것   (B) 느린 속도로 운행할 것

패러 take an alternate route ❯ take a detour

---

6 W-Br

In a moment, I'll pass out these flyers so you can compare the prices.

번역 잠시 후 가격을 비교해 보시도록 이 전단지를 나누어 드리겠습니다.

문제 화자는 무엇을 할 것이라고 말하는가?
(A) 회계 자료를 찾는다. (B) 자료를 나누어 준다.

패러 pass out flyers ❯ distribute information

---

7 M-Au

Our bookcases are easy to put together, so you can start using them after a few minutes.

번역 저희의 책장은 조립이 쉽습니다. 따라서 몇 분 만에 바로 사용하실 수 있습니다.

문제 화자는 어떤 특징을 언급하는가?
(A) 조립하기 쉽다.   (B) 완성품으로 출시된다.

패러 put together ❯ assemble

8 M-Cn

> Just to let you know, light snacks and beverages are available at the on-site cafeteria.

번역 참고로, 간단한 간식과 음료는 현장에 있는 간이 식당에서 이용 가능합니다.

문제 화자는 무엇이 이용 가능하다고 말하는가?
(A) 다과 (B) 제품 샘플

패러 snacks and beverages ❯ refreshments

9 M-Cn

> As the vice president is stopping by next week to check our factory, we should start preparations for his visit.

번역 부사장님이 다음 주에 저희 공장을 확인 차 방문하시므로 방문에 대한 대비를 시작해야 합니다.

문제 다음 주에 누가 공장을 방문할 것인가?
(A) 회사 임원 (B) 잠재 고객

패러 vice president ❯ company executive

10 W-Br

> Join our membership today and take advantage of the extra storage space available at no charge.

번역 오늘 멤버십에 가입하시어 무료로 이용 가능한 추가 저장 공간 혜택을 누리세요.

문제 화자는 무엇이 이용 가능하다고 말하는가?
(A) 추가 할인 쿠폰 (B) 무료 저장 공간

패러 at no charge ❯ complimentary

11 M-Au

> Thanks to the hard work of the organizers, we've made a great deal of progress with planning for the company picnic scheduled for next week.

번역 주최측의 노고 덕분에 저희는 다음 주로 예정된 회사 야유회 계획에 상당한 진전을 이루었습니다.

문제 다음 주에 무슨 일이 있을 것인가?
(A) 공장 견학 (B) 회사 야유회

패러 company picnic ❯ corporate outing

12 W-Br

> Today, Mayor Charles Gregory called a press conference to make a formal announcement.

번역 오늘 찰스 그레고리 시장은 공식 발표를 하기 위해 기자 회견을 열었습니다.

문제 누가 오늘 기자 회견을 열었는가?
(A) 시 공무원 (B) 기업인

패러 mayor ❯ city official

13 M-Cn

> What I like most is that this coffee maker is so easy to use that you don't even need to look at the manual.

번역 제가 가장 마음에 드는 것은 이 커피메이커가 사용이 매우 쉬워 설명서를 볼 필요조차도 없다는 것입니다.

문제 화자는 어떤 특징을 강조하는가?
(A) 견고하다. (B) 사용자 친화적이다.

패러 easy to use ❯ user-friendly

14 W-Am

> After we watch a short instructional video, I'll show you how to use the new cash register.

번역 짧은 교육용 비디오를 본 후에 제가 새로운 금전 등록기를 사용하는 방법을 보여 드리겠습니다.

문제 화자는 무엇을 할 것이라고 말하는가?
(A) 장비를 시연한다. (B) 자금을 배당한다.

패러 show how to use ~ cash register ❯ demonstrate equipment

●UNIT 01 전화 음성 메시지

예제

교재 p. 112

> W-Am Hi, this is Brenda Ahn. I'm scheduled to see the doctor for my annual checkup next month, but I'm afraid I need to cancel. I'll be moving out of state very soon, and I'm quite busy getting ready for the move. Actually, I found a physician in the new city, so I would like you to send him my medical files. Please give me a call back soon.
>
> be scheduled to ~할 예정이다　annual 매년 있는, 연례의
> physician (내과)의사

번역 안녕하세요, 브렌다 안입니다. 다음 달에 연례 건강검진을 위해 진료를 받을 예정인데요. 취소해야 할 것 같아요. 곧 다른 주로 이사할 예정이라 이사 준비에 무척 바쁘거든요. 사실 새로 이사할 도시에서 의사를 찾았으니 그 쪽으로 제 의료 문서를 보내주셨으면 합니다. 다시 전화 주세요.

LISTENING PRACTICE

교재 p. 113

1. (A)　**2.** (B)　**3.** (C)　**4.** (D)

1　M-Cn

> Hello, this is Travis Anderson. I'm calling to let you know I've decided to go ahead with your business, using the terms of the sample contract you gave me. Please call me back to discuss more in detail.

go ahead with ~을 추진하다　terms 조건　contract 계약
in detail 자세히

번역 안녕하세요. 트래비스 앤더슨입니다. 저에게 주신 샘플 계약 조건으로 귀사와 업무를 추진하기로 결정했음을 알려드리고자 전화드립니다. 세부 사항 논의를 위해 전화주세요.

문제 전화를 건 목적은?
(A) 계약을 확정하기 위해
(B) 결제하기 위해
(C) 길 안내를 받기 위해
(D) 주문을 취소하기 위해

해설 **전체 내용 – 전화를 건 목적**
　메시지 중반부에 주신 계약 조건으로 일을 추진하기로 결정했다(I've decided ~ gave me)고 했으므로 정답은 (A)이다.

어휘 agreement 계약　make a payment 지불하다, 결제하다
directions 길 안내

2　M-Au

> Hi, I'm calling from Doctor Benson's office. We faxed you a prescription about an hour ago for one of our patients, Darryl Warren. He notified us that he moved to the other side of town, but we accidentally mailed you the form. If you could give me a call back today to get this straightened out, I'd appreciate it.

prescription 처방전　notify 알리다, 통지하다　accidentally
뜻하지 않게, 잘못하여　get ~ straightened out ~을 바로
해결하다

번역 안녕하세요, 벤슨 박사님 병원입니다. 한 시간쯤 전에 저희 환자 중 한 분인 대릴 워렌 씨의 처방전을 팩스로 보내드렸습니다. 워렌 씨가 다른 곳으로 이사했다고 알려왔어요. 그런데 저희가 서류를 잘못 보내드렸네요. 오늘 바로 전화 주셔서 처리해 주시면 감사하겠습니다.

문제 화자는 어떤 문제를 언급하는가?
(A) 환자가 예약을 어겼다.
(B) 서류가 잘못된 수신인에게 발송됐다.
(C) 약국이 폐업한다.
(D) 전화번호가 연결이 안 된다.

해설 **세부 내용 – 문제점**
　메시지 중반부에 워렌 씨가 이사했다(moved to the other side of town)고 했는데 화자가 서류를 잘못 보냈다(accidentally mailed)고 하며 문제점을 언급하므로 정답은 (B)이다.

어휘 miss an appointment 약속을 지키지 못하다　recipient 수신인　pharmacy 약국　go out of business 폐업하다
disconnected 연결이 잘 안 되는

3　M-Cn

> Good morning, Ms. Hassan. This is Dustin Burns from Louis Contractors. I got your message saying that you're having problems with the air conditioning system that we recently installed for you. I'll send someone to your home to do a check. Please call me back to let me know the time that would be best for you. Thanks.

recently 최근에　install 설치하다

번역 안녕하세요, 핫산 씨. 저는 루이스 컨트랙터스의 더스틴 번즈입니다. 저희가 최근에 설치해 드린 에어컨 시스템에 문제가 있다는 메시지를 받았는데요. 댁으로 사람을 보내 확인하겠습니다. 다시 전화 주셔서 제일 좋은 시간을 알려주세요. 감사합니다.

문제 청자는 왜 화자에게 다시 전화해야 하는가?
(A) 결제 정보를 알려주기 위해
(B) 환불 지침을 받기 위해
(C) 방문 시간을 정하기 위해
(D) 일부 제품 배송을 준비하기 위해

해설 **세부 내용 – 다시 전화해야 하는 이유**
　메시지 후반부에 사람을 보내 확인하겠다고 하며, 좋은 시간대를 알려 달라(Please call me ~ best for you)고 요청하므로 정답은 (C)이다.

어휘 instruction 설명, 지침　set up 준비하다

4　W-Am

> Mr. Ping, this is Ellen Donovan on the assembly floor. One of the conveyor belts stopped working. I have about fifteen workers just standing around, and now I don't know what to tell them. Until I hear back from you, I'm just going to send them to the cafeteria to wait for instructions.

assembly 조립　instruction 지시, 설명

번역 핑 씨, 저는 조립 층에 있는 엘렌 도노반입니다. 컨베이어 벨트 중 하나가 작동을 멈췄어요. 15명의 근로자가 그냥 우두커니 서 있는데 그들에게 뭐라고 해야 할지 모르겠어요. 다시 연락 주실 때까지 카페테리아로 가서 지시를 기다리라고 얘기하겠습니다.

문제 화자가 "그들에게 뭐라고 해야 할지 모르겠어요"라고 말한 의도는?
(A) 유감을 나타내려고　(B) 프로그램을 비판하려고
(C) 초대를 거절하려고　(D) 지침을 요청하려고

해설 **세부 내용 – 화자의 의도**
인용문 앞에서 일을 멈추고 서 있는 직원들을 언급했고 인용문 뒤에서 연락 줄 때까지 지시를 기다리게 한다고 하였으므로 지침을 요청하고 있음을 알 수 있다. 따라서 정답은 (D)이다.

어휘 regret 유감　criticize 비판하다　decline 거절하다
request 요청하다

ACTUAL TEST
교재 p. 114

1. (A)	**2.** (C)	**3.** (A)	**4.** (D)	**5.** (A)
6. (B)	**7.** (B)	**8.** (D)	**9.** (A)	**10.** (C)
11. (A)	**12.** (C)	**13.** (A)	**14.** (B)	**15.** (C)
16. (B)	**17.** (D)	**18.** (C)	**19.** (B)	**20.** (C)
21. (A)				

1-3 전화 메시지

W-Br Hello. I'm calling from Thompson's Removal regarding the request you placed online. You're getting a sofa picked up, right? Just to let you know, **1**there is an extra charge for big items like that, regardless of their weight. You can pay that to the driver when he arrives. **2**Please have the sofa on the curb so he can load it in the van easily. Oh, and I noticed **3**you're not in our Preferred Customer Rewards program. You should join, because you can save some money on this request and others. If you'd like, you can reach me at 555-0111.

---

regarding ~에 관해　request 요청　extra charge 추가 요금
regardless of ~에 상관없이　curb 도로경계석　reward 보상

번역 안녕하세요, 온라인으로 요청하신 건에 관해 톰슨 리무벌에서 전화 드립니다. 소파를 가져가도록 하시는 거죠, 그렇죠? 참고로 그렇게 큰 물품은 무게와 상관없이 추가 요금이 발생합니다. 운전기사가 도착하면 지불해 주세요. 소파를 도로경계석에 두셔서 운전기사가 밴에 쉽게 실을 수 있도록 해 주시기 바랍니다. 아, 저희 우수 고객 보상 프로그램에 가입되어 있지 않으신 걸 알았어요. 이번 요청과 다른 건들에 대해 비용을 아낄 수 있으니 꼭 가입하셔야죠. 원하신다면 555-0111로 전화해 주십시오.

1. 화자는 물품 배송에 왜 추가 요금이 발생한다고 말하는가?
(A) 크기가 크다.　(B) 무겁다.
(C) 깨지기 쉽다.　(D) 값이 비싸다.

해설 **세부 내용 – 추가 요금 발생 이유**
메시지 초반부에 큰 물품은 무게와 상관없이 추가 요금이 있다(there is an extra charge ~ regardless of their weight)고 했으므로 정답은 (A)이다.

어휘 additional 추가의　fragile 깨지기 쉬운

2. 화자는 청자에게 무엇을 하라고 요청하는가?
(A) 온라인으로 결제하기
(B) 종이 문서 제출하기
(C) 가구를 밖으로 내오기
(D) 만날 시간 명시하기

해설 **세부 내용 – 청자에 대한 요청 사항**
메시지 중반부에 소파를 도로경계석에 두라(Please have the sofa on the curb)고 요청하고 있으므로 정답은 (C)이다.

어휘 submit 제출하다　specify 명시하다

3. 화자는 무엇을 추천하는가?
(A) 보상 프로그램 가입하기
(B) 운전기사에게 연락하기
(C) 온라인 서비스 이용하기
(D) 배송 시간 다시 정하기

해설 **세부 내용 – 제안 사항**
메시지 후반부에 우수 고객 보상 프로그램에 가입할 것을 제안(you should join)하므로 정답은 (A)이다.

어휘 reschedule 일정을 변경하다

4-6 음성 메시지

M-Au Thank you for calling Crystal Air Conditioning Services. Please be advised that **4**we are closed this week for the holidays. Call back next week to receive the best prices on air conditioning and the most reliable maintenance and repair services. Or, **5**if you are shopping for a new air conditioning unit, visit our Web site to see a complete list of our inventory. If your existing air conditioning unit is malfunctioning and is still under warranty, **6**please call our customer satisfaction center at 555-0141 to request a repair. Thank you.

---

reliable 믿을 만한　maintenance 유지 보수　complete 완전한　malfunction 제대로 작동하지 않다, 오작동하다
existing 기존의　under warranty 보증기간이 남아 있는

번역 크리스탈 에어컨 서비스에 전화 주셔서 감사합니다. 이번 주는 공휴일로 휴무입니다. 최상의 에어컨 가격과 가장 믿을 만한 보수 수리 서비스를 받으시려면 다음 주에 다시 전화해 주십시오. 새 에어컨을 구입하시려면 저희 웹사이트를 방문하셔서 물품 목록 전체를 확인하세요. 기존 에어컨의 작동이 잘 되지 않는데 아직 품질보증기간 중이라면 저

희 고객 만족센터에 555-0141로 전화하셔서 수리를 요청하세요. 감사합니다.

4. 화자는 크리스딜 에어컨 서비스에 대해 뭐라고 밀하는가?
(A) 특정 상표를 더 이상 판매하지 않는다.
(B) 곧 새로운 지점을 열 것이다.
(C) 공휴일 할인 판매를 하고 있다.
(D) 현재 휴무이다.

해설 **세부 내용 – 언급된 사항**
메시지 초반부에 이번주는 휴무(we are closed this week for the holidays)라고 하므로 정답은 (D)이다.

어휘 certain 어떤   currently 현재

5. 크리스탈 에어컨 서비스 웹사이트를 방문하는 고객들은 무엇을 할 수 있는가?
(A) 상품 살펴보기
(B) 쿠폰 다운로드하기
(C) 소식지 신청하기
(D) 품질보증기간 연장하기

해설 **세부 내용 – 고객들이 할 수 있는 일**
메시지 중반부에 에어컨 구입은 웹사이트의 물품 목록을 확인하라(if you ~ our inventory)고 하므로 정답은 (A)이다.

어휘 merchandise 상품   sign up for ~을 신청하다   extend 연장하다

6. 청자들은 수리 서비스를 받기 위해 무엇을 해야 하는가?
(A) 매장 방문하기
(B) 지원 부서에 전화하기
(C) 기술자에게 이메일 보내기
(D) 온라인 서식 작성하기

해설 **세부 내용 – 청자들이 할 일**
메시지 후반부에 고객 만족센터에 전화해서 수리를 요청하라(please call ~ a repair)고 하므로 정답은 (B)이다.

어휘 technician 기술자   complete a form 서식을 작성하다

7-9 전화 메시지

M-Cn Hello, Ms. Sato. This is Andy Morris calling from Straight Financial. I enjoyed meeting you at last week's interview. I'm pleased to say that **7**we would like to offer you the position of senior accountant. Before we prepare the contract, **8**we'll need to see a scan of your accounting license to prove that you are certified. You may e-mail that to me anytime. I'll be out of town for the next few days, but my colleague, **9**Janet Shim, can handle any inquiries. Her number is 555-0178, extension 436.

accountant 회계사   contract 계약, 계약서   license 자격증   certified 공인된, 자격을 받은   colleague 동료   inquiry 문의   extension 내선번호

번역 안녕하세요, 사토 씨. 저는 스트레이트 파이낸셜의 앤디 모리스입니다. 지난 주 면접 때 뵙게 되어 반가웠습니다. 사토 씨께 선임 회계사 직책을 드리겠다는 말씀을 전하게 되어 기쁩니다. 계약서 준비에 앞서, 사토 씨의 면허 보유를 증명하기 위해 회계 자격증 사본을 확인해야 합니다. 아무 때나 저에게 이메일로 보내주세요. 저는 앞으로 며칠 자리를 비우는데, 저의 동료인 자넷 심 씨가 문의 사항을 처리해 드릴 것입니다. 심 씨 전화번호는 555-0178번, 내선번호는 436번입니다.

7. 화자가 청자에게 전화를 건 이유는?
(A) 청구서를 요청하려고
(B) 일자리를 제안하려고
(C) 연락처를 수집하려고
(D) 인터뷰를 잡으려고

해설 **전체 내용 – 전화를 건 이유**
메시지 초반부에 선임 회계시직을 제안하고자 한다(we would like to offer ~ senior account)고 했으므로 정답은 (B)이다.

어휘 invoice 청구서, 송장   gather 모으다, 수집하다

8. 청자는 무엇을 보내달라는 요청을 받았는가?
(A) 여행 일정
(B) 계약서 사본
(C) 우편 주소
(D) 증명서

해설 **세부 내용 – 청자에 대한 요청 사항**
메시지 중반부에서 회계 자격증 사본(a scan of your accounting license)을 요청했으므로 정답은 (D)이다.

어휘 itinerary 일정   contract 계약서   certification 증명, 증명서

9. 화자가 심 씨에 대해 언급한 것은?
(A) 질문에 답할 수 있다.
(B) 교육을 진행할 것이다.
(C) 청자에게 연락할 계획이다.
(D) 가장 최근에 들어온 직원이다.

해설 **세부 내용 – 심 씨에 대한 언급 사항**
메시지 후반부에 자넷 심 씨가 문의 사항을 처리해 줄 것(Janet Shim, can handle any inquiries)이라고 했으므로 정답은 (A)이다.

어휘 respond to ~에 응답하다, 반응하다   conduct 시행하다

10-12 전화 메시지

M-Cn Hello, this is Carl Russo from Marco Apparel. ¹⁰I see on the order form that the shipping address is in Ottawa, which is different from past orders you've made. We've sent those to Toronto. Please call me back to confirm so I can make sure you don't have any problems with your delivery. ¹¹I'm planning not to go forward until I hear back from you. Also, ¹²we are starting to offer extra-large and double extra-large next month. We hope this better accommodates our client base. I'll talk to you soon.

order form 주문서   delivery 배송   go forward 진척시키다
accommodate (요구 등에) 부응하다   client base 고객층

번역 안녕하세요, 저는 마르코 어패럴의 칼 루소입니다. 주문서에서 배송지가 오타와인 것을 봤는데요. 지난 주문 건들과는 다르네요. 그 동안엔 토론토로 보냈는데 말이죠. 배송에 문제가 생기지 않게 해 드릴 수 있도록 다시 전화해서 확인해 주시기 바랍니다. 연락 주실 때까지 진행하지 않을 계획입니다. 아울러 다음 달에 엑스라지와 더블엑스라지 사이즈 판매를 시작합니다. 이것이 저희 고객층의 요구에 더 잘 부응할 수 있기를 바랍니다. 다시 통화하시죠.

10. 화자가 "그 동안엔 토론토로 보냈는데 말이죠"라고 말한 이유는?
(A) 물건 도착 여부를 확인하고 싶다.
(B) 이미 일부 정보를 보냈다.
(C) 주문서에 오류가 있을지도 모른다고 생각한다.
(D) 지연에 대해 사과하고자 한다.

해설 **세부 내용 – 화자의 의도**
인용문 앞에서 신규 배송지 주소를 언급하며 이전 주문건들과 배송지가 다르다(which is different from past orders you've made)고 하였고 이전 주소지가 토론토였다는 것을 인용문을 통해 알 수 있다. 또한 인용문 뒤에서 배송에 문제가 없도록 확인을 위해 전화를 달라(Please call me back to conform ~ any problems with your delivery)고 했으므로 주문서에 혹시 오류가 있을지도 모른다고 생각한다는 의미로 볼 수 있다. 따라서 정답은 (C)이다.

어휘 dispatch 보내다, 발송하다   apologize for ~에 대해 사과하다

11. 화자는 무엇을 하려고 계획하는가?
(A) 요청 사항이 처리되기를 기다리기
(B) 온라인 주문 검토하기
(C) 일부 환불해 주기
(D) 새 청구서 사본 보내기

해설 **세부 내용 – 화자의 계획**
메시지 중반부에서 연락 줄 때까지 진행하지 않을 계획(I'm planning not to go forward until I hear back from you)이라고 하므로 정답은 (A)이다.

어휘 process 처리하다   partial refund 부분 환불   bill 청구서

12. 화자는 다음 달에 어떤 일이 있을 것이라고 말하는가?
(A) 다양한 색상이 추가된다.
(B) 배송 지역이 확대된다.
(C) 더 많은 사이즈가 구입 가능해진다.
(D) 회원 우대 프로그램이 시작된다.

해설 **세부 내용 – 다음 달에 있을 일**
문제에 구체적인 시점인 next month가 있으므로 이 단어가 언급되는 부분에서 정답의 단서를 찾아야 한다. 지문 후반부에 다음 달에 extra-large와 double extra-large 사이즈 판매를 시작한다고 하므로 정답은 (C)이다.

어휘 a wide range of 광범위한, 다양한   expand 확장하다
loyalty program 회원 우대 프로그램

13-15 전화 메시지

M-Au Hello, I got your contact information from Rio National Park's Web site. It said ¹³you're the head forest ranger there. I'm a photographer for *Nature Awe* magazine. I'm putting together a calendar with photos from various parks in the state, and ¹⁴I'm wondering if you could give me some tips on the best places to shoot. The calendar will be sold this fall, and ¹⁵I plan to give a portion of the proceeds to the park to help with any necessary improvements. Please call me back at 555-0167. Thank you.

forest ranger 삼림 관리자   shoot 촬영하다   proceeds 수익금
improvement 향상, 개선

번역 안녕하세요, 리오 국립공원 웹사이트에서 귀하의 연락처를 구했습니다. 삼림 관리 책임자시라고요. 저는 〈네이처 오〉 잡지의 사진작가입니다. 국내 다양한 공원 사진을 모아 달력을 만들고 있는데, 촬영지로 가장 좋은 곳에 대해 조언을 해 주실 수 있는지 궁금해요. 달력은 이번 가을에 판매될 예정이고, 수익금 일부를 공원 측에 기증해 필요한 곳을 향상시키는 데 쓰도록 도울 계획입니다. 저에게 555-0167로 다시 전화 주십시오. 감사합니다.

13. 청자는 누구이겠는가?
(A) 공원 경비원
(B) 웹사이트 개발자
(C) 전문 사진작가
(D) 연구원

해설 **전체 내용 – 청자의 신분 및 직업**
메시지 초반부에 삼림 관리 책임자(you're the head forest ranger)라고 직접적으로 언급하고 있으므로 정답은 (A)이다.

어휘 professional 전문적인, 직업으로 하는

14. 전화를 건 목적은?
(A) 입장료를 문의하려고
(B) 장소에 대한 조언을 구하려고
(C) 인터뷰를 잡으려고
(D) 단체 여행 일정을 잡으려고

해설 **전체 내용 – 전화를 건 목적**
메시지 중반부에 촬영지로 가장 좋은 곳(the best places to shoot)에 대한 조언을 요청했으므로 정답은 (B)이다.

어휘 inquire 문의하다   entrance fee 입장료

15. 화자는 무엇을 할 계획이라고 말하는가?
(A) 축제 참가하기   (B) 정화 프로젝트 이끌기
(C) 기부하기   (D) 교육 참가하기

해설 **세부 내용 – 화자의 계획**
메시지 후반부에 수익금을 공원에 줄 계획(I plan to give a portion of the proceeds to the park)이라고 했으므로 정답은 (C)이다.

어휘 attend 참가하다   make a donation 기부하다

16-18 전화 메시지

M-Au Hi, Ms. Fletcher. This is David Gifford calling from Royal Insurance. **16**I wanted to thank you again for providing us with a custom decorated cake for our company anniversary party at the last minute. I know you usually require three days, so it was kind of you to make an exception in our case. **17**Everyone really liked the cake. Please let the rest of your team know that. **18**We usually use a bakery downtown, but I was glad to find one closer to our office. We've got lots of events in the coming months. I'll talk to you later.

insurance 보험   custom-decorated 주문 장식한
anniversary 기념일   at the last minute 임박해서   require
필요로 하다   make an exception 예외로 하다

번역 안녕하세요, 플레처 씨. 저는 로열 보험의 데이비드 기포드입니다. 저희 회사 기념 파티에 임박해서 주문 장식 케이크를 만들어 주셔서 다시 한 번 감사드립니다. 보통 3일은 필요하신 것으로 아는데 저희는 예외로 해 주셔서 감사했습니다. 모두들 케이크를 마음에 들어했어요. 팀의 다른 분들께도 알려 주십시오. 저희는 보통 시내에 있는 제과점을 이용하는데 사무실에 더 가까운 곳을 찾아서 기쁩니다. 앞으로 몇 달간 행사가 많이 있습니다. 나중에 연락드릴게요.

16. 화자는 왜 청자에게 감사하다고 하는가?
(A) 기념 파티 기획을 도왔다.
(B) 갑작스럽게 통보했는데 임무를 완수해 주었다.
(C) 보험을 들었다.
(D) 서비스 정상 요금을 면제해 주었다.

해설 **세부 내용 – 감사한 이유**
메시지 초반부에 회사 기념 파티에 임박해서 주문 장식 케이크를 만들어 주셔서 감사드린다(I wanted ~ last minute)고 했으므로 정답은 (B)이다.

어휘 complete 완료하다   on short notice 갑작스러운 통보로
insurance policy 보험 증서, 보험 증권   waive 탕감해 주다

17. 플레처 씨는 무엇을 요청받았는가?
(A) 가능한 한 빨리 화자에게 다시 전화하기
(B) 플레처 씨의 팀에게 새로운 업무 배정하기
(C) 선택사항의 사진 보내기
(D) 동료들에게 칭찬 내용 공유하기

해설 **세부 내용 – 플레처에 대한 요청 사항**
메시지 중반부에 모두들 케이크를 마음에 들어했다 (Everyone ~ cake)고 한 후, 팀의 다른 분들께도 알려 달라(Please let ~ know that)고 했으므로 정답은 (D)이다.

어휘 assign 배정하다, 안배하다   compliment 칭찬
coworker 동료

18. 화자가 "앞으로 몇 달간 행사가 많이 있습니다"라고 말한 의도는?
(A) 마감 기한을 연기하고 싶다.
(B) 너무 바빠서 직접 만날 수 없다.
(C) 향후에 일을 줄 수 있다.
(D) 청자에게 초청장을 보낼 것이다.

해설 **세부 내용 – 화자의 의도**
인용문 앞에서 보통 다른 제과점을 이용하는데 사무실에서 더 가까운 곳을 찾아 기쁘다(We usually ~ closer to our office)고 하며 앞으로 몇 달간 행사가 많다고 했다. 이는 향후에도 거래할 의사가 있음을 밝힌 것으로 볼 수 있으므로 정답은 (C)이다.

어휘 postpone 미루다, 연기하다   in person 직접

19-21 전화 메시지+도표

W-Br Hi, Eric. It's Maria. I've looked over the research you did for the treadmills we're considering for our gym. I think **19**we should purchase the one that has an incline and additional cushioning. The pre-set workout programs would be a waste of money. **20**Do you think the company would give us a better price if we ordered a lot of machines at once? Please find out about this and then fill out the order form. Then **21**you'll need to give it to Ms. Diaz to sign. Thanks.

look over ~을 훑어보다, 살펴보다   treadmill 러닝머신   incline
경사   cushioning 완충   at once 동시에

PART 4

번역 안녕하세요, 에릭 씨. 마리아입니다. 우리가 헬스클럽용으로 고려 중인 러닝머신에 관해 실시한 조사를 살펴보았습니다. 경사와 추가 완충재가 있는 것으로 구입해야 할 것 같아요. 미리 설정된 운동 프로그램은 비용 낭비라고 봐요. 혹시 동시에 많은 기구를 주문하면 좀 더 낮은 가격으로 할 수 있을까요? 확인하시고 주문서를 작성하세요. 그리고 나서 디아즈 씨가 서명하도록 주시면 됩니다. 감사합니다.

기능	C17	LR10	MH4	A9
경사	✓	✓	✓	
추가 완충재	✓	✓		✓
미리 설정된 운동	✓			✓

19. 시각 정보에 따르면, 화자는 어떤 모델이 가장 좋을 것이라고 생각하는가?
(A) C17
(B) LR10
(C) MH4
(D) A9

해설 **세부 내용 – 시각 정보 연계**
메시지 초반부에 경사와 추가 완충재가 있는 제품을 구입해야 한다(we should purchase the one that has an incline and additional cushioning)고 했으므로 정답은 (B)이다.

20. 화자는 무엇에 대해 물어보는가?
(A) 설치 절차
(B) 배송 방법
(C) 대량 주문 할인
(D) 제품 보증기간

해설 **세부 내용 – 문의 사항**
메시지 중반부에 대량 주문 할인 가능 여부(Do you think the company would give us a better price ~?)를 묻고 있으므로 정답은 (C)이다.

어휘 procedure 절차 bulk discount 대량 주문 할인 warranty 품질 보증기간

21. 화자는 디아즈 씨에 대해 뭐라고 말하는가?
(A) 서명을 해야 한다.
(B) 예산에 대해 우려하고 있다.
(C) 배송품을 내릴 것이다.
(D) 공급업체와 만날 계획이다.

해설 **세부 내용 – 디아즈에 대한 언급 사항**
메시지 후반부에 디아즈가 서명을 해야 한다(you'll need to give it to Ms. Diaz to sign)고 하므로 정답은 (A)이다.

어휘 signature 서명 be concerned about ~에 대해 염려하다 unload (짐을) 내리다

●UNIT 02 공지 / 안내 / 회의

예제

W-Am Good morning, everyone. I have a quick announcement to make. We would like to encourage all staff members to start carpooling to the office. By doing so, you can take advantage of saving money on your commute. To help you get organized for this activity, I've put a sheet in the break room where you can sign up if you're interested.

make an announcement 발표하다, 공표하다 encourage 장려하다 take advantage of ~을 이용하다 commute 통근 sign up 신청하다

번역 여러분, 안녕하세요. 간단히 발표할 사항이 있습니다. 전 직원들이 이제 카풀로 출근하시기를 권장드리고자 합니다. 그렇게 하면 차비를 아끼는 이점을 누리실 수 있습니다. 이를 위한 팀을 구성하고자 관심 있는 분이 신청할 수 있는 신청서를 휴게실에 두었습니다.

LISTENING PRACTICE
교재 p. 117

1. (A) **2.** (D) **3.** (C) **4.** (D)

1 M-Cn

Good evening, travelers. Queens Airlines Flight 377 to Dubai, originally boarding at Gate D-12, has moved to Gate A-2 in the international terminal. Please note that Flight 377 passengers will need to have their boarding passes reissued. Speak to an airline representative to receive your updated boarding pass. We apologize for the inconvenience.

originally 원래 boarding pass 탑승권 reissue 재발행하다, 재발급하다 representative 대표, 직원 inconvenience 불편

번역 안녕하세요, 승객 여러분. 원래 D-12 게이트에서 탑승 예정이었던 두바이행 퀸 에어라인 377편은 국제선 터미널 A-2 게이트로 옮겨졌습니다. 377편 승객께서는 탑승권을 재발급 받으셔야 합니다. 항공사 직원에게 말씀하셔서 변경된 탑승권을 수령하십시오. 불편을 드려 죄송합니다.

문제 377편 승객들은 무엇을 하라고 요청받았는가?
(A) 새로운 탑승 서류 수령하기
(B) 보안 검색에 동의하기
(C) 게이트 앞에 줄 서기
(D) 수하물에서 특정 물건 빼기

해설 **세부 내용 – 승객들에 대한 요청 사항**

안내 중반부에 377편 승객은 탑승권을 재발급 받아야 한다(Flight 377 ~ passes reissued)고 하였으므로 정답은 (A)이다.

어휘 security screening 보안 검색   baggage 수하물

2   M-Au

> If there are no further questions, that's the end of our workshop on how to clean necklaces, rings, and bracelets. Remember, these are delicate and expensive items, so if you are unsure about what to do, ask a manager for assistance. I plan on holding more training like this in the future. I hope you'll find it helpful.
>
> delicate 섬세한, 연약한   assistance 도움, 지원

번역 질문이 더 없으시면 목걸이, 반지, 팔찌 세척법에 관한 워크숍을 마칩니다. 섬세하고 값비싼 물품임을 명심하시고, 방법을 모르실 때는 관리자에게 도움을 요청하세요. 이런 교육을 향후 더 많이 열 계획입니다. 여러분께 유익하기를 바랍니다.

문제 화자는 직원들에게 무엇을 하라고 상기시키는가?
(A) 고객에게 빠르게 도움 주기
(B) 서류 제출하기
(C) 가격이 정확한지 확인하기
(D) 관리자의 도움 얻기

해설 **세부 내용 – 직원들에게 상기시키는 것**

담화 후반부에 어떻게 할지 모르면 관리자에게 도움을 요청하라(if you ~ for assistance)고 했으므로 정답은 (D)이다.

어휘 assist 돕다   turn in 제출하다   accuracy 정확, 정확도

3   W-Br

> Hello, and welcome to your first day at Alias Energy. You'll spend the next week going through our orientation program. The first thing we're going to do is introduce ourselves in a fun ice-breaking game. Let's all try to make a good impression. These are the people you'll likely work with for years to come.
>
> ice-breaking 분위기를 누그러뜨리기 위한   make a good impression 좋은 인상을 주다

번역 안녕하세요, 알리아스 에너지에서 첫 날을 맞이하게 되신 것을 환영합니다. 다음 주는 오리엔테이션 프로그램을 진행하며 보낼 것입니다. 첫 번째 할 일은 어색한 분위기를 없애는 재미있는 게임을 통해 자기 소개를 하는 것입니다. 모두 좋은 인상을 주도록 노력합시다. 앞으로 몇 년간 함께 일하게 될 분들입니다.

문제 청자들은 다음으로 무엇을 하겠는가?
(A) 문서 작업 완료하기
(B) 교육용 동영상 시청하기
(C) 동료들 만나기
(D) 제안 사항에 대해 투표하기

해설 **세부 내용 – 다음으로 할 일**

담화 중반부에 어색한 분위기를 깨기 위해 자기 소개를 하자(The first thing we're going to do ~ ice-breaking game)고 하였고, 앞으로 몇 년 함께 일하게 될 사람들이라(These are people you'll likely work with ~)는 말이 이어지므로 정답은 (C)이다.

4   M-Au

> To start off today's meeting, I'd like to congratulate one of our team members. Ms. Bellani was awarded the prestigious Angel Prize for design at an awards ceremony last night. Be sure to check out the photos of Ms. Bellani's winning entry, which are posted on our company Web site. I'm sure you'll easily see why she was selected.
>
> prestigious 명망 있는   awards ceremony 시상식   winning entry 수상작   post 게시하다

번역 오늘 회의를 시작하며 팀원 한 명을 축하하고자 합니다. 벨라니 씨가 어젯밤 시상식에서 디자인으로 명망 높은 엔젤상을 받았습니다. 벨라니 씨의 수상작 사진을 꼭 보도록 하세요. 회사 웹사이트에 게시되어 있습니다. 선정된 이유를 쉽게 알 수 있으실 겁니다.

문제 화자는 청자들에게 무엇을 하라고 권하는가?
(A) 교육 시간 참가하기
(B) 벨라니 씨에게 이메일 보내기
(C) 대회 참가하기
(D) 온라인으로 사진 확인하기

해설 **세부 내용 – 권고 사항**

소개 후반부에서 웹사이트에서 수상작을 확인하라(Be sure to check ~ on our company Web site)고 했으므로 정답은 (D)이다.

어휘 competition 대회, 경연

ACTUAL TEST
교재 p. 118

1. (A)	2. (D)	3. (B)	4. (C)	5. (C)
6. (A)	7. (B)	8. (A)	9. (D)	10. (B)
11. (D)	12. (C)	13. (B)	14. (A)	15. (D)
16. (C)	17. (A)	18. (D)	19. (C)	20. (B)
21. (D)				

1-3 공지

M-Cn **¹This is an announcement for all guests staying at the Retro Inn.** Unfortunately, our swimming pool facilities are closed for urgent maintenance. However, **²I am delighted to announce the start of a new airport shuttle bus service,** which will run every hour between our hotel and Hampton Airport. Simply stop by the desk in the lobby for information on pick-up times and rates. We would also be grateful if you could fill out our survey before you leave. **³This is so that we can further improve our service in the future.**

announcement 발표, 공지   facility 시설   urgent 긴급한
maintenance 유지 보수   be delighted to ~하게 되어 기쁘다
stop by 잠시 들르다   rate 요금   fill out a survey 설문을
기입하다

번역 레트로 인에 투숙하시는 모든 손님 여러분께 알려 드립니다. 안타깝게도 저희 수영장 시설은 긴급 보수로 휴장합니다. 그러나 새로운 공항 셔틀버스 서비스의 시작을 알리게 되어 기쁩니다. 저희 호텔과 햄프턴 공항 간 셔틀버스가 매시간 운행될 예정입니다. 픽업 시간과 요금에 관한 정보는 로비 데스크에 들러 확인하세요. 가시기 전에 저희 설문을 기입해 주시면 감사하겠습니다. 향후 서비스 개선을 위한 것입니다.

1. 공지는 어디서 이루어지는가?
(A) 호텔   (B) 관광정보 안내센터
(C) 컨벤션 센터   (D) 공항

해설 **전체 내용 – 공지 장소**
공지 도입부에 호텔에 투숙하는 모든 손님에게 알린다 (This is an announcement for ~ Retro Inn)고 공지하고 있으므로 정답은 (A)이다.

2. 업체에서 이제 무엇을 제공하는가?
(A) 가이드 투어   (B) 다양한 할인
(C) 푸드코트   (D) 교통 서비스

해설 **세부 내용 – 업체가 제공하는 것**
공지 중반부에 공항 셔틀버스 서비스(airport shuttle bus service)를 시작한다고 했으므로 정답은 (D)이다.

어휘 a range of 다양한   transportation 교통

3. 고객들에게 서식을 기입하라고 요청하는 이유는?
(A) 대회에 참가하기 위해
(B) 의견을 제공하기 위해
(C) 일자리에 지원하기 위해
(D) 결제하기 위해

해설 **세부 내용 – 서식을 기입해야 하는 이유**
공지 마지막에 설문 작성을 요청하며 향후 서비스 개선을 위한 것(This is so that ~ improve our service in

the future)이라고 했으므로 정답은 (B)이다.

어휘 enter a contest 대회에 참가하다   apply for ~에
지원하다   make a payment 결제하다, 지불하다

4-6 회의 발췌

W-Br **⁴Thank you for being here today for our weekly finance meeting.** As some of you may know, the Human Resources department recently conducted an employee survey. There is one request that affects our department. **⁵A lot of people want more options for how the money is invested.** Because of this, we are going to start offering a wider selection of retirement packages for employees. **⁶Jennifer has volunteered to conduct a session to outline the new packages.** If any of you want to help Jennifer make the preparations, please talk to her after this meeting.

finance 재무, 재정   Human Resources department 인사
부서   recently 최근   conduct 시행하다   affect 영향을 주다
invest 투자하다   retirement 은퇴, 퇴직   volunteer 자원하다
outline 개요를 설명하다   make preparations 준비하다

번역 오늘 주간 재무 회의에 참석해 주셔서 감사합니다. 여러분 중 일부가 알고 계신 대로, 인사 부서가 최근 직원 설문 조사를 실시했습니다. 우리 부서에 영향을 미치는 요청 사항이 하나 있는데요. 많은 직원들이 돈을 투자하는 방법에 대해 더 많은 선택 사항이 있으면 좋겠다고 합니다. 이 때문에 직원들을 위한 더 다양한 퇴직금 패키지를 새로 제공할 예정입니다. 제니퍼 씨가 새로운 패키지 개요를 설명하는 시간을 진행하겠다고 자원했어요. 여러분 중 누구라도 제니퍼 씨가 준비하는 것을 돕고 싶다면, 이 회의 이후 제니퍼 씨에게 말씀하세요.

4. 청자들은 어떤 부서에서 일하겠는가?
(A) 구매 부서
(B) 인사 부서
(C) 재무 부서
(D) 품질 보증 부서

해설 **전체 내용 – 청자들의 근무 부서**
담화 도입부에 주간 재무 회의에 참석해 주셔서 감사하다 (Thank you for ~ weekly finance meeting)고 했으므로 정답은 (C)이다.

어휘 purchase 구매하다   quality assurance 품질 보증

5. 화자에 따르면, 직원들은 무엇을 요청했는가?
(A) 휴가일수 증가
(B) 초과 근무 시간 급여 인상
(C) 투자 선택사항 증가
(D) 업무 일정 융통성 확보

해설 **세부 내용 – 직원들의 요청 사항**

담화 중반부에 많은 직원들이 더 많은 투자 옵션을 원한다 (A lot of people want more options for how the money is invested)고 하므로 정답은 (C)이다.

어휘 increase 증가 overtime hours 초과 근무 시간
investment 투자 flexibility 탄력성. 융통성

6. 제니퍼 씨는 무엇을 하겠다고 자원했는가?

(A) 설명회 진행하기
(B) 비정규직 직원 채용하기
(C) 장비 설치하기
(D) 새 설문 조사 실시하기

해설 **세부 내용 – 제니퍼가 자원한 것**

담화 후반부에 제니퍼가 패키지 개요 설명 진행을 자원했 다(Jennifer has volunteered to conduct a session to outline the new packages)고 하므로 정답은 (A)이다.

어휘 temporary 임시의. 일시적인 set up 설치하다

7-9 안내

W-Am As you know, **7**many of our electrical products are stored in the warehouse on Elm Street. This will be closed for refurbishment. **8**As our company grows, we find ourselves in need of a larger space to hold more stock. The work planned to be carried out during this closure will allow us to do this. **9**While the expansion is being completed, which is expected to take three weeks, we hope we will be able to complete all orders on time, so our customers won't notice anything is happening.

electrical product 전자제품 warehouse 창고
refurbishment 정비. 재단장 in need of ~을 필요로 하는
stock 재고 carry out 실행하다 expansion 확장

번역 아시는 대로, 저희 전자제품 중 다수가 엘름 스트리트의 창 고에 보관되어 있습니다. 그런데 이 창고는 재정비로 문을 닫을 예정입니다. 회사가 성장하면서 더 많은 재고를 보관 할 더 큰 공간이 필요하게 됐습니다. 이번 폐쇄 기간 중 실행하 려고 계획한 작업은 이를 가능하게 해 줄 것입니다. 확장이 완료되는 기간이 3주 예상되는데 그동안 모든 주문 건을 늦지 않게 완료해서 고객들이 무슨 일이 있는지 알아차리 지 못하도록 했으면 합니다.

7. 화자는 주로 무엇에 대해 이야기하는가?

(A) 제품 배송비 (B) 창고 폐쇄
(C) 고객 설문 조사 결과 (D) 직원 초과 근무 수당

해설 **전체 내용 – 담화 주제**

안내 도입부에 제품이 창고에 보관중인데, 개조를 위해 문 을 닫는다(This will be closed for refurbishment)고 하므로 정답은 (B)이다.

어휘 rate 요금 overtime 초과 근무

8. 작업을 해야 하는 이유는?

(A) 저장 공간을 넓히려고
(B) 제조 과정을 개선하려고
(C) 건물 이용을 더 쉽게 만들려고
(D) 배송 시간을 줄이려고

해설 **세부 내용 – 작업 이유**

안내 중반부에 재고 보관 공간이 더 필요하다(we find ~ more stock)고 했으므로 정답은 (A)이다.

어휘 enlarge 확장하다 manufacturing 제조 accessible
입장 가능한. 이용 가능한 reduce 줄이다

9. 3주 후에 어떤 일이 있을 것인가?

(A) 일부 물품들이 할인 판매된다.
(B) 새로운 광고 캠페인이 시작된다.
(C) 운영 시간이 변경된다.
(D) 개조 공사가 완료된다.

해설 **세부 내용 – 3주 후 있을 일**

안내 후반부에 확장 완료 기간이 3주 예상된다(While the expansion ~ three weeks)고 했으므로 정답은 (D)이 다.

어휘 operating hours 운영 시간 renovation 개조. 보수

10-12 회의 발췌

M-Cn **10**I know some of you are concerned about the upcoming evaluation, and I wanted to let you know I've been observing our office to look for any problems. Honestly, I can't find any reason to worry. **11**Everyone is very professional, and we've done a good job meeting all of our performance standards. As long as we all keep doing what we're doing, we should get an excellent review on the evaluation. **12**If anyone thinks there is a particular issue we should address before the inspectors visit, write me an e-mail and we can talk more about it.

be concerned about ~에 대해 염려하다. 우려하다
upcoming 다가오는. 앞으로 있을 evaluation 평가 observe
관찰하다 meet a standard 기준에 부합하다 particular
특정한

번역 여러분 중 일부는 다가올 평가에 대해 걱정한다는 것을 압 니다. 저는 사실 우리 부서가 혹시 문제가 있는지 찾기 위 해 관찰했습니다. 솔직히 걱정할 이유가 없습니다. 모두가 매우 전문적이고, 성과 기준을 모두 잘 충족했습니다. 지금 하고 있는 것처럼 계속하는 한 훌륭한 평가 결과를 얻을 것 입니다. 조사관들이 방문하기 전에 해결해야 할 특정 문제 가 있다고 생각하는 분은 저에게 이메일을 보내주시면 그 에 관해 더 얘기 나눌 수 있습니다.

10. 회의에서 어떤 일에 대해 주로 논의하는가?
(A) 다가오는 회의 (B) 업무 평가
(C) 회사 합병 (D) 신규 고객

해설 **전체 내용 - 논의 주제**
담화 도입부에 다가오는 평가에 대해 걱정하고 있는 것을 안다(I know ~ upcoming evaluation)고 했으므로 정답은 (B)이다.

어휘 assessment 평가 corporate 회사의 merger 합병

11. 화자가 "솔직히 걱정할 이유가 없습니다"라고 말한 의미는?
(A) 소문을 믿지 않는다.
(B) 고객이 만족해 한다고 믿는다.
(C) 불평을 이해하지 못하겠다.
(D) 사무실 직원들이 잘 하고 있다고 생각한다.

해설 **세부 내용 - 화자의 의도**
인용문 앞에서 부서의 문제점을 찾으려고 관찰해 왔다(I wanted ~ any problems)고 말한 다음, 솔직히 걱정할 이유가 없다고 했다. 인용문 뒤에서는 직원들의 성과를 칭찬하는 말이 이어지므로 이는 직원들이 문제없이 잘 하고 있다는 것을 말하려는 의도로 볼 수 있다. 따라서 정답은 (D)이다.

어휘 complaint 불평, 불만

12. 화자는 청자들이 문제를 보고하기 위해 어떻게 해야 한다고 말하는가?
(A) 팀장에게 직접 말하기
(B) 조사관 중 한 명에게 연락하기
(C) 화자에게 이메일 보내기
(D) 익명으로 보고서 제출하기

해설 **세부 내용 - 청자들이 해야 할 일**
담화 마지막에 조사관들이 방문하기 전에 해결해야 할 문제가 있다고 생각하는 분은 이메일을 보내 달라(If anyone ~ about it)고 했으므로 정답은 (C)이다.

어휘 file a report 보고서를 제출하다 anonymously 익명으로

13-15 안내

W-Br **13**I'd like to thank you all for coming to this year's National Conference of Newspaper Reporters. We have a number of speakers who are prominent in the field, so I hope you learn a great deal. Just a reminder, you can sign up for membership to our organization. Today is the last day to get the membership at the current rate, which is just fifty dollars for the whole year. **14**After today, it's changing to seventy-five dollars, so I suggest acting quickly. **15**To find out more, visit the registration booth at the rear door. Thank you.

a number of 많은, 다수의 prominent 저명한 sign up for ~을 신청하다 current 현재의 rate 요금 registration 등록 rear 뒤쪽의

번역 올해 전국 신문 기자 회의에 와 주신 모든 분들께 감사드립니다. 이 분야에서 저명한 연사들이 다수 나오시니, 많이 배우시기를 바랍니다. 참고로 저희 단체 회원을 신청하실 수 있습니다. 오늘은 현재 요금으로 회원 자격을 얻는 마지막 날로, 한 해 가격이 50달러밖에 안 됩니다. 오늘 이후에는 75달러로 변경되므로 서두르시기를 권해드립니다. 더 자세한 내용은 뒷문 등록 부스를 방문하세요. 감사합니다.

13. 청자들은 누구이겠는가?
(A) 운동선수
(B) 기자
(C) 화가
(D) 음악가

해설 **전체 내용 - 청자의 신분 및 직업**
안내 도입부에 기자 회의에 참석해 주셔서 감사드린다(I'd like ~ Newspaper Reporters)고 하였으므로 정답은 (B)이다.

어휘 athlete 운동선수 journalist 기자

14. 화자는 왜 서둘러 신청하라고 권하는가?
(A) 가격 인상이 계획되어 있다.
(B) 공급 물품이 한정되어 있다.
(C) 강의가 곧 시작될 것이다.
(D) 일찍 참가하면 무료 선물이 제공된다.

해설 **세부 내용 - 서둘러 신청하라는 이유**
안내 후반부에 오늘 이후 가격이 변경되니 서둘러 달라(After today, it's changing to seventy-five dollars, so I suggest acting quickly)고 했으므로 정답은 (A)이다.

어휘 increase 인상 limited 한정된, 제한된 lecture 강의

15. 청자들은 어디에서 정보를 더 얻어야 하는가?
(A) 프론트 데스크
(B) 무대
(C) 화자의 사무실
(D) 입구

해설 **세부 내용 - 정보를 얻는 곳**
안내 후반부에 자세한 내용은 뒷문 등록 부스를 방문하라(To find out more, visit the registration booth at the rear door)고 했으므로 정답은 (D)이다.

어휘 stage 무대 entrance 입구

16-18 회의 발췌

W-Am Before we start today's meeting, I want to congratulate you all on another profitable quarter. We are growing steadily and **¹⁶**we plan to establish another branch in the southwest region. Some of you will have the option of transferring. **¹⁷**I had hoped to tell you today which of the potential sites we've selected, but I haven't seen them all. So, we'll just move on with the meeting. **¹⁸**Mr. Lobo from the finance team will explain an upcoming change to when you receive your salaries. Mr. Lobo, the floor is yours.

profitable 수익성이 있는   quarter 분기   steadily 꾸준히
establish 설립하다   transfer 옮기다. 이동하다   potential
잠재적인

번역 오늘 회의를 시작하기 전에 다시 수익률 높은 분기가 된 것에 대해 모두에게 축하하고 싶습니다. 우리는 꾸준하게 성장 중이며 남서쪽 지역에 지점을 하나 더 설립할 계획입니다. 여러분 중 일부는 전근을 선택할 수도 있습니다. 여러분께 오늘 후보 부지 중 어느 곳을 선택했는지 말씀드리고 싶었는데 다 보지는 못했어요. 따라서 다시 회의로 넘어가겠습니다. 재무팀 로보 씨가 앞으로 있을 급여 수령 시의 변화에 대해 설명해 드립니다. 로보 씨, 나와주세요.

16. 회사는 무엇을 할 계획인가?
(A) 직원들이 재택 근무를 할 수 있도록 하기
(B) 경쟁업체와 합병하기
(C) 새 지점 열기
(D) 직원 생산성 향상시키기

해설 **세부 내용 – 회사가 계획하는 것**
담화 초반부에 지점을 하나 더 설립할 계획(we plan ~ southwest region)이라고 하므로 정답은 (C)이다.

어휘 merge with ~와 합병하다   competitor 경쟁자
productivity 생산성

17. 화자가 "다 보지는 못했어요"라고 말한 의도는?
(A) 결정 사항은 나중에 알려줄 것이다.
(B) 없어진 문서에 대해 걱정을 하고 있다.
(C) 면접을 진행할 잠재 직원이 더 있다.
(D) 마감 기한 연장을 요청하고 싶다.

해설 **세부 내용 – 화자의 의도**
인용문 앞 문장과 인용문을 연결하면, 후보로 언급된 부지들 중 어느 곳을 선택했는지 알려주고 싶었으나 후보지를 다 보지 못했다(I had hoped to tell ~ I haven't seen them all)는 의미가 된다. 인용문 뒤에는 회의를 계속하자(we'll just move on with the meeting)는 말로 화제가 전환된다. 즉, 다 보지 못했다는 화자의 말은 지금이 아닌 나중에 결정 사항을 알려줄 것이라는 의도로 이해될 수 있다. 따라서 정답은 (A)이다.

어휘 announce 알리다. 발표하다   decision 결정
extension 연장

18. 청자들은 다음으로 무엇에 관해 들을 것인가?
(A) 단체 야유회   (B) 연례 보너스
(C) 장래의 고객   (D) 지불 일정

해설 **세부 내용 – 청자들이 들을 내용**
담화 후반부에 급여 수령 시 변화에 대해 설명하겠다(Mr. Lobo ~ your salaries)고 하므로 정답은 (D)이다.

어휘 outing 야유회   prospective 장래의

19-21 공지+메뉴

M-Cn I have a few announcements for all of you. First, we've had some problems with our fruit supplier, and some items won't be available this week. Unfortunately, that means there'll be no Avocado & Vanilla green smoothie. As a result, **¹⁹**we'll be selling Wednesday's smoothie on Thursday, too. Please apologize to our customers for the inconvenience. Next, **²⁰**it's my pleasure to introduce our new head chef, Catherine Woods. Catherine has already made some improvements to our existing menu. **²¹**I already had the new menus printed and placed by the main entrance. Please familiarize yourselves with the new dishes.

as a result 결과적으로   apologize 사과하다   inconvenience
불편   pleasure 기쁨   existing 존재하는. 기존의   familiarize
oneself with ~을 익히다

번역 여러분 모두에게 알려드릴 내용이 몇 가지 있습니다. 첫째, 과일 공급업체에 문제가 생겨서 이번주에 일부 품목을 이용할 수 없습니다. 유감스럽게도, 아보카도 & 바닐라 그린 스무디를 못 만든다는 뜻이죠. 이에 따라 수요일 스무디를 목요일에도 판매할 예정입니다. 불편에 대해 고객에게 사과드리세요. 다음으로 새로운 수석 요리사 캐서린 우즈 씨를 소개하게 되어 기쁩니다. 캐서린 씨는 이미 기존 메뉴를 개선했습니다. 새로운 메뉴는 이미 출력해서 중앙 출입구 옆에 두었습니다. 새 요리들을 잘 익혀 주세요.

평일 그린 스무디	
월요일	.... 사과 & 케일
화요일	.... 멜론 & 민트
수요일	.... 시금치 & 오렌지
목요일	.... 아보카도 & 바닐라
금요일	.... 케일 & 배

19. 시각 정보에 따르면 화자는 이번 주 이틀 동안 어떤 그린 스무디를 판매할 것이라고 말하는가?
(A) 사과 & 케일   (B) 멜론 & 민트
(C) 시금치 & 오렌지   (D) 케일 & 배

시각 정보 연계 문제 – 이틀 동안 판매할 음료

공지 중반부에 수요일 스무디를 목요일에도 판매 예정(we'll be selling Wednesday's smoothie on Thursday, too)이라고 했다. 시각 정보에서 수요일은 시금치 & 오렌지로 나와 있으므로 정답은 (C)이다.

20. 캐서린 우즈 씨는 누구인가?
(A) 업주   (B) 요리사
(C) 음식 평론가   (D) 고객

해설 **세부 내용 – 캐서린 우즈의 신분**

공지 중반부에 캐서린 우즈를 소개하게 되어 기쁘다(it's my pleasure ~ head chef, Catherine Woods)고 하며 고유명사인 이름 앞에 신분이 언급되므로 정답은 (B)이다.

어휘 critic 평론가, 비평가

21. 화자는 중앙 출입구에 무엇을 두었는가?
(A) 할인 쿠폰   (B) 의견 카드
(C) 홍보 전단   (D) 변경된 메뉴

해설 **세부 내용 – 중앙 출입구에 둔 것**

공지 후반부에 새 메뉴를 중앙 출입구 옆에 두었다(I already had the new menus and ~ main entrance)고 했으므로 정답은 (D)이다.

어휘 promotional 홍보의, 판촉의 flyer 전단

●UNIT 03 여행 / 견학 / 관람

예제

교재 p. 120

M-Cn Welcome to our factory tour. Let me briefly explain today's tour schedule. At 11 o'clock, you'll be taken to our laboratory area, where you can taste some of the new beverages. After this, we will stop for lunch for an hour. Please come back here by 2 P.M. When you come back, we'll watch a video of the history of our company. Okay, I'm going to give you your wristbands next. Please keep these on at all times.

briefly 잠시, 간단히   laboratory 실험실   beverage 음료
at all times 항상, 언제나

번역 저희 공장 견학을 오신 것을 환영합니다. 오늘 견학 일정을 간단히 설명하겠습니다. 11시 정각에 저희 실험실 구역으로 가서서 새 음료를 시음할 수 있습니다. 이후 1시간 동안 점심 식사를 위해 잠시 중단합니다. 오후 2시까지 돌아와 주십시오. 돌아오시면 회사의 역사를 담은 동영상을 시청하실 것입니다. 자, 다음으로 손목 밴드를 드리겠습니다. 항상 착용하고 계시기 바랍니다.

LISTENING PRACTICE

교재 p. 121

1. (C)   **2.** (C)   **3.** (C)   **4.** (C)

1 W-Am

Welcome to our tour of the Pottery Studio. Our facility has in-house artisans specializing in hand-made ceramics. Today they'll demonstrate the craft of making beautiful bowls, mugs, and many others. You will also have the opportunity to mold your own clay pot on the potter's wheel. OK, let's begin.

facility 시설   in-house (회사, 조직) 내부의   artisan 장인
specialize in ~을 전문으로 하다   demonstrate 시연하다
craft 기술   mold 주조하다, (틀에 부어) 만들다   potter's wheel
돌림판

번역 도자기 스튜디오에 견학 오신 것을 환영합니다. 저희 시설은 수제 도자기를 전문으로 하는 소속 장인들을 보유하고 있습니다. 오늘 장인들이 멋진 그릇, 컵을 비롯해 많은 것들을 제작하는 기술을 시연해 드릴 것입니다. 아울러 돌림판 위에서 자신의 도기를 주조할 기회도 있습니다. 자, 시작하시죠.

문제 화자에 따르면, 청자들은 무엇을 할 수 있는가?
(A) 교육용 동영상 시청하기
(B) 간식 먹기
(C) 직접 체험해 보기
(D) 수제 물품 판매하기

해설 **세부 내용 – 청자들이 할 수 있는 것**

안내 후반부에 도기를 주조할 기회가 있다(You will ~ potter's wheel)고 하므로 정답은 (C)이다.

어휘 instructional 교육용의   refreshments 다과   hands-on experience 직접 체험

2 M-Au

Now we are passing through a natural habitat enclosure housing a variety of birds, the final course of our zoo tour today. Here, you can see over 70 species of birds, including parrots that can talk and sing. Please do not feed any of the birds without the permission of the zoo staff members.

pass through ~을 거쳐가다, 지나가다   natural habitat 자연
서식지   enclosure 울타리로 감싼 곳   a variety of 다양한
permission 허가

번역 이제 다양한 조류에게 보금자리를 제공하는 자연 서식지 보호 구역을 지납니다. 오늘 동물원 투어의 마지막 코스죠. 여기에서는 말하고 노래할 수 있는 앵무새를 비롯해 70여 종의 새를 볼 수 있습니다. 동물원 직원의 허가 없이 어떤 새에게도 먹이를 주지 마십시오.

문제 청자들이 허가를 받고 해야 하는 일은?
(A) 플래시 사진 촬영하기
(B) 공연 녹화하기
(C) 동물들에게 먹이 주기
(D) 단체 이탈하기

해설 세부 내용 – 허가를 받아야 하는 일
안내 마지막에 동물원 직원의 허가 없이 어떤 새에게도 먹이를 주지 말라(Please do ~ staff members)고 했으므로 정답은 (C)이다.

3 M-Cn

OK, let's start today's tour. I'm Ted Benson, and I oversee all the operations here at this production facility. This is the Mach Cycle Company's largest assembly plant—it produces more than 400 bicycles per day. First, we'll watch how our popular lines of mountain bikes are built. Come this way.

oversee 감독하다　production 생산　facility 시설
assembly 조립

번역 자, 오늘 견학을 시작합시다. 저는 테드 벤슨이라고 합니다. 이 생산 시설에서 모든 작업을 감독하고 있습니다. 이곳은 마하 사이클 컴퍼니에서 가장 큰 조립 공장으로, 하루에 400대가 넘는 자전거를 생산합니다. 먼저 저희 인기 제품인 산악 자전거가 어떻게 만들어지는지 살펴보겠습니다. 이쪽으로 오시죠.

문제 화자는 누구이겠는가?
(A) 피트니스 센터 강사　(B) 자전거 매장 주인
(C) 공장 관리자　(D) 스포츠 기자

해설 전체 내용 – 화자의 신분
안내 초반부에 화자는 공장의 모든 작업을 감독하고 있다고 본인을 소개(I oversee all the operations here at this production facility)하고 있으므로 정답은 (C)이다.

어휘 journalist 기자

4

W-Br Welcome to tonight's performance. This special benefit concert is an annual event that is organized to benefit the City Music Foundation, which provides financial assistance to aspiring music performers. All of the proceeds from the event are donated to this charitable organization. Alright, let's begin our show.

performance 공연　benefit concert 자선 음악회
foundation 재단　financial assistance 재정적 지원
aspiring 장차 ~이 되려는　proceeds 수익금　donate
기부하다　charitable 자선의, 자선을 베푸는

번역 오늘밤 공연에 오신 것을 환영합니다. 이 특별 자선 음악회는 시티 뮤직 재단을 위해 기획된 연례 행사로, 이 재단은 연주자 지망생들에게 재정적 지원을 제공합니다. 행사에서 얻은 수익금 일체는 이 자선단체에 기부합니다. 자, 공연을 시작합니다.

문제 콘서트를 개최하는 이유는?
(A) 음악 경연대회의 우승자를 가리기 위해
(B) 역사적인 행사를 경축하기 위해
(C) 자선 기금 마련을 위해
(D) 지역에 관광 홍보를 위해

해설 세부 내용 – 콘서트 개최 이유
안내 후반부에 수익금은 자선단체에 기부한다(All of ~ charitable organization)고 했으므로 정답은 (C)이다.

어휘 celebrate 경축하다, 축하하다　raise money 기금을 마련하다　charity 자선　promote 홍보하다

ACTUAL TEST 　교재 p. 122

1. (D)	**2.** (B)	**3.** (A)	**4.** (B)	**5.** (C)
6. (A)	**7.** (B)	**8.** (C)	**9.** (D)	**10.** (C)
11. (D)	**12.** (D)	**13.** (D)	**14.** (A)	**15.** (C)
16. (A)	**17.** (B)	**18.** (B)	**19.** (A)	**20.** (B)
21. (B)				

1-3 여행

M-Cn Good afternoon, all passengers, and [1]welcome aboard our ship, The Blue Royale Deluxe. I'm Brad Kim, and I'm your cruise director. [2]In a moment, I will hand out our daily leaflets, with a detailed schedule of activities on board our vessel. This evening, we'll have three prize drawings in our café on Deck 5. [3]I recommend that all passengers enter their name in a drawing for the chance to win $100 cash. I wish you all a pleasant journey as we head to our destination, the beautiful Emerald Island.

passenger 승객　aboard 탑승한, 승선한　leaflet 전단
detailed 상세한　vessel 배, 선박　prize drawing 경품 추첨
destination 목적지

번역 안녕하십니까, 승객 여러분. 저희 블루 로얄 디럭스호에 탑승하신 것을 환영합니다. 저는 여러분의 항해 감독 브랜드 김입니다. 잠시 후, 선박에서의 활동 세부 일정이 수록된 일일 전단을 나눠드릴 것입니다. 오늘 저녁 5번 갑판 카페에서 3개의 경품 추첨이 있습니다. 모든 승객들은 현금 100달러 당첨 기회를 위해 추첨에 응모하실 것을 권합니다. 목적지인 아름다운 에메랄드 섬까지 즐거운 여행이 되시기 바랍니다.

1. 안내는 어디에서 이루어지는가?
(A) 스포츠 센터　　(B) 공항 터미널
(C) 쇼핑몰　　(D) 유람선

해설　**전체 내용 – 공지 장소**
안내 초반부에 탑승을 환영한다(welcome aboard our ship)고 했으므로 정답은 (D)이다.

어휘　announcement 공지, 발표

2. 화자에 따르면 곧 무엇이 배포될 것인가?
(A) 식사 쿠폰　　(B) 활동 일정
(C) 호텔 쿠폰　　(D) 영화표

해설　**세부 내용 – 곧 배포될 것**
안내 중반부에 곧 활동 세부 일정을 배포할 것(In a moment, ~ schedule of activities on board our vessel)이라고 했으므로 정답은 (B)이다.

어휘　distribute 분배하다, 배포하다　shortly 곧　voucher 쿠폰

3. 화자는 무엇을 하라고 권하는가?
(A) 경품 추첨 응모하기
(B) 건강 음료 구입하기
(C) 현금으로 물건값 계산하기
(D) 단체 사진 포즈 취하기

해설　**세부 내용 – 제안 사항**
안내 후반부에 추첨에 응모할 것을 권한다(I recommend ~ win $100 cash)고 하므로 정답은 (A)이다.

어휘　enter a drawing 추첨에 응모하다, 참가하다　purchase 구입하다

4-6 견학

W-Br　That concludes the guided tour of the National History Museum. [4]I'd like to apologize once again for my broken microphone. I hope you were able to hear all of my explanations despite this problem. Remember to hold onto your entrance ticket, [5]as you can use it for admission to the screening of the film *Mammals Through Time* in Presentation Hall 1. [5]That starts at 2 P.M. [6]I'm also going to give each of you a coupon for our gift shop where you can pick up pictures of the artworks you'll see today. Have a great day!

conclude 끝내다, 마치다　apologize 사과하다　hold onto 계속 보유하다　entrance 입장　admission 입장　screening 상영

번역　이것으로 국립 역사 박물관 가이드 투어를 마칩니다. 다시 한 번 마이크 고장에 대해 사과를 드립니다. 이러한 문제가 있었지만 제 설명을 모두 잘 들으실 수 있었기를 바랍니다. 입장권은 프레젠테이션 홀 1에서 상영되는 영화 〈매멀 즈 스루 타임〉 입장권으로 사용할 수 있으니 꼭 갖고 계십시오. 영화는 오후 2시에 시작됩니다. 여러분 모두에게 오늘 보실 작품의 사진을 구입할 수 있는 기념품점 쿠폰도 드릴 것입니다. 좋은 하루 되십시오!

4. 화자가 청자들에게 사과한 이유는?
(A) 단체 인원수가 너무 많았다.
(B) 일부 장비의 동작이 되지 않았다.
(C) 투어를 금세 끝내야 했다.
(D) 박물관이 있는 지역은 접근이 불가능했다.

해설　**세부 내용 – 사과 이유**
담화 초반부에 마이크 고장에 대해 사과한다(I'd like ~ broken microphone)고 하므로 정답은 (B)이다.

어휘　equipment 장비　cut short 갑자기 끝내다　inaccessible 접근할 수 없는

5. 화자에 따르면 오후 2시에 청자들은 무엇을 할 수 있는가?
(A) 강의 참석하기　　(B) 다른 견학하기
(C) 영화 관람하기　　(D) 과학자를 만나보기

해설　**세부 내용 – 청자들이 할 수 있는 것**
안내 중반부에 입장권으로 영화 관람이 가능하다(Remember to ~ Hall 1)고 했고 영화는 오후 2시에 시작된다(That starts at 2 P.M)고 하므로 정답은 (C)이다.

6. 화자는 무엇을 나눠줄 것인가?
(A) 쿠폰　　(B) 행사 표
(C) 사진　　(D) 엽서

해설　**세부 내용 – 화자가 나눠줄 것**
담화 후반부에 오늘 본 작품 사진을 구입할 수 있는 쿠폰도 주겠다(I'm also ~ see today)고 하므로 정답은 (A)이다.

7-9 관람

M-Au　Ladies and gentlemen, welcome to tonight's performance of *Family Reunions*. [7]As the director of fundraising here at the Community Theater Center, I'm happy to say our budget will allow us to stage six more plays this autumn. And, thanks to your generous donations, we were also able to purchase new lighting equipment. Now, [8]after our play concludes, we invite you to take part in a panel discussion with the performers—they will be happy to answer your questions. [9]Light snacks and bottled juices will be offered free in the lobby during intermission. OK, enjoy the show.

reunion 재결합　fundraising 모금　budget 예산　generous donation 후한 기부　lighting equipment 조명 장비　conclude 끝나다　take part in ~에 참여하다　intermission 중간 휴식 시간

번역 신사 숙녀 여러분, 오늘밤 〈패밀리 리유니언즈〉 공연에 오신 것을 환영합니다. 커뮤니티 극장 센터 모금 담당자로서, 이번 가을에 저희 예산으로 공연을 6회 더 무대에 올릴 수 있다는 사실을 말씀드리게 되어 기쁩니다. 그리고 많은 기부금을 내 주셔서 새 조명 장비를 구입할 수 있게 된 점도 감사드립니다. 공연이 막을 내린 후 출연자들과 함께 하는 토론회에 참석하실 수 있습니다. 출연진이 기꺼이 질문에 답변해 드릴 것입니다. 휴식시간 중에는 로비에서 간식과 병에 든 주스가 무료로 제공됩니다. 자, 공연을 즐겁게 감상하세요.

7. 화자는 누구이겠는가?
(A) 지역 극작가　(B) 모금 관리자
(C) 조명 기사　(D) 사진기자

해설 전체 내용 – 화자의 신분
안내 초반부에 화자가 자신을 모금 담당자(the director of fundraising)라고 했으므로 정답은 (B)이다.

어휘 playwright 극작가　photojournalist 사진기자

8. 청자들은 무엇을 하라고 초청받았는가?
(A) 피드백 설문 조사 작성하기
(B) 동영상 녹화하기
(C) 토론 참여하기
(D) 기념품 책자 구입하기

해설 세부 내용 – 청자들이 할 일
안내 중반부에 공연이 막을 내린 후 출연자들과 함께 하는 토론회에 참석하실 수 있다(after our play ~ the performers)고 했으므로 정답은 (C)이다.

어휘 complete a survey 설문을 기입하다　souvenir 기념품　booklet 소책자

9. 화자에 따르면 무료로 이용할 수 있는 것은?
(A) 좌석 업그레이드　(B) 티셔츠
(C) 잡지　(D) 다과

해설 세부 내용 – 무료 이용 가능한 것
안내 후반부에 간식과 음료가 무료 이용 가능하다(Light snacks ~ during intermission)고 하므로 정답은 (D)이다.

어휘 at no cost 공짜로, 무료로　refreshments 다과

10-12 견학

M-Cn Good morning, and welcome to Hue Bridge Mansion. My name is Gregory, and **10**I'll be telling you a variety of facts about this amazing historical home throughout our tour. Now that I've checked everyone's tickets, we may begin. Our first stop will be the Main Gallery. **11**It houses rare artwork and antiques, so you are required to stay with the group at all times for security purposes. After that, we'll stop by the gardens. There's nothing rare there. You're here at the perfect time because the flowers are in full bloom. **12**We'll meet back at eleven A.M. at the main entrance. Right next to it is a gift shop where you can buy some memorable souvenirs.

historical 역사적인, 역사와 관련된　now that ~이므로　rare 희귀한　antique 골동품　at all times 항상　stop by 잠시 들르다　be in full bloom 만개하다　souvenir 기념품

번역 안녕하세요, 휴 브리지 맨션에 오신 것을 환영합니다. 저는 그레고리라고 합니다. 투어 동안 이 훌륭한 역사적 가옥에 대해 다양한 사실을 말씀드릴 예정입니다. 모든 분의 표를 확인했으니 시작하겠습니다. 첫 번째 목적지는 메인 갤러리입니다. 희귀한 예술품과 골동품이 소장되어 있으므로, 보안상의 이유로 항상 단체와 함께 움직여야 합니다. 이후 정원에 들를 예정입니다. 그곳에는 희귀한 것이 없습니다. 꽃들이 활짝 피어나 방문하기에 완벽한 시기죠. 오전 11시에 주 정문에서 다시 만나겠습니다. 바로 옆에 기억에 남을 만한 기념품을 살 수 있는 기념품점이 있습니다.

10. 청자들은 누구이겠는가?
(A) 신입사원　(B) 정부 조사관
(C) 투어 참여자　(D) 건물 관리자

해설 전체 내용 – 청자의 신분 및 직업
안내 초반에 투어 동안 청자들에게 역사적 가옥에 대해 알려주겠다(I'll be ~ our tour)고 하므로 청자는 투어 참여자임을 알 수 있다. 따라서 정답은 (C)이다.

어휘 government 정부　inspector 조사관, 검사관　participant 참가자, 참여자

11. 화자가 "그곳에는 희귀한 것이 없습니다"라고 말한 이유는?
(A) 구역이 곧 변경된다는 것을 설명하기 위해
(B) 청자들에게 장소가 실망스러울 수 있다고 알려주기 위해
(C) 다른 장소에서 만나라고 권유하기 위해
(D) 청자들이 각자 둘러보라고 제안하기 위해

해설 세부 내용 – 화자의 의도
인용문 앞에서 메인 갤러리에서는 희귀 전시품 때문에 보안상 이유로 단체와 함께 움직이라(It houses rare ~ for security purposes)고 했고 정원에는 희귀한 것이 없다고 했다. 인용문 뒤에서는 정원에 꽃이 만발하여 방문하기에 완벽한 시기(You're here at ~ in full bloom)라고 했다. 이는 갤러리와 달리 정원에서는 자유 투어가 가능하다는 것을 의미한다고 볼 수 있다. 따라서 정답은 (D)이다.

어휘 disappointing 실망감을 주는　suggest 제안하다　browse 둘러보다

12. 청자들은 11시에 무엇을 할 수 있는가?
(A) 시연 지켜보기
(B) 간식 및 음료 즐기기
(C) 역사 관련 강의 듣기
(D) 기념품 구입하기

세부 내용 – 11시에 할 수 있는 행동
안내 후반부에 11시에 정문에서 만나면 바로 옆에 기념품을 살 수 있는 기념품점이 있다(We'll meet ~ memorable souvenirs)고 하므로 정답은 (D)이다.

어휘 demonstration 시연

13-15 여행

M-Cn **13**We hope you are enjoying your experience with Stargaze Travel so far. We still have lots of sights to see around the city. **14**However, I've just received some information that will affect our evening plans. The opera that we have tickets for is now due to start at 8:30 P.M., so we will have an extra half an hour to explore. The show is over two hours long, so **15**I recommend that you buy some snacks to take along. Now, if you follow me, we'll head over to the art museum.

sight 명소   affect 영향을 주다   be due to ~할 예정이다
explore 답사하다   take along 가지고 가다

번역 지금까지 스타게이즈 트래블과 함께 즐거운 시간 보내고 계시기를 바랍니다. 아직 도시에서 둘러볼 명소가 많습니다. 하지만 우리 저녁 계획에 영향을 줄 정보를 입수했습니다. 표를 갖고 있는 오페라가 오후 8시 30분에 시작할 예정이라고 하니 돌아볼 시간이 30분 더 생깁니다. 공연은 2시간 이상 걸리므로 가지고 갈 간식을 구입하시는 것을 추천합니다. 이제 저를 따라오시면 미술관으로 가게 됩니다.

13. 화자는 누구이겠는가?
(A) 미술관 큐레이터
(B) 웨이터
(C) 오페라 가수
(D) 투어 가이드

해설 **전체 내용 – 화자의 신분**
안내 도입부에 스타게이즈 트래블과 즐거운 시간 보내고 계시기를 바라며 둘러볼 명소가 많다(We hope ~ see around the city)고 하므로 정답은 (D)이다.

14. 화자에 따르면 무엇이 변경되었는가?
(A) 시작 시간   (B) 행사 요금
(C) 매표 정책   (D) 메뉴

해설 **세부 내용 – 변경 사항**
안내 중반부에 오페라가 8시 30분에 시작하게 된 것(The opera ~ at 8:30 P.M)과 관련하여 이것이 일정에 영향을 미치는 사항(that will affect our evening plans)이며 30분의 시간이 비게 된 것(so, we will have extra half an hour to explore)까지 앞뒤로 설명이 있으므로 정답은 (A)이다.

15. 청자들에게 무엇을 하라고 권하는가?
(A) 표 예약하기   (B) 사진 찍기
(C) 음식 구입하기   (D) 기념품 구입하기

해설 **세부 내용 – 권고 사항**
안내 후반부에 간식을 구입할 것을 권한다(I recommend ~ take along)고 하므로 정답은 (C)이다.

어휘 reserve 예약하다

16-18 여행

W-Am Okay, everyone. If you look between the apple trees, **16**you will see the new fountain that was installed in the park last month. Next, we'll go to Vermont Lake and take a boat. **17**We used to do this part of the tour last, but we decided it would be better to end up at the Hills Café instead so that you could all get some rest. As the area is quite big, **18**please take a map to avoid getting lost. If you become separated from the group, we won't be able to wait for you.

fountain 분수   avoid 피하다   get lost 길을 잃다   separated from ~에서 떨어진, 분리된

번역 자, 여러분. 사과나무 사이를 보시면 지난 달 공원에 새로 설치한 분수대가 보일 것입니다. 다음으로 버몬트 호수에 가서 배를 탈 예정입니다. 이 부분은 투어 맨 마지막에 하곤 했는데, 여러분이 쉴 수 있도록 힐스 카페에서 종료하는 것이 더 낫겠다고 결정했습니다. 구역이 꽤 넓으니 길을 잃지 않도록 지도를 챙기세요. 일행과 떨어지시면 기다려 드릴 수가 없습니다.

16. 투어는 어디에서 이뤄지겠는가?
(A) 공원   (B) 해변 리조트
(C) 음식점   (D) 쇼핑몰

해설 **전체 내용 – 투어 장소**
안내 초반부에 공원에 새로 설치한 분수대가 보일 것(you will see the new fountain that was installed in the park last month)이라며 투어 일정을 설명하고 있으므로 정답은 (A)이다.

어휘 take place 개최되다, 일어나다

17. 화자는 투어의 어떤 부분이 변경됐다고 말하는가?
(A) 요금   (B) 종료 장소
(C) 이동 방법   (D) 참여자 수

해설 **세부 내용 – 변경 사항**
안내 중반부에서 변경된 투어 마지막 장소를 언급(We used to do ~ end up at the Hills Café instead)하므로 정답은 (B)이다.

어휘 transportation 이동 수단, 교통편   method 방법

18. 화자는 청자들에게 무엇을 제공하는가?
(A) 무료 음료   (B) 구명조끼
(C) 기념품   (D) 지도

해설 **세부 내용 – 청자들에게 제공되는 것**
안내 후반부에 길을 잃지 않도록 지도를 챙기라(please take a map to avoid getting lost)고 했으므로 정답은 (D)이다.

어휘 complimentary 무료의 lifejacket 구명조끼

19-21 견학+도표

W-Br Welcome to the Royce Family Estate. I'm Lilly Lopez, and I'll be your tour guide today. **19**The Royce Family is famous for their contributions of steel mill to our city. They were the main employer for our town for almost thirty years. During that time, the Family also turned their home and extensive grounds into one of the most beautiful gardens in the country. There's so much to see, but **20**I understand you are only with us for an hour. Don't worry. We fit a lot into the hour-long tour. **21**Our first stop will be the Sunrise Lake. You should be able to get some great photos of birds swimming there.

contribution 기여 steel mill 제강 공장, 제철소 extensive 광범위한 fit into ~에 들어맞다, 들어맞게 하다 stroll 산책

번역 로이스 일가 사유지에 오신 것을 환영합니다. 저는 릴리 로페즈라고 해요. 오늘의 투어 가이드입니다. 로이스 가문은 우리 시 제철소에 대한 기여로 유명합니다. 거의 30년 동안 시에서 대표적인 고용주였죠. 이 시기 동안 로이스 가문은 자신들의 집과 넓은 토지를 나라에서 가장 아름다운 정원으로 만들었습니다. 볼거리가 아주 많지만 여러분은 한 시간만 머무시는 걸로 알고 있습니다. 하지만 걱정 마세요. 저희는 한 시간짜리 투어를 알차게 채워 놓았습니다. 처음 들를 곳은 선라이즈 호수입니다. 그곳에서 헤엄치고 있는 새들의 사진을 멋지게 찍으실 수 있습니다.

로이스 일가 사유지 투어

숲과 동굴	30분
토착 야생동물	1시간
역사적인 발걸음	2시간
점심 산책	3시간 30분

19. 로이스 일가는 어떤 종류의 업체를 소유했는가?
(A) 철강 생산 시설   (B) 원예용품 매장
(C) 국립 은행   (D) 연구실

해설 **세부 내용 – 로이스 일가가 소유한 사업체**
안내 초반부에 로이스 가문을 소개하며 로이스 가문은 제철소에 대한 기여로 유명하다(The Royce Family is famous for their contributions of steel mill to our city)고 했으므로 정답은 (A)이다.

어휘 production 생산 gardening 조경, 원예 banking firm 은행

20. 시각 정보에 따르면 청자들은 어떤 투어에 참여하는가?
(A) 숲과 동굴   (B) 토착 야생동물
(C) 역사적인 발걸음   (D) 점심 산책

해설 **세부 내용 – 시각 정보 연계**
안내 중반부에서 청자들이 1시간만 머문다(I understand you are only with us for an hour)고 했고, 시각 정보에서 1시간짜리 투어를 찾아 확인하면 정답은 (B)이다.

21. 청자들은 처음에 어디로 갈 것인가?
(A) 나비 군락지   (B) 수역
(C) 장미 정원   (D) 과수원

해설 **세부 내용 – 처음으로 갈 장소**
안내 후반부에서 첫 방문지는 선라이즈 호수(Our first stop will be the Sunrise Lake)라고 하므로 정답은 (B)이다.

어휘 body of water (강, 호수 등의) 수역 orchard 과수원

●UNIT 04 광고 / 방송 / 보도

예제 교재 p. 124

M-Cn You're listening to Hong Kong's most trusted radio program for food lovers. This week we're talking about the unique recipes, straight from our listeners. If there's a special dish you want to tell me how to make, call me here at the studio. The first recipe is a lasagna made without any cheese. What an idea! I always hear something new.

trusted 믿을 만한, 신뢰받는

번역 여러분은 지금 음식 애호가를 위한 홍콩에서 가장 신뢰받는 라디오 프로그램을 듣고 계십니다. 이번 주에는 청취자들에게서 받은 독특한 조리법에 대해 이야기 나누고 있는데요. 조리법을 들려주고 싶은 특별한 음식이 있다면 스튜디오로 전화해 주세요. 첫 번째 레시피는 치즈 없이 만드는 라자냐입니다. 기발한 생각이죠! 매번 새로운 것을 듣게 되는군요.

LISTENING PRACTICE
교재 p. 125

1. (D)   **2.** (C)   **3.** (B)   **4.** (C)

1 W-Am

This is Gail Rodriguez, with your Boca Raton local update. It's an exciting year for Boca Raton, as a lot of activities are coming up soon. The Latin Food Festival, Summer Outdoor Concert, the annual Big Fish Competition, and more. Visit our Web site for details.

local update 지역 소식   competition 경연

번역 저는 게일 로드리게즈입니다. 보카 레이턴 지역 소식을 전해 드리겠습니다. 보카 레이턴에게는 신나는 한 해입니다. 많은 행사들이 다가오고 있으니까요. 라틴 푸드 축제, 여름 야외 콘서트, 해마다 열리는 대어 낚기 대회 등등이요. 더 자세한 내용은 저희 웹사이트를 방문해 확인하세요.

문제 화자가 "보카 레이턴에게 신나는 한 해입니다"라고 말한 이유는?
(A) 중요한 기념일을 맞아서
(B) 컨퍼런스 센터를 새로 열 예정이어서
(C) 잡지에서 인정을 받아서
(D) 많은 행사를 개최해서

해설 **세부 내용 – 화자의 의도**
인용문 앞에서 보카 레이턴의 지역 뉴스임을 알 수 있고 이 지역에 있어 신나는 한 해라고 하며 인용문 뒤에서 많은 행사들이 있기 때문(as a lot of activities are coming up soon)이라고 이유를 밝히고 있다. 따라서 정답은 (D)이다.

어휘 anniversary 기념일   recognize 인정하다, 알아보다

2 W-Br

Spring is coming, and that means the Auckland Garden Society is busy organizing their annual garden tour. If you live the Historical District and have a yard you want to show off, get in touch with the tour coordinator, Sheila Torres, at 555-0111.

show off 자랑하다   get in touch with ~와 연락하다

번역 봄이 오고 있습니다. 오클랜드 가든 협회가 연례 정원 투어를 기획하느라 바쁘다는 뜻이죠. 역사 지구에 거주하시고 자랑하고 싶은 마당이 있으시다면 투어 담당자인 쉴라 토레스 씨에게 555-0111로 연락하세요.

문제 토레스 씨는 누구인가?
(A) 판매원   (B) 부동산 중개인
(C) 행사 기획자   (D) 뉴스 진행자

해설 **전체 내용 – 인물의 신분**
방송 후반부에 행사 관련 문의처를 알려주며 투어 담당자, 쉴라 토레스(tour coordinator, Sheila Torres)라고 하므로 정답은 (C)이다.

어휘 real estate 부동산

3 M-Cn

If you're looking for a fun adventure for your office, get in touch with Outside the Box. All of our guides are certified by the Alberta Board of Tourism, so you'll be in good hands on your adventure. Sign up now to boost your office's productivity with a unique experience.

be certified by ~에 의해 공인을 받다, 인증을 받다   in good hands 안심하고 맡길 수 있는   sign up 신청하다   boost 신장시키다, 북돋우다   productivity 생산성

번역 회사를 위해 재미난 모험을 찾고 계신다면 아웃사이드 더 박스에 연락하세요. 저희 가이드들은 모두 앨버타 관광위원회의 공식 인가를 받았으니, 안심하고 모험을 즐길 수 있습니다. 독특한 경험으로 사무실 생산성을 향상시키려면 지금 바로 신청하세요.

문제 화자가 아웃사이드 더 박스 직원에 대해 말한 것은?
(A) 다국적 출신이다.
(B) 자격증을 소지하고 있다.
(C) 계절별로 바뀐다.
(D) 사무실을 방문할 수 있다.

해설 **세부 내용 – 직원에 대한 언급**
광고 초반에 남자가 자신의 회사인 아웃사이드 더 박스를 소개하며 회사의 가이드들은 모두 공인을 받았다(All of our guides are ~ of Tourism)고 하므로 정답은 (B)이다.

어휘 certification 증명, 증명서, 자격증

4 W-Br

You're listening to WTRX Radio. Next week, on Thursday at 6 P.M., our station will launch its new talk show, *Public Discourse* with host Tina Brown. This show will cover a variety of topics that affect everyday society. Listeners can call the station to share their inquiries. Up next, let's see how traffic on the roadways is looking with an up-to-the-minute report.

station 방송국   discourse 담론   cover 다루다   a variety of 다양한   inquiry 문의   up-to-the-minute 최신의

번역 WTRX 라디오를 듣고 계십니다. 다음 주 목요일 오후 6시에 저희 방송국은 티나 브라운 씨가 진행하는 새 토크쇼 〈공개 담론〉 방영을 시작합니다. 이 프로그램은 일상 속의 사회에 영향을 주는 다양한 주제를 다룰 예정인데요. 청자들은 방송국에 전화해 문의 사항을 전할 수 있습니다. 다음 순서로 도로 교통 상황을 최신 소식을 통해 알아보시죠.

문제 다음 주에 어떤 일이 있을 것인가?
(A) 모금 행사가 개최된다.
(B) 기념일을 축하할 것이다.
(C) 새로운 프로그램을 처음 방송한다.
(D) 우승자를 발표한다.

해설 **세부 내용 – 다음 주에 있을 일**
방송 초반부에 다음 주 목요일 오후 6시에 티나 브라운이 진행하는 새 토크쇼 〈공개 담론〉 방영을 시작한다(Next week ~ Tina Brown)고 밝혔으므로 정답은 (C)이다.

어휘 fundraiser 모금 행사 announce 발표하다, 알리다

ACTUAL TEST

교재 p. 126

1. (B)	**2.** (A)	**3.** (C)	**4.** (B)	**5.** (C)
6. (C)	**7.** (C)	**8.** (A)	**9.** (D)	**10.** (A)
11. (B)	**12.** (C)	**13.** (A)	**14.** (D)	**15.** (C)
16. (B)	**17.** (D)	**18.** (C)	**19.** (B)	**20.** (C)
21. (C)				

1-3 라디오 방송

M-Au ¹You're listening to Bodybuilding Weekly, the show that gives you workout tips, dietary advice, and other strategies to help you stay in shape. ²My guest today is Roy Benson, a former national champion and the founder of Benson Incorporated. His company's protein shake is one of the most popular brands in the country. ³Today we're giving away a year's supply of this product to one lucky winner of our contest. I'll tell you all about how to enter right after this commercial break from our sponsors, so stay tuned.

workout 운동 dietary 식이 요법의 strategy 전략 stay in shape 건강을 유지하다 former 이전의 founder 창업자 commercial 상업의 sponsor 후원자 stay tuned 채널을 그대로 고정하여 청취하다[시청하다]

번역 여러분께 운동 정보, 식이 관련 조언, 건강한 몸을 유지하는 전략 등을 전해 드리는 보디빌딩 위클리를 듣고 계십니다. 오늘 게스트는 로이 벤슨 씨입니다. 예전 전국 챔피언이자 벤슨 인코퍼레이티드의 창업자이시죠. 벤슨 씨 회사의 단백질 셰이크는 전국에서 가장 인기 있는 제품 중 하나입니다. 오늘 행운의 추첨 당첨자에게 이 제품의 1년치 분량을 제공해 드립니다. 후원업체 광고 후 바로 참가 방법을 말씀드릴 예정이니 채널 고정하세요.

1. 프로그램의 주제는 무엇인가?
(A) 건설   (B) 건강
(C) 의학   (D) 금융

해설 **전체 내용 – 프로그램의 주제**
방송 초반부에 프로그램 주제가 운동과 건강(the show that gives you ~ stay in shape)이라고 하므로 정답은 (B)이다.

2. 로이 벤슨 씨는 누구인가?
(A) 회사 창업주   (B) 정치인
(C) 강사   (D) 비즈니스 컨설턴트

해설 **세부 내용 – 인물의 신분**
방송 중반부에 초대 손님 로이 벤슨이 회사 창업자(My guest today is Roy Benson, ~ founder of Benson Incorporated)라고 하므로 정답은 (A)이다.

어휘 politician 정치인 instructor 강사

3. 청자들은 광고 후 바로 무엇을 듣게 될 것인가?
(A) 채용 공고에 관한 세부 사항
(B) 제품 출시 최신 내용
(C) 추첨에 대한 안내
(D) 사업주와의 인터뷰

해설 **세부 내용 – 광고 후 듣게 될 것**
방송 후반부에 상품 추첨이 있을 것이며 광고 후 참가 방법을 알려주겠다(Today we're giving away ~ from our sponsors)고 하므로 정답은 (C)이다.

어휘 immediately 즉시, 바로 advertising 광고 launch 출시

4-6 교통 방송

M-Au This is your morning traffic update. ⁴The city-wide marathon race starts at 9:00 A.M., and the course takes runners through the downtown area. Expect slower than usual traffic there because of that. ⁵Rides on all city trains will be free during the event, so officials urge commuters to take the subway to central city destinations. Also, Lake Street will be closed to traffic on Friday, as ⁶vendors of organic fruits and vegetables are scheduled to come together there for the City Farmer's Market. It will happen rain or shine.

expect 예상하다, 기대하다 official 공무원 urge 강력히 권고하다 commuter 통근자 destination 목적지 vendor 판매자, 판매업체 be scheduled to ~할 예정이다 rain or shine 날씨에 관계없이

번역 오전 교통 상황 최신 내용을 알려드립니다. 도시 전역에서 펼쳐지는 마라톤 경주가 오전 9시에 시작됩니다. 주자들은 경로를 통해 도심 지역으로 들어가게 되는데요. 이 때문에 평소보다 느린 교통 흐름을 예상하셔야 합니다. 행사 중에는 모든 도시 철도 탑승이 무료입니다. 따라서 공무원들은 통근자들이 도심 목적지까지 지하철을 탈 수 있도록 적극 권고하고 있습니다. 아울러 레이크 스트리트는 금요일에 교통이 통제됩니다. 유기농 과일과 채소 판매상들이 도시 농산물 직거래장을 위해 그곳에서 모일 예정이기 때문인데요. 날씨에 관계없이 진행될 예정입니다.

4. 보고서에 따르면, 도심 지역에 교통 체증을 초래할 수도 있는 원인이 되는 것은?
(A) 비가 오는 지역
(B) 달리기 대회
(C) 도로 확장 프로젝트
(D) 관광 무역박람회

해설 **세부 내용 – 교통 체증 원인**
방송 초반부에 마라톤 경주 때문에 느린 교통 흐름이 예상된다(The city-wide marathon ~ because of that)고 하므로 정답은 (B)이다.

어휘 trade show 무역박람회

5. 통근자들은 해당 일자의 오전에 무엇을 하라고 권고 받는가?
(A) 지정된 주차구역에 차량 두기
(B) 휴대전화용 탑승 공유 앱 사용하기
(C) 지하철로 도심까지 이동하기
(D) 컴퓨터로 재택 근무하기

해설 **세부 내용 – 권고 사항**
방송 중반부에 행사 중에 도시 철도가 무료이니 통근자들은 도심 목적지까지 지하철을 타도록 권고된다(Rides on ~ city destinations)고 하므로 정답은 (C)이다.

어휘 designated 지정된

6. 금요일에 레이크 스트리트에 누가 모이기로 했는가?
(A) 주택 건설자 (B) 교통 공학 전문가
(C) 농산물 판매자 (D) 생태 전문가

해설 **세부 내용 – 레이크 스트리트에 모이는 주체**
방송 후반부에 레이크 스트리트는 금요일에 교통이 통제되며 과일과 채소 판매상들이 시장을 위해 그곳에 모일 것(vendors of ~ Farmer's Market)이라고 하므로 정답은 (C)이다.

어휘 gather 모이다 produce 농산물 ecology 생태, 생태학 expert 전문가

7-9 뉴스 보도

W-Am In local news, **7**officials have confirmed plans to build a Green Line extension to the city's railway system. The work is set to start on June 1. When completed, the line will connect the Chester Shopping Plaza with the Harbor Business District. **8**Paul Jones, director of the Transit Authority, said the extension would help address a past concern for city residents— namely, that the railway system's trains have become too crowded. **9**He also invited residents to make use of the Transit Authority's Web site, which features improvements such as advanced search functions and real-time train tracking.

official 공무원 extension 연장 complete 완료하다 connect A with B A와 B를 연결하다 transit 교통 authority 당국 concern 우려 resident 거주자 namely 즉, 다시 말해 make use of ~을 이용하다 feature 특별히 포함하다 improvement 개선, 향상 advanced 고급의 real-time 실시간의 track 추적하다

번역 지역 뉴스입니다. 공무원들이 도시 철도망에 녹색 노선을 연장하기로 확정했다고 합니다. 공사는 6월 1일에 착수할 예정입니다. 완공되면 녹색 노선은 체스터 쇼핑 플라자와 하버 비즈니스 지구를 연결하게 됩니다. 교통 당국의 폴 존스 국장은 이번 연장으로 시 거주자들에 대한 최근 우려 사항, 즉 철도 교통체계의 열차가 너무 붐비게 된 점을 해결하는 데 도움을 줄 것이라고 밝혔습니다. 아울러 존스 국장은 거주자들로 하여금 교통 당국의 웹사이트를 이용해 달라고 말했는데요. 웹사이트는 고급 검색 기능, 실시간 열차 위치 추적 기능 등이 개선됐습니다.

7. 6월 1일에 무엇을 시작할 예정인가?
(A) 새 교통카드 시스템 도입
(B) 확장된 주차 구역 개장
(C) 새 철도 노선 건설
(D) 쇼핑센터 보수

해설 **세부 내용 – 6월 1일에 예정된 것**
방송 초반부에 철도 녹색 노선을 연장하기로 한 계획이 확정되어 6월 1일에 공사를 시작한다(offices have confirmed ~ on June 1)고 했으므로 정답은 (C)이다.

어휘 introduction 도입, 소개 expand 확대하다 renovation 개조, 보수

8. 존스 씨에 따르면 거주자들에 대한 우려 사항은 무엇이었는가?
(A) 지나치게 붐비는 열차
(B) 열차 서비스 지연
(C) 협소한 주차 공간
(D) 최근 열차 시간표 변경

해설 **세부 내용 – 우려 사항**
방송 중반부에 교통 당국의 폴 존스의 말을 인용하여 이번 연장으로 거주자들의 걱정거리인 열차 혼잡 문제 해결에 도움을 줄 것(Paul Jones, director ~ too crowded)이라고 전하고 있으므로 정답은 (A)이다.

어휘 overcrowded 너무 붐비는 delay 지연 recent 최근의

9. 존스 씨는 거주자들에게 무엇을 하라고 권장했는가?
(A) 피드백 설문 조사 참여하기
(B) 새 기차역 둘러보기
(C) 기차 월 정기 승차권 구입하기
(D) 업그레이드된 웹사이트 이용하기

해설 **세부 내용 – 제안 사항**
방송 후반부에 존스의 말을 이용하여 거주자들에게 개선된 교통당국 웹사이트 이용을 권했다(He also invited residents to ~ Web site)고 전하고 있으므로 정답은 (D)이다.

어휘 survey 설문 조사 explore 탐방하다, 답사하다 monthly 월의

10-12 라디오 방송

M-Cn You're tuned to KBC, Portland's most trusted local news station. [10]The city officials are now working on organizing the event for next year, and they're currently taking applications from those who would like to participate. [11]If your organization wants to sign up to march, get in touch with Kelly Walker. Kelly and her team are always looking for supporters who can represent the city. [12]One of those supporters is actor, Kyle Donovan. He's marching in the parade and actually came into the studio today to talk about it. Stay tuned for the interview.

tune (라디오, TV의 채널을) 맞추다 trusted 믿을 만한 currently 현재 application 신청, 신청서 organization 단체, 조직 sign up 신청하다 march 행진하다 represent 대표하다 actually 사실, 실제로

번역 포틀랜드에서 가장 신뢰받는 지역 뉴스 방송국 KBC를 청취하고 계십니다. 시 공무원들은 내년 행사를 기획하고 있습니다. 현재 참가를 원하는 사람들의 신청을 받고 있는데요. 여러분의 단체가 거리 행진에 신청하기를 원할 경우, 켈리 워커 씨에게 연락하세요. 켈리 씨 팀은 시를 대표할 수 있는 후원자를 계속 찾고 있습니다. 후원자 중에는 배우인 카일 도노반 씨가 있죠. 도노반 씨는 행렬에 참가할 예정인데요. 오늘 이에 대한 이야기를 나누기 위해 방송국에 오셨습니다. 인터뷰가 방송되니 채널 고정하세요.

10. 방송은 주로 무엇에 관한 내용인가?
(A) 다가오는 경축 행사
(B) 새 사업체 개업
(C) 미술 대회
(D) 음악 공연

해설 **전체 내용 – 방송의 주제**
방송 초반부에 시 공무원들이 내년 행사를 기획하고 있다(The city officials ~ next year)고 했고, 그 행사가 거리 행진(march)이라는 것을 알 수 있으므로 정답은 (A)이다.

어휘 upcoming 다가오는, 앞으로 있을 competition 대회, 경연 performance 공연

11. 화자는 청자들에게 무엇을 위해 켈리 워커 씨에게 연락을 취하라고 말하는가?
(A) 특별 할인을 받기 위해
(B) 행사에 신청하기 위해
(C) 표를 구입하기 위해
(D) 후원하기 위해

해설 **세부 내용 – 연락을 취하는 이유**
방송 중반부에 행진에 신청하기를 원하면 켈리 워커에게 연락하라(If your organization wants ~ get in touch with Kelly Walker)고 하므로 정답은 (B)이다.

어휘 receive 받다 discount 할인 register for ~에 등록하다, 신청하다

12. 청자들은 다음으로 무엇을 듣겠는가?
(A) 일기예보 　　　　(B) 행사 일정
(C) 유명 인사 인터뷰　(D) 음악 공연

해설 **세부 내용 – 청자들이 들을 내용**
방송 후반부에 배우를 소개하며 인터뷰가 있으니 채널 고정하라(One of those supporters ~ for the interview)고 했으므로 정답은 (C)이다.

어휘 weather report 일기예보 celebrity 유명 인사

13-15 뉴스 보도

W-Am [13]This is Lydia Hopkins, reporting live from the grand opening event at Weston Stadium. This construction project was made possible through government funds and private donations. [14]Project Manager Todd Green said he was delighted that the team was able to meet the deadline, catching up after bad weather put construction behind schedule. The stadium will host a number of baseball games and concerts, and it will even be used for filming an upcoming movie. Free tours of the facility are available. [15]To check out the times for these tours, visit www.experienceweston.com.

grand opening 개장, 개점 construction 건설, 공사 fund 기금 donation 기부 meet the deadline 마감 기한에 맞추다 catch up 만회하다, 따라잡다 behind schedule 예정보다 늦게 facility 시설

번역 저는 리디아 홉킨스입니다. 웨스톤 스타디움에서 개장 행사를 생방송으로 전해드리고 있습니다. 이 공사 프로젝트는 정부 기금과 개인 기부를 통해 이뤄질 수 있었습니다. 토드 그린 프로젝트 관리자는 악천후로 공사 일정이 늦어진 것을 만회하고 기한을 맞출 수 있어서 기쁘다고 밝혔습니다. 경기상에서 수많은 야구 경기와 콘서트를 개최할 예정이며, 앞으로 나올 영화 촬영지로도 이용될 것입니다. 시설 무료 견학이 가능합니다. 견학 시간을 확인하시려면 www.experienceweston.com을 방문하세요.

13. 화자는 어디에 있는가?
(A) 경기장
(B) 녹음 스튜디오
(C) 영화관
(D) 공원

해설 **전체 내용 – 담화 장소**
방송 도입부에 경기장에서 행사를 생방으로 전하고 있다
(This is Lydia ~ at Weston Stadium)고 하며 자신을
소개하고 있으므로 정답은 (A)이다.

어휘 venue 장소

14. 프로젝트 관리자가 기뻐한 이유는?
(A) 거액의 개인 기부가 이뤄졌다.
(B) 개장일 날씨가 좋았다.
(C) 건물의 에너지 효율성이 높다.
(D) 지연을 피할 수 있었다.

해설 **세부 내용 – 기뻐한 이유**
방송 중반부에 프로젝트 관리자의 말을 인용하여 늦어
진 일정을 만회하고 기한을 맞추게 되어 기쁘다(Project
Manager ~ behind schedule)고 전하고 있으므로 정
답은 (D)이다.

어휘 ceremony 식 energy-efficient 에너지 효율적인
avoid 피하다

15. 화자에 따르면 청자들은 왜 웹사이트를 방문해야 하는가?
(A) 사진을 훑어보기 위해
(B) 제안 사항에 대해 투표하기 위해
(C) 견학 시간을 확인하기 위해
(D) 표를 구입하기 위해

해설 **세부 내용 – 웹사이트 방문 이유**
방송 마지막에 견학 시간 확인을 위해 웹사이트를 방문하
라(To check out the times for these tours, visit ~)
고 하므로 정답은 (C)이다.

어휘 browse 훑어보다, 둘러보다

16-18 광고

W-Br Traveling to Kalamaria? Enjoy a
comfortable stay at the Morris Hotel. **16**We are
popular with out-of-town guests thanks to our
easy access to Kalamaria Regional Airport,
which is just five minutes away. We're also
within walking distance to several shops and
restaurants. **17**We've recently started running a
free shuttle to the city center. **18**Guests should
visit our Web site for a detailed schedule of the
shuttle's operation times. For quiet rooms and
service with a smile, choose the Morris Hotel.
Call 1-800-555-0123 to book your room now.

out-of-town 외지에서 온 within walking distance to ~에
걸어서 갈 수 있는 거리에 있는

번역 칼라마리아로 여행을 가시나요? 그렇다면 모리스 호텔에
서 편안하게 지내세요. 칼라마리아 지역 공항에 단 5분만
에 쉽게 갈 수 있어서 외지에서 온 투숙객에게 인기가 많
습니다. 또한 여러 상점과 음식점에 걸어서 갈 수 있습니
다. 저희는 최근에 도심으로 무료 셔틀버스 운행을 시작했습니
다. 셔틀버스 운행시간에 관한 상세 시간표는 저희 웹사
이트를 방문하셔야 합니다. 조용한 객실과 친절한 서비스
를 찾으신다면 모리스 호텔을 선택하세요. 지금 1-800-
555-0123으로 전화하셔서 객실을 예약하세요.

16. 광고에 따르면, 투숙객들은 모리스 호텔의 어떤 점을 마음
에 들어하는가?
(A) 친절한 직원
(B) 편리한 위치
(C) 적당한 가격
(D) 널찍한 객실

해설 **세부 내용 – 호텔이 마음에 드는 이유**
광고 초반부에 모리스 호텔을 추천하며 공항에 쉽게 갈 수
있어 인기가 많다(We are popular with out-of-town
guests thanks to our easy access to Kalamaria
Regional Airport)고 했으므로 정답은 (B)이다.

어휘 advertisement 광고 convenient 편리한
reasonable (가격이) 적당한, 알맞은 spacious 넓은

17. 호텔은 최근에 무엇을 추가로 도입했는가?
(A) 피트니스 시설
(B) 인터넷 연결
(C) 호텔 내 식당
(D) 교통 서비스

해설 **세부 내용 – 최근에 호텔에 추가된 것**
광고 중반에 최근 무료 셔틀 서비스를 시작했다(We've
recently ~ to the city center)고 했으므로 정답은 (D)
이다.

어휘 on-site 현장의 transportation 이동 수단, 교통편

18. 화자는 왜 호텔 웹사이트를 방문하라고 권하는가?
(A) 고객평을 읽기 위해
(B) 예약하기 위해
(C) 시간표를 확인하기 위해
(D) 사진 갤러리를 살펴보기 위해

해설 **세부 내용 – 방문을 권하는 이유**
광고 후반부에 버스 운행 시간표를 위해 웹사이트를 방문
하라(Guests should visit our Web site ~ operation
times)고 했으므로 정답은 (C)이다.

어휘 make a reservation 예약하다

19-21 광고+가격표

M-Cn Summer has arrived, and **19**we at Zerox
Shoes are celebrating our 10th year in business.
To mark the occasion, we are offering sale
prices on all of our high-quality footwear
products for outdoor and water sports. And
20you can even purchase our latest product

release, the Model TS301, at a sale price of just $70. **These fashionable, lightweight shoes are perfect for wearing at home or in the office. Want to save more money ?** **⁰¹Sign up now for our exclusive e-mail newsletter**—you'll find great deals available only to subscribers.

mark the occasion 행사 등을 기념하다 lightweight 경량의
sign up for ~을 신청하다 exclusive 독점적인 subscriber 가입자, 구독자

번역 여름이 왔습니다. 그리고 저희 제록스 슈즈는 10주년을 맞이하고 있습니다. 이를 기념해 야외 및 수상 스포츠를 위한 고품질 신발 전 제품을 할인가로 제공해 드립니다. 저희 최신 제품 TS301 모델도 단 70달러의 할인 가격으로 구입할 수 있습니다. 패션감각이 돋보이는 이 경량 신발은 집이나 사무실에서 신기에 완벽합니다. 돈을 더 절약하고 싶으신가요? 그렇다면 저희 단독 이메일 소식지를 신청하세요. 구독자에게만 제공되는 큰 혜택이 있습니다.

모델	유형	할인가
TS101	드라이빙 슈즈	50달러
TS201	배구화	60달러
TS301	컴포트 슈즈	70달러
TS401	테니스화	80달러

19. 제록스 슈즈가 특별 할인을 하는 이유는 무엇이겠는가?
(A) 판매되지 않은 재고 물품을 줄이기 위해
(B) 기념일을 축하하기 위해
(C) 피트니스 워킹을 홍보하기 위해
(D) 개업식을 강조하기 위해

해설 **세부 내용 – 할인 이유**
광고 초반부에서 제록스 슈즈가 10주년을 기념해 전 제품을 할인가로 제공한다(we at Zerox ~ water sports)고 했으므로 정답은 (B)이다.

어휘 reduce 감소시키다 inventory 재고, 물품 목록
promote 홍보하다, 판촉하다 highlight 강조하다

20. 시각 정보에 따르면 제록스 슈즈는 최근 어떤 종류의 제품을 출시했는가?
(A) 드라이빙 슈즈 (B) 배구화
(C) 컴포트 슈즈 (D) 테니스화

해설 **시각 정보 연계 문제 – 최근 출시한 제품**
광고 중반부에 최신 제품 TS301 모델도 단 70달러의 할인 가격으로 구입할 수 있다(you can ~ just $70)고 했고 시각 정보에서 TS301 모델을 찾아 확인하면 정답은 (C)이다.

21. 광고에 따르면 청자들은 어떻게 추가 할인을 받을 수 있는가?
(A) 휴대전화 앱으로 결제함으로써
(B) 운동 경기에 참가함으로써

(C) 소식지를 신청함으로써
(D) 설문 조사를 기입함으로써

해설 **세부 내용 – 추가 할인을 받는 방법**
광고 후반부에서 돈을 더 절약하려면 단독 이메일 소식지를 신청하라(Sign up ~ e-mail newsletter)고 했으므로 정답은 (C)이다.

어휘 advertisement 광고 additional 추가의 register for ~에 등록하다, 신청하다

●UNIT 05 인물 / 강연 / 설명

예제 교재 p. 128

M-Cn Welcome to the seminar on business trends. We have several guest speakers today, and we will learn some great tips that you can apply to your own businesses from them. Let me start off by introducing our first speaker, Olivia Gail. She is well known for her best-selling book about how to effectively run a company. Today she'll be telling us about a number of unique approaches to online marketing. Come on up, Olivia.

apply 적용하다 effectively 효과적으로 run a company 회사를 운영하다 approach 접근법

번역 비즈니스 동향 세미나에 오신 것을 환영합니다. 저희는 오늘 여러 명의 객원 연사를 모셨는데요. 여러분 자신의 사업에 적용할 수 있는 훌륭한 조언을 듣게 될 것입니다. 첫 번째 연사이신 올리비아 게일 씨를 소개하며 시작하겠습니다. 게일 씨는 효과적인 회사 운영법에 관한 베스트셀러로 잘 알려져 있습니다. 오늘 저희에게 온라인 마케팅에 관한 독특한 접근법을 다수 알려주실 예정입니다. 올리비아 씨, 나와 주세요.

LISTENING PRACTICE 교재 p. 129

1. (D) **2.** (C) **3.** (C) **4.** (C)

1 M-Cn

Welcome to the workshop, where job seekers learn how to write a good résumé. Let's get started by looking at some of the sample writings which I'll be passing around in a moment. **Please read them through carefully. Also, please note that there is a section where you can mark your top three choices.**

job seeker 구직자 resume 이력서 pass around (여러 사람이 보도록) 돌리다 mark 표시하다

번역 워크숍에 오신 것을 환영합니다. 이곳에서 구직자들은 이력서를 잘 쓰는 법을 배우게 됩니다. 잠시 후 돌릴 예시 글 몇 개를 보시면서 시작하겠습니다. 꼼꼼히 읽어주세요. 또한 여러분이 선택한 베스트 3위를 표시할 수 있는 칸이 있으니 눈여겨보세요.

문제 화자는 참가자들에게 무엇을 주겠다고 말하는가?
(A) 신청서
(B) 시식용 음식
(C) 자신의 저서 사본
(D) 이력서 샘플

해설 **세부 내용 – 참가자들이 받을 것**
초반부에서 워크숍 참가자(청자들)들이 이력서 쓰는 법을 배울 것이라고 한 후 중반부에서 잠시 후 나눠 줄 예시 글을 보면서 시작하겠다고 하므로 참가자들이 이력서 샘플을 받을 것임을 알 수 있다. 따라서 정답은 (D)이다.

어휘 registration form 신청서 template 견본, 본보기

2 W-Am

> We are gathered here tonight to honor our outgoing Marketing Director, Fred Costas. During his tenure at our company, he developed many successful sales strategies—including our award-winning social media campaign. Congratulations, Mr. Costas, on a wonderful career, and best of luck on the next phase in your life.
>
> gather 모이다 tenure 재임 기간 strategy 전략 award-winning 상을 받은 phase 단계, 국면

번역 우리는 오늘밤 퇴임하는 프레드 코스타스 마케팅 부장에게 경의를 표하고자 이곳에 모였습니다. 재직 기간 동안 그는 수상 경력에 빛나는 소셜 미디어 캠페인을 비롯하여 성공적인 판매 전략을 다수 개발했습니다. 코스타스 씨, 훌륭한 경력을 이루신 것을 축하드리며 인생의 다음 막에서도 행운이 함께 하길 바랍니다.

문제 이 모임의 목적은 무엇이겠는가?
(A) 수상 후보를 지명하기 위해
(B) 최근 승진을 알리기 위해
(C) 직원의 퇴직을 기념하기 위해
(D) 판매 캠페인에 대한 조언을 구하기 위해

해설 **세부 내용 – 모인 이유**
담화 도입부에 떠나는 마케팅 부장에게 경의를 표하고자 모였다(We are ~ Fred Costas)고 하므로 정답은 (C)이다.

어휘 nominee 후보 job promotion 승진 retiring 은퇴하는 input 조언

3 M-Cn

> Welcome to my lecture, "Building Negotiation Skills." Today, I will provide you with valuable advice on business negotiations. After I finish my talk, I will divide you into pairs for a role play. Each pair will have a goods "seller" and a goods "buyer", and you will negotiate until you settle on a mutually acceptable price point.
>
> lecture 강연 negotiation 협상 valuable 귀중한 divide A into B A를 B로 나누다 settle on ~을 정하다 mutually 서로, 상호간에 acceptable 받아들일 수 있는

번역 〈협상 기술 개발〉에 관한 제 강연에 오신 것을 환영합니다. 오늘 저는 여러분께 업무 협상에 관한 귀중한 조언을 드릴 것입니다. 제 강연이 끝나면 역할극을 위해 여러분을 두 명씩 나누겠습니다. 각 조는 제품 판매자와 구매자로 구성되며, 서로 수용할 수 있는 가격을 정할 때까지 협상할 것입니다.

문제 화자에 따르면, 청자들은 강연이 끝난 후 무엇을 할 것인가?
(A) 신문 광고 평가하기
(B) 피드백 설문조사 기입하기
(C) 역할극 참여하기
(D) 현지 기업가 만나보기

해설 **세부 내용 – 청자들의 다음 행동**
강연 중반부에 강연 이후 역할극을 위해 두 명씩 나눈다(After I finish ~ a role play)고 했으므로 정답은 (C)이다.

어휘 evaluate 평가하다 entrepreneur 기업가

4 W-Br

> As you will be using a new banking software system starting next week, I invited IT expert James Han who will provide training on the proper operation of the program. Mr. Han has led several training sessions for our company. In fact, his professionalism and friendly attitude were featured in the company newsletter last month. Now, let's welcome James Han.
>
> proper 적절한 professionalism 전문성 attitude 태도 feature 특별히 포함하다 newsletter 소식지

번역 여러분은 다음 주부터 새로운 금융 소프트웨어 시스템을 사용할 예정이므로, 적절한 프로그램 운영에 관한 교육을 해 주실 IT 전문가 제임스 한 씨를 모셨습니다. 한 씨는 우리 회사의 교육 과정을 여러 차례 진행하신 바 있습니다. 사실 그의 전문성과 친절한 태도는 지난달 회사 소식지에 실리기도 했습니다. 자, 제임스 한 씨를 반갑게 맞아 주십시오.

문제 화자에 따르면, 지난 달에 어떤 일이 있었는가?
(A) 연구 결과가 발표되었다.
(B) 광고 캠페인이 시작됐다.
(C) IT 전문가가 출판물에 소개됐다.
(D) 교육이 취소됐다.

해설 **세부 내용 – 지난 달에 있었던 일**
설명 초반부에 교육을 위해 IT 전문가를 모셨다(I invited IT expert)고 했고, 후반부에 그가 지난달 회사 소식지에 실렸다(featured in the company newsletter last month)고 했으므로 정답은 (C)이다.

어휘 findings 연구 결과   release 발표하다   specialist 전문가

ACTUAL TEST
교재 p. 130

1. (B)	**2.** (B)	**3.** (A)	**4.** (C)	**5.** (B)
6. (C)	**7.** (C)	**8.** (A)	**9.** (B)	**10.** (D)
11. (B)	**12.** (A)	**13.** (B)	**14.** (B)	**15.** (C)
16. (A)	**17.** (D)	**18.** (B)	**19.** (B)	**20.** (C)
21. (D)				

1-3 소개

M-Cn Welcome to our employee recognition awards ceremony. Thanks to everyone's hard work and support, **1**we at Canopus Ltd. have seen our company grow to become a leading manufacturer of sports apparel. Now I would like to give special recognition to Ms. Sandy Shields. **2**As a result of her dedication to providing quality customer service, our company has raised its customer satisfaction ratings to their highest level ever. **3**As a token of our gratitude, we are presenting her with two VIP tickets to the City Orchestra's opening night concert. Ms. Shields, congratulations.

recognition 인정, 표창   awards ceremony 시상식   leading 선두의   manufacturer 제조업자   give recognition to ~을 인정하다   dedication 헌신   rating 순위   as a token of ~의 표시로   gratitude 감사

번역 직원 공로상 시상식에 오신 것을 환영합니다. 모두의 노고와 도움 덕분에 캐노퍼스 주식회사는 스포츠 의류 제조 선도업체로 성장할 수 있었습니다. 샌디 쉴즈 씨의 공로를 특별히 인정하고자 합니다. 우수한 고객 서비스를 제공하는 데 헌신한 결과로 우리 회사는 고객 만족 등급을 최상위로 올리게 됐습니다. 감사의 표시로 시립 교향악단의 저녁 개막식 콘서트 VIP 티켓 두 장을 드립니다. 쉴즈 씨, 축하합니다.

1. 캐노퍼스 주식회사는 어떤 회사이겠는가?
(A) 건설회사
(B) 의류 제조업체
(C) 금융기관
(D) 인테리어 디자인 회사

해설 **전체 내용 – 회사의 업종**
담화 초반부에서 회사가 스포츠 의류 제조 선도업체로 성장했다(we at Canopus ~ sports apparel)고 하므로 정답은 (B)이다.

어휘 construction 건설   financial 금융의, 재무의   institute 기관

2. 쉴즈 씨는 어떤 공로를 인정받았는가?
(A) 공장 생산성 증대
(B) 고객 만족도 향상
(C) 접대 비용 절감
(D) 신입사원 채용

해설 **세부 내용 – 쉴즈의 공로**
담화 중반부에서 쉴즈의 공로로 고객 만족 최상등급을 얻었다(As a result of ~ highest level ever)고 하므로 정답은 (B)이다.

어휘 productivity 생산성   reduce 줄이다, 감소시키다   recruit 채용하다

3. 소개에 따르면 쉴즈 씨는 무엇을 받을 것인가?
(A) 음악 공연 티켓
(B) 즉각적인 승진
(C) 현지 상점 상품권
(D) 맞춤형 커피잔

해설 **세부 내용 – 쉴즈가 받을 것**
담화 후반부에서 감사 표시로 교향악단의 콘서트 티켓을 준다(As a token of ~ opening night concert)고 하므로 정답은 (A)이다.

어휘 immediate 즉각적인   job promotion 승진   gift card 상품권   personalized 맞춤형의

4-6 강연

W-Br **4**Welcome to our workshop, "Skills for Job Interviews." It is being offered at no cost as part of the City Public Library's outreach program. As you can see from the schedule, my talks will cover a number of areas. When we get to the topic of non-verbal communication, **5**I'll step down from the stage and show a video that highlights various gestures and body movements. OK, let's start with our topic of answering interview questions. **6**Now, let me give you these print-outs that list common questions interviewers ask job candidates in various industries.

at no cost 무료로   as part of ~의 일환으로   outreach 봉사
활동, 원조 활동   non-verbal 비언어적인   highlight 강조하다
print-out 인쇄물   job candidate 구직자

번역 〈면접의 기술〉 워크숍에 오신 것을 환영합니다. 본 워크숍
은 시립 도서관 지원 프로그램의 일환으로 무료로 제공됩
니다. 일정표에서 보시는 것처럼 제 강연은 많은 부분을 다
룰 예정입니다. 비언어적 의사소통 주제에 이르면 저는 무
대에서 내려가고 다양한 몸짓과 신체 움직임을 강조한 동
영상을 보여드릴 것입니다. 자, 면접 질문에 응답하기라는
주제로 시작해 보죠. 다양한 업계에서 면접관들이 구직자
에게 던지는 일반적 질문을 나열한 유인물을 드리겠습니
다.

4. 화자는 워크숍의 어떤 점을 이야기했는가?
(A) 예정보다 길어질 것이다.
(B) 일련의 워크숍 중 마지막 워크숍이다.
(C) 무료로 제공된다.
(D) 피트니스 센터에서 열리고 있다.

해설 **세부 내용 – 워크숍에 대해 언급되는 점**
강연 도입부에서 워크숍 참석을 환영한 후 무료로 제공
된다(It is ~ outreach program)고 하므로 정답은 (C)
이다.

어휘 free of charge 무료로

5. 동영상에서는 어떤 주제가 강조될 것인가?
(A) 면접 의상
(B) 신체 언어의 유형
(C) 이력서 향상시키기
(D) 자신 있게 말하기

해설 **세부 내용 – 동영상에서 강조되는 주제**
강연 중반부에 다양한 몸짓과 신체 움직임을 강조한 동영
상을 보여주겠다(I'll step ~ body movements)고 하므
로 정답은 (B)이다.

어휘 with confidence 자신 있게

6. 화자는 다음으로 무엇을 나눠줄 것인가?
(A) 간식 상자
(B) 운반용 가방
(C) 인쇄된 목록
(D) 이름표

해설 **세부 내용 – 화자가 나눠줄 것**
강연 마지막에 면접관들의 일반적인 질문을 나열한 유인물
을 주겠다(Now, let ~ various industries)고 하므로 정
답은 (C)이다.

7-9 라디오 방송

W-Am Welcome back to *Books Today*, Seattle's
most popular radio show for news about books
and authors. Today's guest is Tony Pascal,
author of *Chronicle*, this winter's surprise
bestseller. **7**It's an exciting young-adult fantasy
novel that follows the adventures of a high
school student. I loved reading this book. **8**I
can't wait for the sequel, and I know I'm not
alone. Today, **9**Mr. Pascal will tell us about how
he found inspiration to write the novel during
a tour of Iceland, which he has described as
being very similar to a fantasy world. Thanks for
joining us, Tony.

chronicle 연대기   adventure 모험   sequel 속편
inspiration 영감   describe 묘사하다, 설명하다

번역 책과 저자에 대한 소식을 전해드리는 시애틀 최고 인기 라
디오 프로그램 〈북스 투데이〉를 다시 청취해 주셔서 감사
합니다. 오늘의 초대손님은 올 겨울 뜻밖의 베스트셀러에
오른 〈연대기〉의 저자 토니 파스칼 씨입니다. 한 고등학생
의 모험을 다룬 흥미진진한 청소년 판타지 소설이죠. 저도
재미있게 읽었는데요. 속편을 애타게 기다리고 있는데, 저
만 그런 건 아닐 겁니다. 오늘 파스칼 씨가 아이슬란드 여
행 중 소설 집필에 관한 영감을 얻은 이야기를 들려주실 텐
데요. 아이슬란드를 환상의 세계와 매우 유사하게 묘사했
습니다. 토니 씨, 나와 주셔서 감사합니다.

7. 화자는 어떤 종류의 책을 이야기하는가?
(A) 여행 안내서   (B) 자기개발서
(C) 판타지 소설   (D) 전기

해설 **전체 내용 – 논의 중인 책 종류**
방송 초반부에 한 고등학생의 모험을 다룬 흥미진진한 청
소년 판타지 소설이다(It's an ~ school student)라고
했으므로 정답은 (C)이다.

어휘 self-help book 자습서, 자기개발서   biography 전기

8. 화자가 "저만 그런 건 아닐 겁니다"라고 말한 의미는 무엇
인가?
(A) 책이 많은 팬을 보유하고 있다.
(B) 파스칼 씨는 집필을 천천히 하는 것으로 알려져 있다.
(C) 다른 사람들도 헷갈려 한다.
(D) 방송은 많은 청취자를 보유하고 있다.

해설 **세부 내용 – 화자의 의도**
인용문 앞에서 속편을 애타게 기다리고 있다(I can't ~
the sequel)고 말한 다음, 이어서 본인만 그런 것이 아닐
것이라고 한 것으로 보아 속편을 기다리는 사람들이 많다
는 뜻으로 이해할 수 있다. 따라서 정답은 (A)이다.

어휘 confused 혼란스러운   audience 청중

9. 파스칼 씨는 어디서 집필하는 데 필요한 영감을 얻었는가?
(A) 학교 방문 (B) 해외여행
(C) 설문 조사 결과 (D) 영화 개봉

해설 **세부 내용 – 영감을 얻은 곳**
방송 후반부에서 파스칼 씨가 아이슬란드 여행 중 소설에 관한 영감을 얻은 이야기를 들려준다(Mr. Pascal ~ of Iceland)고 했으므로 정답은 (B)이다.

어휘 overseas 해외의 release 개봉, 출시, 발간

10-12 연설

M-Cn Thank you. It's an honor to accept this award for outstanding salesperson. It feels great to receive the recognition for all the hard work I put in. However, it would have been impossible without the fantastic development team. After all, ¹⁰it's easy to sell tents if they're high quality. I also want to thank Edward Phil from Human Resources. ¹¹He helped me arrange a flexible working schedule that was essential to my success. ¹²Now, I'd like to share a brief account about some of the products I sold for the company. Hopefully, it will highlight just how product quality makes selling easy.

outstanding 뛰어난 development 개발 arrange 마련하다. 주선하다 flexible 융통성 있는 essential 필수적인, 극히 중요한 account 설명 highlight 강조하다

번역 감사합니다. 우수한 영업사원에게 주는 이 상을 받게 되어 영광입니다. 제 노고에 대한 인정을 받았다는 사실이 정말 기쁩니다. 하지만 훌륭한 개발팀 없이는 불가능한 일이었을 것입니다. 결국 고품질이기 때문에 텐트를 판매하기가 쉬운 겁니다. 아울러 인사부서 에드워드 필 씨께 감사를 드리고 싶습니다. 업무 일정을 융통성 있게 할 수 있도록 도와주셨는데, 이것이 제 성공에 필수 요인이었습니다. 이제 제가 판매한 제품에 대해 간단히 설명해 드리고자 합니다. 제품의 품질이 판매를 얼마나 용이하게 하는지 부각되었으면 합니다.

10. 화자는 무엇을 판매하는가?
(A) 소프트웨어
(B) 부동산
(C) 자동차
(D) 캠핑 장비

해설 **전체 내용 – 화자가 판매하는 제품**
연설 초반부에 우수 영업 사원에게 주는 상을 받아 영광이라(It's an honor to accept ~ salesperson)고 했고, 중반부에 텐트의 품질이 좋으면 판매하기 쉽다(it's easy to sell tents ~ high quality)고 했으므로 정답은 (D)이다.

어휘 real estate 부동산 gear 장비

11. 화자가 필 씨에게 감사하는 이유는?
(A) 부서 예산을 증액해 주었다.
(B) 일정을 잡는데 도움을 주었다.
(C) 난로를 새로 사 주었다.
(D) 여분의 텐트를 제공해 주었다.

해설 **세부 내용 – 필에게 감사하는 이유**
인사부서 필에게 감사하다고 하며 업무 일정을 융통성 있게 잡도록 도와주었다(He helped me arrange ~ to my success)고 했으므로 정답은 (B)이다.

어휘 budget 예산 spare 여분의

12. 화자는 다음으로 무엇을 할 것인가?
(A) 요점 강조하기 (B) 승인 받기
(C) 제안하기 (D) 의견에 반대하기

해설 **세부 내용 – 다음에 할 일**
연설 마지막에 제품 판매에 대해 간단히 설명한다고 하며, 제품의 품질이 판매를 용이하게 해준다는 것이 강조되기를 바란다(I'd like to ~ makes selling easy)고 했으므로 정답은 (A)이다.

어휘 emphasize 강조하다 approval 승인 proposal 제안 object to ~에 반대하다

13-15 소개

W-Br Thank you for attending this afternoon's lecture by the noted graphic novelist Wendy Sato. ¹³Her talk is the first in our "Great Writers, Great Illustrators" series of programs here at the Central Museum of Art. In a moment Ms. Sato will read passages from her latest graphic novel *The Wind and the Rain*, which she herself illustrated. ¹⁴This children's adventure story has already won great acclaim by literary critics. After the book signing, ¹⁵Ms. Sato will demonstrate the techniques she uses to draw images of nature. Let's now welcome Ms. Sato to the stage.

noted 유명한 illustrator 삽화가 passage 구절 win acclaim 환호를 받다 literary 문학의 critic 평론가, 비평가 book signing 책 사인회 demonstrate 시연하다, 보여주다

번역 오늘 오후 유명한 그래픽 소설가 웬디 사토 씨의 강연에 참석해 주셔서 감사합니다. 사토 씨의 강연은 이곳 센트럴 미술관에서 열리는 〈위대한 작가, 위대한 삽화가〉 프로그램 중 첫 번째입니다. 잠시 후 사토 씨가 자신의 최신 그래픽 소설 〈바람과 비〉의 구절을 읽어 주시겠습니다. 자신이 직접 삽화를 그린 책이죠. 아이들의 모험을 그린 이 책은 이미 문학평론가들에게 호평을 받았습니다. 책 사인회 후 사토 씨가 자연을 그릴 때 이용하는 기법을 보여주실 예정입니다. 이제 사토 씨를 무대로 모시겠습니다.

13. 소개는 어디서 이루어졌겠는가?
(A) 출판사   (B) 미술관
(C) 중고 서점   (D) 영화 스튜디오

해설 **전체 내용 – 담화 장소**
담화 초반부에서 이 강연이 센트럴 미술관에서 열리는 〈위대한 작가, 위대한 삽화가〉 프로그램 중 첫 번째(Her talk ~ Museum of Art)라고 했으므로 정답은 (B)이다.

어휘 publishing 출판

14. 〈바람과 비〉에 대해 언급된 것은?
(A) 실제 이야기를 바탕으로 했다.
(B) 평론가들에게 호평을 받았다.
(C) 영화로 만들어질 예정이다.
(D) 대학생들이 썼다.

해설 **세부 내용 – 언급된 사항**
담화 중반부에서 사토가 〈바람과 비〉의 구절을 읽어 줄 것이라고 했고, 이 책이 이미 문학평론가들에게 호평을 받았다(This children's ~ literary critics)고 했으므로 정답은 (B)이다.

어휘 well received 호평을 받은

15. 책 사인회 후 어떤 일이 있을 것인가?
(A) 연극 공연
(B) 주최자들과 식사
(C) 시연
(D) 가이드와 함께 자연 산책

해설 **세부 내용 – 사인회 후에 있을 일**
담화 후반부에 책 사인회 후 사토 씨가 자연을 그릴 때 이용하는 기법을 보여주실 예정(Ms. Sato ~ of nature)이라고 했으므로 정답은 (C)이다.

어휘 performance 공연   practical 실제적인

16-18 연설

M-Au Thank you for this fabulous dinner. **16**I'm honored that you all gathered to celebrate my retirement. We have so many accomplishments to look back on, but I'm most proud of the work we did on the Hamilton Library. **17**It was a great example of collaboration as a team that I think makes our firm so special. Now, just because I'm retiring, it doesn't mean I won't be keeping busy. **18**I've been creating a Web site that is going to give advice on the construction industry, and it will become available next month. I'll make sure to forward you the whole address when finished.

fabulous 굉장한, 멋진 gather 모이다 retirement 은퇴, 퇴직 accomplishment 성취 look back on ~을 되돌아보다 collaboration 협력 forward 전달하다

번역 멋진 저녁 식사를 마련해 주셔서 감사합니다. 여러분 모두 제 은퇴를 축하하기 위해 모여 주셔서 영광스럽습니다. 회고해 볼 많은 성취가 있었습니다만 해밀턴 도서관에서 했던 작업이 가장 자랑스럽게 남습니다. 우리 회사를 특별하게 하는 팀 협동의 좋은 본보기라고 생각합니다. 이제 저는 은퇴하지만 한가하게 지낼 것이라는 뜻은 아닙니다. 저는 건설업계에 조언을 제공하는 웹사이트를 만들고 있는데 다음 달부터 이용 가능합니다. 작업이 끝나면 전체 주소를 여러분께 꼭 전달해 드리겠습니다.

16. 어떤 행사를 위한 담화인가?
(A) 은퇴 기념 파티
(B) 환영 저녁 식사
(C) 개업식
(D) 회사 합병

해설 **전체 내용 – 담화의 목적**
담화 초반에 은퇴를 축하하기 위해 모여 주셔서 영광스럽다(I'm honored ~ my retirement)라고 했으므로 정답은 (A)이다.

어휘 grand opening 개점, 개업 corporate 회사의 merger 합병

17. 화자는 회사의 어떤 점이 특별하다고 말하는가?
(A) 긴 역사
(B) 세간의 이목을 끄는 프로젝트
(C) 늘어나는 고객층
(D) 증명된 팀워크

해설 **세부 내용 – 특별한 사항**
담화 중반부에 팀 협동이 회사를 특별하게 만든다(It was a great ~ so special)고 했으므로 정답은 (D)이다.

어휘 high-profile 세간의 이목을 끄는 client base 고객층 demonstrated 증명된, 논증된

18. 화자는 다음 달에 무엇을 하겠다고 말하는가?
(A) 책 출판하기
(B) 웹사이트 열기
(C) 관광지 방문하기
(D) 기부하기

해설 **세부 내용 – 다음 달에 할 일**
담화 후반부에 웹사이트를 만들고 있으며 다음 달에 이용 가능하다(I've been creating ~ available next month)고 하므로 정답은 (B)이다.

어휘 publish 출판하다 destination 목적지 make a donation 기부하다

19-21 설명+도표

W-Am Today, we'll practice navigating our upgraded software program. **¹⁹**As we have become the region's top supplier of eco-friendly cooking equipment, we've also invested in streamlining our software to provide faster customer service. First, see this chart of our old login process. We've simplified it by removing a step. Now, when logging in, **²⁰**there is no need to enter your employee e-mail address. Once you've entered your password, you can immediately view client accounts. **²¹**Now, I'll demonstrate how to enter the required data when a first-time customer sets up an account with us.

navigate 다루다, 처리하다   supplier 공급자   eco-friendly 친환경적인   invest in ~에 투자하다   streamline 간소화하다 simplify 단순화하다   immediately 즉시   account 계정 demonstrate 시연하다, 보여주다

번역 오늘은 업그레이드된 소프트웨어 프로그램을 다루는 연습을 하겠습니다. 우리는 지역에 친환경 요리 장비를 공급하는 선도 업체로 자리매김하면서 고객 서비스를 더 빠르게 제공하기 위한 소프트웨어 간소화에도 투자했습니다. 먼저, 예전 로그인 과정 도표를 보시죠. 한 단계를 없앰으로써 로그인을 간단하게 만들었습니다. 이제는 로그인할 때 직원 이메일 주소를 입력할 필요가 없습니다. 비밀번호를 입력하면 즉시 고객 계정을 볼 수 있습니다. 이제 처음 거래하는 고객이 계정을 만들 때 필요한 데이터를 어떻게 입력하는지 보여드리겠습니다.

```
┌─────────────────────────────────────┐
│  [1단계]  직원 ID 번호 입력           │
│    ⇩                                 │
│  [2단계]  사용자명 입력               │
│    ⇩                                 │
│  [3단계]  직원 이메일 주소 입력       │
│    ⇩                                 │
│  [4단계]  비밀번호 입력               │
└─────────────────────────────────────┘
```

19. 청자들은 어떤 종류의 회사에서 일하겠는가?
(A) 인테리어 디자인 업체
(B) 요리 장비 공급업체
(C) 행사 기획업체
(D) 업무용 소프트웨어 제작업체

해설 **전체 내용 – 청자들의 근무지**
담화 초반부에서 우리는 요리 장비를 공급하는 선도 업체로 자리매김했다(As we ~ cooking equipment)고 했으므로 정답은 (B)이다.

20. 시각 정보에 따르면, 로그인 과정에서 어떤 단계가 생략되었는가?
(A) 1단계
(B) 2단계
(C) 3단계
(D) 4단계

해설 **시각 정보 연계 문제 – 생략된 단계**
담화 중반부에 로그인할 때 직원 이메일 주소를 입력할 필요가 없다(there is ~ e-mail address)고 했다. 시각 정보에서 이메일 주소 입력 항목을 찾아서 확인하면 정답은 (C)이다.

21. 화자는 다음으로 무엇을 보여주겠는가?
(A) 고객 문의 응대하기
(B) 잘못 삭제된 파일 복구하기
(C) 컴퓨터 시스템에 로그인하기
(D) 신규 고객 계정을 위한 데이터 입력하기

해설 **세부 내용 – 화자의 다음 행동**
담화 마지막에 첫 거래 고객이 데이터를 입력하여 계정 만드는 방법을 보여주겠다(Now, I'll ~ with us)고 했으므로 정답은 (D)이다.

어휘 respond to ~에 응답하다   restore 복구하다 accidentally 잘못하여   delete 삭제하다

PART 5

문법 편

●UNIT 01 명사

출제 공식 1 CHECK UP
교재 p. 141

1. effectiveness **2.** decision **3.** restrictions

1. 주어 자리

해설 주어 자리이므로 명사가 와야 한다.

번역 신종 플루 치료약의 효과는 과장되었다.

어휘 effective 효과적인 effectiveness 효과(성) remedy
치료(약) exaggerate 과장하다

2. 형용사 수식

해설 형용사의 수식을 받는 자리이므로 명사가 와야 한다.

번역 관리자들은 시기적절하게 올바른 결정을 내릴 것으로 기대
된다.

어휘 supervisor 관리자, 상사 decision 결정 decisive
결정적인, 결단력 있는 on a timely basis 시기적절하게

3. 전치사의 목적어 자리

해설 전치사의 목적어 자리이므로 명사가 와야 한다.

번역 주최 측에서는 우리에게 녹음[녹화물] 사용 제한을 알려왔다.

어휘 organizer 조직자, 주최자 restrict 제한하다
restriction 제한 recording 녹음[녹화](된 것)

출제 공식 2 CHECK UP
교재 p. 141

1. planning **2.** access **3.** funds

1. 불가산명사

해설 careful 앞에 관사가 없으므로 무관사로 쓸 수 있는 불가
산명사가 와야 한다.

번역 신중한 기획은 프로젝트를 반드시 제때에 완료하도록 하는
데 필수적이다.

어휘 plan 기획, 계획 세우기 vital 필수적인 ensure 반드시
~하게 하다 complete 완료하다 on time 제때에

2. 불가산명사

해설 access는 대표적인 불가산명사이다.

번역 오직 소수의 직원들만이 회사 기록 보관소에 접근할 수 있다.

어휘 employee 직원 have access to ~에 접근[출입]할 수
있다 archive 기록 보관소

3. 가산명사

해설 fund는 가산명사이며 앞에 관사가 없으므로 복수형이 필
요하다.

번역 장시간의 토론 끝에, 기금 배정이 마침내 승인되었다.

어휘 lengthy 긴, 장황한 allocation 할당, 배정 fund 기금
approve 승인하다

출제 공식 3 CHECK UP
교재 p. 142

1. Employees **2.** participation **3.** consultation

1. 사람명사

해설 will receive의 주체가 되므로 사람명사가 필요하다.

번역 펜텔사 직원들은 연말에 보너스를 받을 것이다.

어휘 employee 직원 employment 고용

2. 추상명사

해설 '참여에 대해 보상을 받을 것이다'이므로 문맥상 추상명사
자리이다.

번역 설문 응답자들은 참여에 대해 금전적인 보상을 받을 것이다.

어휘 respondent 응답자 financially 재정적으로 reward
보상하다 participant 참가자 participation 참가

3. 추상명사/불가산명사

해설 관사가 없으므로 불가산명사 자리이다.

번역 신입 직원들은 자신들의 직속 상사와 상의하여 일하게 될
것이다.

어휘 recruit 신입 consultant 상담가 consultation 상의

출제 공식 4 CHECK UP
교재 p. 142

1. security **2.** productivity **3.** rental

1. 복합명사

해설 '안전한 이유'라는 해석은 맞지 않으므로 명사를 수식하는
자리가 아니다.

번역 보안상의 이유로, 입력된 모든 데이터는 암호화된다.

어휘 secure 안전한 security 보안, 경비 encrypt
암호화하다

2. 복합명사

해설 employee에 가산명사 처리가 되어 있지 않으므로 복합
명사 자리이다.

번역 기업들은 직원 생산성을 향상시킬 새로운 방법들을 찾기
위해 힘쓴다.

어휘 strive 분투하다 produce 생산하다; 농산물
productivity 생산성

3. 복합명사

해설 '임대 차량'을 뜻하므로 복합명사 자리이다.

번역 그 웹사이트는 가장 좋은 렌터카를 구하는 방법에 관한 몇 가지 유용한 조언을 제공한다.

어휘 useful 유용한 rent 임대하다; (건물) 임대(료) rental 임대, 대여

ACTUAL TEST

1. (A)	**2.** (D)	**3.** (B)	**4.** (C)	**5.** (C)
6. (D)	**7.** (D)	**8.** (B)	**9.** (B)	**10.** (A)
11. (D)	**12.** (A)	**13.** (C)	**14.** (C)	**15.** (B)
16. (C)	**17.** (C)	**18.** (C)	**19.** (B)	**20.** (C)

1. (A) 주어 자리

해설 빈칸은 앞에 정관사 The가 있고, 동사 may change의 주어 자리이므로 명사가 들어가야 한다. 따라서 (A) length가 정답이다.

번역 포터 박사의 연설 길이는 청중이 어떻게 반응하느냐에 따라 달라질 수 있다.

어휘 depending on ~에 따라 audience 청중, 관객 react 반응하다 lengthy 긴, 장황한 lengthen 늘리다, 길어지다

2. (D) 전치사의 목적어 자리

해설 빈칸은 앞에 관사 a와 형용사 brief가 있고, 전치사 Following의 목적어 자리이므로 명사가 들어가야 한다. 따라서 '상담'이라는 뜻의 (D) consultation이 정답이다. (B) consultant는 명사이지만 '상담가'라는 뜻으로 문맥에 어울리지 않으므로 답이 될 수 없다.

번역 짧은 상담 후에, 영양사가 그 환자에게 식단을 추천해줄 것이다.

어휘 brief 짧은, 간단한 nutritionist 영양사 make a recommendation 추천하다 patient 환자 consult 상담하다 consultant 상담가

3. (B) to부정사의 목적어 자리

해설 빈칸은 to부정사 to build의 목적어 자리이므로 명사가 들어가야 한다. 따라서 '지구력, 인내력'이라는 뜻의 (B) endurance가 정답이다.

번역 일부 달리기 초보자들은 훈련 프로그램 초반에 좌절하게 될 수도 있는데, 지구력을 기르는 데 시간이 걸리기 때문이다.

어휘 novice 초보자 frustrated 좌절감을 느끼는 endure 견디다 enduring 오래가는

4. (C) 동사의 목적어 자리

해설 빈칸은 동사 has shown의 목적어 자리이므로 명사가 들어가야 한다. 따라서 '헌신'이라는 뜻의 명사 (C) dedication이 정답이다.

번역 인사부장으로서의 역할에 있어서, 왕 씨는 직장에서 항상 헌신하는 모습을 보여 주었다.

어휘 role 역할 Human Resources 인사부 workplace 직장 dedicated 헌신적인 dedicate 헌신하다

5. (C) 전치사의 목적어 자리

해설 빈칸은 앞에 관사 a와 형용사 new가 있고, 전치사 for의 목적어 자리이므로 명사가 들어가야 한다. 문맥상 '새로운 장소를 찾기 시작했다'라는 내용이 되어야 자연스러우므로 '장소'라는 뜻의 명사 (C) place가 정답이다. (A) placement는 명사이지만 '취업 알선, 배치' 등의 뜻으로 글의 흐름에 어울리지 않으므로 답이 될 수 없다.

번역 현재 사무실 건물의 임대차 계약이 내년에 만료되기 때문에, 매크레이 씨는 이미 새로운 장소를 물색하기 시작했다.

어휘 current 현재의 lease 임대차 계약 expire 만료되다 placement 배치 place 장소; 놓다, 배치하다

6. (D) 전치사의 목적어 자리

해설 빈칸은 전치사 of의 목적어 자리이므로 명사가 들어가야 한다. 따라서 '규제, 제한'이라는 뜻의 명사 (D) restrictions가 정답이다. 동명사 (B) restricting도 전치사의 목적어 자리에 들어갈 수는 있지만 뒤에 목적어가 없으므로 답이 될 수 없다.

번역 이 포스터는 승객들에게 기내용 화물에 들어가는 물품에 대한 규정을 알리기 위한 용도이다.

어휘 intended ~을 위해 만들어진 contain ~을 담다, 포함하다 carry-on luggage 기내 휴대용 수하물 restrict 제한하다 restrictive 제한하는, 제한적인 restriction 제한, 규정

7. (D) 동사의 목적어 자리

해설 빈칸은 형용사 tremendous의 수식을 받고 있고, 동사 has shown의 목적어 자리이므로 명사가 들어가야 한다. 따라서 '헌신'이라는 뜻의 명사 (D) commitment가 정답이다.

번역 영업부장으로서, 루 씨는 자신의 팀에 대한 대단한 헌신과 지속적인 성공을 보여 주었다.

어휘 tremendous 엄청난, 대단한 ongoing 진행 중인 commit 저지르다, 헌신하다

8. (B) 추상명사

해설 빈칸은 앞에 관사 a와 형용사 thorough, complete가 있고, 전치사 after의 목적어 자리이므로 명사가 들어가야 한다. 문맥상 '철저하고 완전한 조사 후에'라는 내용이 되어야 자연스러우므로 '조사'라는 의미의 명사 (B) investigation이 정답이다. (A) investigator는 명사이지만 '조사관'이라는 뜻으로 문맥에 어울리지 않아 답이 될 수 없다.

번역 철서하고 완전한 조사 끝에 누출이 발견되었다.

어휘 leak 누출; 새다 discover 발견하다 thorough 철저한 complete 완전한 investigator 조사관 investigational 조사의 investigate 조사하다

9. (B) 동사의 목적어 자리

해설 빈칸은 동사 recognizes의 목적어 자리이므로 명사가 들어가야 한다. 따라서 '뛰어남, 우수성'이라는 의미의 명사 (B) excellence가 정답이다.

번역 그 회사의 연례 플래티넘 공로상은 경영 관리 부문의 우수성을 표창한다.

어휘 annual 연례의 achievement 업적, 성취 recognize 인정하다, 표창하다 management 경영, 관리 excellent 뛰어난 excel 뛰어나다

10. (A) 추상명사

해설 빈칸은 전치사 for의 목적어 자리이므로 명사가 들어가야 한다. 문맥상 '엘리베이터가 청소를 위해 운행이 중단된다'라는 내용이 되어야 자연스러우므로 '청소'라는 의미의 명사인 (A) cleaning이 정답이다. '청소기, 청소원'이라는 뜻의 명사인 (D) cleaner는 글의 흐름에도 어울리지 않고, 가산 단수명사이므로 앞에 한정사 없이는 빈칸에 들어갈 수 없다.

번역 중앙 로비의 엘리베이터들은 매월 1일에 청소를 위해 일시적으로 운행이 중단된다.

어휘 shut down (기계를) 정지시키다, 문을 닫다 temporarily 일시적으로

11. (D) 불가산명사

해설 빈칸은 동명사 securing의 목적어 자리이므로 명사가 들어가야 한다. 문맥상 '자금을 확보하는 데 어려움을 겪었다'라는 내용이 되어야 자연스럽고, 빈칸 앞에 한정사가 없으므로 '자금'이라는 뜻의 불가산명사인 (D) funding이 정답이다. (B) fund는 가산 단수명사이므로 한정사 없이는 빈칸에 들어갈 수 없다.

번역 공원 확장 프로젝트는 기획자들이 자금을 확보하는 데 어려움을 겪어서 지연되었다.

어휘 expansion 확대, 확장 delay 지연시키다 have difficulty -ing ~하는 데 어려움을 겪다 secure 확보하다 fundraise 기금을 모으다 fund 기금, 자금 fundraiser 모금 행사

12. (A) 동사의 목적어 자리

해설 빈칸은 동사 provides의 목적어 자리이므로 명사가 들어가야 한다. '접근'이라는 뜻의 명사 access는 불가산명사이므로 복수 형태로 쓸 수 없다. 따라서 (A) access가 정답이다.

번역 교내 스포츠 센터는 체력 단련실이 있는 대형 피트니스 시설뿐만 아니라 농구 코트와 배구 코트 이용 권한도 제공한다.

어휘 gym facility 피트니스 시설 weight room 체력 단련실 access 이용(권) accessible 접근[이용] 가능한

13. (C) 전치사의 목적어 자리

해설 빈칸은 전치사 to의 목적어 자리이므로 명사가 들어가야 한다. 따라서 '수익성'이라는 뜻의 명사 (C) profitability가 정답이다.

번역 장기간의 적자 끝에, 워털루사는 이번 분기에 흑자 전환을 예상하고 있다.

어휘 loss 손실 return 복귀; 돌아오다 quarter 사분기 profitable 수익성이 있는 profit 이익; 이익을 얻다

14. (C) 보어 자리

해설 빈칸은 앞에 관사 a, 부사 highly와 형용사 competent가 있고, be동사 is의 보어 자리로, 주어와 동격인 명사 associate가 들어가야 '로드리게스 씨는 매우 유능한 동료이다'라고 자연스럽게 해석되므로 '동료'라는 뜻의 명사 (C) associate가 정답이다.

번역 회계부의 로드리게스 씨는 항상 세부적인 것들까지 최대한의 관심을 보이는 매우 유능한 동료이다.

어휘 highly 매우, 대단히 competent 유능한 utmost 최고의 detail 세부 사항 association 협회, 연관 associate 연관 짓다; 동료

15. (B) 수 일치

해설 「There+be동사/have been」 뒤는 주어 자리이므로 명사가 들어가야 하고, 동사 have been과 수 일치가 되어야 하므로 복수명사가 와야 한다. 따라서 '걱정, 우려'라는 뜻의 복수명사인 (B) concerns가 정답이다.

번역 금융 기관들이 개방형 사무실 콘셉트를 채택한 이래 사생활에 관한 우려가 제기되어 왔다.

어휘 regarding ~에 관하여 privacy 사생활 institute 기관 adopt 채택하다 concerned 걱정하는 concerning ~에 관한

16. (C) 사람명사

해설 빈칸은 전치사 by의 목적어 자리이고, 형용사 medical의 수식을 받았으므로 명사가 들어가야 한다. '전문가'라는 뜻의 professional은 가산명사이고 한정사가 없을 때는 복수 형태가 되어야 하므로 (C) professionals가 정답이다.

번역 〈젊은이를 위한 건강 가이드 잡지〉는 의료 전문가들이 아동 복지 단체와 협력하여 집필한다.

어휘 in cooperation with ~와 협력하여 welfare 복지 organization 단체, 조직 professional 전문적인; 전문가 professionally 직업적으로, 전문적으로 profession 직업

17. (C) 불가산명사

해설 빈칸은 전치사 with의 목적어 자리이므로 명사가 들어가야 한다. 빈칸 앞에 한정사가 없으므로 '허가증'이라는 뜻의 가산 단수명사 (A) permit은 들어갈 수 없고, '허가'라는 뜻의 불가산명사인 (C) permission이 정답이다.

번역 초과 근무는 상사의 승인이 있어야만 허용될 것입니다.

어휘 overtime work 시간 외 근무, 초과 근무 permit 허용하다; 허가증 permissive 관대한, 허용되는

18. (C) 유의할 명사

해설 빈칸은 동사 lacks의 목적어 자리이고, 앞에 관사 the가 있으므로 명사 자리이다. 따라서 '세부 사항'이라는 뜻의

명사인 (C) specifics가 정답이다. (B) specific은 '구체적인'이라는 뜻의 형용사로, 명사로 쓰일 때는 복수형이 되어야 하므로 답이 될 수 없다.

번역 야마모토 씨의 제안은 목표를 예산 내에서 달성할 수 있는지 판단하는 데 필요한 세부 사항이 결여되어 있다.

어휘 proposal 제안 lack ~이 없다, 부족하다 determine 알아내다 achievable 달성할 수 있는 within the budget 예산 내에서 specify (구체적으로) 명시하다 specific 구체적인, 특정한: (복수형으로) 세부 사항 specifically 분명히, 특별히

19. (B) 복합명사

해설 빈칸은 앞에 관사 the가 있고, to부정사 to meet의 목적어 자리로 빈칸 뒤의 명사 schedule과 함께 복합명사를 이룬다. 빈칸 뒤의 명사 schedule과 어울려 '생산 일정'이라는 의미의 복합명사가 되어야 '생산 일정을 맞추기 위해'라고 자연스럽게 해석되므로 '생산'이라는 의미의 명사 (B) production이 정답이다.

번역 모든 조립 라인 노동자들은 생산 일정을 맞추기 위해 추가 근무를 하라는 요청을 받았다.

어휘 assembly line 조립 라인 extra 추가의 produce 생산하다: 농산물 productivity 생산성

20. (C) 복합명사

해설 빈칸은 앞의 명사 price와 함께 '가격 인하'라는 복합명사를 이룬다. 따라서 동사 announced의 목적어로 자연스럽게 연결될 수 있는 '감소, 인하'라는 의미의 명사인 (C) reductions가 정답이다. 해당 절에 이미 동사인 announced가 있으므로 동사인 (A) reduce와 (D) reduces는 빈칸에 들어갈 수 없다. (B) reduced는 '인하된'이라는 의미의 과거분사로 명사 price를 뒤에서 수식하게 될 경우, 가산 단수명사인 price 앞에는 한정사가 와야 하므로 답이 될 수 없다.

번역 Q-렉스 테크사는 최근에 D117 모델의 휴대폰에 대해 가격 인하를 발표했다.

●UNIT 02 대명사

출제 공식 1 CHECK UP

교재 p. 147

1. it **2.** their **3.** theirs

1. 인칭대명사 – 주격

해설 membership을 지칭하므로 단수형인 it이 와야 한다.

번역 귀하의 회원권이 만료되기 전에 갱신하실 것을 권장해 드립니다.

어휘 encourage 권장하다 renew 갱신하다 expire 만료되다

2. 인칭대명사 – 소유격

해설 명사구 original receipt를 수식하므로 소유격이 와야 한다.

번역 소비자들은 전액 환불을 받기 위해서 영수증 원본을 제시해야 한다.

어휘 present 제시하다 original 원래의, 원본의 receipt 영수증 refund 환불

3. 인칭대명사 – 소유대명사

해설 '그들의 경비'를 뜻하므로 theirs(그들의 것)가 와야 한다.

번역 대부분의 부서들은 경비를 절감했지만 영업부는 자신들의 경비를 줄이지 못했다.

어휘 division 부서 expense 경비, 비용 reduce 줄이다

출제 공식 2 CHECK UP

교재 p. 147

1. themselves **2.** themselves **3.** himself

1. 재귀대명사 – 관용 표현

해설 완전한 문장 뒤에 '직접'이라는 의미로 올 수 있는 관용 표현은 by+재귀대명사이다.

번역 때때로 인턴들은 중요한 업무를 직접 수행해야 한다.

어휘 carry out 수행하다, 실행하다

2. 재귀대명사 – 재귀 용법

해설 talk의 주체가 participants이므로 재귀대명사가 와야 한다. (participants = themselves)

번역 설문 조사 참가자들은 서로 이야기하는 것이 허용되지 않았다.

어휘 participant 참가자

3. 재귀대명사 – 강조 용법

해설 '직접', '스스로'를 뜻하므로 강조 용법의 재귀대명사가 와야 한다. his own은 on his own으로 써야 한다.

번역 맥스웰 씨는 그 일을 직접 할 수 없었다.

어휘 be unable to do ~할 수 없다

출제 공식 3 CHECK UP

교재 p. 148

1. those **2.** Those **3.** those

1. 지시대명사 – those + who

해설 관계대명사 who의 수식을 받는 지시대명사 those 자리이다.

번역 회의에 참석하지 않은 사람들을 위해 비디오 녹화본이 있다.

어휘 attend 참석하다

2. 지시대명사 – those + -ing

해설 분사 wishing의 수식을 받는 지시대명사 those 자리이다.

번역 공석에 지원하고자 하는 사람들은 게일 씨에게 연락해야 한다.

어휘 vacant 비어 있는

3. 지시대명사 – those + p.p

해설 분사 interested의 수식을 받는 지시대명사 those 자리이다.

번역 참석에 관심 있는 사람들을 위해 온라인 신청서가 구비되어 있다.

어휘 registration form 신청서

출제 공식 4 CHECK UP 교재 p. 148

1. one **2.** others **3.** another

---

1. 부정대명사 – one

해설 앞에서 언급된 microchip과 동일한 종류를 지칭하므로 one이 와야 한다. that은 the smallest와 같은 수식어구를 앞에 두지 못하며 항상 수식어구가 that보다 뒤에 와야 한다.

번역 샌테크에 의해 개발된 새로운 마이크로칩은 지금까지 만들어진 것 중 최고로 작은 것이다.

어휘 ever 여태껏, 지금까지

2. 부정대명사 – others

해설 주어 자리이므로 other people을 뜻하는 others가 와야 한다. other는 단독으로 쓰이면 형용사이므로 주어 자리에 올 수 없다.

번역 어떤 사람들은 팀으로 일하는 것을 즐기지만 다른 사람들은 그룹 활동을 피한다.

어휘 avoid 피하다 activity 활동

3. 부정대명사 – another

해설 another item(다른 아이템 하나)을 뜻하므로 another가 와야 한다.

번역 만약 제품에 만족하지 못하면 다른 제품으로 교환하실 수 있습니다.

어휘 exchange 교환하다

ACTUAL TEST 교재 p. 150

1. (A)	**2.** (B)	**3.** (D)	**4.** (D)	**5.** (D)
6. (D)	**7.** (C)	**8.** (A)	**9.** (C)	**10.** (D)
11. (C)	**12.** (D)	**13.** (D)	**14.** (A)	**15.** (A)
16. (C)	**17.** (A)	**18.** (A)	**19.** (A)	**20.** (C)

1. (A) 인칭대명사 – 주격

해설 빈칸은 접속사 than 뒤의 절에서 동사 had expected의 주어 자리이고, the crew members를 대신하므로 (A) they가 정답이다.

번역 작업반들은 건물 복구 작업이 그들이 예상했던 것보다 더 오래 걸려서 놀랐다.

어휘 crew 작업반 restoration 복원, 복구

2. (B) 재귀대명사 – 재귀 용법

해설 빈칸은 동사 found의 목적어 자리이고, 주어인 Mr. Rhodes를 대신하여 '로즈 씨는 자신이 심한 스트레스를 받고 있음을 깨달았다'라고 해석되므로 재귀대명사 (B) himself가 정답이다.

번역 새 일자리를 시작하면서, 로즈 씨는 판매 할당량을 채우기 위해 자신이 심한 스트레스를 받고 있음을 느꼈다.

어휘 under pressure 스트레스를 받는 a great deal of 다량의, 많은 quota 할당량

3. (D) 재귀대명사 – 관용 표현

해설 빈칸은 '직접'이라는 의미가 필요하므로 by + 재귀대명사로 관용 표현을 만드는 (D) herself가 정답이다.

번역 벨레즈 씨는 경험이 많아서, 그 거래건을 직접 처리할 수 있다.

어휘 handle 다루다, 응대하다 account 고객, 거래, 계좌

4. (D) 인칭대명사 – 소유격

해설 빈칸 뒤에 명사 cameras가 있으므로 소유격 대명사가 들어가야 한다. 따라서 (D) their own이 정답이고, own은 '자신의'라는 뜻의 형용사로 소유격 대명사와 함께 명사 앞에 쓰여 소유의 의미를 강조하는 역할을 한다.

번역 사파리 공원 관광에 합류하는 호텔 투숙객들에게는 본인의 카메라를 가져오도록 권해 드립니다.

어휘 join 합류하다

5. (D) 인칭대명사 – 소유격

해설 빈칸 뒤에 명사 availability가 있으므로 소유격 대명사가 들어가야 한다. 따라서 (D) their가 정답이다.

번역 가능 여부에 따라, 일부 시간제 직원들은 휴일 동안 초과 근무를 하라는 요청을 받을 수 있다.

어휘 depending on ~에 따라 availability (사람이) 시간이 나는지 여부

6. (D) 지시대명사 – those + who

해설 빈칸은 동사 will be considered의 주어 자리이고 관계대명사절(who have ~ course)의 수식을 받아 '저널리즘 과정을 이수한 사람들'이라고 해석되므로 '~한 사람들'을 뜻하는 (D) Those가 정답이다. (C) Everyone은 '~한 모든 사람'을 뜻하는 말로 쓸 수 있지만 단수 취급해야 하므로 관계절의 동사 have와 수 일치가 되지 않아 답이 될 수 없다.

번역 저널리즘 과정을 이수한 사람이 편집자 자리에 우선적으로 고려될 것이다.

어휘 complete 완료하다 journalism 저널리즘, 언론학 editorial 편집의; 사설

7. (C) 인칭대명사 – 목적격

해설 빈칸은 전치사 for의 목적어 자리이고, 명사 the clients

를 대신하므로 목적격 대명사 (C) them이 정답이다. (A) themselves는 목적어 자리에는 들어갈 수 있으나 for oneself는 '스스로'라는 뜻이므로 적절하지 않다.

번역 고객들은 시의 신규 지하철 노선 탑승에 열광적인 것처럼 보이지만, 그것이 그들이 사용할 수 있는 가장 빠른 선택 사항은 아닐 수도 있다.

어휘 enthusiastic 열정적인, 열렬한

8. (A) 인칭대명사 – 목적격
해설 빈칸은 help의 목적어 자리로 목적격 대명사를 고르는 문제이다. '그(변호사)를 도와줄 조수를 고용했다'라는 의미가 되어야 하므로 목적어 자리에 lawyer를 지칭하는 (A) him이 정답이 된다. help의 주체(assistant)와 목적어(lawyer)가 일치하지 않으므로 재귀대명사 (C) himself는 올 수 없다.

번역 그 변호사는 고객 정보를 디지털로 변환하는 것을 도와줄 조수를 고용했다.

어휘 assistant 조수, 보조원 help A with B A가 B하는 것을 돕다 digitize (데이터를)디지털화하다

9. (C) 인칭대명사 – 목적격
해설 빈칸은 동사 will be joining의 목적어 자리이고, Ms. Browning and Mr. Kato를 대신하므로 목적격 대명사 (C) them이 정답이다. 주어와 목적어가 일치하지 않으므로 재귀대명사 (D) themselves는 답이 될 수 없다.

번역 브라우닝 씨와 가토 씨는 현재 팀으로 일하고 있지만, 다나카 씨가 인턴사원으로 그들과 합류할 것이다.

어휘 intern 인턴사원

10. (D) 대명사 관용 표현
해설 빈칸 앞에 전치사 on이 있으므로 '직접, 스스로'를 뜻하는 관용 표현 on one's own을 넣고 해석해본다. '방문객들은 스스로 역사 지구를 둘러볼 수 있다'라는 해석이 자연스러우므로 (D) their own이 정답이다.

번역 그 지역에 표시된 표지판을 따라가면, 방문객들은 가이드를 쓰지 않고 혼자서 시의 역사 지구를 둘러볼 수 있다.

어휘 mark 표시하다 explore 답사하다, 탐구하다 district 지구, 구역

11. (C) 인칭대명사 – 소유대명사
해설 빈칸은 동사 will lower의 목적어 자리이고, our prices를 대신하므로 소유대명사 (C) ours가 정답이다.

번역 저희 고객 중 어떤 분이라도 다른 곳에서 더 낮은 가격을 찾으실 경우, 그에 맞게 저희 가격을 내리겠습니다.

어휘 low 낮은 elsewhere 다른 곳에서 lower 낮추다 match 대등하게 만들다, 맞추다

12. (D) 인칭대명사 – 소유대명사
해설 빈칸은 동사 expedited의 목적어 자리이고, 문맥상 우리 일(our work)을 대신하므로 소유대명사 (D) ours가 정답이다.

번역 다른 회사들이 여전히 입찰 작업을 하고 있는 반면, 수석 기획자는 우리 일을 신속히 처리했다.

어휘 firm 회사 bid 입찰 expedite 신속히 처리하다

13. (D) 지시대명사 – those + 전치사구
해설 빈칸은 전치사 including의 목적어 자리이고, 전치사구 with particular nutritional needs의 수식을 받아 '영양상 특별 요구 조건이 있는 사람들'을 뜻하므로 전치사구나 관계절의 수식을 받아 '~한 사람들'이라는 의미로 쓰이는 (D) those가 정답이다.

번역 영양상 특별 요구 조건이 있는 사람들을 포함하여 만찬에 참석한 모두가 식사를 즐길 수 있었다.

어휘 including ~을 포함하여 particular 특정한, 특별한 nutritional 영양상의

14. (A) 인칭대명사 – 목적격
해설 빈칸은 to부정사 to give의 간접목적어 자리이고, Ms. Sato를 대신하므로 목적격 대명사인 (A) her가 정답이다. to give의 주체(manager)와 목적어(Ms. Sato)가 일치하지 않으므로 재귀대명사 (C) herself는 답이 될 수 없다.

번역 회계부 신입 직원인 사토 씨는 부장이 자신에게 더 자세한 지침을 주기를 원한다.

어휘 accounting 회계 detailed 상세한 instructions 지시, 명령

15. (A) 지시대명사 – that/those
해설 빈칸은 동사 have surpassed의 목적어 자리이고, 복수 명사 unemployment rates를 대신하므로 주격 대명사 (C) they와 단수대명사 (B) it은 답이 될 수 없다. 빈칸은 또한 전치사구 of the previous year의 수식을 받아 '전년도 실업률'을 뜻하므로 전치사구의 수식을 받을 수 있는 대명사 (A) those가 정답이다.

번역 시 관계자는 올해 실업률이 작년 실업률을 훨씬 뛰어넘었음을 인정했다.

어휘 official 공무원 admit 인정하다 unemployment 실업 surpass 능가하다

16. (C) 부정대명사 – the other
해설 빈칸은 전치사 over의 목적어 자리이다. 앞 절에서 둘이라는 범위(both)가 주어졌고 한 명을 선택할 수 없었다(could not choose one)라고 했으므로 빈칸에는 비교 대상이 되는 나머지 한 명이 들어가야 한다. 따라서 '(둘 중의) 나머지 하나'를 뜻하는 (C) the other가 정답이다.

번역 두 지원자 모두 매우 자질이 뛰어나서, 인사부장은 둘 중 한 명을 선택할 수 없었다.

어휘 highly 매우 qualified 자격이 있는 human resources 인사부

17. 재귀대명사 – 강조
해설 빈칸은 바로 앞 단수명사구 delivery of Mr. Lee's gas stove를 강조하기 위해 쓰였으므로 (A) itself가 정답이다.

번역 리 씨의 가스레인지 배달 자체는 수수료가 없었지만, 전문가의 설치는 소정의 비용을 발생시켰다.

어휘 fee 수수료   delivery 배달   professional 전문적인; 전문가   installation 설치   incur (비용을) 발생시키다   charge 요금

18. (A) 상호대명사

해설 빈칸은 전치사 with의 목적어 자리이고, 내용상 '모든 부품이 서로 호환되도록'이라고 해석되어야 자연스러우므로 '서로'라는 의미의 (A) each other가 정답이다.

번역 주문 제작 컴퓨터를 만드는 사람들은 반드시 모든 부품이 서로 호환 가능하도록 해야 한다.

어휘 custom 주문 제작한   component 부품, 구성 요소   be compatible with ~와 호환되다

19. (A) 부정대명사 – any

해설 빈칸은 동사 have의 목적어 자리이고, 문맥상 '그의 부서에는 하나도 없었다'라고 해석되어야 자연스러우므로 '(부정문에서) 아무것도, 조금도'라는 의미로 쓰이는 (A) any가 정답이다. (B) few는 '소수'라는 뜻으로 문맥에 어울리지 않고, (C) every와 (D) other는 형용사이므로 목적어 자리에 들어갈 수 없다. 참고로, other는 대명사로 쓰일 경우 복수형(others)이거나 앞에 the나 any 등의 한정사가 붙는다.

번역 라울 씨는 교체용 잉크 카트리지를 사러 직접 가게에 들렀는데 자기 부서에는 하나도 없어서였다.

어휘 stop by (~에) 잠시 들르다   in person 직접   replacement 교체, 대체   department 부서

20. (C) 수량대명사

해설 빈칸은 동사 will be sold의 주어 자리이고, 뒤에 「of+불가산명사(of our inventory)」가 있으므로 '대부분'이라는 뜻으로 양을 나타내는 대명사인 (C) much가 정답이다.

번역 가을 창고 정리 세일 동안, 우리 재고품 대부분은 엄청나게 할인된 가격으로 판매될 것이다.

어휘 clearance sale 창고 정리 세일   inventory 재고, 물품 목록   heavily 아주 많이, 심하게   discounted 할인된

●UNIT 03 형용사

출제 공식 1   CHECK UP

1. calm   **2.** impressive   **3.** confidential

1. 주격 보어 자리

해설 2형식 동사 seemed 뒤 보어 자리이므로 형용사가 와야 한다.

번역 직원들은 소방 훈련 동안 침착해 보였다.

어휘 seem ~처럼 보이다   calm 침착한   fire drill 소방 훈련

2. 목적격 보어 자리

해설 5형식 동사 found 뒤 목적격 보어 자리이므로 형용사가 와야 한다.

번역 많은 평론가는 제임스 감독의 새 영화가 인상적이라고 생각했다.

어휘 critic 비평가   impressive 인상적인

3. 목적격 보어 자리

해설 5형식 동사 keep의 수동태이므로 형용사가 와야 한다.

번역 개인 정보는 기밀로 유지될 것입니다.

어휘 personal 개인의   confidential 비밀의

출제 공식 2   CHECK UP

1. fresh   **2.** available   **3.** new

1. 부사+형용사+명사

해설 명사인 design을 수식하므로 형용사 자리이다.

번역 우리는 완전히 새로운 디자인을 채택하기로 결정했다.

어휘 employ 고용하다, 쓰다   completely 완전히   fresh 신선한, 새로운

2. 명사를 뒤에서 수식하는 형용사

해설 options를 뒤에서 수식하므로 형용사가 와야 한다.

번역 시중에서 구할 수 있는 몇몇 소형차 옵션이 있다.

어휘 compact car 소형차   available 구할 수 있는   availability 이용[입수] 가능성

3. 형용사+형용사+명사

해설 consultant를 수식하므로 형용사가 와야 한다.

번역 그 회사는 새로운 법률 컨설턴트를 고용해야 한다.

어휘 legal 법률의

출제 공식 3   CHECK UP

1. All   **2.** A few   **3.** more

1. 가산 복수 명사를 수식하는 수량 형용사

해설 가산 복수명사 orders를 수식할 수 있는 All이 와야 한다.

번역 정오 전에 이루어진 모든 주문은 당일 배송됩니다.

어휘 place an order 주문하다   ship 배송하다

2. 가산 복수 명사를 수식하는 수량 형용사

해설 가산 복수명사 services를 수식할 수 있는 A few가 와야 한다.

번역 일부 인터넷 뱅킹 서비스는 다음 주에 중단될 것입니다.

어휘 electronic banking 인터넷 뱅킹   suspend 중단하다

3. **불가산명사를 수식하는 수량 형용사**

해설 불가산명사 information을 수식할 수 있는 more가 와야
한다.

번역 반품 규정에 관한 더 자세한 내용은 보시려면 저의 웹사이
트를 방문해 주십시오.

어휘 regarding ~에 관하여 return 반품 policy 규정, 정책

출제 공식 4 CHECK UP
교재 p. 154

1. sizable **2.** reliable **3.** considerate

1. **혼동 형용사**

해설 '큰' 회의실을 뜻하므로 sizable이 와야 한다.

번역 그 호텔은 세 개의 큰 회의실이 있다.

2. **혼동 형용사**

해설 '믿을 수 있는' 분석을 뜻하므로 reliable이 와야 한다.

번역 〈이코노미 위클리〉는 믿을 수 있는 시장 분석으로 잘 알려
져 있다.

어휘 analysis 분석

3. **혼동 형용사**

해설 '배려하는'을 뜻하므로 considerate가 와야 한다.

번역 말소리를 낮추어 타인을 배려해 주세요.

ACTUAL TEST
교재 p. 156

1. (B)	**2.** (A)	**3.** (A)	**4.** (B)	**5.** (A)
6. (C)	**7.** (C)	**8.** (B)	**9.** (C)	**10.** (C)
11. (C)	**12.** (B)	**13.** (C)	**14.** (C)	**15.** (A)
16. (C)	**17.** (B)	**18.** (A)	**19.** (B)	**20.** (B)

1. **(B) 형용사 + 명사**

해설 빈칸은 동사 offer의 목적어 역할을 하는 명사 durability
를 앞에서 수식하는 자리이므로 형용사가 들어가야 하고,
문맥상 '우수한 내구성'이라고 해석되어야 자연스러우므로
'우수한, 특출한'이라는 의미의 형용사 (B) exceptional
이 정답이다. (D) excepted는 '제외되어'라는 의미로 명
사를 뒤에서 수식하는 형용사로 쓰이므로 답이 될 수 없다.

번역 젠코사의 손 공구는 독보적인 내구성을 제공한다.

어휘 hand tool 손공구 durability 내구성 exception 예외
exceptionally 유난히, 특별히

2. **(A) 보어 자리**

해설 빈칸은 be동사 are이 보어 자리로 주어인 명사
salespeople을 수식하는 자리이고, 문맥상 '영업 사원
들은 기업 고객들에게 접근하기 쉽다'라고 해석되어야 자
연스러우므로 '다가가기 쉬운'이라는 의미의 형용사 (A)
accessible이 정답이다.

번역 우리 사무실은 상업 지구에 위치하고 있어서, 영업 사원들
은 항상 기업 고객들에게 접근하기 쉽다.

어휘 be located in ~에 위치하다 district 지구, 구역
salesperson (pl. salespeople) 영업 사원 corporate
기업의 accessibility 접근(성) access 이용, 접근

3. **(A) 형용사 + 명사**

해설 빈칸은 주어 자리의 명사 contact를 앞에서 수식하는 자
리이므로 형용사가 들어가면 되고, '잦은 연락'이라고 해석
되어 문맥에도 잘 어울리므로 '잦은, 빈번한'이라는 의미의
형용사 (A) Frequent가 정답이다.

번역 부동산의 매도자와 매수자 양쪽과의 잦은 연락은 양쪽이
완전히 만족하는 결과를 보장한다.

어휘 property 부동산, 재산 ensure 보장하다 satisfied
만족하는 frequency 빈도 frequently 자주

4. **(B) 형용사 + 명사**

해설 빈칸은 주어 자리의 명사 language를 앞에서 수식하는
형용사 자리이고, '묘사적인 언어는'으로 해석되어 문맥에
도 잘 어울리므로 '묘사(서술)하는'이라는 의미의 형용사
(R) descriptive가 정답이다.

번역 그 소설에 사용된 묘사적인 언어는 독자들이 그 장면을 상
상하는 데 도움이 되었다.

어휘 imagine 상상하다 scene 장면 description 서술, 묘사
describe 서술하다, 묘사하다

5. **(A) 형용사 + 복합명사**

해설 빈칸은 동사 offers의 목적어 역할을 하는 복합명사
benefits package를 앞에서 수식하는 형용사 자리이다.
'경쟁력 있는 복지 혜택'이라고 해석되어야 글의 흐름상 자
연스러우므로 '경쟁력 있는, 뒤지지 않는'이라는 뜻의 형용
사 (A) competitive가 정답이다.

번역 바오사는 자질이 뛰어난 지원자들을 유치하기 위해 신입
직원들에게 경쟁력 있는 복지 혜택을 제공한다.

어휘 benefits package 복리 후생, 복지 혜택 attract 끌어
모으다 candidate 지원자, 후보자 compete 경쟁하다
competition 경쟁, 시합

6. **(C) 전치사 + 형용사 + 명사**

해설 전치사 at과 명사 times 사이에서 명사 times를 수식하
기에 적절한 형용사를 고르는 문제이다. all이 들어가면 '항
상'이라는 뜻의 관용 표현을 만들고, 문맥상으로도 '항상
고객 서비스를 이용할 수 있도록 한다'라는 내용으로 자연
스러우므로 (C) all이 정답이다. (A) every는 뒤에 가산 단
수명사가 와야 하고, (B) much는 뒤에 불가산명사가 와
야 하므로 답이 될 수 없다. (D) a lot은 부사이므로 명사
를 수식할 수 없다.

번역 저희 알폰소즈 솔루션즈에서는 항상 고객 서비스를 이용하
실 수 있도록 하고 있습니다.

어휘 available 이용할 수 있는

7. (C) 주격 보어 자리

해설 빈칸은 명사 qualities를 수식하는 관계대명사절 (that are ~)에서 be동사 are의 보어 자리이므로 명사 qualities(자질)를 수식하기에 적절한 형용사 혹은 명사가 들어가면 된다. '존경할 만한 자질'이라고 해석되어야 자연스러우므로 '존경할 만한'이라는 뜻의 형용사 (C) admirable이 정답이다. (A) admiration은 '존경'이라는 뜻으로 qualities와 동격 관계가 아니므로 답이 될 수 없고, (B) admiring은 '감탄하는'이라는 뜻의 형용사로 qualities를 수식하는 말로 어울리지 않는다.

번역 팀원들은 최 씨가 여러 가지 존경할 만한 자질을 갖추고 있기 때문에 그녀를 존경한다.

어휘 respect 존경하다 admiration 감탄, 존경 admire 존경하다, 감탄하다

8. (B) 주격 보어 자리

해설 빈칸은 be동사 is의 보어 자리이므로 형용사가 들어갈 수 있고, '엘리베이터가 작동한다'라는 의미가 되어 문맥도 자연스러우므로 '작동되는'이라는 의미의 형용사 (B) functional이 정답이다. (A) function은 명사로 '기능'이라는 뜻으로 주어인 elevator와 동격 관계가 아니므로 답이 될 수 없고, (D) functioned가 들어가면 수동태(is functioned)가 되는데 function은 자동사이므로 수동태로 쓰이지 않는다.

번역 엘리베이터는 어제 발생한 지진 동안 파손된 후에도 여전히 작동하고 있다.

어휘 damaged 파손된 earthquake 지진 occur 일어나다, 발생하다 function 기능; 기능하다, 작동하다

9. (C) 형용사 + 명사

해설 빈칸은 동사 has created의 목적어 역할을 하는 명사 interest를 앞에서 수식하는 형용사 자리이다. 따라서 '상당한'이라는 의미의 형용사 (C) substantial이 정답이다.

번역 폴 윈터의 새 다큐멘터리 영화는 감독의 전작에 대한 상당한 관심을 자아냈다.

어휘 previous 이전의 substance 물질 substantially 상당히

10. (C) 형용사 + 명사

해설 빈칸은 동명사 supplying의 목적어 역할을 하는 명사 equipment를 앞에서 수식하는 형용사 자리이므로 '믿을 수 있는'이라는 의미의 형용사 (C) dependable이 정답이다.

번역 노박사는 금속 업계에 믿을 수 있는 장비를 제공하는 것으로 명성을 얻었다.

어휘 gain a reputation 명성을 얻다 equipment 장비 depend 의존하다

11. (C) 명사 + 형용사

해설 빈칸은 be동사 is의 보어 역할을 하는 명사구 the best location을 뒤에서 수식하는 자리이고, '신생 기술 업체들이 이용 가능한 최적의 장소'라고 매끄럽게 해석되므로 '이용 가능한'이라는 의미의 형용사 (C) available이 정답이다.

번역 오스틴은 자질을 갖춘 인력을 끌어 모을 수 있는 용이성 때문에 신생 기술 업체들이 이용할 수 있는 최적의 장소이다.

어휘 location 장소 ease 용이함 qualified 자격 있는 workforce 노동력, (기업의) 전 직원

12. (B) 형용사 + 명사

해설 빈칸은 분사 Lacking의 목적어 역할을 하는 명사 efforts를 앞에서 수식하는 형용사 자리이고, '의도적인 노력'이라고 자연스럽게 해석되므로 '의도적인'이라는 의미의 형용사 (B) intentional이 정답이다.

번역 쓰레기 없는 공원을 유지하려는 의도적인 노력 없이 그 문제는 시간이 지날수록 악화될 수 있다.

어휘 lack ~이 없다, 부족하다 free from ~이 없는 litter 쓰레기 intention 의도, 목적 intentionally 고의로 intend 의도하다

13. (C) 수량 형용사

해설 명사구 accounting software를 수식하기에 적절한 수량 형용사를 고르는 문제이다. software는 불가산명사이므로 복수명사를 수식하는 (A) numerous(많은), (B) both(둘 다), (D) few(적은)는 답이 될 수 없다. any는 불가산명사를 수식할 수 있고, '어떠한 회계 프로그램을 설치하든'이라고 자연스럽게 해석되므로 '어떤'이라는 의미의 (C) any가 정답이다.

번역 어떤 회계 프로그램의 설치든 청구서 발부 과정을 간소화시키고 시간을 아껴 줄 것이다.

어휘 installation 설치 accounting 회계 streamline 간소화하다 billing 청구서 발부 numerous 많은

14. (C) 주격 보어 자리

해설 빈칸은 동사 become의 보어 자리로 주어 the weather conditions를 수식하는 역할을 하므로 '위험한'이라는 의미의 형용사 (C) hazardous가 정답이다. 주어 the weather conditions와 명사 hazard는 동격 관계가 아니므로 (A) hazard와 (B) hazards는 답이 될 수 없다.

번역 기상 상태가 더 위험해지면, 경보 메시지가 주민들에게 발송될 것이다.

어휘 alert 경계, 경보 resident 거주자, 주민 hazard 위험

15. (A) 형용사 + 명사

해설 빈칸은 주어 역할을 하는 명사 rooms를 앞에서 수식하는 형용사 자리이므로 형용사인 (A) No가 정답이다. (B) None은 대명사, (C) Never와 (D) Not은 부사이므로 답이 될 수 없다.

번역 현재는 이용할 수 있는 방이 없지만, 이른 오후에 빈방이 좀 있을 것이다.

어휘 currently 현재 vacancy (호텔의) 빈방, 공석

16. (C) 수량 형용사

해설 빈칸은 주어 역할을 하는 명사 vehicles를 수식하는 형용사 자리이고, vehicles는 복수명사이므로 복수명사를 수식할 수 있는 (C) All이 정답이다. (A) Each와 (D) Either는 단수명사를 수식하므로 답이 될 수 없고, (B) Whenever는 접속사 혹은 부사이므로 형용사 자리에 들어갈 수 없다.

번역 자정 이후에 브랙스턴 애버뉴에 놓인 모든 차량은 시에서 견인할 것이다.

어휘 vehicle 차량 tow (차를) 견인하다 whenever ~할 때마다

17. (B) 목적격 보어 자리

해설 빈칸은 동명사 keeping의 목적격 보어 자리로 목적어 자리의 명사구 the financial statement를 수식하는 역할을 하므로 '정확한'이라는 의미의 형용사 (B) accurate가 정답이다. 참고로, keep은 5형식 동사로 「동사+목적어+목적격 보어(형용사)」 순서로 주로 쓰이며, 동명사로 쓰일 때도 동사일 때의 성질을 그대로 유지한다.

번역 재무제표를 정확하게 관리해야 하는 중요성 때문에, 세부적인 것들까지 일일이 주의를 기울여야 한다.

어휘 financial statement 재무제표 accuracy 정확(도) accurately 정확하게

18. (A) 목적격 보어 자리

해설 빈칸은 5형식 동사 proves의 목적격 보어 자리로 목적어 자리의 대명사 himself를 수식하는 형용사가 들어가면 되고, 문맥상 '그리핀 장은 자신이 신뢰할 수 있는 사람임을 증명한다'라는 내용이 되어야 자연스러우므로 '신뢰할 수 있는'이라는 뜻의 형용사 (A) reliable이 정답이다. (C) relying은 현재분사로 '의존하는'이라는 뜻이므로 문맥상 어울리지 않고, (B) relied는 과거분사인데 rely는 자동사이므로 수동 의미로 명사를 수식하는 과거분사로는 쓰이지 않는다.

번역 그리핀 장은 최고의 결과를 만들어 낼 뿐만 아니라 항상 마감 기한을 지킴으로써 자신이 믿을 수 있는 사람임을 증명한다.

어휘 deadline 마감 기한 rely 의지하다, 믿다 reliability 신뢰

19. (B) 형용사+형용사+명사

해설 빈칸은 명사구 15% increase를 앞에서 수식하는 형용사 자리이므로 '인상적인'이라는 의미의 형용사 (B) impressive가 정답이다.

번역 알콘 픽처스사는 새 영화 〈오로라〉 개봉 후에 시장 점유율 면에서 놀라운 15퍼센트 상승을 보였다.

어휘 witness 목격하다; 목격자 market share 시장 점유율 release 공개하다, 출시하다 impress 깊은 인상을 주다 impression 인상

20. (B) 형용사 어휘

해설 명사 authors를 수식하기에 적절한 형용사 어휘를 선택하는 문제이다. 문맥상 '기사에 나온 견해들은 각 저자의 것

이다'라는 내용이 되어야 자연스러우므로 '각각의, 각자의'라는 의미의 형용사 (B) respective가 정답이다.

번역 기사에서 드러난 견해들은 각 저자의 것이며 반드시 〈스타 텔레그래프〉의 입장을 반영하지는 않습니다.

어휘 view 견해, 의견 author 작가 necessarily 반드시, 꼭 reflect 반영하다 position 입장, 태도 successive 연속적인 likely ~할 것 같은 enormous 막대한

●UNIT 04 부사

출제 공식 1 CHECK UP

1. finally **2.** regretfully **3.** thoroughly

1. have+부사+p.p
해설 have와 p.p 사이 부사 자리이다.
번역 두 회사는 마침내 계약에 합의했다.
어휘 final 최종의 finally 마침내 agree on ~에 동의[합의]하다

2. 주어+부사+동사
해설 주어와 동사 사이 부사 자리이다.
번역 유감스럽게도 한 씨가 우리 회사를 떠날 것임을 알려 드립니다.
어휘 regret 후회하다, 유감스럽게 생각하다 regretfully 유감스럽게도

3. 타동사+목적어+부사
해설 타동사와 목적어 뒤 부사 자리이다.
번역 임대차 계약에 서명하기 전에 세부 사항을 철저히 읽어 보십시오.
어휘 details 세부 사항 thorough 철저한 thoroughly 철저히 lease 임대차 계약

출제 공식 2 CHECK UP

1. consistently **2.** Immediately **3.** relatively

1. 부사+형용사
해설 형용사 stable을 수식하므로 부사 자리이다.
번역 건강 음료에 대한 수요는 꾸준히 안정 상태를 유지한다.
어휘 demand 수요 beverage 음료 consistent 일관된, 변함없는 consistently 지속적으로 stable 안정적인

2. 부사+전치사구
해설 after가 이끄는 구를 수식하는 부사 자리이다.
번역 학위를 딴 직후에 테일러 씨는 마케팅 회사에 입사했다.
어휘 immediate 즉각적인 immediately 즉시 earn 얻다 degree 학위 firm 회사

3. 부사 + 부사

해설 부사 easily를 수식하므로 부사 자리이다.

번역 온도는 비교적 쉽게 조절할 수 있다.

어휘 temperature 온도, 기온   relative 비교상의, 상대적인
relatively 비교적   easily 쉽게

출제 공식 3   CHECK UP

1. continually   2. slightly   3. Formerly

1. 부사 + 동명사

해설 동명사 surpassing을 수식하므로 부사 자리이다.

번역 팔머 씨는 지속적으로 판매 목표를 초과 달성한 것에 대해
칭찬을 받았다.

어휘 commend 칭찬하다   surpass 능가하다   goal 목표

2. to부정사 + 부사

해설 to change를 수식하므로 부사 자리이다.

번역 부장은 제1면의 본문을 약간 바꾸기로 결정했다.

어휘 director 감독, 책임자   slight 약간의   slightly 약간
front page (신문의) 제1면

3. 부사 + 분사

해설 분사 located를 수식하므로 부사 자리이다.

번역 예전에는 꼭대기 층에 위치해 있던 영업부가 지금은 7층에
있다.

어휘 former 예전의   formerly 이전에, 예전에   division 부서

출제 공식 4   CHECK UP

1. highly   2. nearly   3. conveniently

1. 뜻에 유의할 부사

해설 '매우 존중받는', '높이 평가되는'을 뜻하므로 highly가 와
야 한다.

번역 제임스 클락은 높이 평가되는 그의 저서 〈우주〉로 가장 잘
알려져 있다.

어휘 regard ~으로 여기다, 평가하다

2. 뜻에 유의할 부사

해설 twice(두 배)를 수식하므로 nearly가 와야 한다.

번역 기자 회견은 예상보다 거의 두 배의 시간이 걸렸다.

어휘 press conference 기자 회견   take (얼마의 시간이)
걸리다

3. 뜻에 유의할 부사

해설 located를 수식하므로 conveniently가 와야 한다.
closely는 '자세히'이므로 located와 어울리지 않는다.

번역 자동판매기는 입구 근처에 편리하게 위치해 있다.

어휘 vending machine 자동판매기

ACTUAL TEST

1. (B)	**2.** (C)	**3.** (D)	**4.** (B)	**5.** (C)
6. (D)	**7.** (C)	**8.** (B)	**9.** (B)	**10.** (D)
11. (D)	**12.** (D)	**13.** (C)	**14.** (D)	**15.** (B)
16. (A)	**17.** (D)	**18.** (C)	**19.** (C)	**20.** (B)

1. **(B)** 주어 + 부사 + 동사

해설 빈칸은 주어 Caron Motors와 동사 recalled 사이에서
동사를 수식하는 부사 자리이므로 '자발적으로'라는 의미
의 부사 (B) voluntarily가 정답이다.

번역 카론 모토즈사는 브레이크 결함 가능성 때문에 자사의 최
신 하이브리드 모델을 자발적으로 리콜 조치했다.

어휘 recall (제품을) 리콜[회수]하다   latest 최신의   fault
결점, 결함   volunteer 자원하다; 자원봉사자   voluntary
자발적인

2. **(C)** 자동사 + 부사

해설 빈칸은 자동사 have responded 뒤에서 동사를 수식
하는 부사 자리이므로 '열광적으로'라는 의미의 부사 (C)
enthusiastically가 정답이다.

번역 소비자들은 새로 나온 딩고 진공청소기의 출시에 대해 열
광적으로 반응했다.

어휘 consumer 소비자   respond 반응하다   release 공개,
출시   enthusiasm 열광, 열정   enthusiastic 열렬한,
열광적인   enthusiast 열렬한 지지자

3. **(D)** be + p.p + 부사

해설 빈칸은 수동 형태의 동사구 may be purchased 뒤에서
동사를 수식하는 부사 자리이므로 '개별적으로, 각각 따로'
라는 의미의 부사 (D) individually가 정답이다.

번역 돌만 리빙사의 주방용품은 낱개 또는 3개들이 한 세트로
구입할 수 있다.

어휘 kitchen utensils 주방용품   individual 각각의, 개개의;
개인   individualize 개별화하다

4. **(B)** 부사 + 동사

해설 빈칸은 등위접속사 and 뒤에 주어 The new parking
fines가 생략되어 있고 동사 divided를 앞에서 수식하
는 부사 자리이므로 '첨예하게, 날카롭게'라는 의미의 부사
(B) sharply가 정답이다.

번역 새로 생긴 주차 위반 벌금은 논란을 초래했고 유권자들을
첨예하게 갈라 놓았다.

어휘 fine 벌금   controversy 논란   divide 나누다   voter
투표자, 유권자   sharpness 날카로움   sharp 날카로운,
선명한

surprise 놀라게 하다

5. (C) 부사 + 분사

해설 빈칸은 과거분사 decorated를 앞에서 수식하는 부사 자리이므로 '매력적으로'라는 뜻의 부사 (C) attractively가 정답이다.

번역 모렐리즈 비스트로는 매력적으로 장식된 식사 공간을 특징으로 하며 특별한 행사에 안성맞춤이다.

어휘 feature ~을 특징으로 하다   decorated 장식된   dining 식사   occasion 때, 경우   attract 마음을 끌다, 끌어모으다

6. (D) 동사 + 목적어 + 부사

해설 빈칸은 that절의 「주어 + 동사 + 목적어」로 이루어진 완전한 문장 뒤에서 동사구 sends out을 수식하는 부사 자리이므로 '자동적으로'라는 의미의 (D) automatically가 정답이다.

번역 모든 회원들께 포니 짐에서는 문자 메시지를 통해 회원 갱신 공지를 자동 발송하고 있음을 알립니다.

어휘 note 주목하다   send out 발송하다   renewal 갱신   notice 공지   via ~을 통해   automate 자동화하다   automatic 자동의   automation 자동화

7. (C) 부사 + 분사

해설 빈칸은 to부정사 to get의 목적격 보어로 쓰인 과거분사 written을 수식하는 자리이므로 부사가 들어가야 한다. 따라서 '전문적으로'라는 의미의 부사 (C) professionally가 정답이다. 참고로, get은 목적어 뒤에 목적격 보어로 과거분사가 와서 '~가 되게 하다'라는 의미로 쓰인다.

번역 설문 조사 결과 많은 청년 구직자들은 자신의 이력서가 전문가에 의해 전문적으로 작성되게 하는 편을 선호하는 것으로 나타난다.

어휘 indicate 나타내다   seeker 구하는 사람   expert 전문가   professional 전문적인; 전문가   professionalize 전문화된, 프로인   professionalism 전문성

8. (B) 조동사 + 부사 + 동사원형

해설 빈칸은 조동사 may 뒤의 동사원형 reduce를 앞에서 수식하는 부사 자리이므로 '상당히'라는 의미의 부사 (B) significantly가 정답이다.

번역 간소화된 제품 개발 공정은 회사의 생산비를 상당히 줄일 수 있다.

어휘 streamlined 간소화된   reduce 줄이다   production cost 생산비   significance 중요성, 의미   signify 의미하다   significant 중요한

9. (B) 부사 + 형용사

해설 빈칸은 형용사 low를 앞에서 수식하는 부사 자리이므로 '놀랄 정도로'라는 의미의 부사 (B) surprisingly가 정답이다.

번역 최근 조사에서 일부 인기 있는 주스 음료에는 놀랄 만큼 적은 양의 영양소가 들어 있는 것으로 드러났다.

어휘 reveal 밝히다   amount 양, 액수   nutrient 영양소

10. (D) 부사 + 분사

해설 빈칸은 과거분사 priced를 앞에서 수식하는 부사 자리이고, '어떤 다른 동일하게 가격이 붙은 모델'이라고 자연스럽게 해석되므로 '상응하여, 서로 맞게'라는 의미의 부사 (D) correspondingly가 정답이다.

번역 아레맥스 A10 디지털 카메라는 같은 가격의 어떤 다른 모델들보다 더 많은 기능을 제공한다.

어휘 feature 기능   correspondence 서신   correspond 일치하다, ~에 해당하다

11. (D) 부사 + 분사

해설 빈칸은 명사 handles를 수식하는 과거분사 designed를 앞에서 수식하는 자리이므로 부사가 들어가야 한다. 따라서 '특별히, 분명하게'라는 의미의 부사 (D) specifically가 정답이다.

번역 리겔 서플라이사는 왼손잡이 사용자들을 위해 특별히 고안된 손잡이가 달린 철물 공구 제품을 제공한다.

어휘 hardware tool 철물 공구   designed for ~을 위해 만들어진   left-handed 왼손잡이의   specify 명시하다

12. (D) 부사 + 형용사

해설 빈칸은 형용사 large를 앞에서 수식하는 부사 자리이므로 '인상적으로'라는 의미의 부사 (D) impressively가 정답이다.

번역 그 회사의 새 공장에서는 놀랄 만큼 대규모로 주방용 가전기기를 생산할 수 있다.

어휘 be capable of ~할 수 있다   appliance 가전기기   on a large scale 대규모로   impress 깊은 인상을 주다

13. (C) be + 부사 + p.p

해설 빈칸은 수동태 동사구 has been ranked 사이에 들어가 동사를 수식하는 부사 자리이므로 '일관되게'라는 뜻의 부사 (C) consistently가 정답이다.

번역 로라즈 비스트로는 일관되게 지역에서 가장 인기 있는 식당 중 하나로 평가받아 왔다.

어휘 rank 평가하다, 등급을 매기다   region 지역   consistency 일관성

14. (D) 부사 + 분사

해설 빈칸은 명사 residents를 수식하는 현재분사 seeking을 앞에서 수식하는 자리이므로 부사가 들어가야 한다. 따라서 '적극적으로'라는 의미의 부사 (D) actively가 정답이다.

번역 적극적으로 일자리를 찾는 주민들의 숫자가 지난 분기에 감소했는데, 이는 건강한 지역 경제의 징후이다.

어휘 seek 찾다, 구하다   employment 직장, 고용   decline 감소하다   activate 작동시키다   active 적극적인, 활동적인   action 행동

PART 5

15. **(B) 부사 어휘**

해설 빈칸에 들어가 해당 절의 내용을 수식하기에 적절한 부사 어휘를 고르는 문제이다. 문맥상 '10시 기차의 1등석 칸 예약이 다 차서, 샤론 씨는 대신에 다음 기차를 타기로 했다'라는 내용이 되어야 자연스러우므로 '대신에'라는 뜻의 부사 (B) instead가 정답이다. (A) seldom은 '좀처럼 ~ 하지 않다'라는 뜻으로 조동사나 be동사 뒤, 혹은 일반동 사 앞에 위치하는 부사로 문장 맨 뒤에는 들어가지 않는다. (C) however(하지만)와 (D) altogether(완전히, 모두 합쳐)는 문맥상 어울리지 않으므로 답이 될 수 없다.

번역 10시 기차의 1등석 예약이 다 차서 샤론 씨는 대신 다음 기차를 타기로 했다.

어휘 fully booked 예약이 다 찬 seldom 좀처럼 ~ 않는 altogether 완전히

16. **(A) 접속부사**

해설 빈칸은 등위접속사 and로 연결된 절(we need ~ to stay afloat)의 앞에 위치해 and 앞에 있는 절과의 의미상 연결 관계를 보여 주는 접속부사 자리이다. 문맥상 '현재 사업 계획이 지속 가능하지 않으므로 좀 더 효과적인 방법을 찾아야 한다'라고 인과 관계로 해석되어야 자연스러우므로 '그러므로'라는 의미의 접속부사 (A) therefore가 정답이다.

번역 우리의 현재 사업 계획은 지속 가능하지 않으므로, 파산을 면할 수 있는 더 효과적인 방법을 찾아야 한다.

어휘 sustainable 지속 가능한 effective 효과적인 afloat 파산은 면한 otherwise 그렇지 않으면

17. **(D) how + 부사 + 완전한 절**

해설 how는 형용사 또는 부사와 결합하여 '얼마나 ~한', '얼마나 ~하게'라고 해석되는데 빈칸 뒤 완전한 절(Bella Son ~ her shoes)과 결합하므로 '솜씨 있게'라는 의미의 부사 (D) skillfully가 정답이다.

번역 디자인 페스티벌 참가자들은 벨라 손이 얼마나 솜씨 있게 자신의 신발에 미술을 접목시켰는지에 깊은 인상을 받았다.

어휘 participant 참가자 incorporate A into B A를 B에 포함[통합]시키다 skillful 솜씨 좋은, 능숙한 skilled 숙련된, 노련한

18. **(C) 부사 + 전치사구**

해설 빈칸 뒤 전치사구 ahead of schedule이 be동사 is의 보어 역할로 쓰여 '좋은 날씨 덕에 예정보다 앞서 있다'라 는 내용의 절이므로 빈칸에는 전치사구를 수식할 수 있는 부사가 들어가야 하며, '현재'라는 의미의 부사 presently 가 들어가면 '현재 예정보다 앞서 있다'라고 해석되어 문맥 도 자연스럽다. 따라서 (C) presently가 정답이다.

번역 건설 공사는 5월까지 완료 예정이지만, 좋은 날씨 덕분에 현재 예정보다 앞서 있다.

어휘 completion 완료, 완성 ahead of schedule 예정보다 빠른 thanks to ~ 덕분에 present 현재의, 참석한; 주다, 수여하다 presence 존재함, 참석

19. **(C) 부사 + 과거분사**

해설 빈칸은 명사구 every guest room을 수식하는 분사구 문(decorated ~ designer)에서 과거분사 decorated 를 앞에서 수식하는 자리이므로 부사가 들어가야 한다. 따 라서 '우아하게'라는 의미의 부사 (C) Elegantly가 정답 이다.

번역 수석 인테리어 디자이너에 의해 우아하게 장식된 에펠 호 텔의 모든 게스트 룸은 충분한 안락함을 제공한다.

어휘 ample 충분한 comfort 안락(함) elegant 우아한 elegance 우아함

20. **(B) 자동사 + 부사 + 전치사**

해설 자동사 focus 뒤의 전치사구(on ways ~)를 수식하기 에 적절한 부사 어휘를 고르는 문제이다. '주로 ~한 방법 에 초점을 맞출 것이다'라는 내용이 되어야 자연스러우므 로 '주로'라는 의미의 부사 (B) primarily가 정답이다. (A) hardly는 빈도부사로 조동사 뒤, 일반동사 앞에 위치해야 하고, (C) formerly는 '이전에'라는 의미이므로 미래 시제 와는 어울리지 않는다.

번역 다가오는 세미나는 사업체들이 지역 사회 번영에 도움을 줄 수 있는 방법에 주로 초점을 맞출 것이다.

어휘 upcoming 다가오는, 곧 있을 focus on ~에 초점을 맞추다 thrive 번창하다 hardly 거의 ~ 아닌 formerly 이전에 relatively 비교적

●UNIT 05 동사

출제 공식 1 CHECK UP

1. includes **2.** have agreed **3.** leads

1. **주어 동사 수 일치**

해설 주어가 단수이므로 단수 동사와 수 일치한다.

번역 각각의 점심은 또한 약간의 샐러드, 바나나, 그리고 에너지 바를 포함한다.

2. **주어 동사 수 일치**

해설 주어가 복수이므로 복수 동사와 수 일치한다.

번역 시 의회 의원 모두가 총회를 개최하는 데 동의했다.

어휘 hold 개최하다 convention 총회

3. **주어 동사 수 일치**

해설 동명사 주어이므로 단수 동사로 수 일치한다.

번역 잦은 회의를 하는 것은 일부 부정적인 결과로 이어진다.

어휘 frequent 빈번한 lead to ~로 이어지다 consequence 결과

출제 공식 2 CHECK UP 교재 p. 165

1. have acted　**2.** is　**3.** operate

---

1. 수량 표현 수 일치
해설 수량 표현 뒤 복수명사와 수 일치하여 복수 동사를 쓴다.
번역 모든 회사 임원들은 심사위원으로서의 역할을 했다.
어휘 executive 임원, 중역　judge 심사위원

2. 수량 표현 수 일치
해설 「each of+복수명사」는 단수 동사로 수 일치한다.
번역 각 교육 세션은 한 시간이 소요될 것으로 예상된다.
어휘 training session 교육 세션　last 지속되다

3. 선행사 수 일치
해설 선행사가 those이므로 복수 동사로 수 일치한다.
번역 복잡한 기계를 작동시키는 사람들만 훈련을 받을 것이다.
어휘 operate 작동시키다　complex 복잡한

출제 공식 3 CHECK UP 교재 p. 166

1. has recorded　**2.** was cancelled
3. has risen

---

1. 능동태
해설 목적어 the meeting minutes가 있으므로 능동태로 써야 한다.
번역 줄리엣은 인터넷에 게재하기 위해 회의록을 기록했다.
어휘 minutes 회의록　post 게재하다

2. 수동태
해설 목적어가 없으므로 수동태로 써야 한다.
번역 프레젠테이션은 저조한 대중의 관심으로 인해 취소되었다.
어휘 cancel 취소하다　public interest 일반 대중의 관심

3. 능동태
해설 자동사이므로 능동태로 써야 한다.
번역 맥퀸사의 주가가 최근에 올랐다.
어휘 share price 주가

출제 공식 4 CHECK UP 교재 p. 166

1. pleased　**2.** equipped　**3.** invited

---

1. 수동태 빈출 숙어
해설 알맞은 숙어 표현은 be pleased to(~해서 기쁘다)이다.
번역 저희는 고객들께 새로운 서비스를 제공하게 되어 기쁩니다.

2. 수동태 빈출 숙어
해설 알맞은 숙어 표현은 be equipped with(~로 갖추어지다)이다.
번역 그 호텔은 큰 세탁 공간이 갖추어져 있다.

3. 수동태 빈출 숙어
해설 알맞은 숙어 표현은 be invited to(~하도록 요청되다)이다.
번역 20명 이상의 저자들이 도서 사인회에 참석하도록 요청받았다.

출제 공식 5 CHECK UP 교재 p. 167

1. will be educated　**2.** decided　**3.** opens

---

1. 미래 시제
해설 upcoming이 있으므로 미래 시제와 어울린다.
번역 엔지니어들은 곧 있을 워크숍에서 교육을 받을 것이다.
어휘 educate 교육하다　upcoming 곧 있을, 다가오는

2. 과거 시제
해설 recently가 있으므로 과거 시제와 어울린다.
번역 최근에 회사는 휴가 정책을 개정하기로 결정했다.
어휘 revise 개정하다

3. 현재 시제
해설 시간을 나타내는 접속사 as soon as절에서는 미래 시제 대신 현재 시제를 써야 한다.
번역 그 역이 생기자마자 교통 혼잡이 완화될 것이다.
어휘 congestion 혼잡　relieve 완화시키다

출제 공식 6 CHECK UP 교재 p. 167

1. are undergoing　**2.** will be visiting
3. is closing

---

1. 현재 진행 시제
해설 currently가 있으므로 현재진행 시제와 어울린다.
번역 현재 우리는 대대적인 개조 작업을 거치고 있다.
어휘 undergo 겪다, 받다

2. 미래 진행 시제
해설 later this month가 있으므로 미래진행 시제와 어울린다.
번역 CEO는 우리의 생산 시설을 이달 중으로 방문할 것이다.
어휘 production 생산　facility 시설

3. 현재 진행 시제

해설 next month가 있으므로 가까운 미래에 예정된 일을 나타낼 수 있는 현재진행 시제와 어울린다. 목적어가 있으므로 수동태인 will be closed는 올 수 없다.

번역 메인 스트리트에 있는 카페는 다음 달에 문을 닫을 것이다.

출제 공식 7 CHECK UP
교재 p. 168

1. has declined   **2.** had lived   **3.** will have been

---

1. 현재완료 시제

해설 「since+과거 시점」이 있으므로 현재완료 시제와 어울린다.

번역 일본의 관광객 수는 작년 이래로 줄었다

어휘 decline 감소하다

2. 과거완료 시제

해설 before절이 과거이므로 그 이전을 나타내기 위해 과거완료 시제가 필요하다. 시간 접속사가 일이 일어난 순서를 밝혀 주므로 과거완료 대신 과거 시제를 쓰는 것도 가능하다.

번역 파스칼 씨는 홍콩으로 이사 가기 전에 싱가포르에서 살았다.

3. 미래완료 시제

해설 By the time절이 현재이면 주절은 미래완료 시제를 쓴다. By the time절에 과거가 오면 주절에 과거완료를 쓰는 것과 구분하자.

번역 리허설이 시작할 무렵 모든 부스는 설치되어 있을 것이다.

출제 공식 8 CHECK UP
교재 p. 168

1. has been delayed   **2.** returned
3. will have signed

---

1. 수동태

해설 목적어가 없으므로 수동태로 써야 한다.

번역 출시일은 예상치 못한 문제로 인해 연기되었다.

어휘 release 공개, 출시   delay 미루다, 연기하다
unexpected 예상치 못한

2. 과거 시제

해설 yesterday가 있으므로 과거 시제와 어울린다.

번역 레이놀즈 씨는 어제 사무실로 복귀했다.

어휘 return 돌아오다

3. 미래완료 시제

해설 「by+미래 시점」이 있으므로 미래완료 시제와 어울린다.

번역 그 고객은 다음 달 말이면 계약서에 서명을 끝냈을 것이다.

어휘 contract 계약(서)

ACTUAL TEST
교재 p. 170

1. (B)	**2.** (D)	**3.** (D)	**4.** (C)	**5.** (B)
6. (B)	**7.** (B)	**8.** (A)	**9.** (B)	**10.** (C)
11. (C)	**12.** (B)	**13.** (B)	**14.** (D)	**15.** (C)
16. (B)	**17.** (C)	**18.** (A)	**19.** (B)	**20.** (B)

1. (B) 동사의 형태 – 수동태

해설 빈칸은 주어 All orders의 동사 자리이고, 뒤에 목적어가 보이지 않고 '모든 주문품은 배송될 것이다'라고 해석되므로 수동 형태인 (B) will be shipped가 정답이다. (D) is shipping은 복수명사 주어(orders)와 수 일치가 되지 않고 ship은 '배송하다'라는 의미로 쓰일 때는 타동사이고 능동 형태일 경우 뒤에 목적어가 와야 하므로 답이 될 수 없다.

번역 모든 주문품은 우리 메인 공장으로부터 가장 효율적인 방법을 통해 배송됩니다.

어휘 via ~을 통해   efficient 효율적인   ship 운송하다

2. (D) 동사의 형태와 시제

해설 빈칸은 주어인 명사구 A cash award의 동사 자리이고, '주다'라는 뜻의 give는 타동사인데 빈칸 뒤에 목적어가 보이지 않으므로 수동 형태가 와야 한다. 또한 '다음 분기 판매 콘테스트(next quarter's sales contest)라면서 미래에 대해 언급하고 있으므로 미래 시제 수동 형태 동사인 (D) will be given이 정답이다.

번역 천 달러의 상금이 다음 분기 판매 콘테스트의 우승자에게 주어질 것이다.

어휘 award 상   quarter 사분기

3. (D) 동사의 형태 – 조동사+동사원형

해설 빈칸은 조동사 must의 뒤에 있으므로 동사원형 자리이고, 뒤에 목적어 original paper receipts를 연결해야 하므로 능동 형태가 되어야 한다. 따라서 능동 형태의 동사원형인 (D) submit이 정답이다.

번역 출장 경비를 환급받기 위해서 모든 직원은 영수증 원본을 회계부에 제출해야 한다.

어휘 reimburse 환급하다, 배상하다   expense 경비   submit 제출하다

4. (C) 동사의 형태 – 수동태

해설 빈칸은 부사절(as soon as ~)에서 주어 payment의 동사 자리이다. 뒤에 목적어도 보이지 않고, '대금이 수령되자마자'라는 내용이 되어야 자연스러우므로 수동 형태인 (C) has been received가 정답이다.

번역 베텔사는 대금을 수령하는 즉시 모든 주문품을 배송할 것이다.

어휘 payment 지불(금), 납입

5. **(B) 동사의 형태 – 능동태**

해설 빈칸은 주어인 Staffing issues의 동사 자리이며, 뒤에 목적어 Silverado Department Store와 목적격 보어 to reduce가 있고 '백화섬이 어쩔 수 없이 냉법 시간늘 술이게 만들었다'라고 능동 의미로 해석되므로 능동 형태의 동사 (B) forced가 정답이다.

번역 직원 채용 문제 때문에 실버라도 백화점은 어쩔 수 없이 주중에 영업 시간을 단축해야 했다.

어휘 staffing 직원 채용   business hours 영업 시간   force 강요하다. 어쩔 수 없이 ~하게 만들다

6. **(B) 동사의 형태 – 수동태**

해설 빈칸은 주어인 Repairs의 동사 자리이며, 뒤에 목적어가 보이지 않고 '수리가 시도되었다'라고 수동 의미로 해석되므로 수동 형태의 동사 (B) were attempted가 정답이다.

번역 노트북 컴퓨터 수리가 시도되었지만, 수리 기사는 그것을 다시 작동시키지는 못했다.

어휘 repair 수리   technician 기술자. 기사   attempt 시도하다

7. **(B) 동사의 형태 – 능동태**

해설 빈칸은 주어인 New Life Pharmaceuticals의 동사 자리이며, 뒤에 목적어 seemingly impossible solutions도 있고 '불가능할 것 같은 해결책을 만들어 냈다'라고 능동 의미로 해석되므로 능동 형태의 동사 (B) has created가 정답이다.

번역 뉴 라이프 제약 회사는 중대한 건강 문제에 대해 불가능할 것 같은 해결책을 만들어 냈다.

어휘 pharmaceuticals 제약 회사   seemingly 겉보기에는   solution 해결책   major 주요한

8. **(A) 동사의 수 일치**

해설 빈칸은 부사절(Now that ~ in London)에서 주어 Mr. Benson의 동사 자리이고, '그의 자리를 채우기 위해 누군가를 승진시켜야 한다'라는 내용으로 보아 벤슨 씨는 이미 전근을 갔음을 알 수 있다. 따라서 현재완료 시제 동사 (A) has transferred가 정답이다. (B) transfer는 3인칭 단수 주어 Mr. Benson과 수 일치가 되지 않아 답이 될 수 없다.

번역 벤슨 씨가 런던에 있는 우리 본사로 전근 갔으므로, 우리는 그의 자리를 채우기 위해 내부적으로 누군가를 승진시켜야 한다.

어휘 now that ~이므로   headquarters 본사   promote 승진시키다   internally 내부적으로   transfer 이동하다. 전근 가다

9. **(B) 동사의 수 일치**

해설 빈칸은 3인칭 단수 주어 Vance Department Store의 동사 자리이므로 (B) provides가 정답이다. (D) are providing은 주어와 수 일치가 되지 않아 답이 될 수 없다.

번역 기온이 영하로 내려갈 때마다, 반스 백화점은 무료로 차를 제공한다.

어휘 subzero 영하의   complimentary 무료의

10. **(C) 동사의 수 일치**

해설 빈칸은 명사 recipes를 수식하는 주격 관계대명사절 (that ~ over many years)의 동사 자리이고, 주격 관계대명사절의 동사는 관계사절의 수식을 받는 명사인 선행사 reciipes에 수 일치되어야 하므로 (C) have been perfected가 정답이다.

번역 세이지 비스트로는 수년에 걸쳐 완성된 조리법을 사용하여 그 식당만의 특별한 요리를 만든다.

어휘 bistro 식당   dish 요리   recipe 조리법

11. **(C) 동사의 형태 – 수동태**

해설 빈칸은 주어 Midas Shopping Mall의 동사 자리이다. 뒤에 목적어도 보이지 않고 '쇼핑몰이 훌륭한 가치와 유명 브랜드로 알려져 왔다'라는 수동 의미로 해석되어야 자연스러우므로 수동 형태가 와야 하고, 지난 '반 세기 동안(For nearly half a century)' 있었던 일을 언급하고 있으므로 현재완료 수동 형태의 동시 (C) has been known이 정답이다.

번역 거의 반 세기 동안, 마이다스 쇼핑몰은 훌륭한 가치와 유명 브랜드들로 알려져 왔다.

어휘 nearly 거의

12. **(B) 동사의 수 일치**

해설 빈칸은 복수명사 주어 The new juice flavors의 동사 자리이므로 복수인 주어와 수 일치되는 (B) appeal이 정답이다.

번역 코웨타 음료 회사에서 선보인 새로운 주스는 천연 재료를 선호하는 젊은 소비자들의 관심을 끌고 있다.

어휘 beverage 음료   consumer 소비자   ingredient 재료   appeal to ~의 관심을 끌다

13. **(B) 동사의 시제 – 현재완료**

해설 빈칸은 주어 Silvia Wedding Gowns의 동사 자리이다. 빈칸 뒤로 「since + 주어 + 과거동사」 절이 와서 '지난 10월에 개업한 이후로'라고 했으므로 빈칸에는 지난 10월, 즉 과거부터 현재까지 해 온 일을 나타내는 현재완료 시제가 들어가 '제공해 오고 있다'라는 내용이 되어야 글의 흐름이 자연스럽다. 따라서 (B) has been offering이 정답이다.

번역 실비아 웨딩 가운즈는 지난 10월에 개업한 이후로 무료 드레스 피팅을 제공해 오고 있다.

14. **(D) 동사의 시제 – 미래**

해설 빈칸은 주어 New computer programmers의 동사 자리이고, 빈칸 뒤 부사절(when ~ next year)에서 내년 초에 있을 일을 언급하고 있으므로 미래 시제 동사인 (D) will be recruited가 정답이다.

번역 우리 회사가 내년 초에 에이스 솔루션즈사와 합병되면 컴퓨터 프로그래머들을 새로 뽑을 것이다.

어휘 merge with ~와 합병되다　recruit 모집하다

15. (C) 동사의 시제 - 과거완료

해설 빈칸은 주어 he의 동사 자리이다. 문맥의 흐름상 빈칸에 들어갈 동사(serve)는 버나드 씨가 COO가 된(became) 과거 이전부터 해당하는 내용으로 '버나드 씨가 최고 운영 책임자가 되었을 무렵, 그는 그 회사에서 거의 25년째 근무해 왔다'라는 내용이 되어야 자연스러우므로 과거완료 동사 (C) had served가 정답이다.

번역 버나드 씨는 최고 운영 책임자가 되었을 무렵, 회사에 재직한 지 거의 25년째였다.

어휘 chief operating officer 최고 운영 책임자

16. (B) 동사의 형태 - 수동태

해설 빈칸은 동명사 주어 Dealing의 동사 자리이다. 동명사 주어는 단수 취급하므로 (B) is considered나 (D) is considering이 답이 될 수 있다. consider는 대표적인 5형식 동사로 「consider+목적어+목적격 보어」의 구조를 가지며 '…을 ~로 간주하다'로 해석되므로 빈칸 뒤에 남은 것이 목적어가 아니라 목적격 보어라는 것을 해석을 통해 알아내야 한다. 여기서는 '간주하다'가 아닌 '간주된다'라는 의미가 되어야 하므로 수동태인 (B) is considered가 정답이다.

번역 불만족하는 고객을 상대하는 것은 가장 힘든 업무 중 하나로 여겨진다.

어휘 deal with 처리하다, 다루다　dissatisfied 불만스러워하는　demanding 까다로운, 힘든

17. (C) 동사의 형태와 시제

해설 빈칸은 부사절(Once ~)에서 주어 an appointment의 동사 자리이며, 빈칸 뒤로 목적어가 보이지 않고 '예약 일정이 잡히면'이라는 수동 의미로 해석되므로 수동 형태의 동사가 와야 한다. 주절의 동사 will receive로 보아 미래에 대한 내용이므로 과거 시제 동사인 (B) was scheduled는 답이 될 수 없고, 시간 접속사 once가 이끄는 절에는 현재 시제가 미래를 대신하므로 미래완료 시제 will have been scheduled 대신 현재완료 형태의 동사인 (C) has been scheduled가 정답이 된다.

번역 일단 예약 일정이 잡히면, 환자는 병원으로부터 확인 공지 이메일을 받게 될 것이다.

어휘 appointment 약속　patient 환자　confirmation 확인

18. (A) 동사의 종류 - 타동사

해설 주어 자리의 동명사 「ailing의 목적어 역할을 하는 to부정사에 들어가기에 적절한 동사 어휘를 고르는 문제이다. 빈칸 뒤의 목적어 food safety regulations를 자연스럽게 연결할 수 있어야 하므로 '준수하다'라는 의미의 (A) observe가 정답이다. (C) remark는 전치사 on 또는 that절과 함께 쓰이므로 맞지 않고, (B) function과 (D)

comply는 자동사이므로 목적어를 연결할 수 없다.

번역 식품 안전 규정을 준수하지 못하면 여러 가지 나쁜 결과가 초래될 수 있다.

어휘 regulation 규정　result in ~을 야기하다　unfavorable 나쁜, 불리한　consequence 결과　function 기능하다　remark 언급하다　comply 따르다

19. (B) 동사의 종류 - 자동사

해설 명사구 a small printing company를 수식하는 관계대명사절(which ~ materials)의 동사 자리에 적절한 어휘를 고르는 문제이다. 빈칸 뒤로 목적어 없이 전치사 in이 있는 것으로 보아 전치사 in과 자연스럽게 연결되는 자동사가 와야 한다. 따라서 전치사 in과 함께 '~을 전문으로 하다'라는 의미로 쓰이는 자동사 (B) specializes가 정답이다.

번역 스피코는 작은 인쇄 회사로, 홍보 자료 디자인 및 제작을 전문으로 한다.

어휘 production 생산, 제작　promotional 홍보의　materials 자료　dedicate 전념하다　display 전시하다

20. (B) 명령문

해설 절에는 반드시 동사가 있어야 하는데 동사가 보이지 않으므로 빈칸은 동사 자리이다. 주어가 보이지 않는 것으로 보아 주어 You가 생략된 명령문이므로 동사원형인 (B) Maximize가 정답이다.

번역 아렉스사의 선반과 수납장으로 여러분 댁의 거실 공간을 최대한 넓게 활용하세요.

어휘 storage cabinet 수납장, 보관함　maximize 극대화하다, 최대한 활용하다

●UNIT 06 to부정사와 동명사

출제 공식 1　CHECK UP　교재 p. 173

1. to support　2. to fill out　3. To regain

1.　명사적 용법

해설 보어 자리에 objective(목적)와 동격을 이루는 to부정사가 와야 한다.

번역 그 모금 행사의 목적은 지역 사업체들을 지원하는 것이다.

어휘 objective 목적　fundraiser 모금 행사　support 지지하다, 지원하다

2.　형용사적 용법

해설 명사 questionnaires(설문지)를 뒤에서 수식하는 to부정사가 와야 한다.

번역 방문객들은 작성할 설문지 한 부씩을 입구 근처에서 가져갈 수 있다.

어휘 questionnaire 설문지   fill out 작성하다   entrance 입구

3. 부사적 용법

해설 동사는 hired이므로 또 다른 동사가 올 수 없다. to부정사가 문두에 쓰이면 보통 '~하기 위해서'라는 목적의 의미로 해석된다.

번역 예전에 누렸던 명성을 되찾기 위해서, 크레스코사는 마케팅 전문가들을 채용했다.

어휘 regain 되찾다   reputation 명성   expert 전문가

출제 공식 2 CHECK UP
교재 p. 173

1. aims   2. to maximize   3. encouraged

1. to부정사를 목적어로 취하는 동사

해설 aim은 to부정사를 목적어로 취하는 동사이며 consider는 동명사를 목적어로 취하는 동사이다.

번역 제안된 계획은 과학 연구 지원을 목표로 한다.

어휘 propose 제안하다   initiative 계획, 사업   aim 목표하다

2. to부정사를 목적격 보어로 취하는 동사

해설 enable은 목적격 보어로 to부정사를 취한다.

번역 새로운 기술들은 우리의 생산 능력을 극대화할 수 있도록 해 주었다.

어휘 enable ~을 할 수 있게 하다   maximize 극대화하다   capacity 능력

3. be + p.p + to부정사

해설 encourage는 목적격 보어로 to부정사를 취하며 수동태로 쓰이면 be encouraged to 형태가 된다.

번역 면접 대상자들은 정장을 입는 것이 권장되었다.

어휘 interviewee 면접 대상자   formal attire 정장

출제 공식 3 CHECK UP
교재 p. 174

1. Meeting   2. parking   3. providing

1. 동명사 - 주어

해설 주어 자리가 비어 있으므로 주어 역할을 할 수 있는 동명사가 와야 한다.

번역 많은 마감 기한을 지키는 것이 출판 분야에서는 매우 중요하다.

어휘 numerous 많은   critical 대단히 중요한   field 분야   publishing 출판

2. 동명사 - 동사의 목적어

해설 avoid는 동명사를 목적어로 취하는 동사이다.

번역 거리 축제 동안은 잭슨 로드에 주차하는 것을 피하십시오.

어휘 avoid 피하다

3. 동명사 - 전치사의 목적어

해설 be committed to의 to는 전치사이므로 명사 역할을 할 수 있는 동명사가 와야 한다.

번역 젠코 일렉트로닉스사는 최상의 기술 관련 서비스를 제공하는 데 전력을 다한다.

어휘 be committed to ~에 헌신[전념]하다   technical 기술의

출제 공식 4 CHECK UP
교재 p. 174

1. returning   2. limiting   3. subscribing

1. 동명사 + 목적어

해설 전치사 뒤 명사 자리이며 the completed form을 목적어로 받는 동명사가 와야 한다.

번역 작성된 양식을 반송하는 데 있어서 편하신 방법을 저희에게 알려 주시기 바랍니다.

어휘 preferred 선호하는   complete 작성하다

2. 동명사 + 목적어

해설 전치사 뒤 명사 자리이며 unnecessary purchases를 목적어로 받는 동명사가 와야 한다.

번역 불필요한 구매를 제한함으로써, JL사는 전체 경비를 줄인다.

어휘 limitation 제한   limit 제한하다   overall 종합적인, 전체의

3. 자동사의 동명사 + 전치사구

해설 전치사 뒤 명사 자리이며 사람명사인 subscriber(구독자)는 가산 처리가 되어 있지 않으므로 정답이 될 수 없다. subscribe는 자동사로 쓰여 목적어가 바로 오지 않고 전치사 to가 뒤따른다.

번역 저희 소식지를 정기 구독하시면 많은 혜택을 누리실 수 있습니다.

어휘 benefit from ~로부터 이익[혜택]을 얻다   subscriber 구독자   subscribe to ~을 정기 구독하다   newsletter 소식지, 회보

ACTUAL TEST
교재 p. 176

1. (B)	2. (B)	3. (A)	4. (C)	5. (C)
6. (C)	7. (C)	8. (C)	9. (D)	10. (D)
11. (C)	12. (A)	13. (A)	14. (C)	15. (C)
16. (C)	17. (C)	18. (D)	19. (B)	20. (C)

1. (B) to부정사 - 명사적 용법

해설 빈칸은 be동사 is의 보어 자리이다. 명사 역할을 하는 to부정사가 들어가면 뒤의 명사 accessibility를 목적어로 연결하면서 주어 The goal과 동격의 의미로 '목표는

141

접근성을 개선하는 것이다'라고 자연스럽게 해석되므로 (B) to improve가 정답이다. 명사절 that절은 완전한 절을 이끌어야 하므로 (C) that improves는 답이 될 수 없고, (D) being improved는 수동 형태로 빈칸 뒤의 명사 accessibility를 연결할 수 없으므로 답이 될 수 없다.

번역 9번가 다리 확장 공사의 목표는 도심 지역으로의 접근성을 개선하는 것이다.

어휘 widen 넓히다   accessibility 접근성

2. (B) 가주어와 진주어

해설 빈칸 앞의 주어 it이 가주어이므로 빈칸에는 진주어 역할을 할 수 있는 to부정사가 들어가야 하고, 빈칸 뒤의 명사구 the company and its corporate values를 목적어로 연결할 수 있어야 하므로 능동 형태의 to부정사 (B) to research가 정답이다.

번역 전문가들은 취업 면접 전에 회사와 회사의 가치에 대해 조사하는 것이 중요하다는 데 동의한다.

어휘 corporate 기업의

3. (A) 동명사 – 주어

해설 빈칸은 동사 has become의 주어 자리이므로 동사인 (B) Approve는 들어갈 수 없다. 빈칸 뒤에 명사구 employees' vacation requests가 있으므로, 이를 목적어로 연결하면서 주어 자리에 들어갈 수 있는 능동 형태의 동명사 (A) Approving이 정답이다.

번역 소프트웨어 업데이트 덕분에 우리 부서장의 입장에서는 직원들의 휴가 요청을 승인하는 일이 훨씬 간편해졌다.

어휘 thanks to ~ 덕분에   approve 승인하다   approval 승인

4. (C) to부정사 – 부사적 용법

해설 빈칸은 뒤의 명사구 renewable energy를 쉼표 뒤의 완전한 절에 연결하는 자리이므로 부사 역할을 하는 to부정사가 들어가야 하고, '재생 에너지를 홍보하기 위해'라는 내용으로 문맥에 자연스럽게 연결되므로 (C) To promote가 정답이다. 쉼표 뒤로 이미 완전한 절이 있으므로 동사인 (B) Promote와 (D) Promotes가 들어갈 수 없고, (A) Promotion은 빈칸 뒤의 명사구를 연결할 수 없으므로 답이 될 수 없다.

번역 재생 에너지를 홍보하기 위해서 공공 도서관 지붕에 태양 전지판이 설치되었다.

어휘 renewal energy 재생 에너지   solar panel 태양 전지판   install 설치하다   promotion 홍보. 승진   promote 촉진하다. 홍보하다

5. (C) 동명사 – 전치사의 목적어

해설 빈칸은 전치사 of의 목적어 자리이고, 빈칸 뒤의 명사 professionalism을 목적어로 취해 '직업의식을 유지하는 것'이라고 자연스럽게 연결할 수 있는 동명사 (C) maintaining이 정답이다. 명사인 (B) maintenance는 빈칸 뒤의 명사를 연결하지 못하므로 답이 될 수 없다.

번역 사원 지침서는 직장에서 직업의식을 유지하는 몇 가지 방법을 기술하고 있다.

어휘 professionalism 전문성. 직업의식   workplace 직장   maintenance 유지. 관리   maintain 유지하다

6. (C) 동명사 – 주어

해설 빈칸은 동사 is의 주어 자리이므로 명사 또는 동명사가 들어갈 수 있다. 빈칸 뒤에 명사 accuracy가 있으므로 이를 목적어로 취해 '정확성을 향상시키는 것'이라고 자연스럽게 연결해 주는 동명사 (C) Improving이 정답이다. 명사인 (B) Improvement는 뒤의 명사 accuracy를 연결하지 못하므로 답이 될 수 없다.

번역 데이터 입력에 있어서 정확성을 향상시키는 것은 매우 중요한데, 단 한 번의 실수로도 회사에 많은 비용을 초래할 수 있기 때문이다.

어휘 accuracy 정확성   entry 입력   costly 많은 비용이 드는   improvement 향상. 개선

7. (C) be + p.p + to부정사

해설 동사 encourage는 to부정사를 목적격 보어로 취해 「encourage + 목적어 + to부정사(…가 ~하도록 권장하다)」로 쓰이는데, 수동태가 되면 「be encouraged + to부정사(~하도록 권장되다)」가 되어야 하므로 동사구 are encouraged 뒤의 빈칸에는 to부정사가 연결되어야 한다. 따라서 (C) to voice가 정답이다.

번역 정부 지원금의 변경으로 피해를 입은 사람들은 시민 초청 간담회에서 자신들의 의견을 개진하도록 권장된다.

어휘 affect 영향을 미치다   funding 자금 (제공)   town hall meeting 시민 초청 간담회   voice (말로) 나타내다: 목소리. 발언권

8. (C) be + p.p + to부정사

해설 동사 expect는 to부정사를 목적격 보어로 취해 「expect + 목적어 + to부정사(…가 ~할 것으로 예상하다)」로 쓰이는데, 수동태가 되면 「be expected + to부정사(~할 것으로 예상되다)」가 되어야 하므로 동사구 are expected 뒤의 빈칸에는 to부정사가 연결되어야 한다. 따라서 (C) to rise가 정답이다.

번역 주택 매매는 벨몬트사가 이 지역에 새로운 유통 센터를 개장하는 이번 봄에 증가할 것으로 예상된다.

어휘 housing 주택   distribution 유통. 배급   rise 증가하다

9. (D) to부정사를 목적어로 취하는 동사

해설 빈칸은 동사 decided의 목적어 자리이므로 명사나 to부정사가 들어갈 수 있다. 빈칸 뒤에 명사구 a two-day marketing conference가 있으므로 이를 목적어로 자연스럽게 연결할 수 있는 to부정사 (D) to attend가 정답이다. 명사인 (A) attendance는 빈칸 뒤의 명사를 연결하지 못하므로 답이 될 수 없다.

번역 우리 영업 사원 일부는 막판에 이틀 간의 마케팅 컨퍼런스에 참석하기로 결정했다.

어휘 salesperson 영업 사원 at the last minute 마지막
순간에, 막판에 attendance 참석

10. (D) 동명사 – 동사의 목적어

해설 빈칸은 동사 avoid의 목적어 자리이고, avoid는 동명사를
목적어로 취할 수 있으므로 (D) accepting이 정답이다.

번역 프리랜서 작가 및 편집자들은 동시에 너무 많은 프로젝트
를 맡지 않도록 해야 한다.

어휘 freelance 프리랜서로 일하는; 프리랜서로 일하다 editor
편집자 at once 동시에

11. (C) to부정사 – 부사적 용법

해설 빈칸 앞에 완전한 절(A private investor ~ dollars)이
있고, 빈칸 뒤로 남은 구문을 연결해 '시의 해안 지역 개발
을 시작할 수 있도록'이라고 해석되므로 부사절 역할의 to
부정사 (C) to begin이 정답이다.

번역 한 개인 투자자가 시의 해안 지역 개발을 시작하기 위해
3백만 달러 이상을 제공하고 있다.

어휘 investor 투자자 waterfront 해안가

12. (A) to부정사 관용 표현

해설 enough는 to부정사와 함께 형용사나 부사 뒤에 위
치해 '…하기에 충분히 ~한'이라는 의미로 쓰이는데,
「large+enough」 뒤에 빈칸이 있으므로 to부정사
가 들어가면 되며, 빈칸 뒤로 남아 있는 명사구 huge
industrial gatherings를 목적어로 연결할 수 있는 능동
형태인 (A) to host가 정답이다.

번역 우리 연회장 중에서 가장 작은 곳도 대규모의 업계 모임을
개최하기에는 충분히 넓습니다.

어휘 banquet hall 연회장 huge 거대한 industrial 산업의
gathering 모임 host 개최하다

13. (A) 전치사 to가 포함된 숙어

해설 is dedicated to의 to는 전치사이므로 빈칸에는 명사나
동명사가 들어갈 수 있다. 빈칸 뒤에 명사구 the highest
level of customer service가 있으므로 이를 목적어로
받아 '최고 수준의 고객 서비스를 제공하는 것'이라고 자연
스럽게 연결해 주는 동명사 (A) offering이 정답이다.

번역 잠비 퍼니처는 최고 수준의 고객 서비스를 제공하는 데 헌
신하고 있습니다.

어휘 be dedicated to ~에 헌신[전념]하다

14. (C) 동명사 – 전치사의 목적어

해설 빈칸은 전치사 by의 목적어 자리이고, 뒤의 명사구 the
most ~ possible을 목적어로 받아 '가능한 한 가장 재
능 있는 고객 서비스 담당 직원을 채용함으로써'라고 자
연스럽게 연결해 주는 동명사 (C) hiring이 정답이다. by
-ing(~함으로써)를 관용 표현으로 알아 두자.

번역 가능한 한 가장 재능 있는 고객 서비스 담당 직원들을 채용
하여 더 적은 노력으로 고객 충성도를 형성하라.

어휘 loyalty 충실, 충성 talented 재능 있는 representative
직원

15. (C) to부정사를 목적격 보어로 취하는 동사

해설 동사 allow는 목적어 다음에 목적격 보어로 to부정사가
들어가 「allow+목적어+to부정사(…가 ~하도록 허락하
다」 순서로 쓰이고, 빈칸은 allows의 목적격 보어 자리이
므로 to부정사인 (C) to enhance가 정답이다.

번역 폴라리스덱 포토 편집 소프트웨어를 이용하여 사용자들은
간단한 몇 단계만 거치면 자신들의 디지털 이미지의 품질
을 향상시킬 수 있다.

어휘 enhancement 향상, 증대 enhance 높이다, 향상시키다

16. (C) 동명사 – 주어

해설 빈칸은 명사절 that절에서 동사 was의 주어 자리이므로
동사는 들어갈 수 없고 동명사인 (C) meeting이 정답이다.

번역 부동산 개발 업자는 각 단계에서 기한을 맞추는 것이 건설
프로젝트의 성공에 매우 중요하다고 말했다.

어휘 property 부동산 developer 개발자 state 말하다
phase 단계, 국면 critical 매우 중요한

17. (C) to부정사 관용 표현

해설 빈칸 앞에 「too+형용사(difficult)」가 있는 것으로 보아 to
부정사가 들어가야 '시행하기에 너무 어려울 것이다'라는
내용으로 자연스럽게 연결되므로 (C) to enforce가 정답
이다. 「too+형용사/부사+to부정사(너무 …해서 ~할 수
없다」라는 관용 표현을 알아 두자.

번역 많은 유권자들은 식품 안전성을 위해 제안된 정책이 시행
하기에 너무 어려울 거라고 여긴다.

어휘 voter 유권자 measure 조치, 정책 enforcement 시행
enforce 시행하다

18. (D) to부정사 관용 표현

해설 동사 have와 to부정사 사이에 빈칸이 있으므로 부사 yet
이 들어가면 「have yet+to부정사(아직 안 했다)」 구문이
되어 '아직 발표되지는 않았지만'이라고 자연스럽게 연결
되므로 (D) yet이 정답이다.

번역 합병 계획의 세부 사항이 아직 발표되지는 않았지만, 분석
가들은 그 거래 가능성에 대해 긍정적이다.

어휘 details 세부 사항 merger 합병 analyst 분석가
optimistic 낙관적인 deal 거래 potential 가능성

19. (B) 동명사 – 동사의 목적어

해설 빈칸은 동사 consider의 목적어 자리이므로 명사 또
는 동명사가 들어갈 수 있다. 빈칸 뒤의 명사구 the
submission deadline을 목적어로 받아 '제출 기한을 연
장하는 것을 고려할 수도 있다'라고 자연스럽게 연결하는
동명사 (B) extending이 정답이다.

번역 사진 콘테스트의 주최 측은 출품 기한 연장을 고려할 수도
있는데, 지금까지 접수된 출품작이 거의 없기 때문이다.

어휘 organizer 주최자 submission 제출 entry 출품작 so far 지금까지 extend 연장하다

20. **(C) 원형부정사**

해설 동사 help는 목적어 다음에 목적격 보어로 to부정사나 원형부정사(동사원형)가 들어가 「help+목적어+to부정사/원형부정사(…가 ~하도록 돕다)」 순서로 쓰이고, 빈칸은 help의 목적격 보어 자리이므로 (C) evaluate가 정답이다.

번역 이번 주말의 교육 워크숍은 관리자들이 모든 회사 직원들의 능력과 가능성을 평가하는 데 도움이 될 것이다.

어휘 evaluate 평가하다 evaluation 평가

●UNIT 07 분사

출제 공식 1 CHECK UP
교재 p. 179

1. remaining **2.** purchased **3.** challenging

1. **분사+명사**

해설 명사 issue를 수식하는 분사 자리이다.

번역 토론 그룹은 다루어야 할 한 가지 사안이 남아 있다.

어휘 debate 토론 remain 남아 있다 deal with 다루다, 처리하다

2. **명사+분사**

해설 명사 items를 뒤에서 수식하는 분사 자리이다.

번역 판촉 행사는 온라인에서 구매된 상품에는 적용되지 않습니다.

어휘 promotion 홍보, 판촉 행사 apply to ~에 적용되다

3. **보어로 쓰인 분사**

해설 2형식 동사 seemed의 보어 자리이다. challenge는 가산명사이므로 관사가 필요하다.

번역 책장을 조립하는 과정은 어려워 보였다.

어휘 procedure 절차 assemble 조립하다 bookshelf 책장 challenging 어려운, 힘든

출제 공식 2 CHECK UP
교재 p. 179

1. desired **2.** written **3.** honoring

1. **과거분사**

해설 우리말로는 '희망하는'이라고 해석되지만 이는 '본인이 희망하는'이라는 우리말 해석에 따른 것이지 수식을 받는 명사인 salary가 희망하는 것이 아니므로 -ing 형태로 쓰지 않음에 유의하자.

번역 대부분의 회사들은 입사 지원자들에게 희망 연봉을 쓰게 한다.

2. **과거분사**

해설 명사 permission을 수식하므로 written(쓰여진, 서면의)이 와야 한다.

번역 세입자는 주택을 개조하려면 서면 허가를 얻어야 한다.

어휘 tenant 세입자 obtain 얻다 permission 허락

3. **현재분사**

해설 명사 banquet을 뒤에서 수식하며 목적어인 our outgoing president를 가지므로 능동 형태가 와야 한다.

번역 우리는 퇴임하는 회장을 예우하는 연회를 열 것이다.

어휘 banquet 연회 honor 기념하다, 예우하다 outgoing 떠나는, 물러나는

출제 공식 3 CHECK UP
교재 p. 180

1. satisfying **2.** disappointing **3.** impressed

1. **감정분사 - 사물 수식**

해설 training session을 수식하므로 감정 분사는 -ing 형태로 써야 한다.

번역 3일간의 교육은 매우 만족스러웠다.

어휘 satisfying 만족스러운 satisfied 만족하는

2. **감정분사 - 사물 수식**

해설 ending을 수식하므로 감정 분사는 -ing 형태로 써야 한다.

번역 그의 최신 소설의 결말은 실망스러웠다.

어휘 latest 최신의, 최근의 disappointed 실망한 disappointing 실망스러운

3. **감정분사 - 사람 수식**

해설 감정의 주체인 interviewers를 수식하므로 감정 분사는 p.p. 형태로 써야 한다.

번역 면접관들은 기포드 씨의 이력서에 매우 깊은 인상을 받았다.

어휘 interviewer 면접관 impressive 인상적인 impressed 깊은 인상을 받은

출제 공식 4 CHECK UP
교재 p. 180

1. Located **2.** reducing **3.** Having exceeded

1. **분사구문 - 수동**

해설 주어인 Vincent Inn이 '위치되어 있다'라는 의미의 수동적 의미가 되려면 과거분사가 와야 한다.

번역 몇몇 명소 근처에 위치해 있는 빈센트 인은 관광객들에게 최적의 선택이다.

어휘 locate ~에 위치시키다 landmark 중요한 건물, 명소

2. **분사구문 - 능동**

해설 '에너지 소비를 줄이다'라는 의미로 쓰이므로 목적어를 받

을 수 있는 현재분사 형태가 와야 한다. 완전한 문장 뒤에 콤마가 오는 형태의 분사구문에서는 현재분사가 주로 출제된다.

번역 그 배치는 더 많은 자연광을 사용할 수 있게 해 주고 이것은 에너지 소비를 줄여 준다.

어휘 layout 배치   consumption 소비

3. 분사구문 – 능동
해설 주어인 Mr. Bauer가 목표를 뛰어넘은 것이므로 능동적 의미로 현재분사를 써야 한다.

번역 판매 목표를 뛰어넘어 바우어 씨는 보너스를 받았다.

어휘 exceed 넘다, 초과하다

ACTUAL TEST

1. (C)	**2.** (B)	**3.** (C)	**4.** (C)	**5.** (B)
6. (A)	**7.** (C)	**8.** (A)	**9.** (C)	**10.** (C)
11. (C)	**12.** (C)	**13.** (B)	**14.** (B)	**15.** (C)
16. (D)	**17.** (D)	**18.** (B)	**19.** (C)	**20.** (D)

1. (C) 과거분사
해설 빈칸은 명사 products를 앞에서 수식하는 자리이고, '완성된 제품'이라는 의미가 되어야 자연스러우므로 '완성된'을 뜻하는 과거분사 (C) finished가 정답이다.

번역 완성된 제품을 보건대 벤슨 씨가 가구 제작자로서 자신의 작품에 대단한 자부심을 가지고 있음이 분명하다.

어휘 from (판단의 근거) ~로 보아   take (great) pride in ~에 (큰) 자부심을 갖다

2. (B) 과거분사
해설 빈칸은 명사 password를 앞에서 수식하는 자리이고, '잊혀진 비밀번호'라는 의미가 되어야 자연스러우므로 '잊혀진'을 뜻하는 과거분사 (B) forgotten이 정답이다.

번역 잊어버린 비밀번호를 되찾으려면 '비밀번호 재설정' 링크를 클릭하여 지시를 따르시오.

어휘 recover 되찾다   instructions 지시, 명령

3. (C) 과거분사
해설 빈칸은 명사구 gaming applications를 앞에서 수식하는 자리이고, '진보된(복잡한) 게임 앱들'이라는 의미가 되어야 자연스러우므로 '진보된'이라는 의미의 형용사(과거분사) (C) advanced가 정답이다.

번역 신종 컴퓨터들은 복잡한 게임 앱들을 원활하게 실행한다.

어휘 smoothly 순조롭게   advance 진전되다   advancement 발전, 진보

4. (C) 과거분사
해설 빈칸은 명사구 several architectural drawings를 뒤에서 수식하는 자리이다. 빈칸 뒤에 목적어도 보이지 않고,

'도시 계획가들에게 제출된 건축 도면'이라는 내용이 되어야 자연스러우므로 '제출된'이라는 의미의 과거분사 (C) submitted가 정답이다.

번역 도시 계획가들에게 제출되는 몇몇 건축 도면에 일부 수정이 이루어졌다.

어휘 revision 수정, 변경   architectural 건축의   drawing 도면   submit 제출하다

5. (B) 현재분사
해설 빈칸은 명사구 beverage products를 앞에서 수식하는 자리이고, '기존의 음료 제품'이라는 의미가 되어야 자연스러우므로 '기존의'라는 의미의 형용사(현재분사) (B) existing이 정답이다.

번역 판매를 향상시키기 위해, 회사에서는 기존 음료 제품 몇 가지를 새로운 맛과 사이즈로 제공할 것이다.

어휘 beverage 음료   flavor 향, 맛   exist 존재하다

6. (A) 감정분사
해설 빈칸은 be동사의 보어 자리로 주어인 명사를 수식하는 형용사(분사) 혹은 주어와 동격인 명사가 들어갈 수 있다. 문맥상 '너무 많은 전문 용어를 사용하는 것은 독자들에게 혼란스러울 수 있다'라는 의미가 되어야 자연스러우므로 '혼란스러운'이라는 의미의 형용사(현재분사) (A) confusing이 정답이다. (D) confused는 '(사람이) 혼란스러워하는'이라는 뜻이므로 답이 될 수 없다.

번역 기자들은 전문 용어를 너무 많이 사용하는 것이 독자들에게 혼란스러울 수 있다는 것을 알아야 한다.

어휘 journalist 언론인, 기자   aware 알고 있는   technical 전문적인, 기술의   term 용어   confusion 혼란   confuse 혼란스럽게 만들다

7. (C) 현재분사
해설 빈칸은 be동사의 보어 자리로 주어인 명사를 수식하는 형용사(분사) 혹은 주어와 동격인 명사가 들어갈 수 있다. 문맥상 '해외 여행이 할 만한 가치가 있지만'이라는 의미가 되어야 자연스러우므로 '~할 만한 가치가 있는, 보람 있는'이라는 의미의 형용사(현재분사) (C) rewarding이 정답이다.

번역 해외 여행은 꽤 할 만한 가치가 있지만, 자국을 둘러보는 것도 많은 이점이 있다.

어휘 overseas 해외의; 해외에   benefit 이점, 혜택   explore 답사하다   reward 보상; 보상하다

8. (A) 과거분사
해설 빈칸은 명사구 quality assurance team을 앞에서 수식하는 자리이고, '공인 받은 품질 보증팀'이라는 의미가 되어야 자연스러우므로 '공인된'이라는 의미의 형용사(과거분사) (A) certified가 정답이다.

번역 당사의 모든 제품은 공인 받은 당사 품질 보증팀의 검사를 통과해야 한다.

9. (C) 과거분사

해설 빈칸은 명사 painter를 수식하는 자리이고, '기량이 뛰어난 화가'라는 의미가 되어야 자연스러우므로 '기량이 뛰어난'이라는 의미의 형용사(과거분사) (C) Accomplished가 정답이다.

번역 뛰어난 기량을 지닌 화가 프레드 오르테가가 자신이 어떻게 대중에게 자신의 미술 작품을 판매하는지에 대해 이야기할 것이다.

어휘 artwork 미술 작품 accomplish 성취하다
accomplishment 성취, 업적

10. (C) 현재분사

해설 빈칸 앞에 부사절 접속사 after가 있고 주어가 생략되어 있으므로 분사가 들어가야 하고, 빈칸 뒤에 명사구 the prototype를 목적어로 받아 '샘플을 테스트한 후에'라고 연결해야 자연스러우므로 능동 의미의 현재분사 (C) testing이 정답이다.

번역 베일리 씨는 샘플 테스트 후에 고객의 피드백에 기반하여 웹사이트 디자인을 약간 수정할 것이다.

어휘 minor 작은, 사소한 adjustment 수정 based on ~에 기반하여 prototype 견본, 시제품

11. (C) 과거분사

해설 빈칸은 명사 costs를 앞에서 수식하는 자리이고, '숨겨진(간접) 비용'이라는 의미가 되어야 자연스러우므로 수동 의미의 형용사(과거분사) (C) hidden이 정답이다.

번역 세금이나 보험료 같은 갖가지 간접 비용은 차량 렌트비를 급격히 증가시킬 수 있다.

어휘 a wide variety of 매우 다양한 insurance fee 보험료
sharply 급격히 hide 감추다, 숨기다

12. (C) 현재분사

해설 빈칸은 명사 popularity를 앞에서 수식하는 자리이고, '높아지는 인기'라는 의미가 되어야 자연스러우므로 '높아지는, 커지는'이라는 뜻의 형용사(현재분사) (C) growing이 정답이다.

번역 도시의 공원에 있는 자전거 도로 숫자가 증가한 이유는 건강을 위한 자전거 타기의 인기가 높아져서이다.

어휘 trail 루트, 코스 popularity 인기 fitness 건강, 체력 단련

13. (B) 과거분사

해설 빈칸은 명사 businesses를 앞에서 수식하는 자리이고, '확실히 자리를 잡은 기업들'이라는 의미가 되어야 자연스러우므로 '확실히 자리를 잡은, 인정받는'이라는 의미의 형용사(과거분사) (B) established가 정답이다.

번역 컨설턴트의 고용은 정착한 기업들이 약점을 파악하고 필요한 개선을 하도록 도울 수 있다.

어휘 consultant 상담사 identify 찾다, 발견하다 weak point 약점 improvement 개선, 향상 establish 설립하다 establishment 설립, 기관

14. (B) 감정분사

해설 빈칸은 and로 연결된 명사구 plot and characters를 앞에서 수식하는 자리이고, '흥미로운 줄거리와 인물들 덕분에'라는 의미가 되어야 자연스러우므로 '흥미로운'이라는 의미의 형용사(현재분사) (B) fascinating이 정답이다. (B) fascinated는 '매료된'이라는 뜻이므로 사물명사인 plot and characters를 수식하기에 의미상 적절하지 않다.

번역 흥미로운 줄거리와 인물들 덕분에 〈월드 저니〉는 모든 관객들에게 추천할 수 있는 영화이다.

어휘 character 등장인물 fascinate 마음을 사로잡다, 매혹시키다 fascination 매력, 매료됨

15. (C) 감정분사

해설 빈칸은 대명사 those를 뒤에서 수식하는 자리이고, '이 학교에 지원하는 데 관심 있는 사람들'이라는 의미가 되어야 자연스러우므로 '관심 있어 하는'이라는 의미의 형용사(과거분사) (C) interested가 정답이다. (B) interesting은 '흥미로운'이라는 의미로 사람들의 관심이나 흥미를 불러일으키는 원인이 되는 명사를 수식하므로 답이 될 수 없다.

번역 센트럴 경영 대학은 장차 이 학교에 지원하는 데 관심이 있는 사람들을 위해 설명회를 개최할 예정이다.

어휘 information session 설명회 apply to ~에 지원하다

16. (D) 현재분사

해설 빈칸은 명사 timeline을 뒤에서 수식하는 자리이고, 뒤의 명사구 famous inventions를 목적어로 받아 '유명한 발명품들을 보여주는 연대표'라는 내용이 되어야 자연스러우므로 능동 의미의 현재분사 (D) showing이 정답이다.

번역 디지털 기술 박물관에는 컴퓨터 공학계의 유명한 발명품들을 보여주는 연대표가 있다.

어휘 timeline 연대표 invention 발명품

17. (D) 현재분사

해설 빈칸은 뒤에 있는 명사구 friendly service and a comfortable atmosphere를 쉼표 뒤의 절에 연결해야 하므로 분사가 들어가면 된다. 빈칸 뒤의 명사구를 목적어로 받아 '친절한 서비스와 편안한 분위기를 제공하여'라고 자연스럽게 연결해 주는 능동 의미의 현재분사 (D) Offering이 정답이다.

번역 친절한 서비스와 편안한 분위기를 제공하는 달리아스 카페는 지역에서 인기 있는 모임 장소가 되었다.

어휘 friendly 친절한 comfortable 편안한 atmosphere 분위기 neighborhood 근처, 이웃 gathering 모임

18. (B) 분사구문 – 수동

해설 빈칸은 뒤에 있는 부사구 nearly 100 years ago를 쉼표

뒤의 절에 연결해야 하므로 분사나 to부정사가 들어갈 수 있다. 빈칸 뒤에 목적어가 보이지 않고, '거의 100년 전에 지어졌지만'이라는 내용이 되어야 자연스러우므로 수동 의미의 과거분사 (B) Built가 정답이다. (A) To build와 (C) Building은 둘 다 능동 형태이므로 뒤에 목적어가 있어야 하고, (A) To build는 '건설하기 위해서'라고 해석되므로 문맥에 어울리지 않는다.

번역 거의 100년 전에 지어졌지만, 로스포트 경기장은 여전히 중요한 스포츠 행사 장소로 쓰인다.

어휘 nearly 거의   venue (행사) 장소

19. (C) 과거분사

해설 help의 목적격 보어 역할로 쓰인 원형부정사(동사원형) stay 뒤에 빈칸이 있고, stay는 뒤에 보어로 형용사를 취해 특정 상태를 계속 유지함을 나타내는 동사이므로 '동기가 부여된, 자극 받은'이라는 뜻의 (C) motivated가 정답이다.

번역 자질 있는 개인 트레이너를 고용하면 체력 단련 목표에 도달하기 위한 동기 부여를 유지하는 데 도움이 될 것이다.

어휘 qualified 자질 있는   motivate 동기를 부여하다
motivation 동기 부여, 자극

20. (D) 감정분사

해설 빈칸은 to부정사 to keep의 목적격 보어 자리이므로 목적어 customers를 수식하는 형용사 또는 동격을 나타내는 명사가 들어갈 수 있다. '고객들이 서비스에 대해 만족하도록 하는 방법'이라는 의미가 되어야 자연스러우므로 '만족하는'이라는 의미의 형용사(과거분사) (D) satisfied가 정답이다. (B) satisfactory와 (C) satisfying은 '만족스러운'이라는 의미로 사람들로 하여금 만족을 느끼게 하는 원인이 되는 명사를 수식하므로 customers를 수식하는 말로 적절하지 않다.

번역 새로운 온라인 세미나 시리즈는 어떻게 하면 고객들이 귀사의 서비스에 만족하는지에 대한 조언을 제공한다.

어휘 satisfaction 만족   satisfactory 만족스러운   satisfy 만족시키다

●UNIT 08 전치사

출제 공식 1 CHECK UP 교재 p. 185

1. before   **2.** within   **3.** Until

1.   시점 전치사

해설 시점 명사에 해당하는 March 5가 있으므로 시점 전치사가 필요하다.

번역 지원자들은 이력서와 자기 소개서를 3월 5일 전에 제출해야 한다.

어휘 résumé 이력서   cover letter 자기 소개서

2.   기간 전치사

해설 기간 명사에 해당하는 48 hours가 있으므로 기간 전치사가 필요하다.

번역 온라인에서 한 모든 주문은 48시간 이내로 발송된다.

어휘 ship 발송하다

3.   시점 전치사

해설 시점 명사에 해당하는 August 31st가 있으므로 시점 전치사가 필요하다. 날짜 앞에 쓸 수 있는 전치사는 on이며, in은 연도와 월 앞에 놓인다.

번역 8월 31일까지 도서관이 공사로 인해 문을 닫습니다.

어휘 renovation 보수

출제 공식 2 CHECK UP 교재 p. 185

1. near   **2.** throughout   **3.** to

1.   장소 전치사

해설 장소 명사 앞에서 전치사 near는 '~ 근처에'를 뜻한다. next는 next to로 써야 정답이 될 수 있다.

번역 안내 데스크는 정문 가까이 위치해 있다.

어휘 entrance 출입구

2.   장소 전치사

해설 장소 명사 앞에서 전치사 throughout은 '전역에'를 뜻한다. past는 '~을 지나서'이므로 의미가 맞지 않다.

번역 우리는 유럽 전역에서 판매를 증가하고자 한다.

3.   방향 전치사

해설 direct가 방향성을 지니는 의미인 '보내다'로 쓰였으므로 방향 전치사 to가 필요하다.

번역 고객들은 모든 문의를 고객 서비스 부서로 보내야 한다.

어휘 direct A to B A를 B로 보내다   inquiry 문의

출제 공식 3 CHECK UP 교재 p. 186

1. except   **2.** as   **3.** through

1.   기타 전치사 – 제외

해설 every라는 범위가 주어지므로 범위에서 제외된다는 의미가 필요하다. except는 all, every, always, no, none과 같이 전체 범위를 나타내는 말과 자주 함께 쓰인다.

번역 그 휴양 시설은 월요일만 제외하고 매일 운영한다.

어휘 recreation 휴양   facility 시설

2. 기타 전치사 – 자격/기능

해설 자격이나 기능을 나타내는 전치사 as가 필요하다. between 뒤에 between A and B 구조가 아닌 단독 명사가 올 때는 복수형으로 써야 한다.

번역 그 소파는 침대로도 완벽하게 기능할 수 있다.

어휘 couch 소파   function as ~로 기능하다

3. 기타 전치사 – 수단

해설 경로나 수단을 나타내는 전치사 through가 필요하다.

번역 티켓 발권은 휴대폰 앱을 통해 가능하다.

출제 공식 4 CHECK UP
교재 p. 186

1. in   **2.** ahead of   **3.** upon

1. 전치사 관용 표현

해설 관용 표현은 in writing이다.

번역 모든 구매 신청은 서면으로 제출되어야 한다.

어휘 in writing 서면으로

2. 전치사 관용 표현

해설 관용 표현은 ahead of schedule이며 beforehand는 부사이므로 뒤에 명사와 함께 쓰지 않고 단독으로 써야 정답이 된다.

번역 도로 공사는 예정보다 일찍 마무리되었다.

어휘 beforehand 미리   ahead of schedule 예정보다 일찍

3. 전치사 관용 표현

해설 관용 표현은 upon receipt이다. as soon as는 접속사이므로 완전한 문장을 이끌어야 한다.

번역 소포를 받자마자 서명 확인이 요구된다.

어휘 confirmation 확인   upon receipt 받자마자   parcel 소포

ACTUAL TEST
교재 p. 188

1. (C)	**2.** (B)	**3.** (C)	**4.** (C)	**5.** (A)
6. (C)	**7.** (B)	**8.** (C)	**9.** (D)	**10.** (C)
11. (D)	**12.** (C)	**13.** (D)	**14.** (C)	**15.** (C)
16. (C)	**17.** (B)	**18.** (D)	**19.** (B)	**20.** (C)

1. (C) 전치사 – 이유

해설 빈칸은 명사구 heavy rain을 절(The autumn music festival was canceled)에 연결하는 전치사 자리이고, 문맥상 '폭우 때문에'라고 연결되어야 자연스러우므로 '~ 때문에'라는 의미의 전치사 (C) due to가 정답이다.

번역 가을 음악 축제는 지역 전체에 내리는 폭우로 인해 취소되었다.

어휘 cancel 취소하다   according ~에 따라서   consequently 그 결과, 따라서   as to ~에 관해서는

2. (B) 전치사 – 양보

해설 빈칸은 명사구 the rainy summer season을 쉼표 뒤의 절에 연결하는 전치사 자리이므로 선택지 중 유일한 전치사인 (B) In spite of(~에도 불구하고)가 정답이다. (A) As a result(결과적으로)와 (D) In contrast(그에 반해서)는 부사 표현이고, (C) Provided that(만약 ~라면)은 접속사이므로 명사를 연결할 수 없다.

번역 여름 장마 시즌에도 불구하고 해변 리조트 업계는 상당한 관광 수익을 발표했다.

어휘 revenue 수익

3. (C) 전치사 – 기타

해설 빈칸은 or로 연결된 명사구 age or hiking ability를 앞에 놓인 절(The City ~ to everyone)에 연결하는 전치사 자리이므로 선택지 중 유일한 전치사인 '~에 상관없이'라는 의미의 (C) regardless of가 정답이다.

번역 시립 자연 센터의 가이드 동반 자연 관찰 산책은 연령이나 하이킹 실력에 상관없이 모두에게 개방되어 있다.

어휘 accordingly 그에 맞춰, 그래서   in case ~한 경우에 대비하여   whereas ~인 반면에

4. (C) 전치사 – 기타

해설 명사 cash를 앞 절에 연결하기에 적절한 전치사 어휘를 고르는 문제이다. 문맥상 '구매를 위해 현금 대신 모바일 지불 앱을 사용한다'라는 내용이 되어야 자연스러우므로 '~ 대신에'라는 의미의 (C) instead of가 정답이다. (A) among은 '~ 중(사이)에'라는 의미로 뒤에 복수명사가 와야 하고, (B) unlike(~와 달리)와 (D) in the event of (~할 경우에는)는 모두 문맥에 어울리지 않으므로 답이 될 수 없다.

번역 점점 더 많은 소비자들이 구매하기 위해 현금보다 모바일 지불 애플리케이션을 사용하고 있다.

5. (A) 전치사 – 목적

해설 명사 a refund를 앞 절에 연결하기에 적절한 전치사 어휘를 고르는 문제이다. 빈칸 뒤의 명사 a refund(환불)는 물건을 반품하는 목적이므로 '~을 위해'라는 의미의 전치사 (A) for가 정답이다.

번역 만약 상품이 어떤 식으로든 파손되어 도착한다면 환불을 위해 반품할 수 있습니다.

6. (C) 전치사 – 기타

해설 빈칸은 명사 research를 절(a high percentage ~ university graduates)에 연결하는 전치사 자리이고, 문맥상 '연구에 따르면'이라는 내용이 되어야 연결이 자연스러우므로 '~에 따르면'이라는 뜻의 전치사 (C) According to가 정답이다. (A) Recent(최근의)는 형용사이므로 명사를 연결할 수 없고, (B) On behalf of(~을 대신하여)와

(D) Along with(~에 덧붙여, ~와 함께)는 전치사이지만 문맥에 어울리지 않으므로 답이 될 수 없다.

번역 연구에 따르면 높은 비율의 그린빌 거주자들이 최근 대학 졸업자들이다.

7. (B) 전치사 – 기타

해설 빈칸 뒤의 명사구 your merchandise를 문맥에 자연스럽게 연결할 수 있는 전치사를 고르는 문제이다. '상품의 배송'이라는 내용이 되어야 자연스러우므로 '~의'라는 의미의 전치사 (B) of가 정답이다.

번역 불완전하거나 부정확한 주소를 제공하는 것은 상품의 배송을 지연시킬 것이다.

8. (C) 전치사 – 시점

해설 빈칸은 명사구 the start를 앞의 절에 연결하는 전치사 자리이고, 문맥상 '근무 시작 전에'라고 해석되어야 연결이 자연스러우므로 '~ 전에'라는 뜻의 전치사 (C) prior to가 정답이다. (A) in that(~이므로)과 (D) as long as(~이기만 하면)는 접속사이고, (B) such as는 전치사이지만 '~와 같은'이라는 뜻으로 문맥상 어색하므로 답이 될 수 없다.

번역 직원들은 근무 시작 전에 새로 생긴 사내 피트니스 센터를 이용하여 운동하도록 권장된다.

어휘 encourage 권장하다 on-site 현장의 workday 평일. 근무 (시간) as long as ~이기만 하면

9. (D) 전치사 – 양보

해설 빈칸은 명사구 the rainy weather를 앞의 절에 연결하는 전치사 자리이고, '비가 오는 날씨에도 불구하고'라는 내용이 되어야 글의 흐름이 자연스러우므로 '~에도 불구하고'라는 의미의 전치사 (D) despite가 정답이다.

번역 시 미술 축제의 모든 자원봉사자들은 비가 오는 날씨에도 불구하고 행사 내내 의욕적이었다.

어휘 volunteer 자원봉사자 motivated 의욕적인. 동기가 부여된 throughout ~ 내내 even if ~에도 불구하고 regarding ~에 관하여

10. (C) 전치사 – 시점

해설 명사구 May 1를 문장의 흐름에 자연스럽게 연결할 수 있는 전치사 어휘를 고르는 문제이다. 글의 흐름상 '5월 1일까지'라는 내용이 되어야 적절하므로 '~까지'라는 뜻의 전치사 (A) until이나 (C) by가 답이 될 수 있다. 동사 must submit은 '제출해야 한다'라는 뜻으로 5월 1일까지 완료해야 할 일을 나타내므로 (C) by가 정답이다. (A) until은 특정 시점까지 계속되는 상태를 나타낼 때 쓰이므로 문맥에 어울리지 않는다.

번역 중앙 우체국에 고용되기 위해서는 모든 지원자들이 자신들의 이력서를 5월 1일까지 제출해야 한다.

11. (D) 전치사 – 기간

해설 명사구 three to four business days를 의미상 자연스럽게 연결할 수 있는 전치사 어휘를 고르는 문제이다. 문

맥상 '영업일 3~4일 이내에'라고 해석되어야 적절하므로 '~이내에'라는 의미의 전치사 (D) within이 정답이다.

번역 웹사이트에 달리 명시되지 않는다면, 모든 주문은 영업일 3~4일 이내 처리 및 발송된다.

12. (C) 전치사 – 분사형 전치사

해설 and로 연결된 명사구 boots and a rain jacket을 의미상 적절히 연결해 주는 전치사 어휘를 고르는 문제이다. 문맥상 '부츠와 비옷을 포함하여'라는 내용이 되어야 자연스러우므로 '~을 포함해서'라는 의미의 전치사 (C) including이 정답이다. (A) about(~에 대한)과 (B) as to(~에 관해서는), (D) notwithstanding(~에도 불구하고)은 의미상 연결이 어색하므로 답이 될 수 없다.

번역 트레킹 투어 참여자들은 하이킹을 위해 부츠와 비옷을 포함한 필요한 모든 장비를 가져와야 한다.

13. (D) 전치사 – 기타

해설 명사 people을 앞 절에 자연스럽게 연결하는 전치사 어휘를 선택하는 문제이다. 문맥상 '모든 연령의 사람들 사이에서'라는 내용이 되어야 자연스러우므로 '~ 사이에'라는 의미의 전치사 (D) among이 정답이다. (A) across from(~의 맞은편에)과 (B) along with(~에 덧붙여), (C) upon(~ 위에)은 문맥에 어울리지 않으므로 답이 될 수 없다.

번역 요가 수업은 모든 연령의 사람들 사이에서 큰 인기 상승을 계속해서 보여준다.

14. (C) 전치사 – 분사형 전치사

해설 빈칸은 명사구 proper completion을 앞의 절에 연결하는 전치사 자리이므로 접속사인 (B) how는 답이 될 수 없다. 문맥상 '올바른 납세 신고서 작성에 관한'이라고 해석되어야 연결이 자연스러우므로 '~에 관한(관련된)'이라는 의미의 전치사 (C) concerning이 정답이다.

번역 시 금융 사무소는 올바른 납세 신고서 작성에 관한 주민들의 질문에 답변하기 위한 상주 안내원을 보유하고 있다.

15. (C) 전치사 – 이유

해설 빈칸은 명사구 the forecast를 앞의 절에 연결하는 전치사 자리이므로 접속사인 (D) as soon as는 답이 될 수 없다. 문맥상 '악천후에 대한 예보 때문에'라는 내용이 되어야 연결이 자연스러우므로 '~ 때문에'라는 의미의 전치사 (C) because of가 정답이다.

번역 주최 측은 궂은 날씨 예보 때문에 금요일 퍼레이드를 연기하기로 했다.

16. (C) 전치사 – 시점

해설 빈칸은 명사구 the completion을 앞의 절에 연결하는 전치사 자리이고, 문맥상 '새로운 패션 구역의 완성 이후'라는 내용이 되어야 연결이 자연스럽다. 동사의 시제가 현재 완료(has increased)인 것으로 보아 '~ 이후('부터')라는 의미의 전치사 (C) since가 정답이다. (A) as a result(결과적으로)는 부사 표현이고, (B) even as(~하는 바로 그

순간에)는 접속사이므로 전치사 자리에 들어갈 수 없으며, (D) beyond(~ 너머)는 전치사이지만 문맥에 어울리지 않아 답이 될 수 없다.

번역 베일리 시로의 관광은 새로운 패션 구역의 완성 이후 눈에 띄게 증가해 왔다.

17. (B) 전치사 – 기타

해설 빈칸은 명사구 recent customer feedback을 쉼표 뒤의 절에 연결하는 전치사 자리이고, 문맥상 '최근 고객 피드백을 바탕으로'라는 내용이 되어야 연결이 자연스러우므로 '~에 근거하여'라는 의미의 전치사 (B) Based on이 정답이다. (A) Inside(~의 안에)는 문맥에 어울리지 않고, (C) Unless(~하지 않는 한)와 (D) Whereas(반면)는 접속사이므로 명사를 연결할 수 없다.

번역 최근 고객 피드백을 바탕으로 달라마트 식품 회사는 유기농 식품군을 늘리기로 결정했다.

18. (D) 전치사 – 첨가

해설 빈칸은 명사구 a souvenir photo를 앞의 절에 연결하는 전치사 자리이고, 문맥상 '기념 사진뿐 아니라'라는 내용이 되어야 자연스러우므로 '~뿐 아니라, ~에 더하여'라는 의미의 전치사 (D) in addition to가 정답이다. (A) within(~ 이내에)과 (C) in case of(~의 경우)는 문맥상 어울리지 않고, (B) as well은 '또한'이라는 의미의 부사 표현이므로 답이 될 수 없다.

번역 모든 듀바닉 레이크 보트 관광 가격은 기념 사진뿐 아니라 점심 식사와 간식을 포함하고 있다.

19. (B) 전치사 – 분사형 전치사

해설 빈칸은 완전한 절(The Lexton Model C ~ limited production) 뒤에 있으므로 동사인 (A) start와 (D) starts는 답이 될 수 없다. 분사형 전치사 starting이 들어가면 '11월부터(11월에 시작하여)'라는 의미로 앞의 절에 자연스럽게 연결되므로 (B) starting이 정답이다. '~부터'라는 의미로 쓰이는 관용 표현 「starting + 시간 표현」을 암기해 두면 편하다.

번역 렉스턴 모델 C 전기 자동차는 11월에 한정 생산을 시작한다.

어휘 electric car 전기 자동차   go into ~하기 시작하다

20. (C) 전치사 – 관용 표현

해설 명사구 further notice를 문맥에 자연스럽게 연결해 주는 전치사 어휘를 고르는 문제이다. 문맥상 '추후 공지 때까지'라는 내용이 되어야 자연스러우므로 '~까지'라는 의미의 (C) until이 정답이다.

번역 장맛비 때문에 저희 식당의 야외 테라스는 추후 공지가 있을 때까지 폐쇄합니다.

●UNIT 09 접속사

출제 공식 1   CHECK UP
교재 p. 191

1. Although   2. as soon as   3. if

1. 양보절 접속사

해설 문맥상 양보의 의미가 필요하다.

번역 콘서트는 무료이지만 좌석은 제한되어 있다.

어휘 seating 좌석

2. 시간절 접속사

해설 문맥상 시간적 의미가 필요하다.

번역 주주 회의는 모든 임원이 도착하자마자 시작될 것이다.

어휘 shareholder 주주   executive 임원

3. 조건절 접속사

해설 문맥상 조건의 의미가 필요하다.

번역 비거주자들은 미리 신청하면 행사에 참여할 수 있다.

어휘 resident 주민, 거주자   register 등록하다, 신청하다
in advance 미리

출제 공식 2   CHECK UP
교재 p. 191

1. While   2. although   3. Once

1. 시간절 접속사

해설 시간절을 이끄는 부사절 접속사가 필요하다.

번역 보수 작업이 진행되는 동안 직원들은 엘리베이터를 사용하지 못할 수도 있다.

어휘 underway 진행 중인

2. 양보절 접속사

해설 양보절을 이끄는 부사절 접속사가 필요하다.

번역 댈러스사에서는 비록 의무적이지는 않지만 직원들이 사내메일을 이용한다.

어휘 interoffice 사내의   mandatory 의무적인

3. 시간절 접속사

해설 시간절을 이끄는 부사절 접속사가 필요하다.

번역 우리가 반품된 물건을 수령하는 즉시, 품질 관리팀에서 그것을 점검할 것이다.

어휘 return 돌려주다, 반품하다   inspect 점검하다

1. When　**2.** since　**3.** Unless

1.　시간절 접속사
해설　문맥상 '기차에서 내린 이후로'보다 '기차에서 내릴 때'가 적절하다.

번역　기차에서 내릴 때 남겨 두는 물건이 없는지 확인하세요.

어휘　make sure 반드시 ~하도록 하다　leave behind 두고 가다

2.　시간절 접속사
해설　현재완료 시제와 어울리는 since가 적절하다. as는 주로 p.p.형 분사와 축약하여 쓴다.

번역　신규 소프트웨어를 사용한 이래로 사무실이 더 생산적으로 변했다.

어휘　productive 생산적인　adopt 쓰다. 채택하다

3.　조건절 접속사
해설　unless는 p.p.형 분사와 함께 주로 축약된다.

번역　달리 명시되지 않는다면 모든 재활용 쓰레기는 녹색 통에 수거되어야 한다.

어휘　unless otherwise 달리 ~되지 않는다면　recyclable 재활용할 수 있는　collect 수거하다

1. so　**2.** both　**3.** not only

1.　등위접속사
해설　앞뒤 문장이 인과 관계이므로 등위접속사 so가 적절하다.

번역　카일 씨가 처리해야 할 긴급한 문제가 있어서 우리는 회의 일정을 변경해야 한다.

어휘　urgent 긴급한　attend to ~을 처리하다　reschedule 일정을 변경하다

2.　상관접속사
해설　and가 있으므로 상관접속사 both A and B 구조가 적절하다.

번역　매장 구매나 온라인 구매 모두에 대해 특별 할인 요금이 이용 가능하다.

어휘　in-store 매장 내의

3.　상관접속사
해설　but also가 있으므로 상관접속사 not only A but also B 구조가 적절하다.

번역　그 수업은 초보뿐만 아니라 중급 학습자를 위한 것이기도 하다.

어휘　intermediate 중급의

1. (B)	**2.** (D)	**3.** (A)	**4.** (C)	**5.** (C)
6. (D)	**7.** (A)	**8.** (C)	**9.** (A)	**10.** (B)
11. (A)	**12.** (B)	**13.** (C)	**14.** (B)	**15.** (D)
16. (A)	**17.** (A)	**18.** (A)	**19.** (C)	**20.** (B)

1.　(B) 부사절 접속사 – 이유
해설　빈칸은 뒤의 절(a heavy snowstorm hit the area)을 앞의 절에 연결하는 접속사 자리이고, '눈보라가 그 지역을 강타했기 때문에'라는 내용이 되어야 문맥의 흐름상 자연스러우므로 '~ 때문에'라는 의미의 접속사 (B) since가 정답이다.

번역　거센 눈보라가 그 지역을 강타했기 때문에 작업자들이 프로젝트를 일시적으로 중단해야 했다.

어휘　temporarily 일시적으로　suspend 중단하다　snowstorm 눈보라

2.　(D) 부사절 접속사 – 양보
해설　빈칸은 뒤의 절(it was quite understaffed)을 앞의 절에 연결하는 접속사 자리이고, 문맥상 '인력이 부족했는데도 불구하고'라는 내용이 되어야 자연스럽게 연결되므로 '~에도 불구하고, ~이긴 하지만'이라는 뜻의 접속사 (D) even though가 정답이다.

번역　제작팀은 인력이 매우 부족했음에도 불구하고 지난달에 모든 마감 기한을 가까스로 맞췄다.

어휘　understaffed 인력이 부족한　as well as ~에 더하여. 게다가　despite ~에도 불구하고

3.　(A) 부사절 접속사 – 시간
해설　빈칸은 뒤의 절(the parade is over)을 앞의 절에 연결하는 접속사 자리이고, 문맥상 '퍼레이드가 끝날 때까지'라는 내용이 되어야 자연스럽게 연결되므로 '~까지'라는 의미의 접속사 (A) until이 정답이다. 참고로, (C) past는 '지나서'라는 의미의 전치사이고, (D) after all은 '결국에는'이라는 의미의 부사 표현이다.

번역　복잡한 교통 때문에 그 버스는 퍼레이드가 끝날 때까지 시 센터에 도착하지 않을 것이다.

4.　(C) 부사절 접속사의 축약
해설　빈칸은 뒤의 절(we receive your payment in full)을 앞의 절에 연결하는 접속사 자리이고, 문맥상 '귀하의 대금을 전액 수령하자마자'라는 내용이 되어야 연결이 자연스러우므로 '~하자마자'라는 의미의 접속사 (C) as soon as가 정답이다. (A) even if는 접속사이지만 문맥에 어울리지 않고, (B) according to는 '~에 따라'라는 뜻의 전치사이고, (D) during은 '~ 동안'이라는 뜻의 전치사이므로 답이 될 수 없다.

번역　고객님의 주문품은 저희가 고객님이 납입하신 대금을 전액 수령하는 즉시 처리됩니다.

PART 5

151

어휘 process 처리하다 in full 전부 even if ~에도 불구하고

5. (C) 상관접속사 – neither A nor B

해설 빈칸 뒤로 상관접속사 nor가 있는 것으로 보아 빈칸에는 neither가 들어가 '일반 대중뿐 아니라 평론가들도 이해하지 못하는 듯했다'라는 내용으로 연결되어야 자연스러우므로 (C) Neither가 정답이다.

번역 일반 대중뿐만 아니라 평론가들도 존 밀러가 감독한 최근 영화를 완전히 이해하지 못하는 듯했다.

어휘 thorough 완전한, 철저한 recent 최근의 direct 감독하다 each other 서로 none 아무도 ~ 않는

6. (D) 부사절 접속사 – 이유

해설 빈칸은 뒤의 절(the city is ~ this Friday)을 쉼표 뒤의 주절(parking ~ very limited)에 연결하는 접속사 자리이고, 문맥상 '시에서 연례 마라톤 경주를 개최하기 때문에'라는 내용이 되어야 연결이 자연스러우므로 '~ 때문에'라는 의미의 접속사 (D) Because가 정답이다. 참고로 (A) In order to는 뒤에 동사원형이 와야 하고, (C) Therefore는 '그러므로'라는 뜻의 부사이므로 절을 연결할 수 없다.

번역 시에서 이번 주 금요일에 연례 마라톤 경주를 개최하기 때문에, 시내에 주차하는 것은 많은 제약을 받을 것이다.

어휘 host 개최하다 annual 연례의 parking 주차 limited 제한된 in order to ~하기 위해서 so that ~하도록 therefore 그러므로

7. (A) 부사절 접속사 – 시간

해설 빈칸은 뒤의 절(your online membership ends)을 앞의 절(The password will become invalid)에 연결하는 접속사 자리이고, 문맥상 '일단 온라인 회원권이 종료되면'이라는 내용이 되어야 연결이 자연스러우므로 '일단 ~하고 나면'이라는 의미의 접속사 (A) once가 정답이다. (B) until은 '~까지'라는 의미의 접속사로 문맥상 어울리지 않고, (C) upon은 on과 같은 의미의 전치사이며, (D) rather는 '다소, 차라리'라는 의미의 부사이므로 절을 연결할 수 없다.

번역 일단 고객님의 온라인 회원권이 종료되고 나면 비밀번호는 무효가 될 것입니다.

어휘 invalid 효력 없는

8. (C) 부사절 접속사 – 조건

해설 빈칸은 뒤의 절(there are ~ available)을 앞의 절(We would take ~ center)에 연결하는 접속사 자리이고, 문맥상 '다른 교통 옵션이 있지 않는 경우에만'이라는 내용이 되어야 연결이 자연스러우므로 '~할 경우에만'이라는 의미의 접속사 (C) only if가 정답이다. (A) except for는 '~을 제외하고'라는 의미의 전치사이므로 절을 연결할 수 없고, (B) whereas(반면)와 (D) until(~까지)은 접속사이지만 의미가 어울리지 않으므로 답이 될 수 없다.

번역 우리는 이용 가능한 다른 교통 옵션이 있지 않는 경우에만 컨벤션 센터까지 택시를 탈 것이다.

9. (A) 등위 접속사 – 역접

해설 빈칸 앞뒤로 동사가 두 개(is attending, can answer) 있으므로 절도 두 개이다. 따라서 두 절을 연결할 수 있는 접속사가 필요하며, 문맥상 '최 씨는 파리 컨퍼런스에 참석 중이지만 이메일 문의에는 답할 수 있다'라는 내용이 되어야 연결이 자연스러우므로 '하지만'이라는 의미의 등위 접속사 (A) but이 정답이다. 참고로, 빈칸 뒤는 주어 Ms. Choi가 생략된 것으로 등위접속사는 뒤 절의 주어가 앞 절의 주어와 중복될 경우 생략할 수 있다.

번역 기술 회의의 조직자인 최 씨는 파리 회의에 참석 중이지만 이메일 문의에는 여전히 답할 수 있다.

어휘 inquiry 문의

10. (B) 등위 접속사 – 결과

해설 빈칸은 완전한 절(Oil paint dries ~ other types of paint) 뒤에 절(it is ~ novice artists)을 추가로 연결하는 접속사 자리이고, '유성 페인트는 천천히 마른다'라는 앞 절과 '초보 미술가들에게 이상적이다'라는 내용의 뒤 절은 인과 관계로 연결되어야 자연스러우므로 '그래서, 그러므로'라는 의미의 등위접속사 (B) so가 정답이다. (D) why는 명사절 접속사 또는 관계부사이므로 완전한 절에 절을 추가로 연결하는 자리에는 적절하지 못하다.

번역 유성 페인트는 다른 종류의 페인트들보다 훨씬 늦게 마르며, 따라서 초보 미술가에게는 이상적인 옵션이다.

어휘 novice 초보자

11. (A) 부사절 접속사 – 이유

해설 빈칸은 뒤의 절(we have ~ our newest products)을, 쉼표 뒤의 주절(we can ~ Web site)에 연결하는 접속사 자리이고, 문맥상 '최신 제품에 대한 디지털 사진이 있으므로'라고 연결되어야 자연스러우므로 '~이므로, ~이기 때문에'라는 의미의 접속사 (A) Now that이 정답이다.

번역 우리는 최신 제품에 대한 디지털 사진이 있기 때문에 드디어 우리 웹사이트에 그것들을 게시할 수 있다.

어휘 post 게시하다 in other words 즉 whereas 반면에

12. (B) 부사절 접속사 – 이유

해설 빈칸은 뒤의 절(the nearby theater ~ this evening)을 앞 절(The restaurant is busy today)에 연결하는 접속사 자리이고, 문맥상 '근처 극장에서 오늘 저녁 공연이 있기 때문에'라는 내용이 되어야 연결이 자연스러우므로 '~ 때문에'라는 의미의 접속사 (B) since가 정답이다.

번역 그 식당은 오늘 저녁에 인근 극장에서 공연이 있어서 오늘 바쁘다.

어휘 nearby 인근의; 인근에

13. (C) 부사절 접속사 – 조건

해설 빈칸은 뒤의 절(the customer is ~ original receipt)을 앞 절(The department store ~ on merchandise)에 연결하는 접속사 자리이고, 문맥상 '고객이 영수증 원본을 제시할 수 있으면'이라는 내용이 되어야 연결이 자연스러

우므로 '(만약) ~라면'이라는 의미의 접속사 (C) provided
가 정답이다.

번역 고객이 영수증 원본을 제시할 수 있어야만 백화점은 제품
에 대한 반품를 받아 준다.

어휘 return 반품   merchandise 상품   present 제시하다
in order that ~하기 위해

14. (B) 부사절 접속사 – 조건/부정

해설 빈칸은 뒤의 절(there is ~ a blizzard)을 쉼표 뒤의 주절
(the tour bus ~ at 8 A.M.)에 연결하는 접속사 자리이고,
문맥상 '극단적인 기상 상황만 아니라면'이라는 내용이 되
어야 연결이 자연스러우므로 '~이 아닌 한, ~하지 않는 한'
이라는 의미의 접속사 (B) Unless가 정답이다.

번역 눈보라 같은 기상 이변이 없는 한, 투어 버스는 오전 8시에
엘튼 역에서 출발할 것이다.

어휘 extreme 극도의   blizzard 눈보라   depart 출발하다
likewise 마찬가지로

15. (D) 부사절 접속사의 축약

해설 빈칸은 뒤에 나오는 과거분사(stated)를 앞 절(Employee
attendance ~ mandatory)에 연결하는 자리이고, 과
거분사를 연결해 '~된 대로'라는 의미로 쓰이는 관용 표현
「as+p.p.(과거분사)」의 as를 빈칸에 대입하면 '직원 지
침서에 언급된 대로'라고 자연스럽게 연결되므로 (D) as
가 정답이다. (A) regarding과 (C) apart from은 전치
사이므로 과거분사 stated를 연결하지 못하고, (B) even
though는 부사절 접속사로 과거분사를 연결할 수는 있지
만 의미가 어색하므로 답이 될 수 없다.

번역 직원들의 월례 부서 회의의 참석은 직원 지침서에 나와 있는
대로 의무적인 것이다.

어휘 attendance 참석   mandatory 의무적인   handbook
안내서   apart from ~ 외에는. ~ 외에도

16. (A) 부사절 접속사 – 목적

해설 빈칸은 뒤의 절(all parts can be equally protected)
을 앞 절(The furniture wax ~ entire surface)에 연결
하는 접속사 자리이고, 문맥상 '모든 부분이 동일하게 보호
될 수 있도록'이라는 내용이 되어야 연결이 자연스러우므로
'~하도록'이라는 의미의 접속사 (A) so that이 정답이다.

번역 가구 왁스는 모든 부분이 동일하게 보호될 수 있도록 전체
표면에 골고루 도포되어야 한다.

어휘 evenly 골고루   surface 표면

17. (A) 부사절 접속사 – 대조

해설 빈칸은 뒤의 절(others require reservations)을 앞 절
(Some of ~ first served basis)에 연결하는 접속사 자
리이고, 문맥상 '일부 캠핑장은 선착순으로 운영된다'라는
앞 절과 '다른 곳들은 예약이 필요하다'라는 뒤 절의 내용
이 서로 대조 관계이므로 '하지만, 반면'이라는 의미의 접
속사 (A) whereas가 정답이다.

번역 일부 지역 캠핑장들은 선착순으로 운영되지만, 다른 곳들
은 예약이 필요하다.

어휘 region 지역   operate 운영되다   on a first come,
first serve basis 선착순으로   reservation 예약   in
case ~인 경우에 대비해서   rather than ~보다는 오히려

18. (A) 부사절 접속사 – 조건

해설 빈칸은 뒤의 절(the items have ~ for delivery)을 앞 절
(Customers can change the shipping method)에
연결하는 접속사 자리이고, 문맥상 '상품이 배송을 위해 포
장되지 않은 상태이기만 하면'이라는 내용이 되어야 연결
이 자연스러우므로 '~이기만 하면, ~하는 한'이라는 의미
의 접속사 (A) as long as가 정답이다.

번역 상품이 아직 배송을 위해 포장되지 않은 상태이기만 하면,
고객들은 배송 방법을 변경할 수 있다.

어휘 shipping 운송. 배송   pack (짐을) 싸다. 포장하다

19. (C) 부사절 접속사 – 조건

해설 빈칸은 뒤의 절(we anticipate ~ an order)을 쉼표 뒤의
주절(we will notify ~ as soon as possible)에 연결하
는 접속사 자리이고, 문맥상 '만약 오랜 지연이 예상된다
면'이라는 내용이 되어야 연결이 자연스러우므로 '(만약) ~
하면'이라는 의미의 접속사 (C) If가 정답이다.

번역 만약 주문 처리가 매우 늦어질 것을 예상할 경우, 가능한
한 빨리 고객에게 알려 드릴 것입니다.

어휘 anticipate 예상하다   notify 알리다

20. (B) 부사절 접속사의 축약

해설 빈칸은 현재분사구 developing the prototype of
our new product를 쉼표 뒤의 절(a major problem
occurred)에 연결하는 자리이고, 문맥상 '신제품을 개발
하는 동안'이라고 해석되어야 연결이 자연스러우므로 '~하
는 동안'을 뜻하는 부사절 접속사 (B) While이 정답이다.

번역 우리의 신제품을 개발하는 동안 심각한 문제가 발생하였고
그것은 상당한 지체를 야기했다.

어휘 prototype 견본. 시제품   cause 야기하다
considerable 상당한

●UNIT 10 관계사

출제 공식 1 CHECK UP
교재 p. 197

1. who   **2.** whose   **3.** that

1. 주격 관계대명사

해설 선행사가 사람이고 동사 앞에 위치하므로 주격 관계대명사
who가 와야 한다.

번역 워크숍에 참석한 대부분의 참가자들은 그것이 도움이 된다
고 생각했다.

어휘 helpful 도움이 되는

2. 소유격 관계대명사

해설 선행사가 사람이고 명사 앞에 위치하므로 소유격 관계대명사 whose가 와야 한다. whom은 목적어가 빠진 문장 앞에 놓일 수 있다.

번역 본인의 그림이 전시 중인 피터 밀러는 자신의 미술 작품을 판매하는 데 동의했다.

어휘 on display 전시 중인　artwork 미술 작품

3. 목적격 관계대명사

해설 선행사가 사물이며 from의 목적어가 빠진 문장 앞에 위치하므로 목적격 관계대명사 that이 와야 한다. 이때 which도 정답이 될 수 있다.

번역 바우어 박사는 자신이 졸업한 대학에서 학생들을 가르치고 있다.

어휘 graduate from ~을 졸업하다

출제 공식 2　CHECK UP
교재 p. 197

1. distributed　2. we　3. searching

---

1. 「주격 관계대명사+be동사」의 생략

해설 문장의 동사는 are guaranteed이므로 빈칸에는 동사가 올 수 없다. 따라서 과거분사인 distributed가 와야 하며 which are가 생략된 형태로 볼 수 있다.

번역 라큐사에 의해 유통되는 유제품은 신선함이 보장된다.

어휘 dairy product 유제품　distribute 유통시키다, 배포하다
guarantee 보장하다

2. 목적격 관계대명사의 생략

해설 동사로 쓰인 discussed 앞에 주어가 빠져 있으므로 주어인 we가 와야 하며, contact와 we 사이에는 목적격 관계대명사 which 또는 that이 생략된 구조이다.

번역 쿠지 일렉트로닉스사는 우리가 지난주에 논의했던 계약에 서명하기로 합의했다.

어휘 sign a contract 계약에 서명하다, 계약을 맺다

3. 「주격 관계대명사+be동사」의 생략

해설 문장의 동사는 should refer이므로 빈칸은 동사가 올 수 없으며 '찾는 사람'을 뜻하므로 능동의 의미인 현재분사가 와야 한다. anyone 뒤에 who is가 생략된 형태로 볼 수 있다.

번역 글 쓰는 직업을 구하는 누구든지 이 웹사이트를 참조해야 한다.

어휘 search for 찾다　refer to 참조하다

출제 공식 3　CHECK UP
교재 p. 198

1. where　2. when　3. why

---

1. 관계부사 – 장소

해설 선행사가 장소이며 완전한 문장 앞에 위치하므로 관계부사 where가 와야 한다.

번역 예전에 공장이 있던 자리에 새 쇼핑몰이 지어졌다.

어휘 site 자리, 위치　located 위치한

2. 관계부사 – 시간

해설 선행사가 시간이며 완전한 문장 앞에 위치하므로 관계부사 when이 와야 한다.

번역 테일러 씨는 그의 고객들이 우리를 방문했던 시간에 출장 중이었다.

어휘 on a business trip 출장 중인

3. 관계부사 – 이유

해설 선행사가 the reason이므로 관계부사 why 자리이다.

번역 그 편지는 우리가 공동 작업을 요청하는 이유를 담고 있다.

어휘 collaboration 공동 작업, 협업

출제 공식 4　CHECK UP
교재 p. 198

1. which　2. how　3. which

---

1. 불완전한 절+관계대명사

해설 관계사절에 주어가 빠져 있으므로 주격 관계대명사 자리이다.

번역 그 강당은 지난달에 건설되었는데, 400명을 수용할 수 있다.

어휘 auditorium 강당　accommodate 수용하다

2. 완전한 절+관계부사

해설 완전한 절을 이어주므로 관계부사 자리이다.

번역 그 웹페이지는 귀하가 계정을 활성화하는 방법을 설명하고 있습니다.

어휘 activate 활성화하다　account 계정

3. 전치사+관계대명사

해설 선행사가 장소이며 완전한 문장 앞에 오므로 관계부사 where를 대신하는 in which가 와야 한다. operate는 자동사로 쓰였다.

번역 우리 회사는 사업을 운영 중인 32개국에 3만 명 이상의 직원을 보유하고 있다.

어휘 operate 영업하다, 사업하다

ACTUAL TEST

교재 p. 200

1. (A)	**2.** (B)	**3.** (D)	**4.** (C)	**5.** (B)
6. (C)	**7.** (D)	**8.** (C)	**9.** (D)	**10.** (C)
11. (C)	**12.** (C)	**13.** (A)	**14.** (B)	**15.** (C)
16. (B)	**17.** (C)	**18.** (B)	**19.** (B)	**20.** (B)

1. (A) 주격 관계대명사

해설 관계사절에 주어가 빠져 있으므로 주격 관계대명사가 들어가야 하고, 선행사인 Jeff Landers가 사람이므로 (A) who가 정답이다.

번역 제프 랜더즈 씨는 최근에 우리 직원 팀워크 강화 워크숍을 이끌었는데, 다음 달에 운영 부서로 옮겨간다.

어휘 teambuilding 팀워크 구축   transfer 이동하다. 전근 가다   operation 운영, 사업

2. (B) 주격 관계대명사

해설 관계사절에 주어가 빠져 있으므로 주격 관계대명사가 들어가야 하고, 선행사인 the best seating arrangement가 사물이므로 (B) which가 정답이다.

번역 이벤트 기획 회사는 우리 연회의 성공을 보장해줄 수 있는 최적의 좌석 배치를 선택할 것이다.

어휘 seating 좌석, 자리   arrangement 배열, 배치   ensure 보장하다   banquet 연회

3. (D) 주격 관계대명사

해설 관계사절에 주어가 빠져 있으므로 주격 관계대명사가 들어가야 하고, 선행사인 a reduced-fare subway pass가 사물이므로 (D) that이 정답이다.

번역 교통국에서는 대중교통 이용을 장려하기 위해 마련된 할인된 지하철 탑승권을 도입했다.

어휘 fare 교통 요금   promote 촉진하다   public transportation 대중교통

4. (C) 주격 관계대명사

해설 관계사절에 주어가 빠져 있으므로 주격 관계대명사가 들어가야 하고, 선행사인 The city's recycling program이 사물이므로 (C) which가 정답이다. (B) that은 콤마뒤에 쓰지 않으므로 오답이다.

번역 시의 재활용 프로그램은 지금까지는 성공적이며, 지금의 높은 참여율을 보일 것으로 예상된다.

어휘 recycling 재활용   success 성공한 것   current 현재의

5. (B) 소유격 관계대명사

해설 관계사절에 주어나 목적어가 빠지지 않았고, 선행사인 Robert Farmer와 tenure가 소유의 관계이므로 소유격 관계대명사 (B) whose가 정답이다.

번역 렉스코사의 신임 CEO는 로버트 파머 씨로, 그의 임기는 다음 주에 시작된다.

어휘 tenure 임기

6. (C) 주격 관계대명사

해설 관계사절에 주어가 빠져 있으므로 주격 관계대명사가 들어가야 하고, 선행사인 a compact travel umbrella가 사물이므로 (C) that이 정답이다.

번역 도나란딕 미니는 소형 여행용 우산으로 기내 반입용 가방 안에 쉽게 들어간다.

어휘 fit ~에 맞다   hand luggage 기내에 휴대할 수 있는 짐

7. (D) 소유격 관계대명사

해설 관계사절에 주어나 목적어가 빠지지 않았고, 선행사 volunteer organization과 members가 소유 관계이므로 소유격 관계대명사 (D) whose가 정답이다.

번역 그리니 클럽은 자원봉사 단체로 회원들은 자연과 관련 있는 여러 관심사를 추구한다.

어휘 volunteer 자원봉사자   organization 단체, 조직   pursue 추구하다   related to ~와 관련 있는

8. (C) 주격 관계대명사

해설 관계사절에 주어가 빠져 있으므로 주격 관계대명사가 들어가야 하고 선행사인 a steep route가 사물이므로 (C) that이 정답이다.

번역 카트만 산악 공원에 있는 블루 트레일은 노련한 하이킹족들에게도 힘든 도전이 될 가파른 코스다.

어휘 steep 가파른   challenge 도전하다   experienced 경험 있는, 노련한

9. (D) 주격 관계대명사

해설 관계사절에 주어가 빠져 있으므로 주격 관계대명사가 들어가야 하고 선행사인 homes가 사물이므로 (D) that이 정답이다.

번역 판매 자료에 따르면, 전문 조경을 한 주택은 재판매 가치가 최대 10퍼센트 더 높아질 수 있다.

어휘 professionally 전문적으로   landscape 조경을 하다   resale 재판매

10. (C) 주격 관계대명사

해설 관계사절에 주어가 빠져 있으므로 주격 관계대명사가 들어가야 하고 선행사인 a package tracking system이 사물이므로 (C) which가 정답이다.

번역 샘슨 익스프레스사는 택배 추적 시스템을 갖추고 있어서 온라인에서 배송 과정을 찾아 볼 수 있다.

어휘 track 추적하다   progress 과정   shipment 운송, 운송품

11. (C) 주격 관계대명사

해설 관계사절에 주어가 빠져 있으므로 주격 관계대명사가 들어가야 하고 선행사인 complementary products가 사물이므로 (C) that이 정답이다.

번역 컴퓨터 하드웨어와 컴퓨터 소프트웨어는 보통 같은 가게에서 판매되는 상호 보완적인 제품들이다.

어휘 complementary 상호 보완적인   typically 보통, 일반적으로

12. (C) 수량표현 + 관계대명사

해설 앞에 수량 표현인 some of가 있으므로 빈칸은 전치사 of
의 목적어 역할을 하는 목적격 관계대명사가 들어가야 하
고 선행사인 sculptures가 사물이므로 (C) which가 정
답이다.

번역 특별 전시에는 진귀한 조각품들이 선보이는데, 그것들 중
일부는 이 박물관에서 한 번도 전시된 적이 없었다.

어휘 exhibit 전시   feature ~을 특별히 포함하다   rare 진귀한.
드문   sculpture 조각품

13. (A) 주격 관계대명사

해설 관계사절에 주어가 빠져 있으므로 주격 관계대명사가 들
어가야 하고 선행사인 a special banquet이 사물이므로
(A) which가 정답이다.

번역 3월 27일에 우리 회사 창립 20주년을 기념하는 특별 연회
가 열릴 예정이다.

어휘 mark 기념하다   founding 창립. 설립

14. (B) 소유격 관계대명사

해설 관계사절에 주어나 목적어가 빠지지 않았고, 선행사인
members와 membership이 소유 관계이므로 소유격
관계대명사 (B) whose가 정답이다.

번역 윙 씨가 맡은 주요 업무는 멤버십이 조만간 만료되는 회원
들에게 갱신 편지를 보내는 것이다.

어휘 responsibility 책임. 책무   renewal 갱신   expire
만료되다

15. (C) 목적격 관계대명사

해설 빈칸에 들어갈 관계사는 앞에 있는 전치사 through의 목
적어 역할을 하고, 선행사인 a staff blog가 사물이므로
목적격 관계대명사 (C) which가 정답이다.

번역 회사는 최근에 직원 블로그를 개시했는데, 이를 통해 직원
들은 다른 사람들과 자신들의 업무 경험을 공유할 수 있다.

16. (B) 주격 관계대명사

해설 관계사절에 주어가 빠져 있으므로 주격 관계대명사가 들어
가야 하고, 선행사인 The X-Through display case가
사물이므로 (B) which가 정답이다.

번역 뛰어난 제품 가시성을 보장하는 X-쓰루 진열장이 한정된
기간 동안 할인 판매될 예정이다.

어휘 display case 진열장   visibility 가시성   limited 한정된

17. (C) 주격 관계대명사

해설 빈칸은 명사구 210 small parts를 뒤에서 수식하는 절
(require special tools to produce)을 연결하는 관계
사 자리이다. 관계사절에 주어가 빠져 있으므로 주격 관계
대명사가 들어가야 하고, 선행사인 210 small parts가
사물이므로 (C)가 정답이다.

번역 고품질의 롤로코니 손목시계는 각각에 210개의 작은 부품
들이 들어 있으며, 이것들은 생산하는 데 특별한 도구를 필

요로 한다.

어휘 high quality 고품질의   part 부품   tool 도구

18. (B) 관계부사

해설 장소 명사를 선행사로 가지며 완전한 절이 뒤따르므로 관
계부사 (B) where이 정답이다.

번역 DMI사 직원들은 교통이 좋지 않은 교외로 통근해야 한다.

어휘 commute 통근하다   suburb 교외   unfavorable 좋지
않은

19. (B) 소유격 관계대명사

해설 관계사절에 주어나 목적어가 빠지지 않았고 선행사인 Ms.
Janssen과 design concept가 소유 관계이므로 소유
격 관계대명사 (B) whose가 정답이다.

번역 얀센 씨는 그녀의 디자인 콘셉트가 새로운 로고에 사용되
었는데, 매력적인 이미지와 그래픽을 창안해 내는 것으로
유명하다.

어휘 be known for ~로 알려져 있다   appealing 매력적인.
관심을 끄는

20. (B) 수량표현 + 관계대명사

해설 앞에 수량 표현인 many of가 있으므로 빈칸은 전치사 of
의 목적어 역할을 하는 목적격 관계대명사가 들어가야 하
고 선행사인 university students가 사람이므로 (B)
whom이 정답이다.

번역 설문 조사 참가자들은 대학생들이었는데, 그들 중 다수는
전에 이와 유사한 활동에 참여한 적이 없었다.

어휘 be engaged in ~에 관여하다. 참여하다

●UNIT 11 명사절 접속사

출제 공식 1 CHECK UP   교재 p. 203

1. that   **2.** that   **3.** that

1.   명사절 접속사 that

해설 indicates의 목적어 자리로 명사절 접속사가 필요하다.

번역 한 조사는 재택 근무가 직원 생산성을 늘릴 수 있다고 나타
낸다.

어휘 indicate 나타내다   productivity 생산성

2.   명사절 접속사 that

해설 announced의 목적어 자리로 명사절 접속사가 필요하다.
what은 완전한 문장을 이끌지 않는다.

번역 켄택사는 자사의 X-시리즈 노트북 컴퓨터 전제품을 회수할
것이라고 발표했다.

어휘 recall 제품을 회수하다

3. **명사절 접속사 that**

해설 be동사 is의 보어 자리로 명사절 접속사가 필요하다. how 는 문맥상 어울리지 않는다.

번역 최근 수세늘 또번 많은 사람들이 선사색을 읽는 것을 선택 한다.

어휘 trend 추세

출제 공식 2 CHECK UP
교재 p. 203

1. whether **2.** whether **3.** if

1. **명사절 접속사 whether**

해설 know의 목적어 자리로 명사절 접속사가 필요하다. or가 있으므로 whether A or B 형태가 어울린다.

번역 올 수 있는지 없는지 우리에게 알려 주세요.

2. **명사절 접속사 whether**

해설 전치사 about의 목적어 자리로 명사절 접속사가 필요하다.

번역 회의는 우리가 아시아 시장으로 사업을 확장해야 하는지 여부에 관한 것이었다.

어휘 expand 확장하다

3. **명사절 접속사 if**

해설 asked의 목적어 자리로 명사절 접속사가 필요하다.

번역 행사 관리자는 시청각 장비가 사용될 것인지 물었다.

어휘 coordinator 진행자, 관리자 audio-visual 시청각의 equipment 장비

출제 공식 3 CHECK UP
교재 p. 204

1. what **2.** how **3.** what

1. **명사절 접속사 what**

해설 find out의 목적어 자리로 명사절 접속사가 필요하며 불완 전한 문장을 이끌고 있으므로 what이 와야 한다.

번역 편집자는 초고에 무엇이 잘못되었는지를 알아내려고 애쓰 고 있었다.

어휘 struggle 분투하다, 애쓰다 first draft 초고

2. **명사절 접속사 how**

해설 explained의 목적어 자리로 명사절 접속사가 필요하며 완전한 문장을 이끌고 있으므로 how가 와야 한다.

번역 건축가는 그 공간을 어떻게 업그레이드할지 설명했다.

어휘 architect 건축가

3. **명사절 접속사 what**

해설 해석상 '다음 단계가 무엇인지'라는 의미가 필요하므로 what이 정답이다.

번역 카토 씨는 문제를 처리하는 데 있어서 다음 단계가 무엇인 지 알고 있다.

어휘 address 다루다, 처리하다

출제 공식 4 CHECK UP
교재 p. 204

1. whatever **2.** whichever **3.** Whoever

1. **명사절 접속사 whatever**

해설 전치사 on의 목적어 자리로 명사절 접속사가 필요하다. whenever는 부사절 접속사로 쓰인다.

번역 설문 조사 참가자들은 자신들이 걱정하는 무엇이든지에 대 해 의견을 말할 수 있다.

어휘 be concerned about ~에 대해 걱정하다

2. **명사절 접속사 whichever**

해설 choose의 목적어 자리로 명사절 접속사가 필요하 며 prefer의 목적어가 빠진 불완전한 문장을 이끄므로 whichever가 와야 한다.

번역 두 손목시계 다 우수하므로, 선호하는 어느 것이든 고르면 된다.

3. **명사절 접속사 whoever**

해설 문장의 주어 자리이므로 명사절 접속사가 필요하며 주어가 빠진 불완전한 문장을 이끄므로 Whoever가 와야 한다.

번역 초과 근무를 원하는 누구든지 그렇게 하라는 승인을 받아 야 한다.

어휘 obtain 얻다 permission 승인, 허락

ACTUAL TEST
교재 p. 206

1. (D)	**2.** (B)	**3.** (D)	**4.** (D)	**5.** (B)
6. (B)	**7.** (B)	**8.** (A)	**9.** (B)	**10.** (C)
11. (A)	**12.** (D)	**13.** (B)	**14.** (C)	**15.** (B)
16. (B)	**17.** (C)	**18.** (D)	**19.** (C)	**20.** (A)

1. **(D) 명사절 접속사 that**

해설 동사 found의 목적어 자리에 빈칸이 있고, 그 뒤로 절 (part-time workers are ~ career progression)이 있 으므로 명사 자리에 절을 연결하는 명사절 접속사 자리이 다. 빈칸 뒤의 절이 완전한 절이고, '시간제 근로자들이 승 진 기회를 잡을 가능성이 더 적은 것'이라는 내용이 되어야 자연스러우므로 (D) that이 정답이다.

번역 조사에서 시간제 근로자들은 승진 기회를 잡을 가능성이 더 적은 것으로 나타났다.

어휘 be less likely to *do* ~할 가능성이 더 적다 career progression 승진

2. (B) 명사절 접속사 whoever

해설 동사 will need의 주어 자리에 동사 is chosen이 있으므로 명사 자리에 절을 연결하는 명사절 접속사가 필요하다. 빈칸 뒤의 명사절에 주어가 빠져 있고, '기획 위원회를 이끌도록 선정된 사람은 누구든지'라는 내용이 되어야 자연스러우므로 (B) Whoever가 정답이다.

번역 기획 위원회를 이끌도록 선정된 사람은 누구든지 월례 회의의 의제를 만들어 내야 할 것이다.

어휘 agenda 의제   monthly 월례의

3. (D) 명사절 접속사 whatever

해설 동사 can provide의 목적어 자리에 빈칸이 있고, 그 뒤로 절(you are looking ~ fashion needs)이 있으므로 명사 자리에 절을 연결하는 명사절 접속사 자리이다. 빈칸 뒤의 절에 전치사 for의 목적어가 빠져 있고, '당신이 찾는 무엇이든'이라는 내용이 되어야 자연스러우므로 (D) whatever가 정답이다.

번역 덱스트론 의류 매장은 여러분의 패션 요구에 맞도록 찾으시는 무엇이든 제공해 드릴 수 있습니다.

어휘 match (요구에) 맞추다, 부응하다

4. (D) 명사절 접속사 how

해설 빈칸은 전치사 on의 목적어 자리이고, 뒤로 절(we can strengthen ~ coming years)이 있으므로 명사 자리에 절을 연결하는 명사절 접속사 자리이다. 빈칸 뒤의 절이 완전한 절이고, '어떻게 우리가 국제 무역을 강화할 수 있는지'라는 내용이 되어야 자연스러우므로 (D) how가 정답이다.

번역 회의는 향후 몇 년간 어떻게 우리가 국제 무역을 강화할 수 있는지에 초점을 둘 것이다.

어휘 focus on ~에 초점을 두다   strengthen 강화하다

5. (B) 명사절 접속사 that

해설 빈칸은 동사 has promised의 목적어 자리이고, 뒤로 절(they will provide ~ library system)이 있으므로 명사 자리에 절을 연결하는 명사절 접속사 자리이다. 빈칸 뒤의 절이 완전한 절이고, '그들(무어 재단)이 자금을 제공할 것을'이라는 내용이 되어야 자연스러우므로 (B) that이 정답이다.

번역 무어 재단은 시의 공공 도서관 시스템의 요구사항을 충족시키기 위해 자금을 제공할 것을 약속했다.

어휘 meet a need 요구를 충족시키다

6. (B) 명사절 접속사 whether

해설 빈칸은 to부정사 to determine의 목적어 자리이고, 뒤로 절(there is ~ bus service)이 있으므로 명사 자리에 절을 연결하는 명사절 접속사 자리이다. 빈칸 뒤의 절이 완전한 절이고, '충분한 수요가 있는지 아닌지를'이라는 내용이 되어야 자연스러우므로 (B) whether가 정답이다. (A) whatever는 명사절 접속사이지만 뒤에 명사가 하나 빠진 불완전한 절이 와야 하고, (C) however와 (D)

whenever는 부사절 접속사이므로 답이 될 수 없다.

번역 심야 버스 운행에 대한 수요가 충분한지 여부를 알아내기 위해서 설문 조사가 시행될 것이다.

어휘 conduct 실시하다   determine 알아내다   demand 수요

7. (B) 명사절 접속사 that

해설 빈칸은 be동사 is의 보어 자리이고, 빈칸 뒤로 절(it has ~ per charge)이 있으므로 명사 자리에 절을 연결하는 명사절 접속사 자리이다. 빈칸 뒤의 절이 완전한 절이고, '한 번 충전으로 배터리 수명이 12시간 지속된다는 것'이라는 내용이 되어야 자연스러우므로 (B) that이 정답이다.

번역 마든 X10 스마트폰의 독보적인 특징은 한 번 충전으로 배터리 수명이 12시간 지속된다는 것이다.

어휘 unique 독특한, 고유의   feature 특징   charge 충전

8. (A) 명사절 접속사 that

해설 빈칸은 가주어 It의 진주어 자리이고, 뒤에 절(computer users save ~ system failure)이 있으므로 명사 자리에 절을 연결하는 명사절 접속사가 들어가야 한다. 빈칸 뒤의 절이 완전한 절이고 '컴퓨터 사용자들이 문서를 자주 저장해야 한다는 것이 권고된다'라는 내용이 되어야 자연스러우므로 (A) that이 정답이다.

번역 컴퓨터 사용자들은 예기치 않은 시스템 오류를 피하기 위해 문서를 자주 저장하도록 권장된다.

어휘 frequently 자주   unexpected 예기치 않은   failure 고장

9. (B) 명사절 접속사 who

해설 동사 has의 주어 자리에 동사 will lead가 있으므로 명사 자리에 절을 연결하는 명사절 접속사가 필요하다. 빈칸 뒤의 명사절에 주어가 빠져 있고, '누가 품질 관리 교육을 이끌지'라는 내용이 되어야 자연스러우므로 (B) Who가 정답이다.

번역 누가 품질 관리 교육을 이끌지는 아직 결정되지 않았다.

어휘 have yet to do 아직 ~하지 않았다

10. (C) 명사절 접속사 how

해설 빈칸은 동명사 주어 Knowing의 목적어 자리이고, 뒤에 to부정사구 to encourage teamwork가 있으므로 명사 자리에 to부정사구를 연결하는 명사절 접속사 자리이다. 참고로, 명사절에서 주어가 생략될 경우 동사는 to부정사로 바뀌어 「명사절 접속사+to부정사구」로 축약될 수 있다. to encourage 뒤에 목적어인 teamwork가 있으므로 to부정사구에 빠진 명사가 없고, '어떻게 팀워크를 장려할지'라는 내용이 되어야 자연스러우므로 (C) how가 정답이다. (B) if와 (D) that은 뒤에 「주어+동사」로 이루어진 완전한 절이 와야 하고 to부정사구를 연결할 수 없다.

번역 팀워크를 독려하는 방법을 아는 것은 모든 관리자들에게 중요한 업무 능력이다.

어휘 supervisor 관리자, 감독

11. (A) 명사절 접속사 where

해설 동사 depends의 주어 자리에 주어(we)와 동사(will hold)가 있으므로 명사 자리에 절을 연결하는 명사절 접속사가 필요하다. 빈칸 뒤의 절이 완전한 절이고, '우리가 연례 연회를 어디서 개최할 지'라는 내용이 되어야 자연스러우므로 (A) Where가 정답이다. (B) What과 (C) Which는 뒤에 명사가 빠진 불완전한 절이 와야 하고, (D) Whenever는 부사절 접속사이므로 답이 될 수 없다.

번역 우리가 연례 연회를 어디서 개최할지는 그 공간을 이용할 수 있는지 여부와 아울러 참석자 수에 달려 있다.

어휘 depend on ~에 달려 있다 availability 이용 가능성

12. (D) 명사절 접속사 whether

해설 빈칸은 동사 will help의 목적격 보어 역할로 쓰인 원형부정사(동사원형) determine의 목적어 자리이고, 뒤에 절(we should continue ~ hair driers)이 있으므로 명사 자리에 절을 연결하는 명사절 접속사가 필요하다. 빈칸 뒤의 절이 완전한 절이고, '우리가 헤어 드라이어 생산을 계속할지 아닌지를'이라는 내용이 되어야 자연스러우므로 (D) whether가 정답이다. (A) whatever와 (B) whichever는 뒤에 명사가 빠진 불완전한 절이 와야 하고, (C) wherever는 부사절 접속사이므로 답이 될 수 없다.

번역 설문 조사를 통해 우리는 우리 휴고 시리즈 무선 헤어 드라이어 생산을 계속할지 여부를 결정할 수 있을 것이다.

어휘 determine 결정하다 wireless 무선의

13. (B) 명사절 접속사 that

해설 빈칸 앞에 「be동사+unaware」가 있고 뒤에 완전한 절(there are ~ the beach)이 있으므로 빈칸에는 명사절 접속사가 들어가야 하며, unaware는 that절을 취하는 형용사 이므로 (B) that이 정답이다.

번역 관광객들은 몬티첼로 섬에서 해변에 가는 것 외에도 할 일이 많다는 것을 모르는 경우가 많다.

어휘 unaware ~을 알지 못하는 besides ~ 외에

14. (C) 명사절 접속사 what

해설 빈칸은 전치사 on의 목적어 자리이고, 뒤에 동사 sets가 있는 것으로 보아 절이 있으므로 명사 자리에 절을 연결해 주는 명사절 접속사가 필요하다. 빈칸 뒤의 절이 동사 sets 앞에 주어가 빠진 불완전한 절이고, '우리 회사를 경쟁 업체들과 차별화하는 것이 무엇인지'라는 내용이 되어야 자연스러우므로 (C) what이 정답이다.

번역 새로운 광고 전략은 우리 회사를 경쟁 업체들과 차별화하는 것이 무엇인지에 초점을 둘 것이다.

어휘 advertising 광고 set A apart from B A를 B와 차별화하다 competition 경쟁, 경쟁자

15. (B) 명사절 접속사 that

해설 빈칸은 동사 explained의 목적어 자리이고, 뒤에 절(the dark stains ~ floor above)이 있으므로 명사 자리에 절을 연결하는 명사절 접속사 자리이다. 빈칸 뒤의 절이 완전한 절이고, '천장의 검은 얼룩은 누수를 나타내는 것'이라는 내용이 되어야 자연스러우므로 (B) that이 정답이다.

번역 배관공은 천장의 검은 얼룩이 위층 바닥의 누수를 나타내는 것이라고 설명했다.

어휘 plumber 배관공 stain 얼룩 ceiling 천장 indicative of ~을 나타내는 leakage 누출

16. (B) 명사절 접속사 how

해설 빈칸은 4형식 동사 show의 직접목적어 자리이고, 뒤에 to부정사구가 있으므로 명사 자리에 to부정사구를 연결해 주는 명사절 접속사 자리이다. to merge 뒤로 목적어가 있으므로 명사가 빠지지 않았고, '어떻게 여러 워드 프로세서 문서들을 하나로 합치는지를'이라는 내용이 되어야 자연스러우므로 (B) how가 정답이다. (A) that은 뒤에 「주어+동사」로 이루어진 완전한 절이 와야 하고 to부정사구를 연결할 수 없다.

번역 사용 지침서 영상은 컴퓨터 사용자들에게 몇 개의 워드 프로세서 문서들을 하나로 합치는 방법을 알려 줄 것이다.

어휘 tutorial 사용 지침서 merge 합치다

17. (C) 명사절 접속사 that

해설 빈칸은 동사 should note의 목적어 자리이고, 뒤에 절(items from multiple orders ~ single package)이 있으므로 명사 자리에 절을 연결하는 명사절 접속사 자리이다. 빈칸 뒤의 절이 완전한 절이고, '복수 주문의 경우 상품이 합쳐져서 하나의 포장으로 배송된다는 점'이라는 내용이 되어야 자연스러우므로 (C) that이 정답이다. (B) which는 뒤에 불완전한 절이 와야 하고, (A) whenever와 (D) however는 부사절 접속사이므로 답이 될 수 없다.

번역 복수 주문의 경우 상품이 합쳐져서 하나의 포장에 담겨 배송된다는 점을 고객들에게 알립니다.

어휘 multiple 많은, 다수의 combine 결합하다

18. (D) 명사절 접속사 how

해설 빈칸은 동사 revealed의 목적어 자리이고, 뒤로 절(she finds inspiration for her writing)이 있으므로 명사 자리에 절을 연결하는 명사절 접속사가 필요하다. 빈칸 뒤의 절이 완전한 절이고, '어떻게 작품에 대한 영감을 얻는지'라는 내용이 되어야 자연스러우므로 (D) how가 정답이다.

번역 〈북스 앤 페이지스 매거진〉과의 최근 인터뷰에서 작가 아만다 웰러는 자신이 어떻게 작품에 대한 영감을 발견하는지에 대해 밝혔다.

어휘 reveal 밝히다 inspiration 영감

19. (C) 명사절 접속사 that

해설 빈칸 앞에 「be동사+disappointed」가 있고, 뒤에 완전한 절이 있으므로 명사절 접속사 that이 들어가야 '긍정적인 피드백을 많이 받지 못해 실망했다'라는 내용으로 자연스럽게 연결될 수 있다. 따라서 (C) that이 성답이다. 참고로 감정을 나타내는 형용사와 함께 that절이 자주 쓰인다.

번역 연구 개발팀은 제품 시험 사용자들로부터 긍정적인 피드백을 많이 받지 못해서 실망했다.

어휘 disappointed 실망한   positive 긍정적인

20. (A) 명사절 접속사 which

해설 빈칸은 동사구 cannot decide의 목적어 자리이고, to부정사구를 연결하는 명사절 접속사이면서 동시에 '어떤, 어느'라는 형용사 역할로 명사 tables를 자연스럽게 연결할 수 있어야 하므로 (A) which가 정답이다. (B) why와 (C) how는 빈칸 뒤의 명사 tables를 연결할 수 없고, (D) if는 뒤에 「주어＋동사」로 이루어진 완전한 절이 와야 하며 to부정사구를 연결할 수 없다.

번역 한나스 카페는 예약을 받기는 하지만, 손님들은 어느 테이블에 앉을지는 결정하지 못한다.

어휘 reservation 예약   occupy 차지하다

●UNIT 12 비교/가정법/도치

출제 공식 1 CHECK UP
교재 p. 209

1. more efficiently   **2.** much   **3.** more flexible

1. 비교급 – 부사 자리

해설 동사 can process를 수식하는 자리이므로 부사가 필요하다. 비교 대상이 언급되지 않을 때는 than을 쓰지 않아도 된다.

번역 저희가 고객님의 문의 사항을 더 효율적으로 처리할 수 있도록 조회 번호를 이용해주세요.

어휘 reference 조회, 참조   process 처리하다

2. 비교급 수식 부사

해설 비교급인 larger를 수식하므로 비교급 수식 부사가 와야 한다. very는 원급 또는 최상급을 수식한다.

번역 실버스톤 경기장은 시에 있는 다른 어떤 경기장보다 훨씬 더 크다.

어휘 stadium 경기장

3. 비교급 수식 부사＋비교급

해설 비교급 수식 부사 much가 있으므로 비교급을 써야 한다.

번역 새로운 고무 파이프는 신축성이 훨씬 더 뛰어나다.

어휘 rubber pipe 고무 파이프   flexible 신축성 있는, 유연한

출제 공식 2 CHECK UP
교재 p. 209

1. most frequently   **2.** promptly   **3.** Even

1. 최상급 – 부사 자리

해설 동사 are asked를 수식하므로 부사가 와야 한다.

번역 가장 자주 문의되는 질문들 목록이 있다.

어휘 frequent 빈번한   frequently 빈번하게, 자주

2. 원급 – 부사 자리

해설 원급 비교 as ~ as 사이에는 형용사나 부사가 올 수 있는데 동사 send를 수식하는 자리이므로 부사가 와야 한다.

번역 가능한 한 빨리 우리에게 견적서를 보내 주세요.

어휘 estimate 견적서   prompt 신속한   promptly 신속하게

3. 최상급 수식 부사

해설 최상급인 the most complex를 수식하며 최상급보다 앞에 위치하므로 Even이 와야 한다.

번역 최신 기술 덕분에 가장 복잡한 업무조차도 간단해졌다.

어휘 complex 복잡한   latest 최신의

출제 공식 3 CHECK UP
교재 p. 210

1. would   **2.** should   **3.** had received

1. 가정법 과거

해설 if절의 시제가 과거이므로 「would＋동사원형」을 써야 한다.

번역 우리 팀에게 시간이 더 있다면, 우리는 더 나은 결과를 낼 것이다.

어휘 come up with ~을 찾아내다, 내놓다   outcome 결과

2. 가정법 미래

해설 주절의 시제가 미래이므로 if절에는 should를 써야 미래를 나타낼 수 있다.

번역 주문을 취소하더라도 예약금은 환불되지 않습니다.

어휘 deposit 예약금, 보증금

3. 가정법 과거완료

해설 주절의 시제가 would have p.p.이므로 if절에는 과거완료를 써야 한다.

번역 보조금을 받았더라면, 우리 프로젝트는 중단되지 않았을 것이다.

어휘 grant 보조금

출제 공식 4 CHECK UP
교재 p. 210

1. Never   **2.** Attached   **3.** Should

1. 부정어구 도치

해설 주어인 Ms. Palmer와 동사인 has가 도치되었으므로 부정어구가 앞에 놓여야 한다.

번역 팔머 씨는 마감 기한이 아무리 빠듯해도 절대 어기는 법이 없었다.

어휘 nearly 거의   miss 놓치다   tight 빠듯한

2. 보어 도치

해설 '첨부된'을 강조하는 보어가 문두로 오고 주어인 sample writings와 동사인 are가 도치된 구조이다.

번역 첨부된 것은 해밀턴 씨가 우리에게 검토하라고 보낸 작문 샘플이다.

어휘 attachment 부착, 첨부 파일

3. 가정법 도치

해설 가정법 미래에서 if가 빠지고 도치된 형태이다.

번역 테일러 씨가 혹시 약속을 취소한다면, 리우 박사가 그를 대신할 것이다.

어휘 appointment 약속   replace 대신하다

ACTUAL TEST

교재 p. 212

1. (A)	**2.** (C)	**3.** (B)	**4.** (A)	**5.** (B)
6. (C)	**7.** (C)	**8.** (C)	**9.** (D)	**10.** (B)
11. (B)	**12.** (B)	**13.** (B)	**14.** (B)	**15.** (B)
16. (D)	**17.** (C)	**18.** (B)	**19.** (B)	**20.** (C)

1. (A) 원급 비교 – 형용사 자리

해설 빈칸은 원급 비교를 나타내는 as ~ as 사이에 있고, be동사 is 뒤의 보어 자리이므로 원급 형용사인 (A) affordable이 정답이다.

번역 로즈데일의 주택은 십 년 전만큼 저렴하지 않다.

어휘 housing 주택   decade 십 년   affordable 알맞은 가격의, 저렴한

2. (C) 최상급 – 형용사 자리

해설 빈칸 앞에 정관사 the가 있고 문맥상 '세계에서 가장 혼잡한 공항 중에 하나로'라는 내용이 되어야 자연스러우므로 최상급 형용사 (C) busiest가 정답이다. 참고로, busiest 뒤의 명사 airports는 중복을 피해 생략되었다고 보면 된다.

번역 시티 국제 공항은 현재 세계에서 가장 혼잡한 공항들 중 하나로, 하루 24시간 운영된다.

어휘 operate 가동되다, 운영되다

3. (B) the + 최상급

해설 빈칸 앞에 정관사 the, 뒤에는 비교 대상을 나타내는 전치사구 of all of them(그것들 모두 중에서)이 있고, '테오 T5가 그것들 모두 중에서 가장 다용도 기기라는 것을 알아냈다'라는 내용이 되어야 자연스러우므로 최상급을 나타내는 (B) most가 정답이다.

번역 30개의 조리용 믹서기를 시험한 후에, 〈프로 키친 매거진〉의 편집자들은 테오 T5가 그것들 모두 중에서 가장 다용도 기기라는 것을 알아냈다.

어휘 versatile 다재다능한, 다용도의

4. (A) 최상급 – 형용사 자리

해설 빈칸은 The banquet facility를 대신하는 대명사 one을

수식하는 형용사 자리이며 앞에 정관사 the, 뒤에는 비교 범위를 나타내는 전치사구 in the region(그 지역에서)이 있고, '그 지역에서 가장 규모가 큰 곳'이라는 내용이 되어야 자연스러우므로 최상급 형용사인 (A) largest가 정답이다.

번역 우리가 시상식을 위해 선정한 연회 시설은 지역에서 규모가 가장 큰 곳이다.

어휘 banquet 연회   awards ceremony 시상식

5. (B) 비교급 수식 부사

해설 빈칸은 비교급 형용사 warmer의 의미를 '훨씬 더 따뜻한'이라고 강조해 주는 부사 자리이므로 비교급 강조 부사인 (B) much가 정답이다.

번역 올 봄 기온은 지역 전체적으로 평균보다 훨씬 따뜻했다.

어휘 average 평균   entire 전체의

6. (C) 최상급 – 형용사 자리

해설 빈칸은 be동사 is의 보어 자리이고, '영업부장은 이메일 서비스가 친숙하다'라며 주어인 명사구 the sales director를 수식하는 내용이므로 형용사가 와야 한다. 따라서 형용사 (C) most familiar가 정답이다.

번역 영업부장은 이메일 서비스가 가장 친숙하지만, 우리는 무엇이든지 고객이 선호하는 커뮤니케이션 수단을 사용할 것이다.

어휘 familiarity 익숙함, 낯익음   familiarize 익숙하게 하다

7. (C) 최상급 – 형용사 자리

해설 빈칸은 명사 sales를 앞에서 수식하는 형용사 자리이며 앞에 정관사 the, 뒤에는 비교 범위를 나타내는 전치사구 in its 25 year history가 있고, '25년 역사상 가장 높은 매출'이라는 내용이 되어야 자연스러우므로 최상급 형용사 (C) strongest가 정답이다. (D) most strengthen의 strengthen은 동사이므로 형용사 자리에 들어갈 수 없다.

번역 작년에 회사는 25년 역사상 최고 매출을 기록했는데, 이것은 예상을 훨씬 뛰어넘은 것이었다.

어휘 surpass 능가하다, 뛰어넘다   expectation 예상, 기대

8. (C) 비교급 수식 부사

해설 빈칸은 비교급 형용사 larger를 앞에서 수식하는 자리이므로 부사가 들어가야 '훨씬 더 많은 양의 쓰레기'라고 자연스럽게 연결된다. 따라서 '상당히'라는 의미의 부사 (C) significantly가 정답이다.

번역 새로운 재활용 규정을 시행하기 전에는, 그 지역에서 훨씬 더 많은 양의 쓰레기가 배출되었다.

어휘 implement 시행하다   regulation 규정, 규제   trash 쓰레기   significant 중요한   significance 중요성, 의미

9. (D) 가정법 과거완료

해설 빈칸은 주어 we의 동사 자리이고, if절의 동사가 had received로 과거완료 시제이므로 가정법 과거완료 시제

가 들어가야 '우리는 더 많은 시간이 필요했을 것이다'라고 자연스럽게 연결되므로 (D) would have needed가 정답이다.

번역 건설 프로젝트를 위해 많은 견적을 받았더라면, 우리는 도급 업체를 선정하는 데 더 많은 시간이 필요했을 것이다.

어휘 contractor 계약자, 도급 업체

10. (B) 비교급 수식 부사

해설 빈칸은 비교급 형용사 older의 의미를 '훨씬 더 오래된'이라고 강조하는 부사 자리이므로 비교급 강조 부사인 (B) a lot이 정답이다.

번역 현재 50년째 사업을 해 오고 있는 아트랙스 햇 회사는 시에 있는 많은 다른 업체들보다 훨씬 더 오래되었다.

어휘 operation 사업, 영업

11. (B) 부정어구 도치

해설 주어 the Art Museum 앞에 동사 does가 있는 것으로 보아 주어와 동사가 도치되었음을 알 수 있다. 도치 구문이 되려면 앞에 부정어가 필요하므로 '좀처럼 ~ 않는'이라는 의미의 부정어 (B) Seldom이 정답이다.

번역 그 미술관은 로버트 바니니 같은 저명한 강사를 초청하는 영광을 갖는 일이 좀처럼 없다.

어휘 lecturer 강사, 강연자   distinguished 유명한, 뛰어난

12. (B) 가정법 도치

해설 빈칸이 있는 절은 쉼표 뒤의 절 앞에 붙어 절의 내용을 부연 설명하는 부사절이고, 주절의 동사가 미래 시제 will이며, 문맥상 '주민 누구라도 재활용품 쓰레기통을 추가로 요청하면, 무료로 제공받을 것이다'라는 내용이 되어야 자연스러우므로 미래 시제 가정절임을 알 수 있다. 단수 주어인 any resident의 동사가 수 일치되지 않고 동사원형(require)인 것으로 보아 접속사 If가 생략된 가정법 도치 구문임을 파악해야 한다. 「주어+should+동사원형」이 도치되면 「Should+주어+동사원형」 형태가 되므로 (B) Should가 정답이다.

번역 페어델 시 주민 누구나 추가로 재활용품 쓰레기통을 요청하면, 하나가 무료로 제공될 것이다.

어휘 additional 추가의   bin 쓰레기통   recyclables 재활용품   free of charge 무료로

13. (B) 가정법 과거완료

해설 빈칸은 If절의 동사 자리이고, 가정법 과거완료 시제인 주절의 동사 could have displayed와 시제를 일치시켜 주어야 '10월 5일까지 완성되었더라면, 그것들을 전시할 수 있었을 것이다'라는 내용으로 자연스럽게 연결되므로 (B) had been completed가 정답이다.

번역 시제품이 10월 5일까지 완성되었더라면, 우리는 가을 박람회에서 그것들을 전시할 수 있었을 것이다.

어휘 trade show 박람회   complete 완료하다, 완성하다

14. (B) 비교급 관용 표현

해설 명사구 May 10을 자연스럽게 연결해 주는 전치사를 고르는 문제이다. '늦어도 5월 10일까지는'이라는 내용이 되어야 글의 흐름이 자연스러우므로 '늦어도 ~까지는'이라는 의미의 (B) no later than이 정답이다.

번역 지역 의료 학회(RMC) 참석에 관심 있는 사람들은 늦어도 5월 10일까지는 등록해야 한다.

어휘 register 등록하다   at least 적어도   lately 최근에

15. (B) 최상급 강조 부사

해설 빈칸은 최상급 형용사 best를 강조하는 부사 자리이다. very는 정관사 the 뒤에 와서 the very의 형태로 '단연코'라는 의미의 최상급 강조 부사로 쓰이므로 (B) very가 정답이다.

번역 소프트 디자인사는 지난 10년간 단연코 최고의 디자인 솔루션을 제공하는 데 전념해 왔습니다.

어휘 solution 해결책, 해법

16. (D) 최상급 관용 표현

해설 완전한 절 뒤에 자연스럽게 연결될 수 있는 수식어를 고르는 문제이다. '늦어도 12월 10일까지는'이라는 내용이 되어야 자연스러우므로 '(아무리) 늦어도'라는 의미의 전치사구 (D) at the latest가 정답이다.

번역 개인 행사를 위해 여러분이 요청한 모든 대여 물품은 늦어도 12월 10일까지는 반환해야 합니다.

어휘 rental 대여, 임대

17. (C) 보어 도치

해설 해당 문장은 a welcome packet is enclosed에서 enclosed가 문장의 앞으로 나오면서 주어와 동사의 순서가 바뀐 도치 구문이므로 보어인 (C) Enclosed가 정답이다. (A) Enclosure는 '동봉된 것'이라는 뜻의 가산 단수명사이므로 앞에 한정사가 와야 한다.

번역 컨퍼런스 참석자로서 필요하실 자료가 들어 있는 환영 패키지를 동봉합니다.

어휘 packet 꾸러미, 뭉치   attendee 참석자   enclosure (편지에) 동봉된 것   enclose 동봉하다

18. (B) 비교급 관용 표현

해설 be동사 is와 보어 자리의 형용사 available 사이에 들어갈 알맞은 부사 어휘를 고르는 문제이다. 문맥상 '우리 메뉴에 더 이상 없다'라는 내용이 되어야 자연스러우므로 '더 이상 ~ 않다'라는 의미의 부사 표현인 (B) no longer가 정답이다.

번역 우리 식당의 많은 손님들은 우리 메뉴에 더 이상 없는데도 여전히 스파이시 치킨 요리를 요청한다.

어휘 diner 식사하는 사람   spicy 양념이 강한, 매운   platter 서빙용 접시, 요리

19. (B) 부정어구 도치

해설 주어 the amusement park 앞에 동사 has가 있는 것으로 보아 주어와 동사가 도치되었음을 알 수 있다. 도치 구문이 되려면 앞에 부정어가 필요하므로 '거의 ~ 않다'라는 의미의 부정어 (B) Hardly가 정답이다.

번역 그 놀이공원은 토요일에는 붐비지 않는 날이 거의 없었다.

어휘 amusement park 놀이공원

20. (C) 비교급 관용 표현

해설 명사 luggage를 앞에서 수식하는 자리에 들어갈 적절한 수량 형용사를 고르는 문제이다. 쉼표 뒤의 절이 「the+비교급(the more)」으로 시작한 것으로 보아 「the+비교급 ~, the 비교급(더 …할수록 더 ~하다)」 구문임을 알 수 있고, 빈칸 뒤의 명사 luggage는 불가산명사이므로 양을 수식하는 비교급 형용사 (C) less가 정답이다.

번역 대개 가지고 다니는 짐이 적을수록 여행은 더 편해진다.

어휘 in general 보통, 대개

어휘 편
●UNIT 01 빈출 명사 어휘 1
ACTUAL TEST
교재 p. 215

| **1.** (C) | **2.** (B) | **3.** (A) | **4.** (B) | **5.** (C) |
| **6.** (D) | **7.** (C) | **8.** (B) | **9.** (C) | **10.** (B) |

1. (C) access

해설 선택지의 명사 중 (A) approach와 (C) access는 '~에의 접근(권)'이라는 뜻으로 주로 전치사 to와 함께 쓰이며 빈칸 앞의 수식어인 unlimited와도 잘 어울리므로 정답 후보가 된다. (A) approach는 가산명사이므로 한정사가 없을 경우 복수 형태로 쓰여야 하므로 답이 될 수 없고, approach와 뜻은 같지만 불가산명사인 (C) access가 정답이다.

번역 디지털 구독을 하면 〈더 뉴스 트리뷴〉의 모든 인터넷 콘텐트를 무제한 이용할 수 있다.

어휘 subscription 정기 구독   unlimited 무제한의   content 내용, 콘텐트   approach 접근, 접촉   reservation 예약   publication 출판

2. (B) expertise

해설 주어인 기조 연설자(keynote speaker)가 '보도 및 기사 작성에 관해(on reporting and writing)' 공유할 수 있는 것이 목적어로 들어가야 내용상 자연스러우므로 '전문 지식'을 뜻하는 (B) expertise가 정답이다.

번역 우리 기조 연설자이자 수상 경력에 빛나는 기자인 제니 허프만 씨가 보도 및 기사 작성에 관한 그녀의 전문 지식을 공유해 줄 것입니다.

어휘 keynote speaker 기조 연설자   prize-winning 입상한, 수상한   journalist 언론인, 기자   capacity 용량, 능력   insurance 보험   deadline 마감 기한

3. (A) scope

해설 보수 공사(the renovation project)와 관련된 것들 중에서 includes의 목적어로 온 '건물의 전기 시스템 개선'을 포함할 수 있는 명사가 주어로 와야 하므로 '범위'를 뜻하는 (A) scope가 정답이다. (B) inside(내부)는 주로 위치를 나타낼 때 쓰는 말이므로 문맥에 어울리지 않는다.

번역 보수 공사 범위에는 건물의 전기 시스템 개선도 포함된다.

어휘 renovation 수리, 보수   electrical 전기의   inside 내부   enrollment 등록   director 감독

4. (B) phase

해설 순서와 관련된 형용사인 final(최종의)의 수식을 받았으며, '장식용 분수를 설치하는 것'은 건설 공사의 단계 및 순서에 해당하므로 '단계'를 뜻하는 (B) phase가 정답이다.

번역 쇼핑몰 건설 공사의 최종 단계에는 장식용 분수 설치가 포함된다.

어휘 final 최종의   construction 건설, 공사   involve 수반하다   install 설치하다   decorative 장식용의   fountain 분수   impact 영향   posture 자세

5. (C) recognition

해설 '매장 관리자가 매출을 증가시킨 것에 대해 빈칸을 얻었다(earned)'는 내용이므로 '공로를 인정받았다'로 연결되어야 가장 자연스럽다. 따라서 '(공로 등에 대한) 인정, 표창'을 뜻하는 (C) recognition이 정답이다.

번역 우리 매장 관리자는 분기별 매출을 10퍼센트 증가시킨 공로를 인정받았다.

어휘 earn 얻다   increase 증가시키다   quarterly 분기별의   exception 예외   diversity 다양성   vacancy 공석, 빈방

6. (D) priority

해설 5형식 동사 make의 목적격 보어 자리에 적절한 명사 어휘를 택하는 문제로, 5형식 동사의 목적격 보어 자리에 들어가는 명사는 목적어와 동격이 되어야 한다. 신임 시장이 내건 공약에 대한 내용으로 make의 목적어인 '일자리 창출(job creation)'과 동격이 될 수 있는 명사가 답이 되어야 하므로 '우선 사항'을 의미하는 (D) priority가 정답이다.

번역 새로 선출된 게리 라이트풋 시장은 일자리 창출을 최우선 과제로 삼겠다고 말했다.

어휘 elect 선출하다   mayor 시장   job creation 일자리 창출   shortage 부족   incident 사건   manner 방식, 태도

7. (C) components

해설 be동사 are의 보어 자리에 명사가 왔으므로 주어 자리에는 보어와 동격이 되는 명사를 고르면 된다. 선택지 중에서

보어인 '제품(product)'과 동격이 될 수 있는 명사는 '부품'을 뜻하는 (C) components이며, '엘튼사의 부품들은 항공 우주 산업에 선택된 제품이다'라고 자연스럽게 해석되므로 (C) components가 정답이다.

번역 최고 수준으로 제작되어, 엘튼사의 부품들은 항공 우주 산업에 선택된 제품이다.

어휘 engineer 제작하다   aerospace 항공 우주
suggestion 제안   evaluation 평가   policy 정책

8. (B) initiative

해설 to부정사 to take의 목적어 자리에 적절한 명사 어휘를 고르는 문제로, 문맥상으로 '바워즈 씨가 동료들을 종종 나서서 도와주는 것으로 보아, 직장에서 솔선수범하는 것을 좋아한다'라고 자연스럽게 연결되므로 (B) initiative가 정답이다. '솔선수범하다'를 뜻하는 관용 표현 take initiative를 알아 두자.

번역 바워즈 씨가 종종 동료들의 프로젝트를 나서서 도와주는 것으로 보아, 그는 확실히 직장에서 솔선수범하는 것을 좋아한다.

어휘 clearly 분명히   volunteer 자원하다   colleague 동료
relaxation 휴식   absence 결석, 부재   compensation 보상

9. (C) references

해설 동사 made의 목적어 자리에 적절한 명사 어휘를 고르는 문제이다. 명사 reference는 주로 전치사 to와 함께 쓰여 '~에 대해 언급하기'라는 뜻으로 쓰이며, '빌리 도우의 음악에 영감을 받은 작가가 자신의 소설에서 그를 여러 번 언급했다'라고 자연스럽게 해석되므로 (C) references가 정답이다.

번역 그의 음악에 확실하게 영감을 받아서, 작가는 자신의 소설에서 빌리 도우를 여러 번 언급했다.

어휘 inspire 영감을 주다   author 작가, 저자   numerous 많은   permission 허락, 허가   perspective 관점, 시각

10. (B) revision

해설 계약서에 대해 무언가를 요청했는데, 그 이유가 원래 양식이 잘못된 정보를 포함하고 있기 때문이라고 했으므로, 내용상 '수정'을 뜻하는 (B) revision이 들어가야 자연스럽다. (D) relocation은 전치사 to와 잘 어울리기는 하지만 '이동, 이전'을 뜻하므로 적절하지 않다.

번역 샌더즈 씨는 신규 고객을 위한 계약서 수정을 요청했는데, 원래 양식에 잘못된 정보가 있었기 때문이다.

어휘 original 원래의   inaccurate 부정확한   presentation 프레젠테이션, 제출   nomination 지명, 추천   relocation 이전

●UNIT 01 빈출 명사 어휘 2

ACTUAL TEST

교재 p. 217

1. (B)	2. (C)	3. (A)	4. (D)	5. (B)
6. (D)	7. (C)	8. (A)	9. (C)	10. (D)

1. (B) shortage

해설 '~에도 불구하고'라는 뜻의 despite의 특성상, despite 뒤에는 문장 내용에 걸림돌이 되는 명사가 와야 연결이 자연스럽다. '프로젝트를 제때 끝낼 수 있었다'고 했으므로 일을 완수하는 데 걸림돌이 되는 '부족'이라는 뜻의 (B) shortage가 빈칸에 들어가야 '직원이 부족한데도 불구하고'라는 뜻으로 문장의 연결이 자연스럽다.

번역 사내 직원의 부족에도 불구하고, 우리는 제때에 프로젝트를 완료할 수 있었다.

어휘 in-house 회사 내부의   complete 완료하다   on time 제때에   privilege 특권   atmosphere 대기, 분위기

2. (C) basis

해설 basis는 '기준(단위)'을 의미할 때 'on a ~ basis(on a regular basis 정기적으로 / on a weekly basis 일주일 단위로)'의 형태로 쓰인다. '재활용 쓰레기 수거는 일주일 단위로 시행된다'라는 해석이 자연스러우므로 (C) basis가 정답이다.

번역 재활용 쓰레기 수거는 주민들에게 비용 청구 없이 시에서 매주 시행한다.

어휘 recyclable waste 재활용 쓰레기   weekly 매주의, 주 1회의   charge 요금   quantity 수량   focus 초점   approach 접근(법)

3. (A) intention

해설 명사 intention은 to부정사의 수식을 받아 '~하려는 의도'로 자주 쓰이며, 빈칸에 들어갔을 때 '박 씨가 은퇴하려는 의사를 발표했다'라는 내용으로 연결이 자연스러우므로 (A) intention이 정답이다.

번역 지난 금요일 직원 회의에서 박 씨는 공식적으로 은퇴 의사를 발표했다.

어휘 officially 공식적으로   retire 은퇴하다   structure 구조   completion 완료, 완성   employer 고용주

4. (D) reputation

해설 다나 디즈 비스트로가 훌륭한 음식을 제공한 것에 대해 얻어낸(earned) 것이므로 '명성'을 뜻하는 (D) reputation이 내용상 연결이 가장 자연스럽다.

번역 영업한 지 4개월밖에 되지 않았지만, 다나 디즈 비스트로는 이미 훌륭한 음식으로 명성을 얻었다.

어휘 operation 영업, 사업   acquisition 습득   privilege 특권   feature 특징

5. **(B) factor**

해설 신공항은 클로버 시에 지점을 개설하기로 한 아미텍사의 결정에 있어 중요한 이유가 되므로 '요인, 인자'를 뜻하는 (B) factor가 정답이다.

번역 아미텍사는 클로버 시에 지점을 개설하겠다는 자사의 결정에 신공항이 중요한 요소였음을 확인해 주었다.

어휘 confirm 확인해 주다 decision 결정 branch 지점 title 제목 supply 공급 replacement 대체(물)

6. **(D) emphasis**

해설 빈칸 뒤 전치사구 on simplicity와 어울려 '단순함에 중점을 두어 디자인되었다'라는 내용으로 자연스럽게 연결되는 (D) emphasis가 정답이다. (C) comment는 전치사 on과 함께 쓰여 '~에 대한 논평[언급]'을 뜻하므로 문맥에 어울리지 않는다.

번역 신상품 가구들은 단순함에 중점을 두고 멋지게 디자인되었다.

어휘 attractively 멋지게 simplicity 단순함, 간소함 combination 조합 procedure 절차 comment 논평, 언급

7. **(C) consent**

해설 앞 절에서 '진료 기록이 기밀이다'라고 했으므로 '환자의 동의 없이는 공개될 수 없다'라고 연결되어야 자연스러우므로 '동의'를 뜻하는 (C) consent가 정답이다.

번역 진료 기록은 기밀이라서 환자의 동의 없이는 공개할 수 없다.

어휘 medical record 진료 기록 confidential 기밀의 release 공개하다, 발표하다 patient 환자 merger 합병 sensitivity 민감성 reward 보상

8. **(A) coverage**

해설 빈칸에 들어갈 명사는 휴대폰 손상에 대해 품질 보증 서비스가 제공하는 것이어야 하므로 '보장·보상'을 뜻하는 (A) coverage가 정답이다. (B) prediction(예측), (C) consumer(소비자), (D) defect(결함)는 품질 보증 서비스가 제공하는 것이 될 수 없으므로 답이 될 수 없다.

번역 품질 보증 서비스는 휴대폰의 손상에 대해 전면 보상을 제공한다.

어휘 warranty 품질 보증 damage 손상, 피해 prediction 예측 consumer 소비자 defect 결함

9. **(C) alternative**

해설 자전거로 출근하는 것은 차를 운전하는 것에 대해 '건강한 대안'이 되었다고 해야 의미상 연결이 자연스러우므로 '대안'이라는 의미의 (C) alternative가 정답이다.

번역 통근하는 많은 사람에게 자전거를 타고 출근하는 것이 자동차를 운전하는 것에 대한 건강한 대안이 되었다.

어휘 commuter 통근자 cycling 자전거 타기 restriction 제한 discovery 발견 timetable 시간표

10. **(D) patronage**

해설 for는 이유를 나타내는 전치사로, 내용상 for 뒤에는 단골 고객에게 감사하는 이유가 와야 하므로 '애용'을 뜻하는 (D) patronage가 정답이다.

번역 쿠폰을 발송하는 것은 매장의 단골 고객들에게 지속적인 이용에 대해 감사하는 간단한 방법이다.

어휘 loyal 충성스러운 shipment 운송, 배송 reduction 감소

●UNIT 01 빈출 명사 어휘 3
ACTUAL TEST
교재 p. 219

1. (B)	**2.** (C)	**3.** (D)	**4.** (A)	**5.** (B)
6. (B)	**7.** (D)	**8.** (D)	**9.** (D)	**10.** (C)

1. **(B) setting**

해설 전치사 in의 목적어 자리에서 lab(실험실)과 자연스럽게 복합명사로 연결될 수 있는 명사를 고르는 문제이다. 문맥상 '~에서 작업하다'로 장소를 뜻하는 말이 와야 연결이 자연스러우므로 '환경'을 뜻하는 (B) setting이 정답이다.

번역 연구 보조직에는 실험실 환경에서 화학 물질을 가지고 작업하는 일이 수반된다.

어휘 assistant 조수, 보조 chemical 화학 물질 discovery 발견 explanation 설명

2. **(C) assessment**

해설 conduct의 의미상 목적어 자리에 실행할 수 있는 대상이 와야 하므로 (B) proof(증거)와 (D) standard(기준)는 적절하지 않다. (A) tour(여행, 방문)와 (C) assessment(평가) 중에서 문맥상 '부동산의 상태에 대한 철저한 평가를 시행해야 한다'라는 내용이 되어야 자연스러우므로 정답은 '평가'를 의미하는 (C) assessment이다.

번역 사업체를 위한 새로운 장소를 임차하기 전에, 건물 상태에 대한 철저한 평가를 시행할 필요가 있다.

어휘 conduct 행하다 thorough 철저한 property 부동산, 부지 proof 증거

3. **(D) proximity**

해설 빈칸의 명사를 뒤에서 수식하는 전치사구 to the airport가 위치를 나타내는 말이며, 문맥상 '공항에 가깝기 때문에 노스 스타 호텔을 선호한다'라는 내용이 되어야 자연스러우므로 '가까움(근접)'을 뜻하는 (D) proximity가 정답이다.

번역 출장차 방문하는 사람들은 공항이 가깝기 때문에 노스 스타 호텔을 선호하는 경우가 많다.

어휘 business traveler 출장자 elevation 승진, 증가 selection 선발 luxury 사치

4. **(A) enthusiasm**

해설 빈칸이 들어 있는 to부정사구는 내용상 평소 하는 운동에 다양성을 추가해야 하는 이유가 들어가야 하므로 '운동에 대한 열정을 유지하기 위해'라고 해석되어야 자연스럽다. 따라서 정답은 '열정'을 의미하는 (A) enthusiasm이다.

번역 운동에 대한 열정을 유지하기 위해, 규칙적으로 하는 운동에 다양성을 추가하는 것이 바람직하다.

어휘 maintain 유지하다 advisable 권할 만한, 바람직한 variety 다양성 character 성격, 특징 completion 완료 occasion 때, 행사

5. **(B) portion**

해설 전치사구 of ~ entrance fee의 수식을 받으면서 동사구 will go의 주어 자리에 적절한 명사 어휘를 고르는 문제이다. (A) promise(약속), (C) seller(판매자)와 (D) coverage(범위, 보도)는 '입장료의'라는 뜻의 전치사구 (of ~ entrance fee)의 수식을 받는 말로 적절하지 않다. '입장료의 일부는 하이킹 코스를 관리하는 데 쓰일 것이다'라는 내용이 되어야 자연스러우므로 '일부, 부분'을 뜻하는 (B) portion이 정답이다.

번역 국립공원 입장료의 일부는 하이킹 코스를 관리하는 데 사용될 것이다.

어휘 entrance fee 입장료 trail 오솔길, 코스 promise 약속 seller 판매자 coverage 범위

6. **(B) approach**

해설 4형식 동사 give의 직접목적어 자리에 적절한 명사 어휘를 고르는 문제이다. 빈칸에 들어갈 명사는 뒤에 온 전치사 to와 잘 어울리면서, 내용상 개인 트레이너를 쓰는 것이 줄 수 있는 이점이 들어가야 자연스러우므로 '평소 하는 운동에 대한 새로운 접근법'이라고 해석되는 (B) approach가 정답이다.

번역 개인 트레이너를 쓰면 규칙적으로 하는 피트니스 운동에 새로운 접근법을 제시해 줄 것이다.

어휘 neighborhood 이웃 collection 수집

7. **(D) nature**

해설 빈칸 앞 명사구인 any written information을 자연스럽게 수식할 수 있는 명사를 고르는 문제이다. '성격, 성질'이라는 뜻의 (D) nature가 빈칸에 들어가면 '기밀 성격을 띤 서면 정보는 책상 위에 두지 않도록 한다'라는 내용으로 자연스럽게 연결되므로 (D) nature가 정답이다.

번역 직원들은 기밀 성격을 띠는 서면 정보를 절대로 책상 위에 내놓지 않도록 해야 한다.

어휘 employee 직원 ensure 반드시 ~하게 하다 recognition 인정 advice 충고 importance 중요성

8. **(D) setbacks**

해설 '~에도 불구하고'라는 뜻의 despite는 문장의 내용에 부정적인 의미의 명사가 와야 연결이 자연스럽다. '지역 최대의 기업이 되었다'고 했으므로 기업이 성장하는 데 걸림돌이 되는 '난관, 차질'이라는 뜻의 (D) setbacks가 빈칸에 들어가야 '초기의 난관에도 불구하고'라는 뜻으로 문장의 연결이 자연스럽다.

번역 초기에 약간의 난관에도 불구하고, 델코 매뉴팩처링사는 지역 최대의 기업 중 하나로 성장했다.

어휘 region 지역 membership 회원권 distance 거리 ability 능력

9. **(D) service**

해설 전치사 of의 목적어 자리에 적절한 명사 어휘를 고르는 문제이다. '박 씨의 20년 간의 회사 근무를 축하하고자 파티가 열렸다'라는 내용이 되어야 문맥이 자연스러우므로 '근무'라는 의미의 (D) service가 정답이다.

번역 박 씨의 회사 재직 20주년을 기념하기 위해 기념 파티가 열렸다.

어휘 celebrate 기념하다, 축하하다 distance 거리 element 요소 process 과정

10. **(C) correspondence**

해설 동사구 respond to의 목적어 자리에 적절한 명사 어휘를 택하는 문제이다. 문맥상 '고객에게서 온 모든 서신에 신속히 응해야 한다'라고 해석되어야 자연스러우므로 '서신'을 뜻하는 (C) correspondence가 정답이다.

번역 고객 서비스 담당 직원들은 기존 고객 및 잠재 고객들의 모든 연락에 신속하게 대응해야 한다.

어휘 representative 직원 respond to ~에 대응하다 current 현재의 potential 잠재적인 processing 처리 incentive 장려책 participation 참여

●UNIT 02 빈출 형용사 어휘 1

ACTUAL TEST
교재 p. 221

1. (A)	2. (C)	3. (A)	4. (D)	5. (A)
6. (A)	7. (C)	8. (B)	9. (C)	10. (C)

1. **(A) fragile**

해설 파손되지 않도록 포장할 때 특별히 주의를 기울이라는 내용으로 보아 items(물품)를 수식하는 형용사로는 '파손되기 쉬운'이라는 뜻의 (A) fragile이 정답이다.

번역 파손되기 쉬운 물품을 포장할 때는 운송 중에 깨지지 않도록 특별히 주의하세요.

어휘 pack 싸다, 포장하다 shipping 운송 casual 평상시의 productive 생산적인 extensive 광범위한

2. **(C) substantial**

해설 계산대에서 줄 서는 시간을 줄이는 일이 고객 만족도를 향상시킬 수 있다는 내용의 문장에서 improvements(향상)를 수식하는 형용사로는 향상의 정도를 나타내는 말이 자연스럽다. 따라서 '상당한'이라는 뜻의 (C) substantial이 정답이다.

번역 계산대 줄에서 기다리는 시간을 줄이는 것은 고객 만족도를 상당히 향상시킬 수 있다.

어휘 shorten 단축시키다   check-out line 계산대 줄
Improvement 개선, 향상   satisfaction 만족
anonymous 익명인   impatient 조급한   contingent 불확정의, 우연의

3. (A) competent

해설 '전문가'라는 뜻의 사람명사인 professional을 수식하기에 적절한 형용사는 선택지 중 '능숙한'을 뜻하는 (A) competent 뿐이다.

번역 넓은 집이나 사무실을 페인트칠하려면 능숙한 전문가를 고용하는 것이 최선이다.

어휘 professional 전문가   repeated 반복되는
widespread 광범위한   removable 제거할 수 있는

4. (D) unattended

해설 5형식 동사 leave의 목적격 보어 자리에 적절한 형용사 어휘를 고르는 문제이다. '항공사 휴게실에서조차도 방치된 채로 짐을 두어서는 안 된다'고 해석되어야 자연스러우므로 '방치된'이라는 뜻의 (D) unattended가 정답이다.

번역 항공사 휴게실에서조차도 여행자들은 짐을 방치해 두어서는 안된다.

어휘 luggage 여행용 짐   unfolded 접히지 않은, 펼쳐진
unfinished 완료되지 않은   unopened 열리지 않은

5. (A) sizable

해설 '박람회에서 전시하는 것은 돈이 들 수 있다'는 내용의 문장에서 돈의 '액수(amount)'를 수식하기에 적절한 형용사는 선택지 중 '상당한, 꽤 큰'이라는 의미의 (A) sizable뿐이다.

번역 박람회에서 전시하는 데는 상당한 돈이 들 수 있는데, 숙소가 비싼 도시들에서는 특히 더 그렇다.

어휘 exhibit 전시하다   trade show 박람회   lodging 숙소
rentable 임대할 수 있는   stylish 유행을 따른, 멋진

6. (A) exceptional

해설 '투어 참가자들이 일몰을 즐길 수 있다'는 내용의 문장에서 '일몰(sunsets)'을 수식하기에 적절한 형용사는 선택지 중 '특출한, 매우 우수한'이라는 뜻의 (A) exceptional뿐이며, '특별한 일몰을 즐길 수 있다'로 해석도 자연스럽다.

번역 투어 참가자들은 블루 마운틴 산맥의 산등성이를 따라 트레킹을 하면서 특별한 일몰을 즐길 수 있다.

어휘 participant 참가자   sunset 일몰   trek 트레킹하다
ridge 산등성이   tentative 잠정적인   progressive 점진적인

7. (C) confidential

해설 접속사 and는 양쪽에 비슷한 형태 또는 의미를 연결하는 접속사이다. 따라서 and 앞에 있는 passwords(비밀번호)와 유사한 의미로 연결될 수 있는 어휘를 골라야 하므로 '기밀의'라는 의미의 (C) confidential이 가장 적절하다. 참고로, 명사 앞에는 「형용사+형용사+명사」와 같이 명사를 수식하는 형용사를 여러 개 올 수 있다.

번역 시큐어링 플러스 애플리케이션은 여러분의 비밀번호와 기타 개인 기밀 정보를 모두 보호해줄 것입니다.

어휘 punctual 시간을 엄수하는   proficient 능숙한
unauthorized 공인되지 않은

8. (B) durable

해설 선행사인 명사 luggage를 수식하기에 적절한 형용사 어휘를 고르는 문제이다. '내구성이 있는, 견고한'이라는 뜻의 (B) durable은 등위접속사 and 앞에 있는 형용사 lightweight(가벼운)와 함께 '여행용 가방(짐)'을 의미하는 luggage를 자연스럽게 수식하므로 (B) durable이 정답이다.

번역 비행기 여행을 자주 하는 사람들은 가볍고 견고한 여행 가방을 선택해야 한다.

어휘 frequent 잦은, 빈번한   lightweight 경량의   swift 신속한   eventual 궁극적인   customary 관례적인

9. (C) profitable

해설 문맥상 새로운 식당이 불과 몇 주 만에 이뤄낸 변화를 나타내는 말이 들어가야 적절하다. 따라서 '새 식당이 불과 몇 주 만에 수익이 나게 되었다'라고 자연스럽게 연결되는 '수익이 나는'이라는 뜻의 (C) profitable이 정답이다.

번역 1번 가에 있는 그 새로운 이태리 식당은 불과 몇 주 만에 수익을 내게 되었다.

어휘 deliberate 고의적인   leisurely 한가한, 여유로운
respective 각각의

10. (C) renowned

해설 건축가들(architects)로 구성된 팀을 수식하기에 적절한 어휘는 '유명한'을 뜻하는 (C) renowned 뿐이다. (A) scenic(경치가 좋은), (B) habitual(습관적인)과 (D) spacious(넓은)는 사람으로 구성된 팀을 수식하기에 어색하다.

번역 스카이모어 타워 사무용 건물은 일류 회사의 유명한 건축가 팀이 디자인한 것이다.

어휘 architect 건축가   firm 회사   scenic 경치가 좋은
habitual 습관적인   spacious 널찍한

●UNIT 02 빈출 형용사 어휘 2

ACTUAL TEST
교재 p. 223

1. (A)	2. (A)	3. (C)	4. (B)	5. (C)
6. (C)	7. (A)	8. (D)	9. (C)	10. (A)

1. (A) spacious

해설 주어인 '연회장'을 수식하는 말로는 '넓은'을 뜻하는 (A) spacious가 가장 적절하며, 빈칸 뒤 내용도 '최소 100명을 수용할 수 있다'라며 공간의 크기에 대해 이야기하고 있으므로 (A) spacious가 정답이다.

번역 그 호텔의 모든 연회장은 최소 100명을 수용할 수 있을 정도로 충분히 넓다.

어휘 banquet room 연회장 eventful 다사다난한 separate 분리된 rewarding 보람 있는

2. (A) sufficient

해설 명사 funds를 수식하기에 적절한 형용사 어휘를 고르는 문제이다. (B) economical(경제적인), (C) foreseeable(예측할 수 있는), (D) definite(분명한)은 '돈'을 뜻하는 funds를 수식하기에 적절하지 않다. '충분한'이라는 뜻으로 '충분한 기금 덕에 무료 강좌가 곧 열린다'라며 문맥을 자연스럽게 연결해 주는 (A) sufficient가 정답이다.

번역 충분한 기금 덕분에 무료 공예 강좌가 조만간 시작될 예정이다.

어휘 arts and crafts 공예 be set to do ~할 예정이다 economical 경제적인 foreseeable 예측할 수 있는 definite 분명한

3. (C) prolonged

해설 도로 건설 공사로 인해 발생될 수 있는 상황이 목적어로 와야 하므로 '장기화된 도로 폐쇄와 지연'이 가장 문맥상 적합하다. 따라서 정답은 (C) prolonged이다.

번역 워털루 가의 공사 작업은 장기화된 도로 폐쇄와 교통 지연을 유발시켰다.

어휘 cause 유발하다 closure 폐쇄 dissatisfied 불만스러워하는 expandable 확대할 수 있는 insufficient 불충분한

4. (B) designated

해설 명사 extensions는 '내선 전화'를 뜻하므로 '회사 전화 시스템에는 주 회선이 있고, 각 부서 사무실 별로 지정된 내선이 있다'고 연결되어야 내용이 자연스러우므로 (B) designated가 정답이다.

번역 그 회사의 전화 시스템에는 안내용 주 회선과 각 부서 사무실 별로 지정된 내선이 있다.

어휘 extension 내선, 구내 전화 department 부서 approving 승인하는 competitive 경쟁적인 hesitant 주저하는

5. (C) Accessible

해설 빈칸은 Being으로 시작하는 분사구문에서 Being이 생략되고 난 보어 자리에 들어가 주어 Cadic Supermarket's delivery service를 수식하기에 적절한 형용사 어휘를 고르는 문제이다. 빈칸 뒤에서 빈칸을 수식해주는 전치사구 via mobile phone과 주어 delivery service를 '휴대폰을 통해 이용 가능한 배송 서비스'라고 자연스럽게 연결해주는 '이용(접근) 가능한'이라는 의미의 (C) Accessible이 가장 적절하다.

번역 휴대폰을 통해 이용할 수 있는 카딕 슈퍼마켓의 배송 서비스는 빠르고 이용하기 쉽다.

어휘 via ~을 통해 reversible 되돌릴 수 있는 necessary 필요한 ultimate 궁극적인, 최고의

6. (C) proficient

해설 지원자가 갖추어야 할 자격 조건에 대해 이야기하고 있으므로 '다양한 소프트웨어에 능숙해야 한다'라고 해석될 수 있는 (C) proficient가 정답이다.

번역 행정 보조직 지원자는 다양한 사무용 소프트웨어 프로그램에 능숙해야 한다.

어휘 candidate 지원자, 후보자 administrative assistant 행정 보조 outgoing 외향적인 streamlined 간결한

7. (A) Extensive

해설 명사 renovation work를 수식하기에 적절한 형용사 어휘를 택하는 문제이다. (B) Skilled(숙련된), (C) Vacant(비어 있는), (D) Inviting(매력적인)은 '보수 작업(renovation work)'을 수식하는 말로 적절하지 못하다. renovation work 뒤의 전치사구(including ~ systems)에서 보수 작업에 수반된 여러 작업을 나타내고 있으므로 '광범위한 보수 작업'이라고 연결되어야 내용이 자연스럽다. 따라서 (A) Extensive(광범위한)가 정답이다.

번역 배관 및 전기 시스템 개선을 포함한 광범위한 보수 작업이 DRM 타워에 예정되어 있다.

어휘 plumbing 배관 skilled 숙련된 vacant 비어 있는 inviting 매력적인

8. (D) persistent

해설 명사 stains를 수식하기에 적절한 형용사 어휘를 고르는 문제이다. '얼룩'을 뜻하는 stains를 꾸미는 말로 (A) innovative(혁신적인), (B) efficient(효율적인), (C) supportive(지원하는)는 어울리지 않는다. persistent는 '끈질긴'이라는 뜻으로 '끈질긴 얼룩', 즉 '잘 지워지지 않는 얼룩'이라고 해석되며 stains를 수식하는 말로 적절하므로 (D) persistent가 정답이다.

번역 약한 옷감의 잘 지워지지 않는 얼룩을 제거하려면, 전문 클리닝 서비스를 이용하는 것이 최선이다.

어휘 remove 제거하다 stain 얼룩 delicate 섬세한, 연약한 professional 전문적인 innovative 혁신적인 efficient 효율적인 supportive 지원하는

9. (C) vulnerable

해설 vulnerable은 주로 전치사 to와 함께 '~에 취약한'이라는 의미의 vulnerable to로 쓰이며, '공원의 초목은 하이킹족들의 훼손에 취약해서'라는 내용으로 문맥을 자연스럽게 연결하므로 (C) vulnerable이 정답이다.

번역 공원의 초목은 하이킹족들의 훼손에 취약하므로, 우리는

모든 방문객에게 표시된 길에서 벗어나지 말라고 당부한다.

어휘 vegetation 초목 mark 표시하다 considerate 사려 깊은 attentive 배려하는

10. (A) punctual

해설 '투어 버스는 정확히 오전 9시에 출발한다'라며 시간에 대해 이야기하는 내용이므로 '시간을 엄수하는'을 뜻하는 (A) punctual이 들어가면 '모든 참가자들은 시간을 엄수해야 한다'라고 해석되어 문맥이 자연스럽다. 따라서 (A) punctual이 정답이다.

번역 투어 버스는 정각 오전 9시에 출발하므로, 모든 참가자는 시간을 엄수해야 합니다.

어휘 exactly 정확히 automated 자동화된 recurrent 재발되는 seasonable 계절에 맞는

●UNIT 02 빈출 형용사 어휘 3

ACTUAL TEST
교재 p. 225

1. (C)   **2.** (C)   **3.** (C)   **4.** (B)   **5.** (C)
6. (C)   **7.** (A)   **8.** (C)   **9.** (B)   **10.** (B)

1. (C) welcome

해설 be welcome to는 '~해도 된다'는 뜻으로 주어의 행위를 흔쾌히 허락하는 의미로 쓰인다. (A) possible은 주어가 사람인 경우에 쓰지 않으며 가주어 it을 두어 「it is possible for you to do」 형태로 쓴다. (B) exciting은 사람의 감정을 나타낼 때는 excited의 형태로 써야 하고, (D) pending(미결의, 임박한)은 의미가 맞지 않는다.

어휘 annual 연례의 pending 미결의, 임박한

번역 설령 여러분이 윌포드 예술대 학생이 아니더라도 연례 학생 영화제에 참석하셔도 좋습니다.

2. (C) genuine

해설 명사구 designer handbag을 수식하기에 적절한 형용사 어휘를 고르는 문제이다. (A) courteous(정중한), (B) grateful(고마워하는)은 handbag을 수식하는 말로 적절하지 못하다. '모조품과 차이를 구별하기 어렵다'는 내용이므로 모조품과 반대 의미인 '진품의'라는 뜻의 (C) genuine이 적절하다.

번역 유명 브랜드의 진품 핸드백과 모조품 간의 차이를 구별하기가 가끔 어려울 때가 있다.

어휘 distinguish 구별하다 designer 유명 디자이너가 만든, 유명 브랜드의 imitation 모조품 courteous 정중한 grateful 고마워하는 sturdy 견고한

3. (C) equivalent

해설 결함이 있는 제품에 대해서 고객이 받을 수 있는 것으로 환불 혹은 일정 금액의 상품권이 있다고 설명하는 내용으로, '환불 혹은 그에 상응하는 금액의 상품권'이라는 내용이 되어야 적절하므로 '금액(amount)'을 꾸미는 형용사로는 '(가치 등이) 동등한'을 뜻하는 (C) equivalent가 적절하다.

번역 고객들은 결함 있는 세품을 받을 경우 환불을 받거나 또는 그에 상당하는 금액만큼의 상품권을 받을 수 있다.

어휘 be entitled to do ~을 할 권리가 있다 faulty 결함이 있는 pleasant 즐거운 wishful 소원하는

4. (B) imperative

해설 be동사 is의 보어 자리에서 진주어인 that절의 내용을 수식하기에 적절한 형용사 어휘를 고르는 문제이다. that절의 내용이 바이러스 방지 프로그램을 설치한다는 것이므로 imperative(반드시 해야 하는)가 들어가야 '바이러스 방지 프로그램을 반드시 설치해야 한다'는 내용으로 자연스럽게 연결된다. 따라서 (B) imperative가 정답이다.

번역 새 컴퓨터는 어떤 것이든 반드시 바이러스 방지 프로그램을 설치해야 한다.

어휘 voluntary 자발적인 ambitious 야심 있는 considerable 상당한

5. (C) versatile

해설 사람의 감정을 나타내는 어휘인 (A) optimistic(낙관적인)과 (B) satisfied(만족하는)는 '기기(device)'를 수식하는 말로 부적절하다. 명사 devices를 뒤에서 수식하는 관계사절(that ~ make calls)이 전화를 거는 것보다 훨씬 많은 것을 할 수 있다는 내용이므로 '다용도의'의 뜻을 지닌 (C) versatile이 정답이다.

번역 오늘날의 스마트폰은 전화를 거는 것 이상의 기능을 할 수 있는 다목적 기기이다.

어휘 device 장치, 기기 make a call 전화를 걸다 optimistic 낙관적인 satisfied 만족하는 unavailable 이용할 수 없는

6. (C) relevant

해설 사람을 채용할 때 고려하는 핵심 요인이 되는 지원자의 경험에 대한 내용이므로 '지원자의 관련 분야 경험'이라고 해석되어야 자연스럽다. 따라서 '관련 있는, 적절한'을 의미하는 (C) relevant가 정답이다. (B) numerous(많은)는 many와 동의어로 불가산명사인 experience를 수식할 수 없고, (A) adjacent(가까운)와 (D) impartial(공정한)은 의미상 experience를 수식하는 말로 적절하지 않다.

번역 지원자의 관련 분야 경험이 새로운 소프트웨어 개발자를 채용할 때 고려하는 핵심 요인이다.

어휘 factor 요인 adjacent 인접한 impartial 공정한

7. (A) unforeseen

해설 빈칸의 상황 때문에 연설자가 컨퍼런스에 참석하지 못한나고 했으므로 '뜻밖의, 예측하지 못한'이라는 의미의 (A) unforeseen의 수식을 받아 '예측하지 못한 상황 때문에'라는 내용이 되어야 자연스럽다. 따라서 (A) unforeseen이 정답이다.

번역 예측하지 못한 상황 때문에 기조 연설자는 목요일 컨퍼런스에 참석하지 못할 것이다.

어휘 circumstance 환경, 상황   occasional 가끔의   sound 견실한, 타당한

8. (C) distinguished

해설 '성공한, 뛰어난'이라는 뜻의 (C) distinguished는 전문가들(professionals)을 수식해 '그들의 분야에서 가장 뛰어난 전문가들'이라는 자연스러운 내용을 만들어 준다. 따라서 (C) distinguished가 정답이다. (A) seasonal(계절에 따른), (B) extensive(광범위한)와 (D) reliant(의존하는)는 의미상 '전문가들'을 수식하는 말로 적절하지 않다. 참고로, seasoned(숙련된), reliable(신뢰할 만한) 형태로 쓰면 사람을 수식하는 형용사가 될 수 있다.

번역 디지털 마케팅 컨퍼런스의 연설자들은 자신들의 분야에서 가장 뛰어난 전문가들이다.

어휘 field 분야   reliant 의존하는

9. (B) pending

해설 빈칸 뒤의 절에서 거래가 아직 완료되지 않았다고 했으므로 '부동산 매매가 여전히 진행 중이다'라는 내용으로 연결되어야 자연스럽다. 따라서 '미결인, 미정인'이라는 의미의 (B) pending이 정답이다.

번역 부동산 매매는 아직 진행 중이라 거래가 아직 완료되지 않았다는 점을 알고 계셔야 합니다.

어휘 property 부동산   transaction 거래   complete 완료된   searching 엄중한   incoming 새로 선출된, 들어오는   resist 저항하다

10. (B) certified

해설 명사구 yoga instructor를 수식하기에 적절한 형용사 어휘를 고르는 문제이다. 요가 강사(yoga instructor)를 꾸며 주는 말로는 '공인의, 자격증을 가진'이라는 뜻의 (B) certified가 가장 적절하며, '자격증을 갖춘 요가 강사가 되려면, 교육 과정 이수가 요구된다'라고 해석되어 내용도 자연스럽다. 나머지 보기는 의미상 강사(instructor)를 수식하는 말로 어울리지 않는다.

번역 자격증을 가진 요가 강사가 되려면 200시간의 교육 과정 이수가 필수다.

어휘 instructor 강사   completion 완료, 완성   prolonged 장기적인   projected 예상된   assorted 여러 가지의

●UNIT 03 빈출 부사 어휘 1

ACTUAL TEST

교재 p. 227

1. (C)	2. (A)	3. (D)	4. (A)	5. (B)
6. (C)	7. (C)	8. (B)	9. (C)	10. (A)

1. (C) fairly

해설 (A) some과 (B) much는 관사 a와 함께 쓸 수 없고, (D) closely는 '면밀히, 밀접하게'라는 뜻이므로 simple(간단한)과 의미상 어울리지 않는다. '상당히, 꽤'라는 의미의 fairly는 정도를 강조하는 말로 '아주 간단한'이라고 해석되어 simple과 잘 어울리므로 (C) fairly가 정답이다.

번역 프린터에 새 잉크 카트리지를 넣는 것은 10분 정도 걸리는 아주 간단한 일이다.

어휘 task 일, 과제   closely 면밀히

2. (A) frequently

해설 문맥상 '영업 사원들의 사기 진작을 위해 이토 씨가 자주 목표를 설정하고 인센티브를 제공한다'라는 내용이 되어야 자연스러우므로 '자주'라는 뜻의 (A) frequently가 정답이다. 동사가 현재 시제일 경우 빈도부사가 자주 답이 된다는 것도 알아 두자.

번역 영업 사원들의 사기를 진작시키기 위해서, 이토 씨는 자주 목표를 설정하여 실적이 가장 뛰어난 사원들에게 인센티브를 제공한다.

어휘 motivated 동기가 부여된   incentive 인센티브, 장려금   performer 성과를 내는 사람, 성과자   extremely 극도로   subsequently 그 뒤에, 나중에   greatly 대단히

3. (D) rarely

해설 '박물관이 도심에서 멀리 위치해 있기 때문에'라는 이유를 댔으므로 문맥상 '거의 방문하지 않는다'라는 내용이 되어야 자연스럽다. 따라서 '드물게, 좀처럼 ~하지 않는'이라는 의미의 (D) rarely가 정답이다.

번역 관광객들은 시의 산업 박물관을 방문하는 일이 거의 없는데, 박물관이 도심 지역에서 멀리 떨어진 곳에 위치해 있기 때문이다.

어휘 located 위치한   nearly 거의   locally 지역에서

4. (A) properly

해설 '편집부 인턴은 제대로 교육을 받으면 업무를 배정받을 수 있다'는 내용이 되어야 자연스러우므로 '제대로, 적절히'라는 뜻의 (A) properly가 정답이다.

번역 모든 편집부 인턴은 제대로 교육을 받으면 보도 자료 작성 같은 업무를 배정받을 수 있다.

어휘 editorial 편집의; 사설   assign 맡기다   press release 보도 자료   probably 아마도   severely 심하게

5. (B) routinely

해설 빈칸이 들어있는 that절은 명사 products(제품)를 수식하는 관계사절로, 주절의 주어인 essentials(필수품)에 대해서 설명하는 내용이다. 따라서 '쇼핑객들이 계획 없이 일상적으로 구매하는 제품들'이라는 내용이 되어야 문맥상 적절하므로 '일상적으로'라는 뜻을 가진 (B) routinely가 정답이다.

번역 '필수품'이라는 말은 쇼핑객들이 계획하지 않고 일상적으로 구입하는 제품들을 가리킨다.

어휘 term 용어, 말 essential 필수품; 필수적인 refer to ~을 가리키다 lately 최근에 unusually 평소와 달리 inaccurately 부정확하게

6. (C) Typically

해설 쉼표 뒤의 부사절에서 '가끔 야외 정원 구역이 유지 보수 때문에 폐쇄된다'라고 했는데, 이 절을 연결하고 있는 접속사 although는 '(비록) ~이긴 하지만'이라는 뜻이므로 주절에 반대되는 내용이 와야 한다. 따라서 '보통 도브 맨션 투어에는 야외 정원 방문이 포함된다'라는 내용이 되어야 적절하므로 '보통'을 뜻하는 (C) Typically가 정답이다.

번역 보통 우리의 도브 맨션 투어에는 야외 정원 방문이 포함되지만, 가끔 이 구역은 유지 보수로 인해 폐쇄됩니다.

어휘 outdoor 야외의 maintenance 유지 보수 productively 생산적으로 largely 대체로 easily 쉽게

7. (C) lately

해설 문맥상 '최근에 인기가 많아졌다'가 적절하고, 현재완료 시제와도 잘 어울리는 (C) lately가 정답이다. (D) shortly는 '곧'이라는 뜻으로 주로 미래 시제와 어울리므로 답이 될 수 없다.

번역 유기농 과일 및 채소가 최근에 점점 더 인기가 많아졌다.

어휘 organic 유기농의 freshly 신선하게 newly 새로 shortly 곧, 조만간

8. (B) promptly

해설 부사 promptly는 '즉시, 신속하게'라는 의미로 주로 동사를 수식하지만, 시간을 나타내는 전치사구 앞에 쓰여 '정확히 제시간에'라는 뜻으로 전치사구를 수식하기도 한다. '정확히 저녁 7시에 시작할 것이다'라고 해석되어 문맥도 자연스러우므로 (B) promptly가 정답이다.

번역 시상식이 정확히 저녁 7시에 시작될 예정이니, 그 시간에는 모두가 착석해주셔야 합니다.

어휘 award ceremony 시상식 be seated 앉다 extremely 극도로 solely 오로지, 단지 markedly 현저하게

9. (C) relatively

해설 문맥상 '역사 지구를 제외한 시 모든 지역에서 호텔 요금이 비교적 저렴하다'라고 해석되어야 자연스러우므로 '비교적'이라는 뜻의 (C) relatively가 정답이다. 나머지 보기는 inexpensive(비싸지 않은)를 꾸미는 말로 의미상 적절하지 않다.

번역 호텔 객실 요금은 역사 지구를 제외하고는 시 모든 지역에서 비교적 저렴하다.

어휘 rate 요금 inexpensive 비싸지 않은 except for ~을 제외하고는 approximately 대략 repeatedly 되풀이하여 exactly 정확히

10. (A) briefly

해설 동사 explain을 수식하기에 적절한 부사를 고르는 문제이다. '간략히 설명해 줄 것이다'라고 자연스럽게 해석되므로 '간단히'라는 뜻의 (A) briefly가 정답이다. (B) previously는 '이전에'라는 뜻이므로 미래 시제 will과 어울리지 않고, 주로 접속사로 쓰이는 (C) whenever는 동사를 수식하는 부사 자리에는 적절하지 않다. (D) alongside는 부사로 쓰일 때는 '나란히'라는 뜻으로 문맥에 어울리지 않는다.

번역 웹사이트의 '회사 소개' 란은 우리 조직의 목표 및 가치관에 대해 간략히 설명해줄 것이다.

어휘 section ~란, 항목 organization 조직, 단체 objective 목표 values 가치관 previously 이전에 whenever ~할 때마다 alongside ~와 나란히, ~와 함께

●UNIT 03 빈출 부사 어휘 2

ACTUAL TEST

교재 p. 229

1. (D)	**2.** (B)	**3.** (C)	**4.** (B)	**5.** (D)
6. (D)	**7.** (B)	**8.** (B)	**9.** (D)	**10.** (B)

1. (D) entirely

해설 문맥상 '지역 주민들의 기부에 전적으로 의존한다'라고 자연스럽게 연결되므로 '전적으로'라는 의미의 (D) entirely가 정답이다.

번역 청소년 오케스트라의 자금은 지역 주민들의 기부에 전적으로 의존한다.

어휘 funding 자금 depend on ~에 의존하다 donation 기부 local 지역의 accurately 정확하게 carefully 조심스럽게 finely 정교하게

2. (B) steadily

해설 steadily는 증가나 감소 등의 변화 추이를 나타내는 말로 잘 어울리고, '부동산 가격이 꾸준히 떨어지고 있다'라고 자연스럽게 해석되므로 '꾸준히'라는 의미의 (B) steadily가 정답이다.

번역 작년과 달리 올해 부동산 가격은 꾸준히 하락하고 있다.

어휘 contrary to ~와 반대로 agreeably 기분 좋게 resistantly 저항하여 potentially 잠재적으로

3. (C) Ideally

해설 문장 앞에서 문장 내용 전체를 수식하기에 적절한 부사 어휘를 고르는 문제이다. 문맥상 새로운 식당을 열기에 가장 적합한 장소를 제안하고 있는 내용이므로 '이상적으로는'을 의미하는 (C) Ideally가 적절하다. (A) Virtually의 '사실상'이라는 뜻은 '거의'와 비슷해 'virtually all(사실상[거의] 모든)', 'virtually impossible(사실상[거의] 불가능한)' 등으로 쓰이므로 여기서는 어울리지 않는다.

번역 이상적으로 말하면 우리는 해안가의 유흥가에 새 식당을 열어야 한다.

PART 5

어휘 waterfront 해안가, 강가   entertainment 오락, 여흥
district 지구, 구역   virtually 사실상   habitually
습관적으로, 늘   barely 거의 ~ 아닌

4. (B) occasionally

해설 문맥상 '신상품을 위한 공간을 마련하기 위해 가끔 할인가에 상품을 제공한다'라고 해석되어야 적절하므로 '가끔'이라는 뜻의 (B) occasionally가 정답이다. 현재 시제의 동사를 꾸미는 말로는 특히 빈도부사가 잘 어울린다는 점을 알아 두자.

번역 그러니 식료품점은 신상품을 위한 공간을 마련하기 위해 가끔 할인가에 상품을 제공한다.

어휘 grocery 식료품점   reduced 감소한, 할인한   new arrival (입고된) 신상품   tightly 단단히, 빽빽이 carelessly 부주의하게   respectively 각각

5. (D) seldom

해설 운동 장비 구매 시 나타나는 고객들의 성향에 대한 시장 조사 결과를 설명하는 내용으로 문맥상 '고객들이 브랜드 선호를 거의 드러내지 않는다'라는 내용이 되어야 자연스러우므로 '거의 ~ 않는'이라는 뜻의 (D) seldom이 정답이다. (A) slightly는 어떤 상태의 정도를 나타내는 말이므로 주로 형용사를 수식하고, (C) moderately는 동사를 수식할 때 '적정하게, 알맞게'라는 뜻으로 해당 문맥에 어울리지 않는다.

번역 시장 조사 결과 고객들은 운동 장비를 구입할 때 거의 브랜드 선호를 드러내지 않는 것으로 나타난다.

어휘 indicate 나타내다   specify 명시하다   preference 선호   equipment 장비   slightly 약간   recently 최근에 moderately 적당히

6. (D) solely

해설 빈칸이 있는 절은 관계사절로 명사구 a customized training program(맞춤형 훈련 프로그램)을 수식하는 내용이고, 문맥상 '오직 지구력 향상에만 중점을 둔 훈련 프로그램'이라고 해석되어야 자연스러우므로 '오로지'라는 의미의 (D) solely가 정답이다.

번역 그 마라톤 주자는 오로지 지구력 향상에만 중점을 둔 맞춤형 훈련 프로그램을 요구했다.

어휘 customized 맞춤형의, 주문 제작한   endurance 인내, 지구력   adversely 불리하게, 반대로   quarterly 분기별로 nearby 인근에; 인근의

7. (B) exclusively

해설 문맥상 '유기농 식품 제조사들과만 거래한다'라는 내용이 되어야 자연스러우므로 '오직 ~만'의 의미로 쓰이는 (B) exclusively가 정답이다. (C) markedly는 주로 증감의 변화나 어떤 특징 등을 비교하는 데 있어 '두드러지게, 현저히'라는 뜻으로 쓰이므로 해당 문맥에는 어울리지 않는다.

번역 잠재 공급 업체들은 프레시 슈퍼마켓이 오로지 유기농 식품 제조사들과만 거래한다는 것을 유념해야 한다.

어휘 deal with 다루다, 취급하다   maker 제조사   organic 유기농의   previously 이전에   markedly 두드러지게

8. (B) formerly

해설 카라 루미즈는 신임 영업부장인데, 과거에 대해 이야기하고 있으므로 '이전에 제품 관리자였다'라는 내용이 되어야 자연스럽다. 따라서 '이전에'라는 뜻의 (B) formerly가 정답이다.

번역 우리 회사의 신임 영업부장인 카라 루미즈는 이전에 기술 부서의 제품 관리자였다.

어휘 division 부서, 국   perfectly 완벽하게

9. (D) significantly

해설 형용사 overpriced를 수식하기에 적절한 부사를 고르는 문제이다. (A) remotely(원격으로), (B) distantly(멀리), (C) negatively(부정적으로)는 '가격이 비싸게 매겨진'을 뜻하는 overpriced와 의미상 어울리지 않는다. significantly는 '가격이 상당히 비싸게 매겨진'으로 의미가 자연스럽게 연결되므로 (D) significantly가 정답이다.

번역 투카나의 일부 제품은 아시아 국가들에서 상당히 비싸게 가격이 책정되었다.

어휘 goods 제품   overpriced 값이 비싸게 매겨진   remotely 원격으로   distantly 멀리   negatively 부정적으로

10. (B) customarily

해설 동사 visit을 수식하기에 적절한 부사를 고르는 문제이다. (A) exceedingly(극도로), (C) vaguely(모호하게), (D) slightly(약간)는 동사 visit을 수식하는 말로 의미상 어울리지 않는다. customarily는 '으레, 통상적으로'라는 뜻으로 '으레 아침에 바닷가 지역을 방문한다'라고 자연스럽게 수식해 주므로 (B) customarily가 정답이다.

번역 투어 단체는 일출을 보기 위해 으레 아침에 바다 가까이 있는 지역을 방문한다.

어휘 oceanfront 바다 가까이 있는   sun rise 일출 exceedingly 극도로   vaguely 모호하게

●UNIT 03 빈출 부사 어휘 3

ACTUAL TEST

교재 p. 231

1. (B)	2. (A)	3. (C)	4. (B)	5. (A)
6. (C)	7. (A)	8. (B)	9. (C)	10. (A)

1. (B) unexpectedly

해설 동사 canceled를 수식하기에 적절한 부사 어휘를 고르는 문제이다. (A) greatly(대단히), (C) biweekly(격주로), (D) loosely(느슨하게)는 동사 canceled와 의미상 어울리지 않는다. unexpectedly는 '예정된 사찰을 갑자기 취소했다'라는 내용으로 자연스럽게 수식하므로 (B) unexpectedly가 정답이다.

번역 회사 사장은 피츠버그에 있는 새 생산 시설의 예정된 사찰을 갑자기 취소했다.

어휘 cancel 취소하다   production 생산   facility 시설   greatly 대단히   biweekly 격주로; 격주의   loosely 느슨하게

2. (A) noticeably

해설 비교급 형용사 higher를 수식하기에 적절한 부사 어휘를 고르는 문제이다. '항공권 가격은 성수기 동안 (평소보다) 확연히 더 높다'는 내용이 되어야 적절하므로 '눈에 띄게, 현저히'를 뜻하는 (A) noticeably가 정답이다. (B) extremely는 '극히'라는 뜻의 강조 부사로 비교급 형용사를 수식하는 말로 적절하지 않다.

번역 항공권 가격은 붐비는 여름 휴가 시즌 동안 현저히 더 비싸다.

어휘 air ticket 항공권   favorably 호의적으로, 유리하게   generously 관대하게

3. (C) arguably

해설 명사구 the city's best new restaurant를 수식하기에 적절한 부사를 고르는 문제이다. (A) gradually(점차), (B) portably(휴대용으로), (D) neutrally(중립적으로)는 의미상 '최고의 식당'을 수식하는 말로 어울리지 않는다. '퓨전 맥스는 단연컨대 우리 시 최고의 새로운 식당이다'라고 자연스럽게 해석되는 '단연컨대, 거의 틀림없이'라는 뜻의 (C) arguably가 정답이다.

번역 유명 셰프인 드루 칸 소유의 퓨전 맥스는 단연컨대 우리 시 최고의 새로운 식당이다.

어휘 own 소유하다   celebrity 유명 인사   gradually 점차   portably 휴대용으로   neutrally 중립적으로

4. (B) simultaneously

해설 문맥상 '행사 내내 공원의 여러 지역에서 동시에 연주하는'이라는 내용이 되어야 자연스러우므로 (B) simultaneously가 정답이다.

번역 음악 축제에는 두 개의 밴드가 출연해 행사 내내 시립 공원의 여러 지역에서 동시에 연주할 예정이다.

어휘 feature 주인공으로 출연시키다   throughout ~ 내내   accidentally 우연히, 실수로   doubly 두 배로   precisely 정확히

5. (A) initially

해설 앞뒤 문맥을 대조 관계로 만들어 주는 등위접속사 but에 주목하여 의미상 대조 관계를 갖는 어휘를 선택하면 된다. '지금은 높이 평가되고 있다'는 것과 대조를 이룰 수 있는 의미가 되려면 '처음에는 비판을 받았다'이므로 정답은 (A) initially이다. (C) conversely는 앞에서 말한 것을 반대로 말하고자 할 때 쓸 수 있는 부사이므로 맞지 않다.

번역 투스칸 모터사의 GR-6 승용차는 처음에 단조로운 외관 때문에 비판을 받았으나, 지금은 높이 평가되고 있다.

어휘 bland 특징 없는, 단조로운   conversely 정반대로   superbly 최고로

6. (C) intentionally

해설 과거분사 designed를 수식하기에 적절한 부사 어휘를 택하는 문제이다. '공동 작업을 촉진하기 위해'라는 특정한 목적을 위해 사무실이 설계되었다(designed)고 했으므로 문맥상 '의도적으로, 일부러'라는 의미의 (C) intentionally가 가장 적절하다.

번역 큰 탁자들과 탁 트인 공간을 지닌 새 사무실은 공동 작업을 촉진하기 위한 의도로 설계되었다.

어휘 promote 촉진하다   collaboration 공동 작업   simultaneously 동시에   similarly 유사하게, 마찬가지로   namely 즉, 다시 말해

7. (A) enormously

해설 동사 vary를 수식하기에 적절한 부사를 고르는 문제이다. '생활비가 차이 날 수 있다'라는 내용이므로 차이의 정도를 나타낼 수 있는 '엄청나게'라는 의미의 enormously가 들어가야 문맥이 자연스럽다. 따라서 (A) enormously가 정답이다.

번역 생활비는 지역에 따라 엄청나게 차이가 날 수 있는데, 작은 마을이 가장 비용이 적게 드는 곳이다.

어휘 vary 서로 다르다, 달라지다   affordable 가격이 알맞은   consequently 따라서   purely 순전히

8. (B) altogether

해설 동사 eliminate는 '없애다, 제거하다'라는 뜻이므로 어느 정도를 제거할 수 있다는 것인지를 나타낼 수 있는 '전적으로, 완전히'라는 뜻의 altogether의 수식을 받으면 '휴대폰 결제 기술 덕분에 지폐를 완전히 없앨 수도 있다'라고 해석되어 문맥이 자연스럽다. 따라서 (B) altogether가 정답이다. (D) ever since는 '그(과거) 이후로 줄곧'이라는 의미이므로 주로 현재완료 시제와 함께 사용된다.

번역 모바일 결제 기술 덕분에 일부 국가들은 앞으로 지폐를 완전히 없앨 수도 있다.

어휘 eliminate 없애다   paper money 지폐   rather 오히려   freely 자유롭게   ever since 그 이후로 줄곧

9. (C) preferably

해설 빈칸 뒤 전치사구 within two weeks와 잘 어울리는 부사 어휘를 고르는 문제이다. '가능한 한 빨리 면접을 시작하고 싶어 한다'는 내용에 추가적으로 '2주 이내에'라며 구체적인 시일을 제시한 것이므로 '가능한 한 빨리, 가급적 2주 이내에'라는 내용이 되어야 문맥이 자연스럽다. 따라서 '가급적'이라는 의미의 (C) preferably가 정답이다. (A) immediately는 '즉시'라는 뜻이므로 '2주 이내에'라는 내용과 어울리지 않는다.

번역 인사팀은 가급적이면 2주 이내에 가능한 한 빨리 지원자들 면접을 시작하고 싶어 한다.

어휘 within ~ 이내에   immediately 즉시   willingly 자진해서, 기꺼이

10. (A) subsequently

해설 문맥상 '수 씨가 보관 공간 몇 군데를 둘러보고, 큰 곳을 임차하기로 결정했다'는 내용이므로 '둘러보고 그 후에 결정했다'로 시간의 순서를 나타내 줄 수 있는 '그 후'라는 의미의 (A) subsequently가 정답이다. (C) timely는 형용사로 동사를 수식할 수 없고, (D) currently는 의미상 과거 동사를 수식할 수 없다.

번역 수 씨는 우리 보관 장소 몇 군데를 둘러보고 난 후 가장 큰 장소를 임차하기로 결정했다.

어휘 storage 보관, 저장 unit (건물) 한 채 timely 시기적절한 currently 현재

●UNIT 04 빈출 동사 어휘 1

ACTUAL TEST

교재 p. 233

1. (B)	2. (A)	3. (B)	4. (A)	5. (A)
6. (D)	7. (C)	8. (B)	9. (A)	10. (B)

1. (B) generate

해설 빈칸의 to부정사구는 매주 브레인스토밍 시간을 갖는 목적을 나타내는 구문이고, 브레인스토밍은 아이디어를 구상하는 회의 방식을 의미하므로 '아이디어를 내기 위해 브레인스토밍을 한다'는 내용이 되어야 자연스럽다. 따라서 '만들어 내다'라는 뜻의 (B) generate가 정답이다.

번역 편집팀은 미래의 콘텐츠를 위한 아이디어를 만들어 내기 위해 매주 브레인스토밍 시간을 갖는다.

어휘 weekly 매주의, 주 1회의 brainstorming 브레인스토밍(자유롭게 아이디어를 내놓는 회의 방식) prove 증명하다 conduct 행하다 dispose 배치하다

2. (A) accommodate

해설 문맥상 '연회장은 최대 50명의 단체 손님을 수용할 수 있다'는 내용이 되어야 자연스러우므로 '수용하다'라는 의미의 (A) accommodate가 정답이다.

번역 스프링필드 연회장은 최대 50명의 단체 손님이 식탁에 앉아서 식사할 수 있다.

어휘 up to 최대 ~까지 sit-down meal 식탁에 앉아서 하는 식사 measure 측정하다 transport 수송하다 request 요청하다

3. (B) surpass

해설 to부정사의 목적어 their previous sales record를 자연스럽게 연결하면서 '혁신 기술 덕분에'라는 긍정적인 내용과 어울리는 어휘를 골라야 한다. '혁신 기술 덕에 영업 사원들은 이전 판매 기록을 초과할 것으로 기대한다'라는 내용이 되어야 자연스러우므로 '초과하다'라는 뜻의 (B) surpass가 정답이다.

번역 혁신적인 기술 덕분에 영업 사원들은 자신들의 이전 판매 기록을 거의 20퍼센트나 초과할 것으로 기대한다.

어휘 innovative 혁신적인 salesperson 영업사원 previous 이전의 nearly 거의 overhaul 점검하다 compile 편집하다 solicit 간청하다

4. (A) encounter

해설 앞 문장 내용이 고속도로를 폐쇄한다는 내용이고 빈칸이 있는 절은 그 결과 운전자들이 하게 될 일에 대해서 이야기하고 있으므로, detours(우회로)를 목적어로 '우회로를 타게 될 것이다'라고 해석되어야 자연스럽다. 따라서 '접하다, 맞닥뜨리다'라는 의미의 (A) encounter가 정답이다.

번역 15번 고속도로는 확장 공사로 인해 폐쇄될 예정이므로 운전자들은 공사 기간 동안 우회로를 이용하게 될 것이다.

어휘 expansion 확장, 확대 motorist 자동차 운전자 detour 우회로 duration 지속 기간 relocate 이전하다, 이전시키다 occupy 차지하다

5. (A) specify

해설 목적어인 '모든 색상 및 스타일 선택 사항'은 주어인 '제품 안내책자'에 포함되어야 할 사항이므로 '(구체적으로) 명시하다'라는 의미의 (A) specify가 정답이다.

번역 제품 안내책자는 신상품 사무용 의자들의 모든 색상 및 종류별 선택 사항을 명시해야 한다.

어휘 brochure 안내책자 option 선택(권) attain 획득하다 exceed 초과하다

6. (D) notify

해설 문맥상 '지연이 예상되면 고객들에게 통지할 것이다'라는 의미가 자연스러우므로 (D) notify가 정답이다. (A) rely는 자동사로 뒤에 목적어가 올 수 없고, (C) strive는 자동사로 뒤에 주로 to부정사구가 연결된다.

번역 우리는 제품 배송에 있어서 어떠한 지연이라도 예상된다면 고객들에게 항상 통지할 것입니다.

어휘 delay 지연 rely 의지하다 qualify 자격을 얻다 strive 분투하다

7. (C) specializes

해설 빈칸 뒤에 목적어가 없고 전치사 in이 연결되어 있으므로 전치사 in과 어울려 '~를 전문으로 하다'라는 의미를 나타내는 자동사 (C) specializes가 정답이다. (B) appeals는 주로 전치사 to와 연결되는 자동사이다.

번역 30년 이상 믿을 수 있는 포장재 공급 업체로서 넬슨사는 배송 상자와 편지 봉투를 전문으로 한다.

어휘 trusted 믿을 수 있는 supplier 공급 업체 packaging 포장재 envelop 봉투 draw 그리다, 끌어당기다 appeal 관심을 끌다 appear 나타나다

8. (B) accompany

해설 목적어 every tour group을 자연스럽게 연결할 수 있는 동사 어휘를 고르는 문제이다. 따라서 목적어를 취할 수 없는 자동사 (A) participate, (C) emerge, (D) consist는 답이 될 수 없다. '전문 가이드가 모든 투어 단체에 동

행할 것이다'라고 목적어인 every tour group과 자연스럽게 연결될 수 있는 '동행하다'라는 뜻의 타동사인 (B) accompany가 정답이다.

번역 유서 깊은 블랑 하우스를 방문하는 모든 투어 단체들에는 전문 가이드가 동행할 것입니다.

어휘 expert 전문가; 전문적인   historic 역사적으로 유명한. 역사적인   participate 참가하다   emerge 생겨나다. 부상하다   consist 구성되다

9. (A) exceed

해설 주어 The costs와 목적어 our current budget을 자연스럽게 연결하는 동사 어휘를 고르는 문제이다. '모든 박람회 참석에 드는 비용은 예산을 초과할 수도 있다'라고 해석되어야 자연스러우므로 (A) exceed가 정답이다.

번역 지역 박람회 전부에 참석하는 비용은 우리의 현재 예산을 초과할 수도 있다.

어휘 regional 지역의   trade show 박람회   current 현재의   budget 예산   compete 경쟁하다   analyze 분석하다   evaluate 평가하다

10. (B) retain

해설 '부서에서 가장 귀중한 직원들'을 목적어로 연결하면서 동시에 '새 전략'을 수식하는 말로 적절한 동사를 택해야 한다. 따라서 '유지[보유]하다'라는 의미의 (B) retain이 정답이고, '직원들을 계속 보유할 수 있는 새 전략을 개발 중이다'라는 내용이 되어 자연스럽다.

번역 관리자로서의 역할에 따라, 베일리 씨는 그의 부서의 가장 귀중한 직원들의 이직을 방지할 수 있는 새로운 전략을 개발하고 있다.

어휘 role 역할   strategy 계획. 전략   valuable 귀중한   resume 재개하다   connect 연결하다   delegate 위임하다

●UNIT 04 빈출 동사 어휘 2

ACTUAL TEST
교재 p. 235

| 1. (B) | 2. (B) | 3. (C) | 4. (D) | 5. (B) |
| 6. (C) | 7. (B) | 8. (C) | 9. (B) | 10. (A) |

1. (B) consult

해설 문맥상 '휴가 규정에 대한 정보는 직원 지침서를 참고하세요'라는 내용이 되어야 자연스러우므로 '참고하다'를 뜻하는 타동사인 (B) consult가 정답이다. (C) exist는 자동사로 뒤에 목적어가 올 수 없고, (A) educate와 (D) shift는 문맥상 어울리지 않는다.

번역 회사의 휴가 규정에 관한 정보는 직원 지침서를 참고하세요.

어휘 regarding ~에 관한   manual 설명서   educate 교육하다   exist 존재하다   shift 바꾸다

2. (B) utilize

해설 가주어 It 구문에서 진주어 자리의 to부정사구에 들어갈 알맞은 동사 어휘를 선택하는 문제이다. (C) respond는 자동사로 뒤에 목적어가 올 수 없으므로 답이 될 수 없다. 문맥상 '마케팅 캠페인을 기획할 때는 소셜 미디어를 활용하는 것이 중요하다'라는 내용이 되어야 자연스러우므로 정답은 (B) utilize이다.

번역 신규 고객을 끌어모으기 위한 마케팅 캠페인을 기획할 때 소셜 미디어를 활용하는 것이 중요하다.

어휘 attract 끌어모으다   excel 뛰어나다   respond 대답하다   yield (수익·결과를) 내다. 양보하다

3. (C) undergo

해설 '모든 고객 서비스 직원은 교육을 받아야 한다'라는 내용이 되어야 자연스러우므로 '겪다(받다)'라는 뜻의 (C) undergo가 정답이다. (B)는 자동사로 뒤에 목적어를 연결할 수 없고, (A) assist(돕다)와 (D) spend(쓰다)는 의미상 '교육 과정'을 목적어로 연결하기에 부자연스럽다.

번역 모든 고객 서비스 담당 직원들은 커뮤니케이션 능력에 중점을 둔 교육 과정을 거쳐야 한다.

어휘 assist 돕다   depend 의존하다

4. (D) accelerate

해설 회사의 새 공장이 자동화 조립 라인을 사용하는 목적에 대한 내용이 들어가야 하므로 '생산을 가속화하기 위해'라고 해석되어야 자연스럽다. 따라서 '가속화하다'라는 뜻의 (D) accelerate가 정답이다. 나머지 보기는 모두 자동사로 뒤에 목적어가 올 수 없으므로 답이 될 수 없다. 참고로, (B) retreat은 타동사로 쓰이는 경우도 있으나 '(가치가) 떨어지다'라는 뜻으로 문맥상 어울리지 않는다.

번역 회사의 최신 공장에서는 생산을 가속화하기 위해 자동화된 조립 라인을 사용한다.

어휘 automated 자동화된   assembly line 조립 라인   production 생산   rise 오르다   retreat 후퇴하다   interfere 간섭하다

5. (B) features

해설 feature는 '~를 포함하다, ~를 특징으로 하다'라는 뜻으로 '요리책에는 50여 개 이상의 조리법이 포함되어 있다'라고 주어와 목적어를 자연스럽게 연결하므로 (B) features가 정답이다.

번역 〈영양가 높은 식단〉 요리책에는 건강에 좋은 채식 요리에 대한 50여 개의 창의적인 조리법이 실려 있다.

어휘 nutritious 영양가 높은   creative 창의적인   recipe 조리법   vegetarian 채식주의자   reach ~에 이르다   perform 행하다

6. (C) terminate

해설 빈칸 뒤의 명사구 the lease agreement를 자연스럽게 연결할 수 있는 동사를 골라야 한다. 문맥상 '세입자가 임대차 계약을 조기에 종료하기를 원한다'라는 내용이 되어야 하므로 '종료하다'라는 의미의 (C) terminate가 정답이다. 특히, 계약이나 합의 등을 종료할 때는 terminate를 쓴다는 것을 알아 두자.

번역 세입자가 임대차 계약을 조기에 종료하기를 원할 경우 집주인의 서면 허가가 필요하다.

어휘 landlord 집주인   tenant 세입자   lease agreement 임대차 계약   concentrate 집중하다   disconnect 연결을 끊다   remain 남아 있다

7. (B) finance

해설 문맥상 '워킹 홀리데이 프로그램은 젊은 여행자들이 체류 비용을 조달하는 것을 도울 수 있다'라는 내용이 되어야 자연스러우므로 '비용을 조달하다'라는 의미의 (B) finance가 정답이다.

번역 워킹 홀리데이 프로그램은 젊은 여행자들이 해외 도시 체류 비용을 조달하는 데 도움을 줄 수 있다.

어휘 overseas 해외의; 해외에   assemble 모으다, 조립하다   enlarge 확대하다   occupy 차지하다

8. (C) restored

해설 빈칸 뒤의 '전선이 수리되자마자'라는 내용과 어울리려면 '전력 서비스가 복구될 것이다'라고 해석되어야 자연스럽다. 따라서 '복구하다'라는 뜻의 (C) restored가 정답이다.

번역 폭풍 후에 전선이 수리되는 대로 전력 서비스가 복구될 것이다.

어휘 in the wake of ~에 뒤이어   interrupt 방해하다   diversify 다양화하다   intend 의도하다

9. (B) solidify

해설 부사적 역할로 쓰인 to부정사구에 들어갈 동사 어휘를 고르는 문제이다. XP 게이밍사가 레오 테크사를 인수한 목적에 대한 내용이 와야 하고 목적어인 its position(그것의 자리)과도 잘 어울릴 수 있어야 한다. '최고의 업체로서 자리를 굳히기 위해'라는 내용이 되어야 자연스러우므로 '굳히다'라는 뜻의 (B) solidify가 정답이다. (C) consent는 자동사이므로 뒤에 목적어가 올 수 없다.

번역 XP 게이밍사는 최고의 비디오 게임 개발 업체로서의 자리를 공고히 하기 위해 최근에 레오 테크사를 인수했다.

어휘 acquire 획득하다   donate 기부하다   consent 동의하다

10. (A) settled

해설 문맥상 '날짜가 정해지자마자 회의장을 예약할 것이다'라는 내용이 되어야 자연스러우므로 '결정하다'라는 뜻의 (A) settled가 정답이다. (D) appear는 자동사로 수동태로 쓰이지 않는다.

번역 우리는 날짜가 정해지자마자 회의를 위해 회의장을 예약할 것이다.

어휘 reserve 예약하다   depart 출발하다

●UNIT 04 빈출 동사 어휘 3
ACTUAL TEST
교재 p. 237

1. (C)	2. (A)	3. (C)	4. (D)	5. (C)
6. (C)	7. (B)	8. (B)	9. (B)	10. (C)

1. (C) strive

해설 빈칸 뒤의 to부정사구와 자연스럽게 연결될 수 있는 동사 어휘를 고르는 문제이다. strive는 to부정사와 함께 쓰여 '~하려고 애쓰다'를 의미하며, 문맥상 '전문 가이드가 모든 여행을 기억에 남는 여행으로 만들려고 애쓴다'가 자연스러우므로 (C) strive가 정답이다.

번역 저희 지오 어드벤처 투어의 전문 가이드들은 모든 여행을 기억에 남는 여행으로 만들기 위해 애씁니다.

어휘 memorable 기억에 남는   handle 다루다, 처리하다   undertake 떠맡다, 착수하다

2. (A) emerge

해설 빈칸 뒤에 목적어가 없으므로 자동사가 들어가야 한다. 따라서 '부상하다'라는 의미의 자동사인 (A) emerge가 정답이며, '에너지 회사들의 주식이 인기주로 부상할 수도 있다'는 내용이 되어 해석도 자연스럽다.

번역 유가 인상으로 인해 에너지 회사들의 주식이 투자자들에게 인기주로 부상할 수도 있다.

어휘 stock 주식   favorite 좋아하는 것, 인기주   investor 투자자   operate 운영하다   reveal 밝히다, 드러내다   enable 할 수 있게 하다

3. (C) coincides

해설 빈칸 뒤에 목적어 없이 전치사 with로 연결되었으므로 '동시에 일어나다, ~와 일치하다'라는 뜻으로 주로 전치사 with와 함께 쓰이는 자동사 (C) coincides가 정답이고, '우기의 시작이 여름 방학 기간과 일치한다'라고 문맥도 자연스럽다.

번역 그 지역 우기의 시작은 종종 대학들의 여름 방학과 겹친다.

어휘 rainy season 우기   demand 요구하다   activate 활성화하다

4. (D) confront

해설 문맥상 '선수들은 경기 내내 바람 부는 날씨와 맞서야 했다'라는 내용이 되어야 자연스러우므로 '맞서다'라는 의미의 (D) confront가 정답이다. (B) refrain은 '삼가다'라는 뜻으로 주로 전치사 from과 함께 쓰이는 자동사이므로 답이 될 수 없다.

번역 밸리 시 골프 시합에서 선수들은 전체 시합 내내 바람 부는 날씨와 맞서야 했다.

어휘 **windy** 바람이 부는 **entire** 전체의 **annoy** 짜증나게 하다
refrain 삼가다 **sacrifice** 희생하다

5. (C) convene

해설 빈칸 뒤에 목적어가 없는 것으로 보아 자동사를 골라야 한다. 자동사 convene은 '모이다'라는 뜻으로, '전문가들이 컨퍼런스에 모일 것이다'라는 내용으로 문맥이 자연스럽게 연결되므로 (C) convene이 정답이다. 참고로 convene은 '소집하다'라는 의미의 타동사로도 쓰일 수 있다.

번역 올 봄에 700명 이상의 정보 기술 전문가들이 데이터 보안 컨퍼런스에 모일 것이다.

어휘 **hold** 개최하다 **arrange** 배열하다, 마련하다
accumulate 모으다, 축적하다

6. (C) appointed

해설 주어가 사람이고 동사는 수동태 자리이므로 사람이 주어일 때 수동태로 쓸 수 있는 동사 어휘를 선택해야 한다. 즉, 능동태로 썼을 때 목적어로 사람을 쓸 수 있는 동사인지 판단하면 된다. 따라서 능동태일 때 '(사람을) 임명했다'로 해석되는 (C) appointed가 정답이다. 나머지 보기는 목적어로 사람을 쓰면 어색하므로 오답이다. 참고로, 동사 appeal은 전치사 to와 함께 쓰여 appeal to(~에게 매력을 끌다)로 주로 출제된다.

번역 와이어트 골드버그는 최근 이사회 의장으로 재직하도록 임명되었다.

어휘 **serve as** ~로서 일하다 **chairperson** 의장 **board of directors** 이사회

7. (B) delegates

해설 동사 어휘를 고를 때는 동사 자리 뒤에 오는 전치사가 큰 단서가 될 수 있다. 목적어 뒤에 전치사 to가 있으므로 'delegate A to B(A를 B에게 위임하다)'의 형태로 자주 쓰이는 delegate부터 확인해 보면, '우리 부서장이 윤 씨에게 특정 문서 작성 업무를 맡겼다'라고 자연스럽게 해석되므로 (B) delegates가 정답이다.

번역 우리 부서장은 윤 씨에게 특정 문서 작성 업무를 맡겼는데, 그녀가 글 쓰는 능력이 뛰어나기 때문이다.

어휘 **engage** 관심을 사로잡다, 고용하다 **approve** 승인하다
assist 돕다

8. (B) direct

해설 목적어 뒤에 전치사 to가 있으므로 'direct A to B(A를 B로 보내다)'의 형태로 자주 쓰이는 direct부터 확인해 보면, '모든 청구서 발부 관련 문의는 고객 서비스 부서로 하세요'라고 문맥이 자연스러우므로 (B) direct가 정답이다.

번역 청구서 발부에 관한 모든 문의는 우리 고객 서비스 부서로 하세요.

어휘 **billing** 청구서 발부 **inquiry** 문의 **cause** 초래하다
instruct 가르치다 **encourage** 장려하다

9. (B) dispose

해설 빈칸 뒤에 목적어가 없고 전치사 of가 있는 것으로 보아 전치사 of와 함께 '~을 없애다[처리하다]'라는 의미로 쓰이는 (B) dispose가 정답이고, '시에서 주민들이 폐전자 제품을 처리할 수 있는 재활용 센터를 새로 열었다'라는 내용으로 문맥도 자연스럽다.

번역 시에서는 재활용 센터를 새로 개설했는데 그곳에서 주민들은 원치 않는 폐전자제품을 처리할 수 있다.

어휘 **recycling** 재활용 **unwanted** 원치 않는 **electronic** 전자 장비의 **reduce** 줄이다 **delete** 삭제하다

10. (C) thrive

해설 빈칸 뒤에 목적어가 없으므로 자동사를 골라야 한다. 따라서 '번창하다'라는 의미의 자동사 (C) thrive가 정답이다. (A) shorten(단축하다), (B) compile(편집하다), (D) oversee(감독하다)는 모두 타동사로 목적어가 와야 하므로 답이 될 수 없다.

번역 지원을 아끼지 않는 환경에서 사기가 올라가고 직원들이 직장에서 일을 잘 해낼 수 있을 것이다.

어휘 **supportive** 지원하는 **environment** 환경 **morale** 사기, 의욕 **oversee** 감독하다

●UNIT 05 빈출 어구/명사

ACTUAL TEST
교재 p. 239

1. (C)	**2.** (B)	**3.** (D)	**4.** (B)	**5.** (C)
6. (B)	**7.** (B)	**8.** (C)	**9.** (A)	**10.** (C)

1. (C) effort

해설 effort는 'in an effort to(~해 보려는 노력으로)'의 형태로 자주 쓰이며, 문맥상 '고객 서비스를 향상시키려는 진심 어린 노력으로'라는 내용이 되어야 자연스러우므로 '노력'이라는 뜻의 (C) effort가 정답이다.

번역 진심으로 고객 서비스를 향상시키고자 하는 노력으로, 던-테크사는 이메일을 통해 피드백 설문지를 배포했다.

어휘 **sincere** 진실된 **force** 힘, 영향력 **stress** 압박

2. (B) response

해설 response는 in response to(~에 대응·대답하여)의 형태로 자주 쓰이며, 문맥상 '증가한 수요에 대응하여, 회사가 생산을 늘릴 것이다'라는 내용이 되어야 자연스러우므로 '대응, 응답'의 뜻을 지닌 (B) response가 정답이다.

번역 수요 증가에 대응하여 베바딕 오토사는 자사의 전기차 모델 생산을 증가시킬 것이다.

어휘 **demand** 수요 **boost** 증대시키다 **ceremony** 의식
opportunity 기회

3. (D) notice

해설 notice는 'until further notice(추후 통지가 있을 때까지)'의 형태로 자주 쓰이며, 문맥상 '미술관이 추후 통지가 있을 때까지 문을 닫을 것이다'라는 내용이 되어야 자연스러우므로 '공지, 통지'라는 의미의 (D) notice가 정답이다.

번역 시립 미술관은 그곳의 갤러리를 개조하기 위해서 추후 공지가 있을 때까지 폐관할 것이다.

어휘 renovate 개조하다 circulation 순환, 유통 removal 제거 invention 발명(품)

4. (B) advantage

해설 advantage는 'take advantage of(~을 이용하다)'의 형태로 자주 쓰이며, 문맥상 '세일 기간 동안 할인된 가격을 활용하도록 장려된다'라는 내용이 되어야 자연스러우므로 '이점, 장점'을 뜻하는 (B) advantage가 정답이다.

번역 쇼핑객들은 창고 정리 세일 동안 할인된 가격을 활용하도록 장려된다.

어휘 discounted 할인된 clearance sale 창고 정리 세일 nomination 지명, 추천 permission 허가 inquiry 문의

5. (C) receipt

해설 「(up)on + 명사 / 동명사(-ing)」는 '~하자마자'라는 뜻으로 문맥상 '투어 비용을 전액 받자마자'라는 내용이 되어야 자연스러우므로 '받기, 수령'이라는 의미의 (C) receipt이 정답이다.

번역 투어 비용이 전액 입금되는 대로 여행 일정표가 이메일로 발송될 것입니다.

어휘 itinerary 여행 일정표 security 보안 ambition 야망 honor 명예

6. (B) supervision

해설 supervision은 under the supervision of의 형태로 '~의 감독 하에'라는 의미로 쓰인다. 문맥상 '실험실 보조원들은 정규직 연구원들의 감독 하에 일한다'라는 내용이 되어야 자연스러우므로 '감독, 관리'라는 뜻의 (B) supervision이 정답이다.

번역 유니버시티 테크 센터의 실험실 보조원들은 정규직 연구원들의 감독 하에 일한다.

어휘 assistant 보조원, 조수 extension 확대

7. (B) compliance

해설 compliance는 'in compliance with(~에 응하여)'의 형태로 자주 쓰이며, 문맥상 '시의 환경법을 준수하기 위해 필요한 모든 조치를 취한다'라는 내용이 되어야 자연스러우므로 '준수, 따름'이라는 뜻의 (B) compliance가 정답이다.

번역 핸드렉스 케미컬 매뉴팩처링사는 시의 환경법을 준수하기 위해 필요한 모든 조치를 취한다.

어휘 take measures 조치를 취하다 environmental 환경의 transfer 이동; 이동하다 allowance 용돈

8. (C) exchange

해설 exchange는 'in exchange for(~ 대신에, ~에 대한 교환으로)'의 형태로 자주 쓰이며, 문맥상 '주말 동안 근무한 대신에'라는 내용이 되어야 자연스러우므로 '교환'이라는 의미의 (C) exchange가 정답이다.

번역 매장 경영진은 휴일 주말 동안 일한 대가로 일부 직원들에게 초과 근무 수당을 줄 것이다.

어휘 management 경영진 associate 직원 overtime pay 초과 근무 수당 postponement 연기 revision 수정

9. (A) range

해설 range는 'a range of(다양한)'의 형태로 자주 쓰이며, 문맥상 '다양한 제품을 구비하고 있다'라는 내용이 되어야 자연스러우므로 '다양성'이라는 의미의 (A) range가 정답이다.

번역 덴털즈 스포츠 매장은 자전거부터 운동복에 이르기까지 다양한 제품을 구비하고 있다.

어휘 have ~ in stock ~의 재고가 있다 workout apparel 운동복

10. (C) preparation

해설 preparation은 'in preparation for(~에 준비·대비하여)'의 형태로 자주 쓰이며, 문맥상 '발표에 대비하여, 마틴 씨는 차트와 그래프를 검토 중이다'라는 내용이 되어야 자연스러우므로 '준비'라는 의미의 (C) preparation이 정답이다.

번역 영업 프레젠테이션을 준비하기 위해, 마틴 씨는 사용할 도표와 그래프를 검토하고 있다.

어휘 availability 입수[이용] 가능성 excitement 흥분 strictness 엄격함

●UNIT 06 빈출 어구 / 형용사

ACTUAL TEST
교재 p. 241

1. (B)	2. (A)	3. (B)	4. (D)	5. (C)
6. (C)	7. (B)	8. (C)	9. (D)	10. (A)

1. (B) eligible

해설 eligible은 'be eligible for(~에 대한 자격이 있다)'의 형태로 자주 쓰이며, 문맥상 '직원들은 매장 제품 구입 시 할인 받을 자격이 된다'라는 내용이 되어야 자연스러우므로 '(자격 등이 맞아) ~할 수 있는'이라는 뜻의 (B) eligible이 정답이다.

번역 녹턴 숍스 사의 모든 직원들은 어떤 매장 제품을 구입하든지 할인을 받을 수 있다.

어휘 discount 할인 possible 가능한 flexible 융통성 있는, 유연한 essential 필수적인

2. (A) eager

해설 eager는 'be eager to부정사(~하고 싶어 하다)'의 형태로 자주 쓰이며, 문맥상 '많은 주민들이 시립 공원의 확장된 하이킹 코스를 이용하고 싶어 한다'라는 내용이 되어야 자연스러우므로 '간절히 바라는'이라는 뜻의 (A) eager가 정답이다.

번역 최근 설문 조사에 기반하여, 많은 주민들은 올 여름에 시립 공원의 확장된 하이킹 코스를 이용하고 싶어 한다.

어휘 based on ~에 기반하여 expanded 확대된, 확장된 costly 비용이 많이 드는 sympathetic 동정적인

3. (B) likely

해설 likely는 'be likely to부정사(~할 것 같다, ~하기 쉽다)'의 형태로 자주 쓰이며, 문맥상 '곧 새 뮤직 비디오를 공개할 것 같다'는 내용이 되어야 하므로 '~할 것 같은'이라는 의미의 (B) likely가 정답이다.

번역 포크 가수인 카트리나 카일리는 자신이 조만간 새 뮤직 비디오를 공개할 가능성이 있다고 발표했다.

어휘 release 공개하다, 발표하다 insist 주장하다 evident 분명한

4. (D) devoted

해설 devoted는 'be devoted to(~에 전념하다)'의 형태로 자주 쓰이며, 문맥상 '광고 예산의 절반 정도가 온라인 마케팅 광고에 주로 쓰여진다'라는 내용이 되어야 하므로 '전념하는, 헌신하는'의 뜻을 지닌 (D) devoted가 정답이다.

번역 보통 우리 광고비의 약 절반 정도가 온라인 마케팅 광고에 쓰여진다.

어휘 in general 보통, 대개 advertising 광고 caring 배려하는 claim 주장하다 deny 부인하다

5. (C) exempt

해설 exempt는 'be exempt from(~에서 면제되다)'의 형태로 자주 쓰이며, 문맥상 '외국인 방문객들은 부가가치세 납입이 면제된다'라는 내용이 되어야 자연스러우므로 '면제되는'이라는 뜻의 (C) exempt가 정답이다.

번역 국가의 새로운 세금 제도에 따라 외국인 방문객은 대부분의 구매에 대해 부가가치세 납입이 면제된다.

어휘 sales tax 판매세, 부가가치세 eliminated 제거된 distinct 뚜렷한 deducted 공제된

6. (C) subject

해설 subject는 'be subject to(~의 대상이다)'의 형태로 자주 쓰이며, 문맥상 '불법적으로 취득한 물품은 세관 직원에 의한 압수 대상이 된다'라는 내용이 되어야 자연스러우므로 '~될 수 있는'이라는 뜻의 (C) subject가 정답이다.

번역 본국에서 합법적으로 취득하지 않은 물품은 세관 직원에게 압수당할 수도 있다.

어휘 legally 합법적으로 seizure 압수 customs agent 세관 직원 opposed 반대하는 reluctant 꺼리는 admitted 공인된

7. (B) hesitant

해설 hesitant는 'be hesitant to부정사(~하는 것을 주저하다)'의 형태로 자주 쓰이며, 문맥상 '일부 소비자들은 온라인으로 옷을 구매하는 것을 주저할 수도 있다'라는 내용이 되어야 자연스러우므로 '주저하는'이라는 뜻의 (B) hesitant가 정답이다.

번역 미리 제품을 점검할 수 없기 때문에, 일부 소비자들은 온라인에서 옷을 구입하는 것을 주저할 수도 있다.

어휘 inspect 점검하다 beforehand 사전에, 미리 consumer 소비자 sizable 꽤 큰 neutral 중립의 apparent 분명한

8. (C) limited

해설 limited는 'be limited to(~에 한정되다)'의 형태로 종종 쓰이며, 문맥상 '카노프 씨의 러시아어 능력은 불과 몇몇 단어 및 구문에 한정된다'라는 내용이 되어야 자연스러우므로 '한정된, 제한된'을 의미하는 (C) limited가 정답이다.

번역 카노프 씨는 자신의 러시아어 구사 능력이 불과 몇몇 단어와 구에 한정된다고 말했다.

어휘 phrase 구 prevent 막다 relaxed 느긋한, 편안한

9. (D) bound

해설 bound는 'be bound to(틀림없이 ~하다)'의 형태로 자주 쓰이며, 문맥상 '더 높아진 환경 인식 덕에, 친환경 제품의 수요가 틀림없이 증가할 것이다'라는 내용이 되어야 자연스러우므로 '꼭 ~할 것 같은'이라는 뜻의 (D) bound가 정답이다.

번역 더 높아진 환경 인식 덕분에, 친환경 제품에 대한 수요가 증가할 것이 확실하다.

어휘 awareness 인식 eco-friendly 친환경적인 equal 동등한 be subject to ~의 대상이다, ~을 조건으로 하다 visible 눈에 보이는, 가시적인

10. (A) compatible

해설 compatible은 'be compatible with(~와 호환되다)'의 형태로 자주 쓰이며, 문맥상 '프로텍 플러스 바이러스 퇴치 프로그램은 거의 모든 컴퓨터 운영 체제와 호환된다'라는 내용이 되어야 자연스러우므로 '호환이 되는'이라는 뜻의 (A) compatible이 정답이다.

번역 프로텍 플러스 바이러스 퇴치 프로그램은 거의 모든 컴퓨터 운영 체제와 호환 가능하다.

어휘 nearly 거의 sociable 사교적인 achievable 성취할 수 있는 capable 할 수 있는, 유능한

●UNIT 07 빈출 어구/동사

ACTUAL TEST

교재 p. 243

1. (B)	2. (C)	3. (D)	4. (A)	5. (B)
6. (C)	7. (D)	8. (A)	9. (B)	10. (A)

1. (B) inform

해설 inform은 'inform A of B(A에게 B에 대해 알리다)'의 형태로 자주 쓰이며, 문맥상 '음식 공급 업체 직원에게 어떠한 식단 제한 사항에 대해서라도 알리는 것이 중요하다'라는 내용이 되어야 자연스러우므로 '알리다'라는 의미의 (B) inform이 정답이다.

번역 연회 참석자들에게 있을 수 있는 식사 제한은 어떤 것이든지 음식 공급 업체 직원에게 통지하는 것이 중요하다.

어휘 catering 행사 음식 공급 dietary restriction 식사 제한 banquet 연회 attendee 참석자

2. (C) refer

해설 refer는 'refer A to B(A를 B에 위탁하다)'의 형태로 쓰일 수 있는데, 빈칸 뒤에 전치사 to가 있으므로 refer를 대입해 본다. 문맥상 '우리는 더 이상 휴대폰을 수리하지 않으므로, 모든 서비스 요청은 지역 기사에게 위탁할 것이다'라는 내용이 되어 자연스럽다. 따라서 '위탁하다, 맡기다'라는 의미의 (C) refer가 정답이다.

번역 우리 가게에서는 더 이상 휴대폰을 수리하지 않으므로, 모든 서비스 요청은 지역 기사에게 보낼 것입니다.

어휘 no longer 더 이상 ~ 않는 technician 기사 vary 달리하다, 달라지다 seek 찾다, 구하다 moderate 완화하다

3. (D) prevent

해설 prevent는 'prevent 사람 from -ing(~가 -ing하는 것을 막다)'의 형태로 자주 쓰이며, 문맥상 '허가받지 않은 직원들이 건물에 들어오는 것을 막기 위해'라는 내용이 되어야 자연스러우므로 '막다, 방지하다'라는 의미의 (D) prevent가 정답이다.

번역 출입 카드 시스템은 허가받지 않은 직원들이 건물에 들어가는 것을 막기 위해 고안된 것이다.

어휘 access 출입 unauthorized 허가받지 않은 personnel 직원들 caution 주의를 주다 circle 빙빙 돌다 modify 수정하다

4. (A) reimbursed

해설 reimburse는 'be reimbursed for(~에 대해 환급받다)'의 형태로 자주 쓰이며, 문맥상 '직원들은 연료비에 대해 환급받을 것이다'라는 내용이 되어야 자연스러우므로 (A) reimbursed가 정답이다. (B) exchanged도 be exchanged for의 형태로 쓰이지만 '~로 교환을 받다'라는 뜻으로 문맥상 어울리지 않는다.

번역 직원들은 업무차 지점에 가기 위해 자신의 차를 사용할 경우 연료비를 환급받게 된다.

어휘 expense 비용 on business 업무로 influence 영향을 끼치다

5. (B) transform

해설 transform은 'transform A into B(A를 B로 변형시키다)'의 형태로 자주 쓰이며, 문맥상 '낡고 비어 있는 공장을 현대적인 미술관으로 바꿔 놓다'라는 내용이 되어야 자연스러우므로 (B) transform이 정답이다.

번역 데크론 부동산 개발은 비어 있는 오래된 공장을 현대적인 미술관으로 탈바꿈시킬 준비를 하고 있다.

어휘 modern 현대적인 eliminate 제거하다 substitute 대체하다 replace 대신하다

6. (C) discourage

해설 discourage는 '의욕을 꺾다, 좌절시키다'라는 뜻으로 'discourage 사람 from -ing'의 형태로 자주 쓰이며, 문맥상 '일부 여행객의 방문 의욕을 꺾을 수도 있다'라는 내용이 되어야 자연스러우므로 (C) discourage가 정답이다.

번역 관광 비자 발급을 위한 그 나라의 복잡한 자격 요건 때문에 일부 여행객들은 방문하는 것을 포기할 수도 있다.

어휘 requirement 자격 요건 tourist visa 관광 비자 afford ~할 여유가 되다 avoid 피하다, 막다 terminate 끝내다, 종료하다

7. (D) familiarize

해설 familiarize는 '익숙하게 하다'라는 뜻으로 'familiarize yourself/사람 with ~'의 형태로 자주 쓰이며, 문맥상 '당신이 새 도시에 빨리 익숙해지는 방법'이라는 내용이 되어야 자연스러우므로 (D) familiarize가 정답이다. (A) cooperate도 전치사 with와 자주 쓰이지만 자동사이므로 뒤에 목적어 없이 cooperate with의 형태로 쓰인다.

번역 이삿짐 업체의 웹사이트에서는 새로운 도시에 빨리 익숙해지는 법에 관한 조언을 제공한다.

어휘 tip 조언 cooperate 협동하다 accompany 동행하다 standardize 표준화하다

8. (A) honor

해설 honor는 'honor A for B(B에 대해 A에게 상을 주다)'의 형태로 자주 쓰이며, 문맥상 '협회가 작가인 애나 그리스데일에게 상을 수여할 계획이다'라는 내용이 되어야 자연스러우므로 (A) honor가 정답이다.

번역 도서관 협회는 아동 문학에 기여한 공로로 작가인 애나 그리스데일에게 상을 수여할 계획이다.

어휘 author 작가 contribution 기여 literature 문학 happen 발생하다 express 표현하다 deserve ~을 받을 만하다

9. (B) account

해설 account는 take ~ into account의 형태로 쓰여 '~을 고려하다'를 의미하며, 문맥상 '일기 예보를 반드시 고려하라'는 내용이 되어야 자연스러우므로 (B) account가 정답이다.

번역 야외 피크닉을 계획할 때는 반드시 일기 예보를 고려하라.

어휘 outdoor 야외의 be sure to *do* 반드시 ~하다 weather forecast 일기 예보 storage 저장, 보관 transcript 기록, 원고

10. (A) refrain

해설 빈칸 뒤에 목적어가 없이 바로 전치사 from이 있으므로, '삼가다'라는 의미로 refrain from의 형태로 쓰이는 자동사 refrain을 대입해 본다. 문맥상 '관객들은 오케스트라 공연 중 말하는 것을 삼가야 한다'라는 내용이 되어야 하므로 (A) refrain이 정답이다.

번역 관객들은 오케스트라 공연 도중에는 말하는 것을 삼가도록 요청된다.

어휘 audience 관객, 청중 oppose 반대하다 escape 탈출하다

●UNIT 08
빈출 Collocation / 동사 + 목적어

ACTUAL TEST

교재 p. 245

1. (D)	**2.** (B)	**3.** (B)	**4.** (B)	**5.** (C)
6. (A)	**7.** (B)	**8.** (A)	**9.** (A)	**10.** (B)

1. (D) issues

해설 coupon을 목적어로 받을 수 있으며 전치사 to와 의미적 관계를 이루는 동사를 고르는 문제이다. 전치사 to 뒤에 사람(대상)이 나오므로 '…에게 ~을 발행하다'로 쓸 수 있는 (D) issues가 정답이다. (A)는 'allow 목적어 to부정사(목적어가 ~하는 것을 가능하게 하다)'로 쓰이며, (B)는 'exchange A for B(A와 B를 교환하다)'로 쓰인다. (C)는 목적어로 coupons를 받을 수 있지만 의미상 「to + 대상」과 연결되지 않으므로 오답이다.

번역 조아니 의류 회사는 구매 금액이 50달러 이상인 첫 고객들에게 쿠폰을 발행한다.

2. (B) assume

해설 assume은 '(직책·책임 등을) 맡다'라는 뜻으로 '린치 씨는 최고 마케팅 관리자직을 맡을 것이다'라는 내용이 되어 문맥이 자연스럽다. 따라서 (B) assume이 정답이다. (A) react와 (D) arrive는 자동사이므로 뒤에 목적어가 올 수 없다.

번역 최근의 승진으로 린치 씨는 최고 마케팅 관리자직을 맡을 것이다.

어휘 latest 최근의 promotion 승진 react 반응하다 decrease 줄다, 줄이다

3. (B) express

해설 타동사 express는 '표현하다'라는 뜻으로 목적어 concerns와 어울려 '주민들이 관심을 표현할 수 있다'라고 자연스럽게 해석되므로 (B) express가 정답이다. (A) comment(논평하다), (C) speak(말하다), (D) remark(언급하다)는 모두 자동사로 뒤에 목적어가 올 수 없으므로 답이 될 수 없다.

번역 시민 초청 간담회는 주민들이 여러 사안들에 대한 관심을 나타낼 수 있는 토론의 장을 제공한다.

어휘 town hall meeting 시민 초청 간담회 concern 걱정, 관심사 various 여러 가지의 comment 논평하다

4. (B) determine

해설 whether to로 시작하는 명사구를 목적어로 자연스럽게 연결할 수 있는 동사 어휘를 고르는 문제이다. '소기업 소유주들은 사무용 장비를 대여할지 혹은 구입할지 결정해야 한다'라는 내용이 되어야 문맥이 자연스러우므로 '결정하다'라는 뜻의 (B) determine이 정답이다.

번역 소기업 경영주들은 자신들의 기업을 위해 사무용 장비를 대여할지 아니면 구입할지를 결정해야 한다.

어휘 lease 대여하다 enterprise 기업 hesitate 주저하다 stimulate 자극하다 repair 수리하다

5. (C) simplify

해설 문맥상 일부 고객이 온라인으로 주문하기가 복잡하다고 지적한 것에 대해 해야 할 일을 언급하는 내용이 와야 하므로 '과정을 간소화해야 한다'라는 의미가 되어야 적절하다. 따라서 '간소화[단순화]하다'라는 뜻의 (C) simplify가 정답이다. (A) consist는 자동사로 뒤에 목적어를 연결할 수 없다.

번역 우리 고객들 일부가 온라인으로 주문하는 것이 복잡하다고 지적했기에, 우리는 그 과정을 간소화해야 한다.

어휘 place an order 주문하다 complex 복잡한 consist 구성되다

6. (A) address

해설 address는 '(문제 등을) 다루다'라는 뜻으로 '무니 씨는 팀에게 동기를 부여하는 문제를 다룰 계획이다'라고 해석되어 문맥이 자연스러우므로 (A) address가 정답이다. (D) insist는 자동사이므로 목적어를 연결할 수 없다.

번역 자신의 강연에서 무니 씨는 직장에서 팀에게 동기를 부여하는 문제를 다룰 계획이다.

어휘 motivate 동기를 부여하다 workplace 직장 enroll 등록하다 speculate 추측하다 insist 주장하다

7. (B) implement

해설 문맥상 '지방 정부 보조금 덕에 새로운 재활용 프로그램을 시행할 것이다'라는 내용이 되어야 자연스러우므로 '시행하다'라는 의미의 (B) implement가 정답이다.

번역 로젠 국립 대학은 지방 정부로부터 받는 보조금 만 달러 덕분에 새로운 재활용 프로그램을 시행할 것이다.

어휘 grant 보조금 reduce 줄이다 transport 수송하다 succeed 성공하다

8. (A) imposes

해설 impose는 '(힘들거나 불쾌한 것을) 부과하다'라는 뜻으로 '시에서 쓰레기를 버리는 행위에 대해 벌금을 부과한다'라고 해석되어 문맥이 자연스러우므로 (A) imposes가 정답이다. (C) intervene은 자동사이므로 목적어를 연결할 수 없다.

번역 방문객들은 어떤 공원에서든 쓰레기를 버리는 행위에 대해 시에서 벌금을 부과한다는 것을 유념해야 한다.

어휘 fine 벌금 litter 쓰레기를 버리다 resource 자원을 제공하다 intervene 개입하다 confront 맞서다

9. (A) extend

해설 extend는 '주다, 베풀다'라는 뜻으로 격식을 차려 환영·환대·초대·감사 등의 뜻을 전달할 때 종종 쓰인다. 문맥상 '자원봉사자들에게 감사의 뜻을 전하고 싶다'라고 해석되어야 자연스러우므로 (A) extend가 정답이다. (B) notify는 '통지하다'라는 뜻으로 의미의 연결이 어색하고, (C) comply와 (D) specialize는 자동사이므로 목적어를 연결할 수 없다.

번역 축제 주최자인 싱 씨는 행사 동안 도와준 자원봉사자들에게 감사를 표하고 싶어 한다.

어휘 organizer 주최자 gratitude 감사 volunteer 자원봉사자 notify 공지하다 specialize 전문적으로 다루다

10. (B) renewed

해설 be동사 뒤에 과거분사로 수동태 구문을 만들어 주어와 의미가 자연스럽게 연결될 수 있는 동사 어휘를 고르는 문제이다. '해지를 원한다는 통지를 받을 때까지'라는 내용으로 보아 현재 소프트웨어를 이용 중인 것을 알 수 있으므로, '소프트웨어 정기 이용(subscription)이 자동으로 갱신될 것이다'라는 내용이 되어야 가장 자연스럽다. 따라서 '갱신하다'라는 뜻의 (B) renewed가 정답이다.

번역 귀하의 바이러스 퇴치 프로그램 정기 결제 서비스는 귀하가 서비스 해지를 원한다는 통지가 접수될 때까지 자동으로 갱신될 것입니다.

어휘 subscription 구독, 정기 결제 서비스 이용 automatically 자동으로 notice 통지, 공지 suspend 유예하다 correct 바로잡다

●UNIT 09
빈출 Collocation / 동사+부사

ACTUAL TEST
교재 p. 247

1. (B)	2. (B)	3. (C)	4. (C)	5. (B)
6. (D)	7. (B)	8. (C)	9. (B)	10. (C)

1. (B) closely

해설 closely는 '면밀히, 주의하여'라는 뜻으로 '보다'라는 의미를 지닌 동사들과 잘 어울려 쓰이고, 문맥상으로도 '우리는 모든 서비스 제안서를 면밀히 검토할 것이다'라고 해석되어 자연스러우므로 (B) closely가 정답이다. (C) recently는 과거 또는 현재완료 시제와 어울려 쓰인다.

번역 우리는 어떤 것이 우리의 요구에 가장 적합한지를 결정하기 전에 모든 서비스 제안서를 면밀히 검토할 것이다.

어휘 review 검토하다 proposal 제안 suitable 적합한 durably 튼튼하게 respectfully 공손하게

2. (B) thoroughly

해설 동사구 was examined를 수식하기에 적절한 부사 어휘를 택하는 문제이다. '회의에서 철저히 검토되었다'라는 내용이 되어야 문맥이 자연스러우므로 '철저히'라는 의미의 (B) thoroughly가 정답이다.

번역 우리가 의제에 포함시킨 것의 대부분은 지난주 회의에서 철저히 검토되었다.

어휘 agenda 의제 examine 조사하다, 검토하다 relatively 비교적 exceedingly 극도로

3. (C) slightly

해설 형용사 thicker를 수식하기에 적절한 부사 어휘를 선택하는 문제이다. 완두콩 수프의 질감 상태를 나타내는 '더 걸쭉한(thicker)'과 어울리려면 상태의 정도를 표현하는 부사인 '약간'이라는 의미의 slightly가 가장 적절하다. 따라서 (C) slightly가 정답이다.

번역 차갑게 먹으면 완두콩 수프는 약간 더 걸쭉한 질감과 더 부드러운 맛이 난다.

어휘 pea 완두콩 thick 두꺼운, 걸쭉한 texture 질감 mild 부드러운 exclusively 독점적으로, 오로지 deliberately 고의로

4. (C) evenly

해설 동사구 are distributed를 수식하기에 적절한 부사 어휘를 고르는 문제이다. '공정성을 위해서'라고 언급한 것으로 보아 '업무가 균등하게 분배되어야 한다'는 내용이 되어야 앞뒤 문맥이 일치하므로 '균등하게, 대등하게'라는 의미의 (C) evenly가 정답이다.

번역 공정성을 위해서, 관리자들은 팀원들 간에 업무를 균등하게 분배해야 한다.

어휘 in the interest of ~을 위하여 fairness 공정성 supervisor 관리자, 감독 distribute 분배하다 firmly 단호하게 noticeably 눈에 띄게 apparently 보아하니

5. (B) accordingly

해설 동사구 should plan을 수식하기에 적절한 부사 어휘를 고르는 문제이다. accordingly는 앞서 언급된 상황에 '부응해서, 그에 맞춰'라는 뜻이고, 문맥상 '퍼레이드 동안 교통이 복잡할 것이므로, 운전자들은 그에 맞춰 계획을 세워야 한다'라는 내용이 되어야 자연스러우므로 (B) accordingly가 정답이다.

번역 도심 지역의 교통이 퍼레이드 동안 복잡할 것이므로 운전자들은 그에 맞춰 계획을 세워야 한다.

어휘 traffic 교통 eventually 결국 constantly 끊임없이

6. (D) generously

해설 동사 offer를 수식하기에 적절한 부사 어휘를 선택하는 문제이다. 문맥상 '뮤지컬 감독이 질의응답 시간을 기꺼이 마련하겠다고 했다'라는 내용이 되어야 자연스러우므로 '관대하게, 기꺼이'라는 의미의 (D) generously가 정답이다.

번역 뮤지컬 감독은 금요일 공연 후에 질의응답 시간을 기꺼이 마련하겠다고 발표했다.

어휘 host 주최하다, 열다 performance 공연 overly 너무, 지나치게 partially 부분적으로 correctly 정확하게

7. (B) collaboratively

해설 동사 work를 수식하기에 적절한 부사 어휘를 고르는 문제이다. 전치사 with의 목적어로 사람명사가 나오므로 '~와 일하다'로 해석되며 이에 어울리는 부사는 '~와 협력하여 일하다'라는 의미를 만드는 (B) collaboratively이다. (A) hardly는 뜻에 유의할 부사로 be동사 뒤, 조동사 뒤, 일반동사 앞에 위치하여 '거의 ~이 아니다'로 해석되므로 정답이 될 수 없다. (C) extremely는 정도를 수식하고 동사는 수식하지 않는 부사이며 (D) previously는 과거 시제에 어울리는 부사이므로 오답이다.

번역 인턴들은 디자인 과정의 모든 단계에서 제품 개발자들과 협력해서 일할 기회를 가질 것이다.

어휘 hardly 거의 ~이 아니다 extremely 극도로 previously 이전에

8. (C) punctually

해설 to부정사구 to arrive를 수식하는 말로 적절한 부사 어휘를 택하는 문제이다. 문맥상 시간에 대해 이야기하고 있으므로 '참가자들은 제시간에 도착해야 한다'는 내용이 되어야 자연스럽다. 따라서 '정각에, (시간을) 엄수하여'라는 의미의 (C) punctually가 정답이다.

번역 우리 워크숍은 오전 10시 30분에 시작하며 참가자들은 제시간에 도착할 것으로 예상된다.

어휘 confidently 자신 있게 alongside 나란히 extensively 널리, 광범위하게

9. (B) substantially

해설 to부정사구 to increase를 수식하기에 적절한 부사 어휘를 선택하는 문제이다. substantially는 증감의 변화 상태를 수식하는 부사로 자주 쓰이며, 문맥싱으로도 '연료비가 상당히 오르고 있기 때문에'라고 해석되어 자연스러우므로 '상당히, 많이'라는 의미의 (B) substantially가 정답이다. (C) largely와 (D) mainly는 '주로'라는 뜻의 부사이고 '주로 오르고 있다'라는 말은 어색하므로 정답이 될 수 없다.

번역 연료비가 계속 많이 오르고 있기 때문에 그 택배 회사는 배송비를 인상할 예정이다.

어휘 raise 올리다, 인상하다 fuel cost 연료비 restrictedly 제한적으로 mainly 주로

10. (C) expressly

해설 동사 state를 수식하기에 적절한 부사 어휘를 고르는 문제이다. 문맥상 '회사의 교환 규정은 분명히 명시하고 있다'라고 해석되어야 자연스러우므로 '분명히'라는 뜻의 (C) expressly가 정답이다. (A) either와 (B) neither는 부정문에서 쓰는 부사이고, (D) scarcely는 보통 일반동사 앞에 쓰이므로 답이 될 수 없다.

번역 그 회사의 교환 규정은 주문 제작 상품은 반품이나 환불이 되지 않을 수 있다는 것을 분명히 명시하고 있다.

어휘 exchange 교환 state 명시하다 customized 주문 제작한 return 반품하다 scarcely 거의 ~ 않는

●UNIT 10
빈출 Collocation / 기타 형용사 및 부사

ACTUAL TEST
교재 p. 249

1. (B)	**2.** (D)	**3.** (B)	**4.** (C)	**5.** (B)
6. (D)	**7.** (C)	**8.** (D)	**9.** (D)	**10.** (D)

1. (B) welcome

해설 명사 addition을 수식하기에 적절한 형용사 어휘를 고르는 문제이다. addition은 '추가된, 즉 새로 합류한 직원'을 뜻하며 인턴 모두가 열심히 일했다고 긍정적으로 평가한 내용으로 보아 '환영받는 직원'이라고 해야 문맥상 자연스럽다. 따라서 '환영받는, 반가운'이라는 의미의 (B) welcome이 정답이다.

번역 하계 인턴 모두가 열심히 일했으므로 그들은 우리 직원들에게 환영받는 충원 인력입니다.

어휘 addition 추가, 부가 mutual 상호간의 fascinated 매료된

2. (D) tentatively

해설 형용사 scheduled를 수식하기에 알맞은 부사 어휘를 선택하는 문제이다. 빈칸 뒤쪽으로 추후 확인을 받아야 한다고 언급했으므로 5월 7일로 잡혀 있는 일정은 확정된 일정

PART 5

이 아님을 알 수 있다. 따라서 '잠정적으로'라는 의미의 (D) tentatively가 정답이다.

번역 관리자 회의는 잠정적으로 5월 7일로 잡혀 있는데, 추후에 확인을 받아야 한다.

어휘 be scheduled for ~로 예정되다 subject to ~을 받아야 하는 confirmation 확인 gradually 점차 impressively 인상적으로 unknowingly 모르고

3. (B) consistently

해설 형용사 high를 수식하기에 적절한 부사 어휘를 고르는 문제이다. 문맥상 '지속적인 고품질 서비스로 긍정적인 고객 평가를 받았다'라는 내용이 되어야 자연스러우므로 '꾸준히, 지속적으로'라는 의미의 (B) consistently가 정답이다.

번역 알파 이삿짐 센터는 지속적인 고품질 서비스로 긍정적인 고객 평가를 받아 왔다.

어휘 earn 얻다, 받다 positive 긍정적인 potentially 잠재적으로 eventually 결국 adversely 불리하게, 반대로

4. (C) reasonably

해설 형용사 priced를 수식하기에 적절한 부사 어휘를 택하는 문제이다. priced는 '값이 매겨진'이라는 뜻으로 가격에 대해 수식하는 말로 가장 자연스러운 부사를 골라야 한다. 따라서 '합리적으로, 적정하게'라는 뜻의 (C) reasonably가 정답이다. 참고로, 가격을 수식하는 말로 자주 쓰이는 형용사 'affordable(가격이 알맞은)', 'reasonable(적정한, 합리적인)', 'competitive(경쟁력 있는)'도 함께 알아 두자.

번역 가정용 베이직 패키지는 줌 텔레콤에서 가장 가격이 저렴한 케이블 TV와 인터넷 패키지이다.

어휘 readily 손쉽게 barely 거의 ~ 아닌

5. (B) primarily

해설 주격 보어 자리에 쓰인 전치사구 due to the rainy weather를 수식하기에 적절한 부사 어휘를 택하는 문제이다. 문맥상 '저조한 참석률은 주로 비 오는 날씨 탓이었다'라는 내용이 되어야 자연스러우므로 '주로'라는 의미의 (B) primarily가 정답이다.

번역 지난 가을 음악 축제의 저조한 참석률은 주로 비 오는 날씨 때문이었다.

어휘 attendance 참석, 참석률 highly 대단히, 매우 popularly 일반적으로

6. (D) rigorous

해설 명사 inspection을 수식하기에 적절한 형용사 어휘를 선택하는 문제이다. inspection은 '점검'이라는 뜻이므로 '엄격한'이라는 의미의 형용사와 가장 잘 어울리므로 (D) rigorous가 정답이고, 나머지 보기는 '점검'을 수식해주는 말로 의미상 부적절하다.

번역 우리가 판매하는 모든 중고차는 먼저 숙달된 정비공의 엄격한 점검을 통과해야 한다.

어휘 inspection 점검 mechanic 정비공 wealthy 부유한 polite 예의 바른 luxurious 호화로운

7. (C) readily

해설 형용사 accessible을 수식하기에 적절한 부사 어휘를 고르는 문제이다. 문맥상 '우리 창고에 있는 재고 대부분은 손쉽게 접근할 수 있다'라는 내용이 되어야 자연스러우므로 '손쉽게'라는 의미의 (C) readily가 정답이다.

번역 우리 창고의 재고 대부분은 손쉽게 접근할 수 있어서 손이 닿기 위해 사다리를 사용할 필요가 없다.

어휘 stock 재고품 warehouse 창고 accessible 접근 가능한 ladder 사다리 loudly 큰 소리로

8. (D) highly

해설 형용사(과거분사) regarded를 수식하기에 적절한 부사 어휘를 고르는 문제이다. 관계대명사 who절에서 티나 칼로의 업적에 대해 언급하고 있으므로 문맥상 '존경받는, 매우 인정받는 교육자'라고 해석되어야 자연스럽다. 따라서 '매우, 대단히'라는 의미의 (D) highly가 정답이다.

번역 티나 칼로는 수상 이력이 있는 아동 도서들을 집필한 존경받는 교육자이다.

어휘 regard (높이) 평가하다, 존경하다 educator 교육자 profitably 유익하게 densely 빽빽이

9. (D) immediately

해설 전치사구 after the afternoon seminar를 수식하기에 적절한 부사 어휘를 선택하는 문제이다. after the afternoon seminar는 시간대(순서)에 대한 표현이므로 시간 관련 수식어인 '즉시'라는 의미의 immediately의 수식을 받아야 자연스럽다. 따라서 (D) immediately가 정답이다. (B) presently는 시간 관련 수식어이긴 하지만 '현재'라는 뜻으로 미래 시제와 어울리지 않으므로 답이 될 수 없다. immediately는 before나 after와 함께 쓰여 '직전', '직후'라는 의미로 쓰인다.

번역 오후 세미나 직후에 간식과 다과가 제공될 것이다.

어휘 refreshments 다과 historically 역사적으로 presently 현재 mannerly 예절 바르게

10. (D) otherwise

해설 접속사 Unless와 어울리며 과거분사 instructed를 수식하기에 적절한 부사 어휘를 택하는 문제이다. 문맥상 '달리 지시받은 바 없으면'이라는 내용이 되어야 자연스러우므로 '다르게'라는 의미의 (D) otherwise가 정답이다. (A) else는 '(이미 언급된 것에 덧붙여) 또 다른'이라는 의미로 what이나 anything, somebody 등의 대명사 뒤에 붙어 쓰이므로 답이 될 수 없다.

번역 별도의 지시가 없는 한 인사부에 지원서를 제출하세요.

어휘 unless ~하지 않는 한 instruct 지시하다 employment application 입사 지원서 else 또 다른 diversely 다양하게 moreover 게다가

PART 6

● 풀이 전략

1-4 안내

교재 p. 256

월-데일 마트 배송 규정

보통의 경우 고객님이 구입하신 상품은 영업일 1일에서 5일 이내에 [1]도착할 것입니다. [2]하지만 부피가 큰 물품의 경우 고객님께 이메일을 드려 배송 날짜와 시간을 확인합니다. 만약 해당 날짜가 맞지 않으실 경우에는 저희 고객 서비스 센터로 연락하셔서 배송 [3]일정 변경을 요청하실 수 있습니다.

모든 배송에는 성인인 수령인의 서명이 필요합니다. [4]배송을 수령할 수 있는 분이 반드시 계셔 주시기 바랍니다. 서명을 받지 않은 물품은 고객님 댁의 문 밖에 놓아 두지 않습니다. 상품에 손상이 있는지 점검하신 후에 인수증에 서명하셔야 합니다. 배달한 사람이 댁을 떠나기 전에 반드시 상품을 확인해 주시기 바랍니다.

policy 규정, 방침 business day 영업일 confirm 확인하다
inconvenient 불편한, 맞지 않는 shipment 수송 recipient
수령인 delivery receipt 인수증 inspect 점검하다 ensure
반드시 ~하게 하다

번역 (A) 고객님의 제품 배송 지연에 대해 사과드리고자 합니다.
(B) 아동은 어른의 관리하에서만 이 제품을 사용해야 합니다.
(C) 배송을 수령할 수 있는 분이 반드시 계셔야 합니다.
(D) 저희는 모든 포장재에 재활용품을 사용합니다.

어휘 delay 지연 supervision 감독, 관리 available 시간이
나는 recycled product 재활용품 packaging 포장재

●UNIT 01 접속부사 문제

예제

교재 p. 258

소포를 해외로 배송하는 규칙은 국가마다 다르다. 따라서 고객들이 규칙에 따라 소포를 준비하는 것이 중요하다. 이름과 주소 외에 글씨가 소포 겉면에 있으면 안 된다. 추가 글씨는 배송 과정을 느리게 할 수 있다.

READING PRACTICE

교재 p. 259

1. (B) **2.** (A) **3.** (C)

1 접속부사

매트록 주철 프라이팬을 구입해주셔서 감사합니다. 매번 사용한 후에 제대로 세척해서 관리해야 팬의 성능이 유지됩니다.

세척을 위해서는, 먼저 종이 타월로 내부를 닦아서 기름이나 남은 음식물을 제거하세요. 그 다음에는 뜨거운 물로 팬을 헹구세요. 그리고 나서 종이 타월을 이용해서 팬의 물기를 완전히 닦으세요. 아니면 가스레인지를 중불로 놓고 그 위에서 팬을 건조시키세요. 마지막으로 다음 번 사용에 대비해 기름 반 티스푼으로 팬의 표면을 코팅하세요.

purchase 구입 cast-iron 주철로 만든 care for 관리하다
properly 제대로, 적절히 performance 성능 wipe 닦다
rinse (세제 없이) 씻다, 헹구다 coat 막을 입히다, 코팅하다

해설 빈칸 앞 문장에서 종이 타월을 이용해 팬의 물기를 닦으라고 했는데, 뒤 문장에서 가스레인지를 중불로 놓고 그 위에서 팬을 건조시키라며 앞서 말한 팬의 건조 방법 외에 쓸 수 있는 다른 방법을 제시하고 있으므로 두 번째 대안을 소개할 때 쓰는 '아니면, 그 대신에'라는 뜻의 (B) Alternatively가 정답이다.

어휘 if so 만약 그렇다면 thus 따라서, 그러므로
consequently 그 결과, 따라서

2 접속부사

골드 사이언티픽 서플라이는 선도적인 과학 기기 제조 업체로서, 영광스럽게도 자사의 VS-7 뷰 모델의 현미경이 국제 디지털 현미경 박람회(IDMTS)에서 최고 디자인상을 수상했음을 알립니다. 이 상은 독창적인 디자인 요소와 사용 편리성에 대해 시상합니다. 특히 VS-7 뷰는 고난도 작업 조건에서의 안정성에 대해 호평을 받았습니다. VS-7 뷰에 대한 더 자세한 정보를 보시려면 www.ende-mark.com을 방문하십시오.

leading 선두적인 manufacturer 제조자, 생산 회사
instrument 기구, 악기 microscope 현미경 trade show
박람회 recognize (공로를) 인정[표창]하다 original 독창적인,
원래의 element 요소 praise 칭찬하다 stability 안정성
challenging 도전적인, 힘든

해설 빈칸 앞 문장에서 일반적으로 적용되는 심사 포인트에 대해 설명했는데, 뒤 문장에서 VS-7 뷰는 고난도 작업 조건에서의 안정성에 대해 찬사를 받았다며 VS-7가 수상을 하게 된 포인트에 대해 다시 한번 구체적으로 강조하고 있으므로 빈칸에는 강조의 의미를 부여해 줄 수 있는 접속부사가 들어가야 자연스럽다. 따라서 '특히'라는 뜻의 (A) In particular가 정답이다.

3 접속부사

7월 1일부터 드림 오피스 프로덕츠는 메이플 가 160번지에 있는 그린뷰 쇼핑 플라자에 위치하게 됩니다. 더 넓은 매장과 주차 공간으로, 이 새로운 시설은 고객들에게 더 다양하게 엄선된 제품들과 더 편리한 쇼핑을 제공해 드릴 것입니다. 이번 확장을 기념하여, 6월 21일부터 시작되는 주에 예전 매장에서 재고 정리 세일을 합니다. 최고 40퍼센트까지 특별 할인된 제품들을 가져가세요! 게다가 메이플 가에서의 대개장을

홍보하기 위해 7월 3일 주말에 또 한 번의 세일을 합니다. 조만간 뵙기를 바랍니다!

---

floor space 바닥[매장] 면적   parking 주차   facility 시설   goods 제품   expansion 확대. 확장   clearance sale 재고 정리 세일   promote 홍보하다

해설   빈칸 앞에서 6월에 재고 정리 세일을 한다(we will hold a clearance sale ~ during the week of June 21)고 했는데, 뒤에서 7월에 또 세일을 한다(we will have another sale on the weekend of July 3)고 언급했으므로 유사한 내용을 추가할 때 쓰는 접속부사가 들어가야 글의 흐름이 자연스럽다. 따라서 '게다가'라는 의미의 (C) Moreover가 정답이다.

어휘   nevertheless 그럼에도 불구하고   specifically 특별히   in addition to ~에 덧붙여. ~ 외에도

●UNIT 02 어휘 문제

예제

교재 p. 260

KG 전동 드릴을 구매해 주셔서 감사합니다. 이 제품은 설명서대로 사용하는 경우, 구매 후 1년간 결함이 생기지 않음을 보장합니다. 이러한 제한적 보증은 잘못된 사용이나 관리로 인한 피해에 대해서는 보상하지 않습니다. 이 경우 고장이 발생한 제품은 수리 또는 교체를 위해 서비스 센터로 보내실 수 있습니다.

READING PRACTICE

교재 p. 261

1. (C)   **2.** (D)   **3.** (A)

1   동사 어휘

델빈 쇼어즈 항구는 대대적인 확장이라는 기쁜 소식을 알리고 있다. 항구 소유주인 델빈 쇼어즈 포트 조합(DSPC)은 최근에 인접한 블록의 공터를 매입했다. 이 부지는 이전에 론데일 밀즈 공장으로 사용되던 곳으로, 그것은 작년에 철거되었다. "해운업계의 높은 성장세에 부응하기 위해, 우리는 항구 시설을 확장해야 합니다."라고 DSPC의 제프 리 의장은 말했다. 부지 개발 일정은 DSPC 기획 책임자들이 논의 중이다.

---

port 항구   purchase 구입하다   adjacent 인접한. 가까운   vacant 비어 있는   previously 이전에   demolish 철거하다   shipping 해운. 운송   timeline 일정표

해설   첫 문장에서 대대적인 확장을 발표한다고 했고 그 다음 문장에서 항구 소유주인 DSPC사가 최근에 공터를 매입했다며 사업 확장에 수반되는 내용을 덧붙인 것으로 보아, 해당 문장 또한 '높은 성장세에 부응하기 위해, 항구 시설을 확장해야 한다'라는 내용이 되어야 문맥이 자연스럽다. 따라서 '확장[확대]하다'라는 의미의 (C) enlarge가 정답이다.

어휘   relocate 이전하다   sell 매각하다   lend 빌려주다

2   명사 어휘

쓰레기 매립지에 관한 최근 연구에서 재활용 가능한 것들이 쓰레기의 거의 70퍼센트를 차지하는 것으로 드러났습니다. 하지만 우리 지자체는 가정용 쓰레기의 약 30퍼센트만을 재활용하고 있습니다. 우리는 전국 평균 재활용 수치인 40퍼센트와 같아지도록 이 수치를 늘리고자 합니다. 지역민들이 이러한 목표를 달성하도록 돕기 위해, 도로변 재활용 물품 수거를 10월 1일부터는 일주일에 한 번으로 늘릴 예정입니다. 시 웹사이트에서 재활용품 관련 규정 목록을 열람할 수 있습니다.

---

landfill 쓰레기 매립지   reveal 드러내다. 밝히다   recyclable 재활용할 수 있는   account for 차지하다   approximately 대략   household 가정; 가정의   trash 쓰레기   increase 늘리다   in line with ~와 비슷한[일치하는]   assist 돕다   resident 주민   curbside 차도 가장자리   pickup 수거   regulation 규정

해설   앞 문장에서 가정용 쓰레기의 약 30퍼센트만 재활용하고 있다라고 했으므로, this 뒤에는 앞에서 언급된 30퍼센트를 대신하는 명사가 들어가 '이 수치를 늘리길 원한다'라는 내용이 되어야 한다. 빈칸 뒤의 '전국 평균 재활용 수치인 40퍼센트와 비슷해지기 위해서'라는 내용과도 자연스럽게 연결되므로 '수치'를 뜻하는 (D) figure가 정답이다.

어휘   aim 목적. 목표   promise 약속   change 변화. 변경

3   명사 어휘

캐스틸로 은행을 대표하여, 지난해 우수 고객이 되어 주신 데 대해 감사드립니다. 고객님께서는 실버 고객 등급의 자격을 얻으셨음을 알려 드리고자 연락드립니다. 고객님께서는 이제 캐스틸로 은행 신용카드로 자격 조건이 되는 구입 시 1달러 당 1포인트를 받으실 수 있습니다. 고객님의 등급은 자동으로 업그레이드될 것이므로, 고객님께서 추가로 하셔야 하는 일은 없습니다. 아무때나 온라인 계정에 접속하셔서 고객님의 포인트가 얼마인지 확인해 보시기 바랍니다. 잔여 포인트는 메인 화면에 나타납니다.

---

on behalf of ~을 대표[대신]하여   loyal customer 단골 고객   inform 알리다   qualify 자격을 얻다   reward 보상   status 지위. 상황   be eligible to do ~할 자격이 있다   earn 얻다   automatically 자동으로   further 추가의   log on to ~에 접속하다   account 계정

해설   앞 문맥에는 해당 고객이 은행의 실버 등급이 되어 받게 된 보상 포인트 제도에 대해 설명하는 내용으로 구성되어 있고, 빈칸의 바로 앞 문장에서 언제든 온라인 계정에 접속해 포인트가 얼마나 쌓였는지 확인해 보라고 했으므로, 메인 화면에 보이는 것은 '적립되어 남아 있는 포인트'가 되어야 내용상 적절하다. 따라서 '잔액. 잔고'라는 의미의 (A) balance가 정답이다.

●UNIT 03 시제 문제

예제

교재 p. 262

레드우드 하이츠 (4월 7일) – 남서 지역에서 가장 큰 미술관인 반 크로프트 미술관이 아마추어 화가들에게 자신의 작품을 선보일 수 있는 발판을 제공할 예정이다. 5월 1일부터 5월 14일까지 해당 미술관은 각 수준의 화가들로부터 공개적으로 작품을 받는 전시회를 개최할 것이다. 작품들은 미술관의 정규 운영 시간에 일반인이 볼 수 있도록 전시된다.

READING PRACTICE

교재 p. 263

1. (B)　　**2.** (A)　　**3.** (C)

1 시제

비즈니스 전문가들은 빠듯한 마감 시간에 맞춰 일하는 것이 스트레스이며, 기기 고장으로 인해 파일을 날리거나 단어 저장을 깜박 잊어 버리면 상황이 더 악화된다는 것을 알고 있습니다. 가넷 클라우드 스토리지가 바로 여러분에게 필요한 해결책입니다! 저희 시스템은 최신 기술을 사용하여 여러분 자료의 안전을 보장하며, 그 과정이 자동으로 이루어지므로 여러분은 더 이상 데이터 백업에 대해서 걱정할 필요가 없습니다. 기본 설정 시, 열려진 파일은 15분마다 저희 서버에 저장됩니다. 이 시간은 여러분의 필요에 맞게 조정될 수 있습니다. 오늘 www.garnet.com을 방문하셔서 무료 체험을 신청하세요.

professional 전문가; 전문적인　tight 빠듯한, 빡빡한　deadline 마감 시간, 기한　equipment 장비, 기기　malfunction 고장　latest 최신의　guarantee 보장하다　security 보안, 경비　no longer 더 이상 ~ 않는　automatic 자동의　default setting 기본[초기] 설정　suit ~에게 맞다　sign up for ~을 신청하다　trial 시험, 체험

해설 해당 지문은 광고문으로서 가넷 클라우드 스토리지라는 서비스에 대해 현재 시제로 홍보 및 설명하고 있는 내용이다. 따라서 빈칸에도 현재 시제로 설명하는 내용이 들어가야 문맥이 자연스럽게 연결되므로 '조정될 수 있다'를 의미하는 (B) can be adjusted가 정답이다.

2 시제

저희는 항상 저희 컨트리클럽 회원들과의 소통을 향상시키고자 애쓰고 있기에, 이메일을 통해 배포하게 될 새로운 소식지의 창간을 기쁜 마음으로 알려 드립니다. 일부 다른 회원들과 마찬가지로, 고객님께는 이메일 주소를 제공하지 않으셨습니다. 저희 웹사이트의 '회원 정보란'에 고객의 개인 기록을 업데이트하시거나, 아니면 저희 관리 사무소를 직접 방문하시어 이를 바로잡으실 수 있습니다. 저희 사무 직원이 고객님을 도와 드릴 수 있습니다.

strive 애쓰다, 노력하다　launch 개시, 출시　brand new 새 것인　newsletter 소식지　distribute 나누어 주다, 배포하다　rectify 바로잡다　administration 관리, 행정　in person 직접　clerical assistant 사무 보조원

해설 앞 문장에서 새로운 소식지가 이메일을 통해 배포될 것이라고 했는데, 뒤 문장에서 이 점을 바로잡아 달라(You can rectify this)고 했으므로 빈칸에는 '제공하지 않았다'가 들어가야 '소식지가 이메일로 배포된다 → 이메일 주소를 제공하지 않았다 → 이를 수정해 달라'와 같이 자연스럽게 연결될 수 있다. 따라서 (A) have not provided가 정답이다.

3 시제

플로레스 대로가 도로 재포장 작업으로 약 닷새 동안 교통이 폐쇄될 예정이다. 그 동안에 해당 거리에 사는 주민들은 대체 주차장을 찾아야 한다. "시에서 이 작업을 한 번에 통째로 하는 대신 구획별로 하도록 계획했으면 좋았을 텐데요."라고 인근 주민인 재키 포드 씨는 말했다. "사람들이 몇 블록 떨어진 곳에서부터 걸어가야 할 테니까요." 교통국 담당 직원인 레지나 크로프트 씨는 혼란을 줄이기 위해 최선을 다하겠다고 밀했다. "작업이 모두 완료되자마자, 주민들은 매끄러운 도로 표면을 환영할 것이라고 생각합니다."

repave (도로를) 재포장하다　meanwhile 그 동안에　alternative 대안이 되는; 대안　section 부문, 구획　in one piece 통째로　neighborhood 이웃, 인근　Transit Authority 교통국　representative 직원, 담당자　limit 제한하다　disruption 혼란, 분열　complete 완료하다　smooth 매끄러운

해설 지문 초반에 도로 재포장 작업으로 플로레스 대로가 폐쇄될 예정이며 주민들이 대체 주차장을 찾아야 할 것 (residents ~ will have to find alternative parking)이라며 미래에 일어날 일에 대해 언급했으므로, 빈칸은 이로 인해 주민들이 앞으로 받게 될 영향에 대한 내용이 되어야 자연스럽다. 따라서 '걸어가야 할 것이다'라는 의미의 (C) will have to walk가 정답이다.

●UNIT 04 문장 고르기 문제

예제

교재 p. 264

제 27회 연례 밀턴시 미술 박람회를 놓치지 마세요. 200명 이상의 지역 화가들이 참석할 예정이며 박람회 참가자들에게 직접 미술품을 판매할 것입니다. 전시하는 화가들을 위한 부스 공간이 아직 남아 있습니다. www.fair.org에 더 많은 정보가 있습니다. 모든 작품은 반드시 실제 화가에 의해 디자인되고 만들어진 것이어야 합니다. 복제품의 전시나 판매는 허용되지 않습니다.

READING PRACTICE

교재 p. 265

1. (D) **2.** (B) **3.** (A) **4.** distinguishes
5. (B) **6.** (C) **7.** features **8.** (C)
9. Furthermore **10.** ensures **11.** (D)

1 문장 고르기

이 지역 작가인 켄 스피나 씨가 이번 주 토요일인 4월 23일 오후 2시에 셸비 시립 공공도서관에서 강연을 할 예정이다. 그는 새로 출간된 자신의 소설 〈선샤인 메모리즈〉를 발췌하여 낭독하고, 그 소설을 집필하는 동안 겪었던 어려움에 대해서 이야기할 예정이다. <u>그는 물론 청중들의 질문도 받을 것이다.</u> 참석자들은 '틀림없이' 스피나 씨의 창작 과정에 대해 더 많이 알고 싶어 할 것이라고 포젠 씨는 말했다.

challenge 어려운 도전, 시련 face 맞닥뜨리다 attendee 참석자 no doubt 틀림없이 creative 창조적인

번역 (A) 서명이 담긴 이 책들은 참석자들 일부에게 증정될 것이다.
(B) 그는 가능한 한 빨리 이 작문 강좌를 들을 계획이다.
(C) 더 최근에 나온 많은 책들도 재활용 종이로 인쇄된다.
(D) 그는 물론 청중들의 질문도 받을 것이다.

해설 바로 앞 문장에서 작가인 켄 스피나가 신작 소설을 낭독하고 자신이 집필하는 동안 겪은 어려움에 대해 이야기할 것이라고 했으므로, '그는 청중들의 질문도 받을 것이다'가 들어가야 강연의 구성에 대해 소개하는 내용으로 자연스럽게 연결될 수 있고 뒤 문장과도 어울린다. 따라서 (D)가 정답이다.

어휘 sign 서명하다 participant 참석자 writing course 작문 강좌 audience 청중, 관객

2 문장 고르기

프리스콧 음악 축제는 프리스콧에서 열리는 연례 행사로 전국의 음악 단체들이 모여듭니다. 매년 축제에 대한 많은 호평들은 행사 기획자들이 언제나 밴드를 제대로 선정한다는 것을 보여 주는데, 올해도 예외가 아닙니다. <u>대표적인 장르는 재즈, 팝, 그리고 포크 뮤직 등입니다.</u> 따라서 누구에게나 뭔가 즐길거리는 반드시 있을 것입니다. 밴드를 위한 몇 자리가 아직 이용 가능합니다. 공연을 할 의향을 전하려면 director@prescottmusic.org로 이메일을 보내 주십시오.

annual 연례의 attract 끌어 모으다 numerous 많은 review 평가 year after year 해마다, 매년 be no exception 예외가 아니다 consequently 결과적으로, 따라서 slot (프로그램 등에 들어갈) 자리, 틈 give a performance 공연하다

번역 (A) 표는 미리 구입하거나 입구에서 구입할 수 있습니다.
(B) 대표적인 장르는 재즈, 팝, 그리고 포크 뮤직 등입니다.
(C) 밴드 최종 명단은 행사 웹사이트에 게시되었습니다.
(D) 날씨가 안 좋으면 취소될 수도 있습니다.

해설 바로 뒤 문장에서 따라서 누구에게나 즐길거리가 반드시 있을 것이라고 했으므로 빈칸에는 뒤 문장의 원인이 되는 내용을 골라야 한다. '대표적인 장르는 재즈, 팝, 그리고 포크 뮤직 등이다'가 빈칸에 들어가면 여러 장르가 제공되므로 누구나 즐길 수 있다는 인과 관계가 자연스럽게 성립되므로 (B)가 정답이다.

어휘 purchase 구입하다 in advance 미리 entrance 입구 final 최종의 post 게시하다 cancellation 취소 take place (일이) 일어나다, 벌어지다

3 문장 고르기

가끔 저희가 전시장에 진열하는 가구를 할인가에 구입 가능할 때가 있습니다. 이 상품들은 전혀 손상되거나 결함이 있는 것들이 아닙니다. 하지만 진열 상품들은 모두 일단 판매되면 취소가 안 됩니다. 이 가구에 대해서는 반품이나 환불 요청을 받지 않습니다. <u>유감스럽게도 진열 상품에 대해서는 배달 서비스를 해 드리지 못합니다.</u> 고객들이 직접 이 상품들을 싣고 운반해야 합니다.

on occasion 가끔 display 전시하다 showroom floor 전시장 reduced 감소한, 할인한 in no way 결코[조금도] ~ 않은 damaged 손상된 defective 결함 있는 final 변경할 수 없는 return 반품 refund 환불 load (짐을) 싣다 transport 운반하다 on one's own 혼자, 직접

번역 (A) 유감스럽게도 진열 상품에 대해서는 배달 서비스를 해 드리지 못합니다.
(B) 이 진열 상품들에 대해서는 신속한 판매를 위해 대폭 할인을 제공합니다.
(C) 또한 저희 직원이 재활용을 위해 진열 상품들을 가져올 것입니다.
(D) 저희는 자부심을 가지고 실내 디자인에 대한 컨설팅 서비스를 제공합니다.

해설 빈칸 뒤 문장에서 고객들이 직접 이 상품들을 싣고 운반해야 한다며 물품의 배송 방법에 대해 구체적으로 언급하고 있으므로 고객이 직접 배송해야 하는 이유가 될 수 있는 '진열 상품에 대해서는 배달 서비스를 제공하지 않는다'는 내용이 들어가면 연결이 자연스럽다. 따라서 (A)가 정답이다. However 뒤로는 진열 상품 구매 시 단점이 될 수 있는 내용들이 나열되고 있으므로 나머지 보기는 문맥상 적합하지 않다.

어휘 regret 유감스럽게 생각하다 generous 후한, 너그러운 encourage 권장하다, 조장하다 in addition 게다가, 또한 pick up 찾아오다, 수거하다

4-5

셔틀 서비스에 관하여

에어허브스-익스프레스사는 이 지역의 국제 공항과 시내를 오가는 저렴한 이동 수단을 제공합니다. 저희는 승객들이 탑승을 요청하기 전에 항상 정확한 요금을 말씀드립니다. 그렇게 함으로써 과정에 대한 불확실성을 모두 없애고 예상과 달라 놀랄 일도 전혀 없도록 합니다. 게다가 저희의 수준 높은

고객 서비스는 다른 셔틀 회사들과 **4**차별화됩니다. 저희의 '사용 후기' 페이지를 방문하여 에어허브스-익스프레스사에 대한 고객들의 긍정적인 경험에 대해 읽어 보십시오. **5**그러고 나서 다음 셔틀 탑승을 저희에게 예약하십시오. 재희가 기하의 교통편을 제공해 드리기를 기대합니다.

---

affordable 저렴한 가격의 region 지역 international 국제적인 rider (탈것을) 타는 사람 exact 정확한 fare 교통 요금 remove 없애다 uncertainty 불확실성 what's more 게다가 testimonial 추천의 글. 사용 후기 look forward to doing ~하기를 고대하다 transportation 교통. 차량 이동

4. 동사 어휘

해설 문맥상 회사의 장점을 홍보하는 내용이고, '우리의 수준 높은 고객 서비스는 다른 셔틀 회사들과 차별화된다'는 내용이 되어야 자연스러우므로 '구별 짓다'는 뜻의 distinguishes가 정답이다. transform은 '다른 회사로부터 우리를 변형시키다'라는 내용이 되어 문장이 어색해진다.

어휘 distinguish 구별 짓다 transform 변형시키다

5. 문장 고르기

번역 (A) 이 자리에 지원하시려면 이력서를 제출하십시오.
(B) 그리고 나서 다음 셔틀 탑승을 저희에게 예약하십시오.
(C) 일부 비행편은 취소될 수도 있음을 알려 드립니다.
(D) 차에 귀중품을 두지 마십시오.

해설 앞 문장에서 후기 페이지를 방문해 당사를 이용한 고객들의 긍정적인 경험에 대해 읽어 보라고 했고, 뒤 문장에서 귀하의 교통편을 제공하기를 기대한다며 고객에게 회사의 서비스를 홍보하고 서비스 이용을 권장하는 내용이 이어지고 있으므로 비슷한 내용이 들어가야 연결이 자연스럽다. 따라서 '그리고 나서 다음 셔틀 탑승을 저희에게 예약하세요.'라는 내용의 (B)가 정답이다.

어휘 apply for ~에 지원하다 résumé 이력서 book 예약하다 valuables 귀중품

6-7

고객들께 알립니다

저희 페니 레인 서점은 고객들에게 최선의 서비스를 제공하기 위한 새로운 방법들을 끊임없이 모색하고 있습니다. 일례로, 저희는 새로운 모바일 앱을 개시하여 유명 저자들의 매장 특별 방문은 물론 매장 판촉 행사 및 할인 판매에 대해서도 고객들에게 지속적으로 알려 드리고자 합니다. **6**이것은 일반 앱 소스에서 무료로 다운로드할 수 있습니다. 사용자 이름과 비밀번호를 정하시고 나면, 앱의 모든 **7**기능에 자유롭게 접속하실 수 있습니다. 궁금한 점이 있으시면, 앱에 포함된 FAQ(자주 묻는 질문들) 코너를 방문하시면 됩니다.

---

announcement 발표. 안내 continuously 끊임없이 for instance 예를 들어 launch 시작하다 promotion 홍보. 판촉 행사 in-store 매장 내의 appearance 등장. 나타남 have access to ~에 접속하다

6. 문장 고르기

번역 (A) 저희는 고객들의 의견을 소중히 여기며 여러분의 의견에 대단히 감사드립니다.
(D) 앱스토어 중 하나에 후기를 남기셔서 그렇게 하실 수 있습니다.
(C) 이것은 일반 앱 소스에서 무료로 다운로드할 수 있습니다.
(D) 검색을 더 용이하게 하기 위해 저희 웹사이트 디자인을 바꿨습니다.

해설 앞 문장에서 새로운 모바일 앱을 개시할 계획이라고 했는데, 뒤 문장에서는 앱의 사용법에 대해 언급하고 있으므로 빈칸에는 앱을 다운로드하는 내용이 들어가야 연결이 자연스럽다. 따라서 '이것은 일반 앱 소스에서 무료로 다운로드할 수 있습니다.'는 내용의 (C)가 정답이다.

어휘 value 소중히 여기다 appreciate 감사히 여기다 review 평가. 후기 free of charge 무료로 redesign 다시 디자인하다 navigate 항해하다. (인터넷에서) 탐색하다

7. 명사 어휘

해설 문맥상 '앱의 모든 기능에 접속할 수 있다'는 내용이 되어야 자연스러우므로 '기능'이라는 의미의 features가 정답이다. models는 상품의 모델 혹은 디자인을 의미하므로 문맥에 어울리지 않는다.

어휘 feature 기능 model (상품의) 모델

8-9

리지무어 직원들에게 드리는 공지

9월 1일부터 근무 시간 후에 비스카운트 타워의 출입은 오로지 정문을 통해서만 허용됩니다. 다른 출입구의 열쇠를 가진 사람들도 마찬가지입니다. 다른 출입구에서 주차장이 가깝기 때문에 처음에는 이런 규정 변경에 반대했습니다. **8**하지만 새로운 규정으로 회사의 경비가 줄어들 것으로 예상됩니다. 경비 절감책에 관해 전문가에게 컨설팅을 받았는데, 야간 경비원의 숫자를 줄이라고 권고했습니다. 정문을 통해서만 이동하면 같은 수준의 보안을 유지할 수 있습니다. **9**뿐만 아니라 근무 시간 후에 오는 배달원의 혼란도 줄일 수 있는데, 그들은 직원의 위치를 찾는 가장 빠른 방법을 알아 내는 데 종종 어려움을 겪기 때문입니다.

---

after-hours 근무 시간 후의 permit 허용하다 solely 오로지 entrance 출입구 resist 저항하다. 반대하다 proximity 가까움 expert 전문가 cost-cutting 경비 절감 measure 조치. 정책 overnight 야간의 security guard 경비원 maintain 유지하다 confusion 혼란 courier 배달원. 택배 회사 have difficulty -ing ~하는 데 어려움을 겪다 determine 알아내다. 결정하다 locate ~의 위치를 찾아내다

8. 문장 고르기

번역 (A) 한편, 나눠 드린 열쇠들은 수리가 끝난 직후 다시 쓸 수 있게 될 겁니다.
(B) 시설 일부에는 새로운 상가 세입자들을 위한 빈자리가 몇 곳 있습니다.

(C) 하지만 새로운 규정으로 회사의 경비가 줄어들 것으로 예상됩니다.

(D) 옆문의 새 열쇠를 발급받으려면 경비실로 연락하기 바랍니다.

해설 앞 문장에서 처음에는 규정 변경에 반대했다고 했는데, 빈칸 뒤에서는 이와는 반대로 경비 절감 대책에 관해 전문가에게 컨설팅을 받았다며 규정 변경으로 인한 경비 절감 효과를 설명하고 있다. 따라서 서로 상반된 내용을 연결해 줄 수 있는 접속부사 However(하지만)로 시작하고 경비 절감 대책에 관한 내용과도 자연스럽게 이어질 수 있는 (C) '하지만 새로운 규정으로 회사의 경비가 줄어들 것으로 예상됩니다.'가 정답이다.

어휘 meanwhile 그동안에, 한편 distribute 나누어주다
opening 빈자리 commercial 상업의 tenant 세입자
expense 경비 issue 발급[발부]하다

9. 접속부사

해설 빈칸 앞에서 근무 시간 후 정문 출입만 허용된다는 규정 변경으로 인해 회사의 경비를 줄일 수 있다는 장점에 대해서 언급했는데, 빈칸 뒤에서도 근무 시간 후에 오는 배달원들의 혼란도 줄일 수 있다며 장점을 추가로 언급했으므로 유사한 내용을 연결하는 접속부사가 들어가야 글의 흐름이 자연스럽다. 따라서 '뿐만 아니라'라는 의미의 Furthermore가 정답이다.

어휘 in contrast 대조적으로 furthermore 뿐만 아니라, 게다가

10. 동사의 형태 – 시제

해설 빈칸은 주어 The Warehouse Manager의 동사 자리이며, 해당 지문은 구인 광고문으로 빈칸의 앞뒤 문장에서 모두 창고 관리자직에 대해 현재 시제로 설명하고 있으므로 빈칸도 '창고 관리자는 ~을 책임집니다'라며 업무 내용을 현재 시제로 설명하는 내용이 되어야 문맥의 흐름이 자연스럽다. 따라서 ensures가 정답이다.

어휘 ensure 확실하게 하다, 책임지다

11. 문장 고르기

번역 (A) 앞으로 결원이 생길 경우 귀하에게 기꺼이 연락드리겠습니다.

(B) 시로코 전자의 일자리를 수락하신 것은 옳은 선택이십니다.

(C) 시로코 전자의 신상품에 관한 자세한 정보는 저희 영업팀에서 얻으실 수 있습니다.

(D) 위에서 소개한 자리에 지원하려면, 지원서에 조회 번호 WM053을 입력하십시오.

해설 빈칸 앞 문장에서 지원하려면 회사 고용 센터를 방문하라며 창고 관리자직에 지원하기 위해 할 일에 대해 서술하고 있으므로 이와 관련된 내용이 연결되는 것이 문맥상 자연스럽다. 따라서 지원 방법에 대해 좀 더 구체적으로 명시한 (D)가 정답이다.

어휘 open up (기회 등이) 생기다 obtain 얻다 outline
개요를 서술하다 reference number 조회[참조] 번호

10-11

> ### 창고 관리자 구함
>
> 시로코 전자는 현재 웨스트브룩에 있는 유통 시설의 창고 관리자 자리에 공석이 있습니다. 창고 관리자는 상품의 인수 및 보관, 운송이 적절하고 효율적으로 수행되는지를 [10]책임집니다. 이 자리는 관리직이기는 하지만, 채용되면 무거운 물건을 들어올리거나 도움을 받지 않고 사다리를 올라가는 일도 요구되므로 지원자는 신체적인 능력도 뛰어나야 합니다. 회사에서 면접하기를 원하며 채용 가능성이 있는 대상은 동종 직종에서 최소 5년간의 경험이 있는 사람입니다. 따라서 지원서를 작성할 때 근무 경력을 빠짐없이 제출하는 것이 중요합니다. 지원하려면 회사 고용 센터인 www.sirocco.com/careers를 방문하면 됩니다. [11]위에서 소개한 자리에 지원하려면, 지원서에 조회 번호 WM053을 입력하십시오.
>
> ---
>
> warehouse 창고 currently 현재 vacancy 결원, 공석
> distribution 분배, 유통 storage 보관 shipping 운송
> merchandise 상품 carry out 수행하다 properly 적절하게
> efficiently 효율적으로 management 관리 candidate
> 지원자, 후보자 lift 들어올리다 unassisted 도움을 받지 않는
> applicant 지원자 physically 신체적으로 capable 유능한
> potentially 가능성 있게, 잠재적으로 accordingly 그래서
> employment history 근무 경력 fill out 작성하다
> application form 지원서

PART 7

● 풀이 전략

1-2 구인 광고

교재 p. 278

신문사 새 부서장 모집

〈볼더 포스트-가제트〉는 역량 있는 기자를 구합니다. **1**저희는 웹사이트에 게시할 영상물이나 기타 게시물 수를 늘리는 데 힘쓰고 있으므로 영상 캡처링과 편집 능력은 상당한 가산점이 됩니다.

2업무는 기사 교정 및 수정, 당선자나 다른 지역 인사들을 인터뷰하는 것, 그리고 볼더 지역 주민들이 관심을 가지는 행사를 최대한 보도하기 위해 기자단을 관리하는 것입니다.

지원에 관심 있으시면 비키 그라임스에게 (791) 555-5122번으로 연락 바랍니다.

seek 찾다 division 부서 qualified 자격을 갖춘 raise (양·수준 등을) 올리다 piece (신문·잡지 등에 실린) 기사[글] proofread 교정하다 revise 수정하다

● 패러프레이징

READING PRACTICE

교재 p. 282

1. (B) **2.** (B) **3.** (A) **4.** (B) **5.** (B)
6. (B) **7.** (B) **8.** (A)

1

저는 귀사의 잡지 〈에브리 위크엔드〉를 애독하고 있습니다. 특히 신참 여행자들을 위한 조언이 담긴 글들을 즐겨 읽고 있습니다. 현지인처럼 도시를 탐방하는 방법에 관해 귀중한 의견을 제시해주고 있거든요.

valuable 소중한, 귀중한 suggestion 제안, 의견 explore 답사하다, 탐구하다 local 현지인; 지역의

문제 〈에브리 위크엔드〉에 관해 시사되는 것은?
(A) 현지인이 쓴 잡지이다.
(B) 여행 관련 조언을 해준다.

해설 **Not / True**
마지막 문장에서 잡지 〈에브리 위크엔드〉는 도시를 탐방하는 방법에 관한 의견을 제시해준다(It gives valuable suggestions on how to explore cities like a local)고 했으므로, 여행 관련 조언을 준다는 것을 알 수 있다. 따라서 (B)가 정답이다. 현지인처럼(like a local) 도시를 탐방하는 방법을 제시해 준다고는 했으나, 현지인이(by a local) 쓴 잡지인지는 알 수 없으므로 (A)는 정답이 될 수 없다.

패러 지문의 suggestions on how to explore cities
❷ 정답의 travel tips

2

저는 제 신용 한도를 늘리고 싶었는데, 전화를 걸어야만 신용한도를 늘릴 수 있다는 안내를 받았습니다. 저는 이것이 이해되지 않습니다. 콜 센터에 전화를 걸어서 할 수 있는 것과 마찬가지로 온라인 지원 센터를 통해서도 같은 업무를 볼 수 있어야 한다고 생각합니다. 정말 유용한 서비스가 될 수 있도록 온라인 지원 센터의 기능을 확대하실 것을 권해 드립니다.

extend 연장하다, 확대하다 credit limit 신용 한도
place a phone call 전화를 걸다 make sense 이해가 되다, 타당하다 accomplish 완수하다, 달성하다 expand 확장하다
capability 능력, 역량

문제 글쓴이가 회사에게 하도록 제안하는 것은?
(A) 지원 센터의 운영 시간 늘리기
(B) 온라인 지원 센터에서 더 많은 서비스를 제공하도록 하기

어휘 hours of operation 운영 시간

해설 **세부 사항**
마지막 문장에서 유용한 서비스가 될 수 있도록 온라인 지원 센터의 기능을 확대할 것을 권한다(I recommend you expand the online support center's capabilities)고 했으므로, 글쓴이는 온라인 지원 센터에서 더 많은 서비스를 제공할 것을 제안하고 있음을 알 수 있다. 따라서 (B)가 정답이다.

패러 지문의 expand ~ capabilities
❷ 정답의 offer more services

3

여러분이 경주를 좋아하시든 산악자전거 타기를 좋아하시든, 딕비는 가장 인기 있는 브랜드의 최신 자전거들을 가장 좋은 가격에 보장해 드립니다. 만약 더 싸게 파는 곳을 찾으실 경우, 그 가격에서 10%를 할인해 드립니다.

racing 경주 latest 최신의 guarantee 보장하다
a good deal 싸게 잘 산 것, 좋은 거래 beat 낫다, 기록을 깨다

문제 딕비 자전거 가게에 대해 명시된 것은?
(A) 최저가 제공을 약속한다.
(B) 자전거 제품을 10% 할인해준다.

패러 지문의 at the best prices, guaranteed
❷ 정답의 offer the lowest prices

해설 **Not / True**
딕비 자전거 가게는 가장 좋은 가격에 자전거를 제공하며, 더 싸게 파는 곳을 찾을 경우, 그 가격에서 10% 할인해준다(If you find a better deal, we'll beat it by 10%)고

했으므로, 딕비 자전거 가게는 최저가 자전거를 제공한다는 것을 알 수 있다. 따라서 (A)가 정답이다. we'll beat it by 10%는 '더 싼 가격에서 10% 할인해 준다'는 의미이지 자전거 제품가에서 10% 할인해 준다는 것은 아니므로 (B)는 정답이 될 수 없다.

4

아래 설문을 작성하셔서 도서관의 서비스 향상에 도움을 주시기 바랍니다.

도서관 직원들은 친절하고 정보를 잘 갖추고 있습니까?	★★★★★
도서나 기타 자료를 찾기 쉽습니까?	★★★★☆
열람실은 시설이 잘 갖춰져 있습니까?	★★★★★
도서 대여료가 적정합니까?	★★☆☆☆

fill out (서식을) 작성하다 knowledgeable 잘 알고 있는 materials 자료 well equipped 시설이 잘 갖춰진 rental 대여(료) reasonably 합리적으로

문제 도서관에 대해 암시되는 것은?
(A) 모든 열람실에서 무선 네트워크 접속이 가능하다.
(B) 도서 대출에 수수료를 청구한다.

해설 추론
설문의 마지막 항목을 보면 도서 대여료의 가격이 적정한지(Is the book rental reasonably priced?)를 묻고 있으므로, 도서 대출 시 비용이 청구된다는 것을 추론할 수 있다. 따라서 (B)가 정답이다.

어휘 wireless 무선의 accessible 접근[접속] 가능한 charge 청구하다 fee 수수료 check out (도서를) 대출하다

5

자격 요건
· 국가 공인 마사지 치료 유효 면허증 필수
· 스파, 클리닉 또는 유사 시설에서 12개월 이상 근무 경력 필수

requirement 자격 요건 state-issued 국가에서 발행된 therapy 치료 setting 환경, 장소

문제 이 직책에 요구되는 것은?
(A) 석사 학위
(B) 최소 1년 경력

어휘 master's degree 석사 학위

해설 세부 사항
12개월 자격 요건으로 공인 자격증과 경력을 언급하고 있다. 반드시 12개월 이상의 경력자여야 한다(Must have worked ~ for no less than twelve months)고 했으므로 (B)가 정답이다. 학위에 대한 언급이 없으므로 (A)는 정답이 될 수 없다.

(패러) 지문의 no less than twelve months
➡ 정답의 A minimum of one year

6

비컨 아파트 세입자들은 A타워 1층에 있는 레크리에이션실을 개인 행사를 위해 사용할 수 있습니다. 이곳은 평면 TV, 테이블과 의자들, 그리고 세 개의 소파를 갖추고 있습니다. 이전에 이 장소는 부동산 관리 사무실에 전화하여 예약이 가능했습니다. 그러나 오늘부터 세입자들은 예약을 위해 온라인 시스템을 이용하셔야 합니다.

tenant 세입자 recreation 레크리에이션, 오락 function 행사 be equipped with 갖추다 property 부동산 management 관리

문제 레크리에이션실에 변경된 것은?
(A) 세입자에게 제공되는 장비
(B) 예약 방법

해설 세부 사항
이전에는(previously), 오늘부터(starting from today)와 같은 대조를 나타낼 수 있는 부사(구)를 사용하여 달라진 점을 언급하고 있다. 예약을 관리 사무실이 아닌 온라인으로 해야 하는 점이 바뀌었으므로 (B)가 정답이다.

7

저희는 늘고 있는 고객층과 친근한 업무 환경을 가지고 있습니다. 성과 목표치 달성 시 주어지는 보너스 및 넉넉한 시급을 제공합니다. 또한 직원들은 고객에게 판매한 모든 상품 판매액의 10퍼센트를 받게 됩니다.

client base 고객층 generous 후한, 관대한, 넉넉한 performance 업무, 성과 target 목표(치)

문제 어떤 혜택이 언급되는가?
(A) 넉넉한 유급 휴가 기간
(B) 상품 판매에 대한 수수료

해설 Not / True
고객에게 판매한 모든 상품 판매금의 10퍼센트를 받는다(Employees also receive ten percent of all ~ customers)고 하였으므로 (B)가 정답이다.

어휘 commission (실적에 따른) 수수료, 중개료

(패러) 지문의 ten percent of all product sales
➡ 정답의 Commission on merchandise sales

8

부재중 메시지

받는 사람: 에이미 프레스턴
보낸 사람: 고든 리브스
회사명: 알파 세일즈
연락처: 555-0195
날짜: 9월 4일
시각: 오후1:05

전화하였음 [ ]　　직접 방문하였음 [✔]
전화 주세요 [✔]　　전화할게요 [ ]

메시지: 리브스 씨는 다음 무역 박람회에서 배포할 책자를 만드는 중입니다. 연간 판매량을 준비하여 책자에 포함될 수 있도록 해주세요.

brochure 안내 책자　pass out 나누어주다. 배포하다
trade fair 무역 박람회

문제 리브스 씨에 대해 언급된 것은?
　(A) 사업체를 직접 방문하였다.
　(B) 무역 박람회를 참석할 수 없다.

해설 **Not / True**
메시지를 남긴 사람이 리브스 씨이며 직접 방문했음을 알 수 있는 체크 표시가 있으므로 (A)가 정답이다. 리브스 씨가 무역 박람회에서 책자를 나누어준다고 하였으므로 (B)는 정답이 될 수 없다.

어휘 in person 직접　stop by 방문하다

패러 지문의 visited ➡ 정답의 stopped by in person

●UNIT 01 주제 / 목적 문제

예제

교재 p. 284

줄리엣 씨께

우리 사무실의 직원 생산성을 향상시키기 위한 아이디어를 모색 중이시라고 들었습니다.

제 생각에는 현재의 칸막이형 배치를 개방형으로 바꿔 보면 어떨까 합니다.

제가 가능한 구도를 그림으로 만들어 봤습니다. 휴게실 게시판에 붙여 두었습니다. 한번 보시고 의견 주세요.

문제 편지는 왜 작성되었는가?
　(A) 사무실 배치 변경을 제안하기 위해
　(B) 잠재적인 고객을 소개하기 위해
　(C) 가구 주문에 대해 후속 조치를 하기 위해
　(D) 업무 평가 결과를 보고하기 위해

READING PRACTICE
교재 p. 285

1. (B)　　**2.** (C)

1 문자 메시지

자동 발송 메시지. 회신하지 마세요.

오전 9시 5분에 출발하는 보스턴행 RW509편 승객 여러분께 출발 탑승구는 이제 C24가 아님을 알려 드립니다. 대신에 C30 게이트에서 출발 시간 약 한 시간 전에 탑승이 시작됩니다. 이 비행편의 추후 변동 사항은 터미널 곳곳에 있는 전광판에 뜰 것이니, 그것을 보고 비행 세부 사항을 확인하시기 바랍니다.

automated 자동화된　depart 출발하다　board 탑승하다
commence 시작되다　approximately 대략　throughout
도처에　refer to (정보를 알아내기 위해) ~을 보다

문제 메시지를 보낸 이유는?
　(A) 출발 지연에 대해 사과하기 위해
　(B) 탑승구 변경을 통지하기 위해
　(C) 승객이 탑승 수속을 했음을 확인해주기 위해
　(D) 비행기 탑승이 시작되었음을 알리기 위해

해설 **주제 / 목적**
지문 서두에서 오전 9시 5분에 출발하는 보스턴행 RW509편의 탑승구는 C24가 아니라 C30 게이트로 변경되었다(the departure gate is no longer C24 ~ before the departure time at gate C30 instead)고 했으므로, 탑승구 변경을 통지하기 위해 보낸 메시지임을 알 수 있다. 따라서 (B)가 정답이다.

어휘 delay 지연　notification 통고. 통지　confirm 확인하다
check in 탑승 수속하다

2 편지

산체스 씨께,

레이크 펜로즈 지역의 뉴스 및 사건을 다루어 주신 데 대해 감사드립니다. 저는 지난 수년간 귀하의 기사를 애독해 왔습니다. 그런데 유서 깊은 존 헤비 로지의 복원을 다룬 귀하의 12월 9일자 기사에서 오류가 한 가지 눈에 띄었습니다. 그 프로젝트가 전적으로 공적 보조금으로 지원되고 있었다고 하셨는데, 사실 그 복원 사업에 조달되는 자금의 거의 50%는 개인 기부자들이 아낌없이 지원해주신 것입니다. 이 프로젝트를 지원해주신 분들의 공로를 인정하고 감사드리는 것은 중요합니다. 내일 신문에서 정정기사를 볼 수 있기를 바랍니다.

감사합니다.

레이크 펜로즈 역사학회
재무책임자, 이모진 핀리 드림

coverage 보도   restoration 복원, 복구   notice 알아차리다
entirely 전적으로   fund 자금을 대다   subsidy (국가) 보조금
grant (정부나 단체에서 주는) 보조금   financing 자금 조달
generously 후하게, 너그럽게   donor 기부자   give credit
공로를 인정하다   correction 정정

문제 핀리 씨가 편지를 보낸 이유는?
    (A) 심층 기사의 소재를 제안하기 위해
    (B) 행사에 초청하기 위해
    (C) 사실과 다른 오류를 알리기 위해
    (D) 기부를 요청하기 위해

어휘 in-depth 심도 있는, 면밀한   extend an invitation
초대하다   identify 확인하다, 알리다   factual 사실과
관련된, 사실에 기반을 둔   donation 기부

해설 **주제 / 목적**
편지 중반부에서 12월 9일자 기사에 오류가 있다(I noticed
a mistake in your December 9 article)면서, 프로젝
트가 전적으로 공적 보조금으로 지원되고 있다고 기사에
언급되어 있는데, 사실은 조달 자금의 거의 50%는 개인
기부자들의 후원금이라(You stated that the project ~
generously provided by private donors)고 했다. 또
마지막 문장에서 내일 신문에서 정정 기사를 볼 수 있기를
바란다(I look forward to seeing your correction in
tomorrow's paper)고 했으므로, 핀리 씨는 사실과 다른
오류를 정정하기 위해 편지를 보냈음을 알 수 있다. 따라서
(C)가 정답이다.

●UNIT 02 세부 사항 문제

예제
교재 p. 286

저희 심사위원들이 귀하를 우승 후보 중 한 명으로 선정하게
되었음을 알리게 되어 기쁩니다. 축하합니다!

귀하를 수상 연회에 초대합니다. 3월 3일 오타와에 있는 로
얄 리셉션 홀 수상식에서 우승자가 발표될 것입니다.

행사 초대권을 동봉했습니다.

문제 3월 3일에는 무슨 일이 일어날 것인가?
    (A) 대회 우승자가 발표될 것이다.
    (B) 심사위원들이 인터뷰를 실시할 것이다.
    (C) 제출 기간이 끝날 것이다.
    (D) 미술 전시회가 개최될 것이다.

READING PRACTICE
교재 p. 287

1. (C)   **2.** (D)

1 일정표

클레어몬트 도서관 특별 활동 일정표

일	폐관
월	오전 10시: 동화책 읽어 주기 오후 4시: 숙제 봐주기
화	오후 7시: 청소년 독서 교실
수	오전 10시: 동화책 읽어 주기 오후 4시: 숙제 봐주기
목	오전 11시: 어르신 컴퓨터 기초 교실
금	오전 10시: 동화책 읽어 주기 오후 4시: 숙제 봐주기
토	오후 1시: 공예 활동 오후 3시: 셰익스피어 작품 읽기

모든 활동은 무료로 도서관 이용객들에게 제공됩니다. 도서
관 카드가 없을 경우, 등록 접수처에서 카드를 신청할 수 있
습니다. 시간을 내어 활동을 이끌거나 도움을 주고 싶으시면,
555-0132번으로 론다 스튜어트에게 연락 주십시오.

basics 기본, 기초   senior citizen 어르신, 고령자   craft 공예
patron 고객, 후원자   at no charge 무료로   sign up for ~을
신청[가입]하다   registration 등록   assist 돕다

문제 특별히 노인들을 위한 행사가 있는 요일은?
    (A) 월요일
    (B) 화요일
    (C) 목요일
    (D) 토요일

해설 **세부 사항**
질문에서 elderly people을 키워드로 삼고 단서를 찾으
면 동의어인 senior citizens를 포착하여 해당 사항을 확
인할 수 있다. 노인을 위한 컴퓨터 기초 수업이 있는 날은
목요일에 해당하므로 정답은 (C)이다.

2 기사

라몬디 리조트가 몇 주간의 지연이 있은 후 마침내 이번 시즌
을 위해 개장했다. 라몬디 리조트는 보통 11월 중순에 개장
하지만, 이번에는 그럴 수 없었다. 기온은 영하로 꽤 내려갔
지만, 스키를 탈 정도로 충분한 눈을 만들어 낼 만큼 강우량
이 충분하지 못했던 것이다.

"이제 스키 애호가들을 위해 리조트를 개장하게 되어 기쁩니
다."라고 리조트 매니저인 빌리 에스테스 씨는 말했다. "눈의
바닥층이 탄탄하게 다져졌으므로, 이번 시즌 남은 기간 동안
스키 타기 좋은 환경을 기대하고 있습니다."

에스테스 씨는 내년에 추가로 스노 머신을 구입할 자금을 이
미 할당해 두었다고 말했다. 그 기계들을 사용하여, 이 리조
트에서는 날씨가 충분히 추워지자마자 인공눈을 만들기 시작
할 수 있다.

문제 에스테스 씨에 따르면 리조트는 이미 무엇을 했는가?
(A) 일일 운영 시간을 연장했다.
(B) 입장료를 올렸다.
(C) 더 많은 장비를 설치했다.
(D) 구매를 위해 예산을 잡았다.

해설 **세부 사항**
질문에서 Mr. Estes와 already를 키워드로 삼고 단서를
찾으면 세 번째 단락에서 정답의 근거를 찾을 수 있다. 리
조트가 스노 머신 추가 구매를 위해 자금을 이미 할당했다
(the resort has already allocated ~ next year)고
했으므로 정답은 (D)이다.

● UNIT 03 Not / True 문제

예제
교재 p. 288

내부 마케팅 매니저 직이 공석으로 있습니다. 해당 직책에 검
토 대상이 되기 위해 지원자는 3년 또는 그 이상의 경력이 있
어야 하며 최소 한 번의 팀장 역할을 해 본 적이 있어야 합니
다. 직속 상관의 추천서 또한 필요합니다.

본인이 이에 해당한다고 생각하시면, 이력서와 추천서를 그
레고리 씨에게 보내 주세요.

문제 지원자의 기본 자격 요건으로 언급된 것이 아닌 것은?
(A) 경력   (B) 상관의 서면 보증
(C) 리더 경력   (D) 과거 업무 포트폴리오

READING PRACTICE
교재 p. 289

1. (C)   **2.** (A)

1 기사

**안토니오 레스토랑의 개업 40주년을 기념하는
요리 경연대회**

레드빌(8월 30일) – 안토니오 레스토랑의 오랜 주인인 안토
니오 보렐로 씨가 개업 40주년을 기념하여 일련의 행사들을
개최한다. 보렐로 씨는 10년 전에 〈레드빌 가제트〉에서 서비
스 우수상을 받은 것에 특히 자부심을 갖고 있는 것으로 알려
져 있다. 아들이 주방에서 일하고 부인이 현재는 홀서비스를
맡고 있어, 안토니오 씨는 자신의 높은 수준이 유지될 수 있
다고 확신한다.

보렐로 씨는 기념행사 동안 메인 이벤트로 요리 경연대회를
생각하고 있다. 지역 주민들은 심사를 위해 레시피 아이디어

를 제출할 것을 요청받으며, 상위 3개의 레시피 아이디어의
주인들은 안토니오 레스토랑에서 자신들의 음식을 요리하도
록 초청받는다. 이 경연대회에 대한 더 자세한 사항은 시청
홈페이지에서 찾아볼 수 있다.

문제 기사에 따르면, 안토니오 레스토랑에 대해 사실인 것은?
(A) 곧 있을 수상의 후보로 지명되었다.
(B) 다양한 나라의 음식을 제공한다.
(C) 보렐로 씨의 가족이 이 식당에서 일한다.
(D) 그동안 주인이 여러 명이었다.

어휘 nominate 후보(자)로 지명하다   upcoming 곧 있을,
다가오는   a range of 다양한

해설 **Not / True**
기사문 첫 단락의 마지막 문장에서 안토니오 보렐로 씨
는 아들이 주방에서 일하고 아내가 홀서비스를 맡고 있
어 높은 수준의 서비스가 유지될 수 있다(With his son
working ~ high standards are maintained)고 했으
므로, 보렐로 씨의 가족이 안토니오 레스토랑에서 일한다
는 것을 알 수 있다. 따라서 (C)가 정답이다.

2 공지

선베리 지역 주민들께 알립니다:

파인 시티 도시 계획 위원회에서는 선베리 토지 용도 지정 분
류를 '주거용'에서 '상업용 및 주거용'으로 바꾸는 것을 고려
하고 있습니다. 이러한 변화는 이 지역 주민들에게 상당한 영
향을 끼칠 수 있습니다. 잠재적 영향들로 지금까지 언급된 것
들은 다음과 같습니다:

긍정적 영향	부정적 영향
• 사업체에 편리한 접근성 • (D)버스 운행 증가 수반	• (B)교통량 증가 • (C)새로운 건설 공사로 인한 소음

이 사안에 관해 설문조사에 응하시려면 www.rcpc.gov/
tfzs를 방문하세요.

문제 선베리 지역에 일어날 수 있는 변화로 언급되지 않은 것은?
(A) 주택 가격이 상승할 수 있다.
(B) 더 많은 차량이 도로를 사용할 수 있다.
(C) 건설 공사들이 시작될 수 있다.
(D) 대중교통이 개선될 수 있다.

선베리 지역에 일어날 수 있는 변화의 긍정적인 영향과 부정적인 영향을 제시한 항목을 보면, 긍정적인 영향으로는 사업체에 편리한 접근성과 버스 운행 증가(Accompanying increase in bus service)를 들었고, 부정적인 영향으로는 교통량 증가(More car traffic)와 새로운 건설 공사로 인한 소음(Noise from new construction projects)을 들고 있다. 주택 가격이 상승할 것이라는 내용은 언급되어 있지 않으므로, (A)가 정답이다.

어휘 vehicle 차량 public transportation 대중교통

●UNIT 04 추론 문제

예제

교재 p. 290

코웰 씨께

최근 저희 제품을 구매해 주셨기에 귀하와 동반인 1인을 저희 본사 특별 행사에 초대하고자 합니다.

행사에는 간단한 음식과 라이브 음악, 그리고 저희 엔지니어들에 의한 다양한 제품 시연이 있을 예정입니다. 입장을 위해 행사에 이 카드를 가져오세요.

자세한 사항을 위해 저희 웹사이트를 방문해 주시기 바랍니다.

문제 행사에 대해서 암시된 것은?
(A) 연례 행사이다.
(B) 사전 등록이 요구된다.
(C) 개인적인 장소에서 개최될 것이다.
(D) 초청객에 한한다.

READING PRACTICE

교재 p. 291

1. (C) **2.** (C)

1 광고

탑 마크스 마켓을 이용해 주셔서 감사합니다!

고객이 되어 주신 데 대해 대단히 감사드리며 특별한 혜택을 드리고자 합니다. 다음 주문시 쿠폰코드 WELCOME15를 이용하셔서 15% 할인을 받으십시오. 저희 사이트에서 결제 시 '특별 혜택'이라고 나와 있는 박스 안에 이 쿠폰코드를 입력하시기만 하면 됩니다. 이 할인은 화이트보드 마커 같은 작은 필수품부터 교내 인기 순위 1위 교실을 만들어 주는 신나는 교육용 소프트웨어 프로그램에 이르기까지, 카탈로그상의 모든 매장 상품에 대해 유효합니다.

* 쿠폰은 할인 적용 전에 총 합계가 300달러 이하인 주문에 대해서만 사용할 수 있습니다. 쿠폰 만료기한은 1월 1일이며, 무료 배송 주문에는 사용할 수 없습니다.

customer 손님, 고객 check out 계산하다, 결제하다 valid 유효한, 효력 있는 entire 전체의 essential 필수적인; 필수적인 것 dry erase marker 화이트보드 마커 educational 교육적인 total 합계가 ∼이 되다 apply 적용하다 expire 만료되다 be combined with ∼와 결합되다 free shipping 무료 배송

문제 탑 마크스 마켓에서 쇼핑을 할 것 같은 사람은?
(A) 작가   (B) 화가
(C) 교사   (D) 운동선수

해설 **추론**

광고문 두 번째 단락의 마지막 문장에서, 탑 마크스 마켓에서는 화이트보드 마커 같은 필수품부터 교내 인기순위 1위 교실을 만들어 주는 신나는 교육용 소프트웨어 프로그램 등을 구입할 수 있다는 것을 알 수 있다. 화이트보드나 교육용 소프트웨어 프로그램의 사용자들은 교사일 것임을 추론할 수 있으므로, (C)가 정답이다.

2 양식

소렌토 엔터프라이즈: 환급 신청서

직원	리처드 도노반	직원번호	01468
날짜	11월 20일	금액	237.5달러

경비 종류(해당 사항 모두에 표시)
[ ] 항공 [✔] 식사 [✔] 택시 [ ] 장비 [ ] 기타

세부 사항: 델라노 인더스트리즈 사와 합병 협정을 체결하기 위해 애틀랜타 출장에 쓰인 경비임(영수증 첨부함)

담당자 기입란
승인 담당자: 스티븐 트레조
지급 예정일: [ ] 즉시 [✔] 다음 급여일
[ ] 기타 _____

reimbursement 상환, 환급 request 요청 expense 비용, 경비 equipment 장비 receipt 영수증 merger 합병 agreement 합의, 협정 approve 승인하다 issue 발급하다, 발부하다 payday 급여 지급일

문제 지급에 대해 암시된 것은?
(A) 특정 금액을 초과할 수 없다.
(B) 관리자의 승인을 받아야 한다.
(C) 급여와 함께 지급될 것이다.
(D) 장비 구입에 쓰인 것이다.

해설 **추론**

양식의 마지막 항목인 지급 예정일을 보면, 경비는 다음 급여일(On next payday)에 지급될 것임을 알 수 있다. 따라서 (C)가 정답이다.

어휘 exceed 초과하다 certain 특정한 purchase 구입

●UNIT 05 문장 삽입 문제

예제

교재 p. 292

일정을 조정해 주셔야 할 것 같습니다.

금요일에 커피 콩 배송이 있습니다. 알고 계실지도 모르겠지만, 그 트럭이 아침 5시경에 도착합니다.

보통은 레지나가 기사님을 마중 나가지만 지금 출장을 갔어요. 오셔서 받아 주실 수 있을까요?

가능한지 퇴근 전에 제게 알려 주세요. 감사합니다.

문제 [1], [2], [3], [4]로 표시된 곳들 중 다음 문장이 들어가기에 가장 적절한 곳은?

보통은 레지나가 기사님을 마중 나가지만 지금 출장을 갔어요.

(A) [1]　　　　　　　　(B) [2]
(C) [3]　　　　　　　　(D) [4]

READING PRACTICE

교재 p. 293

1. (A)　　**2.** (B)

1 기사

보스톤 비즈니스 인사이더

맥코이 홈 솔루션즈사는 조만간 최고급 가구 신상 라인을 선보일 예정이다. '리얼 스타일'이라는 명칭을 단 이 제품 라인은 맥코이사의 일반적인 저가 제품들과 차별성을 띠고 있다.

맥코이사의 CEO인 제니 아야 씨는 그 계획을 상세히 밝히고 있다. "우리 회사는 저렴한 가격대의 가구 생산 업체로서 전국 1위로 자리잡았으며, 이제 새로운 시장과 틈새시장으로 확장할 때입니다."라고 아야 씨는 말한다.

'리얼 스타일' 제품은 올해 사사분기에 공개될 예정이다.

release 공개하다, 발표하다　**high-end** 최고급의　**strategy** 계획, 전략　**establish oneself as** ~로서 자리를 잡다　**producer** 생산자, 생산회사　**affordable** 가격이 저렴한　**furnishing** 가구　**niche** 틈새시장　**quarter** 4분기

문제 [1], [2], [3], [4]로 표시된 곳들 중 다음 문장이 들어가기에 가장 적절한 곳은?

'리얼 스타일'이라는 명칭을 단 이 제품 라인은 맥코이 사의 일반적인 저가 제품들과 차별성을 띠고 있다.

(A) [1]　　　　　　　　(B) [2]
(C) [3]　　　　　　　　(D) [4]

해설 **문장 삽입**

제시문에서 the line이라고 지칭했으므로 앞 문장에서 line에 대한 언급이 있어야 한다. 지문의 첫 문장에서 고급 가구 신상 라인을 곧 출시한다고 했으므로 바로 뒤에 제시문을 삽입해볼 수 있다. 제시문의 내용이 저가 제품과의 차별성에 대한 것이므로 제시문 다음 문장의 the strategy(그 계획/전략, 여기서는 고급 가구도 진양한 것을 지칭)와 자연스럽게 연결된다. 따라서 정답은 (A)이다.

어휘 **usual** 평상시의, 보통의　**cost-conscious** 비용을 중시하는, 저가의

2 편지

스피로스 씨께,

영국 예술 재단(FBA)에서는 귀하의 보조금 신청서를 검토하여 귀하에게 글로버 보조금을 수여하기로 결정했음을 알려드리게 되어 기쁩니다. 아시겠지만, 이 보조금은 젊은이들이 언제라도 예술에 대해 공부할 기회를 가질 수 있도록 하기 위해 45년 전에 글로버 씨가 창설한 것입니다. 젊은이들이 무대 연극을 창작하고 연출하도록 돕는 귀하의 방과후 프로그램은 이러한 목표에 완벽히 부합합니다.

저희는 귀하가 글로버 보조금을 받을 자격이 충분하다고 확신합니다. 귀하가 지금까지 해오신 일련의 프로그램 작업은 정말로 감동적이었습니다.

귀하와 귀하의 학생들이 또 어떤 것을 해낼 수 있는지 지켜보고 싶습니다.

감사합니다.

의장, 주드 에르완 드림

inform 알리다　**foundation** 재단　**review** 검토하다　**grant** 보조금　**application** 신청서　**award** 수여하다　**found** 설립하다　**ensure** 보장하다　**confident** 확신하는　**worthy** 자격이 있는　**recipient** 수령인　**inspiring** 고무적인, 감동적인

문제 [1], [2], [3], [4]로 표시된 곳들 중 다음 문장이 들어가기에 가장 적절한 곳은?

젊은이들이 무대 연극을 창작하고 연출하도록 돕는 귀하의 방과후 프로그램은 이러한 목표에 완벽히 부합합니다.

(A) [1]　　　　　　　　(B) [2]
(C) [3]　　　　　　　　(D) [4]

해설 **문장 삽입**

제시문에서 this goal이라고 지칭했으므로 앞 문장에서 목표에 대한 언급이 있어야 한다. 두 번째 문장에서 보조금 지원이 창설된 목적(to ensure ~ opportunities to learn about art)이 나오므로 이 목적에 부합한다는 제시문이 들어갈 수 있다. 따라서 정답은 (B)이다.

어휘 **create** 창조하다, 창작하다　**produce** 제작하다, 연출하다　**stage play** 무대 연극　**perfectly** 완벽하게　**be in line with** ~와 일치하다

●UNIT 06 동의어 문제

예제
교재 p. 294

게일 씨, 안녕하세요, 귀하의 리겔 Q3 세단이 빌트모어 가 14번지에서 대기 중입니다. 자동차 키를 받기 위한 비밀번호는 7513입니다.

언제든지 주저 말고 저희에게 연락 주세요.

하몬드 렌탈 카를 선택해주셔서 감사합니다!

문제 3단락 첫 번째 줄의 단어 'choosing'과 의미상 가장 가까운 것은?
(A) 임명　　　　　　(B) 자원봉사
(C) 시상　　　　　　(D) 거래

READING PRACTICE
교재 p. 295

1. (B)　　**2.** (A)

1 편지

레이놀즈 씨께,

귀하께 RSI의 수석 소프트웨어 개발자 자리를 제안하게 되어 기쁩니다. 자격을 갖춘 많은 프로그래머들이 이 자리에 관심을 보였으며, 많은 후보군 중에서 단 한 명만 선발하기가 쉽지 않았습니다. 하지만 결국 전문가로서의 뛰어난 귀하의 경험이 돋보였습니다.

저희 제안 조건을 상세히 열거한 서류를 동봉합니다. 검토하시고 문의 사항이 있으시면 555-0136으로 저에게 전화 주십시오.

position 자리, 직위　qualified 자격이 있는　select 선발하다
in the end 결국　stellar 뛰어난　professional 직업의,
전문적인　stand out 두드러지다, 눈에 띄다　detail 상세히
열거하다　terms 조건

문제 1단락 세 번째 줄의 단어 'field'와 의미상 가장 가까운 것은?
(A) 풀밭
(B) 지원자 집단
(C) 학문적 주제
(D) 텍스트 입력 상자

해설 **동의어**
명사 field는 '밭, 들판, 분야, 영역, (모든) 경기자[참가자]' 등의 의미가 있다. 여기에서는 '수석 소프트웨어 개발자 자리에 지원한 많은 후보자들(the large field) 중 한 명만 선발하기가 쉽지 않았다'라는 의미로, 이 문장에서 field는 '후보군, 후보자들'의 뜻으로 쓰였다. 따라서 (B) applicant pool이 정답이다.

2 이메일

발신: ⟨barrysherrill@tcc.edu⟩
수신: ⟨esmerelda@esmereldaspottery.com⟩
제목: 훌륭한 강의!
날짜: 10월 12일

안녕하세요, 로페즈 씨

저를 기억하실지 모르겠지만, 저는 토요일 귀하의 무료 강좌에 참석했습니다. 강사로서의 귀하의 열정과 예술가로서의 능력에 깊은 인상을 받았기에, 톨레도 기술 전문대학의 채용 담당자로서 저희 학교 야간 과정에서 강의를 해주시기를 요청하고 싶습니다. 지역민들에게 귀중한 시간이 됨과 더불어 귀하의 업체를 알릴 수 있는 좋은 기회가 되리라고 생각합니다.

의향이 있으시면 직접 만나서 더 얘기를 나누고 싶습니다. 귀하의 작업실로 찾아뵙기에 언제가 좋으시겠습니까?

배리 셰릴 드림

impressed 깊은 인상을 받은　enthusiasm 열정, 열의
instructor 강사　hiring director 채용 담당자　valuable
귀중한　exposure 노출, 알려짐　in person 직접

문제 1단락 네 번째 줄의 단어 'exposure'와 의미상 가장 가까운 것은?
(A) 홍보　　　　　　(B) 위험
(C) 풍경　　　　　　(D) 발견

해설 **동의어**
명사 exposure는 '노출, 폭로, 홍보, 광고' 등의 의미가 있다. 여기에서는 '지역민들에게 귀하의 업체를 알릴 수 있는 좋은 기회(good exposure)가 될 것이다'라는 의미로, 이 문장에서 exposure는 '알리기, 홍보'의 뜻으로 쓰였다. 따라서 (A) publicity가 정답이다.

●UNIT 07 의도 파악 문제

예제
교재 p. 296

[오전 9:44] 게리, 제 비행기가 지연되었어요.

[오전 9:45] 사울, 언제 도착할 예정이에요?

[오전 9:47] 12:10분에서야 도착할 거 같아요. 최대한 빨리 택시를 잡아타고 갈게요.

[오전 9:49] 그건 걱정 마세요. 제가 데리러 갈게요.

[오전 9:52] 정말 고마워요.

문제 오전 9시 49분에 게리 씨가 "그건 걱정 마세요"라고 말한 의미는 무엇이겠는가?
(A) 회의가 취소되었다.
(B) 차량을 렌트할 필요가 없을 것이다.
(C) 사울이 택시를 탈 필요가 없다.
(D) 사무실이 매우 가깝다.

READING PRACTICE

교재 p. 297

1. (A)   **2.** (A)

1 문자 메시지

> **첸 닝 [오전 9:45]**
> 프랭키, 휴이트 씨가 당신에게 회사 차가 있다고 하던데요.
>
> **프랭키 카터 [오전 9:48]**
> 네. 제품 사양서를 전달하러 엘모어 가에 있는 우리 공장을 방문 중이에요. 차 필요하세요?
>
> **첸 닝 [오전 9:48]**
> 그게, 고객과 점심 미팅이 있는데, 차를 가지고 갈까 생각했거든요.
>
> **프랭키 카터 [오전 9:49]**
> 아. 그런데... 적어도 2시까지는 여기 있을 거라서요.
>
> **첸 닝 [오전 9:50]**
> 알겠어요. 그럼 택시를 부를게요.
>
> product specification 제품 사양서

문제 오전 9시 49분에 카터 씨가 "적어도 2시까지는 여기 있을 거라서요"라고 말한 의미는 무엇이겠는가?
   (A) 닝 씨는 차를 사용할 수 없다.
   (B) 그녀는 회의에 참석할 수 없다.
   (C) 그녀는 닝 씨를 기다리는 것을 개의치 않는다.
   (D) 닝 씨는 그녀를 위해 식사를 주문할 필요가 없다.

해설 **의도 파악**
오전 9시 48분에 닝 씨가 고객과의 점심 미팅에 차를 가지고 가려고 했다(I thought I might drive)고 했고 9시 49분에 현재 차를 이용 중인 카터 씨가 현장에 2시까지 있을 것이라고 했으므로 이는 닝 씨에게 차를 줄 수 없다는 뜻으로 이해할 수 있다. 따라서 (A)가 정답이다.

어휘 vehicle 차량   mind 꺼리다

2 온라인 채팅

> **일레인 알베스 [오후 2:03]**
> 진우, 테오 씨가 방금 대량 주문에 대해 무료 배송을 받을 수 있는지 물어보러 전화했어요.
>
> **진우 강 [오후 2:04]**
> 하지만 그 판촉 행사는 지난주에 끝났는데요.
>
> **일레인 알베스 [오후 2:05]**
> 저기, 테오 씨는 오랫동안 우리 회사를 이용해 왔잖아요.
>
> **진우 강 [오후 2:06]**
> 당신 말이 맞아요. 단골 고객을 지속적으로 만족시키는 것도 중요하죠. 전산에 그 변경 사항에 대해 확실히 기록을 남겨 두는 것만 해줘요. 그렇지 않으면 다른 직원들이 혼동할 수도 있으니까요.
>
> **일레인 알베스 [오후 2:07]**
> 문제 없어요. 지금 처리할게요.
>
> free shipping 무료 배송   bulk order 대량 주문   promotion 홍보, 판촉 행사   loyal customer 단골 고객   make a note 메모[기록]하다   otherwise 그렇지 않으면   confuse 혼란스럽게 만들다   employee 직원   take care of ~을 처리하다

문제 오후 2시 5분에 알베스 씨가 "테오 씨는 오랫동안 우리 회사를 이용해 왔잖아요"라고 말한 의미는 무엇이겠는가?
   (A) 그녀는 수수료를 면제해 줘야 한다고 생각한다.
   (B) 테오 씨는 승진할 자격이 있다.
   (C) 그녀는 착오가 있었다는 것에 놀랐다.
   (D) 테오 씨는 정책에 대해 알아야 한다.

해설 **의도 파악**
고객 주문 건에 대해 무료 배송 가능 여부를 논의했고 판촉 행사 기간이 지나서 해당 사항이 없음을 알자, 단골 고객임을 언급한 상황이다. 2시 6분 대화를 보면 단골 고객을 우대해야 하는 데 동의하고 있으므로 판촉 행사 기간 만료와 상관없이 무료 배송을 해주자는 의미로 이해할 수 있다. 따라서 정답은 (A)이다.

어휘 fee 수수료   waive 면제해주다   be qualified for ~의 자격이 있다   promotion 승진   policy 정책, 방침

● UNIT 08 이메일 / 편지 지문

예제

교재 p. 298

> 수신: 그레이엄 빈센트 〈g-williams@info.com〉
> 발신: 제인 리스턴 〈jliston@odelaudio.com〉
> 날짜: 12월 2일
> 제목: 초대 요청
>
> 빈센트 씨께
>
> 저는 귀하의 마케팅 관련 책을 재밌게 읽었습니다. 유용한 팁이 많이 있었어요. 시애틀에 있는 저희 사무실에서 강연을 해주실 수 있는지 궁금합니다. 첨부한 지도를 참고하시기 바랍니다.
>
> 연락을 원하시면 본 이메일 또는 555-0168, 내선번호 47번으로 회신 주세요. 이 사안을 구체적으로 논의할 수 있기를 바랍니다.
>
> 제인 리스턴
> 오델 오디오 인사부장

문제 리스턴 씨는 왜 이메일을 보냈는가?
   (A) 빈센트 씨를 강연에 초대하기 위해
   (B) 빈센트 씨가 회사를 도와준 것에 감사하기 위해
   (C) 빈센트 씨에게 정규직을 제안하기 위해
   (D) 빈센트 씨에게 인터뷰에 참석할 것을 요청하기 위해

ACTUAL TEST

교재 p. 299

1. (B)	**2.** (C)	**3.** (D)	**4.** (A)	**5.** (B)
6. (B)	**7.** (D)	**8.** (C)	**9.** (B)	

1-2 이메일

수신: 창고 직원
발신: 조 카디먼
제목: 최근 행사들
날짜: 10월 3일

모든 직원들의 최근의 노고에 감사드리고 싶습니다. **¹**우리 창고의 침수로 인해, 다른 시설에서 일하느라 쉽지 않은 몇 달간이었습니다. 하지만 청소 작업이 완료되어 이제 물품 보관을 위해 창고를 다시 이용할 수 있게 되었다는 것을 알려 드리게 되어 기쁩니다.

그 덕분에 우리는 주문을 더 신속하게 처리하고 우리 영업 정상화에 대한 고객들의 믿음에 따른 주문량 증가에 대처할 수 있게 되기를 기대합니다. 그런 의미에서 우리 경영진은 이번 기회를 우리 회사의 미래를 위해 중대한 시점으로 여기고 있습니다. 이번의 중대한 사건을 기념하고 여러분의 노고에 감사를 표하기 위해, **²**다음 주 화요일 퇴근 후에 구내식당에서 축하 행사를 열 예정입니다. 여러분 모두 그곳에서 뵙기를 바랍니다. 다양한 다과 및 음식이 제공될 것입니다.

시설 관리자
제인 돕슨

warehouse 창고 flooding 홍수, 침수 work out of ~에서 일하다 alternative 대안이 되는 storage 저장, 보관 facilities 시설 delighted 매우 기뻐하는 operation 작업, 작동 house 보관하다, 저장하다 goods 물품, 제품 anticipate 예상하다, 기대하다 deal with 처리하다 volume 용량 faith 믿음 as such 그런 의미에서 significant 중대한 celebrate 기념하다 landmark 획기적인 사건 dedication 전념, 헌신 a wide range of 다양한 refreshments 다과

1. 창고에 대해 이메일이 시사하는 것은?
(A) 재고가 바닥났다.
(B) 몇 달 동안 폐쇄되었다.
(C) 최근에 확장했다.
(D) 새로운 장소로 이전했다.

해설 추론
첫 단락의 두 번째 문장에서, 창고의 침수로 인해 몇 달 동안 대안으로 다른 보관 시설을 이용했다(Due to the flooding of our warehouse, ~ alternative storage facilities)고 했으므로, 창고가 몇 달 동안 폐쇄되었다는 것을 추론할 수 있다. 따라서 (B)가 정답이다.

어휘 run out of ~이 다 바닥나다 **stock** 재고품 **enlarge** 확대하다 **relocate** 이전하다

2. 다음 주 화요일에 일어날 일은?
(A) 대량 주문이 처리될 것이다.
(B) 교육 워크숍을 위해 직원들이 모일 것이다.
(C) 직원들을 위한 파티가 열릴 것이다.
(D) 고객들의 회사 건물 출입이 허용될 것이다.

해설 세부 사항
질문의 next Tuesday가 문제 해결의 단서로, 지문에서 next Tuesday가 언급된 부분을 찾아본다. 두 번째 단락 후반부에서 창고 직원들의 노고에 감사를 표하기 위해 다음 주 화요일 퇴근 후에 구내식당에서 축하 행사를 열 예정(we will hold a celebration in the cafeteria next Tuesday after work)이라고 했다. 따라서 (C)가 정답이다.

어휘 process 처리하다 **gather** 모이다, 모으다 **premises** 건물에 딸린 부지, 구내

3-5 이메일

수신: 아니타 데이비스 〈a.davies@smart-clips.com〉
발신: 브라이언 니콜즈 〈b.nichols@smart-clips.com〉
날짜: 1월 28일
제목: 대기실 개조

아니타,

우리 미용실 대기실을 개선하기 위한 준비 작업이 원활하게 진행되고 있어요. 우리가 이렇게 하기로 결정해서 다행이에요. **³**길 건너 새로 개업한 미용실의 대기실이 아주 멋지거든요. 우리도 그 수준에 맞먹을 정도로 세련될 필요가 있어요. 낡은 커피메이커는 개별 컵으로 커피를 내릴 수 있는 새것으로 바꿨어요. **⁵**직원과 고객 모두 다양한 향을 음미하게 될 거고, 마실지 안 마실지도 모를 커피를 커피포트에 계속 새로 내릴 필요가 없을 거예요. 그렇게 하면 불필요한 낭비도 줄일 수 있을 거예요.

⁴새 소파와 오크 소재의 사이드 탁자 두 개를 주문했는데, 금요일 점심때쯤 도착할 거예요. 지금 있는 안락의자는 스팀 청소를 맡기면 보기 좋을 것 같아요. 다음 주에 스팀 청소기를 대여할게요. 분명히 모두가 우리 미용실의 산뜻한 새로운 모습을 좋아할 거예요.

브라이언

waiting area 대기실 preparation 준비 smoothly 원활하게 impressive 인상적인 match 맞먹다, 필적하다 sophistication 세련됨 brew (차를) 끓이다 appreciate 감상하다, 고마워하다 wider variety of 더욱 다양한 consume 먹다, 마시다, 소모하다 current 현재의 steam-clean 스팀 청소하다

3. 업체가 변화를 주는 이유는?
(A) 더 많은 고객들을 수용하기 위해
(B) 재능 있는 직원들을 유치하기 위해
(C) 고객의 요구에 부응하기 위해
(D) 경쟁 업체에 뒤처지지 않기 위해

해설 **세부 사항**

첫 번째 단락 두 번째 문장에서 길 건너 새로 개업한 미용실의 대기실이 아주 멋지니 우리도 그 수준에 맞먹을 정도로 세련될 필요가 있나(as the newly opened salon ~ to match their level of sophistication)고 했으므로, (D)가 정답이다.

어휘 accommodate 수용하다   attract 끌어 모으다   talented 재능 있는   respond to ~에 대응하다   keep up with ~에 뒤떨어지지 않다   competitor 경쟁자

4. 이번 주 후반에 있을 일은?
(A) 가구 몇 점이 배송될 것이다.
(B) 니콜즈 씨가 물품을 스팀 청소할 것이다.
(C) 기계가 설치될 것이다.
(D) 데이비스 씨가 계획을 승인할 것이다.

어휘 install 설치하다   approve 승인하다

해설 **세부 사항**

두 번째 단락 첫 문장에서 새 소파와 사이드 탁자 두 개를 주문했는데, 금요일 점심때쯤 도착할 것(I've ordered ~ arrive on Friday around lunchtime)이라고 했다. 따라서 (A)가 정답이다.

5. [1], [2], [3], [4]로 표시된 곳들 중 다음 문장이 들어가기에 가장 적절한 곳은?

그렇게 하면 불필요한 낭비도 줄일 수 있을 거예요.
(A) [1]   (B) [2]
(C) [3]   (D) [4]

해설 **문장 삽입**

제시문은 '그렇게 하면 불필요한 낭비도 줄일 수 있을 것이다'라는 의미로, That way와 also로 보아 불필요한 낭비를 줄일 수 있는 방법 뒤에 들어가야 한다는 것을 알 수 있다. 따라서 마시지 않을지도 모를 커피를 커피포트에 계속 새로 내릴 필요가 없을 것(we won't have to keep making new pots of coffee that may or may not be consumed)이라는 내용 뒤인 (B)가 정답이다.

어휘 reduce 줄이다   unnecessary 불필요한

6-9 이메일

데이비드 파텔
밀턴 호텔
242 캐니언 로드
웰링빌, 캘리포니아

파텔 씨께,

최근 제가 귀 호텔에 숙박한 것과 관련하여 귀하에게 연락하라는 조언을 받았습니다. **7**저는 보통 업무차 웰링빌을 방문할 때는 언제나 밀턴 호텔에 묵는데 대개 기분 좋게 머무릅니다. **6**그런데 이번에는 몇 가지 문제가 저를 불만족스럽게 만들었습니다.

우선, **8(D)**침실에 딸려 있는 욕실의 샤워기는 제가 처음 도착했을 때는 뜨거운 물 공급이 되지 않았습니다. 이것은 결국은 수리되었지만, 다소 불편했습니다. 또한 **8(B)**수영장 시설을 이용할 수 없어서 실망스러웠는데, 보수 관리 문제로 폐쇄되었더군요. **8(A)**테니스 코트는 제가 직접 이용하지는 않았지만, 제대로 관리되는 것처럼 보이지 않았습니다. 그 때문에 머무르는 동안 제가 늘 하는 운동을 계속하지 못했습니다.

동료가 다음 주에 웰링빌을 방문할 예정입니다. **9**귀 호텔에서의 제 경험이 너무 안 좋아서 동료에게 플라자 호텔에 묵으라고 권할까 심각하게 고려 중입니다. 인터넷을 보니 그곳이 귀 호텔보다 공항에서는 더 멀지만, 회원 포인트 방식을 제공해서 무료 숙박을 받을 수 있더군요.

위 문제에 대해 논의하고 싶으시면 언제든 저에게 연락 주시기 바랍니다.

카라 리처즈

regarding ~에 관하여   normally 보통, 일반적으로   occasion 경우, 때   unsatisfied 불만을 느끼는   en suite 딸려 있는   eventually 결국   fix 수리하다   inconvenience 불편   disappointed 실망한   maintenance 유지, 관리   workout 운동   colleague 동료   negative 부정적인, 나쁜   redeem (쿠폰 등을) 상품으로 교환하다   accommodation 숙박   hesitate 주저하다

6. 편지를 보낸 이유는?
(A) 호텔 요금을 문의하기 위해
(B) 불만을 제기하기 위해
(C) 예약을 변경하기 위해
(D) 호텔 업그레이드를 요청하기 위해

해설 **주제 / 목적**

첫 단락에서 보통 업무차 웰링빌을 방문할 때는 밀턴 호텔에서 머무르는데, 이번에는 몇 가지 불만족스러운 문제가 있었다(However, on this occasion, there were a number of issues that left me unsatisfied)고 했으며, 두 번째 단락에서는 불만 사항을 구체적으로 언급하고 있다. 따라서 (B)가 정답이다.

어휘 inquire 묻다, 알아보다   rate 요금   complaint 불평, 불만

7. 리처즈 씨에 대해 암시된 것은?
(A) 전에 이 호텔에서 일했다.
(B) 웰링빌로 이사할 계획이다.
(C) 숙박하는 동안 테니스를 쳤다.
(D) 전에 웰링빌을 방문한 적이 있다.

해설 **추론**

첫 단락 두 번째 문장에서 리처즈 씨는 보통 업무차 웰링빌을 방문할 때(every time I visit Wellingville on business)는 언제나 밀턴 호텔에서 기분 좋게 머문다고 했으므로, 리처즈 씨는 전에 웰링빌을 방문한 적이 있음을 추론할 수 있다. 따라서 (D)가 정답이다.

8. 밀턴 호텔의 특징으로 언급되지 않은 것은?

  (A) 스포츠 시설   (B) 수영장

  (C) 공항 셔틀버스   (D) 침실에 딸려 있는 욕실

해설 **Not / True**

두 번째 단락에 밀턴 인의 특징이 구체적으로 언급되어 있다. 침실에 딸려 있는 욕실(my en suite bathroom)은 처음 도착했을 때 뜨거운 물 공급이 되지 않았다고 했으며, 수영장 시설(the swimming facilities)은 보수 관리 문제로 폐쇄되어 이용할 수 없었고, 테니스 코트(The tennis courts) 역시 관리되지 않는 것처럼 보였다고 했다. 따라서 언급되지 않은 (C)가 정답이다.

어휘 feature 특징

9. 이메일에 따르면, 플라자 호텔 웹사이트에 명시된 것은?

  (A) 밀턴 호텔보다 더 저렴한 객실 요금을 제공한다.

  (B) 고객 보상 제도를 운영한다.

  (C) 충원하려고 하는 공석이 몇 개 있다.

  (D) 공항 옆에 위치해 있다.

해설 **Not / True**

세 번째 단락에서 리처즈 씨는 플라자 호텔이 회원 포인트 방식을 제공해서 무료 숙박을 제공한다(they offer a member point system ~ for free accommodation)고 했다. 따라서 (B)가 정답이다

어휘 operate 운영하다 reward scheme 보상 제도 job vacancy (일자리) 공석 fill 채우다 be located 위치하다

●UNIT 09 광고 / 공지 지문

예제
교재 p. 302

> **구인**
>
> 낮과 저녁 교대로 울프펜 카페에서 파트 타임 서버로 일하실 분이 필요합니다.
>
> 낮, 저녁, 주말, 휴일에 근무가 가능해야 합니다. 서빙 경험, 특히 빠른 근무 환경에서의 경력이 우대됩니다.
>
> 주요 업무는 손님을 맞이하고 주문을 받고 결제를 담당하는 것입니다.
>
> 모든 서버는 시급과 팁을 받습니다. 3개월 근무 후 정규직으로의 승격이 가능합니다.
>
> 직접 방문해서 지원하시면 매니저와 예비 현장 인터뷰를 가질 것입니다.

문제 이 직책에 대해 자격 요건으로 언급된 것은?

  (A) 공휴일 근무 가능 여부

  (B) 경력

  (C) 특정 학력 수준

  (D) 무거운 물건을 들어올릴 수 있는 능력

ACTUAL TEST
교재 p. 303

1. (B)	**2.** (D)	**3.** (C)	**4.** (A)	**5.** (D)
6. (A)	**7.** (C)	**8.** (D)	**9.** (A)	

1-2 광고

> **지오반니 사진관**
>
> **1(A), (D)** 지오반니가 이끄는 전문 사진가 팀은 자부심을 가지고 15년 동안 스트랜턴에서 서비스를 제공해 오고 있습니다. **2**저희는 얼굴 사진과 단체 사진, 그리고 여러분의 회사 모습을 최상으로 담은 자연스러운 사진을 촬영합니다. 모든 사진을 벽에 걸어 둘 정도의 멋진 출력물로 받아 보시거나, 또는 **1(C)** 추가 비용 없이 정식 출판물이나 홍보 자료용으로 편리한 디지털 파일 형태로 받아 보십시오.
>
> 오늘 555-0163으로 저희에게 전화 주셔서 저희 업체 서비스에 대해 더 알아보시고 견적서를 받아 보세요!

skilled 숙련된, 전문적인 photographer 사진가 headshot 얼굴 사진 portrait 초상화, 인물 사진 candid photo 포즈를 취하지 않은 자연스러운 모습의 사진 portray 그리다, 묘사하다 publication 출판, 출판물 promotional 홍보의 material 자료 obtain 얻다 price quote 견적서

1. 지오반니 사진관에 대해 명시되지 않은 것은?

  (A) 많은 사진가들이 그곳에서 일한다.

  (B) 한 출판물이 특별상을 받았다.

  (C) 사진의 디지털 복사본을 제공한다.

  (D) 10여 년 전에 설립되었다.

해설 **Not / True**

첫 문장에서 지오반니가 이끄는 전문 사진가 팀(Giovanni and his team of skilled photographers)은 15년 동안(for 15 years) 스트랜턴에서 서비스를 제공해 왔다고 했으며, 마지막 문장에서는 추가 비용 없이 정식 출판물이나 홍보 자료용으로 사용할 수 있는 편리한 디지털 파일(convenient digital files)을 제공한다고 했으므로, 언급되지 않은 (B)가 정답이다.

어휘 multiple 많은, 다수의 recognition 인정, 표창

2. 지오반니 사진관이 전문으로 할 것 같은 것은?

  (A) 가족 사진   (B) 학교 사진

  (C) 패션 사진   (D) 기업 사진

해설 **추론**

첫 단락 두 번째 문장에서 얼굴 사진, 단체 사진과 회사의 모습을 최상으로 담은 자연스러운 사진을 촬영한다(We can take ~ in its best light)고 했으므로, (D)가 정답이다.

3-5 공지

[3]헤일 미술관: 관람객 공지 사항

헤일 미술관은 사진가들에게 인기 있는 장소로, 전세계 현대 미술 작품들을 폭넓게 소장하고 있습니다. [3]모든 관람객들에게 미술관 내에서 사진 촬영이 허용되지만 몇몇 예외 조항이 있음을 알려 드리고자 합니다. 플래시는 항상 꺼 두셔야 하고 삼각대는 허용되지 않습니다.

관람객들은 상설 소장품은 모두 촬영할 수 있습니다. [4]하지만 특별 전시품에 대해서는 사진 촬영이 금지됩니다. 이 작품들은 다른 미술관들로부터 대여한 것들로, 헤일 미술관에는 소유권이 없기 때문입니다. 이 경우에는 표지판이 눈에 띄게 걸려 있을 것입니다.

헤일 미술관에서 촬영한 사진들은 사적인 용도로만 가능합니다. 판매 및 어떤 종류의 상업적 용도로도 사용되어서는 안 됩니다. 이는 부분적으로는 일부 작품들을 위해 필요한 저작권 보호 때문입니다. [5]또한 그러한 행위는 미술관 1층 기념품점에서 판매되는 포스터, 그림 액자, 기타 상품들로부터 얻는 미술관의 수입에 피해를 줄 수 있기 때문이기도 합니다. 이 수입은 지속적으로 발생하는 비용을 위해 자금을 모으는 데 필요합니다. 미술관에서 사진을 촬영함으로써, 여러분은 위와 같은 규정에 동의하시게 됩니다. 감사합니다.

---

house 소장하다 extensive 폭넓은. 광범위한 collection 수집품. 소장품 contemporary art 현대 미술 inform 알리다 photography 사진 촬영 exception 예외 turn off 전원을 끄다 at all times 항상 tripod 삼각대 permanent 영구적인. 상설의 prohibit 금하다 exhibit 전시품; 전시하다 on loan 대여하여. 차용하여 ownership 소유(권) prominently 두드러지게. 눈에 띄게 commercial 상업의 copyright 저작권 protection 보호 additionally 게다가. 또한 harm 해를 끼치다 income 소득. 수입 merchandise 물품. 상품 ongoing 계속 진행 중인 consent 동의하다 regulation 규정

3. 공지의 목적은?
(A) 미술관의 역사를 설명하기 위해
(B) 좋은 사진을 찍기 위한 조언을 주기 위해
(C) 미술관 규정을 간략히 설명하기 위해
(D) 이용 불가능한 서비스에 대해 사과하기 위해

해설 주제 / 목적
공지문의 제목(Hale Art Museum: Notice to Visitors)에서 미술관에서 관람객에게 보내는 공지문임을 알 수 있으며, 첫 번째 단락의 두 번째 문장에서 미술관 내에서 사진 촬영이 허용되지만 몇몇 예외 조항이 있다(photography is allowed within the museum, with some exceptions)고 했다. 따라서 미술관 관람객에게 미술관 규정을 설명하기 위해 보낸 공지문임을 알 수 있으므로, (C)가 정답이다.

어휘 tip 조언 outline 개요를 서술하다 unavailable 이용할 수 없는

---

4. 일부 품목의 사진 촬영이 제한되는 이유는?
(A) 미술관 소유가 아니다.
(B) 현재 팔려고 내놓은 것이다.
(C) 매우 민감한 부품들을 가지고 있다.
(D) 개인 소유의 공간에 보관되고 있다.

해설 세부 사항
두 번째 단락에서 특별 전시품들은 다른 미술관들로부터 대여한 것이기 때문에 헤일 미술관에 소유권이 없으므로(the Hale Art Museum has no ownership rights) 사진 촬영이 금지된다고 했다. 따라서 (A)가 정답이다.

어휘 restrict 제한하다 belong to ~의 소유이다 currently 현재의 up for sale 팔려고 내놓은 delicate 민감한. 섬세한 component 요소. 부품 store 보관하다

5. 헤일 미술관에 대해서 암시된 것은?
(A) 고대 미술과 현대 미술을 모두 소장하고 있다.
(B) 기금 모금 목표를 달성하지 못했다.
(C) 더 많은 자원봉사자들을 찾고 있다.
(D) 미술관 내에 판매용 그림들을 가지고 있다.

해설 추론
세 번째 단락에서 미술관에서 촬영한 사진을 상업적 용도로 사용하는 것은 미술관 1층 기념품점에서 판매되는 포스터, 그림 액자, 기타 상품들로부터 얻는 미술관의 수입에 피해를 줄 수도 있다(this practice could harm the museum's income ~ sold in our first-floor gift shop)고 했다. 따라서 미술관 내의 기념품점에서 판매용 그림을 갖추고 있다는 것을 추론할 수 있으므로, (D)가 정답이다.

어휘 ancient 고대의 meet a goal 목표를 달성하다 fundraising 기금 모금 volunteer 자원봉사자 on site 현장에

6-9 광고

에르고 퓨처

[9]하루에 여섯 시간 이상 책상에 앉아 있는 사람이라면 누구나 기이한 각도로 키보드를 치고 컴퓨터 스크린을 응시하며 불편한 의자에서 시간을 보내는 것으로 인한 통증에 익숙할 것입니다. 에르고 퓨처는 이러한 문제를 잘 알고 있으며 해결책을 가지고 있습니다.

[9]에르고 퓨처는 여러분이 더 오랫동안 더 편안하게 작업하실 수 있도록 여러분의 신체에 맞춰 제작한 의자와 책상을 판매하고 있습니다. [6]저희 전문가와 짧은 면담을 마친 후에, 여러분의 고유한 척추 모양에 맞춘 의자와 여러분의 신장에 완벽하게 맞는 높이에 놓이는 책상을 제작해 드립니다. 장인이 공들여 제작한 저희 사무용 책걸상 세트는 획일적인 일반 작업 내와는 비교가 되지 않습니다.

저희는 건강 전반을 지지하는 오래가는 제품을 만듭니다. [7]실제로 저희는 모두가 에르고 퓨처 제품을 사용하는 것이 중요하다고 생각하기에 다른 어떤 가구 회사보다 더 많은 결제

방식을 제공합니다. 저희 영업 사원이 귀하나 귀사에서 저희 제품을 구입할 수 있도록 방법을 찾아 드릴 것이며, 제품을 구매하시면 다른 가구 제조업체와 동일한 수준의 품질 보증 서비스가 제공됩니다. 운동선수들은 품질이 떨어지는 장비에 결코 만족하지 않을 것인데, 사무실 근로자들은 왜 그래야 합니까?

[8]오늘 (820) 555-0139로 저희에게 전화 주셔서 이 광고를 보셨다고 말하시고 첫 번째 주문에 대해 10% 할인을 받으세요.

be likely to *do* ~할 것 같다, ~하기 쉽다   be familiar with ~에 익숙하다   ache 통증(= pain)   uncomfortable 불편한   angle 각도   stare at ~을 응시하다   custom-fitted 고객에게 맞춘   session (특정 활동을 위한) 시간[기간]   specialist 전문가   conform to ~에 따르다   spine 척추   comparison 비교   master-crafted 장인이 공들여 제작한   generic 일반적인   one-size-fits-all 획일적인, 천편일률적인   workstation 작업대   long-lasting 오래 지속되는   overall 종합적인, 전체의   goods 제품   payment plan 결제 방식   sales representative 영업 사원, 판매원   warranty 품질 보증   guarantee 품질 보증   manufacturer 제조업자   athlete 운동선수   settle for ~에 만족하다   inferior 하위의, 열등한

6. 에르고 퓨처는 어떤 종류의 제품을 만드는가?
(A) 사무용 가구
(B) 스포츠 장비
(C) 개인용 컴퓨터
(D) 가전제품

해설 **세부 사항**
두 번째 단락 두 번째 문장에서 에르고 퓨처에서는 척추 모양에 맞춘 의자와 신장에 맞는 높이의 책상을 제작한다(we'll build you a chair ~ at the perfect level for your height)고 했으므로, (A)가 정답이다.

7. 광고에 따르면, 에르고 퓨처의 특별한 점은?
(A) 원자재를 구하는 방법
(B) 만족도 보장 정도
(C) 지불 방식의 다양성
(D) 직원 교육량

해설 **세부 사항**
세 번째 단락에서 모두가 에르고 퓨처 제품을 사용하는 것이 중요하다고 생각하기 때문에 다른 어떤 가구 회사보다 더 많은 결제 방식을 제공한다(we offer more payment plans than any other furniture company)고 했으므로, (C)가 정답이다.

어휘 acquire 획득하다   raw material 원자재, 원료   extent 정도   satisfaction 만족(감)   financing 자금 조달

8. 고객들이 할인을 받을 수 있는 방법은?
(A) 보상 프로그램에 가입함으로써
(B) 에르고 퓨처에 친구를 추천함으로써
(C) 물품을 대량 구입함으로써
(D) 광고를 언급함으로써

해설 **세부 사항**
마지막 단락에서 오늘 전화해서 광고를 봤다고 말하면 첫

주문에 대해 10% 할인을 받을 수 있다(Call us today ~ to receive 10% off your first order)고 했다. 따라서 (D)가 정답이다.

어휘 refer A to B A를 B에게 추천하다   mention 언급하다

9. [1], [2], [3], [4]로 표시된 곳들 중 다음 문장이 들어가기에 가장 적절한 곳은?

에르고 퓨처는 이러한 문제를 잘 알고 있으며 해결책을 가지고 있습니다.
(A) [1]
(B) [2]
(C) [3]
(D) [4]

해설 **문장 삽입**
제시문에서 this issue라고 했으므로 문제점이 언급된 이후에 들어가야 한다. 첫 번째 단락에서 책상에 오래 앉아 있는 사람이 가질 수 있는 문제점을 나열하고 있으므로 이어서 제시문을 삽입해 볼 수 있다. 또한 제시문에서 해결책이 있다(we have a solution)고 했으므로 뒤따르는 내용이 해결책인지 확인해 보면, 삽입문 이후부터 에르고 퓨처의 특징점이 언급되므로 자연스럽게 이어진다. 따라서 정답은 (A)이다.

어휘 solution 해결책

●UNIT 10 문자 / 채팅 지문

예제
교재 p. 306

셜리 로웰 [오전 9:38]
찰스, 바빠요?

찰스 밀러 [오전 9:38]
아니요. 무슨 일이에요?

셜리 로웰 [오전 9:39]
중요한 문서를 깜빡하고 가져오지 않았어요. 아마 제 책상 위에 문서가 있을 거예요. 스캔해서 보내 주실 수 있나요?

찰스 밀러 [오전 9:40]
네. 사무실에 들어가기 위해 보안팀에서 열쇠를 받아올게요.

셜리 로웰 [오전 9:41]
문은 잠그지 않았어요.

찰스 밀러 [오전 9:42]
그렇군요. 지금 바로 처리할게요.

문제 오전 9시 41분에 로웰 씨가 "문은 잠그지 않았어요"라고 쓸 때, 그 의도는 무엇인가?
(A) 밀러 씨가 집에서 일할 수 없다.
(B) 밀러 씨는 열쇠가 필요 없다.
(C) 밀러 씨가 엉뚱한 사무실에 있다.
(D) 밀러 씨가 문을 잠가야 한다.

1. (C)　　**2.** (A)　　**3.** (D)　　**4.** (C)　　**5.** (C)

6. (A)　　**7.** (D)　　**8.** (D)　　**9.** (B)　　**10.** (D)

1-2 문자 메시지

아셀라 멜피 [오후 1:25]
오늘 사무실을 비우시나요? 자리에 들렀는데, 안 계셔서요.

패트릭 발데즈 [오후 1:26]
새로 계약한 고객인 하이랜드 사 담당자들을 만나기 위해 공항에 가는 길이에요. **¹**오늘 저녁에 그들에게 저녁식사를 대접하는 일을 맡았거든요.

아셀라 멜피 [오후 1:27]
그건 깜박했네요.

패트릭 발데즈 [오후 1:28]
추천할 만한 괜찮은 식당 있어요? 그들에게 좋은 인상을 주고 싶거든요.

아셀라 멜피 [오후 1:31]
²제가 직접 간 적은 없지만, 이토가 스시 바가 시내에 막 개업했는데, 그에 관한 좋은 후기들을 많이 읽었어요.

패트릭 발데즈 [오후 1:32]
저한테는 그거면 충분해요. 고마워요!

on one's way to ~로 가는 길에　representative 대표자, 담당자　account 고객　suggestion 제안　downtown 시내에　numerous 많은　review 평가, 후기

1. 발데즈 씨가 맡은 일은?
(A) 직원들 모집하기　　(B) 항공권 예약하기
(C) 고객들 접대하기　　(D) 은행 계좌 개설하기

해설 세부 사항

오후 1시 26분 메시지에서 발데즈 씨는 새로 계약한 고객인 하이랜드 사 담당자들을 만나기 위해 공항에 가는 길이라면서, 오늘 저녁에 그들에게 저녁식사를 대접하는 일을 맡았다(I'm responsible for taking them out to dinner this evening)고 했다. 따라서 (C)가 정답이다.

어휘 recruit 모집하다　book 예약하다　entertain 접대하다　bank account 은행 계좌

2. 오후 1시 32분에, 발데즈 씨가 "저한테는 그거면 충분해요"라고 말할 때 암시하는 것은?
(A) 새로운 업체를 기꺼이 가 볼 의향이 있다.
(B) 몇몇 물품의 품질이 마음에 들었다.
(C) 멜피 씨의 서류 작업이 만족스럽다.
(D) 후기를 출력할 준비가 되었다고 생각한다.

해설 의도 파악

추천할 만한 괜찮은 식당이 있는지를 물은 발데즈 씨의 말에, 멜피 씨는 오후 1시 31분 메시지에서 자신이 직접 간

적은 없지만 시내에 막 개업한 이토가 스시 바에 관한 좋은 후기들을 많이 읽었다(I haven't been there myself, but Itoga Sushi Bar downtown just opened, and I've read numerous positive reviews about it)고 했다. 따라서 '그거면 충분하다'는 발데즈 씨의 의도는 멜피 씨가 추천한 식당에 가 볼 의향이 있다는 것이므로, (A)가 정답이다.

어휘 be willing to *do* 기꺼이 ~하다　be pleased with ~에 만족하다　paperwork 서류작업

3-6 온라인 채팅

[오전 10:15] 포드 창
³여러분 모두 스미스 앤 글래스 제약회사가 새로운 광고 대행사를 찾고 있다는 소문 들었어요?

[오전 10:16] 와이어트 쏘프
아니요, 못 들었어요. 그게 사실이에요?

[오전 10:17] 리사 예이츠
저도 들었어요. **³**우리는 그들과 접촉해서 제안을 제시해야 해요. 그들은 우리 회사로서는 큰 고객이 될 테고, 우리는 그들의 요구를 감당하기에 적합한 능력을 갖추고 있다고 생각해요.

[오전 10:20] 와이어트 쏘프
저도 동의해요. **⁴**리사, 당신은 전에 새로운 고객을 설득해서 우리에게 기회를 주도록 하는 데 성공한 적이 있잖아요. **⁵**그 회사에 누군가와 연락을 취할 수 있어요?

[오전 10:21] 포드 창
잠깐만요, 다니엘, 거기 임원들 중 한 명을 알지 않아요?

[오전 10:22] 다니엘 클리프
⁵네, 헤더 파텔이에요. 우리는 월터 사무용품 업체에서 함께 일한 적이 있어요. 몇 년간 왕래가 없었지만, 제가 연락하면 싫다고 하지는 않을 거예요.

[오전 10:24] 와이어트 쏘프
좋아요. **⁶**그녀에게 연락해서 당신을 만나 점심식사를 할 수 있는지 알아봐 주지 않을래요?

[오전 10:25] 다니엘 클리프
그럴게요.

rumor 소문　pharmaceuticals 제약회사　advertising agency 광고 대행사　approach 접근하다, 접촉하다　proposition 제의, 제안　be equipped to *do* ~할 능력을 갖추다　handle 다루다, 처리하다　persuade 설득하다　make contact with ~와 연락[접촉]하다　executive 간부, 경영진　reach out to ~에게 연락하다

3. 채팅 참가자들은 어디서 일할 것 같은가?
(A) 제약회사　　　　　(B) 채용 대행업체
(C) 사무용품 판매 업체　(D) 광고 회사

해설 추론

오전 10시 17분 대화에서 그들이 우리의 큰 고객이 될 것이다(They'd be a great client for us)라고 했을 때 가

리키는 대상은 10시 15분 첫 번째 대화에서 등장했던 스미스 앤 글래스 제약회사이며, 이 제약 회사가 광고 대행사를 찾고 있다고 했으므로 채팅 중인 사람들이 광고 회사 직원들임을 알 수 있다. 따라서 정답은 (D)이다.

어휘 employment 고용, 채용   vendor 판매회사

---

4. 예이츠 씨에 대해 암시된 것은?
   (A) 몇몇 회사에서 일한 적이 있다.
   (B) 창 씨로부터 소식을 들었다.
   (C) 과거에 새로운 고객을 확보한 적이 있다.
   (D) 제안서 작성을 끝냈다.

해설 **추론**
오전 10시 20분 메시지에서 쏘프 씨는 리사 씨가 전에 새로운 고객을 설득하는 데 성공한 적이 있다(Lisa, you've had success persuading new clients to give us a try before)고 했다. 따라서 정답은 (C)이다.

어휘 secure 확보하다   draw up 작성하다   proposal 제안, 제의

---

5. 오전 10시 21분에, 창 씨가 "다니엘, 거기 임원들 중 한 명을 알지 않아요?"라고 말한 의미는 무엇이겠는가?
   (A) 클리프 씨가 서류에 중요한 세부 사항을 포함시키지 않았다.
   (B) 클리프 씨는 선발 위원회에 들어가면 안 된다.
   (C) 클리프 씨가 이전 동료에게 연락해야 한다.
   (D) 클리프 씨가 기업 문화를 말해 줄 수 있다.

해설 **의도 파악**
오전 10시 20분 메시지에서 쏘프 씨가 스미스 앤 글래스 제약회사의 누군가에게 연락을 취할 수 있는지 묻자, 창 씨가 클리프 씨에게 그 회사의 임원들 중 한 명을 알지 않냐고 확인 차 물어본 말이다. 이에 10시 22분 메시지에서 클리프 씨는 그 임원이 헤더 파텔 씨라고 대답하며 월터 사무용품 업체에서 함께 일한 적이 있다(Yes, her name is Heather Patel. We used to work together at Water Office Supplies)고 했다. 따라서 클리프 씨가 이전 동료에게 연락해 보아야 한다는 의미가 되므로 (C)가 정답이다.

어휘 detail 세부 사항   selection committee 선발 위원회   former 이전의   coworker 동료   corporate culture 기업 문화

---

6. 쏘프 씨가 마련하라고 제안한 것은?
   (A) 업무상 점심식사   (B) 장비 점검
   (C) 기획 회의   (D) 사무실 둘러보기

해설 **세부 사항**
오전 10시 24분 메시지에서 쏘프 씨는 클리프 씨에게 헤더 파텔 씨와 연락해서 점심식사를 함께할 수 있는지 알아보라고(Why don't you reach out to her and see if she'll meet you for lunch?) 제안하고 있다. 따라서 쏘프 씨가 마련하라고 제안한 것은 점심식사이므로, (A)가 정답이다.

어휘 arrange 마련하다   inspection 점검, 검사

7-10   문자 메시지

> **클레어 산체스 [오전 8:24]**
> 안녕하세요, 마이클. 지금 우리 프레젠테이션에 사용할 슬라이드 작업을 하고 있는데요. 끝나면 바로 보내 드릴게요. **7**계획대로 어제 보내지 못해서 미안해요.
>
> **마이클 터너 [오전 8:41]**
> 걱정하지 말아요. **8**오늘 오후나 되어야 필요하니까요. 그리고 제가 라우리 스위트를 대여해 놓았어요.
>
> **클레어 산체스 [오전 8:48]**
> 알겠어요. 로버트 딘도 올 거라고 들었어요. 그가 지난번에 우리 작업에 대해 피드백을 했다고 들었는데요.
>
> **마이클 터너 [오전 8:54]**
> 네, **9**그는 좀 까다로울 수 있어요. 하지만 분명히 이번에는 훨씬 나을 거예요.
>
> **클레어 산체스 [오전 9:06]**
> 그러길 바랍시다. 좋아요, **10**점심식사 후에 라우리 스위트에서 만나요. 현재는 가구가 비치되어 있지 않으니까, 우리가 회의실 준비를 해야 해요.
>
> **마이클 터너 [오전 9:11]**
> 알겠어요, 12시 정각에 출발해서 준비하는 것을 도울게요.

sweat it 애태우다, 걱정하다   book out 대여하다   come along 함께 오다[가다]   please 기쁘게 하다, 기분을 맞추다   currently 현재   unfurnished 가구가 비치되어 있지 않은   head over ~로 향하다   sharp 정각   set up 설치하다

---

7. 산체스 씨에 대해 암시된 것은?
   (A) 일찍 출근했다.
   (B) 일부 파일에 접근할 수 없었다.
   (C) 그녀의 제안이 받아들여지지 않았다.
   (D) 그녀의 작업이 예상보다 오래 걸렸다.

해설 **추론**
오전 8시 24분 메시지에서 산체스 씨는 프레젠테이션에 사용할 슬라이드 작업을 하고 있는데 예정대로 어제 보내지 못해서 미안하다(I'm sorry they weren't with you yesterday as planned)고 했다. 따라서 산체스 씨의 슬라이드 작업이 예상보다 오래 걸렸다는 것을 알 수 있으므로, (D)가 정답이다.

어휘 access 접근[접속]하다   disapprove 찬성하지 않다, 인정하지 않다

---

8. 오전 8시 41분에, 디니 씨가 "걱정하지 말아요"라고 말한 의미는 무엇이겠는가?
   (A) 산체스 씨가 프레젠테이션에 빠지는 것을 허락하겠다.
   (B) 산체스 씨가 휴가를 낼 것을 권한다.
   (C) 산체스 씨가 조사를 더 하기를 원한다.
   (D) 프레젠테이션에 사용할 슬라이드를 서둘러 받으려고 하지 않는다.

해설 **의도 파악**

오전 8시 24분 메시지에서 산체스 씨가 작업을 예정대로 어제 보내지 못해서 미안하다고 하자, 터너 씨는 오늘 오후나 되어야 필요하니(we don't need them until this afternoon) 걱정하지 말라고 했다. 따라서 '걱정하지 말라'는 터너 씨의 말이 의미하는 것은 슬라이드를 서둘러 받지 않아도 된다는 것이므로, (D)가 정답이다.

어휘 miss 놓치다, 빠지다　take leave 휴가를 내다
in a hurry 서둘러

9. 로버트 딘에 대해 암시된 것은?
(A) 회의에 참석하지 않을지도 모른다.
(B) 꽤 비판적일 수 있다.
(C) 터너 씨와 공동 작업한 적이 있다.
(D) 회사 소유주이다.

해설 **추론**

오전 8시 48분 메시지에서 산체스 씨가 지난번에 피드백을 준 로버트 딘도 프레젠테이션에 올 것이라고 하자, 오전 8시 54분 메시지에서 터너 씨는 그가 좀 까다롭지만(he can be a bit difficult to please), 분명히 이번에는 훨씬 나을 것이라고 했다. 따라서 로버트 딘이 까다롭게 비판할 수도 있다는 것을 알 수 있으므로, (B)가 정답이다.

어휘 critical 비판적인　collaborate with ~와 공동 작업하다

10. 라우리 스위트에 대해 암시된 것은?
(A) 꼭대기 층에 위치해 있다.
(B) 근처 화장실이 고장이다.
(C) 열 명 이상을 수용할 수 있다.
(D) 현재 내부에 의자가 없다.

해설 **Not / True**

오전 9시 6분 메시지에서 산체스 씨는 현재 라우리 스위트에는 가구가 비치되어 있지 않으니(It is currently unfurnished, so we'll need to get the room ready), 점심식사 후에 만나 회의실 준비를 해야 한다고 했으므로, (D)가 정답이다.

어휘 nearby 인근의　out of order 고장 난　hold 수용하다
inside 내부에

●UNIT 11 기사 지문

예제
교재 p. 310

지역 여성 정부상 수상

알링턴 (3월 10일) – 어제 기자회견에서 로펌 니콜스 앤 말론의 대변인은 레나 맥키니 카이상 수상자라고 발표했다.

이 영예로운 상은 언어 교육에 헌신한 교육자에게 매년 수여된다.

맥킨은 그녀의 노고와 자신의 수업에 대한 헌신을 인정받았으

며 그녀가 근무하고 있는 기관은 현금 만 달러를 받게 된다. 이곳이 공립이기 때문에 납세자들은 3월 17일 지역 회의에 참여하여 수상금이 어떻게 쓰일지에 대해 논의하게 될 것이다.

문제 납세자들은 무엇을 하도록 권장되는가?
(A) 수상 후보를 지명한다.
(B) 새로운 지역 대표자를 선출한다.
(C) 프로그램에 기부한다.
(D) 지출 계획에 대해 바라는 바를 말한다.

ACTUAL TEST
교재 p. 311

| 1. (D) | 2. (B) | 3. (B) | 4. (A) | 5. (C) |
| 6. (B) | 7. (C) | 8. (D) | 9. (D) | |

1-2 기사

바턴 시 미술 작업실

바턴 시(5월 7일) – [1]도나 로페즈는 자신만의 도자기 공예 작업실을 경력상 그렇게 일찍 개시할 생각이 없었다. 하지만 포터 물류 단지에서 저렴한 값으로 임대되는 작업실을 보고 다시 생각하게 되었다. "그동안 작품을 만들기 위해 시내에 있는 아츠 센터의 시설을 이용해 왔어요. 앞으로 몇 년 동안은 나만의 공간을 감당할 형편이 안 될 것 같았는데, 포터의 제 작업실 공간은 거의 횡재였죠"라고 로페즈 씨는 말했다.

[2]로페즈 씨는 접시나 그릇, 기타 주방용 도자기의 온라인 판매와 자신이 하는 일련의 강좌들로부터 나오는 수익으로 작업실 경비를 충당하고 있다. 그 강좌들 중에는 주중에 도자기 공예 고급 기술을 가르치는 '실습 교실'과, 도자기 공예 입문자들을 위한 무료 강좌인 '기초반' 등이 있다. 더 자세한 내용은 그녀가 운영하는 사이트인 www.esmereldaspottery.com에서 찾아볼 수 있다.

ceramics 도자기 공예, 도자기류　workshop 작업실, 일터　at a bargain price 싼 값으로　reconsider 재고하다　piece (예술) 작품 한 점　afford (~할 금전적·시간적) 여유가 되다　a great deal 엄청 수지 맞는 거래　fund 자금을 대다　proceeds 수익 bowl 그릇　practicum 실습　advanced 고급의　foundation 토대, 기초　enthusiast 애호가

1. 로페즈 씨가 예상보다 일찍 미술 작업실을 열 수 있었던 이유는?
(A) 대출을 받았다.
(B) 경연대회에서 우승했다.
(C) 대학을 일찍 졸업했다.
(D) 비싸지 않은 공간을 발견했다.

해설 **세부 사항**

기사문 첫 단락 첫 번째 문장에서 로페즈 씨는 일찍 공예 작업실을 열 생각이 없었는데, 포터 물류 단지에서 저렴한 값으로 임대되는 작업실을 보고 다시 생각했다(when she saw a workshop for rent at a bargain price in Porter Warehouse Complex, she reconsidered)고 했다. 따라서 (D)가 정답이다.

어휘 grant 승인하다 **loan** 대출(금) **competition** 경연대회
inexpensive 비싸지 않은

2. 기사에 따르면, 로페즈 씨가 만드는 것은?
(A) 스테인드 글라스 (B) 식기류
(C) 조각상 (D) 타일 모자이크

해설 세부 사항
두 번째 단락 첫 문장에서 로페즈 씨는 접시나 그릇, 기타 주방용 도자기의 온라인 판매(selling her plates, bowls and other kitchen ceramics on the Internet)와 자신의 강좌 수익으로 작업실 경비를 충당한다고 했다. 따라서 (B)가 정답이다.

3-5 기사

데니턴 랩스, 오하이오 미래 협회로부터 13만 달러를 수령하다

데이턴 – 오하이오 미래 협회(COF)는 제약회사인 데니턴 랩스사를 13만 달러의 보조금 수령자로 선정하여 고교생들이 졸업 후에 성공적으로 취업할 수 있도록 하였다. **3**COF가 맡은 임무는 학생들이 미래에 대비하도록 돕는 것이며, 론다 레이놀즈 의장은 이러한 목표 아래 협회에서는 항상 협력자를 찾고 있다고 말한다. "**4**데니턴 랩스사는 상당수의 오하이오 학생들을 고교 졸업 후에 바로 고용해 온 이력이 입증되었으며, 따라서 우리는 이 회사가 귀중한 협력자가 될 것이라고 믿습니다."라고 레이놀즈 씨는 설명했다.

5데니턴 랩스사는 주말 강좌를 마련하여 학생들이 전문 기술을 익히고 졸업 후 직장 생활에 대한 조언과 방향성을 제시할 워크숍에 참가할 수 있도록 하는 데 이 보조금을 사용할 예정이다.

첫 강좌는 11월 5일에 시작된다. 이 강좌는 몽고메리 카운티 학군에 속한 모든 고교생들에게 개방되어 있다. 학생들은 데니턴 랩스사 홈페이지에서 직접 신청하여 등록할 수 있다. 참가 비용은 없으며, 식사가 제공된다.

---

council 위원회, 협회 **manufacturer** 제조사 **recipient** 수령인 **grant** 보조금 **enable** 할 수 있게 하다 **graduation** 졸업 **mission** 임무 **assist** 돕다 **chairperson** 의장 **proven** 입증된 **employ** 고용하다 **large numbers of** 대단히 많은 **directly** 바로 **ally** 협력자 **participate in** ~에 참여하다 **direction** 방향, 목표 **post-school** 졸업 후의 **register** 등록하다 **sign up** 신청하다

3. COF가 도우려고 하는 사람들은 누구인가?
(A) 과학자 (B) 학생
(C) 교사 (D) 사업가

해설 세부 사항
기사문 첫 번째 단락의 두 번째 문장에서 COF의 임무는 학생들이 미래에 대비하도록 돕는 것(The COF's mission is to assist students to prepare for the future)이라고 했다. 따라서 (B)가 정답이다.

4. 데니턴 랩스사가 보조금 수령자로 선정된 이유는?
(A) 많은 고교 졸업생들을 채용한다.
(B) 교육적인 제품을 만든다.
(C) 중요한 주제에 관한 공개 강좌를 개최한다.
(D) 지역사회 발전을 위한 프로젝트에 자금을 지원한다.

해설 세부 사항
첫 단락 후반부 레이놀즈 씨의 말에서 데니턴 랩스사는 상당수의 오하이오 학생들을 고등학교 졸업 후에 바로 고용해 온 이력이 입증되어(Denniton Labs has a proven history ~ from high school), 귀중한 협력자가 될 것이라고 믿는다고 했다. 따라서 (A)가 정답이다.

어휘 hire 채용하다 **graduate** 졸업생 **hold** 개최하다 **finance** 자금을 대다

5. 기사에 따르면, 11월 주말에 데니턴 랩스사에서 일어날 일은?
(A) 기사들이 새 기계들을 설치할 것이다.
(B) 발명품들이 전시될 것이다.
(C) 진로 지도가 제공될 것이다.
(D) 직원들이 특별한 기술 교육을 받을 것이다.

해설 세부 사항
두 번째 단락에서 데니턴 랩스사는 주말 강좌를 마련하여 학생들이 전문 기술을 익히고 졸업 후 직장 생활에 대한 조언과 방향성을 제시할 워크숍에 참가할 수 있도록 할 것(Denniton Labs will use the funds ~ for their post-school work lives)이라고 했으며, 세 번째 단락에서 첫 강좌가 11월 5일에 시작된다(The first course will begin on November 5)고 했다. 따라서 (C)가 정답이다.

어휘 technician 기술자, 기사 **install** 설치하다 **machinery** 기계류 **invention** 발명, 발명품 **exhibit** 전시하다 **guidance** 지도

6-9 기사

윌셔홀, 대변신을 추진하다

테니 하이츠, 4월 5일 – 2년 간의 기획 끝에 윌셔홀이 마침내 야심 찬 개조 작업에 들어갈 준비가 되었다. 이 프로젝트의 목표는 윌셔홀을 현대적인 공연장으로 변모시키는 것이다. **6**18개월 동안 폐쇄되며, 정확한 개장 날짜는 추후에 발표될 것이다.

민간 및 기업의 기부금, 정부의 예술 보조금, 티켓 요금을 모두 합쳐 윌셔홀은 공사를 위해 1,850만 달러를 모을 수 있었다. 극장 관리자인 데이비스 팔머 씨는 새 객석을 설계한 건축가, 존 레이놀즈 씨의 노고를 칭찬했다. "**7(D)**공사가 완료되고 나면, 관객을 위한 좌석 수가 거의 두 배가 될 겁니다."라고 팔머 씨는 설명했다. "**7(B)**또한 더 많은 공연을 수용할 수 있도록 무대도 확장됩니다. 그렇게 되면 영향력이 큰 공연을 놓치게 되지 않을 겁니다. **8**예를 들어 작년에 아리아나 폰테인은 전국 콘서트 투어 중에 테니 하이츠에는 들르지 않았습니다. 우리 무대가 그녀의 무대 장치를 수용할 정도로 크지 않았기 때문이죠. 개조 후에는 그런 문제가 없을 겁니다."

7(A) 내부 개조뿐만 아니라 건물 외부에도 개조 작업이 시행되는데, 정문 근처에 화단 조성하기와 부지 내 주차장에 새로 아스팔트 깔기 등도 포함된다.

9 폐쇄되기 전에 월셔홀의 마지막 공연은 〈길 건너에〉라는 제목의 연극이다. 공연 주체는 월셔홀 소속 극단이다. <u>이는 확실히 이 장소의 제1기 시대에 어울리는 결말이다.</u>

---

transformation 변화, 변신 go forward 진전되다 undergo 겪다 ambitious 야심적인 be aimed at ~을 목표로 삼다 performance venue 공연장 closure 폐쇄 combination 조합, 결합 corporate 기업의 donation 기부 federal 연방 정부의 charge 요금 praise 칭찬하다 architect 건축가 auditorium 객석, 강당 accommodate 수용하다 miss out on ~을 놓치다 potential 가능성 있는 in addition to ~외에도, ~뿐 아니라 exterior (건물) 외부 flower bed 화단 on-site 현장의 parking lot 주차장 layer 층, 겹 entitled ~라는 제목의 in-house (조직) 내부의 troupe 공연단, 극단

---

6. 월셔홀은 얼마나 오랫동안 폐쇄되는가?
(A) 6개월 동안
(B) 1년 반 동안
(C) 2년 동안
(D) 3년 동안

해설 **세부 사항**
기사문 첫 번째 단락에서 월셔홀은 보수 공사로 18개월 동안 폐쇄될 것이라고(The closure will last for 18 months) 했으므로, (B)가 정답이다.

7. 공사 작업의 일부로 언급되지 않은 것은?
(A) 주차장 재포장
(B) 무대 확장
(C) 음향시스템 개선
(D) 좌석 추가

해설 **Not / True**
두 번째 단락의 팔머 씨의 말에서 공사가 완료되고 나면, 관객을 위한 좌석 수가 거의 두 배가 될 것(we will have nearly double the number of seats for audience members)이며, 더 많은 공연을 수용할 수 있도록 무대도 확장될 것(the stage will be expanded to accommodate more performances)이라고 했다. 또 세 번째 단락에서 정문 근처 화단 조성과 주차장에 새로 아스팔트 까는(covering the on-site parking lot with a new layer of asphalt) 외부 공사가 진행될 것이라고 했으므로, 지문에 언급되지 않은 (C)가 정답이다.

어휘 repave 재포장하다 enlarge 확대하다 add 추가하다

8. 아리아나 폰테인은 누구일 것 같은가?
(A) 여배우 　　　　(B) 건축가
(C) 극장 관리자 　　(D) 뮤지션

해설 **추론**
두 번째 단락에서 무대가 확장되면 큰 공연을 놓치지 않게 될 것이라면서, 그 일례로 작년에 아리아나 폰테인은 전

국 콘서트 투어 중에 테니 하이츠에는 들르지 않았다(For example, ~ not large enough for her set)고 했다. 따라서 아리아나 폰테인은 뮤지션임을 알 수 있으므로, (D)기 정답이다.

9. [1], [2], [3], [4]로 표시된 곳들 중 다음 문장이 들어가기에 가장 적절한 곳은?

이는 확실히 이 장소의 제1기 시대에 어울리는 결말이다.
(A) [1] 　　　　　(B) [2]
(C) [3] 　　　　　(D) [4]

해설 **문장 삽입**
제시문은 '이는 확실히 이 장소의 제1기 시대에 어울리는 결말이다'라는 의미이므로, 월셔홀을 폐쇄하기 전에 마지막으로 있을 일 뒤에 들어가는 것이 적절하다. 따라서 마지막 공연인 〈길 건너에〉에 관한 내용 뒤인 (D)가 정답이다.

어휘 certainly 틀림없이, 분명히 fitting 어울리는, 적합한 phase 단계, 국면

●UNIT 12 웹페이지 / 기타 양식 지문

예제 　　　　　　　　　　　　　　　　교재 p. 314

www.thefreelancerpenplus.com

| 소개 | 일자리 | 멤버십 | 연락처 |

환영합니다!
프리랜서 펜플러스는 글쓰기 실력을 연마하고 다른 작가들과 소통할 수 있는 최고의 웹사이트입니다.

프리랜서 펜플러스를 최대한으로 활용하려면 유료 회원이 되세요.

멤버십 혜택은 다음과 같습니다.
• 포럼에서 답변을 달거나 여러분의 포럼을 열 수 있습니다.
• 누구보다 먼저 관련 일자리 정보를 알 수 있습니다.
• 회원 전용 스마트폰 앱을 사용할 수 있습니다.

가입에 관심이 있으신가요? '멤버십 탭'을 클릭하세요.

문제 멤버들이 할 수 있는 것으로 언급된 것이 아닌 것은?
(A) 비회원보다 일자리 목록 미리 보기
(B) 메시지 창에서 새로운 토론 시작하기
(C) 모바일 장치를 위해 고안된 소프트웨어 사용하기
(D) 다른 회원들과 개인적으로 연락하기

ACTUAL TEST 　　　　　　　　　교재 p. 315

| 1. (C) | 2. (C) | 3. (D) | 4. (B) | 5. (D) |
| 6. (D) | 7. (C) | 8. (D) | | |

PART 7

209

1-2 양식

> **바오 컴퓨터 수리점**
>
> 컴퓨터 수리 의뢰일: 10월 14일
> 수리 기사: 압둘 칸
> 수리 전표: 1114BL3
> 고객: 도니타 패트리지
> 전화번호: (413) 555-0189
>
> > **문제:**
> > 컴퓨터에서 가끔 시끄러운 소음이 남. 사용자가 대용량 앱을 실행할 때 주로 문제가 발생함.
> >
> > **[1]진단 및 수리 과정:**
> > 냉각팬 중 하나가 조정이 맞지 않아, 전원을 켤 때마다 이상한 소리가 났음. 앱 실행으로 인한 시스템 부하가 팬을 작동시킨 원인이었음. 냉각팬을 교체하자 문제가 사라짐.
> >
> > **특이사항:**
> > [2]본 컴퓨터는 우리 가게의 보증 연장 기간에 해당하여 이번 수리 비용 전액이 보험으로 보장됨.
>
> 완료일: 10월 14일
> 기사 서명: 압둘 칸
> 고객 서명:
>
> ---
> drop-off date 인계일 generally 대개, 보통 load (프로그램을) 로딩하다 diagnosis 진단 procedure 과정, 절차 out of alignment 조정이 되어 있지 않은, 어긋나 있는 turn on (전원이) 켜지다, 켜다 strain 부담, 압력 replace 교체하다 disappear 사라지다 extended 연장된 warranty 품질 보증 cover (보험으로) 보장하다

1. 양식의 한 가지 용도는?
(A) 지불을 요청하기 위해
(B) 새로운 시스템의 문제점을 설명하기 위해
(C) 시행한 작업의 세부 사항을 전달하기 위해
(D) 게시물에 대한 피드백을 하기 위해

해설 **주제 / 목적**
바오 컴퓨터 수리점의 수리 작업 명세서로, 양식 중반부에 컴퓨터의 문제점(Problem), 진단 및 수리 과정 (Diagnosis and repair procedure), 특이사항(Notes) 등이 제시되어 있다. 따라서 시행한 작업의 세부 사항을 전달하기 위한 양식임을 알 수 있으므로, (C)가 정답이다.

어휘 details 세부 사항 carry out ~을 수행하다 posting 게시물

2. 수리에 대해 명시된 것은?
(A) 완료하는 데 며칠이 걸렸다.
(B) 복잡한 과정이 요구되었다.
(C) 고객에게 비용 청구 없이 이루어졌다.
(D) 보고된 문제점을 해결하지 못했다.

해설 **Not / True**
양식 후반부의 Notes 부분을 보면 컴퓨터는 가게의 보증 연장 기간에 해당하여 이번 수리 비용은 전액 보험으로 보장된다(The computer is ~ fully covers the fee for

---

this repair)고 했다. 따라서 (C)가 정답이다.

어휘 complicated 복잡한 at no charge 무료로

3-5 웹페이지

> www.healthstory.ca
>
> | 소개 | 동영상 | 레시피 | 회원 가입 | 연락처 |
>
> **헬스 스토리**
>
> 여러분이 자신의 건강을 진지하게 생각할 준비가 되셨다면, 헬스 스토리를 시작할 준비가 되신 겁니다. [3]헬스 스토리는 오타와 건강 협의회의 정식 승인을 받은 유일한 건강 관련 민간 단체로, 오타와 건강 협의회는 건강 및 피트니스와 관련된 정책을 세우는 정부 기관입니다. 그러니 전혀 놀랄 일이 아닙니다!
>
> 저희가 보유하고 있는 폭넓은 레시피는 어떤 식이요법이라도 지원하며, [4]저희는 건강한 몸매를 유지하는 데 도움이 되는 상세한 운동 동영상도 보유하고 있습니다.
>
> 한 달에 단돈 4.99달러로, [5]전 세계 의사나 간호사, 그 밖의 건강 관리 전문가들이 기고한 통찰력 있는 글들을 통해 피트니스 전반에 대해 알아야 할 모든 것을 습득하실 수 있습니다.
>
> 회원 가입을 하시려면 여기를 클릭하세요, 결정할 준비가 되지 않으셨다면 아래에 이메일 주소를 입력하셔서 저희 무료 우편물 수신자 명단에 가입하세요. 피트니스 입문자를 대상으로 하는 간단히 읽을 수 있는 이메일로 헬스 스토리가 제공하는 것들을 경험해 보실 수 있습니다.
>
> | 고객 이메일: | 제출 |
>
> ---
> wellness 건강 earn 얻다 stamp of approval 승인 extensive 폭넓은, 광범위한 detailed 상세한 workout 운동 stay in shape 건강한 몸매를 유지하다 insightful 통찰력 있는 professional 전문가: 전문의 commit (공개적으로) 의사[결정]를 밝히다 newcomer 신참자

3. 헬스 스토리에 대해 명시된 것은?
(A) 텔레비전 방송에 나왔다.
(B) 원래 의사들을 위한 소셜미디어였다.
(C) 체험용 회원권을 할인해준다.
(D) 정부 기관의 승인을 받았다.

해설 **Not / True**
첫 번째 단락 두 번째 문장에서 헬스 스토리는 오타와 건강 협의회의 정식 승인을 받은 유일한 건강 관련 민간 단체이며, 오타와 건강 협의회는 건강 및 피트니스와 관련된 정책을 세우는 정부 기관이라고 했다. 따라서 (D)가 정답이다.

어휘 feature 특집으로 다루다 originally 원래 trial membership 체험용 회원권 endorse 승인하다

4. 웹페이지에 따르면, 헬스 스토리 동영상에서 볼 수 있는 것은?
(A) 유명인사 인터뷰 (B) 운동 모습
(C) 요리 강습 (D) 보도 기사

해설 **세부 사항**

두 번째 단락에서 헬스 스토리는 건강한 몸매를 유지하는 데 도움이 되는 운동 동영상을 보유하고 있다(we have detailed workout videos)고 했으므로, (D)가 정답이다.

어휘 celebrity 유명인사

5. 헬스 스토리 기고 글의 출처는?
   (A) 다른 웹사이트에서 링크된 것들이다.
   (B) 인기 있는 포럼 게시물에서 선정한 것들이다.
   (C) 경연대회 우승자들이 제공한 것들이다.
   (D) 건강 관리 전문가들이 기고한 것들이다

해설 **세부 사항**

세 번째 단락에서 전 세계 의사, 간호사, 그 외의 건강 관리 전문가들이 기고한 글을 통해 피트니스 전반에 대해 알아야 할 모든 것을 습득할 수 있다(you'll learn everything ~ other healthcare professionals from around the world)고 했으므로, (D)가 정답이다.

어휘 link 연결하다 post 게시물 competition 경연대회
submit 제출하다 expert 전문가

6-8 설문 조사

트래블 월드의 모바일 앱을 이용해주셔서 감사합니다!
잠시 시간을 내어 다음 설문을 작성해주십시오.

트래블 월드 앱을 어떤 용도로 사용하십니까? 해당되는 것 모두를 선택하세요.

□ 호텔 예약하기	□ 항공권 구입하기
⁶☑ 식당 정보 얻기	□ 지상교통을 이용한 여행 준비하기

다음 내용에 동의하시는지 여부를 표시해주세요.

트래블 월드 앱은 사용하기 쉽다.	☑ 네
	□ 아니요
트래블 월드 앱은 여행에 관한 나의 모든 요구를 충족시킨다.	☑ 네
	□ 아니요
⁷트래블 월드 앱은 가격이 적절하다.	□ 네
	☑ 아니요

기타 의견 및 제안 사항 있으십니까? 있다면 아래에 작성해 주세요.

귀사의 앱의 다양한 기능은 편리하지만, 기능성은 한 가지 기능에만 주력하는 앱이 더 뛰어나다고 생각합니다. ⁸실제로 저는 귀사의 앱의 기능 대부분을 사용하지는 않기 때문에, 앞으로 사용하려고 하는 용도에 더 명확하게 들어맞는 다른 앱으로 바꿀 계획입니다.

고객님의 의견에 감사드립니다! 이 설문에 대한 고객님의 응답과 관련하여 연락을 드려도 되겠습니까?
☑ 네   □ 아니요
이름: 제인 프레티
이메일: j.peretti@cnkomail.com

---

fill out (서식을) 작성하다 apply 적용되다. 해당되다 obtain 얻다 arrange 마련하다. 준비하다 ground travel 지상교통을 이용한 여행 indicate 나타내다 statement 성명. 진술 reasonably priced 석당한 가격의 suggestion 제안 range 다양성. 범위 feature 기능 functionality 기능성 superior (보다 더) 우수한 dedicate oneself to ~에 전념하다 switch 바꾸다 tailored to ~에 맞춘 specifically 명확하게

6. 프레티 씨는 트래블 월드 앱을 이용하여 무엇을 할 것 같은가?
   (A) 숙소 예약하기
   (B) 항공 여행 조사하기
   (C) 운전 도로 계획하기
   (D) 식사할 곳 결정하기

해설 **추론**

설문지에서 트래블 월드 앱의 용도를 묻는 첫 번째 질문에 프레티 씨는 식당 정보 얻기(Obtaining dining information)에 체크 표시를 했다. 따라서 (D)가 정답이다.

어휘 lodging 숙소

7. 트래블 월드 앱에 대해 암시된 것은?
   (A) 모든 모바일 기기와 호환 가능하다.
   (B) 자주 업데이트된다.
   (C) 이용이 무료가 아니다.
   (D) 일부 국가들에서는 도움이 되지 않는다.

해설 **추론**

설문 중반부에 트래블 월드 앱의 가격이 적절한지를 묻는 항목(The Travel World app is reasonably priced)을 보면, 트래블 월드 앱의 이용료가 있음을 추론할 수 있다. 따라서 (C)가 정답이다.

어휘 compatible 호환이 되는 device 기기 frequently 자주

8. 프레티 씨가 트래블 월드 앱 사용을 중단하겠다고 말한 이유는?
   (A) 앞으로는 여행을 덜 다닐 계획이다.
   (B) 최신 버전에는 특정 기능이 들어 있지 않다.
   (C) 그녀의 회사에서 다른 앱을 구입했다.
   (D) 더 전문화된 앱으로 바꿀 것이다.

해설 **세부 사항**

설문 후반부에서 프레티 씨는 트래블 월드 앱의 대부분의 기능을 사용하지 않기 때문에, 앞으로 용도에 더 명확하게 들어맞는 다른 앱으로 바꿀 계획(I'm going to switch ~ what I'll use it for)이라고 했다. 따라서 (D)가 정답이다.

어휘 latest 최신의 specialized 전문적인. 전문화된

●UNIT 13 이중 연계 지문

READING PRACTICE

교재 p. 319

웹페이지 + 편지

---

www.redhillroofing.net

| 홈 | 사진 갤러리 | 제품 | 팀 소개 | 연락처 |

레드힐 루핑은 이 지역 최고의 지붕 공사 업체입니다. 저희는 지난 25년간 주택 및 사업체 건물 모두에 최고 품질의 서비스를 제공해 왔습니다.

저희는 최근에 지인 추천 프로그램인 루핑 커넥트를 도입했습니다. 현재 또는 이전 고객들은 지인들에게 저희 업체에 대해 알려 주시고, 그들에게 고유 추천 코드를 제공하실 수 있습니다. 지인은 청구서 요금에서 50달러를 할인받게 됩니다.

새 지붕은 건물의 가치를 올리고, 주택의 에너지 효율을 향상시키며, 곰팡이와 같은 건강상 해를 끼칠 가능성이 있는 요소를 막는 데 도움이 될 수 있습니다. 679-555-0133으로 오늘 저희에게 전화 주시거나, 다른 연락 방법을 보시려면 상단의 '연락처'란을 클릭하십시오.

---

premier 최고의 **roofing** 지붕 공사 **top-quality** 최고 품질의 **residential** 주택지의 **property** 부동산, 건물 **launch** 시작하다 **referral** 추천, 소개 **previous** 이전의 **bill** 청구서 **energy efficiency** 에너지 효율 **potential** 잠재적인 **hazard** 위험 **mold** 곰팡이 **get in touch** 연락하다

A.J. 코스탄자, 3007 베스타 애버뉴
메리스빌, PA 17053
10월 12일

코스탄자 씨께,

어제 만나뵙고 귀하의 주택 지붕 교체에 관해 논의할 수 있어서 반가웠습니다. 이 작업에 대한 대략적인 비용 내역서를 동봉합니다. 이 가격은 차고를 포함하여 건물 지붕 전체를 교체하는 비용이 반영된 것임을 알아 두시기 바랍니다. 루핑 커넥트 프로그램을 통해 공사에 대해 50달러의 할인을 받으시게 되며, 이는 동봉한 서류에 나와 있습니다.

작업반은 언제라도 일을 시작하는 것이 가능합니다. 공사 일정을 잡으시려면 550-0158로 저희에게 전화 주십시오.

---

replacement 교체 **Enclosed you will find** ~을 동봉합니다 **statement** 내역서 **approximate** 대략적인 **be aware that** ~을 알다 **reflect** 반영하다, 반사하다 **count** 계산에 넣다, 포함시키다 **garage** 차고 **crew** (작업) 반, 팀 **available** 시간이 나는

문제 코스탄자 씨에 대해 암시된 것은?
(A) 그가 요청한 공사는 60일 정도 소요될 것이다.
(B) 현재 그의 주택 지붕에 쓰인 타일은 아직 보증 기간이 끝나지 않았다.
(C) 자신의 사업체를 위해 새로 지붕을 해야 한다.
(D) 친구를 통해 이 업체에 대해 알게 되었다.

해설 연계

웹페이지의 두 번째 단락에서 레드힐 루핑은 최근에 지인 추천 프로그램인 루핑 커넥트를 도입했으며, 지인은 청구서 요금에서 50달러를 할인받게 된다(The friend will be given $50 off their bill)고 했다. 또 편지 첫 번째 단락의 마지막 문장에서 코스탄자 씨는 루핑 커넥트 프로그램을 통해 공사에 대해 50달러의 할인을 받게 된다(Through the Roofing Connect program, you will receive a $50 discount on the work)고 했다. 따라서 코스탄자 씨는 친구를 통해 레드힐 루핑에 대해 알게 되었다는 것을 추론할 수 있으므로, (D)가 정답이다.

어휘 under warranty 보증 기간 중인 find out 알아내다

ACTUAL TEST

교재 p. 320

1. (C) **2.** (B) **3.** (C) **4.** (D) **5.** (A)
6. (C) **7.** (C) **8.** (B) **9.** (A) **10.** (D)

1-5 웹페이지 + 이메일

URL: https://www.dancewithharley.com

할리 댄스 교실

할리 댄스 교실은 성인들을 위한 모든 단계의 강습을 제공합니다. 저희 강습의 전체 목록을 보시려면 아래 항목들을 클릭하세요.

항목 1 볼룸댄스	누구라도 이 고전적인 스타일의 댄스를 알아야 합니다. **1(D)** 파트너를 데려오시거나 혼자 오셔서 새로운 친구를 사귀세요.
항목 2 뮤직 비디오	**1(A)** 최신 유행하는 뮤직 비디오에서 그대로 따온 춤 동작으로 사람들에게 깊은 인상을 주고 싶으신가요? 이 강습은 여러분이 가장 좋아하는 가수와 똑같이 춤을 출 수 있는 능력을 여러분께 드립니다.
항목 3 운동	**1(B)** 속도가 빠른 이 강습을 통해 자신이 깨닫지 못하는 사이에 힘과 체력을 기르게 됩니다.
4항목 4 고급반	전문 댄서이거나 그렇게 되기를 원하신다면, 고급 단계의 이 강습을 수강하실 것을 고려해 보세요.

2정식 교육을 받은 댄서이며 여분의 수입을 얻기를 원하시나요? 본인이 직접 댄스 강습을 하며 즐기면서 일해 보세요! 더 자세한 내용을 원하시면 연락 주세요.

---

complete 완전한, 전체의 **ballroom** 볼룸댄스, 사교댄스 **classic** 고전적인 **impress** 깊은 인상을 주다 **straight** 곧장, 바로 **trendy** 최신 유행하는 **performer** 연기자, 연주자 **fast-paced** 속도가 빠른 **strength** 힘, 기운 **stamina** 체력, 스태미나 **realize** 깨닫다, 알아차리다 **advanced** 고급의, 상급의

발신: 〈harley@dancewithharley.com〉
수신: 〈anad@esbez.net〉
제목: 회신: 문의
날짜: 4월 12일

디아즈 씨께,

³저희 댄스 교실에 연락 주셔서 감사드리며 플래그스태프 지역에 오신 걸 환영합니다. 이곳에 잘 정착하시기를 바랍니다. 로스앤젤레스에서 이사오셨다니 적응하시는 데 어려움이 많지 않을까 생각되네요.

보내 주신 이메일을 통해 과거 10년 동안 뮤지컬 공연에서 전문 댄서이셨다는 것을 알게 됐습니다. ⁴다행히도 귀하와 같은 수준 높은 수강생들이 선택할 수 있는 적절한 강습들이 있다는 것을 알려 드립니다. 자세한 사항을 보시려면 이 링크를 클릭하세요.

⁵등록하시기 전에 어떤 강습이든 자유롭게 참관해 보시기 바랍니다. 그래야 수강료를 지불하시기 전에 귀하에게 맞는 강습을 확실히 찾아 낼 수 있으니까요. 목록에 있는 강습 중 관심이 가는 것이 있으면 제게 알려 주시기만 하세요. 그러면 저희가 귀하의 방문 일정을 잡겠습니다. 조만간 뵙기를 바랍니다!

할리 브라운 드림

inquiry 문의 reach out to ~에게 연락을 취하다 settle in 정착하다. 적응하다 adjustment 적응 selection 선발, 선택 가능한 것들 appropriate 적절한 feel free to *do* 편하게 ~하다 sit in 참관하다. 청강하다 sign up 등록하다 suit ~에게 맞다. 어울리다

1. 댄스 강습 수강의 이점으로 언급되지 않은 것은?
(A) 인상적인 기술 습득
(B) 신체 건강 향상
(C) 일시적인 스트레스 완화
(D) 더 폭넓은 인간관계

해설 Not / True
할리 댄스 교실 웹페이지의 Category 1을 보면 파트너를 데려오거나 혼자 와서 새로운 친구를 사귀라(Bring a partner or make new friends)고 했으며, Category 2에서는 강습을 통해 최신 유행하는 뮤직 비디오에서 따온 춤 동작으로 사람들에게 깊은 인상을 줄 수 있으며, 가장 좋아하는 가수와 똑같이 춤을 출 수 있게 된다(These classes will give you the ability to dance just like your favorite performers)고 했다. 또, Category 3을 보면 속도가 빠른 강습을 통해 힘과 체력을 기르게 된다(Any one of these fast-paced classes will have you building strength and stamina)고 했다. 따라서 웹페이지에 언급되지 않은 (C)가 정답이다.

어휘 acquisition 습득 **temporary** 일시적인 **relief** 경감, 완화

2. 웹페이지에서 할리 댄스 교실에 대해 시사한 것은?
(A) 온라인에 댄스 동영상을 게시한다.
(B) 새 직원들을 구하고 있다.
(C) 새로운 장소에서 문을 열 것이다.
(D) 대중에게 공연을 선보인다.

해설 Not / True
웹페이지 후반부에서 본인이 직접 댄스 강습을 하며 즐기면서 일해 보라(Have fun while you work by teaching your own dance class!)며 더 자세한 내용을 원하면 연락 달라고 했다. 따라서 할리 댄스 교실에서 강사를 구하고 있다는 것을 알 수 있으므로, (B)가 정답이다.

어휘 employee 직원 **location** 장소 **put on** 무대에 올리다 **public performance** 공연

3. 디아즈 씨에 대해 사실일 것 같은 것은?
(A) 강사직에 지원하고 있다.
(B) 자신의 댄스교실을 운영하고 있다.
(C) 최근에 새 도시로 이사했다.
(D) 연예기획사에서 일하고 있다.

해설 Not / True
할리 브라운 씨가 디아즈 씨에게 보낸 이메일 첫 번째 단락에서 로스앤젤레스에서(move from Los Angeles) 플래그스태프 지역으로 온 것을 환영한다(welcome to the Flagstaff area)며 이곳에 잘 정착하기를 바란다고 했으므로, (C)가 정답이다.

어휘 apply for ~에 지원하다 **recently** 최근에

4. 브라운 씨는 어떤 강습의 링크를 제공했을 것 같은가?
(A) 항목 1   (B) 항목 2
(C) 항목 3   (D) 항목 4

해설 연계
이메일 두 번째 단락에서 브라운 씨는 디아즈 씨에게 수준 높은 수강생들이 선택할 수 있는 적절한 강습들이 있다(we do have a selection of classes appropriate for high-level students like you)면서 링크를 제공했다. 웹페이지를 보면 전문 댄서이거나 전문 댄서가 되기를 원하는 사람들을 대상으로 하는 고급 단계의 강습은 Category 4이다. 따라서 (D)가 정답이다.

5. 브라운 씨가 디아즈 씨에게 하도록 장려하는 것은?
(A) 무료로 강습 참가해보기
(B) 몇몇 강사들에게 이메일 보내기
(C) 몇몇 수강생 후기 읽기
(D) 오디션 참가 신청하기

해설 세부 사항
이메일 마지막 단락에서 브라운 씨는 디아즈 씨에게 수강료를 지불하기 전에 자신에게 맞는 강습을 찾아 낼 수 있도록 등록 전에 어떤 강습이든 자유롭게 참관해보라(Please feel free to sit in on any class before signing up)고 했다. 따라서 (A)가 정답이다.

어휘 try 시험 삼아 해 보다 instructor 강사

6-10 웹페이지+영수증

www.armstronginst.com/awakeretreat

어웨이크 리트리트를 통해 여러분의 비전을 되찾으세요!

어웨이크 리트리트는 암스트롱 협회의 후원을 받아, **6(B)**교사 및 교수들이 열정을 되찾고 자신들의 일에서 새로운 목적을 발견하도록 도와 드립니다. **6(D)**이 프로그램은 전문가들이 지도하며, 그들의 통찰력과 경험을 바탕으로 참가자들이 강의실에서 자신들의 능력을 최대한 발휘하도록 인도해 드릴 것입니다. 어웨이크 리트리트는 이틀 간에 걸쳐 진행되는 프로그램으로 소규모 토론, 강의, 자아성찰 시간이 포함되어 있습니다.

고도의 자격을 갖춘 저희 네 명의 정규직 강사들 중 한 명이 전체 프로그램을 이끌게 됩니다. 저희 강사들은 패트릭 암스트롱과 제니스 쉴즈(암스트롱 협회의 공동 설립자들), **9**한나 김(프로그램 진행자), 가브리엘 멜로(수석 교관)입니다. **7**프로그램에서, 여러분은 예전 경험을 이용하여 정책 변경을 추진하는 법, 여러분이 뛰어난 능력을 보이는 리더십 영역을 발견하는 법, 직원들을 위해 업무를 창출하는 법 등에 대해서 배우게 됩니다. **8**저희는 프로그램을 이수한 후에 저희들이 보낸 설문지를 작성한 참가자들의 의견을 토대로 계속해서 프로그램을 개선하고 있습니다. 여러분의 커리어를 다음 단계로 올릴 이 기회를 놓치지 마십시오!

6(C)어웨이크 리트리트의 참가비는 저희 숙소에서의 1박과 식사 일체를 포함하여 **10**595달러이며, **6(A)**3회 할부도 가능합니다.

reconnect 다시 연결되다 sponsor 후원하다 passion 열정 renewed 새로워진 specialist 전문가 insight 통찰력 participant 참가자 maximize 극대화하다 effectiveness 효과, 능력 self-reflection 자아성찰 retreat 수행, 수련 cofounder 공동 설립자 facilitator 조력자, 진행자 identify 찾다, 발견하다 excel 뛰어나다, 탁월하다 continually 계속해서 based on ~에 근거하여 questionnaire 설문지 complete 이수하다, 마치다 accommodation 숙박 be divided into ~로 나누어지다

암스트롱 협회 고객 영수증

고객: 브루노 카도소
프로그램명: 어웨이크 리트리트
일시/강사: 5월 7-8일 / **9**한나 김
10지불액: 595달러
지불 수단: 로얄카드: XXXX-XXXX-XXXX-7638

프로그램 수속 시 지불 증명서로 본 영수증을 지참하시기 바랍니다. 예약을 취소하시려면 555-0161로 제니스 쉴즈에게 연락 주십시오.

receipt 영수증 proof 증명 check in 수속하다 cancellation 취소

---

6. 어웨이크 리트리트에 대해 사실이 아닌 것은?
(A) 참가비는 분납 가능하다.
(B) 참가 대상자는 교육계 종사자들이다.
(C) 참가자들은 프로그램 장소에서 2박을 한다.
(D) 프로그램은 전문가들이 인솔한다.

해설 **Not / True**
웹페이지 마지막 단락에서 어웨이크 리트리트의 참가비는 숙소에서의 1박과 식사 일체를 포함하여 595달러라고 했으므로, 참가자들이 프로그램 장소에서 2박을 한다는 (C)는 지문의 내용과 일치하지 않는다. 따라서 (C)가 정답이다.

어휘 pay in installments 분납하다 target audience 주요 대상

7. 프로그램에서 다루는 주제로 언급된 것은?
(A) 효율적으로 시간 관리하기
(B) 정책에 대한 피드백 받기
(C) 리더십 강점 찾기
(D) 숙련된 직원 채용하기

해설 **Not / True**
웹페이지 두 번째 단락에 프로그램에서 다루는 주제가 언급되어 있다. 예전 경험을 이용하여 정책 변경을 추진하는 법(using your past experiences to drive policy changes), 자신이 뛰어난 능력을 보이는 리더십 영역을 발견하는 법(identifying the leadership categories in which you excel), 직원들을 위해 업무를 창출하는 법(creating a mission for your staff) 등에 대해서 배우게 된다고 했으므로, (C)가 정답이다.

어휘 efficiently 효율적으로 strength 강점, 장점 experienced 경험 있는, 능숙한

8. 암스트롱 협회에서 참가자들에게 보내는 것은?
(A) 다른 프로그램에 쓸 수 있는 쿠폰
(B) 프로그램 관련 설문 조사
(C) 수료증
(D) 참가자 명단

해설 **세부 사항**
웹페이지 두 번째 단락 후반부에서 암스트롱 협회에서는 프로그램을 이수한 참가자들에게 보낸 설문지(the questionnaire we sent to them after completing the program)를 토대로 프로그램을 개선하고 있다고 했다. 따라서 (B)가 정답이다.

어휘 follow-up 후속의 certificate 증명서 completion 완료, 이수

9. 카도소 씨에 대해 암시된 것은?
(A) 프로그램 진행자로부터 교육을 받을 것이다.
(B) 프로그램에 대해 할인을 받을 수 있었다.
(C) 전에 암스트롱 협회 워크숍에 참가한 적이 있다.
(D) 처음의 예약을 취소하고 싶어 한다.

해설 연계

영수증을 보면 카도소 씨의 강사는 한나 김(~ Instructor: ~ Hannah Kim)이며, 웹페이지를 보면 한나 김은 프로그램 진행자(program facilitator)이다. 따라서 카도소 씨는 프로그램 진행자인 한나 김으로부터 교육을 받을 것임을 알 수 있으므로, (A)가 정답이다.

어휘 be eligible for ~의 자격이 있다

10. 영수증에 명시된 것은?
(A) 쉴즈 씨가 카도소 씨의 예약을 도왔다.
(B) 카도소 씨는 동료와 함께 행사에 참가할 것이다.
(C) 카도소 씨의 회사에서 등록을 했다.
(D) 금액은 전액 지불되었다.

해설 연계

웹페이지 마지막 단락에서 어웨이크 리트리트의 참가비는 1박과 식사 일체를 포함하여 595달러(The fee for the Awake Retreat ~ is $595)라고 했으며, 영수증을 보면 카도소 씨는 595달러를 지불(Amount paid: $595.00)했다. 따라서 카도소 씨는 참가비 전액인 595달러를 지불했음을 알 수 있으므로, (D)가 정답이다.

어휘 coworker 동료   registration 등록   pay in full 전액 지불하다

●UNIT 14 삼중 연계 지문

READING PRACTICE
교재 p. 325

안내책자 + 공지 + 고객 상품평

> ### 아트무어 가구 / 빅토리아 풍의 탁자
> ### (제품 번호 2NJI890)
>
> - 제품 상세: 견고한 소나무 재질의 식탁으로, 다리가 섬세하게 세공되어 있음. 여섯 명이 편안하게 앉을 수 있고, 선택적으로 사용할 수 있는 확장용 덧판을 확장하면 8명까지 앉을 수 있음.
>
> - 규격: 63 X 36 X 31 (인치)
> - 마감재: 오크목, 체리목, 자연목, 메이플
> - 교체/ 부속 부품:
> • 탁자 다리 (부품 번호 100-A)
> • [1]확장용 덧판 (부품 번호 103-A)
> • 의자 (제품 번호 N220)
> • 설치용 부품 (부품 번호 101-A와 102-A)
>
> Victorian 빅토리아 풍의   description 서술, 묘사   sturdy 견고한   pine 소나무   elegant 우아한, 섬세한   carved 조각된   optional 선택적인   extension leaf 탁자를 넓게 쓸 수 있도록 펴게 되어 있는 덧판   finish 마감재   replacement 교체   mounting hardware 설치용 부품

> 영업팀에게 알립니다:
>
> 빅토리아 풍의 탁자, 제품 번호 2NJI890에 관한 최신 업데이트 정보가 있습니다. [2]제조 업체에 연락했더니, 오크목 마감재를 쓴 탁자가 전국적으로 기대 이상으로 판매되고·있는 것으로 보여, 그 제품을 주문한 모든 고객들에게는 주문 처리가 지연될 것 같습니다.
>
> [1]그리고 제조 업체에서 선택적으로 사용할 수 있는 덧판 제작을 중단했다고 알려 왔으므로, 홍보 문구에서 그 부분은 삭제해 주시기 바랍니다. 질문 있으시면 알려 주세요.
>
> 라울 산티아고
>
> contact 연락하다   manufacturer 제조 업체   apparently 듣자[보아]하니   beyond expectation 기대 이상으로   fulfillment 이행, 고객의 주문 처리   notify 알리다   sales pitch 판매 권유, 홍보

> www.artmoorfurniture.com/reviews
>
> 바네사 아야 – 3월 20일
>
> 저는 빅토리아 풍의 탁자가 정말 마음에 듭니다! 많은 손님들이 그 탁자가 정말로 멋지다고 말씀해 주셨습니다. [2]제가 선택한 마감재 소재의 제품이 재고가 없어서 주문이 밀린다는 소식이 당연하게 느껴집니다.
>
> 탁자에 대해 유일한 단점은 일반 사람들이 조립하기에 쉽지 않다는 것입니다. 저에게도 너무 어려워서 외부의 도움을 받아야 했습니다.
>
> 그럼에도, 저는 그 탁자를 적극 추천합니다!
>
> multiple 다수의   comment 언급하다   attractive 멋진   backorder (재고가 없어) 처리 못한 주문, 이월 주문   average 보통의   put together 조립하다   complicated 복잡한   outside 외부의   highly 대단히, 매우

1. 탁자 제조 업체에서 생산을 중단한 것은?
(A) 부품 번호 101-A
(B) 부품 번호 102-A
(C) 부품 번호 103-A
(D) 제품 번호 N220

해설 연계

공지문 두 번째 단락에서 제조 업체에서 덧판 제작을 중단했다고 알려 왔다(they stopped making the optional leaf)고 했으며, 안내책자에서 확장용 덧판의 부품 번호를 보면 103-A(Extension leaf (part no. 103-A))이다. 따라서 (C)가 정답이다.

2. 아야 씨가 선택한 탁자의 마감재는?
(A) 오크목
(B) 체리목
(C) 자연목
(D) 메이플

해설 연계

고객 상품평을 보면 아야 씨는 자신이 선택한 마감재 소재의 제품이 재고가 없어서 주문이 밀린다는 소식이 당연하게 느껴진다(I'm not surprised to hear there is a backorder on the finish I got)고 했으며, 공지문을 보면 오크목 마감재를 쓴 탁자가 기대 이상으로 판매되어 주문 처리가 지연될 것 같다(the oak-finished table ~ delay for any customers ordering that one)고 했다. 따라서 이야 씨가 오크목을 마감재로 쓴 탁자를 선택했다는 것을 알 수 있으므로, (A)가 정답이다.

ACTUAL TEST

교재 p. 326

1. (C)	**2.** (A)	**3.** (B)	**4.** (B)	**5.** (D)
6. (A)	**7.** (D)	**8.** (C)	**9.** (D)	**10.** (B)
11. (D)	**12.** (C)	**13.** (C)	**14.** (A)	**15.** (C)

1-5 광고+편지+이메일

무료로 공간 사용 가능합니다!

[1]파크데일 도서관 꼭대기 층의 500제곱피트 규모의 회의실이 이제 1회, 혹은 정기적 사용을 위해 예약 가능합니다. 창문을 통해 파크데일의 멋진 전경이 보일 뿐만 아니라, 화이트보드와 25석의 좌석, 필요에 따라 붙이거나 분리할 수 있는 4개의 탁자도 제공됩니다.

[3]파크데일 도서관은 파크데일 시민들의 공동체 의식 고취에 전념하는 바, 이러한 목표를 공유하는 개인 및 단체들의 예약 신청서만을 후보로 고려하겠습니다. 여러분의 신청서에 이 점을 입증해 주시기 바랍니다. 신청서는 저희 지역 지원 활동 담당자인 린다 아미슨 씨에게 직접 또는 아래 주소로 제출하실 수 있습니다:

파크데일 공공 도서관
메인 가 312번지
파크데일, WI 53090

available 이용할 수 있는   reserve 예약하다   one-time 1회의   regular 정기적인   in addition to ~뿐 아니라, ~ 외에도   separate 분리하다   be committed to ~에 전념[헌신]하다   promote 촉진하다   a sense of community 공동체 의식   application 신청서   organization 단체, 조직   evidence 증거   submit 제출하다   outreach 지원[봉사] 활동   coordinator 진행자, 담당자   in person 직접

린다 아미슨
파크데일 공공 도서관
메인 가 312번지
파크데일, WI 53090

아미슨 씨께,

〈파크데일 데일리 리더〉에 광고하신 회의 장소 예약을 신청하기 위해 편지 드립니다. 저는 파크데일 테이블탑 게임 클럽

(PTG)의 회장이며, 이 클럽은 토요일 오후에 모여 보드게임이나 카드게임을 즐기는 지역민들의 친목 및 화합 모임입니다. [5]우리가 10개월 전에 첫 번째 모임을 가진 이후로, 우리 모임의 총무가 고맙게도 매주 자신의 집에 우리를 초대해 왔습니다. [2]하지만 그룹 규모가 커져서 이제는 더 큰 장소가 필요합니다. 귀 도서관의 회의실이 바로 우리가 찾고 있는 것입니다.

이 편지에 신청서를 동봉합니다. [3]요구하신 특별한 요건을 충족하기 위해 〈파크데일 가제트〉가 우리 모임에 대해 쓴 기사도 첨부했습니다.

감사합니다.

파크데일 테이블탑 게임 클럽 회장
키미 강 드림
동봉

apply 신청하다   advertise 광고하다   treasurer 회계 담당자, 총무   graciously 상냥하게, 고맙게도   host 주최하다   enclose 동봉하다   requirement 필요조건, 요건

발신: 〈cjacobi@rz-com.net〉
수신: 파크데일 테이블탑 게임 클럽 회원
제목: 이번 주 토요일 새로운 모임 장소!
날짜: 11월 14일

안녕하세요, 회원 여러분!

기쁜 소식이 있습니다. 우리가 매주 토요일 오후 3시부터 7시까지 파크데일 도서관에 상설 모임 [4]장소를 확보했습니다. [5]그동안 여러분 모두를 저희 집 거실에 모시는 것도 정말 기쁜 일이었지만, 이 새로운 장소 덕분에 모두가 더 편해질 것이라고 생각합니다. 더불어 우리 모임도 더 확장할 수 있을 테고요.

이번 주 토요일에 도서관 로비에서 몇 분 일찍 만나서 함께 회의실로 이동합시다. 이번 주 게임은 블록 브레이커로, 그렌리 게임즈에서 개발한 속도감 있는 전략 게임입니다. 자유롭게 친구분도 데려오세요!

클레이 자코비 드림

secure 확보하다   permanent 영구적인, 상설의   spot 장소   delight 기쁨, 크게 기쁜 일   expand 확장하다

1. 파크데일 도서관에 대해 암시된 것은?
(A) 주말에는 운영 시간이 다르다.
(B) 직원들이 소식지를 발간한다.
(C) 건물에 여러 층이 있다.
(D) 회의실에 프로젝터가 있다.

해설 추론

광고문 첫 단락에서 파크데일 도서관 꼭대기 층에 있는(on the top floor of Parkdale Library) 회의실 사용 예약이 가능하다고 했으므로, 파크데일 도서관 건물에 여러 층이 있다는 것을 알 수 있다. 따라서 (C)가 정답이다.

어휘 newsletter 소식지, 회보

2. 강 씨가 PTG에 대해 변화했다고 언급한 것은?

(A) 회원 수
(B) 회비
(C) 모임 횟수
(D) 게임 종류

해설 **Not / True**
강 씨가 보낸 편지를 보면, 파크데일 테이블탑 게임 클럽 (PTG)은 총무의 집에 모여 게임을 즐겨왔는데, 그룹 규모가 커져서 이제는 더 큰 장소가 필요하다(our group has grown, and now needs a larger space)고 했다. 따라서 (A)가 정답이다.

어휘 membership fee 회비

3. 강 씨가 보낸 첨부 문서에는 PTG에 대해 뭐라고 나와 있을 것 같은가?

(A) 지역 기업의 후원을 받고 있다.
(B) 파크데일 주민들에게 유익하다.
(C) 회원 가입 요건이 까다롭다.
(D) 보험에 가입되어 있다.

해설 **연계**
편지의 두 번째 단락에서 강 씨는 도서관에서 요구하는 특별한 요건을 충족하기 위해 〈파크데일 가제트〉가 모임에 대해 쓴 기사를 첨부했다(I have also attached ~)고 했다. 광고문을 보면 두 번째 단락에서 파크데일 도서관은 파크데일 시민들의 공동체 의식 고취에 전념하며, 이러한 목표를 공유하는 개인 및 단체들의 예약 신청서만을 후보로 고려하겠다(As Parkdale Library is committed to ~ share this goal)고 했다. 따라서 강 씨가 보낸 첨부 문서에는 PTG가 파크데일 주민들에게 유익하다는 내용이 나올 것임을 추론할 수 있으므로, (B)가 정답이다.

어휘 sponsor 후원하다 **beneficial** 유익한, 이로운 **strict** 엄격한 **insurance policy** 보험

4. 이메일에서 1단락 첫 번째 줄의 단어 "spot"과 의미상 가장 가까운 것은?

(A) 광고 방송   (B) 장소
(C) 얼룩   (D) 시야

해설 **동의어**
spot은 명사로는 '장소, 얼룩'이라는 의미가 있으며, 동사로는 '찾아 내다, 발견하다'라는 의미가 있다. a permanent meeting spot은 '상설 모임 장소'라는 뜻으로, 여기에서 spot은 '장소'라는 의미로 쓰였다. 따라서 (B) place가 정답이다.

5. 자코비 씨는 누구인가?

(A) 게임 회사의 홍보 담당 전문가
(B) 도서관의 지역 지원 활동 담당자
(C) 지역 단체 설립자
(D) 게임 클럽의 총무

해설 **연계**
강 씨가 보낸 편지에서 모임의 총무가 자신의 집에 우리를 초대해왔다(our treasurer has graciously hosted us in his home every week)고 했다. 또 자코비 씨가 PTG회원들에게 보낸 이메일의 첫 번째 단락을 보면 '그동안 여러분 모두를 저희 집 거실에 모시는 것이 정말 기쁜 일이었다(While it has been a true delight having all of you in my living room)'라고 했으므로 그가 PTG 클럽의 총무임을 알 수 있다. 따라서 (D)가 정답이다.

어휘 **public relations** 홍보 **founder** 설립자

6-10 이메일 + 이메일 + 안내문

수신: 아이코닉 전자 〈inquiries@argentielec.com〉
발신: 레나 폴리 〈foleyl@toledo-mail.com〉
날짜: 10월 7일, 오전 8:29
제목: 아이코닉 5

관계자분께:

10제 아이코닉 5 스마트폰에 문제가 있는데, 저는 그것을 캔톤 몰에 있는 아이코닉 매장에서 지난달에 구입했습니다. **6** 전원 버튼을 누르면 화면이 밝아지는 데 몇 분이 걸립니다. **7(A)**별도의 보조 배터리를 판매하나요? **7(C)**만약 그렇다면 새 배터리로 이 문제가 해결될지 궁금합니다. **7(D)**또 소프트웨어의 다음 업데이트는 언제가 될지 알 수 있을까요? **7(B)**제가 전화기를 반송하면 회사에서 배송비를 지불하게 되나요, 아니면 제가 이 비용을 내야 하나요? 조속한 답변 부탁 드립니다.

감사합니다.
레나 폴리

retail store 소매점 light up 밝아지다 separate 분리된, 별개의 resolve 해결하다 shipping cost 배송비

수신: 레나 폴리 〈foleyl@toledo-mail.com〉
발신: 케네스 닉슨 〈kennethnixon @argentielec.com〉
날짜: 10월 7일, 오전 11:54
제목: 회신: 아이코닉 5

폴리 씨께,

전화기에 문제가 있으시다니 죄송합니다. **7(A), (C)**보조 배터리 재고가 있기는 하지만, 배터리를 교체하는 것만으로 문제가 해결될 것 같지 않습니다. **7(B)**대개 고객께서 제품을 반송하는 데 드는 배송비를 지불해야 하지만, 고객님의 경우에는 그에 해당하지 않습니다. 마침 저희가 이와는 다른 문제로 이 전화기를 리콜 조치했는데, 전원을 켜면 전화기가 너무 과열된다는 문제입니다. 그러므로 고객님께서는 첨부한 문서에 설명된 지시 사항을 참조하셔서 전화기를 반품하고 전액 환불을 받으실 수 있습니다.

감사합니다.

아이코닉 전자 고객 서비스 담당자 128번
케네스 닉슨 드림

리콜 제품: 아이코닉 5
기기 반품 방법

제품 회수 박스를 요청하시려면, 저희 웹사이트 www. argentielec.com을 방문하십시오. [8]아래 열거된 구성품들 중 하나라도 회수 박스에 들어 있지 않을 경우 1-800-555-0167로 전화 주십시오.

1. 이송 중에 배터리가 사용되지 않도록 반드시 전화기의 전원을 꺼 주십시오.

2. 특별히 제작된 내열성 재질로 내부가 감싸져 있는 내부 박스를 개봉하세요. [9]어떤 분들은 이 재질에 민감할 수 있으니, 장갑을 끼셔야 하며, 또는 그것을 만지지 않도록 주의하십시오.

3. 비닐봉투 안에 전화기를 넣고 내부 박스에 넣어, 박스 뚜껑을 테이프로 밀봉하십시오.

4. 내부 박스를 배송 상자에 넣고 테이프로 밀봉하십시오.

5. 미리 인쇄된 배송 전표를 붙이십시오. 아니면, [10]아이코닉 매장에서 제품을 구입하셨을 경우, 그 매장에 제품을 가져다 주셔도 됩니다.

6. 폴리 씨가 언급한 문제점은?
   (A) 전화기의 전원이 켜지는 속도가 느리다.
   (B) 전화기가 사용 중에 과열된다.
   (C) 전화기 부품 몇 개가 없다.
   (D) 전화기 액정이 깨졌다.

해설 **세부 사항**
폴리 씨가 아이코닉 전자에 보낸 이메일의 두 번째 문장에서 전원 버튼을 누르면 화면이 밝아지는 데 몇 분이 걸린다(When I press the Power button, it takes up to a minute for the screen to light up)고 했다. 따라서 (A)가 정답이다.

어휘 overheat 과열되다   miss 놓치다

7. 폴리 씨가 제기한 내용 중 닉슨 씨가 언급하지 않은 것은?
   (A) 제품 구입 가능성
   (B) 배송비
   (C) 배터리 교체
   (D) 소프트웨어 업데이트

해설 **연계**
폴리 씨가 보낸 이메일을 보면, 폴리 씨는 별도의 보조 배터리를 판매하는지(Do you sell separate battery packs?), 새 배터리로 문제가 해결될지(I am wondering purchasing a new battery would resolve this issue), 다음 소프트웨어 업데이트가 언제인지(could you tell me when the next software update is), 전화기 반송 시 배송비 지불 여부(If I do send back ~ cover those costs myself?)에 대해 문의했다. 닉슨 씨가 보낸 이메일을 보면, 보조 배터리 재고는 있으나(we do have battery packs in stock), 배터리를 교체하는 것만으로 문제가 해결되지는 않을 것이며(the problem would not be resolved simply by changing the battery), 대개 제품을 반송하는 데 드는 배송비는 고객이 지불해야 하지만, 이 경우에는 그에 해당하지 않는다(Normally, customers do have to pay ~ not be the case for you)고 대답했다. 하지만 다음 소프트웨어 업데이트가 언제인지를 물어본 질문에는 답변하지 않았으므로, (D)가 정답이다.

어휘 availability 입수[이용] 가능성

8. 고객들이 제공받은 전화번호로 전화해야 하는 이유는?
   (A) 환불 상황을 확인하기 위해
   (B) 회수 박스를 요청하기 위해
   (C) 빠진 물품을 신고하기 위해
   (D) 과정에 대해 문의하기 위해

해설 **세부 사항**
안내문의 두 번째 문장을 보면, 구성품들 중 하나라도 회수 박스에 들어 있지 않을 경우 1-800-555-0167로 전화하라(Please call 1-800-555-0167 if any of the components listed below are not in your recovery box)고 했으므로, (C)가 정답이다.

어휘 status 상황, 상태   missing 없어진, 빠진

9. 전화기 반품의 준비 단계 중 하나로 언급된 것은?
   (A) 비닐봉투를 테이프로 밀봉하기
   (B) 반품 배송 전표 출력하기
   (C) 전화기 배터리 분리하기
   (D) 특정 재질 만지지 않기

해설 **Not / True**
안내문에서 전화기 반품 시 준비 단계를 보면, 두 번째 항목에서 내부 박스는 특별히 제작된 내열성 재질로 내부가 감싸져 있는데, 어떤 사람들은 이 재질에 민감할 수 있으니, 장갑을 껴야 하며, 또는 그것을 만지지 않도록 주의하라(Some people may be sensitive ~ be careful not to touch it)고 했다. 따라서 (D)가 정답이다.

어휘 preparation 준비   remove 없애다, 꺼내다   material 재료

10. 폴리 씨에 대해 사실인 것은?
(A) 기기 교환을 요구할 것이다.
(B) 제품을 직접 반품할 수 있다.
(C) 닉슨 씨에게 영수증을 보내야 한다.
(D) 10월에 자신의 스마트폰을 구입했다.

해설 연계

첫 번째 이메일의 첫 번째 문장에서 폴리 씨는 지난달에 아이코닉 5 스마트폰을 캔튼 몰에 있는 아이코닉 매장에서 구입했다(~ my Iconic 5 smartphone, which I purchased last month at the Iconic retail store in the Canton Mall)고 했다. 안내문의 마지막 문장을 보면, 아이코닉 매장에서 제품을 구입한 경우, 그 매장에 제품을 가져다 주어도 된다(if you purchased the item at an Iconic retail store, you may drop it off at the store)고 했다. 따라서 폴리 씨는 제품을 직접 구입한 아이코닉 매장에 반품할 수 있다는 것을 추론할 수 있으므로, (B)가 정답이다.

어휘 permit 허용하다

11-15 광고+이메일+일정표

노스라인 컨트리 클럽

노스라인 컨트리 클럽은 18홀의 완전한 골프 코스와 올림픽 경기장 규모의 실내 수영장, 현대적인 클럽하우스 등을 갖추고 있습니다. 저희 골프장은 3년 연속 '메인 주 최고의 골프 코스'로 선정되었습니다. **11**골프장 내 식당은 회원 및 회원의 손님들만 이용하실 수 있으며, 개인 행사를 위해 예약하실 수 있습니다(최고 레벨 회원만 가능).

피크타임 제외 회원권: 한산한 시간대(주중 오후 2시 이후, 주말 오후 6시 이후부터 폐장 시간까지)의 골프 코스 이용권 [월 175달러]

일반 회원권: 모든 개장 시간 동안 골프 코스 이용권, 클럽하우스 바 5% 할인 [월 275달러]

고급 회원권: 모든 개장 시간 동안 골프 코스 이용권, 피크타임 제외 회원 및 일반 회원보다 예약 우선권, 클럽하우스 바 10% 할인 **12**[월 300달러]

최고급 회원권: 모든 개장 시간 동안 골프 코스 이용권, 다른 모든 회원보다 예약 우선권, 클럽하우스 바 15% 할인, 개인 행사 예약 가능 [월 375달러]

house 소유하다   indoor 실내의   rate 평가하다, 등급을 매기다
consecutive 연속의   on-site 현장의   exclusively 독점적으로
ultimate 최고의, 최상의   off-peak 비수기의   access to
~에의 접근[이용]권   enhanced 향상된, 높인   priority 우선[권]
ahead of ~보다 앞서

수신: 스펜서 모리스 〈s.morris@pinepost.ca〉
발신: 피터 벤슨 〈bensonp@northlinecc.com〉
날짜: 6월 24일
제목: 노스라인 컨트리 클럽 레슨

모리스 씨께,

13귀하께서는 저희 클럽에 처음 가입하셨을 때 라이언 브로디 씨의 골프 레슨 대기 명단에 이름을 올려 놓으셨는데, 기쁘게도 이제 자리가 났다는 것을 알려 드립니다. 내기 명단에 오른 분들이 많았는데, 귀하께서 비어 있는 시간대에 시간이 되시는 유일한 분이라서 정말 운좋게도 이 자리를 얻으실 수 있었습니다. **15**브로디 씨의 다른 수강생들은 모두 최소 24개월 동안 그에게 레슨을 받아 오고 있으며, 이 레슨을 통해 인상적인 결과를 내오고 있습니다. 그들은 다음 달에 지역 골프 토너먼트에 참가할 준비를 하고 있습니다. 브로디 씨의 목표는 그들이 자신들의 능력을 최대한 발휘하도록 **14**만드는 것입니다.

귀하의 첫 레슨은 7월 1일 오후 3시에 있습니다. 클럽하우스에서 브로디 씨를 만나시면 됩니다.

두 시간 레슨에 175달러가 청구된다는 것을 알려 드립니다.

12이것은 회원 가입으로 지불하시는 월회비 300달러에 추가되는 것입니다.

감사합니다.
피터 드림

waiting list 대기 명단   time slot 시간대   minimum 최소한(의)
yield (결과를) 내다   compete 경쟁하다, (시합에) 참가하다
reach one's full potential 능력을 최대한 발휘하다   take
place 열리다   bill 청구서를 보내다

노스라인 컨트리 클럽

골프 레슨 일정표: 7월 1일 화요일

시간 및 강사	도로시 산티아고	라이언 브로디	에이버리 월시
오전 8시	엘리자베스 퍼거슨	도나 카렌	사라 와그너
오전 10시	—	**15**앤 커티스	—
오후 1시	마이클 스미스	제시카 황	—
오후 3시	—	스펜서 모리스	—
오후 5시	십 대 그룹 레슨	윌 스턴	멜라니 그레넌

모임 장소: 고객과 따로 약속을 잡지 않는 한 클럽하우스.

unless otherwise 달리 ~하지 않는 한   arrange 마련하다,
주선하다

11. 노스라인 컨트리 클럽에 대해 사실인 것은?
(A) 회원들에게 골프 카트 무료 이용권을 제공한다.
(B) 클럽 수영장은 겨울에는 문을 닫는다.
(C) 최근에 클럽하우스를 확장했다.
(D) 회원들은 식당 시설을 이용할 수 있다.

해설 Not / True

광고문 첫 번째 단락의 마지막 문장에서 골프장 내 식당은 회원 및 회원의 손님들만 이용할 수 있다(Our on-site restaurant is available exclusively to members and their guests)고 했으므로, (D)가 정답이다.

어휘 **golf cart** 골프 카트(골퍼와 골프백을 나르는 전동차)
dining facility 식당

12. 모리스 씨는 어떤 회원권을 가지고 있을 것 같은가?
(A) 피크타임 제외 회원권
(B) 일반 회원권
(C) 고급 회원권
(D) 최고급 회원권

해설 **연계**
이메일 세 번째 단락을 보면 모리스 씨는 월회비가 300달러인 회원권(the $300 in monthly fees that you pay for your membership)을 구입했다는 것을 알 수 있다. 광고문을 보면 월회비가 300달러($300/month)인 회원권은 고급 회원권(Enhanced Membership)이므로, (C)가 정답이다.

13. 벤슨 씨가 브로디 씨에 대해 암시하는 것은?
(A) 모리스 씨 이후에 클럽에 가입했다.
(B) 일부 레슨을 취소해야 했다.
(C) 그가 제공하는 서비스에 대한 수요가 많다.
(D) 그의 레슨은 단체 및 개인을 대상으로 한다.

해설 **추론**
벤슨 씨가 모리스 씨에게 보낸 이메일의 첫 번째 단락을 보면, 브로디 씨의 골프 레슨 대기 명단에 오른 사람들이 많은데(there are a lot of people on the list) 운좋게 자리를 얻었다고 했다. 따라서 브로디 씨가 제공하는 서비스에 대한 수요가 많다는 것을 알 수 있으므로, (C)가 정답이다.

어휘 **cancel** 취소하다 **in high demand** 수요가 많은

14. 이메일에서 1단락 여섯 번째 줄의 단어 "drive"와 의미상 가장 가까운 것은?
(A) 동기를 부여하다 (B) 휘두르다
(C) 이동하다 (D) 운영하다

해설 **동의어**
동사 drive는 '운전하다, 몰다, (사람을 ~하도록) 만들다' 등의 의미가 있다. 여기에서는 '브로디 씨의 목표는 그들이 자신들의 능력을 최대한 발휘하도록 만드는 것이다'라는 의미로, drive는 '(사람을 ~하도록) 만들다'의 뜻으로 쓰였다. 따라서 (A) motivate가 정답이다.

15. 커티스 씨에 대해 암시된 것은?
(A) 그녀의 레슨 시간이 최근에 변경되었다.
(B) 그녀의 회원권으로 우선 예약권이 제공된다.
(C) 최소 2년 동안 브로디 씨로부터 레슨을 받아 왔다.
(D) 작년에 지역 골프 토너먼트에서 우승했다.

해설 **연계**
일정표를 보면 커티스 씨는 브로디 씨에게 레슨을 받는 회원임을 알 수 있으며, 이메일 첫 번째 단락의 중반부를 보면 브로디 씨의 다른 수강생들은 모두 최소 24개월 동안 그에게 레슨을 받아 오고 있다(All of Mr. Brodie's other students have been training with him for a minimum of 24 months)고 했다. 따라서 브로디 씨에게 레슨을 받는 커티스 씨는 최소 2년 동안 브로디 씨로부터 레슨을 받아 왔음을 추론할 수 있으므로, (C)가 정답이다.

YBM
단기토익
700+